HUGH
GAITSKELL

by the same author

POLITICS IN POST-WAR FRANCE
DE GAULLE'S REPUBLIC
(with Martin Harrison)
CRISIS AND COMPROMISE
THE FRENCH PARLIAMENT, 1958–67
FRENCH POLITICIANS AND ELECTIONS
(with Martin Harrison and David Goldey)
WARS, PLOTS AND SCANDALS IN POST-WAR FRANCE
POLITICS AND SOCIETY IN DE GAULLE'S REPUBLIC
(with Martin Harrison)

HUGH GAITSKELL

A Political Biography

PHILIP M. WILLIAMS

JONATHAN CAPE
THIRTY BEDFORD SQUARE
LONDON

First published 1979
© 1979 by Philip M. Williams
Jonathan Cape Ltd, 30 Bedford Square, London WC1

British Library Cataloguing in Publication Data
Williams, Philip
Hugh Gaitskell.
1. Gaitskell, Hugh 2. Statesmen – Great
Britain – Biography
941.085'5'0924   DA566.9.G3

ISBN 0–224–01451–X

Printed in Great Britain by The Anchor Press Ltd
and bound by Wm Brendon & Son Ltd
both of Tiptree, Essex

To the memory of
Charles Anthony Raven Crosland
admired and beloved friend for forty years

CONTENTS

ILLUSTRATIONS

Cartoons appear on pages 287, 321, 416 and 561

The endpapers are a previously unpublished cartoon by Vicky of the 1952 Party Conference at Morecambe

TABLES

PREFACE

THIS is a book about the life and thought of one of the chief political leaders of post-war Britain, the most influential exponent of the democratic Socialist ethos. It sets the career of Hugh Gaitskell in the context of the political system and culture of his day. Dramatic though it was at times, his life is not merely interesting in its own right, or because of his national and international impact. Before 1951, his career throws light on the workings of government during the war and the subsequent Labour attempt to reconstruct British society more humanely and justly. In the long opposition years which followed, his activities afford an excellent window on the Labour Party, its characteristic methods of operation and its distinct traditions and pathology. But though it illustrates some broad themes, the book is not a general account of post-war Britain, and issues and individuals from Winston Churchill to Harold Wilson appear in relation to Hugh Gaitskell and not to their wider role.

It is a political biography. I have avoided amateur psychology, and do not consider it appropriate for an outsider to explore Gaitskell's more intimate relationships while most of his family and close friends are still alive and entitled to their privacy. But I think I have omitted no important influences on his intellectual and political development.

I knew Hugh Gaitskell only slightly, just enough to form an impression of him as a man. In building up a picture of his personality and the development of his political views and style, I have been generously helped by his family and by friends from both early and late in his life. The book has benefited greatly from that, but its essential theme is the public life of a public figure.

From 1945 to 1956 he kept intermittently a diary about public events, which has survived. I have found it factually reliable and have quoted many brief extracts; the whole diary is to be published later. A number of other private diaries have also been generously made available to me; so have some private letters to friends, one or two of whom prefer to remain anonymous; official papers have not. I have treated fully a number of episodes which were important in his life and are inadequately or misleadingly recounted elsewhere; and over such forgotten periods as his conciliatory role in the Party early in his leadership, I have felt my interpretation so unfamiliar today as to require rather ample evidence.

A political biographer should show how the world looked to his subject, in order to explain why he took the decisions he did; and should assess as objectively as possible his proper place in the history of his country and his times. It is not easy to be both interpreter and judge. I have tried to understand and not denigrate his opponents, but political judgments cannot hope to command universal acceptance. Mine are those of an old sympathiser with Gaitskell's views and an old admirer of the man: better qualifications no doubt for the first role than for the second. I began my task expecting to find my broad concurrence tempered by many specific disagreements: those remaining are not concealed, but I have been impressed at how often, on thorough examination, his case proved stronger than I had anticipated. I have tried to be a fair-minded advocate and an honest as well as a sympathetic judge; others must assess the outcome.

· P.M.W.

Oxford
January 1978

ACKNOWLEDGMENTS

MY first debt is to Baroness Gaitskell and to her husband's literary executors, the Rt Hon. Roy Jenkins and the late Rt Hon. Anthony Crosland, for selecting me to write his biography and giving me the run of Hugh Gaitskell's voluminous papers and his diary. Other members of his family have been very helpful, particularly his brother, Sir Arthur Gaitskell, his sister, Lady Ashton, and his daughter, Mrs McNeal.

My colleagues the Warden and Fellows of Nuffield College, Oxford, provided a very convenient and congenial environment and the Social Science Research Council helped financially in the early stages. Librarians were helpful at Transport House, at the BBC Written Archives Centre at Caversham, at the LSE, and at the *Daily Telegraph* and *Daily Express* press-cutting libraries, as well as at my own college. I am grateful to my successive research assistants, Christine Woodland, Mary Tyerman, Tony Humphris, John Allt and Andrew Cleaver; and to my incomparable secretary Jean Brotherhood.

Many people in politics, the Civil Service and elsewhere (named in the list of interviews) were generous with their time. I am greatly obliged to them all, and especially to those whose personal political views were different from Gaitskell's or from my own. In addition several of them kindly gave me useful original material—batches of his letters, or memoranda or contemporary diaries of their own which they allowed me to use: particularly Austen Albu, Sir Vaughan Berry, the Rt Hon. Lord Boyle, Dr F. E. Budd, Dr D. E. Butler, Lady Cannon, Sir Norman Chester, Richard Cleaver, Mrs Durbin, the Rt Hon. Lord Gordon Walker, Mrs Grant, George Martelli, the Rt Hon. Christopher Mayhew, J. B. Orrick, the Rt Hon. Lord Pannell, Lord Roberthall, Cyril Robinson, the Rt Hon. William Rodgers, Professor Arthur Schlesinger Jr, the Rt Hon. George Strauss, Sir Vincent Tewson, Mrs Watson (for photographs) and the Rt Hon. Sir Kenneth Younger. I am grateful to the British Library of Political and Economic Science at LSE for permission to use and quote from Hugh Dalton's unpublished diaries which are deposited there. I have also seen a number of letters and jottings in the possession of a close friend of his later years. Three sources were quite invaluable: Sir Arthur Gaitskell provided several of his brother's forty-year-old letters; Alastair Hetherington, as editor of the *Guardian*, had records of his frequent conversations with the Leader of the Opposition which he made available to me; and the late Rt Hon. Richard Crossman gave me free access to his back-bench diaries, saying that there would be no point in keeping them and then withholding them from the biographers of major figures. I am grateful to the Labour Party for permission to reproduce the 1960 statement on Party Objects intended to reaffirm, amplify and clarify Clause IV.

I wish to thank Hugh Gaitskell's family, Mrs Sam Watson, Mr George Martelli, Mrs Anthony Crosland, Mr Geoffrey Goodman, the Rt Hon. Douglas Jay, the Rt Hon. Roy Jenkins, and the Labour Party Library at Transport House for kindly supplying illustrations, and also acknowledge the following for permission to reproduce plates as listed: Erich Auerbach, ARPS, 45; Black Star, 36; Camera Press, 40; Central Press Photos, 14; *Evening Standard*, 26; Express Newspapers Ltd, 56; Edith Tudor Hart, 24; Keystone Press Agency Ltd, 16, 17, 23, 25, 29a, 54, 61; LIFE © Time Inc. 1979, 41 (photo by Mark Kauffman), 50 (photo by Larry Burrows); *Newcastle Chronicle and Journal*, 46; Ivor Nicholas Photography, 47; *Northern Echo*, 19; Lawrence Parton, Grimsby, 58; Petrochemicals Ltd, 18; Popperfoto, 9, 28, 42, 44, 48, 59; Portman Press Bureau Ltd, 34; Press Association, 29b, 32, 52; Punjab Photo Service, New Delhi, 39; Radio Times Hulton Picture Library, 8, 15, 27; Sport and General Press Agency Ltd, 49; Syndication International Ltd, London, 22, 37, 55, 57, 63; Three Star Press Agency, 53; Topix, 64; UPI/Popperfoto, 31, 35, 62; Verity Press Features, 30; George Wimpey and Co. Ltd, 43. Cartoons on pp. 287 and 321, and the endpapers, by Vicky, are reproduced by kind permission of Mirror Group Newspapers, on p. 416 by Abraham Abu, and on p. 561 by Emwood and the *Daily Mail*.

Lastly, I am grateful for the helpful comments of many people who have read the MS in whole or large part at various stages: the Rt Hon. Lord Armstrong, Vernon Bogdanor, Lord Briggs, Michael Brock, David Butler, Martin Cannon, the late Rt Hon. Anthony Crosland, Elizabeth Durbin, Lawrence Freedman, Lady Gaitskell, David Goldey, A. H. Halsey, David Henderson, the Rt Hon. Roy Jenkins, Mrs McNeal, Sir Leslie Murphy, Patrick Renshaw, Lord Roberthall, David Robertson, Robert Skidelsky, John Street, Nita Watts and Laurence Whitehead. I owe a great debt to Eleanor Brock for volunteering to compile the index, and to her, Stephen Reilly and John Street for reading the proofs. They have frequently saved me from mistakes and infelicities, for those that remain in the wording the responsibility is entirely mine.

ABBREVIATIONS

The following abbreviations occur in the text (see also p. 793 for source abbreviations):

AEU	Amalgamated Engineering Union (now AUEW)
ARP	Air raid precautions
ASSET	Association of Supervisory Staffs, Executives and Technicians (now ASTMS)
CAP	Common Agricultural Policy (of the EEC)
CDS	Campaign for Democratic Socialism
CIA	Central Intelligence Agency (of the United States)
CIGS	Chief of the Imperial General Staff
CLP	Constituency Labour Party
CND	Campaign for Nuclear Disarmament
CP	Communist Party
ECA	European Co-operation Administration (of the United States)
ECOSOC	Economic and Social Council (of the United Nations)
EDC	European Defence Community
EEC	European Economic Community (the Common Market)
EFTA	European Free Trade Area
EOKA	Greek Cypriot guerrilla movement
EPC	Economic Policy Committee (of the British Cabinet)
EPU	European Payments Union
ERP	European Recovery Program (of the United States)
ETU	Electrical Trades Union (now EEPTU)
ICFC	Industrial and Commercial Finance Corporation
ICI	Imperial Chemical Industries
ICS	Indian Civil Service
ILO	International Labour Organisation
ILP	Independent Labour Party
IMF	International Monetary Fund
ITV	Independent Television
LLY	Labour League of Youth
LSE	London School of Economics and Political Science
MEW	Ministry of Economic Warfare
MFP	Ministry of Fuel and Power
MoI	Ministry of Information

NCB	National Coal Board
NEC	National Executive Committee (of the Labour Party)
NEDC	National Economic Development Council
NFRB	New Fabian Research Bureau
NHS	National Health Service
NOP	National Opinion Polls
NUDAW	National Union of Distributive and Allied Workers (now USDAW)
NUGMW	National Union of General and Municipal Workers
NUJ	National Union of Journalists
NUM	National Union of Mineworkers
NUPE	National Union of Public Employees
NUR	National Union of Railwaymen
OEEC	Organisation for European Economic Co-operation
PLP	Parliamentary Labour Party
PPE	Philosophy, Politics and Economics (at Oxford)
PPS	Parliamentary Private Secretary
PWE	Political Warfare Executive
RPM	Resale Price Maintenance
RSA	Rest of the Sterling Area (apart from the United Kingdom)
SCUA	Suez Canal Users Association
SEATO	South East Asia Treaty Organisation
SLE	Systemic *Lupus erythematosus*
SOE	Special Operations Executive
SSIP	Society for Socialist Information and Propaganda
T&GWU	Transport and General Workers Union
TSSA	Transport Salaried Staffs Association
TUC	Trades Union Congress (and by extension its General Council)
UCL	University College, London
UNRRA	United Nations Relief and Rehabilitation Association
USDAW	Union of Shop, Distributive and Allied Workers
VFS	Victory for Socialism
WEA	Workers Educational Association
Y voters	Persons becoming qualified by age to vote during the life of the current electoral register

INTRODUCTION

HUGH Gaitskell had led the Labour Party for exactly seven years when, almost on the threshold of 10 Downing Street, he was struck down by a fatal illness. His ministerial experience was very limited: a year and a half in junior office, two and a half as head of a Department, less than two at the Treasury, only one in the Cabinet. He led his Party in but one general election: to a heavy defeat. Yet he was honoured at his death as no mere Leader of the Opposition had been before, and is still remembered with a respect by many opponents, and a devotion by many admirers, that is unmatched among his contemporaries.

His career was short but meteoric. He had sat in the House for only five years when he became Chancellor of the Exchequer, the shortest such parliamentary apprenticeship since Pitt; and for only ten when he was elected to lead his party, the shortest in modern times. Since Labour became a major party, he is the only leader chosen by a substantial majority – and the only one ever challenged subsequently for re-election.

The paradoxes go further back. Born to a family of soldiers and empire-builders, his strong sense of fairness and equality made him a Socialist. Unsuccessful in competing for scholarships to Winchester and Oxford, he became a university teacher, then a rare academic achievement. Undistinguished and unobtrusive at school, he was to be one of the most embattled and controversial of politicians. Keen on golf and literature as an undergraduate, he worked for the TUC in the General Strike; and the shy and sensitive public-schoolboy depended politically on the confidence and loyalty of trade unionists, especially the miners who preferred him to a man of more dazzling gifts from among their own ranks. A Socialist, Gaitskell risked his political life for the American alliance; an admirer of the United States, he favoured a controlled economy; an ardent libertarian, he believed in strong disciplined political parties; the least insular of Labour leaders, he became the hero of the Party's Little Englanders. His public image was one of cold aloofness: it was less like his true personality than that of almost any other major political figure of the century. No 'desiccated calculating machine', Hugh Gaitskell in private was lively, warm and pleasure-loving. In public affairs his problems came from too much emotionalism rather than too little. He always detested trimming, and sometimes gambled to the point of recklessness for causes he thought right. Temperament made him seek drastic solutions, but reason made him mistrust extremes; and in rejecting the narrower values and prejudices of his class, he never became a vengeful apostate.

He led an argumentative and indeed fissiparous Party in the difficult conditions of apparently unsuccessful opposition, and only at the very end did his reward come within sight. His turbulent reign as Party leader illustrates the problems of one who tries to use his authority creatively, rather than merely registering conflicting pressures. Gaitskell was a leader of principle, and a committed educator. To become an effective instrument of 'conscience and reform', his Party had to shake off the outlook of a band of propagandists without acquiring that of a mere machine to administer the existing order. He endangered his own position to make his followers face the implications and responsibilities of that difficult trans-formation. He insisted that the Party must attend to the concerns of ordi-nary people, and faced imperturbably, though not with indifference, the charge of betraying purposes which few of its voters had ever demanded.

His political style can be criticised, as well as his policies. A passionate man himself, he often misjudged or offended the emotions of others. Thoroughly professional in equipping himself with the necessary skills for political leadership, he was not always an adroit tactician. Well aware that governments must act in circumstances which can rarely be foreseen, he could be pedantic about detailed policy-making in advance. Judicious and careful in weighing up the consequences of action, his final commitments were so wholehearted and so forcibly expressed that his attitudes were frequently misunderstood. Out of office, he would not propose policies he could not carry out in power; Harold Macmillan, who found his style as uncongenial as his views, said he missed all the fun of opposition by behaving as if he were in government.

He believed that the aim of political activity was to win power in order to govern according to clear values and principles. But the clarity and candour which impressed his admirers were sometimes found abrasive and divisive by others, for he would not bend before breezes of short-term sentiment in either Party or electorate, and took great political risks when he thought principle required it. He lived up to his family motto, *Fortitudo et Integritas* – and sometimes seemed to be trying to impose it on the whole Party. He sought to win power by convincing people through reasoned argument that his purposes and policies were right and relevant; for he despised the professional public relations techniques of exploiting the irrational, as well as more traditional forms of demagogy. Accused of elitism, in fact he paid voters the compliment of taking seriously their judgment, intelligence and capacity for idealism. Britain since the second world war has rarely (if ever) found political leadership to match the quality of inspiration which, towards the end, Hugh Gaitskell offered.

PART ONE

THE MAKING OF A DEMOCRATIC SOCIALIST

'A life of Hugh is bound to be dull, because he was so damned blameless'
(A COLLEAGUE OF HG IN THE 1930s, TO THE AUTHOR)

THE MAKING OF A
DEMOCRATIC SOCIALIST

CHAPTER 1

'SEEKING SOMETHING TO FIGHT FOR' 1906–28

'I always regarded you as a dreamer and not a do-er'
(A BOYHOOD FRIEND WHEN HG BECAME CHANCELLOR)

i Childhood: Homeless but Happy

HUGH TODD-NAYLOR GAITSKELL was born on 9 April 1906 at 3 Airlie Gardens, Kensington, the son of an Indian civil servant. His family originally came from Cumberland, and derive their name from a local word which meant a sheiling (enclosure) for goats. His middle name came from his godfather who was in the ICS; he dropped the hyphen in boyhood. The Gaitskells included mercers, curriers, clergymen and a Whitehaven sea-captain. An older branch lived at Yeorton Hall near Egremont (from which Hugh's widow was to take her title); it was sold around 1870 to pay racing debts.[1] Those relatives dispersed to California and South America. When Hugh's elder brother visited Medellin in Colombia for the International Labour Organisation in 1963, he was given the wrong key for his hotel room and found it belonged to Maurice Gaitskell, a distant cousin speaking only Spanish.

A younger branch moved to Bermondsey as distillers, and one of them, Thomas (who had once eloped to Gretna with an heiress), raised a regiment of Surrey Yeomanry in the Napoleonic Wars. Among its officers was his younger brother, Henry, Hugh's great-grandfather. Most of Hugh's immediate forebears served in the Regular Army, often in India, and their descendants settled round the Empire. Henry's son, Colonel James Gandy Gaitskell, retired to Cheltenham. His own son Arthur, Hugh's father, went to a school for officers' sons there, and then to New College, Oxford. Arthur Gaitskell senior abandoned the military tradition, and joined the Indian Civil Service without taking his degree. Apart from occasional furloughs, he spent the rest of his short life in Burma, where he arrived at nineteen in 1889 – four years after annexation – and left in August 1914 as Commissioner for Settlement and Land Records in Rangoon. He then came home on sick leave suffering from sprue, a tropical disease from which he died in Scotland on 1 December 1915 at forty-five.

Everyone describes Arthur Gaitskell as a model of integrity, and he left a strong impression on his children even though they were not often together. He was a loving father to them by the standards of the day, particularly affectionate to his daughter; but his other juvenile relatives regarded with awe this good-looking, intelligent, serious and silent man, who gave up playing bridge because he was winning too much money at it. Responsibility and conscientiousness, devotion to the public service and the sense of an obligation to work for the less fortunate were qualities inherited by both his sons and translated into different circumstances and values: for Arthur junior, the difficult start and successful management of a famous peasant co-operative in the Sudan; for Hugh, workers' education and, later, politics.

There was another side to Arthur Gaitskell senior, whom the Burmese called 'Tiger Gaitskell'.[2] In 1898, on his first furlough, he met on the boat to Japan the young daughter of the Consul-General in Shanghai, George Jamieson, who came from a farming family on Speyside in Banffshire. A poor but able youth, Jamieson had been encouraged by his village schoolmaster to go on to Aberdeen University, and had risen to one of the top posts in the Consular Service, where he also became a distinguished Chinese scholar, as well as winning a prize – open to world-wide competition – for an essay on bi-metallism. After a romantic pursuit to Scotland, Arthur Gaitskell married Adelaide Mary ('Addie') Jamieson. She was much younger than he was, and lived until 1956. Two of their three children were born in Rangoon: Dorothy Margaret (Jane to her brothers and Bunty to everyone else) in 1899 and Arthur in 1900; Hugh, nicknamed Sam, came five and a half years later.

Their mother was a very different character from their father: vivacious, charming, sociable and – from natural high spirits rather than social rebellion – often highly unconventional. She once embarrassed her husband by absenting herself from her own dinner party and, when a prominent leader of Rangoon society, she went out one night and mixed up all the street signs. Though quite conservative, and with a strong sense of social hierarchy, she made many Burmese friends when that was very unusual. She was devoted to her children, especially her sons, and when she came home to England their normal orderly life was disrupted, they were indulged with sweets and all discipline was thrown to the winds. To her Hugh owed the gaiety and friendliness which were so familiar to those who knew him.

The family had many links with Burma. Harry Todd-Naylor, Hugh's father's cousin, whose Yorkshire gentry forebears had fought for Charles I, served out there as a Deputy Commissioner and became Hugh's godfather. At thirteen Hugh acquired a stepfather who was in business in Burma: Gilbert Wodehouse, first cousin of P.G., nephew of Graham Wallas the early sociologist, and schoolfellow of Clement Attlee. A third link was Hubert Ashton, Cambridge triple Blue and President of the MCC, who married Hugh's sister in 1927; after many years in the Burmah Oil Company he became after the war Conservative MP for Chelmsford and Parliamentary Private Secretary to R. A. Butler. Hugh was not indifferent to Burma (he was asked to read a book on it before publication in 1938) but the strong connections had – surprisingly – no apparent influence on his life, outlook or policy.

Separation from his parents possibly did have such an influence, though if so it should have had more impact on his brother and sister. The children had no home life in the ordinary sense. Their father died when Hugh was nine and for most of those years they were in different continents, together only when Arthur Gaitskell had his long leaves in England. Their mother came back rather more frequently, but apart from one exceptional year Hugh's entire childhood from the age of two and a half was spent boarded out with relations or at boarding schools. Hugh's life shows no sign of neurotic striving; 'entirely natural and straightforward,' wrote Maurice Bowra, who knew him from the age of eighteen, 'he lacked those inner conflicts which disturb so many young people.'[3a] Yet it is striking that a very large number of famous leaders, notably British Prime Ministers and other prominent politicians, have had a childhood bereft of parents.[4]

Hugh spent his first winter in Burma, where a fine family photograph shows him in the arms of an aunt, with his parents and a dozen servants. Then his father came home on leave, bringing with him the child's devoted Indian nurse 'Mary Ayah', and they lived for fifteen months in Cheltenham. Revisiting it forty years later, Hugh thought it an attractive town, though he found it 'still full of faint, early childhood memories, not particularly pleasant ones. Staying with stuffy relations and going to church in a stiff sort of way.'[5] During school terms the three children went to live with their father's first cousin, Mrs Pike, in a large North Oxford house. 'Cousin May', who came from Achill Island where she was the local squiress, was kind but strict, and her household was disciplined and fairly puritanical. One pot of jam had to last a week; and there was much stress on truthfulness, good manners and consideration for social inferiors. The austerities were tempered by Cousin May's daughter Kathleen, whom the children adored, and by a sprightly young nanny, who used to play with them and sing to them at bedtime: old Scots ballads for Bunty, music-hall songs for Arthur, and hymns for Hugh. (He once startled a strange lady in the street by chanting to her from his pram: 'Soon shall you and I be lying/Each within our narrow tomb'.)

For holidays they went to other relatives. Often they spent Christmas with their maternal aunts in rather grand detached houses in London, ruled by strange nannies. The older Gaitskell children felt themselves somewhat poor relations (they were given five shillings between them to buy presents for eighteen people); and Hugh, as the youngest of all, was much teased by his cousins. At Easter, and some Christmases, they would go to their mother's aunt and uncle who lived at Kinermony, a farm near Aberlour on Speyside. Later in life Hugh often recalled those holidays: 'Some of my happiest memories are of night train journeys to Scotland, of breakfast in the train crossing the Forth Bridge ... [and] playing for hours beside a burn that splashed down the hillside into the Spey.'[6] Summer was best of all. Every year until 1919 George Jamieson, their only living grandparent, took the dower house at Brancaster Staithe on the Norfolk coast – the house that they thought of more than any other as home. On rare, treasured occasions their parents would join them; more often their mother alone did so. They bicycled, fished and played with their cousins who stayed near by.

The Gaitskell children did not question the frequent separation from their parents, and their childhood was happy in spite of it. For the two older ones it meant a good deal of responsibility as well as more autonomy than was normal for children then; Hugh was the cherished baby of the family, relatively sheltered until he went to Winchester. Family relationships were warm when they were all together, and, with the parents so often away, the three children were deeply attached to one another. Arthur was always the leader and Hugh his devoted champion and follower. Nearly fifty years later he wrote to a friend: 'when I was a boy I loved my brother, no one else, and no one else would do.' Arthur was the more fiery and volatile, Hugh much more placid. But also stubborn. Arthur, fearing to be late for school, would be driven frantic by Cousin May's table rules about finishing everything on your plate; Hugh, too young for school, would sit it out until a hot plate had to be brought for his meal, and sometimes he even won. Later, a game of bridge occasionally led to a row, with both the elder children marching off and leaving Hugh to play all four hands. Though their paths diverged later in life, the close relations between the three were never broken.

When Hugh was five, he, his sister and their nanny (Arthur was left behind) went out to Burma for a year, to the hill station at Maymyo where their father was working. It was a great change from the relatively secluded life at Oxford, with other colonial children to play with, parties to go to and ponies to ride furiously. Mary Ayah returned to help with the children, while their parents pursued a gay social life. In 1912 the whole family returned and took rooms in Oxford for a few weeks. Arthur Gaitskell senior bought from the bicycle shop of William Morris (later Lord Nuffield) a temperamental motor-car, which disliked steep hills and would climb them only by zigzagging backwards – still possible when roads were quite empty. Then the parents returned to Burma. Cousin May had gone home to Ireland and the children stayed with her unmarried sister, Cousin Cis (Miss Todd-Naylor), at another North Oxford house. Hugh went as a day-boy to the Dragon School (known as Lynam's) from six to eight, and was a boarder from eight to thirteen.[7]

Later he described the Dragon as a highly unorthodox and notably unconventional preparatory school.[8] C. C. ('Skipper') Lynam, the headmaster, was an ardent radical, devoted to the memory of Gladstone, who wore a red tie and seaman's jersey and concentrated on encouraging independence and self-confidence in his 200 pupils. Unlike Summerfields, the rival and more conventional Oxford prep school to which Harold Macmillan went, Lynam's admitted a few girls (unheard-of then) and the sons of local tradesmen as well as those of dons and professional people. Masters were called by their nicknames and formal discipline was little stressed, though classroom work was taken seriously. Everyone there then remembers it as a very friendly place. Hugh followed his brother and inherited Arthur's nickname, the Goat. Like Arthur, he and his best friend Charles Plumb (son of a bishop and later a civil servant) were favourites of the Skipper, whose tastes for loud ties and boating they shared. To one sporting friend Hugh was 'a nice little chap, quiet and unassuming ... rather friendless'. But another had a stronger impression of him as 'the personification of decency', the natural arbiter in any quarrel between boys, and the leader in a protest against some injustice by a master.[9] Later in life, too, his qualities were slow to reveal themselves to everyone.

He discovered quite young in various ways that his own situation, far from being typical, was one of exceptional privilege. Searching for early signs foreshadowing the future, friends later recalled some of his juvenile encounters with poverty;[10] and he himself never forgot the friend's father who, hearing he was going to Winchester, told him: 'You don't know how lucky you are—only one boy in ten thousand is going to have the opportunities which lie before you.'[11] It shocked him, he claimed, into 'the first awareness of a social problem'.[8] But at this tender age he was an ordinary typical little boy who showed no sign of becoming a fledgling politician (though there were a few at the school, and Hugh did come second to one of them, J. P. W. Mallalieu—son of a Liberal MP—in a public-speaking contest). Contemporaries commented, however, at prep school, Winchester and Oxford alike, that he was unusually unpossessive and behaved as a 'natural socialist', treating everyone as equal and everything as held in common.[12]

ii Winchester: Quiet Rebel

Hugh followed his brother to Winchester as he had to the Dragon School. He was never obviously unhappy but clearly found it much less congenial, though it left many enduring marks. The problems of adolescence were more than usually acute for him, for even the limited family life he had known was now wholly disrupted. His mother had stayed in England for four years after Arthur Gaitskell senior died in 1915, but then she returned to Burma to remarry. Then when grandfather George Jamieson died, the children lost the adult relative who meant most to them, and with whom they had so often stayed in London and Norfolk. Bunty looked after Hugh at first, but in 1921 she also went out to Burma, returning periodically mainly for his sake. Arthur was at Oxford, and then went off to the Sudan in 1923, and for the first time Hugh was entirely alone.

Before the other two went abroad, the young Gaitskells had spent their holidays together. In 1919 they stayed in County Kilkenny with Protestant Irish family friends from Burma (where Hugh defied their hostess, whose temper was legendary, in defence of his brother who had spilt some water on the stairs – she astonished and relieved them all by bursting out laughing). After 1920 they discovered Exmoor – where Canon Wodehouse, father of their mother's second husband, had been a rector – and rejoiced in the contrast to the flat Norfolk countryside. About that time Hugh picked up dancing at a Christmas party;[13a] he always remained a passionate enthusiast for it, 'dancing himself to death like a dervish', as Harold Macmillan is supposed to have said. After Arthur's departure, Hugh sometimes holidayed with school friends, or invited one of them to accompany him to stay with his Martelli cousins at Brancaster. The Royal West Norfolk Golf Club, close to Sandringham, was an elite preserve which the youngsters had had to themselves during the war, but where they were not made very welcome after it; but at nineteen, against strong competition from his seniors, Hugh won the Prince of Wales Cup. He and his cousin George became attached to a red-haired local belle, Felicity Cory-Wright (a daughter of Sir Herbert Beerbohm Tree, she appears in a well-known poem of Rupert Brooke); years later, to his daughter, Hugh called her 'the adored of my youth'. He taught her children to play cricket (a game he never himself enjoyed). He acted with enthusiasm in charades, and showed considerable talents at pencil games as well as golf. His idealistic side was apparent, too, and, when he became Chancellor, Felicity – a staunch Tory – wrote 'I always regarded you as a dreamer and not a do-er'.[14]

At Winchester his career began inauspiciously, in the sanatorium with mumps before his official admission, and it continued without distinction. The intellectual star of the school in his day was his junior Richard Crossman, his classroom neighbour one year; the sporting heroes were the Ashtons, one of whom married Hugh's sister. Chatting to them once at a cricket match, Bunty vividly recalls Hugh saying, 'I hope all my friends see Claude Ashton talking to us'. He became a prefect in H House, Culver's Close, where the prefects' room contains a plaque in his memory ('greatly honoured ... for his courage and integrity'). But he made much less mark there than Arthur, recently head of the house.

Winchester was a nursery for the professional upper-middle class, and has been called 'of all public schools the most aloof and intellectual'.[15] It educated rather fewer sons of old pupils and far more university scholarship winners than its leading rivals, and it instilled a strong sense of public service in its future judges, administrators, ambassadors and professors. A high value was placed on intellectual honesty, coherence and clarity, none at all on idle aristocratic eccentricity or commercial thrusting. Sometimes socially shy but always intellectually self-confident, Wykehamists have been stereotyped as high-minded, argumentative proselytisers — or as prim and dedicated prigs. Reinforcing his strict upbringing, Winchester's heavy emphasis on self-restraint helped Hugh to keep under firm control the strong emotions that seethed beneath a placid surface; so that an American who was a close friend at New College could call him 'a very thorough Wykehamist though superficially rebellious'.[16a] That was only partially true, for his reaction against one side of Winchester was lasting. But in other aspects the discipline served him well in politics; and in many ways — his high-minded sense of duty, his notable courtesy and self-control, his rational style — he fitted the ideal mould.

Though far more conservative then than today, the school was slowly changing.[17] One quite critical contemporary of Hugh's called it

> much less philistine than most of its contemporaries. Intellect was not despised as at Rugby or Harrow. You could reach the top of the school and be respected if you had a good brain, even if you couldn't lift a cricket bat off the ground.[18]

Boys could now specialise in science or history as well as in classics; and there was an active cultural life, with flourishing musical, archaeological, natural history and debating societies, and crowded lectures on Italian painting by the headmaster, which inspired among others the future Lord Clark. Hugh was best at history, for which he won a prize. The Dragon School, which sent many boys to Winchester, heard reports of him 'working very hard, as usual'.[19] He played football with and other sports without enthusiasm, but (like Mrs Iremonger's Prime Ministers) he much preferred individual games such as golf and tennis. One terrible disappointment was to do badly through illness in a senior steeplechase he had been tipped to win. His fellows found him more serious-minded than most, notably fair and honest, unusually friendly to his juniors, and a relaxed and amusing companion. Only very occasionally did a streak of ruthlessness show.[20] He was quite popular, without enemies;[21] but no one ever expected great things of him. 'Quiet, gentle, charming and very honest ... but one wouldn't look to him for any fireworks or leadership', was the view of a senior. The housemaster later wrote of 'a quiet, modest, studious and undemonstrative boy of whom no one could have predicted his future'; though as a prefect (by his appointment) he felt Hugh 'made his weight felt by quiet determination and a certain sweet reasonableness and sense of justice'.[22a]

The houses (of about forty boys) were very self-contained, for juniors were expected to make friends only in their own house.[23] Fortunately Trant's (as Culver's Close was usually known, after its founder) had and has a reputation for being 'more liberal, more grown-up and civilised' and less rigidly disciplined than any other.[24a] Plays were produced in alternate years, and Hugh's poetic and theatrical interests lasted all his life. Acting as a woman in Sophocles' *Antigone* (translated by his housemaster), he was stiff, awkward and over-rational; he sent his sister a photograph of himself, commenting (justly), 'Don't I look an idiot!'. A group of seniors read papers on literary subjects, and occasionally invited some prominent public figure to talk, such as Mrs Asquith, or John Drinkwater the poet. Hugh was active in house discussions, with a strong taste for argument and a combativeness in it which surprised and puzzled his friends. His brother and sister had always found him 'slightly annoyingly the man who was right – annoying because he usually *was* right'.[25] Now, a contemporary in the same house was exasperated by the mental agility with which he would 'frequently get the better of an argument, although he knew as well as you did that he was in the wrong!' Others remember his sarcastic, acid, inflammatory style, his bitterness about social inequality, and his liking for unpopular causes – defending trade unions, or criticising hunting, or attacking landlords or capitalists.

He was not explicitly political, though he himself believed that at Winchester his 'Liberal sympathies were quite evident'.[8] He is recorded as speaking three times in the school debating society, defending democracy in March 1923, and the next year supporting a vote of confidence in the first Labour Government – arguing that whatever the next one might be like, this one depended on Liberal support and was bound to be moderate.[26] He himself recalled only the third occasion, when in October 1923, soon after Italy invaded Corfu, he denounced Mussolini as a tyrant, an enemy of Britain and a likely architect of a new world war. His first political interest was in international affairs, and he was responsible for founding a branch of the League of Nations Union at Winchester. He later wrote – incidentally implying that he carried more weight than his contemporaries recall – that he had

used his influence with the leading figures in the school – the popular games-playing element, school prefects, etc., – to induce them to join. This made it fashionable and before long it had a membership of over 100 – a quarter of the whole school.[13b]

he really felt liberated. Many years later he wrote to a friend: ' "To thine own self be true" was the great creed of my developing phase at Oxford. And I still believe it is the most important thing of all.' His total change of life-style had for two years no overt political content at all, but he was quietly working out for himself the personal values to which he adhered for the rest of his life. When the moment of decision came in the General Strike, he knew without a moment's hesitation which side he was on.

He later painted his own picture of the university scene:

> Oxford in the middle twenties was gay, frivolous, stimulating, and tremendously alive ... it was a brief, blessed interval when the lives of the young were neither overshadowed by the consequences of the last war nor dominated by the fear of a future one. Most of us sighed with relief and settled down to the business of enjoying ourselves ... Politics, to tell the truth, were rather at a discount. We were in revolt all right — against Victorianism, Puritanism, stuffiness of any kind, but most of us weren't sufficiently bitter — or perhaps sufficiently serious — to be angry young men ... [in] the heavenly freedom of Oxford [revolt] took the form of an outburst of scepticism, a mistrust of dogma, a dislike of sentimentality and of over-emotional prejudices or violent crusades.
>
> We were, therefore, suspicious of general ideas, especially when these involved some mystical, collective, common good. We professed the happiness of the individual as the only acceptable social aim. As for personal values, truth was our supreme object and intellectual integrity was the greatest of virtues.[32b]

A good-looking, curly-haired, friendly youth with a charming smile, unobtrusively intelligent and highly gregarious, Gaitskell deliberately broke away from the narrow clique of New College Wykehamists and made friends elsewhere in the college and — unusually for those days — in the university. As he later wrote to his daughter, there was a sharp split 'between the "hearties" who played games and were dull, & the aesthetes who didn't and weren't'.[38a] By taste and by friendships he was close to the latter, soon adopting their conventions, abandoning the sober suit and flower in buttonhole for the fashionable wide 'Oxford bags' and even puce ties. His tastes were literary and artistic, though not musical. He read widely and discriminatingly. Housman was a favourite poet, Proust and D. H. Lawrence his most admired authors (he later read Lawrence's letters through twice over as soon as they came out); and he was sensitive to literary style, though his own was notable for precision and lucidity rather than elegance. As secretary of the Mermaids, the New College play-reading society, he broke with custom by bringing in modern authors like Ibsen and Strindberg; more frivolously, he kept up his liking for elaborate

charades (a favourite pastime in school holidays) through another flourishing college society.

He made friends in many different circles, though (then, as later) he
would not mix them up. He was to describe his first year as 'fairly normal
— playing golf, making friends, amusing myself ... I did not do a great deal
of work either in my first or second year, but enjoyed myself at parties
quite a lot'.[8] He played tennis frequently and cards occasionally, punted
on the river and took long walks in summer, and went often to the theatre
or cinema (though not to concerts).[39] One ambition was to win a golf
Blue; and he joined an exclusive dining club, the Gridiron. He had a little
money, and he was anxious to break with public school constraints and
extend his social contacts. Years later he wrote to his brother:

> I think it was your experiences at Winchester that stopped you getting
> what you might have done out of Oxford. You say Poverty interfered
> with your social life. Only a Wykehamist would allow it too [*sic*]. It is
> true that I was better off than you were but the fact that I joined the
> Grid was never of any importance at all. Plenty of well off Wykeham-
> ists joined too and because they remained Wykehamists never had a
> proper social life.[35a]

Hugh was determined that artificial barriers should not restrict that:
'He had no sense of social distinctions, and this was not the result of intellectual conviction but the cause of it. He was a natural democrat who took
people on their merits.'[3f] While he regarded having a wide range of
acquaintances as part of his emancipation, his more conventional friends
thought some of the others distinctly scruffy. He delighted in the eccentrici-
ties of John Betjeman, whom he knew from the Dragon School, and he
moved occasionally on the fringe of a homosexual set whose tastes were
then quite prevalent among the aesthetes. At one of his first meetings with
Elizabeth Harman (now Countess of Longford), they sat under a haystack
talking about Oscar Wilde. Finding her sympathetic, he said: 'I'm so glad.
If you hadn't thought that way, I don't think we could have gone on being
friends.'

In practice Gaitskell spent much more time with girls than most undergraduates did. They were still new in Oxford, and even chaperones had not
entirely vanished. But he sharply denied having been a ladykiller, saying
that like most Wykehamists he 'was far too diffident and shy'.[8] Years later
he told his daughter: 'emotionally it was chiefly romantic, divine, most
pure calf love for women older than myself!'[38a]

Though he was on the aesthetes' side of the great Oxford divide, he was
not firmly in any one camp. He persuaded one friend to stand (successfully)
for office in the Junior Common Room as someone acceptable to both
parties, and light-heartedly told another (twice) that they qualified only as

semi-aesthetes because they both disliked striped ties. He took one close friend – Jim Orrick, a Maryland postgraduate student of English literature who was years older than himself – for all-day walks on the Downs to cure him of being too thorough an aesthete. He seems to have been the sort of person to whom others took their troubles;[3f] and though no prig, he already displayed the conscientious prefect's concern for his friends' right development – which Orrick called long afterwards 'a passion for improving the human race, beginning with me'.[16b]

Among senior members Hugh's first close friend was Maurice Bowra. He had been up at New College with Arthur and was now Dean (later Warden) of Wadham, an overwhelming personality and for years one of Oxford's most prominent figures. Largely through him, Gaitskell met literary lions like Auden, Connolly, Day Lewis and Pryce-Jones. Bowra stimulated his frivolous, exuberant side (and also his lasting interest in and admiration for the ancient Greeks). Yet the influence was not all one way, for in the General Strike it was to be the undergraduate who altered the behaviour of the don.[3g]

Even in those carefree first two years, there was a strong serious element. 'You could almost feel your mind unfolding,' said Gaitskell later;[40] and again: 'The great thing for me was the flowering of intellect and personality – much repressed at Winchester. Feeling oneself develop was exciting – also getting rid of a lot of adolescent shames.'[38a] It was a time of self-discovery in many ways, particularly in developing his own philosophy of life: 'We *did* think & talk a *lot* about morals including basic politics, but more I think *individual* morality, sex etc.'[38b] He was never to change the fundamental outlook which he worked out then and immediately afterwards: 'out of all the confusion of adolescence values *do* emerge – at least they did for me – but not until I was in my early 20s. And on the whole I have stuck by them.'[38c]

Absorbed in his personal intellectual and moral development, Gaitskell had no time for undergraduate politics. His brother had told him that the Union, the famous debating society, was a waste of time and so he never became a member. Though political clubs flourished, he was slow to join the Labour Club and took no active part. Even when friends with whom he had dined went on to a political meeting, he did not always accompany them.[39a] Nevertheless, his adventurous choice of an academic subject was a sign of the way his interests were moving. 'Modern Greats', now usually called PPE (Philosophy, Politics and Economics), was newly established; and when Gaitskell took Finals in 1927 he had fewer than 200 predecessors. Many traditionalists had stoutly opposed its introduction, making its tutors and students determined to show that relevance was not incompatible with rigour.

Gaitskell had no time for metaphysics, and little interest in philosophy.

'I never really took to it,' he wrote long afterwards to his younger daughter.[41] About this time he wrote to his brother:

> You seem to worry a great deal about things to which there never will be an answer—I mean Ultimate Objects, the Good, God etc.; as you know I never bother much about such things but try to confine myself to questions which can be answered in some way ... After all in spite of its philosophical unsoundness utilitarianism has a good deal to be said for it and serves as a good enough basis for practical affairs.[35b]

In his first term he went for elementary economics to Lionel Robbins, who called it 'a subject deadly for both teacher and taught'. He would sit on Robbins's sofa reddening with suppressed mirth at the mild impertinences of his Australian fellow-pupil until his decorous Wykehamist reticence broke down in peals of helpless laughter.[42] Later his economics tutor was the young, eccentric and stimulating Harold Salvesen, with whom he became friendly. In political organisation, he wrote essays for the Warden, H. A. L. Fisher; the treatment was competent, high-minded and far from radical. Yet, although the solemn and uninspiring subjects gave little scope for showing it, Gaitskell's outlook was already shifting.

Early in the summer of 1925, sitting on the Downs with their mother on his first home leave from the Sudan, Arthur was happily holding forth about his triumphs at polo and his dinner with the Governor-General when to his astonishment his young brother and devoted admirer told him forcefully that his life and values were altogether futile and worthless. That first challenge to his inherited imperialist attitudes was to have a lasting impact on him.[43] Later that summer at Brancaster, Jim Orrick had an absurd but violent argument with Hugh about snobbery, over the appropriate address for a letter to his staircase servant.[16b] A year afterwards, at the start of the summer term in 1926, Hugh tried in vain to explain his changing outlook to his friend Frank Pakenham, then an ardent Tory.[44] Just a week later the change became a matter of public commitment when the General Strike provoked a dramatic break in Gaitskell's Oxford existence. It was the first major turning point in his life.

iv   *The General Strike: Commitment to the Labour Movement*

The strike was a clash between the confused trade-union leadership of a united working class, and a narrow-minded but determined government. The coalowners were truculent, short-sighted and inefficient employers; the miners worked for poor pay in bad and dangerous conditions, and after years of bitter industrial struggle they preferred fighting to negotiation,

were proud of their own solidarity, and expected workers in more vulnerable occupations to follow their lead without much question. Those workers, and a good many middle-class people too, had a bad conscience about
them. The cautious, rather short-sighted leaders of the TUC therefore
supported the miners in what they thought was an unusually large industrial dispute, and found themselves in a situation with no issue except
capitulation – or the attempted revolution which they did not want, had
not prepared, and could not have carried out. In contrast, the government
knew its own mind and meant to smash the trade union militants once for
all. The Prime Minister, Stanley Baldwin, was conciliatory in language but
determined in resisting compromise moves by the dangerous characters
like the Archbishop of Canterbury, and skilful in presenting the strike as
a challenge to the constitution. It was called off in nine days, but the miners
fought on alone for six months. Winston Churchill, hitherto the most intransigent Minister, now tried to bully the colliery companies into accepting reasonable terms, but against the rapacious and vengeful coalowners
Baldwin's skill and determination evaporated.[45]

In Oxford the strike and the government's appeal brought an immediate
response from the upper-middle-class undergraduate body.[46] Class bitterness was then intense, and at a college ball the year before, the young
gentlemen in their white ties and flowered buttonholes had been jeered by
rows of angry workers shouting 'enjoy yourselves while you can, it won't
last much longer'.[16b] Many students went off to drive trains or act as special
constables in order to defend the social order or save the nation from destruction, though many others did so rather in a spirit of fun or adventure.
The Vice-Chancellor even contemplated conscripting the undergraduate
population, and the hearties attempted to break up a rowdy protest meeting of the Labour Club (Gaitskell's presence is not recorded). But other
senior members were, like the Archbishop, thoroughly unhappy at the
bitter and divisive conflict.

Gaitskell had no doubts:

> I had been reading some Socialist theory ... but I did not follow day to
> day politics at all closely. Thus ... the impact of the Strike was sharp
> and sudden, a little like a war, in that everybody's lives were suddenly
> affected by a new unprecedented situation, which forced us to abandon
> plans for pleasure, to change our values and adjust our priorities.
>
> Above all we had to make a choice, and how we chose was a clear
> test of our political outlook ... all my sympathies were instinctively on
> the side of the miners, the unions, the Labour Party and the Left
> generally. It was their cause I wanted to help.[32c]

When Bowra protested that the strike would do the miners more harm than
good, the undergraduate replied firmly that he would not 'desert his side

just because it had miscalculated its means';[3c] and impressed the don enough for Bowra to go round vainly lobbying in favour of conciliation.[39] To Gaitskell, as Hugh Dalton wrote later, 'it was impossible for any generous spirit to be emotionally on the side of "the masters" '; and he had little tolerance for his many friends who saw matters differently.[47]

When Gaitskell sought leave to go off and work for the TUC, Warden Fisher refused, saying (according to Gaitskell at the time): 'Your arguments are well put and you have a strong case. But I have the power to prevent you going down and I propose to exercise it.' Furious, Gaitskell on his way out ran into Jim Orrick, told his tale, and asked what his friend meant to do. Nothing, replied Orrick, since Mr Baldwin's pretence that this was a revolution was blatantly fraudulent; but had it been true, he would have felt obliged to support the government. 'That's sheer vulgarity,' cried Gaitskell, angrier than ever: and did not speak to Orrick for a month. It was their only quarrel.[16b]

At G. D. H. Cole's house in Holywell, a dozen or so undergraduates had met to offer their services to the TUC. Gaitskell later described his enrolment:

> What could I do? Precious little. Speak at meetings? God forbid! Organise? Absolutely no experience. Had I got a car? No. Could I by any chance drive a car? Yes, I had learnt the year before. Then perhaps I could drive John Dugdale's ... as ... he could not spare much time ... I went off to the Oxford Strike Committee headquarters, got myself enrolled as a driver and received my instructions.[32c]

With a paid-up trade union card as a papermaker, he drove undergraduate speakers like Evan Durbin and John Parker to village meetings around Oxford, carried messages to Didcot with John Betjeman, who thought it all a great lark, and maintained liaison with London by ferrying Margaret Cole to and fro and bringing back copies of the TUC paper, the *British Worker*. Returning at night, she recalled with alarm his disconcerting speed at the nine right-angled turns in Benson village, 'most of which we seemed to take on two wheels', since returning after midnight might involve being confined to college at night. Once he did arrive late, failed to climb in, and was fined £1 despite 'a fierce verbal protest to the Warden ... that he was shockingly biassed'.[32d] His contemporaries could absent themselves with impunity on the other side, and that injustice still rankled decades later.[48]

Waiting about for hours in London, Margaret Cole took her young chauffeur to meet Labour personalities and intellectuals like R. H. Tawney, who later had a profound influence on him but at the time merely remarked on his driving: 'How dangerous it is to let young men take charge of projectiles.'[33a] The General Strike was an impressive introduction to the Labour Movement, reinforcing Gaitskell's developing outlook. After it

ended, he worked at raising money for the miners, locked out for another
terrible six months, and was proud of extracting 10s. from a staunchly Tory
old schoolfellow, David Eccles.[13b] Subsequently he came to see the strike
as demolishing 'the absurd "myth" of syndicalism', and its collapse as a
permanent warning that unplanned, emotional revolutionary activities led
to disaster.[49] But at the time, as he later recalled:

> It is wholly untrue that I deplored the strategy of the strike. I did not
> honestly think a great deal about it. I knew that once the chips were
> down my part was on the side of the strike. I considered the Govern-
> ment had behaved badly to the miners and that was that.[8]

His family were appalled. One cousin said over dinner: 'What we can't
forgive Hugh is betraying his class.'[50] But his mind was made up, and he
wrote to an astonished aunt: 'Henceforth my future is with the working
classes.'[8] [40]

For Gaitskell the strike was no nine days' wonder. Its impact was immediate as well as lasting, and it transformed his Oxford life. Determined
to escape from the conventional middle-class career mould expected by his
family and his school, he set out to obtain First Class Honours in order to
acquire the independence that would allow him to choose. Both in and out
of term he now began working very hard to make up for lost time. Spending an industrious Christmas vacation with the family friends in Ireland,
he rather resented their emphasis on grimy manual labour and the 'feeling
that I was regarded as "a lily of the field" '.[51a] In Oxford he was still able
to enjoy himself, for he was good at organising his time, but his priorities
were quite changed. He gave up serious golf, got down to his books by
9 a.m., and always seemed to be busy when friends visited his lodgings.[52]
Unlike most undergraduates he made no secret of his hopes.[16b]

The direction of his work changed as well as the intensity. He chose as
his special subject the history of the Labour Movement, finding in it the
same romantic appeal that Pakenham, his room-mate, found in Irish
Nationalism; one of his undergraduate essays on Chartism (finished at
4 a.m.) was published as a tiny book by the WEA in 1928.[53] He also became
active in a weekly discussion group for Socialist undergraduates which Cole,
his tutor, inaugurated and presided over until long after the war. They took
themselves very seriously, taking on the roles of Ministers in a Labour
government, and trying to visualise and handle for themselves the practical
problems of transforming society.

Cole was a good deal older than Bowra, and had a great influence on
Gaitskell. He was 'a wonderfully stimulating' tutor who 'treated one as
completely adult—a research worker rather than someone to be pushed
through an examination'.[32f] Hugh learned much from him, culturally and
aesthetically as well as politically. They went for long country walks to-

gether (though his brother and friends deny Hugh's claim that it was Cole who taught him to like walking). Cole was an expert on wine, fine glass and poetry, and his public-school pupil with the aesthetic tastes was re-assured to discover that 'you could be a Socialist without being a clod-hopper'.[54]

In some ways the senior man became a surrogate father to Gaitskell, but again the influence was by no means only one way. In the summer of 1928 Cole wrote to his former pupil about the new book on Labour policy he was starting, which 'hasn't got far yet, partly because you will get into it, and my mind insists on arguing with you instead of the world at large. It is, in spirit, dedicated to you.'[55] Later, after a 'tremendous argument' one evening about Guild Socialism, in the morning Cole admitted himself convinced; Gaitskell was 'deeply touched and absurdly pleased'[32g] by a reference to it in the preface.[56] Gaitskell's impact on his tutor was not lasting, but Colin Clark, who knew them both well, wrote:

> By 1929, strange but true – I witnessed it myself – the roles had been reversed and Gaitskell was leading Cole. Gaitskell persuaded him to abandon his Guild Socialist ideas and turn his attention to ordinary parliamentary politics.[57]

Friends who knew Gaitskell in his final year thought that, as his political values crystallised, he was not only applying himself assiduously to aca-demic work and developing new interests, but becoming fundamentally more serious. He remained as cheerful and amusing and attractive as ever, but Elizabeth Harman, who was in her first year at Lady Margaret Hall and knew him well, could not believe he was the same Hugh who had taken a childhood delight in riding pillion on Arthur's motorbike, and had loved golf or punting. Now they endlessly discussed life and literature and art and sex, though not politics or religion. The teacher in him was coming out, and he was eager to improve his friends' taste in everything from dress to literature to personal relationships. Women, he held firmly – despite his own flamboyant ties – must wear sober and well-tailored clothes, nothing gaudy. Proust must be read in French – 'and such was the force of his personality that you did it because *he* wanted you to'. Following his creed of self-realisation, he admired every sign of independence, unconvention-ality and escape from the normal way of doing things. Total realism and candour was his goal: the worst of sins was to 'dramatise the situation', but the changing nuances of a personal relationship must always be out in the open, never covered up – a characteristic not recognised at all by his male friends. That summer he took her to a college ball where she met Frank Pakenham, her future husband; a year later Hugh planned – most unconventionally! – to propose to her at a dinner party for six in Paris, but it was not a success.[58]

Hugh's sister had become engaged the year before to her cricketing celebrity, and he wrote congratulating her:

> I'm willing to forgive you for condemning me always to be known as Hubert Ashton's younger brother-in-law ... I had my fortune told by Lady Morgan and am to have an unsuccessful life but two children ... may you keep life for ever as a Romance and not a 'Reality'.[51b]

The family came together in 1927 for the marriage, and for Hugh's twenty-first birthday. He celebrated with his Oxford friends at the Clarendon Hotel (no dinner jackets and a white woolly sweater for the host), and with his family in Venice, where he teased Arthur who had sent a telegram from Shepheard's in Cairo to meet at the Danieli – the two most expensive hotels in the Mediterranean. The brothers then went off on holiday to the Tyrol. Germany and Austria were Hugh's favourite foreign countries then, and – fearing French influence like most liberal Englishmen – he sympathised with the idea of *Anschluss* (union between them, assumed to be voluntary).[3d] He was there three times over the year 1926–7, 'climbing mountains by night in the Black Forest and watching the dawn rise from the top'.[51b] He was in Italy, too, and earlier in France, which he liked less; and after his Finals he went with Bowra on an Adriatic holiday, acquiring a lifelong love of that coast and especially Dubrovnik.

It was a good deal more foreign travel than was usual for undergraduates in those days, and Gaitskell was 'for his age and time, remarkably cosmo-politan'.[54] His many foreign friends included Victor Raul Haya de la Torre, the leading South American left-winger of the next generation, who spent some years in England. Yet Gaitskell shared, without the insular prejudice, the intense Englishness of the three mentors who, he claimed, later did most to influence his early development as a Socialist: Cole, Tawney and Dalton.[59] Of Cole he was to write, starting with a sentence equally applicable to himself:[32h]

> However much on the intellectual plane Douglas was an international-ist, emotionally – and he never attempted to hide it – he was pro-foundly attached to England. He was not even a little Englander – really a little Southern Englander!'[60]

Tawney once spoke in 1933 of his humiliation at seeing 'his fellow-Englishmen' in dreadful conditions in the Manchester slums before the war; when a friend remarked afterwards on his not saying 'fellow human beings', Gaitskell thought about it and said he too would have used Tawney's words.[33b] Where his father and brother had followed the family tradition of service abroad, Hugh felt it his vocation to work for better conditions at home.

Committed but not sectarian, he shared lodgings that final year with two

Conservatives, Frank Pakenham and Roger Nickalls, at 2 Isis Street near Folly Bridge; in 1952, Nickalls was taken back twenty-five years at hearing the familiar voice and characteristic phrase, 'It's not fair', in Gaitskell's first Budget broadcast as Shadow Chancellor.[61] A young Fellow of New College of those days still remembers the excitement of his economics colleague realising that in an otherwise poor year Pakenham and Gaitskell might actually get Firsts.[62] Both did, Pakenham without a serious viva, Gaitskell after a very long one indeed, in which he came up on the historical subjects at which he did best.[63] Most of his examiners called him an excellent examinee who was rather lucky, but the economist, A. J. Jenkinson, was most impressed.[64]

His mother was keen for him to join the ICS, but had reluctantly accepted that he need not do so if he took a First; and he firmly resisted her attempt to change his mind.[65] Distressed as she was at his determination, she would have paid for him to stay on to do research. Cole had him to dine in Soho and offered to get him a scholarship to write a life of Feargus O'Connor, the Chartist leader. But Cole also proposed an alternative at which Gaitskell jumped: an adult education job in Nottingham:

> I was tremendously pleased with this second idea. Having heard Douglas [Cole] talk about the WEA I had sometimes wondered if I could do this sort of job but thought it probably beyond me. Yet there I was being offered a start at once. I plumped for it, and on the strength of Douglas' recommendation, got the Nottingham post. It was my experiences there — especially in the coal fields — which were to turn me later towards active politics.[32i]

v   Nottingham: The Miners in Defeat

Although working-class conditions shocked Gaitskell in Nottinghamshire, it was far from a depressed area.[66] The town was prosperous in 1927–8, and the coalfield was one of the least badly hit. But with the owners pressing for district agreements, a breakaway union, led by the former district secretary George Spencer, tried to take advantage of the area's comparative profitability to work in collaboration with the owners at the expense of solidarity with their fellows in other coalfields. Miners who had been active in the strike, or had stayed loyal to the Notts Miners Association, were victimised quite ruthlessly and persecuted in all sorts of petty ways. Bitterness was intense: 'to call a man a Spencer was like calling him a Nazi,' said one loyalist many years later.[67] Gaitskell wrote anonymously about it in his first published article, explaining the social background and the forms of economic pressure used, and concluding that the Spencer Union was too artificial to establish itself permanently.[68] (He wrote the article with the help of his unemployed miner friend George Keeling, who was desperately badly off; was paid three pounds for it; and without asking Keeling gave the money to the Miners' Federation. Yet a few weeks later Gaitskell, when his friend came to say goodbye to him just after he had drawn his last quarter's salary, tried to give or lend the money to Keeling — who refused.[69])

If Oxford had been intellectual emancipation for Gaitskell, Nottingham was the time of liberation from the personal constraints of colleges and landladies. He took a small two-roomed flat 'right in the centre of town above shops and offices and very convenient and nice ... I have had it done up a good deal myself'.[35c] The untidy establishment was entered through a small kitchen where he experimented disastrously with 'disgusting stews'. Until Christmas he shared the flat with his Oxford friend Jack James; afterwards he was able to put up occasional visitors, who recalled with distaste the squalid conditions, with unwashed cutlery from which to select a knife and fork, and none too clean sheets to sleep in.[70]

His mood of bohemian revolt implied no conventional breach with his family, to whom he remained deeply attached. But he totally repudiated their values and style of life and those of his peers. When his cousin George Martelli left the Navy, Hugh was delighted; and on the day when University College, Nottingham, acquired its charter, he refused to attend the ceremonies and took a girlfriend out for the day instead. (He was very attached to her, and twenty years later as a Minister wondered with wistful bewilderment why she did not write to him.) Now that he was in D. H. Lawrence country he became even keener on that author, trying (vainly) to arrange a meeting through James; he sometimes stayed up all night reading Proust; and the local *palais de danse* played a very major part in his existence. His one friend at the university was Sebastian Sprott, a young psychology lecturer, and in contrast to Winchester's litany of 'it isn't done', they both enthusiastically preached 'the virtues of scepticism'.

Gaitskell always felt depressed on starting a new job, and when he began at Nottingham the psychological strains were particularly acute. His family were scattered across the continents, his friends were living in a quite different world, and his colleagues were uninspiring. He told his brother gloomily that

> perhaps a lot of [my news] centres around the feeling and fact of stagnation ... there are no proper library facilities. No one to discuss one's subject with, no one one wants to talk seriously too [sic] & a general atmosphere of depressed defeat. The University does seem to be full of people ... who have ended up by staying here indolent & depressed & almost becoming provincial.[35c]

Few of his colleagues took him seriously, and some were actively jealous of the shy, sensitive young public-school and Oxford Socialist.[71] While delighted to take the post, he had been far from confident that he could do the work well, and in the same unhappy letter to his brother he wrote:

> At first I was very depressed and felt that probably I was a failure but now I've ceased to worry—I am afraid I am just hardened and insensitive though for a time petty slights, not exactly personal ones, were very painful. It is not very satisfying because so many of the people are really too old to learn much & so many others ... hope vaguely that if they sit there long enough they'll suddenly find themselves educated, others just don't bother to come.[35c]

In these first lonely and depressing weeks Gaitskell found some release with the other sex. He told his friends that Nottingham was the most libertarian town in the country, particularly uninhibited by class constraints, and he found plenty of girls from the dance hall or shops or railway booking offices to take out to dinner or on long country walks. His motto was 'act first and think afterwards', he told his brother, confessing after a few months,

> I was afraid that my existence here was becoming too much sex without the essential intellect but I'm not afraid now of [that] ... when I feel like treating the thing as an art and a game that's rather fun, like Swann before he falls in love with Odette. Probably after a few unsatisfactory evenings I shall settle down to work and then suddenly fall in love after I've forgotten all about it.[35d]

He soon entered on his first mature relationship with a steady girlfriend, which was to continue for a time after his move to London. But for some years before and after Nottingham he rejected marriage as a bourgeois convention. At his last college ball he had been much excited by a lady who had left her husband—'a thin stick-like haggard creature' whom he clearly saw as an early heroine of 'women's Lib'.[72] In 1932 he assured his brother that marriage was 'becoming less and less essential in England'.[35a]

Professionally, his start at Nottingham was not at all easy. With people of his own class, in familiar surroundings, he had acquired plenty of self-confidence in his last year at Oxford. At his first meeting with Hubert Ashton's father he cheerfully expounded the problems of India to a man who had gone out there forty years before.[65] But the assurance was backed by knowledge, mental agility and serious thought; at one dinner party at Bowra's where Gaitskell had a vigorous argument with a young coalowner, he impressed his host (a stern judge) by his formidable controversial powers.[3a]

At Nottingham it was a different story. The miners were a tough lot, who had had a very bad time in the strike. Half of them were unemployed, blacklisted by the owners. They were, as Gaitskell wrote later, 'naturally extremely bitter';[8] or as one of them put it, 'hostile and aggressive to everyone'.[69] Gaitskell came from another class, had obviously never gone hungry, and gave at first a slightly effeminate impression; he had no experience of lecturing, and started off badly, 'tentative, hesitant and stuttering'.[69] Many years later he still shuddered at the memory.[73] He was acutely conscious of the incongruities both between his own background and that of his pupils, and between their daily problems and the subjects he was supposed to teach them. His very first lecture was on Saving and Economic Progress. 'Looking back,' he remembered, 'I am surprised at my audacity. For I gave them ... the full classical doctrine in which thrift ... is crucial.'[74] Not surprisingly, they gave him a hammering.

He had to learn up banking and currency, which he had not previously studied, in order to persuade enough unemployed miners to take his class to qualify it for a grant. It was demanding in time and intellectual energy as well as emotionally.[75] But Gaitskell was both a stubborn man and a very patient and lucid teacher who took trouble to make his material relevant and interesting. He was, as Keeling put it, 'constitutionally incapable of a snobbish thought, word or deed'.[22b] With his own love of frankness, he found the candour of his pupils refreshing, and he wrote to his brother that the miners were:

> the nicest sort of people – indeed I like very much all the working people I have met ... more honest and natural than the Middle Class who are always trying to be something they aren't & who are never quite sure whether they are saying the right thing.[35c]

In 1927 victimised miners from the loyalist union did not often find well-educated middle-class young men coming to teach in their area and wholeheartedly taking their side, and he won their confidence because, as one of them said years later, 'he was so obviously sincere'.[22c] He attracted 'fantastic loyalty and affection in the mining villages – they adored him'.[76]

He never forgot them, and the impact of that first contact with working-class life was profound. It 'brought him down to earth with a damned shock', said Keeling, and afterwards Gaitskell frequently told his friends how very deep an impression the conditions had made on him: 'He thought of poverty, inequality, unemployment and slums with emotion and spoke of them with heat.'[77] It gave a new and far more personal dimension to what had been an intellectual commitment. In that early, jaundiced letter he answered Arthur, who had 'rather offensively' rebuked him for 'grinding a Labour axe', by quietly insisting on the miserable conditions while vigorously rebutting any suggestion of sentimentality:

I am as scrupulously honest as I can be and that is not difficult because I am so cold-blooded that I'm only too glad to calm the excitement of some of my pupils and induce them to revel in that doubtful pleasure the scientific attitude. I find to my surprise that on the whole its easier to excite one's moral indignation by reading "The decay of capitalist Civilisation" by Sidney Webb than by hearing as I do at times that someone has been living on bread and beetroot or that the children have no shoes and very few clothes.[35c]

Yet in their frequent long talks at this time about the shape of a Socialist society, Keeling described him as displaying an almost childlike nostalgia for the lost simplicities of Merrie England; and both Keeling the miner[69] and Bowra the don characterised Gaitskell as a 'William Morris Socialist.'[3h] A society that was more just to human beings was essential, he told Keeling, even though it was likely to be somewhat less efficient economically. To his brother he wrote: 'Laziness is a vice but I think too much stress on efficiency is also one ... [both] apt to create a feeling of dissatisfaction in one which spoils the harmony of one's existence.'

In the same letter he went on: 'there is far too much poverty and in-equality ... to remedy (without imagining that thereby you reach the millennium). It seems to be a question apart from one's own ambitions. It is simply a judgement.'[35d] The reference to the millennium was typical. Discovering how the private owners treated their workers (and how short-sightedly they exploited the natural resources) convinced Gaitskell that the need to nationalise the mines was blatantly obvious; but even in those early days he never shared the common Socialist illusion that a change of ownership would end the workers' sense of alienation.[69]

Nottingham meant for Gaitskell getting to know working-class people as well as working-class conditions, and making the exhilarating discovery that the enormous differences of background and tastes between him and them did not preclude completely uninhibited human contact — with his girlfriends, or his washerwoman, who would occasionally drop in to tea to the embarrassment of visitors from Oxford, or the miners with whom friendships extended far beyond the classroom; they came to his flat, took him off to football matches, and went on camping expeditions with him. It was a great transformation in the shy young man who, at the start of the year, found it so uncomfortable to be among the workers with whom he sympathised but could not mix, that he avoided them by travelling first class on trains.[78] But he did not pretend to himself that he and they were really just the same; on the contrary, he was fascinated to find out how differently his new friends thought and felt and judged from his familiar upper-middle-class acquaintances:[79]

I am very interested in the question of 'class'. I would like to write something on it some time. It's quite extraordinary how important the thing is as a whole and historically though it does not exactly make my work difficult [*sic*]. But of course meeting so many people who have lived and do live so utterly differently from oneself is peculiar.[35c]

Above all with his strong sense of fairness and justice ('a bee in his bonnet about it,' said Keeling) Gaitskell was impressed by the intense and selfless loyalties for which mining communities are famous.[66a] All his life he was to preach the need for team work and solidarity in the Labour Movement, and the miners were a living example. A quarter of a century later, when he moved the third reading of the Bill to nationalise the mines, he referred to his Nottingham experiences – to stress not the economic misery, but the ruthless treatment of human beings. Often he said later that it was those miners who made him a Socialist, and he told the House of Commons: 'They taught me what economic feudalism was. They taught me what the naked exercise of arbitrary power meant. They taught me what it was to be victimised.'[80] The effect on him was startling and profound and permanent, as Keeling insisted:

This tentative, shy, stuttering young man – this academic Socialist vaguely interested in helping the poor, became a real fighting politician. It really seemed to change his very soul ... it was a complete and utter change in a human personality.[69]

Gaitskell now had his mission in life: to use his excellent mind and the educational benefits he had acquired from his own class background to help people with fewer advantages than himself to struggle against the forces of power and privilege. The arena for that struggle was politics not adult education, though at this period his friend Orrick expected his engagement to take a different form. 'I thought he was going to be an agitator. It never occurred to me he would be a really serious politician.'[16b] His upper-middle-class origins had seemed likely to prove a barrier in the Labour Party of the 1920s, but now that he had discovered how easily he could leap that barrier in making personal friendships, it did not look so insurmountable in public life. Indeed, he was worried at Nottingham that he might have, not too much money, but too little to be able to devote time to politics instead of earning his living.[81]

It was his miner friends who urged him to make his first political speeches, who encouraged him to try to enter Parliament himself, and who asked him back to Nottinghamshire to make his first general election speeches in 1929.[82] Hugh's very first venture was to speak with Keeling from a water-trough in the Derby Road, Nottingham; a more important occasion was the adoption meeting for a new Labour candidate, Seymour Cocks, in the small, smoke-filled anteroom of the Co-op Hall at Hucknall.[83] Years later he called Hucknall 'a very ugly town for which I have a nostalgic affection'.[84] He started the WEA class there himself and always liked it best of his classes; the first one of all was held 'on a Sunday morning in the room which, having been the ladies' cloakroom the night before, retained a curious smell of tobacco and a rather strong scent'.[85] He had four classes in all, which took him all round the county and to the Derbyshire border; on one of these expeditions he met in a miner's cottage near Worksop the rising young politician who was to do most to promote his early career: Hugh Dalton. Dalton found him 'very emphatic and delightfully unrespectful. He was out to change society from top to bottom. He was against all privilege and social injustice ... for real social equality.'[86]

Though Nottingham widened Gaitskell's outlook in so many ways, intellectually he feared it would have the reverse effect. For all his personal modesty, he was conscious of his own abilities; perhaps he was the more afraid of slipping backwards because his progress was so recent. 'I see tremendous danger of stagnating here,' he told his brother in December 1927: 'I went to London a few days ago. The difference is quite remarkable — there is so much more vigour and better taste and better intelligence and more personality in the atmosphere.'[35c] By the spring he was sounding much happier, more relaxed and self-confident, planning future research (unexpectedly, in Tawney's field of seventeenth-century economic history) and

> doing a little lecturing and coaching and working on my own. All quite nice — I am playing a good deal of tennis and leading a *slightly* more sociable existence. I lecture at the Prison once a week which, in a way, is interesting, though there is nothing especially peculiar about the prisoners.[35d e]

But by then he had already been offered and accepted a new job, for motives which as usual he scrutinised critically:

> I think it is absolutely essential never to deceive oneself ... it is true that the problem of self-cultivation v. self [sic] for the community does appear — personally I compromise — I go to London next year but hope to go on doing this work a little and at least write books which may be of some use — Of course I *want* to but that doesn't matter unless you're a puritan and religious which I am not.[35d e]

He was still determined to avoid conventional paths. That summer he revisited Oxford, found the ordinary undergraduate frivolities in full swing, and told Elizabeth Harman most vehemently that the bubble had broken and he had nothing now in common with those who led that life.[87]

Gaitskell's new post was at University College, London, where Noel Hall had just been appointed to revive the Economics Department. Advised by his former tutor at Brasenose (A. J. Jenkinson, the examiner whom Gaitskell had so impressed), Hall asked Gaitskell over lunch in Charlotte Street to come to UCL as his assistant.[64] Gaitskell had already been urged by Warden Fisher not to stay too long at Nottingham, and now on Lionel Robbins's advice he accepted Hall's offer.[88] The shy youth who had arrived there a year before 'was almost unrecognisable when he went back to London ... as if he [came] seeking something, and now he had found something he was going to fight for'.[69]

CHAPTER 2

AIMING AT A CLASSLESS SOCIETY 1928–34

'I think life would be more amusing if one was ambitious'
(HG, 1928)

i *'Low Bloomsbury': Bohemian Lecturer*

GAITSKELL spent eleven years at University College, London, arriving in the autumn of 1928 as the junior in a department of two, with only seventeen students, and ending as head of a staff of six.[1] In economics UCL was overshadowed by the massive presence of the London School of Economics close by, where students went for their advanced lectures; the UCL staff originally performed a mainly tutorial function.[2] During Gaitskell's time violent debate was raging over both the fundamentals of economic theory, and the propriety of academic economists taking public stands on policy issues. Keynes was at the heart of both controversies, and the centre of orthodox resistance to him was at the LSE, dominated by Professors Hayek and Robbins.[3] Strongly committed politically and less concerned with the theory of his subject than with its practical application, Gaitskell was somewhat (though not wholly) sheltered by being in a separate institution.

With such small numbers, relations with both colleagues and students became unusually close at UCL. Talking to his chairman after one Labour meeting at the LSE in about 1951, Gaitskell launched into an 'extraordinarily impassioned tirade' against big departments and in favour of small intimate ones.[4] But the friendly relations did not occur automatically, for UCL had a 'stiff and starchy' tradition. Gaitskell ignored it, taking trouble to get to know his undergraduates. One of the first of them recalled that at their very first meeting, when she saw him to get a reading list, he went out of his way to make friends – a habit she found to be typical. That student eventually married Evan Durbin, who came briefly to UCL a year later; Gaitskell, who loved to tease his earnest young colleague, invented a mythical college rule against any fraternising with undergraduates.[5]

Gaitskell still felt himself to be a student, attending Robbins's lectures at the LSE to learn the technique. In his own lectures he was very shy at first, and stuttered badly. That soon disappeared. He always prepared his material thoroughly and organised it admirably, as he did his political speeches later on. He also had a humorous, lighter touch which he did not always retain later, but which at this period made him a popular after-dinner speaker. Years afterwards one student of his recalled:

As a lecturer Hugh Gaitskell combined lucidity of exposition and elegance of language with a certain diffidence which manifested itself in the frequent use of his hands ... [to] drive home a point. His lectures bore the stamp of meticulously careful preparation and were always stimulating ...

It was as a tutor rather than a lecturer that Hugh Gaitskell excelled. He was in his element in the small discussion group and the seminar, where his acute mind was quick to pinpoint flaws in an argument and, above all, in the private tutorial where students' written work was searchingly but gently criticised and ... difficulties cleared away.

What distinguished his tutorials from any others was the wide range of topics he would discuss with, and the genuine personal interest he showed in, his students. It was this which for many of us, made these scheduled fortnightly half-hourly visits to his room more than simply 'tutorials' and caused us to look on him not as a tutor only but as a friend as well. With whatever problems or even personal worries we went to him, we could always count upon a sympathetic understanding, helpful counsel, and not seldom, practical assistance.[6]

His teaching style in classes was unusually imaginative for that time. He escaped the textbook approach, inviting City visitors to explain gold prices or using a serious new non-party study to introduce the steel industry. A colleague in another department said he had a reputation as the best teacher in the college; a junior lecturer found him in seminars 'a bit of an inspiration — very agile, very good at following undergraduate thought'; and the published account is confirmed by other former students. Some of them liked him for special reasons of their own — the many Indians, or the Civil Service candidates whom he was responsible for advising, or the girls who found him 'a gorgeous dancer' and an attractive figure with his polite Wykehamist manners and his elegant dress. Most of all the personal interest was appreciated, and the fact that he was quick to notice and offer help when they were worried or in trouble.

The post suited him intellectually as well as personally, for the courses he was teaching integrated economics with other social studies in a way more characteristic of Oxford PPE than of the modern specialised professional discipline. Noel Hall in his very first approach had said that he wanted someone 'interested mainly in the social side'. The principal subjects Gaitskell taught at first were Comparative Social Institutions and Political and Social Theory (which included British Government). He was actively encouraged to work closely, as indeed he wished, with the LSE sociologists and anthropologists, in whose areas he did most of his early reading.[7]

Living near by and often teaching the same students, economists and historians were in frequent contact. Gaitskell made friends outside his own discipline with teachers of history and government like Walter Adams and Denis Brogan, and particularly with M. M. Postan, the economic historian. Postan, also a new arrival at UCL, was eight years older than Gaitskell. They argued about Russia (from which Postan had escaped) and about Marxism in various private conversations and lively discussion groups. Another friend was John Macmurray, whose lectures Hugh had attended at Balliol, and who was the first person in Britain to study seriously the ideas of the young Karl Marx.[8] When he came to UCL as Professor of Philosophy he fascinated Gaitskell and Evan Durbin, helping them to sort out their ideas and evolve a moral basis for non-Marxist Socialism.

Durbin, the most intimate of all, was like Gaitskell an economist with friends mainly from other disciplines. They had known each other at New College, where Durbin was an active Socialist politician and Gaitskell thought him 'a bit of a prig and a puritan'.[9] He came to UCL a year after Gaitskell, and moved on after a year to the LSE. Until his tragically premature death in 1948, they were the closest of friends and the staunchest of political allies. They were very different people, and Gaitskell loved teasing Durbin about the contrasts. Son of a Baptist minister who had become a pacifist in the First World War, Durbin had been brought up in the radical anti-Establishment tradition of West Country Nonconformity, and pulpit experience made him a far more accomplished speaker than Gaitskell. Durbin was earnest, Gaitskell light-hearted; Durbin reputedly lazy, Gaitskell energetic; Durbin rooted in the values of the lower-middle class, Gaitskell in revolt against those of the upper; Durbin a product of the radical-liberal tradition, Gaitskell a rebel against the Tory ethos;[10-11a] Durbin supplying the common sense ballast and applying with assurance a clearly thought-out philosophy, Gaitskell more tolerant but intellectually not so solidly anchored. Gaitskell thought of himself as a rationalist, in contrast to the emotionalism of G. D. H. Cole; but Durbin 'had such firm views that for anybody who had any doubts at all it was like grabbing a priest'.[12] Their friendship began in innumerable intellectual discussions, but soon concentrated on political thought and action.

Some friends realised that Gaitskell's heart was always in politics, and years later his brother wrote to him: 'I know how much this has really been the mainstream in your mind all your life.'[13] Yet other friends thought differently, and Hugh himself wrote to Arthur in 1932:

Perhaps I am too complacent about myself and my life. Of course I have intense periods of depression, but I have never seriously contemplated any other kind of existence for it is so clear to me that I should only be more unhappy. If you really believe I was right about my career — and you have said so often — why not follow me a little? ... You see I'm a real crusader about this kind of thing: but after all I do believe in it if in nothing else and always have done so ever since Oxford.[14a]

At UCL his main role was as a teacher. As an administrator his early reputation was mixed;[15] and he confessed later that the attraction of a don's life was its lack of discipline.[16] He never looked like making a major contribution to economic theory. His talents as an academic writer, like Cole's and Tawney's, were best displayed in economic and social history or in the lucid exposition of difficult arguments. He knew it, keeping up his WEA activities, writing mainly works of serious popularisation, and using his skills increasingly as a policy adviser to the Labour Party.[17] His teaching was never just disguised propaganda; and though everyone knew his views, undergraduates and professors agree that he did not try to impose them, so that they could not (like those of some of his colleagues) be inferred from his students' examination answers. But while a respectable minority of his colleagues thought he could have risen high in the profession, that was never the centre of his attention.

Apart from his formal duties, he played a very active part in numerous little discussion groups of colleagues and friends, which proliferated in university circles at that time.[18] Durbin was a close friend of the psychologist Dr John Bowlby, a strong Freudian; Gaitskell became a friend, too, and indeed at this period the two allies were concerned with psychology almost as much as politics. One important forum was a group of economic and social historians, led by Postan and his wife Eileen Power (a well-known medieval historian), who went for long walks in the country or met over dinner; Gaitskell concerned himself particularly with the attitude of different social classes to the advent of Socialism. Another was Tots and Quots, a small dining club of scientists and other intellectuals who met monthly on Saturday nights to argue in congenial company, over good food and drink, about 'the unity of scientific method'. It began at the end of 1930, with Gaitskell as one of the four founders and principal recruiter; he dismayed some of the others by ensuring serious discussions. The scientists included J. B. Bernal, P. M. S. Blackett, J. B. S. Haldane, Lancelot Hogben and Solly Zuckerman, one of the young founders; others who came were G. P. Wells (H.G.'s son), Henry Mond (Lord Melchett), Roy Harrod occasionally, Richard Crossman later, Frederick Lindemann (the future Lord Cherwell), Postan and Gaitskell. Zuckerman believed that these discussions accounted for Gaitskell's later sympathy for scientists in public life. His distrust for those who were committed Marxists—as many of them were—may also have originated there. The most important of these groups were directly concerned with working out Socialist economic policy, and are dealt with later.*

These multifarious activities developed gradually, often at Gaitskell's own initiative, over the first few years at UCL. In the brief period before they began, he felt rather lonely as he often did in a new job, though his Nottingham girlfriend came to stay for a short time.[19] He spent Christmas of 1928 on his own, cooking his own meals and reading Lytton Strachey's *Elizabeth and Essex* (following Aldous Huxley, Virginia Woolf and Evelyn Waugh).[20] But now that he was in the big city, his social life soon developed.

He had found a large white-panelled flat in a Queen Anne house at 12 Great Ormond Street (now an estate agent's office), which he took great trouble decorating; he was proud of his apple-green curtains, his carpets and chintz, and his original drawing by Meninsky. Penniless Oxford friends like Lionel Perry and John Betjeman stayed with him sometimes, and the Coles had his back room as a *pied-à-terre*. He and John Bowlby shared an excellent cook, and his students as well as friends came to lunch at the flat, in what was then an unheard-of gesture from a tutor. (But after one lot of visitors almost jumped through his new bed, he was more circumspect about his invitations.)

His more frivolous activities centred on the Cave of Harmony at Seven Dials (later the Gargoyle Club) where he indulged his love of late-night dancing. At this time he was keen on radio entertainers, liked musical comedies even more than the straight theatre, and enjoyed the antics of his more outrageous friends; one evening in Trafalgar Square when Betjeman mounted on a lion to deliver a Socialist soap-box oration, Gaitskell was as delighted as their companion was embarrassed. He became a familiar figure in the Bloomsbury set around Francis Meynell, more actively political than those at the court of Virginia Woolf. He joined (though Evan Durbin never would) the 1917 Club in Gerrard Street, a cheap social and political centre—at a time when most clubs were expensive, socially exclusive and single-sex—where the impecunious young intellectual and professional Left met for lunch and gossip until it went bankrupt in 1931. It was named after the (first) Russian Revolution, its founders were mostly pacifists, and its assorted patron saints were H. G. Wells, Ramsay MacDonald and George Lansbury, though it had some Communist members. Many scientists and actors joined, along with civil servants and poets; while the atmosphere was serious, the prevailing life-style anticipated the

* Below, Sections ii (social classes), v (economic policy).

permissive society of a later generation, and there was much overlap between the less earnest membership and the Cave of Harmony crowd.[21]

These young intellectuals of Charlotte Street Bloomsbury, lived '500 yards from the Gordon Square Bloomsbury, and in a different world'.[22] They met informally at Bertorelli's restaurant, with its excellent cheap dinners, and at the Fitzroy Tavern on the corner of Windmill Street, better known as Kleinfeld's. The most bohemian pub in London, it was so much a club for its large and devoted clientèle that the regulars could always find a friend there and the newcomer stepping inside felt 'a sense of adventure — and one of intrusion'.[22] Originally the regulars had been mainly artists both struggling and successful (headed by Augustus John and Nina Hamnett); later also writers, poets, journalists, dons, scientists and budding politicians, many of whom became famous: Jacob Epstein, Dylan Thomas, Solly Zuckerman, Emlyn Williams, Tom Driberg, Ian Mackay, and 'Popski' of the Western Desert. Many were hard up, but when anyone sold a picture or a story, everybody celebrated.[23]

Gaitskell was a frequent though not a regular customer at Kleinfeld's. To his staider academic friends at this time he seemed 'rather gay and fast with lots of girl friends and a *slight* touch of the enfant terrible'.[24] But at the Fitzroy Tavern the dashing blade of UCL was thought a quiet, gentlemanly, rather reserved young fellow, who was never drunk and never involved in the political arguments. Early in these Bloomsbury years, in 1930, he was depressed by a persistent toothache. A doctor friend sent him to Sir Thomas Horder, 'said to be the best diagnostician in London', who told him it was due to a small tubercular gland and successfully prescribed a long Swiss holiday.[14d] That trouble never recurred, though a little later, as his political interests developed, some of his friends did wonder needlessly whether he was robust enough for so strenuous a life.[25]

Foreign travel was very cheap, and unlike Durbin (who disliked 'abroad'), Gaitskell went to Europe often. At home his holidays were not particularly austere. Twice he stayed in Scottish castles — briefly in 1930 at Forfar with the Finlays (Burmah Oil friends of his mother), and for a longer period in 1931 at Craignish in Argyll with Naomi Mitchison, who was already known as a novelist, and her husband Dick, a rising young Socialist lawyer. Close friends of the Coles and now of Gaitskell's, they shared his characteristic mixture of seriousness and gaiety. At Craignish he went for twenty-mile walks, swam a good deal and acted in his favourite charades, once appearing as a Roman emperor in a bath-towel looking 'remarkably dissolute'.[26a] Never fond of the grouse moor, he could not abide dead birds; after one quarrel Naomi Mitchison (who was briefly in love with him) threw a bloody pheasant at him. Though he wrote indignantly to Margaret Cole, 'I will *not* be a character in one of Naomi's novels', he did not entirely escape that fate.[27]

One of the best-loved characters in those circles was Amyas Ross, who became Hugh's intimate friend.[28] He had been a contemporary of Arthur's at the Dragon School and then at New College. In between he was an anti-war schoolboy with revolutionary views at Repton, where Victor Gollancz was a radical member of the staff.[29] At New College he instigated a strike of college servants, and was a founder of the Oxford University Labour Club. Now he was a brilliant, impulsive, unpredictable entrepreneur of bright ideas, as well as an improbable WEA tutor in economics and a Labour candidate.

Between Evan Durbin and Ross there could hardly have been a sharper contrast in personality. Gaitskell's friends were as varied as his interests, and he always kept them in separate compartments: Bowra, for instance, complained that at Oxford, he 'was not allowed to meet' Durbin.[30] This eclecticism was perfectly conscious. Gaitskell wrote to Cole in September 1928:

> I can't change myself even if I wanted to – I can't honestly tie myself down either to one thing or one person or more, but to be true must be one individual with a number of contacts in different places reflecting the different parts of my personality ... I may, as you suggest, find the one person in the world to combine my different selves into one. At the moment, however, she does not exist.[31]

He was to meet Dora Frost for the first time a few weeks later. In the spring of 1929, Amyas Ross was Labour candidate in a by-election in the Tory stronghold of St Marylebone, and she and Hugh were both among his active helpers in the campaign. That first encounter took place at Kleinfeld's when Hugh looked in to fortify himself before the ordeal of speaking at an outdoor meeting. At the end of 1950, Hugh Gaitskell the new Chancellor of the Exchequer dropped in at the Fitzroy Tavern to wish the proprietors a happy New Year, and recorded in their visitors' book, 'This is where I met my wife'.

Dora was an old friend of Amyas and Peggy Ross. Her background was very different from Hugh's. Her father, Leon Creditor, was a Jewish writer and Hebrew scholar who had emigrated from Russia in 1903. He was a delightful man of saintly good temper, generosity and gentle wit, adored by his family. The Creditors first settled in the East End of London, where he taught Hebrew and wrote regularly for the only 'quality' Yiddish newspaper, the *Jewish Times*. He was devout and the three elder children, two girls and one boy, learned to speak and read Hebrew fluently; but though Dora enjoyed this, she was never religious. Their mother, uneducated herself but with five well-educated brothers, was ambitious for her son and daughters to acquire an education and a profession. Dora went to an excellent grammar school in Bow Road, and wanted to take a degree in

English and French and go in for teaching. But she was ineligible for a
grant, and was persuaded by her mother—much to her later regret—to
switch to medicine. Just before her nineteenth birthday she married a young
doctor, David Frost, who specialised in psychiatry and biochemistry. (It
was he who called in Horder, his old tutor, about Hugh's gland.) Their son
Raymond was about four years old when Dora first met Hugh early in
1929.

The friendship quickly took root. She was five years older than Hugh
and soon became his confidante. They had many interests in common—
in literature (especially modern fiction), in psychology, and not least in the
Labour Party which Dora had joined at sixteen. She had no idea of going
into politics, for she was happy with her job in publishing. When Hugh
first came to London the Frosts were living in Gower Street. Later they
rented a big house just north of Regent's Park, where they let the top floor,
often to young university lecturers; after giving up his flat, Hugh had a
room there for a time before he went to Vienna. The Frosts had always
had their own separate circles of friends, a style which Hugh admired. His
friendship with Dora flourished and grew closer over the years, and she
discovered long afterwards that he had once said to Peggy Ross: 'If Dora
were free I'd marry her.' But he was still expressing himself strongly and
articulately against matrimony, and if anyone had suggested that outcome
to Dora at this period, she would have thought they were mad.

With Amyas Ross, Hugh's relationship was deeply but not exclusively
political. The Rosses had just started a business in Soho Square, selling
foreign prints. Through a chance street conversation in January 1930,
Gaitskell discovered that they were desperately short of capital—with
plenty of orders but no petty cash to buy stamps to deal with them. After
consulting Dora, he asked the Rosses to lunch next day at Bertorelli's and
offered to put in £750. It was a generous gesture rather than an investment;
he had never had much money of his own, and had just—disastrously—
allowed another friend to risk most of it (£1,500) on the Stock Exchange,
where it was rapidly lost.

The Soho Gallery was at the start an 'extraordinary scatter-brained
organisation'.[32] Its main activity was to sell, particularly to schools, good
reproductions—at first principally of Impressionists and later of Old
Masters. It organised school exhibitions, displays of original work and a
loan club for pictures. Gaitskell rather prided himself on his knowledge
of modern art; though he was never a genuine connoisseur, he gave a
friend a Matisse long before they became fashionable, and he liked Van
Gogh, Paul Klee and Picasso. But the Soho Gallery did not cater primarily
for those tastes, and Gaitskell's main motive was to help a friend.

His connection drew some lofty criticism from the artistic snobs of UCL
—which he would meet by smilingly changing the subject.[33] He became

honorary chairman, and found the business experience useful and fascinating, though 'the worry and anxiety ... [of having] all one's eggs in the same basket' could be 'very upsetting'.[14e] Yet quite unexpectedly the gallery proved a great success, spawning three allied companies during the 1930s and in ten years expanding its turnover from £500 to £33,000. Most of his loan was repaid in 1937, the rest – which he had waived – after the war, in which the business, oddly, had boomed. He remained chairman until he took office in 1946, and did not sever his connection finally until he sold his shares for £500 in 1952.[34]

Gaitskell's speech for Amyas Ross in the St Marylebone by-election was his very first serious outdoor meeting. It began badly. But as he was struggling to interest a tiny handful of people in the naval estimates, a tramp began to heckle; the exchanges grew lively, and a respectable crowd of 200 gathered. When the speaker concluded triumphantly, the tramp came up to him: 'Well guv'nor, I reckon that was worth half a crown, don't you?' Gaitskell gave him 5s.[35]

All his early speeches were made on behalf of his friends, like Ross or Durbin or his Notts comrades. He was impelled into politics, too, by the hardship and oppression he had found among the miners. But he was also beginning to be attracted to it for its own sake, as he explained to his brother with his usual introspective anxiety to explore his own attitudes:

> Personally I find myself concerned primarily with my own happiness (really non-unhappiness would be more accurate) and also to some extent with other people's. At least if you like to include it all under own happiness you can – it's certainly true that I'm not happy unless at least I successfully deceive myself into thinking that I'm doing something towards making other people happy.[14b]

A few weeks later he exploded:

> How I loathe the conceited ineffective snobbish rich! I suppose I have been insulted by them so often, and to be insulted by people one despises is intolerable. It is ghastly to think that people of our generation will be like that too – there is no doubt that equal education is essential.

He softened that tirade by adding, 'I hope you will be amused by this, as you are meant to be'. In the same letter he confessed to another kind of motive:

> one must have drama in one's life ... this for me is rather revolutionary – I have always opposed dramatisation because of its hypocrisy. But now cynically I see that there may be much to be said for it ... I think I have decided that I really do want to be a great man – this is

not a burning passion – but rather that I think life would be more amusing if one was ambitious ... By great I simply mean powerful, in the public eye, important ... My motives may be mostly egoistical but because of a controlling altruism, my actions may lead to excellent results for society.

There is another point, perhaps the most important of all. I want to live at a higher rate, to exercise my vitality ...

I am quite aware that I have no exceptional ability so that there really is no reason why I should be successful (except that *exceptional* ability really has little to do with it). But I want more vitality.[14c]

With all his other outlets, he found that stimulus most of all in politics.

ii *'Straight Out for Socialism'*

During Gaitskell's first five years in London, from 1928 to 1933, the political situation changed dramatically, and among the young Socialist intellectuals, excitement and enthusiasm gave way to disillusionment and resentful gloom. At first the smug insular passivity of Baldwin's Conservatism was offset by optimism about the prospect of a new government. Hugh told his brother at the very end of 1928: 'I think that soon things will be more exciting here – the Conservative govt is such a fog – I hope it will be lifted altogether at the election.'[14c] When Labour was returned he was overjoyed, as he wrote later:

The election of 1929 seemed to us at the time a wonderful, almost miraculous victory. We had done so much better than I (perhaps because most of my speaking had been in Marylebone!) had thought possible. We paid little, no doubt far too little, attention to the absence of a clear majority. It was enough for us that Labour was in power again, and for the first time held the largest number of seats. Our hopes for peace could be high, we would clear the slums – and, above all, tackle the unemployment...[11b]

Then the world depression struck, and the government stood helplessly by as the numbers out of work mounted steadily. Labour supporters soon became disillusioned. In the 1931 financial crisis, the Labour Party lost its three leading Ministers when Snowden and Thomas joined MacDonald's National Government as an emergency combination for a few weeks to save the pound. It promptly abandoned the gold standard, reduced unemployment benefit, and then went to the country; Labour was reduced to a miserable rump of fifty MPs and the Conservatives were installed in power until the war. Most of Labour's parliamentary leadership – for the only time in the Party's history – swung briefly to the Left in resentment and alarm at the defection of the leaders of the Labour government, the electoral catastrophe brought on by its sterility, the demagogy of the other side, and then the advent of Hitler at the beginning of 1933. Even Clement Attlee was talking of emergency powers acts and local government commissars. That temporary mood influenced Hugh Gaitskell, too. He was furious at the defections, he welcomed as thoroughly justified the naval mutiny at Invergordon in September 1931,[36] and he was left stunned and bitter by Labour's electoral catastrophe. Concern that Labour would never be allowed to come to power democratically was so general at that time that even Hugh Dalton was talking of bringing the Durham Light Infantry to London to replace the Brigade of Guards;[24] and long afterwards Gaitskell told a profile writer that it was 'the only time I have ever questioned the practicability of democratic Socialism'.[16]

Although he told another journalist that his Left leanings began at the beginning of 1932,[37] they were already apparent in his 1931 election speeches. At an inquest on the election results at Digswell Park in November, with Ernest Bevin in the chair, a pencil note of the proceedings records laconically '*Gaitskell* emphasised necessity for liquidating the opposition'.[38] Then, lunching one day in Bloomsbury in 1932, Gaitskell ran across for the first time for years his old Dragon schoolfellow Lance Mallalieu, now a pro-government Liberal MP—and treated him with blistering contempt for naively trusting the Tories.[39] As usual, he had no truck with half-measures. He vigorously defended the Soviet regime against charges of dictatorship, he saw the Communist Party as just a bunch of impatient comrades, he talked freely to his friends of the revolution and the proletariat, the class war and the class enemy, and he struck more than one of them as temperamentally a natural revolutionary.[40a]

Before long, he and Evan Durbin were both to be selected as Labour candidates for neighbouring Medway towns. At the time their attitudes contrasted sharply. Gaitskell said in his very first press briefing:

> I think the time has come when the Labour Party must go straight out for Socialism when it is returned to power. But I do not believe in joining 'Left-Wing' organisations which are not part of the official Labour Movement. We cannot afford to have sectionalism at this stage.[41]

At Gaitskell's adoption meeting three days later, Cripps said Labour should not take office again unless it had a majority to introduce Socialism immediately.[42a] The new candidate for Chatham entirely agreed, saying shortly afterwards:

> The Labour Party had ... tried to get better conditions out of capitalism ... leaving the economic power in the hands of the same people

as before ... [W]ere ... that policy to be pursued [again], it would have a second collapse much more serious than the first.

The only way in which Socialism could be got was shortly and fairly sharply ... [T]hey should get the power, proceed with measures of Socialisation, and smash the economic power of the upper class. When they had the power he believed they would be in a position to carry into action measures which were essentially revolutionary ... much better than by staying outside and trying to organise revolution.[42b]

Five months later, Durbin was selected next door at Gillingham after a speech which put preserving political democracy as Labour's first objective, ahead even of Socialism and peace.[43a]

Throughout that year Gaitskell's speeches used strong language and struck a bitter note. Unemployment, he told his adoption meeting, could not be cured 'until they had got rid of the rich altogether';[42a] slums, he said a year later, would remain as long as property-owners sat on the local council.[42c] He set out his outlook more fully in a 1933 manuscript on wages policy. It opens: 'the destruction of this inequality, the creating and maintaining of a society in which it cannot exist becomes the essential and direct purpose of all Socialist activity'. That was the ultimate aim alike of the Communists, of the old Ramsay MacDonald evolutionary school, and of the Labour Party. The latter was also obliged to offer answers to immediate problems, but in so inegalitarian a society that involved dangers:

Faced with this sentiment and lacking the support of a well nourished class hatred, many English Labour leaders have been inclined to put in the forefront ... purely material advantages ... Equality is degraded from its rightful place and allowed in, if at all, only when heavily disguised ... [hiding] the essential aim of a Socialist party not only from the general public ... but ... from the members of that Party itself ... [creating] a false sense of security and a blindness to the opposition and conflict which a redistribution of wealth involves ... A Socialist party is different from other parties not because it offers a different mechanism for the same object, but because the object itself is different. Even economic planning ... can exist without Socialism. Still more is this true of a particular monetary policy or the public control of an individual industry ... [T]he fundamental objective and criterion by which policy must be judged [is] the achievement of Economic Equality ... [W]ithout it Labour policy becomes merely opportunist, distinguishable only from the policies of other parties by the suggestion of attractive means to 'Prosperity',[44] a greater humanitarianism, and, as some would have it, far less favourable circumstances in which to take action ... A failure to advance in the direction of that ideal [of social justice] is bound to appear little short of a betrayal.[45]

Tawney's influence is evident in that equality (not public ownership) was already the centre of Gaitskell's commitment and loyalty. But the tone and style—the emotive terms, the suspicion of leaders, the warnings against compromise—are enduring characteristics of the Labour Left.

Gaitskell was never a trimmer, always a man for total engagement. Where Durbin already judged events in the light of a carefully worked-out philosophy, Gaitskell's was still fluid, and he reacted violently to dramatic incidents such as the General Strike, the collapse of the Labour government, the repression of the Austrian Socialists. Politically inactive in Oxford, Gaitskell had missed the student socialist arguments about democracy and revolution, and so came to a considered position later than many contemporaries.[46] But even in his left-wing period, he combined almost fanatical commitment with a contempt for wishful thinking, an insistence on rigorous rational argument, and a concern for practical results. Once he came to think through the means of achieving Socialism, he firmly rejected the hope of spontaneous revolution as a myth, the strategy of organised revolution as leading to the wrong end, the tactic of forming dissident groups outside the Labour mainstream as a futile diversion of energy, and the underlying Marxist analysis of society and history as false in theory and detrimental in practice.

Gaitskell's excellent short account of Chartism, written before the crisis in late 1928, discusses how the problems of power were faced by a radical movement frustrated by its impotence to influence the government. That weakness was cause even more than consequence of its factional divisions. Chartism, he wrote,

> might have become purely proletarian—in which case there would always have been a tendency towards revolution—or it might have progressed by a middle and working class alliance—in which case a pacific policy was almost essential. In fact ... the extremists undermined the case of the moderates and the moderates queered the pitch of the extremists. Nevertheless it is unlikely, even if their respective fields had been clear, that either could have succeeded.

He went on to make a point that was obviously true of the 1840s: 'The success of the middle class alliance depended on the acceptance by the working class element of middle class leadership and middle class ideas.' (Years later, one profile-writer after another misquoted him as saying that working-class movements without middle-class leadership and ideas would always fail.) His own leanings were rather more to O'Connor than to the moderate Lovett, but he thought no proletarian revolution conceivable then without a Lenin or Napoleon to lead it.[47]

Another question arising from this work also troubled him: the discovery that the revolutionary army was made up not of a growing skilled working class produced by the new forces of production, but of the shrinking labour force in declining and obsolete trades, with some déclassé individual allies — by no means the socially indispensable creators of wealth whom Marxist theory saw as the carriers of historical progress. He worried over that problem for years in those long discussions with Postan and his historian friends about social classes and their role in history, and it was one major reason for his rejection of the theory.[48a]

The dream that mass discontent alone could produce an unplanned, spontaneous, successful revolution had been doomed to failure in the nineteenth century, as he had argued in *Chartism*. The lesson was borne out, nearer to his own day, by the short-lived wave of syndicalist agitation before and just after the First World War. That agitation ended in disaster in 1926 when, partly because of the expectations it had aroused, the wholly unrevolutionary trade union leaders found themselves engaged in a hopelessly ill-considered challenge to the government. Gaitskell had been unthinkingly loyal at the time of the General Strike, but once he did think about it his sympathy for the wretched condition of the miners did not predispose him to favour the self-consciously irrational doctrine which had largely contributed to their defeat. As an ultimate aim, Guild Socialism was more sophisticated, but even it, as he argued (successfully) with its main author and his own former mentor Douglas Cole, was 'both unrealistic and really directed to false aims. One must always, I said, come back to the happiness of the individual.'[11c] As a strategy, syndicalism was a recipe for disaster, the kind of left-wing movement expressing emotions without considering consequences which he always detested. Even in his own left-wing period he saw the General Strike as 'merely the last explosion of a firework which failed in 1921'.[45] Later on he came to regard it as the most vivid and complete exposure of 'the absurd "myth" of syndicalism ... of its emotional anti-rational outlook ... contrast[ing with] ... the ruthless logic and professional techniques of the Bolshevists'.[49]

That last alternative was equally unappealing, though for quite different reasons. One of those reasons was his abhorrence of splinter groups, shown repeatedly in these years. Sir Oswald Mosley's revolt within the Labour Party had attracted many discontented young Socialists (notably Aneurin Bevan up to the very moment of Mosley's breaking off to form the New Party, and John Strachey even afterwards, until it turned towards Fascism). Gaitskell may never have felt the attraction at all;* if he ever did, he swung sharply away as soon as Mosley left the Labour Party.[51] Only a few weeks later he wanted a pamphlet produced at once 'to counteract the Mosleyite swing towards Jingoism'.[52] That conviction of the need for unity, solidarity

* Dame Margaret Cole, Mrs Durbin and Sir Noel Hall thought he did; Lady Gaitskell was quite sure he did not. (Among non-Labour people tempted by the New Party programme were Harold Macmillan and J. M. Keynes.)[50]

and discipline was just as strong in his left-wing youth as it was later when he became leader of the Party. He had not forgotten how the Chartists ruined their slender chances by frittering away their energies in fighting one another, or how, after 1918, most European Socialist parties had been paralysed by disastrous splits. He was always wary of Communist efforts to divide the Labour Party in the name of Left unity, and he had far too acute a sense of power ever to be tempted into sects or sideshows.

He rejected the ends of Communism as much as the means. He had defended the Soviet Union enthusiastically, explained its faults as the product of Russian circumstances, and doubted the reality of dictatorship. But the great famine of 1933 came as an eye-opener, for he was never a man who allowed his faith to blind him to unwelcome evidence.[53] He followed later developments closely, especially the purge trials, but continued to favour a defensive alliance with the USSR, and (unlike Durbin) never before the war equated Nazism and Communism.* But while he still saw their economic and social aims as entirely opposed, his notes for a speech on Fascism at Chatham on May Day 1935 contain the grudging words: 'It must be admitted that *politically* communism is the same.'[54]

Intellectually, too, Marxism did not tempt Gaitskell for long. In their very first conversation Postan was struck by 'the note of doubt he sounded every time he brought out a stock idea'.[48b] Such a questioning mind could never be entrapped within a closed system of thought, and Gaitskell's examination of Marxism led him to repudiate it as old-fashioned, false and intellectually crippling. From his study of history, he rejected as untrue the class analysis culminating in inevitable proletarian revolution. In arguments with Marxist intellectuals, especially in Tots and Quots, he found them sterile and dogmatic purveyors of a 'hollow and boring' system of dialectics.[55] Through following world events he came first to question the way the Soviet Union was developing, and then to discover in Vienna that Marxism did not aid but impeded his left-wing friends in assessing their own predicament. That experience both reinforced his emotional commitment to Socialism and anchored him firmly on the moderate wing of the Labour Party.

iii *Socialist Think-tank*

During Gaitskell's left-wing period as well as later, he was busy preparing seriously behind the scenes for the practical problems which a Labour government would face: work which was the centre of his activity throughout the decade, and which has had no real parallel in the Party before or since.[56]

* After Durbin's death, he confessed to John Bowlby that he had been wrong about Russia and that Evan was always absolutely right.

1 Hugh Gaitskell (left) with his undergraduate brother, Arthur

2 His father in 1889, just before leaving for Burma   3 His mother

4 His parents' household in Burma, with baby Hugh in the arms of his aunt (Mrs de Burgh Griffiths) and Mary Ayah standing by

Quite early in the disappointing life of the Labour government, Cole had inspired a series of meetings of discontented intellectuals ('loyal grousers' as one of them put it) at Easton Lodge, home of the Countess of Warwick. Gaitskell was present from the start. At the first meeting, John Strachey was 'full of the Mosley manifesto, which was strongly criticised and found no real friend';[57] but Strachey soon wore out his welcome and came no more.

From these gatherings eventually emerged two distinct but closely linked organisations with a largely overlapping membership: the Society for Socialist Information and Propaganda (SSIP) and the New Fabian Research Bureau (NFRB). The first was a propaganda body, with an executive full of Gaitskell's friends, including the Coles, Dick Mitchison, and Colin Clark. Started in June 1931 with Ernest Bevin as chairman, it lasted little more than a year, becoming absorbed by that minority wing of the old ILP which stayed in the Labour Party when the rest left in 1932. Durbin opposed the absorption entirely, while Gaitskell tried to insist on safeguards: only individual Labour Party members to be admitted to the new body, and no electoral activity. His amendment (moved by H. H. Elvin) was lost by 45 to 64; the SSIP then voted to dissolve itself.[58] The ex-ILPers insisted on replacing Bevin as chairman (thus reinforcing his deep distrust of intellectuals), and the new Socialist League soon became under Sir Stafford Cripps the main organisation of the Labour Left, until the leadership obliged it, too, to dissolve itself in 1937.

The NFRB, prudently kept separate at Cole's insistence, was a research organisation set up in March 1931 to take the place of the moribund Fabian Society (with which it merged in 1938). Attlee was chairman, Cole honorary secretary, and Gaitskell both assistant honorary secretary and chairman of the economic section; later he also became vice-chairman of the foreign affairs group. He was efficient at administration, organising Cole's gigantic research programme, drafting reports and managing committees: by 1933 the economic section had eleven all working well (though not all at once).[59] It may also have been his and Durbin's doing that, to discourage Communist attempts to capture it, the NFRB adopted a rule (still retained by the Fabian Society) that it would adopt no resolutions of its own on policy.[60] He was good at smoothing over internal tensions, and soon became almost as influential as Cole himself. Years later Gaitskell wrote that the NFRB

harness[ed] the intellectual energies of many younger socialists to the practical issues of policy confronting the party ... brought them together and put them in touch with the older leaders ... [In] post-war years ... [many] who had been connected with it were members of the Labour Government.[11d]

C

The NFRB was nothing if not ambitious. Its economic inquiries sprang from a double disappointment. The Labour government had failed not only to move an inch in a Socialist direction, but even to govern effectively —tackling neither the long-term catastrophe of unemployment nor the immediate threat of financial panic. The aim was to organise serious thinking on both fronts. Gaitskell started off the committee on Socialist economics on a series of broad topics: criticism of the individualist organisation of resources; how far Socialism should employ, or abandon, the price mechanism; problems of efficiency and incentives, of saving and spending, of the direction of investment, of trade unions, wages and labour mobility, and finally of the conditions on which any form of private enterprise might be allowed.[61]

One of the most controversial of those topics among academic economists at that time was the use of the price mechanism under Socialism. Outside the NFRB, Gaitskell and Durbin organised a separate circle of colleagues to discuss it, which met in Bogey's Bar (a restaurant run by Durbin and Bowlby in a hotel basement). They also held discussions introduced by people of sympathetic views with experience of finance, like Bill Piercy, or of industry, like Austen Albu or Anthony Bowlby (John's brother).[62]

Another general subject came up through the NFRB's committee on currency and the price level, of which Durbin was convenor. The depression had brought new interest in the rapid remedies promised by monetary heretics like Major Douglas, the Social Credit leader. Gaitskell wrote a remarkably lucid and penetrating analysis of Major Douglas and three others, which formed a chapter in Cole's collection, *What Everybody wants to know about Money*;[63] in the year in which Keynes first used a multiplier analysis, it was groping towards a similar approach. Later, Gaitskell and Durbin, with a colleague, W. R. Hiskett, carried out an official inquiry into Social Credit for Hugh Dalton's Labour Party Finance and Trade Committee. It was published as a pamphlet and was reported to the Party Conference in 1935. Durbin and Hiskett spoke in the brief debate, and all three were much in demand as lecturers on the topic around the country.[64]

The main theme of anti-Labour propaganda at that time was to stress the difficulties which a Labour government would face in dealing with the financial community.* In 1935, Gaitskell contributed a chapter to *New Trends in Socialism*, edited by George Catlin.[65] He argued in detail that a government which knew its own mind could easily overcome financial sabotage of all kinds, from a run on the banks to a flight from the pound.

* An implied restriction on democratic choice arousing no alarm in respectable circles, unlike suggestions forty years later that a government of the Right might face difficulties with the trade unions.

The subject remained one of his major preoccupations until just before the war.

On financial questions the most important group was XYZ, a select dining club founded in January 1932 by a few Labour sympathisers in the City – very rare birds at that time – to prevent the Party ever again being entrapped by its ignorance of finance. Inspired by H. V. Berry, the assistant manager of the Union Discount Company, and warmly welcomed by J. S. Middleton, the Party's general secretary, its members became the anonymous advisers ('my experts') of Hugh Dalton, Labour's financial specialist and probable future Chancellor. The slightly conspiratorial title was chosen to protect its City members' careers – and twenty years later was to awaken the ever-ready suspicions of the Labour Left.

XYZ began with a few financial editors and 'City people mostly young but sometimes of surprising rank and seniority'.[66] Labour leaders like Attlee came as guests, and among the regular members were Dalton, Pethick-Lawrence and Charles Latham, chairman of the LCC's finance committee from 1934. About that time XYZ added its first economists: Durbin, Jay and Gaitskell. It 'provided memoranda for Transport House … policy statements for annual Conferences and occasionally pamphlets.'[67] It met fortnightly or monthly in a pub over a City alley deserted by night, and later at a Charing Cross hotel. During 1934 it discussed Stock Exchange reform, compensation when industries were nationalised, a Socialist Budget, and finance by bank credit; in 1935, Labour banking policy, bank nationalisation, a draft Bill for a National Investment Board, and measures against financial panic. It drafted the Bill for nationalising the Bank of England in 1946, and Francis Williams, an early member, credits it with having

> in a quiet way more influence on future government policy than any other group of the time … without attracting publicity … a democratic Socialist 'cell' which far exceeded in its success anything that the numerous much-vaunted communist cells of the time managed to achieve.[68]

Problems of immediate policy occupied Gaitskell, too, always linked to the central issue of unemployment. Again the NFRB was one main forum, but not the only one. He wrote with Durbin a substantial manuscript on wages;[45] but failed to get it published because it was thought to be too political for the academic profession and too academic for the politicians.[69] He was convenor of the wages committee, and also involved with one on taxation, and another (Durbin's) on currency and the price level. Many economists outside the Labour Party felt that these were areas of policy in which action could be taken against unemployment, and occasional ineffective efforts were made to influence government policy by collective letters to *The Times*. In June 1932 James Meade tried to recruit support for a plea for an expansionist policy, but neither Cole nor Gaitskell would sign, because the draft letter wanted a government promise not to increase taxation. Gaitskell argued that an explicit call for an unbalanced Budget would have been preferable, since without that the letter would merely reinforce pressures to cut expenditure. While admitting that his own alternative might well be politically impossible, he said it was not

> my business to make the best of the National Government but rather to point out to everybody that their actions are neither morally nor economically justifiable ... so long as we only do what the business world likes we shall never get anywhere near a classless society.[70]

He did, with 36 other economists, sign a letter in favour of expansion shortly before the next Budget, which drew from Neville Chamberlain, the Chancellor of the Exchequer, a 'resounding negative'.[71] Six weeks earlier he had said publicly that the Government's mania for economy was 'bound to intensify the depression ... Yet it was just at this moment that the State would be right to spend the money to continue with its public works ... this was the only way out of the depression.'[42b] But elsewhere he wrote that such limited objectives were not enough:

> [A] 'Prosperity' policy is essential.[44] But ... its achievement need [not] necessarily imply anything socialistic. The 'controlled inflation' of which we hear so much need not involve in any way a diminution of inequality or an attack on the class structure. Such policies must therefore be supplemented or related to the true socialist objectives.[45]

iv   *Chatham: United Front Candidate*

While busy on these back-room activities, Gaitskell kept up his WEA work as well. The college authorities encouraged him;[72] and he himself told friends that he found it more rewarding than his university teaching.[73] For some years he took classes at Shoreditch, Gravesend and Eltham, most of the students continuing to attend over a three-year period. One colleague called him a brilliant teacher who gave the most lucid lecture she had ever heard; another (not particularly friendly) thought him as much superior to Crossman as a teacher as he was inferior as a lecturer. His Shoreditch students were immensely impressed with him, and told a friend who stood in one month when he was ill that they thought him a future Chancellor of the Exchequer. Like many Oxbridge Socialists at that time, Gaitskell found it the most natural way to make contact with intelligent workers, and it was to prove very important later on in making it easy for him to meet trade unionists on friendly terms.[74] It also contributed directly to his budding political career. It was through the secretary responsible for the Shoreditch class, Harold Ceeney, that Gaitskell met George Dexter, WEA organiser for Kent; and through taking classes for Dexter, who was chairman of the Chatham Labour Party, that he first became a parliamentary candidate in 1932.

By the time he was accepted for Labour's parliamentary panel he had become quite an experienced speaker. In 1929 he had spoken in Notts again, making a good impression but perhaps foreshadowing a future weakness, for the miner friend who had asked him wrote afterwards telling him (cryptically) not to worry about the emotional side of a speech.[75] He spoke frequently also for Amyas Ross in St Marylebone. In 1931 he was again active on behalf of friends—for Dick Mitchison at King's Norton in Birmingham,[76] and for Durbin at East Grinstead in Sussex against 'rowdy but good-natured Tory opposition'.[9] Even in those discouraging circumstances—a Conservative stronghold in a Conservative year—he impressed a critical academic colleague with his ability to arouse enthusiasm without descending into rhetorical nonsense.[40] His vigorous left-wing appeal impressed Durbin's agent, Tom Baxter, who urged Gaitskell to put his name on the parliamentary panel.[77]

That first step towards Westminster was relatively easy, though Socialist intellectuals of the previous generation—like Cole and Laski and Tawney—had rarely taken it. Many of Gaitskell's contemporaries did, but then found the next stage difficult; only one (John Parker at Romford) became an MP before the war. The Labour Party expected young men to work their way up from a hopeless seat to a marginal; when they were qualified to look for a winnable constituency, they had to compete with trade-union-sponsored candidates who appealed to the local Party's soul, its pocket-book, and often its reverence for seniority also. Meanwhile young middle-class Socialists found it hard to combine earning their living with a Labour candidature. In business, particularly in the City, they dared not let their views be known; less intolerant professions, too, often considered the two occupations incompatible. Evan Durbin would not renounce his parliamentary ambitions and lost an Oxford fellowship as a result; Robert Fraser, a close friend, once had to abandon his in order to keep his job on Labour's own newspaper, the *Daily Herald*. Gaitskell was remarkably lucky: the first seat he fought had previously been won by Labour, and the second had been safe (except in 1931) ever since 1922. Meanwhile, University College gave him a base at the centre from which to operate.

Its tolerance was rather grudging. Its century-old charter flatly banned all political activity from college premises. After the 1931 election, when the left-wing students wanted to form a Socialist society, the Provost refused to lift the ban. The students were determined, and one evening Gaitskell went to tell his head of department that they were about to meet in his room to form the society. When Noel Hall said the defiance could not possibly be overlooked and the consequences might be very serious, Gaitskell answered: 'That's why I'm telling you.' Hall spent an anxious night, but next morning his junior considerately came in two hours earlier than usual to tell him they had met after all in a pub across the road.[33] Though Gaitskell had second thoughts about risking his job for a pointless gesture, he took a leading part:

> The formation of this Society owed a great deal to the backing and active support of Mr. Gaitskell. He presided at several meetings (if I remember aright he was its first president) and it was largely due to him that such prominent [speakers came] ... as John Strachey and Stafford Cripps.[6]

The authorities agreed with reluctance to Gaitskell's standing at Chatham, and there were some mutterings about his taking time off to campaign in the 1935 election (though not from his students who, far from feeling neglected, often went to help).[78]

The opportunity at Chatham came because Frank Markham, Labour MP from 1929 to 1931, was one of the handful who followed MacDonald, becoming his PPS; in the 1931 election Markham moved elsewhere, and a Tory won with a majority of 9,054 over Labour (represented by Oliver Baldwin, son of the Conservative leader), with 1,135 votes for Mosley's New Party. In reaction against Markham, the local Labour Party was looking for a left-wing candidate, and for the one and only time in his life Gaitskell filled that bill.[79] A strong left-winger himself, Dexter pressed so hard for Gaitskell that he would have resigned the chair if anyone else had been selected.[80] The CLP interviewed one trade unionist and three dons (the others were Durbin and Colin Clark), and were so unanimous that Gaitskell's name was the only one put forward.[81] At the adoption meeting, Dexter told the others that they had picked a future Prime Minister.

Technically Chatham and Gillingham were divisions of Rochester, and Chatham included middle-class parts of that town as well as the dockyards. There, wages were low – £3 a week was typical – and Gaitskell could never see how anyone could survive on it. The Party chairman during the 1935 election was a railwayman about to retire on 4s. a week pension. At public meetings, collections of 6s. 7d. or 4s. 6½d. would be reported with pride.[82a] There was a combined Trades Council and Labour Party (including the Co-operatives, which were politically active locally) but no organised trade union domination. On the contrary, there was some class tension between the aggressively proletarian unskilled men, especially from the Workers' Union and the Transport & General, and the numerous and able 'intellectuals' (teachers, engineers and civil servants) who largely ran the

Labour Party. The former resented the latter and would not work for them in local elections – and found no readier a welcome in the active local Communist Party, dominated by schoolteachers. Some of the class-conscious unskilled never quite lost their suspicions of Gaitskell's cultured accent, but most Party workers were quickly won over by his regular activity, his friendliness, his interest in people and his willingness to undertake tedious chores. Among the survivors, his popularity has lasted for forty years and he is still spoken of with pride. One of them called him 'the best candidate to work for we ever had', immediately correcting herself: 'You didn't work for him, you worked with him.'[79a]

In the summer, he came every Friday night for three open-air meetings; at one, he was always introduced as 'our prospective candidate Mr Huge Gaitskell', at another they had to get to the pitch before either the Salvation Army or a business propaganda body, the Economic League. In winter they met on Sunday evenings. Gaitskell carried their portable platform round from meeting to meeting and then back to Party headquarters at midnight. He was punctilious and – for him – unnaturally punctual, frequently missing his meals rather than be late. He managed to avoid talking like a lecturer or over the heads of the audience, and no longer despised the tricks of the public speaker's trade. As always he prepared carefully, showed concern for the individuals he spoke to, and so was at his best in personal canvassing or in his Saturday meetings with small groups. On Sunday afternoons there were indoor discussion meetings at Party headquarters, followed by chats to more small groups of Party faithful – a very successful way to keep them satisfied and likely to continue active.

The most distinctive feature of Gaitskell's candidature was his lavish attention to the Labour League of Youth. On summer Saturdays he went with them on midnight rambles, talking politics, and often ending up with political chores into the small hours. On Sunday mornings they had regular classes on Socialist problems. At twenty-six he was of their generation but a little older, able to lead political discussions and offer personal advice. His admirers proudly claim that that local branch was reputed the best in the country, and say 'they worshipped him'. His interest in the LLY was as an educator concerned about his young friends, not because it offered an organisational springboard. He played no part in it outside Chatham, regarding its activities as a diversion from serious politics, and knowing that an active and influential left-wing youth organisation would soon be curbed by Transport House; for he always disliked factional disputes, and thought his efforts best spent in the adult Party.[83]

In 1933 those disputes often turned on relations with the Communist Party, which was still pursuing its 'class against class' line, denouncing the social democratic politicians and trade union leaders as 'social fascists' and as the workers' most dangerous enemies: the same disastrous policy which had led the infatuated German Communists to collaborate tactically with Nazis against democrats, and to greet Hitler's advent to power as the last gasp of German capitalism before its inevitable collapse. The British Communists always sought to detach the Labour Party's following from its leaders through a 'united front from below', and found many Labour sympathisers – including Gaitskell – who saw them as merely headstrong, dedicated Socialists. They had an appealing cause in anti-Fascism, and in Chatham they set up a committee to enlist non-Communists, especially trade unionists, Labour and ILP supporters, and Jews.[82c] Gaitskell's two closest friends in the local Party were Dexter and Charlie Macey, both strong United Front advocates though loyally anxious not to let that campaign embarrass the candidate. Gaitskell seems to have warned Macey of the risks of being manipulated by the Communist Party;[82b c] but he was quite sympathetic to the campaign, and willingly spoke on the same platform with Communists (for example debating with their local leader on compensation or confiscation when industries were nationalised).

The Chatham Party was bitterly divided, for many members – including the secretary (Eric Cash, a dockyard worker), a new chairman and the leaders of the women's section – were very suspicious of the Communists. It came close to splitting, but Gaitskell kept friendly with both camps by concentrating on organisation and membership drives, leading a week's campaign of canvassing and open-air meetings at the height of the dispute.[43b] Already he differed from most left-wingers in his abhorrence of factionalism, and his willingness to subordinate his personal preferences in the cause of Party unity and discipline. He therefore tried to minimise the damage to the local Party by promising to respect the decision of the majority. They decided to reject the United Front and ban appearances by the candidate on a platform with Communists; Macey, Dexter and another leading member resigned from the Party, and four more offered to do so.[43c]

The effect was soon felt. At Gaitskell's adoption meeting the main speaker had been Sir Stafford Cripps, the new flamboyant leader of the Labour Left; eight months later that other left-wing hero Harold Laski was 'not considered suitable'. Shinwell would do 'if no one better is available', but Attlee (then deputy leader of the Party) was much preferred.[84] Attlee came, and Gaitskell also spoke at the meeting:[42c] a last appearance before leaving England for a year abroad. Through Noel Hall, an adviser to the Rockefeller Foundation, Gaitskell had been offered a fellowship to Vienna – and the college expected him to give that offer priority over his candidature.[85] His experience in Vienna was to prove as decisive as the General Strike and Nottingham, making him a lifelong and unshakeable supporter of collective security abroad and of parliamentary democracy at home.

v   *Red Vienna's Scarlet Pimpernel*

Gaitskell took his holiday in Austria in the summer of 1933, before spending the next academic year in the capital. Vienna in the 1930s was a mecca for Gaitskell's political friends and for his professional antagonists, the classical economic theorists, as well as for its famous psychologists and philosophers.

In economics the Austrian school was the main inspiration of the orthodox resistance to Keynes, and Vienna produced many economists of worldwide reputation: among them Haberler, Hayek, Machlup, Morgenstern, as well as Mises in an older generation. In a badly paid profession in a poor country, they often earned their living by day and taught by night. In the coffee-houses — warm and well lit and supplied with leading European papers — the impecunious intellectuals would sit gossiping for hours over a cup of coffee. Many foreign economists visited Vienna, and their local colleagues made a fuss of them.[86]

The advanced foreign students were among the chosen few invited by Ludwig von Mises to his private seminar or 'inner circle'. In this select gathering, Gaitskell noted (with some exaggeration, for argument was lively): 'there is no discussion. He is just incapable of it. There's one exception — the *English* are allowed to speak ... but if any Austrian or German student raises his voice Mises shuts him up at once.'[87] Gaitskell took advantage of the exception, volunteering almost at the first meeting to present — in German — a paper refuting Mises's own recent book arguing that a Socialist state could not have a rational pricing system: 'I was a little nervous for, of course ... Mises is not exactly good at taking criticism. However, it went off better than I expected. He was very polite, and Haberler and Strigl both came firmly to my rescue.'[87] A visiting American economist recalls that Mises thanked the speaker only for his excellent *German*, though he himself had found the paper 'a quite convincing demonstration of a workable price system under socialism ... a compelling piece of argumentation'.[88] It was a bold undertaking for a young man of twenty-seven, and after the ordeal was over Hugh wrote to his brother that he was 'feeling very happy and relieved and lazy'.[14f]

Gaitskell found some individual economists (notably Haberler) 'absolutely first class', but professionally he was disappointed in Vienna: 'One is inclined to be lazy (which the Viennese certainly are) and to spend hours a day in coffee-houses ... as a teaching and learning place Vienna is simply not to be compared with London.'[87] The teaching had no effect on his own views, except to make him react against it.[89] But he took his work seriously, and professionally it was a fruitful period, inspiring his only substantial academic work. This was on capital theory, a fashionable subject among the Austrians, and considered important in studying the causes of un-employment. He eventually published in a German periodical what he called 'two rather extraordinarily high brow articles' on it, and several years later (when he had just become Chancellor) was delighted when they were republished in a textbook edited by Oskar Morgenstern, a prominent ex-Viennese American economist.[90] The exposition is so clear, in an area where clarity is rare, that after thirty years it was still heavily relied on in discussions of capital theory.[91] He was among the translators of Haberler's theory of international trade;[92] and he began translating a major work on capital theory by an important Austrian economist, Böhm-Bawerk, author also of one of the first full criticisms of Karl Marx. Gaitskell's lucid and readable version would, unlike the translations then available, have made it accessible to the English-speaking public. But the war and then political preoccupations prevented the translation ever being finished – as Böhm-Bawerk's own academic work had come to an end when he became Austrian Minister of Finance.

As in London, Gaitskell's life in Austria had its frivolous side. Red Vienna preserved a gaiety and liveliness sharply contrasting with both the grim ruthlessness of Communist regimes and the virtuous solemnity of much of the British Labour Movement, which he had once called 'that horrible strain of puritanism in us'.[14g] Of all foreign cities the Austrian capital was his favourite, and though his London habits had not been austere, Viennese friends after seeing him at home commented on how much livelier was his life out there. In an early letter he wrote to his brother:

[T]here is probably no place in Europe where the standard of women's looks is so high and their morals at the same time pleasantly loose. Not that I have so far had any great experience, but ... if one had the inclination one's social life could be very well looked after here ...

... most people here are quite crazily Anglo-Phil – they are in any case very nice to foreigners – so that one's path is really rather strewn with primroses.

God – But Vienna *is* charming – really absolutely unique – the whole atmosphere is quite peculiar. I know that if I were not attracted to Dora or if she were here, I should not want to go back to England. In the first place it is quite small – I live very much in the centre of the town and for the most part walk ... [O]ne keeps coming across the most lovely buildings and squares tucked away quietly behind the main streets. Secondly it is very easy to get to ... very good country ... the last few days everyone has rushed off to ski ...

Then it is so easy and cheap to amuse oneself in the evening. There are masses of dancing places and if one goes to the Viennese instead of the international ones it is really charming – everybody is so very gay — although most of them haven't a bean and can afford only a glass of wine ... a mixture of charm, gaiety, kindliness etc.

... I have picked up a rather nice Viennese girl who ... looks after children in one of the famous Vienna municipality (Socialist) kindergarten — she dances quite incredibly well and it's all nice and light and romantic and entirely without foundation which is exactly what I want ... I am really too lucky, for Dora will probably be arriving here on Christmas Day.[14f]

For Gaitskell's future outlook, the crucial impact of Vienna was political. Controlled ever since the war by a Socialist Party with two-thirds of the votes, one of the least healthy cities in Europe, once notorious for its tuberculosis rate, had been wholly transformed by democratic political action, and now provided 'the most exhilarating social monuments of the post-war period in any European country'.[93] The splendid new workers' flats offered not only collectively organised cultural facilities, but the physical and family amenities taken for granted by the middle classes. To the Viennese workers they were a source of immense pride. But the upper classes were grimly resentful at losing not only most of the empire, but even political hegemony in their own capital; and they and the lower-middle-class now found their personal living space (above a bare minimum) attracting heavy municipal taxation to pay for housing the lower orders who had suddenly come to power.

Vienna brought Gaitskell into contact with a Central European Marxist tradition which was predominantly Jewish, and so doubly unfamiliar. Its revolutionary past was not far behind it. Elwyn Jones, coming out after the crisis, met a gentle, white-haired old Socialist who warned him that he would meet many extremists in Vienna; he told Gaitskell, who replied, roaring with laughter, 'Of course you realise he's an assassin?'[94] (He was Friedrich Adler, who in 1916 had shot the Austrian Prime Minister.) The leaders still often used Marxist revolutionary language, though in practice they were firmly committed to democracy. That meant seeking power by winning a majority (they already had over 40 per cent of the national vote) but not blurring the sharp lines separating their own closed society from that of their political opponents.[95]

The Republic of Austria was the politically disgruntled and economically precarious remnant of the old Habsburg Empire — a great capital and a rural countryside deprived of its industrial areas where the ethnic minorities lived. In 1919 the Allies had stopped the Austrian Socialists from carrying out the *Anschluss* with Germany, where Hitler now ruled with the seizure of his Austrian homeland as his foremost objective. Two parties in the rump state had a very strong popular base, the Socialists among the Viennese workers and the Nazis among the peasants and middle class;

but the much smaller conservative Catholic minority was in power, propped up by Fascist Italy. Members of the three parties did not mix much in their daily existence: each tried to provide for its followers, materially and culturally, throughout their lives. To the Viennese workers their Party was no mere electoral organisation, but the equivalent at once of a church, a welfare state, a university, an army and a way of life.

Gaitskell was fascinated by the world of Viennese Socialism. He took long tram-rides to the suburbs on Saturday nights to learn about its history from his friend and teacher Karl Polanyi (whom he had met in London through Cole) over the minute dinners, one egg and one spoonful of spinach per head, which were all his hosts could afford. He sometimes attended editorial conferences of the journal of which Polanyi was foreign editor. Living at first in a centre for foreign students run by an eccentric Austrian Socialist, Dr Oskar Bock, and his English wife, Gaitskell extended his friendships quickly in Party circles. Political commitment and social enjoyment were thus reinforced by the personal links which meant so much to him. Within a few months that entire world was smashed to pieces by Fascist artillery, and he saw at first hand the savage repression and suffering that followed from military defeat. The experience marked him for life.

The Austrian Party had proportionately the world's largest membership, and was proud of having preserved its solidarity – unique on the Continent – by avoiding both timid Social Democratic compromise and wild Communist adventurism. (During the 1920s Vienna was the headquarters of the 'Two-and-a-half International', to which the British ILP belonged.) But the Party kept its left wing within the fold only by renouncing coalition and going into opposition, leaving an army and police force which they felt sure would never fire on the workers. They organised their own private army, the *Schutzbund*, for protection not aggression – but it still alarmed the other side. Intransigence bred intransigence, and occasional muscle-flexing on the Left gave influence and a pretext to their extreme as against their moderate adversaries;[96] while the 'mindless militarisation' of the Party, against the warnings of its best-qualified leaders, reinforced its separatist and isolationist tendencies.[97]

At first the Socialists felt secure, believing as good Marxists in their inevitable victory. But their clerical conservative opponents, alone in power, gradually purged the armed forces which, in 1927, did fire on a spontaneous demonstration which had got out of hand. The Socialists' position weakened especially after 1933 when Austrian democracy was precariously wedged between mighty Fascist neighbours both north and south. Their leadership tried hard to avoid civil war, for they foresaw all the consequences of defeat – including the impossibility of escaping Nazi rule for long. But Chancellor Dollfuss, instead of compromising with them against

Hitler, began from 1933 gradually but systematically to erode their positions of strength. Ten weeks before the climax Gaitskell wrote to his brother: 'One is witnessing the slow, very slow, depression and extermination of the socialist movement. Fascism in Austria is certainly milder than elsewhere but its existence can't be denied.'[14f]

The likelihood of a clash brought tensions among Socialists. The leaders still hoped to strengthen the moderates in the government by avoiding provocations; they knew that if they struck first they would be condemned in the Western democracies; and they believed that the working class could fight effectively only if united in outrage against some blatant act of oppression—which Dollfuss carefully avoided.[98] The younger generation feared that he was successfully whittling away the Socialist capacity to resist. Gaitskell knew everyone who mattered in both wings: 'As the danger of a confrontation drew nearer, Hugh became ever more involved. Sometimes he argued that he should after all be also working on his Thesis. Nobody quite believed that.'[99] But (as in Chatham) his close personal friends were among the left-wing opposition, including the Kulcsars, an ex-Communist couple who started before the clash a new underground group named—like Lenin's paper—the Spark. In the endless arguments about revolutionary strategy he tried to warn his young friends that they were rash in overestimating their own strength, naive in imagining that a violent conspiratorial seizure of power could ever lead to democracy, and foolish in allowing hatred for the domestic enemy to blind them to the risk of total obliteration by the Nazis.[100] Nevertheless, when the clash came he seems to have thought their resistance might after all have succeeded.[101] But after some final provocations from hotheads in the provinces (mainly Heimwehr Fascists, but also Socialists at Linz), the government struck first and ruthlessly, arresting the Party and *Schutzbund* leaders before they could even tell their men where the arms were hidden.

On the night of 11 February 1934 Gaitskell, returning from a lively party, saw machine-guns being set up in the streets. During coffee in the Bocks' dark sitting room next morning, all the lights went out; the general strike had begun. 'Blood will flow on the streets of Vienna tonight,' he said—for unlike the other English there, he knew that was the signal for the Schutzbund's last stand.[102] That day he stood with a visitor from the Rockefeller Foundation watching the government's artillery pound the prized new workers' flats; forty-eight hours later the military and political power of the Viennese workers had been crushed by the heavy guns. The Socialists mourned 1,500 dead and 5,000 wounded.[103] Their leaders were in exile or gaol (several were to be hanged); breadwinners lost their jobs and families all their meagre possessions (down to underclothes). Occasionally starving children were rescued by Catholic charities—and put in convents.[104]

Execrated by most Austrians, the clerical-fascist regime survived the Nazi murder of the Chancellor in July 1934 but succumbed in 1938, after Mussolini lost interest in his puppet state.

As soon as the fighting ended Gaitskell threw himself into furious activity. From the *Daily Herald*'s Vienna office, where communications would not be intercepted, he telephoned to the Coles in London to alert British opinion; thanks to him the Labour Movement sent out Elwyn Jones to watch conditions in trials and prisons, Walter Citrine to represent the trade unions, and Naomi Mitchison to help, alongside the Quakers who had been doing relief work in Vienna ever since the war, to manage the hardship fund organised in London at Gaitskell's suggestion. Gaitskell got the Coles to arrange meetings for an Austrian economist friend who was in Britain to reveal what was going on, and tried to stir up public opinion at home through his journalistic friends — G. E. R. Gedye, John Gunther, Vernon Bartlett, Philip Gibbs — and on his own Easter visit to England. He sent Transport House reports on particularly shameful cases of brutality and oppression, and promoted a petition to Dollfuss from foreign residents in Vienna, urging an end to the executions; eventually he and others persuaded the British authorities to intervene.[105]

Personally, he kept in touch with distressed Socialist families in need of help — carefully, to avoid attracting police attention. He

> was a leader, a counsellor, who constantly accompanied delegations into town halls and prisons. He was the organiser of innumerable secret meetings, of talks with clandestine Austrian Socialists, of activities to enlighten the public in the West. Gaitskell the courageous friend played an important part in kindling the spark of freedom into a flame so quickly among Austrian workers after the February days.[106]

He sheltered refugees (including Ilsa Kulcsar) in his own flat, and gave 'manifold assistance' to various clandestine groups:

> An Englishman was almost beyond suspicion in those days. I remember running across Hugh one morning ... in his shirt-sleeves, carrying a laundry-basket. 'I'm turning stoker,' he said. He was taking a load of compromising papers from [his] centrally-heated flat ... to his former digs ... where there were honest stoves to burn them in.[99]

Speaking German, but a foreigner, he kept contact between sections of the party, warned Socialist friends not to go home on nights when massive police raids were expected, and acted as courier to the exile capital of Viennese Socialism at Brno. Immediately after the fighting, on 14 February 1934, he accompanied three Socialist leaders to Prague by train and there met a young Socialist student, Josef Simon, who was to organise escapes (using professional pepper smugglers). He made frequent trips across the border to Brno and Prague, sometimes accompanying refugees by train, sometimes taking a wanted person out by car (each carrying the other's passport in case of arrest). He may have arranged false passports, especially for Socialist children. He was the first and a main source of funds for Simon to pay the smugglers and the families sheltering refugees; eventually 170 people, including some quite prominent politicians, escaped through that network.[107*]

Gaitskell's activities can be known only in outline, for they took place long ago, and even at the time the less one knew what one's friends were doing, the safer for everybody. One British associate of those days thought Gaitskell very innocent and unsuitable for clandestine work.[109] If so, he learned quickly. An Austrian who saw him at close quarters found him 'very active and resourceful, always very quiet and calm. I admired him very much because he seemed to take risks with equanimity'. Another, whom he met on many street corners to pass on names, addresses and money, called him 'an idealist and a good organiser. One could rely on his help.' A third, then abroad, remembered that 'Viennese friends told me at the time that Hugh was absolutely fearless and had an uncanny ability to unmask traitors and spies'. A British friend said he was at his best in those days: 'ingenious and devoted and very brave'.[110]

For the second time in his twenties, Gaitskell had become emotionally wholly committed to a side which had miscalculated its means. He returned to England angry and frustrated at his own impotence, and seemed to his constituency workers for the first time capable of violence.[111] He certainly approved of it in some circumstances, telling the Labour Party in 1935: 'Socialists should understand that it is their duty to do anything in their power directly or indirectly to assist the revolutionary opposition within fascist countries.'[112] He was always prepared to fight a domestic Fascist threat by any means necessary, and warned a public meeting in Chatham on May Day 1935 of the need, even with the 'Conservative' type of Fascism, for 'Clarity about ultimate possibility of need for Revolutionary action e.g. General Strike'. But pending that desperate last resort, his opening themes to the same meeting were: 'Our duty here — Maintenance of Democracy — The Tradition of Liberty – The Use of Political Freedom.'[54] Earlier, he had told the Chatham Party in his New Year message 'I was a witness of two civil wars and their ghastly and tragic consequences, and I learnt, as never before, to value the freedom of British political institutions.'[43d]

---

* Among those Hugh helped to escape were the Young Socialist leader Dr Ludwig Wagner, and the author Adolf Sturmthal. Back in London, he was very active in helping refugee scholars.[108]

CHAPTER 3

'A PROPER SOCIAL DEMOCRAT' 1934–9

'Hatred of inequality and the Class Structure – the germ of all Socialist feeling'
(HG, 1934)

i *Constitutionalism and Collective Security*

During 1933 and 1934 the Labour leadership (except Cripps) abandoned the vaguely revolutionary rhetoric in which they had briefly indulged, and with the great bulk of the Party set out again on the parliamentary road to power. More hesitantly, they also began renouncing the pacifism to which most Socialists had been emotionally drawn, and making a new commitment to collective security. Gaitskell participated in both movements – without the hesitation – and found himself in the mainstream of Party opinion.

He returned from Vienna in the summer of 1934 bitter about the undeserved fate of his comrades; you could no longer joke with him about political matters, said Noel Hall, who provoked an explosion from him by setting an examination paper which treated Communism and Fascism as equivalent. Yet Hall also commented that it was not until after his return to England that Gaitskell became 'a proper social democrat'.[1] The downfall of Austrian democracy had shown him that Socialists must choose. Its powerful enemies on the Right were strengthened by the Austro-Marxists' unwillingness to repudiate revolutionary aspirations clearly and unequivocally. That ambivalence was understandable in Vienna, for reasons which did not apply in England. There, Gaitskell now insisted, support for parliamentary democracy and rejection of revolutionary rhetoric must be absolutely specific. For, though both in Britain in 1926 and in Austria in 1934 the Left were victims far more than aggressors, the revolutionary talk of the previous generation had played a part in both countries in making the clash inevitable and in inhibiting the leadership from making the best of a bad situation.

In the six months after his return, Gaitskell debated these problems of political strategy in his usual way in a small group of a dozen friends who systematically sought to discover how the institutions of a Socialist Commonwealth can be set up after the acquisition of political power – the undemocratic opposition of Capitalism overcome with the preservation of continuous General Elections – and how a Dictatorship of the Left can be crushed.[2a d]

They went thoroughly into the risks of repression while the Labour Party was in opposition, of sabotage after it won power, or of prior Conservative moves to rig the constitution to prevent it winning; and agreed – usually unanimously, occasionally with a couple of dissenters – on the ways Labour would be justified in resisting.[3]

Part of Gaitskell's revulsion from the Left was a change of attitude towards the Communist Party. Although never naive about it, at Chatham he had been relatively sympathetic. But in Austria the tiny CP had devoted its energies to attacking the beleaguered Socialist leadership; and now, back in Britain, Gaitskell was as impressed by their futility and irrelevance as by their underhand methods.[4] He agreed to the Socialist strategy group's conclusion that Labour's case was best argued 'on grounds of social justice and economic efficiency not ... of class struggle'.[2c] His disenchantment with Marxism was directly derived from his Austrian experience. Already sceptical on many grounds about the doctrine, he concluded in Vienna that as a guide to practical action it was positively harmful, diverting the faithful away from harsh realities into sterile attempts to apply rigid, irrelevant categories. While he had no time for the Communists, he found the moderate Marxists absurd.[5] Once while there, provoked by a passionately anti-Marxist Englishman, he is recorded as having 'put the Marxist case';[6] but after his return, 'In his frequent conversational inquests on the Austrian Social Democrats he invariably spoke of their Marxism as one of their afflictions'.[7a] Contact with their dogmatic British counterparts – as in Tots and Quots – only made him more distrustful.

So thorough-going were his rejection of revolutionary Marxism and his acceptance of constitutionalism that acquaintances from the NFRB or the 1917 Club, or close but new-found friends like Douglas Jay, could not believe he had ever taken a different view.[8] In February 1936 Gaitskell (along with Eileen Power) paid an overnight visit to Beatrice Webb and tried in vain to shake some of the misconceptions of his hostess. Irritated that he had not read her recent eulogy *Soviet Communism: A New Civilisation*, and did not believe that its triumphs in Russia would lead to a growth of Communism among the British trade union rank and file, she recorded an unflattering portrait:

> [H]e is said to be one of the rising young men in the socialist movement. Like Durbin he is fat and self-complacent; clever, no doubt, but not attractive; like Durbin he is contemptuous of Cripps and a follower

of Morrison and Dalton, and, I think, he is anti-communist ...
Gaitskell altogether demurs to our view that the young generation are
going definitely communist. 'They pass through a stage of communism; but they find that the working class are unaffected by communist
propaganda and they drift back to the labour party ... [or] become ...
uninterested in politics' is his verdict ... the professed Marxists don't
count in the constituencies ...

The Trade Union Movement is today, he thought, stale-mated as a
progressive force in Great Britain as it is in the U.S.A. ... [W]ith a mass
of unemployed, strikes are of no avail. Political action of a reformist
character – including municipal administration, was the one and only
way according to Gaitskell: he was in fact an orthodox Fabian of the
old pre war school. What is wrong about this group of clever and well
meaning intellectuals ... is the comfort and freedom of their own
lives; they have everything to gain and nothing to lose by the peaceful
continuance of capitalist civilisation.[9a b]

Vienna taught a harsher lesson, which rarely entered into the personal
experience of British politicians: the impotence of good intentions and
majority votes against superior force. The British Left, unlike Continental
Socialists, had the false sense of national security of an island people
sheltered from invasion for centuries. That sense was reflected in the
different forms of pacifist illusion voiced by Lansbury, Maxton and Cripps;
and in the insistence of the official Labour Party on continuing to register
its hostility to the Tory government by voting against armaments. Having
seen for himself what the military triumph of evil entailed, Gaitskell had
little patience either with those at home who talked glibly of violence
without thinking out the consequences, or with those whose wishful thinking blinded them to the dangers of allowing the Fascist countries to acquire
military predominance. He did not openly challenge Party policy, which
indeed he would have thought improper for a parliamentary candidate.
But privately he was already persuaded that war was coming and that
Britain must rearm.[10]

As early as December 1933 he had written from Vienna:

politically everything is just too bloody ... no one here seems to have
any doubt that Germany is simply preparing for war ... they naturally
think our policy since Germany left the League completely mad – and
so I'm afraid it is. I feel so ashamed of it and especially the way we
have simply given everything up and gone back to a sort of shifting
[sic] isolationism. Everything is just ghastly.[11]

Early in 1935 he publicly put the chance of a European war within five or
ten years at more than 2 to 1.[12] In 1935, too, his Chatham hostess Mrs

Grieveson recalls Gaitskell and Durbin discussing in her sitting room when the European war would begin: one said 1938, the other 1939. To her surprise, none of Gaitskell's young LLY friends became pacifists, but all entered the armed forces to work within them as Socialists.

Collective security had been Gaitskell's first political interest, and his mood of desperation about the worsening international situation provided another ground for mistrusting Cripps — who in 1935 was talking of the League of Nations as part of the international burglars' union, and proposing to stop Mussolini's impending invasion of Abyssinia by sanctions imposed by 'the workers' (who were nowhere listening).[13] For his part, Gaitskell, like most advocates of collective security, exaggerated what a different British policy could achieve, and apparently believed — like the Foreign Office — that Italy could be recruited to the anti-German camp. In arguing with the Left, his first ground for supporting collective security was the need to defend the USSR against German attack. His opponent, Dr Edward Conzé, claimed that British workers were being lured into a war solely to safeguard French predominance and 'the investments of our employers' when they should be building 'a free and happy socialist Britain'.[14]

Trying to wake up some of the younger denizens of this left-wing dreamland, in the summer of 1935 the Labour Party organised at Geneva a fortnight's summer school on foreign affairs.[15] Among the 28 students were 9 prospective candidates at the coming election, 13 future MPs and 6 future Ministers, including 2 Foreign Secretaries, George Brown and Michael Stewart. Gaitskell wrote a thirteen-page summing-up, which condemned Labour's now discarded policy of a general strike against all wars as 'an invitation to the fascist aggressors'.[16]

The League of Nations, he said, should be seen as no longer a capitalist but an anti-Fascist combination, 'one-third socialist' with the USSR in. (He did not hint at special problems with Russia, but when Ted Willis — then close to the Communist Party — argued that an international armed force should include the Red Army, Gaitskell replied that in some countries Soviet defenders might be as unwelcome as Fascist invaders.)[17] Though capitalism was largely blamed for both war and Fascism, the inference that nothing could be done till it was abolished was on many grounds 'both wrong and dangerous'. That approach offered Socialists no policy for the present day, when 'for most governments — especially those threatened with attack from Fascist neighbours — isolation is impossible, and so is unilateral disarmament'. It would lump together all capitalist governments, ignoring 'that there are degrees of temperature even in hell'; it would undermine collective security, the only hope of averting a war ending with 'civilisation and capitalism (and Socialism) in ruins'; and it would not be understood by the man in the street. Finally, Gaitskell's note attacked Lansbury and Cripps ('certain Labour politicians who appear unwilling or unable to understand the policy to which their party is committed') and admonished Labour's National Executive: 'Greater discipline must be insisted upon among the leaders who speak on Foreign Affairs. It is just as serious to give a wrong impression of Party policy on this matter as it is on the "United Front" or anything else.'[16]

The students lived in a large old Geneva house, went round the ILO and the League of Nations, and attended outdoor lectures (though Ted Willis found another student much more absorbing than the lectures). The liveliest arguments were often informal: wandering round Geneva one velvety August night and finding a fruit stall open but unattended, they took some peaches and left some money—and, starting from this uncapitalistic confidence in mankind, argued long into the small hours over Socialist aims and how to achieve them. Willis attacked Gaitskell for his caution about the Labour League of Youth and the Communist Party, and was told they were quite irrelevant to the real problems of the Labour Movement and the trade unions—'where power lies, and where my work lies'. When they next met twenty-five years later, Gaitskell greeted his rebellious student (long since expelled from both the Labour and Communist Parties) with no inquiry about his colourful political past, but by asking: 'Hallo Ted, how are you? Whatever did happen to that girl? ... I wonder if we left enough money for those peaches.'[17]

The director of the school was a League of Nations official, Konni Zilliacus. Gaitskell became very friendly with him then, though a target long afterwards of his bitter hostility as a left-wing Labour MP. In 1935 Zilliacus was pseudonymously pamphleteering against the National Government's foreign policy, and supplying the Labour Party with material which, he believed, would ensure that it won the coming general election.[18] But in the same city a week or two later, the British Foreign Secretary Sir Samuel Hoare pledged British support for collective resistance to aggression, and the League's cumbrous machinery creaked into action, imposing sanctions on all Italy's imports except the one which would hurt—oil. Such half-measures were sure to fail, but Britain would not risk provoking Mussolini into striking against the British Navy; and on 9 December the world learned that Hoare and Laval had agreed to Italy acquiring half of Abyssinia. Sanctions had by then achieved their one success: the re-election of the British National Government on the collective security policy it had taken up two months before, and abandoned three weeks later.

Gaitskell predicted that reversal beforehand to sceptical friends,[19] and denounced it afterwards in public: 'The Conservative candidate made great play with the Union Jack. No party has so disgraced or besmirched the Union Jack as this National Government.'[20a] But like another Conservative Prime Minister a generation later, Baldwin saved himself by sacrificing his closest colleague – and by postponing the abandonment of Abyssinia for five months. In March 1936 the Germans marched into the demilitarised zone of the Rhineland: the longest single step towards the Second World War, yet the hardest to challenge for a peaceful nation and a Party mistrustful of *realpolitik*. Even Dalton argued in the House of Commons that Britain could only acquiesce in the German occupation of a part of Germany.

Gaitskell gave his personal view of the situation in the *Daily Herald* on 1 April 1936.* He favoured the government's military staff talks with France, which would show Hitler that Britain would oppose any aggression against Germany's neighbours. But the talks, and Britain's concern, should not be limited to Germany's western frontier, excluding Eastern Europe; and Italy should not be treated as a partner, but instead subjected to oil sanctions while she continued with her war in Africa. The need was for a European pact of mutual assistance for all European frontiers, with Germany if she accepted the terms, otherwise without her. Three months later Gaitskell repeated these views in arguing against Cripps (who had said he preferred total opposition and encouraging strikes in arms factories, but that for the sake of unity he would reluctantly agree to a Labour offer to support the government conditionally – provided the conditions were absolutely impossible of fulfilment). Gaitskell replied:

> He did not agree either that we should not support the Government, even if they were on the side of France and the U.S.S.R. ... If France and the U.S.S.R. went to war against a Fascist Germany, he would not be prepared to stay out just because Churchill was a member of the British Government that went to their assistance.[21a]

A few years later the Labour leadership, the Labour Left and the Communist Party (though not the semi-pacifist ILP) were all giving top priority to defence against European Fascism, and to foreign affairs over domestic. Hugh Gaitskell saw that need years earlier than most political figures on the Left – or elsewhere.

ii *Socialism Before the Deluge*

In his own subject of economics Gaitskell was less prescient. He always favoured policies of expansion; but in economic theory, lacking self-confidence, he remained more orthodox than Keynesian until 1937, a year after the *General Theory* came out. His colleague Rosenstein-Rodan influenced his ideas and his reading, introducing him to the Swedes like Wicksell and to J. R. Hicks.[22] Senior Labour politicians were suspicious

---

* Not now a prospective candidate, he no longer felt inhibited from doing so.

of Keynes for having worked with Lloyd George, but the attitude of the young Labour economists was quite different. Not only did they, like Keynes, attribute the trade cycle (in 1935) to changes in the relationship between savings and investment, but they named him as the appropriate economist to advise a future Labour Minister responsible for measures to restore prosperity.[2b] However, their detailed work on employment policy was a sophisticated analysis of traditional Labour measures, rather than a new Keynesian approach. In 1936 (before the *General Theory* was available) an Economic Group — Gaitskell, Durbin, Jay and Colin Clark — wrote a long memorandum on these lines, apparently the first of several on different economic topics, for Dalton's Finance and Trade Sub-committee of the Labour Party Executive.[23]

These young Socialist economists also still differed from Keynes in thinking that no expansionist economic policies could be carried out until the country's financial structure was changed, above all by nationalising the joint stock banks.[2b] Like iron and steel later, in the early 1930s that item was the main ground of domestic controversy within the Labour Party. G. D. H. Cole was the main intellectual advocate of nationalisation; among the politicians Attlee and Cripps supported it, but Dalton opposed it as unnecessary for effective control of the economy, and as politically dangerous because it would expose Labour to the kind of scaremongering tactics used in 1931. It was approved by Labour's Leicester Conference in 1932, but dropped from the 1937 'Immediate Programme'. Gaitskell stood with the Left, arguing for it not only in *New Trends* (1933) but also in 1935 at a NFRB conference on banking,[21b] where he 'attacked with great ferocity' a defence of traditional policy by a senior representative of the Westminster Bank.[24] On the other flank, one of his main points against the Social Credit spokesmen was that their plans could not be carried out without nationalising the joint stock banks (which they did not propose).[25] Insurance companies were also among his main targets.[21c]

Bank nationalisation was discussed exhaustively in XYZ, which carefully assessed the need to take over major financial institutions and worked out practical means of doing so. As we have seen, the Bill nationalising the Bank of England was drafted there; and Gaitskell and his friends gradually came round to the view (which post-war experience proved correct) that that was the only indispensable prerequisite for economic expansion. This conclusion emerged from long talks in yet another political discussion group, led by Hugh Dalton, about the growing influence of the Bank and Treasury over the City;[22a] the young economists were moving from the orbit of Cole the academic to that of the practising politician. At the end of 1936 Durbin wrote to Dalton saying he no longer wanted nationalisation of the joint stock banks in Labour's Immediate Programme; and Gaitskell certainly agreed.[26]

Arguments about economic structure and long-term questions of power were among the reasons why Gaitskell was not an instant convert to Keynesianism. Its preoccupation with short-run macro-economic management contradicted the instinctive Labour presumption that the ills of capitalism were too acute to be met by palliatives addressed only to symptoms. Moreover, as a modern writer points out, Keynes's approach 'suggested an alternative economic strategy to the one outlined by the Labour Party ... avoided having to choose between capital and labour ... [and implied] indirect and general, as opposed to direct and detailed economic control by government'.[27] But in 1936 Gaitskell still fully expected that a Labour election victory would open the struggle for power and not conclude it. Far from trying to temper Labour policies to what capitalists would concede, he spent much of his energies on considering possible undemocratic forms of resistance—from the anticipated financial panic to Conservative measures to strengthen the House of Lords—and planning how to counter them. The argument about bank nationalisation was entirely about power, and he and his friends favoured doing it immediately until they became convinced that effective power could be obtained without it.[28]

Defeating financial panic in different forms remained a serious concern until the war; Gaitskell drafted the last of many memoranda on it for Dalton's Finance and Trade Sub-committee in 1938. He dealt very thoroughly with the dangers of a flight from sterling, a collapse of security prices, a run on the banks and a flight from currency into goods.[29] Cripps had cheerfully assumed that such a crisis was bound to accompany the advent of a Labour government, but Gaitskell thought an effort must be made to avert this, since it might well ruin both the Party at the polls and the workers through unemployment.[30] Weakness in coping with inflation was a longer-term financial threat to a progressive government. His worry about that threat was not due to special foresight about problems with the trade unions, for he was sure there would be none[1a] (and in his own time, rightly sure) and their bargaining power was still small.[9a] It arose instead from the crude lessons widely drawn from experience abroad, notably in France, where a divided left-wing government had been disastrously weakened by its failure in this area; Gaitskell replied that in Sweden a united Socialist Ministry had managed monetary policy with striking success.[31] But his justified concern about inflation indicated no move to the Right; on the eve of war he told a Labour League of Youth school at Godalming that a Labour government must at once nationalise the Bank of England and set up a National Investment Board, and that 'budgetary policy must take steps as soon as possible to reduce social and economic inequality. That, I take it, is the major aim of Socialism.'[30]

*   *   *

Gaitskell was an active lecturer. In November 1936 he spoke to trade union officials on financial and monetary policy at Wellingborough; on becoming Chancellor of the Exchequer fourteen years later, he chose as his PPS Arthur Allen who had organised that meeting. He was on the London Labour Party's 1938 list of speakers on finance and economics and on foreign affairs. By then candidate for South Leeds, he spoke in the West Riding on similar topics, most ambitiously at a day school on 'The Coming Slump' in April 1938. Less publicly, he remained a mainstay of the NFRB, attending every meeting of the executive, becoming vice-chairman of its international section, and chairing or speaking at conferences on various subjects (agriculture, defence, propaganda). From 1935, he also sat on various Labour Party advisory committees; Dalton's on finance; Shinwell's on Trade and Preferences, dealing with the Ottawa agreements; and one with Ernest Bevin on international questions.

Before the threat of immediate war overshadowed everything, he outlined his expectations for 'The Next Ten Years in Britain' at the beginning of 1935, on what he already called the very unlikely assumption that peace was preserved. He forecast (protesting at the absurdity of doing so) a Conservative victory at a 1936 election, a possible split, and a good Labour majority in 1938 or 1939. He fully expected to see a National Investment Board set up (it was a Keynesian as well as a Labour proposal), and also nationalisation of the Bank of England, the electricity supply, the railways and probably the mines; and he saw a 50 per cent prospect of extending nationalisation much wider than any Labour government had yet envisaged, to land, cotton, insurance and the joint stock banks.* He did not see much chance of any substantial change in the distribution of wealth, or of 'permissive' reforms in areas like divorce, abortion, obscenity and the death penalty – calling all these 'improbabilities'.[12]

While equality was always his fundamental aim, public ownership was his chosen instrument. In his first article in South Leeds after becoming its Labour candidate in 1937, he wrote: 'So long as production is left to the uncontrolled decisions of private individuals, conducted, guided and in-inspired by the motive of profit, so long will Poverty, Insecurity and Injustice continue.'[32] Soon afterwards, he supplied notes for lectures to the Labour League of Youth, in which he said social justice must mean ending the scandalous inequality which 'will exist so long as private ownership of means of production is general'.[33]

His fullest surviving statement on this subject is a lecture in December 1935, where he said four advantages could be expected from socialisation:[34]

---

* The Socialist strategy group discussed these and one other, iron and steel (which had more support than any of the first three).[2b]

'Equality'.	1. Through Public Ownership to lay the foundations of a classless society.
'Internal Efficiency'.	2. Through Coordination to remove 'internal' wastes and increase the efficiency of the industry.
'National Planning'.	3. As a necessary accompaniment to effective national planning, to eliminate unemployment, insecurity and waste.
'Workers Position'.	4. To improve the status and position of the workers.

He opposed confiscation on grounds of both principle and practice, saying it was appropriate in a revolutionary situation but not in a democracy; but if compensation were paid, then the change of ownership would not lead to a rapid advance to equality, and consequently 'Socialisation as such is not Socialism'. He favoured workers having full control, if they wished, over workshop conditions, including discipline; but he opposed a syndicalist structure giving them power to raise prices or restrict output as they chose. Instead, 'What is needed is to get rid of the class distinctions' — and of spokesmen for capitalist interests at the top.[35] As always, he based his views on a fundamental assumption: 'an underlying hatred of inequality and the Class Structure ... [is] the *germ* of all Socialist feeling.'[36]

All these problems of Labour's political and economic programme and foreign policy were thoroughly discussed in a small group of close friends who met informally, perhaps as often as once a fortnight, in one or another's house or sometimes at the LSE, with Durbin as the moving spirit. The membership varied somewhat with the topic, and besides Gaitskell it included Robert Fraser, leader writer on the *Daily Herald*, Douglas Jay of *The Economist*, Colin Clark, Ivor Thomas and (out on the fringe, not being a Londoner) Richard Crossman. The group produced two books both edited by their most senior member, Professor George Catlin: *New Trends in Socialism* (1933) and *War and Democracy* (1938); Gaitskell's contribution to the latter was too long and did not appear. Jay's book *The Socialist Case* and Durbin's *The Politics of Democratic Socialism* were also extensively discussed there. As with XYZ there was a faint whiff of conspiracy, for they tried to avoid attracting attention: the preface to *War and Democracy* rather fraudulently stresses their 'spontaneous consensus'. Here Gaitskell was in strictly social-democratic company, dedicated to strengthening the intellectual foundations of orthodox Labour politics.[37]

These personal associations were reinforced when Gaitskell acquired a new patron, far closer to the centre of Party power than Cole or Tawney: Hugh Dalton. Thirty years later Gaitskell was to call those three the men who most influenced his pre-war political development.[38] Though he had held only a junior post as Parliamentary Secretary to the Foreign Office, Dalton was universally regarded as a future Chancellor or Foreign Secretary. Out of Parliament from 1931 to 1935, he first sat on Labour's National Executive in 1926–7, and then continuously from 1928 until the Bevanite sweep of 1952. Unusually among senior men in politics (or elsewhere) and far more than any of his colleagues, he had an abiding, life-long and selfless interest in encouraging able young newcomers and helping their careers. Unlike Morrison, Dalton had been active in the talks from which the SSIP emerged, but he withdrew in 1932 on discovering that official NEC responsibilities could not be combined with unofficial ginger-group activity. Cut off from the intellectual Left, he found a natural alternative in the social democratic group.

They became his political protégés, especially Gaitskell, whom he privately saw, as early as November 1933, as a potential Party leader in twenty years' time if his health proved good enough.[39] The two men met first in a miner's cottage near Worksop when the younger man was teaching at Nottingham,[40] and next in 1930 at dinner with Postan and Eileen Power; there, after Gaitskell and Durbin left, Dalton characteristically upbraided his hosts for 'hoarding these charming young Socialists' for their exclusive enjoyment.[7b] The friendship soon ripened between two men both of whom were upper-middle-class public school Socialists, taught economics at London University, and were as interested in foreign affairs as in finance. Besides their contacts in town, 'Little Hugh' stayed twice (in October 1932 and September 1935) at 'Big Hugh's' country cottage in Wiltshire.[41a] Gaitskell, like Dalton's other young disciples, followed their mentor in Party matters, notably over the leadership at the end of 1935 – all favouring Herbert Morrison against Attlee and Greenwood.[42]

The younger men also shared Dalton's contempt for Cripps, who resigned the deputy leadership a few months before the election to be freer to indulge in the semi-revolutionary rhetoric which so delighted the Tories. There was a striking contrast between those public posturings and the private (and radical) constructive hard work of Dalton's young friends. No wonder Gaitskell told Beatrice Webb:

> The one hopeful institution in the labour movement is the Fabian Research Bureau ... the younger men like Maurice Webb and Durbin and Parker and himself ... with Dalton and Morrison will be the intellectual leaders of the future ... Like everyone else he deplored the inferiority of the Labour Party staff at Transport House and the over-whelming influence of Citrine over the Trade Union Movement.

She found him as scornful of Cripps's movement as of the man, dismissing the Socialist League as 'purely mischievous' but fortunately quite unimportant.[9a]

Even when closest to them in his own views, Gaitskell had been wary of the quarrelsome factionalism of the Left and their endless revolts. Always a party man, in 1932 he told his selectors at Chatham that he had no use for splinter groups, and warned his friends who wanted a United Front with the Communists not to let themselves be used to split the Labour Party instead. He distrusted the sectarianism of the old ILPers, and vainly tried to guard against the Socialist League taking a separate line of its own. In 1935 he told Ted Willis he would have nothing to do with the factional disputes in the Labour League of Youth, and he criticised the Party leaders for insisting publicly on their own individual viewpoints on foreign affairs. All Socialist parties had always believed – in principle if not in practice – in the doctrine (now obsolete in Britain) that political action must be united and disciplined to be effective. Gaitskell's generation were the more conscious of the need for teamwork after seeing the harm so recently done by futile fragmentation: on the Left by Communists and ILP, on the Right by National Labour and New Party, and by the unpredictable Cripps who was consistent in nothing but his hostility to the leadership (within a couple of years he was to switch from preaching half-baked revolution and half-hearted pacifism to calling for alliance with anyone, however anti-Socialist, who would oppose Chamberlain).

By 1935 Gaitskell's position was thus clear. Politically the Labour Movement was moving away from pacifism and revolution towards collective security and constitutionalism, the Labour Left was busily discrediting itself, and the leadership was open to constructive suggestions on policy. Intellectually, he was becoming increasingly impatient with the Left's abstract theorising; in 1935 when Postan sent him an offprint on Marxism, he replied that he had lost interest in the subject and implied it was high time his friend did so too.[7a] Personally, he was in touch with the Party leadership through the friendship of a senior politician, and among his own generation he associated through Durbin with a group of intellectuals whose views were more orthodox and stable than his own had sometimes been.

After the war, he wrote that that group 'marked ... the transition from the pioneering stage to that of responsibility and power'. His friends, he wrote, were – unlike Laski, Cole and Tawney –

> not content to be merely intellectual advisers ... separated too much from the main stream of the political movement because they did not accept ... responsibility.
>
> They broke away ... from any kind of Marxist doctrine. They believed as passionately in democracy as they did in socialism ... [seeing] the spectacle of Fascism rising on the Continent.
>
> [Their] economics ... [were] based on the work of Tawney and ...

Keynes ... They were not just interested in protesting against the ills of the present, they wanted to get rid of them in a practical kind of way ...

... they were, before everything, realistic. They were not interested in Utopianism. They believed that if you accepted democracy as the best and only tolerable form of government, you had ... to accept and understand [its] limitations ... People had to be persuaded, and their views and emotions ... taken into account.

They believed in making the economy more efficient; they believed in the possibility of full employment; they believed in social reforms which would gradually undermine the class structure, so that in due course a happier and more socially just society emerged. These were the ideals they held in front of them, and it was in order to advance these that they had gone into politics.

On their outlook, he wrote elsewhere:

They were realistic in politics and critical of armchair politicians who, not understanding what the British electorate were really like, were forever making bad political judgments. Above all, while accepting the ultimate emotional basis of moral valuation, they had great faith in the power of reason both to find the answers to social problems and to persuade men to see the right. They were for the pursuit of truth to the bitter end, through the patient and unswerving application of logical thought. They wanted no barriers of prejudice to obstruct the free working of the mind or blunt the sharp edge of intellectual integrity.[43]

iii   *From Southern Marginal to Northern Stronghold*

By the time Gaitskell went to Vienna the National Government had shed the Liberals and Snowden, and had lost much ground in the country. 'In England, of course,' he wrote in December 1933, 'things are going pretty well for the L.P. and I suppose there's a chance of my getting in at Chatham next time. But then I haven't much faith in the Party doing much as it is at the moment.'[11] In April 1934, on a brief visit to England, Gaitskell told a public meeting: 'the shoddy façade with which the government deceived the electorate in 1931 was crashing and crumbling wherever and whenever the workers had an opportunity.'[44] Under Herbert Morrison, Labour for the first time won control of the London County Council that spring; in the Medway Towns they gained seven council seats in 1933–4. As always, the prospect of electoral success invigorated and unified the Party, restoring its confidence in itself and its leaders.

From Vienna, Gaitskell had kept in touch with Chatham by a regular correspondence with Mrs Grieveson, as well as by meetings on his brief visit home in April 1934. Soon after his return that autumn, he officially attended his first Labour Party Conference at Southport as Chatham's delegate. A few weeks later he accompanied Mrs Grieveson to a Mosley meeting in Gillingham — where, having warned her against interrupting, he was himself provoked into accusing the Fascist leader of 'telling abominable lies' about events at the Southport Conference. Hecklers of Mosley risked being beaten up for much less, but Gaitskell was not molested; and on their emerging to face the huge hostile crowd outside, a local Communist called out: 'Let them alone, they're two of ours!'[45] If he had ever felt that Communists were 'ours', he did so no longer. He told a meeting at Gillingham in December 1934: 'The only way to combat Fascism was to stand firmly by democracy. They could not get votes by shouting.'[46a] Like Durbin earlier, he too now put the preservation of democracy in Britain first of his three political objectives, along with Socialism and peace.[20b]

Since 1933 Durbin had been prospective candidate for Gillingham. Though next door to Chatham, it was very different: less hopeful (Tory in 1929), more of a dormitory suburb, and with fewer left wingers — Durbin told his wife he would have been unhappy fighting Chatham. The two friends conducted many constituency activities together, each speaking frequently in the other's division, and writing jointly to the local press. (In the election they arranged to go together to a boxing match at the naval barracks, hunting sailors' votes; the unpunctual Gaitskell thought it an excellent idea but arrived very late — and met the Durbins, who had hated the whole thing, on their way out early.)

They both followed the Party line on foreign and defence matters, denouncing the government for its betrayal of collective security, accepting military sanctions if necessary, repudiating 'one-sided disarmament' by Britain, but saying they would as MPs certainly have voted against increased arms estimates. As candidates in a dockyard town, they ingeniously claimed, using many statistics, that Labour would restore prosperity to the Admiralty yards by bringing back work handed over by the Tories to private contractors — yet that these would not suffer since Labour would also get rid of Tory protectionist policies, encouraging a revival of trade and so of commercial shipbuilding.[47]

Parliament was dissolved in October 1935 and Gaitskell was plunged into the first of his six general elections. Besides his energetic local party, he had numbers of his students helping at weekends, several Austrian Socialist refugees who kept discreetly in the background, and many personal friends and relatives (including his Tory cricketing brother-in-law, and his mother who worked in the committee rooms and sat prominently on the platform, loudly announcing every now and then: 'I'm not a member of the Labour Party, you know.')[48] While Durbin fought 'a very candid, very educational, very W.E.A. type of campaign', Gaitskell was more effective – with a lighter touch, and rather more willing to play politics.[49] But he too was fundamentally serious, perhaps not bitter enough for the class-conscious unskilled workers; and he discouraged his supporters from using bad puns on his own name ('Get-skill') or that of his Conservative opponent Lionel Plugge ('Pull the Plug out').[50] He protested at his adoption meeting of rumours being spread that he was a German Jew, a Russian or an Italian;[46b] but there was so little bitterness in the campaign that he complained of the lack of heckling.

For some time he had been busily cultivating non-Labour personalities, particularly the many Liberals in the educational and Church world of Rochester; and he annoyed some Labour people by deciding on the very morning of nomination day to have several Liberals sign his first paper, somehow delaying the nominations for half an hour until Mrs Grieveson arrived with the signatures. He showed his usual talent for getting help from his influential seniors by attracting an impressive array of speakers for a first-time candidate. They ranged from a prominent trade union leader, George Hicks, to politicians like Cripps and Dalton, and intellectuals like Tawney, Cole and Laski – who, according to Party workers, made the best speech of the lot. (A more frivolous source claims that Amyas Ross stole the show by hilarious imitations of Stanley Baldwin, the Prime Minister.)

At the eve-of-poll rally in the Rochester Casino, Gaitskell's students carried him in on a chair decorated with the Labour colours. Publicly he told his supporters there: 'Whether we win or lose tomorrow is not of vital importance. The election is merely another stage in the struggle which has been going on for the last century.'[20c] Privately he confessed to student friends that he had no chance of success; but at the count he was less philosophical, and became very wrought-up, saying later that the result was like a kick in the stomach.[51]

Capt. L. Plugge (Cons.)	19,212
H. Gaitskell (Lab.)	13,315
Majority	5,897

Gaitskell had polled 2,500 more than Labour had ever previously obtained in the constituency. He did a bit better than in other naval seats where Labour was strong, exactly the same as in similar seats in the south of England.[52] His biggest disappointment was the total failure of his generation – apart from John Parker at Romford – to penetrate that stronghold of the elderly, the Parliamentary Labour Party.[53]

A few weeks later Gaitskell was one of those contributing to the NFRB's inquest on the election at Maidstone. He was still anxious to avoid mere MacDonaldite palliatives:

> [W]e wanted neither revolution nor reform. The centre of the pro-
> gramme must be socialisation, but we needed a short term programme
> ... [We] had nothing to offer in time of boom, but ... if another de-
> pression came, people would want big changes.[21d]

He nearly became an MP in 1936, instead of 1945. In October 1936 there was a by-election in the mining stronghold of Clay Cross, Derbyshire (once Arthur Henderson's seat), close to Gaitskell's old Nottinghamshire lecturing ground. He was runner-up but lost to George Ridley, a trade union member of the NEC, after a 'protracted meeting'.[54] Had Gaitskell entered the House then, he would certainly have been in the government in 1940 and (health permitting) in the Cabinet by 1945, with incalculable consequences.

In 1936 Gaitskell, after a year away in Vienna, and then a term away contesting the general election, had fences to mend at UCL. In November he decided not to stand again at Chatham, and received in reply the warmest tribute a CLP in a marginal seat can bestow: 'the whole of the Party in Chatham would be pleased if you were offered a "safe" seat in the near future.'[55] For domestic reasons he was not anxious to find a new constituency at once, for Dora was getting divorced. Even after that was settled and they were free to marry, he remained hesitant about a candidature.* He found a letter from the agent in South Leeds ('a first rate seat')[56] awaiting him on returning from his honeymoon in April 1937 — and had doubts about following it up since he 'had intended to concentrate on academic work and drop politics for the time being'.[57]

South Leeds had a solid working-class population employed in small engineering and textile factories and railway engine sheds. Labour's municipal leader in Leeds was a well-known pre-war housing reformer, the Reverend Charles Jenkinson, a parish priest from that constituency with a mission to demolish it. The area was largely self-contained and surprisingly isolated from Leeds north of the river. It had its own community life; Richard Hoggart wrote his paean of praise to traditional working-class communal values after growing up in the constituency.[58] Socialist Sunday Schools still flourished between the wars, and every Sunday morning in summer 60 or 80 (occasionally even 200) people came to a Labour outdoor meeting on 'The Stones', in Cross Flatts Park in the centre of the constituency. The speakers were usually local councillors and party workers, quite often the MP, and occasionally visitors.

In 1904 Labour won some of its first municipal Leeds victories there,

---

* Gaitskell's marriage and home life are discussed in the next Section.

and in 1922 one of its first two parliamentary seats (out of six). The MP was Harry Charleton (an NUR engine-driver on the London to Leeds run) who lost by 700 votes in 1931 and returned to the footplate, then regained the seat in 1935. But his majority was down from 8,000 in 1929 to only 1,000, since – owing to his age – many Labour voters supported a local man who polled 3,600 as a Social Credit candidate, the only one in Britain.[56] (Ironically, Social Credit's main intellectual antagonist was later to represent them.) By the next election in 1939 or 1940, Charleton would be past the NUR retiring age for MPs, so the union would no longer sponsor him and subsidise the constituency. In 1936 George Brett, the secretary-agent, told Charleton that South Leeds would have to look for a new candidate, and the MP did not demur. But Brett did not add that he thought the CLP could if necessary afford to do without the NUR sponsorship money. A forceful and intelligent man (whose daughter Marjorie later founded the Leeds Fabian Society), he was determined to choose a first-class candidate.

The local party invited several potential nominees to speak from The Stones that summer. Gaitskell, in sharp contrast to his Chatham experience, was the only intellectual. His name came from John Parker, MP, secretary of the NFRB, who was a keen talent-spotter of young middle-class Labour supporters, and a friend of Brett's daughters through the University Labour Federation. Parker heard from Dick Mitchison, who spoke in Cross Flatts Park late in 1936, that South Leeds was looking for a candidate; and on 20 October 1936 he wrote suggesting Gaitskell, Durbin, Tom Reid (later MP for Swindon), and two women who were promptly ruled out.[59] Brett heard well of Gaitskell from both Harold Laski and Hugh Dalton (who spoke in Leeds soon afterwards), met him after some delay on 22 May, and took to him at once.

Gaitskell's competitors were all trade unionists: two from Charleton's NUR – Councillor Dai Jones of Pontypridd and W. T. Proctor of Pontypool – and two from NUDAW (the distributive workers' union): Evelyn Walkden and Hyman. All but the last were short-listed, though Gaitskell and Dai Jones had made much the best impression (and Walkden had not spoken owing to shortage of time).[60] But now trade union politics intervened. NUR delegates from all over Leeds decided to send only one of their members, Tom Proctor, before the selection conference – so that South Leeds was forbidden by people from outside the constituency even to consider Dai Jones. Naturally the locals were indignant, especially Brett, who thought Gaitskell best but would have been perfectly happy with Jones – though, for his own good reasons, not with Proctor. From that moment the agent went all out for Gaitskell's nomination even though it would mean losing the trade union money on which his own salary depended. He had no regrets, writing years later when Gaitskell became

5 With Mary Ayah   6 As a boy

7 A shooting party before the First World War at Staithe House at
Brancaster, Norfolk, rented by Hugh's uncle Ernest Martelli (far left).
Hugh, aged 6 or 7, is standing in front of his grandfather George Jamieson,
and his father is on the far right

8 End of the General Strike, May 1926. Police clearing the streets in London for the first tram

9 Vienna, February 1934. Austrian troops engaged in street fighting against the Socialists

Chancellor of the Exchequer that he was delighted that 'all the risks I took to keep Bro. Proctor out [have proved] worthwhile'.[61a]

He gave Gaitskell good advice before the selection conference:

> Proctor and his friends are getting the backs up of the purely Labour Party members and are blundering in tactics all along the line ... confine yourself to how you would tackle the Division — the time you could spend, the personal canvas [sic] you would be able and willing to do ... that you could get valuable platform assistance from political friends of importance. Stress your experience in nursing Chatham and your increased vote ... [and] support from young people. Mention that you were the runner-up at Clay Cross. Hammer facts like these into them, together with your firm belief in the cause of Socialism.[61b]

All delegates to the previous AGM were invited to the selection conference on 3 September 1937, and three nominees spoke. Gaitskell followed Brett's advice closely. He returned in the train with Walkden who, he wrote to Brett, seemed a formidable competitor.[62] But the real battle was with Proctor, and Gaitskell won.

Furious, the NUR claimed that the selection conference was invalid, since Brett had not sent credentials to those affiliated organisations which had ignored the AGM but had now suddenly become active. The NUR was then a very powerful union within the Party nationally, and was bitterly resentful of the growing independence of the constituency parties (which, actively encouraged by Dalton, had just won the right to elect their own NEC members). Its allies on Labour's National Executive may well have been joined by enemies of Dalton, whose friendship for Gaitskell was well known.[63] The National Executive upheld the complaint, and on 7 November a new selection conference was held. Walkden withdrew to avoid antagonising the NUR, who tried hard to maximise their strength and were backed by some local trade unionists wanting a sponsored candidate. Brett again sent good advice.[61c] Before the voting, Gaitskell refused to offer to offset the trade union money, saying he wanted a choice on merit; only after his nomination was narrowly confirmed did he promise to pay £100 towards Party funds and £200 to election expenses, enabling Brett to remain as part-time agent. (Proctor became an MP in 1945, and Walkden in 1941 — before Gaitskell.)

Worse embarrassment followed. Harry Charleton had assumed that the constituency were looking for a new candidate because they could not afford an unsponsored MP, as he himself would soon become. But when they chose one, he thought he should have remained as MP on new financial terms. So he too complained to the NEC because he had not been called to the first selection conference. Thinking him too old anyway, the CLP still did not invite him to the second one.[64] He took umbrage, broke off

D

relations with Brett, demanded to see the local executive without the agent, refused to attend Gaitskell's adoption meeting, and ignored Herbert Morrison's mediation.

Charleton had no personal resentment against Gaitskell, who went to see him twice.[65] But in his wrath at Brett and the local party, the MP boycotted the constituency altogether, and for four years would not come near it. So, having offended the NUR and been a subject of NEC intervention, Gaitskell had become candidate for a safe seat – but one where the sitting MP would have nothing to do with him or it or the CLP, but was determined to cling on at Westminster. Instead of an uncomfortable couple of years before Hugh Gaitskell could take his assured place in the House of Commons, he had eight years to wait.

For the next two years of peace he was there regularly, and faced some mildly unpleasant opposition. He was denounced by the prospective Conservative candidate in August 1938 in the local Tory paper as a warmonger, an intellectual, and a Londoner; Brett protested and the author privately apologised, saying he had not realised Gaitskell was a public school boy.[66] The Fascists were active elsewhere in Leeds, with its large Jewish population; Holbeck Moor, where a Fascist march was stopped in a once-famous pitched battle, lies within the constituency. Gaitskell was himself once a target for anti-semitic rumours. But within the local Labour Party the new candidate soon overcame his inauspicious start. Though a middle-class intellectual in a working-class constituency, chosen in competition with working-class rivals in succession to a working-class MP, he quickly attracted and always retained the enthusiastic loyalty of South Leeds.

That was partly because he was so assiduous in constituency work, just as in Chatham – far more so than Charleton had ever been. He wrote regularly for the local party papers – less for the *Citizen*, pride of the Leeds city party, than for the *South Leeds Worker* and the *Beeston Democrat*. He came regularly, canvassing, visiting the working men's clubs on Saturday nights as he enjoyed doing for the rest of his life, speaking from The Stones on Sunday mornings and attending the General Committee in the afternoons. The local Party soon discovered his unassuming friendliness and pleasure in mixing with ordinary people and in constituency work. He would never stay in hotels, always with his agent or chairman (insisting on paying). George Brett was his first host; then Harold Watson on the Middleton Estate, or Billy Goodwill in his little back-to-back with the toilet four doors up the street; finally George Murray.[67] He quickly became known, and quickly loved. When war came, he knew he could rarely visit and doubted if he could continue his financial contribution, but the Party was determined to keep him on; in 1945 he was ill at the moment of the election, but the selection conference knowingly renominated – unopposed – a candidate who might well be unable to campaign at all. Such was the reputation he had earned among his constituents in the last twenty months of peace.

iv *Marriage, and Professional Promotion*

Gaitskell's connection with South Leeds began at the very same moment as another lifelong bond, even more important: his marriage. The passionate friendship with Dora had ripened long before. The Frosts separated in 1933, and but for the 'utterly shameful and disgraceful' state of the divorce law — so Dora told the House of Lords much later — the Gaitskells would have married then or soon afterwards.[68] It was also in 1933 that Dora suffered a crushing blow when her publishing firm was taken over and she lost her cherished job. She went out to Vienna to join Hugh for the last five months of his stay there. On their return in the summer of 1934, he rented 24 Harley Road, an agreeable three-storey Victorian house near Swiss Cottage, shaken by trains which ran beneath the building. He was active in these years in helping to find jobs and asylum for persecuted refugee scholars, and he played his own part by sharing his house with friends from Vienna like Julius Braunthal, later secretary of the Socialist International, and Fritz Hirsch, an *Arbeiter Zeitung* journalist, with his family. Hugh and Dora went around together; she joined him in all the UCL outings, and saw much more of his political friends outside the Bloomsbury world.

Divorce still presented enormous problems. Until A. P. Herbert's Act of 1937, legal proceedings could be very slow, humiliating and precarious, and even afterwards it carried, for everyone involved, a stigma hard to imagine today. They wanted to avoid damaging either David Frost's professional career or Hugh's political prospects: very regretfully, Dora thought it unwise even to help Hugh in Chatham. The waiting was particularly hard for her, since she had lost her financial independence and was anxious about the effect of the separation on her son, Raymond. By 1936, however, her divorce was under way, and when it was completed — without the difficulty or deceit they had feared — they were at last able to announce their forthcoming marriage to their friends at Kleinfeld's.

Hugh and Dora were married in the Registry Office in Hampstead Town Hall on his thirty-first birthday, 9 April 1937. Evan Durbin was best man, and only a few relatives and very close friends were present. They spent their honeymoon in Normandy, and returned to Harley Road where they lived until the war began. After all his scorn for bourgeois family life, Hugh was soon writing to a friend about to marry: 'As a husband of almost exactly 3 months standing and after a distinctly protracted engagement, I can confidently recommend respectability when one has reached the thirties!'[69] A UCL colleague noticed that Hugh 'carried himself better, looked healthier, life was ... less full of devils around the corner'.[1a] The secure home life he had never known before had a tranquillising influence, giving him (said the same colleague) an impressive combination of 'ballast and buoyancy'.[1a] The partnership was an exceptionally successful and happy one. Twenty years later, Hugh explained his change of mind about marriage in a letter to his stepson Raymond Frost, who had just become engaged:

> I do think honestly you are wise to take the plunge. A bachelor's life is bound to become less and less satisfactory ...
>
> I agree too ... about the advantage of having someone with whom one can share all one's problems & worries as well as one's successes & plans ... someone on whose personal loyalty & affection one can always rely. Certainly in politics life would be very grim indeed without this.[70]

Their domestic circumstances did not change much until a few months before the outbreak of war. Their enthusiasm continued – for convivial friendship, reading and walking; their literary tastes were so similar that Hugh soon left Dora to choose his non-political books for him. Throughout the gathering gloom of the 1930s, they escaped as often as possible for walking weekends in the Chilterns, the South Downs and Dorset, staying cheaply in pubs. Sometimes they met the Durbins, but joint holidays were not easily arranged – for Evan was a planner in advance, while the Gaitskells liked to dash off on impulse. Their favourite haunt was Abbotsbury in Dorset, from which they explored the Hardy country. In March 1938 they bought their first house: a cottage, Sweatmans, in the village of Milland just across the Hampshire border from Liphook: 'a pink washed house ... reached through most lovely country ... H.G.'s mother lives close by'.[71] It was here that Hugh developed his passion for gardening, at which he became expert.

About the same time his friend George Wansbrough, who was a director of Reyrolles, brought him on to the board of a subsidiary, the Eureka Vacuum Cleaning Company. Gaitskell was delighted to get the business experience, and his colleagues found he made many very useful and sensible contributions.[72] His financial circumstances changed too, for he inherited a legacy from his aunt in Malta, Mrs De Burgh Griffiths, who died in April 1938 leaving some £14,000 to each of her Gaitskell nephews. Later on this money was shrewdly invested on Hugh's behalf by a friend in the City and multiplied several times over. Hugh's attitude seems to have been to ignore this personal capital. Certainly Dora was not aware until after his death how much it had grown: and it had little if any direct effect on their style of life. Another old acquaintance, who lived in the house for a couple of years, wrote when Gaitskell became Leader of the

Opposition: 'He had an excellent sense of humour, and was economical in every day matters: a good budgeteer.'[73]

As his wife, Dora could now take an active part in Hugh's political work. She accompanied him regularly to South Leeds, and wrote occasional pieces for the constituency Labour paper. But, contrary to what some of their friends suspected, she was not the driving force and did nothing to push him in the direction of a political career. She would have been happy if he had decided to remain as an academic Socialist; but she was equally prepared for the more exacting life of a politician's wife, and was to be Hugh's most enthusiastic ally in his chosen field. For the time, however, she was plunged into domesticity by the birth of their two daughters, Julia in April 1939 and Cressida three years later.

At this period Gaitskell also took on new responsibilities at UCL. On Noel Hall's departure in 1938, he was promoted to Reader and appointed to head the department jointly with his close friend and economic mentor, the Austrian economist Paul Rosenstein-Rodan. (They both forgot to attend a formal university dinner to celebrate their appointment.)[51b] In practice Gaitskell did all the administration, scrupulously carrying out the invidious tasks of hiring and firing with the utmost concern for individual feelings. Some colleagues and friends were annoyed that he was not offered a chair. His academic productivity had not been high, and with the strong competitive winds blowing from the LSE, there was still doubt about the future of economics at UCL. But it seems that the decisive factor was his unwillingness to give up his parliamentary candidature, which was not a statutory bar but was deemed by the authorities (as in other cases) to be incompatible with a professor's duties.[74]

Had Gaitskell returned to UCL after the war he was given to understand that he would have been appointed Professor.[75] No doubt the same condition would have been posed;[76] and though at one point he seems to have thought he might go back, that was never likely. He was an excellent teacher, who was anxious to do his best for his students, and who struggled and suffered with the difficulties of teaching a subject whose basic theory was in total flux, so that every lecture had to be revised afresh every year. But he lacked the mathematical equipment to go deep into economic theory, on which he had little that was original to say. He worked at it conscientiously for a time, but it was torture.[77] He was still much happier writing works of serious popularisation like the short book on *Money in Daily Life* which he began for the new Labour Book Service, whose Advisory Council he joined. To a colleague who knew him both at the NFRB and on the University Board of Studies, he seemed an intelligent and reasonable man who made sensible suggestions, but just 'a nice ordinary competent economist, we all meet dozens of them'.[78] His academic career was respectable but he would not have become distinguished in economic theory. When he visited UCL not long after the war, he was surprised to find himself 'very unmoved'.[79]

Gaitskell in the 1930s was greatly appreciated by his friends, but those who claim to have foreseen his public eminence are very few. Casual acquaintances who had to do business with him sometimes found him rather priggish, though those who met him socially were often struck by his frivolous side. Eric Roll, a young economist who became very friendly with him at one weekend conference, and later knew him well in Whitehall, was 'tremendously impressed'. Gaitskell seemed well established in both the academic and the political worlds, with lively cultural interests, and a 'glamorous young man ... he took great care of his clothes, was elegantly dressed, good-looking with wavy hair, scholarly *and* worldly ... not a drunkard but one who went in for worldly pleasures – dancing, the girls, food and drink'.[80]

All his friends remarked upon his considerateness, courtesy and charm, as well as his lively sense of humour. Often they stress how very speedily first acquaintance turned into real intimacy. The wife of one wartime colleague said:

> It was absolutely magical. You felt at once he was somebody you knew ... he had a wonderfully sympathetic understanding of people; unlike some of his clever friends, Hugh always made *you* feel clever too ... he was like a magnet. When you were with him everybody felt sunny.[81]

All competent politicians display a superficial warmth and a carefully cultivated memory for people, and Gaitskell did that too. But his interest in others was far more than a public relations device or a veneer of good manners, for he had a kind of 'fanatical gregariousness' – a positive appetite for meeting new people and discovering their ideas and experiences. If he saw a young acquaintance with a girl, he would inquire about her next time he met the man – sometimes years or even decades later.[82] Not only did his friendships ripen very quickly, they usually lasted for life; one of his nicest traits was that he never forgot those who had helped him when he was unimportant. Those who knew him well, however critical of his political weaknesses, remember him as a human being only with loyalty and affection.

Though polite in expressing his opinions, he was firm and very outspoken about them. But he did not obtrude his own aesthetic and other tastes on his friends. 'If you sat next to him at lunch,' said Noel Hall, 'the conversation lit up. He was so unobtrusive; he assumed you shared his pleasures and values ... he was a very sensitive man.'[1a]

Unlike Durbin at times, he was quite tolerant of disagreement. He enjoyed arguments but not quarrels, and on some sensitive subjects he protected his own integrity by silence. On religion he was 'totally uncommunicative — a very clammy clam' because he tried neither to pretend not offend.[1a] So the gap that later yawned between the public image and the private man exists even among those who knew him personally. Usually he was very open and uninhibited, a hater of humbug, with an 'incurable directness' and with strong emotions which he often showed.[83] But in circumstances where he was not really at home he was armoured in an impenetrable reserve, a determination not to give himself away. Even intimates met that reserve occasionally if they differed from him on a subject like religion, or a great political crisis like Munich.

Privately he was introspective, and insistent on being brutally honest with himself, but he revealed these deep self-criticisms only to his beloved — and distant — brother. He was not arrogant, but was aware of his own abilities and without false modesty; occasionally he displayed his frustration and irritation with the elderly and ineffective Labour MPs of that period. He was rather attracted to the limelight and did not despise worldly success, but was much more concerned to try to influence events and policies. Many friends did not even think of him as a prospective politician, or as ambitious at all, and hardly any of them imagined he would rise so high in the political world — though he was publicly mentioned as one of Labour's potential leaders as early as 1939, in an anonymous study by a Conservative MP containing many very shrewd personal judgments on politicians of the day.[84] He was saved from most of the occupational faults of the political profession by the integrity which, when friends sum him up, is nearly always the first quality they emphasise.

He had thrown over the creed and values of his class and family, and to his colleagues like Hall 'his pride in his emancipation from his inheritance came flooding through'.[1a] His generation rejected conventional morality as humbug; but the same colleague saw no 'ambition in the sense of personal aggrandisement ... [but he was] desperately ambitious as one might be ambitious to be a bishop, or St. Francis'.[1a] For on fundamentals — courage, loyalty, integrity — he retained and reinterpreted the values of his upbringing. Where his military forebears had stressed physical courage, Gaitskell respected the same quality in moral and intellectual terms, fighting wholeheartedly for the side to which he committed himself. Loyalty to country remained, in the old-fashioned sense, but not to empire. That was replaced by a new loyalty to the Labour Movement and its standards of collective action; years later he told his daughter that Socialism was his religion.[85] In day-to-day struggles, too, he prized loyalty not to great abstractions but to persons, and felt a strong sense of solidarity with colleagues and allies who fought on the same side. First of all came intellectual integrity: a rigorous honesty in making up his own mind, a fastidiousness about candour in persuading others, an obstinacy about getting the argument exactly right, which could often infuriate — and sometimes inspire. To this personal moral code he adhered all his life, and he wrote twenty years later that he was 'much more likely ... [to] be a failure than a sham'.[86a]

That code helped make him intellectually impressive, too. A Fabian acquaintance was struck then as later by his disciplined intelligence, his insistence on thinking a subject through before making up his mind, and his determination in sticking to it when he had done so. He was most frequently criticised for being too rational, especially in expecting problems of value-judgment to be solved by rigorous economic thinking; Colin Clark ironically recalls being attacked by Gaitskell in 1936 for taking too political an attitude to economics. Others felt that his strong emotions sometimes impaired his judgment of a situation. Misled by his mildness of manner, some people at the university were astonished at the determination and authority he showed during the war. To his political friends it was not so surprising; Barbara Wootton said he had 'a backbone of steel'. On one point everyone agreed: Gaitskell was never a trimmer. Whatever view he took his engagement was total. 'A more committed man it would be hard to find.'[87]

v   *The Shadow of Hitler*

Those first two years of Gaitskell's married life were overshadowed by the coming war. His own activities had already expanded beyond economic policy. He was vice-chairman of the NFRB's international section from 1934, did much of his speaking and lecturing on foreign topics, and wrote a book on the breakdown of the League of Nations. As usual he was unlucky about publication, for the readers thought it too historical and insufficiently analytical, and he never found time to revise it.[88]

It was a decade, wrote Quentin Bell, of 'mounting despair ... unable to shake the complacency of a torpid nation, we saw the champions of war, tyranny and racial persecution winning ... it was bloody to be alive and to be young was very hell.'[89] Gaitskell's reactions were identical.[86b] He wrote in the summer of 1938 that he felt 'continuously angry about the Chamberlain policy — especially in respect of Spain'.[90] Austria had succumbed to Hitler in March 1938, and Czechoslovakia — once refuge for his Austrian friends — fell a year later. In those days he was never accused, as he sometimes was after the war, of showing too much sympathy for the men in power. 'The motive was not only stupidity and fear but *Capital's Class Prejudice and Economic Interest*.'[91] That was one item of Marxist analysis which he still accepted, writing in other lecture notes that year: 'Fascism has become the last defence of a crumbling economic system. It is the last bulwark of Capitalism.'[33] Twenty years afterwards, he still recalled his impotent rage at 'the horrors of that time and the incredible obstinate stupidity of the crowd who were in power'.[92]

For him and for those who thought like him, Munich was shame and shipwreck. Just before it, when the schools were being evacuated from London, he took Raymond and the Hirsch children down to Milland by car. He evidently wrote to Dalton urging parliamentary co-operation with Churchill, Eden and the Liberals.* Publicly, he thought that the mobilisation of the British fleet had deterred Hitler, who wanted to avoid fighting on two fronts, and that Chamberlain had nevertheless capitulated out of 'admiration for Fascism and hatred of Russia'.[93] His vehemence caused a temporary breach with Robert Fraser, who was passionately pro-Chamberlain, and severely strained relations with Evan Durbin, who felt there was no strong strategic, diplomatic or moral case for war with Germany over the Sudetenland. But Durbin was over-optimistic;** and Gaitskell had good grounds for writing: 'I think events will do more to persuade you than anything I can say.'[95a]

Czechoslovakia, he told Durbin a week after Munich, would 'either be overun [sic] or broken to pieces by Germany, or else turn Fascist herself'; democratic forces would collapse and friends of Germany come to power in Poland, Romania and Yugoslavia. A German ultimatum to France would now find the victim isolated:

> Russia in my opinion would not move ... Germany has achieved her goal of being able to fight a one front war. I think that the threat will probably be sufficient to induce France and Great Britain to make further extensive concessions ... which may ultimately affect the internal form of Government.

In armaments he thought that Britain's position would improve absolutely but might not do so relatively, and that the sacrifices required – including conscription – would be harder to get accepted, since Neville Chamberlain's policies had divided the country: 'while prepared to fight for the democratic ideal as such and for the ideal of collective security as such there is little to attract us in fighting merely to preserve the territorial integrity of the British Empire.'[96] Durbin wrote at the New Year that they did not disagree in their judgment of political regimes or of the probable future

* Dalton's reply expressed willingness, but scepticism about the Liberals and contempt for Eden – though not for Churchill.[41b]

** Durbin thought Munich might avoid the partition of Czechoslovakia or the invasion of France, and assumed the Anglo-French guarantee to the rump Czechoslovakian state would be implemented.[94]

'(except that I think you are a bit cracked about fascism in this country)'. But

> Clearly we differ about the number of things for which we are prepared to die ... I think you would also die to support the idea of democracy [outside Britain, and] ... to destroy the present regimes in Italy and Germany (though not those of Russia and Japan).[97]

Three weeks after Munich Hugh Dalton called a dozen political friends to his flat to discuss foreign policy. That meeting filled anti-appeasers like Douglas Jay with 'the blackest despondency'.[98a] Fraser and Durbin advocated colonial and other concessions to Germany, and were joined by John Wilmot, Ivor Thomas and Herbert Morrison. Kingsley Martin was at his silliest: 'while we cannot stand up to Germany', yet 'Broadcasts in foreign languages moderate and instructive about democracies, German literature of the past, etc., might do much'. Dick Crossman, shrewdly anticipating the Nazi–Soviet pact, thought no effective resistance to Germany possible for three or four years. Gaitskell was one of only four who remained resolute:

> It would be fatal to oppose arms. Distinguish arms votes completely from foreign office votes. Concentrate on ARP [air raid precautions] and air defence. Expansionist monetary policy. Loan of 300 to 400 million pounds for ARP, etc., would give much employment and we need not fear immediate inflation. Demand conscription of wealth. Scheme for large incomes. Stress nutrition. If shortage of labour and capital use control to prevent production of luxuries. In Leeds, as against Wellingborough, they all say 'Let's stick to our guns and don't be frightened of public opinion'. The women are still very pacifist, but H.G. disagrees profoundly with Bob Fraser on moral issues. Our problem is how to combine a cunning foreign policy with moral uplift.[99*]

The succinct summary conveys nothing of the atmosphere of desperation which oppressed Gaitskell and those who thought like him. A few days later he wrote to Durbin:[100]

> I suppose you just don't realise how deeply some of us feel this business nor how hopeless we feel about the future. As I see it this means *at best* [sic] for me the end of my life and activities in Britain — a change-over which even I cannot face without gloom, at worst it means that I am compelled to go on struggling hopelessly and vainly against all that I most despise and detest ... I can understand, you see, those who

* Bob Fraser, the leading appeaser, was prospective candidate for Wellingborough and had cited public opinion there.

say that strategically we had to give way because of the arms position
— I can understand the pure pacifists who will not fight for anything.
But I cannot understand those who thought it *morally* right ... I do
not often cry — but I did after Berchtesgaden — the last time was on
February 14th 1934 [the defeat of the Austrian Socialists].[95b]

On this life and death issue, Gaitskell now found some of his closest
political friends taking a view he saw as disastrously mistaken, while some
violent Tories — whom he had thought misguided or even malevolent —
were on his own side. That made him feel more tolerant towards members
of the other party.[101] Yet though he recognised the anti-appeasers outside
the Labour Party as potential allies, and he had no doubt of the desperate
need to change the country's policy quickly, he did not join Cripps's
Popular Front campaign to unite all Chamberlain's critics. Twenty years
later Gaitskell explained his attitude to John Strachey — in 1938 a leading
fellow-traveller of the Communist Party, which vociferously supported the
Popular Front:

> [M]y criticism ... was not that they were in favour of collective security
> together with Russia — we were *all* in favour of that — but rather that
> this was so hedged about with 'ifs' and 'buts', because of the pacifist
> elements and the difference between 'capitalist' and 'non-capitalist'
> worlds, that it confused the issue. I recall having a debate with Stafford
> at a Fabian Summer School in 1937 in which I was advocating collec-
> tive security and he was opposing it![102]

Again, at a meeting early in 1939 at the Garden House Hotel in Cambridge,
Cripps[103] shocked Gaitskell's friends by arguing 'that of the two evils,
imperialism and fascism, imperialism was the more abhorrent, and that a
successful war against Hitler would ... strengthen British imperialism'.[7c]

It was not just a matter of rhetoric. The Popular Front spokesmen — including Cripps and Bevan as well as the Communists — were strong opponents of rearmament under the deeply distrusted Tory government. Gaitskell
knew that an armaments programme takes four years to develop, and
unless it began at once, a better government would be unable to defend
the country (let alone conduct a bolder foreign policy). Nor would there
be a better government while the Opposition's foreign and defence policies
remained so incoherent that the Labour leadership (and the Left even more)
seemed to ordinary voters to advocate both 'standing up to the dictators'
and denying weapons to the armed forces.* Gaitskell did not incur that
charge, or allow ideological passion to blind him to the obvious need. He

---

* From the spring of 1937 Dalton persuaded the Parliamentary Labour Party
to abstain on defence estimates instead of voting against them, as the Left (and
Attlee) still wanted to do.

told his constituents of his 'dismay and anxiety and not a little disgust at the Government's policy of surrender to blackmail and bullying'—but added:

> Peace can only be secured by re-establishing the rule of law in inter-
> national affairs ... neither a neo-nationalism nor a cowardly surrender
> to Fascism will be accepted by the vast mass of our people. For the
> moment rearmament is also essential ... the scandalous gaps in our
> defences have become a byword.[104]

The need to make rearmament more acceptable led Gaitskell into a major effort to influence Labour Party policy. With the Nazi occupation of Prague in March, the Chamberlainites had at last recognised the menace and begun desultory negotiations for a Russian alliance. Plainly the government would soon have to break every pledge and precedent, and introduce military conscription in peacetime. Labour was likely to oppose that, for besides the semi-pacifists who loathed it, the trade unions suspected that it was a preliminary to industrial conscription. Yet its opposition would discredit the Party, which had so long been demanding resistance to Fascism.

Gaitskell and his friends, encouraged by Dalton, did all that a group of political nobodies could do to persuade their seniors to take a more constructive course. As after Munich, Gaitskell suggested that Labour should propose 'conscription of wealth' (an annual 'wealth tax', which Douglas Jay was already advocating) and agree in return to accept 'conscription of manpower'.[105] With Durbin and Jay, he was received in the Leader of the Opposition's room by Attlee, Morrison, Dalton, Alexander and Shinwell, and persuaded them to put the idea to the Parliamentary Labour Party, which narrowly turned it down.[98b] Meanwhile, throughout 1939 Gaitskell and his friends in XYZ were preoccupied with preparing practical schemes to spread the burden of rearmament more fairly. If war came, his memorandum said, 'we have in mind far more drastic proposals'.[106] He outlined those at a Fabian conference in February 1939, proposing 'to put the country on an allowance basis, control unearned income at source and fix the rate of earned income'.[21e]

Two months later Gaitskell wrote to George Brett:

> It has been beautiful weather here the last few days. I have done a lot
> of gardening & alternate that with writing the book on Money. But the
> situation is pretty disturbing. Whenever I hear the news I drop the
> book & get on with the digging. It seems a good deal more impor-
> ant![107]

After Munich he at once abandoned his previous optimism that Russia would fight against Hitler, and in August 1939 he was 'among the very few ... neither surprised nor unduly shocked by the Molotov–Ribbentrop agreement'.[7d] Yet even with war inevitable, and all previous hopes submerged in the desperate struggle for survival, he did not feel that his activities had been futile. Twenty years later an old antagonist, Ted Willis of the Labour League of Youth and the Young Communist League, who had seen himself as a leading political spokesman of his own generation, told Gaitskell of his shock, on joining the army, at discovering that no one had ever heard of him. With better judgment, and more awareness that politics plays little part in the lives of ordinary people in ordinary times, Gaitskell was not surprised. But unlike Willis he did not think the activity had just been pointless froth on the surface:

> You didn't waste your time. The generation that went into the Forces was quite different from the generation that went in in 1914, because subconsciously and without knowing it ... they had been politically won over against Hitler ... they were politically *more* conscious and less like sheep than the generation [of] 1914.[17]

Munich was the fourth great event in Gaitskell's early development. The General Strike had committed him to the side of the workers. The shelling of the Vienna flats had given him his lifelong loathing of repression and dictatorship (even in countries calling themselves socialist). For his own inner security and stability, marriage was the decisive change. Now, over Munich, he advocated a course that to many ordinary people seemed likely to increase the risk of war which, led or misled by their government, they still desperately hoped to avoid. As he wrote to Durbin:

> Democracy certainly involves tolerance ... but it requires many other things too — especially just now it needs people who have strong convictions and independence and courage to express what they believe without always wondering whether the electorate will like it.[95b]

Once again, as in his breach with his family, this emotional and warm-hearted man was in disagreement on a major issue with people who were close to him, and had to choose between his public convictions and his private affections. It was an experience with which he was to become familiar, from which he suffered exceedingly, and through which he would emerge a far more formidable political leader than his friends had ever imagined.

There were already a few signs, as Douglas Jay realised after Dalton assembled his friends in his flat for their gloomy talk after Munich. Returning home in the Underground, Jay said to Gaitskell that, if that was how the saner half of the Labour Party felt, everything looked pretty hopeless:

He replied, with the utmost confidence, that a few of us would stiffen the Labour Party; that the Labour Party and Churchill would stiffen the country; that this country would stiffen France; and that we should then survive until Roosevelt joined in one day ... it was spoken with such force, clarity and conviction that I was not merely reconvinced of the impossibility of acting on any other assumption, but travelled home astonished that I could have known someone apparently so well for five years without recognizing his extraordinary reserve of under-lying strength — 'Will like a dividing spear', as John Strachey aptly quoted from Matthew Arnold after Hugh's death. To me it illumin-ated, once for all, what the next twenty-five years gradually unfolded to a larger audience.[98c]

PART TWO

PRACTISING GOVERNMENT

'A man who had been biding his time, blossoming with the power'
(A UNIVERSITY ACQUAINTANCE ON HG IN 1940–1)

'A first-rate administrator [who] still has to show ... qualities of leadership'
(*New Statesman* ON HG'S APPOINTMENT AS MINISTER, 1947)

CHAPTER 4

COALITION POLITICS: SERVING DOCTOR DALTON 1939–42

'These old gentlemen, with their optimistic twaddle, can never win the war.'
(HG, MARCH 1940)

i The Ministry of Economic Warfare

GAITSKELL'S wartime role had been settled early, for German-speaking economists were few and in demand, and his old chief Noel Hall was active in recruiting them. In later years, Hugh often told Dora that he regretted having missed serving in the armed forces through being conscripted for Whitehall well before hostilities began;[1] but with his rational outlook, he does not seem to have questioned a decision which so plainly made the best use of his skills.[2] Long afterwards he recalled: 'I was put in a reserved occupation before the war and asked ... to join the Ministry of Economic Warfare ... on the very first Monday [I] turned up ... as one of the founder members.'[3]

In September 1939 everybody expected the war to open with devastating bombing raids on London. Dora took Julia to the cottage at Milland, the first of several successive retreats in the country, which Hugh, visiting on his day off, found very overcrowded and depressing.[4a] He himself moved in to 20 Mecklenburgh Square as a paying guest of his old friends Eileen Power and her husband M. M. Postan, who had also been recruited into MEW. At first he feared that as a civil servant he would have to give up South Leeds; and though that proved unnecessary, his links with the constituency were now limited to letters to his agent and very rare visits.[5]

The Director of Intelligence at the new Ministry was Churchill's friend Major Desmond Morton, who had warned Gaitskell just before war was declared to be ready to start work — in familiar surroundings, for MEW began life in the building of the London School of Economics.[6] There were a few permanent civil servants on its staff, but the vast majority were temporaries from the City, universities or the legal professions.[7] Most were serving for half or less of their previous earnings:[4b] 'the intelligence work of the Ministry was dependent upon the good will of individuals who were willing to accept a lowly status and low pay, or upon employers who were willing to make up the difference in salaries';[8a] after a month Gaitskell learned that UCL would make his up to the full £800.[4c]

He entered on his Whitehall task with high expectations and a sense of vast relief to be working actively against Hitler at last.[9a] But reality was often frustrating, and at first he found it 'all a bit chaotic', and 'difficult to get used to a subordinate position and all the red tape in matters where one thinks one knows better!'[4a][b] His best language was German, but Noel Hall was in charge of German Intelligence; so Gaitskell was attached to the Neutral Countries section of the Ministry's Intelligence Department with the job of analysing the information about France. This introduction to Whitehall, he wrote later, 'did not seem very sensible to me: firstly because my French was, and still is, very bad; secondly, because I didn't think France was a neutral country'.[10]

After about a week Gaitksell took over responsibility for Belgium and Holland, Germany's neutral neighbours and a channel for her imports:

> Ships bound for neutral ports had first to be brought into our contra-band bases and the manifests examined. Then we had to decide what was to be let through and what was to be seized. That was the Ministry's job ... detective work done with the help of the famous black lists.[7]

At the start of the war the Ministry was also busy negotiating War Trade Agreements with the neutrals, restricting all their supplies to prevent their own products or any surplus imports being shipped to Germany. That involved 'hours of keen bargaining and poring over the trade returns'; before long the blitzkrieg came, and it looked 'all very academic'.[7] He would himself have preferred a much tougher approach, rationing the neutrals instead of bargaining with them;[11a] and he knew what that might mean:

> I am frankly pessimistic about the war. It isn't going to be easy to blockade Germany properly – which I think is the only way to win the war – without risking a big extension of the war with many of the present neutrals drawn in on one side or the other.[4a]

The work was demanding, never finishing before 8 p.m.[12] It left Gaitskell frustrated as well as exhausted. The official historian of the blockade contrasts 'the offensive spirit and sense of innovation which inspired the group of enthusiasts which founded the Ministry of Economic Warfare' with the 'more conservative and cautious elements ... from some of the older government departments'; and records 'bickering and discordance' between the brilliant band of junior temporaries and their seniors seconded from the Foreign Office and elsewhere.[8b]

These internal frustrations were somewhat relieved by a palace revolution in December 1939. Morton became Deputy Director-General under Sir Frederick Leith-Ross; Noel Hall succeeded him as Director of Intelligence; and Gaitskell once again stepped into his old chief's shoes, as Director of Intelligence with Enemy Countries. He was still bitterly critical of the Foreign Office people in his own Ministry, but now even more irritated at the obstruction of the blockade by more powerful Departments in White-hall. 'The temporaries,' he wrote later,

> had to accommodate themselves to a vast government machine and a Civil Service hierarchy and learn to put up with Foreign Office control — a perpetual irritant to men who were mostly strongly anti-Munich and straining to impose a tough blockade.

For serious interference with the trade of neutral countries might jeopardise their goodwill, which it was the task of diplomats to cultivate. Moreover, the appalling lack of co-ordination among economic Departments was the despair of those who took the war seriously. When MEW wanted to buy up foreign materials to keep them out of German hands, 'little could be accomplished ... because of the opposition of the Treasury and other departments',[7] which saved trivial sums of money by purchasing oil from South America instead of from Romania, whose supplies went to fuel the German war effort instead.[13] Gaitskell found a ready outlet for his impotent fury in his old patron Hugh Dalton, now the Labour spokesman on economic warfare, to whom he exploded: 'What can we do about the neutrals? The Foreign Office won't let us bully them and the Treasury won't let us bribe them.'[11a]

These contacts with Dalton were approved by his own Minister, Ronald Cross;[14] but they were resented in other Departments. Soon a senior Treasury official, whom Gaitskell had severely criticised, was telling him pointedly that Dalton was going about blaming the Treasury for obstructing economic warfare.[15a] It was the first instance of Gaitskell's wartime professional dilemma: how to reconcile his zeal to use every channel to speed up the war effort with the need to keep the goodwill of a powerful routine-minded bureaucratic hierarchy. He managed that problem with surprising success.

Gaitskell partly resisted MEW's natural temptation to overestimate the immediate impact of blockade, which was later to harm its reputation and that of its Minister. In March he explained to Dalton that Germany would suffer less heavily from the blockade in this war than in the last: the regime was much stronger, the civilian standard of life was much lower, the overland supplies through adjacent neutrals were much greater, and above all no important military activity was using up her stocks, which indeed were increasing. That meant she could hold out indefinitely, and neither allies nor neutrals would remain convinced for long that we could win. Against this background Gaitskell was tempted by the abortive expedition to help Finland against Russian invasion: he thought it might weaken Germany, cutting off her iron ore supplies, obliging her to fight and depleting her stocks. But he soon concluded that it would be a dangerous diversion.[16]

Above all he was alarmed at the slow pace of Whitehall in the phoney war, the lack of urgency, and even the tendency in some high official quarters to conclude that, since the blockade was going badly, it might become necessary to make peace. A coalition government was essential, he told Dalton: these old gentlemen with their optimistic twaddle could not win the war.[15b] In the next two months the Norwegian fiasco so deepened his gloom that he feared it would be lost unless we pulled ourselves together. At breakfast on 8 May 1940, he wondered whether any preparations had been made if Hitler went for Holland and Belgium.[11b] Two days later he had his answer – and, very soon, his coalition government.

The massive German attack made glaringly obvious the desperate need for new political leadership. On 10 May Winston Churchill became Prime Minister and asked for Dalton as one of his Labour colleagues, offering him on 14 May (against some opposition) the post he sought as Minister of Economic Warfare. Dalton summoned Gaitskell to his flat at midnight and told his young friend that he

> wanted him to be, in fact, a good deal more than a Private Secretary, more like a *Chef de Cabinet* in France. He should be fully in my confidence, and feel free to advise me on all questions, both of policy and persons. This invitation, after a night's reflection, he accepted.[11c]

ii   *Corridors of Power:* Chef de Cabinet

The appointment seemed to Gaitskell's friends 'an exhilarating piece of good fortune'.[9b] He himself saw another side of it, telling a colleague that 'this is not really the job I want, but I feel I have to do it because I have a certain sense of loyalty to Hugh Dalton'.[17] He understood that a civil servant, snatched from the ranks to become the confidant and adviser of a Minister he knew well, might incur the suspicion and dislike of his former colleagues; and that the Minister's personality would not minimise friction either within his own Department or with others.

Hugh Dalton was fifty-two, a large man with hooded eyes, a loud voice, and 'an excess of boyish vitality'.[18] He had done several great services to his Party, notably in organising the back-bench revolt against the leadership's policy of voting against arms estimates, and in his lifelong preoccupation with spotting able young men and fostering their careers. Intellectually capable, politically astute but often abrasive, and a voracious empire-builder, he meant to extend the operations of the Ministry of Economic Warfare into adjoining fields cherished by other Departments – the Foreign Office, the War Office, the Ministry of Information. Within his own domain Dalton was determined, as he once put it, 'to divide or to educate, but in any case to rule'.[15c] He expected quick, efficient, politically sensitive advice at the most improbable hours, for like Winston Churchill he was a night-owl who, after a good dinner, would summon his staff at 11 p.m. to work on into the small hours. And if he felt the quality of the advice deficient, if it were slow in coming, above all if he suspected official obstruction or opposition, then his devastating temper would flare in a memorable scene. Like his hero Sir William Harcourt (or like George Brown in a later day), Dalton was a bit of a bully who usually meant no real harm, and quickly recovered from his tantrums. Like Harcourt also, he had no idea, and was often astonished and occasionally even contrite to be told, of the bitter humiliation and resentment of civil servants so treated by their Minister. Gaitskell was now to serve this formidable master as confidential adviser, as buffer against the outside world, and especially as a channel of communication with the officials.

Gaitskell's appointment was disliked by the Ministry's Director-General, Sir Frederick Leith-Ross, who feared being shunted aside;[19] and by the Foreign Office, who 'were horrified at a temporary getting such a position. They complained that I wouldn't know my way about Whitehall.'[3] Dalton soothed the Director-General's wounded feelings, said he 'knew Gaitskell well enough to be sure that he would have no difficulty in personal relations with other Private Secretaries', and suggested the appointment of an assistant from the Foreign Office.[11d] They sent Patrick Hancock to undertake the chores from 'buying [Dalton's] railway tickets to scouring the town for sherry!' – and to 'drafting letters to the Minister's satisfaction', which was no easy task.[20] Dalton had a Labour MP, John Wilmot, as PPS, and a Liberal, Dingle Foot, as Parliamentary Secretary – for in the coalition government junior ministers were not drawn from the Minister's party or selected by him. Despite his partisan reputation, Dalton was always on good terms with his parliamentary secretaries, and assigned 'My Foot', as a lawyer, to deal with the many legal problems besetting the Ministry in managing the blockade.

With the Germans in France cargoes had to be checked not in the Channel as in the past, but in their ports of origin. That could be done effectively only with American consent, fortunately forthcoming now that Britain's position had become desperate.[7] There were difficulties with the courts, and more troubles with the Foreign Office as neutral ships were stopped and neutral traders blacklisted;[21] the system had only tenuous foundation in international law, but Dalton – and Gaitskell – thought that 'utterly pedantic ... till Hitler's neck has been broken'.[15d] But Dalton's total dedication to winning the war overrode any consideration of foreign susceptibilities, humanitarian scruples, administrative routines or party politics, and the Ministry owed a great deal to him. Dalton

> placed on all its work the stamp of his buoyancy, originality and courage. If the innovations in policy seem today to be an inevitable response to changed circumstances, they did not always appear so at the time; and in the summer of 1940 it needed some persistence and faith to maintain the blockade at all.[8c]

The prerequisite of such a policy was a reorganisation giving 'less power within the Ministry to the fearful and more to the bold'. Within his first two weeks Dalton had Gaitskell arrange a series of conferences where he could hear his top advisers talk, and form quick judgments about them. The senior of those seconded Foreign Office officials, of whom Gaitskell had complained, resigned after a fortnight on grounds of health. Apparently to the regret of the Foreign Office, the Minister appointed two vigorous temporaries, Lord Drogheda and Noel Hall, as joint directors under Leith-Ross.[11e] The men now running the MEW were kept furiously busy developing the new blockade system. They ate in the office, worked nights and Sundays and slept in bunks in the basement. Politicians, temporaries and career civil servants were thrown constantly into one another's company, soon came to know one another, and developed a strong and cohesive loyalty to the Department's personnel and policies.[22a]

The day-to-day management of the blockade kept the officials fully occupied. But once Dalton had determined the main lines of policy and reorganised the Ministry to implement them, it no longer required much attention from him.[8d] Within a month Gaitskell was telling him that he would soon have too little to do, and might take over economic general staff work from his Labour colleague Arthur Greenwood.[15e] But Dalton's restless energies were turning in a different direction. He wanted the responsibility for running propaganda and organising subversion in enemy-occupied Europe – a job, he claimed, for a politician of the Left rather than a professional soldier. There was a short, sharp battle with the War Office, and some obscure opposition to overcome from within the Prime Minister's entourage.[23] Then Dalton triumphantly expanded his empire, adding to the MEW what Winston Churchill called the MUW (Ministry of Ungentlemanly Warfare). Gladwyn Jebb, his former private secretary at the Foreign Office in 1929–31, became his chief assistant for this work and – with Gaitskell and Wilmot – one of the 'three attendant sprites' on whom Dalton relied for confidential advice.

A couple of days after his appointment Dalton observed contentedly that Hugh Gaitskell was 'well in charge'. From the start he was used not merely as a private secretary but as confidential political counsellor and executive spokesman for the Minister: the *chef de cabinet* role Dalton had assigned to him. He dissuaded his master from talking Sir Stafford Cripps out of going to Moscow as Ambassador; conveyed from Dalton to Attlee warnings about prominent German sympathisers; expressed alarm – in July 1940 of all times – at symptoms of the class war in Britain; and reminded the Minister, who had quite forgotten, that he had recently sent 'a most abusive letter' on quite a trivial matter to a powerful colleague from whom he was about to seek a favour.[24] Gaitskell found working for Dalton

> exhausting, exhilarating and instructive. He taught me a lot, especially how to write Cabinet papers and draft letters. He hated slipshod English, sentences that meant little and added nothing ... He used to keep a 'prod list' on his desk so that he could follow up all the things he had started. Many ministers I have known have bright ideas but never follow through. This was not true of Dalton ... He had tremendous drive. He enjoyed power and getting things done. He was most impatient with difficulties.[25]

Gaitskell proved adept at handling this difficult master. Very early on he brought in some draft with which Dalton was dissatisfied. The Minister threw it on the floor. The private secretary knew he was lost for ever if he picked it up – and in the end Dalton did so himself.[26] In his obituary of Dalton, Gaitskell recalled:

> He could be exceedingly bad-tempered. He was apt to bully and shout at people. He got angry unreasonably when it was not really the fault of the officials. I found an easy way of dealing with this. I just shouted back. I remember once we had a shouting match; it must have lasted at least 5 minutes. At the end of it a sly grin spread over his face. 'Well, well', he would say, 'perhaps there is something in your point of view'. He liked this sort of encounter and respected people who stood up to him.[25]

Not many did. On another occasion when Dalton was bawling out a whole roomful of his staff, it was Gaitskell who interrupted him: 'Look here, Hugh, you are not to talk to civil servants like that – I won't have it.'[27]

This new self-assurance transformed Gaitskell's personality and astonished people who had known him well at UCL. One of them said:

> I was seeing a man who had been biding his time. Toughness, determination and ability shone out then – in that order – which I hadn't experienced before. He struck me then as quite ruthless, that I was seeing the real Hugh for the first time. I could see him absolutely blossoming with the power of the Minister's secretary – a job which you can make what you will of ... He had enormous confidence. Previously

he was diffident and would make suggestions; that all vanished overnight ... He didn't strike you as being an ordinary Private Secretary
but very much more. I never met another one like it in that department or any other. His bearing, the way he spoke, everything – he
sloughed off a skin that had been a disguise. Of course he couldn't
have taken that authority, it had to be given him, but he obviously
seized everything that *was* given; some people wouldn't have. He
almost forgot to say: 'The Minister would like you to ... ' – not quite
but almost. Previously his speech had been very quiet, now it became
almost brusque. But he wasn't unpopular – people admired his
ability.[28]

Not for the last time, Gaitskell's personality flowered in response to a
challenge, and he shouldered wider responsibilities not merely as capably
as before, but much more so.

Dalton treated his trusted advisers, after his own peculiar fashion, as
personal friends He frequently invited them to dinners, private as well as
official, gloomy as well as gay (once when a distinguished American
diplomat was the guest of honour, his neighbour John Wilmot fell asleep
and snored at the table). Occasionally the Minister would invite one of his
secretaries to his rural retreat in Wiltshire, delighting in his 'favourite
trick' of insisting on very long country walks at a very fast pace until his
junior had to ask him to slow down.[15f] In September 1940, when Gaitskell
was the victim of his master's inexhaustible energy, they returned to
London to find that the Ministry had been badly bombed in their
absence.

Just after the war began Gaitskell had written to Brett that he had 'given
up worrying about Air Raids. London is very well defended and besides,
I don't think we shall have anything serious for the present.'[4b] Now a very
different period was beginning, in which raids frequently occurred while
the Minister's staff was working at night; and though Gaitskell did not
share his master's taste for excitement for its own sake, he was among
those who joined Dalton's rush to the roof to see what was going on.[22a b]
His own temporary home was one of the first places in London to
suffer. 'I have been having a rather exciting time,' he wrote to George
Brett:[4d]

The third night of the Blitz ... they came pretty close to us. They began
with a hit on a gas main and some buildings about 150 yards away:
this started a fire and half an hour later, attracted no doubt by the
blaze, they got a direct hit on nos. 30 and 31 Mecklenburgh Square –
10 houses down on our side: they were just rubble when we saw them
the following morning. Finally, just to wind things up, they dropped
a time bomb on the square garden on top of the public shelter. The

consequence was that just after the all clear when I was hoping we would get some sleep, the police ordered us out of the house in ten minutes. The bomb eventually stayed there for a week (no one allowed back all the time) and was then exploded by the R.E. ... every window in our house facing the square is gone and various other things including front door damaged. While we were waiting for the old time bomb and sleeping elsewhere they dropped a lot more in the neighbourhood.'

His companion's account supplements his own:

The air-raid wardens told us to get out of the house immediately, and wouldn't even give us time to get dressed. So with overcoats over our pyjamas we walked through the air raid to the Lyons Corner House in Coventry Street, which at that time stayed open all night. We found it filled with people like ourselves, refugees from bombed or unsafe homes. Some of them slumped drowsily over their cups of tea, others talked and joked with conspicuous gusto, but of complaints, self-pity, there was not even a suspicion.

In response, 'Hugh ... revealed more openly than ever before how deeply he felt at that time his involvement with England and her collective future' and why he 'worked and slaved during the war ... with concentration, indeed dedication'.[29] That intensity of work was a matter of comment among his colleagues;[30] and on weekends, relaxing with his family, he 'used to look tired and thin and strained'.[31]

After Mecklenburgh Square was bombed, he and Durbin lodged in Foot's flat in Tufton Court, Westminster; later he moved to Devonshire Place with Robin Brook, a banker and Jebb's personal assistant, who became a lifelong friend. All overworked and without their families, they spent little time at home; and Gaitskell struck some of his new associates as rather reserved, disinclined to gossip even about politics, and quite hard to get to know.[22] He was largely cut off both from his family and from the close friends with whom he felt at home. One of these was the gentle and feckless Amyas Ross, who through Hugh's own good offices had been recruited to MEW and even persuaded to keep office hours and wear a suit. But in that cold winter Ross caught pneumonia after a car accident, and was found dead in his freezing, slummy flat off New Oxford Street: another of the early bereavements which saddened Gaitskell's life.

With the invasion scare of the summer of 1940, Dora and Julia had moved to Jaylands, a house in Worcestershire which Hugh's sister had found, which the two families shared, and to which they welcomed relatives. There were always at least three children to keep them busy. 'Julia is very energetic,' Hugh wrote, 'walking everywhere all the time and she also has quite a few words. I must say I think she is very attractive.'

But though the house was 'reasonably comfortable', he found it 'very remote';[4d] and he did not much enjoy the local society.[15g] Early in 1941 he took a house at Woburn, which he had to visit regularly since it was the headquarters of the propaganda activities for which Dalton now shared responsibility. Dora and Julia now moved there, and Hugh was able to see a little more of them. It was not much. One official who lodged in the house recalls that Hugh appeared only at breakfast (which Dora rose at 6.30 a.m. to provide) because the Minister kept him busy the rest of the day. The lodger was struck by his kindness to the children (including Raymond when he was home) and by the strenuous life he was leading: 'he could never have stood that pace without her'.[32] (But in one side of the strenuous life at Woburn he would not participate, refusing Dalton's frequent demands for 'some of the younger men to run round the whole of Woburn Park with him'.[25])

iii *'Ungentlemanly Warfare': The Control of Propaganda*

Woburn, wrote Dalton, was 'an active outpost in the Whitehall war'.[11g] It was the headquarters for part of the 'MUW', the second, clandestine area of responsibility which that restless Minister had now eagerly annexed. At first the Special Operations Executive (SOE) had three branches. One, SO2, dealt with the cloak-and-dagger activities of organising sabotage and subversion; Gaitskell had no concern with it.[33] Another, SO3, was organised by Gaitskell in late July 1940 as a planning and Intelligence staff for SO2, to comprise regional and country research bureaux; it did not survive.[34] His main task was building up and dealing with the remaining branch, SO1, which after some bitter political battles was to be absorbed into the Political Warfare Executive (PWE).

SO1 was controlled from London, and carried on secret propaganda to enemy and enemy-occupied countries from its country headquarters at Woburn.[35] It was troubled by a series of distinct but overlapping conflicts. There were differences about the content of propaganda between Left and Right; personal rivalries among the propagandists, among the bureaucrats and between the two groups; and clashes between the staff and the Minister. There was departmental friction between traditional Whitehall Ministries and new wartime outfits; between the Foreign Office, which was 'slow to realise the importance of broadcasting', and the Woburn enthusiasts with their 'tendency to try to make foreign policy by means of propaganda';[36a] and above all between MEW and the Ministry of Information, which had been left in charge of open propaganda – an arrangement supposed to last only until the subversive side of SOE had been organised, but which Duff Cooper, the Minister, was determined to maintain.[37a]

Divided ministerial control of propaganda was a recipe for ineffectiveness; of subversion, a recipe for disaster. Since only the 'Ministry of Ungentlemanly Warfare' dealt with both, Dalton's claim that he should be responsible for both was well justified.[38] But as a Labour Minister in a predominantly Conservative coalition his position was weak, especially after July 1941 when Churchill made his own crony, Brendan Bracken, Minister of Information; and Dalton's abrasive personality did not win the loyalty of his senior officials.

The Woburn propagandists, wrote Dalton later, were 'a mixed lot, with much talent and much temperament[36b] ... I owed much, in handling the many diverse and highly individual characters in SO1, to Hugh Gaitskell'.[11g] Among them were Gaitskell's cousin George Martelli and his old school-fellow Richard Crossman, whom he characterised to Dalton as 'brilliantly able, immensely energetic, and overwhelmingly ambitious ... completely loyal, for the time being, to any Chief who he thinks will aid his ambition'.[15h] Gaitskell's old Vienna acquaintance Kim Philby used to consult him, over sausages and mash in a Berkeley Square pub, about the political content of their propaganda; Philby felt that Gaitskell and Dalton would have liked to be more revolutionary, but were constrained by the Foreign Office.[39] The personal assistant was kept busy smoothing over several internal rows: there was a bitter one in the summer of 1941 between SO1 and SO2 over a Middle Eastern appointment, and another between Woburn itself and the Minister's Whitehall entourage.

Friction between Ministers became even worse when Bracken replaced Duff Cooper, and set out aggressively to regain the ground abandoned by his predecessor;[40] MoI and SOE staffs were not even allowed to talk to one another.[37b] In August and September 1941, therefore, control over political warfare in enemy and occupied territory was transferred from individual Ministers to an imposing but ineffective committee of Dalton, Bracken and Eden.[41] The three leading officials working on propaganda then proposed that the Ministers should jointly supervise a new Political Warfare Executive, amalgamating SO1 with sections of the MoI and the BBC;[37c] so that in practice the PWE should be managed by themselves— the Three Peawits as Dalton privately called them — without the constant intervention of Doctor Dynamo — as they called him. Dalton's alternative plan for overcoming the friction was to fuse the staffs of different Ministries in each region of the world, and wherever possible to insist that outside Britain, political warfare should be conducted only through SOE agents. Regional fusion was opposed by the Three Peawits but it delighted the Woburn propagandists, who hoped to get control over the BBC; and Gaitskell tried to use Martelli and Crossman to organise a local counter-revolution there, backing the Minister against the Three Peawits.[42] Dalton serenely summed up his long report as showing a state of 'indiscipline bordering on riot'.[15i]

Dalton also appealed for support to his Party leader,[15j] writing to Attlee:

I am ... faced by a combination of two Conservative Ministers and three principal officials, all of whom are anxious to reduce my influence over the new PWE to a minimum ... There is a set being made in certain influential quarters, some political and some official, against Labour Ministers.[43]

This was not merely self-serving, for even after he knew he was to leave MEW, Dalton urged Attlee to see that SOE went to a man of the Left, like Cripps.[44] But though his case was good, he could not – as Gaitskell saw – threaten to resign over an obscure issue on which he would not carry conviction outside.[15j k] So, in return for joint ministerial control which he knew would fail, he demanded and gained concessions on regional fusion of staffs. The wrangling persisted at the committee of Ministers;[45] and at Christmas 1941 one of Dalton's staff presented his master with a book called *How to Get Rid of Bracken*, on which Dalton commented: 'the trouble is that it takes seven years, and then the bloody stuff may grow again'.[15l] A month later the Prime Minister, bored by the constant rows, promoted Dalton to a new office.

The struggle was a deplorable diversion of energy, as Gaitskell and many other participants knew.[46] The constant friction and manoeuvring between Ministers came as a shock, and one day he said innocently to Dalton: 'I had no idea that it would be all like this.'[11h] But Gaitskell loyally served his master's interests without becoming subservient to his whims. To one official he was 'a devil incarnate, always pulling strings'; to another, an indispensable check on the Minister's tendency to approve any wild scheme in order to win popularity among the staff; a third very critical observer feared that a departmental defeat for Dalton would deprive the propagandists of both the 'galvanic stimulus of ministerial control' and 'the steady, sensible and subtle aid of H.G.'.[47]

Gaitskell was influential partly because he alone in MEW dealt with both Dalton's regular and clandestine activities.[48a] He undertook such humdrum tasks as preparing a successful talk by Dalton to the office staff: ' "He has forgotten nobody," said one of the young ladies coming out afterwards.'[15m] The blockade sometimes raised questions which were not routine; in July 1941 Gaitskell was inquiring into a failure to brief the Minister properly about Spanish ships. A fortnight later he was summoned at midnight to redraft a paper for the next day's Cabinet on European food supplies for the coming winter. Always a hard-liner on blockade policy, Gaitskell argued strongly that concessions would certainly benefit the Germans rather than the captive nations; Churchill and the Cabinet warmly agreed. But Dalton[49] was still complaining two months later that he had 'to be constantly vigilant ... If the Foreign

Office had had their way, the blockade by now would be leaking like a sieve.'[43]

Once, MEW found itself politically isolated. The Germans were punishing resistance in Greece by tolerating widespread starvation there, and British humanitarians were pressing hard for relief supplies to be let through. Unusually, Dalton was disinclined to oppose the Foreign Office. But all his subordinates were intransigent, and after Foot and Drogheda had failed, Gaitskell succeeded in stiffening the Minister. Though Dalton argued that the Germans would reap the advantage and exploit the precedent, he was overruled almost unanimously, and a wheat ship was sent — to the benefit of both the occupier and the starving Greeks.[50] Yet, unlike many senior men at MEW, Gaitskell kept good enough relations with the Foreign Office[48a] for one of its officials whom he saw frequently to call him 'a perfect Private Secretary to a Minister. There is something velvety about Gaitskell'.[15n]

A *chef de cabinet* always fits uneasily into Whitehall, and 'Big Hugh's' personality did not help. But Gaitskell succeeded in interpreting the Minister to his officials, and vice versa, without arousing resentment among his seniors against a junior suddenly thrust into a position of power. His private office colleagues thought well of his judgment, though he may have protected the Minister too much from advance rumblings of trouble.[48a b] They were impressed with his toughness rather than his tact, and saw his greatest service as directing the Minister's immense energies into useful channels.[51]

That was never easy. Dalton found Gaitskell 'much the most mercurial of my three sprites'.[15j] With the new arrangements at Woburn, Gaitskell became 'rather bored' with a job he had never sought;[3] indeed the future of MEW was in some doubt.[4e] He would have liked to move to an expanding Department active in the war effort, such as the Ministry of Supply which had a vacancy dealing with manpower problems; but that fell through.[9c] Then on a dreadful day in December 1941, when the Japanese had sunk two British battleships, a depressed and exhausted Hugh Gaitskell had a great quarrel with his master — not for the last time — for working the staff far too long into the night.[52]

In February 1942, Dalton's fortunes suddenly changed and Gaitskell's with them. Winston Churchill, who cared very little for propaganda and not at all for the departmental wrangles over it, was determined on a change at MEW. Dalton longed for the Foreign Office, but was offered only the Board of Trade. He had not wanted it when it was talked of a year earlier;[15o] but now he accepted, and as usual was eager to take with him 'my trusted inner circle'.[11i]

Gaitskell was very reluctant. He had just been invited to become deputy to Leith-Ross—who was himself moving to the Board of Trade to plan post-war supplies and food relief—as a Principal Assistant Secretary and the second man in what became the British section of UNRRA.[53] It would mean 'a vast increase in salary, and work which I believed would be extra-ordinarily interesting'.[3] It might also mean giving up politics.[10] But Gaitskell was very tempted to follow his family tradition of service in poor countries in this form acceptable to a twentieth-century Socialist. As he later told a reporter, he went down to his mother's cottage at Milland to write out his resignation:

> The telephone rang. Dalton wished to see me urgently. I saw him in London. He told me he was going to the Board of Trade and urged me to go with him. I told him I was about to resign.
>
> It was a Sunday. We talked very late and drank a lot of whisky. Dalton said I could go as his 'personal assistant'.
>
> Early in the morning I got up and went from the basement in the Ministry and wrote a note to Dalton, setting out my conditions: 1) the UNRRA job remained open for three months. 2) I was to go as personal assistant. 3) No more late nights with Dalton. He accepted my conditions.[54]

Dalton genuinely cared for his subordinates' interests as well as his own:

> It had long been understood between Gaitskell and me that, after his heavy term in my Private Office he should have whatever good chance of promotion came along and caught his fancy. Next day we signed a treaty. He came with me to the Board of Trade. But I promised that he should not have too many late nights, and that, after a month, he should be available for promotion ... To go on with me in an active home Department full of economic problems would, I thought and told him, be much better training, and a much surer road to the House of Commons, than an international prospective food relief organisation.[11J]

Dalton took a civil servant as private secretary, and Gaitskell became his personal assistant—for six months instead of one. Once again, in his new as in his old Department, a suspicious Permanent Secretary was won over by his efficiency and charm, and soon offered him a permanent post.

iv *The Coal Scuttle*

The Board of Trade was the custodian of all the economic functions of the state that belonged to nobody in particular, the most sprawling and im-penetrable tract of the Whitehall jungle. Gaitskell's first task was to map the territory and introduce the new President to the leading fauna in two very candid memoranda. The first described the Board of Trade itself, and the other the Mines Department, one of its three subordinate Ministries along with Petroleum and Overseas Trade.[55]

The first listed five major problems for the Minister's attention, four of which were soon to occupy Gaitskell himself: one as Dalton's personal assistant, spending almost his whole time on fuel;[56] three of the others later, as a regular civil servant. They were post-war reconstruction, on which 'the Board of Trade have been very obstructive'; the attempt to release building space and labour for war work by concentrating retail distribution into fewer shops; curtailing civilian goods, from cigarettes to furniture; and a review of the need for all present exports:

[A] great deal of the work is squeezing home consumption still further, and doing this in the most efficient and economical way. This involves severe conflict with vested interest [sic] who will undoubtedly make as much trouble as possible, but it also offers scope for economic planning and successful Government Control which will be highly popular with the Left.

The President, if he is to be successful, *must* himself be prepared to go into the burning issues, partly because many of these are political, e.g. should tobacco rationing be introduced? Can we ration fuel? He will be met with excuses for inaction from so called experts, often really vested interests, and this opposition will have to be broken down. Moreover, not only must the President be in a position to judge the practicability of particular schemes for reducing consumption, concentrating industry, but he must also push them through if he approves and then keep an eye on the administration, so long as there is any danger of it going wrong.[55a]

To succeed, Dalton would need to improve the Department's deplorable publicity; to assert his influence in the Lord President's Committee, the real domestic Cabinet; and to introduce a 'brains trust' of reliable advisers such as Evan Durbin and Douglas Jay. The memorandum was scathing about the leading Board of Trade officials. One or two were characterised as 'very able and energetic', but most were dismissed in such terms as: 'pleasant weak character: not much good'; or 'described as "wet" No. 1 in the Government Service'; or even 'One of the real enemies of the war effort'. Dalton at once set out to recruit new blood, an enterprise in which for once he enjoyed the sympathy of his colleagues. Sir Kingsley Wood, the Conservative Chancellor, blamed Dalton's predecessors for not doing so long before.[15p]

The memorandum on the Mines Department was in similar vein. Gaitskell derived his impressions from a dinner with four of its officials whom he knew, and the appropriate official historian confirms their harsh verdict.[57a] They were particularly critical both of David Grenfell, the weak and ineffective Labour Secretary for Mines, and of Sir Alfred Hurst the Permanent Secretary, who was considered an able and dangerous advocate of the coalowners' views. But they spoke well of some of their colleagues, especially the statistician whom they called:

> extraordinarily able. He is only twenty-six, or thereabouts, and is one of the most brilliant younger people about ... he has revolutionised the coal statistics ... The great thing about him is that he understands what statistics are administratively important and interesting. We must on no account surrender him either to the Army or to any other department.

His name was James Harold Wilson.

On their advice and Gaitskell's recommendation Lord Hyndley, for years the government's commercial adviser on coal, was appointed Permanent Secretary;[58] five years later those two were to work together as Minister of Fuel and Power and chairman of the National Coal Board. Sir Alfred Hurst was moved, to take charge of post-war reconstruction. Gaitskell had the invidious task of breaking the news to him — and of telling Sir Horace Wilson, the head of the Civil Service (once Neville Chamberlain's closest adviser and still the *bête noire* of all opponents of Munich), that his Minister wanted the victim out of office next day. Sir Horace protested and was 'very hoity-toity'; Gaitskell, looking at two enormous photographs of Baldwin and Neville Chamberlain, 'only just refrained from reminding him that there was a war on and unsuccessful Generals were fired even quicker than this'.[15a]

The political head was not changed. Churchill wanted to remove Grenfell, but to Dalton's dismay Attlee felt that he could not sacrifice another Labour Minister when the Party's deputy leader Arthur Greenwood was being dismissed. Dalton therefore felt obliged to take over this most controversial and time-consuming area of policy himself.[15a] Grenfell stayed in office three more months. Though an administrative nonentity, he proved a political disaster, and in two great battles his stubborn opposition to change undermined Labour policies. For over coal, party and class antagonisms still went deep; and though Labour was often defending the national interest, the Conservatives had an overwhelming majority at Westminster and their party leader in Downing Street.

The sober official historian records the background of twenty years of bitter strife and mismanagement, which were now taking their toll.[57b] Having won in 1926, the owners had imposed longer hours and lower wages instead of undertaking structural change or technical re-equipment, so that compared with its Continental competitors British coal-mining became increasingly technically obsolescent. They resisted outside inter-

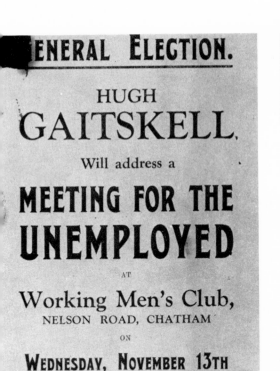

HUGH
GAITSKELL,
Will address a

MEETING FOR THE
UNEMPLOYED
AT

Working Men's Club,
NELSON ROAD, CHATHAM

ON

WEDNESDAY, NOVEMBER 13TH
At 12 Noon.

Printed by Stafford & Son (T.U.), 258, High Street, Chatham and
Published by T. E. Reader, 32, New Road, Rochester.

South Leeds Parliamentary Election 1945

Vote Labour

GAITSKELL X

Printed by Tillotson & Firth Ltd., Morley and
Published by G. Brett, Central Committee Rooms,
4 Cambrian Terrace, Leeds

10 A campaign poster for his first election,
Chatham 1935

11 Candidate for South
Leeds, 1945

12 With Labour Party friends in Chatham, 1935. Mrs Grieveson is on
Gaitskell's right

13 With Dora at a Fabian Summer School at Dartington Hall, 1938

14 Ernest Bevin (*centre*), the new Foreign Secretary, arriving at the Beaver Hall meeting of new Labour MPs on 28 July 1945

vention in war as they had in peace, and after thirty months of it had made no 'serious attempt to improve the efficiency of the available labour'.[55b]

To do so was not easy, for the inter-war battles had left the miners understandably bitter and sullen. Their numbers were inadequate, for sons were now reluctant to follow their fathers down the pit.[59] Besides, in the first two years of the war the armed forces called up 80,000 younger miners who the Mines Department had decided could not be spared.[57c] By 1942 two-fifths of the labour force were over forty and one-fifth over fifty;[11k] so that lengthening the working week to counter absenteeism led only to fatigue and more absenteeism – quite apart from the miners' 'strong sense of wrongs unremedied'.[57d*]

This inefficient, undermanned industry, with its ageing and discontented labour force unable to produce enough coal, seemed ripe at last for reorganisation; meanwhile only rationing could ensure that limited supplies were fairly distributed. Every Minister on the Lord President's Committee accepted the first, and all but one the second.[61] But the mineowners still hoped to avoid reorganisation and many Conservative MPs detested rationing; both urged the recall of miners from the forces instead. The Ministers accepted that too. Then all three proposals met a major obstacle: the Prime Minister. Alone, he successfully opposed any release of fighting soldiers. Aided by his party, he blocked rationing. Dalton eventually sacrificed that to achieve reorganisation; but though the owners lost some of their power to obstruct, Churchill absolutely vetoed nationalisation.

At several stages of Gaitskell's political life the miners played a crucial role. They had impelled him to join the Labour Movement in 1926; later on he made his reputation handling their problems as Minister of Fuel and Power, and he enjoyed their steady support both before and after he became leader of the Labour Party. It was as Hugh Dalton's assistant in 1942 that he made his first contacts with their leaders, and had his official introduction to their turbulent industry.

His first memorandum to Dalton set out the issues:

(1) *Fuel*   This is the most urgent problem of all. We have just scraped through this Winter, largely owing to the exceedingly warm Autumn, but the prospects for next Winter are not bright, and a failure of fuel supplies would do great damage to the war effort. Politically the fuel position is obviously full of dynamite. What is needed is an immediate survey of the position next winter well in advance, so that action can be taken early. But it must be a survey of all fuel, together with coal,

* Some owners had learned nothing; when a miner just back from the Army was killed on his fifth day in the pit, the company deducted half that day's wages.[60a]

E

gas and electricity. Effective action has so far broken down due to the failure to take these together. There are three particular problems –

(i)   Coal production. This raises the issue of nationalisation, which, combined with successful concentration of production is much favoured by some. (There is no need for me to say anything about the politics of this.)

(ii) Bottle-necks in coal conversion plant and transportation.

(iii) Problem of rationing. It must be done for all fuel, and there is a conflict of views. Opinion in the Board of Trade has been against, no doubt influenced by vested interest. Outside opinion in Whitehall is unanimously in favour. Can you ration fuel? This is the biggest question you will have to face, and you will have to go into it in great detail yourself.[55a]

Even more urgently, Gaitskell warned that the 'very grave' manpower situation needed the instant attention of the Lord President's Committee.[55b] On 6 April 1942 its chairman Sir John Anderson told the War Cabinet that of the 720,000 men needed to meet the nation's coal needs for the coming year, only 705,000 were still in mining.[57e] Of the 15,000 deficiency, other industries could at most supply 3,000, and the Army had only 5,000 miners not serving in field force units; even if the Cabinet released 7,000 fighting soldiers, by next winter normal wastage would reduce numbers to 705,000 again. Churchill, on his own, prevented releases. Overruled, Dalton loyally defended that decision in the House the following month; but he became wary of letting other essential industries like clothing lose men who could never be retrieved.[62]

Enough men were found from industry and the non-field forces to postpone the crisis, which in the end was unsatisfactorily met by training unskilled and unwilling conscripts (nicknamed 'Bevin boys'). Meanwhile, with labour short and stocks inadequate, Dalton and Gaitskell for three months concentrated exclusively on two problems: rationing fuel, and reorganising coal production to improve efficiency and regain the miners' confidence. Already the miners' leaders 'regarded Hugh Gaitskell as an old friend and comrade. They always liked him to be present when we met'. Soon the mineowners came to ask for more money, and for the first time he met face-to-face the men whose conduct had so outraged him sixteen years before; 'never', he said, had he 'seen such a collection of hard-faced twisters', and he called their leader 'a pure Galsworthy type'. Dalton too thought that most of them 'could be dealt with only by orders, not by persuasion; and finally only by liquidation'; and would not let them raise prices without concessions in return on the long-overdue reorganisation of the industry.[63]

While these major plans were brewing, Dalton turned his attention to what Gaitskell had called 'the biggest question you will have to face'. In the losing battle for fuel rationing Gaitskell played a central role. He suggested using Sir William Beveridge, who devised a complex but (in Dalton's view) 'very clever and perfect plan'; his amendments helped make it 'a beautifully simple scheme'; and he, with Beveridge, remained its staunchest defender.[64]

Rationing was neither administratively nor politically simple, though Whitehall opinion was overwhelmingly favourable, and so were not only the Labour leaders and Cripps, but non-political Ministers like Sir John Anderson and Lord Leathers. It is far from clear that public opinion was hostile; one early survey found 70 per cent in favour and only 10 per cent against.[65] But there were genuine doubts about how much it would save;[55b] and problems both of staffing and of guaranteeing delivery if transport were dislocated.[66] Politically, some miners hesitated, fearing for their concessionary coal;[11l] and the Minister of Mines himself was against it.[67]

The opposition was vociferous if not representative. On 21 April Dalton announced plans to save 10 million tons of coal annually by allocating a fuel ration to each house and each individual – and met 'a most surprising uproar ... from all parts of the House ... many [lobby correspondents] think that the scheme is already dead'.[68] Over the next ten days Gaitskell warned his master that 'through the press the vested interests are working like tigers against fuel rationing', and Dalton observed 'that the coal-owners are spending a lot of money trying to get rid of me!'[15r] Gaitskell and many others (including R. A. Butler) thought that the Tories feared not getting enough for their country houses.[69] Dalton thought they objected equally to rationing, coupons and officials, to the miners for not working harder, to the feeble Grenfell, and to himself for plotting nationalisation.[15s] A friendly Conservative MP told him that the Tory back-benchers' 1922 Committee 'acted as they did because they felt that the Labour Party in the Government was getting too much of its own way'.[70] A decade later the official historian explained the storm as

the opposition of industrial and class interests – of all those who felt that the ration would be inconvenient ... Fairly heavy sacrifices were being demanded of the middle classes and the larger houses. The public utilities also were no better pleased ... the rationing plan became a sort of unacknowledged test of the relative strength of parties and interests within the Coalition Government and in Parliament.[57f]

It gave the Conservatives their greatest political victory of the war.[71]

The Left blamed the Labour Ministers for not arousing Labour back-benchers and the movement outside.[72a] But Dalton and Gaitskell, trying to do so through Brett, found the movement outside entirely sluggish:

There is at present a campaign against rationing conducted most un-
scrupulously by the capitalist press, partly because the coal-owning
interests are anxious to damage and, if possible, get rid of Dalton;
partly because the gas and electricity interests hate the idea of rationing; and partly because the richer classes are going to suffer under
rationing ...

Rationing in the present circumstances is the only way by which
working people will get a fair deal ... the poorer and smaller house-
holds will not suffer ... The burden will be placed, where it can most
easily be carried, on the larger houses and the wealthier people.

Unfortunately, the Labour Party seems to be a bit slow in realising
this. I therefore ask you to do everything you can in Leeds to wake
people up to the great dangers which will certainly follow a failure to
get the rationing scheme through, and to the very close interest which
working people have in avoiding the chaos and injustice of no
rationing.[4f]

He asked Brett (without revealing his inspiration) to organise letters to the
press, Party resolutions sent to MPs, action in the city council, and pressure
from industrialists whose supplies might be in danger if rationing failed.
But after three weeks the only reaction from Leeds was a pro-rationing
resolution from the city Labour Party, and Brett wrote 'wondering what
is going to happen about it and if your department are going to have to
climb down'.[73] Dalton was wondering, too.

Gaitskell was strongly against any concession. He feared that the summer
was the last chance, for after that, even if rationing proved necessary, the
stocks would already be dispersed in private cellars beyond government
control.[74] But the more experienced Dalton doubted if he could beat the
big battalions of the majority party, backed by a Prime Minister who
loathed all rationing schemes and had accepted them even for food and
clothes only with the utmost reluctance.[75] Dalton used his PPS to organise
and brief Labour MPs, and tried to moderate the hostility of the 1922
Committee;[76] but he was seeking a line of retreat. On 12 May he had 'a
bathroom brain-wave!' Any Cabinet crisis on coal should come over the
whole problem, including reorganisation, where all the Labour Ministers
would have to stand together. He therefore proposed to postpone the
rationing debate until a complete coal programme could be presented after
Whitsun.[11m]

On the same day James Stuart, the Conservative Chief Whip ('a poor,
wispy creature') warned Churchill that 100 Tories might vote against the
government and many more would abstain.[15t] Then Oliver Lyttelton, the
Minister of Production, came round to accept reorganisation, and Dalton
grasped at the new suggestions – including a better wage system – as offer-

ing him an honourable way out. Gaitskell was still producing material for endless ministerial meetings on rationing, but politically it was dead. On 1 June when the War Cabinet discussed reorganisation plans, the Prime Minister was interested only in the statement that rationing would not be introduced immediately.[77]

It never was. Gwilym Lloyd George inherited the problem on his appointment to the new Ministry of Fuel and Power, and in September 1942 he decided on restricting supplies instead – balancing, as the official economic historians put it, 'heavy risks ... against political expediency and administrative complexities'.[78] That winter was exceptionally mild, and with an allocation scheme for industrial coal, and a good public response to appeals for fuel economy, the stocks proved adequate. But next winter 'squeezing of the consumer was the main factor in balancing the coal budgets', and in January 1944 severe month-to-month restrictions of supplies became necessary. Consumption of electricity and gas rose while that of coal, the fuel of the poor, was falling.[79] 'The well-to-do, if they were patriotic, suffered with the poor. If they were not, they connived with the coal merchant.'[80]

As compensation for the abandonment of rationing, Dalton's 'bathroom brain-wave' enabled the Labour Ministers to make some progress over reorganisation, and Gaitskell was again involved in the struggle as his confidential adviser. This new conflict, probably the first in which he and Aneurin Bevan were active on opposing sides, provided another instructive lesson in the realities of political power.

Nationalisation of the mines was favoured not only by all Socialists but by Dalton's non-political expert advisers, Sir Ernest Gowers and Lord Hyndley, but since the War Cabinet would never accept it, the problems of presentation were delicate:

> I have seen Gaitskell ... come out of Dalton's room with tears in his eyes – all because Dalton had rejected two successive drafts which Gaitskell had prepared on the nationalisation of the mines and finally told him that it was useless to ask him to write anything.[81]

Prudently, Dalton and Ernest Bevin pressed only for the pits to be requisitioned for the duration of the war. Even so, many miners disliked the objective of concentrating production, and Grenfell as usual reflected the views of the most cautious – making it easy for the Conservative Ministers to evade discussing the question of ownership. As Dalton put it: 'we met great resistance, some from most surprising quarters, and had to fall back on a second-rate compromise'.[82] But he and Bevin felt 'sure that if the owners lost control of the pits now, they would never get it back.'[11n] They were better prophets than Aneurin Bevan, who predicted that if the pits were not nationalised in war, they never would be in peace.[60d] When the compromise was accepted, Dalton commented on that uncompromising attitude. At long last, he wrote, 'The miners' leadership ... have learned the lesson that their traditional policy of "all or nowt" always ends in nowt. This time they have gone to the other extreme ... "Keep on nibbling at the cheese, boys".'[15u]

The compromise was far from satisfactory. The companies kept financial responsibility and the mine managers remained their employees, but subject to the orders of the Minister's Regional Controllers; for disobedience 'there is the sanction ... of taking over the pit'.[60e] Gaitskell disliked the plan, fearing that with 'the wrong kind of Minister and the wrong kind of Regional Controllers, the scheme [might] make no difference at all'.[15v] Bevan went so far as to call it a Nazi or Fascist scheme giving the Minister 'unknown powers of patronage and corruption' – though not so far as to vote against the government.[60f]

Early in 1942 there had been widespread unofficial strikes in the coal-fields, which Dalton met by setting up a strong independent board of inquiry into miners' wages. On Gaitskell's advice he appointed Harold Wilson as its secretary.[83] Within two weeks it had accepted their claim for a national minimum wage, which the owners had defeated in 1926 and were still contesting, and raised their wages from fifty-ninth among industrial earners to twenty-third.[84] The settlement not only ended the strikes, but won the union executive over to the reorganisation scheme. The miner MPs then agreed too, with three dissenters including Bevan;[15w] and so, after three long meetings, did the Parliamentary Labour Party.[11o] Both in the government[15x] and in the House Conservative opposition was less than Dalton and Gaitskell had expected, and 'all the Government spokesmen's persuasions [were] addressed to the Labour Party'.[15y]

The results of the compromise were mixed. Speaking for the miners, Will Lawther told the next Party Conference after a year's experience of it that Bevin and Dalton had done more for the mining industry than all their predecessors.[85] But Labour critics like Bevan complained that if Labour Ministers had shown more 'energy', and Labour MPs acted 'more robustly', they could easily have won both the fuel-rationing and the re-organisation battles.[72b]

That was soon disproved. In October 1943 Gwilym Lloyd George, the Liberal Minister now responsible for the mines, was backed by every one of his Regional Controllers when he told the War Cabinet that 'dual control' was working badly, and that effective operational control was impossible unless, as Bevin and Dalton had proposed, the state became the owner of the mines as long as the war continued. But Winston Churchill flatly refused to contemplate nationalisation, and explicitly threatened a general election on it.[86]

No one took up the challenge. For once in a coal debate, Aneurin Bevan was silent. 'For the rest of the war, nationalisation of the mines was not an issue.'[87] It was not robustness or energy that Dalton had lacked, but a sufficient power base. Though Labour's goodwill was indispensable to the war effort, industrial sanctions were an unusable weapon, effective only in so far as they helped Hitler. Politically, a party in a minority in the House and the government could not impose its policies on its majority partner; and if it considered withdrawing from the Coalition, the Prime Minister could threaten Labour with another 1931 election in which the rebellious MPs would be 'blown away like feathers before a tempest'.[15z]

With two conceptions of Labour politics in conflict, the limits of agitation and protest had been clearly demonstrated. A politician concerned with achievement rather than gestures needed parliamentary and public support which in 1942–3 were not available for domestic disputes. Dalton had had a good case, first over control of propaganda, then over fuel rationing, and now over the mines. But sound policies were not enough, and no amount of robust and energetic agitation could replace the missing parliamentary majority. Gaitskell's experience under Dalton drove those lessons firmly home.

CHAPTER 5

FROM WHITEHALL TO WESTMINSTER 1942–7

'How fascinating … the attraction of administrative power'
(HG, 1945)
'We've defeated the doctors — now we can smash the Tories'
(HG ABOUT HIS ILLNESS, 1945)

i Board of Trade Civil Servant

THOUGH preoccupied with fuel, Gaitskell continued for six more months of 1942 as Dalton's personal assistant over the whole diverse Board of Trade empire. It was an invidious position which at once provoked the usual bureaucratic friction over his rank, functions and even accommodation. The Permanent Secretary, Sir Arnold Overton, was able to block his promotion to Principal Assistant Secretary, but not to restrict his field of operations. He was suspected of being too much of a politician not only by the Board of Trade civil servants, but also in anti-Labour quarters outside. A week after the fuel-rationing storm began, Conservative Central Office apparently planned a parliamentary attack on him, but it was poorly prepared and Dalton skilfully diverted it.[1a]

In June Dalton relinquished responsibility for coal, and Gaitskell had five days' well-earned leave. On his return they had a long talk, and the personal assistant suggested that 'external economic relations' offered his Minister an opportunity to influence policy on a wide front. The Economic Section of the Cabinet Secretariat was seeking allies for a proposal (drafted by James Meade) for a post-war Commercial Union of states, designed as a complement to Keynes's currency plans and to any future political association of the United Nations type. Gaitskell approved, and redrafted Meade's paper as a 'quite bright' memorandum phrased to attract Dalton's backing.[2] It argued that while Britain would benefit from freer world trade, Russia must be brought into the new Union and state trading must be recognised as legitimate. Dalton approved, encouraging the academic temporaries against some official obstruction.[3a*]

* In September 1943 an International Trade Charter was drafted, emphasising freer trade and full employment. But after the war the Russians stayed out, and

One of these temporaries described Gaitskell as: 'extremely able at seeing the larger issues. He had an immediate grasp of policy and administrative matters; could see the problem, convey it, and get something done. He had drive.'[5] In his last two months as personal assistant, he was also working on retail trade problems and as a talent scout, seeking recruits to strengthen the higher ranks of Board of Trade officialdom. That role did not endear him to the senior administrators, who obstructed and delayed such appointments as Douglas Jay's dealing with post-war reconstruction.[3b][c] He minimised but could never eradicate their suspicion of a *chef de cabinet*:[6a] 'I was impressed by the way he got over his impossible situation,' said another colleague. 'We were at first told not to talk to him because it would make difficulties with Overton who was horrified at the appointment, but within a few months he and Overton were on the best of terms.'[7] The civil servants were persistent and in August Overton proposed to Dalton that Gaitskell should take over a regular administrative post, with promotion at last to Principal Assistant Secretary. Dalton tried instead to keep him as personal assistant for post-war reconstruction,[3b] but this time — to the Minister's fury — Gaitskell was adamant.[6a][b]

Under G. L. Watkinson, the official in the Department whom he most respected, Gaitskell was responsible for 'half a dozen of the dirtiest jobs in the office ... not unimportant but politically unexciting':[6a] price control, retail trade, the film industry and, for a brief period, post-war reconstruction.[8] The division's main activity, price control, was by now a reasonably routine operation.[9a] But concern to keep down the prices of essentials still had to be balanced with the need to keep the producer interested in making them; and production was dealt with by another division. When Gaitskell later as a Minister defended the use of controls as an instrument of economic policy, he knew from his own experience that this was the major problem.[10]

At first his main preoccupation was the retail trade. The government knew too little about the statistical situation in shopkeeping, too much about the political. Hungry for additional labour for the armed services and the war industries, it would have liked to require distribution as well as manufacturing to be concentrated on the most efficient units. But it was hampered by lack of information, by the shopping difficulties of people engaged on essential work, by uncertainty about where labour could be released, and by the fear of howls of parliamentary protest. Dalton was sensitive to political dangers after his buffeting over fuel, and in his speech in the House on 23 July (based on material collected by Gaitskell) he was careful to show great sympathy for the small shopkeeper. To his delight,

---

the General Agreement on Tariffs and Trade — devised to satisfy the US Congress and reflecting American trading interests — was adopted instead as a supposedly temporary stopgap.[4]

he found that the government could most easily meet its needs for labour and for office and storage space at the expense of the larger shops and chains, and he began a new policy of deliberate discrimination in favour of small traders.[9b]

Gaitskell was actively involved, holding 'ticklish conferences' with the interests, being sent to 'nobble the National Chamber of Trade', and ingeniously selling Dalton's policies to the multiple stores which would suffer from them. He prepared Dalton's statement of 13 October 1942, which was well received even by Labour MPs from whom Dalton had expected criticism. Dining with Gaitskell two months later to discuss the replies to some planted parliamentary questions, the Minister concluded happily: 'For the time being, I have quite extinguished all press and parliamentary agitation in favour of small shops.'[11] But again politics had triumphed over economic efficiency, for the retail trades kept too much labour; according to the official historians this was the biggest failure of the wartime Board of Trade.[9c]

With his departure from Dalton's private office, Gaitskell—in the words of a close friend—

> disappeared as it were into a tunnel of steady, efficient, laborious administration ... working on the same floor of the same building, I seemed to see less of him than at any time in the previous ten years or next fifteen ... we were all so desperately busy with our own responsibilities in working hours, and with fire-watching and flying bombs out of them.[12]

At the beginning of 1943 Dalton told him he 'should turn increasingly' to post-war work, and at Easter Gaitskell agreed to work out schemes for his Minister to 'stimulate selected sectors of the Home Front, as I did with Commercial Union'.[3d] He was to find it a frustrating experience:

> If you are interested in ideas and plans alone, it's quite fun, but of course it's far harder to get any decisions & when it comes to long run issues almost impossible. So one is apt to be very discouraged. One of the alarming things I notice is the very great gap between what I believe is the popular attitude to postwar—which is now much more socialistic & the attitude of the business men we have to deal with which is for the most part reactionary & capitalistic ... there is such a very real struggle for industrial *power* ... the Director class ... are really much less concerned with maximising profits than with just exercising arbitrary power. They regard shareholders as a bore ... and ... the state as a menace. *They* want to be allowed to decide for themselves what is in the public interest.[13]

Businessmen were not the only opponents. Gaitskell represented the Board of Trade in the preparatory talks preceding the White Paper on full employment in May 1944, and argued strongly for maintaining consumer demand by running budget deficits where necessary. Even the dry official records show how profoundly he shocked the orthodox Treasury spokesman, Sir Wilfred Eady.[14] (The feeling was mutual, and in 1945 Gaitskell, at his first encounter with Dalton as Chancellor, warned him against Eady.)[15a] Gaitskell was also active over location of industry policies — which always preoccupied Dalton, whose constituency was in the depressed Durham coalfield — insisting that after the war the Board of Trade rather than other Departments should have responsibility for the problem;[16] and participating in ministerial as well as official meetings about it, as Dalton's confidant.[17]

He played a more personal role over another post-war problem: anti-monopoly policy. He chaired a small informal committee on it, including James Meade from the Cabinet Office; and with G. C. Allen he prepared a draft working paper which one sardonic official compared to 'a tract on the drink trade written by a couple of teetotallers'.[18] Gaitskell's colleague stressed his skill in arguing the case against monopolies both within the Board of Trade and with the Treasury; and pointed out that his dinners with Dalton enabled the Minister to know when papers from junior officials were being quietly blocked by a senior man who did not like their content — for many permanent civil servants were still wedded to pre-war restrictive devices. Dalton did not wholly share Gaitskell's enthusiasm for forbidding all these restrictive agreements, but he was determined to have the subject taken seriously;[3e] and in 1948, as a result of these discussions, the Monopolies Commission was set up. The talks also opened a long campaign by Dalton and Gaitskell to interest the Labour Party in consumer problems, especially resale price maintenance. But it met resistance from outside interests and the Civil Service, and indifference from two Labour Presidents of the Board of Trade;* in the end a Conservative Minister and government won the credit for abolishing RPM.

Of all his administrative tasks, Gaitskell was most fascinated by the film industry, with its exotic personalities, its crazy economics — for films tended to make either a loss or a huge profit — and its tangled problem of resisting American cultural domination without falling into insularity, or inefficiency, or British monopoly control. (J. Arthur Rank already owned 600 cinemas, distribution companies, and half Britain's studio space.) Gaitskell wrote Dalton's briefs and conducted 'quite tough bargaining' with the two principal interests, Rank and the (partly American) Associated British

* Harold Wilson and Sir Hartley Shawcross (see Chapter 9).

Picture Corporation.[3f] He helped the industry – potentially so important for exports – to prepare for post-war developments, notably by getting studio space released; and was, a former colleague wrote later, 'one of the few people in B.O.T. who ... enthusiastically aided my somewhat tough methods of getting results.'[19]

Less serious contacts with the industry included complimentary invitations to premières and private showings, dinners with Rank or Korda or Skouras (the Greek-American magnate, who 'said nothing worth remembering all night')[3g] and agreeable lunches with Vivien Leigh and Ingrid Bergman.[20a] Gaitskell made many lasting friends in the film world, and when he was ill in 1945 his old colleague Lord Drogheda, now chairman of the Films Council, wrote that he was 'sadly missed' there.[21] When he entered the House, Rank and Korda invited him to become vice-president and economic adviser of the British Film Producers' Association at £1,000 a year plus expenses, with an office and a secretary available for his parliamentary work.[22a] Having consulted Dalton and Cripps, and ensured that his independence was safeguarded, he agreed.[15b] He soon found that he could not give enough time to justify the stipend, but he continued as an honorary vice-president until he joined the government.[22b]

At the Board of Trade Gaitskell had at first as little family life as ever. The lease of the Woburn house ran out in February 1942, and he then arranged for Dora to go to stay with his mother at Milland for a few months. On 23 July 1942 his second daughter was born in a near-by nursing home, and named after Cressida Bonham Carter, who had been billeted on them at Woburn. They then returned to their own cottage, to Hugh's delight, 'because, of course, I love Sussex and being in my own house and garden – but I'm afraid it may be pretty lonely for Dora'.[23a] He saw them only at weekends and the separation became increasingly galling, while the cottage was very cramped when he came.

In March 1943, therefore, Dora and the children moved back to London. The Gaitskells rented the lower floors of 21 Well Walk, with another family living upstairs in the 'huge 1880 baronial house in Hampstead'.[13] The rooms were very cold, the ceilings very high, and the house very run-down and hard to manage. Once again they were sharing – with two of Dora's sisters and their small children, and with Evan Durbin. But the family was reunited and Hugh was now able to see more of them than before.

In January 1944 he wrote happily to Brett that Cressida was 'getting to the nicest age of all – which I put, so far, at 18 months to 3. Julie is as sweet as ever.' Less happily, he recorded 'a good deal of talk about the secret weapon and the bombardment of London from the French coast, but beyond making arrangements to send the family away if it ever starts and clearing the cellar, we are not taking it too seriously'.[23b] Luckily, the children were away during a heavy raid a month later, which caused several local fires, and again at the end of the year when a flying bomb landed at the end of their road and smashed most of their windows. 'I'm afraid,' he wrote ruefully,

> my prophecies about the end of the war were not too accurate! But I was in good company in making them, and if the Arnhem thing had come off and the weather had not been so foul, it might have been a different story.[23c]

Looking forward to the return of peace, he kept up his close relations with Dalton. They dined regularly, together celebrating Evan Durbin's selection for a safe Labour seat at Edmonton, and lamenting the badly handled dispute between Government and Party over Beveridge's great social security report.[24] Gaitskell helped with occasional political tasks, drafting a resolution for the Labour Party on international policy, which was accepted by the 1942 Party Conference, and in 1943 a paper on post-war employment and finance. In October 1943 Dalton organised a discussion on post-war Labour foreign policy among his coterie, like the one after Munich just five years before; Durbin struck one participant as very right-wing, but Gaitskell's views are not recorded.[25] A year later Gaitskell was concerned that the use of British troops against Greek Communists would provoke at home both left-wing hostility to the government and non-party quasi-isolationist resentment in the country.[3h]

Though as friendly as ever, his relations with Dalton were subtly changing as Gaitskell acquired some of the administrator's attitudes towards politicians. Early in his term at the Board of Trade he said that when he got into the House, he would propose that only junior ministers should answer MPs' letters, so as to stop 'a shocking waste' of Cabinet Ministers' time. When Gladwyn Jebb told Dalton that Foreign Office officials 'spend all their time slaving away and then ministers either do nothing or do it all wrong', Gaitskell added 'that all civil servants in *all* Departments ... often feel like this!'[3i] Like many wartime acacemic recruits to Whitehall, he was happier there than as a don;[26a] and he found executive work, unlike Dalton's private office, 'wholly absorbing and satisfying'.[12] Cool, intelligent and rational in his appraisal of issues, good-tempered and skilful at managing men, full of enthusiasm and energy for the job, he was widely regarded as potentially a great civil servant, and to some old friends and new colleagues, he seemed to have found his true metier.[26a b]

Some regular civil servants had more doubts. Sir Herbert Andrew, then his subordinate (and later a Permanent Secretary without much love for temporaries) felt that Gaitskell was too concerned with intellectual and social principles rather than their practical application, too willing to believe that inefficient controls would be an effective instrument of economic policy, and too convinced that once the policy was right, the realities would conform.[27]* Yet Gaitskell had no love of controls for their own sake; he criticised Dalton for damaging morale by restricting too severely the production of toys.[18] Andrew also felt that Gaitskell was too inclined to get into excessive detail and, as head of a Department, might not have reserved himself sufficiently for the broader issues: that criticism we shall meet again. But Watkinson, Gaitskell's immediate superior, whom he thought the ablest and most progressive senior man in the Board of Trade, had only praise for his work. He was effective and successful in dealing with other Departments;[3j] and the industry with which he had most to do — the film trade — was eager to secure his services after the war was over.

Within his own division, impressions were mixed. His secretary was devoted to him, like all her successors: 'I don't want to attract attention to my chiefless state until you know what your future is to be; it would be too awful to find myself permanently saddled with a new boss and then for you to return!'[28] His colleagues, following a pre-war custom, met daily in his room for 4 p.m. tea and a talk about the day's work: 'always a fruitful occasion of good talk and valuable exchanges', wrote one of the temporaries.[29] A career civil servant complained that he did not relax or give himself away, and would never gossip about politics; he seemed at first very self-possessed and ponderous, almost the 'desiccated calculating machine' of later years. Yet people liked him much better as they got to know him, and outside the office soon discovered the relaxed and gregarious Hugh Gaitskell his friends knew, so that on his departure he left no one feeling any antagonism and resentment towards him.[27]

He was still impatient with the ponderous pace of Whitehall, which 'gives one the feeling of swimming in treacle';[20b] and if the thought of an administrative career seriously crossed his mind, he did not entertain it for long. He had little time to think about the future, but assumed that he would return to UCL, and Overton recalled his having once 'suggested that irrespective of the date of the Election you might wish to get back to your academic work well before the beginning of the Michaelmas Term'.[30] UCL tried to make that easy, offering him a chair and allowing him to wait until the election before deciding.[31] Early in 1945 he walked round Milland with a friend 'weighing the attractions of academic life and the occupational hazards of politics'.[32] He also had a renewed offer from Leith-Ross of a senior post with UNRRA, the international relief organisation.[29] But that die had been cast in February 1942, when Dalton persuaded him

---

* Andrew had to administer a White Paper, written by Gaitskell, on the distribution of war-surplus goods to the public. Orderly and fair-minded, it did not anticipate the actual chaos. The first major item delivered from the armed services included bloodstained blankets, supposed to be sold to the trade as new.[27]

to remain in the political race; and the subsequent three years confirmed his decision as he discovered 'how fascinating was the attraction of administrative power'.[33]

ii South Leeds: Elected from a Sick-bed

While normal political activity was suspended during the war, Gaitskell did his limited best to keep up his links with South Leeds. But twice the constituency nearly lost him altogether: at the very beginning of the war, when he entered the Civil Service, and at the very end, when he was incapacitated at the time of the 1945 election.

At the outbreak of war, Gaitskell was worried that his Civil Service post would oblige him to withdraw. On 8 September 1939 he wrote to his agent that he could not make speeches, or do much as a candidate, or—on his reduced salary—continue paying his £100 a year subscription to the constituency Party. But 'I do *not* want to sever all connection with S. Leeds'.[34a] Evidently the executive committee were eager to keep him, and a week later Gaitskell wrote again appreciating their support, and hoping 'that while I could not very well address public meetings, I might come up and see as many as possible of our people some time'.[23d] The following month he learned that UCL would make up his salary, and wrote promising to continue his annual payment, hoping that the executive would (as they did)[35a] use it to retain Brett as part-time agent, since 'it is extremely important that Party activities and organisation should be maintained despite the war'.[23e] That concern often recurs later in the correspondence.

The local Party remained solid. 'We have the usual grousers inside the Leeds Lab. Party Communist inspired,[36] but they never get away with anything—in my own Division I have no trouble.'[35b] Meetings were badly attended, but the constituency stalwarts continued to keep contact through social activities, and Alderman Brett (now working full-time but unpaid on air-raid precautions) was among the Labour leaders who played a prominent part on the Council. During 1941 one little local difficulty was cleared up at last when, responding to mounting criticism of the absentee MP, the Labour Party National Executive belatedly intervened. Charleton agreed to resume constituency activities and help at the next election; Gaitskell arranged to see him, and soon the MP was again writing to the agent as 'Dear George'.[37] But two years later Gaitskell was still lamenting to Brett: 'There appears to me to be no prospect that he will resign, though of course I do think myself that a lot of the older ones in the party ought really to make way now so as to get the average age down a bit!'[23f] At the time of the election his brother commiserated with him on his 'bad luck in having an old man blocking your way for so long in S. Leeds.'[20c]

The troubles of the South Leeds Party were financial rather than political. Subscriptions were falling off, and George Brett feared they would face the next election penniless. In 1942 he took a job offered by a wealthy Leeds clothing manufacturer and Labour sympathiser, and so saved the cost of his salary. Gaitskell agreed, provided that his own £100 p.a. subscription should be reserved for a special election account.[35c] Brett remained part-time agent, though ill for much of 1943. Subsequently Gaitskell was able to go to Leeds a little more frequently, alternating his visits with those of Charleton and of candidates in near-by seats; he attended occasional socials, and talked to the active party workers about both organisation and policy. But there were practical and also political difficulties. On one return train journey to London he had to stand for eight hours; and another time, having volunteered to speak to party activists on full employment, he had to suppress the title because 'of trouble going on about candidates in the Civil Service arising largely out of Evan Durbin's adoption ... this happens to be the subject about which we have been told to be particularly cagey'.[38] However, by the beginning of 1945 Gaitskell's parliamentary prospects seemed excellent: a safe Labour seat, a loyal constituency Party with sound finances and its local squabbles settled, and a general election due before long. Then, at almost the last moment, the prize was nearly snatched from him by the only serious illness of his working life.

At the Board of Trade, as at the MEW, Gaitskell had continued 'grossly overtiring himself'. Political friends visiting Leeds told Brett so;[35d] and Gaitskell referred to the load in several letters: 'for some weeks past I am overworking and have to spend a good part of every weekend working ... [on] a new job';[23g] 'terribly busy again'; '*very* overworked at present'.[23c] It was 'the only period between 1933 and 1963 when he seemed basically tired'.[12] Then, when Dora came to London one day in early March 1945, they went to the Gargoyle Club in Soho for their first evening's dancing for years. Hugh felt ill at the club, had a bad night and the next morning, walking to the tube station, suffered a pain in his chest which recurred when running or walking up hills. After a week he went to see his doctor, who fixed him an appointment with a heart specialist on 4 April.

Next weekend, he was with the family in the country when he came down with bad neuralgia and a persistent temperature. It kept him from work for the first time for over ten years, and though he returned briefly to the office, the specialist decided that he had suffered a minor coronary thrombosis.[39] He was promptly packed off for three weeks in bed with complete rest—he was not to write letters or even shave himself—to be followed by two more months away from work. Dora wrote to Brett on his behalf:

one of the blood vessels supplying my heart is not functioning properly. This produces a sort of cramp which brings on the pains and sensations and seems to have caused some damage ... [it] happens quite often to older men but is unusual in someone of my age. I imagine it is simply the result of five years overwork and strain.

The doctors could not promise future immunity, only that the two months' rest would improve his chances. They discouraged him from fighting the election,

> though not to the extent of positively forbidding me ... To give up now would be a bitter blow and not only to me but to you as well who have helped me so much ... I realise ... that if I have to drop out, the Party must be given time to find someone to take my place, but I think it is reasonable to let me have just a week or two and perhaps more if the war does not go too fast.[40]

Brett's reply conveyed the good advice and sympathy of a man who recalled that, after his own more serious coronary, 'my doctors would have had me pack up everything — they have an idea that politicians foam at the mouth & are always in a state of turmoil.'[35e] Gaitskell was now so popular with the local party workers that Brett 'was ready, if necessary, to fight the election without the candidate being there'.[34b] He welcomed Dora's suggestion of consulting Lord Horder, who was experienced in assessing the strain of political activity,[39] and he hoped to get Transport House support over speakers;

> if you were well enough to be in the Constituency you would with big backing from Head Office be a better proposition than any new candidate. I ... will go to any lengths to keep Hugh in the field but I think we must begin to act and Horder seems the first move ... to safeguard both Hugh and myself with the Division.

On 11 May Brett at last revealed the candidate's condition to his party executive, who voted without dissent or abstentions to send a message of sympathy and continued support in the election 'if he can come to the constituency even although he can take no physical part'. The agent was 'naturally delighted ... the circumstances will make our people work like elephants'. As it turned out, it was the Conservative candidate (Donald Kaberry, later Sir Donald and MP for Leeds North West) who had to withdraw at the last minute.[41]

Dalton, enlisted by Brett, at once promised to help with speakers. At his request Horder examined Gaitskell at Milland on 22 May, and reported that, given three months' limitation of effort, the patient could resume political activities. But he must stay away from South Leeds until the last fortnight, and appear only twice daily, and only once at an indoor public meeting.[42] Gaitskell sent these terms to Brett on a postcard, and then — finding it still a strain to walk or even talk — went off to Sandown in the Isle of Wight for a short holiday (promptly ruined when Julia caught whooping cough). On 28 May he wrote hoping the General Management Committee had not had to decide on his candidature before they knew the worst:

> I would much have preferred and still prefer that they should have had a full opportunity of doing so with all the facts known. If anything went wrong this would be much better from everyone's point of view and prevent recriminations.

But Brett had received the postcard ('more than we expected') and an unprecedentedly large GMC on 27 May had unanimously agreed to fight with Gaitskell even if he could not participate at all. That decision, wrote the agent, 'has never been questioned by anybody'. He added, 'we shall take great care of you & fight like tigers to win the seat'; and the candidate replied, 'We've defeated the doctors — now we can smash the Tories!'[43]

Gaitskell remained in the south for two more weeks, receiving almost daily letters from his agent and sending almost as many back. Marjorie Brett wrote encouragingly to Dora of 'the affection and loyalty of all party members to him'.[44] Her father proudly recorded that 'Our people packed like sardines the largest first meeting of Workers I have ever seen in the Division', and that Attlee was to open the campaign in South Leeds with Dalton and Ivor Thomas also speaking there; and Bevin and A. V. Alexander in the city. Mostly their correspondence dealt with the mundane but often tricky problems of Gaitskell's accommodation, photograph blocks, petrol coupons and poster space. The candidate took an active part, suggesting the slogans for the posters, writing his election address in a couple of days ('It has nearly killed me to do it so quickly') and hoping to counteract the Conservatives' appeal to patriotism by displaying the Union Jack alongside the US and Soviet flags:

> We have *got* to spike the Tory's 'national' fun. Use Red White and Blue wherever you can. If you can get the flags done, *use them everywhere with my photo.* Here again *don't* worry too much about expense. I feel it will be a very close fight in S. Leeds.[45]

Cheating the doctors slightly, Gaitskell moved north nearly three weeks before the poll, but kept to Horder's conditions by staying outside the constituency. Brett had promised not to make the candidate work, but wanted him present at Attlee's two meetings on the 16th, and generally available to encourage the party activists. His host was an old school friend, the Reverend John Beloe, Vicar of Morley, who recalled that

Gaitskell 'spent nearly all the time lying on our spare-room bed', and that as neither Hugh nor Dora could tie a red rosette 'my wife obliged, having made many blue ones in Huddersfield for her father'.[46a] Gaitskell moved into South Leeds ten days before polling day and went round with a loudspeaker in the afternoons, appearing briefly before his one audience a night; he spoke for five minutes at the big rally in Leeds Town Hall before being whisked off by his protective supporters 'to another meeting'.[47] Fortunately it was a sedate campaign and he faced virtually no heckling.[48]

In heavy type Gaitskell's election address proclaimed:

On the vital issues – Jobs, Homes and Fair Shares – continuing the Coalition would have meant knuckling under to the reactionary Conservative majority ... Never less than a million without jobs and in most years far more. This was the result of Conservative Rule and Private Enterprise ... HOUSING ... a Labour Government will tackle it with the same public enterprise, efficiency and drive which produced our bombers, guns and tanks.

Nationalisation was mentioned but not emphasised under WHAT I STAND FOR on the back page:

1. JOBS FOR ALL.
2. A NATIONAL INDUSTRIAL POLICY.
3. DECENT PENSIONS AND HEALTH SERVICES.
4. A GOOD EDUCATION FOR OUR CHILDREN.
5. FAIR SHARES AND NO PROFITEERING.
6. FRIENDSHIP WITH RUSSIA AND AMERICA TO PREVENT WAR.

His Conservative opponent was a Huddersfield solicitor, Brigadier A. M. Ramsden, who had fought in the First World War and held an anti-aircraft command in the Midlands in the Second; Brett described him as 'a decent sort ... I don't think he is really political'. There was no animosity in his campaign, and he became a great admirer of Gaitskell's, sending charming letters of congratulation at each step of Hugh's ascent of the political ladder.[49] The Liberal was a schoolmaster, William Barford, whom Gaitskell expected to take mainly Conservative votes.[23h] Some Labour people feared that Gaitskell's civilian status would count against him but, just in time for inclusion in his election address, he was awarded the CBE for his wartime services.[50] His supporters underlined this in meetings, somewhat to his embarrassment, and also quoted a message from Harold Laski, Chairman of the Labour Party, stressing the 'contribution of quite special value' Gaitskell could bring to Parliament.[51]

Mild though the campaign in South Leeds had been, the sick man found it a very heavy strain. 'I was thoroughly alarmed in the last few days,' wrote Brett, 'but you came through splendidly.'[35f] On the return journey the Gaitskells' car broke down on Hampstead Heath, half a mile from home, and was then so incompetently repaired that it vibrated very badly when he retired to his mother's house at Milland a few days later. The pain came back, he had to return to bed under sedation for several days, and he feared he might need an operation.[23i] His wife, too, had been having a very difficult time, and when he returned to Hampstead at the end of the month conditions were far from easy: 'We are in rather a mess here – everything very dirty and untidy. No help in sight. Dora very tired with a bad cold and the children coming back on Tuesday!' But by then he knew he was Member of Parliament for South Leeds.[23j]

In 1945, because of the armed forces' ballots from overseas, the votes were not counted for three weeks after polling day. But experienced electioneers on both sides in Leeds had already correctly concluded that Labour had taken five of the six seats.[35g f] Although Gaitskell had earlier spoken pessimistically of his own chances,[46a b] he was now reasonably confident: 'My sober judgment is that after counting in the Forces we might get a majority of 5,000 which is quite good enough for me!'[23i] In fact his majority was twice that, with a swing almost identical to that in Leeds as a whole.

H. Gaitskell (Lab.)	17,899	1935: Lab.	15,223
A. Ramsden (Cons.)	7,497	Cons.	14,207
W. Barford (Lib.)	3,933	Ind.	3,642
Majority	10,402		1,216

Ten days earlier he had written to thank George Brett[34c]

whatever the future may bring (including even the return of Brigadier Ramsden on the 26th July to Parliament!) ... Good advice, kindness, sympathy, encouragement – all have been showered upon me. And at the end, I know quite well it was *you* who were taking the really serious risks ... you must now leave this particular ship to make its own way – having so to speak piloted it down the river to the open sea.[23k]

iii   Back-bencher and Under-Secretary

Immense hopes were placed in the Labour Government which came to power in July 1945. The war had just ended in Europe, and was about to end in the Far East. Like most wars it had radicalised popular expectations, and distressed areas, dole queues and glaring social inequalities now seemed intolerable. The Conservatives suffered from this mood; they had been in power before the war, and were grudging about the reforms proposed during it, especially Beveridge's social security scheme. Labour, long committed to greater social justice and stricter government control of the economy, was seen as the appropriate party to handle the post-war difficulties.

Those difficulties were enormous. Industry had been converted far more thoroughly to war production in Britain than in Germany or the United States, and could be reconverted only gradually to peacetime activities. The transition was not cushioned by the invisible exports – shipping, insurance and overseas investments – which had for decades masked the country's unfavourable balance of trade. For in the war, besides losing her old markets, Britain had sold off foreign assets and incurred debts; so that exports paid for only a quarter of her imports, and investment income for only 2 per cent (as against 22 per cent before the war).[52a b] To pay her way abroad, Britain had now to increase exports from 5 per cent of GNP (10 per cent before the war) to no less than 15 per cent.[53] But since the prices of exports had risen less than those of imports, that would mean increasing their volume by two-thirds. It was a most ambitious target, yet it was achieved in only five years, with industrial production rising by an annual average of 6 per cent.[52b] For food and raw materials to keep her industries working during this dramatic recovery, Britain had expected that the United States would temporarily continue Lend-Lease supplies. But with the end of the war these were cut off almost literally overnight. Until the Marshall Plan three years later, Britain depended for her basic needs on hard and humiliating negotiations with a demanding American administration, constrained by a mistrustful and hostile Congress.[54]

In those daunting circumstances, keen supporters expected the first majority Labour government to carry out a domestic revolution, while Conservative opponents blamed it for difficulties and austerities they had themselves long known to be inevitable. That campaign of recrimination, assisted by some notorious indiscretions on the Labour side, provoked class bitterness among the comfortably-off against both the Government and the unions. But by 1945 the Labour Party had much governmental experience and a new political self-confidence. There were hidden conflicts in the Cabinet, and a few open revolts among the swollen ranks of back-benchers, but the Party in those years was singularly free from its inveterate factionalism. Its supporters, too, saw that sacrifices really were being shared, so that in 1950, after five years of stringent austerity, its working-class vote remained almost solid; and the trade unions, enjoying unprecedented bargaining power under full employment, exercised responsible restraint in the long-term interest of their own members, of the Government, and of the country's economic recovery.

In 1945 Gaitskell shared and expressed the euphoria characteristic of Labour's enthusiastic young newcomers to Parliament. After the results were declared he participated in a motorcade round Leeds, and toured his constituency to thank his helpers. Next day he and Dora lunched with his friendly Conservative opponent, and he then returned to London for the first meeting of the new Labour MPs at the Beaver Hall. He thought Attlee and Bevin spoke well there, and commented sadly on Morrison's 'frantic and rather absurd efforts to wrest the Party leadership away for himself ... Ambition driving the most intelligent people mad as usual, I suppose'.[15a] Two days later he attended Dalton's 'young victors' dinner at St Ermin's Hotel,[1b] where the discussion made him feel comparatively elderly and experienced.[55] His own contribution stressed the need to deal with housing by giving skilled building workers higher priority in demobilisation; to meet any obstruction from the House of Lords by a well-timed general election; and to subsidise coal prices, as well as food and clothing, in order to permit the raising of miners' wages.

The new MPs were naturally agog to learn the composition of the new Government, and Gaitskell and Durbin were rather shocked to find Dalton assuming that no newcomer would get a post. Nevertheless Gaitskell was seriously considered for a Parliamentary Secretaryship to Cripps at the Board of Trade;[56*] but Horder advised him not to take office as yet, and they consoled themselves with happy XYZ dinners discussing how to nationalise the Bank of England. Then the Far Eastern war ended with unexpected suddenness and horror. When Durbin heard that the first atomic bombs had been dropped, he gloomily predicted that 'Europe is finished, possibly parts of North and South America may survive'.[15c]

When Parliament met, Gaitskell was greatly impressed by Churchill, mildly disappointed in Attlee, and utterly horrified at a false alarm that he had been prematurely called to make his own maiden speech. With some trepidation, he delivered it on the finance day, 21 August 1945, with hardly a Tory present: the only speech he ever declaimed beforehand to his wife. He expressed surprise at the mildness of Conservative opposition to nationalising coal and the Bank, advocated action against monopolies and against restrictive practices by trade associations, praised the hard-pressed Civil Service, and urged moderation upon the House of Lords. He felt that 'it went off well — as indeed it should have done in view of the immense amount of trouble I took in preparing it'.[15d] Some of his colleagues later claimed to have seen him from that moment as a future leader of the Party.[58]

Gaitskell no longer had the cottage at Milland which — to Dora's later regret — he had sold in July (characteristically refusing to maximise his profit).** When the House adjourned he took the girls off for a holiday with the Durbins at their Cornish farmhouse, where the two new MPs

---

* Wilmot, Minister of Supply, would also have liked him as a junior. Harold Wilson thought Gaitskell should have been the one exception to Dalton's rule.[57]
** It fetched £2,400[15e], and was resold two years later for £6,000.[59]

spent hours writing in longhand to constituents, mostly about demobilisation troubles.[60] In the new session Gaitskell, still careful about his health, played no conspicuous part. He was used occasionally as an unofficial government spokesman outside Westminster: broadcasting to the armed forces on the post-war British economy; defending the Government— lucidly, logically and without humour—at the Oxford Union's first post-war debate; and joining the Advisory Council to the Post Office. Along with Sydney Silverman ('calculated to irritate anybody') he sat on a Select Committee which proposed reforming parliamentary procedure by sending much more legislation to committees. Gaitskell wanted these to meet on Wednesday mornings, which would mean limiting the Party meeting to an hour. But the older members disliked the extra work and, he feared in Silverman's case, the reduced opportunities for making trouble at the Party meetings.[15b]

Gaitskell's parliamentary commentaries in the *Leeds Weekly Citizen* condemned the Opposition for confusion, frivolity, and ignorance of the lives of ordinary people; singled out for particular praise three Labour Ministers—Shawcross, Cripps and Aneurin Bevan; and predicted a 'big future' for one back-bencher, Jim Callaghan. He displayed his familiar concern for consumers (over agricultural policy) and regretted Bevan's decision to let National Health Service doctors take private patients.[61] Wisely, he himself spoke seldom, and only on subjects with which he was familiar: the administrative difficulties of price controls, and the bill nationalising the Bank of England which he had helped to draft, first in XYZ and then on the Select Committee. He defended the Government against the first Conservative censure motion, challenging the Opposition to accept or repudiate Bevin's demobilisation plans which Churchill was demagogically criticising, warning of the urgent need to increase exports, and stressing the pragmatic grounds for nationalisation. Four months of silence followed; for he failed to catch the Speaker's eye in a big debate on manpower. Then he defended Dalton's Budget, urging 'a really hard blow at inheritance for the sake of social justice', and warning that pay-as-you-earn income tax might be dangerously damaging to the production drive.[62] He was to return to both themes later.

He had nearly become Attlee's PPS in February 1946, and was being tipped for promotion in the press: he spent less than a year altogether on the back benches.[63] Later, that was to prove a handicap in opposition and as leader, since his political experience was unlike that of nearly all his followers. But no such thoughts crossed his mind at the time, for he had decided early on to accept anything offered, however unattractive.[15f] A vacancy arose in May 1946, just after his fortieth birthday, for a Parliamentary Secretary at the Ministry of Fuel and Power. It was a crucial Department both economically—since Britain's industrial recovery depended overwhelmingly on the revival of coal production – and politically – because it was responsible for three of the first four industries to be nationalised. That strategic position guaranteed difficulties, and opportunities, to the Ministers responsible for it.[64]

Gaitskell had short and undramatic interviews with the Prime Minister and Chief Whip, and then an unpromising telephone conversation with his new chief, Emanuel Shinwell:

S. 'I understand you're going to be my new Parliamentary Secretary.'
G. 'Yes, I understand so.'
S. (after a pause) 'Well, that's all right. We've got this Bill on Monday but you won't be able to do much.'
G. 'No, I suppose not.'
S. 'There's a meeting this evening with the Attorney General and the Financial Secretary – you can come and listen if you like.'
I said I did like.

The beginning was rather typical of what my experiences at F & P were to be for some time. Good publicity opportunity combined with a far from easy Ministerial position.[15f]

Emanuel Shinwell was a veteran who had joined the ILP in 1903, before there was a Parliamentary Labour Party, and had entered the House with the Clydeside rebels in 1922. He had been Minister of Mines in 1929, later changing from the Prime Minister's leading admirer to the bitter critic who captured MacDonald's own seat at Seaham in 1935. His 'chief claims as a Labour Leader', felt Gaitskell after a year's experience of him, 'are oratory, strength of personality and quick wits. He is certainly a good speaker of the platform type – at his best when he prepares nothing.'[15f] But his improvisations got him into constant scrapes, to which he reacted with legendary pugnacity. In the office his bonhomie won the affection of his civil servants, who did not find him hard to manage – though there was friction with his PPS, George Wigg, who resented being excluded from policy-making. Gaitskell had known him slightly since 1937 (through serving on a Labour Party committee on Empire trade, which he chaired) and thought him 'ravaged by suspicion'.[15f] Shinwell had never trusted anyone, and was not about to start with the new young middle-class Labour MPs.

Other circumstances, too, were unpropitious. Gaitskell's post had originally been intended for Harold Wilson, whom he would himself have replaced as Under-Secretary for Works; probably wrongly, Gaitskell suspected that Shinwell chose him instead as knowing less about mining than the former Ministry of Mines statistician and author of *New Deal for Coal*.[65] Then the Prime Minister, who took an unusual interest in junior appointments, was deliberately keeping the young Labour intellectuals out of the obvious economic and financial slots, and sending them to 'learn the facts of life' in dealing with the trade unions: a policy which irritated the miners, an important section of the Parliamentary Labour Party (PLP):[66]

> There was much jealousy among the Miner M.P.s about my appointment and I learnt later that a deputation had even gone to the Chief Whip about it. But it got nowhere, and fortunately I did not know what was happening. They regarded this job, however, as open only to them, and since it was for about all of them the only one they could possibly hope even to be considered for, their dismay and resentment can be understood.[15f]*

Finally, Shinwell heard Gaitskell's name before Attlee proposed it, when Hugh Dalton (whom he cordially loathed) boomed confidentially in a railway carriage full of northern MPs that Fuel and Power was at last to receive an urgently needed ministerial reinforcement.[67]

Gaitskell described his new job to his cousin as 'the sort of post of honour offered to a too successful man in the hope that he will not return from it alive'.[68] His first weekend was busy, for the next three parliamentary days were devoted to the report stage of the coal nationalisation bill with its 60 clauses, 4 schedules, and 107 amendments from the Minister alone:

> I decided fairly quickly [wrote Gaitskell later] that I could *not* sit through 3 days and say nothing and therefore asked Shinwell to let me take some of the amendments. He agreed. I chose a few fairly simple but controversial ones and made, on the first, a successful maiden speech. This was quite easy as I was well briefed and the questions were not technical. But everybody thought it remarkable to be able to do well at such short notice![15f]

A week later he wound up the third reading debate, defending the autonomy of the National Coal Board, the compensation arrangements, and the criteria of operation: not maximum profits, but maximum output while covering costs. He argued that two essential changes were both blocked by the coalowners: a technological revolution, for which they could neither attract capital nor develop unified management; and decent relations with the workers, who would never be reconciled to their old masters after the kind of treatment meted out to his own miner friends in Nottinghamshire. He wrote to the best of those friends, George Keeling: '*You* should have been standing there making that speech.'[69] A BBC commentator called it 'a real Parliamentary triumph ... that brought him congratulations from all the veterans'.[70]

* After Gaitskell's own period as Minister, the miners (then a larger parliamentary force than ever before or since) became his most loyal supporters in the PLP.

Once his parliamentary baptism of fire was over, he soon discovered how remote – even physically – was the Parliamentary Secretary's office from the Minister's and how awkward was his position, particularly as an interloper in the difficult relationship between the Minister and the Permanent Secretary. He 'usually feels himself excluded from the important decisions ... the Minister assumes the P.S. knows nothing about anything'.[159] In Fuel and Power, which had not had able junior men, the Parliamentary Secretary traditionally took charge of health and safety. He also dealt with most parliamentary correspondence from MPs, and chaired a committee on the Department's delegated legislation. Gaitskell fought long battles with civil servants, insisting that MPs needed replies to forward direct to their constituents, couched in human terms and not in bureaucratic jargon; and that the aim of explanatory memoranda was not to obfuscate departmental orders, but to help ordinary people understand them.

Parliamentary Questions were an area in which Shinwell prided himself on his ability to improvise. Gaitskell took them without incident some three weeks after his appointment – but not again for nearly a year. He made six speeches in the House, one winding up on the Coal Bill, but most quite unimportant. Outside Westminster, he occasionally spoke beyond his departmental brief; housing was his main constituency problem, and he agreed with the Minister responsible, Aneurin Bevan, that new houses must be built for durability and quality, not just cheapness. He visited many pits, talking to the workers and Coal Board staff. When speaking on the coal industry, he did not spare the old management, and defended the miners against 'white-collar snobbery' in two of his rare memorable phrases (both soon borrowed by his seniors[71]); he called the coal-face workers 'the fighter pilots of the 1946 Battle of Britain' and said that their absence from work attracted attention because they were essential, whereas if 30,000 people went to Ascot or the Derby, 'nobody gives a tinker's cuss'.[72]

For an able man who felt underemployed, it was a frustrating period. Then suddenly the humdrum life of the Ministry of Fuel and Power erupted into a great crisis, when the power stations were shut down for lack of coal, industry was halted, and 2 million men were abruptly thrown out of work.

iv   *The Fuel Crisis and After*

For five winters coal stocks had been precariously low, and with the end of the war the demand for coal soared (especially for electricity) just as the reluctant miners were hoping to escape from the pits. Output was rising nevertheless, but not nearly as fast as had been hoped. Attlee and Morrison had been worried for many months, and so were the electricity undertakings. But Shinwell suspected the companies of seeking a pretext to defer nationalisation. He advised the Prime Minister not to rely too much on statistics or forget 'the imponderables'.[73a] His ebullient temperament made him overconfident that his miner friends would respond to his exhortations, and predisposed to accept the optimistic advice coming from a senior official. Six months before the great shut-down he rashly said in public that everyone was expecting a fuel crisis except the Minister of Fuel and Power.[74] Though the crisis of February 1947 was not wholly his fault, it was hardly surprising that his colleagues had not always given his departmental problems priority over their own; or that many of them, as well as the public ('shiver with Shinwell and starve with Strachey'), later blamed him for the catastrophe.[75]

Gaitskell was put in an acutely embarrassing position. He had confidence in the advisers – Douglas Jay and James Meade – whose forecasts had so alarmed Attlee; and he never found 'imponderables' much of a refuge from uncomfortable facts. But Shinwell mistrusted him both as a Wykehamist intellectual and as a protégé of the detested Dalton: 'I have found', Gaitskell wrote later, 'that if I do not see him frequently his suspicions of me begin to grow ... [But as] I never really enjoy his company it is an effort for me to see him.'[15f] To some officials and to close friends his worry was obvious.[76] But he felt it would be improper and disloyal to gossip against Shinwell with political colleagues outside the Department, or to contradict the Minister in the weekly departmental meetings.[77] Nor did his superior welcome private advice, for as a private secretary put it: 'Shinwell wouldn't allow him to express a view because he felt that *he* knew the miners and that Hugh hadn't ever been down a mine in his life.'[78]

Shinwell's big gamble is still justified by some thoughtful officials (though for the delay in giving priority to power stations there can be little excuse). Full advance precautions against a catastrophic winter would have meant most severe restrictions on the power stations and on industry, deliberately imposing shut-downs and unemployment to guard against a hypothetical disaster.[79] In the long years of shortage no Minister of Fuel took that course, and Gaitskell certainly thought Shinwell the last man to do so:

As an administrator, however, S. is hardly a starter. He has no conception at all of either organisation or planning or following up. Everything is done by fits and starts, and on impulse. The best you can say is that he contributes at intervals a kind of rugged force and drive which stimulates the officials ... He will always try and evade an unpopular decision, procrastinate, find a way round, etc. Of course there often is a case on political grounds for this. But S.'s hesitations go beyond natural prudence and amount to sheer weakness and moral cowardice.[15f]

In mid-November 1946 Shinwell's officials pressed for compulsory restrictions on industry's fuel consumption; he sent their paper to the Cabinet accompanied by his own reservations, but some limits were imposed.[80] On 3 January 1947 he belatedly warned his colleagues of the risk of a breakdown of electricity supplies: that eleventh-hour decision was perhaps precipitated by Gaitskell who, returning from Manchester, reported that the situation was far worse than had been thought.[81f]* A few days later Gaitskell was sent to a Cabinet Committee (chaired by Dalton) to plead for one month's absolute priority on the railways for coal trains, as for military traffic before D-Day—but the Cabinet did not agree.[83] Then on 30 January came the worst snow blizzard for fifty years, inaugurating the worst winter weather for a century. The transport was blocked, the inadequate stocks soon exhausted. Yet the worried Cabinet was so little informed that on Thursday 6 February Dalton noted: 'coal and electricity supplies are in a pretty poor way. It will be a great relief to get through *March*.'[73b] On the very next day, in a minor debate of the kind usually arranged for a Friday, Shinwell told an astonished House of Commons of the great shut-down:[84]

> Today, at this morning's Cabinet, [Shinwell] suddenly asks for permission to tell the House of Commons this afternoon that all electricity must be cut off from industry in London, South-East England, the Midlands and the North-West, and from all domestic consumers between 9 and 12 and 2 and 4 each day. This is a complete thunder clap, following on the usual rather hopeful tales we have had from this man during the past week.'[73b]

London's power stations were so short of coal that, unless it could be shipped in within three days, the Ministry feared that sewerage and water supplies would break down and the capital might have to be evacuated.[85]

During the fuel crisis 'Gaitskell really emerged as a decisive force in the Department'.[86] He was an experienced administrator when urgent administrative decisions were desperately needed. He and the Permanent Secretary (Shinwell played no part) spent all the first weekend drafting instructions for the 580 electricity undertakings when they reopened on the Monday. Attlee made him chairman of a committee of officials from eleven Departments, which met from 2 to 6 p.m. daily—including Sundays—for three weeks to apply these restrictions; all Permanent Secretaries had its minutes on arriving for work next morning. It decided which industries were essential, how much non-industrial users could have, and how the restrictions could gradually be relaxed:

* Finding that repeated alarm signals from the regions had not been heard, Gaitskell had switched coal stocks from domestic to industrial use, and brought in supplies from across the Pennines.[82]

[Gaitskell] liked administration, giving his decisions then and there across the table, as to who could be switched on. And the Central Electricity Board representative would often leave the table straightaway to phone through the necessary instructions.

He found that essential industries were inseparably interlocked with others — milk required bottles and bottles required tops — and those in real difficulties got 'compassionate and helpful decisions, after spirited argument'. But some powerful institutions were firmly turned down: the Bank of England was amazed to be denied electricity to print dividend warrants; weekly journals were cut off for a fortnight. The secretary of the committee remembers no appeals against Gaitskell's decisions, but thought them unnecessary because he took such trouble to meet departmental views and revise burdensome decisions as soon as possible. Wigg, Shinwell's defender and no friend of Gaitskell, pays warm tribute to the Parliamentary Secretary's role in the crisis.[87]

Gaitskell recorded later that:

the P.M. during and after the Fuel Crisis (and perhaps before) did not conceal his distaste for E.S. ... criticising and questioning everything he said ... through the Cabinet Fuel Committee, where these scenes used to occur, the Office of Minister of F. & P. was virtually put in commission.[15f]*

This Cabinet Committee under Attlee himself allocated the available coal to transport, electricity, and other major categories of users.[88] Within 'general industry', it was assigned by a Fuel Allocations Committee, again composed of departmental officials and chaired by Gaitskell, who sent its minutes direct to the Prime Minister. Though its work soon diminished as the weather improved and stocks recovered, here too his chairmanship impressed both the officials and his political seniors.[89]

On 1 January Gaitskell had become the first ministerial chairman of yet a third committee of departmental civil servants, again reporting direct to the Cabinet. This was an upgraded version of the wartime Materials Committee of officials, which was still meeting quarterly to allocate supplies of raw materials like steel, timber, paper, cotton and tin plate. Its new secretary wrote later that Gaitskell 'was the first and best of my chairmen'; and the new system, unlike the old, appears to have given general satisfaction. Separate meetings were held for each material, sometimes lasting all day. The Departments stated their case but the chairman

* The Permanent Secretary chaired an Emergency Committee dealing with building coal stocks at the power stations. The Minister had little role; he took a first press conference on 9 February, but a senior civil servant took all the subsequent ones, and important parliamentary statements were made by the Prime Minister.

had sole executive authority; his decision could be queried in Cabinet, but never was. 'He ruled it with a rod of iron,' said his private secretary.[90] Occasionally he would argue out a difficult decision with an aggrieved senior colleague, but his verdict was accepted every time, not only by lesser Ministers like Charles Key at Works, but by powerful figures like Aneurin Bevan. 'They obviously respected his judgment.'[91]

He was highly regarded, too, by the committee members – civil servants and industrialists manning the controls. When he became Chancellor one of them recalled that 'From the moment when you ... penetrated with ease into the dark, fearsome jungle of timber technicalities I tipped you for the highest office'.[92] Such committees including both politicians and officials are rare in Whitehall, and old-style civil servants, like Gaitskell's own Permanent Secretary, disapproved of them. Gaitskell dissented, calling them

> among the most businesslike and useful bodies I have ever been con-
> nected with. At Ministerial Committees there tends to be too much
> bickering, talking, woolliness, ignorance and personal feeling. At
> purely official committees there tends to be too little drive. The com-
> bination of a Minister and officials may give you the drive combined
> with the expertise, and without the personal feelings and ambitions
> being too prominent.[15g]

Clearly he was delighted to take responsibility himself at last.

He was not allowed much of it in his departmental duties. The officials took him more seriously after the fuel crisis, and his life became much busier; no longer could he take the children to school every morning (though he still did so twice a week).[93] At his many meetings with the departmental 'big-wigs', another private secretary records, 'Mr. Gaitskell always gave me the impression of being the ablest man present, and thoroughly in command ... always calm, never flustered. A wonderful man!'[89] But relations with the Minister became more difficult than ever, for Shinwell knew that several senior colleagues wanted to get rid of him, and was in the worst of moods:

> Suspicion and aggression went – as usual – together ... Shinwell did
> not just pass [the buck]. He picked it up and hurled it ... More than
> one of his colleagues has said to me, 'The Cabinet is really a remark-
> ably harmonious affair, except for S. His presence spoils the atmo-
> sphere. He throws apples of discord the whole time.'[15f] *

* Dalton found Shinwell 'by far the least attractive member of the Government, always looking round for someone to whom to pass the blame. [MS addition: no team spirit] He is always trying to pretend that it is Alf Barnes' fault for

Knowing that he was losing the confidence of the Prime Minister while Gaitskell was gaining it, Shinwell seems to have suspected his young subordinate of intriguing to take over his job.[94] There was no truth at all in this, and Gaitskell himself wrote later that he would not have wanted to remain as Shinwell's Parliamentary Secretary, but never expected to succeed him.[95] Civil servants remember that the Minister used to 'treat him as a little office-boy' and rap him sharply over the knuckles if he questioned the official advice which Shinwell so readily accepted; while Gaitskell, acutely sensitive to his senior's mistrust, was concerned to be seen giving the Minister all the help he could.

Shinwell's resentment may have been accentuated by policy differences. After the crisis, fuel rationing was again seriously considered as in 1942, though eventually dropped for administrative reasons.[96] Instead, heating by gas or electricity was banned in the summer months, a policy which Gaitskell defended so loyally in the House that one senior official (who liked neither him nor it) thought it showed his doctrinaire liking for restrictions.[97] In fact the incident illustrates his difficult relationship with Shinwell. He had strongly opposed the Minister's original policy of continuing the ban on such heating at specified hours of the day, and without asking him, Shinwell had told the Cabinet that he was unwilling to defend it in Parliament. After Gaitskell assured his superior that that was quite untrue, Shinwell relaxed and thereafter gave him more chances of speaking in the House.[15f]

Already, just before the fuel crisis, Gaitskell had wound up the second reading debate on the Bill nationalising electricity with 'probably the most accomplished performance by a junior minister in this Parliament'.[98] Dalton noted proudly that he was 'making his mark ... as a sure-footed and efficient Minister, and a very effective parliamentarian';[73c] though another listener thought him very dull.[99] In April he justified the independent corporation structure for the nationalised industries, and in May he defended Shinwell's electricity restrictions. Soon afterwards the Minister delegated to him most of the committee stage of the Electricity Bill. Gaitskell's private secretary was struck by his self-confidence in selecting which amendments to deal with himself and which to leave to Shinwell. He did so on unexpected lines, as another civil servant recalls: 'The difficult ones Gaitskell took. I remember his great courtesy and mastery. He went down very well with the committee ... There was a sharp contrast between Shinwell's bluster and Gaitskell's extremely rational approach and persuasive power.' The self-confidence was reflected also in his winding-up

---

not moving the coal. Barnes, on the other hand, has done not at all badly.'[3k] Transport, Barnes's Ministry, was Fuel and Power's traditional Whitehall enemy; and Dalton was Shinwell's other main scapegoat.

speech, which he wrote himself and did not show to his resentful civil service adviser on electricity.

A sympathetic commentator described his style:

> He talks, not like a politician, but like the modern type of young English professor – quietly, unassumingly, without bombast or any air of superiority, but clearly, measuring his statements, marshalling his facts and his arguments, taking note, as he goes along, of his opponent's viewpoint, answering it dispassionately, and all the time taking the listener to the conclusion *he* thinks is the right one. He never batters or bullies an opponent in argument, but rather meets him half-way and then leads him gently off along the Gaitskell path. He has a sense of humour, too, and ... his allusive jokes and very gentle ironies go down well.[70]

On becoming Minister himself, Gaitskell wrote a tactful letter of thanks to his old chief: 'If it is thought that I have been a success in Parliament it is mainly due to the many opportunities you gave me, especially the Electricity Bill.'[100] That summer he was briefly left in charge of the Department, and relations had improved enough for him to persuade a reluctant Shinwell, against the Department's advice, to break a holiday to intervene and help settle a troublesome strike in Yorkshire.[101]

Coal recovered quite quickly, but the fuel crisis was not the last of that appalling year. The Americans were eager to remove any obstacle to the sale of their goods abroad, and had insisted during the 1945 loan negotiations that sterling must be made fully convertible within fifteen months of the money becoming available. That meant 15 July 1947, a date which Keynes had valiantly but vainly resisted as far too early. The war had left Britain with heavily depleted reserves and an immense load of foreign debt: £3,500 million worth of sterling balances were held abroad. Their holders' wants could be supplied at once only by United States industry, relatively little affected by the war; so, if the overseas holders of sterling were allowed to convert the loan into dollars, it might rapidly evaporate instead of allowing Britain time to reconvert from war to peace.

Now the Bank and the Treasury – rashly, as Gaitskell believed – persuaded the Chancellor and Cabinet that the commitment could safely be implemented on time.[102] Within six weeks of 15 July, an immense run on the pound by all its foreign holders had wiped out most of the loan, and forced the suspension of convertibility. For years afterwards, fear of the threat to the currency posed by the sterling balances was to constrain British economic policy; immediately, the Cabinet at the end of August halted all currency allowances for foreign travel and abolished the basic petrol ration – of all the government's unpopular measures, the one most

15 1947—the year of the fuel crisis. Emanuel Shinwell, Minister of Fuel and Power (*left*); a miner; Lord Hyndley, Chairman of the Coal Board; and (*right*), Aneurin Bevan, Minister of Health

16 Photographing his daughters at home, 1947

17 With his family at home in Frognal Gardens, Hampstead, just after
becoming Minister of Fuel in October 1947

infuriating to the middle class. That autumn marked the government's lowest point in that Parliament, with the Conservatives leading by eleven points on the Gallup poll and winning, in the municipal elections in November, one of their greatest victories ever.

The Labour Party often reacts badly to adversity, and the Cabinet was shaken by the disasters.[103] Cripps and others plotted to replace Attlee by Bevin, but were foiled by the latter's refusal. Dalton reported Aneurin Bevan threatening to lead a left-wing revolt over nationalisation of steel (which Dalton also championed). Gaiteskell commented:

> Bevan's head had swollen enormously ... his bluff about resignation has been called ... All the same ... it would be a great mistake to assume that this is more than a set-back for Bevan. He still leads in the race for Labour Prime Minister in 1960! 'Very like LL.G.', says Evan. Yes, but I can't help wondering whether LL.G. was really quite so unscrupulous![15f]

Outside the Cabinet, the first dissident left-wing manifesto (the pamphlet *Keep Left*) was published in April, and in August an irritable PLP meeting on steel nationalisation foreshadowed another future battle. Gaitskell was surprised how often MPs for marginal seats

> are most unrealistic about the Left Wing character of the electorate ... identifying their own keen supporters – politically conscious and class-conscious Labour men – with the mass of the people, who are very much against austerity, utterly uninterested in nationalisation of steel, heartily sick of excuses and being told to work harder, but probably more tolerant of the Government and appreciative of its difficulties than many suppose.[15f]

Gaitskell sympathised with the resentment of ordinary workers at exhortations from the well-off – though not with middle-class complaints against the form-filling necessary to provide 'fair shares' in scarce goods. The austerities of 1947 changed his personal habits, for he gave up smoking when Dalton raised the tobacco tax, and – since he was constantly urging the public to economise on fuel – imposed a spartan regime on his suffering household: electric fires were banned, and Raymond, when home from Oxford, hardly dared use an electric razor.[104] In the previous summer he had moved from Well Walk to 18 Frognal Gardens, a big, rambling house with a private drive at the top of a steep Hampstead hill, which had once been the home of Sir Walter Besant, and was now to be Gaitskell's for the rest of his life. Various people, including his mother and his brother, shared it at different periods, and at this time he had as tenants Evan Durbin and two civil servants: his assistant private secretary Muriel Loosemore, and his old schoolfellow Charles Plumb. When any of them wanted a bath,

F

Dora had to use her own scanty coke ration to stoke the kitchen boiler, which Hugh sometimes made up at 8.30 a.m. before leaving for the office. In the country, at Milland, he had sold Sweatmans but still went to stay with his mother at Tuxlythe, where 'he chops his own firewood and gropes his way to bed by candlelight. His mother cooks breakfast by marsh gas ... Milland has no piped water and the Gaitskells and I share supplies from the same meagre spring'.[105] At weekends in the early post-war months he worked hard on the weeds and bracken to create a productive garden and orchard. But in office the opportunities grew rare, and even in opposition he reckoned himself lucky to escape there on one weekend in four.[106]

His private secretaries stood in some awe of his impressive intellectual equipment, but were reassured by his personal modesty – and by some signs of practical incapacity. A keen but not always successful photographer, he delighted them by seeking their advice on where he was going wrong; and when he wanted to buy his children a model boat to sail on the Hampstead ponds, and was so busy that Miss Loosemore had to get it for him, she also had to show him how to put up the sails. Even in public life his self-confidence came only gradually. Just before taking office, he wrote to the producer who had invited him to take part in a BBC Brains Trust:

> As regards subjects, I feel profoundly ignorant of everything, but perhaps less so in the fields of economics, politics and social questions generally. As for your last paragraph, I am more than doubtful whether I shall enjoy the experience. In fact, at the moment it seems positively terrifying![107]

Pomposity was the last vice he could be accused of. A journalist covering one of his first meetings as a junior minister noticed how completely he was at home in the fish and chips bar afterwards. That meeting was in Chatham, for Gaitskell always tried to keep up links with old friends.[108] In October 1947 he visited the South Yorkshire and East Midland coalfields and made sure of seeing his old Notts and Derby students.[109] His last meeting of that tour was at Swadlincote, a mile or two from the scene of those early lectures to miners which had first impelled him into politics. The journalists came to it to photograph the new Minister of Fuel and Power.[110]

CHAPTER 6

MINISTER OF FUEL AND POWER 1947–50

'The most overworked man in Britain'
(HERBERT MORRISON ON HG, 1948)

i *'Unenviable Post'*

THE ministerial reshuffle of October 1947 was long overdue and had been expected for weeks; Gaitskell found 'quite an unpleasant atmosphere' when he met the 'excited and jealous' MPs in the dining rooms at the House.[1a] Besides winning Attlee's confidence as a committee chairman, Gaitskell had the strong backing of Dalton, Morrison and Cripps – and would have received the same office if the latter had succeeded in making Ernest Bevin Prime Minister.[2] He was tipped in the press, and picked up hints from associates, but was sceptical until the Prime Minister summoned him. Attlee

> smiled and said in his clipped, muttering way, 'I am reconstructing the Government. I want you to be Fuel & Power'. I said, 'Oh! Well!' He said, 'It is not a bed of roses.' I said, 'I know that already.' Then I asked about the Parliamentary Secretary. They have given me Robens and I am pleased.[1a]

He determined to give Robens a better deal than he himself had had.[3]

With coal and electricity nationalised, Attlee had decided to leave both the new and the old Minister of Fuel and Power out of the Cabinet. Shinwell reluctantly accepted the War Office, where he was to be happy and successful, but was furious at being the only Minister so demoted.[1a] He used George Wigg to inspire an editorial attack on Dalton in the *Daily Mirror*;[4] and did not soon forgive his young successor. Neither he nor Wigg would speak to Gaitskell or Robens in the Westminster corridors, and all the civil servants knew of the bad blood.[5] However, in mellow old age Shinwell, though still bitter against Dalton and Cripps, denied having ever felt any animosity towards Gaitskell, who had shown him nothing but friendliness and had been a 'first class' Parliamentary Secretary.[6]

Elsewhere, the new Minister met with a gratifying receptior from his seniors. On the very day he heard of his appointment he met the formidable Ernest Bevin, who was not supposed to cherish middle-class intellectuals. Fed up like all his colleagues with Shinwell's bombastic speeches, Bevin advised: 'Don't speak for six months, don't say a bloody word, not even good morning.'[7] The Foreign Secretary said that with 40 million more tons of coal, the extra exports would transform Britain's political position; and Gaitskell tactfully asked if he could come to Bevin for advice on the problems. 'He beamed about this and said, "Well, certainly, if the old war horse can help some of the younger ones he would be only too glad to".'[1b]

Gaitskell had more regular dealings with Sir Stafford Cripps, who had just taken over from Morrison responsibility for co-ordinating economic policy:

> Cripps wants to run the thing with H[arold] W[ilson], R[ussell] S[trauss] and myself as his lieutenants …[8] He is very friendly and very helpful so far. The only danger is of bees in his bonnet. There have been plenty in the past but certainly fewer and fewer in recent years.

But he was happier about personal relations than he was with the official machine:

> The Cabinet Committee meetings which I have attended have been harmonious and friendly. The Big 5 are all without exception very well disposed to me and I think to the other young Ministers. There is no jealousy … Sometimes Cabinet Meetings horrify me because of the amount of rubbish talked by some Ministers who come there after reading briefs which they do not understand … A smaller Cabinet, mostly of non-departmental Ministers, would really be able to listen and understand more easily and hear the others arguing the matter out.[1a*]

Gaitskell's appointment was generally well received in very diverse quarters.[9] The miners regretted Shinwell's departure, but no longer wanted a miner as Minister, fearing he would not dare show generosity towards his mates. The Leeds Tory paper gave the newcomer a charitable headline: 'Unenviable Post'.[10a] The *New Statesman* felt: 'Mr. Gaitskell has proved himself a first-class administrator: he has still to show that he possesses the qualities of leadership necessary for this job.'[11a]

After the first week Gaitskell wrote in his diary that 'becoming a full Minister is a great step and a great change. Much more so indeed than I expected earlier'.[1b] Traditionally, that Department expected its political masters to know little about the business and to take official advice. By

---

* Gaitskell attended Cabinet for his own departmental business.

the end of the war it was almost a diarchy, with the Permanent Secretary doubling with the Controller-General who ran the unsatisfactory dual control scheme of 1942.[12] In 1945 a new Permanent Secretary, Sir Donald Fergusson, a short and formidable civil servant of the old school, reluctantly moved in from Agriculture to pull into shape this notoriously weak Ministry, now destined for so central a political role. Fergusson had found

> all the troubles that usually occur in a new Department ... people whom [other] Departments could best spare ... an enormous proportion of temporary staff ... a great deal of favouritism ... widespread disgruntlement, friction and inefficiency. It takes years of work to remedy such a state of affairs and endless patience.[13a]

He had strong views on most subjects, particularly on the need for the new nationalised industries to be free of ministerial interference with their day-to-day work; and on the role of Ministers. They should deal with the big political, parliamentary and interdepartmental questions, stay out of detailed administration, and pay attention to the advice which the departmental hierarchy would send up to them through the proper source, the Permanent Secretary.

Hugh Gaitskell's outlook was very different for, unlike most new Ministers, he knew the machine from inside. At his first meeting with the Ministry staff, he said that as an old civil servant he understood their problems.[14] From his wartime work in Whitehall, he thought much better of them than of either businessmen or Coal Board officials.[15] And after seventeen months in the Department as a junior Minister, he was familiar with both its personnel and problems, and impatient to put his own ideas into practice. Hugh Dalton had taught him the importance of getting good civil servants, and he had himself seen how bad official advice had contributed to the failure to anticipate the fuel crisis. Fergusson sensed what was coming, and his letter about the Department's weaknesses was designed to warn his new Minister against unduly rapid and sweeping changes.[16]

Most civil servants at Fuel and Power came to feel for Gaitskell much more respect and admiration, but perhaps less personal affection, than for Shinwell or Robens. To his private secretaries he was kind and considerate, though occasionally rough in moments of stress; they usually became warm admirers. One junior official in the private office was vainly looking for a new flat when he was appointed; not liking what she had heard of his reputation with Dalton, she decided to leave. Gaitskell did not try to stop her, but he offered her accommodation in his own Hampstead house, gave her lifts home from the office, and scrupulously kept his promise not to inflict business on her out of hours; she stayed in the private office for five more years. Leslie Murphy, the principal private secretary for all but the last few months of Gaitskell's term, promised on quitting the Civil Service to return to Whitehall whenever his old master came back to office, to do any job the latter wanted. Gaitskell took a lot of trouble choosing presents for his private secretaries, and showed a Wykehamist zeal for improving them. To Murphy, whose literary tastes he found insufficiently developed, he gave a dozen carefully selected major modern works (including *Of Human Bondage*, *To the Lighthouse*, and *Portrait of the Artist as a Young Man*). Another secretary, who asked for something reflecting Gaitskell's own tastes, was given *Pilgrim's Progress* and also Shakespeare's *Sonnets* — 'the poetry I like best and which I think the most beautiful ever written'.[17]

He took time to get to know his staff, and on first meeting did not always put them at their ease. His first sherry party for them was a wooden affair. Some of his civil servants felt he was too impatient and short of time, or irritable with bad drafting, or unwilling to suffer fools gladly. Once he dismayed a departmental conference by publicly expressing no confidence in Coal Division, which had so badly advised Shinwell; and one (very untypical) high official thought him 'incredibly arrogant' and 'a block of ice'. But others found he was friendly, saw things in perspective, and — though exacting — was conspicuously more considerate and courteous to civil servants than many of his colleagues. The hostility of a very few seems to have been a reaction to a Minister who knew far more about the subject than the politicians were expected to, who sought advice from capable administrators irrespective of rank, and who provoked resentment among the older, less flexible men by shaking their settled habits and assumptions.

Gaitskell did not operate at all as the traditional civil servants expected: 'He found out straight away where the wisdom — such as it was — was to be found and insisted on going there directly without any intermediaries ... and then he would by-pass the top people and disregard their advice.'[18] His private secretary gives a similar picture:

> He wanted to get into the running of the Department and to be part of the decision-making process along with the civil servants ... He would bring in the Under-Secretary, Assistant Secretaries, even Principals, and have a debate from which policy emerged ... Many permanent secretaries would say, 'it's my job to lead this sort of discussion and to produce recommendations to you'.[19]

Gaitskell thereby ensured a hearing for ideas and advice from the junior ranks, but at a price: he was a Minister fascinated, almost obsessed, with detail. To most (not all) of his civil servants then and later, this habit seemed a serious weakness. His immense capacity for work, and for absorbing complicated briefs, meant that it did not distract him from general policy; and it did help him to probe and assess the capacity of his advisers. But he carried it to extremes on almost every front:

It was very difficult to produce a letter that Gaitskell would sign without altering. He was very good at introducing the personal note, so that you got a letter from Hugh Gaitskell, not from a secretary. But it wasn't always worth it, it took too much of his time.[19]

Over the House of Commons, where ministerial reputations are so easily lost: 'He was very concerned about his image ... made terrific preparation for any appearance ... with Parliamentary Questions, extraordinary preparation to make sure he could answer every conceivable supplementary' — at perhaps excessive cost in civil servants' time.[19] In the statistical forecasts, he

> absolutely wallowed with delight, going through all the little workings. So these meetings which ought to have been dealing with high policy, resolved into a very detailed discussion. The Permanent Secretary fumed, the Under-Secretaries fumed, the meetings lasted two or three hours.[18]

His civil servants were quite unaccustomed to a Minister who never thought it inappropriate or beneath his dignity to add up a column of figures. He was 'a ferret' who, when sent a file, 'instead of just reading the top [minute] would go through the lot and pick up things which officials sometimes hadn't intended to bring to his notice'. He had a grip on everything that was going on, but he risked both inhibiting the officials and imposing too much on them. 'He's another under-secretary and not my best either — he'll break the Department,' complained Fergusson early on.

The Permanent Secretary would have preferred files going up to the Minister to show only his own recommendations, without conflicting minutes (and so arranged matters when the next Minister of Fuel and Power took office). He could not make that change in Gaitskell's day. But he was determined not to have his own proposals subsequently questioned and criticised by his juniors, whose views the Minister insisted on hearing; the conflicting demands of these two strong-willed men were reconciled by Murphy (who had been Fergusson's private secretary before becoming Gaitskell's) organising meetings to discuss the problems before any recommendation went forward.[19] On some minor issues the Permanent Secretary had his way; when Gaitskell early on contemplated controlling the price of logs (an administrative nightmare, for the 80,000 sellers included many fly-by-night 'spivs'), Fergusson was able to delay and consult until the fuel scarcity eased and the proposal perished. On major matters, they mostly saw very much eye to eye; and where they did not it was the Minister who prevailed.[20] And whatever the early tensions, these two powerful personalities soon reached a *modus vivendi* and, to the credit of both, came to feel the warmest mutual admiration. 'I really am blessed with a most admirable Permanent Secretary,' wrote Gaitskell after eight months as Minister. 'The more I see of D.F. the more I like him. He is very shrewd and wise and yet not in the least obstructive ... what an enormous difference it makes to my life.'[1c] And Fergusson – who had worked for Sir John Anderson, Neville Chamberlain, Winston Churchill and Philip Snowden – was later to describe Gaitskell as 'the most efficient Minister I ever served'.[21]

ii　*Pitmen, Publicity and Petrol*

The Permanent Secretary wrote to 'Dear Hugh' on his first day in office in October 1947, setting out both the immediate problems of staffing and policy and 'the major tasks that lie ahead over the next 2 or 3 years and the best way of tackling them both in the national interest and in your own interest'. Before a co-ordinated fuel policy could be developed, the relations between the Ministry and the Coal Board had to be worked out, the right men found to run the newly nationalised electricity industry, and gas brought into public ownership in the next session. That was 'vital' – and 'would immensely strengthen your own personal position in the Party, Parliament and the country'. The immediate policy problems were the rapid rise in domestic electricity consumption, which must be restricted to avoid a strain on coal supplies, and the danger of trouble in the pits. But, though it was essential to get more coal, the Minister should stop constantly intervening and leave the Board to do its job: 'action by the Ministry will only do harm ... [and] play into Horner's hands'.[13a*]

Gaitskell sent his own initial agenda to Fergusson, concentrating on the immediate issues. He wanted all pending unpopular decisions announced quickly; a high-level scientist appointed (a proposal not much loved by the Permanent Secretary); better departmental statistics; better handling of petroleum; and above all a quick improvement in both the Ministry's and the Coal Board's dreadful public relations. They agreed on the need to limit electricity consumption, to make early appointments to the electricity boards, and to bring in the Gas Bill.[22] That measure was still competing with steel for a place in the legislative programme. Two weeks later Gaitskell steered it through the Cabinet Committee;[1b] and five weeks afterwards he announced the names of the area electricity board chairmen.[23a] Meanwhile, the new Minister's early days were dominated by two urgent problems. One was coal production – crucial for industrial output, employment, the domestic consumer and even British influence abroad. The other was petrol for private motorists – inescapable politically because of the motoring organisations' furious campaign to restore the 'basic

---

* Arthur Horner, general secretary of the National Union of Mineworkers, was a leading Communist.

ration', and administratively because it provoked nearly 2 million applications for special treatment.

At the end of the war, demand for British coal was insatiable both at home and abroad. But the price for past mishandling of the industry's affairs now had to be paid: the National Coal Board took over an industry in desperate straits, with 85,000 fewer workers than in 1938, output 46 million tons lower, capacity and equipment badly run down, and productivity 10 per cent below the pre-war level.[24] Though the Coal Board was criticised for failing to recover the output of a vanished past, its real task was to offset a downward trend which had begun well over a generation earlier.[25]

Gaitskell was responsible for dealing with the immediate consequences of these longstanding problems. Everyone was clamouring for more coal: the domestic householder, cut to two-thirds of pre-war needs; manufacturing industry, which got only 85 per cent of its claims, the minimum to avoid economic disaster and unemployment; the booming electricity industry; and the insatiable export demand of a war-damaged Continent. Bevin had impressed on Gaitskell the desperate need for producing 40 million more tons;[1b] and Gaitskell said publicly that 'In all trade negotiations with other countries the one question that was always put to Britain was: "Have you the coal?" '[26a] To regain any of the lost output quickly, the goodwill of the mineworkers was indispensable. Considering the generations of ill-treatment, the sellers' market they now enjoyed, and the wails of the middle class at austerity, the miners displayed astounding moderation and responsibility.

To demonstrate to the union that a new deal was intended, the five-day week was promised for May 1947, the miners undertaking that production would not fall.[27a] The decision caused much anxiety, but Gaitskell had defended it by pointing to the recovery of production from the fuel crisis and to satisfactory recruitment.[28] The miners kept their word and output did not decline — but the urgent need was to increase it. In October a new agreement was negotiated to lengthen hours again; each area could choose either to restore Saturday shifts or to add half an hour to the working day.[29] There was more publicity over another labour problem: absenteeism. It was far better documented than in any other British industry, but may have been no greater; and it was probably slightly lower than among European miners, and 'not extraordinarily high' in comparison with Americans (whose working conditions are quite different).[30a] But Shinwell's exhortations had failed to check it, and with the five-day week was introduced an attendance bonus, to be forfeited if any of the five shifts were missed. The union wanted only one-fifth of the bonus to be forfeit for each lost shift, but the Cabinet (overruling Shinwell) had rejected this as eliminating any incentive effect.[27b] Gaitskell continued to resist this demand, which his Tory successors eventually accepted. His own solution – with which to his delight Ernest Bevin agreed – was to exempt overtime earnings from income tax.[31] But Dalton ruled that out as administratively unworkable.[32a]

The Ministry of Fuel and Power had long suffered from appalling public relations. Gaitskell's realism and honesty at once created a good impression. Within a week the very critical *Economist* was praising his 'straightforward clarity' in producing 'at last, a coal budget which is intelligible and reasonable'.[33a] With exports slashed and consumption low over the fine summer of 1947, distributed stocks were 40 per cent above 1946, and industry and the power stations were to get priority. The target of 200 million tons in 1947 (which the gloomy *Economist* had thought impossible) was missed only by a whisker. Hailing that 'milestone on our journey', Gaitskell immediately insisted that next year's production must add another 10 million tons for export.[34] Serious critics welcomed his candid approach, which soon earned him the confidence his predecessor had never enjoyed.[23b]

Relations with the general public went less smoothly. The winter coal budget projected a 10 per cent saving in gas and electricity by household consumers, and Gaitskell, who set a good example in his own home, regularly called for fuel economy in his speeches. This led to the first celebrated gaffe of his public life, when he told a municipal election meeting at Hastings:

> It means getting up and going to bed in cold bedrooms. It may mean fewer baths. Personally, I have never had a great many baths myself and I can assure those who are in the habit of having a great many baths that it does not make a great deal of difference to their health if they have fewer. And as far as appearance [goes] – most of that is underneath and nobody sees it.

As he wrote later, it was meant and taken simply as a joke – 'the kind of thing I have said again and again at open-air meetings to liven things up'.[1d] The press reported it only briefly. But Winston Churchill could not resist the opportunity:

> When Ministers of the Crown speak like this ... [they] have no need to wonder why they are getting increasingly into bad odour. I had even asked myself ... whether you, Mr. Speaker, would admit the word 'lousey' as a Parliamentary expression in referring to the Administration ... purely as one of factual narration.[35]

Sensitive though he was, Gaitskell was not worried at first: but the publicity convinced him that it had been unwise – especially for the

successor of 'somebody who always said the wrong thing'.[1d] He received
a few anonymous letters and a protest from a remote relative, while his
old nurse, from whom he had not heard for thirty years, sent an indignant
denial. Even a quarter of a century later a school friend told the author:
'He washed well!'

Those early weeks as a Minister were a difficult period. Hugh Dalton
had to resign, after an innocent but monumental indiscretion;* and though
expecting that he would — as he did — return to the Government before
long, Gaitskell felt depressed again by the 'no friends at the top' reaction
of other politicians like Bevin and Cripps.[36] The latter

> showed no remorse and I could not help feeling that he had now
> satisfied one more ambition by becoming Chancellor ... it is a rather
> horrid prospect. Ambition certainly does seem to kill the pleasanter
> aspects of human nature. But H.D. is certainly just the same.[1d]

In his own Department, Gaitskell recorded in his diary, 'I am faced with a
series of insoluble problems, one major administrative nightmare and much
public criticism'. The last two reflected 'the perpetual, dreary row about
petrol'.[1e]

In August 1947, to the dismay of Fergusson, who was on holiday, the
Cabinet had abolished the basic petrol ration to which every motorist had
been entitled. They hoped to save $36 million, and did not foresee the
hurricane of middle-class fury blown up by the motoring organisations.[37]
Gaitskell loyally defended a hated policy not of his own making, optimistically claiming that no fair-minded driver would prefer pleasure
motoring to a better meat ration or to timber imports for desperately
needed houses.[23c] But he did all he could administratively to reduce the
odium. On taking over he found that the huge flood of correspondence
about it had fallen six weeks into arrears, and took enormous pains to
have letters answered promptly and sympathetically.[38] Six out of seven
applications for 'supplementary rations' were granted (even for hunting)
and years later grateful writers still recalled the trouble he took.[39] *The
Economist* complained bitterly of a class vendetta by the government, yet
it praised Gaitskell's own ministerial broadcast[40] for 'sweet reasonableness,
manly sympathy, confidential frankness and firm hand', conceded his 'very
strong case', and recognised that he 'has served the Government well — on
previous form, astoundingly well'.[33b] But in his next effort in public relations on this subject he authorised, against his own better judgment, a news-
reel film which was booed and hissed in some West End cinemas. He was
sitting in one of them himself, and

* Entering the House to introduce his autumn Budget, he had revealed its
main outlines to a journalist he knew well — and they appeared in print before he
had finished speaking, with the Stock Exchange still open.

felt horribly embarrassed and really suffered agony ... I felt the film was ridiculous and cursed myself for agreeing to its release ... this is the horrid side of politics – ... continual criticism to face and one's own infirmities in being sensitive to it ... Altogether I very much doubt if I am really suited to this kind of thing.[1e]

Gaitskell had already decided that he would have to struggle against the Chancellor to 'get some sort of basic ration restored in the summer ... The present thing is administratively a horror'.[1e] A couple of weeks later he was criticised[33c] for rashly hinting at these hopes in the House, just before a grim warning by Cripps on the economic situation – a warning for which Gaitskell had 'been begging ... for some time to ease my position on basic [petrol] ... the job of public relations for a politician is appallingly difficult. In a sense it is *the* problem. How not to say the wrong thing and how to get the right thing across.'[1f] But Cripps proved open to persuasion, and Gaitskell was soon able to announce a new 'standard' petrol ration for everyone. His critics resented his avuncular references to a 'bonus' and a 'concession', and especially his refusal to allow successful applicants for supplementary rations to draw the standard ration as well, for that would have left nothing worth having for those who had had to lay up their cars. *The Times* tempered its approval of 'a sporting attempt to by-pass austerity' by attacking 'the April foolery of administration'.[41]*

Before any general petrol ration could be restored, the black market had to be beaten. Measures against it were recommended by the Russell Vick Committee, but Gaitskell had a hard fight to force them through. Commercial petrol was to be dyed red, and any private motorist driving with red petrol in his tank was presumed to have acquired it illegally – to the dismay of the oil companies, the road transport industry, the lawyers and the police. The scheme had a mixed reception.[42] But six months later Gaitskell could happily record:

> I managed to persuade the Cabinet to let me give back some of the savings made beyond expectations from suppressing the Black Market. So we are beginning to stop the tiresome business of deducting the standard ration from supplementary allowances. This has got me a tolerably good press.[1h]

That transitional solution saved 250,000 tons a year over a crucial two years (far more than the Ministry's estimate of 100,000 tons); and it greatly relieved the intolerable political and administrative strain.[43]

*Gaitskell wrote that they 'are grumbling, but I am fairly certain that they will settle down. However, my political instincts in this were quite right; better than those of my Civil Service advisers who wanted me to make a new philosophy out of deducting the standard ration from the supplementary coupons.'[1g]

iii *The Gas Bill, the Coal Board and the Miners' Union*

That outcome lay far ahead. As 1948 began, Fergusson had sent him a friendly warning not to 'take on more than human strength can manage ... you can't go on at the tempo of the last 3 months'.[13b] But Gaitskell had no chance to relax. He wrote in his diary soon afterwards: 'The prospect ahead is pretty grim. Indeed, without Marshall Aid it is ghastly and there is no certainty about that. What will happen if there is a Republican victory and Taft is President in 1949?'[1e] Apart from coal production, the departmental outlook was 'horrible';[1e] and even a few weeks later, when he appeased much of the hostility by restoring the petrol ration, he still found that

> I am grossly overworked again. Everything is happening at once. The Gas Bill—now three days a week, mornings and afternoons in Committee; the new petrol scheme and all its repercussions; a crisis in the Coal Board; some horrible problems of coal quality and exports, and rather a heavy list of speaking engagements. And then finally the grim world oil situation with all its repercussions on our plans here.[1g z]

The Gas Bill should have been the least contentious of all the nationalisation measures, but it had become the target of a determined Opposition filibuster.[27c] The Conservatives always favoured a decentralised structure for the nationalised industries, and in December 1945 the Heyworth Committee on gas (set up by Gwilym Lloyd George under the wartime coalition government) had recommended public ownership through regional boards. Both the Ministry of Fuel and Power and the Cabinet approved, though both thought a supervisory national board necessary too. After long talks with Morrison, Gaitskell had himself[44a]—in his first two weeks in office—found a 'rather ingenious' way to stop the national board encroaching, with which he felt 'quite pleased'; and he did not expect any very serious opposition from the industry.[1b] In February he introduced the Bill in a 'rather dull opening speech, primarily for the record ... one must sacrifice parliamentary effects for security, at least until one has a great more [sic] experience than I have. We start the Committee stage next week.'[1f]

Not the content but the context of the Bill explains the sequel. In the previous session the Government had been denounced for guillotining the Transport Bill; in this one they had decided after long argument to give priority to gas and defer steel to next year, just because they expected gas to be uncontentious.[27d] Therefore—and also perhaps recalling the recent fuss over transport—they sent the Gas Bill to standing committee without a guillotine resolution. That gave the Opposition a chance to block it for that session, after which it would have to start again—and so might again crowd out the hated Steel Bill. The Conservatives mounted a massive campaign of obstruction, producing over 800 amendments; obliging the Committee to sit not only mornings but three afternoons a week when the House also met; interrupting its proceedings by futile divisions – both in the committee (five times as many as on its 'model', the Electricity Bill) and in the House itself;[45] and solemnly debating whether nationalisation should be spelt with an 's' or a 'z'.[46] Their spokesman, Brendan Bracken – Dalton's old enemy and Churchill's crony – threw himself zestfully into the operation. As it was purely tactical, there was no bitterness;[47] and Gaitskell's burden was relieved by the admirable lucidity and patience of Sir Frank Soskice, the Solicitor-General. But he soon found it

> a most abominable bore to have to sit for five hours a day opposite Bracken, while the Opposition delay and obstruct ... He likes to make irrelevant, colourful and sometimes entertaining speeches ... I ... find it hard to hide my distaste and keep my temper ... I believe he himself would be prepared to do a deal with me but he ... seems terrified of his own supporters, which is all bound up with his weak position in the Tory Party.[1i j]

Just before Whitsun, Gaitskell and his Labour colleagues on the committee decided to end the farce. They sat without stopping for fifty hours, through two consecutive nights, with only half-hour breaks for breakfast and with an all-night buffet outside the committee room door; some of the suffering civil servants still remember the 'indescribable' sight of the bristly MPs in the morning. 'I do not think we should ever have got through the Bill without this', wrote Gaitskell; and though the Opposition members were both younger than the Government's cohort, and able to risk a shift system, it was their stamina that finally collapsed. It was a 700-year record, for there has been no single all-night committee sitting before or since.* Flushed with victory, Gaitskell made a good-humoured farewell speech, praising his own side and teasing the Tories, but forgetting to thank the long-suffering staff – a sad lapse for which at least one senior civil servant never forgave him. He took a Parliamentary Question that afternoon, then went home to bed and slept for sixteen hours.[1j k] Next month on the third reading he provoked 'uproar' by comparing Bracken's 'screeching, raucous voice' to Hitler's:

> I had determined to insult Bracken to make up for the offensiveness he had displayed upstairs, also to satisfy the outraged feelings of our own people. He, himself, took it quite well, but his side (the House was packed) got annoyed and decided to shout me down.[1c]

---

* The chairman, who had to sit throughout, woke guiltily from a doze at 5 a.m. to find Soskice, lucid as ever, addressing an entirely somnolent committee.[48]

After a more reasoned speech on coal ten days later, he concluded: 'I am afraid most people think I am much better at solid arguments and statistics than at political invective and I am afraid they are quite right.'[1l]

During these debates Herbert Morrison, himself heavily burdened, had – with Bracken's cheerful assent – called the Minister of Fuel and Power 'the most overworked man in Britain'.[45b] Gaitskell, carrying the filibuster on top of his serious responsibilities, wrote gloomily to Dalton: 'I have myself had a pretty tough time in the last six months – enough work and worry to last a long time – and now just as I thought the worst was over coal has begun to give trouble again.'[49] When the obstruction began, the new petrol rationing scheme was being mooted; as it ended, a long-developing crisis erupted in the Coal Board with the dramatic resignation of Sir Charles Reid, the mining engineer whose wartime committee had provided the technical case for compulsory reorganisation of the industry.

Gaitskell, like Reid, was critical of the structure of the Board, on which Shinwell had insisted: only full-time members, with specific functional duties.[27e] He felt it blurred management responsibilities and provoked friction at every level from the Board downwards.[44b] But as Minister, believing in the principle of Board autonomy, he chose to work by informal persuasion. Every Monday he dined with the chairman, Lord Hyndley, often with Robens or Fergusson present, to talk over the problems.[50] The slow process of conversion was suddenly accelerated by Reid, who shared Gaitskell's views but not his patience.[19] Reid demanded an inquiry by outside businessmen, but the labour director Ebby Edwards, the former general secretary of the NUM, would not hear of it. Gaitskell tried in vain to act as 'an appeaser',[51] choosing as chairman of the inquiry a very new part-time member of the Board, Sir Ronald Burrows. But Reid resigned in a letter 'so plainly insulting to the rest of the Coal Board that I clearly had to accept it ... in many ways I regret not having accepted his resignation months ago.'[1k]

Offstage noises came at the most delicate moment with a sudden burst of trumpeting from a familiar rogue elephant: the Secretary for War, Emanuel Shinwell:

> That man has entered my life once more to my considerable regret. He has started making speeches about coal ... calculated to make trouble with the Coal Board ... I sent a violent minute to the P.M. asking him to stop this business ... The P.M. then saw him ... [and he] promised to behave in future. Notwithstanding this, however, he plunged in far worse over the weekend and made an extraordinary speech more or less admitting the failure of nationalisation. This has caused great indignation in the Party.[1j]

Vigorously rebuked in the PLP by James Callaghan, now a junior minister,

Shinwell – assuming the attack was instigated by more senior enemies – inspired a newspaper story that he alone had dissuaded Gaitskell from accepting Reid's outside inquiry.[52a b]

The unhappy legacy of the past meant that nationalisation faced special problems in the mines. The historic mutual suspicion between union and management affected organisational problems and appointments to the boards as well as industrial relations; and Conservatives, who had been so bitterly attacked for the failures of private ownership, naturally exploited these teething troubles.

They had an opportunity when the Burrows Committee concluded its inquiry. Fergusson was so worried about 'headlines in the Opposition press' and 'a tremendous public row' that only the recommendations were published instead of the full report. Reid then intervened again with three articles in *The Times*, and a Conservative MP, Colonel Lancaster, called for the Coal Board to be split up into two dozen independent boards – at once reviving the NUM's memories of regional competition driving down wages.[1m] Gaitskell vigorously denounced these proposals in the House, warning that if areas had to pay their way, some would need to raise prices and close pits.[53a] Years later he wrote privately to an academic expert on nationalisation that the decentralised structure appropriate to gas would not only have been quite unsuitable for coal, which needed 'national decisions', but could never have been adopted because, 'Apart from anything else, the miners would never have tolerated it'.[51]

The union's goodwill was indispensable for maintaining production:

> Reid would not matter at all if only output were better, but it has been very disappointing since Easter and I am now alarmed. To-day we had a meeting with the N.U.M. and the N.C.B. ... but ... nobody knows of anything which is fairly easy to do and can be done.[1k]

Recruitment was slackening off again and, with the return to Saturday morning working, absenteeism was slightly up. Quality was poor, and Gaitskell was always carefully sympathetic to irate persons who brought him samples of worthless coal.[54] Exports had improved – to 16 million tons in 1948, treble the 1947 figure – but were still only one-third of pre-war. Gaitskell was desperate to increase them, and when on 7 October 1948 he met the Board and the NUM he warned them frankly that, as the union's general secretary put it, 'there could be no further concession to the miners unless it came about as a consequence of increased output'.[55]

The general secretary was Arthur Horner, a prominent Communist. Not surprisingly the Communist Party had always recruited relatively well among the miners, and as its line veered with the onset of the cold war its influence began to preoccupy the Ministry of Fuel and Power.[13a b] But while they showed no enthusiasm for the production drive, the British

Communists – unlike their far stronger French comrades – never tried to exploit massive industrial action for political ends; indeed Gaitskell himself believed that 'the mining industry has been given a sort of exemption by Pollitt from the general attack which the C.P. is going to make'.[56]* If so, that no doubt reflected the Party's reluctance to risk losing such an important post as Horner's. For experience had made the other leaders of the union so anti-Communist that they mistrusted not only Horner himself but the Coal Board too, since its labour director was his friend and predecessor Ebby Edwards, who would deal with nobody else.[1n] Gaitskell found it easy and congenial to work with these other leaders, and became particularly friendly with those from the northern coalfields: Sam Watson of Durham, Jim Bowman of Northumberland and Ernest Jones of Yorkshire. After delivering his October 1948 warning to the union, he felt fairly satisfied that the majority would back

> a concentrated drive against absenteeism ... A year ago this would hardly have been possible ... the politics of the thing from now onwards will be an alliance between myself and them behind the scenes...
>
> I particularly picked out one or two lines that I knew the Communists were running, e.g. subsidy of the industry, higher prices, etc., and ruled them out completely. All this is bound to sharpen the conflict within the Union and, of course, we run the risk of local trouble with the C.P. at any time now.[1o]

That same meeting in October 1948 set up a joint production committee which (rather remarkably) the miners and the Board asked a reluctant Sir Donald Fergusson to chair. It reported three weeks later with

> proposals on attendance [which] bring the Union for the first time firmly behind the drive against absenteeism ... Most probably, however, the Communists will not come out against the production drive but will content themselves by doing very little about it, and continue to press for higher wages and other improvements which the industry cannot afford.[1h]

Gaitskell toured the coalfields, speaking bluntly to large private meetings of managers and delegate conferences of miners. In Durham, where joint consultation really worked effectively, he was enormously heartened by the excellent relations between miners and management. Nor did he get on only with his moderate allies, for in Scotland he found the Communist leaders 'surprisingly friendly', their relations with the Board quite good, their president's speech unexpectedly reasonable, and their Gala 'most impressive – a good bit of modern democracy'.[57] Some areas rejected the proposals on absenteeism, but Gaitskell believed that he had had some

* Harry Pollitt was general secretary of the Communist Party.

success in getting higher output, 'not through public meetings but through the private delegate conferences with the lodge officials which I have held all over the country'.[1m] James Griffiths, an old leader of the union and now his ministerial colleague, confirmed that impact;[58]* and in May 1949 Gaitskell persuaded the NUM executive to continue the agreement for longer hours which they had adopted in his first days in office.[1p]

Gaitskell made an excellent impression on ordinary miners on his constant visits. He had no patience with middle-class censoriousness about the pitmen, and when mining executives complained about high wages, he told them there were plenty of vacancies at the coal face if any of them cared to apply. At one Durham mine, a 'very tough and loyal' pit committee were themselves tackling unjustifiable absenteeism. Having travelled overnight, Gaitskell

> went down [the] pit on the Friday morning. When we got near the coal face we had to do the last 200 yards with a roof of about 3 foot 6 inches. Of all the various forms of exercise one has to take in a pit this is the worst, and I was very exhausted by the time I got to the 18 inch face where the men must lie on their sides to throw the coal on to the belts. I referred to this when talking to the press and spontaneously said that I could understand a bit of absenteeism in such conditions.[61–2a]

In South Wales, the miners at one pit (Penallta) threatened to boycott his visit, thinking he would be taken to an area dressed up for the occasion. Instead, he asked advice from the union lodge secretary, visited the most difficult section, and was afterwards told that his action and his 'free and easy manner' had won the miners' complete confidence and would long be felt in the work of the colliery.[63]

Often the miners' suspicions, as the Penallta incident shows, were directed at the local staffs whom the boards had recruited from within the industry, and they won some sympathy from Gaitskell. But they were not all so reasonable. There were complaints against the appointment of new officials, for which the union itself was pressing so as to improve health and safety and training; and against the cost of the administration, which was below 1 per cent—official salaries at national and divisional level cost less than directors' fees (their salaries excluded) before the war. 'Ironically, the Coal Board has not spawned a burdensome bureaucracy, though it has not been able to avoid a widespread feeling among the mineworkers that it has.'[30b] Gaitskell thought that its bad public relations were largely to blame, and made it difficult for the Minister to stay in the background as Fergusson[13a] (and he himself)[1b] would have wished. But he was indignant

---

* Gaitskell often consulted Griffiths privately about coal. He had been Dalton's candidate to succeed Shinwell[59] and was at one time tipped to succeed Gaitskell.

when outsiders sought to exploit these unjustified charges. In one of his last speeches as an under-secretary, he lashed out at 'the slanders' of Tory speakers like Churchill and Boyd-Carpenter.[10b] After seeing for himself the excellence of industrial relations in the north-east, he was angry—and a little naive—at the purely destructive attitude of the press.[1a] In this context he was exasperated when his old Fabian friends joined the chorus, publishing in May 1949 a pamphlet summarising many complaints from the coalfields. They testified to the miners' deep loyalty to the government, and agreed about the NCB's bad public relations: in his view they blamed the Board members when the 'Real Problem is lower down'.[64] But he resented their supplying ammunition for Bracken and other Tories in the House, and wrote to a former miners' agent who supported him against the critics: 'I *was* extremely angry about the Fabian pamphlet, and have told some of those concerned privately what I thought'. His wrath made a lasting—and unfavourable—impression.[65]

Like Aneurin Bevan,[66a] Gaitskell had no patience with the 'rather apologetic and timid attitude' of some of their colleagues, which let the government's case go by default: 'This is not only politically extremely dangerous but also thoroughly bad for the morale of the members of the Boards and their staffs ... [doing] ourselves considerable political damage and encouraging trouble in the industries concerned.'[44d] If the Ministers responsible thought criticism justified, they should raise it informally with the boards, otherwise 'they should be ready to defend them'.[44e] No doubt referring to Shinwell who had recently attacked as too high the very salaries he had when Minister sought to increase,[67] Gaitskell added acidly: 'they may reasonably expect that other members of the Government will do likewise'.[26b] But for the same reason—maintaining morale in the industries —he tried to avoid starting polemics himself, for he feared that the violent Opposition attacks on the boards and their members made it even harder to attract first-rate people. His conscientiously uncontroversial presentation of the National Coal Board's first annual report to the House, in what he justly called 'a rather plodding, extensive kind of speech', drew a small attendance and little interest; he lamented that 'the Debate just cannot be carried on in an atmosphere of complete impartiality'.[68]

For while Gaitskell sought and earned the workers' confidence, he knew that the ordinary consumer and voter had also to be convinced of the success of nationalisation. It would be judged, he told the NUM's annual conference at Whitley Bay, by six criteria: adequate supplies for industry; enough for exports; more for the domestic consumer; better quality; paying its way; and reasonable prices so that the consumer as well as the worker should gain from technical improvements.[69] By the end of his term of office, performance was improving. Output per man-shift reached the pre-war level in September 1949, far ahead of all other European countries.

Production was rising, though not fast enough, and domestic consumption was well up, though still rationed for the sake of exports. Fatal accidents in 1948 were fewer than ever before, and fewer still in 1949. The miners had trebled their wages (while other wages had doubled); but prices had risen less than for many commodities, and the Board made a profit where the old owners took a subsidy (£27 million in their last year).[70]

There were still serious problems. Voluntary absenteeism fell every year from 1946, but was naturally higher than in the depression. Small strikes were still frequent, though man-days lost in the three post-war years were fewer than 2 per cent of the corresponding figure after 1918. Recruitment fluctuated, but after a worrying phase, 'the first seven years of nationalisation had seen the industry stem what threatened at one time to be an almost fatal erosion of its labour supply'.[30c] Under the old owners, economic recovery would have been impossible. But the Board succeeded in reversing the steady decline over which the companies had for so long presided.

iv   *New Colleagues, and a Lost Friend*

The constant crises of his first nine months had put a heavy strain on Gaitskell. His close friends had known he was exhausted and worried about his heart, and an alarmed Evan Durbin urged him to take a long complete rest at Whitsun 1948 so as to 'be fit for months and alive for years' — tragically ironical advice from one with only four more months to live.[71] But after that the pressures became less intense, and Gaitskell was able to lead a more relaxed life. He went on an NUM outing from the unexciting Labour Party Conference at Scarborough, and was photographed with Aneurin Bevan in the unlikely setting of a Butlin's camp at Filey. He enjoyed his coalfield visits, especially one in Scotland taking in the Scottish Coal Board and hydro-electric stations, and returning by air. He commented happily,

> civil engineering is so simple. Driving tunnels to let water go through and then making artificial waterfalls is in the literal sense child's play ... Flew in the pilot's seat on the way back for the first time and was astounded to find they never use the controls at all ... Every now and then they turn a knob slightly ... rather like a radio.[1t]

When he and Dora went to the NUM conference at Whitley Bay, as usual he spent much of his time convivially with the miners' leaders, singing songs until midnight after a bibulous dinner with their executive.[1s]

On his next trip to Northumberland, to speak with Michael Foot and Aneurin Bevan at the Miners' Gala, Gaitskell felt 'ridiculously pleased' when Jim Bowman called his speech the best he had ever heard there. The social ambience was different this time, for he stayed the previous night at Wallington where Sir Charles Trevelyan, a Minister in the first two Labour governments, kept open house for visiting Socialists. The place was to go to the National Trust on Sir Charles's death and though Gaitskell approved, he had a feeling of slight dreariness — 'that … tradition and continuity seemed to be dying'.[1r] But sentiment did not dull his critical faculties. In the best bedroom where he slept hung a painting, said to portray a Trevelyan lady on her deathbed in the same room. Alf Robens, who later slept there, said in the morning, 'I was careful not to roll over so as not to disturb the lady'; Gaitskell's comment was, 'If you look carefully you will see that the windows aren't the same, nor is the four-poster bed the same as in this room. I don't believe it's a Trevelyan lady at all.' With a touch of exasperation, his private secretary added: 'He was quite right. He was always right.'[38]

As a Minister he was now a guest in grander circles. He attended the wedding of Princess Elizabeth and Prince Philip (although 'I find it difficult to take these things seriously');[1u] and a dinner at No. 10, with some of his younger colleagues, to meet the royal pair. He talked to her about fuel economy, 'and she said that Queen Mary's house was the coldest she knew; she hardly ever had a fire anywhere. I asked if this was because she was spartan or because of the house, but she said, "no" — it was because of her national duty.'[1g]

A few months later the Gaitskells went to their first Buckingham Palace dinner:

> We ate off the famous gold plate. It was queer having no toasts, not even 'The King', so smoking started at once. Also queer that before we had time to get on with the port or liqueurs we all had to get up and go into another room. Later I was led round the various female royalties and did my five minutes with each. It seems to me a most barbarous custom to condemn the wretched Princesses to nothing but tête-à-tête conversations, so that there is an endless flow of small talk.

The Queen told Dora 'that she thought I was a good Minister because I do not make many speeches'.[1r]

He was finding more time to meet colleagues and follow affairs outside his own Department. He saw a good deal of his fellow economic Ministers, who dined together each Thursday to chat and iron out minor departmental conflicts. Their host was Sir Stafford Cripps, Minister of Economic Co-ordination and Chancellor as well since Dalton's fall, who now dominated the Government's domestic policies. A vegetarian who symbolised austerity in material things, and a devout Christian who believed that political leadership should appeal to the best in human nature and not truckle to group or individual selfishness, he enjoyed remarkable moral authority during three critical years. Gaitskell quickly developed immense admiration for him. He was no judge of men – 'some rogues and crooks have fascinated him' – and he seemed unable to relax. But he had a very keen intelligence, patience, kindliness and, above all,

> courage which is closely combined in his case with superb self-confidence ... This is where he differs from most politicians. Most of us, I think, are cowards in the sense that we are always counting the political difficulties and probably tending to exaggerate them. You feel with Cripps that almost nothing is politically impossible. He sails on simply concerned with what is the best solution from every other point of view and ignoring all the rocks which lie ahead.[1f]

As usual, Gaitskell's comments on the character of others reveal a good deal about his own.

These weekly dinners soon expanded beyond strictly economic business, for Cripps began inviting two colleagues who had been his allies in the pre-war Popular Front campaign. The first was John Strachey, Minister of Food, and in the 1930s the most persuasive of Communist propagandists (though never a Party member):[72]

> I reserve judgment about him. He is still, I think, much too inclined to abstract theory. At the moment he is a deflationist and rather anti-control. I think this is rather a rationalisation of the difficulties he has in introducing and maintaining certain controls in his own field. But it is also due to half-baked economics which he learned in the past. At the same time I think he is a very able negotiator, and fairly influential at Cabinet meetings – states his case forcibly, though with exaggeration. Is he to be trusted? Probably not.'[1u]

Four months later Cripps introduced a second old associate:

> [L]ast night Aneurin Bevan was also present and appears to have joined the group. I must say that Stafford is showing much more political acumen than I expected. He is obviously anxious to have Bevan as an ally. And the group is now fairly powerful consisting as it does, apart from the Chancellor and myself, of the Ministers of Health, Supply, Food, the Economic Secretary, Paymaster-General and President of the Board of Trade.[*] I could not help feeling that Stafford was surveying his future Cabinet. It would be surprising if he did not himself expect to be Prime Minister one day. But these things depend more on accident of age and health than anything else.[1g]

* Those six Ministers were Bevan, Strauss (another old Popular Front campaigner), Strachey, Jay, Marquand and Wilson.

Following an argument a few weeks afterwards, Gaitskell saw another potential premier there:

> Personality is a funny thing. Bevan, of course, has it very decidedly. He is powerful, though maddening as well. But I feel pretty sure he will be Prime Minister one day and probably at that level will be a good deal better than now.[73] I would not, however, have him as Foreign Secretary, he is much too unscrupulous and would involve us in much too much trouble with other countries.[1c]

Barely a fortnight later, Bevan marred his triumphant inauguration of the National Health Service with a celebrated lapse, calling the Tories 'lower than vermin'. Gaitskell disapproved, without being unduly prim. When he, Bevan and Michael Foot all spoke at the Northumberland Miners' Gala, he found Foot

> rather strange. He never seems to talk except when making speeches, and was most silent and reserved all the time. Jennie Lee ... and Bevan now positively defend the policy of insulting one's opponents. 'Aggression is what will get us votes' – and suchlike nonsense. It would be much better if A.B. simply said that he was Welsh; he spoke as he felt, and sometimes he felt very strongly ... Jennie Lee said she was worried about the fire going out of the miners because they were getting such a lot. I am afraid I have little sympathy with such attitudes.[1r]

Gaitskell's relations with Bevan's friends were amiable. In one coal debate he went out of his way to praise only one back-bench contribution, an 'impressive and most attractive speech' by Jennie Lee;[53b] Michael Foot wrote asking him to advertise *Tribune* – then loyally supporting the government to which Bevan belonged – from his platform at meetings. He probably did so, for he had suggested it – along with *The Economist* – to an old Chatham party worker, now in Australia, as a 'readable and useful' source for keeping in touch with Labour Britain.[74]

He and Bevan did not always see eye to eye, for their style and temperament were altogether dissimilar – especially over foreign affairs, in which Gaitskell now had time to take an interest again. In October 1948 both men, with Cripps and two other Ministers, lunched with five Americans involved in Marshall Plan affairs – who surprised Gaitskell by their sympathy for the current Communist-led miners' strike in France:

> The lunch ended with a wordy argument between Bevan and myself about the use of the word 'democracy', to which everybody else listened in silence. It looked as though it had been staged between the left and right wing of the Government, but it was in fact purely accidental, and

provoked by Bevan talking about the Russian peasant's idea of democracy, about which I felt quite certain he knew as little as I did! Strachey and Strauss vaguely supported him, as they would from pre-war days.[1h]

At a similar lunch at the American Embassy to meet Kenney, the new representative of the Economic Co-operation Administration,

> Nye typically opened his conversation with the gentleman on whom we depend for dollars by describing his experiences in the great San Francisco Dock Strike of 1933, and made it quite plain, quite pleasantly but unmistakably, that he held the lowest opinion of American Justice. (Mr. Kenney is a lawyer.)[1v]

Yet on the major issues the future rivals were not far apart. Bevan was convinced that the American alliance was indispensable, while Gaitskell, its determined champion politically, was as firm as Bevan in resisting economic pressures from across the Atlantic.[75] In Europe Bevan resolutely stood up to Soviet pressure – and went beyond any of his colleagues in demanding a guarantee to Yugoslavia against Russian aggression, and in arguing forcefully in the Cabinet for the relief of Berlin – blockaded in the summer of 1948 – by a tank convoy instead of an airlift.[66b]

Those events led to a review of British policy in Germany which divided Gaitskell's friends. Dalton, with his violent national prejudices, was an unrepentant anti-German. But H. V. Berry, the founder of XYZ, was now regional commissioner at Hamburg, and on a visit to England diverted the club from its usual financial agenda to talk about the problem:

> Berry wants us to make an ally of Western Germany, allow them to rearm and build them up. This horrified Chris Mayhew. I did not go as far as Berry but I think the Foreign Office policy of continuing to blow up air-raid shelters in Western Germany while apparently worrying about Russian aggression all the time is really absurd. Incidentally, Frank P[akenham] feels very, very strongly about this and was recently on the verge of resigning. I not unsuccessfully persuaded him out of it.[76]

Bevan, like Pakenham, strongly opposed the dismantling policy.[66c] But again he went further. On 22 December 1948, after previous arguments, Dalton reported another inconclusive Cabinet discussion:

> S.C. said we ought to make up our minds whether we regarded the Germans as still a danger, or as an ally in building W. Europe. E.B. said he was trying to steer a middle course. A.B. said we ought to build them up as much as we could. They were a better barrier against

Communism than the French. I [Dalton] ... spoke sharply against the German danger.[77]

Outside Europe, the great issue at that moment was Palestine, where Ernest Bevin's policy outraged Labour's Zionist traditions. Here Gaitskell, in his moderate fashion, sympathised with the feelings which at least once led Bevan to consider resignation.[32b] After a private talk in which the latter attacked Bevin and criticised Attlee, Gaitskell commented:

Part of this, of course, is just ambition and jealousy, but it really is impossible to defend the situation we have got ourselves into in the Middle East now ... I think they must realise in the F.O. they have gone a bit too far lately.

At a Cripps dinner soon afterwards, Bevan claimed that the Foreign Secretary had first got a vote of confidence in his Palestine policy in return for agreeing to recognise Israel, and had then tried to slip out of that decision. 'Nye came out quite openly against Bevin and seemed to be anxious to start an intrigue to get rid of him. While nobody else joined in, I think most of us feel fairly critical of the foreign policy.' When the House debated the policy, no adequate promise of recognition was given and sixty Labour MPs abstained. 'I think a good many ... did not realise they were really risking the fall of the Government. On the other hand I must confess to some sympathy with their point of view.'[78]

Whatever his own differences with other Ministers, Gaitskell always felt strongly the need — for decades appreciated by most Conservative Cabinets and no Labour one — for solidarity in public and reasonable mutual understanding in private. He had been indignant at Shinwell for breaching the former convention, and was mildly shocked at Bevan's contempt for the latter. After one Cripps dinner he wrote:

The Minister of Health [Bevan] is in some ways a very simple person. He has no scruples about denouncing his colleagues. The other evening he launched attacks on the Prime Minister, the Lord President and the Minister of Defence, and of course on previous occasions he has frequently attacked the Foreign Secretary. When this happens everybody becomes embarrassed. Either you remain silent in which case you feel 'pi' which is not a pleasant feeling — you are the good boy, not slandering your colleagues — or you also say what you think, probably in much more moderate terms than the Minister of Health; but this of course makes you feel rather a cad. Stafford [who] usually remains silent ... [said that] the Party could not continue to be run in the new Parliament by the old men at present at the top ... We younger ones sat back rather primly and said nothing ... Stafford also revealed the interesting and curious fact that he had never had a private meal with the Prime Minister since the Government was formed—meaning by that a meal at Number 10 where he and some of the other Party Leaders could meet and talk.[1n]

Among the 'younger ones' of his own generation, Gaitskell's closest personal friend and political ally throughout his working life had been Evan Durbin, whose sudden death in the summer of 1948 was the saddest of his bereavements. During that recess, he and Dora had gone down to Milland to open the new village hall and revisit his old house and garden. They then went off on three weeks' holiday to their favourite haunt of those years, Abbotsbury on the Dorset coast (about which Hugh laid down the law to Ronald Edwards's wife who had been born and brought up there, just as he once had to Hubert Ashton's father over India).[79] On 3 September, after a long walk with the Edwards, they had just finished dinner when the telephone rang, and Gaitskell learned from his private secretary that Durbin had been drowned saving his daughter and another girl on a dangerous Cornish beach:

> I do not want to write here and now about Evan [he noted a fortnight later] ... I record simply that physically the feeling I most had was one of cold, as though I had had something stripped from me and was exposed much more than before to the elements ... Grief affects people very differently. For me it is sort of chemical in its action. I find it impossible to control my tears ...[80]
>
> I still cannot get it firmly into my head that he has gone. Every now and then I think about it again. I suppose one's personal loss declines as time passes, at least one will feel it less frequently. But the full loss to his friends and to the country will be there, sure enough. There is nobody else who had his peculiar combination of theoretical and practical knowledge of Labour policy and the intelligence and will-power needed. And, there is nobody else in my life whom I can consult on the most fundamental issues, knowing that I shall get the guidance that I want.[1q*]

In many subsequent conflicts he found friendly seniors, capable lieutenants, valued allies, and able and devoted young admirers. But he was never again to enjoy the close companionship of someone of similar outlook and standing in the Party, with whom he could share all his burdens and battles in complete trust and intimacy. On becoming Chancellor he wrote sadly: 'It would be so much less lonely if he were here.'[81] Always inclined to do far too much himself, he might not have worn himself out so thoroughly if Durbin had survived. Much more emotional and impulsive than his

* He organised a trust fund, soliciting contributions from friends, to take care of Durbin's family and the education of his children.

friend, he might have been restrained by Evan's calmer advice from some of his more foolhardy acts. Evan might even have been able to modify Hugh's famous obstinacy. The clarity, realism, courage and intellectual honesty of Durbin's mind and character were in themselves a sad loss to the Labour Party. But the close partnership of the two men might have been a good deal more than the sum of two impressive parts.

v *Minister for Nationalised Industries*

Gaitskell did not advocate public ownership on purely practical grounds, but he knew that these were indispensable to convince others. He told the Oxford Union at its first post-war debate: 'Ultimately it is our aim to socialise the means of production and exchange. For this Parliament we have set ourselves a limited task ... we shall nationalise the three major industries and one institution, the Bank of England.'[82] Early in 1949, with the experience of office, he set out his views on nationalisation to another student audience.[83] 'Not an *end* in itself,' say his notes.

'Our Socialism is much wider. Described in negative terms – the *three* evils of individualism – *Inequality, Insecurity, Inefficiency*. Therefore primary aim to *remove these*.'

Two other evils against which criticism is directed.

(a) *Concentration of economic power exercised without responsibility*. Now much modified by (i) Govt. Controls (ii) Trade Union strength. It *still* counts.

(b) *Spiritual* aims – undesirability of concentrating on *material ends*, maximise wealth and income, etc. This probably appeals to relatively few people & is mixed in origins – *objection* to competitive struggle as such – [word illegible] *or* desire for different *motive* and *incentive*. But doubtful how far this changes except at top under nationalisation. All the same desire to serve community important. Whole subject deserves much closer study – incentives, ideals, and happiness in work.

But first three for *most* people more important.

Before going further – make *democracy* an end in itself and need to acknowledge this in our policy.

He argued again that since payment of fair compensation was essential in a democratic society, nationalisation would not directly reduce present inequalities; that it could help substantially to promote economic security, especially in the heavy investment industries; that natural monopolies should be in public hands; but that nationalisation could contribute most to Socialist aims by improved efficiency ... through e.g. better industrial relations, a larger unit of administration or production, technical reconstruction & a much higher level of investment'. That criterion implied a large role for the managers, who must be chosen for ability and not by patronage, adequately paid, and not subjected to constant interference. However, those engaged in the industry – managers as well as workers – inevitably had a limited perspective, against which it might be the Minister's duty to assert the need for a broader view.

In Gaitskell's personal creed, inequality was the worst of the 'three evils of individualism'. But his ministerial responsibilities concentrated his attention on problems of efficiency. Managers had to be found for the industries who had the workers' confidence and were good at their job; they had to be given enough freedom to do it well, without being allowed to impose their own judgment on matters outside their proper sphere.

At the end of 1948, Gaitskell was half way through his term at Fuel and Power. His old civil service chief from the Board of Trade, now serving in his own Department, sent him a greeting suggesting 'that over Christmas you should think back a bit over the tremendous successes you have had over the past year'.[84a] Gaitskell's characteristic response was to draw up an enormous balance-sheet, setting out twenty-two accomplishments and a future agenda of ten items.[85] He counted as his main achievements his handling of the petrol problem, which had ended the quarrel with the motoring organisations without increasing the country's import bill; much better relations in coal, accompanied by higher production and a trebling of exports; the introduction of high-level scientific advice to the Ministry; and progress on major legislation. Over electricity, he had made some of the changes he wanted, but was very far from satisfied. He was still unhappy about the organisation of the Coal Board, and he recognised that he had hardly begun to establish a co-ordinated fuel policy for his various and often rival industries.

The problem of relations between Minister and boards, where Gaitskell had no useful precedents to guide him, was most acute in electricity. That of appointments to the boards was difficult everywhere but worst of all in the mines, where production directors drawn from the old management, and labour or welfare directors who were former union officials, were the carriers of generations of mutual mistrust.[27f] There were, Gaitskell admitted privately, 'too many people in managerial positions who are still strongly opposed to nationalisation and quite willing to make trouble with the Coal Board and the N.U.M. The Coal Board has not yet won their loyalty'.[1w] All the first chairmen of divisional boards came from outside the industry, partly to escape these suspicions and partly because no one from within it had experience of running a big organisation.[44c]

These considerations encouraged a peculiar vogue for appointments from the Services. Gaitskell approved of the practice, and visiting a happy modern pit in Kent, whose divisional chairman was a rear-admiral, he commented on its advantages: 'doing something for its own sake and because it is their job comes naturally. They have been brought up to believe in service and so, as it were, take to nationalisation.'[1s] Moreover, a famous chairman from the armed forces might help to take the boards out of politics. Knowing that Hyndley might have to retire on health grounds, Gaitskell thought of choosing 'a really national figure who would disarm the Opposition by merely being Chairman. Someone like Mountbatten or Montgomery. He would not need to be much more than a figure-head.'[1c]

Attlee and Morrison quickly disposed of this notion—to Gaitskell's relief when, at a Palace dinner six weeks later, the Field-Marshal bored Dora, and appalled Hugh by boasting of trying to persuade one of his ex-generals, who was just leaving the South Wales Coal Board, to denounce the NCB publicly:[86]

> I was really shocked by this deliberate acknowledgement of disloyalty. How right the P.M. and Lord President were ... It really is extraordinary that such an unattractive person should have achieved such things. But I fancy these traits—extreme egotism, lack of humour and being a bore—are not uncommon amongst successful leaders.[1f]

Nevertheless when he had to propose a successor for Hyndley, Gaitskell wrote to Morrison that the Government would probably have to choose between two types:

> the popular figure-head, which might be very useful to us politically at the moment, and might also be valuable from the point of view of the morale of the industry. Or we can go for administrative capacity, organising ability etc., which may produce better results in the rather longer run. Ideally, of course, we want someone who combines both types.

Morrison had suggested Sir Andrew Duncan, Churchill's former Minister of Supply, who was rather old and unlikely to accept—though Gaitskell felt it would be 'Politically ... brilliant ... would really succeed in taking the Coal Board right out of politics'. His own short-list was headed by Field-Marshal Lord Alexander:

> a magnificent appointment from the figure-head point of view ... His mere name is bound to stave off a good deal of criticism in the Press and from the Opposition. Whether he would really have the necessary administrative qualities; whether he would be able to be sufficiently tough with the N.U.M. I do not know.[87a]

In the end, after a friendly refusal from Sir Geoffrey Heyworth of Unilever, he persuaded Hyndley to continue until after the election.[1x]

Gaitskell was responsible for far more appointments to the boards of nationalised industries than any other Minister: counting only full-timers, about seventy. Industrial relations were better in gas and electricity than in coal, but there was still resentment against the appointment of Conservatives or former managers, especially opponents of nationalisation, and also against high salaries. Gaitskell rejected these complaints, writing to Michael Young, research secretary of the Labour Party:

> Anything in the nature of political patronage in this sphere could only create insecurity within the industry and thoroughly discredit the Boards with the general public. All that matters really is that the Boards should work well. If inefficient people are appointed on political grounds they will not work well. I know perfectly well, of course, that in practice some political concessions in this field have to be made. But we are always being pressed for more.[88]

He told a Labour MP who protested about gas and electricity appointments that there were among former managers a 'great many able people ... opposed to the change, [who] are quite prepared to accept it once it has been made.'[89a b]

At the Labour Party's Blackpool conference in June he was again 'worried by the failure of the leaders to defend nationalisation adequately. They are much too apologetic ... this is thoroughly bad politics and quite unjustified'.[1w] In a paper to the Cabinet's Socialisation of Industries Committee, he urged a more robust attitude by Ministers over both appointments and salaries. Critics complained about appointments of both insiders (former managers) and outsiders (to part-time posts). But the former were needed, and were keen to make a success of their jobs; and the nationalisation Acts rightly required the latter to ensure administrative and other skills in some non-technical posts. Political discrimination would not only be wrong, but would eliminate able people, provoke severe criticism, and have utterly 'demoralising and discreditable' results if a Tory government imitated it. Moreover, boards must pay enough to recruit good men. Owing to the constant public and press criticism, the posts were far less attractive than comparable business jobs, yet tenure, pensions and expense allowances were much less generous, and salaries very little above those of their own managerial employees:

> It would be quite disastrous to the whole national economy as well as to the success of the nationalised industries if our coal, electricity and gas industries were to be staffed by second-raters and the best administrative and engineering brains were to be deterred from seeking careers in these industries.[44f]

Gaitskell was always delighted to appoint able trade unionists to the boards, and even after leaving office he helped to persuade James Bowman to become chairman of the National Coal Board itself.[90] He did not find it easy. When a full-time post on the NCB was vacant:

> I offered the job to two of the best NUM officials ... and both refused largely, I think, on personal grounds. [One] was all set to accept but his wife almost had hysterics at the prospect of leaving North Wales and moving so far up in the economic and social scale that he decided that he could not do it. How few people would expect this sort of thing to happen.[1r y]

But he flatly refused to appoint official spokesmen of the unions to run the industries in which their own members worked. Many unions did not want that: the Miners were so hostile to the idea that their general secretary Ebby Edwards lost his union membership the moment he joined the Coal Board. Others like the Railwaymen were in favour, and the Communist Party—which controlled the Electrical Trades Union—also took up the theme.

Gaitskell met their challenge head on, telling his colleagues, 'I regard the syndicalist tendencies now being encouraged by the Communists as exceedingly dangerous and requiring very firm handling.'[44g] He warned the ETU conference at Worthing that the government would not accept the proposal. Full-time workers' representatives would become managerial spokesmen and cease to be workers; while part-timers could not maintain a dual loyalty over, say, wage negotiations. If working-class people were trained to take over managerial jobs, as of course they should be, then the unions must change their attitude to promotion and stop regarding them as going over to the other side. The electorate would judge the nationalised industries on their service to the general public, not only to their own workers. He had a chilly and unresponsive reception; the well-disciplined conference by a large majority condemned the selection of old reactionary managements for executive jobs, and unanimously passed a motion in favour of direct union representation moved by Les Cannon, then a leading Communist.[52c]

Gaitskell's mistrust of syndicalist militancy went back to his first formative political experience in the General Strike, which was in part the outcome of a generation's preaching by a dedicated activist minority. It had led the trade union movement to a catastrophic dead end, shattered its bargaining power until the war, and brought terrible suffering to the miners and their families. Now, as Minister of Fuel and Power, he took a firm stand against any manifestation of it. Later on he was to show interest in any practical scheme for workers' participation in running their firms;[91] but he regarded the co-partnership schemes which had flourished in the gas industry as perhaps suitable for private companies, but quite inappropriate in a publicly owned enterprise.[27g] In all the industries for which he was responsible, he was concerned both to ensure a fair deal for their workers and to protect the legitimate interests of the rest of the community. On price policy, for example, he privately warned the Labour Party: 'The real danger ... is likely to be a syndicalistic one...that any surplus there is will be absorbed by wage demands which have no relation to the general situation of the country.'[88]

Hostile both to syndicalist militancy and to the Communist Party, he clashed again with the ETU in December 1949, when a long-threatened unofficial strike at the power stations broke out just before the general election. Warned by Lord Citrine, chairman of the British Electrical Authority, Gaitskell had in advance secured Cabinet authority to use troops, which were put in at once when the strike began without warning at four power stations ten days later. He thoroughly mistrusted the ETU, for

> although it denounced the strikers officially, we are perfectly certain the unofficial elements are largely guided and controlled by the Communists as well.[92]
>
> I saw a great deal of Citrine during the strike and was much impressed by his determination and firmness ... the Ministry of Labour ... were concerned almost wholly with ending the strike; whereas we were concerned with smashing the strikers. I wrote a long minute to the P.M. ... but ... the fundamental issue is still unresolved ... It is quite possible that the C.P. would not mind in the least landing this sort of thing on us just before the Election.
>
> When the Election is over the Government ought really to face up to the issue of Power Station strikes, and decide whether they can afford to treat them as ordinary industrial disputes. In my view they cannot.[1y]

Governments were still asking that question a quarter of a century later.

Managers no less than workers might be parochial in judging the interests of their industry, yet good men would not be recruited or retained if they were subject to constant interference by Ministers claiming a wider view. The idea of autonomy for the boards was in theory accepted by the Labour Party, which had for years been committed to Herbert Morrison's conception of the independent public corporation. One of its strongest defenders in Whitehall was Gaitskell's Permanent Secretary, and on the whole Gaitskell shared that view. He told his colleagues in May 1949 that so long as the boards had statutory responsibility to pay their way and manage detailed administration, they must be left considerable latitude.

The Minister must not duplicate their staffs, remove their power of decision, or try to teach them how to do their job.[44h]

However, Parliament held him broadly responsible for their record, and he had his own statutory responsibilities, which he had power to enforce by giving the boards a General Direction in the national interest. He should not use it frequently, for that would discourage able men from serving, by frustrating them or making them feel unduly dependent. But he was fully entitled to intervene on matters going beyond the responsibility of the boards.[93] He had done so on three recent occasions: to stop the National Coal Board fixing wholesale margins with the coal merchants and cutting off supplies to any who sold cheaper;[94] to persuade them to sell anthracite to Canada for dollars when the European price was higher; and to insist on a higher charge for electricity in winter:

> [S]ome overriding consideration lying outside the strict responsibility of the Boards was, in every case, involved — the principle of preventing restrictive practice in coal distribution, the importance of exporting in the national interest to the right destination, the need to diminish the risk of load shedding and obtain the full assistance of industry in staggering hours.

Though willing to issue a Direction, he had not needed to do so. He preferred frequent informal discussions with the chairmen — weekly for coal, less frequently for electricity and gas. The government might need greater powers to control prices (the Coal Board had voluntarily agreed not to raise domestic prices without the Minister's consent, but there was no such arrangement in electricity or gas); and to guarantee subsidies for investments about which a board was hesitant (as over the coke oven programme).[27h] But wider powers of direction would be of little use; Ministers would rarely use them for fear of bad publicity and obstruction by the board.[44h] As he wrote privately a few years later:

> It is true that in theory a Minister can exercise power without responsibility if he has a very weak Board. But generally speaking, if he ... succeeds, he has no particular motive for hiding his light under a bushel; and I can only say it is an extremely difficult thing, in my experience, for the Minister to get his way with the Board in a matter which they really object to, without the whole affair coming to the surface.[51]

Gaitskell's successors did not adhere to the principles he tried to establish. Conservative Ministers set, sometimes for purely electoral reasons, and later Labour ones followed, a bad example of political interference with the nationalised industries which was usually unavowed. With responsibility for their management hopelessly blurred, and accoun-

G

tability impossible to enforce, the public corporations have attracted much justified criticism – frequently misdirected against a form of organisation which has never, since those early days, been allowed to work as its originators intended.

His main battle on this front came with the electricity industry, as aggressive as any private firm in its determination to sell its product. When the crisis over coal production was at its worst, consumers burned 15 million tons more in 1948 than in 1947, and of them all the most insatiable were the power stations. Domestic consumption of electricity had doubled since 1938, and demand still soared;[95] private enterprise vigorously sold electric fires, though at peak hours power could not always be supplied.[96] To the industry, this proved that its need for new generating plant deserved priority over competing claims for investment capital – while Gaitskell believed that consumers should pay the real cost of their demands (kept artificially low for years) through a surcharge at peak periods.[27i] His frequent clashes with Citrine as the chairman of the British Electricity Authority show the problems of that relationship:* the more so because the latter, whose firmness he so admired in the power-station strike, had for twenty years been general secretary of the TUC and wielded far more influence than Gaitskell in the Labour Movement. The two men got on well personally, lunching regularly together to discuss mutual problems. But inevitably their perspectives were quite different.

Citrine was now as uncompromising an advocate of priority for investment in electricity as he had apparently been for coal when he was on the Coal Board:[1v]

> I had a few trenchant arguments about this with Hugh Gaitskell ... I took the line that we must aim at supplying consumers with all the power they needed, whatever might be the state of the weather ... But Gaitskell was adamant that this policy was economically unjustified ... Right through my Chairmanship the policy of restricting our capital development was continued.[98]

Nevertheless, at Fuel and Power Gaitskell was a vigorous defender of the industry's legitimate investment interests;[27j] and at the Exchequer, when Citrine appealed against him to Attlee, it was the Chancellor who won. But the pressure was intense, for by 1951 the industry, producing 250 per cent of its 1938 output, still fell far short of the demand;[99] so that a powerful chairman using all his influence and ingenuity was able to capture a huge share of investment resources – twice as much as coal and gas combined, almost one-third as much as all manufacturing industry. No wonder

* Other Ministers suffered too; 'it's far easier to get cooperation out of ICI than out of Walter Citrine,' said one of them at one of Cripps's dinners.[97]

that the leading analyst of fuel policy called the electricity authorities 'extremely greedy claimants on our capital resources'.[100]

On the consumption side, the boards were even more successful in frustrating a ministerial policy better adapted than their own to the interest of the British economy. Gaitskell on taking office had at once to face the need to restrict electricity consumption in the home:[13a] otherwise industry and the unions would rebel against the voluntary load-spreading agreements which restricted their own supplies. Besides, the Minister of Fuel told Ernest Bevin, 'if he was to get his exports I must have some means of stopping domestic electricity demand, and [I] gave him a rough idea of the tax proposal. He seemed to swallow it quite well'.[1b] (A tax on consumption was one of many expedients discussed in the Ministry, or with Cabinet committees.)[27k] Before the fuel crisis Shinwell had considered controlling the sales of electrical fires — on which the tax was doubled in 1947 — and afterwards there were new proposals to introduce rationing; but both were found administratively too difficult. The tax scheme itself was soon superseded by the plan of charging more at peak hours and seasons, which Gaitskell had put forward earlier but Shinwell had turned down.[101] He revived it as Minister, appointing in February 1948 an advisory committee to report in three months on electricity pricing. Chaired by a former Governor of Assam, Sir Andrew Clow, it was dominated by an old UCL colleague, Professor Ronald Edwards.[102] (Gaitskell told Edwards, with whom he had often discussed the economics of public utilities: 'I can't have you as chairman, I've got to have somebody distinguished!')[79] It duly recommended a differential tariff, higher in winter, lower in summer, and so provoked an angry storm:

> This has always seemed to me common sense and I had no difficulty in getting it through the Cabinet. Also easily persuaded Citrine some time ago. But then suddenly, after it had been through the Cabinet, was informed that all his experts were violently against it ... The meeting with the Area Board chairmen was an uproar ... unbelievably stupid and muddled arguments ... they are all madly keen to sell electricity and just cannot get used to the idea that at the moment they should stop people from buying it ... but ... Citrine got them round to accepting the principle of the thing only with a differential which I regarded as far too small.[1r]

Before doing so, Citrine challenged Gaitskell to issue a General Direction to the board — a legal power which had been used by no Minister then, and very few since — to impose a plan so unpopular that Gaitskell told Edwards its only supporters were 'you, and perhaps me'.[79] It took almost reckless courage for the Minister to tell so powerful a chairman that he would; but when he did, Citrine agreed to comply without it.[27l] Indeed more than once Citrine seemed to be convinced, telling Gaitskell apologetically that he was 'very much suspected by the Area Board chairmen and regarded as a politician ... They would never have [confidence in him] if he did not speak up for them'. He was explaining why he had done that so ferociously, 'losing his temper and accusing the Ministry of trying to dominate the Board and put things across them'.[1t] Gaitskell concluded that Citrine's compromise would have to be accepted, but he persuaded the chairman to reconsider the size of the differential. A week later, with no further contact, Citrine announced one far too small to be effective.[103a] Then the area Boards failed to explain it, and even reduced consumers' bills just when the scheme intended to raise them (by repaying deposits in the first quarter under the new charge). Their opposition, as Gaitskell told his colleagues, 'certainly made it far more difficult to get it accepted by public opinion'.[44i] He still wanted to 'stand firm even if we do lose a few votes';[1x] but the half-hearted scheme made too little difference to justify its unpopularity, and was abandoned the following winter.[27i] The industry had got its way, and official and unofficial commentators lamented for years afterwards the failure to adopt Gaitskell's policy.[104]

Before this defeat, Gaitskell had temperately defended the orthodox Morrisonian view against Aneurin Bevan at a Cripps dinner:

> Being, of course, a glutton for power he does not like the present policy of setting up the semi-autonomous Boards. He wants to control and answer for them; in fact to have them under him like departments. There is of course a good deal in what he says. Certainly it is no easy job to try and establish just the necessary degree of control without going too far. Also it is irritating not to be able to keep them on the right lines all the time. On the other hand there would, I think, be even greater dangers if, for instance, the Coal industries were run entirely by the Department. In any case we are now committed in the case of my industries to the principle of the semi-independent Board, and that being so one must give this particular form and relationship a fair trial.[1c]

But Gaitskell liked to get his own way as much as anyone, and his tussle with the electricity boards made him think again:[105]

> Yesterday I discussed with D[onald] F[ergusson] the general problem and even he I think is having to come round to the view that the Minister really must have a closer contact and more powers. It is really very unsatisfactory having to deal with the Boards as though they were independent authorities with no special obligations to the Government. Yet if they choose that ... without a major and public row there is

very little the Minister can do about it. A possible solution might be to have a Board but make the Minister Chairman of ... it so that it was ... openly under his control.[103a]

He did not change his basic view. His main concern was still with the efficient running of the industries, and other devices were subordinate to that. So he was cautious about consultative councils, which he saw as 'more a safety-valve than anything else'.[51] In coal, for instance, he thought they should deal with the price structure (at which different grades were sold to different consumers) but not the price level (which was not for them, since it depended on the wages of the men and the efficiency of the Coal Board).[44j] He regretted that parliamentary debate was ineffective, but felt that that was 'not particularly important. M.P.s are far too busy to do this properly. What they can do is to serve as a mouthpiece for complaints and criticisms and help to keep Minister and Boards on their toes'.[51]

When MPs did complain, however, Gaitskell remained above all concerned to preserve the morale of the boards; and so remained even after leaving Fuel and Power. He was worried that concessions would discourage their members and encourage Labour's political opponents. Morrison had, since 1947, been keen to fend off public and parliamentary criticism by setting up an 'efficiency unit', nominated by the various boards, to advise them all.[106] He had tried it out on the chairmen at a dinner at the Bank of England in May 1948, which Gaitskell attended.[1g] They objected, but Morrison persisted, steering it through the relevant sub-committee of Labour's National Executive in the autumn;[107] and again urging it on his colleagues after the 1950 election. Gaitskell demurred:

> We must somehow or other avoid giving the Boards of the socialised industries the impression that we believe they are inefficient and that we really have not sufficient confidence in those we appointed to do the job properly ...
> It is even more important to avoid giving the public or Parliament the impression that we have lost confidence in the Boards ... we are trying to achieve at the same time two rather different aims:
> (1)   An improvement in the actual efficiency of the Boards and,
> (2)   an increase in their public accountability ...
> If you try and add — in order to satisfy the public — some superior body continually investigating the activities of the Boards to see whether they are efficient ... it is bound to look like a criticism of the Boards and evidence that the Government do not really trust them.[87b]

Recalling the Burrows Committee, Gaitskell feared that to ensure public confidence the government would appoint outsiders, risking embarrassment whether their reports were published or withheld; while private efficiency checks, perhaps linked with the O&M branch of the Treasury, would not extend public accountability:

> I beg you not to think that the reaction against the efficiency unit proposals is entirely due to tiresome obstinacy on the part of the Chairmen ... We might find ourselves doing most serious damage not only to the reputation of the socialised industries, but also to their efficiency – which is the last thing in the world you would wish.[87b]

Morrison replied that only outside scrutiny would make monopolies attend to public opinion and consumer needs or face unpleasant decisions; and that Parliament would be hard to satisfy: 'if the Chairmen want to avoid [a Select Committee] in the near future they really must help us in putting forward a positive alternative'.[87c] They preferred the Select Committee, which some years later, under the improbable joint aegis of Colonel Lancaster and Ian Mikardo, unexpectedly succeeded in taking the nationalised industries out of the daily political battle.

It was not easy to draw the line between fussy political interference, damaging to the boards' efficiency, and timid political abdication, leaving them as autonomous state monopolies answerable to no one. Though doubtful about institutional checks, Gaitskell – with no precedents to guide him – developed as a Minister a successful middle course. When he left the Department Sir Geoffrey Vickers, one of the ablest members of the National Coal Board, sent him a warm tribute: 'you will be missed here ... we have been properly hotted up, adequately backed up and sufficiently left alone ... if you have set a pattern, everyone will owe you a lot.'[108] For Gaitskell approached the problem as a man deeply committed, both from conviction and for the sake of his own reputation, to making a new industrial experiment work successfully. As a practising politician, he knew that most Labour supporters as well as uncommitted voters would judge success by the kind of practical standards he had set for the coal industry at Whitley Bay.[109] As a Minister, he was familiar with the difficulty of recruiting to run these enterprises the able men without whom they were sure to fail. As a Socialist intellectual, who had thought out his position with his usual thoroughness, he believed that nationalisation of these basic industries would contribute to Socialist aims, not directly by promoting equality, but by improving efficiency.

He attributed current criticisms largely to misunderstanding. Discussing the familiar list in July 1949 with the National Council of Labour – some thirty leaders of the Party and trade union and co-operative movements – he explained the disappointments over appointments, salaries, consultation and centralisation by:

(a) *Expectations* based on
    (1) failure to realise the primarily *technical* nature of case for nationalisation
    (2) failure to apprehend the economics of the position
    (3) failure to understand problems of administration
    (4) failure to understand politics of socialisation.
(b) Hard luck—i.e. Rising Costs.
(c) *Propaganda* against nationalisation—Hatred of size—Effects of limelight.
(d) Weakness in Administration—*Public Relations* all round.[110]

It was a coherent if rather narrow managerial outlook, understandable in a Minister struggling to overcome the teething troubles of new organisations by whose success nationalisation, and even the Labour government, would shortly be judged by the electorate. It explains his fear that elaborate supervisory arrangements would deter good managers from taking on responsibility. It accounts for his curious liking for figurehead appointments, intended to shield the boards from purely partisan attack. It is some excuse for his excessive exasperation at the Fabian pamphlet on the mines which seemed to play into the hands of the opponents of nationalisation; and at the critics of high salaries, on both Left and Right, who threatened to condemn the nationalised industries to second-rate staffs and board members. He himself when out of office always tried to follow the line he would have taken in government; so he was shocked at the irresponsibility of the Conservative Opposition, and innocently believed that they could not expect to win the next election—otherwise they would not attack the boards so much.[111a] Early in his term as Minister, he denounced the 'persistent "smear" campaign by sections of the diehard Press and reactionary elements in the Tory Party';[26b] and at the end of it he exclaimed angrily in an election speech:

> They have obstinately resisted all the Government's efforts to take the nationalised industries out of politics. They have shown bitter hostility ... scoffed and sneered ... belittled every achievement and magnified every weakness. How can you trust them ... [after] such an orgy of slander ... ?[26c]

vi   *Politics and Social Life*

'An orgy of slander' was not too strong a phrase for the bitterness displayed on domestic matters by the Attlee Cabinet's opponents. Social tensions were acute, and much of the middle class bitterly resented Labour controls, Labour austerity and the very existence of a Labour government. A generation later a leading political correspondent wrote that he had 'never known the Press so consistently and irresponsibly political, slanted and prejudiced' as it was at this time.[112]

A fairly flourishing black market enabled many 'spivs' to make a dishonest living by evading the controls: the slender foundation for a shameful whispering campaign against Socialist corruption. It led to the Lynskey Tribunal of Inquiry, which reported at the beginning of 1947 on allegations against Ministers, civil servants and public figures who had had dealings with a flamboyant contact man, Sydney Stanley. Both Gaitskell and Bevan detested this method of investigation, for reasons now generally familiar. Bevan characteristically wanted to counter-attack with a Bill requiring disclosure of the source of all Party funds, and Gaitskell wrote equally characteristically, 'If this is practical there is certainly something to be said for it'.[103b] Gaitskell found that lawyers were increasingly coming to see the Tribunal as 'abominably unfair', and that the Ministers at Cripps's dinners felt it quite the wrong way to deal with matters of great political importance.

He was himself departmentally involved, for one of the two men censured was the trade unionist George Gibson, a director of the Bank of England and chairman of the North-Western Electricity Board. His case greatly troubled Gaitskell, who read the evidence by and about him and believed he had behaved foolishly but in no way discreditably:

> Reading the evidence made me more and more furious about the unfairness of the Enquiry. People are de facto put in the Dock but not given the right to defend themselves freely ... it is absolutely intolerable that three lawyers, advised by three other lawyers, should be laying down rules as to what is etiquette for Ministers and public men. Their complete ignorance of the machine and other worldly matters comes out very clearly in the questions put.[103c]

After discussions with Attlee, Morrison, Cripps and the Chief Whip it had been agreed to leave Gibson's fate until the Tribunal reported; when he was censured, Attlee and Morrison felt that he had to go. Gaitskell, like Citrine, thought that wrong, but Robens convinced him that a Minister could not challenge the Tribunal's verdict. He was saved from an unhappy dilemma – which might have had to go to Cabinet – by Gibson's own decision to resign. Gaitskell was 'very upset', and seriously considered speaking in the debate.[113] But

> I cannot very well denounce the Tribunal without bringing some discredit on the Party because it will be said that one Member of the Government wanted to whitewash the sinners ... I still believe that the procedure is very unfair. I told the Chief Whip I cannot vote for the Government motion, and he accepted that. He did not want me to

speak, but I warned him that I might if Gibson was attacked ... I
wish I was better at making up my mind on these difficult conscience
issues.[103d]

The great exposure of Socialist corruption ended with revelations of some
dubious business practices, full vindication of the civil servants, and
the ruin of an indiscreet trade unionist and an imprudent junior
politician.[114]

A supposedly respectable form of this unsavoury campaign was to
attack Labour appointments as 'jobs for the boys'.* Gaitskell, who had
been criticised by MPs on his own side for refusing to bestow political
patronage, was one of the victims. Two BBC comedians, the Western
Brothers, broadcast on 9 October 1948 on Saturday night's 'Music Hall' —
a regular 'platform for Tory propaganda', as one listener complained.[115]
They told a 'joke' which began: 'Did you hear about the new job advertised
by the National Coal Board? Well, there were many thousands of applicants'; and ended: 'Now, who do you think got the job? Mr. Gaitskell's
nephew.' (Various acquaintances asked Gaitskell if he had a nephew
working for the board; in fact he had over-scrupulously discouraged his
stepson Raymond Frost, who was keenly interested, from even applying.)[116]
Senior Ministers very seriously considered legal proceedings. The Solicitor-
General advised that Gaitskell could obtain damages, and the Lord Chancellor and Cripps both wanted him to sue.[1h] Sir Donald Fergusson saw it as
'a glaring case in a series of insinuations which are constantly being made
in "Music Hall jokes" ', and advised consulting Herbert Morrison and the
Prime Minister, but doubted whether the Government would gain in the
long run from a lawsuit: 'comedians would never forget and they might do
you a lot of harm'.[13c] Morrison minuted: 'Personally I'm not necessarily
averse [to legal action]. But the tradition is that Ministers don't.' He
advised suing only if the BBC or the comedians refused to make an ample
public apology, to which in fact they consented.[117]

A few months later Gaitskell was again the victim of distasteful publicity.
The prospective Liberal candidate for South Leeds alleged that an attendant asked him to move when he sat down opposite Gaitskell (who had
never met him) in a dining car on the London train. Gaitskell thought the
attendant might have acted without his knowledge.[118a] The Hotels
Executive (responsible for dining cars) said that he had never requested or
received preferential treatment, and after solemn enquiry found no trace
of the incident. The charge was quite implausible, for no public figure had
better manners than Gaitskell, and less pomposity or 'side'. That very
week he had given up his own reserved compartment to a family without

* Many fewer Labour politicians received paid public employment from Attlee
after the war than Conservatives from Churchill during it.

seats;[119] and one night around this time, when Jim Orrick was coming to stay, Gaitskell met him at Victoria – rightly guessing his old Oxford friend would lose the address and forget the time difference between Paris and London.[120]

By 1949 Gaitskell was no longer overworking and had time for holidays. Before Easter he spent a few 'exquisite' days at Abbotsbury with Dora, then opened a miners' convalescent home at Swanage: 'They were all very friendly but the speeches after the dinner in the evening lasted for $3\frac{1}{2}$ hours. I spoke for ten minutes.'[1p] At Whitsun he went on a strenuous expedition to the Lake District with Dalton, now back in office, and he and Alf Robens lost themselves and their wives in the neighbourhood of Langdale Pikes.[84c] In the summer an old 1917 Club acquaintance ran into him on holiday in Jersey, 'in shorts, climbing cliffs with the children and having a wonderful time ... he was a very unstuffy person'.[121] He was also meeting the Establishment, gossiping at a Royal Naval College Services dinner with the C-in-C Mediterranean, a popular admiral 'with shocking views about almost everything but I believe very good at his job', then attending a Peterhouse Feast as the guest of his old friend M. M. Postan, and talking at length to Canon Raven, the pacifist Vice-Chancellor of Cambridge. In London he noted a subtle change:

> There has been the usual run of social engagements, Buckingham Palace parties and garden parties, etc. The general feeling seems to be that the shadow of the coming election was visible. The parties seemed to be more Tory and less democratic than before. I do not think this is entirely imagination – all my colleagues seem to have the same opinion.[1v]

That did not make him at all inclined to political compromise. Like both Cripps and Dalton, usually keen nationalisers, he was against the proposed takeover of industrial insurance.[122] But in principle he remained a convinced egalitarian, and privately at this time would argue seriously for complete, universal, Shavian-style equality of incomes.[123*] Publicly, he told the Oxford University Labour Club that though the government had done much to make incomes more equal, 'Property is still very unequally divided, and that is a problem which has got to be tackled [by the] taxation of inheritance on a still larger scale'.[23d] The press gave it a little publicity, and Cripps asked him how his Budget was getting on. The Budget season was the wrong time to mention taxation, but Gaitskell felt privately that 'really a Socialist Minister must occasionally be allowed to draw attention to the unequal distribution of property'.[1x]

---

* As Chancellor he modified this to: no one should get over £5,000 a year.[123]

He would have liked to keep the beer tax, raise the petrol tax and limit the increase in food prices. Instead, Cripps cut both beer tax and food subsidies:

> For once in a way I found myself agreeing with Bevan ... that the Budget was ... regrettable, chiefly because it would weaken Stafford's position in the Party. I am not sure whether he really minds about this. It is just possible that he regards Stafford as a very much better future Prime Minister than Morrison, and does not think of himself as competing just yet.[1x]

Owing to flu, Gaitskell missed the secret conclave in the Isle of Wight where the Labour Ministers and National Executive met to discuss the future. Like Bevan, he strongly favoured an autumn election; unlike Bevan — and unlike most of the Party — he was far from sure that Labour would win by fifty seats.[103e] The complacent mood was soon to be shattered by a new dollar crisis leading to the devaluation of sterling, in which Gaitskell emerged for the first time in a central political role.

In the shadow of that mounting crisis, not yet realised by the man in the street, Gaitskell again attracted the unwelcome attentions of the press when the emotions that seethed behind his front of rational intellectuality broke through for the first time in public. On 6 July 1949 he was speaking to the NUM's annual conference at Porthcawl, three hours before the Chancellor was to make a statement in the House on the dollar situation.[62] He dealt at length with mine safety and with Coal Board appointments, then suddenly dropped his script to talk of 'a moment of supreme crisis for the Government', and of his pride in his experiences as a Minister visiting the coalfields. 'Mr. Gaitskell was overcome with emotion,' wrote one journalist; 'tears welled in his eyes, his voice faltered';[124] and another: 'His face was deathly white, and for a moment he staggered as if he was about to collapse'.[52d] As Gaitskell himself recorded:

> [T]ears came into my eyes and I had to stop speaking for a few seconds and have a drink of water. From the point of view of the speech it was, I suppose, extremely effective. Emotion is infectious, and as somebody said to me afterwards when I apologised, it was what really made the speech ...
>
> Some of the comments I must confess turned my stomach and made me hate journalists even more.* And I feel that way because as a speech it was a very good one ...
>
> I also believe it may materially have affected the subsequent debates

---

* For instance, the suggestion that the government had staged the incident, choosing Gaitskell to perform because as a university lecturer he must have 'great histrionic ability'.[125]

in the Conference about the Coal Board and about wage demands.

... I rather expected that the Chancellor or the P.M. might tick me
off because I had got out of step but ... subsequent events have so
much proved me right that in the long run it was probably not a bad
thing for me to have spoken as I did.[1v]

As these events developed into a major crisis, Gaitskell—not yet even in
the Cabinet—was given partial and temporary responsibility for the
Treasury. As in the fuel crisis, but now on a larger stage, he rose to the
challenge and played a decisive role which was soon to bring him to the
Chancellorship, and eventually to the leadership of the Party.

vii   *Minister for Energy*

Overworked eighteen months before, Gaitskell could be spared from his
Department in the summer of 1949 because by then its work was completely under control. That meant much more than routine administration
on the lines suggested by civil servants or boards of nationalised industries.
Most Ministers of Fuel and Power before and since have been—as one
senior civil servant put it—'blown about by the industries'. Gaitskell, however, had set as one of his mid-term aims the development of a coherent
fuel policy, and saw it as his function to represent the wider public interest
as interpreted by government policy, and to ensure that the narrower perspectives of the industries themselves did not prevail over it.

That outlook brought him into conflict with some powerful forces. The
NUM won very substantial and overdue improvements for its members,
but eventually had to be warned that there could be no more without real
gains in production; and his appeals had a real impact because the union's
leaders were convinced that the government was genuinely trying to share
resources fairly, and therefore recognised the state of the economy, saw
their own interests in long-term perspective instead of short, and used their
tremendous bargaining power responsibly. The electricity boards, led by
an able man of great influence in the Labour movement, acquired a share
of investment resources which seemed vast to outsiders but quite inadequate
to themselves because Gaitskell would not back their full demands—
though they did successfully obstruct his unpopular attempt to make
tariffs bear a proper relationship to costs. More formidable still were the
oil companies, backed by the Foreign Office and by the Oil Division of his
own Ministry.

Oil was the subject of Gaitskell's first paper to the Cabinet, written in
the crowded weeks after he became Minister, and of fifteen of the ninety-
six that followed it.[126] He himself discovered the large, hidden drain of
dollars through Bahrain and he actively encouraged a thorough inter-

departmental investigation of the problem, characteristically insisting on reading all the *official* working papers himself; it found that the three British oil companies made a positive contribution to the balance of payments so huge that some of his colleagues thought a couple of noughts had been added to the figures by mistake.[21b]

Before the war, Britain had imported 82 per cent of her oil as finished products, nearly half of it from the Caribbean. Vital dollars could be saved by purchasing Middle East crude from new fields in the sterling area, if only the oil companies would refine in Great Britain instead of on the oilfields themselves. That aim was actively favoured by the Marshall Plan authorities and, encouraged by new technical developments, American companies as well as British ones had by 1953 invested over £150 million in refineries, notably at Fawley in Hampshire. Gaitskell vigorously promoted the policy, successfully fighting for steel in the Production Committee. By 1951 the new refineries enabled Britain to export more oil than coal.[127]

The Ministry of Fuel and Power was anxious to keep the goodwill of the American companies, for the British government had no statutory powers and could only coax them into home refining, buying their tankers from British yards, or contributing in other ways to the British balance of payments. The companies were keen to return to competition and get rid of the Petroleum Board, which during and after the war distributed 'pool' petrol to consumers and allocated the proceeds to producers under an agreed scheme. On efficiency grounds there was quite a good case for nationalising oil distribution, but 40 per cent of it was in American hands. After a thorough investigation the Department ruled out that solution because of international complications, and therefore favoured dissolving the Board.[128] Gaitskell was reluctant, turning down the first draft Cabinet paper proposing it as far too favourable to private enterprise, but he agreed in the end, and in July 1948 the Petroleum Board was dissolved.[129] In December, Morrison's NEC sub-committee on the next Party programme also suggested nationalising oil distribution in Britain, and asked Gaitskell for his view – within three working days.[130] For once his reply simply reproduced (with one trivial grammatical amendment!) a minute from Fergusson urging 'two overwhelming objections ... so long as we are dependent on Marshall Aid and have not solved our balance of payments problem'. To take over the American share of distribution in Britain

would cause an uproar in the U.S.A., not only in itself but because of the effect it might have in encouraging other Governments to nationalise ... The whole Marshall Aid Plan would be jeopardised, not only because of American objections to the economic aspects of the policy ...but because Americans would ... regard it as threatening American as well as British command of oil resources and trade throughout the world.[131]

Moreover, if British companies elsewhere 'were nationalised by foreign Governments we should lose an immense amount of invisible exports .We cannot afford to risk this loss by setting an example of nationalisation'.[131]

Gaitskell clearly foresaw the danger for the British economy of dependence on Middle Eastern oil:

> Should Russia over-run this area there would not merely be insufficient oil for Britain but for a large part of the rest of the world. And, even without Russia it is difficult enough. The Arab States are making difficulties about the pipeline because of the Palestine question. God knows when we shall really get our expansion programme going there, and how precarious it will all be even when the output is doubled as we plan in the next four to five years.[1e]

But there was no simple way to replace dollar oil by sterling oil, as Gaitskell's detailed inquiries soon ascertained.[1f] When he left the Department, a prominent oilman called him 'the Minister who absorbed more quickly than any other the intricate problems of the oil industry'.[132]

That was not a euphemism for a man bemused by the experts or captured by the companies. Contrary to official advice, he kept up energetic pressure on the American firms, which operated in the sterling as well as in the dollar area, to switch the oil they sold to Britain to sterling sources. That, he wrote, was

> a great and important issue which is going to loom larger and larger in the next months and perhaps years. Fundamentally there is a conflict between the American desire to help Europe become independent of dollar aid, which really involves the switching from dollar to nondollar sources, and the desire of the American exporters, such as the Oil Companies, to continue to supply Europe.[1x]

The conflict would become acute as soon as the British oil companies had a surplus. Under the loan agreement, which forbade discrimination, Britain would not be allowed to exclude oil which cost dollars and import only oil which could be paid for in sterling; so that unless a compromise could be negotiated in Washington, British consumption would still need to be restricted in order to save dollars – which were being spent unnecessarily when alternative supplies were available. In the worst phase of the currency crisis:

> Where it was expected that we could save 85 million dollars – we cannot without 'discrimination' save more than 30. But all efforts on my part to have this problem discussed and resolved have been blocked by the

Foreign Secretary who is terrified of the reactions of the U.S. Oil Companies. I hope to return to the attack before long.[103f]

And early the following year:

The Americans are being extremely tiresome ... [over] the vested interests of the U.S. Oil Companies resisting like hell the policy of H.M.G., which is to save dollars by substituting sterling for dollar oil ... American policy [is] to grant E.C. [European Co-operation] Aid in order to help us overcome the dollar crisis; but to resist like anything our efforts to do so if these involve displacing American exporters from overseas markets.[1y]

In the long run, however, Gaitskell was successful, for the dollar share of British oil imports fell from 52·6 per cent in 1947 to 32 per cent in 1950 and −largely because of policies he had initiated−to only 19 per cent late in 1953, at an annual saving of £150 million.[133]

Some supposed friends of Britain proved even more difficult than the Americans. The Australian Labour Government, 'extremely loyal and firm', had declined to damage sterling by de-rationing petrol, but the Liberal Opposition promised to do so and (so Gaitskell understood) won the election largely by that rash and irresponsible pledge. Despite many telegrams, talks at the Colombo conference, and a British offer of a Commonwealth Conference to discuss oil consumption, the new Prime Minister Robert Menzies, for fear of splitting his Cabinet, used 'completely specious arguments' to insist on de-rationing. Gaitskell was angry. 'We have prepared what I regard as a rather masterly statement which appears to be extremely courteous and polite and high minded, but in fact thoroughly blackens the Australian Government as they deserve to be blackened.'[103g]

Meanwhile Gaitskell was trying to negotiate an agreement in Washington by which the American companies, operating in both currency zones, would take sterling instead of dollars and would be allowed a larger share of the market in compensation.[134] The State Department seemed to him heavily influenced by the companies and afraid of the political trouble they could make, but in May 1950−when he had moved from Fuel and Power to the Treasury−a compromise was reached: both British and American companies produced extra supplies, in return for de-rationing petrol throughout the sterling area.[103h] His immediate reaction was: 'I've got to say "Snap!" to this.'[135]

The principles of Gaitskell's domestic fuel policy were that the industries should be co-ordinated to secure maximum efficiency at the lowest cost; and that the consumer should then choose the fuel he preferred at a realistic price, allowing for damage inflicted on other people and reflecting, for example, the real cost of electricity at peak periods.[26d] He had no love for controls for their own sake. He defended petrol rationing when it was most unpopular, but got rid of it as soon as he could. He thought Harold Wilson's 'bonfire' of controls in 1949 unwise, because it would have been more advantageous politically to drop them gradually over the year.[1x] But wherever possible the consumer should have a free choice. After six years of restriction Gaitskell allowed him to change coal merchants — which meant overruling the Coal Board, who had agreed to enforce fixed margins for wholesalers by boycotting any merchant who undercut. At a dinner for junior Coal Board staff, he interrogated them on the point, then gleefully told Hyndley: 'Your young men agree with me and not with you';[136] and he would not authorise the proposed monopolistic arrangement.

He took more interest than most Ministers of Fuel and Power in the contribution of science, and viewed it in a longer-term perspective than most of his advisers. As Parliamentary Secretary he had no impact, for Fergusson took the administrator's view that scientists should be 'on tap not on top', and Shinwell dissolved his advisory committee of distinguished scientists when it tried to move beyond discussing the best appliances for domestic grates. But on becoming Minister Gaitskell took the matter up again, appointing a strong Scientific Advisory Council, and overruling Fergusson to bring in Sir Harold Roxbee Cox (later Lord Kings Norton) as Chief Scientist with executive powers. That was a unique position for a scientist in Whitehall, and it continued after Gaitskell's time; even in 1963 when Sir Burke Trend's committee reported, Fuel and Power was well in advance of other Departments. The new Chief Scientist had the full backing of his Minister in carrying out experimental work likely to yield results only in the long term: on the gas turbine, where it helped improve the industry's sluggish technological record, or on deriving oil (and gas) from coal, which might have made the whole economy less vulnerable to a Middle Eastern crisis. Most of this work was to be abandoned before it could have come to fruition.[137]

Like Dalton, Gaitskell was ahead of his time in attaching importance to 'quality of life' issues. On some environmental questions such as Oxford's perennial road problem, he was in the mainstream of the Establishment, telling Jay once in their official car from Hampstead to Whitehall: 'If they spoil Christ Church Meadow, I won't move the gas works!'[138] He disliked the open-cast coal programme, and insisted that the ruined land must be properly restored. He cancelled some open-cast operations on amenity grounds, and reduced the scale of others;[23e] and would have abandoned the policy entirely had not Douglas Jay persuaded him that would be too risky.[21c] He was keen on smoke abatement during his own term at Fuel and Power, and he strongly supported his successor's measures on it after becoming Chancellor; out of office he made further speeches about it, and as Party leader he once asked an amazed Cecil King if it would be a vote-winner.[139]

*   *   *

Gaitskell was an excellent Minister of Fuel and Power. He knew all the Department's varied activities in such detail as greatly to impress a sceptical City audience: 'He could tell them where every tanker was on the high seas.'[140] The command of and interest in detail was no bar to delegation; his Parliamentary Secretary had a full say on general departmental policies, but Gaitskell never interfered with Robens's handling of any specific assignments like the administration of petrol rationing, or fuel conservation. His 'fantastic industry' and 'prodigious capacity' for 'absorbing material like blotting-paper' allowed him to penetrate into detail without losing sight of long-term policy.[141]

In spite of his later reputation for obstinacy, he was eager to seek advice. He was delighted when a visitor from the north brought a point of view unfamiliar in Whitehall.[142] When the Coal Board put forward a technical proposal with unwelcome political implications, Gaitskell asked for the technical reasons without trying at all to edge towards a more palatable conclusion, then accepted the advice without more ado, saying it was his task as Minister to take care of the political consequences.[143] Nor was he too stubborn to change his mind, as Douglas Jay induced him to do over open-cast coal. He would yield to argument, but not to political seniority or the weight of the Whitehall machine. When the high officials of the Investment Programmes Committee put forward to the Production Committee of the Cabinet an allocation which Gaitskell had not seen, he flatly refused to accept it—and Cripps, the chairman, gave way and agreed to reconsider.[21d] Indeed his views carried so much weight in the Chancellor's eyes that Gaitskell could tell one journalist:

> Sometimes we disagreed on something and it went to the Cabinet, but on more than one occasion when it got there he deliberately refrained from opposing me, and indeed sometimes supported me, feeling that as I was the Minister concerned I must really decide.[144]

Gaitskell's decisions were his own, but he was skilful at winning assent to them without either offending or capitulating to those affected. The former managing director of the Gas Light and Coke Company wrote when he left the Ministry regretting 'losing such an admirable Minister ... It has been a great pleasure to serve under you as we knew that you had the interest of the Gas Industry always in mind and this did a great deal to take away the bitterness of nationalisation'.[145] He could stand up to the unions when necessary, refusing (unlike his Tory successors) to abandon the incentive element in the attendance bonus for miners.[30d] But he still established excellent relations with the General and Municipal Workers, who were dominant in the gas industry;[146] and Dalton—whose constituency was in the Durham coalfield—rightly told the Prime Minister that

Gaitskell 'had done jolly well with the miners, who now much preferred him to his predecessor'.[111b]

By his civil servants he was universally respected – but less often called by his Christian name than Shinwell had been. A few of the older men resented his independence of mind, his willingness to seek advice from juniors, his determination not to be run by the industries. But others maintained stoutly that when he disagreed with his advisers he was almost always right. And however they found him as a person, all his civil servants recognised and admired his qualities: inordinate industry; businesslike habits; persistence and intelligence in dealing with other Departments; clarity of mind; incisiveness and decisiveness; drive; intellectual courage; and integrity.[147] 'We get rare pleasure', wrote one who knew him well, 'out of seeing you take hold of all sorts of bowling.'[84b] Apart from the concern for detail he approached the administrator's ideal of a Minister. Fuel and Power was a difficult Department in which to enhance a political reputation. But when Gaitskell left it, Fergusson wrote welcoming the 'wide public recognition of your great success' in the office – and already saw him as a future leader of his Party.[13d]

Outside the Department, his personality had made no great impression. The storm over petrol rationing had died down; and while the serious papers regarded him as a successful and competent administrator, readers of the popular press knew him best from a series of unhappy accidents – the baths episode, the Western Brothers 'joke', the dining-car incident, the tears at Porthcawl. In the House he had a few devoted admirers and much goodwill, notably among the miner MPs. He took immense trouble with his parliamentary correspondence and with parliamentary questions, and handled those ordeals, especially difficult for a young Minister, with considerable success. Later on, as a Party leader who worked far too hard, he was often accused of inadequate contact with his parliamentary followers; but as a Minister he frequented the tea-room most assiduously and kept in careful touch with back-benchers.[148] He was courteous and persuasive in ordinary committee debates, and coped very successfully with the extraordinary challenge of the Gas Bill filibuster. But his major speeches showed little trace of the two whiskies he took beforehand to steady his nerves. An intelligent new Labour Member, elected in 1949, found them 'deadly dull'; a civil servant, who approved of his policies, called his style 'if not "right but repulsive", at least "right but not very attractive" '. Most of his speeches were lectures, well-organised and thorough, informative and fair-minded, without much humour, sparkle or punch.[149] But as one trade union MP, who had been very critical of Gaitskell, shrewdly observed: 'It was always to your advantage when the Opposition went for you ... it brought the best out of you to reply to them, without referring to your prepared brief ... severe tests ... bring the best out of you'.[89c]

Within a year, and with only five years' parliamentary experience, Gaitskell became Chancellor of the Exchequer. This meteoric success he owed partly to the exhaustion of the senior Ministers whose health was shattered by ten gruelling years in high office. He owed it partly to the first-class administrative competence that had made him a success in a Department where another accident-prone Minister, like his predecessor, might have brought the government into serious disrepute. His economic expertise was a help. But above all he owed his promotion to his handling of a major crisis. Like the fuel crisis of 1947, devaluation in 1949 enabled Gaitskell to demonstrate his rare ability to meet a greater challenge even more successfully than he had dealt previously with lesser ones. The general public, the Party and Parliament were unaware of it. But in the summer of 1949 the tribal chiefs of Whitehall and the senior men in the government – Attlee, Cripps, Morrison and Bevin – discovered Hugh Gaitskell's most important quality: his capacity for growth.

Appendix

The following note appears in HG's handwriting (Papers, file P.19):

Looking backward.

A. Achieved since becoming Minister in October 1947.
Petrol black market abolished.
Small basic Ration restored to all and some contribution to Defence but no higher imports.
Dissolution of P[etroleum] B[oard] carried out without trouble or criticism.
Coal/Oil conversion halted and kept under control without serious trouble.
New Petroleum Industry C'ttees set up.
Better relations with motoring organisations established.
Electricity Area Boards and (nearly all) Consultative Councils – apparently working successfully.
Clow Committee and Report – Winter Differential introduced.
Realistic Generating Programme laid down and Progressing arrangement nearly settled.
Load spreading by commercial consumers introduced.

Coal Output increase doubled in 1948.

Exports trebled   „ „

Coal budgeting and Statistics on a proper basis.

Disposal of low quality coal (partial success only).

Better relations with N[ational] C[oal] B[oard] and N[ational] U[nion of] M[ineworkers].

J[oint] P[it] P[roduction] C[ommittee].

Burrows Committee trouble overcome.

Coal Bill drafted and in Committee.

Gas Bill drafted and passed.

Main Gas Appointments made.

Coke Oven Programme tackled.

Appointment of S[cientific] A[dvisory] C[ouncil] and Chief Scientist.

B.   Not achieved since becoming Minister.

N[ational] C[oal] B[oard] not really developing fast enough — too little enterprise and drive — Board itself not right — Nothing much done here, though relations with Ministry good.

B[ritish] E[lectricity] A[uthority]   Relations with us not satisfactory — too distant and hostile — suspicious — ? Meeting with Boards.

Public Relations though improved still not wholly satisfactory.

Fuel and Power Coordination — not much done here.

Coal Distribution — nothing here except some more freedom.

Lighting Controls —

So it really amounts to this.

Chief jobs in 1949 are:

Reorganisation of N[ational] C[oal] B[oard]

Better and closer relations with B[ritish] E[lectricity] A[uthority]

Coordination of Fuel and Power

Coal Distribution inquiry

Lighting controls

to which should be added

Gas Boards in action

Subsidence

Mineral development

Refining Programme

Coke Oven Programme.

PART THREE

TWO YEARS AT THE CENTRE

'Such wonderful talent ... such a difficult team worker'
(HG ON ANEURIN BEVAN, 1951)
'He's nothing, nothing, nothing ... The Party will sweep him away'
(BEVAN ON HG, 1950 AND 1951)

CHAPTER 7

THE TREASURY: SUBSTITUTING FOR STAFFORD CRIPPS 1949–50

'Being in the centre does ... appeal to me'
(HG ON GOING TO THE TREASURY, MARCH 1950)
'Opportunity is carrying you forward on a great wave'
(DALTON TO HG, SEPTEMBER 1950)

i Devaluation: 'Vice-Chancellor of the Exchequer'

FOUR years after the end of the war, Labour Britain had made an impressive economic recovery. Exports (by volume) were at a record level, up by half in two years, so that overseas trade was almost in balance.[1a] Since 1945 they had risen from 50 per cent below pre-war to nearly 55 per cent above, and paid for 85 per cent of imports instead of one-third:[2] the best performance in Europe. Industrial production by volume in the first half of 1949 was 30 per cent above 1938; and output per man-hour had since the war increased faster than in the United States.[3] These achievements depended on strict controls at home, to direct resources into essential activities, and abroad, to check flights of capital and to use scarce gold and dollar reserves only for food and raw materials. Wherever possible non-dollar supplies had to be found, exports channelled to dollar markets, and 'hard currency' conserved for indispensable needs. But that involved discrimination offensive to the Americans' interests and ideology, and to the commitments they had extracted in return for Lend-Lease and the 1945 loan. After the loan agreement, sterling had for the moment seemed secure, as it did again once Marshall Aid was settled: 1946 and 1948 were favourable years. But in 1947 American insistence led to the disastrous experiment in convertibility of sterling, which dissipated most of the loan; and in 1949 a sharp recession in the United States curtailed her purchases abroad, reduced the outflow of dollars, and at once revealed the precariousness of the pound.

The acute crisis which followed led to a sharp struggle over economic policy. Many, though not all, of the government's official and financial advisers disliked the restrictions on trade and capital movements and were, like the Americans, eager to reintegrate Britain into the international economy, for reasons often political as much as economic. But with the gold and dollar reserves dangerously low, dismantling controls would make the stability of the currency dependent on the goodwill of foreign investors and bankers, and thus would strengthen overwhelmingly those domestic forces which were calling for severe deflation and heavy cuts in public expenditure, especially on social services and food subsidies. Labour Ministers believed those expenditures both desirable in themselves and necessary to retain trade union goodwill under the full employment which they were determined to preserve.

Nor did they believe with the foreign and domestic bankers that the problem was due to inflation within Britain, curable in orthodox fashion by deflating the domestic economy until the foreign account balanced at a low level of activity. The great export drive could not have succeeded so spectacularly if British costs and prices had been severely out of line; and it was not the United Kingdom but the rest of the sterling area which suffered the greatest fall in dollar earnings when the United States recession reduced that country's purchases everywhere. Douglas Jay maintained that the imbalance between North America and Europe was structural, going back to 1914, but that it had long been masked by the European reserves which had now vanished.[4] The devaluation of the pound in September 1949, in the long run inevitable, was precipitated by the reluctance of foreigners who anticipated it to hold sterling. But in those days of political and economic uncertainty, devaluation was a traumatic as well as a dramatic step. For conservative men it still reeked of immorality; for chauvinists (or politicians who worried about them) it spelt national or party humiliation; for the cautious it was a leap in the dark — though, once decided upon, it had to be on a large enough scale to leave no expectation that another might follow. In all these debates Hugh Gaitskell was a central figure.

Gaitskell took on extra responsibilities at the Treasury in the summer of 1949. Cripps was away ill in Switzerland, and his duties were nominally taken over by Attlee, officially assisted by a youthful 'triumvirate'. The senior was Harold Wilson as a member of the Cabinet, but he had a heavy load as President of the Board of Trade; Douglas Jay was one of the junior Treasury Ministers (and the other, Glenvil Hall, would also have been involved had not he too fallen ill); Gaitskell, still Minister of Fuel and Power, played the principal role. He took up these new duties at a crucial moment, when a recession in the United States was making dollars desperately short. His conduct during the crisis made his reputation among senior men in Whitehall and in the Cabinet.

Treasury views were divided. Some officials found in the currency crisis an opportunity to press for major policy changes and sharp deflation at home. Gaitskell, while recognising the need for limited cuts in public expenditure, was primarily responsible for frustrating the pressures for a more extreme course; for he was a staunch defender of import and currency controls and he would have resigned if the government had again accepted a return to convertibility. There were other high officials who had long seen devaluation as the only remedy for the dollar shortage. Once convinced of that, it was Gaitskell – still outside the Cabinet – who gave them the necessary political backing, and successfully urged the policy on the senior Ministers and especially the sick and reluctant Chancellor. 'In effect, at the moment of crisis, he took charge as the man who knew what needed to be done and was able to do it.'[5a]

The dollar problem and the American pressures had alarmed him before he took up his Treasury assignment in mid-July. The threatened United States recession was reducing her purchases and therefore the flow of dollars, and no one could be sure how much Marshall Aid Congress would vote.[6a] At one Thursday dinner when Cripps was away, the other economic Ministers were determined not to deflate and as yet unconvinced of the need to devalue; they preferred to seek alternative supplies, available only by making arrangements – bilateral pacts at first, multilateral trading between non-dollar countries later – which would discriminate against the United States. To Gaitskell's surprise and pleasure, at the Cabinet's Economic Policy Committee (EPC) Cripps and Bevin also endorsed those views – though unlike Gaitskell Bevin remained fairly hopeful of persuading Washington. Experience was later to soften Gaitskell's suspicions of the Americans, but in 1949 he was gloomy about them, writing in June:

> They want to force us to make all the effort to push our exports into the United States, and no doubt if necessary would say that we ought to deflate ourselves to achieve this. Nevertheless, if we were to succeed they would probably be demanding higher tariffs! ... They complain that our exports replace theirs in non-dollar areas but will not take the only step to prevent this which is to lend or give away dollars.[6b]

A week later, just before the EPC meeting, he wrote that the crisis had worsened, and

> we are at the parting of the ways. If we continue to aim at convertibility and multilateralism, I do not see how we can avoid deflation and devaluation now that the American slump is deepening. But if we do neither and go in for ... trade discrimination in a big way against dollars and a great effort to replace dollar supplies with supplies from other areas, we risk the cutting off altogether of Marshall Aid.[6c]

That was the context of his emotional reference at Porthcawl to 'a moment of supreme crisis for the Government'.

Gaitskell had wondered if that incident would damage his political prospects. Instead, a few days later he was for the first time brought into the very centre of policy-making as a result of the multiple illnesses which forced Cripps to take leave in 1949 (and to resign late in the following year). At the beginning of 1949, Harold Wilson would have seemed a much likelier successor. It was Gaitskell's leadership over devaluation which so impressed his seniors that he became the preferred choice of both the Prime Minister and Cripps. In Jay's words, he

> made up his mind clearly and decisively what needed to be done; convinced the doubters ... and supervised all the arrangements ... [persuading] those few who knew the facts that, if Cripps' health failed, Hugh Gaitskell was the only possible Chancellor ... [and] determining the subsequent leadership of the Labour Party and so much else.[5a]

Gaitskell wrote, in two instalments on 3 August and 21 September 1949, a full narrative of the crisis. This account is based on it, together with that of another diarist, Hugh Dalton, and the recollections of other leading participants.[7] Between the end of June and Cripps's departure for Switzerland on 18 July, there were four meetings of the EPC to discuss the steady drain on the reserves.[8a b] The Chancellor was too ill to give an effective lead, and though in theory import savings of $700 million were agreed, Gaitskell doubted whether any of the sterling area countries, even Britain, would achieve them in practice. There was no agreed long-term line, and while Cripps and Bevin were still opposed to convertibility, Gaitskell was acutely worried by those Treasury officials for whom it was the main long-term objective, with devaluation and heavy deflation at home as the immediate steps. Bevin, records the diary,

> while opposed instinctively to any 'cuts' at home – he hates austerity – and opposed also instinctively to 'The Gold Standard' is also determined to rescue the world by successful negotiation in Washington ... Undoubtedly the danger is that these two most powerful Members of the Government on their own in Washington and advised by the Treasury, whose views are 'liberal' will agree to long term ties which will be eventually ruinous to us for the sake of some short term gain. They may indeed be driven to this because of the state of the reserves by the autumn.[6d]

At one of these early July meetings, Cripps himself surprised Gaitskell by saying when the civil servants had left: 'One of my difficulties is that my official advisers are all "liberals" and I cannot really rely on them to carry through a "socialist" [sic] policy in these negotiations.'[9] At Dalton's suggestion Douglas Jay was brought into the talks with the Commonwealth Finance Ministers and with the US Secretary of the Treasury, John Snyder.[10] That counterweight to the official advice proved crucial later on.

Talk of a coming devaluation, in Washington and London, was one of the major reasons for the run on the reserves. That step had for some time seemed inevitable to two high officials: Sir Edwin Plowden, head of the planning staff, and Robert Hall, director of the Economic Section of the Cabinet Office. By the end of June, Attlee and Morrison had broadly come round to their view, but Cripps and Bevin had not.[8a c] As Gaitskell recorded:

> Harold Wilson now says he also favoured it then, but if so he certainly did not say so. Others were against — Hugh Dalton especially strongly — on the logical grounds that it would widen not narrow the gap. Others ... thought ... devaluation was just another way of reducing the standard of living of the working class.[6d]

Gaitskell did not share the worries about consequences at home, but he doubted whether British exports to the dollar area would expand sufficiently to justify devaluation. At the start of July he still hoped to rely on discriminatory arrangements with other suppliers, backed in the short run by strict exchange controls — though Cripps and Bevin 'smothered' his efforts to insist on trading with Canada only in sterling.[6d] Then, in the next two weeks, the reserves fell sharply as world-wide recession damaged Britain's exports and traders anticipating devaluation added to the pressure on the pound. After eighteen months in which the dollar deficit had steadily fallen, in the second quarter of 1949 it doubled and cost Britain £160 million in gold.[11] With plenty of surplus capacity available in the export industries, Gaitskell and Jay separately but simultaneously decided that devaluation was inevitable;[12] and when Nicholas Kaldor flew in from Geneva to lobby them for it over lunch on Monday 18 July, he was preaching (though they did not say so) to the converted.[6d]

An hour later Attlee, sitting next to Gaitskell on the Treasury bench, muttered: 'Oh, by the way, I am mentioning you in this statement.' It was the first time Gaitskell had heard directly that he was to substitute for Cripps. Jay lunched with him on Wednesday 20 July, and they rehearsed the arguments which had won them both over to devaluation:

> (a) because exchange control had clearly not been able to prevent the continuation of the capital drain; devaluation on the other hand would not only check it, but bring the money back.
> (b) The U.S. Government were clearly not going to be able to do anything in the short term to help us and might insist on very stiff terms for the long term.

(c) The Commonwealth countries were obviously influenced in their import policy by the relative prices of sterling and dollar goods. Thus the control over dollar expenditure was clearly much looser than we had supposed.

(d) The prospect of expanding exports to dollar areas was probably greater than we had at first supposed – because of the great profitability of exporting to these areas as a result of devaluation.

(e) To delay devaluation might be exceedingly dangerous because as the reserve fell we should find it more and more difficult to carry out the operation without risk of a 'collapse of the currency': in consequence we should be completely dependent on the U.S.A. and be at their mercy.[6d]

Within both the Treasury and the government matters now moved quickly. On the Thursday, Gaitskell and Jay first saw Harold Wilson, who appeared to agree with them, and then easily won over Bevan, Strachey and Strauss at one of their regular dinners. On Monday the 'triumvirate' met three leading Treasury officials, and went on to see Attlee, Morrison and Dalton. They found that everyone now recognised that devaluation had become inevitable.[13] The Cabinet met twice that week but, as Dalton shows, the matter was not decided there. Morrison had put in a paper saying there was a 'close relation' between high public expenditure and dollar difficulties, which Dalton challenged. Morrison was strongly backed only by Hector McNeil, Minister of State at the Foreign Office, who wanted to conciliate foreign – especially American – critics.[8d] Gaitskell too (though Dalton's account does not say so) vigorously criticised Dalton's 'very rosy view' that public expenditure and the balance of payments were quite unrelated;[6e] some cuts in spending, and therefore in taxation, would make it much easier to free more resources to exploit the new export opportunities. According to Dalton's report: 'Deval^n isn't discussed, but is mentioned, approvingly by H.M[orrison], myself, A.B[evan] and J.S[trachey]. (Only C.A[ttlee] & A.V.A[lexander] were in the Cab in 1931. How differently we Ministers are reacting now! No flicker of surrender.)'[8d]

Gaitskell had disagreed with Dalton at that meeting, but on most matters they stood together against the Treasury:

H.G. and D.J[ay] come again to see me after this. H.G. says he'll resign if we commit ourselves again to convertibility. They say there is still very heavy [sic] from all official quarters 'to do something else' as well as devaluation. We agree that we should reduce investment programme, & tell banks to reduce personal advances ... What they all want is a slash in public expenditure on social services.

H.G. and D.J. both express distrust of H.W[ilson]. They don't know what he's up to. They think he's currying favour with Bridges and Treasury officials ... [Wilson] says S.C[ripps] reacted very strongly at the end against the very heavy pressure being brought to bear on him.

Two other points emerged from Cab talks. (1) Canadians must be made to face facts ... (2) Though we won't retreat on social services, it is agreed that P.M. should ask all Dept^{al} Ministers to cut down expenditure by, say, 5% ... without undue publicity.[8d]

There was a prolonged argument about the date of the devaluation. To avoid international dislocation and resentment the Treasury officials — backed by Harold Wilson — wanted to wait until early September when Cripps would be in Washington for a regular meeting of the World Bank and International Monetary Fund.[14] Morrison and Jay favoured acting at once to reduce pressure on the pound, and for fear the news would leak.[15] Attlee and Gaitskell preferred an intermediate date — before Washington to demonstrate that the decision was not imposed from abroad, but after Cripps's return to England so that he could explain it to the country — and their dissenting colleagues came round to that view on Thursday 28 July, just after the Cabinet. Attlee was to write to Cripps in Zürich. The letter was drafted by Jay, and he and Gaitskell took it to the Prime Minister next evening.[16] They found two senior Treasury officials also waiting; 'the underground Civil Service had been busy!'. These two — Sir Edward Bridges the Permanent Secretary, and Sir Henry Wilson-Smith the head of Overseas Finance — asked for the letter to set out more strongly the case for waiting until Washington, and were invited to amend it accordingly.

After the weekend, however, the officials came back with their own completely redrafted version of the letter. Gaitskell was appalled.

When I read this I exploded and made a scene. I said that they had gone far beyond the Prime Minister's instructions; that I totally disagreed with their approach and we must go back to the original draft by the Economic Secretary [Jay]. They crumpled up after this and we compromised by adding one or two paragraphs to the Economic Secretary's draft, emphasising more strongly the need for restricted Government expenditure. (It was interesting that later on I heard that this was the one passage of the letter to which the Chancellor strongly objected.) It only shows how hopelessly bad the judgement of the officials was about the way to influence their Minister.[6e]

Gaitskell and Jay lunched at Chequers next day to deliver the letter for Attlee to sign. It was taken on to Wilson, who was holidaying in Switzerland, by his private secretary and Wilson took it to Cripps without arousing journalistic suspicions.[6e*] He saw both Bevin, who was now inclined to favour devaluation in due course, and Cripps, who was far from convinced it was necessary. Until a devaluation is decided on, any finance minister has to deny that it would ever enter his head (for otherwise it would instantly become inevitable); and Stafford Cripps hated breaking his past commitments. The whole case would have to be argued out again when the sick Chancellor returned.

The Washington talks were now not far off. Gaitskell's suspicions of the Treasury and Foreign Office officials were confirmed when he read the draft brief prepared by the latter,[17]

> the first part of which might have been written by someone who was completely schooled in the anti-British American press. I got very angry about this – and ... said ... I would ask the Economic Secretary [Jay] to do a redraft ... The fear of the Economic Secretary's draft being the winner had a most useful effect. Bridges, in fact, rewrote the whole thing and an entirely different impression was created.[6e]

Dalton's account – derived from Douglas Jay – is characteristically more highly coloured:

> In the absence of H.M. [Morrison] and me and Strachey – and S.C. in Switzerland – the old fight had gone on. *In spite of all our Cabinet discussions and decisions,* the officials ... put up a brief for Ministers, immediately before they were due to leave for W'ton, with all the old stuff about the 'need to restore confidence', and hence to make large reductions, including changes of policy, in public expenditure ...
>
> H.G. and D.J. fought this out. D.J. praised H.G. *most* highly. He acted as 'Vice-Chancellor of the Exchequer' and attacked the officials, both on intellectual grounds and on tacking on decisions already taken ... under H.G.'s attack, the officials retreated ... If S.C. had had the wrong paper put up (but it wasn't), he might, having been out of touch and ill, have weakened. If the P.M. had weakened ... the Labour Party [might] be breaking up as in 1931.
>
> H.G. and D.J. saw eye to eye throughout. H.W. was away at this point, but D.J. doesn't trust him. He trims and wavers, and is thinking more of what senior Ministers – and even senior officials – are thinking of him than of what is right.[8e]

The official advice to Cripps and Bevin was now settled, but the Ministers themselves still had to be convinced. When Cripps came back on Thursday 18 August, Gaitskell sent him a ten-page memorandum on the

---

* Gaitskell's own covering letter to Wilson told him (to pass on to Cripps) which advisers favoured which date, and ended mysteriously: 'The figure last week was 46.' This was a cricket score required by the President of the Board of Trade.

case for devaluation, and a copy of a shorter note to the Prime Minister arguing for an election preferably in November 1949, possibly in the following summer, but not in between.[6e*] Next day, the Chancellor saw Bevin and the Prime Minister at Chequers, and Gaitskell and Harold Wilson were also invited. Gaitskell recorded:

> It was a depressing occasion. The argument rambled along; some-times about devaluation itself; sometimes about the date. The P.M. did not intervene at all but sat at his desk doodling and listening to the argument. It was obvious that Stafford was quite out of touch and I felt that I had completely failed to put anything across to him at all. I was, of course, myself arguing both for devaluation and for the earliest date. H. argued strongly against the early date – although on the last occasion when we had met he had appeared to accept it. The Foreign Secretary swayed this way and that, and every now and then we were treated to a long monologue on … 1924 … 1931, etc. It was very hot and the room is a very small one. Bridges said little and was quite fair and objective.[6e]

Bevin promised to support devaluation and Cripps reluctantly agreed, though insisting – as indeed his health made inevitable – on waiting until Washington before he would undertake to defend the decision publicly.

Gaitskell went off on holiday to Jersey, returning late (his plane was delayed) for the Cabinet on 29 August which confirmed the decision to devalue and the need to take strong consequential measures against inflation: 'the Chancellor seemed calmer and better, though still looking very thin. He said to me then as he had said at Chequers, "I have not slept".'[6e] Cripps and Bevin then left for Washington, where they settled on a devaluation of the pound from $4·03 to $2·80.

No one now doubts that the policy was right and inevitable, but the long delay probably forced them to fix too low a rate.[18] Gaitskell certainly wanted a readjustment large enough to be quite clearly final;[19a] but he had wanted to act sooner, and would very likely have preferred a rate of $3·00.[20] Following Cripps's return, the Cabinet met in secret on Saturday 17 September, using the back entrance to Downing Street. Cripps briefed Churchill as Leader of the Opposition, who complimented him warmly on a brave and correct decision but warned that 'I shall make the utmost political capital out of it'; his denunciation of Cripps for breaking commitments was so harsh that the Chancellor later refused to accept an honorary degree at his hands.[21a] Next day, Sunday, after an impeccable operation combining full international consultation with total secrecy, the pound was devalued by 30 per cent.

* Both went to Attlee, Cripps, Morrison, Bevan and Strachey; the former also to Jay and Plowden, and the latter to Dalton.

ii   *Cabinet Controversy, and the 1950 Election*

The Government held together over the devaluation of September 1949, but the need to tackle the inflationary consequences – strongly urged in Gaitskell's economic memorandum – soon produced ominous divisions among Ministers. At the end of October he succinctly summarised the outcome:

> Most people would say that things have not gone too well. We have produced our economy cuts and they have had a bad reception. The gold drain has certainly been stopped but the building up of reserves has been very slow. There is to be no Election until next year.[6f]

After Cripps's return in September the official briefs, no longer vetted in advance by Ministers, were still arguing for large economies on the basis of figures some of which Jay and Wilson contested. At the EPC, Dalton sounded a warning. 'I said that officials served Ministers well so long as they thought the Govt. would go on. If they had doubts on this, they wavered and were tempted to make Minutes for the record, to show to successors.'[8f] Cripps threatened to resign unless economies of nearly £300 million[22] were agreed, at which Bevan 'launched forth into a diatribe' with what Gaitskell thought rather dishonest backing from Dalton.[6f] The latter criticised Cripps's figure, while the former went further, wanting economic affairs removed altogether from the Treasury.[23a] He 'thought S.C. would resign rather than give up his main proposals for economy. Others, including himself would resign rather than agree. One catalyst was a quick election.'[8g]

Next day there was another battle over the detail of the cuts. The Foreign Secretary and Minister of Defence fought hard for the Service estimates.[24] Cripps and Bevan, though old allies, clashed again – over the extent of inflationary pressure – and again both hinted at resignation. Cripps was thinking of a shilling increase in National Insurance contributions;[25] and Bevan was 'making it quite clear that he would have no interference with the Health Service'.[6f] The result 'after a multitude of meetings' was a series of compromises, with cuts agreed at the rate of £280 million a year – half from government expenditure, and half from the capital investment programme including £35 million off housing.[8h] The decision was poorly received, with even the government's middle-class sympathisers like Hyndley and Fergusson 'violently critical'. Gaitskell thought the policies reasonable and the political outcome not too bad:

> I do not believe this middleclass reaction at all typical throughout the country, and I doubt if we have lost much ground as a result, despite

the terrific onslaught on the part of the press. Even papers like the Mirror, friendly to Labour, have been critical because they have failed to get any of the sensations which they love. How I detest them![6f]

With its threats of resignation from Bevan if cuts were made in the health service and from the Chancellor if they were not, the 1949 Cabinet clash strikingly resembles the battle over the 1951 Budget. It provoked no less tension, for Douglas Jay found 'S.C. very messianic and A.B. very ideological about what are practical administrative questions not really lending themselves to either form of high emotion!'[8g] Yet in this earlier conflict, Bevan's antagonist was the man he admired as the best Chancellor Britain ever had, Sir Stafford Cripps.[26]

Plainly, then, the 1951 clash was not simply due to the stubborn personality of Gaitskell, who in 1949 was not even in the Cabinet and played no important part. But his sympathies were already strongly with Cripps. Dalton talked to him after one EPC meeting:

He is now very frightened of 'inflationary pressure' and says that, if we don't deal with it, we shall have another dollar crisis in the spring. If this morning's clash came to a break, he would be with S.C. against A.B., and so he thinks would the country, and most of the Party. A.B., he thinks, should have been moved by the P.M. before now from a spending Dept. to, say, the Ministry of Labour, where he would do very well ... he finds A.B. very difficult.[8g]

Specific disagreements did not preclude friendly relations between the future rivals, and the Minister of Health was among the very few recipients of Gaitskell's two memoranda during the crisis. When Thomas Balogh asked him to choose a colleague to lunch with a visiting American economist, Bevan's was the first name he proposed.[27] No doubt he recalled a recent ministerial dinner for another American, Senator Pat McCarran:[28]

He is a typical U.S. politician type; extreme right wing Republican [sic], Irish and a bit of a rascal. Nye Bevan was an immense success with him and not because he said nice things. He was extremely rude about Americans but the Senator lapped it up because of the way it was done. There is no doubt that Nye is really a natural witty and amusing conversationist. If his speeches are brilliant they are not the brilliance of carefully prepared, painstaking research, but something much more spontaneous. The remarks which he is famous for in public are equally made in private, as I have often heard at Cabinet meetings and similar occasions.

I think he is also a more profound thinker than he is sometimes given credit for. The other evening after a Group Dinner we drifted

H

into a discussion about religion and philosophy. In this Nye started
attacking religion, not as one might have expected on Marxist
grounds, but far more on rationalist grounds—very sympathetic to
me. It was a little embarrassing because of the Chancellor's religious
views, but did reveal I think that Nye had really read and thought
about these matters fairly deeply. I said to him afterwards, 'The other
day you called me an "arid intellectual", and I wrote you off as a
hopeless nineteenth century mystic but I am glad to welcome you
back into the eighteenth century fold after your performance tonight'.

It is refreshing to find that one's colleagues can talk about these
subjects in this way. We are all so busy as Ministers we tend to get into
a terrible rut and talk shop. John Strachey said he had just finished
reading Toynbee's great six volume history. I am really positively
ashamed, amongst these friends, not to have read anything worth
reading for such a long time.[6g]

A few weeks later Gaitskell contrasted his problems with Harold Wilson
with his pleasant relationship with Strachey and other colleagues,

with whom one can have that emotional and intellectual intercourse
which is really the stuff of ... friendship ... such as Douglas [Jay] and
Frank Pakenham, and even to some extent Nye Bevan ... Frank ...
does not like Bevan and was rather horrified when I said that I thought
Bevan would almost certainly be leader of the Party and therefore
P.M. sometime.[6h]

After months of argument the date of the general election was finally
decided on in December 1949. All the seniors, expecting the next Budget
to be unpopular, had for months seen February as the latest possible
date.[29] For months, too, Cripps, Bevan and Gaitskell had been urging
Attlee to go to the country before the winter. At one Thursday dinner of
economic Ministers on the evening of the devaluation debate, 29 September, everyone except Jay agreed with them, and Cripps and Bevan pressed
the Prime Minister to announce a dissolution that very night in his winding-up speech. But Attlee and Morrison both demurred, Bevin was
abroad, and the Ministers who favoured an early poll ('all the intellectuals',
said Attlee) were outweighed by its opponents.[30]
Gaitskell blamed the bad reception of the government's cuts on the
uncertainty about the election, causing delay which 'enabled the press to
build up an impression that there were to be tremendously severe cuts.[31]
It is quite possible that it was deliberate policy on the part of the Opposition press ... to make the whole plan appear a flop.'[6f] The Cabinet discussed it for an hour on 13 October and decided to wait until 1950, as
Attlee strongly urged. Bevan and Cripps dissented and Wilson was 'half

against';[8i] while Gaitskell, waiting outside, thought it 'a great mistake' when he was told.[6f] Six weeks later, six senior Ministers – Attlee, Morrison, Cripps, Dalton, Bevan and Addison – met with the Chief Whip to decide between February or June. (Bevin left it to them, saying he was 'no politician'.) Pressed by the Chancellor, who said that he could not hold sterling beyond February, all but Morrison agreed on the season which Gaitskell – worried about the power-station strike and the risk of another fuel crisis – had so strongly opposed.[32]

Gaitskell celebrated the New Year with a great party – 'an enormous success' – for Hampstead and ministerial friends, though

> I missed the highlight of the evening when Eva Robens ... restive because of what she regarded as the phlegmatic behaviour of those present, looked hard at Harold Wilson and said, 'You come from north of the Trent, don't you? Surely you know how to behave!' and then proceeded to fling her arms around him and kiss him passionately, to his very great embarrassment. As he had previously been giving a lecture on why the ladies could not obtain nylons – which was full of statistics but all very sober, this incident gave great pleasure.[6i]

At a rather dreary dinner party given by Cripps, after the dissolution, the Production Ministers and their wives bet 1s. a head on the result 11 of the 14 predicting a clear Labour majority of at least 70. But Gaitskell feared losses due to redistribution of seats, Liberal defections to the Tories, and a big swing against government interference in people's lives. He bet on a Labour majority of 30, won the pool, and preserved Cripps's cheque for 14s. as a memento.[33]

During the first week of the election Gaitskell stayed in the south, speaking for other candidates – including left-wingers like Hugh Delargy at Thurrock and Tom Braddock at Mitcham, as well as old friends like Frank Hardie at Epsom and Elizabeth Pakenham at Oxford. 'What a pleasure', he wrote, 'to have such friends in the middle of all this political struggle ... It would be nice to think that I had disproved the Thomas Morley saying, "There are no friends at the top".'[6h] He spent the remaining three weeks in his own constituency, with enough forays out into the West Riding for a neighbour to comment on his generosity with his time.[34] It was the only general election in which he was really active in South Leeds, for in 1945 he had been ill, and later he was everywhere in demand. He attracted national publicity only when he clashed with Churchill, who had committed the Conservatives to end petrol rationing as soon as possible. On 10 February, Gaitskell replied that unless prices were raised (perhaps trebled) to discourage consumption, that would cost $40–50 million for the United Kingdom alone – and 'it is better to go easy on petrol than be short of bread'. But for the Socialists' 'usual ineptitude and incompetence', answered Churchill, we would now have the refineries to take advantage of the 'vast masses of petrol in the sterling area'; next day Gaitskell replied that these resources did not exist, for the British oil companies operated in Persia and Venezuela, which were outside the sterling area. But if Washington agreed to allocate Britain more petrol without demanding more dollars, then the prospects of an increased ration were 'not bad'.[35]

Attlee told Gaitskell afterwards that he had spoken entirely without notes in the election, which he had positively enjoyed. The younger man felt quite differently. 'When one has to make say 50 speeches in all, it is impossible not to be bored with the sound of one's own voice long before the end. Indeed, if one were not bored it would only show what an intolerable character one was.' He thought the audience reactions similar to those of 1945, but showing signs of both

> additional confidence in the capacity of Labour to govern, and ... a collection of grievances against us for the way some aspects of government had affected them ... especially among the lower middle class and middle class who had been offended by our words and ... suffered considerable economic disadvantages by our actions.[6k]

Austerity, petrol rationing and Aneurin Bevan's 'vermin' speech[36a] had indeed taken their toll in the commuter belt, where Labour's middle-class gains of 1945 were lost for twenty years. The swing to the Conservatives was around 8 per cent in the suburban counties of Greater London, only 2 per cent over the rest of the country. Bevan was held largely to blame by Attlee[8j] and Cripps, and by 'general feeling' in the Labour Party; but, as Gaitskell had expected, his reputation quickly recovered when Parliament met: 'He is so much the best debater, so much the most effective speaker on the Front Bench, indeed in the House.'[6k]

There was no serious defection among working-class voters like those of South Leeds. The Gallup poll found Labour won an even higher proportion of working-class voters in 1950 than in 1945, while the small parties and left-wing independents who opposed Labour candidates were decimated (many Communists polled only a quarter of their 1945 vote). A solid Labour ward had been added to Gaitskell's constituency and, on a far higher poll than in 1945, he found himself with much the safest Labour seat in the city and a result 'certainly quite up to my best expectations'.[6k*]

But the redistribution which helped Gaitskell had severely — and predictably — damaged the Party as a whole.** Labour still polled 800,000 more

---

* See Table 1.
** That had not deterred Churchill from denouncing it as Labour gerrymandering.

TABLE 1   *South Leeds: Voting in 1945, 1950*

	1950	%		1945	%
H. Gaitskell (Lab.)	29,795	61·1	H. Gaitskell	17,899	61·0
B. H. Wood (Cons.)	14,436	29·6	A. Ramsden	7,497	25·6
E. Meeks (Lib.)	4,525	9·3	W. Barford	3,933	13·4
Majority	15,359			10,402	

votes than the Conservatives, a lead in votes which would have given the latter an overall majority of sixty-nine seats. But it gave Labour a majority of only five.[37]

Beforehand, Bevan had thought the election quite likely to produce a weak Conservative government which 'wouldn't last long'.[8f] Dalton, too, would have preferred that to a weak Labour one:

> The thought of a small Labour majority depresses me deeply, with all the economic difficulties ahead, and added strains on tired men, and an unpopular Budget, and the Govt. at the mercy of any small disloyal clique ... Would, perhaps, a small Tory majority be better, with the prospect of an early election resulting in a *good* Lab majority?[8k]

Bevan had been dismayed at Gaitskell's prediction of a Labour majority of thirty, saying: 'I would rather not be in power at all'.[6i] For in those days a working majority was supposed to be around forty, and though a few twentieth-century minority governments had survived thanks to precarious backing from another party, a nominal but tiny majority was quite unprecedented. The prospect looked daunting, especially since many Labour MPs were tired and elderly. Gaitskell faced it robustly. At worst, a Conservative government after the next election would have a hard time and last only one Parliament; at best, fear of the Tories might enable Labour to recover Liberal votes, provided 'we can avoid giving unnecessary offence and quietly improve the economic position'.[6k] World events were soon to dash any such hopes.

iii   *Minister of State: The First Clash with Bevan*

Gaitskell had early warning that if Labour won the 1950 election he would not return to Fuel and Power. Attlee meant to send him to the Treasury as Minister of State for Economic Affairs to help Cripps, whose health was still poor.[8n] Dalton told Gaitskell, wanting to make sure he would accept, and was reassured that he was most unlikely to decline anything and that, though 'happy and reasonably comfortable' at Fuel and Power, he was now ready for a change:[38]

[O]ne is always in a way glad to leave a Ministry because you leave behind unsolved problems and some skeletons in cupboards and shed a load, and you walk into the other job with a free mind without ... responsibilities for what has been done beforehand ... being in the centre of the financial and economic policy does appeal to me. I feel there is quite a lot which could be done if one had the opportunity, and if one were helped by the right people.[6h]

Attlee promised to make it clear that the new post was no demotion, but warned that it carried a lower salary—which Gaitskell assumed was 'a deliberate test of my loyalty' but was in fact a prime ministerial muddle.[6k] Years later Gaitskell, in a television interview, told his old friend Malcolm Muggeridge that though it 'appeared to be a down-grading ... I didn't mind that, I can honestly say that, I was pleased to be moved to a sphere I was very interested in'.[39] Dalton assured him that not being in the Cabinet 'isn't a serious drawback for you; you are on EPC—which often matters more—as a Foundation Member'.[40a] Congratulations came from the senior men in both parties, including Churchill and Macmillan, Bevan and Butler, and from several left-wing MPs. There were also many regretful letters from MFP civil servants and members of boards of nationalised industries.

Dalton had proposed his name, telling Attlee that a Treasury Minister needed 'not only keen intelligence or bright ideas, or diligence, or methodical adm^n, but power to resist high powered advice'.[8n] Gaitskell hoped to bring into his new Ministry a few trusted friends from the old one like Fergusson and Murphy;[41] but peacetime Civil Service practice prevailed.[19a b] In his first week he was laid low by flu, and wrote to one of his party workers in South Leeds: 'Just at present I feel in a thorough muddle and rather lonely and depressed. But this always happens in a new job & I suppose I shall settle down in time.'[42-3a] Before long he was showing, as a journalist noted,

> a quiet determination to run this most ancient department that shook some of its officials. In discussion, he was able to match them in objectivity and analytical power, and ... no administrative convolutions would deter him from getting to the bottom of a question.[44a]

Being their intellectual equal, Gaitskell knew they could not pull wool over his eyes; so, though initially suspicious of the official case, he was open to conviction once he had investigated it thoroughly and made up his own mind about it. Again he disconcerted senior officials by his probing into detail, his disregard for hierarchy and protocol, his liking for long 'seminars' where a problem could be argued out with what they often thought excessive thoroughness.[45]

As Cripps's understudy Gaitskell was involved in the later stages of the Budget arguments, which brought the first rumblings of a great storm. For to Gaitskell's dismay the post-election reshuffle had not touched the Cabinet's most turbulent member. Bevan

certainly wanted to move and in my view it was imperative from the point of view of finance that he should be moved. Apparently under the influence of Bevin the P.M. decided he must go back to clear up the mess he created.[23b] It only means the mess will not be cleared up ... It is a great mistake and one which may cost us very heavily.[6k]

Gaitskell's view was not due to personal animosity. He was working hard (and successfully) to persuade Cripps to cancel the recent £25 million cut in Bevan's housing programme;[4b] and the Department to which he would have liked Bevan to move[6k] was the latter's own choice, the Colonies.[8l] The Minister of Health had exasperated his Cabinet colleagues by 'the mess he created' long before Gaitskell figured in the dispute at all.

The reasons went back to the beginnings of Bevan's great achievement, the National Health Service. When it was introduced in July 1948, no one could predict the demand, or tell how many doctors and dentists would join; and their pay had not been decided. Understandably, the first estimates proved much too low and a large supplementary, of £59 million or nearly 30 per cent of the original estimate, had to be voted.[47] Less excusably, just as that was going through the House in February 1949, the estimates for 1950/51 were budgeting for a reduced annual rate of expenditure.[48] In the Budget speech, the Chancellor warned that supplementaries had to be confined to rare cases such as a major change of policy; and specified that, failing economy in the use of the National Health Service over the next year, a special tax or charge might become necessary.[49] In May 1949 the all-party Select Committee on Estimates unanimously drew attention to the pharmaceutical services and the 'need for public recognition that abuse of their facilities constitutes a grave threat to their maintenance and further expansion'; and by a majority recommended deterring it by 'such regulations as are practicable to prevent excessive or wasteful prescriptions'.[50] With the post-devaluation economy drive, authority to impose a charge for prescriptions was announced by the Prime Minister on 24 October 1949 and piloted through the House by Bevan himself on 9 December.[51]*

* It passed by 138 to 9. The 138 included 10 future Bevanites, among them Jennie Lee and Ian Mikardo, and 100 other Labour MPs; the opponents (counting tellers) were 5 Liberals and 1 Conservative, 1 Communist and 3 Independent Labour pro-Communists, and 1 Labour man, Walter Ayles. Bevan told the PLP of 'cascades of medicine pouring down British throats — and they're not even bringing the bottles back';[21b] and more sedately claimed in the House that since

By the New Year, the Estimates Committee had unanimously agreed that 'it should be possible to make reasonably accurate forecasts of expenditure'.[53] Yet in March 1950, a year after the Chancellor's ban on supplementary estimates, the Ministry of Health presented one for nearly £100 million – about 37 per cent of the original estimate for the NHS, and not far short of half the entire estimate for education. Moreover, by the Minister's own decision its presentation was delayed long after the Department knew it would be necessary, provoking the all-party Public Accounts Committee to protest unanimously against 'a serious impairment of the system of Parliamentary control'.[54] While the wilder Tory charges of widespread extravagance were false, Bevan's 'verbal pyrotechnics' in sweeping them aside also covered up his own administrative laxity.[55]

This was Gaitskell's first appearance in the dispute. He successfully urged Cripps to insist that NHS spending must come under Treasury control like all other expenditure and that its total must be limited; and tried to have the limit set below the next year's estimates, so that Bevan would face the choice between making economies or imposing charges. That did not succeed. 'As usual, there was a policy compromise because of the threat of Bevan's resignation and the unwillingness of the Cabinet to accept the principle of charging just yet ... Personally, I think politically ... cuts would have done us a lot of good.'[6k]

The 'compromise' was negotiated, according to his own claim, by Harold Wilson.[56] It fixed a generous ceiling, well above current expenditure, with measures to enforce it; and in return again deferred the charges suggested by Cripps in March 1949, hinted at by the Estimates Committee in May, authorised by Bevan's own Act in December, and again discussed by the Cabinet in March 1950. For as Gaitskell saw, Cripps was inhibited both by his old friendship with Bevan and by his decision to allow the supplementary estimate, which he defended against the Tory assault by arguing that it had averted closure of hospital beds and restriction of services. Nevertheless, the Chancellor knew that it had made a mockery of his statement a year before, and was determined that that should not happen again, repeatedly emphasising that the estimate for 1950/51 – £34 million above the final total for 1949/50 – must really be 'a ceiling beyond which we must not be carried'.[57]

Bevan never meant to carry out his side of the bargain. As his biographer puts it, 'the charges ... had been stopped and Bevan lived to threaten resignation another day'.[36b] He denied his colleagues' right to criticise his departmental expenditure. On 13 March 1950 the Cabinet minutes recorded that Ministers 'agreed to resume at a later date their

---

people knew of the 'abuse' of 'unnecessary expenditure' on prescriptions, the charges aroused little indignation.[52]

discussion on the finances of the National Health Service'. Next day — the very day that Cripps rescued him in the House over the supplementary estimate — Bevan challenged this minute in a letter to the Prime Minister. 'I do hope', he wrote a little petulantly, 'that I can have some peace to get on with my proper work without this continual nibbling.'[36b c] It soon became clear that he accepted the concession (no charges yet) but meant to ignore the counterpart (an effective ceiling).

His colleagues, however, were also anxious for the well-being of the services for which they were responsible. Already one-third of all expenditure on social services went to the NHS; if Bevan were granted sovereign rights and a blank cheque, all economies must be made at others' expense. So Cripps was not speaking only for a parsimonious Treasury in his Budget statement[58a] that there could be

> no excuse for exceeding the estimates in the coming 12 months ... further measures of control must be exercised ... Any expansion in one part of the [Health] Service must in future be met by economies or, if necessary by contraction in others ... should these [powers of control] prove to be insufficient, an Amending Act will be introduced. It is not proposed to impose any charge immediately in connection with prescriptions, since it is hoped that a more easily administered method of economising in this branch of expenditure can be introduced shortly. The power to charge will, of course, remain so that it can be used later if it is needed.[36d]

Above all the Cabinet would no longer rely on Bevan to enforce the ceiling. Like Shinwell after the fuel crisis, he had to put up with 'a barely sufferable indignity, the surveillance of Health Service finances by a special weekly Cabinet Committee, presided over by the Prime Minister'.[36b]

When these decisions were being made, Gaitskell was still outside the Cabinet, and when they were finally settled he had been in the Treasury barely a week. As yet, Bevan was not hostile to him or even to the Treasury. Gaitskell had the idea of

> preparing and circulating a forecast of the national income, investment, saving, taxation, revenue and expenditure for the next two years ... Nye, difficult enough on his own Department, was delighted with it and has really given us quite good support on the general theory of preventing inflation.[6j]

Even the health service conflict at first aroused no bitterness:

> Relations with Nye have settled down again after the great row about the Health Services. There also seems to be more harmony in the Party as a whole, although Nye still looks on himself as a sort of

leader of the Left-wing, his actual attitude on the essential points of policy is not nearly so far removed from Herbert's as it used to be. Curiously enough too he seems to have accepted his present position in the Party ... Perhaps somebody really has told him that he nearly lost us the Election.

The thing I like about him is that one can have a terrific row with him in a Cabinet Committee and yet remain on quite cordial terms with a good deal of friendly back-chat. Another endearing characteristic is that he does not really make much effort to collect around him a lot of supporters in the Cabinet or Government, though his enemies would say that was only because he could not find any.[6j]

The antagonism arose quite specifically from the attempt to enforce the ceiling on NHS expenditure to which Bevan had nominally agreed. On the night the Prime Minister's committee was set up he had come home 'white with passion';[36e] and his wrath fell on Gaitskell, whom Cripps had appointed 'as Treasury prosecutor'.[6l m] Though Cripps had been explicit in announcing the 'compromise' to the House, Bevan was exasperated above all by any mention of charges, and so came to look on Gaitskell 'as the pedantic spokesman of the Treasury's most arid doctrines'.[36b] From Gaitskell's side it was

> One of the more unpleasant jobs I have been made to do ... The Committee was set up to see the ceiling was observed and there were not any supplementary estimates. The Chancellor['s] ... position would certainly be a most difficult one if there has to be a supplementary estimate of anything but a nominal size ...
>
> The meetings are not exactly easy or comfortable, and on one occasion the Minister of Health, provoked by something I had said, slammed his papers down and started to walk out of the room. The P.M., however, summoned him back and smoothed him down ... It is a very wearing affair—always having to nag one's colleagues, and especially when they are as slippery and difficult as the Minister of Health.[6m*]

This incident, which seems to have occurred on 28 June, had lasting consequences. A day or two later Bevan complained angrily to the Chancellor that, knowing he would resign rather than accept charges, 'spokesmen of the Treasury and you have not hesitated to press this so-called solution upon the Government ... really you must not go on treating every issue as of the same importance. Some go too near the bone and this is one.' At the hated committee 'last Wednesday, under what I consider to have been

---

* This entry does not suggest that charges were 'a mission or an obsession' with Gaitskell, as Harold Wilson later alleged.[59]

unjustifiable needling, I gave way to an outburst of resentment'. Blaming Cripps himself, Bevan would attend no more Thursday dinners, since 'it can hardly create friendly relations if you continue to press it. I am not such a hypocrite that I can pretend to have amiable discourses with people who are entirely indifferent to my most strongly held opinions.'[60] Those dinners were soon to end anyway owing to Cripps's illness. But Bevan's explosion was not his first or his last, and according to John Strachey the dinners had already become tense occasions:

> Aneurin Bevan began to lash Hugh with the fury of his tongue. Hugh would sit rather silent under it, occasionally replying with a dry, factual contradiction. When this had happened several times I walked away from one of the dinners with Bevan and asked him why he was doing it. 'Why', I said, 'are you going out of your way to make a rift between yourself and one of the really considerable men of the Government?' '*Considerable!*' Aneurin replied. 'But he's nothing, nothing, nothing!'[61]

iv *Minister for Overseas Finance*

Most of the senior members of that Cabinet had held office for ten gruelling and anxious years. Early in 1950 Gaitskell assessed them all. Morrison had been desperately ill in 1947, but was now active again – prone to intrigue, but

> mostly on the side of the 'angels', especially where public expenditure is concerned ... [Attlee] seems to me to have more political sense than almost everybody else. Undoubtedly, too, his position in the Government is stronger than it has ever been ... I think history will record that he was among the more successful British Prime Ministers.

Bevin was remarkably resilient, one day 'hardly capable of coherent speech and the next ... shrewd, sensible, imaginative – all his old, best qualities'. Cripps's health might not be quite as bad as he claimed, for when Bevin's decline seemed evident, 'I know that ... Stafford was greatly attracted by the idea of becoming Foreign Secretary'.[6j]

Sir Stafford Cripps, a left-wing rebel in the 1930s, was now the champion of national unity and the most respected preacher of austerity and sacrifice as indispensable to Britain's recovery. Deeply religious, in a devout Anglican and not Nonconformist tradition, he held his new views with all his old certitude and singlemindedness.[62] They carried weight in the House, the Party and the country thanks less to his 'superb intellect' than to his 'moral strength and serene integrity'. So noble a figure sounds a hard man to work with, but 'he had not only admirers but friends everywhere ... those who served him loved him'. For Cripps was exceptionally considerate to his staff, and Gaitskell later recalled 'often going to see him feeling depressed and worried over some difficult problem, and coming away with a wonderful renewal of confidence'.[63]

Yet their co-operation could easily have been spoilt by the junior man feeling resentment at being neglected, or provoking it by aggressiveness. Gaitskell had been unsure about the move: 'I do not want to be a kind of superior Under-Secretary to the Chancellor and it is essential that I should retain the right to take any dispute between him and me to the Cabinet.'[6h] But no friction developed. Gaitskell avoided publicly contradicting his superior in Cabinet or in EPC (and so, seeing no point in repeating Cripps's views, kept 'too silent for my liking').[6k] Their relations turned out to be excellent, though quite unexpected. Cripps left technical and complicated matters to Gaitskell, and frequently took his advice. To the younger man's surprise,

> in bargaining either with his colleagues or with outsiders ... we all of us are nervous ... lest he gives way too much. I find myself ... having to stiffen him up on almost every occasion ... he is undoubtedly mentally tired and perhaps physically not well also. But I suspect that his strong point was not so much ... just being tough with everybody but rather accepting sound advice and then having the courage to put it across to the country.[6j]

The Budget of 1950 was unexciting: income tax down, petrol tax up, and the standard ration doubled as Gaitskell had hoped for a long time.[6j] In the House, he spoke after Churchill and, like so many Labour Ministers over the years, attacked the Opposition for wanting total government expenditure cut, and more spent on every separate service. He defended the welfare state, high taxation, and especially full employment. 'We recognise that it is the major economic problem of democracy to hold full employment without inflation.' Unless the Conservatives meant to break trade union bargaining power by deflation and unemployment,

> we must have some arrangement under which increased earnings, justified by an increase in output, are distributed among the various classes of workers. The Opposition say 'no, we do not even want to contemplate this problem. We would rather it were not there at all.' How do they propose to get rid of it? We shall have an answer no doubt this evening.[58b]

Before going to the Treasury, he had given his own answer. Dalton's account of it brings out the economic and political climate of those days:

> Last week at E.P.C. H.G., in agreement with D.J., put in a first class

paper on Controls and Liberalisation. The first part is an admirable statement of economic doctrine. Don't rely mainly on financial controls to prevent inflation. Always keep demand just above supply, in order to hold full employment, and rely on *physical* controls— especially on total imports, capital export, building location and essential material—even when no longer 'in short supply'—to hold inflation. Really, therefore, though this is not the way anyone puts it, always have a bit of inflationary pressure, but use physical controls to prevent it breaking through.[8m]

A few days later Dalton told Attlee that the author of this 'masterly' paper should in due course become Chancellor.[8m] Their colleagues approved these principles as 'guidance to official advisers, who keep on giving advice which runs contrary to H.M.G.'s view of things'.[8n] But as Gaitskell knew, that strategy could be undermined by economic pressures from abroad.

When he went to the Treasury in March 1950, Gaitskell acted as understudy to the Chancellor on every front. Both he and the officials disliked that arrangement, which did not ease Cripps's burden and could not last. After the Budget, therefore, Cripps gave his Minister of State full responsibility for overseas finance, with the difficult task—among others—of trying to persuade other countries to adopt the same economic priorities as Britain. Five years earlier, as an optimistic back-bencher, Gaitskell had written on the American loan agreement:

It is recognised, at last, that the expansion of international trade depends on the maintenance of Full Employment—and not the other way round ... From this follows the idea of an undertaking by each nation ... *that it will not seek 'to maintain employment through measures which are likely to create unemployment in other countries'* ... i.e. a solid foundation on which we could build a *positive international full employment policy*. This, in my view, transcends in importance all else ... These risks [of non-discrimination] will be enormously diminished if at the forthcoming international conference we can really get agreement on an International Full Employment Policy. To this great task the skill and energies of our representatives should now be primarily directed.[64]

Now that was his own mission as Minister of State, speaking for Britain when the Economic and Social Council of the United Nations met at Geneva that summer to discuss international measures to ensure full employment.

Gaitskell spent much time preparing for this meeting, where the Government hoped to persuade the participants to legislate for corrective action once unemployment reached 3 per cent.[23c] (Britain wanted 2 per cent but agreed to 3 per cent in hopes of United States co-operation.)[65] The agenda was set by 'an extremely progressive report' by several economists, mostly written by Nicholas Kaldor,[6m] which called on creditor countries (i.e. mainly the United States) to lend abroad through the Bank and Fund in order to correct incipient depressions. Similarly Gaitskell's speech urged them to plan for full employment by creating demand at home, and to run down their balance of payments surpluses rather than impose deflation on their neighbours. Britain, he promised, would join an international agreement to avoid undue fluctuations in capital exports especially to developing countries.[66]

> We were able to make quite a splash with the speech both with the press here and at Geneva. But the atmosphere there was not very encouraging ... I was the only Minister present, which was perhaps an indication of the kind of attitude adopted by most Governments towards ECOSOC.[6m]

There was opposition from the United States Treasury, and especially from the Fund's president Camille Gutt, the ultra-orthodox Belgian ex-Minister of Finance, who directly attacked Gaitskell's speech. The latter was not too despondent: 'I do not see why there should be any difficulty about the Full Employment business ... one of the few good things about the Council of Europe is that M. Gutt has nothing to do with it!'[67] However, the pressure of the Korean war and the rearmament crisis forced even the British government to abandon its Bill, though Gaitskell as Chancellor responded to the final ECOSOC resolution by announcing that Britain would take 3 per cent as a 'standard'.[68]

With no international commitment to full employment, Gaitskell feared to let Britain become exposed to strong deflationary pressures from abroad. World trade in 1950 was still largely conducted under bilateral agreements setting quantitative limits on imports from one country to another, which gave both the means and the incentive for manipulation by governments. American foreign economic policy concentrated on removing quantitative restrictions ('liberalisation'), on forbidding discrimination, and on working towards convertibility of currencies – the so-called 'fundamentals' to which Britain was committed under (and indeed before) the loan agreement, but from which she had retreated in 1947. As her economic situation improved with Marshall Aid and the devaluation of sterling, the Americans again began pressing for some progress in meeting these obligations. Gaitskell's paper on Controls and Liberalisation, in January 1950, shows that, as Dalton's diary indicates, he came into the Treasury in a very wary frame of mind. 'On "liberalisation" we have gone about far enough. But we have done it for political reasons – U.S. and

Europe.'[8m] To the dismay of the Treasury officials, he wanted to tell the Americans that they could expect no movement on the 'fundamentals' until it was clear that they could avoid a slump with its disastrous consequences for the British economy; and, since the civil servants felt some concessions to the United States pressure would be necessary, Gaitskell was determined to keep tight control over any negotiations at their level. Cripps generally supported him, though other senior Ministers were more dubious. Then in the summer the Korean war transformed Washington's priorities, and her anxiety to encourage British rearmament superseded her concern for British progress towards freer world trade.[69-70]

While there was no change on that front, a major breakthrough was achieved in more limited talks on an allied, 'very abstruse but very important subject',[6m] the proposed European Payments Union.[71] That success was mainly due to Gaitskell—surprisingly, since at first sight the issues seemed similar in the two cases. It was essential to protect the reserves of gold and foreign currency, which were dangerously low; those five disastrous weeks of convertibility in 1947 had shown how quickly they might vanish, leaving us 'starving slaves of the U.S.'.[72] There must be exchange controls to stop transfers of capital abroad, and Gaitskell worried constantly about their adequacy.[6a d*] There must also be measures to limit imports, and to channel exports wherever possible towards dollar markets, and these aims were achieved by bilateral agreements with each European country, fixing quantitative limits for most of its trade with Britain. When Gaitskell came to the Treasury he simply saw these as defences not to be dismantled; gradually he became convinced that some satisfaction must be given to Britain's trading partners.

The pressure came not only from the Americans but from the Continental members of the Organisation for European Economic Co-operation (OEEC). Weak countries resented Britain's superior bargaining power, which meant that Italy could not get a bilateral agreement allowing her fruit into the British market unless she agreed to hold unwanted sterling. Creditor countries like Belgium wished to spend on dollar goods the surplus they earned in Europe, and were aggrieved at British discrimination against them. For unfortunately,

> Belgium, Switzerland and Germany ... economically ... belong to the dollar area and the difficulty has been to reconcile this with a conception of European co-operation, in which on political grounds it was essential to include at any rate Belgium and Germany.[73]

---

* But the Bank of England was always concerned to enhance the role of sterling as an international trading currency, which enabled Britain both to earn foreign exchange for various 'invisible' services, and to hold in London the reserves of all the sterling area countries.

This argument did not much move Gaitskell,[74] who always doubted – as over the Common Market in 1962 – whether political friendship between countries need have much to do with the state of their economic relations.[75]

Britain's own economic interests were not clear, for the existing ramshackle arrangements were unsatisfactory. The lubricant of the system was a supply of Marshall Aid dollars, intended to stimulate purchases of American goods; recipient countries in surplus were required to share these dollars with their debtors. But since currencies were not convertible, every country had to settle – every month – its individual bill with each other country. For all of them the outcome was 'as unpredictable and haphazard as that of the better known Monte Carlo roulette';[76] in 1948–9 Britain had had to pay £73 million in gold to Belgium and Switzerland, yet received none for her (larger) surplus with the remaining OEEC countries.[77] Few of these, moreover, would benefit as much as Britain from an expansion of total trade – which required a multilateral payments scheme, allowing surpluses with some neighbours to be offset against deficits with others so that only the net balance with the whole group had to be settled. Provided the Treasury's fears about a possible drain of gold could be met, and the Bank satisfied about the role of sterling, there could be big economic gains from going into such a scheme.

Britain, however, jealously protected her reserves against any consumption of inessential dollar goods by her own people, and feared to throw them open to finance either luxury imports into the rich Continental creditor countries (against whose goods she would no longer be allowed to discriminate) or the deficits of other countries with them. That risk would be dangerously increased if the £400 millions worth of sterling balances held in Europe on account of past (not current) transactions, were also made available. So Cripps had warned in February that Britain could neither accept the multilateral payments scheme, nor abandon the right to reintroduce quantitative restrictions if she ran into balance of payments difficulties. In March he put forward Britain's alternative plan, offering concessions in return for retaining all the existing bilateral agreements which enabled Britain to discriminate.

On first moving to the Treasury, Gaitskell was extremely suspicious of all these plans. On 15 March 1950 he wrote Cripps a short note warning that even the new British proposals meant too much risk of losing gold:

> I do urge that you should play this hand as long as possible ... It is after all just possible that it might be better for us if the present negotiations were to break down ... I am sure that it will pay us to gain time and not be rushed.[78]

A week later he wrote in his diary that before long 'we shall have to have a complete showdown with them [the Americans] on their whole approach to the world's economic problems'.[6k] Yet within two months he was working closely with them, and had become one of the chief architects of the new system.

Several factors changed his mind. First, devaluation dramatically improved the position of sterling both on current and on capital account.[79] As each new figure became available, the reserves looked more secure and the British negotiators breathed easier. (Furthermore, the creditor countries had devalued less, or not at all, and the Belgian and Swiss surpluses, through which British dollars and gold might have drained away, themselves soon evaporated.) Secondly, progressive Europeans like Robert Marjolin, the secretary-general of OEEC, persuaded him how deep was the Continentals' resentment against discrimination, which they saw merely as a device to maximise British bargaining power.[74] Thirdly, Treasury views, though far from unanimous, helped to bring home to him how much Britain could gain economically from joining a successful payments scheme, and lose politically by staying out of it to the exasperation of both Americans and Continentals.[80*] 'When he came to the Treasury', recalled one adviser with whom he became close, 'he was very doctrinaire and had had very little background about international economic relations ... experience of operating at these levels [showed him] that some factors were less vital than he had thought, and others more so.'

Above all Gaitskell discovered that as usual the United States Administration was divided against itself. Only a week after looking forward to 'a complete showdown with them', he concluded from a long talk to the Economic Co-operation Administration representatives, Averell Harriman[83] and Milton Katz, that 'in the battle we shall have to fight with [the IMF and the US Treasury] ECA might become our allies'; and that then, if the Europeans could be brought in too, by a British pledge to drop unilateral discrimination, 'it would be very difficult for the U.S. Government to resist'.[74] Harriman and Katz were to fulfil his highest hopes. When it was all over he wrote:

> It is rather odd that after acquiring a reputation within the U.K. Government for objecting to so much of what the Americans were trying to do in Europe I should yet have been able to get on well with them. I think the explanation is that most of them had fundamentally the same outlook as I had. They were and are economist new-dealer

* Official Europeanism had strict limits, and did not take seriously the Schuman Plan for a Coal and Steel Community, launched by France in May 1950 and destined for a far more successful future than Whitehall ever supposed. Years later Gaitskell attributed Britain's rejection of it to its supra-national character, and to the extraordinary French demand for a reply in principle within twenty-four hours.[81]

types, and anxious to get the same kind of payments system going as we were ourselves. [6m]

They willingly introduced safeguards into the multilateral structure to avoid the risks Britain feared, defended the agreed plan in Washington against the US Treasury and the IMF, and prevailed upon Congress to appropriate $500 million.

Gaitskell's revised view of the Americans was confirmed increasingly as he saw their attitude from the centre of policy-making. Their demands in these years, he wrote later, were

> informal, rather timid ... [and] politely but firmly brushed off. The *real* pressure for relaxations came, (a) from the dominions, especially after the victory of the Tories in Australia, and (b) from other Ministries in the U.K. whose demands for dollar imports were never satisfied. [84]

Both in London and Paris, Gaitskell managed the British case in the EPU discussions. Even within the official machine the head of the Overseas Finance Division, Sir Henry Wilson-Smith, 'retired from the field and left it all to me'. [6j] And since Cripps was overworked, in poor health and pre-occupied with the Budget, the whole subject was 'almost entirely handed over to me, and the eventual settlement is in fact a result of a series of negotiations which I conducted personally'. [6m] In Paris he was not only the chief United Kingdom delegate but usually the chairman too, and Harriman attributed the final success largely 'to your sympathetic understanding of the problems of all concerned, and the kindly but firm manner in which you forced a facing up to the real issues'. [85] Gaitskell penetrated into detail like an official or expert adviser rather than a ministerial head of delegation, and wholly disregarded status and protocol – appalling his more solemn and stuffy officials, but delighting the Americans. [86] (Katz in particular became a close friend.) He found that nothing was ever settled at formal Executive Committee meetings, though they were private and few countries were represented; to make progress, the same people had to move upstairs to the overcrowded quarters of the British delegation, where little groups retired to the balcony outside when difficulties arose. [6m]

Gaitskell's main aim was to secure liberal credit facilities and so make the liability to pay out gold and dollars as remote as possible. At first he had argued that gold payments would force each country to protect its reserves and so slow down liberalisation, and should therefore be excluded entirely. Harriman and Katz disagreed, but 'vigorously disavowed any intention of forcing deflation on anyone'. [74] During a long negotiating session with them in London in May, Gaitskell once got up at 6 a.m. and scribbled down his view of Britain's essential conditions, which corresponded closely to the government's final proposals:

The officials were I think at first all quite horrified and regarded me as much too inflationary, but it was necessary to condition the Americans to our point of view ... after that weekend the attitude of the officials to me changed decisively and for the better.[6j]

The British Government, in return for concessions by the Americans on the arrangements for gold and credit, let them have their way on the technical methods of bringing sterling into the new system.[6j] The real difficulties over gold were with some of the Continentals:

> In contrast to the Anglo-American economists, with whom we might associate the Scandinavians, we had the Belgian, French and to some extent Swiss banker outlook, who invariably took the side of the creditor and wanted a much tighter system of credit. It is indeed an extraordinary situation that the bankers should have so much power ... They virtually control the financial system of Belgium and have a considerable influence on that of France. No doubt this is partly due to the extent of inflation that there has been in these countries vieing with a dislike of control ... We are much more frightened of deflation and unemployment and are quite prepared to impose controls to prevent inflation ... Hence their insistence on keeping the volume of credit down.[6m]

The final arrangements brought in the entire sterling area, and not just the United Kingdom. The participating countries agreed to free a progressively higher proportion of their (private) trade from quantitative restrictions, to reimpose these only in exceptional conditions, and then not to discriminate. All current transactions were to go through a fully multilateral payments scheme. All participants agreed to lend to the Union, and became entitled to borrow from it up to their quota (which was based on their trade turnover). Within that figure, no gold was to pass for small net debts and credits, but larger debtors had to pay out gold on a sliding scale, so increasing the pressure on them to get out of debt; while creditors received only half in gold, to discourage large surpluses and encourage more expansionist policies. Gaitskell struggled, with the ECA's goodwill and against creditors' opposition, to increase quotas (eventually settled at 15 per cent of turnover with Europe) and reduce the gold element. The Bank was satisfied by an agreement (in the event, inoperative) allowing countries to opt to hold sterling; and Britain won Continental goodwill by allowing existing sterling balances in Europe to be drawn upon by countries in net deficit with the Union. With stronger reserves, a limited liability to pay out gold, and a United States guarantee (the Katz-Gaitskell agreement) to reimburse any gold she did lose by this undertaking, it seemed a safe concession. The scheme went 'farther than any previous international monetary mechanism in placing responsibility to maintain international balance on the creditor as well as on the debtor'.[87] Gaitskell would have liked to go further, but wrote later:

> Unfortunately none of the major European countries agreed and it was only with some difficulty and the support of the Americans that we managed to get any substantial amount of credit in the system. It cannot of course be overlooked that countries like Switzerland are quite unwilling to join in a system in which incorrigible debtors like Turkey and Greece can simply go on living at the expense of others.[88]

He seems to have played a major part in getting the British Government to accept the plan.[89] It satisfied the Labour Party and, on the whole, the Opposition;[90] though the Bank of England continued to worry that the new EPU 'currency' might threaten the special position of sterling. Most of the Continentals were favourable, though Belgium and Switzerland were very reluctant. The US Treasury and the IMF thought it too soft on debtors, too tolerant of economic sin in reimposing quantitative restrictions, and too likely to encourage trade expansion within Europe rather than with the rest of the world. But the ECA representatives realised that the alternative to the EPU was not the instant world-wide liberalisation of which some Washington doctrinaires still dreamed, but continued restrictions all round.

The OEEC countries reached unanimity in early July 1950, and the EPU agreement was signed in September. Once the Korean crisis was over, the EPU made it possible to free most imports from quantitative restrictions; it enabled a much smaller injection of United States aid to finance a much faster expansion of European trade; and it survived the Korean war, Western rearmament, and the commodity boom, with their huge distortions in trade patterns and rapid and violent swings in national positions. Before being wound up on the return to world-wide convertibility in 1959, it had made 'a notable contribution to European recovery',[91] and proved 'one of the major achievements of post-war European cooperation'.[18b]

The episode had a lasting effect on Gaitskell, who had felt uncertain of the outcome.[6J] 'It is rather fun having participated in something which has really actually happened. I mean a new economic system which is definitely going to make some difference, whatever they may say.'[6m] The talks themselves undermined his deep suspicion of the Americans on economic policy, showing him that they could be invaluable allies for a Labour Britain. He wrote to Harriman towards the end:

> [O]n the really important issues we just naturally find ourselves thinking along the same lines. And since, like you, I believe that just about

the most important thing in the world is for the United States and Britain to work along together, this experience has been wonderfully encouraging.[92]

Undoubtedly it helps to explain his attitude to the rearmament gamble a few months later.

In September, he shifted from the problems of Europe to those of the Third World, when he deputised for Cripps in presiding over the Commonwealth Finance Ministers' Conference in London. This meeting approved the arrangements for the 'Colombo Plan', adumbrated in Ceylon in January. The Asian countries had now produced their detailed development plans for improving communications, electricity and agriculture, costing £1,868 million over 6 years for India, Pakistan, Ceylon and Malaya. Britain's contribution was to run down their sterling balances (already depleted by £340 million in 1946–9) by a further £250 million, reducing them by 1957 to a normal currency reserve. A few days later Gaitskell, lobbying in Washington, wrote: 'if the Congressional elections go reasonably well for the Government there is a pretty good chance that the U.S. will come in.'[70] Though the Republican gains a month later severely limited the Administration's freedom of manoeuvre, the United States did join in 1951 and made substantial sums available. The Colombo Plan attracted several non-Commonwealth Asian countries in the 1950s and 1960s, suggesting that it played—against the daunting scale of Asia's problems—a modest but useful part.

The Commonwealth Finance Ministers were evidently impressed with Gaitskell;[44b] and his friend and colleague Douglas Jay was surprised to find him again revealing unsuspected powers.[5b] Gaitskell himself told a City audience that the meeting had been 'a most exhilarating experience'.[93] Privately he described it as:

Hard work but I enjoyed it. I like being Chairman. It is a thing I do very easily and without much effort ... here were these seven or eight totally different people—a fiery Ceylon Nationalist, a wise and sensible Indian Administrator, a clever but slightly doubtful character from Pakistan, a pushful politician from Australia, a nice elderly man from New Zealand, another rather similar (Mayhew from Canada) and ourselves—all sitting round and talking about affairs of some importance to some 600 million people, and doing so in a sensible, friendly way without any signs of racial feelings or prejudices or argument or anger. In a way it was quite moving.[6n]

v *Korea and Rearmament 1950: 'The Maximum We Can Do'*

In April 1950 Gaitskell was sent as a 'Treasury watchdog' to a meeting of the Western European Union, which discussed without much result the means of financing defence, and tried to persuade the United States to pay part of the cost. There was friction and buck-passing between different governments and different Ministries within the same government, including Britain's:

> The Delegation was led by Shinwell as Minister of Defence ... his chief officials made a determined effort to go back on a Defence Committee decision as soon as we arrived in Brussels, and I had to be very firm indeed. Having won this particular battle, Shinwell was as quiet as a lamb and seemed quite willing to say at the Conference the various things I ... [wrote] down on pieces of paper and passed to him. [6J]

During the summer, Cripps's health deteriorated again, and again Gaitskell ran the Treasury in his place. In June the Chancellor even wrote a letter of resignation, but Gaitskell and Plowden with difficulty persuaded him to go away for three months instead. 'Meanwhile, I have been left in charge, and in order to impress outsiders and officials, at his suggestion, have moved into his enormous room.' [6m] Then on 24 June North Korean tanks crossed the 38th Parallel and invaded South Korea, and all the familiar economic problems were abruptly overshadowed by a new one which dominated Gaitskell's own Chancellorship: rearmament. On 26 July Shinwell told Parliament that £100 million were to be spent on re-equipping the armed forces. But on the very same day Washington urgently asked its allies how much, given United States assistance, they could step up their defence expenditure over the next three years.

Observers interpret events in the light of their own experience, and especially since Vietnam much has been made of local factors in the peninsula and of the defects of the South Korean regime. But at the time Western minds were haunted by the Communists' rapid elimination of all their rivals in Eastern Europe. Socialists above all were sensitive to the Prague putsch, the threats against Yugoslavia and the Berlin blockade. In Washington, a major analysis by the National Security Council had recently anticipated a world-wide Soviet offensive over the next few years. [94] A few weeks later came Korea, the first Communist military invasion of a neighbouring country since 1945, and everyone – in power or out – knew what had followed the indifference of governments in the 1930s to acts of aggression in remote places. Within four days President Truman, with almost unanimous approval in Britain, had decided to intervene.

Nobody could then know what part the Kremlin had played, beyond supplying arms on a huge scale.[95] Some people feared a Soviet march to the Channel. Others, who thought that idea alarmist, still took very seriously the risk of another Communist satellite army attacking a neighbour: Yugoslavia, Scandinavia, West Germany or Iran were identified as possible targets not only by American intelligence sources, but also by Aneurin Bevan, Richard Crossman and the Yugoslav government.[96-7a] So, in late July, the Americans offered to contribute to strengthening Western Europe's defences, provided her allies helped themselves also. Britain, apart from her wartime record, had in 1950 the most stable political system and the most flourishing economy; as the expected leader, she was the key to the others' response.

The British government, which had originally expected to spend £2,300 million on defence over the next three years, already knew that re-equipment would require another £300 million. It was calculated that the economy could produce a further £800 million of military equipment without going over to a war footing. Replying within ten days as requested, Britain therefore, on 4 August, offered to spend on defence in the next three years — conditional on the promised American aid — an extra £1,100 million, of which the United States was asked to provide half.[98] The three-year total would thus be £3,400 million: the British paying £2,850 million of it and, it was hoped, the Americans £550 million.[99]* A later decision to raise the pay and numbers of Servicemen put the total up to £3,600 million.

The Korean war and consequent rearmament were to transform the British economy, British politics, and Gaitskell's career. For him, its first impact came through a humiliating Cabinet defeat at the hands of his old chief, Shinwell: not over the big increase, for the £1,100 million was accepted without much dispute, but over the little one — the extra £200 million on pay.[100] Everybody agreed to some increase, and the Treasury had allowed £30 million a year for it. But the Ministry of Defence were quietly planning to spend nearly twice as much. Cripps's last official act had been to protest angrily to Shinwell at the Ministry of Defence making proposals without consulting the Treasury. Gaitskell discovered that they were demanding £55 million, but argued the Service Ministers into compromising at £40 million:

> Meanwhile, however, they had circulated — contrary to an understanding with us — their original proposals to the Cabinet ... and I had a strong suspicion that they had been round to the P.M. and got him to

* Originally the figure for Britain was £900 million per year; Gaitskell told Cripps he thought the calculation dubious and the sum inadequate, and Cripps said he meant £950 million — which the Cabinet accepted.[99]

surrender ... It was a bad Cabinet, many of the more responsibly minded Ministers being away, such as the Lord President [Morrison] and Dalton, Harold Wilson and Patrick Gordon Walker. And, of course, it was flooded out with Service Ministers and Chiefs of Staff, so perhaps it was not surprising that I was routed. But I fear that this will ... give the Defence Ministry the idea that they can spend anything they like and get away with it ... I was horrified by the entirely casual attitude to the £15 million ... adopted by many of the Cabinet ... I am all for spending money if we can get good value for it in the way of strong defences ... but that is no reason for pouring money down the drain.[6m]

Clearly, long before the 1951 Budget crisis, Gaitskell was trying to keep control over expenditure by fighting about marginal increments;[101] and contrary to Bevan's view,[36f] the Treasury was not specially tender to any military demands.

Gaitskell's defeat leaked to the press;[102] and he 'complained bitterly' to Attlee of having to do the Chancellor's job without having his authority or knowing what the Prime Minister wanted. Attlee would not let Cripps be disturbed, but he did promise better consultation in future.[6m] Three weeks later Gaitskell felt more philosophical about his defeat:

I agree that the decision *may* be right – What annoyed me was not that it was taken but that I had persuaded Shinwell to accept a good deal less – so that the Chiefs of Staff (having I suspect got the ear of the P.M. in advance) really got a very weak sort of Cabinet to overrule this agreement – and that is bad. Politicians should keep on top! Also it is not a good thing that our colleagues should get into the habit of thinking that £15 million is just 'a ha'porth of tar'! However I can hardly imagine a more unsuitable issue to resign on – apart from the fact that I don't feel very strongly on the substance (it was a reasonable gamble) and anyhow why resign from an Acting-post?[67a]

The change of Ministry also affected Gaitskell's private life. Where the Ministry of Fuel and Power had often taken him to distant coalfields and hydro-electric stations, he was now constantly conducting international negotiations, often abroad. These were sometimes exhausting, and on his first trip to Paris he had only forty minutes to himself.[6j] But now and then they gave an opportunity to relax. Dora came with him for the final EPU meeting, when he amused the officials by getting sudden urges to dine in a garish restaurant, and to visit Montmartre.[86a] At the ECOSOC conference he found Geneva beautiful but 'very hot' and 'fiendishly expensive',[6m] went off dancing and swimming and hunting for cheap cafés with his civil servants, and delighted them by his unpretentious modesty.[86c d] The international talks had drawbacks for private life too, combining with family illnesses and foul weather to interrupt his 'entirely inadequate and improvised holiday' in the late summer, as he lamented to Dalton when he had to go to Paris for the regular Bank and Fund (World Bank and IMF) meeting. His old patron had written that 'opportunity is carrying *you* forward on a great wave',[40b] and Gaitskell replied:

> Who wants to see these stiff-shirted bourbon bankers anyway when I might continue the marked progress I have made in surf-riding? ... the sensation of being carried literally on the wave forward remarkably fast is far keener than that of the metaphorical career wave of which you wrote so nicely – though the prospect of suddenly finding oneself ... submerged by the succeeding wave is very real in each case![67]

Gaitskell had to interrupt his holiday again to go to Paris on 'my first trip in what is called a "V.I.P." plane, which was beautifully fitted up with curtains, armchairs, mahogany panelling, etc.'. A car came to collect him at 6 a.m.:

> I managed to wake in time, shave, dress and even have some breakfast, and then saw the car standing in the pouring rain outside, and found to my despair that I could not get out of the hotel. The doors seemed to be locked; it was pitch dark inside, and I did not know where the keys were. Everybody else was asleep. Finally in desperation I opened the dining-room window from the top – the bottom would not move – and clambered up and out – all in my best overcoat and black hat.[6n]

This time it was not a routine Treasury occasion, but another consequence of the insistent American pressure for rearmament. The French were strongly resisting Washington's demand for rebuilding German armed forces; but Britain sent a delegation, led by Shinwell and including Gaitskell, to persuade them to follow her example and lengthen the term of military service to two years. Gaitskell found them 'completely obstructive' and 'very unconvincing', though he did reach some common ground with their Finance Ministry over problems of rearmament finance.[6n]

Parliament was recalled on 12 September 1950 to pass the Bill lengthening national service. The Prime Minister in opening the debate stressed that the rearmament programme was dependent on American assistance:

> This great expenditure represents the maximum we can do ... without resorting to the drastic expedients of a war economy[*] ... we are reaching the limit of what we can do unaided without impairing our

---

* 'Drastic expedients' meant direction of labour and requisitioning of premises.[103]

economic position ... before we can decide the exact extent of our effort we must know what assistance will be forthcoming from the United States of America.[97c]

Gaitskell spoke on the economic aspects, stressing that an increase of over 50 per cent in defence spending had serious implications for both the balance of payments and domestic consumption. Since exports, investment and the Colombo Plan commitments must not be sacrificed, the standard of living might well have to fall. He too took care to emphasise the dependence of the programme on American help, to qualify his forecasts ('*if* the full production programme is carried out ... '), and to reaffirm that the British people should not undertake 'burdens unduly heavy in relation to their resources' or to those borne by their allies.[97d] 'I have never had more trouble with any speech,' he wrote. 'When I began work on it nobody had really settled any line of policy at all ... I knew subconsciously that it would be of very great importance to my own personal career. No doubt this worried me.'[6n] It was a great success, taking him 'a long step towards establishing himself as Sir Stafford Cripps's successor'.[104]

Tensions within the Labour Party were still muted, except for the few unhappy pacifists. Harold Wilson and John Freeman, who were both to resign with Bevan the following year, spoke a few days later to justify the government's ban on exporting machine tools to Eastern Europe.[97f] Richard Crossman cautiously supported the programme:

> if we want to influence American policy we have to contribute to the defence of the West ... this has taken us far beyond the present level of our resources ... we have gone far ahead of the Americans. I think we were right to do so. But we cannot go beyond a certain limit.[97b]

But warning notes were now appearing in *Tribune* (which had supported the Berlin airlift, the Atlantic Pact and the Korean intervention);[105] and Jennie Lee suggested that Britain was doing too much and the United States too little.[97e] Across the Atlantic the view was naturally different, as Gaitskell was soon to discover when, at his own request, he went to Washington to put the British case: against convertibility and immediate trade liberalisation, for which the Americans did not press; for their participation in the Colombo Plan, where the Administration showed goodwill; and on two rearmament problems, raw materials and financial assistance.[70]

Raw material prices were soaring as the United States and the European countries competed for defence supplies. Absurdly, the Americans were pressing hard for a great allied rearmament effort, yet impeding it by their own purchasing programme, which was raising prices and creating shortages in Europe and especially in Britain (where stocks had been run down owing to restrictions on dollar imports, and on credit after devaluation). The British would have liked to set up commodity committees of producing and consuming countries, co-ordinated by the United States, France and the United Kingdom; but the other European countries were unwilling. In principle the Americans accepted Gaitskell's approach, but the seven United States agencies concerned were not brought together until December, following Attlee's visit. Even then long delays continued, because of 'the chaotic nature of the administration in Washington [and] the extraordinary fear the Americans have of giving any offence to the smallest possible power'. By March 1951 a cumbrous organisation was at last in place – and raw material prices were falling from their peak.[106]

The talks on financing rearmament proved no more satisfactory. In conveying the first United States approach in late July, the American Ambassador had given definite but not specific assurances of financial help. When the British Government responded by asking the Americans to pay half of the £1,100 million increase:

> They received our proposals very coldly and seemed to expect that we ought to be doing a lot more ... They are curious people to deal with – nice, well-intentioned but, I think, often lacking in judgement. And whereas most high officials here are pretty shrewd [politically,] ... their counterparts in the American Civil Service are often very much at sea.[6m]

Such frustrations were soon to be repeated on a larger scale, for British politicians (and officials) normally served a government with a parliamentary majority which could fulfil any commitment it made; they found it hard to appreciate that no US Administration could do the same, and that its promises of assistance, even when genuinely meant, could never be more than pious hopes.

Gaitskell found out in October 1950 that the Administration could not deliver on its pledges, for Congress had severely restricted non-military aid under the Mutual Defence Assistance Act, and had forbidden its use to compensate for lost exports.[107] American public opinion was quite unsympathetic, for Britain's reserves had doubled in the past year, following devaluation and economic recovery in the United States. They were still far too low, and were threatened by worsening terms of trade;[93] but Americans observed the improvement and disregarded the qualifications. The political climate in Washington was appalling, with newspapers treating as blackmail the British warning that her rearmament must depend on the size of the American contribution. Even her Administration sympathisers thought her claims exaggerated, while in the less friendly US Treasury officials believe it is time that Britain chose between a suitable posture of defence and a continuation of her present high standard of living ... It is wondered here whether Britain may not be subordinating the immediate task of financing her rearmament to that of strengthening her position in the sterling bloc.[4c]

It soon became known that Britain would not get more than one-third of the $1,500 million she was requesting; so that the Americans were demanding even more from Britain while no longer offering much themselves. As Gaitskell wrote, it was

> a rather awkward situation. We had said in public that we would carry out this programme given substantial dollar aid. It was evident that the Americans would not be able to give us that aid. It was, however, equally apparent that some considerable speeding up in defence was necessary.[70]

Gaitskell was warned on arrival by all his hosts — Snyder, Secretary of the Treasury, Foster, head of ECA, and Harriman, head of the Mutual Security Agency and responsible for foreign aid — that Britain could no longer expect Marshall Aid.[6n] The promised financial help over rearmament, too, would have to wait until the deteriorating terms of trade showed up in the balance of payments. Bevin had persuaded the Americans in September to discuss the long-term problem with Britain and France, and meanwhile to make a contribution to the first £200 million of extra spending to which Britain was already committed; but where Britain had asked for 50 per cent of it in dollars, they offered only 20 per cent — which Gaitskell tactfully welcomed as a first instalment.[70]

The long-term prospects seemed somewhat more hopeful. During the tripartite discussions, Paul Nitze, Assistant Secretary of State, suggested that instead of the United States making bilateral grants to each of her allies, NATO should consider how far the defence burden was being fairly shared among the European countries and between them and the United States. The British proposed that this 'burden-sharing exercise' should be carried out in stages: first a military plan for NATO and for each member; then a NATO decision on where the equipment was to be produced, which could be costed; and then arrangements to compensate for any inequality of burdens, either by adjusting the production programme, or by having countries carrying too light a share pay sums of money. That second alternative should

> not entitle the country which supplied the money rather than equipment to any particular control over the way the recipient country, which was carrying the heavier burden relatively in terms of equipment and manpower, spent the money it received.

The Americans, worried about Congress, demurred to that. Gaitskell felt that while

> for our own political purposes we must present the Nitze exercise as a new look where we would no longer be in the same relationship as we had been under E.R.P. [European Recovery Program], we would have in practice to be reasonable and not pedantic ... the sensible way out of the difficulty was probably to try and get NATO missions set up in the different countries in which the U.S.A. ... would really be acting in and on behalf of NATO.

He also thought the Americans recognised – without eagerness – the need to assess the equity of the distribution of the burden; and he returned reasonably optimistic:

> [T]he Americans probably start with the idea ... that we ought to be able to carry ... the £3,600 million programme without much financial assistance. We can, however, reasonably expect that they will be open to argument as a result of considering the whole question of equality ... We may have ... to adjust our ideas as to the form ... [of aid], in particular as between military production and dollars. From the point of view of Congress (and incidentally the point of view of economic interest) the former is greatly to be preferred.[70]

Apart from business Gaitskell enjoyed his first trip across the Atlantic – 'an event in anybody's life,' he wrote. He had tried to arrange a lecture tour before the war and had again hoped to go both as a back-bencher, and as Minister of Fuel and Power.

> I was determined at the Treasury to get there ... I felt quite boyish, the same as we used to when we went to Scotland as children, starting out on this trip ... On arrival we found that our luggage was not there. We had been treated as so much VIP that they managed to put it on the wrong plane, and that meant waiting. So we decided to go into New York for lunch.

He was struck by the number of Blacks, and by the 'endless streams' of cars delaying his Sunday afternoon flight on to Washington. He found the capital 'attractive ... in its domestic architecture ... big white Ministry buildings stand in a kind of park; and then the trees, mostly fully grown and just with autumn tints on them'.[6n] From Washington he had a bumpy, uncomfortable flight to Ottawa for talks with the Canadian Ministers of Finance and Commerce. He found that transition rather 'like moving from the south of England to the north', and the Canadian capital less congenial than the American, lacking in subtlety and charm – though the civil servants and Ministers with whom he mixed were capable and helpful.

After three days in Canada Gaitskell took the train to New York, where he had little to do but enjoy himself and did so thoroughly – except at the United Nations, which he thought depressing and 'excruciatingly dull'. Returning to his hotel on the second night, he found a message to telephone the British High Commissioner in Canada. He put through the call from his bedroom, and the voice told him to prepare for a shock:

> I thought, 'Oh God! what awful brick have I dropped in Ottawa – are the Canadians going to claim that we have agreed to import far more?' Then he went on 'I have a message for you from the P.M.' I thought that he meant the Canadian Prime Minister ... Then he read ... that Stafford was not going back for a year and that after consulting with his colleagues, the P.M. wanted me to take his place. Would I agree to having my name submitted to the King? I can never think of the right thing to say ... So I just said ... 'Yes I will do it and I will send him a a message myself soon'.[6n]

Unable to locate any New York friends to celebrate with, he summoned his official advisers (one of them from bed) to take advantage of his last few hours before the press arrived. 'A rather pathetic procession moved slowly up Broadway', the officials prudently dissuading the new Chancellor from entering each dubious establishment marked 'Dancing' and 'Girls', so that dissipation was confined to buying ties at the all-night shops and visiting a nightclub with a political cabaret (where they were mistaken for actors). They were very short of money, and on finding that Gaitskell's whisky and soda had cost $10, Plowden forbade a second – to his master's chagrin when they discovered too late that the price covered several drinks.[108] Next evening:

> My last night in New York while it was still secret was especial fun ... I went with my friend, Jim Orrick and 'did the town', the best part being dancing with his sister-in-law in Greenwich Village at a ... most excellent cabaret of informal character.[6n]

He told Orrick of his promotion as they said goodnight, and went to bed at 4.30 a.m.; yet he was down for breakfast with a senior adviser who was catching a very early plane.[109] The news broke that afternoon.

> I am getting quite used to being approached by journalists. It is rather like the novelette business of two detectives waiting for you. They step out and confront you, and ... I gave them a quick message and was photographed – horrible photos – and had to pack.[6n]

In his exhilaration on first hearing the news, he poured out to William Armstrong – Cripps's private secretary and now to be his own – his hopes for the rejuvenation of the Labour government with the arrival of his generation in positions of power.[108a] But by the time he landed at London Airport more sober thoughts prevailed, and when his own private secretary congratulated him he replied: 'No it isn't good news — it is ten years too soon.'[86c] As he wrote a few days later, he was used to the Treasury by now, but not to the public side of his new job, where 'It's roses to begin with but not for more than a day or two'.[43b] His first call was on Cripps, who was charming and did all he could to smooth Gaitskell's path; his next on Attlee, who advised reassuringly: 'don't worry, my boy, it may never happen'.[39] As Gaitskell recorded it:

> one's interviews with him are never very exciting or long. But I made sure that I really was to be Number 4 in the Government as Stafford had been. He warned me about Shinwell and Bevan, but told me that he was going to move Nye from the Ministry of Health to the Ministry of Labour — something I had been hoping for and in my quiet way pushing for a long time. But ... he told me a day or two ago that there had been difficulties. So he was letting it rest for the moment ... inflation and rearmament [are m]ore difficult in some ways, though less critical, than the 1947–49 problems. So far everybody is being very nice but that will not last for long.[6n]

CHAPTER 8

CHANCELLOR OF THE EXCHEQUER: BEVAN AND THE BUDGET 1950–1

'A high snow peak ... [and] a steaming tropical swamp'
(DALTON COMPARING HG AND BEVAN, APRIL 1951)
*'One or other of us is not going to be a member of the Government tomorrow –
I am not sure which it will be'*
(HG TO THE KING ABOUT BEVAN, JUST BEFORE THE BUDGET)

i *Unknown Chancellor*

BECAUSE of Cripps's state of health, senior Ministers had known for months that a new Chancellor might be needed. Dalton, who did not want the post himself, had urged Gaitskell's eventual claims on Attlee in January 1950, in the summer, and again in October when he heard that Cripps had finally resigned – only to find that the decision he wanted had already been taken.[1] The decisive influence was Cripps[2] [3a] [4a] himself, who further insisted that Gaitskell, though young and little known in the Party, must replace him also as the fourth senior Minister, after the Prime Minister, Morrison and Bevin.[5] Those senior colleagues also approved of Gaitskell[6] and much preferred him to Bevan.[7] [8a] [f] Morrison did not think himself qualified, turned down various unofficial approaches, and was quite content at the choice of a man too young, as it then seemed, to be a dangerous rival.[9a]

Lobby gossip had tipped Bevan or Morrison himself, assuming Gaitskell would lack weight.[10] He was only forty-four, the second youngest Chancellor of the twentieth century, with the least parliamentary experience since Lord Henry Petty at the beginning of the nineteenth. He had little standing with the Labour rank and file. Yet his promotion was well received in the PLP, and James Callaghan, who often acted as an additional PPS to Gaitskell, wrote: 'I have not heard a single word of criticism about your appointment, because it is regarded as a natural and inevitable step. There was no one else. That is a remarkable tribute.'[11a] [c] One commentator found approval among most MPs but unhappiness on the Left; Richard Crossman agreed, but thought Gaitskell more willing to listen and much

18 Visiting an oil refinery in 1948. Leslie Murphy, Gaitskell's private secretary, is behind his right shoulder looking down

19 With Herbert Morrison (*left*), Prime Minister Clement Attlee, and Sam Watson (*right*) in Durham, 1949

20 Douglas Jay

21 Jim Griffiths and Patrick Gordon Walker (*right*), Colonial and Commonwealth Secretaries, at a conference with their officials

22 With housewives in his Leeds constituency

shrewder than Cripps.[12] The one really hostile comment came from the Beaverbrook press, pursuing a long flirtation with the Labour Left. The political correspondent of the *Daily Express* discovered more back-bench and ministerial opposition than anyone else.[13] He also recalled Porthcawl, to suggest that Gaitskell might 'crack emotionally under the strain of having to introduce a rearmament budget', and the Service pay battle with Shinwell, to predict that the authority of the Treasury, asserted under Cripps, would now crumble if it were challenged.[14]

Such challenges were not hard to foresee. Gaitskell himself hopefully felt it 'so important ... to give the lie to the famous saying ... that "there are no friendships at the top" ';[15] but the rearmament programme made friction inevitable between the Chancellor and the Minister of Defence, quite apart from the latter's personal antagonism. As Gaitskell wrote:

> I have not had much trouble with any of my colleagues. Shinwell is the most difficult. Obviously my promotion over his head went very deep. He never loses an opportunity of picking a quarrel with me, sometimes on the most ridiculous grounds. In any case there are often very good grounds for it in view of the terrific defence expenditure.[16a]

Shinwell had told Attlee in advance that he disapproved of Gaitskell and favoured Morrison.[8a f] More ominous was the wrath of Aneurin Bevan, whose selection was opposed by senior Ministers[4b] and trade union leaders[8b] and, in Attlee's view, would not have carried confidence abroad.[3a]

Bevan had been restive for some time, and plenty of journalists knew it. He had stayed too long at the Ministry of Health, where his creative work was done. He was unhappy with Morrison's policy of 'consolidation', and preferred rousing the Labour faithful to cosseting the floating voter. Such differences over political strategy become acute when a precarious government must soon face the electorate.* As the Party Conference opened at Margate, a political correspondent drew attention to their

> duel for the future and not the present leadership of the party ... the Minister of Health is manoeuvring for support ... assuming for himself the role of defender-in-chief of the social services, especially the National Health Service, against any economy measures which may be hatching in the Treasury.[18]

Weakened in the PLP by his 'vermin' speech, Bevan still appealed to the Party activists, and hoped that an early election would return either a Labour government strong enough to ignore Morrison's electoral

---

* As with Chamberlain and Gladstone in 1885, Gladstone and Rosebery in 1894, Chamberlain and Balfour in 1903 — and Carrington and Whitelaw seventy years later.

I

calculations, or a Tory one which would soon be ousted by a more left-wing Labour opposition.[18]

The battle lines were thus already drawn six months before the crisis over Gaitskell's Budget and three weeks before his appointment as Chancellor. That promotion touched off a major explosion. Bevan had apparently expected Cripps to recommend him for the succession;[19-20] when Woodrow Wyatt told him Cripps was proposing Gaitskell, 'he went very red in the face, said "Disgraceful, monstrous", and rushed out of the room'.[21a b] When the appointment was announced, he launched a torrent of abuse against the Prime Minister in the hearing of the policemen, the officials of the House, and Tory MPs, until Douglas Jay pushed him into the Chancellor's room and shut the door.[22a]

Several of Bevan's colleagues concluded that he had wanted the Exchequer for himself; friends of his thought he hoped for the Foreign Office, where Ernest Bevin might be obliged by ill health to resign at any time.[23] Bevan was fully entitled to aspire to these major offices, and might well resent the elevation of a man his junior in age by nine years and in parliamentary experience by sixteen, with far lower Party and national standing — and with whom he was having 'frightful wrangles'[24a] on the Cabinet Committee on Health Service financing. He sent the Prime Minister, instead of his promised note on reorganising Whitehall departments, a petulant letter expressing

> consternation and astonishment ... it is impossible to give advice and counsel about Government policy when only a part at a time is disclosed to me ... I have no complaint that you have not thought it prudent or wise to consult me ... but ... I think the appointment of Gaitskell a great mistake ... [which] must necessarily change my attitude to the new office which you suggested for me.[25a]

There followed 'a tremendous row with Clem' over the appointment.[24b] The intended reshuffle had to be postponed, for as Dalton heard, 'Nye is being very difficult and behaving very badly and alienating many friends and sympathisers'.[24c]

Gaitskell learned or judged that Bevan was 'not so much jealous but humiliated', Shinwell similarly put out, and Wilson 'inordinately jealous, though in view of his age there is really no reason for it'.[16b] Outside Westminster his appointment drew approval from an immense variety of people, from film stars to Gas Board members and from the chairman of the Stock Exchange to the secretary of the Beeston Working Men's Club and Institute. Leslie Murphy, Gaitskell's former private secretary, was so thrilled that he forgot to shave. Sir Donald Fergusson had hoped for it

> because of my admiration for your courage & sense of proportion ...

[and of] a national as opposed to a purely party interest. That was where I think Dalton failed and Cripps succeeded.

But please remember you have 20 or 30 years before you ... take a long view and don't wear yourself out.[26]

That note recurred over and over again.

On becoming Chancellor Gaitskell did not much change his ministerial style.[16b] He did not move into 11 Downing Street but stayed in Hampstead, mainly because of the children's schooling. Again his civil servants found him fascinated by detail and determined to ensure that he fully understood the complexities of every issue. Again he took immense pains with Parliamentary Questions, going through each in detail and frequently siding with the critical MP against the office; it took time, but gave Gaitskell a much better understanding of the House of Commons. Behaving more like a fellow-administrator than a senior Minister, he would spend hours talking over problems with junior officials, or holding 'seminars' on the economic implications of policy. Senior and traditional Treasury men resented the time involved, the attention to juniors, or the questioning of the established policies of Whitehall's premier Department; at first some also found his manner brusque and imperative. But some able younger officials, later holding high responsibilities themselves, saw matters differently. His questions on detail were shrewd and probing and enabled him to judge which advisers to rely on. As Gaitskell held his own with the ablest civil servants, the arguments advanced the discussion and gave him a full grasp of the problems.

As at Fuel and Power, he had had months to get to know the senior officials before taking responsibility for the Department. Again there was an early malaise, soon dispelled:[27]

I cannot say that I am entirely happy about the officials ... they have such a keen sense of their own independent departmental position as apart from serving me ... buttressed up by such institutions as the Budget Committee, which is purely official ...

... The machine can get so easily slack if you leave them alone. But if you harass them then they complain bitterly that you are interfering too much and not delegating, etc.[16a]

Gaitskell knew that a Chancellor submerged by minor problems would have no time for major ones. He had no Minister of State, but delegated heavily to the Economic Secretary (John Edwards) and Financial Secretary (Douglas Jay), urging them repeatedly to refer upwards as little as possible.[5] Dalton noted at the New Year that Gaitskell 'said he wasn't feeling too overworked ... He has got D.J. & J.E. to take over a lot of work and relieve him of many minor decisions.'[28] But the probing and harassing had their price. As always the civil servants felt he wanted to do too much himself. His insistence on redrafting major speeches was the despair of his advisers.[29] He was bad at keeping appointments – seeing too many people, letting discussions run long over time and disrupting his daily timetable. He put too much faith in the accuracy of the estimates he tried so hard to improve, and some shrewd civil servants – though not all – felt that he was too interested in the economic aspects, too confident that there was a right economic answer, and so somewhat distracted from the Minister's role of exercising political judgment. But almost every survivor who served under him in the Treasury thought him, in a difficult year, an exceptionally intelligent, courteous, clear-sighted and courageous chief.[30] An unofficial historian of the Treasury writes that Gaitskell

> probably understood his job better than any Chancellor we have had before or since ... His officials had a great respect for him, but they complained that he insisted on doing other people's work for them – a complaint that may simply mean that he wanted to run his own policy.[31]

On first learning that he was to take Cripps's place, Gaitskell had told William Armstrong that over the next few years the principal task of a Socialist Chancellor would be the redistribution of wealth, which unlike the greater equalisation of incomes was not yet generally accepted; once that was accomplished, the philosophical differences between the parties would gradually diminish and their rivalry would turn increasingly – as in the United States, he said – into a competition in governmental competence.[32a d] He did not tackle it in his first and only Budget, for that was designed to combat inflation by reducing consumption.[33a] But for his second he was planning a capital gains tax;[24d*] and both before and after the 1951 election he urged the need for Labour to think out its policy on the subject.[34]

More immediately he was concerned, like later Labour Chancellors, with the pressures of trade unionists and of bankers. In his first major speech in the House he addressed the former in terms that were to become painfully familiar, and was praised for his realism in the *Financial Times* (then very partisan). Acknowledging that 'the remarkable stability of wages over the last 12 months [cannot] be continued indefinitely', he warned:

> Higher incomes, unaccompanied by increases in production, will certainly lead to higher prices: and higher incomes in one group will

---

* He also wanted extra surtax on unearned income; a capital levy when the political climate was right; and a Party decision on whether to allow people to buy private education for their children.

lead to demands for higher incomes elsewhere, which, in turn, will lead to higher prices for everyone ... We cannot by manipulation of personal income, get more out of the national product than is available ... The Government must, as far as possible, so control through its budgetary and credit policy the flow of money as to reduce pressure provided this does not of course lead to unemployment.[35a]

But the qualifications mattered, and he was no less firm with the bankers. Cobbold, Governor of the Bank of England, had been pressing for a higher bank rate ever since Dalton's day. Gaitskell thought it a costly and 'completely antiquated' alternative to more direct methods of credit control,[36] but found their discussions 'rather sticky' and the Governor, though not trying to pursue an independent policy, 'somehow uncooperative'. Gaitskell found most of the Bank spokesmen 'singularly bad at putting their case, and ... usually wrong in their conclusions'.[16c]

There were also a few problems with his fellow Ministers, and when Dalton praised Gaitskell's Cabinet statement on the forthcoming Economic Survey as better than Cripps's had been, he added: 'You also treated very patiently the theoretical rigmarole of one who was very peeved not to have been offered the job!'[37a] Departmental friction occurred with the Board of Trade, whose senior officials were still unwilling to act against monopolies, consumer grievances and resale price maintenance. Gaitskell had long been anxious to do so, as had Dalton – who, seeking new issues for the Labour Party after the deadlocked 1950 election, chaired a Cabinet Committee on these problems. But Dalton claimed that he met constant foot-dragging from officials, abetted by their political chiefs, at the Board of Trade, Agriculture and Food. Harold Wilson saw no economic or political urgency; after Wilson resigned in April, his successor Sir Hartley Shawcross remained timid, and nothing was done about RPM until Edward Heath abolished it in 1964.[38]

These discussions were confined to Whitehall. Beyond, intense controversy developed over relations with several foreign countries. One was the Argentine, where the Ministry of Food had overestimated Britain's bargaining position in negotiations over meat and had had to cut the ration to 8d. Gaitskell had repeatedly tried to persuade them to settle, but loyally took responsibility for a thoroughly unpopular policy.[39] Publicly, his winding-up speech in the House was made inaudible by 'Tories yelling all the time. This is now normal in every Government last speaker. And Mr. Speaker makes no effort to check it'.[24e] Privately, his wife impressed the housewife's resentment on the Chancellor by keeping him on fish, which he did not like.[40] Conservatives also repeatedly urged scaling down the sterling balances and so repudiating Britain's debts (at least in part) and her promises to the Asians under the Colombo Plan. At Churchill's sixth such question Gaitskell was stung into replying – to the delight of the Labour benches[16a] – that his 'attitude to India ... has always been unrealistic and ... totally lacking in humanity'.[41] He had even more trouble over an agreement with Egypt, which halved the current rate of repaying British debts and avoided a disastrous economic war.[42]

There were faint tremors of the coming domestic earthquake:

> Outwardly Nye Bevan is quite friendly again, and at least he gives a much more honest view of things than Shinwell does. I do not really feel with him that he is insincere and for long going to take a view simply because of his personal likes or dislikes.
>
> Harold Wilson is probably still exceedingly jealous, but I must say I have had no great difficulty with him. But all this is rather premature because the real struggle will come when we try and settle expenditure policy and get nearer to the Budget.[16a]

Prospects of a peaceful settlement of that coming struggle were not improved by the end of Marshall Aid – formally on 1 January 1951 but in fact six weeks earlier. Knowing that Britain's balance of payments surplus made this inevitable, Gaitskell made the best of it by ensuring maximum publicity for her impressive economic improvement. 'In a little over two years', he claimed, 'we have done a job ... for which four years were originally allowed.'[43] The two governments agreed that aid was suspended not abolished, and would be restored if the British economic situation or balance of payments deteriorated seriously. But that commitment was not to be fulfilled.

ii Korea and Rearmament 1951: 'To the Limit of the Resources under our Control'

The joint statement specified that Marshall Aid was ending because of Britain's rapid recovery, but also owing to new burdens on the United States arising from her own and allied rearmament. For by December 1950 the Chinese had entered the Korean conflict, in which the U.S. was to incur very heavy casualties. General MacArthur had driven back the North Koreans in September, advanced beyond the 38th Parallel and then, to Britain's dismay, approached the Chinese frontier. That 'prancing proconsul' already alarmed many Americans, including President Truman; but to dismiss him too soon would only play into the hands of a growing and furious Republican opposition. Confident to the last that the Chinese would not intervene, MacArthur swept on to the Yalu – and was thrown back in disarray by a massive Chinese offensive on 24 November which nearly drove the United Nations forces out of Korea.

After Truman's supposed hint that the atomic bomb might be used against China, Attlee flew to Washington on 4 December 1950 for a famous meeting, at which they differed sharply. The British still held, as the Americans recently had, that China could be kept out of the Soviet orbit by sympathetic treatment over Formosa (Taiwan) and UN represent-ation.[44a] But the Americans — engaged in a desperate war, and with the Republican hawks strengthened in Congress — now argued that United States opinion would not understand a policy of opposing aggression in Europe while appeasing it in the Far East.[45-6]

Besides differing with them over China, the Labour Government wanted to keep in step with the Asian Commonwealth, particularly India. But American support was vital both to economic recovery and to balance Soviet military power in Europe; and a rebuff to the friendly Truman Administration would strengthen the Republicans who were isolationist in the West and adventurist in the East. The dilemma became acute after Peking brutally rebuffed two conciliatory UN resolutions, one (the 'Five Principles') largely inspired by the Commonwealth Prime Ministers. The United States had — under strong criticism at home — accepted the Five Principles (hoping that the Chinese would reject them);[47] she now pressed for reciprocal concessions from her allies, urging the UN to declare China an aggressor and to prepare sanctions against her. The Senate voted for that (the 'Brand China' resolution) with no dissenter, the House of Representatives with only two. By tabling it at the UN on 20 January 1951, the United States divided the British Cabinet not over its merits — for no one wanted it — but over whether the United Kingdom could risk a break with Washington.

Gaitskell played a major part in this controversy. On 10 January, just before the Five Principles were voted, he was very worried: 'the inter-national outlook gets gloomier and gloomier'. The British government feared, he wrote, that if the Chinese were bombed or blockaded they would retaliate by seizing Hong Kong and attacking Indo-China and Malaya. 'The awful dilemma is that if we cannot restrain the Americans then we have to go in with them in China, which nobody wants, or desert them ... [with] very serious consequences in their participating in Euro-pean defence.'[16c] Bevin's policy had been to make every effort to delay matters and moderate the Americans, but in the last resort accept the 'Brand China' resolution. Then on 25 January the Cabinet, with Bevin away ill, were told they 'must assume the resolution would be put in an unpalatable form'. The Foreign Office spokesman and Minister of State, Kenneth Younger, wanted to vote against the United States. Only Hector McNeil, his predecessor in the post, advocated supporting Washington; as the Cabinet clearly would not agree to that, Gaitskell proposed absten-tion — which was also preferred by Attlee, Morrison and Jowitt. But

Younger said it was really no different from an adverse vote, on which course the majority decided. Gaitskell was appalled. It meant opposing all the white Dominions, but far worse:

> I thought this decision might have the most fatal consequences on Anglo-American relations, and that it would enormously strengthen the anti-European block in the U.S.A. It might lead to their virtually coming from Europe which would, in my opinion, be the end for us.[16d] [l]

Discovering next day the dismay of the Treasury and Foreign Office officials, which they felt sure Bevin would share, Gaitskell privately warned the Prime Minister that he might have to resign if the decision was maintained:[16d] a very bold stand for a young Minister with no popular following.

Events at once made it pointless, for Washington agreed after all to consider an amendment (inspired by Gladwyn Jebb the British Ambassador to the UN, and Lester Pearson the Foreign Minister of Canada) which deferred discussing sanctions till after a new attempt to conciliate China.[48] The Cabinet rescinded its previous decision, which four Ministers still supported.[49] It agreed to cast its vote for the resolution if the proposed amendments were accepted, and if not to let Attlee decide; Gaitskell felt confident 'he would not go further than abstention'.[16d] The United States did agree to delay any decision on the sanctions which so alarmed all their allies, and on 1 February, a week after the UN forces resumed the offensive, the amended resolution was voted by 44 to 7.*

The American Administration was still under heavy pressure from the Republican hawks to break free from European entanglements and fight an all-out war in the Far East, a course which seemed very dangerous not only to the Labour Government, but also to Winston Churchill and President Truman. Advised by the CIA that the Russians hoped for a free hand in Europe while American troops were tied up in Asia, Truman publicly called war with China 'a gigantic booby-trap'.[51] But to persuade domestic opinion to continue supporting American aid to Europe, the Administration needed evidence of the Europeans' readiness to contribute to their own defence. In exerting pressure on them, Washington was no more sensitive to their political than to their economic complaints. The Department of Defense, overriding the State Department,[46c] insisted on bargaining American commitment in Europe (more United States troops

---

* India and Burma joined the Soviet block against it, while Sweden, Yugoslavia and seven Arab and Asian countries abstained. Foot, in one page on this affair, badly misquotes his sources and makes twelve errors, six of them substantial; all six are damaging to Gaitskell. Roth repeats most of them, including the untruth that Gaitskell called this clash 'a battle for power' between Bevan and himself.[50]

and a United States supreme commander) against European acquiescence in immediate rearmament, including that of West Germany.[53]

Any Administration sympathy for Europe's needs and difficulties was soon swept aside by the impatient and suspicious congressional Republicans, increasingly aggressive after their gains in the November mid-term elections. Dean Acheson abandoned his previous policy of detaching the U.S.A. from Chiang Kai-shek and trying to wean the Chinese Communists away from the USSR; and the Korean invasion was taken to confirm the National Security Council's alarms and to show, contrary to the advice of the State Department's Russian experts, a new Soviet willingness to use armed force to achieve her objectives.[54] Both the State Department and the military believed that a massive Soviet attack on the West was a serious and perhaps even an imminent possibility; and against NATO's 12 divisions the Russians had 175, with 27 (plus 60,000 militarised German police) in East Germany alone.[46d] On 6 December 1950, during Attlee's visit, the American joint chiefs of staff sent out a general war warning to all unified commanders.[55] The British War Office, too, warned the Cabinet early in the New Year: 'war possible in 1951, probable in 1952'.[24f]*

In this mood of crisis German rearmament was reluctantly accepted 'in principle'. The main opposition came from the French, but the British government was unhappy too, and divided over Germany as well as China; 'there is to some extent the same cleavage', noted Gaitskell.

> The anti-Americans ... will not admit now the Russian menace. This leads them to oppose a lot of things which the Americans want to do ... [like] rearming Germany. It leads to accepting ... an agreement with Russia which ... might be extraordinarily dangerous.[57] ... [Some] believe it their duty and the right policy to follow opinion in the Party which certainly is pretty anti-American, and still rather pacifist.[16d]

He was among those who disagreed, and believed the Labour activists untypical of the country on such issues, and anyway prepared to follow a Government lead. He added:

> One cannot ignore the ... personal ambitions and rivalries at work. H.W. is clearly ganging up with the Minister of Labour, not that he

---

* Apparent corroboration for those fears emerged years later from Communist sources when Karel Kaplan, a Czech historian who defected after having had access to all Party archives, disclosed a secret Kremlin meeting in January 1951 at which Stalin revealed plans to overrun Western Europe within three or at most four years, and his hearers (the Defence Ministers and First Party Secretaries of the satellite countries) agreed in writing to place their forces under Russian command in the coming war.[56]

cuts very much ice because one feels that he has no fundamental views of his own, but it is another voice. The others on Bevan's side are very genuine. Jim Griffiths for pacifism; Chuter Ede because he is anti-American and Dalton because he hates the Germans.[16d]

Differences in the Cabinet still turned on foreign policy – attitudes towards Germany or China – rather than on the need to rearm. That need was not seriously contested, for if Europe failed to respond to the Americans, it risked being left alone face to face with the USSR. The pressure for even faster rearmament was now insistent, and Britain still held the key. Continental recovery was far behind hers, and political stability and determination were far less. Germany was shattered and disarmed; France was undermined by neutralism and defeatism; weak French and Italian governments faced aggressive Communist oppositions. Without a British lead, there would be no significant European contribution; without that contribution there could be no hope of convincing Congress or the American public to help defend the Continent (while still fighting in Korea) by assembling sufficient forces to deter an attack.[58] Substantial financial aid would come only if the 'burden-sharing' proposals were agreed and then Congress voted them – as it never would if Britain balked at faster rearmament.[59]

Even before the Chinese entered the Korean war, the American soldiers had sought from Britain a programme costing £6,000 million in three years. That estimate was endorsed by the British chiefs of staff;[60] and apparently accepted in principle by Shinwell, the Minister of Defence, in Washington just after Gaitskell became Chancellor.[61] When Attlee visited Truman in December, the British chiefs of staff helped the Americans to press their point upon him.[46e] At the NATO Council in Brussels two weeks later, Bevin announced the British government's decision to rearm faster. On 29 January Attlee told the House of Commons that the Cabinet had decided on an expansion from £3,600 million to £4,700 million over the next three years.[62a]

This, the third increase in a year, was a very big one. In August the government had already agreed to raise defence spending by £1,100 million over three years; now it proposed to double that expansion. The earlier proposal had depended on American help, covering (the Government hoped) half the original amount; but by December it knew that aid would come only slowly and uncertainly through 'burden-sharing'. The extra load on British resources had thus trebled in six months, and the share of GNP going to defence was to rise from 8 per cent before the crisis to 14 per cent after it – a proportion exceeded in NATO only by the United States. No longer did the Prime Minister warn of reaching Britain's economic limit;

instead he promised 'to carry out this production programme to the limit of the resources under our control'.[62b]

In early January Gaitskell had recorded 'something like a panic developing about our defence programme ... the atmosphere becomes more and more like 1940'.[16c] In this mood the Cabinet accepted the £4,700 million programme on 25 January with little dissension: less, over a decision which would have repercussions and provoke controversy for years, than over that crucial UN vote on the 'Brand China' resolution. Gaitskell's diary describes the atmosphere.

> The storm is blowing up harder. We have had a bad week. The meat ration cut to eightpence; the announcement of the rearmament programme and the rise in the price of coal. The general feeling is that we should suffer a pretty heavy defeat if there was to be an Election now.
>
> We got the rearmament programme through however rather more easily than might have been expected ...

With Bevin, Shinwell and the CIGS away, Gaitskell was its main advocate.

> It was expected that Bevan would put up a lot more resistance. I never thought so myself ... We were committed to some acceleration – we could hardly start arguing with the Chiefs of Staffs about what was essential and what was not essential. Both the President of the Board of Trade [Wilson] and Minister of Supply [Strauss] made some effort to resist it, partly I think on political grounds (they are linking up with the Minister of Labour) and partly just as an alibi in case the programme could not be fulfilled or exports dropped catastrophically.[16d]

This contemporary account was confirmed by G. R. Strauss:

> I went to see Aneurin Bevan and said: 'This is much too big ... ' He made sympathetic noises but I was surprised he wasn't more enthusiastic ... I made a speech against it to the Cabinet. Nye never opened his mouth, or if he did he didn't say anything worth saying. Only Harold Wilson and I were against it.[63a b]

Strauss's Parliamentary Secretary, John Freeman, mentioned his Minister's opposition soon afterwards to Dalton.[64] Wilson also thought the programme impracticable, and his biographers say that Bevan dissuaded him from resigning in February over the raw materials situation; though at the time Strauss found him, as well as Bevan, lukewarm.[65]

In the Cabinet, Bevan merely cast doubt on the military intelligence estimates.[66] Many of his colleagues – whom he had never previously left unaware when he seriously disapproved – have testified that he did not challenge the programme until two months later.* His general unhappiness had often been leaked to the press;[69] but those familiar rumblings fore-shadowed a coming battle over paying for rearmament, not an attack on the policy itself as unnecessary, undesirable or impracticable. Besides, Bevan did not just silently and reluctantly acquiesce; shortly before the programme was agreed, he at last accepted his long-suggested transfer to the Ministry of Labour, which was directly involved with it. Gaitskell expected that he would there maintain 'his reputation of being radical in everybody else's Ministry except his own. He will probably be more cautious about wages policy and the direction of labour[70] than he has ever been in the past'.[16e] At his own request,[21c] Bevan wound up the defence debate on 15 February 1951; and he made a categorical public commitment, which Attlee and Gaitskell were careful to avoid, to the full rearmament programme:**

> we do beg that we shall not have all these jeers about the rearmament we are putting under way ... We shall carry it out; we shall fulfil our obligation to our friends and Allies, and at the same time we shall try to ... give mankind another breathing space.[71b]

Many agreed with Gaitskell that it was one of Bevan's best speeches, and it won acclaim even from diehard Tories.[20c d]

> Nye gave one of [his] most brilliant performances ... glittering with striking phraseology ... What a tragedy that a man with such wonderful talent as an orator and such an interesting mind and fertile imagination should be such a difficult team worker, and some would say even worse – a thoroughly unreliable and disloyal colleague. Will he grow out of this? Will he take on the true qualities that are necessary for leadership? Who can say? Time alone will show.[16f]

---

* Dalton reports Crossman saying later: 'Nye's mistake was not to break on armaments, when programme enlarged in February [sic]. I say he made no move.' (Strachey, a Bevan sympathiser who attended these Cabinets as War Minister, was there and did not demur.)[24g] Gordon Walker noted on 9 April 1951: 'Bevan now said that he disliked the whole defence programme.'[67a b] Shinwell wrote later, 'there was never a murmur of protest' from Bevan.[8a d] This is confirmed by Attlee, Freeman, Younger (present on 25 January 1951), and both Gaitskell's and Attlee's private secretaries. These recollections must be treated with caution: Strauss forgot Gaitskell's active part, Wilson forgot Strauss's, and Shinwell and Younger forgot Wilson's.[68]

** Attlee: 'If the programme is fully achieved, the total defence budget over the next three years ... may be as much as £4,700 millions ... limitations on production ... may make it impossible to spend this sum within that period.'[62c] Gaitskell used identical words.[71a] Credit for the qualification was later claimed by Bevan, who had himself omitted it;[72a b] and more plausibly by Strauss, who had queried the programme from the start.[63b]

On 9 March Ernest Bevin was at last moved from the Foreign Office and replaced by Morrison. Because of Bevin's precarious health the Prime Minister had had time to consult widely about the succession.[73] Attlee would have liked to appoint a trade unionist;[24h] but Bevan was never mentioned.[74] He had thus been passed over for both the senior offices, despite his ability and standing in the Party.[75] As early as Christmas, his unhappiness with the Administration had led him to canvass potential allies in resignation;[76] and the choice of Morrison, further weakening his power in the Cabinet, may have been decisive. He doubtless feared his support for rearmament would alienate his following among back-benchers and activists in the country;[77] and thought by resigning he could mobilise them against the 'disastrous and accelerating drift to the right'. From 9 March, wrote Leslie Hunter, he was looking for a pretext to resign;[4c] and many of Bevan's colleagues concurred.[78] Others felt sure that, had he been offered either the Exchequer or the Foreign Office, he would not have resigned a few weeks later.[79] Bevan became more critical in Cabinet after Morrison's appointment, and in discussions on rearmament 'the superficial cordiality between Gaitskell and himself ... reported by members of the TUC economic committee ... rapidly disappeared'.[8b] He soon began to sound his first notes of doubt about arms expenditure – though according to Wilson's biographer it was only after the die was cast that, persuaded by his two fellow-resigners, he broadened the issue beyond teeth and spectacles and 'became a Wilsonite' about the defence programme.[80] For his disappointment had come just as all the tensions and frustrations were mounting to their long-foreseen crunch: the rearmament Budget.

iii   The Cabinet and the Health Charges

The Budget was presented on 10 April 1951, and within a fortnight Bevan, Wilson and Freeman resigned. Gaitskell recorded the developing crisis in two long entries in his diary upon which, with those of other participants, the following account is based.[16g h] He knew early on that he would have to find between £100 and £200 millions, of which – to make the inevitable extra taxation more acceptable – he hoped to get half from economies. But since old age pensions had to be increased, he soon discovered that simply to hold the social services bill constant would involve very drastic cuts in the health service, entirely eliminating free dental and optical services. The Ministers responsible, Hilary Marquand for Health and Hector McNeil for Scotland, quickly dissuaded him from that. When he informed Attlee, Morrison and Bevan of his modified plans, he met 'no adverse reaction' on health charges but 'no enthusiasm at all' on tax increases. 'The P.M. said, "Well! We shall not get many votes out of this".'

During February the health service estimate had to be settled. The previous amount was £393 million; the Ministry wanted £30 million more; Gaitskell persuaded Marquand to try to keep within the old figure, provided the Prime Minister's committee on health service finance were told and accepted the consequences, which they did.[81] In mid-March they approved Marquand's scheme for keeping within the ceiling by imposing some dental and optical charges, and also the prescription charge authorised in Bevan's Act of November 1949. Gaitskell asked Attlee to convene a further *ad hoc* meeting of interested Ministers, particularly Bevan, to give them early warning. There the Prime Minister did not defend the proposals of his own committee, which Bevin now joined Bevan in attacking;[82] anxiety was felt about the prescription charge rather than teeth and spectacles, but a majority backed the Chancellor. Both he and Bevan hinted at resignation. That evening McNeil promised to go with Gaitskell if necessary.[83]

The four senior Ministers met on Tuesday 20 March, and Ernest Bevin proposed compromising on £400 million for the health service. Knowing that that meant no prescription charge, Gaitskell at once accepted providing all others did. Morrison agreed and so (in writing) did Attlee.[84] Next day, the Prime Minister entered hospital with an ulcer. On Thursday 22 March the Cabinet spent an hour and a half on health charges. Bevan again threatened to resign, and indeed to walk out of the meeting, though he was persuaded not to. Although the Home Secretary, Chuter Ede, and Jim Griffiths 'were a little doubtful, all but Bevan and Wilson concurred ... the decision was a perfectly clear one – to proceed with the preparation of the Bill on the lines of the Bevin compromise.' The main clash came 'between Shinwell and Bevan when Bevan began to attack the arms programme in the middle of the discussion': the first contemporary reference to Bevan opposing rearmament itself.[16h]

Over the next fortnight other features of the Budget were being decided and Gaitskell was preparing his speech. There were constant appeals to him to compromise with Bevan, and by him to Morrison to call another Cabinet or smaller meeting of Ministers to settle the matter. Morrison would not do so, and Gaitskell, bereft of any political advice from his senior colleagues, found it an agonisingly lonely period.[32b c]

Bevan went public on 3 April, telling a Bermondsey heckler that he would not remain in 'a Government which imposes charges on the patient'. To Gaitskell and others it seemed 'a blatant threat' to intimidate the Cabinet into reversing its decision;[16g] and at first the Chancellor showed astonishment, wrath and defiance.[32a] He exploded to Dalton: 'Nye's influence was very much exaggerated ... If we didn't stand up to him, Nye would do to our party what L.G. had done to the Liberals. It would, he thought, do us good in the country to make a stand on this.'* But that intemperate

* He added that if Bevan, Wilson and Strachey [*sic*] did resign: 'We'd be well rid of the three of them.'[24i]

mood soon passed.[32a]

On Monday, April 9th, my birthday, I went to the Cabinet where the only item on the agenda was the Budget ... There was little comment on the Budget as a whole, what there was being favourable ... all the taxation side went through easily. But there was another very long discussion on the Health charges ... Bevan himself did not raise [any other] objections ... Of course, everybody was aware ... [and resented] that he had deliberately put himself in a position ... to say ... he was forced to resign.

During the discussion that morning I did not say anything about resignation myself.[16g]

Apart from the two dissidents and George Tomlinson, Minister of Education, who was willing to pay any price to keep Bevan, everyone agreed to reaffirm the Easter decision; Ede, who liked Bevan's arguments, was put off by his threats.[67c] But the repeated appeals to Bevan made him more intransigent, and at lunchtime the meeting adjourned until 6.30 p.m. That gave time to consult Attlee in hospital, and allowed Gaitskell to go home for a birthday party. His private secretary recalls:

The girls had made an enormous cake and were tremendously proud of their father about to introduce his first Budget, which he knew, and no one else did, might never happen at all. In the end he broke down completely and had to leave the party altogether — and I almost broke down too.[32a]

At 5.30 Gaitskell went to tell the King about the Budget and the clash with Bevan:

He said, 'He must be mad to resign over a thing like that. I really don't see why people should have false teeth free any more than they have shoes free'; waving his foot at me as he said it. He is, of course, a fairly reactionary person. As to the rest of the Budget the King did not comment on it and never does. So I left him, saying, 'Well! it looks as if one or other of us is not going to be a member of the Government to-morrow. I am not sure which it will be'.[16g]

Meanwhile Morrison and Whiteley, the Chief Whip, had visited Attlee; and when the Cabinet resumed, 'Morrison read out a message from the P.M. which in effect gave his vote to me and urged the Cabinet to stand by me.'[85] This evening meeting lasted till 9 p.m.:

This time, though very quietly, I did bring my own position in. I simply said that it would be impossible for me, having had a Cabinet decision in favour of this just before Easter, to have it reversed at the last minute. I said that if I resigned I would make no trouble whatever and would always support the Party.[16g]

Dalton confirms his promise 'to go quietly, and not to attack the Government afterwards. This is a high moral attitude compared with Nye.'[24J] Addison, Dalton and Shinwell vociferously supported Gaitskell; Ede and Griffiths felt bound by the previous decision; only Tomlinson voted with the two dissidents.[16g]

Before the vote there was pressure on the Chancellor too. Tomlinson suggested retaining the £400 million ceiling but omitting the charges — precisely the formula which, a year earlier, Bevan had nominally accepted from Cripps but made no effort to observe. Gaitskell resisted it as a dishonest dodge to avoid the charges — without which the Health Ministers knew they could not keep within the ceiling, and which he knew would never be accepted except in the Budget speech. But Morrison liked the formula and kept bringing it up. He pressed it directly, after the Cabinet and again next morning; got Gordon Walker to phone Gaitskell and urge it;[86] and put the idea to the Prime Minister, who was to see Bevan and Wilson at 10.30 a.m. and the Chancellor afterwards.

Gaitskell had worked on his speech at home with his private secretaries until 1 a.m. on Budget day, Tuesday 10 April. Ten hours later:

I went along to the hospital [where] ... he had been kept fully in touch with everything ... he tried to get me to accept some form of words ... which [Bevan and Wilson] would accept, to the effect of a ceiling of 400 millions and if charges were necessary then they would have to be passed. But I had made up my mind that I would announce the charges and I refused to give way. I offered my resignation several times, and I thought as I listened to his arguments that he was going to accept it.[16g]

Attlee urged that something might turn up, and questioned the Chancellor's view that if no one resigned there would be no trouble in the PLP. Gaitskell replied that 'my position would be impossible' unless the charges went through.

Finally, he murmured what I took to be 'Very well! You will have to go.' In a split second I realised he had said 'I am afraid *they* will have to go'.

Just then the Home Secretary [Ede] and Chief Whip came in ... knowing the Home Secretary was very much a wobbler, I felt very depressed. However, there was no need to be. The ... P.M. ... turned to the Chief Whip and said, 'Well, Willy can we get this through the Party?' 'Not the slightest doubt if there are no resignations — No difficulty at all.' They both expressed the view that they thought Bevan wanted to resign in any case.[16g]

Gaitskell then offered to drop his proposal for the charges to come into force at once, so that the Bill need not be retrospective and could be delayed a little. His three hearers thought it would make no difference, but at the very last minute Morrison decided it might.

Gaitskell told Dalton next day: 'Up till noon he hadn't known whether he was going to make a Budget speech or not.[87] He had twice offered to resign, and not to attack the Government.'[24g] After a quick lunch in the Treasury with his wife, Gaitskell walked across to the House escorted by his PPS and private secretary—and found Morrison coming out of the chamber to urge him to make the change after all.[5a] He 'struck out the [relevant] sentence at 3.28 p.m. ... [and] began to deliver the speech'.[16g]

As usual on Budget Day, the House was packed. Wearing an outsize red carnation given him by Felicity Cory-Wright,* Gaitskell began at a tremendous pace. Churchill intervened to tell him to take his time, and his speech lasted 133 minutes, but it won universal acclaim. He 'rose a comparative tyro', wrote one Tory paper, and 'sat down an acknowledged star'.[88] Churchill complimented him on his lucidity and 'evident lack of hatred and malice', and Clement Davies, the Liberal leader, on his thoroughly deserved personal triumph: 'Never in my experience has there been such a chorus of congratulations.'[89a] Long afterwards Lord Boyle called it 'the best [presentation] I have heard [in] twenty years';[90] and an academic study writes of 'a *tour de force* in analysis and exposition' which 'stands out from those before and since'.[91a]

The content had a more mixed reception. Gaitskell earned Labour congratulations and Opposition criticism by not cutting social services, and by laying almost all the fiscal burden on the better-off.[92] Rearmament involved spending on defence nearly £1,500 million in 1951/52, an increase of over £500 million. The Chancellor's tasks were to find the real resources for defence production; to finance the programme without inflation; and to prevent excessive strain on the metal and engineering industries on which the main burden would fall. Gaitskell's plans, more precisely set out than those of any predecessor, were to be spectacularly frustrated, through circumstances which could not be foreseen, by a great balance of payments crisis. No future Chancellor gave hostages to fortune by taking the public so fully into his confidence.

The extra resources needed for defence were expected to come mainly from an increased Gross Domestic Product, with a small reduction in personal consumption and a smaller amount from higher imports.[93] The new government expenditure would wipe out the previous huge Budget surplus, and so slash the government's big contribution to savings. To stop

* The flower was the old symbol of the Austrian Socialists, who were touched that he wore it.

consumers having too much to spend and draining away resources, the new Budget must therefore close an emerging inflationary gap between total savings and total investment. That gap was calculated at £140 million, after allowing for two changes in the Budget itself (higher pensions, which widened it, and higher taxes on distributed profits, which narrowed it by encouraging company savings). Gaitskell filled it entirely by raising more revenue: £73 million from income tax (with better marriage and child allowances to ease the burden on wage-earners); £35 million from petrol tax; £20 million from purchase tax (though he took it off essentials such as kitchen utensils); and the last £10 million from cinema-goers and from the profits tax changes whose full effect would be felt later.[94]

He dealt in two ways with the metals and engineering bottleneck, crucial for exports, investment and now rearmament. Purchase tax was doubled on major consumption items competing with defence; and civilian investment was discouraged from absorbing these scarce resources by suspending the 'initial allowances' by which the cost of new plant and machinery could be partly offset against income and profits taxes.[95] That was the most damaging long-run feature of the Budget, contributing to industry's chronic reluctance to invest, and Gaitskell himself said he hoped it could soon be reversed.[89c] It was little criticised by Tories and not at all by the Labour Left.

The Chancellor had conceded nothing to the Conservative clamour for cuts in government expenditure which, with prices rising fast, would have meant big changes in policy. Half that expenditure was for defence or interest on the National Debt; £1,615 million for social services; less than £400 million for other domestic items (already, despite rising costs, well below the previous year). The social services fell into four equal groups: food subsidies, pensions and insurance benefits, the health service, and the rest (education, housing and local grants). Gaitskell did not cut them, but limited their expansion to the £26 million increase in their estimates — including £8 million for education, with more children in schools, and £7 million for the health service. With the £20 million increase in pensions, even in this rearmament Budget estimated expenditure on social services was up by nearly £50 million. Food subsidies were unchanged: the consumer was to bear the cost of future but not past increases in prices. (While the Budget was later criticised for not relieving the poor of that burden of rising prices, Bevan had never made the criticism in Cabinet.)[16g]

Those measures bore an 'almost uncanny similarity'[33a] to the recommendations of Tribune — far closer than to those of Hugh Dalton.[96] Edited by Michael Foot and Jennie Lee, the journal wanted increased old age pensions, national assistance, and perhaps family allowances — to be paid for by higher direct taxes on unearned incomes and distributed profits, and by heavier purchase tax on luxuries.[33b] It differed with Gaitskell on only one item; but for that it did not forgive the Chancellor. The health service was to keep within a ceiling of £400 million, having only £7 million more instead of the £30 million for which its Ministry had asked. Since hospital costs were rising and standards should not be reduced, the difference was to be made up by charging half the cost of false teeth and spectacles, which would bring in £13 million in 1951/52 and £23 million in a full year.* At this point in the Budget speech a lone 'Shame!' came from Jennie Lee, listening beside her husband in the shadows behind the Speaker's chair. 'Bevan, red in the face and breathing like an angry bull ... was standing as inconspicuously as possible'; he walked out when Gaitskell finished that passage.[97] His wife's 'muffled cry' was, in Michael Foot's words, 'the only hostile demonstration Gaitskell received that afternoon'.[25b]

iv *The Parliamentary Labour Party*

Bevan and his wife were entirely isolated. The Budget of April 1951 was warmly and enthusiastically received in the PLP, even by his sympathisers.[98] All the parliamentary correspondents confirmed Dalton:[99] 'the Party are very pleased & the Tea Room is full of his [Gaitskell's] praise ... it is practically all one way'.[24k] Chuter Ede, very often a critic, told Gaitskell: 'This is just what the Party wanted. It will make all the difference.'[16h] Stanley Evans, then quite friendly with Bevan, spoke of the 'tonic effect on my Party. Indeed, I do not remember the PLP being so perky, united and harmonious for a long time'.[89d] In the debate, 20 out of 28 Labour backbenchers applauded the Budget and not one attacked it.** Detailed criticism fastened not on health charges, but on the conditions – meant to discourage early retirement – attached to the increased old age pensions. Four Members regretfully approved the charges and three did not. But the three all welcomed the Budget, one (John Baird) affirming the support of both the PLP and the country and another (John McGovern) calling it 'one of the best ... for years ... can be defended from any angle'.[89e f] As the Chief Whip had told Attlee,[16g] and as outsiders knew, even on its slender majority a united Cabinet could have carried it with no difficulty at all.[100] The charges began a long crisis, but not because they provoked any spontaneous revolt in the Labour Movement, in the PLP or even in a dissident minority. Their impact demonstrated the individual influence, and was due to the individual reaction, of one man alone.

That reaction was delayed. On the morning after the Budget most com-

---

* Children were exempt from both, and expectant and nursing mothers from the former; those in hardship would be reimbursed from national assistance; dental treatment was not affected.

** Of the 8 others, 1 (Keenan) was mildly critical, 3 implied approval and 4 were silent – 2 later critics and 2 later supporters.

mentators expected Bevan to take the escape route he had left himself at Bermondsey by claiming that part-payments for dentures and spectacles were not 'charges on the patient'.[101] He told the PLP amid applause 'that he had decided not to take a certain course'.[102] In Cabinet next day, Wednesday, he and Wilson tried again to get the charges postponed.[16h] They claimed that Attlee had told them he was planning a June election;[25c] Morrison denied that;[24m] and Ministers decided to bring in the Bill the following Tuesday and take the second reading a week later. Glaring at the silent Gaitskell, Bevan exploded as they dispersed, 'Why should I have to put up with these bloody absurdities?'[103]

There were two efforts at compromise. Three trade-unionist Ministers – Griffiths, Isaacs and Tomlinson – revived the 1949 idea of increasing the national insurance contribution in lieu of the charges; both Bevan and Gaitskell refused.[104] Then the Cabinet on Thursday 19 April confirmed that the Bill would be taken the following Tuesday, and Bevan said he would resign on the third reading.[16h] Dalton recorded

> a general impatience in the Cab with this continual nerve war – first he threatened to resign before the Budget, then on Budget day, then if the charges were brought in, then he wouldn't vote on a second reading & now this.[24m]

But when Shinwell suggested announcing that the charges might be temporary, Bevan replied 'that would make a great deal of difference' – and Gaitskell agreed to say they need not be permanent.[16h] Bevan threw a note across the table to Wilson, 'We've got them on the run.'[105] That afternoon Shinwell put up a formula, 'should not be permanent';[106] Gaitskell changed 'should' to 'need not necessarily'; and the paper was handed to Bevan:

> He read it and tossed it aside contemptuously, calling it 'a bromide'.
>
> He then went on to say that he would not be satisfied ... [unless we] left it open whether the charges ever came into force at all. He followed this up with a long and rather excited statement that the arms programme could not be carried out ... I gather he had this impression from a meeting of the Defence Production Committee which had taken place that day.
>
> I said that of course if there were to be a complete change in the Defence programme we should need a completely new Budget ... but until ... [then] I was not prepared to budge on the Health Bill. Shortly after there was a Division and we did not see Bevan again. He had, however, been asked by the Home Secretary to produce an alternative form of words, and in fact never did so.[16h]

Exasperated by Bevan's renewed intransigence, the leading Ministers –

Morrison, Gaitskell, Ede and the Chief Whip—now decided that the Prime Minister must be informed.[107]

Meanwhile Gaitskell had 'confirmed his triumph' in his Budget broadcast and his winding-up speech in the debate, emerging as 'a new force in politics'.[108] But Bevan, busily lobbying against the Bill in the tea-room where he was never normally seen, had infuriated Ede, the Leader of the House and his former sympathiser.[16h] The final straw was that evening's *Tribune*, savagely attacking Gaitskell personally as well as the Budget.[33c] It probably swung several Ministers away from compromise:[16h] notably Dalton who called it 'a most wicked publication'.[24n] Among them was the Prime Minister. In his hospital bed on the Friday afternoon, listening to Ede, Attlee finally said: 'Well, we cannot go on like this. He must behave properly if he is to remain a Member of the Government.'[16h] He then sent what he called an 'ultimatum' that he hoped to hear before the weekend that Bevan would loyally accept and carry out government decisions.* Next day Bevan resigned.

Tribune, founded by Cripps in 1937, was edited by Bevan during the war and then, when he took office, by Jennie Lee and Michael Foot—the only two of his associates who wanted him to resign. Loyal to the government while Bevan was a member, it had lately been restive, rejecting an article by a regular contributor, Woodrow Wyatt, for praising Bevan's speech in the February defence debate.[21a] Its financial state was always precarious, and a few days before the Budget Foot thought it would have to close; he foresaw, however, that Bevan's resignation might 'save' it, offering it 'new opportunities, a new lease of life'.[109a] He therefore approached Lord Beaverbrook, with whom he had formerly been friendly. That Tory magnate, who published his newspapers to make propaganda rather than money, was happy to supply the sinews of factional war within the Labour Party by keeping *Tribune* alive, unknown of course to the constituency activists who read it. He had often hired away its talented left-wing journalists to run his own right-wing press empire; and when his manager objected to the use of *Daily Express* funds to pay the subsidy, he retorted: 'Where would we get our recruits without *Tribune*?'[110]

This was the journal which, on 20 April 1951, ended several years of reasonable harmony in the Labour Party and resumed the fratricidal civil war which has lasted on and off ever since. Its editorial claimed that not since 1931 had Conservatives so warmly applauded a Labour government. Blandly quoting himself twenty years later, Michael Foot called that charge 'undeniable';[25e] and R. J. Edwards, a future Beaverbrook editor, wrote of a 'Festival Budget for the City'. The charge was false, for only the *Daily*

* Foot quotes it as a gratuitous item in a conspiracy to drive Bevan out—but omits both the Bevin and the Shinwell compromises.[25d]

Express leader-writer (a Beaverbrook-Bevanite?) cynically applauded Gaitskell for taking Tory measures.[109b] Where *Tribune* wanted more government expenditure at home, the entire Opposition press clamoured for less — while also condemning the Chancellor for overburdening the better-off. So did the Conservatives in the House.*

Tribune, however, denounced 'the Gaitskell dictate' as 'contemptible', 'timid and squalidly inadequate', and 'another 1931'; twice accused him of having 'deserted Socialism at the moment of crisis'; and compared him directly to the former Labour Chancellor Philip Snowden.[112] That was a deliberate imputation of bad faith and betrayal, for to its readers Snowden was Judas: the Chancellor who allied with the Tories, slashed working-class standards, accepted a peerage and turned bitterly against his lifelong associates. Yet from start to finish Gaitskell had the support of *Tribune*'s own founder, whom Bevan regarded as the best Chancellor Britain ever had.[113] Cripps wrote to his successor early on: 'Stick to what you believe to be right and don't allow anyone to divert you by arguments of political expediency'; and told his wife to reassure Gaitskell after the resignations: 'Stafford ... says he is sure you have done the right thing.'[114]

On Saturday 21 April, eleven days after the Budget and just after the *Tribune* assault, Bevan sent the Prime Minister a resignation letter which, as Attlee tartly replied, 'extended the area of disagreement a long way beyond the specific matter'.[115] Bevan had known quite well that teeth and spectacles were too narrow an issue to resign on, telling a sympathiser who said so: 'Don't you worry, I'll broaden it all right.'[20b c] Harold Wilson and John Freeman, Parliamentary Secretary to the Ministry of Supply, soon followed him. Both had been worried for much longer about the scale of rearmament, and both advised him to base his dissent on that issue;[116] as Freeman used to put it later, admitting some exaggeration: 'When Nye had finally determined his course of action, Harold and I made up Bevanism to give him a justification for it.'[117] Yet Bevan hesitated to the end, for only his wife and his future biographer pressed him to go;[118] most of his friends 'were dubious about or, more usually, bitterly critical of his tactics'.[25f] He did not try to win over other doubters;[119] and at the last minute he pressed even Wilson and Freeman to remain.[120a] But Free-

---

* 'Almost any cut in expenditure would have been preferable ... Industry is likely to be staggered' (*The Times*). 'Taxes to pay for Socialism rather than rearmament' (*Dispatch*). 'Niggling, tinkering, juggling ... mediocre' (*Mail*). The end of the Robin Hood road' (*Graphic*). 'The middle and upper classes are bearing a disproportionate share of the cost of the Government's schemes' (*Scotsman*). The *Daily Telegraph* and the *Financial Times* wrote in much the same vein.[111] Reginald Maudling said: 'I think the reason the party opposite are so strongly in favour of the Budget is that its proposals are so obviously designed to soak the capitalist, or to place the burden on the middle and upper ranges of income.'[89g]

man was incensed by Dalton's clumsy talk of promotion, which he interpreted as a simple bribe to keep him;[117] though in fact both Dalton and Gaitskell favoured his advancement on merits even if no one resigned, and Gaitskell particularly wanted another left-winger (preferably him) in the Cabinet.[25n] It is said that in the end Wilson proved the most resolute of the three.[120a b]

Bevan's resignation speech on the Monday was preceded, to the delight of the House, by a Parliamentary Question from George Thomas on the perils caused by straying sheep in South Wales. Gaitskell wrote mildly of Bevan's 'extraordinary performance, totally lacking in any understanding of what people expected, [which] turned opinion even more sharply against him – on top of the Tribune article'.[16h] Moving far beyond teeth and spectacles, Bevan criticised the British rearmament programme as impracticable, and the American programme as a greater threat to the West than the Russians themselves, for it risked mass unemployment and imperilled even 'the foundations of political liberty and Parliamentary democracy'.[121a] He turned to denounce the Budget for not restraining inflation, and for having 'united the City ... and disunited the Labour Party' in the interest of the United States. He attacked the Treasury for having too many economists, 'and now we have the added misfortune of having an economist in the Chancellor of the Exchequer himself'. He charged Gaitskell with political dishonesty, arousing furious Labour resentment – for he knew Gaitskell could not reply since personal statements are not debatable:

> [T]he Chancellor ... said that he was now coming to a complicated and technical matter and that if Members wished they could go to sleep. They did. Whilst they were sleeping he stole £100 million a year from the National Insurance Fund ... so that the re-armament of Great Britain is financed out of the contributions that the workers have paid into the Fund in order to protect themselves.'[122]

Bevan went on to attack the health charges as the first pebble of an avalanche that would sweep away the welfare state – and to explain why he had set an earlier pebble rolling himself. 'I had to manoeuvre, and I did manoeuvre and saved the 25,000 houses and the prescription charges.'[123]

When he sat down a moment later, wrote Michael Foot: 'not a touch of warmth alleviated the universal coldness. No single cheer greeted his peroration ... it certainly appeared that he had made a ruinous error'.[25g] Bevan's was the only resignation speech for thirty years or more to show no regret at the breach with old colleagues;[124] and though he drew sympathy and attention at first, he lost both by the boast about his own 'manoeuvre' and the personal attack on Gaitskell.[125]

Harold Wilson next day covered similar ground without bitterness or personal invective,[121c] and 'in a third of the time ... won three times as much sympathy'.[126] Freeman made no statement, but wrote to both Attlee and Gaitskell. Just after the Budget he had told the Chancellor he stood with Bevan, but that 'breaking up the government on such a narrow issue appeared to me the height of folly' and that he had worked whole-heartedly against a split; he hoped their good relations would continue, and was delighted 'to see ... how clearly the mark of greatness sits upon you'. On the Monday he wrote again to say that despite 'Nye's outburst' he would resign too, but with no 'animosity or vendetta against your-self'.[127]

At the PLP meeting next day the spirit was different. It opened with 'restrained' statements by Wilson and Freeman. Gaitskell then rose to a 'pretty considerable ovation' which he attributed to resentment against *Tribune*. On his friends' advice he ignored the personal attacks and defended himself calmly.[128] He denied knowing (as Bevan had charged in the House) that the amount allotted to defence spending was already 'unrealisable' — though he was so innocent of the new standards of contro-versy that he would not repeat that denial publicly lest it damage the Party.[129] He warned that if raw material shortages did occur they would hamper civilian as well as defence production, add to inflationary pressure, and so require a tougher Budget not an easier one.[24v] He sat down to tremendous applause.

> Bevan made things even worse for himself by following this with a shocking outburst of bad temper which was evidently a revelation to many people in the Party. He almost screamed at the platform. At one point he said, 'I won't have it. I won't have it.' And, this of course was greeted with derision. '*You* won't have it?' called other Members of the Party. Of course in the Cabinet we have had this on [sic] a number of times but they had not seen it before.[16h l]

Other eye-witnesses were less restrained. One spoke of Bevan as hysterical and almost screaming; another, Dalton, as 'soon quite out of control ... sweating & screeching, & seemed on the edge of a nervous breakdown'.[130] A Conservative recalls:

> Several Labour M.P.s said to me at the time that what Bevan could never forgive was the fact that Hugh Gaitskell, on an objective assess-ment, really did beat him in argument at the party meeting. Bevan was a *terribly* bad loser in debate.[90]

Dalton and Ede, MPs in 1930, were both reminded of Mosley; in winding up from the chair, Ede said so.[130] But Gaitskell, unlike some of his friends, never thought that meeting would prove decisive.[16h]

Michael Foot wrote that Labour MPs afterwards were 'aghast at what they had seen' (though without explaining why).[131] One constant theme of his book is the loathing of Bevan and his friends for that forum. For it was in the PLP that the Bevanites discovered how they were seen by the ordinary Labour MP who, unlike the readers of *Tribune*, knew their characters so well: as elitist sectarians who posed as the sole guardians of Socialist principle, while seeking personal publicity and factional support at the expense of the Party. Bevan himself all too obviously despised the mass and all too often insulted the individuals who followed those he thought lesser men. No wonder he hated an arena where he was so tempted to destroy himself.[132]

Bevan had greatly overestimated his own influence. Gaitskell, whose political antennae were not always sensitive, had underestimated it immediately after the Bermondsey speech. His friends soon corrected that mistake: Dalton told him he thought too much of the electorate as a whole rather than the Party;[24i] and Callaghan warned: 'Oh! Boy, these temperamental Celts!! Wilson doesn't matter either way — Nye does.'[11b] Gaitskell listened to them, quickly recognised Bevan's strength outside the House, and by May thought the rebel might well win within the Labour Party — and so condemn it to opposition 'for years and years'.[16h] But the Bevanites wholly misjudged the mood of the PLP. Even the usually realistic Freeman thought the Government could not survive Bevan's resignation by more than eight or ten weeks.[24o] Bevan himself, unlike Gaitskell, brushed aside Callaghan's friendly warning that his rival was stronger than he thought, exploding: 'The Party will sweep him away!'[133]

Despite the enthusiasm for the Budget and the lack of real hostility to the health charges, he predicted to Dalton that the Bill would fail: 'The Party will be a rabble, and you won't carry it.'[24k g] His resignation brought a new bitterness into the debate on it. But its second and third readings, on 24 April and 7 May, were both unopposed. In the one division in committee, the government won by 262 to 3; Harold Wilson, Barbara Castle and other future Bevanites voted with the majority, but there were thirty or forty abstentions, which worried the Leader of the House 'because it made our loyal people so unhappy. It was a humiliating spectacle to see the Labour Party quarrelling while the Conservatives looked on and laughed'.[16j] In 1951 angry quarrels in the PLP were unfamiliar: a different world.

The Bill included a time limit, which had been offered to Bevan without changing his mind, but might have altered Wilson's.[121d] 'We made two small concessions ... to make the charges maximum charges ... [and] limit the Bill to three years unless an affirmative resolution was passed.'[134*] There was as yet no feeling in the constituencies.[135] Both the TUC and

* Attlee and Ede (joined, for the only time, by the Chief Whip) favoured compromise on a two-year limit.

the trade union MPs—especially the miners—felt more anxious to shield old age pensioners from rising prices than to keep dentures and spectacles free.[136]

On pensions there was real, widespread and spontaneous feeling among back-benchers. Where only three of the twenty-eight who spoke in the Budget debate criticised health charges, a majority pressed for the higher pensions to be paid at a lower age than seventy (sixty-five for women), or before 1 October, or both. The Trade Union Group had three meetings with Ministers, once including Attlee. At the first, Gaitskell saw them alone 'on the Budget as a whole and found that the pensions were the only thing they were worried about. They were quite solidly behind me on the teeth and spectacles'. Ministers feared the Opposition would support a pensions revolt, and the Whips 'all said that the feeling was very strong in the Party as a whole'. Gaitskell agreed to pay the increase to those who had already reached sixty-five and retired, but not to those who would do so later and could stay at work. 'The Trade Union Group accepted it with much gratitude. It ... went through quite calmly ... this is not an issue on which I have ever felt very strongly ... [or was] prepared even to contemplate resignation.' The pressure neither surprised nor upset him: 'I had always expected this and indeed said in the Cabinet and the Party Meeting that if there were any more money available I would not have put it into the Health Services but done better for the pensioners.'[16j] That would both give help to the neediest, and respond to working-class preferences. But it was not Bevan's priority; and his approach to the crisis is sadly illuminated by his biographer, twenty years later, calling Gaitskell's remark a 'gratuitous provocation'.[25c]

v   *Merits, Manoeuvres and Men*

The argument over the scale of British rearmament is assessed in the next chapter. It was to continue for many years. But in the spring of 1951 a Chancellor preparing a Budget had to take it as given, the basic policy he was expected to finance by colleagues none of whom (*pace* Michael Foot) had as yet challenged its necessity or threatened to resign over its size. Facing that huge extra expenditure, no Chancellor could have failed to seek economies in a departmental budget so large, so long immune and so steadily growing as that of the health service. Certainly Gaitskell was very stubborn about health charges, thinking them right and not just a sad necessity; his Treasury advisers would have been quite content to raise the money differently.[32a] That did not mean that he was impervious to reason as Foot implies, or hostile to the health service as Bevan assumed.[121g] Past abuses were admitted by a Labour dentist[89f] and an optician,[121h] both opposed to the charges; and Attlee wanted charges justified on those grounds as well as for economy.[16g] But Gaitskell never endorsed the sweeping accusations made by the Conservatives – and decisively repudiated by the Guillebaud Committee which they themselves set up in 1953.[137] The Ministers responsible for the Service easily convinced him that his initial suggestions would be too damaging, and one of them, Hector McNeil, wrote to thank him for his 'sympathetic and understanding frame of mind'.[138]

In 1951 the cost of the service was still £11 million below the estimate, thanks to the hated weekly Prime Minister's committee – though Bevan took the credit.[121i] It remained well above Cripps's original ceiling, imposed long before rearmament. To avoid restrictions on the hospitals, Gaitskell let the estimates for 1951/52 (a rearmament year) exceed expenditure the year before by £41 million gross and, under Ernest Bevin's compromise, by £18 million net. He protected the new ceiling of £400 million by reclaiming £23 million where payment (in part) would cause least hardship. False teeth and spectacles were required infrequently, and the sick, needy, and children were exempt. Indeed according to the Guillebaud Committee (unanimously) the denture charge positively improved the service by diverting dentists back to school and conservation work (previously 61 per cent of their expenditure had been on dentures); though the charges on spectacles deterred sight-testing.[139]

Bevan's objection was not to the specific charges but to renouncing an entirely free health service. He had not been such a purist earlier, when he had felt that broader political considerations required him to remain in the government. It was he who stopped free transport for rural patients attending hospital regularly – later described by an official Labour spokesman as, for some people, 'one of the most onerous ... Health Service charges'.[140] In piloting the Act authorising prescription charges he had told the House they were 'a very small aspect indeed of the whole administration ... We must keep our sense of proportion, because ... [this] is not a considerable retreat.' But when others chose the same priority, he implied that they would sacrifice their principles 'for a miserable £5,000 a year'.[141]

Conservatives could of course use the Labour charges to justify their own harsher measures: as Bevan put it in his resignation speech, 'are you going to take your stand on the upper denture?' But that was only a debating point, for their policy had been determined long before 1951; as one government supporter asked, 'Do hon. Members on this side of the House never listen to the party political broadcasts?'[121j] Bevan, as Dalton had warned him,[24j] by splitting the Labour Party helped to give the Tories their first opportunity; and they did not even rely on Gaitskell for debating points in defending their later increases, for in 1961 they quoted him less than Attlee, Bevan himself or Cripps.

On Bevan's reasoning in 1949, the sum involved did not justify his resignation. That argument cut both ways: it was also a small point for the Chancellor to stick on, and £13 or £23 million was well within the margin of error of the notional figure for defence. But once that huge sum was laid open for raiding, every spending Minister would claim his share of the spoils. Other Ministers, too, had had to reduce their estimates.[142] Most of them already felt that 'Nye is getting away with murder'.[143] So while Gaitskell readily conceded that a new defence policy would mean a new Budget, until the present policy was changed he had to carry it out. Like every Chancellor, he had to fight over small sums, just as he had recently been shocked by his colleagues' insouciance over £15 million for armed forces pay.

The case for giving way to Bevan on health charges in 1951 was based entirely on a political calculation. It was not that he held a more principled view than his critics, or championed a policy to which all Socialists had long been devoted, or had convinced the Labour Movement that the health service should be exempt from normal financial constraints, or could avert a threatened Tory 'avalanche' sweeping away the welfare state. It was that, like Joseph Chamberlain in 1886, he was a commanding political figure, capable of raising a revolt large enough to split his party for years. Bevan might not have resigned if his great achievement had been left untouched, and no serious revolt would have been likely without him; so that his colleagues, however good their case and bad his behaviour — indeed just because it was likely to be bad — might have been wise to let the rogue elephant have his way, if by doing so they could have avoided civil war in the Party.

The calculation depends on hindsight about troubles which occurred later on in opposition. Gaitskell's whole case was that Labour had to prove itself a responsible party of government — an opportunity the Party was soon denied by electoral defeat, so that the future he envisaged was unattainable in 1951. Thus, even if Bevan had had his way over health charges and remained, it might have made very little difference if, as seems likely, he would have rebelled in any event as soon as Labour went out of office.

Two conceptions of the Party's future were in conflict. Bevan foresaw Labour's defeat with equanimity, and indeed as we have seen would have preferred that to victory by a majority he thought inadequate (meaning one of thirty not of five). Gaitskell already saw Labour as a reforming party of government, not as a movement of impotent protest; he was not at all defeatist about the next election, believing it could be won if Labour proved its competence in running the country. He saw his own stand as essential to demonstrating that conception of the Party, telling Gordon Walker early in the struggle: 'We must show that we administer responsibly.'[67d]

Bevan cherished at the time, and his biographer still repeats, a theory that Morrison and Gaitskell brought up health charges as a deliberate plot to drive him out.[144] That is demonstrably false. First, Gaitskell had no animosity against Bevan; we have seen that his comments had been appreciative as well as critical, and that he viewed without dismay the prospect of Bevan as Labour's next Prime Minister. Second, Gaitskell was one of the many Ministers who did not expect Bevan to resign, rashly discounting as bluff his threats which had perhaps been devalued by their frequency.[145] Third, Morrison at the end pressed hard for compromise: so much so that that hardened intriguer developed a conspiracy theory of his own to explain Gaitskell's intransigence, attributing it to a calculated bid to polarise the Party and lead the right wing which was sure to win.[146]

This second conspiracy theory cannot so simply be disproved, but there is no scrap of evidence for it and it is not taken seriously by surviving politicians, or by officials who were close to Gaitskell.[147] As a gamble it would have been insanely reckless, for he had no certain ally and could never – from the first clash until four hours before the Budget – count with confidence on the Prime Minister's backing.[148] His diary shows, and his private secretaries recall, that his mood was altogether different.[5] To the shock of Bevan's Bermondsey threat of resignation Gaitskell reacted, first with anger, but then with deep concern lest a split keep Labour out for a generation and frustrate all he cared for in politics.[32a] No loyal official could help him judge that. He wrote:

> In a situation of this kind it is impossible not to feel ... that perhaps after all you were really being too stubborn, that you had got the thing out of perspective and that you were really risking too much not for yourself, but for the Government ... no other Member of the Cabinet ... would give [political] advice. I had it from one other Minister, Alf Robens.[16h]

After it was over he thanked a supporter in his constituency:

> [I]t really meant a great deal to me – coming from you who are not only one of our best people in S. Leeds but also know such a lot about the Health Services. It has been a very heavy strain – emotionally as well as intellectually – fighting this battle and letters like yours just make me feel that it *was* worth while taking all the risks and facing all the brickbats and beastliness.[149]

To deny the conspiracy theories is not to pretend that he was innocently unaware of the personal aspect of the contest: he was a politician, not a don or a preacher. Those surviving associates do recognise that he was very conscious of his exposed position as a young man, junior in his Party and suddenly promoted to high office, whose authority as Chancellor would soon vanish if he retreated under fire, as commentators had expected when he was appointed.[150] Nine years later he summed up to George Brown: 'It was a battle between us for power – he knew it and so did I.'[151]

Bevan's discontent had been well known for months, especially since he had been passed over for both the Exchequer and the Foreign Office. Yet if as many colleagues believed he was simply looking for a pretext to resign, it is hard to explain his prolonged hesitation. He must have found it unthinkable that Gaitskell ('nothing, nothing, nothing') could prevail over health charges where Cripps had given way.[25h] After losing the battle at the Easter Cabinet, Bevan at Bermondsey publicly threatened resignation; if he could not be Chancellor, he would show himself more powerful than the Chancellor.[152] When that failed, he felt he would be stronger outside than in, and so it was time to go.[153]

Bevan was uninhibited in expressing his personal feelings.[154] When the Cabinet accepted Ernest Bevin's compromise, he protested at the policy but also that 'his own personal position would be rendered impossible; his prestige would be undermined ... It will be known that he has been over-ridden'. After Bermondsey he said to Dalton: 'If it is such a small thing, why not give way? The compensation of giving way would be me. Is that a very small thing?' He asked the whole Cabinet the day before the Budget, 'aren't I worth £23 millions?'[155] After his resignation, he told the PLP meeting, 'But for *my* Health Service he would never have been Chancellor'; and offended his audience by claiming to have been 'martyred' for his principles.[25i] Understandably (*pace* Michael Foot) Dalton concluded that 'Megalomania and jealousy govern him', and wrote to the absent Prime Minister: 'Hugh's ... attitude to resignation, as compared with Nye's, was like a high snow peak compared with a steaming tropical swamp!'[156] Big men have big faults – which can alone explain why the legitimate policy dispute provoked such vituperative ferocity, and why Bevan aroused such resistance in his colleagues.

It was only reluctantly that the Cabinet supported Gaitskell, the junior and far less powerful figure, and his unpalatable proposals. The 'majority overwhelming and unshakable', imagined by Michael Foot, did not exist until Bevan's miscalculation, intransigence and bullying created it. At first several colleagues sympathised with his dislike for health charges. But they also recalled the repeated postponements in Cripps's day, when Bevan's ceilings were disregarded while other Ministers had to cut their estimates. Later, Gaitskell won their approval by showing loyalty and goodwill, accepting Ernest Bevin's compromise, and promising that if he resigned he would make no difficulties for the Government. But Bevan provoked them by seeking to force their hand in public – so that Chuter Ede[22a] felt it would be intolerable for Cabinet majorities of 18 to 2 to be overridden because 'X' was one of the 2.[22b] Bevan was, wrote Dalton, 'determined to bend the Cabinet to his will or break it ... He showed, [colleagues] thought, unbearable conceit, crass obstinacy and a totalitarian streak'.[157]

Clement Attlee was not affected by this atmosphere, for he had entered hospital three weeks before the Budget. He was regularly consulted, and whenever obliged to decide he supported Gaitskell. But his physical absence permitted not a timely intervention from Olympus but — in his usual style — a calculated detachment until events dictated an apparently ineluctable outcome, only four hours before Gaitskell was due to bring in his Budget. No one could suppose a Prime Minister (least of all one with a single-figure majority) would accept his Chancellor's resignation so late. Expecting and hoping to the last that one man would give way, Attlee must have known much earlier that in a crunch Bevan would be the one to go.[158]

Attlee's tactics were faulty, for as the dispute dragged on it became harder to settle. At the very start, Gaitskell might have given way under strong pressure; if not, he would have resigned alone and at a much less disastrous moment. But Attlee, who had chaired the Cabinet Committee, tried neither to reverse its decision nor to defend it; and once Gaitskell had accepted Bevin's compromise and won Cabinet endorsement for it, he would not himself retreat, and he would no longer have resigned alone.

Bevan was the more frustrated and resentful of the two, but the less determined either to win or resign. Having failed in private persuasion he publicly challenged his colleagues: so that Attlee could no longer let Gaitskell go without open capitulation and grave loss of prestige. Now that the Prime Minister could not afford to appease Bevan, the last hope of keeping him was by a decisive intervention, insisting that the Cabinet decision of 22 March must be upheld, while offering every help to save his face. Instead, Attlee went on waiting vainly until the last moment for someone to crack — thus minimising both his personal involvement in the quarrel and his chance of solving it.

Even after Budget day Bevan's colleagues — Gaitskell and Morrison included — were still hoping to extricate him from the embarrassment they thought he had put himself in at Bermondsey.[4d] Only after he rejected Shinwell's compromise did even Chuter Ede insist to Attlee that Bevan must play with the team or go. Measuring the exasperation of his colleagues, the Prime Minister could see at last where the balance of forces lay.

Gaitskell was expecting soon after Bevan resigned that he would organise revolt at the October Party Conference, and exploit all the uneasiness of Party members whose political experience had been almost exclusively in opposition. Gaitskell believed such a revolt could be defeated with 'strong and firm' leadership from the Prime Minister, but he now knew better than to count on that; and if Attlee sought to compromise and patch things up, 'then I think we shall probably lose. I cannot carry on the fight alone. I have not the standing or the experience'.[16h] In the event, Attlee remained non-committal in public, and would never appeal to the confused and unhappy Labour activists to support his own defence policy. By the summer Gaitskell thought, and said Morrison agreed,

> that the P.M. has taken a very weak line about Bevan. He is very careful not to come out fully and firmly in the open against him, nor has he really given in our view much lead to the country on rearmament, though it was he and Bevin who initiated the new programme.[16k]

Attlee blamed Morrison as acting Prime Minister for the resignations,[159] became 'pretty cool' towards Gaitskell, and did not welcome their good relations.[16k] In May, Gaitskell had summed up:

> [A]lthough I ... [knew] it would be a hard struggle I did not think it would be quite so tough. I suppose that if I had realised that there were so many things which could have meant defeat, I might never have begun; or at least I would have surrendered early on. If Ernie had not suggested the compromise; if some of the Cabinet had been more frightened; if Bevan had played his cards better; if the Budget speech had not been a success; if the Broadcast had been a flop; if I had not won the battle decisively in the Party meeting. If any of these things had not happened it might have meant failure ...
>
> All the same, with all the risks I think I was right. I said ... [once] to Hugh Dalton, 'It is really a fight for the soul of the Labour Party' ... I am afraid that if Bevan [wins] we shall be out of power for years and years.[16h]

23 Reading to his children, 1950

24 Raymond Frost, his stepson

25 Cutting comics with his family, 1950

26 Met by his wife on returning from New York as the new Chancellor
of the Exchequer, October 1950

CHAPTER 9

CHANCELLOR OF THE EXCHEQUER: THE ECONOMY 1951

'He probably understood his job better than any Chancellor before or since'
(SAM BRITTAN ON HG, 1970)
'A gay man ... who would jive about the house in the morning'
(A SCHOOLBOY WITH WHOSE PARENTS HG STAYED, 1951)

i *Inflation, Incomes and Iranian Oil*

GAITSKELL'S last six months in office were dominated by the repercussions of the Western world's rearmament. Bidding against each other in a mad scramble for raw materials, the NATO countries contrived a wild commodity boom on a 1973 scale. First, Britain's precarious wage and price stability was severely threatened; then in the autumn she suffered a balance of payments crisis as sudden as it was massive. Politically the Labour government thus became vulnerable in the Party to the Bevanite attack on its defence and foreign policy, and in the country to the Conservatives, who narrowly won the November 1951 election, with more seats than Labour but fewer votes.

From the moment he became Chancellor Gaitskell had been concerned about inflation. At first he thought income tax would have to go up by 1s. in the pound instead of 6d.;[1] he was afraid that the Budget might have been too mild, not too harsh; and he rejected higher food subsidies as adding to the inflationary danger.[2] [3a] [b] Thus prices were allowed to rise, pressure for wage increases mounted, and two years of trade union restraint (responding to Cripps's astonishingly successful appeals) were coming to an end. Already in December 1950 Gaitskell had sent the Cabinet's Economic Policy Committee a paper on incomes policy.[4] By April he had 'spent a great deal of time and thought' on proposals for wages to be compulsorily linked to the cost of living, or to production or productivity; but he concluded that they all 'involve far-reaching risks and difficulties, some economic, some psychological' and would not be acceptable to either side of industry.[5a]

The Treasury did not yet appreciate the strength of the pressures for

K

higher wages, or the ease of financing spending above current incomes, in response to a cost inflation injected from outside the British economy.[6a] In the first five months of the year consumption, far from falling, was 5 per cent above that of 1950, and by the summer Gaitskell was worried.[7a] In late July he restored some controls consumed in Harold Wilson's bonfire.[8] He limited bank advances, again finding the Bank of England 'very uncooperative'.[9a] He hoped to appease trade union pressure for equal pay for women by 'some small gesture to the Civil Service Unions ... but the Cabinet, led on by Herbert, turned even this down'.[7a]

The unions also complained at increases in dividends which, despite the Budget's differential tax on distributed profits, rose in June (net of income tax) by 14 per cent. Gaitskell at first hoped to use the issue to bargain with the unions;[10] instead, on 26 July, he announced that for the three re-armament years dividends were to be limited by law to the average of the last two years, to encourage 'reasonable restraint in the field of wages' and prevent 'the wage-price spiral ... set in motion by external forces last year ... continu[ing] of its own momentum'.[3c] The government fell before the law could be passed, but the prospect of it helped resist the Bevanites within the Labour Party. Dalton had warned that the NEC's forthcoming election manifesto would call for dividend limitation, and that to refuse would risk defeat at Conference. On merits, Gaitskell was mildly in favour in any case. The announcement brought him no credit from the Bevan-ites;[11] and met 'most furious and violent abuse from the Right wing press and a positive torrent of nonsense, as well as a few good arguments'. He recorded his reactions:

> [I]t is difficult not to be upset by the intensity and violence of the criticisms ... [or] to have doubts about the wisdom of your own policy, and so ... [lose] self-confidence. However, I am certainly a good deal tougher than I was, and it is just as well because I am in a very much more exposed position – detested by the Left and now very much out of favour with the Right.[7a]

In September 1951 Gaitskell engineered an invitation to speak to the TUC at Blackpool.[12] He spent three whole days in preparation.[13] It was more time than he gave any speech but the Budget, yet he thought it well spent and his best performance, 'because it was very, very frank and con-firmed my view that people will take the truth so long as you put it across in the right way'. Without suggesting 'a wage freeze or rigid restraint', he warned that disastrous inflation was inevitable if incomes rose faster than productivity, and appealed for moderation in wage claims in the interest of the export drive. He said that life was 'thinner, poorer, harder' than necessary because production was cramped and held back by fear, and by deeply embedded habits of thought ... created by fear ... fear of the machine ... fear of the lost job, fear of letting unwanted men go ... fear of better methods, fear of letting someone else share in the work.

He used unpalatable and as yet unfamiliar figures to show that subsidies could not be financed from higher taxes on the rich, or wages raised at the expense of dividends. But he recognised that while wage increases forgone were lost to the worker for good, dividend limitation piled up undistributed profits for the future.[14] These could not be raided for immediate consumption, but the Labour Movement urgently needed to devise a policy for reducing inequalities of property.[15a]

One experienced correspondent called his reception 'a personal triumph'. Another thought his speech better than that of Cripps, and saw him then and there as Labour's next leader.[16] Congress voted, most unusually, to print and circulate it;[17] and the president of the NUGMW thought it among the half-dozen best speeches ever given to the TUC.[15b] Gaitskell, who had been nervous, called it 'a pretty good reception, and all the people on the platform were overjoyed'; and hoped it had cemented his relations with the trade union leadership.[7b]

Domestic economic problems were soon overshadowed by a major balance of payments crisis aggravated by an external factor: the first major move from the oil-producing Middle East against the industrialised West. On 1 May 1951 the Iranian Parliament, which Gaitskell thought 'corrupt and incompetent', passed a law scrapping the British concession and nationalising the oil wells and refineries. It threatened to be costly in dollars, since that was the main source of oil under British rather than American control; and it might well tempt Iraq to seize her own oil, or Egypt the Suez Canal. The Cabinet was divided. Backed by the Services and by Herbert Morrison, Shinwell called loudly for a show of force. Attlee agreed with Gaitskell and Noel-Baker, his former and present Ministers of Fuel, who wanted to keep the oil flowing and therefore to negotiate a settlement, but would not rule out using force in the last resort. 'The rest of the Cabinet were a good deal more pacifist ... they do not realise how serious the loss of the oil would be.'[7c]

In the Middle East the Americans blamed British troubles on the past record and intransigence of the Anglo-Iranian Company and the Foreign Office, while the latter and the Services suspected that they simply wanted to take Britain's place. (There was some justice on both sides.)[18] Gaitskell thought a revolutionary coup might lead to a partition re-creating the wartime spheres of influence, with the British occupying the southern oilfields and the USSR seizing Azerbaijan in the north; the Americans were very wary that any intervention might 'end up with the British out and the Russians in'.[19a] Gaitskell, too, suspected their motives – an oilman was Under-Secretary of State – and he once hinted so publicly.[20] But he had thought for years that Anglo-American co-operation in the region was as essential as it was difficult.

The British chiefs of staff also knew that no action was possible without the United States.[7c] They kept reassessing their resources and their advice – from 'extremely warlike' to 'outright appeasement' and back to 'a much stronger line'.[7d] Shinwell switched, too, becoming 'an extreme appeaser';[21] though Morrison remained bellicose.[22] [23a] [b] Attlee, Gaitskell and Noel-Baker wanted to refuse to pay cash for the oil and to withdraw British tankers (since the Iranians could not market it on their own) while preparing 'particularly if a pretext existed for military action'. The Opposition leaders were consulted, and insisted on holding the island of Abadan to use in the last resort to refine oil from Kuwait.[7d]

President Truman sent Harriman out to mediate, and Gaitskell met his old friend secretly in Paris and urged the dangers of an outright Iranian victory or an Anglo-American split. Both the Americans[19b] and Morrison then wanted Gaitskell himself to go out, but he was reluctant and could not be spared; Stokes, Minister of Materials, went instead.[24] In September, Morrison again wanted to use force to stop the Iranians expelling British technicians from Abadan, but was opposed by the Cabinet, including Gaitskell (and by the Americans).[25] Attlee's government fell before Mossadeq's was pushed; and in the election Gaitskell justified reliance on the United Nations and temperately criticised Conservative belligerence.[26] As at Suez later, he was by now convinced that Britain must not break with the United States, and that except to save lives the use of force would be illegal, immoral and politically unwise.

ii   *The Balance of Payments Crisis*

The direct cost of replacing the oil from Iran was between $300 and $400 million a year.[27] That seemed bearable in the first half of 1951, when the balance of payments looked healthy; the reserves reached a post-war peak on 30 June.[28a] [b] Britain was benefiting from devaluation in easier export sales, and from high raw material prices for the products of the RSA (Rest of the Sterling Area). But in the second half of the year the British economy had both the biggest trade gap and current-account deficit for any half-year, and the biggest deterioration between one half-year and the next, that it had ever experienced.[6b]

The Government and its advisers had little warning of the coming storm. The initial forecasts had been somewhat optimistic.[6c] But they still seemed attainable until the situation changed with catastrophic suddenness, reflected only belatedly in the statistics.[29a b] Trade figures for each month became available only a month afterwards, and were known to exaggerate the trade gap, so that early signs of trouble were discounted. The economists plausibly expected import prices to level off (as they did), and the sterling area reserves to be maintained because, if the terms of trade moved against the United Kingdom, the RSA primary producers would gain. Export earnings and invisibles were doing well. The dollar surplus in the first six months of 1951 was half that for the same months of 1950—yet the official target was not to add to the reserves, only to break even.[6d]

At the end of August the July figures brought some cause for concern, made worse by the August figures a month later; if September proved as bad, the reserves would fall to the level forecast for the end of the year. But even that might have been borne but for a new crisis in the fourth quarter. A bad trend turned into a catastrophe when the RSA suddenly and without warning vastly increased its dollar purchases, and turned in a dollar deficit instead of the expected surplus.[6e]

Gaitskell took the initiative early on the long-term problems. In mid-June 1951 he urged the OEEC Ministers in Paris to start new discussions with Washington over stabilising commodity prices, to prevent inflation being induced from outside. He told the next OEEC Council that since 1950 prices of Britain's exports had risen 18 per cent, of all her imports 42 per cent, and of imported raw materials only, 72 per cent. He suggested that the International Commodity Conference, which was meeting in Washington to allocate scarce materials, might handle price questions as well, and that countries which agreed with his views should work together in that forum. 'He could not have invited European support for his case more plainly.'[30a] But the Europeans were afraid that visible American leadership was politically dangerous even though American co-operation was vital; and that to act through NATO would give an impression that the Americans were running them, which the Communists would exploit. Belying their reputation then and since, the Americans were equally timid about taking the lead, especially publicly.[31]

As for Britain's own problem, Gaitskell told the House just before the recess that the coming quarter might well be difficult owing to special and seasonal factors which should not affect the last quarter.[3d] He took measures to limit dollar imports, to cut some food rations and to tighten control over steel and other allocations, and he tried vainly to arrange a Commonwealth Finance Ministers' meeting for September.[32a c] Two weeks later, just before his Jersey family holiday, he recorded that 'the balance of payments was worsening because the rise in import prices was more rapid than expected and the export drive very slow to start'.[7a] He was still unaware of the imminence of the crisis; as he wrote years later to Strachey, 'the change in the situation was anticipated, but not the speed with which it took place'.[33] Indeed his main immediate worries were quite different: domestic inflation, the cost of living, and dividend limitation. But late in August after his holiday: 'I found to my dismay that ... the dollar deficit in the third quarter would be at least 500 million dollars ... [and] likely to continue ... unless energetic steps were taken.'[7b] After speaking to the TUC in Blackpool in the morning of 4 September 1951, and attending Cabinet in the afternoon, he flew off that night to New York and Washington.

Gaitskell had a hard case to argue there, for at first the Americans insisted yet again that European rearmament was inadequate.[7b] No one could speed up without much more dollar aid, which the Continentals were still receiving and wanted increased. But Britain had recently renounced it altogether, and knew that Congress, despite the assurances then given, was unlikely to resume it. In any case, the British Government did not want to return to dependence, and therefore preferred multilateral aid through the 'burden-sharing' plan which the United States had adumbrated. That meant prolonged discussions — which at first the Americans would not even begin until Britain accepted the bigger military programme and an increased share in it.[34-5a]

Gaitskell had two tasks: first in Washington, negotiating privately and directly on Britain's behalf; then at the NATO Council in Ottawa, becoming Europe's spokesman in publicly challenging extravagant American assumptions. He was surprisingly successful in both:

> My first job was, of course, to impress on the Americans the seriousness of the dollar situation which was developing so that they could consider giving us various forms of help. As usual, it was necessary to tell the same story to different Ministers.[36-7]

On his return he told the Cabinet that the Americans had been, 'As usual, "taken by surprise" at our account of our troubles, but terrified of Congress, and, in any case, won't settle anything till after an election'.[9b] There were pressures to resist from various agencies and politicians, each with its own objective: the military using NATO to demand a bigger defence effort, the Treasury pressing in the IMF for quicker trade liberalisation, Congress threatening sanctions against countries which tried to obtain non-dollar supplies by East-West trade — all operating independently and oblivious, as the very pro-American *Economist* put it, of the 'dangers of pushing everything and everybody too far'.[38]

Besides opposing United States proposals which would have made Britain's situation worse, Gaitskell sought concessions from them on 'steel, a more helpful purchasing policy as regards raw materials by their agencies, and some kind of device whereby though we might not receive direct economic aid we could be helped by other means':[36] in other words, burden-sharing. He made no progress over the violent and damaging oscillations in the Americans' raw material purchasing policy, for they had their own complaints against 'price gouging' by Commonwealth suppliers, who in turn rejected Gaitskell's cherished stabilisation schemes.[30b] Over steel, Congress was prejudiced against Labour for nationalising the industry, and the Conservatives were to be treated somewhat better.[39] The US Treasury was not at all friendly; John Snyder, the Secretary, suspected Gaitskell's intentions and blocked him from seeing the President.[40] Snyder would not let the IMF be used — as the British wanted — to help nations in exchange difficulties, but only 'to bully or bribe countries into getting rid of restrictions'. After a silly row on a trivial matter (pensions for the IMF directors) in which Gaitskell played no part, Snyder got very drunk at dinner, reproached all the other governments for treating the United States as a milch cow, and generally 'revealed himself as a pretty small minded, small town, semi-isolationist'.[7b]

Fortunately the Departments directly concerned soon came 'to understand and take seriously our economic plight'; the State and Defense Departments and the ECA were friendly and helpful. In particular Gaitskell was impressed by Dean Acheson, the Secretary of State, 'a sensitive and cultured man' with whom he argued constantly.[7b] The arguments began over the Americans' insistence that European rearmament was still inadequate, and their refusal to talk about 'burden-sharing'.[35a b] Gaitskell, however, as he told Dalton on his return to London,

> said that we could not, as U.S. were pressing us to do, go beyond £4,700 million (rearm^t in 3 years) and could only reach it, if certain conditions as to supply of materials, etc., were fulfilled. Other European countries were doing much less than we, both absolutely and in relation to their paper programmes. French and Italians were very weak and mendicant. H.G. asked whether U.S. Treasury screened demands of Armed Forces, as we did. He gathered not. He urged them to.[9c]

According to Acheson, Gaitskell told them that Britain's balance of payments deficit would amount to $1,000 million, half of it due to the frantic United States purchases of raw materials driving up prices, and much of the rest to the diversion of manufacturing resources from exports to arms. He concluded:

> The British were already behind in their own program for 1951; the increased requests of General Eisenhower were out of the question. Not only was it impossible for them to do more, but they could not long continue the present rate of rearmament.[19c]

Whether or not the Secretary of State was as 'prepared and sympathetic' as he later blandly claimed, the Administration's attitude to 'burden-sharing' now changed abruptly. Though it had itself initiated the idea a year earlier, before Gaitskell's visit it would not even allow discussions to begin; after the visit a 'thoroughly convinced' Acheson got President Truman to authorise a full review of the economic capacity of the NATO countries.[19c] Eventually 'burden-sharing' was to ease Britain's difficulties – but too late to help the Attlee Government.[41]

After his return, Gaitskell still officially maintained that though the £4,700 million programme could not be increased, it would be carried out if supplies were available.[42] Far from rigidly insisting on an impossible programme, he did more than anyone else to persuade the Americans to scale down their objectives. But unlike his critics he knew that private explanations of Britain's problems caused least offence and were most effective:

> I had once more explained [to Harriman] the gravity of the dollar situation and made it plain, as I had done on several previous occasions, that if they did nothing about it we should not be able to carry through the defence programme – we should have to give priority to exports. I never, of course, said anything of this kind in public.[36]

Conversely, he was outspoken, courageous and influential where he thought public criticism appropriate. From Washington he accepted a lift in the Canadian Finance Minister's plane to the NATO Council's Ottawa meeting: the first attended by the Finance Ministers, who often seemed allies against their own Foreign Office and Defence colleagues.[43] Gaitskell felt it was this confrontation that made the conference useful.[7e] If so, that was thanks to himself. Acheson made one 'impressive and very lucid' speech on foreign affairs, and one impossible demand: that military and civilian production must be simultaneously increased. Gaitskell replied bluntly that the United States, by refusing to contemplate the slightest cut in her own civilian consumption, was cornering available world supplies and stopping her European allies from getting enough to increase their production. Flatly contradicting General Eisenhower's call in Paris for a 'burst of speed', he urged the need over a long period for strong defences and a 'steady pull'. His speech made a tremendous impact, for all the Finance Ministers agreed; but few were willing to speak out publicly.[44]

> I was at first depressed by the feebleness of the Finance Ministers ... some of them seem to say nothing whatever, presumably for fear of the Americans ... [I said] it was absolutely out of the question for us to do any more unless we were to have a war economy both internally and

in our relationship between each other. I criticised Acheson for appearing to suggest that we could have guns and butter as well. This was one of the things which continually irritated me—a sort of ganging up between the Americans who always wanted promises of tremendous programmes for Congress and the mendicant Europeans who would promise anything so long as they thought they could get some dollars. However, I think ... [we] made a considerable impression, as subsequent events showed ... even before we left Ottawa the American Ministers—Acheson, Foster and Snyder—had all begun to talk of screening down the military requirements rather than following the only other alternative which was to give us a great many more dollars. And by the time the enquiry [into burden-sharing] began I think this was their accepted idea.[7e]

The French, keen on supranational solutions because of their own government's instability, wanted that inquiry conducted by three experts.[7e] The Americans suggested that the three should include Gaitskell, and should serve in a personal not an official capacity: a remarkable effort to have him represent Britain even if her government changed.[30c] But he himself felt, like most others, that the 'three wise men' must on so crucial an economic and political problem enjoy the full confidence of their governments, and in the end Harriman, Monnet and Plowden were chosen.[45]

After two days in New York, Gaitskell returned to Britain and a worsening economic crisis. The sterling area's balance of payments with Europe was going wrong, the deficit for the third quarter (always the worst) was likely to rise to £600 million, and the remedial measures were not ready.[7e] At the time he told the Cabinet that the causes were: '(1) Lesser U.S. buying of wool, rubber and tin; (2) Increased U.K. purchases, not for re-armament — (3) Persia.'[46] The purchases were unexpected because the statistics were inadequate, and Whitehall did not know how far stocks had run down in the previous year which now were being replaced—at inflated prices.[47] Conversely, the sales and prices of raw materials were dropping at a disastrous moment. For the RSA countries had been selling at the top of the market, and now began to spend the proceeds; in the second half of 1951 they earned only half as many dollars as in the first half, but they imported at double the 1950 rate.[48] Normally they offset the United Kingdom's dollar deficit with a surplus, but now they aggravated it with an equal deficit of their own. Moreover, controls over capital exports to the sterling area were insufficient, and British private investment was financing large current deficits in both Australia and South Africa.[49*]

* These countries were very slow to take or even discuss any corrective action.

Gaitskell had to explain the crisis publicly in the context of an election, called by Attlee in his absence. He spent much of the week after his return preparing a party political broadcast which 'caused endless trouble'; and on 3 October 1951 he gave the Chancellor's traditional Mansion House speech. As usual his approach was reasoned and unemotional, and he told one adviser that he could not change his own personality: 'I haven't got Aneurin Bevan to give them.'[50] But 'It was quite clear to me that ... it would be quite fatal to attempt to hide any of the facts. It was very fortunate indeed that I took this line, as after events showed.'[7e] Though he left late, was caught in a traffic jam and arrived very late indeed at the Mansion House (where 'food is not easily produced warm'),[50] he felt that 'The penguins were not so frigid as they might have been (perhaps they were cheered considerably by the prospect of our losing the election)'.[7e] He gave a frank account of the state of the reserves and the heavy impact on them of adverse price changes; of the difficulties of the engineering industry faced with the competing claims of domestic investment, exports and rearmament; and of the need for the defence burden to be more equally shared within NATO. As R. A. Butler made clear,[51] the speech was based 'on the best information then available';[52] and it disproved the Conservative charge that Labour Ministers had concealed the situation from the country during the election. Moreover, the policies announced by Butler after the election were, except over bank rate, in Gaitskell's words 'exactly what we would have done'.[53]

iii   *The Defence Burden*

The balance of payments crisis imposed cuts in the defence programme, which Labour prepared and the Conservatives implemented. Those cuts naturally reinforced the Bevanite view that the original programme had been mistaken. Gaitskell had ardently supported it in public: and in private perhaps too ardently for a Chancellor of the Exchequer.[54] But its initiators were Attlee, Bevin and Shinwell; and responsibility was shared by Bevan, Wilson and the whole Cabinet.

The debate became confused in several ways. First, critics made three distinct assumptions. One view was that the policy was unnecessary in that the Soviet threat was exaggerated, and even dangerous in tying Britain too closely to a reckless America; that opinion, never held by the Bevanite Ministers before they resigned, hinted at in Bevan's resignation statement but never endorsed by Harold Wilson, gradually came to predominate in their camp.[55] The second view was that the programme, however desirable, was impracticable and might seriously damage the British economy; Wilson and Freeman had held it throughout the ministerial discussions but Bevan not until the very end. Thirdly the critics (after they resigned) took for granted that the economic costs of agreeing to an excessive programme outweighed the political costs of refusal. There were other confusions. The situation changed rapidly during 1951, and the balance of argument shifted from January to April, to September, to November. Moreover, Ministers' actions indicate that they had much more in common with their critics than either would admit; but their speeches do not, for they could not risk the international repercussions of saying so.

The first assumption cannot be conclusively disproved. We cannot know how far Western rearmament dissuaded the Russians from asserting their overwhelming conventional military superiority. They neither marched across Europe nor encouraged their satellites to pick off exposed salients; but then, by 1952 and 1953 the vacuum was not quite so tempting. Bevan argued on 15 February 1951 that Russia would not take such risks with such low steel production:[56] an undoubted deterrent to a long war, but not against a short, sharp strike to the Channel with her 175 divisions against NATO's twelve, before the United States could move. The State Department believed that danger to be real and some recent evidence appears to support them. Bevan and some of his followers themselves feared a Korea-type satellite operation. No responsible administration could prudently disregard such formal warnings as 'war possible in 1951, probable in 1952'; only a dozen years before, men like Gaitskell had despaired to see their predecessors neglecting similar dangers.[57] Had they known in 1951 of Stalin's paranoia in his last years, their alarm might have been even greater.

Conversely the political perils of the American alliance were unconvincing. Rearmament never did endanger Western democracy as Bevan predicted it would.[58] Allied or not, Britain would suffer from any dangerous tendencies in American foreign policy; but a breach with the United States in 1951 would only have increased them, for the danger of American adventurism lay in the Far East, not in Europe.[59] That danger was much reduced when Truman (three days before Bevan resigned) courageously dismissed General MacArthur. But the Republican Right were still wedded to an Asia First policy, and would have been reinforced if Europe had refused to contribute to her own defence.[60]

The economic argument was much stronger, especially when the incoming Conservatives cut the programme back after ten months. But that decision is not conclusive. The cut was made in response to a situation which British rearmament had not caused and which the Bevanites had not foreseen: for many of their predictions were not borne out. The programme was sometimes said to be physically unattainable for lack of essential raw materials and machine tools; sometimes to be economically unwise, leading to mass unemployment, wrecking the balance of payments, and endangering Britain's hard-won economic recovery; and sometimes to impose too great a strain on one crucial sector, metals and engineering.

The Government always recognised that the programme would require raw materials and machine tools from abroad. Officially it was conditional on these supplies – a reservation for which Bevan perhaps disingenuously claimed the credit – and Attlee and Gaitskell carefully said so in their speeches though, curiously, Bevan did not. The possibility of a cut was always present in the minds of Ministers who stayed, as well as those who resigned.[61] As Morrison's journalist confidant put it:

> In public, ministers were forced to show an inflexible determination to go through with the programme at all costs. Nothing less would create the climate of opinion in which Congress would vote the neces- sary supplies. In private, they knew that if the Americans failed to deliver the goods, it would be the rearmament programme and not the British economy which would suffer. And Bevan knew it too.[62]

Genuine economic dangers had to be weighed against the political risks of refusing to step up the defence effort. No defence plans could either be effective or appear to be so without American participation. The North Atlantic Treaty secured that on paper, but it would be without substance until the United States sent more troops to Europe and appoin- ted an American supreme commander for NATO. Today, after decades of continuous, active and sometimes clumsy American involvement in Europe, we forget how hard it was for the Administration to persuade public and congressional opinion to accept a policy so contrary to United States traditions. It had no hope of success without signs of similar seriousness in Europe, where any response was known to depend on a British lead. In January 1951 the British government whittled down the proposed three-year programme from £6,000 million to £4,700 million. Had they instead refused any significant increase at all, the consequences might have been very grave: similar refusal by other allies; rejection of the European commitment in Congress; reinforcement of the Asia First, Fortress America wing of the Republicans, perhaps electing Senator Taft to the Presidency; gloomy defeatism in France and Germany; and a vacuum across the Elbe tempting the Russians to believe that the United States (just as in Korea before the attack) had lost interest in Europe's fate.

Though not certainties, for a responsible government such risks had to outweigh equally hypothetical economic losses. So on 25 January the Labour Cabinet – with no talk of resignation from Bevan – resolved to carry out the £4,700 million programme 'to the limit of the resources under *our* control' – while warning the Americans that their resources would also have to contribute to it.[63] Ministers may have relied too much on assurances from the United States, but even if they suspected that those assurances would not be carried out, they could neither be sure in advance nor say so publicly. In conditional acceptance they chose the least damaging response.

When Bevan issued his challenge in April 1951, the programme was less than three months old. The raw materials situation was somewhat worse and the production Ministers were already concerned about its practicability.[64] But far from suggesting that the original figures were unrealisable, they told Gaitskell – who had asked them – that these 'were still the best available estimates'.[65] It was indeed too early to be sure that a three-year programme could not be fulfilled;[6f] and in any case it would have been imprudent to announce that publicly. Commodity boards had just been set up to plan raw materials distribution;[6g] Britain would not have got better treatment from them by abandoning her commitment. The burden-sharing exercise, assessing the economic load on each country and the compensation for those worst affected, was still only a promise – and one dependent on the Americans considering the European programme adequate. In addition to January's political worries about Congress and the Continent, the Cabinet now had reason to fear that any economic gains from a cut-back in April would be offset by losses through reduced offers of assistance in both raw materials and finance.

While the Bevanites pointed with relish to any signs of production falling short, these only increased Gaitskell's worry about inflation. For civilian goods as well as armaments would be held back by shortages of raw materials, worsening the inflationary pressure. Failure for economic reasons to fulfil the defence programme, far from releasing more for social services, would require a tougher Budget – either heavier taxation or real cuts in domestic spending. To this argument the Bevanites found no satisfactory answer.[66]

In the end extra defence expenditure over the first year was slightly short of the £1,250 million planned.[67] The shortfall was £120 million, far less than the Bevanites' proposed £300 million cut.[68] No doubt a smaller programme would have meant less industrial dislocation than the large one did. Yet by the middle of 1951, when Bevan had predicted mass unemployment in industrial areas, those out of work were only 1 per cent.[69-70] Even in August, Gaitskell still feared that inflationary pressure had been underestimated 'partly because the impact of the defence programme, through contracts placed, has been rather greater than we allowed for. At any rate, the level of unemployment has fallen sharply to the 1945 figure'.[7a]

Within the whole economy, engineering was the sector crucial to defence production. There the critics' case was strongest. Rearmament would absorb metal goods and leave an export gap, which it had been hoped would be filled by textiles; by the end of 1951 these were clearly performing disappointingly – the first signs of the decline of the woollen industry.[6h]

At first engineering carried the increased burden, quite unexpectedly keeping up its 1950 level of exports. Its main competition came from West Germany, whose factories had no defence orders to fulfil – because of understandable political fears of a new German army, notably in France and on the British Left. The main economic drawback of British rearmament was that loss of an export opportunity;[71-2a] ironically it was partly due to the long rearguard action by the Bevanites and other opponents of German rearmament.

The Bevanites early drew attention to the problem of engineering exports. By the end of 1951 this acquired new importance for reasons neither they nor anyone else had foreseen. Gaitskell's export target was met, not pushed far out of reach by defence demands as they had expected.[73] Instead the strain on the dollar reserves came largely from the rest of the sterling area; the United Kingdom contribution to it was not through low exports but high imports (largely for stockpiling, which was in part for defence).[74] Its full dimensions were not apparent until the autumn.[75]

The critics had foreseen the new situation though not the reasons for it. Gaitskell's response was the same as theirs. He warned the Americans privately that Britain could not fulfil the programme without a bigger contribution from them, and publicly that they were expecting far too much from Europe. 'Half way to Bevan,' commented one Canadian on his Ottawa speech; 'Has Gaitskell joined the Bevanites?' chortled *Tribune*.[76] Yes, in that the balance of payments crisis now led him to use their arguments in Washington;[77] no, in that his public statements were constrained both because he was friendly to the Americans and because he was a responsible Minister seeking concessions and therefore needing their goodwill. The Bevanites profited politically by ignoring these constraints – and gave Ministers a useful argument in Washington (just as the Communist threat was an invaluable dollar-earner for the French and Italians, and an implacable Congress often convenient to the US Administration).[6i] In the September talks Plowden warned Harriman,

> if you let [the Chancellor] down now you will be playing straight into Bevan's hands. Moreover, don't imagine that if the Labour Party lose the Election it will help at all ... Bevan may capture the whole Labour movement in opposition.[7b]

Had Labour won the election, they would have benefited as the Conservatives did from the turn of the economic tide. Certainly they too would have spread the British defence programme over an extra year.[78] The political as well as the economic situation had changed: Congress had authorised the United States commitment, the Administration had agreed to a slower pace, and the European countries had undertaken (though not carried out) their own defence programmes — which in February 1952 were co-ordinated into a big international effort, for once achieved on time in 1953.[79] Alarms about Soviet intentions were less urgent, as Churchill — presumably reflecting Intelligence reports — said in December 1951.[80] The cut was made when the economic case for it had become far stronger, and the political and military cases against it no longer relevant.

In a broader sense the Bevanites did anticipate some future developments. In the next decade, reluctance to abandon overseas commitments was to play a major part in Britain's slow economic decline. In 1951 Britain took some economic risk to continue in a Great Power role which, as Gaitskell knew, could not indefinitely be sustained. He wrote in 1952: 'in our military and political association with America we generally try and hold a status which ... [implies] a 2 to 1 power ratio but just does not fit the real ratio of — say — 7 to 1 ... we find it a heavy burden to carry'.[81] Yet at that time and relative to her neighbours Britain still really was a Great Power whose abdication might have had far-reaching consequences. The Bevanites were right about the long-run need to cut commitments, wrong to ignore the immediate danger of abandoning them prematurely.

iv *Last Days in Office*

Gaitskell, Morrison and Shinwell were at the Ottawa conference when they learned to their dismay that the Prime Minister had decided to go to the country. Back in May 1951 Attlee had tentatively planned for an October election despite Morrison's doubts;[23c] and like Dalton and others, Gaitskell had then agreed because of 'the narrow majority and the Bevanites'.[9d] But in Ottawa in September, his private secretary recalled, 'To Hugh it came as a thunderclap. He was very very upset by it, and they sent messages back saying: "for God's sake don't announce it while we are here or you will destroy our negotiating position".'[82] Gaitskell himself wrote in his diary that it had done so, though fortunately most of the important decisions had already been taken.[7e] On his return he told Dalton that the case for October was now much weaker, for they had earlier hoped for settlements in Korea and Iran which had not occurred; and that 'we should be badly beaten, and one hated not to win, and to hand over power to the enemy'.[83] This casts great doubt on the Whitehall rumour that before leaving he had urged on Attlee the need for a new mandate to impose the austerity required by the economic crisis.[84] That worry was only just becoming acute when he left on 4 September; and he cannot have discussed dissolution, for Attlee would not have concealed his intention to dissolve.[85]

Gaitskell left Ottawa on 21 September for New York, where to his amusement bankers and industrialists competed to entertain him at dinner. He kept up his contacts with the media as he had in Washington, where he became the first Chancellor to appear on television, making an excellent impression on the 10 million viewers.[86] 'One could not help feeling nervous ... [but] by the end of the half hour one ... only wanted more time to explain everything to the questioners.'[7b] He had very little time off on the trip, but told Dalton on his return 'that American girls were much better looking', and that he had enjoyed himself and 'had some wonderful meals'.[9c] Just before leaving he went very late to the office to thank the unfortunate typists — who throughout these meetings had nothing to do all day but worked all night. A civil servant was impressed:[87] 'most such people don't realise they've got any typists.'[34a]

On his return he was occupied by party politics as well as Treasury duties. He found the Labour Conference at Scarborough 'a very depressing affair'. In the constituency section of the National Executive, Bevan came top and Shinwell lost his seat to Barbara Castle. Gaitskell was particularly shocked that Driberg polled more than Jim Griffiths;* for he learned[88] that Griffiths's vote was down because of 'pretty shameful canvassing' by the Bevanites, who had told delegates to plump to vote only for their four factional candidates.[7e] Now a national speaker, Gaitskell was busy electioneering in Scotland, the Midlands and London, condemning the use of force in Iran, and clashing with Lady Violet Bonham Carter when he doubted if the Tories, so long associated with the mineowners, could encourage higher coal production. He found it 'intolerably boring having to say the same thing so many times', but thought his stolid Yorkshire folk very different from audiences elsewhere.[7e]

His faithful local Party ran the campaign, as in all later elections, with the candidate arriving only for the last few days. Redistribution had made South Leeds safer than ever, and even without a Liberal, his majority was hardly dented.

Hugh Gaitskell (Lab.)	30,712
Winifred Brown (Cons.)	16,493
Majority	14,219

But a tiny national swing against the government brought the Conservatives back to power, though much more narrowly than he had expected. He had thought at the start that they would win by 75, at the end by nearly 50;[7e] but in fact they polled fewer votes than Labour, and their majority

* Driberg had been severely censured by the PLP for absenting himself unpaired on a long journalistic trip when, with a majority of only five, sick MPs had to attend every division.

was only 17 seats.[89] Few observers thought they would retain power for thirteen years.

Gaitskell returned to the Treasury to say goodbye, his successor R. A. Butler courteously insisting on working from the Parliamentary Secretary's room:

> The leave taking itself was quite short and unsentimental ... Civil Servants in this country, thank goodness, have to be hardened to changing Governments and changing Ministers. It is rather remarkable what close and intimate relations one manages to develop despite this.[7f]

He charmed several officials by his careful choice of farewell presents — Housman's poems for one, an Elizabeth Bowen novel for another, a Dostoevsky for a third.[90]

When he left the Treasury the tributes again poured in. The Canadian Finance Minister had 'enjoyed ... working with you more than I can say'; Gaitskell's own private secretary felt 'sure that you have left an enduring mark on the Treasury and the whole Government machine — in fact I am continually struck by the extent of your influence'; Winston Churchill 'very warmly ... appreciated [how] you had used that [economic] knowledge for the service of the State'.[91] In less exalted quarters he left attractive memories. George Brett's schoolboy grandson recalled him as 'a gay man — the sort of man who would jive about the house in the morning'.[92] An old lady from Kingston had written to him because her husband, being under seventy, was not entitled to the higher old age pension; but they were entitled to National Assistance, and while her own MP did nothing, the Chancellor had ensured that they obtained it.[93]

He did not simply follow the rules, either in policy or administration. On behalf of the Arts Council his old schoolfellow Sir Kenneth Clark wrote later: 'You have been in the past, and may again become, our chief protector.'[94] Long before Bevan spoke of the desiccated calculating machine, Gaitskell told the Royal Scottish Academy that 'Chancellors are hard-faced, gloomy men, good at counting and sums ... lacking in imagination ... essentially low-brow people' — before proclaiming his eagerness to encourage the arts, assist the National Trust, promote the Festival of Britain, and preserve great houses, while avoiding 'the obvious dangers of uniformity and conventionality' in state patronage, and of philistine reaction if public opinion was not kept sympathetic.[95] Nor would he always submit to 'precedent and the awful Whitehall logic about endless repercussions'. When independent India insisted on taxing ICS pensions, already eroded by inflation, and the Treasury refused to reimburse the pensioners, the Dominions Office cunningly sent an old student of Gaitskell's to persuade the Chancellor to overrule his advisers.[96] He did so from a sense of justice, not from family sentiment for ICS officials; for though the family connection with Burma was so strong, his only row with the Prime Minister came when he agreed with his officials in opposing a loan to that country.[7a]

When Gaitskell became Chancellor he was a competent departmental Minister little known to the public, and his qualities were appreciated only by a few in the Cabinet and Whitehall. A year later he had become an international figure. He was inexperienced and had minor failings, from chronic unpunctuality to pernickety redrafting. But he was a quick learner, rapidly improving in handling the press or the House of Commons; and a Minister who knew his own mind, understood and tried to overcome the difficulties of applying his policies, was effective in persuading Cabinet and Parliament, and was always willing to take responsibility.

Abroad, where he had no pre-Treasury experience, he proved a skilful negotiator, so that the Americans wanted him as British representative both in Iran and for the burden-sharing inquiry. Having decided that the United States was indispensable to British and European security, however awkward her economic policies, he defended the alliance without flinching from the political costs. The rearmament programme was initiated by Attlee and Bevin, but Gaitskell undertook the main burden of defending it. He knew the economic risks, and while never condemning the United States publicly for letting Britain down, he worked hard behind the scenes to limit the burden without straining relations with Washington; and he succeeded, though too late for his own government or Party to reap the benefit.*

At home, his bitter dispute with a formidable colleague split the Labour Party for years. Yet his proposals were at first warmly welcomed on the government benches. There would have been no revolt but for the resignations, and then no bitterness but for the tone adopted by Bevan and his journal. No one else thought the health charges justified a split; Gaitskell may have been too stubborn about them, but he was not acting at all like Snowden in 1931, or 'deserting his Socialism in time of crisis', or 'dismantling the welfare state'. Nor can he reasonably be blamed for the balance of payments crisis. For its causes were largely outside the United Kingdom and overwhelmingly outside his control; its development was wholly unforeseen and unprecedentedly sudden; and it was met by measures prepared under his auspices.

Politically, he plotted no manoeuvre to drive out Bevan, whom he had rather admired; on the contrary, the clash seemed likelier to terminate his own ministerial career. But it was not he who alienated his colleagues, for

* 'A brave and very responsible man, who had been misled but would not defend himself because he thought his country's needs should take precedence.'[97]

he never personalised the conflict in Cabinet; he always promised loyal support from the back benches if the decision went against him; and though for the first time he faced bitter personal hostility, yet in the hope of healing the split he carefully refrained from replying in kind to his opponents, and would not give the struggle within the Labour Party priority over that against the Tories.

Gaitskell was in politics to achieve the power to put his ideas into practice, and had no patience with those (familiar on the British far Left and the American far Right) who would willingly see their opponents taking the decisions affecting men's lives, rather than infringe the purity of the opposition's party principles. When one Treasury adviser once asked how he could stand his intolerable life, overworked all week and speech-making or fence-mending at weekends, Gaitskell replied: 'I love it. It's the power.' He was 'desolated', felt another, at losing the Chancellorship.[98] Yet when he deemed it necessary he did not hesitate to put at risk both the office and the influence which he properly prized so highly. But when the government fell, he could not have imagined that neither he nor—with only three exceptions—any of his Cabinet colleagues would ever hold office again.*

In the three great controversies of his Chancellorship, Gaitskell's judgment may be challenged over health charges, over rearmament, and over the balance of payments. But no reasonable critic of his policies would deny his outstanding political honesty and courage (qualities less rare among politicians than cynics maintain, but not universal). Once again Gaitskell, confronted with wider responsibilities, in Attlee's words 'rose to the occasion splendidly'.[99] In the perpetual parliamentary reassessment of political reputations, he was for the first time being discussed as a potential leader of his party and of the nation.

* The three were Patrick Gordon Walker, James Griffiths and Harold Wilson.

PART FOUR

THE WAR OF ATTLEE'S SUCCESSION

'One would get no fun out of politics if one spent all one's life thinking of one's own political success'

(HG, 1955)

'Achieving Socialist goals under democratic conditions...the only thing really worth talking about'

(HG, 1958)

290

CHAPTER 13   Labour's New Champion

CHAPTER 10

OPPOSITION FRONT BENCH
1951–4

'A desiccated calculating machine'
(BEVAN ON AN UNNAMED RIVAL, 1954)
'We must earn their respect and gain their confidence'
(HG ON THE VOTERS, 1952)

---

i *The Labour Coalition*

WHEN the House met in November 1951, Hugh Gaitskell sat on the Opposition front bench which he was to occupy for the rest of his life. The Labour leaders had both to mobilise their forces against the new Tory government with its narrow majority, and to meet a vigorous assault from their own dissidents, concentrated against Gaitskell. The dispute partly diverted his attention for the next four years, under Attlee's leadership, and for two more under his own in 1959–61. We must therefore examine the structure and traditions of the party through which both he and his critics hoped to achieve the power to put their political principles into practice.

In origins and organisation the Labour Party is unlike the Conservative in being the political wing of an industrial movement. Because of that relationship, the emotions of the faithful are stirred by myths and memories older than the Party, reflecting uphill struggles against employers and sometimes the state itself. Conservatives and Liberals were organised from above, to mobilise support in the country for an established parliamentary leadership. But the Labour Party was built up from below in protest against a Parliament unresponsive to working-class concerns, as an alliance of the trade unions with the societies of Socialist propagandists. Since the allies differed greatly in outlook and interest, it took the form of an elaborately structured federal coalition, on to which the Parliamentary Party, born in 1906, had to be awkwardly grafted.

While the Labour Party was developing into the alternative government of the country, its federal structure remained but the components changed. The (Marxist) Social Democratic Federation withdrew very early on, and its various Communist and Trotskyite successors have normally been excluded. The Independent Labour Party, which once assembled most active British Socialists, declined in the late 1920s into a small sectarian Left opposition, half revolutionary and half pacifist, and broke away in 1932. The Socialist League organised the dissidents in the next five years, then dissolved itself under threat of disaffiliation. Thus the Socialist societies, except for the Fabians, disappeared from the coalition, while after 1918 local Constituency Labour Parties (CLPs) took their place.

The unions still provided the big battalions, dominating the annual Conference with 5 million votes to the CLPs' nearly 1 million (in 1950); by long-standing custom (not rule) affiliated organisations cast their votes as a block, so that six large unions alone could out-vote the rest of the Conference.[1] Between Conferences the Party in the country is represented by the National Executive Committee (NEC), elected by Conference each year in 'divisions': 12 representatives of the unions, 1 of the Socialist societies, 7 of the CLPs, 5 women, and the Party treasurer. Since 1937 the first three divisions have elected their own representatives, but all affiliated organisations could still nominate and vote for the others, while the Party leader, chosen by the PLP, served *ex officio*. Thus in 1950 eighteen of the twenty-seven NEC members were chosen by trade-union votes.

Since 1922, Labour has been either in office or the official Opposition. Its front-benchers were the best-known spokesmen of the Party, expressing its views in Parliament, and forming the team which would govern the country if Labour won an election. Yet, despite the growing prominence and importance of the PLP, it chose only one representative on the NEC, the leader (though individual MPs were always elected by the divisions). The two bodies—the NEC representing Conference which settled Party policy, and the PLP leadership representing Labour voters and views in the House and the country—each had a claim to legitimate authority. Conflict between them might embarrass the Party in its battle for public support, as when Winston Churchill in 1945 suggested that the NEC might unconstitutionally try to dictate to a Labour Cabinet (incurring a memorable rebuke from Attlee). Various devices were adopted to prevent clashes: an item could become Party policy only if Conference voted it by two-thirds; the election manifesto was drawn up jointly by the NEC and the PLP; and the timing of its implementation was left to the latter. But the only real safeguard was a common outlook among members of both bodies.

For most of the Labour Party's history up to the 1970s, harmony was maintained because the front-benchers and the trade union majority generally agreed. The parliamentary leaders were responsive to the needs of government and to the ordinary Labour and uncommitted voters; the secretaries of the big trade unions were concerned with the influence of their organisations on public policy, and with the standard of living of their members. Political and industrial leaders had more in common with one another than either had with the ardent ideologists among the constituency activists (for whom that was proof that the industrial 'bosses' were out of touch with their members). The union leaders were natural defenders of a party constitution which ensured their own predominance in Conference; while the constituency parties had ensured since 1937 that, besides the principal PLP leaders, a few left-wing critics – Cripps, Laski, Bevan – sat on the NEC to act as a ginger-group.

The leaders could usually rely on a majority of the Parliamentary Party, for most MPs always doubted whether either internal dissension or left-wing politics would help to defeat the Conservatives. But they could ignore neither their active constituency workers nor the electoral damage done by open disputes, so that a revolt in the local Parties or the unions put the PLP under effective pressure. In those days, however, the trade union leaders rarely had to face any political demands from the mass membership, and always resisted those of unofficial activists. Experience of industrial battles and negotiations had taught them the need for solidarity, for acceptance by minorities of unwelcome majority decisions; and in politics too they preached loyalty to the leadership, and sustained it in Conference and on the NEC. Often they were blunt men, trained in a hard school, who had little patience with tiresome rebels in union or Party.

Structure and traditions allowed rival tendencies to control different segments of the coalition. Critics were strong in the constituency Parties where many besides the perpetual malcontents instinctively felt that the leaders needed an occasional prod. The front-benchers had to accommodate their policies to a political and economic situation which they could not control, and to the need to win over uncommitted voters if they were ever to implement those policies. But the Labour Party was always receptive not only to opponents of specific proposals, but also to rebels against the whole outlook of a leadership which they always accused of lacking determination or vigour or Socialist principles.

These systematic critics ranged from the Communist Party, whose small but dedicated and disciplined forces were important in some trade unions, to the fervent and impatient idealists, far more numerous but often less effective. Those temperamental rebels were given to utopianism and wishful thinking, certain of their own unblemished rectitude, suspicious of all compromise and all authority. They never forgot the temptations of power that afflict some front-benchers, or recognised the temptations of purity to which critics succumb – as Aneurin Bevan in the 1930s warned Jennie Lee:

Yes, you will be pure all right. But, remember, at the price of impotency. You will not influence the course of British politics by as much as a hair's breadth. Why don't you get into a nunnery and be done with it?[2]

Their outlook reflected the old radical, provincial, Nonconformist tendency to see Westminster politicians as willing victims of the aristo-cratic, or the parliamentary, or the Whitehall embrace. All those suspici-ons were so stimulated by the trauma of 1931 that even a generation later the most influential figure in the Labour Movement was said to be the ghost of Ramsay MacDonald. Of course many active constituency workers passionately wanted their Party to come to power, and usually gave the leadership the benefit of the doubt. But every election defeat brought Labour's deep-rooted opposition-mindedness to the surface, and gave the PLP minority their chance. They could appeal to ancient traditions, blame the leaders for excessive moderation, and present themselves as the exclusive guardians of principle—even as simple rank and filers, keeping a watchful eye on the careerists at the top. But they too were politicians, disagreeing with the leaders perhaps on the extent of necessary compro-mise; perhaps on electoral strategy, wanting to rally the active party workers and not worry about the floating vote; or perhaps aiming at a change of leadership, and meanwhile seeking Party status and public prominence not in the Shadow Cabinet, but as constituency representatives on the National Executive.

The Front Bench faced such opposition from the ILP in the late 1920s, and from the Socialist League and the Popular Front campaigners in the 1930s. But from 1939 to 1951 dissent had generated no sustained attack on the leadership or its policies. As the elections of 1950 and 1951 showed, the Attlee government retained its solid working-class following, absorbing or wiping out all the splinter groups on its Left—Communists, ILP and Common Wealth. Yet the responsibilities of office had entailed supporting some unpopular policies, especially over defence where Labour's pacifist tradition had deep roots. Once out of government, with the leaders' prestige eroded by defeat, many CLP activists were relieved to revert to a more familiar stance.

Bevanism thus revived a tradition which had seemed to be disappearing. To Gaitskell and his associates, it threatened not only their policies and their own positions of leadership, but also Labour's prospects of power. Before the war, Labour's criticisms of Chamberlain's appeasement policy were discredited by its votes against defence estimates; now as the Bevan-ites came to question any need for rearmament at all, Gaitskell feared they would threaten Labour's credibility as well as Britain's security. As he wrote for an American journal in 1952, drawing an analogy with the Republican Right in the United States:

An Opposition that is continually taking the easy line ... may evoke much enthusiasm among its own supporters, but it is most unlikely to win the confidence of the electorate as a whole. And even if it does, its failure to live up to what was said earlier will soon lead to its downfall.[3]

Frequently in his first year out of office, he warned against demagogy, pointing out the

> extraordinary contrast between what the Tories now say and do as a Government and what they preached and promised when in Opposition.
>
> We do not intend to follow this very bad example ... If we [do] ... we may temporarily enlist the support of some sections or interests and we may enjoy a shortlived emotional satisfaction, but we shall certainly suffer in our reputation with the country and weaken our chances of getting back into power.[4]

The argument was sharpest on foreign affairs and defence, but was not confined to them. For Labour was still a rather new party needing to establish its credentials as a serious instrument of government. Uncommitted voters, Gaitskell wrote, 'are interested not only in policy but in whether we shall govern the country honestly, efficiently and in a truly responsible manner ... By our bearing we must earn their respect and gain their confidence.'[5] But as Roy Jenkins once put it years later, 'Fighting Opposition or Alternative Government?' was a false dilemma for Labour, since it was easy to be neither and difficult to be both, but impossible to be the one without the other.

ii Revolt at Westminster: A Party Within the Party

Labour had been in office for eleven years. The ex-Ministers who dominated the Parliamentary Committee (or Shadow Cabinet) were concerned to defend their own records and sympathetic to their successors' problems. But in November 1951 many MPs wanted more aggressive opposition than Gaitskell seemed willing, or some others able, to provide; and hoped to disengage from some governmental policies which were unpopular among Party workers in the constituencies. So, though the Bevanites were few in the PLP, they found much sympathy when they sought to push it as a body towards the Left – but none when they divided it by pursuing, at Westminster and in the weekly press, a bitter feud against the frontbenchers.

The problem of leadership was in everyone's mind, for Attlee's successor would have to be chosen before long. Morrison, his deputy, had neither his backing nor that of the unions, and handled foreign affairs badly in opposition as in office. Bevan had plenty of sympathisers, and on the whole behaved moderately until 1954; even so he often alienated them by emotional outbursts as he had in 1951. In 1954–5 he forfeited their goodwill by his sustained intransigence; and his friends' unrelenting vendetta against the leadership did him further harm. Though Gaitskell made bad mistakes too, by 1955 both his rivals had thoroughly discredited themselves and gave him a very comfortable victory.

His insistence on responsible opposition appealed more to intelligent voters unimpressed by the routine Party dogfight than to strong partisans. Within the PLP, it proved a heavy political handicap. He had thought the official economic spokesmen a capable team easily able to resist Bevanite criticisms.[6a] But in one early PLP argument over the Chancellor's economy cuts, he himself spoke (as he admitted) 'rather pedantically';[6b] and Bevan won great sympathy with a moderate and effective reply urging that to conceal its own divisions Labour must launch a frontal attack.[7] 'Bevanites pushing,' wrote Dalton. 'Weak opposition. H.G. not sufficiently combative against the Tories.'[8a] In the House next day Gaitskell did better, defending his own health charges while criticising the increases the Government proposed.* But he would make no concessions to demagogy:

> [W]e do not intend, now that we are in opposition, to follow the bad example which the [Conservatives] set ... [to] object to actions which we ourselves would have taken [or] pretend, as they constantly did, that we can do something which we know all the time is not really possible.[9]

As he insisted soon afterwards to a trade union audience: 'We should never stifle the still small voice that whispers to us: "yes, but what would you do if you were the Government now?" That is something precious, that voice ... the conscience of an Opposition Party, and we should cherish it.'[10]

Within the Party, Gaitskell was most vulnerable over defence, though at first even that controversy was subdued. As the burden-sharing exercise got under way at last, the Bevanites argued against taking dollar aid for the rearmament programme lest political dependence follow. Gaitskell refuted their case in a long memorandum to the Parliamentary Committee, arguing that it would bring quite small economic benefits but large political drawbacks: 'we should have gravely weakened our military position, seriously damaged Anglo-American relations, and of course left ourselves fundamentally far more dependent on America.'[11] The PLP twice voted heavily against it.[12] But the government's cuts in the defence programme

---

* He argued that his had been put on temporarily when both taxes and consumption were rising fast; theirs were permanent, with consumption falling and taxes about to be cut. His charges, unlike theirs, did not fall on the sick or discourage preservative dental work. Prescription charges, dropped by Labour to avoid hardship to old age pensioners, were now imposed on everyone.[9]

revived the Labour quarrel; and its presentation of them, as a foreign observer noted, 'misses no opportunity to envenom a conflict which perfectly serves [its] interest'.[13] Churchill especially annoyed Gaitskell (and others) by going 'out of his way in the most mischievous manner to pat Bevan on the back ... to stir up trouble in the Labour Party'.[14-17a*]

Despite their dark suspicions when other Labour leaders earned Tory praise, the Bevanites welcomed Churchill's approval as willingly as Beaverbrook's money, and gleefully resumed their attack on the ex-Chancellor and his friends whom they presented to Labour Party workers as simply Tories in disguise. Gaitskell did not retaliate. He defended his own record vigorously, never publicly attacked his critics, and even appealed to them to call off the vendetta for the sake of the Party.[18a] Gaitskell had defended Bevan during the election against the Tory charge of spreading class hatred.[19] Like some of Bevan's own associates, Gaitskell believed that he would be satisfied only by the Party leadership;** but nevertheless hoped he and Wilson might 'work their passage' back to the Front Bench.[6a] Dalton too was eager for that, and Douglas Jay still saw Bevan as a possible future leader.[8b]

Hoping to restore unity, Gaitskell refrained from starting polemics himself or even answering those directed against him. He had no idea of trying to drive the Bevanites out of the Party. But believing them to be a small minority, he would not make large policy concessions to them; and he did insist that once the PLP had debated and settled its tactics, all MPs must support the decision — as they always had in the past, and still did in Socialist Parties elsewhere. In that distant and different world, regular revolts or ostentatious abstentions by dissident groups of Labour MPs were very rare; there had been only a couple of peacetime cases in twenty years. Front-benchers who were more flexible on policy than Gaitskell were often even stronger than he over enforcement of majority decisions.

The call for discipline posed two questions for the Left: whether their leaders should stand for the Shadow Cabinet, and whether their organised group should continue. Election to the Shadow Cabinet would give a chance of influencing policy at the price of sharing responsibility; after long arguments, no Bevanite stood.[21a] James Griffiths came top with 195 votes and Gaitskell third with 175, far ahead of Dalton and Shinwell.[6b] But Wilson would still have liked to return to the Front Bench, and in some moods so would Bevan. Bevan was violent in private, and talked (though he did nothing) about organising in their constituencies against

* His unscrupulousness (for of course he approved of Gaitskell's policy not Bevan's) horrified some senior civil servants and official advisers.

** Crossman too thought Bevan 'almost exclusively concerned to be Leader of the Labour Party rather than to formulate Left-wing policy'.[20a]

MPs who opposed him. But he was active in neither the House nor the PLP, and in public he was restrained.[22]

Many of the left-wing MPs had been associated in the old Keep Left group ever since 1946. But this organised parliamentary faction raised different issues.[23] For the Bevanites made it the spearhead of a campaign against the leadership among Labour MPs – and, since its functions were tactical, admitted members to it only after careful screening.[24] Since the disaffiliation of the ILP twenty years earlier, there had been many differences of opinion among Labour MPs but no organised group seeking to use the differences to raise mutiny – or revolution – in the ranks. The Bevanites therefore provoked great resentment, as well as some effort by their younger opponents to organise the other side in the PLP.[6b] Churchill did all he could to exploit Labour's split: opposing a motion of censure in February, he broke normal conventions by revealing that Labour Ministers had agreed with the United States to bomb Chinese airfields in Manchuria if UN troops in Korea were attacked from them.[25] Gaitskell thought it was 'a particularly dirty trick', showing Churchill's 'complete unscrupulousness' and intended – successfully – to 'spread suspicion and confusion in our ranks'.[6b] On 2 March 1952 the Bevanites carried Labour's divisions beyond the privacy of the PLP to the floor of the House by ostentatiously abstaining on the Service estimates.

It was the very question on which the Party had discredited itself before the war. But in the 1930s a more divided PLP had acted in unity; first the large minority in favour of rearmament accepted the whip and voted against the estimates; then, when they became a majority in 1937, the rest honoured the new decision to abstain. In 1952 one-fifth of the Party (christened from their number 'the 57 varieties') publicly underlined the split. The Shadow Cabinet (against Gaitskell's wishes) had put down a rather absurd amendment approving the defence programme but attacking the government's incapacity to carry it out; the Bevanites' substitute proposal was turned down in the PLP by 115 to 41 (their defeat would have been worse in a bigger meeting).[26] Next day, defying a three-line whip, they abstained on the Labour amendment and then voted against the estimates.

Most Labour MPs were enraged. Rebellion against government policy had been organised by the ILP in the 1929 Parliament, and had occasionally erupted spontaneously in that of 1945. But open rejection of majority PLP decisions in opposition was unheard-of. Every Labour candidate had signed the PLP's standing orders, which forbade voting against those decisions and allowed abstention only on grounds of conscience; but since 1945 these had been suspended. Now the Shadow Cabinet recommended that they should be reimposed;[27] every MP should promise to observe them; and the rebels should be censured.[6b] That was a compromise, for the Chief Whip William Whiteley, a solid Durham miner, had wanted the rebels to lose the Labour whip at once. He feared the Party would go the way of the Liberals unless the solidarity of the trade union movement was observed at Westminster. He was supported in the Shadow Cabinet by Robens and Callaghan;[6b] and outside it by the TUC chairman, Arthur Deakin, Bevin's successor as the Transport Workers' general secretary, who expected the backing of the trade union MPs.[28a]

A new faction – nicknamed the 'Keep Calm' group – sought a compromise, hoping both to limit the Bevanites' revolt and to check any strong action against them. It was led by three ex-Ministers: G. R. Strauss and John Strachey, who had campaigned with Bevan for the Popular Front before the war, and Kenneth Younger. They, and most of their followers such as Michael Stewart and Kenneth Robinson, had much sympathy with Bevan's policy views (though two supporters, Hilary Marquand and Hector McNeil, had been among his targets a year before). This impeccably middle-class leadership group, allied to the mainly middle-class Bevanites, soundly defeated Whiteley, Robens, Callaghan and the trade union MPs.[29]

Wrath cooled over the weekend before the crucial PLP meeting, and many MPs became worried at the prospect of Bevan being driven out. Gaitskell was not among them.[6b] Dalton found him 'very strung up against Bevanites. Wants a show down!'[8c] But Strauss rallied strong support for a compromise resolution merely restoring standing orders. Shadow Cabinet members did not canvass for their own motion, and Attlee spoke for it very feebly.[30–1a] 'Bevan made a violent speech, of nauseating egoism, and sweating with hatred.'[32] Even so Strauss's resolution passed easily, 163 to 74.[31a] The Bevanites supported it, then a week later tried (vainly) to obstruct the only action it proposed.[6b]

The Keep Calmers had averted an open and immediate clash, but they had also convinced dissidents that open rebellion was quite safe, ensuring a continuing public struggle within the Party. After a truce when Gaitskell became leader, the fight broke out again bitterly in 1960. The ex-mediators did not resume conciliatory efforts as Wilsonite compromisers; six of those seven Keep Calmers survived, and all were staunch Gaitskellites.[33] Like Bevan in the Cabinet, his friends on the Left constantly alienated their would-be sympathisers.

For doing that, eventually they paid the price in the choice of a successor to Clement Attlee. In 1952 few people believed that choice could be long delayed. Attlee was sixty-nine. He had been elected leader in 1935 as a stopgap whose tenure was expected to be short. Even after sixteen years this taciturn man, with his public-school and military values, had very few close friends and no personal faction. But he was now respected by his opponents as a man of integrity and an efficient Prime Minister, and admired by his followers as the leader who had brought Labour to power and carried out its policies. To his colleagues he had been and still was preferable to any rival, for he was skilled at balancing between strong personalities and conflicting tendencies. Armed with the prestige of the Premiership, the massive backing of Ernest Bevin, and Labour's (then) reliable loyalty to its own government, he had hitherto combined tactical flexibility with strategic direction. Now Bevin was dead, the Party out of office, and Attlee concerned only to keep it together. His style had always been that of a chairman reflecting majority views; and in opposition, faced with a bitter internal feud, he preserved his own position and the Party's unity by giving no lead at all.

His likeliest successor seemed to be his deputy Herbert Morrison, five years his junior, his chief opponent back in 1935, and the other survivor of Labour's inner cabinet. A shrewd, cheerful cockney who understood the British electorate, a superb organiser, master of the London County Council in the 1930s, a courageous wartime Home Secretary, and then a most effective leader of the House of Commons, he was the natural beneficiary of Labour's strong sense that great service deserves great reward. But he could be a ruthless party manager, and he had made many enemies. His vision was narrow, and his naked ambition appeared unseemly even to hardened colleagues. The trade unions had no love for him, the Left detested him, and even his friends thought him ultra-cautious about the floating voter. He suffered too from Attlee's personal dislike, and from his own catastrophic performance from both Front Benches on foreign affairs. Gaitskell respected him as honest and courageous, 'the nearest we have to a Scandinavian Socialist leader', who 'really understands the working of democracy'.[6c] He and others easily persuaded Attlee that Morrison should revert to party management.[34]

In the spring of 1952 Attlee told Leslie and Margaret Hunter he might retire at seventy, when Morrison would certainly succeed him. 'I'd go at once if I thought Morrison could hold the party together, but I don't think he can. He is too heavy-handed ... I may have to hang on for a bit and see.'[28b]* About the same time several anti-Bevanite ex-Ministers had the leader to dine at the House to persuade him to intervene more actively. As Gordon Walker recorded:

> Attlee was rather casual. Bevan would fade out as a menace: it had often happened before. The thing was to give him time ... suddenly Attlee said that no one ought to be P.M. after 70. Had it not been for the split in the Party, he wd certainly have made up his mind to go. We should give our mind to finding the next leader.[35a]

* He inclined to Bevan, ignored Gaitskell, and later turned even more against Morrison.[28b]

He then departed abruptly, leaving the others discussing a succession which
might now be quite close, for his birthday was in January – only eight
months away.

Gaitskell thought James Griffiths (a Welsh miner who was himself
present at the dinner) might well get Bevanite, Keep Calm and many trade
union votes and win an immediate leadership election: whereupon Bevan
would become deputy, since Morrison would not serve. In the next House,
Gaitskell hoped and assumed Morrison would be sure to win (though the
Chief Whip disagreed); and therefore wanted to persuade Attlee to stay
for four or five years, provided he would take the lead against Bevan.[36] But
if Attlee would not lead, then he should retire quickly; the ex-Ministers
thought he confirmed, when asked, that he would go at seventy.[37-8] Instead the leader suddenly announced 'in the most hole in the corner way'
(at a meeting of Labour agents, some of whom missed the point) that he
hoped to go on into the next Parliament. But he would not lead as Gaitskell
wanted. He lunched with the ex-Ministers at Stokes's house at the end of
July, and Gordon Walker recorded:

> We all said we could not attack Bevan without leadership. Gaitskell
> said that it all turned on whether Attlee would make a strong speech
> about the Party in the Party. I said that this would be enough to beat
> Bevan ... Morrison said he had often attacked rebels. And would do so
> again if Attlee wanted. But he did not want to be left out on his own ...
>   Attlee did not commit himself at all. He would certainly speak out
> if this were the best way to beat Bevan. But he had been advised by
> 'people close to the rank & file' not to attack. Bevan would hang him-
> self in time.[35b]

Another man in the middle was Dalton, who now found Gaitskell 'very
tense and unsmiling ... in danger of having an obsession about the
B[evanite]s'.[39] But Bevan was impossible, and Dalton feared the feud was
'getting worse & more & more personal ... the only thing that can endanger victory'.[8d] Bevan's bitterness constantly embarrassed his sympathisers, like Younger. Crossman too complained of his determination 'to
down-grade Hugh Gaitskell to ... junior clerk in the next Labour Government';[20b] and recorded that in one debate, after Gaitskell had done 'a
brilliant job' of exposing Churchill, 'Nye rose in a good House ... [to
make] a personal attack on Gaitskell ... [heard] with enormous relief by
the Tories and icy silence by our own benches'. Boothby said it was Bevan's
first speech for twenty years to help the Tories, and Dalton called it disgraceful.[40]

Thus in the House Bevan did seem likely to 'hang himself in time', and
Attlee's technique was quite effective. Elsewhere it was a different story.

L

iii   *Revolt in the Constituencies: Morecambe and Stalybridge*

Attlee's advisers proved as wrong about Party workers in the country as they were right about the MPs;[41] for no one else knew about the tantrums and personalities at Westminster, or noticed Gordon Walker and Stokes who, in default of the leader, condemned the 'party within a party'. Gaitskell was almost alone in speaking out in defence of the rearmament programme with unpopular forthrightness, taking great risks with his own political future. Well before his first public blast against the dissidents, he was becoming recognised as Bevan's chief antagonist.[42]

That blast was a sequel to the 1952 Party Conference at Morecambe. The Bevanites used the elections for constituency representatives on the NEC — hitherto a contest among individuals seeking to influence Party policy — for an organised factional campaign to discredit the parliamentary leadership.[43] Sensationally they took six of the seats.* As Bevan put it later, these elections 'served their purpose as a symbol'.[20c] Gaitskell had intended to wait for a better year, but decided that having been so violently attacked he ought to stand.[44–5] Some of his friends were absurdly optimistic, and even good judges like Callaghan and Dalton thought he might just scrape on;[46] though Dalton was among the few who expected his own seat to be lost and feared for Morrison's.[47]

The swing was massive, and organised. The Keep Calm leader John Strachey did disastrously badly. The veteran left-winger Sydney Silverman lost votes, while his views progressed and the Bevanite newcomers polled five times his score (three Bevanites, most unusually, had almost identical totals). Morrison came slightly and Dalton badly behind the winners. Gaitskell was next, doing far better than Shinwell (a member of the Executive till 1950); but with only one-third of Bevan's vote and half that of Wilson and Crossman. Thanks to Labour's fondness for familiar faces, the Bevanites now had a permanent institutional base in the Party.[48]

The results brought an explosion of cheers. Demonstrations from the galleries and from some of the delegates gave the conference what Michael Foot called its 'ugly, raucous features'.[49a] Spokesmen of the leadership were loudly booed, often before they had even opened their mouths.[45b c] At the time Dalton called it the worst Conference 'for bad temper & general hatred' of the last twenty-five years;[8e] later on, younger men thought it the worst of the next twenty-five.[50–2a] Arthur Deakin, giving his 'fraternal' address from the TUC, furiously denounced the Bevanites against 'Vesuvian' interruptions;[49b] he was angry at Attlee's silence and very nearly said so.[28c] One of the winners called it 'a ghastly conference, doomed from the

* See Table 2.

TABLE 2   *NEC Constituency Section Voting, 1952*

		Votes (*in thousands*)	
	1952	Since 1951	Since 1950
Elected			
Bevan (outgoing member)	965	+107	+116
Castle (outgoing member)	868	+192	—
Driberg (outgoing member)	744	+ 98	+156
Griffiths (outgoing member)	700	+103	− 81
Wilson	632	+236	—
Mikardo (outgoing member)	630	+ 69	+267
Crossman	620	—	—
Defeated			
Morrison (outgoing member)	584	− 11	− 87
Dalton (outgoing member)	437	−108	−217
Gaitskell	330	—	—
Callaghan	196	+ 54	+ 12
Shinwell	146	−264	−458
Greenwood	141	—	—
Mrs Braddock	130	—	− 47
S. Silverman	129	− 56	—
Noel-Baker	118	−131	−245
Robens	92	—	—
Strachey	59	−120	—

(Nine others polled under 50)

beginning'.[53] The weather was wet and blustery, the accommodation poor, the hall too small. Labour had never been to Morecambe before. It has never returned since.

It was the first Conference for twelve years with Labour not in government. Though the galleries were rowdy, there were serious and lively debates on unanimously agreed NEC resolutions about foreign policy and defence; USDAW (a union with an old ILP-pacifist tradition) proposed defence cuts, but lost by over 3 to 2. Gaitskell voted for all the successful resolutions,[54] and privately was pleased with the outcome.[55-6] Morrison accepted rejection with dignity, winning a tremendous ovation when he promised to continue to serve loyally.[38b] His defeat and the violence of the galleries produced a reaction, as Crossman had feared, both in the Conference and among Labour's supporters in the country.[57] Morrison's friends deeply resented the tone of the Bevanite campaign, and Crossman found that 'the bitterness increased steadily ... with really nice people telling you how unfair the demagogy was'.[20d] In Birmingham, wrote Roy Jenkins, the local leaders, 'who were rather wobbly beforehand, have been so shocked by Morecambe as to be driven very hard our way'.[58] Bevan's following among Labour voters fell to 22 per cent (against 51 per cent for the leadership), and among Party members to 40 per cent (against 48); only 11 per cent of the voters and 22 per cent of the members welcomed Morrison's defeat, which 40 and 55 per cent respectively deplored.[59]

The leadership thus still had far more support in the electorate and even in the Party than its critics, and had carried its policies. But, unchallenged among the activists, the Bevanites had scored a spectacular success; and Gaitskell feared that if Attlee's tactics of silence continued to prevail, the morale of their opponents would collapse.[60] When the results were announced, he told a journalist: 'There is only one thing we have to do in the next few years, and that is to keep the Labour Party behind the Anglo-American alliance.'[61] Since the Bevanites so willingly pandered to anti-Americanism and neutralism, he wrote: 'it is clear to me now that we must fight. The worm must turn'.[56] Before the Conference he had cooled down local Party workers in Leeds who urged him to pull no punches against the Bevanites.[62] Now, one of them drove him back from Morecambe and begged him to speak out, and two more confirmed that advice.[63] He had consulted no Westminster colleague.[64] But his mind was made up when, on Saturday morning, he came to the *Leeds Citizen* office to draft what to say in Cheshire next day.[65] It was to be 'what was for me an unusually violent speech ... a call to battle'.[6c]

Gaitskell found 450 people waiting for him in the small old-fashioned theatre at Stalybridge, and warned them to expect a shock: 'I know you will not find it easy to applaud or laugh but I only ask you to sit and listen.' He condemned the 'gross political ingratitude' and 'blind stupidity' of rejecting Morrison, 'the principal architect of efficient organisation and realistic policy ... a loyal colleague, wise counsellor, and fearless administrator'. He alleged that many resolutions and speeches were promoted by the Communist *Daily Worker*:[66]

> I was told by some well-informed correspondents that about 1/6th of the Constituency Party delegates appeared to be Communists or Communist inspired. This figure may well be too high. But if it should be one-tenth, or even one-twentieth, it is a most shocking state of affairs to which the National Executive should give immediate attention.[67–8]

He welcomed the Morecambe policy decisions, which all loyal Labour supporters would now accept. He protested that the CLPs had been badly misled by the Bevanite press pouring out

> a stream of grossly misleading propaganda with poisonous innuendoes

and malicious attacks on Attlee, Morrison and the rest of us ... because of a distaste for public rows inside the Party, we endured it for
the most part in silence. But it is now quite clear ... that we were wrong.

To reply was not

endangering the unity of the Party. For there will be no unity on the
terms dictated by *Tribune*. Indeed its ... vitriolic abuse of the Party
Leaders is an invitation to disloyalty and disunity. It is time to end the
attempt at mob rule by a group of frustrated journalists and restore
the authority and leadership of the solid sound sensible majority of
the Movement.

If we don't or can't do this we shall not persuade, and shall not
deserve to persuade, our fellow citizens to entrust us once again with
the Government of the Country.

The hitherto silent audience gave him a loud round of applause at the end. [45b]

The speech was injudiciously phrased. The much-resented words 'mob
rule' may have echoed Jay, who had told Hugh and Dora that he had never
understood their meaning, or imagined the effects produced by Hitler and
Goebbels, until he heard the 'organised Communist screams from part of
the gallery'. [69–70] Gaitskell had not meant to attack the delegates themselves, but was entirely to blame for not making himself clear. Communist
infiltration was indeed a danger; [71] and the Communists themselves emphasised that many Bevanites were far more anti-American than their leader,
for 'most of those who support Bevan are deeply suspicious of the alliance
... [and reject] Government policy in Malaya, in the Middle East and in
Korea. THIS GOES FAR BEYOND BEVANISM'. [72] But Gaitskell was most unwise to publicise a very exaggerated estimate of it which he neither publicly endorsed nor privately believed. Ironically, his suggested NEC inquiry was to be proposed by Harold Wilson (to discredit him) and seconded
by his own ally Sam Watson; the NEC voted 16 to 7 to let sleeping dogs
lie. [73]

The 'frustrated journalists' were particularly indignant at becoming
targets themselves. Kingsley Martin, editor of the *New Statesman*, threatened to sue for libel. Gaitskell replied with appropriate caution, and Martin
then said he would publish the correspondence to allow 'the Labour
Movement as a whole to judge between us'. But Gaitskell justified his
charges with a long dossier of quotations compiled by Dora; Crossman
feared the journal would suffer 'irreparable damage'; [20f] and Martin conveniently ruled that publication would bore the readers. [74]

Other politicians besides the Bevanites resented Gaitskell for hitting
back – after eighteen months – at those who had systematically denigrated
him and his colleagues. When Strachey and other Keep Calmers rebuked

him, he challenged them to cite their protests against the Left's attacks on him.[75] But to critical rank and file Labour workers, sick of bickering politicians who damaged morale in their local Parties, Gaitskell replied most patiently. A local secretary from Somerset urged 'the likes of you' to go out to the backwoods to make your 'suicidal speeches' – and was astounded when Gaitskell accepted this as an invitation to speak. 'I am somewhat chastened by your kind letter to me', he apologised. 'Dulverton are almost stupefied with delight by the news that you will come.'[76a b]

Stalybridge did not prevent a 'post-Morecambe accommodation';[49c] *pace* Michael Foot, it led to one. For everyone wanted to end the feud, and no one but the Bevanites thought it could be ended on their terms. Gaitskell said the obstacles were two:[77] the personal attacks and, at Westminster,

> the Bevanite group – meeting beforehand to decide their attitude and tactics at Parliamentary Labour Party meetings, seeking to win prestige victories on this or that issue, boasting when concessions were made to them, and threatening mutiny when they were not, trying at all times to discredit and weaken the official leadership in the Party.
>
> I do not think that either the Bevanites or those outside Parliament realise just how much soreness and bitterness this has caused among other Labour M.P.s. If it goes on, it is hopeless to talk of unity.[70a]

His judgment proved correct. Immediately after Stalybridge the Bevanites had rejoiced, believing he had weakened his own side.[78] But they had no idea how much resentment they had aroused, or how others saw their activities. Where Michael Foot had found the past year 'exhilarating',[49d] to Clem Attlee it was the unhappiest of his long leadership,[20g] and to Jim Griffiths it had almost caused the Party 'irrevocable harm'.[70b] When Parliament reassembled, Crossman found 'the atmosphere ... worse than I have ever known it ... such hostilities in the air that you sweated before you got hot'.[20h] As Dalton sadly noted:

> More hatred, and love of hatred, in our Party than I can ever remember. Nye's defects of character, and of entourage, are growing on him. Arrogance, conceit, personal animosities – & the entourage egg him on. Now Mikardo & Co. are trying to undermine non-Bevanite M.P.s in their constituencies.[8f]

A chorus of respected Labour voices promptly endorsed Gaitskell's remedies for the trouble. Griffiths, the one leader without enemies, condemned 'the intolerance, the personification of differences, the singling out of colleagues ... for attack'. Morgan Phillips, the cautious secretary, called for 'privately-organised factions' to disband.[70c] Dalton concurred;[79a] and so, in his careful balancing act, did Strachey[70b]. Even Attlee at last abandoned his silence:

What is quite intolerable is the existence of a party within a party with separate leadership, separate meetings, supported by its own press ... I say ... 'Work with the team. Turn your guns on the enemy, not on your friends' ... The most brilliant player on the left wing [would be] no use if he ... put the ball through his own goal.[80]

Bevan's concern for party unity was limited; he was against well-meant compromises over the leadership.[81] But unlike his irreconcilable entourage he did not confuse a handful of *franc-tireurs*, firing as often as not at their own officers, with an effective political army. He and Harold Wilson decided to open up the Bevanite group — without consulting it — to all Labour MPs.[82] It was not enough.

At the PLP on 23 October 1952, Attlee refused to 'create a rival Party Meeting'. In the sole reference to Stalybridge, Crossman reported Morrison saying: ' "Considering what Gaitskell had had to put up with for a year, he couldn't blame him if he didn't choose his words quite right." This produced an enormous round of applause for Gaitskell.' From the chair, Attlee, having at last made up his mind, demanded a vote — as a question of confidence — on disbanding unofficial groups and ending personal attacks; declined to call the Keep Calm leaders Strachey, Strauss and Younger; refused any postponement; and succeeded by 188 to 51 with a dozen abstentions.[83]

Gaitskell promptly welcomed the PLP resolution: having 'been on the receiving end for the past 18 months and recently done some fairly vigorous hitting back ... I am all for bringing this kind of thing to an end.'[84] The Keep Calmers feared that a complete ban on groups would be too restrictive[31b] (and Tom Driberg actually compared the Bevanites to the Parliamentary Christian Socialists).[85a] But Bevan himself overruled 'some of his closest friends' — according to Michael Foot — and decided to co-operate.[49d] 'To continue the Group now is to perpetuate schism,' he told Crossman:

'If you were to continue the Group in these conditions and I were the Leader, I would have you expelled. The Group is intolerable.' I then asked, 'Then why hasn't it been intolerable for the last six months?' 'Well of course it's been intolerable,' he said, 'we've got away with it. And we needed it then. We don't need it now ... if we go on with it we shall alienate the people in the Parliamentary Party we are trying to win.'[86]

Not even irreconcilables like Mikardo would defy a PLP resolution.[20i] So the Bevanites, protesting at such illiberal interference with the freedom of association among MPs, agreed to disband.[18b]

To show independence, Bevan stood against Morrison for deputy leader, polling more than expected (82 to 194). To show reasonableness he then stood for the Parliamentary Committee of twelve. A new electoral system (which he assumed was a plot against him) had been devised by Attlee for his benefit;[28d] as in many trade unions, candidates with less than half the votes were to go to a second ballot, while (to avoid plumping by minorities) everyone must vote for twelve names. On the first round, six of the old committee won a majority. Gaitskell, despite Stalybridge, again came third with 179 — 4 more than in 1951. Bevan was twelfth with 108, and on the second ballot again twelfth with 137, so that he would have been elected under either system. Wilson polled 91, but other Bevanites far below the group's strength.[87]

Both at Westminster and in the country the mood was transformed. Even in Bevanite constituencies, Crossman found that 'Attlee's counter-attack has been extremely successful' and the 'whole atmosphere has changed'.[20j] In the PLP, the end of the Bevanite group and Bevan's return to the Front Bench dispelled much suspicion and animosity:

> Mysteriously, and with astonishing rapidity, the mood of the Parliamentary party has changed. The Bevanite and anti-Bevanite feeling has melted away and ... everyone is rather shamefacedly aware that both sides are on the same side after all ... this couldn't have happened if there had been real fundamental issues of policy dividing the two sides ... the enormous desire of the Labour Movement for unity, and therefore the enormous fear of any contestant of being blamed for disunity, [is] at least a partial explanation.[20k]

Gaitskell conceded privately that the Stalybridge speech was badly worded and the Communist passage a mistake;[88] but he always maintained that in the long run his stand had been necessary and healthy for the Party.[20l] It affected his own position too. Arthur Deakin was impressed by the first politician to challenge the Bevanites, and mistakenly thought he had found a true hatchet-man of the Right. His enthusiasm was both to promote and to embarrass Gaitskell's career.[89]

iv   *A Solid Bastion: South Leeds*

Gaitskell's West Riding base influenced his political attitude — for instance to the Liberals, no friends of Labour in that part of the world. His working-class constituency kept him in touch with grass-roots opinion and confirmed his own suspicion of the far Left's factional activities. But its staunch support was not typical of a city where Labour politics were particularly turbulent, and social and geographical divisions were sharp. North of the river were the business and civic headquarters, the university, the prosperous residential areas, the flourishing Jewish community. South Leeds always felt neglected, even complaining that local Labour leaders moved north on becoming JPs. The southern wards, quite recently separate villages, were kept distinct by distance and poor transport — especially Middleton, which with its miners became part of South Leeds only in 1948. With their fierce sense of identity and deep-rooted working-class culture, Labour voting was still an expression of local as well as class solidarity; in some areas canvassers did not knock on doors but rang handbells to bring whole streets to the polls. The city cherished a peculiar local form of electoral organisation until well into the inter-war years: electors went to their Party committee rooms to collect their polling number, often believing they could not otherwise vote.[90]

Always a safe seat except in 1931, after the war South Leeds was impregnable to Tory attack. Gaitskell's assiduous attention to it was due not to political prudence but to temperamental thoroughness and real feeling for the people he had gone into politics to serve. As back- or front-bencher, Chancellor of the Exchequer or Leader of the Opposition, his monthly weekend visits had top priority even if he had to fly back from abroad; he is said to have missed only once in his whole parliamentary career.[91] Usually he came up by train, writing a speech on the way. He lodged (and insisted on paying) with a local supporter, generally his agent: Brett or Goodwill at first, George Murray after 1950. At election times, needing space and quiet, he went further afield, staying with Mrs Duffield, Brett's daughter;* and later in North Leeds with his prosperous friends the Gillinsons — who occasionally put him and Dora up at other times, and often loaned him a car. They provided an escape from endless politics, and the opportunity to meet Leeds writers and artists such as Terry Frost. But he always felt guilty at being out of the constituency.

Usually he held Saturday, 'surgeries', and brought his agent or a local councillor along to help deal with constituents' problems. Among the commonest were pensions and military service matters, and especially complaints against landlords or property companies or estate agents, since local housing was appalling; at one time he had fifty letters a day.[92] That was local council business, but an MP's intervention could sometimes speed things up. If he could help he would take endless trouble; if not he would say so straightforwardly. Early in the evening he would relax, often watching a cowboy film on television, and then tour the workingmen's clubs where he was completely at home. He might see more people on Sunday morning, then have a good traditional Yorkshire lunch at the Goodwills' or the Murrays'. The general committee met on Sunday afternoons for his convenience, and he often caught a teatime train back to London. Whenever possible he came for social events, and in September 1953 he spent a full week canvassing the area, which he always enjoyed. He would linger chatting with the housewives so that fellow-canvassers

* He amazed Mrs Duffield by going to bed on whisky and chocolate biscuits.

would find themselves two or three streets ahead and have to slow down. But his Party workers knew that 'somehow he was always there in the next street. You could always find him when you wanted him'; and that at election time voters would say, 'Oh yes, we know him well, he's been here to tea'.

These working-class people never understood the notion that Hugh Gaitskell found it hard to mix with or talk to ordinary folk:

> He was pleasant, friendly, you never felt he was talking down to you. The whole division was fond of him ... the sort of approach that encourages people to talk helps a person who is perhaps a bit nervous, draws people out ... not necessarily about politics,

said a woman trade unionist. 'I never met anyone so brilliant and yet so friendly,' echoed a shop steward. 'It's very difficult to find people with the level of intelligence he had and yet who had so obviously the common touch and who was so ready to learn from things he had done wrong himself.' To a third party worker 'he didn't seem an intellectual, he was down to earth, never up in the clouds about realities, it didn't matter what company he was in, he was just the same to the people who knew him ... He talked with you, he didn't talk down to anybody.' The Middleton miners seemed a closed and impenetrable group to other trade unionists in the constituency, but not to Gaitskell: 'he was their idol', said their spokesman. An occasional young lower-middle-class left-winger never felt at ease with him and doubted if others did either – though readily admitting it was not for want of effort on Gaitskell's part, and affirming that he was 'a much-respected man'. But nearly everyone else used words like 'loved' or 'adored' or 'worshipped', often carefully denying that these were euphemisms for deference.

Solid Labour constituencies, with no real electoral contest, often have weak local Parties. South Leeds was active enough but rather narrowly based, never building up much of a women's section or a youth movement. Gaitskell was attentive to the fairly small devoted band, mostly councillors, who ran it for years. He always showed appreciation of their work, kept in close touch, gave them a good time when they came to London or to a Party Conference, and often quietly helped with their own or family problems. In 1961 he suggested and paid for an annual dinner-dance for the 100-odd collectors of subscriptions; it was a huge success, and the constituency has held one ever since. His reward was unshakeable personal loyalty, buttressed by the intense if rarely displayed local pride of good Yorkshire folk who knew they were sending Britain's next Prime Minister to Parliament.

In all the post-war struggles Gaitskell never had to worry about their backing. In 1952 they made him a delegate to allow him to stand for the

National Executive, defeating by 13 to 6 a procedural move to block this. Before Stalybridge they were keener than he to denounce the Bevanites; and after it they gave him a unanimous vote of confidence and loyalty. In 1954 he was unanimously nominated as Party treasurer. They unanimously congratulated him over Suez (not to be taken for granted in a working-class area where feelings ran high).[93a] The one occasion on which they ever disavowed his policy was when he attacked Clause Four; the city Party reaffirmed the Clause, and the divisional Party concurred with it by 17 to 12 — though a personal vote of confidence in Gaitskell was at once passed by 30 to 2.[93b] Over the defence battle in 1960, Dalton's first question was whether South Leeds was reliable.[8g] It supported its member throughout,[93c] and became a bastion of the Campaign for Democratic Socialism.[94]

Like so many local Labour Parties, in NEC elections South Leeds was amiably tolerant and frequently voted for representatives with whose views it disagreed. Gaitskell did not try to influence its choice, even before Morecambe;[8h] though he called it 'absurd' that the NEC was chosen by people who had no idea of the 'real relative merits' of the candidates.[95] Of its 7 votes, the Left had always had at least 3;[96] even in 1960 South Leeds endorsed Gaitskell's policies but supported 5 of his opponents (and 2 more in the women's section) for the NEC. In 1961 it rejected all 7.

Though Gaitskell was meticulous in telling his local Party about current Westminster controversies, that sympathetic audience gave him something of a holiday from politics. For Labour's internal battles had little echo in South Leeds. The harmony was rarely disturbed — in the late 1950s by a couple of middle-class ex-Communists who had left the CP over Hungary, and occasionally by a youthful left-winger who grew up in South Leeds but soon moved on to redder pastures. Gaitskell coped with exemplary patience with the very few critics, though the officers might sometimes act more authoritatively.

The rest of Leeds was very different, for Trotskyists were active in the Labour Party there twenty years before they appeared elsewhere. Throughout the 1950s there were constant clashes in which, though the South Leeds CLP was not directly engaged, its local stalwarts were. In the early 1950s some prominent Leeds Labour women courted expulsion by attending a Soviet-sponsored peace congress. There were moves to proscribe the Trotskyists in 1954 and in 1959. During the 1960–1 battles Gaitskell was twice the target of ugly demonstrations. In the university, where the far Left had its headquarters, Gaitskell had a few good friends, although he never had much to do with the place. But he had excellent relations with the Leeds unions, especially the engineering shop stewards; indeed, astonishingly, though not a member of the AEU, he once presented their annual award of merit when their president Bill Carron was ill.[97]

As South Leeds was geographically separate, socially homogeneous,

fiercely self-contained and suspicious of outsiders, the quarrels of the rest
of the city rarely penetrated there. Local people, asked why they had so
much less political strife than their neighbours, always explained that they
were entirely a working-class party, and that all the university lecturers
lived north of the river. No wonder, perhaps, that Gaitskell once wistfully
wished the constituency formed a separate borough of its own.[98]

v   *Shadow Chancellor and the 'Butskellite' Myth*

When a moderate Conservative succeeded a moderate Labour man at the
Treasury in November 1951, *The Economist* light-heartedly invented a
composite Chancellor-figure. 'Mr Butskell' became a target for those in
both Parties who advocated polarisation politics. Gaitskell never believed
that the Conservatives would follow that course, since it would be as
disastrous for them as for Labour. Traditional fears – of unemployment
at home and risky adventures abroad – had kept their majority down to
seventeen; unlike Bevan, he was not at all sure that they would lose the
next election if they could lay those fears to rest. So he expected no attack
on the welfare state, and doubted if they would even cut food subsidies:

> Butler is on the extreme left of the Tory Party and is shrewd enough
> to understand that they have got to ... live down the reputation in-
> herited from ... the thirties ... to be able to say to the electorate when
> the election comes, 'no war: no unemployment: no cuts in social
> services. Just good Government'. If I am right about this they will
> want to stay in power for three or four years, and I don't really see why
> they should not.[6a]

He and Butler agreed in favouring a moderate electoral strategy, in
disliking violent abuse of opponents, and in treating issues seriously. Both
were respected by people exasperated at 'the barren and moribund sterili-
ties of Party conflict'.[99] There were other superficial personal resemblances
between two able intellectuals in politics, with similar family backgrounds,
many enemies as well as admirers in their own parties, and high reputations
outside them.[100] Gaitskell himself found Butler more congenial than other
Conservative leaders.[20m] But his economic training, his emotional temperament and his 'unquenchably Socialist' opinions were alien to Butler.[101a]
Gaitskell's actions were sometimes reckless. He prized loyalty to colleagues
highly. In private he put the same views to everyone, and in public he
sought to convince people by freely revealing his mind and motives. The
two personalities had little in common.

There was a little more justification for the concept of Butskellism, for
in those days there was among informed people widespread agreement
both on economic techniques – approving the use of Keynesian tools – and

on some major purposes: maintaining full employment without inflation or sterling crises. That allowed people in the extreme wings of both Parties to develop a polemical myth for use against their moderate colleagues, falsely postulating a much fuller consensus on a supposedly objective, neutral view of politics which the Treasury mandarins were often alleged to inspire. In fact, Gaitskell and Butler differed quite sharply both in their policies and in their judgment of the mandarins. Gaitskell had worked in the administrative machine, and was never taken in by those public servants who equated their personal values with impartial economic expertise. As Minister of State he was wary of advice from some of his own officials and from Continental right-wing experts; he had flatly vetoed the French choice of one of the latter as chairman of NATO's Financial and Economic Board. As Shadow Chancellor, he prevented Churchill appointing Lord Waverley chairman of the Royal Commission on Taxation. Formerly Sir John Anderson, Waverley had been a formidable Whitehall figure who became Chancellor during the war, sat as an Independent MP in the Tory Shadow Cabinet, opposed all Labour's welfare policies, and deplored the 'premature' establishment of the health service. Only a week before his new appointment he had attacked food subsidies in his maiden speech in the Lords. When Gaitskell insisted on debating the choice, Waverley resigned, still claiming bitterly to be an independent non-party man.[102a]

Churchill tried to exploit that familiar type of bogus independence by appointing non-party conservative 'overlords' to supervise the politicians who ran the ordinary Departments. The device offended Gaitskell as an orderly administrator, and it offered him a political opportunity. On first handing over to Butler, he privately urged his successor to defend the Chancellor's prerogatives against either an economic 'overlord' (Waverley was being suggested)[102b] or Churchill's crony Lord Cherwell.[6a] In public he mounted effective attacks with which many Tories agreed;[20n] he blamed these elderly peers for causing 'frustration, muddle, vacillation and delay', and later for so cluttering up the Cabinet that there was no one in the Commons to answer on either foreign affairs, defence or the Commonwealth when Churchill and Eden both fell ill.[103]

Gaitskell defended the Treasury, and valued advice from economists and civil servants who worked within his own fundamental political and social assumptions. But those were quite different from Butler's. They disagreed on the role of monetary policy; on the distribution of budgetary burdens and benefits; and on convertibility of sterling. Calling Butskellism a silly catchword used to minimise big and growing Party differences, Gaitskell wrote later that he was much more willing than the Chancellor to use the Budget as an instrument of control over the economy, and to retain some direct controls. Above all they differed completely about the distribution of wealth.[104]

From the start Gaitskell thought Butler too responsive to the restriction-ist bankers,[105] and too willing – as *The Economist* put it – 'for the first time since 1931' to allow financial stringency 'to undermine the foundations of cheap money'.[106] Urged by Dalton to attack the Tories more vigorously, Gaitskell delighted his old mentor by seizing on the issue. Already, he said, he had seen Treasury officials at Butler's invitation, and warned them of 'a hell of a row if unemployment goes above 500,000. They must rely, to get a switch of labour, more on direct physical controls, and less on credit restriction'.[8i] He was not opposed to monetary restriction in all circum-stances.[107-8] But he was deeply suspicious of it as a jerky and unpredictable mechanism discouraging investment rather than consumption, and bound to end in unemployment.[109]

Gaitskell preferred to use budgetary adjustments. Since these had their technical side, he detested having to respond to the Chancellor without access to the full Treasury information.[110] He therefore attempted to work out his own analysis very fully in advance;[70d] and could assess from his own experience the quality of the advice going to the Chancellor – and of the advisers.[111] Conservative Chancellors found that his wide contacts beyond the Party made his speeches well-rounded and unpredictable, so that in answering them 'they had to think a lot, unlike Harold Wilson's which were just party points. His views might be party or not, but were always thought out, there were no cheap points'.[112]

Budgetary policy involved inescapable political choices as well as eco-nomic technicalities. In March 1952 Butler reduced income tax, increased social benefits, and cut food subsidies by one-third (£160 million). Gaitskell felt Labour could have had no better target than that cut;[6b] and showed – without challenge – that the package would benefit most of the well-to-do but hurt two-thirds of those earning less than £10 a week. Coming a week after the '57 varieties' rebelled, his attack reunited the feuding PLP;[113] and in committee Labour secured many more amend-ments than usual.[114] (*Tribune*'s contribution was a headline, 'End the Sham Fighting', and two articles praising the Tories at Gaitskell's expense.)[18c d]

Butler was anxious to avoid parliamentary rows;[111] so that Gaitskell could often insist successfully on choosing times and subjects of debates to suit the Opposition. In the negotiations he could usually 'call the tune ... was tough but reasonable';[115*] and his Finance Bill team were brilliant at 'exposing and inflaming underlying Tory dissensions'.[116a b] Carefully chosen, excellently organised and full of talent, it included six ex-Ministers and eighteen younger MPs who were to hold high office under Harold Wilson years later. Gaitskell himself was much keener than his colleagues on broadening its base by bringing Wilson back to the Front Bench.[117]

* Gaitskell negotiated through his sister's husband Hubert Ashton, Butler's PPS – a symbol of Butskellism.

As the first gleams of affluence appeared, Gaitskell insisted that its benefits must be fairly distributed. In 1953 the terms of trade were much improved and rearmament slowed down. Butler got rid of much taxation imposed in 1951, and took 6*d.* off income tax. Replying to this popular Budget in circumstances particularly unpropitious (through an accident of procedure) Gaitskell's effective speech again united his Party.[118] He claimed that Butler had done most for the better-off instead of concentrating on those at the lowest tax levels, whose need was greatest. Moreover, the better balance of payments was a windfall not due to the government; and its tax changes indicated failure not success, since they were necessary to stimulate flagging production.

The following year Butler, just because his 1953 tax concessions had so stimulated the consumption of the well-off, would not restore the purchasing power of old age pensions.[119-20] Gaitskell, whose Budget speeches had become an annual parliamentary event, warned that full employment meant great bargaining power for trade unions, which could set off a vicious spiral of wage and price inflation; they would not continue their present restraint if shareholders alone benefited through higher dividends or capital assets swollen by undistributed profits.[121-4]

As savings, those profits were necessary to the national economy. Gaitskell always insisted on the need for investment. After a visit to Israel he warned that her resources should be used 'for fundamental economic development and not frittered away in protecting a standard of living which could not in the long run be maintained without that development'.[108] He constantly reminded the House that better terms of trade brought Britain only a precarious surplus, which must be devoted to industrial investment not consumption.[125] Bevan, as a prospective Minister after their reconciliation, was to say that persuading people of that necessity was the central problem of democracy.[126]

Gaitskell was always a teacher, and carried out the task of persuasion with less eloquence but more consistency:

> The acid test of social democracy is whether the community can have enough self-discipline. Such discipline involves many different things — a readiness to pay taxes and develop the habit of saving, a real effort of partnership on both sides of industry for greater production, a spirit of tolerance and compromise in politics; restraint in wage claims which only lead to all round price increases, a refusal to press sectional advantages against the interests of the nation.[127]

He was delighted that Labour's 1953 domestic policy statement, *Challenge to Britain*, concentrated on the balance of payments problem and therefore stressed the need to increase exports and investment rather than consumption, and to organise the sterling area more effectively. He felt it was the best analysis of the issue ever produced in a Party statement – yet it still failed to face the full implications for wage claims and social services increases.[128] The next Labour government must not be committed to incompatible objectives – more consumption, investment and aid to under-developed countries all at once, when it could be sure neither of higher productivity nor of stable terms of trade.[129] Morrison was also worried, and together they convinced the NEC – through its economic sub-committee – not to extend the commitments; Bevan tried but failed to expunge their warning paper from the records.[130]

It was on that issue rather than on nationalisation that Gaitskell objected to *Challenge to Britain*.[131] The Bevanites had welcomed with delight its rather vague proposals for public ownership in chemicals, machine tools and mining machinery; Gaitskell did not criticise these, but welcomed the pragmatic approach.[132] Indeed it was he who pointed out, as the Left did much later, that capitalism would never generate the necessary savings:[133]

> I do not believe that we shall get industrial investment on the scale and in the directions that the nation requires without far more State participation, initiative and influence ... [as] experience will teach us even more vividly in the next few years.[134]

He foreshadowed a controversial Labour manifesto of twenty years later by advocating a development plan for the basic industries,

> making plain the part to be played by the State ... We cannot rely any longer on the surplus income of wealthy men to provide capital for investment ... *the State must provide the savings for investment* ...
> Why not take over shares in payment of death duties? Why not let the State put up part of the capital for the young and enterprising firm that wants to expand? Why not more cooperative production ... [and] greater workers' participation in the ownership and control of the firms where they work?[85b]

As the need to invest ruled out a 'Christmas tree programme', so 'the Socialist policy of fair shares' was all the more necessary. He wanted to tackle inequalities in the educational system, and in property;[135] and he favoured drastic fiscal reforms.

These reforms were meant to prevent the well-off avoiding death duties by gifts and by spending from capital;[136] and Gaitskell positively welcomed the strong opposition they would evoke. He was indignant that Butler would not let the Royal Commission on Taxation investigate a tax on dis-saving.[137] The rejection of that proposal – devised by Kaldor – was lamented two decades later by a Conservative financial spokesman: 'If 20 years ago, we had ... kept the main tax burden away from savings ... and concentrated it on the spending side, this country would be a far more

27 With Sir Stafford Cripps (*seated, right of table*), at a NATO Finance Committee meeting in March 1950

28 Rearmament and the economy. In his private office with George Strauss, Minister of Supply (*left*), and Harold Wilson, President of the Board of Trade (*centre*), just after the decision to rearm in January 1951

29a His own Budget, April 1951

29b His successor's Budget: R. A. Butler, April 1953

30 A clutch of Chancellors at a dinner in May 1952: (*left to right*) Hugh Dalton, Rab Butler, Winston Churchill, Hugh Gaitskell, John Anderson and John Simon

31 Fortunate defeat. Hugh Gaitskell and Alice Bacon after voting to expel Bevan from the Labour Party in March 1955

32 Trade union leaders meet during the newspaper dispute of 1955: (*left to right*) Charles Geddes, chairman of the TUC; Ernest Jones, president of the NUM; and Arthur Deakin, general secretary of the T&GWU

33 Family holiday in Jersey, 1951

34 At his nephew's wedding, September 1956. *From the left:* Hugh, Julie, his mother Mrs Wodehouse, his sister 'Bunty', her husband Hubert Ashton MP, and Cressida

prosperous and peaceful place than it is today.'[138] At the time it was far more controversial, and Gaitskell believed that the combination of a capital gains tax, a reform of inheritance law to stop evasion, and Kaldor's expenditure tax instead of surtax would provide 'a most interesting and exciting fiscal policy ... much of it worked out in XYZ ... If ... we can really save a vast amount of money for the revenue, one can see the opportunity of a tremendous and exciting political row.'[139]

Abroad, his differences with the Chancellor were quite as sharp, and Butler wrote, justly: 'If the pound had been set free in 1952 the word "Butskellism" might never have been invented.'[101a] That policy (called Operation Robot) was rejected by the Conservative Cabinet in February 1952.[140-1] It would have introduced sterling convertibility at a floating rate, which would dismantle the principal government controls over the British economy and, Gaitskell thought, subordinate domestic growth to international pressures. He was against convertibility until dollars were plentiful, since it would rule out trade discrimination.[142] He had hoped during the 1951 sterling crisis that the Commonwealth countries, which had incurred half the deficit, would co-operate to save the pound. But their Finance Ministers did not meet until February 1952, and then followed where the Tories led in approving convertibility and non-discrimination; Australia promptly seized on that excuse to change previous policy and restrict sterling as well as dollar imports.[143] Gaitskell was bitterly critical, and Ministers were very evasive, about that sacrifice of British interests to the dogma of economic liberalisation.[144]

Another Commonwealth Conference, in December 1952, did nothing effective to organise the sterling area, plan its investment policies, or enable the United Kingdom to keep a check on its capital exports. Gaitskell again raised the issue repeatedly in the House and the country, expressing 'anxiety, misgiving, disappointment and scepticism' at the renewed talk of convertibility — emotions widely shared on the other side of the House as well as his own.[145] He argued that convertibility and non-discrimination would frustrate dollar-saving developments by emphasising *laissez-faire* not government action; by discouraging private investors from producing dollar substitutes, since they would soon lose the protection afforded by import controls; and, amid pious calls for the right kind of investment, by flatly refusing to prevent the wrong kind.[146]

A year later he was again stirring up imperialist back-bench Tories against the government's eagerness for freer international trade; and using the latest Commonwealth Finance Ministers' Conference to show the divisions of interest within the sterling area, the weakness of its economic defences and the continuing drain on United Kingdom capital.[147] But where the Tories were mostly anti-American, Gaitskell sharply distinguished — as he always had — his economic worries about the United States from his political sympathies. He stoutly denied that a strong sterling area would undermine the Atlantic alliance, and called it a major fallacy to think political co-operation between countries must imply free trade.[148] Thus in foreign economic policy, where Butler gave priority to convertibility, Gaitskell defended exchange controls and the sterling area (foreshadowing later arguments over the Common Market).

Poor Mr Butskell: a short life, wrecked by schizophrenia.

vi   *Labour's Truce and the Irreconcilables*

In the early 1950s the conflict between Labour's two wings was not over domestic policy at all. Neutrals like Younger detected 'scarcely even a difference of emphasis' and thought it was 'the absence of a real issue to fight about' which made the dispute 'squalid'.[31c] Gaitskell always stressed that the quarrel was quite artificial (underlining his own commitment to more nationalisation).[149] Talking to him after Morecambe late in 1952, Crossman found the same, and foresaw

> no serious difficulty in reaching agreement on a Labour party pro-
> gramme ... The real disagreements are ... about relations with
> America, military commitments etc. ... Douglas Jay and Harold
> Wilson really want the same policy and ... there are really only
> differences of emphasis, temperament and will as regards domestic
> policy between Nye and Hugh Gaitskell.[20k]

This ally of Bevan's thought that on foreign policy Labour divisions were 'really basic', but that luckily Bevan felt domestic issues to be far more important;[20k] indeed at this period 'Nye used to tell me I shouldn't concentrate on foreign affairs and that every Left movement had to be based on domestic, working-class issues.'[20o]

After the battles of previous years, 1953 proved a welcome lull in Labour's civil war. There would be no general election, for the Conservative majority was small but safe; and no leadership election in the Opposition, since Attlee stayed on. Bevan was back on the Front Bench and his group dissolved. Domestic policy aroused no acrimony;[21b] the Party Conference at Margate was called in retrospect a 'harbinger of ... revisionism'.[150] The atmosphere, Gaitskell wrote to his agent, was 'a great improvement' on Morecambe.[95] *Challenge to Britain* was comfortably approved, and seven motions for more nationalisation were lost, all but one (on armaments) by two-thirds majorities. Gaitskell spoke twice from the floor, choosing subjects with little appeal on which Labour policies needed thinking out: taxation of capital, and the public schools.[151] Privately, he recruited the Steelworkers' leader Harry Douglass (in a hotel bathroom) for a TV programme against denationalising steel.[152] South

Leeds had unanimously nominated Gaitskell as delegate and NEC candidate, and he was runner-up, increasing his vote from 330,000 to 533,000 – so that, after Stalybridge, he won over half the CLP votes.

Herbert Morrison now rejoined the Executive in a manner which greatly influenced Gaitskell's future. Immediately after Morecambe the major union leaders decided to back Morrison for Party treasurer instead of the ailing incumbent Arthur Greenwood, a veteran long past useful service. But Greenwood, who was to chair the coming Conference, flatly refused to resign; and if he lost, Morrison was warned that he might collapse and die on the platform. At the very last minute the Executive proposed that the deputy leader should be a member *ex officio*, and Morrison withdrew from the treasurership contest. His union sponsors, especially Arthur Deakin, saw that as a belated defection which reawakened their old doubts about him; and it allowed them, when Greenwood died a few months later, to bring Gaitskell on to the NEC as treasurer – and perhaps as a younger contender for Attlee's succession.[153-4] In the annual PLP election Morrison beat Bevan for deputy leader by 181 to 76.[155] For the Shadow Cabinet, Gaitskell came second with 176 (3 down), Bevan ninth with 126 (18 up), and Wilson runner-up with 105 (15 up).[156]

The Bevanite irreconcilables – Jennie Lee, Barbara Castle, John Freeman, Ian Mikardo – wanted, unlike Bevan himself, to revive the banned group and resume open warfare within the Party.[8j k] After Gaitskell's Conference speech on public schools, 'Jennie rushed to the mike to annihilate him, only to find herself howled down'.[20p] Soon after Margate she seemed to be seeking a pretext for her husband to quit the Front Bench;[8f] and a few weeks earlier, while Gaitskell was abroad, Mikardo had tried to get him off the Fabian executive by abolishing co-option.[157] But other Bevanites deplored such activities. Wilson was still hoping for the compromise – Morrison as leader, Bevan as deputy – which the latter had contemptuously rejected at Morecambe.[8l] Crossman was dissatisfied with the Front Bench, but felt that the Left 'or should one still call it Bevanism, is also collapsing as a force'.[20q] The working-class Bevanite MPs, too, were 'horrified' by the intransigence of their colleagues.[20r]

The irreconcilables kept the feud alive in their two weekly journals. *Tribune* provoked successful suits for libel or heavy-handed pressure from Labour's NEC (in which Gaitskell took no active part) by its repeated acts of aggression – mainly vituperative attacks on trade union leaders. These were condemned both by Keep Calmers like Younger and by Bevanites like Crossman and Wilson.[158] Just after Margate, *Tribune* attacked the PLP over the Shadow Cabinet election, which showed such a striking difference between the verdict of the Labour MPs, who were familiar with their colleagues' personality and usefulness, and that of the CLPs who were not; the author J. P. W. Mallalieu infuriated members by suggesting that MPs talked Bevanite to their local Parties, but voted the other way at Westminster.[159*]

The *New Statesman* also did its bit to try to destroy the truce, publishing a vicious anonymous profile of Gaitskell as 'The Gentleman from Whitehall', 'the embodiment of the new bureaucratic man', dominated by 'cold and methodical ambition for Party power'.[116c] It did not print a protest from R. H. Tawney, but did allow two others:[160] Mrs Durbin, who denied the lie that Gaitskell nearly followed MacDonald in 1931, and Frank Pakenham, who justly called the portrait 'totally unrecognisable ... malevolent ... [full of] envy, hatred and malice'.[116d] Gaitskell refused to be upset by it. But at the next New Year when – most unusually – he attended three parties in a week, he wrote wryly to Dalton: 'You see how hard I am trying to combat the impression spread around by the "New Statesman" profile.'[139a]

Gaitskell's only factional activity was to try to counteract the Bevanite propaganda machine. As Dalton wrote, that

> was never idle – *Tribune*, the *New Statesman*, *Reynolds'* (with Driberg's weekly column), Crossman's column in the *Sunday Pictorial* and, perhaps, more than a fair share for Michael Foot and some others on the air.[161] This was now a formidable instrument for influencing Labour opinion.[79a]

After Morecambe, Gaitskell had optimistically suggested that *Tribune* might become 'a vehicle of propaganda for Party policy and an open forum for discussion ... without the vitriol';[70a] and wondered, when Michael Foot declined because its aim was Socialist education, why that aim should rule out the inclusion of different points of view.[162] He put much time and energy into trying to launch a journal for Labour moderates. As early as July 1952 there was talk of trying to buy *Forward* (which his friends acquired a few years later) or the *Spectator*.[163] Meanwhile he persuaded several union leaders to back *Socialist Commentary*.[164] After Sydney Elliott became editor of the *Daily Herald* late in 1953, Gaitskell feared that the Party's official paper, the leadership's one forum, was also sliding to the Left. He mobilised the trade union members of the *Herald* board to resist some proposed changes, and complained that the paper was becoming 'anti-American and pro-Russian on every possible occasion'.[165] He took great precautions to keep these activities secret.[166]

The continued Bevanite sniping pushed Gaitskell closer to Deakin than he wished.[20r] He spoke as readily for left-wingers – Ted Castle at an Abingdon by-election, Lena Jeger at Holborn and St Pancras, Norman

---

* Crossman's diary records no instance of that, but does record the opposite – MPs voting in secret with the Bevanites upstairs, but publicly with the leadership on the floor.[20s]

VICKY, SCARBOROUGH, Oct. 1. 54.

"O, WE **DID** LIKE TO BE BESIDE THE T.U.C. SIDE..."

Mackenzie at Hemel Hempstead—as for orthodox Labour candidates.[167] In private, a *Times* lunch at the Margate Conference became 'a silent conflict between Gaitskell and Morrison, with Morrison talking all the time in terms of how to defeat the left and Gaitskell very statesmanlike and controlled'.[168] In public, another profile writer noted four days before the *New Statesman*'s attack on him that, though well known as an anti-Bevanite he 'says little if anything on that score nowadays. The pact of party unity has been well kept'.[169]

Nevertheless, too many of his own wing thought Gaitskell 'too rigid' to be a coming Party leader or deputy.[8m] In 1954 as in 1951, Bevan's errors in polarising the Movement and personalising the issue again unwittingly built up Gaitskell's stature. For Labour's uneasy truce depended precariously on Bevan's political sense restraining his own emotional instincts and those of his followers. His personal animosity towards Gaitskell went deep. In India that spring, he had a very friendly dinner conversation with an American working for the UN, which died on the spot when he said 'you seem to know England very well', and his neighbour replied, 'yes, Hugh Gaitskell is one of my oldest friends'.[170] Again, defending Mallalieu in the Shadow Cabinet after the latter's article on the PLP elections, Bevan spoke of the dangers of discipline; and 'When Gaitskell quite mildly refers to "the dangers of indiscipline" Bevan fixes him ... with a glare of concentrated hatred & says, "You're too young in the Movement to know what you're talking about" '.[171] But when it was suggested that Bevan was looking for a pretext to resign again, he indignantly denied that imputation.[79b]

Bevan's abrupt change of course in April 1954 was quite unexplained. Some of his friends attributed it to his poor showing in the PLP elections.[172] Certainly the defeats rankled, for he always attributed these mainly self-inflicted wounds to the corruption of back-benchers hungry for office.[154] Yet in March 1954, only three weeks before the break, Bevan seemed to one sympathetic observer to have renounced factionalism and become 'very moderate' and 'very responsible'.[31d] Suddenly, and with no warning even to close friends who welcomed the change, he reopened Labour's civil war.[173] The next twelve months were the only post-war period in which Bevan normally followed the advice of his irreconcilable rather than his moderate friends. During that year he finally destroyed his chance to lead the Labour Party.

CHAPTER 11

FOREIGN AFFAIRS AND THE DISINTEGRATION OF BEVANISM 1954–5

'I don't see how one can have strong loyalties ... and continually refuse to do any of the dirty work'
(HG, 1955)

i *Indo-China: Bevan Resigns Again*

As Gaitskell had always claimed, Labour conflicts in these years were not about domestic policy. The real difference was over attitudes to the United States, and found expression over rearmament. The Bevanites had accepted the old £3,600 million defence programme in 1950, and in 1951 began by attacking only the speed-up agreed in that January. But a year later in 1952, just as the programme was slowing down to the original pace, they were becoming critical of any rearmament at all. Gaitskell thought their outlook as dangerous to the country's safety and the Party's credibility as Labour's opposition to defence estimates had been in the 1930s. He had shed all pacifist illusions in Vienna in 1934, and had sought as a young candidate to persuade his leaders not to oppose conscription in 1939. He never equated Stalin and Hitler, but he feared that any dictatorial regime might exploit a tempting military vacuum, and he now took the lead in publicly defending rearmament; if there was now less danger of war, he argued, that very fact was 'its overwhelming justification', showing that a stronger West was inducing caution in Moscow.[1] Military strength must of course be balanced against economic, but the critics seemed to want to cut any defence programme at all. So would pacifists, American isolationists or the Communist 'instruments of Russian imperialism';[2] but not Marshal Tito, who spent 23 per cent of Yugoslavia's national income on defence compared to Britain's 12 per cent, and evidently did not 'think that the best protection against Russia is just a high standard of living'.[3]

Without American power the Central European vacuum could not be filled. Gaitskell was therefore alarmed by the growing hostility towards the United States, which by 1952 the Bevanites were exploiting. Bevan, while denying that he was anti-American, denounced American fiscal policies for 'doing more harm to Western Europe than Stalin can ever do', asking: 'when are we going to have some sense of nati lonapride and tell the United States that she cannot have Great Britain on any terms?'[4] Gaitskell pointed out in reply that those who demanded, simultaneously defence cuts, and independence of the United States, were pursuing incompatible aims. If Britain refused co-operation in European defence, at worst America's isolationism might revive, and at best we would become more dependent on her and less able to affect her policy.[1] He warned against the 'dangerous game' of stirring up anti-American feelings, and attacked those who

> seem to face both ways. They declare in favour of alliances like NATO to defend Western democracy, but they do not want to pay the cost.
>
> They know we must co-operate with the Americans, but spend time abusing them.
>
> They admit the need for rearmament but always demand cuts in the programme ... playing up to the sentiments of pacifists, neutralists and fellow-travellers and fanning the flames of anti-Americanism in order to get the support of people with whom they really disagree.[5]

Privately he analysed the sources of anti-Americanism as including differences over the Far East, some American economic policies, her bombastic generals, and Senator Joe McCarthy. But he rightly emphasised British resentment at the changing power relationship, and perceptively predicted that though so far expressed only on the Left, it might soon be echoed on the Right.[6*]

He was exasperated when the new Republican Administration and Congress abandoned burden-sharing, treating aid as an expression not of solidarity among allies, but of American charity.[7] He had always known that their economic and foreign policies would be more damaging to Britain, Europe and the underdeveloped countries than those of the Democrats.[8] He visited the United States a few months after they came in, already feeling that the maladroit moralising of John Foster Dulles, the new Secretary of State, was inflaming both anti-Americanism in Britain and anti-British feelings among Americans.[9] But the domestic American criticism of Dulles was so widespread that Gaitskell told the British Ambassador on his return: 'you are still the only person I found ready to defend the Secretary of State'.[10]

As in 1950–1, suspicion of American policy was most evident over Germany and over the Far East. In Indo-China the war against the French was coming to its climax in early 1954. The United States saw it as a struggle against Communist aggression, the Asians as a revolt against European imperialism: to them NATO was an alliance of colonialists.

* As it was after Suez.

Gaitskell sympathised with them, favouring Indo-Chinese independence, and partition to end the war. He thought the settlement would probably collapse without a defence treaty; but that treaty must include Asians, be acceptable to India, and exclude Chiang Kai-shek.[11-12]

On those conditions, the British Government and Opposition were in agreement.* Britain was still fighting the communist Chinese in Malaya, and was willing as the Americans wished to form a regional defensive alliance modelled on NATO, provided it was acceptable to the Asian Commonwealth countries. Eden welcomed Labour pressure in support of policies he was privately urging on the United States – as when Attlee on 13 April 1954 appealed to the willing Foreign Secretary to ensure that any alliance should include Asians and reject colonialism. At that moment Bevan, in Michael Foot's words, 'almost trample[d] on his diffident leader' in his haste to get to the dispatch box and denounce the treaty as a surrender to the American pressure, which would be deeply resented both in Britain and in Asia.[13]** He argued that the treaty meant 'encirclement' of China, a view which Gaitskell, without naming Bevan, scathingly attacked.[12] Bevan's interpretation of United States policy is derived by Michael Foot (who calls it the Dulles doctrine) exclusively from subsequent developments – in the coming crisis over the besieged French fortress of Dien Bien Phu.[15] But the outcome of that crisis showed that Bevan's alarm was unjustified, for the United States would not enter the war to save the French.

Two weeks after Bevan's clash with Attlee, at the end of April 1954, Dien Bien Phu was attacked and Paris appealed for American intervention. The French government and the American 'hawks' were opposed by many compatriots in both counties and by all the other allies. The Administration faced strong opposition in Congress, notably from the Senate Democratic leader Lyndon Johnson. After briefly hinting at token British participation, it declined to act without British moral support, which was withheld.[16] Rejecting the advice of the 'hawks', President Eisenhower then left the fortress to its fate, and accepted a Geneva conference.[17-18] That decision seemed to Crossman, Bevan's principal ally on foreign affairs, to demolish Bevan's ground for quarrelling with the Shadow Cabinet.[19a]

It also demonstrated a political truth of less parochial significance. The President of the United States had asked the British Government for its moral approval of American intervention, and had invoked its dissent to override his own chief military adviser. No foreign leader who had chosen

* That agreement included Gaitskell's last two points, which Dulles loathed.

** Bevan's credentials to speak for Asia were dubious. After he addressed the Indian Parliament, Nehru had publicly rebuked him, saying peace was best served 'without too much shouting'; and Gaitskell's friend in New Delhi, who worked for the UN and knew Nehru well, wrote that 'He is, of course, far closer in his views to you and Mr. Attlee than to Aneurin Bevan'.[14]

for the past two years to win easy cheers at home by strident anti-American-ism could have won that influence in Washington. Eisenhower was willing and able to act as he did only because Churchill and Eden were seen as reliable allies, who might disagree with United States policy but sympa-thised with her problems and took co-operation seriously. Attlee and Gaitskell shared many of their views, enjoyed a similar reputation, and might in office have wielded similar influence. Bevan never could. It was that British influence, so Michael Foot contends, that 'possibly stopped the third world war'.[20a]

Bevan's challenge to Attlee was apparently spontaneous, after a good lunch at Crossman's house with his friends 'steaming Nye up' to take a strong line.[19b] To interrupt his own leader and contradict him flatly on a major issue was, wrote Gaitskell, 'a clear attempt to step up in front of C.R.A., and was so regarded by everybody'.[21] At the Shadow Cabinet that evening Bevan's behaviour was criticised in moderate terms by Shinwell, Soskice, Morrison and Gaitskell, with no reaction from Attlee.[22a] Bevan, according to Dalton, 'shouts with eyes goggling ... "*I* address meetings, very big meetings, and *I* know what people are thinking ... *I* know the mind of this country" '.[23] When the Shadow Cabinet met again next day before the Party meeting, Attlee gave his view on the policy. Bevan walked out, announcing that he would leave the Front Bench after Easter. Usually a chorus appealed to him to come back and be sensible; but in-stead, Gaitskell recorded:

> Clem said in his most Haileybury military accent, 'Why can't you be a man and face the music?' One or two other people murmured, 'Let him go' ... We then went upstairs to the meeting, which was pretty crowded, and Clem ... to our astonishment, proceeded to speak with the utmost vigour and indignation about A.B.'s behaviour on the Front Bench ... I have often wondered whether Clem did this deliberately, knowing that it would provoke A.B. into an immediate resignation.[24]

Bevan at once declared that he had already abandoned the Committee. Downstairs: ' "What a wonderful Easter egg!" said a Tory at the tape'.[25]

The moment, as Bevan knew, was very badly chosen, just after an out-standingly good speech by Attlee on the hydrogen bomb and two good by-elections. 'Just when we were beginning to win the match', complained the leader, 'our inside left has scored against his own side'.[26] Bevan's resignation enraged the Right of the Party and 'a great majority of the middle-of-the-roaders'.[19b] Since the United States did not intervene in Indo-China, it baffled his followers in the country;[27] and at Westminster it alarmed some of his closest friends.[28] He gave no explanation to the next PLP meeting—since a close ally moved the adjournment without warning him, lest he harm himself by speaking.[19c] Luckily for him, Morrison provided a diversion by a personal attack on him in *Socialist Commentary*.[29]

The Bevanite divisions now became public, for Harold Wilson as runner-up was entitled to Bevan's vacant Shadow Cabinet seat, and accepted it in the name of Party unity. Bevan told Crossman that was 'gross personal disloyalty' and 'would be the end of Wilson's political career'; when Crossman asked if Wilson then was expendable, Bevan replied: 'Of course he is. You're all expendable.'[30] Most of the Bevanite MPs condemned Wilson's 'betrayal'. But elsewhere Bevan had done himself 'incalculable harm'.[31]

ii *The Treasurership, German Rearmament and Party Discipline*

The Bevanite split in April 1954 was not over policy (where Wilson claimed he agreed with Bevan) or over tactics (where hardly anyone did so), but over a long-standing dispute about long-term strategy, in which Bevan now suddenly changed sides.[20b] In the next few days he urged his friends first 'to attack the Right wing of the Party all along the line', next to 'destroy the bogus reputation of Clement Attlee', and finally to seize the parliamentary initiative from the 'hopeless' Front Bench.[19b d] At Westminster the Bevanites were alienating support by their 'tactics, conduct and highly organized disunity';[32] and in the country, a 'very carefully selected' Second XI (their name) of candidates and hopefuls began to meet monthly to organise resolutions for Conference and selections for Parliament.[33]

Bevan took a far more serious step when he deliberately decided to divide the industrial as well as the political Movement. On 6 May 1954, learning that Arthur Greenwood was dying, he resolved to stand for treasurer against Gaitskell – expecting to lose but hoping that his opponents would 'split every union and expose Deakin and Tom Williamson by making them prefer an intellectual like Gaitskell to a miner like me'.[34] He would give up his safe seat on the NEC, where – since the majority were against him – he had no interest in trying to shape Labour policy.[19e] To him the Party was still a battleground, not an army fighting the Tories for power: and its institutions were not forums for comrades to agree on strategy, but enemy forts to be conquered. Just before Greenwood's death he had told his friends that

> an electoral success would be disastrous until it [the Front Bench] had been completely changed as the result of a mass movement in the constituencies ... Nye said twice that he didn't care one halfpenny about the Labour Party in its present form, and also mentioned Mac-Donaldism in close connection with Harold ... Of course, this is a

view which, when he is in a different mood, he can annihilate just as easily, and often has.[19d]

In July he revealingly decided not to make a major foreign affairs speech, telling Crossman: 'There is nothing left for me to say. Attlee has delighted the whole party. If I attack him, I shall make us all unpopular; and if I support him, what's the point?'[19f]

Bevan and the irreconcilables always overestimated their followers' resentment against the leadership. The constituency activists elected rebels to the NEC to keep the front-benchers on their toes and urge them into more intransigent opposition, rather than to drive them out and install a new lot. Morrison's reception after his defeat at Morecambe showed the delegates' eagerness to see their leaders co-operating. Gaitskell had exaggerated their hostility at Stalybridge; now Bevan and his friends were behaving as if he had been right. But unlike a few of the left-wing MPs, most ordinary Party supporters wanted to heal the split rather than widen it; they put Labour's interests before those of the party within the Party. In that mood it seemed natural to them for Labour's financial spokesman to seek a place on the NEC as treasurer – but not for a rival leader to abandon a safe Executive seat simply to keep him out.[35–6a] Without knowing that Bevan cared not a halfpenny for the present Labour Party and did not desire its victory over the Tories, the activists could sense from his conduct – from his quitting the Shadow Cabinet without an issue, and from the tone of his treasurership campaign – that he would willingly disrupt the Movement from top to bottom in order to win control of the rump.

Bevan attributed his defeats to a conspiracy of bureaucratic leaders frustrating the rank and file, and hoped by polarising the Movement to undermine their power within three years.[20c] It was an error of judgment in both the short and the long term. In the next few months, his actions alienated his own following in the constituency Parties instead of Gaitskell's in the industrial wing; and a year later, his second attempt forfeited instead of attracting support in the unions. Consequently, his defeats were to be much heavier than his most pessimistic friends had feared.

Greenwood died on 9 June. By chance Gaitskell, who had not seen Deakin for some time, had already asked him to lunch. Early in the meal Deakin proposed to nominate Gaitskell for treasurer, and it was only later that Gaitskell was surprised to hear rumours that Bevan would stand.[22a]* His

---

* Foot insinuated that Deakin's price was Gaitskell's support for expelling Bevan – who had still been in the Shadow Cabinet when Deakin first proposed Gaitskell. He wrote: 'whether a compact in this sense was concluded with Gaitskell is unknown'.[20d] Serious writers usually base serious charges on evidence, not on its absence. There is none.

victory was not predetermined by the trade union steam-roller; in July he still saw the contest as 'a pretty close thing',[37a] and thought he might well lose the Engineers, the Miners and the election.[36b] Two days later he won both nominations.

The Bevanites claimed with little cause that his success was a blatant defiance of the rank and file and denounced as undemocratic the normal rule that union executives made the nominations – though approving it in the six unions proposing Bevan. (Three of those six – Electricians, Fire Brigades and Foundry Workers – had executives under strong Communist influence and not very responsive to the members' political views.) Strife was most acute in the AEU, always a cockpit not a bastion, with its strong left wing, partly Communist, and a right-wing with some very wily leaders struggling to keep it behind Party policy. The union had had no one on the NEC since 1949, and it nominated Gaitskell partly to attract Deakin's support for its NEC candidate;[38] besides, several AEU MPs lobbied members of their executive on his behalf.[22a] The executive's right to nominate, now contested for the first time, led to a 'long wrangle' in which 'there was no evidence which side really spoke for the ordinary member'.[39] Few branches complained;[40] but the executive eventually lost in the union's appeal court.

The furious recriminations about undemocratic wire-pulling could not apply to the Miners, Bevan's own union, whose executive made no recommendation. On the House of Commons terrace on 23 June 1954, Bevan told Sam Watson he counted on their vote:

> Sam said he didn't know, but Durham were voting for H.G. Very angry, N[ye] said he would denounce S. at the Gala. This was a conspiracy by bureaucrats, not a democratic decision.
>
> S: When you win an election you call it a democratic decision. When you lose you call it a conspiracy.[41]

Bevan replied furiously: 'How can you support a public school boy from Winchester against a man born in the back streets of Tredegar?'[42] At their conference in July Gaitskell won by 505,000 to 233,000, thanks in his own view to Sam Watson, Ernest Jones of Yorkshire, and his many contacts from his days at the Ministry of Fuel and Power.[22a] Bevan won only in South Wales, his home district; in Scotland, the other Communist stronghold; and (surprisingly) in Northumberland.[25b]

For propaganda purposes the struggle for nominations continued, with Gaitskell's collecting 9 trade unions to Bevan's 6, 29 CLPs to Bevan's 57, and the Royal Arsenal Co-operative Society.[43] But the AEU and NUM votes would clearly be decisive. Bevan had plenty of time to drop out and return to his safe seat in the CLP section. He did not do so. Gaitskell concluded that he cannot retreat of his own volition. So a story is invented to cover up his action, that he intends to go on challenging the power of the block vote, and run against me year by year. Maybe he will. But I am pretty sure this was not his original intention ... [he is said to be] completely browned off with his own crowd and ... all he wants to do is to go and bury himself in the country.[22a]

At the same time as he abandoned the NEC, Bevan bought a Chiltern farm. Crossman felt that he did so as 'a reinsurance against failure'.[19g] The failure was to be resounding.

Bevan's heavy defeat for the treasurership was the more surprising since the vote was to coincide with the climax of the debate on the very issue where he was strongest: the rearmament of Western Germany, the most unpopular aspect of American policy. To the dismay of the State Department, the Pentagon insisted on it from the start, only five years after Hitler's war, as a condition of American participation in European defence.[44] It was detested by both British and French opinion. Ernest Bevin dragged his feet over it; Herbert Morrison was less reluctant, but Dalton and other critics were able to confine Cabinet acceptance to the 'principle'. Gaitskell, wrote Dalton in 1951, was 'always very careful to balance bet^n H.M. & me on this'.[45]

Some of his colleagues shunned in opposition policies which they had accepted in office, but Gaitskell — typically — moved the other way. When the Conservatives brought up the treaties for ratification, he had made up his mind. In the Shadow Cabinet Dalton wanted to oppose outright; Gaitskell was 'very obstinate' at first in resisting that suggestion, though when the government motion was published he raised no objection to voting against it.[46] To Dalton's reproach that he was becoming 'H.M.'s Jack in the Box', Gaitskell retorted heatedly:

You sit on the fence. You used not to like people who sit on the fence ... there was a bitter struggle for leadership going on. It might last several years. The B'ites might win. Then he'd have to consider whether he could go on in public life. I said there were a lot of people in the middle, who wanted these personal hatreds suppressed. He said this rested with the B'ites. He was very tense and unsmiling.[25c]

Dalton was only the most committed of the many non-Bevanite politicians who shared — or feared — the violent anti-German emotions widespread in a Labour Movement as insular in reality as it was internationalist in rhetoric. Those feelings were even stronger in France, whose government tried to contain them by proposing to incorporate Germany into a European Defence Community (EDC).[47] The reluctance of French opinion and of the National Assembly led to prolonged delay, and to the defeat of EDC on 30 August 1954. Meanwhile the Labour Party was so closely divided that the NEC abandoned normal collective responsibility. In the PLP the leadership's majority fell in February 1954 to only two.[48]

Gaitskell wrote to one Labour MP: 'I have never been a fanatic either way. It has always seemed to me a profoundly difficult issue ... The military side is probably less important than the political and psychological.'[49] But as usual his balanced view did not preclude an active commitment once he had decided. When the NEC launched an 'educational' campaign of twenty-five regional conferences, Gaitskell spoke at five (more than Morrison) – knowing that he was damaging his prospects for the treasurer-ship.[50] He argued that only military occupation could prevent Germany rearming; but since the Americans would not co-operate, that was bound to fail – with disastrous results: 'to start on it without carrying it through ... would create a fire of German militarism ... which might be impossible to control.'[51-2] But she should rearm in voluntary association with the Allies, not unilaterally. To a Labour opponent of the policy shocked to find that her fellow-delegates 'simply hated the Germans', he replied:

No doubt the Germans are dangerous, but the only way to handle them is to offer them friendship. I do not think you can offer them friendship without offering them equality, and that means similar rights in relation to defence as other countries.[53]

He fought the 'most dangerous illusion' that the West could accept Russian terms for neutralising Germany, which risked both American withdrawal from Europe and Russian control of all Germany. For an unarmed Germany would be a source of instability, vulnerable to 'infiltration, bribes, threats and even military action to put the Communists in control'; while an armed one would be far less dangerous in association with the West than alone – when she would always be tempted to regain her lost eastern territories by a new pact with Russia.[54]

Gaitskell had hoped that France would accept EDC. When it failed, he lobbied the Socialist International to support 'parallelism' – German re-armament concurrent with talks with the Russians. He hoped to influence the vote at the Labour Conference at Scarborough.[55] For the leadership might well lose, having had only 53 per cent of the TUC votes in early September; and it had little room for manoeuvre. Gaitskell himself was willing to compromise to avert defeat, but he found at the TUC that the union leaders might not agree.[56] Attlee opened the Scarborough debate by saying that emotional hostility to Germans was natural but irrelevant, like American emotional hostility to the Chinese who had killed their soldiers in Korea.[57] A few unions switched, especially the Woodworkers who 'wanted to be the cabinet-makers'; and the official policy was carried by 3,270,000 to 3,022,000.[58]

Twenty years later the high passions aroused over arming Germans against Russians – though natural so soon after Hitler's defeat, and even closer to the Communist seizure of Czechoslovakia and blockade of Berlin – seem much exaggerated on both sides. The Pentagon felt it urgent to fill the gap in Central Europe with German divisions; but Stalin died and the early 1950s passed with no German troops and no Soviet drive to the Channel. The alarms of the opponents proved unreal too. The Russians were not provoked into stopping negotiations or launching preventive war; and the new German army did not undermine democracy as the critics were sure that it would.

Gaitskell was elected treasurer at Scarborough by 4,338,000 to 2,032,000 for Bevan: more than his friends ever hoped or his opponents feared.[59]* He even won between one-third and a half of the CLP vote.[60] The results in the constituency parties section again showed that Bevan, who was retiring from it, misunderstood the people he claimed to represent. In April when he quit the Shadow Cabinet and Harold Wilson took his place, he had predicted that that would finish Wilson's career; and his friends had threatened to throw the defector off the NEC.[62] Instead Wilson came in first, while Anthony Greenwood – now backed by the Bevanites but not identified as a factional candidate – gained sensationally and finished third.[63]

Bevan reacted furiously to his defeat. At the *Tribune* meeting on the Wednesday night he denounced the new NUM president Ernest Jones by name for misrepresenting the miners: 'He had better learn to behave himself. That is blunt.' His next target was unnamed. We now know, he said, that

> the right kind of leader for the Labour Party is a desiccated calculating machine who must not in any way permit himself to be swayed by indignation ... [at] suffering, privation or injustice ... for that would be evidence of the lack of proper education and absence of self-control.[20e]

Those present were not sure whether he meant Attlee, as the context suggests, or Gaitskell as was later supposed;** Gaitskell himself was

---

* In the train back to London, Arthur Deakin told a Tory journalist that he hoped Gaitskell would succeed Attlee – who hoped so too, and would time his retirement accordingly.[61]

** Members of the audience held both views. Reporters on *The Times* and the *Guardian* thought Gaitskell, on the *Telegraph* Attlee. One prominent Bevanite suggested it was Wilson. Prudently, Bevan's public relations adviser Ted Castle doubtful.[65-6] The speech went down badly, and Bevan's conduct in defeat was compared adversely with Morrison's two years before.[67] Gaitskell was not surprised by it:

> It is quite wrong to think of him as a scheming careful plotter. He schemes only at intervals, and his actions are determined far more by emotional reactions, particularly anger and pride, than anything else. Although softened by British environment, and having a much more attractive side to his character in private, there are distinct similarities to the way he behaved [sic], and the way Hitler behaved during the war. When Hitler lost one campaign after another, having gone against the advice of his generals, he never said, 'I was wrong', and that, I think is rather the way that A.B. reacts too.[22a]

Immediately after Scarborough Gaitskell publicly predicted that the narrow decision would be accepted and that the German rearmament controversy was over.[66] Surprisingly, he proved right;[68] and only two years later Aneurin Bevan was privately 'accusing the Germans of trying to blackmail us into defending them without their doing their share'.[69] There was one final splutter in November 1954, when the Government brought to the House of Commons the treaties on rearming Germany within NATO, which replaced the EDC. The PLP accepted them by a majority of fifty (as against only two in February).[70] But feelings ran deep and dangerous, and everyone knew it; so that when in the Shadow Cabinet Callaghan proposed that Labour should abstain, to his surprise Morrison and Gaitskell at once supported him.[71]

The debate showed wide differences, for in winding up Attlee astonished his own Front Bench by hinting at talks with the Russians before ratification.[72] Earlier Gaitskell, making his first major foreign policy speech, angered Bevan[18c] when he said that 'neutralism and defeatism' would have the same results as in the 1930s, and suggested that delay might revive American isolationism and German nationalism, and destroy the 'hopeful' new French government.[18d] Not long before, indeed, he had written that 'a great party, Her Majesty's Opposition ... cannot weakly and unworthily abstain';[52] and apparently the TUC leaders still felt the same.[19h] But it is very unusual for an Opposition to vote with the Government. (For example, the Conservatives abstained over the American loan and ratifying Bretton Woods; and only eighty of them voted for NATO.) For the sake of Labour unity Gaitskell and his friends 'were prepared to sink our individual point of view in order to make it easier for other people to sink theirs. Many of them did so'.[73] But a few did not.

---

told the press it was Gaitskell not Attlee. Bevan always said publicly it was a 'synthetic leader' — and privately that of course it was not Gaitskell, who was highly emotional, and couldn't count.[64]

M

Every Labour candidate was pledged to accept majority decisions of the PLP. Its standing orders allowed MPs on grounds of conscience not to vote for a Party decision, though never to vote against one. The Bevanites were warned that they would be expelled if they divided the House.[74] But no reminder or appeal or persuasion could deter 'half a dozen pacifists, egotists and crackpots'—as Gaitskell described them—from calling a division.[75] The PLP withdrew the whip from them (though not for long) and the press at once denounced Labour for excessive discipline.[76]

Herbert Bowden, the Deputy Chief Whip, was sure the Bevanites wanted to establish a precedent for unpunished defiance and so make the standing orders unenforceable.[22b] Gaitskell told several critics that not to withdraw the whip would have reduced the Party to a rabble and played into the Bevanites' hands. To have voted with the Government would have exposed Labour's division and enabled them to abstain ostentatiously under the conscience clause, while the abstention of the whole PLP 'smothered the Bevanites', and the disciplinary action would deter them from constant rebellions.[77] He repeated his case for disciplined parties in a lecture 'In Defence of Politics' at Birkbeck College.[78]

There he defended the system against charges that the issues between the Parties were either excessive ('why can't they agree?') or trivial ('there's no difference between them'); that the party battle drove politicians into insincerity; and that it crushed independents and dissidents. He explained that Party leaders had to reconcile the demands of their own active workers with those of the floating voters. He maintained that individual politicians had plenty of freedom to speak their mind (subject to collective responsibility, as is usual in executive posts everywhere), but that voting was different. For 'a Government depends upon votes not words' and could take a long view only if it could rely on its followers in the lobby, while an Opposition must convince the electorate that it could form a stable government:

> Moreover, while we all admire a man who follows the dictates of his conscience, I cannot myself agree that the man who puts his own views first and the loyalty to the group second is necessarily right, or better than the man who sacrifices his own point of view for the sake of the group.

It was a view congenial to those in the majority rather than the minority, and Michael Foot replied in *Tribune* that decisions reached in private Party meetings frustrated debate and imposed a 'masquerade ... as the substitute for genuine democracy'.[79] Foot defended an MP's unlimited right of self-expression by vote, and ignored the doctrine (today apparently obsolete in Britain) on which all Socialist parties had previously insisted: that political parties pledged to changing society cannot be effective unless their parliamentary representatives accept majority decisions. *Tribune* had reason for reviewing Gaitskell's lecture three months late, for in March 1955 Labour's disciplinary crisis reached its climax over Aneurin Bevan himself.

iii *The Bomb, and the Bevanite Break-up*

During these early Opposition years, Gaitskell co-operated regularly with three groups of political associates—later adding the moderate Bevanites, to whom he gradually drew close. First were his own political generation of ex-Ministers, who had met in 1952 to resist Bevan and plan for Attlee's succession, and who were often associates of Herbert Morrison rather than Gaitskell. In later years a few of them continued to play a big part as individuals: James Griffiths as a respected figurehead deputy leader, Alf Robens and Sir Frank Soskice as trusted advisers, Patrick Gordon Walker after 1959 as unofficial chief of staff. Dalton, more senior and not politically in that set, also remained influential. A second group comprised the young MPs whom Gaitskell encouraged in the Dalton tradition. Crosland and Jenkins were economic specialists on the Finance Bill team; so was Jay from an older generation; the better-known Wyatt was not. The link to this group was personal friendship rather than economic expertise or parliamentary collaboration. Lacking status outside Westminster, these allies could not share Gaitskell's burdens (e.g. on the National Executive). They had a common Oxford background and a similar intellectual and political outlook, though each disagreed with Gaitskell at times. They were close because he found them congenial companions, with whom he could relax and enjoy himself, and because they all displayed the two qualities he valued most: courage and loyalty.

That was true too of the third group, his allies among the leaders and parliamentary spokesmen of the trade union movement. On the political side there were two of his Leeds neighbours: Alice Bacon, a member of the National Executive; and Charlie Pannell, who a little later became an important leader of the trade union MPs along with George Brown. Beyond Westminster the most prominent were the general secretaries of the two great general unions, Arthur Deakin and Tom Williamson. Until his death on May Day 1955, Deakin had for years dominated the industrial movement by the force of his personality and the power of his union. He was one of those vigorous, boisterous, extroverted and intolerant working-class characters whose bullying and crudity are readily excused by intellectuals who like their politics, but never forgiven by those who do not. He was the chief of a group of trade union leaders who, in the precarious economic situation after the war, had used their great bargaining power with restraint—and had had to fight bitterly against the militant or demagogic minority who challenged that policy. This earned those leaders a bad press on the Left in their own day and since, and their heritage has been ostentatiously repudiated by many of their successors. Yet they improved their members' real standard of living substantially, without imposing the arbitrary injustice of inflation on the poor and weak; and they made it possible under the Attlee Cabinet to reconstruct the economy and lay the foundations for lasting prosperity on which future governments failed to build.

Among this group of union leaders the closest to Gaitskell, and a crucial figure in all the crises of the 1950s, was Sam Watson of the Durham miners, the uncrowned king of the county. The miners' union was an old federation of districts, in which the Communists had a secure foothold in Scotland and South Wales. The struggle against them in the NUM was perpetual, and since 1926 the suspicion of them among other miners' leaders was profound. Watson was quite a different type from Deakin: a personal friend of Bevan as well as Gaitskell, keen on adult education, a man of broad interests and great intellectual ability. He was Gaitskell's staunch ally both in the union and on Labour's National Executive, where he was chairman of the international sub-committee. He was no power-seeker, and repeatedly refused to move from Durham to London. Like Pannell and Alice Bacon, he began as Gaitskell's valued political supporter and became his intimate friend.

Conflicts in the unions were often bitter and neither side was always scrupulous about means. Preoccupied with the problems that concerned them directly, the union leaders expected help from Labour politicians who were normally their allies. When Gaitskell as Party treasurer sought higher subscriptions from them, the general secretary of the TUC told him that 'the best way to get the Unions to pay up was to make it clear to them ... that the Labour Party machine would ... [help] against Communist candidates at Union elections'.[80] It was not just an organisational matter. The trade unionists in the PLP and on the NEC usually voted with Gaitskell against the Bevanites. His approach often differed from theirs, but when they called on him in turn for support, he did not feel they should be left to fight disagreeable battles alone. That sense of solidarity and obligation was to lead him into his worst blunder: his backing – after great hesitation – of the move to expel Aneurin Bevan in March 1955.

As Gaitskell hoped and expected, Bevan's Scarborough outburst in October 1954 provoked a hostile reaction among Labour MPs;[37b] and his later conduct brought him more humiliation and bitterness. The back-benchers came down heavily against him on foreign policy, only about fifteen dissenting from a PLP decision not to vote against SEATO. Bevan shouted that he would do so anyway, but then stayed away from the debate.[22c] His failure to lead did both himself and the Left 'catastrophic' harm.[81] *Tribune* harmed him too, pursuing its violent attacks on trade union leaders by a denunciation of Deakin which many Bevanites considered indefensible;[82] 'Bevanism', said Harold Wilson, 'would be far better without *Tribune*.'[83] At the end of 1954 the *Daily Mirror* planned an article on 'The Flop of the Year: Aneurin Bevan'.[84]

At the New Year, Bevan tried to retrieve his position by reviving the argument over German rearmament, again urging immediate talks with the Russians before ratification. But the German Socialists and the International had now accepted the policy, and even former Shadow Cabinet critics like Dalton strongly resented efforts to reopen the old divisions.[22d] When Bevan put his motion to the PLP on 9 February, he lost by 93 to 70. But he then mustered over 100 MPs, including old Keep Calmers like John Strachey and Michael Stewart, for a similar motion contradicting the PLP decision, on which he demanded time for a debate. Crossman, 'delighted' at the prevailing harmony on domestic issues, was dismayed to find this move producing in the PLP 'an atmosphere of division, disunity, hatred and all uncharitableness which I have rarely known'.[19i] A week later, on the evening of 24 February 1955, Attlee on behalf of the Shadow Cabinet moved that Bevan's conduct 'makes a farce of Party Meetings and brings the Party into disrepute'. He said the motion was directed to the future, not the past, and carried it by 132 to 72.[85-6*]

Within a week of this formal warning Bevan led another spectacular revolt – against Labour's acceptance of the hydrogen bomb, of which he had himself approved only a fortnight earlier. At their weekly lunch on Tuesday 15 February, Crossman had wondered whether the Bevanites should oppose its manufacture by Britain:

> Nye was emphatic that we should not, on the ground that the British people were not prepared to see themselves denied a modern weapon[87] ... not the H-bomb, but our strategy and foreign policy were the real issues ... I was extremely impressed by his argument that public opinion was not ripe for it.[19l q]

Bevan did not see the H-bomb as morally different from the A-bomb or even saturation bombing;[88a] and on request, explicitly approved of Crossman and Wigg publishing a forthcoming *New Statesman* supplement on these lines.[89] But at lunch a week later he agreed to their doing so only 'grudgingly', and 'was obviously evasive'.[19k]

On the morning of 24 February, a few hours before censuring Bevan, the PLP debated its attitude to the government announcement that Britain would make the H-bomb. Attlee had already approved, and Crossman and some other Bevanites justified the decision by the need to remain indepen-

* The same meeting of the PLP, which Bevan and Foot thought so vindictive, also restored the whip to the seven November rebels.

dent of the United States. The Shadow Cabinet knew their views when it proposed a motion of censure (on a three-line whip) but explicitly accepted the H-bomb as a deterrent to aggression. In Bevan's absence the morning PLP approved with very few dissentients;[90-3] and unanimously agreed to Fred Peart's motion asking the government for talks with Russia without referring to Germany.[22d]

Bevan met his friends again on Tuesday 1 March. He avoided the subject of the bomb till the very end of their lunch, when he said he could not vote for the Labour motion accepting the deterrent strategy. That evening Crossman persuaded him to do so, but next day,

> Jennie ... had changed his mind again ... he left fairly determined to lead a new split. In the House he met George Wigg, who ... swung him back again. We went into the debate together, and as we entered the Chamber he said to me, 'I'm still completely in two minds which I should do'.[19k q]

The White Paper said the alliance would retaliate with nuclear weapons against an attack even by conventional forces. Neither the government nor the Opposition leaders were willing to specify the circumstances more precisely, and so tell the Russians just how far they could safely go. Attlee was asked to do so by Warbey at the Party meeting on defence,[19k] and in the House by Silverman and Pargiter; he did not reply, and Strachey said the government should not reply either.[88b] During the debate Bevan repeated the question about using the bomb first, and made three attacks on his own leaders.[93] First he complained that Attlee and Morrison were absent (at the weekly Shadow Cabinet, as he knew). Then he said he would not vote for the Labour censure motion if it implied approval of the White Paper statement, and demanded their assurance that 'their Amendment, moved on our behalf, does not align the Labour movement behind that recklessness; because if we cannot have the lead from them, let us give it ourselves';[94] The Shadow Cabinet had (from Leslie Hunter) a verbatim report of Bevan's speech, and decided not to air Labour's differences in public;[92b] so Attlee sat down without replying, and evaded an answer when Bevan intervened – in his third attack – to demand one.[88d]

Bevan had neither attended the PLP meeting on the subject nor tried to raise the question with the Front Bench in the five days since then.[86] Instead he embarrassed Attlee on the floor of the House as he had over his SEATO challenge just a year before, and led sixty MPs in ostentatious refusal to vote for the censure motion. Younger, long sympathetic to him, saw 'no shadow of justification either for his offensive conduct to Clem in the House or for abstaining ... he has behaved throughout like a spoilt child and richly deserves anything that comes to him'.[91] A dozen old Bevanites refused to follow his lead: not just Wilson and Crossman but devotees like

Delargy, Freeman, Hale and Swingler.[19k] 'We reminded him', wrote Crossman to a bewildered Party worker, that

> he had no moral scruples about the H-bomb and was indeed a member of the Labour Government which started making nuclear weapons ... at the end of his speech he seemed almost deliberately to pick a quarrel with Clem Attlee and to find a most unconvincing reason for not supporting the vote of censure.[95]

iv   *Painful Epilogue: 'If thy Nye Offend Thee, Pluck it Out'*

Labour MPs generally were indignant at Bevan's disruptive activities. In 1952, after losing over arms estimates in the PLP, he had instigated the first mass abstention in the lobby. At Westminster he had repeatedly offended his colleagues by abusing some harmless back-bencher; and in the country both he and *Tribune* had kept fanning the flames of Labour's internal feud, and trying to spread them to the industrial wing. In the last twelve months he had challenged Attlee on the floor of the House over SEATO, and resigned from the Shadow Cabinet in a fit of petulance; declared war on the union leaders when he failed to win the treasurership; and done his best to reopen the German rearmament wound as soon as it began to heal. Finally, within a week of being warned for that, and without even attending the meeting which decided Party policy, he had again challenged the leader in public and staged an open split in the House. No one at all defended his conduct.

Back-bench MPs were demanding a special Party meeting, and many felt the PLP could not do its job while he was a member.[25d] But Gaitskell was not among the fire-eaters. Late in February 1955, just before the clash, he had lunched with Dalton and played at Cabinet-making, thinking of Bevan as Minister of Defence or Colonies.[96] After it he had serious tactical doubts, both about the formal grounds for sanctions and about the effect on the treasurership contest. But when on 7 March 1955 the Shadow Cabinet held a special meeting to discuss the issue, to his astonishment Ede and Callaghan — neither of whom was a stern disciplinarian, and both of whom opposed German rearmament — insisted that Bevan must forfeit the Party whip.[97]

Withdrawal of the whip — expulsion from the PLP — was a sanction for misdeeds at Westminster, imposed by vote of all the Labour MPs. But only the National Executive could expel from membership of the Labour Party in the country, and then the victim could appeal to Conference — as Cripps had vainly tried to do in 1939, and Bevan might do successfully in 1955. If a rebel MP was expelled from the Party he would face opposition from an official candidate at the following election and probably lose his seat; but if not, losing the whip would relieve him of his promise to observe the obligations imposed on Labour MPs by the standing orders he had signed, while leaving him the right to stand for any Party office.

Gaitskell therefore warned his Shadow Cabinet colleagues that it would be foolish to deprive Bevan of the whip unless they were both willing to expel, and able to carry both NEC and Conference.[98] He thought 'that sooner or later [Bevan] would have to go, but I was not sure whether this was the right moment', and advocated strong censure instead. But Attlee was the aggrieved party, he concluded, and the leader's view should prevail.[99] Attlee and four others spoke mildly for censure, three of them giving tactical reasons and saying they would accept the majority view. That view, because of demoralisation in the Party in the country, was strongly for withdrawing the whip.[100] In the end ten members voted for that course, including Gaitskell who said that once the process was begun it must go right to the end. 'I do not recall throughout this that Attlee said anything. Certainly ... [nothing] heard by the Committee generally.'

The vote in the PLP was postponed because Bevan was (probably diplomatically) ill.[19ł] The Bevanites used the delay to mobilise pressure.[25ʄ] In the country they had some success, though fewer protested at this point than in November over the pacifist rebels. Canvassers were being asked whether they were for Attlee or Bevan; and Crossman found his disheartened Party workers as critical of Bevan as they were reluctant to see him expelled. At Westminster the agitation failed. Bevan and his irreconcilable advisers hoped that 130 MPs would sign a round robin, but had to drop the idea after a discouraging canvass; and hoped too that their six NEC members would threaten to resign, but found no enthusiasm for that.[101] Crossman told Bevan bluntly at one of their lunches: 'you're being advised by suicide maniacs. The basic thing to realise is that you were wrong last week and everybody knows you were wrong except the people in this room.'[102]

Bevan issued a statement denying any challenge to Attlee's authority, which made Gaitskell decide he must mention the row in his next public speech.[103] He told his Doncaster listeners that the issue was 'standards of loyalty' among Labour MPs:

> Mr. Attlee was subjected ... to a hostile interrogation in language which might have come from the leader of another Party ... even an implied threat that if his answers were unsatisfactory another lead would have to be provided ... a direct challenge to the elected Leader of our Party ... this kind of behaviour ... has been getting more not less frequent. Effective leadership and good team work becomes impossible if all the time we have to face disruption from within.[104]

There was no hint of criticism from the audience.[105]

Nevertheless the Shadow Cabinet knew that withdrawal of the whip from Bevan would alarm many MPs, some of whom would vote for it only if the leaders made it a matter of confidence. All the whips intended to resign if the proposal was rejected, and at two meetings on 7 and 9 March most of the Shadow Cabinet agreed that they would do so too—with Attlee and Morrison reluctant, and Griffiths and Wilson absent. At the PLP on 16 March Attlee carefully avoided hinting that the issue was one of confidence, even when—as he was speaking—all but two of the Shadow Cabinet signed a note urging him to say clearly that they would all resign if they lost.[106] Bevan denied challenging Attlee and denounced Gaitskell for saying what he 'must have known was a lie'.[107] Dalton records 'his voice rising to the familiar scream, "there are the men who are working against the leadership, those hatchet-faced men sitting on the platform".' He said others had conspired against Attlee in 1947—and two MPs (Alice Bacon and Percy Daines) reminded him that he had himself lobbied them against Attlee at that time.[108] Gaitskell thought it quite a powerful speech with no trace of apology or repentance.[109]

Fred Lee then proposed to censure Bevan instead of withdrawing the whip. He began by saying everybody would 'agree that Nye had behaved outrageously, to which there was no dissent whatever'.[19m] Elaine Burton, whose left-wing CLP had threatened not to readopt her if she voted to withdraw the whip, asked Attlee if it was a question of confidence. The leader replied, 'Yes, necessarily so', in a voice so weak that half the meeting could not hear him. Lee's amendment was lost by only 124 to 138, and Attlee's motion carried by 141 to 112. It was exactly the result Gaitskell expected. The Chief Whip had predicted a majority of eighty for the platform, but both Gaitskell and Dalton put the margin at less than half that because they foresaw Attlee's hesitancy in putting the case.[110] Gaitskell concluded, and his trade union friends concurred, that Bevan could not now be expelled unless, on being asked for assurances about his future conduct, he refused to give them.[111]

Attlee now busily set about disclaiming responsibility. He showed 'frigid hostility' to Gordon Walker, Stokes and George Brown, who went to see him on 17 March, and then had an unpleasant and unfriendly interview with Gaitskell and Robens, complaining at being made 'the spearhead of a policy in which I did not believe'. They both protested that he had never made his disbelief clear at the time; for had he done so, their own attitude would have been different.[112] Gaitskell argued that Bevan would be in a strong position if he lost the whip while keeping his Party membership;[113] but that instead of expelling him his membership might be suspended for six months—a period which would be up before Conference—in order to deny him a clear victory. Attlee considered the idea but rejected it. The trade union leaders had been willing to settle for that, but both

Deakin and Williamson now publicly called on the leader to take a firm stand.

Bevan still had support in the CLPs which, as constituencies were currently being redistributed, were able to bring more pressure than usual on many MPs.[22e] Protests against expulsion came from 150 local Parties, of which about a quarter had anti-Bevanite Labour MPs—who risked being reported to their caucuses, and complained of 'spying and pressure' at PLP meetings.[114]* But many MPs were themselves very unhappy, and some of Gaitskell's close friends—and his wife—told him he was going much too far. On 21 March Crosland, Jenkins and Wyatt jointly wrote to say they had frequently voted for the Shadow Cabinet while doubting its wisdom, but could no longer do so out of loyalty and contrary to their own views; and warned him that no one could lead the Party unless, like Attlee and unlike Morrison, he enjoyed solid support from people in the centre who had opposed withdrawing the whip.[115]

Now the affair became entangled with Gaitskell's job as treasurer, in which capacity he was asking the unions to agree to higher affiliation fees which would, he hoped, raise the income of the Party by 50 per cent. They negotiated over dinners at the St Ermin's Hotel in Victoria, and the next one was fixed for Monday 21 March. Gaitskell asked Attlee to come, but the leader feared he would be spotted and his presence misunderstood. His absence was to prove crucial.

On that evening, the union leaders agreed as Gaitskell wished to raise the affiliation fee from 6d. to 9d.; and both Deakin and Williamson of the General and Municipal Workers had already offered to affiliate their unions to the Party on a much higher membership. At the dinner they initiated, and others supported, a call for Bevan's expulsion even against Attlee's wishes. Gaitskell did not conceal either from the leader or from the Bevanites that his own attitude was influenced by his need as treasurer to keep the unions' goodwill; he said so to Attlee on 17 March, and was reported by Crossman as saying on the evening of Tuesday 22 March,

> we must consider money, and many of our big backers were asking why we hadn't acted three years ago. I then said we knew about his meeting at St. Ermin's Hotel and he said 'Oh, that's a pure phoney, we've been having regular meetings on the National Agency service and last Monday happened to be the last of them. But I don't deny that, in discussing the money, this issue of Bevan has been not un-important'.[19n]

The more lurid versions alleging decisive financial pressure can be dis-

* Half the 150 CLPs were in Tory seats.

counted, however, for Deakin at no time talked to his own executive or to his crucial ally Tom Williamson of reducing the unions' contribution to Party funds.[116] He was capable of dropping an elephantine hint, but Gaitskell would not have taken that very seriously.*

Nevertheless it was at this St Ermin's dinner that Gaitskell made up his mind that he must keep solidarity with his trade union allies. They checked the names of the Executive and found only 12 definite opponents of expulsion out of 27: Attlee, Griffiths, the 6 Bevanites, and 4 trade unionists —2 moral rearmers, and 2 from unions which Gaitskell called 'Communist-dominated'.[118] Morrison and Dalton agreed to support expulsion even against Attlee, and for the first time Gaitskell became fully committed, finding a mover and seconder and canvassing the trade union members who complained that Attlee should lead, not they.

On the other side, Bevan again asked his NEC supporters to resign if he were expelled, but only two of the six promised to do so.[19n] Crossman, who would not promise, invited Gaitskell round for a drink on Tuesday 22 March—the night after the St Ermin's dinner and before the NEC met—and tried to change his mind, warning him that he was appearing to be 'a stooge for big forces outside'. Gaitskell denounced Bevanism as 'only a conspiracy to seize the leadership', which his host denied. Allegedly he found parallels between Nye and Adolf Hitler as demagogues; he admitted 'minor differences' such as Bevan's concern for parliamentary liberty! (Gaitskell's account omits Hitler; the silly analogy was in his mind but not his considered view.)[119]** Gaitskell was bitterly critical of Attlee, thought Bevan's influence would wither in the wilderness, and concluded that the main Tory issue in the next election would be undermined if Bevan were expelled, and underlined if he were not. Crossman summed up their

* Deakin told Leslie Hunter that he had warned at the dinner that unless Bevan was expelled the unions would not give the Party any more money than hitherto and might give less. Other union leaders agreed; and Hunter says Gaitskell gave way rather than lose 'the personal support of the unions and their financial support for his plans to strengthen the party'.[92c] Lord Williamson flatly denied such a threat, and others thought that though Deakin might have growled he would not have meant it.[117] Gaitskell, who talked so freely to Crossman, would not have omitted it from his diary if he took it seriously. Hunter had previously understood Gaitskell to be against expulsion; now exaggerated his change of mind; and, seeking to explain it, may have put Deakin's dark mutterings into a precise form, date and place. As a loyal Labour man writing just before a general election, he was perhaps trying clumsily to protect the Party leader's reputation by saying 'Gaitskell had to choose between two evils'.

** After one great row with Bevan — probably this one — Gaitskell was escorting a friend to an XYZ ladies' night in the House when Bevan passed them on the stairs and she made a very derogatory comment. 'It was the only time Hugh ever ticked me off. He said, "Helen, that's not the way to talk about a great man and a great politician" — although he was fighting him. He really gave me a lecture.'[120]

talk: 'He drank a great deal of whisky ... We both promised not to tell our closest friends, and I think I can now occasionally repeat this.'[19n]

Next day, Wednesday 23 March 1955, the NEC met. Attlee said Bevan might claim that his expulsion was a breach of parliamentary privilege, which Sir Frank Soskice (consulted by Gaitskell) thought 'inconceivable'.[121] One of the two moral rearmers, James Haworth, moved and the other seconded an amendment seeking from Bevan undertakings to which, in Gaitskell's view, no one could seriously have expected him to agree. Attlee proposed that Bevan should be seen before the final decision, and Gaitskell said that would ensure no expulsion. They exchanged sharp words over the meaning of the PLP's vote.[22f] Trade union members of the NEC on both sides were under pressure from their unions;[122] and Attlee won by 14 to 13.

Bevan was seen by a sub-committee of 8 of whom 3 had voted to expel and 4 had voted against (plus the chairman).[123] He told his friends he would not answer questions and 'be cornered by Gaitskell'. Crossman warned him that he would then stand no chance at Conference, and he agreed to clear his statement with Attlee. He offered a 'really abject apology' which at first infuriated the Bevanite irreconcilables;[19n] but even they had seen it to be necessary by the time he met the sub-committee on 29 March.[19o]

There, Gaitskell recorded, he was quite unrepentant:

> There was a general effort to keep the temperature down. In accordance with this I said very little. Most of the questions came from Jim Haworth and Jack Cooper ... The only time I did intervene nearly led to a row. I said, 'Would you agree that it was a bad thing for the Party if members attack the leaders, and if so, will you agree not to do this in future?'
>
> He said, 'I refuse to answer that question. It is a trap.'
>
> Whereupon there was a sort of uproar and everybody tried to rush in to keep us apart.
>
> Edith [Summerskill] ticked him off gently for being so suspicious. But in general he evaded every question of this kind.[22e*]

Haworth thought Bevan's behaviour truculent and his assurances worthless, and switched to support expulsion. But the moment had passed. With Attlee abstaining the NEC voted to endorse the action of the PLP and to 'note' Bevan's assurances. Because of the news of an imminent election, Bevan regained the whip at once as Gaitskell had expected. The latter

---

* Gaitskell's contemporary account, confirmed by the few surviving eye-witnesses, cannot be reconciled with Michael Foot's story that he 'seemed to nominate himself as chief inquisitor'.[124]

summed up succinctly and accurately: 'nobody has really come out of it very well'. Attlee had lost support on the Right, Bevan in the PLP as a whole, and he himself in the centre, where he was again suspect as a rigid right-winger after a year in which he had begun to live down that reputation:

> [M]ost of my friends think I was very foolish to allow myself to be carried on by the 'right wing', with the inevitable result that the Bevanites 'framed' me as the 'Chief Prosecutor' ... I always find it difficult to behave in these matters in the subtle way which my own friends seem to expect. I don't see how one can have strong loyalties with people like George Brown and Alf Robens, not to speak of the T.U. leaders, and continually refuse to do any of the dirty work for them and with them ... my own position is no doubt weaker ... [but I] cannot regard that as the only thing that matters. One would get no fun out of politics if one spent all one's life thinking in terms of the single object of one's own political success.[22e]

All the protagonists also came out badly in showing very poor judgment. Bevan's behaviour so outraged everyone that even the irreconcilable Bevanites did not defend him at the time, but waited twenty years for memories to fade.[125] One Keep Calmer sent Attlee a resolution criticising Bevan; another said Bevan had been 'hopelessly wrong'; a third felt: 'He'll have to be sensible for at least a year before anyone will take him seriously again.'[126]

Attlee was hailed as the saviour of the Party from a disaster principally of his own making; for, since Bevan's sin was an offence against the leader, no one would have suggested expulsion if Attlee had said from the first that he would not go beyond a motion of censure. For the third time in four years—just as over the 1951 Budget and the 1952 Morecambe revolt—he abdicated the responsibility of leadership by allowing matters to rot before showing his hand.

Gaitskell always saw that the worst of outcomes was to fail in attempting extreme measures: unless both NEC and Conference would vote to expel, it was a mistake to withdraw the whip. He put the right alternatives, then—as he himself recognised—made the wrong choice: 'undoubtedly had I foreseen, as I should have done, where Clem's original attitude would lead us, I should have thrown my weight on the first day against withdrawing the Whip and in favour of the censure motion.'[22e] (So much for Foot's conspiracy theory, and Hunter's blackmail theory.) But while a word from Attlee could have prevented the crisis, he was not exclusively to blame. The Shadow Cabinet hardliners should have been warned by their own assessment that they could not carry the PLP convincingly without a collective threat of resignation. Misconduct in the House always arouses more indignation inside than out, and most Labour voters opposed expulsion.[127] If as in this case the MPs themselves were doubtful, either from principle or prudence, then the leadership would fail to force it through. The Shadow Cabinet, demanding what Hunter called 'shot-gun divorce', won an inadequate majority at the cost of widespread resentment.[92d]

Both sides had their conspiratorial interpretations. The Bevanite view, that Attlee would be the next victim after Bevan, was the exact reverse of the reality.[128] If Bevan had gone, Attlee's position would have been unchallenged; the leader was criticised only after he struggled to save Bevan, and then not so much for doing that as for vacillating while others were committing themselves to unpopularity on what they thought to be his behalf. Conversely, Gaitskell exaggerated the cohesion and organisation of Bevan's supposed conspiracy to seize the leadership, and his own hard line helped the disintegrating Bevanites briefly to patch up the deep divisions between the *Tribune* irreconcilables — Michael Foot, Jennie Lee and J. P. W. Mallalieu — and most of the rest. But though they all opposed the expulsion, after Easter their Tuesday lunches were never resumed, and Bevanism was no more.

Crossman had been right to warn Bevan:

> [Y]our strategic aim is fantastically over-ambitious: my own is limited to trying to restore a proper balance between Right and Left in the Party ... your general line in the last few months has taken you further from effective power and nearer to the danger you mentioned of becoming a Jimmy Maxton.[129]

That reference to Maxton, the lovable but futile ILP rebel of the 1930s, gives a clue to the attitudes of both Bevan and his opponents. The idea of a Labour Party which could not accommodate Aneurin Bevan seems absurd today, as it would have done in 1951 or 1959, given his record over the previous few years. But after 1954/5 even his admirers feared he was becoming a perpetual dissident, effective at disruption but with nothing to offer a Labour Party preparing for power.

His critics thought that Bevan in the wilderness would either fade away like Maxton, or return chastened to the fold. Expulsion had never been a political death sentence for Labour MPs (except for four who seemed indistinguishable from Communists).[130] Nearly all the rest came back in time; and after rejoining they were not penalised but often held high office.* Those who merely lost the whip have all regained it before the

---

* For instance: Cripps, Bevan and Strauss, who suffered expulsion in 1939 over the Popular Front; Ellen Wilkinson, who renounced to avoid it; George Buchanan, the former ILP MP.

following election. Except for fellow-travellers, the NEC used expulsion as a sanction not to destroy rebels politically, but to enforce on them minimal standards of co-operation with Party colleagues, on pain of going it alone in an electoral climate deadly for independents.[131] As that climate has changed since, parliamentary discipline has loosened considerably.

Thinking of Maxton and Cripps, the leadership doubtless underestimated the unpopularity of Bevan's expulsion. But he was very lucky to escape so lightly. The NEC majority wanted him out but never all voted together. A newspaper strike saved him from humiliating public dissection of his apology. Above all Churchill's retirement heralded an early election and persuaded Labour to close ranks.[132] Yet the electoral advantages of reprieving Bevan were not wholly clear.[19p] Churchill and Beaverbrook were among the astute Tories who publicly encouraged Bevan and helped build him up;[133] and just as Gaitskell had predicted, the Conservatives presented him as the real Labour leader, one famous cartoon showing his face emerging from behind Attlee's.[134] But that was partly Gaitskell's own fault, reflecting the attempt to expel no less than its failure. Above all the harmful impression of Labour's disunity and quarrelsomeness was revived, and that was mainly but not only owing to Bevan.

An unsuccessful move to expel, disillusioning Labour activists without reassuring floating voters, was the worst possible prelude to the election campaign. Yet for Labour's longer-term health that may have been the best outcome of the clash. Without the damaging consequences of expulsion, it brought about the change in Bevan's conduct which the threat of it was meant to achieve.[135] He was never again to follow the advice of the 'suicide maniacs' who had led him so close to disaster. Gaitskell too learned a lesson: using mistaken tactics in a vain effort to obtain a dubious objective, he had harmed himself with his closest friends, with uncommitted MPs, and with Attlee. The 1955 election therefore reopens the forgotten chapter in Gaitskell's life in which he conscientiously conciliated the moderate Left—a course he had begun earlier, only to be diverted by Bevan. The expulsion crisis put an end not only to Bevanism, but to Gaitskell's Stalybridge period too.

CHAPTER 12

LEADER BY A LANDSLIDE
1955

*'I am a Socialist because I want to see fellowship ... [while preserving]
the liberties we cherish'*

(HG AT CONFERENCE, 1955)

i *Party Treasurer, and the 1955 Election*

DURING 1955 Gaitskell's position in his Party was dramatically transformed.
He began it as a respected politician of high intelligence and great courage,
who seemed too rigid for party leadership. For, since the rival coalitions
in a two-party system are so broad and so severely penalised for splitting,
they need leaders who can hold them together. In that skill, so conspicuous
in his predecessor and so obsessive in his successor, Gaitskell seemed
deficient even to some of his friends: too inflexible intellectually, too strict
a disciplinarian, with too insensitive political antennae, too narrow a base
at Westminster and among the trade union leadership, and too little appeal
to Party workers in the country. Over Bevan's expulsion, these doubts
crystallised so sharply that Gaitskell's prospects of leading the Labour
Party might well have been destroyed. Yet only nine months later he was
chosen to do so by a margin far more impressive than in any comparable
contest. His two opponents had lost both prestige and reputation, and he
had himself worked hard to meet the criticisms. During 1955 he broadened
his base in the Party; improved its organisational efficiency; co-operated
increasingly with the moderate Left; and proved that he could appeal
effectively to Labour's rank and file both in the House and the country, and
satisfy (as he did for four years) their overwhelming demand to end the
feuding.

The first step was his election as treasurer in 1954. It was his first extra-
parliamentary office, making him the one member chosen for the National
Executive by Conference as a whole. The post had been honorific for
decades, but the election had symbolic value — which was why Bevan persistently contested it. For Gaitskell it had a practical advantage too, for
it gave him an Executive seat. But he was incapable of treating any job as
a sinecure.

The office offered plenty of scope for useful work. Labour's activities had always been hampered both by shortage of money and by deep-seated conservatism. In his short tenure Gaitskell carried out several reforms. He brought in an outside adviser with Labour sympathies, Desmond Hirshfield, to report on the (low) managerial efficiency of the office. He improved its financial procedures, and began to mechanise its accounting. He transferred part of the pension funds from very low-yielding government stocks into equities, and found better investments, partly through the Co-operatives, for some of the political funds. He was keen to raise the poor salaries of the staff, and began a review of their inadequate pensions. Above all he sought to revive Labour's dilapidated local organisation, especially the declining agency service.[1-2] That meant money; and the unions, generous at election times, were tight-fisted over financing the humdrum running costs like salaries, rent, printing and telephones.[3-5]

From the first, he wrote, Sam Watson was pressing him to

> start taking the lead in all sorts of ways, and particularly ... about the finances ... not through messing about with the administration of Transport House and the Regions, but through talks with the Unions and speeches in the country. I think his advice is probably sound.[6a]

But Gaitskell was uncomfortable in these negotiations, for 'the job of Treasurer has simply not been done for ten years', so that no one agreed on what it entailed, especially in relation to the NEC's finance committee. He would have liked to take over the chair from Jock Tiffin of the T&GWU, but foolishly said so to Deakin instead of to Tiffin himself—whom he had to mollify by dropping the idea.[7]

The negotiations took place over a series of dinners, beginning on 26 October. Besides Gaitskell and Phillips the Party secretary, the main union leaders attended: Deakin, Tiffin and Williamson from the general unions; Ernest Jones and Sam Watson from the NUM; Birch from USDAW, Openshaw from the AEU, Stafford (a left-winger) from the NUR, and Poole from the Boot and Shoe Operatives. Deakin had told Gaitskell at Scarborough that the two big general unions meant to affiliate over 400,000 more members to the Party.[8] That would both help the funds and strengthen the platform against the Left, providing 'a complete safeguard, certainly against the Engineers going wrong and possibly the Miners, though I am not too worried about this at present'.[6a]

Now the others urged the general unions to affiliate even more members. To Gaitskell's pleasure and surprise the others also agreed with him and Phillips on the need to raise the affiliation fees,[9-10] which since the war had fallen both as a percentage of wages and in purchasing power (though elections were costing more).[4] Fees were to go up from 6d. to 9d., despite Deakin's and Williamson's reluctance to increase their very low political levy. Into this delicate situation erupted, at the start of the talks, *Tribune*'s vitriolic attack on Deakin over the dock strike; and at the end, the Bevan expulsion crisis in which Deakin behaved heavy-handedly. Nevertheless, at Southport before the TUC in September 1955, the executives of eighty affiliated unions agreed to increase the affiliation fee from 6*d.* to 9*d.*, raising the Party's income by 50 per cent and allowing it to start remedying the worst organisational deficiencies.[11]

The agreement brought in £75,000. That amount sharply limited the reorganisation the Party could afford, for even without higher salaries a full-time agency service throughout the country would cost over £300,000 per annum.[12] Gaitskell told David Ginsburg (then at Transport House) during the talks that 'the best we can hope for is a scheme which concentrates a good deal more money and control in marginal constituencies'.[10] Before the final agreement, Labour's electoral defeat in May 1955 had precipitated a more sweeping organisational inquest by a committee, chaired by Harold Wilson, which condemned the 'penny-farthing machine'. Advocated by a new alliance of Gaitskell with Wilson and Crossman, the inquiry was opposed by some NEC traditionalists.[13a b] Gaitskell encouraged it; though he might have preferred another chairman, and he would not use it to undermine Morgan Phillips.[14a b] Gaitskell and Wilson again worked together to reorganise the structure, first of the Shadow Cabinet, and later of the NEC's sub-committees.[11c] The press noted their excellent relations, and *The Economist* wrote that ' "Nye's little dog" of a few years ago is now Hugh's most important retriever'.[15]

The new treasurer's unprecedented activity was not welcome everywhere. Opponents of Deakin and Williamson deplored their increased influence. Some senior traditionalists in Transport House resented the new broom;[5] though juniors noted that Gaitskell was often in the office and, unlike most politicians, greeted them in the corridors.[16] Colleagues on the National Executive thought he interfered too much on too many subjects. One opponent claimed that the newcomer was

> losing ground rapidly ... because he [has] been chucking his weight about at Transport House ... he has a Treasury mind – he goes to *all* the committees – things the Treasurer formerly never dreamed of attending – and sits there like a supercilious school master bossing everybody about ... he's getting everybody's back up.[17a e]

His own political friends were sometimes irritated too. He protested early on at inadequate publicity for a policy statement on agricultural marketing;[18-19] later he criticised a party pamphlet for being far too complicated – provoking George Brown (Labour's spokesman) to complain bitterly that 'Gaitskell wants to be bloody Minister of Agriculture as well as Chancellor'.[17a f] Ironically, this first reproach at his passion for redrafting was due not to his donnish perfectionism but to his efforts to make the propaganda 'as light and simple as possible'.[20] More seriously, Gaitskell annoyed his trade union allies by trying as Dalton had done to help able young politicians like Anthony Crosland and Woodrow Wyatt, whose seats had vanished in the current major redistribution of constituencies.[21] Such efforts continued to do him harm with the unions.[22] But he never shared the objections then being put by people like Peter Shore and Anthony Benn to union sponsorship of candidates;[17b c] on the contrary, he lamented to the national agent that some local Parties preferred middle-class candidates to good union men.[23]

On balance Gaitskell gained much political benefit from his organisational activities. They gave him closer contact with the union leaders, for purposes cherished by constituency Party workers. They also aligned him with the moderate Bevanites on the Executive in a spirit of co-operation which was soon to extend beyond organisation to policy.

Gaitskell had always maintained that Labour would find no problem in reaching agreement on domestic issues, and the shrewder Bevanites soon concurred. At the 1954 Conference, with its battles over the treasurership and German rearmament, even *Tribune* criticised Gaitskell on home affairs only for his allegedly lukewarm advocacy of comprehensive schools.[24a] Just before the 1955 election *Socialist Commentary* wrote: 'Bevan ... has no alternative home policy ... we hear very little about [nationalisation] nowadays'.[25a] Just after it Bevan himself, complaining that Labour was too close to the Government on foreign affairs, commended its 'good [domestic] programme'. which if not 'exciting or ambitious, nevertheless was definite and practical'.[24b] As Crossman mused when he read those words: 'How things have changed since three or four years ago.'[26a]

In the Shadow Cabinet election in November 1954, Bevan did not stand and Gaitskell was top along with James Griffiths; each polled 170 (down by 6 and 10 respectively). Gaitskell suspected Bevan of trying to set the miners against the other unions — with an eye on the next year's treasurership contest — over an Insurance Bill.[27] But all Bevanites were not suspect; Gaitskell proposed Crossman — to his great surprise — as one of the Labour Party negotiators with the TUC,[26b] and they formed 'a common front' at those talks.[26c] So began what later became Crossman's most creative policy-making activity: and, more immediately, began (as he wrote)

the harmonious relations between Wilson, Gaitskell and myself in trying to make the best of Challenge to Britain ... Nye's absence makes that much easier, and ... Gaitskell is easier to work with than Morrison ... younger and more ambitious and anxious to get a policy.[26c]

After the final drafting committee with Gaitskell, Crossman confirmed that 'on home electoral policy there is nothing dividing the Party.[28] I went out of the meeting really delighted'.[26d]

Gaitskell bitterly denounced Butler's April Budget for purchasing political popularity by economic improvidence, to the advantage of the well-off and to the detriment of the poor.[29] To the new Prime Minister, Eden, it was a speech inspired by 'newly-acquired class-war hatred';[30b] to some Tories it was an unscrupulous attempt to outdo Bevan.[31] But the Opposition were overjoyed at 'the most powerful debating performance that has come from the Labour Front Bench for a long time', and his peroration was interrupted 'by storming cheers from behind ... [a] prolonged explosion on the Labour benches'.[32] His analysis was not confined to his own Party. The *Manchester Guardian* summed up:

> Mr. Butler may indeed have cause to regret his generosity later in the year ... And then the laugh would really be with Mr. Gaitskell. But the prospect of Mr. Butler 'eating his words' at some time in the autumn is not going to win this election.[33]

Gaitskell had wound up his Budget speech by 'eagerly, gladly' welcoming the election challenge. But the Labour leaders would have preferred delay, and had told Churchill that 'a quick election wouldn't be playing the game'.[34a] Gaitskell himself — unlike Transport House[13a] — had no illusions, knowing that 'The circumstances could hardly have been worse for us or better for the Tories'.[35] Labour's handicaps were severe, if often self-inflicted. As he had foreseen, it was now paying for the extravagant propaganda of 1951, pretending that a Tory government would endanger peace, full employment and the welfare state.[36-7] Better terms of trade had enabled the Conservatives to relax austerity and to profit at the polls, channelling the extra resources to consumption instead of investment or exports — while the bills came in much later. Nor could Labour credibly claim to provide a viable alternative to the government with its new and popular Prime Minister. For just before the dissolution Bevan had almost been expelled, while the Opposition leadership was certain soon to change hands.

The expulsion crisis did not hamper Labour's campaign planning. Gaitskell and Crossman collaborated amiably on drafting the manifesto, which the Bevanites did not try to alter. At the NEC, 'sweetness and light ruled', and Crossman found he had 'greatly under-estimated the good will and co-operative spirit engendered by the election' in the constituency Parties.[26e] The reconciliation was not complete: Bevan fixed all his own speaking arrangements without contact with Transport House[2b] — which settled all Gaitskell's and, for the first and last time in a general election, did not send him to speak for Bevanites.[38]

Gaitskell was used in marginal East Anglia (which proved Labour's best English region), in rural Lincolnshire, and on the north-east coast. For the last ten days he was based in his own constituency, but spoke daily for Yorkshire colleagues, and returned once to London to dominate Labour's liveliest television broadcast. Answering Tory attacks on the cost of the Labour programme, he

> accused the Tories jauntily of having thought of a number and multiplied it by 10 ... he was not in the least worried about the financing of it if production went up steadily ... saw no reason why they should put up taxes and hoped there would be some margin to enable them to reduce taxes on lower incomes.[39]

A friendly paper called it 'a wonderful piece of conjuring'.[39] Earlier, he had fought against overloading the programme with expensive commitments; now he defended its practicability in the press, and in a briefing session for candidates.[40] 'You are really the only person who has helped other candidates with new and splendid stuff', wrote Philip Noel-Baker.[41] Nothing in the reception of his argument in 1955 forewarned him of the devastating Conservative counter-attack when he repeated it in 1959.

Leeds forfeited a seat in the 1955 redistribution;[42] but its new boundaries left Gaitskell's rather isolated constituency unchanged, as safely Labour as ever, with its loyal little band of experienced workers to run the campaign before the MP arrived.[43] (When he did, the press proved so demanding that his agent insisted he must have a public relations man next time to fend them off.)[44] In a straight fight against the same opponent, he marginally improved his share (65·2 per cent) of a smaller poll:

Hugh Gaitskell (Lab.)	25,833
Winifred Brown (Cons.)	13,817
Majority	12,016

Before the election Gaitskell had been 'quite sure that ... the less we bring foreign policy in the better'.[19] On the Left, Barbara Castle and Ian Mikardo had hoped to win the election on the Bomb. But only one Labour candidate mentioned it at the briefing session, and Crossman wrote 'in the campaign the issue was a complete flop'.[45] Gaitskell's experience was similar, as he told the national agent: 'I found almost no interest in foreign affairs or the hydrogen bomb. I don't think I can have had more than three questions on them both throughout the whole campaign, and those came mostly from Tories.'[23a] His audiences were detached though not unfriendly. But 'whereas the middle classes do broadly fear the return of a Labour Government ... the working classes do not feel the same about the return of a Tory Government.'[23a] Consequently, he wrote to his former secretary who knew the constituency well: 'We suffered from the general indifference and apathy. The meetings were smaller and the collections were quite sharply down from 1950 & 1951.'[46] In home policy,

> nationalisation made no appeal at all. This, I think, is partly our fault, because we have not done enough propaganda about the success of nationalisation where there have been successes, but it is very unsatisfactory to be on the defensive even with workers in the industries concerned.[23a]

He cited chemical workers, noting that Labour did extremely badly in Middlesbrough and Cleveland.[37a] Among many other Labour MPs, Harold Wilson drew the same conclusion.[26a]

Both Griffiths and Wilson thought the Labour split more damaging still;[47] and Gaitskell suspected that it had forfeited Labour votes to the Liberals.[23a] It hurt all candidates alike. Not long before the election, a Gallup poll had found that a Labour Party led by Aneurin Bevan would have alienated 27 per cent of Labour supporters and 54 per cent of Liberals.[48] The election results seemed to bear that out. In straight fights in unchanged seats, the median swing against all Labour MPs was 1·2 per cent, against leading left-wingers 1·6 per cent.[2e] In Gorton and Salford East, safe seats with new candidates from the far Left, reliable majorities evaporated.[49] The lowest big-city swing was in Leeds with a solid phalanx of orthodox MPs; the highest in Coventry with the best-known left-wing party in the country.[2f] Elaine Burton, whom it had tried to reject, did much better than either Crossman or Edelman, her left-wing neighbours, because, Crossman thought, the voters consciously reacted against those views.[50] The lesson was so clear that, to Gaitskell's own surprise, 1955 was the only post-war election defeat which did not swing Labour to the Left.[51]

Gaitskell drove that lesson home.[52] To those who wanted sharper 'differentiation from the Tories', he replied that the parties had been no further apart when turnout was high in the 1950 and 1951 elections; and that if either put forward more extreme proposals it might raise the total vote only to its own disadvantage—as Labour would by adopting the Communist line, or the Tories by advocating their pre-war policies. Young working-class voters, he said, no longer feared the Conservatives and wanted more material goods[53]—and better-off people who moaned about that attitude were being 'odiously hypocritical'. He warned that Labour must never become 'a sterile dogmatic group, living on our own illusions', and emphasised the fundamental need for

> keeping the outlook of the Labour Party and its members sufficiently near to that of the electors ... [To] win support for our views ... we [must] understand those whom we wish to carry with us, and adapt

our approach to them accordingly ... *Our local parties must be truly representative of the ordinary Labour voter.*[25b]

It was, he wrote, 'the most important subject of all ... to make the constituency parties keep in closer touch with Labour supporters in general and the electorate as a whole ... [and] not relapse into isolationism again'.[54]

ii *Margate, and the Demise of Mr Butskell*

When Parliament met in June 1955, Hugh Dalton, the enthusiast for youth, retired from the Shadow Cabinet and so shamed his contemporaries into following his example.[55] Hoping to postpone a leadership election, he astutely excepted Attlee from this pressure, for every delay would diminish Morrison's chances and Dalton wanted Gaitskell to be the beneficiary. The calculation was equally plain to Bevan's friends — and to Morrison's. The latter wanted Attlee to bow out gracefully in July, allowing their man to take over for the new session in October. But the Conservative Government ran a single session straight through to the summer of 1956, so that the new PLP officers elected in July 1955 would serve for over a year. Attlee at once agreed when Dalton and Bevan called vociferously, first in the Shadow Cabinet and then in the PLP, for him to stay on without a time-limit. Morrison's prospects were dashed again.[56]

With Dalton's coup, five of the old Shadow Cabinet had gone. In a smaller PLP Gaitskell won his best vote, 184 — 2 behind Griffiths, the only other to reach 150. Wilson was fifth with 147, and Bevan (who had regained the whip when the election was called) was seventh with 118. Previously Bevan had earned warm approval from the PLP by deciding (against the advice of the usual irreconcilables) not to oppose Morrison for deputy leader. But that moderation was a tactical move in the leadership contest to win centre support away from Morrison — or from Gaitskell, who seemed to Bevan's shrewder friends the greater threat.[57]

Bevan still saw the struggle for the treasurership as a way to detach the union rank and file from their bosses. Gaitskell had originally been sponsored for the office by Deakin, but was now so independent of him that Deakin's death on May Day 1955 made no difference.[58] Jock Tiffin, the new T&GWU general secretary, easily beat off a left-wing attack on the executive's right to nominate for treasurer; the NUGMW leaders faced no opposition to it; the AEU executive manoeuvred ruthlessly to retain it.[59] The Miners' delegate conference again proposed Gaitskell by a slightly smaller majority, 457,000 to 271,000.[60] Two of the 'big six' unions, the NUR and USDAW, had supported Bevan in 1954; both now switched to the incumbent.[61] Many constituency party voters also appreciated Gaitskell's work as treasurer and were fed up with the feud. Half their votes now went against their former idol;[62] Bevan polled only 1,225,000 in all, to Gaitskell's 5,475,000.[63] His campaign against the bosses had detached not their rank and file, but his own.

Speculation about the leadership had been rife ever since the general election. It was stimulated by Attlee's illness in August and by an interview in September, when he told Percy Cudlipp he wanted to hand over to a man brought up in the present age, not Queen Victoria's 'as I was'.[64a] (So was Morrison.) On 10 October 1955 the Party Conference opened at Margate, portrayed in the *New Statesman* as a kind of American convention where 'the contestants for leadership paraded in their ideological bikinis, manoeuvring to give the judges a more favourable view'.[65] Gaitskell was indignant at the gossip. He still did not believe that Attlee was going, that he himself should stand, or that he could win.[66]

Conference began very badly, first for himself, then for the Party. He displayed his inexperience at the Sunday night demonstration before it opened, with a Front-Bench kind of speech which was received with impatience, unlike Morrison's 'knock-about attack on the Tories'.[67] The Wilson report was discussed on Tuesday afternoon, after the treasurership announcement; and

> a time-bomb went off with a shattering explosion. It was the fearful noise of Mr. Bevan blowing his top at what was comically called a private session. As every window was open and the loudspeakers on, even the quiet fisherman at the end of the pier could catch every word.[68]

Ignoring the report, Bevan denounced the debates as charades, the union leaders as oligarchs, and his NEC opponents – whom he blamed for the election defeat – as bad Socialists. Even MPs who had supported him in March condemned him for reopening the feud, and at the *Tribune* meeting next evening the audience resented efforts made by Ian Mikardo and Bryn Roberts of NUPE (though not by Bevan) to keep it alive.[69]

Bevan's targets were quicker than he to assess the mood, and avoided answering his outburst in kind. Morrison's reply pointed modestly to the government's achievements after 1945. Walking back to lunch, Gaitskell told Hunter he greatly admired the reply, and doubted whether he could or should try to match it – exasperated though he was with Bevan's claim to be 'the sole guardian of the Ark of the Covenant'. He was to make his own platform début that afternoon in a debate on the nationalised industries. Saying their achievements had been insufficiently publicised, he corrected that mistake with all too plentiful statistics down to nett ton-miles per engine-hour – until a wry sentence delighted his bored audience: 'You even need a calculating machine to work it out!' Suddenly spotting Bevan laughing with his friends at the back, Gaitskell dropped his notes and changed his tone.[64c] We have to persuade the voters, he said, that nationalisation was relevant to a better standard of living, economic security, greater equality and planning. But the need to do so did not affect the quality of his own convictions:

I am a Socialist and have been for some 30 years. I became a Socialist quite candidly not so much because I was a passionate advocate of public ownership but because at a very early age I came to hate and loathe social injustice, because I disliked the class structure of our society, because I could not tolerate the indefensible differences of status and income which disfigure our society ... because I hated poverty and squalor ... Pay people more if they do harder, more dangerous, and even more responsible work; pay people more if they have larger families. But the rewards should not be, as they still are, dependent upon the accident of whether you happen to be born of wealthy parents or not ... I am a Socialist because I want to see fellowship, or if you prefer it, fraternity ... [while preserving] the liberties we cherish. I want to see all this not only in our country but over the world as a whole.

These to me are the Socialist ideals. Nationalisation ... is a vital means, but it is only one of the means by which we can achieve these objects.

He wound up by quoting Clause Four of the Party constitution in order to distinguish the aim, namely 'To secure for the workers ... the full fruits of their industry', from 'the common ownership of the means of production which is the means'.[70]

Aneurin Bevan, 'red-faced and furious' at the back of the hall, muttered 'sheer demagogy, sheer demagogy'.[64b] But even *Tribune* wrote that 'After [Gaitskell's] performance, perhaps public ownership will cease to be a wall between Right and Left';[24c] Attlee was enthusiastic;[64b] and the applause of the delegates lasted for nearly a minute (three times as long as for Morrison).[71] The press thought his performance the better of the two.[64b] One American observer found it

breathtakingly brilliant, the British press didn't begin to do justice to it ... while asserting his personal dedication to socialism [he] did not give an inch in matters of doctrine. Significantly, the ovation he received was universal and not partisan. It was the first time in his career that Gaitskell had been so applauded.[72]

Gaitskell did more than win goodwill for himself, for it was largely his achievement that the Margate mood changed in mid-week, so that delegates dispirited by the bad start went home in good heart.[73] Once again he had risen to an occasion and demonstrated new capacities with which his friends would not have credited him. Moreover, the new alignment survived the conference, as Crossman noted.[74] When the new NEC met,

> the division, which had begun to arise on the Wilson report, became clear. It is a division between a young guard, who want efficiency, and an Old Guard, afraid that efficiency means giving the Young Guard power. There is no doubt whatsoever that Jack Cooper is now ready to work with Harold Wilson and myself, that Gaitskell is ready to work with us, and it is probable that the new T & G member, who replaces Tiffin, will do the same.[*] In fact, there is a new centre of the Party forming, which is trying to create a policy and a leadership not subservient to the Unions on the one side or appeasing Bevan on the other. There is no doubt, however, that if Herbert succeeds Clem in the near future, he will fight this new centre for all he can.[26f]

Gaitskell's triumph at Conference was soon followed by another in the House. That was the last of a series of clashes with Butler, whose chickens were now coming home to roost.

With his radical proposals for tax reform, his professional concern for sound economic forecasting and his political interest in demolishing the Butskell bogy, Gaitskell had every incentive to oppose the Chancellor in 1955. The grounds were obvious. In February Butler checked demand, restoring the hire purchase restrictions he had lifted six months before and raising bank rate to $4\frac{1}{2}$ per cent, its highest level for over twenty years. Less than eight weeks later, he expanded demand again in his Budget. In May the government was re-elected; in July he imposed new restraints on credit and capital expenditure; in October he was forced into a crisis Budget. That deplorable record was a gift to Gaitskell, who gained stature with every speech – as Morrison quite failed to do.

In February, Gaitskell warned in the press of a coming crisis.[75] He was 'going out on a limb with a vengeance ... moving to the Left to save his position' within the Party, thought Crossman, who assumed that the government would either check inflation and bring in a soft Budget, or fail to do so and postpone the election.[26g] Even cynical Labour politicians did not yet foresee that the election date might determine the content of the Budget, and not the reverse (though some were quick to learn the lesson). In 1954 Butler had justified a neutral Budget by the precarious state of the economy; in 1955, facing worse inflation and a worse balance of payments, he took 6d. off income tax. Repeatedly challenged, he never revealed what economic improvements since February had justified his decision.[30e] When the official forecasts are released, the best clue may turn out to be his confession twenty years later: 'Churchill once told me that his knowledge of

* This obscure gentleman was named Frank Cousins.

economics was as follows: "You can cook your Budget, my boy, but you can't cook the balance of payments." It was on that basis that I conducted myself as Chancellor.'[76]

Gaitskell's criticisms were summed up in his attack on the April Budget. Not mentioning rearmament, he claimed that Labour had restrained consumption to build up exports and investment — both now booming in other countries but stagnant in Britain:

> When the Government came into power, the worst strain of the post-war period was over ... the build-up of exports, the rebuilding of industrial equipment, was all finished ... Now was the opportunity to construct on a sound basis an even more flourishing export trade, an adequate surplus for investment abroad, reasonable gold reserves, and, above all, a high level of home investment ... this opportunity has been missed.[30a]

Butler was giving nearly £140 million in income tax reliefs, nearly half to companies, and more to well-off individuals living off investments than to those on low or earned incomes.[77] But rising consumption depended so precariously on better terms of trade that a small setback — only one-third of the improvement since 1951 — drove Britain into crisis measures:

> The Chancellor is in a dilemma. If he turns the credit screw hard enough ... he ... creates unemployment. If he keeps full employment he risks a balance of payments crisis. If he imposes direct control on the less essential imports he eats a whole mouthful of words. So ... he asks ... the Prime Minister to have an early General Election.[30a]

Gaitskell's criticisms were echoed elsewhere at the time, and confirmed by all later critics.[78] Within three weeks of polling day the *Telegraph* was stressing Butler's concern about inflation, a word which 'at the time of the Budget he studiously avoided'.[79] Gaitskell again warned of a precarious balance of payments, prices rising faster than elsewhere, the worst strikes since the war — and the biggest Stock Exchange boom in history: the fruits of 'trying to preserve full employment but removing the defences against inflation', while encouraging an unfair distribution of wealth. In the House, Butler was characteristically cautious, but Peter Thorneycroft (President of the Board of Trade) welcomed higher consumption and decried too much emphasis on exports.[80] Then, when the Chancellor restricted credit and capital expenditure in July, Gaitskell accused him of 'deliberately deceiv[ing] the electorate'; and though Butler tried to blame the recent dock strike, Gaitskell drove him to admit that that was no explanation, for the 'fundamental causes' were 'that we have been consuming too much at home'.[81]

To that excess consumption his April Budget had given a stimulus.

Gaitskell had warned that the Conservative electoral prospectus was fraudulent and the bills would soon have to be paid. Early in October Butler spoke at the Mansion House of more restrictions to come, and his Shadow charged him with the 'biggest act of political deceit since ... Stanley Baldwin sealed his lips on defence in 1935'.[82a b] Gaitskell was furious too at the injustice of the proposals.[83a] 'I am not easily roused to anger,' he confessed, 'but I must say that this latest cry to cut back the spending of worse off people to cure a crisis mostly caused by too much spending by better off people is intolerable.'[82a] The moment Parliament resumed, an autumn Budget withdrew £38 million from companies and £110 million from individuals – almost exactly the amounts each category had received in the spring.[83b] But instead of reversing his income-tax concessions, Butler imposed purchase tax on household necessities (for the first time for a decade, or in some cases ever), raised postal charges, and severely cut capital expenditure by the nationalised industries and local authorities.[84] Some Labour colleagues as well as Tories suspected Gaitskell of simulating wrath with an eye on the leadership contest.[85] But they were genuine feelings, expressed for months, about social justice and political standards.

Discussing Butler's case for his proposals – the 'emergence' of inflation, the need to rebuild reserves, overseas burdens and costly social services – Gaitskell saw nothing changed since April: 'There is no new element. The deterioration was clear enough in the spring. The dangers were pointed out to him again and again, but he remained obstinately complacent ... Always an expert in evasion, he has now become an addict of the easy half-truth.' The point of the April Budget, said Gaitskell,

> was not the incentive to people to produce more, it was the incentive to vote Conservative ... He has persistently and wilfully misled the public about the economic situation and he has done it for electoral reasons ... the April Budget – a masterpiece of deception – certainly encouraged instead of damping down additional spending. Now, having bought his votes with a bribe, the Chancellor is forced – as he knew he would be – to dishonour the cheque ... He has behaved in a manner unworthy of his high office. He began in folly, he continued in deceit, and he has ended in reaction.[83d]

Labour was delighted, and the Tories deeply embarrassed.[86] Not without malice, Wilson then urged an immediate censure motion – to be moved by Herbert Morrison.[87] Everything had been said already, and the deputy leader's long, hesitant, inconsequential ramblings came as a sad anticlimax.[88]

Butler hit back hard in the censure debate, telling Bevan that after Gaitskell's speech 'he will ... no longer need to "stoop to conquer" '[83f] – and, to the Tories' delight, the member for Ebbw Vale vigorously nodded his agreement.[90] Apart from Party feeling, they sympathised with Butler (who had recently lost both wife and father), and felt their usual class rancour against a Wykehamist on the other side.[91] The press also thought Gaitskell had gone too far, though the Conservatives had hurled far wilder (and less justified) charges at Attlee's government.[92a] But even in private Gaitskell was utterly unrepentant. H ewrote to Douglas Jay in the United States:

> I launched a ferocious attack on Butler and deeply shocked the prim Manchester Guardian and other similar papers. Nevertheless, I think it was justified, and as you can imagine the Party approved ... It really is staggering what they [the Government] have the face to say and do.[93]

The Opposition kept up a prolonged campaign against the Finance Bill which delighted their rank and file, and forced an all-night sitting from which they snatched one of those tactical triumphs which enormously raise Opposition morale. 'Gaitskell made no attempt to hog everything for himself, but led a team that kept continuously on the offensive ... and had by far the best of the battle.'[94] The struggle had far-reaching repercussions. For Gaitskell's assault finished Butler as Chancellor; as Roy Jenkins perceptively predicted, he never introduced another Budget and Harold Macmillan soon replaced him as the dominant influence in Eden's government.[83c] On the other side, it affected the leadership. The close collaboration between Gaitskell and Wilson was suspect to some senior trade unionists in and out of Parliament.[26h] But Attlee told the Chief Whip that with those two in harmonious alliance he could safely retire at last.[95-6]

iii *Attlee Takes His Time*

Gaitskell did not campaign for the Party leadership, and was indeed reluctant to stand in 1955. He was always a political professional, seeking power to put his principles into practice, not a preacher spreading the word in the wilderness. But ambition never consumed him, and he would willingly have served under another acceptable leader. He was still young, and until the last minute hoped only to replace Morrison as deputy leader when the latter succeeded Attlee. Even in October 1955 he agreed with Gordon Walker that that outcome would be best for both the Party and himself.[97]

That was not false modesty. He had considered standing for deputy leader in 1953 if Morrison did not;[34b] and from 1954 he was talked of as the next leader but one.[98] On 15 December 1954 he and Arthur Deakin lunched at the St Ermin's Hotel with a maverick right-wing Labour MP, Stanley Evans, and agreed that Morrison was still their candidate when Attlee retired.[99] By June there was a strong demand for a younger successor, and Gaitskell was tipped;[100] but he still 'argued most determinedly' that

Morrison should have a turn first.[101] The pressure continued over the summer.[102a b] When supporters appealed to him 'to dish Bevan by settling the leadership once for all', he answered that he would play no part, and he would not commit himself either way.[103] Just before the Margate Conference a Gallup poll found that if Attlee retired, Morrison and Gaitskell would be equally acceptable, with Bevan far behind among supporters of all parties.[104] At the same time, Gaitskell told the Chief Whip that Morrison should have his turn.[105]

The trade union leaders had never loved Morrison, but during the Bevan expulsion crisis he was still their candidate.[106] That affair had turned them against Attlee, and their rumblings continued at Margate,[64e] where some hardliners like George Brown suspected Gaitskell of moving too far to the Left in quest of the leadership.[107] But Gaitskell's main aim was to stop Bevan, and he consented to stand himself only when Morrison's parliamentary reputation and performance declined so fast that this became the best way of doing so.

The possibility was in his mind early in the recess, for he had warned Morrison then that he 'wd certainly [stand] if there were any chance of Bevan winning. This was before the slump in Bevan's position had become clear'.[103] By September his tactical analysis had changed, for after Attlee ruled out a 'Victorian' successor, Gaitskell still said firmly that he would not split Morrison's vote; he might have to reconsidei if drafted by a great many MPs, but 'I don't think that likely'.[64f] He changed his mind only when 'with the greatest difficulty he was persuaded that Morrison might well be a loser, and, even if not so, a played-out and inadequate leader';[102b] and that Bevan's only hope lay in Morrison's failings.

Bevan had wrecked his chances by quitting the Shadow Cabinet in 1954 and by his intransigence in the subsequent year. As Attlee told Crossman the day the PLP had voted to withdraw the whip, 'Nye had the leadership on a plate. I always wanted him to have it. But you know, he wants to be two things simultaneously, a rebel and an official leader, and you can't be both.'[108] Many of Bevan's followers knew it. A few, like Crossman and Wilson, now thought Gaitskell far preferable to Morrison;[26i] most did not. Hunter recalled that after Attlee said he did not want a successor from the Victorian age,

> the Bevanites began, with that unanimity which so oddly marked their opinions long after their group had been disbanded, to discover that 'poor old Herbert' was getting a raw deal ... Passionately Barbara Castle explained to me that, though she had disagreed with so many of Herbert's ideas on policy in the past, his record had earned him the right to a short period of leadership.[109]

Had they previously shown such touching concern for the deserts and reputations of the Labour leaders, the Party would have been a far happier and more effective organisation.

The Party Conference helped to crystallise opinion. Morrison and Gaitskell both did well, and many journalists left Margate convinced that the former would soon succeed.[110] But Gordon Walker 'found a strong trend amongst M.P.s in Hugh's favour';[97] and the Chief Whip even told Gaitskell that Morrison was slipping so fast that Bevan might win.[111] On Friday 14 October, Gaitskell drove Harold Wilson home to Hampstead after they had done an end-of-Conference broadcast together. They stopped in a side street in Soho, and Wilson promised to support Gaitskell as the only possible leader now that Bevan had ruled himself out — provided he would seek 'accommodation not constant confrontations; which he took very well'.[96a b] Two nights later Gordon Walker reported visiting Gaitskell at home:

> I asked Hugh about Wilson as No. 2. He had made a deal with him (as George Brown had told me). We must break up the Bevanites, but Wilson was quite unreliable — an envious enemy of Hugh. He wanted Alf Robens ... I said I thought Wilson would beat Alf. It would therefore be better to put up Jim Griffiths as a caretaker. Hugh did not agree with this. But we both felt we must test out opinion in Parl.[112]

That same weekend, Robens said in Manchester that Attlee would retire in ten days when Parliament reassembled. Eight Labour MPs wrote from the Council of Europe at Strasbourg urging Gaitskell to stand; he replied that he did not believe the story.[113] On 25 October the *Daily Herald* published a curiously equivocal denial from Attlee in Malta. Morrison was urged by his friends, who were worried by Gaitskell's growing support and feared another delaying move, to tell Attlee that unless he resigned most of the Shadow Cabinet would do so. But though keen for Attlee to go, Morrison would not himself lead a split.[64g] That hesitation, and then his lamentable failure in the censure debate, suddenly eroded his remaining support.[114] In early November, under pressure from more and more MPs, Gaitskell decided to stand when the time came. Roy Jenkins recalled:

> He only swung because he was convinced by me and others that Herbert's position was very *weak*. Then he said: 'I must see him alone and tell him'. He had lunch with Herbert when he told him; he was in a great state before it; said it would be the most difficult meal of his life. He came back in a state of high euphoria, saying it was terribly easy because Herbert was euphoric too, and said: 'Of course, my boy, you go ahead if you want to, you'll be out on the first ballot'.[115]

Privately Morrison was resentful but still confident, expecting that whether

Gaitskell or Bevan was eliminated, that vote would switch to himself.[116] Gaitskell rather agreed, telling Leslie Hunter:

> At the moment he thought Herbert would just about get it, but he himself would probably have a large enough vote to make his subsequent election to the deputy leadership a certainty. But, he said, feeling was changing very rapidly and anything might happen in the next month or so.[117]

Morrison refused to recognise the decisive factor — the PLP's determination to settle the issue by choosing a younger man.[118] That factor meant that if Gaitskell did not stand, another contender of his own generation was likely to appear;[119] so that without helping Morrison, he might wreck his own prospects of succeeding later. He told the only correspondent who reproached him for denying Morrison his turn that he shared her high regard for his senior, but

> the members of the Party made up their minds that they wanted a younger man to lead them at the next Election. If I had myself refused to stand against the very strong pressure to do so, it is quite likely that somebody else would have been put up. Even if this had not happened there would undoubtedly have been a very bad affect [sic] on the morale of the Party.[120]

Gaitskell still did not think a contest imminent. On 2 November he wrote to Douglas Jay in the United States: 'There is a continual fuss going on about the leadership but as far as I can see, Clem has no intention whatever of moving on and in consequence the discussion is all rather academic as well as being regrettable.'[121] Three days later Attlee lunched with Leslie Hunter on Guy Fawkes Day and let off his own fire-cracker by revealing that he was retiring forthwith. He professed 'a savage animosity little short of sheer hatred' for Morrison, regret that Bevan had ruled himself out, and willing if not enthusiastic acceptance of Gaitskell as his likely successor.[64h] Assuming correctly that he meant to go at the beginning of December, Hunter promptly told Gaitskell who was incredulous: for Attlee had said nothing about it in their many talks at Margate, and had just agreed to his visiting the United States over the Christmas recess.[122]

Gaitskell still refused to canvass support in the PLP as all but two of his friends wanted him to.[123] They did so instead, led by Dalton, who revelled in political intrigue and operated (so his wife said) 'like elephant going through jungle — clumsy, trumpeting but sly'.[34c] Confidently he assured Attlee's PPS Arthur Moyle, 'Your old man should retire now, we've got it all sewn up for Hugh Gaitskell.'[124]

Attlee's departure was probably quite unaffected by Dalton's booming forays (which may not have helped Gaitskell's cause). Nor, despite Bevan's conspiratorial nightmares, was the leader forced out in December by the very unions and the very newspaper he had effortlessly thwarted in June and again in October.[125] The paper was the *Daily Mirror*, which did now favour Gaitskell, but which Attlee never read.[126a] The trade union pressures came from Morrison's supporters.[127] But they miscalculated badly, for Attlee leaked his intention to Hunter only ten days after his latest denial, just when the autumn Budget debate had given Gaitskell an immense advantage.[128]

Bevan as well as Gaitskell gained from the collapse of Morrison's prestige.[129] Moderate Labour MPs became alarmed that in a straight fight Bevan, backed by the Left, the miners, the Welsh and Morrison's many dedicated enemies, might even win;[130] while if Morrison won, four years under a leader so far past his best would demoralise his own wing, to Bevan's great benefit.[102a b]

By the time the House met, the Bevanites' preference for Morrison over Gaitskell was widely taken for granted.[131] It was encouraged by others, as one acquaintance testified.

> I was one of those whose advice Nye Bevan sought, at a difficult moment in his career, as to which line he should take to counter Hugh Gaitskell's bid for leadership ...
>
> I pointed out to him that he and Gaitskell were the younger of the three starters ... [so] his policy must be to disentrench his troops opposing Morrison and realign them in support of the older man in order to defeat Gaitskell. Then, when Herbert would have to hand over to a younger man, he should have a straight fight against Gaitskell, which, by that time, he might win.
>
> He did not contradict me, but remarked upon the difficulty of disentrenching your army suddenly in order to face the other way and support the enemy whom you really wished to defeat. I, in turn, could not deny this, but said that I saw no alternative — upon which we parted amicably.

This adviser to the champion of red-blooded socialism was James Stuart, Chief Whip of the Tories whom Bevan had called 'lower than vermin'.[132]

iv *Defeat of the Unholy Alliance*

On 3 November the hatchet was solemnly buried. The two old enemies met over a drink in the smoking room.[133] Morrison had authorised first Eddie Shackleton, then Dick Stokes to negotiate for him with Bevan's spokesman Leslie Hale. The terms were never defined but it was understood that Bevan would offer his support in return for second place and eventually the

N

Foreign Office.[134a b] Morrison based his strategy on picking up Bevanite votes at the second ballot;[64i] and during November his need for them increased as his support ebbed away to Gaitskell—so completely that Stokes told Hale that their talks had lost their point since he could no longer promise anything.[134a c] But the Bevanites desperately needed Morrison to split their opponents on the first round. Many close friends vainly urged him to withdraw with dignity, and Sir Hartley Shawcross wrote sadly to Gaitskell: 'He would spare himself an unhappy defeat and regain the affections of the Party if he were to do so, but I fear that he will receive contrary advice from the Bevanites.'[135] George Wigg and Emanuel Shinwell were also busy 'working up working-class sentiment against a Winchester intellectual'—so helping Bevan too, for he had a great success at the trade union group.[136]

On the morning of Wednesday 7 December, Attlee, without trying to warn Morrison, announced his retirement.[137] That night Morrison and Bevan dined together.[138] Nominations were due by 11 a.m. on Friday, and on Thursday afternoon their last 'curious and desperate manoeuvre' was mounted.[89d] Bevan told the press that he would willingly accede to the proposal of ten MPs (mostly ageing advocates of seniority)[139] that the younger men should withdraw and give Morrison an unopposed return.[140] The ten sponsors included four Bevanite sympathisers;* and also Morrison's most ardent supporters, Shinwell and Stokes. They both canvassed actively for it, as did Bevanite irreconcilables like Mikardo.[142] Several signatories had expected the rivals to be approached privately, and were astonished to see their names in print.[126c] Public pressure was no way to persuade Gaitskell, but his enemies doubtless hoped his refusal would cost him votes.

Their misjudgment was complete. The reputations that suffered were those of his two opponents, cynically allied after years of mutual hatred. Twenty MPs, many of them old Morrison men, came up to Gaitskell on the Opposition Front Bench to urge him not to withdraw.[143a b] Then 'a swarm of his backers tackled him urgently in the [division] lobby'.[126c] From the other camp, a 'nauseated' Harold Wilson warned that if Gaitskell withdrew, he would frustrate the deal by standing himself.[96a b] Desmond Donnelly wrote hastily: 'This has decided it conclusively. I have just talked to 2 Bevanites who are outraged and are voting for you, so don't have a single doubt of any kind.'[144] Crossman 'rang up Barbara and found she was as wild as I was', discovered that his local activists felt the same, and wrote a special column for Saturday's Mirror to denounce the pact.[145] Moderate left-wingers like Anthony Greenwood and Kenneth Robinson felt equally strongly.[146] James Griffiths summed up: 'It was altogether too

* Foot's list omits those four—Hale, Sir Fred Messer, Walter Monslow and W. T. Paling—and adds Tom Williams, who did not sign.[141a]

Machiavellian and created cynicism, and finally decided many to turn and vote for Hugh Gaitskell.'[147] Only *The Times* (normally so distrusted by the Bevanites) sagely commended experience and condemned sweeping change – provoking more letters urging Gaitskell to ignore it;[148] and a Beaverbrook-Bevanite hopefully predicted that Bevan might stand annually for the leadership and perhaps 'democracy will win in the end'.[149]

Gaitskell's press statement said that despite his high regard for Morrison, he felt the Party should choose.[140] When voting ended at noon on Wednesday 14 December, he was expected to win easily on the first ballot. Chuter Ede (no Gaitskellite) said on his way to the 7 p.m. announcement that he was going 'to the political funeral of two of the greatest publicity mongers I've ever known, who will be left at the post by a man who never courted publicity in his life'.[150] Virtually every available vote was cast:[151] Gaitskell had 157 to 70 for Bevan and only 40 for Morrison – by far the most convincing victory any new Labour leader has won.* It was partly a tribute to his own hard work and his recent efforts at conciliation; partly a reaction against his opponents, reflecting Bevan's contempt for Party unity and for the Labour MPs, and Morrison's dismal performance; and most of all a sign of hope that the dreary feud could be ended by settling the leadership for many years.

Gaitskell's response was impeccable. He thanked the Party and said how humble and responsible he felt.[152] Then he made a moving appeal to the man whose hopes had been so cruelly extinguished. The vote, he said, represented only their ages which they could not control: 'Herbert, you are the greatest living Socialist, there are only the years between us. I could not have done in the years given to me all that you have done in the years given to you.'[153] Saying the Movement needed Morrison's services, he begged his senior not to resign the deputy leadership. But Morrison had made up his mind beforehand – without waiting for Shinwell's call, 'Don't take it, Herbert'.[154] Gaitskell brought the meeting to its feet for Morrison's departure, then spent over half his press conference repeating his tribute. He still thought the veteran might replace him as treasurer and (as Gordon Walker had suggested)[97] become a Labour Lord Woolton to overhaul the Party's organisation – an idea which apparently did not appeal to Morgan Phillips.[89f] But until the New Year Gaitskell continued hopeful.[155]

The usual flood of congratulations recalled every period of his life. From his own class, there were a Tory MP from the Dragon School, his old Winchester housemaster Cyril Robinson, a tennis-playing neighbour from his Norfolk boyhood, and Maurice Bowra from Oxford: 'Look after your

---

* Those elected by more than 60 Labour MPs were Attlee, Wilson and Callaghan, who went to more than one ballot, and MacDonald who won by 5 in a straight fight.

health and drive Sir Antony [*sic*] to a loony bin as soon as you can before he drives everyone else.' Bowra's friend Mrs Ian Fleming drily supposed that 'If we *have* to have a labour party, it is as well you should lead it'. Among the prominent were Sir Donald Fergusson from Fuel and Power, Sir Kenneth Clark of the Arts Council, and Lord Cobbold of the Bank of England; abroad, Douglas Abbott the former Canadian Finance Minister, Averell Harriman the Governor of New York, and Tage Erlander the Swedish Socialist Prime Minister.[156]

Among Labour friends, R. H. Tawney wrote:

> The decisive majority ... made me feel a stronger confidence in the future than recently I have. And, on more personal grounds, it was a great pleasure to know that one whose courage, in addition to other qualities, I admire is to be in command.

A venerable retired Labour couple – who had heard Keir Hardie and known John Burns 'before he deserted us for Asquith' – echoed Tawney rather touchingly: 'I express the thoughts of all of *our* generation ... We both hope to be spared, to enjoy another 1945, with yourself at Downing Street, and somehow, by your Leadership now, we feel a sense of new political security.' Elizabeth Pakenham struck a similar note: it had been 'so dreary working for Labour the last few times, but now all is energy and confidence again'. There were old friends like George Keeling from Nottingham days, and Mrs Grieveson from Chatham, and casual acquaintances like the Balliol undergraduate he had met at dinner, or 'the woman you shared tea with in a café' in Norfolk.[156] Here was the friendly, approachable man, intensely interested in everyone he met – so familiar to his constituents and so misunderstood by the metropolitan journalists and by parliamentary rivals; the fallible individual who had forgotten to pay his subscription to the Party of which he had just become leader; the unassuming character who was speaking to the WEA in his constituency only two days later.[157]

Gaitskell did not win the leadership by being a nice man who made friends easily. He reaped the reward of years of hard work, arguing assiduously and persuasively in the PLP, and becoming in the House itself 'the mainstay of the Opposition. Bevan lost primarily because he treated the parliamentary Labour Party with barely concealed contempt'.[158] Having always dismissed the Labour MPs as irrelevant, in June 1955 Bevan suddenly discovered, as Crossman noted, that they mattered after all.[26l] He had waited too long.

Gaitskell's personality helped, however; for 'The House of Commons always judges a member by his character rather than by his intelligence or his opinions. What it is trying to do is to find the men whom it can trust in a crisis.'[92c] But his vote surpassed most prior estimates.[159] It was so impressive because of a political factor: the urge to settle the debilitating succession struggle. Feeling that urge too, Labour supporters in the country probably shared the MPs' preference.[160] When Crossman announced the result at a Devon by-election meeting, 'there was a spontaneous round of cheers, and this means that every Labour person now feels we have a Leader and can say who the next Prime Minister will be and feels that makes a difference'.[26J]

In the House, Gaitskell carried the northerners and over two-thirds of the Scots, and cut into Morrison's London base.[161] The campaign against Wykehamist intellectuals failed, for 'the trade union group were behind him [almost] to a man'.[123a] Determined anti-Bevanites appreciated 'your steadfastness and courage. You have been a rock in moments of despair. Without you the Parliamentary Party would have jumped off the deep end as well as the rank and file'.[162] But the centre of the Party, so suspicious of both intransigent groups, had recently come to see him as a conciliator with 'a great power of adjusting different points of view'.[126d] Only three years after Morecambe, most constituency party representatives on the NEC voted to be led by the author of the Stalybridge speech; and the editor of *Reynolds*, who had denounced him then, now wired: 'particularly glad that the majority is convincing'.[163] In Gaitskell's first press conference he showed his current mood if not his settled opinion: for when asked what he thought of Attlee's comment that the leader should be 'a little left of centre', he replied: 'That suits me.'[164]

His two principal ex-Bevanite supporters sent characteristic messages. Crossman wrote:

> I am *unqualifiedly* glad that you are now the Leader. I am also even gladder that there is now no fence with each of us on his own side. Personally – and because I like Dora very much – it is nice to feel we can be friends again.
>
> But I want you also to know that I am not a bandwaggon kind of person. My value to the Party, so far as I have one, is as an awkward independent ideas man who can always be relied on to chase an idea further than is convenient.
>
> Be that as it may, yesterday was a very good day for the Party.

Gaitskell replied, to Crossman's delight:[165]

> Nobody in their senses could possibly accuse you of jumping on to band-waggons. On the contrary I could make out something of a case against you for jumping *off* rather than *on* at some moments during the last 10 years! ... God knows we want the ideas ... and I know you'll play a big part in providing them. But we also need more skilled but straightforward on-the-Party-line anti-Government debating in the House.[166]

Wilson paid tribute to his 'superb speech from the chair', shrewdly warned that there might now be a slight reaction, and promised the

> fullest loyalty. In my view, the issue of the leadership is settled for twenty years (though this does not rule out a possible extension). We cannot afford during those years the intrigues & 'Attlee-must-go' type of manoeuvres that have characterised the past. I think that those of us who will be closely associated with you really owe you a pledge that they will have none of it or be associated with backstairs intrigues. For my part, you have that pledge. If ever I felt – for reason of developments which I certainly can't foresee – that any change were required, I would tell you frankly & not listen to any one else's views on the subject ... above all we will keep in closest touch. You start off with the full support of all men of goodwill.[167]

Others from the Left greeted the result in the friendliest terms, often referring to Gaitskell's work in the House. Anthony Greenwood said that thanks to him and Wilson:

> It is many years since the P.L.P. was in such good heart and many of us are happier than we have been for a long time. The Party seems at last to have shaken off its preoccupation with its own internal problems and to have gone all out for an attack on the Tories ...
>   Everybody with a contribution to make, whether they are usually regarded as being Left, Right or Centre, have [sic] been brought into play.[168]

The moderate Left alone could not end Labour's feud. That depended on Bevan, who as usual was ambivalent. With the PLP tide running strongly, he had told Crossman earlier: 'You can't force the Party to accept Gaitskell, and I must warn you that, if he is Leader, I might not be able to collaborate'. But he added cautiously: 'Gaitskell might be more acceptable in nine months' time than now'; and Crossman concluded: 'once the change has taken place, he will accept it'.[26k] Gaitskell did his best, saying as soon as Morrison walked out: 'Nye, we haven't got on in the past, but if you will accept this vote, as I would have had to accept it if it had gone the other way, I promise you I will not be outdone in generosity.'[153] (Charlie Pannell thought it his finest moment.) Bevan replied offering congratulations and support, and wishing Gaitskell 'higher office'.[169]

Those first seeds of reconciliation took a year or two to flower, yet on the very next day, 'Nye was already busy finding out if he stood a chance of being elected Deputy Leader ... despite the fact that only a fortnight ago [he] had been talking of walking out of the Party if Gaitskell was elected.'[170] He contested the vacancy in order to show his willingness to serve under

Gaitskell; and his high poll again showed the MPs' eagerness to end the feud.[171]

Attlee summed up with his famous terseness:

> I was delighted with your vote which was just about what I had anticipated. It was a pity that Herbert insisted on running. He had, I think, been warned of the probable result.
>
> I hope that Nye & Co will now go all out to support you. I think that there was a good deal of 'gesture' in his vote ...
>
> I wish you and Dora all happiness and success & if there is anything which I can do to help, you may be sure I will.[172]

The tone shows no trace of the animosity implied in the Bevanite version of Attlee's attitude.[141b] But their relationship still had a curious edge. Gaitskell had recorded a year earlier that Attlee

> remains as inscrutable as ever. He has still got extremely good political judgment. His idea of leadership, of course, is more that of an Eisenhower than a Truman ... He is very much concerned with Party unity, and this leads him to make concessions to the Left. He is sometimes, I think, not as honest as he should be in opposition, regarding it as quite reasonable to take a line which he knows he would not take in Government. For this, of course, there are plenty of precedents, and nobody has been worse at it than Churchill. He is still unapproachable, difficult to talk to, and without, so far as one can see, any intimates at all.[6c]

At the Gaitskells' usual noisy and crowded New Year party in the rambling Frognal house, Attlee sat quietly in a corner with perhaps 100 people milling about in the big room. Suddenly he called for silence and offered a toast: 'To the Leader of the Labour Party!' Blushing furiously, Gaitskell rushed in from next door to thank him: 'I'm very touched, Clem. I wasn't expecting anything like that.' *Sotto voce* but not quite inaudibly, his predecessor muttered: 'You'd no right to, either!'[173]

A few years later, just before the 1959 election defeat and the crisis of his career, Gaitskell gave his own assessment in a letter to a friend who thought his triumph astonishing:

> It isn't really. It was forecast over 20 years ago that I would be Foreign Secretary or Chancellor. The leadership came my way so early because Bevan threw it at me by his behaviour. Ask yourself about the Labour Party now — if not me then who?
>
> Qualities? Perfectly ordinary ones — intelligence, hard work, capacity for getting on easily with people — and — which is what always surprises people — some moral courage. Of course there are great weaknesses — don't I know it! But the whole subject is boring.

CHAPTER 13

LABOUR'S NEW CHAMPION

'Compared with Attlee I am a furnace'
(HG ON HIS ALLEGED COLDNESS)
'It is much more likely that I shall be a failure than a sham'
(HG, 1958)

---

i *The Man and His Friends*

HUGH GAITSKELL was forty-nine, the youngest Party leader that twentieth-century Britain had yet seen. He was one of the least known to the public, for his rise had been very rapid: it was only ten years since he had entered Parliament, eight since he had become a Minister, five since he had joined the Cabinet. He was also the least understood; his personality was less like the public impression of him than that of any other front-rank political figure (except perhaps for his opposite number, Sir Anthony Eden). Being best known as actual or Shadow Chancellor, he could not shake off the label of the desiccated calculating machine: 'about as big a misjudgment', wrote a very old journalistic friend, 'as anybody could make of a man, most of whose political weaknesses came from too much emotionalism'.[1] It was equally inappropriate to the private individual, who enjoyed life thoroughly, was an enthusiastic dancer, found official functions boring, and was quite determined not to subordinate personal friendships to the pursuit of political advantage.

Physically Gaitskell was not particularly imposing: a well-built energetic man of medium height, with curly brown hair, blue eyes, a fresh complexion, and no very prominent features for the cartoonists to seize on. Rebecca West had once cattily said that if he entered a room with someone else, eyes turned to the other person;[2] and his PPS thought that Gaitskell himself felt he lacked presence.[3a b] He was never obsessed with politics like some of his colleagues. He liked going to the theatre and opera. His literary tastes extended from Shakespeare to P. G. Wodehouse and Simenon. On holiday he went back to old favourites like Proust, Hardy and his wartime discovery, Henry James; and all the great Russians, Tolstoy, Chekhov, Turgenev, Dostoevsky. He kept up with new novels, which Dora used to select for him; and his range impressed a friendly publisher.[4] Like so many politicians he enjoyed Trollope, but his reading was less confined to history and biography than that of many colleagues. Most of all he adored poetry, invariably reading a little every night before going to bed. Shakespeare's *Sonnets* came first in his affections, and then Yeats, though he had nineteenth-century favourites too. There was great excitement when he found a copy of Meredith's sonnet sequence *Modern Love* in Norman's Hampstead secondhand bookshop; in 1959, he wrote quite a long comment on an analysis of it by an Oxford undergraduate friend of Julie's.[5]

His home life was happy—especially so, in the view of some MPs, for a prominent politician.[6] Yet during the week he saw almost nothing of his family. Domestic weekends were rare, often only one in four or seven.[7–8a] He loved his garden, especially his irises; and once replanned it, turning all the lawns into flowerbeds and vice versa.[9] He worked at it strenuously, and said gardening had ruined more men than drink.[10] In less energetic moods he was fond of listening to great jazz singers like Ella Fitzgerald and Billie Holliday; he was once buying records in Oxford Street with Cressida, who had gone off for more, when to his mild embarrassment a lady MP (Elaine Burton, who had been told 'the Chancellor of the Exchequer is here') entered the cubicle where the new Leader of the Opposition, alone, was cheerfully dancing to the music.[11a] He was a great fan both of Greta Garbo and—unlike his wife—of Mae West. Though for years he had no television set either at home or in his room at Westminster, in the constituency friends arriving to talk politics might be firmly shushed until the end of the Western he was avidly watching.[12]

The Gaitskells lived comfortably but not extravagantly in a prosperous, cultured suburban environment. They ran no car when Hugh was in office, and bought only one new one during the next eleven years; a Wolseley acquired before the 1959 election, number VLX1—a happy symbol, said someone, for 'Vote Labour X'. The house was always full, with Hugh's mother and stepfather living there; and an old schoolfellow Charles Plumb and his wife on the top floor. Hugh was not allowed to help in his years of overwork and eminence; Dora did all the cooking and ran the household and family affairs with a daily help and a friend to garden twice a week. Hugh confessed to conservatism only over food and women's clothes: 'I like good roast beef, best English sausages, potted shrimps, apple pie, ginger cakes. And it always takes me time to adjust to any new fashion—especially in hats.'[10]

The girls went to school first at King Alfred's on the edge of the Heath, a co-educational school with an old if somewhat muted progressive tradition; and then to Queen's College, a day school in Harley Street, from which Cressida later transferred to North London Collegiate at Edgware. Middle-class Labour politicians of that generation often sent their children to private schools; it seems to have aroused little domestic argument or public criticism. But Gaitskell found it embarrassing. He called it a transitional problem which parents must decide in the children's interests:

> I don't think it reasonable to criticise parents for doing that ... [or] inconsistent to say we wish to ... not be faced with this extremely difficult choice ... we ought to have such a good state system of education that in fact private schools just didn't come into the picture ... But ... unless you happen to have a very good state school fairly near it is difficult.[13]

Gaitskell was most scrupulous over financial matters great and small. On becoming leader, when the Co-operative Societies still wished to pay him the agreed retainer for chairing a committee of inquiry into their affairs, he declined because he would have much less time for it. When he consented to sign an election article for the *Mirror*, written by a member of its staff, he insisted that the fee must go to the Labour Party.[14] He set an example to other ex-Ministers from economic Departments by avoiding any entanglement with business,[15] turning down all offers of directorships or consultancies,[16] and declining a gift of shares worth £30,000 from his old Nottingham friend George Keeling, the ex-miner who had become a wealthy manufacturer.[15] During the early 1950s he was not particularly well off, kept quite a careful eye on expenses, and was glad to earn a little extra by his articles and lectures both abroad and at home: in 1954 he wrote to a friend of 'the 101 things one has to do, some for money, mostly for nothing'.[17] But (unlike so many Bevanites who accused him of lack of principle) he would never take money from Lord Beaverbrook.[11b] Subsequently he was economical more from upbringing than necessity, for later in the decade his financial situation improved substantially.[18]

Election to the leadership limited but otherwise did not much affect his home life. The Gaitskells entertained from time to time and were excellent hosts. Hugh still kept his diverse friends in compartments, mixing them up only occasionally at a big party. There might be a lunch or an evening for trade union leaders, a foreign ambassador and his wife, or a visitor like Adlai Stevenson or Kwame Nkrumah, with interested political colleagues. But he would not use his home as an annex of his office, and he always insisted that politicians were human and needed some private life. Few of his guests at Frognal Gardens were there because of their political status; and those parliamentary colleagues who came were those he found congenial rather than those he calculated could be useful. Most Labour Premiers have entertained little, and Crossman thought that with Gaitskell in Downing Street and Chequers, social life would have been skilfully used to smooth over tensions in the Party.[19] Some close friends felt he did not use it enough, and some touchy political associates felt they deserved more frequent invitations to Frognal Gardens. But grumbles against the

'Hampstead set' reveal the social weaknesses of Labour personalities rather than the political weaknesses of the Party leader.

The close personal friends of the 1950s were not, as his opponents supposed, the secret inspirers of his political outlook; that had been fixed long before he met them. They were not a kitchen cabinet of the all too familiar kind, or a substitute for the professional staff he lacked until 1959, for their talents and interests did not lie in that direction. Nor were they sycophantic courtiers hoping to ingratiate themselves – for this monarch was entirely surrounded by candid friends. They were simply a number of young, very able, like-minded individuals with whom he associated in Parliament, and whom he admired for their intelligence, culture and character. Anthony Crosland practised astringent intellectual puritanism and preached unabashed libertarianism and private enjoyment – a combination particularly attractive to Gaitskell as it recalled his own youth. Roy Jenkins, cultivated and urbane but also politically courageous, seemed to Gaitskell to show sounder judgment and was also an attractive companion. The leader was aware of their weaknesses and occasionally not quite sure of their seriousness. But he insisted on the primacy of personal relationships, and would not give them up when they later became, as he knew, a political embarrassment. 'Kings who had favourites were never popular', he wrote privately in June 1960, listing among the sins which were held against him 'kicking against the pricks of loneliness – in other words wanting to continue to have friends – real ones ... I put that as something I want especially to try & keep.'

Gaitskell's mother, Mrs Wodehouse, died suddenly and painlessly on 14 October 1956. She was, wrote her cousin who had been 'proxy grandfather' at Hugh's christening, 'one of the gayest and at the same time the kindest person that I have ever met ... I think the parson thought it [the christening ceremony] was a little too frivolous.' Hugh owed to her much of his zest and vitality; and they had been far closer latterly than in his youth when they were usually separated, he in England and she in Rangoon, an enthusiastic social leader of the local community. During and after the war she was home again, and Hugh's career gave her an interest in politics she had never shown before: from a non-voter she became a Labour loyalist, called her son 'the Minister' even to close friends, and frequently attended the House of Commons.[20] She had a flat during the week in his Frognal Gardens house, and he was often with her at Milland.

Her death marked a double break, for besides the sadness of the bereavement itself, it cut his last link with that village, to which for twenty years he had occasionally managed to flee. He had disposed of his own house, Sweatmans, in 1946 (without making any profit on it).[21] But he had retained thirty acres next door to his mother's, with a picturesque but condemned old cottage farmhouse called Maysleith, which he had bought in 1941 hoping to renovate it or build on the site. In 1954 he sadly abandoned the idea, and two years later, just before she died, he sold the land (again for no more than he had paid for it).[22] Apart from Milland, he and Dora liked to escape for weekends to Abbotsbury in Dorset, or Washington in Sussex, or to stay in Kent with old friends like the Balcons or the Brooks. They played a lot of croquet, and in the evenings indoor games like L'Attaque: 'he always knew all the rules, he was frightfully good, he was always *determined* to win'.[23a] Real holidays, in the summer, were entirely carefree but by no means inactive, for he believed that expeditions made a vacation seem longer. He was keen on swimming and boating, exploring all the local scenic beauties and historical attractions, and — as always — making new friends. In the early 1950s the Gaitskells were particularly fond of Pembrokeshire; later they went abroad — to Italy and Yugoslavia — partly for the sake of privacy. On holiday he was always totally relaxed, forgetting his public responsibilities and cherishing the rare opportunity to see his family.[5a b]

As a guest the Leader of the Opposition is much in demand, and Gaitskell rather enjoyed being lionised. After 1955 his social activities expanded markedly. He had always found parties irresistible, especially if they included dancing; he and Dora liked good food and wine and conversation; he would flirt light-heartedly for an evening with a pretty woman. He wrote to his daughter at Oxford in 1958:

> You know what a pleasure lover I am. So you must not expect a puritan outlook from me! Pleasure is not only all right but good so long as it is not too selfish or too undermining of one's capacity to do whatever it is one *can* do ... if you have too much of it (in the crude sense) you react against it & look round for a little monasticism.[8b c]

He and Macmillan were about to be given honorary degrees at Oxford (by accident on the same day), and though he found stuffy official functions tedious, he was looking forward to staying with Bowra and to 'lots of junketing'.[8d] He perhaps felt it was a side of life he had neglected, and seems to have consciously striven to make up for lost time.[24] He was confident in his own integrity, and imprudently indifferent to the reactions of others.

His enjoyment of social life was not confined to London society, though like most of us (and like almost all politicians) he enjoyed gossip and found plenty of it at these dinner parties, which might even yield useful political intelligence. But he was happy too with accidental and unknown acquaintances — hitchhikers to whom he gave a lift, neighbours on a flight, people in a railway waiting room.[25] Staying with friends in a village 'he charmed everyone, he was so interested in everybody and everything they were doing—whoever he was talking to was the only person in the world for him'.[23][a][b][c]

He never forgot people he had known long before he became famous. He had not been a close friend of Eric Cash, the Party secretary at Chatham, but Gaitskell went out of his way to help when Cash asked his advice twenty years later.[26] At an export promotion conference in the 1950s, he spotted the civil servant who had been his secretary on the Materials Committee eleven years before, and deserted the dignitaries to go and chat.[27] He was concerned about his political colleagues simply as people, and sat for two hours in the hospital when Crossman's wife was dying, in case he might be needed.[28a]

The Winchester motto is 'Manners Makyth Man', and Gaitskell was renowned among friends and opponents alike for his courtesy and considerateness. As a civil servant and Minister, he had earned goodwill for 'doing the unpleasant thing in a pleasant manner'.[29] As a party politician he often astonished peevish correspondents on both Left and Right by the patience and thoroughness of his replies.[30] 'His gift of getting along with all kinds of people', wrote one journalist, 'is his main political capital.'[31] Emanuel Shinwell spoke of his 'inordinate and phenomenal politeness';[32] and the Liberal leader Jo Grimond said he had 'the best political manners of anyone I have known'.[33]

Now and then he could be insensitive. A young Fabian official (an admirer and later a valued supporter) was upset when Gaitskell said publicly that the many misprints in his Fabian pamphlet were not his fault (after he had been late with the proofs). When after many talks Kenneth Younger finally gave up his Grimsby seat, Gaitskell after only perfunctory regrets at once inquired whether Crosland could win it. But more typical were the Labour candidate in 1950, harassed by criticisms of the Government's fuel policies, who was impressed by the Minister's understanding of the questioner's worry as well as by the thoroughness of his answers; the close Jewish friend in Leeds whom he phoned on the night of his Suez broadcast to reassure her that he was not turning against Israel; the inexperienced author of another Fabian pamphlet on which he performed necessary and devastating surgery with extreme kindness.[34]

He was insistent on maintaining the dignity of his office as leader. He declined to speak on a Liberal motion at the Oxford Union, or indeed at all except against one of the four senior Conservative leaders: 'If I were to debate against Macleod who is Minister of Labour—very pushing—it would *downgrade* the whole party.'[8c][e] Even for close colleagues, a summons to Gaitskell's room at the House had some flavour of an invitation to the headmaster's study.[35] Back in 1945 he had rather disliked his supporters' exploitation of his wartime CBE in the campaign;[36] but as leader he made sure that the letters followed his name on the report of the Co-operative inquiry.[37] Crossman even wrote once of his 'naive self-importance'.[28b]

Off duty he was quite different. One lady who had known him since the 1930s thought of him as one of the very few politicians who 'never turned into a balloon';[38a] another, a later but closer friend, said much the same:

> He had *absolutely* no side at all. I've never in my life met anybody else who wasn't altered by his position ... who didn't get a tremendous weight of importance on their shoulders. It was a completely individual characteristic of Hugh ... at the dinner table he would sit completely silent while two other people were talking about a subject that he knew about and they didn't. He was absolutely unassuming ... he was a very good listener and he didn't have that thing of getting the conversation round to him, unlike anybody else.'[38b c]

He was indeed an excellent listener, particularly with the young.[39] Yet even quite close associates, who had known him for years, felt they could not penetrate the curtain of reserve behind the courteous affability. (A few emphatically denied its existence: usually women.)

His dislike of privilege and pomposity persisted after he became leader of his Party. When he next visited the United States, the official American brief described him as 'Totally devoid of pretentiousness and self-importance';[40] and he insisted on flying tourist to the dismay of his wealthy trade union sponsors.[41a] In Milan, the Congress for Cultural Freedom allotted him an expensive luxury hotel, from which he and the family promptly moved. Meeting new acquaintances at the annual Anglo-German encounters at Koenigswinter, he would introduce himself quite naturally, never expecting them to know he was Leader of the Opposition.[42]

On holiday abroad he valued privacy above all. He would ask friends to suggest good cheap obscure restaurants in France;[15] and on official visits he eagerly escaped from constraints, and dismayed his younger companions by his nocturnal energy and enthusiasm.[43] Leslie Hunter recalled:

> One week-end he had left home at dawn, flown to Copenhagen and spent the whole day at an extremely tricky meeting of the Socialist International. It was followed by an official dinner which broke up about midnight. My wife and I were sneaking off when Gaitskell caught us and demanded to be taken somewhere to dance. For the next three hours he was giving brilliant expositions of 'jive' and 'bepop' with a crowd of youngsters ... though some years younger than Gaitskell, I felt balding and middle-aged beside him in this company. He was very much at home.[44]

As Leader of the Opposition, doing far too much himself and with a jealously guarded timetable, he found it far harder to keep spontaneous contact with ordinary people. Political opponents on the Left therefore reproached him with being cold and remote—at which he once privately protested: 'Compared with Attlee I am a furnace'. But he did his utmost to keep in touch with the working-class roots of the Party. He was always welcome and at ease in the flourishing workingmen's clubs of the West Riding; he enjoyed and drew strength from meeting ordinary Labour supporters on provincial tours,[*sf*] and in time became much more relaxed and spontaneous in those surroundings.

It was not an impression he always managed to convey from the platform or the television studio. People brought into direct contact with him, after knowing him only as a public figure, were struck time and again by the niceness of the man:

> he tends at a distance to create an impression almost wholly different from that he does in his direct personal relations.
>
> His friendliness, warmth and humour are veiled by distance. The intellectual ability and integrity, the logic and power of objective judgment, communicate. But not the emotional fire that gives them life.[45]

ii *The Politician and His Style*

Gaitskell worked himself far too hard. He managed his time better than he had as Chancellor, no longer letting his appointments run later and later during the day. But he still would never waste a moment, and did everything at the last possible minute—notably catching trains, which he always ran recklessly close.[46] On the way to a meeting he would compose his speech, and in a slow question time he might write a newspaper article.[47] If he had his secretary in Leeds he would dictate correspondence to her in the car. (Sometimes he drove up, and in his careful way he worked out the least time-consuming route—that later adopted for the M1.)[48] Friends warned him constantly to slow down, drop trivial engagements, run a marathon not a sprint, conserve his energies for the long haul.[49] The worst strain, emotional as well as physical, came later when his leadership was threatened; but from the start he took on much too much.

One typical week, about a year after he became leader, began at 10.15 on Monday morning with a study group discussing policy for the nationalised industries. He lunched with Leslie Murphy, his former private secretary, to talk about the oil industry where Murphy now worked (it was soon after Suez). In the afternoon he attended three sub-committees of the National Executive, and went on to a trade union dinner. On Tuesday and Wednesday there were four more sub-committees, an all-party committee on broadcasting, an appointment with a trade union leader, meetings of the

PLP and the Shadow Cabinet—the House was sitting—and a Downing Street dinner for the Crown Prince of Iraq; the previous evening the leader had dined with the government's Chief Scientific Adviser, his old friend Sir Solly Zuckerman. On Thursday he met in turn a Transport House official, a journalist, the Prime Minister of Malta, a Manchester civic dignitary, and the parliamentary lobby; he lunched with the editor of the *Manchester Guardian*, and dined with Crosland. On Friday, when he did not have to be at Westminster, he had three long morning appointments (one with a difficult Co-operative Commission member); spoke that evening at a meeting of a London local Party; and afterwards, accompanied by Dora and Julie, had dinner with an MP. Both the previous and the next weekend were fairly free; on the Saturday he was dining with an economists' club in Oxford, and visited Crossman's near-by farm on the way. Most weekends were busier than that, but sometimes the week itself was broken up by provincial rallies and meetings, short trips abroad, and receptions for distinguished foreign visitors—or interrupted by a call on the Prime Minister, a session of the Independent Co-operative Commission, or a meeting of the House of Commons Privileges Committee.

Correspondence was substantial. Constituency cases were no longer a flood as they had been just after the war, but they still generated about twenty letters a month. Routine mail flowed in from the general public, and from people concerned with current problems. Some problems attracted enough attention to be filed separately: for instance prisoners in Hungary, the crisis in Cyprus, Labour's big policy-making exercise, the reform of the Co-ops, the affairs of the Socialist International, politics in Scotland. Apart from all these, he would receive on average more than one letter a day of a serious kind. Over half of those came from a variety of sources—foreign ambassadors or British diplomats, Transport House officials and local Labour worthies, prominent foreign Socialists, British journalists or academics or former MPs, an occasional Gaitskell relative, or a professional organisation with a problem. The rest were from parliamentary colleagues, discussing an item of domestic policy, writing informatively from abroad about the situation in a foreign country, giving advice or praise or criticism about his handling of that week's parliamentary crisis (if it were a serious one, there would be twice as many letters from MPs). He was scrupulous in replying, and also in sending condolences to the sick or bereaved.

His tiny staff were also worked hard. On a senior level he had no one until 1959, when John Harris came for the election campaign. Harris stayed on afterwards as personal assistant, public relations adviser and link-man with the press. Gaitskell's PPS was normally a fairly elderly trade unionist MP (he briefly had two PPS's towards the end) and was used as a sounding-board for opinion in the PLP but not much for substantive

35 Hugh Gaitskell is elected Leader of the Party in December 1955. At
that evening's press conference at Transport House

36 Suez demonstration in Trafalgar Square, November 1956, with Bevan as the main speaker. When Gaitskell spoke at a mass meeting in the Albert Hall two nights later, the cease fire had been announced

37 Underground with Nottingham-shire miners in 1957

38 With President Tito in Yugo-slavia, 1957

39 In Delhi, with the President of India (*left*) and Prime Minister Nehru in December 1957

40 Homework with his daughter Julie, 1957

41 With Prime Minister Harold Macmillan, receiving honorary degrees at Oxford in 1958. His old schoolfellow John Sparrow, Warden of All Souls, is on his left

matters. The leader took advice on specific subjects from the Shadow Cabinet colleague or Transport House official concerned, and sometimes even accepted their drafts. But his confidence in Party headquarters was limited, and in particular those who differed from him politically found him hard to work for, feeling he would never leave them alone. Indeed, his redrafting itch was a trial to everyone, and a serious misuse of his time and energy;[50] though it did usually lead to genuine improvements.[51] He had a secretary as Leader of the Opposition, Mrs Skelly, whom he inherited from Attlee and who came from the Labour Party staff; she found him 'a marvellous boss' who gave you a job to do and left you to get on with it. But when asked about Suez being a specially hectic time, she replied that she could not remember a period that wasn't. Gaitskell's wife felt exactly the same.[52]

Some people thought him a worrier, and everyone remembers his fussiness over detail. Yet he would deal easily with several problems in quick succession, switching his orderly mind from a major academic lecture to a constituency visit and then to a personal letter to a fretful colleague.[46] Off duty, he forgot his problems at once and relaxed completely. And he never worried in the least about his capacity to carry the responsibilities of government. In his day Conservative leaders still felt born to rule, and their supporters saw Labour administrations as passing aberrations. Even on the Labour benches those feelings were widely shared. Attracting natural critics and gadflies, used to opposition and its familiar outlook, the Labour Party had – like the Republicans in the United States – developed deep-seated psychological reflexes which still operated when it astonished itself by winning an election. Defeatism and opposition-mindedness were so widespread that a sympathetic Transport House official thought Gaitskell the only Labour leader who genuinely felt far better qualified to run the country than the men in power.[53]

Yet he was born, one profile-writer wrote, with one skin too few.[54] As he wrote about the daughter of a Hampstead friend: 'I quite understand her being sensitive to aggression from others. This one has to overcome, and does in time, though it is a painful process.'[55] He cared a great deal about his friends and their opinions, and took immense time and trouble to explain his own views to unknown correspondents. His thin skin, and his consciousness of his own ability and integrity, help explain his occasional unwise concern at attacks in the press – which he himself once attributed to his knowledge of his own inadequacies. Most political leaders react irritably to the media – Kennedy and Johnson no less than Wilson and Heath (to say nothing of Nixon); and Gaitskell would sometimes write an enormous letter to the offending journalist, both correcting error and explaining the rectitude of his own stand.[56]

He was a thoroughly professional politician, who used the public relations salesmen but kept them in their place. After one favourable interview
which he found 'rather nauseating', he promised his daughter:

> [A]bove all, you need never worry that I shall be 'merely the man they
> attempt to put over' ... the one thing that matter[s is] 'to be oneself'.
> I have never changed my mind about that and I really don't have any
> fears that I ever shall do. It is much more likely that I shall be a failure
> than a sham.[8g]

He kept his sense of balance, and never shared Bevan's intense suspicion
of advertising men and all their works. Indeed he welcomed their technical
help in campaigns, and overcame the Labour Party's deep distaste for
public opinion research.[57] Again unlike Bevan, he saw that mastering television technique was now indispensable to a politician, and patiently spent
many weary hours in rehearsal.[28c] But he detested the whole notion of
manipulating personalities in order to improve the 'image' of public
figures, and would never dream of lending himself to such an operation.[58]
The Party leader traditionally read the lesson in church on the morning
before Conference; Gaitskell, because his friends knew he was not religious,
was most reluctant even to attend[59] — though once persuaded, he characteristically sought advice on how to read the lesson.[47]

Gaitskell was quite a shrewd judge of character. He leaned towards in-
dulgence, particularly perhaps with women; though when he met Jacqueline
Kennedy at the zenith of the Camelot myth, he thought her shallow and
superficial.[23b] He felt serious doubts about endorsing as a Labour candidate a businessman of acceptable views and excellent sponsorship, who
later acquired a wider but mixed reputation as an MP.[60] The chairman of
a pro-Labour popular newspaper found Gaitskell 'a most difficult, butt-
oned-up character';[61] many political colleagues must have regretted not
having made the same impression on Cecil King when he promptly bared
their private confidences to the nation in his famously indiscreet memoirs.
In Transport House, as earlier in Whitehall, Gaitskell generally picked
good advisers; and some doubts about his judgment reflect the disappointment of Labour MPs whom he did not favour, and their resentment of
those he did. The younger politicians whom he encouraged — despite
charges of cronyism — later made their own way to the very front rank
under a Labour leader with no personal inclination to help them. But
friendship alone gave their views no extra weight in Gaitskell's mind, and
when colleagues trusted in one field advised on another, they would be told
firmly: 'That's not your subject.'[62]

His highest priority was his conviction that people should be themselves.
He assured the worried young daughter of his Hampstead friend that not

being too sure of her political views was 'a sign of political integrity –
almost the most important quality in public life'.[55] That did not impair
his dedication to his own fundamental values. Their emotional roots
had been part of him always; their intellectual foundation, solidly laid
before the war, did not shift after it.* But when this committed man dealt
with others who had a different commitment, his touch was not always
assured. He gave great weight to what he called 'the mysterious but vitally
important quality of judgment ... the highest, the most important quality
of all, which means very largely knowing what other people are thinking
and feeling and how they are going to behave'.[64] (Bevan too regarded it as
a Prime Minister's most crucial need.)[65] Yet he was very resistant to
pressures, which he often failed to anticipate. Despite – or because of – the
strength of his own emotions, he easily misunderstood or disregarded the
emotional commitments of others. So, having always believed in public
ownership just as one desirable means to accomplish Socialist ends, he
failed to foresee either the numbers or the intensity of feeling of those who
saw in it the essence of Socialism.

He prized intellectual honesty highly, and was conspicuous among public
men for his willingness to face rather than fudge difficult issues, and to
explain his reasons candidly. After he accepted an illogical compromise
motion on bomb tests in 1957, he agreed with his fellow-Wykehamist
Kenneth Younger that 'a Winchester education is a grave handicap for
this sort of operation, by making one attach too much importance in *all*
circumstances to intellectual clarity and consistency!'[66] As his troubles
mounted in January 1960, he wrote to Anne Fleming:

> I still tend to assume that people are rational & that if you go on telling
> the truth as you see it you convince them. You once lectured me on the
> need to dissemble, but I never really learnt the lesson. Someone said
> to me the other day that Macmillan obviously loved saying one thing
> and doing another – and I'm sure that's true & no doubt in politics the
> corkscrew is really what you need. It's no use being superior & goody
> goody about this, when it's really just that you can't do it that way.

One friendly journalist wrote during the 1959 election campaign: 'I have
never known him soften the uncomfortable truth to win the easy approval
of his audience.'[67] Applied to Gaitskell, that sweeping statement was less
rose-tinted than to most political figures; but he too was well aware that

---

* In a long 1955 essay by him on the ideology of British Democratic Socialism,
the latest writers given thorough treatment were Cole, Tawney, Dalton and
Durbin. Jay was mentioned as an interpreter of Keynes, and four other economic
books were given a short footnote; Strachey as a Marxist, and Laski as a writer
influential outside Britain, were quickly dismissed. Crosland's *The Future of
Socialism* came out a few months after this essay.[63]

politicians must simplify their message to reach a large audience, and that 'It's no use trying to go on being 100% academic when one is in politics.'[68] Over the years he condoned a few party propaganda statements at which the pure searcher after truth would have jibbed. Crossman, the eager practitioner of psychological warfare, records them all with reproachful surprise—reflecting Gaitskell's personal reputation rather than ordinary political standards.[28d] He was probably the 'prominent Bevanite' who told Henry Fairlie in 1955 that Gaitskell lacked 'the toughness or capacity for self-deceit which was needed in a party leader'.[69a] Soon after Gaitskell's death he said with intent to shock: 'At last we have a leader who can lie.'[70]

Crossman too was a Wykehamist; indeed their relationship was always warped, as Crossman (typically) recognised, by his own far more glittering record at the school.[28e] After supporting Gaitskell for the leadership, he wrote:

> I do know Gaitskell better than most people and realise how wrong people get him. He is not a cold man, but a person of competence with an enormous lot of rather vague emotions, which lead him often to burst into tears, a man not at all sure of himself outside his special subject, a man who felt himself a hero and a St. Sebastian when he stood up to Nye and, most serious of all, someone who takes a moralising and reactionary attitude, which is almost instinctively wrong in my opinion, on every subject outside economics. But he is also an extremely honest man and a sensible man, with the kind of mind that will take advice, who might become a very good Leader.[28f]

Gaitskell was indeed more 'moralising' than Crossman over Suez or immigration, but hardly more 'reactionary'. The casual dismissal of 'a person of competence' reflects some contempt for an utterly different intellectual style. Crossman could instantly justify by dazzling intuitions each rapid shift of political front; what the diarist saw as Gaitskell being uncertain and not knowing his own mind was rather his insistence on thinking things through before making it up. When he had done so, his views were far more stable and solidly based than Crossman's, and he was most reluctant (perhaps too much so) to sway with short-term political breezes. Whatever tactical problems that style entailed, it was much likelier than Crossman's to inspire confidence.

In pointing to Gaitskell's sense of becoming a martyr to duty, Crossman drew attention to an attitude apparent later as well as earlier in the new leader's career. At the start of 1951 Gaitskell had thought it likely that he not Bevan would have to resign office; subsequently, feeling himself much too junior to carry the burden of fighting the Bevanites in the country, he expected them to win control of the Party unless Attlee spoke out—an improbable event which occurred only after Gaitskell had again risked his own political life at Stalybridge. More than once in 1960 and 1961 he thought the next Party Conference might well be his last as leader. Nor was he buoyed up (like so many of his enemies) by any zest for that kind of battle, for he loathed faction fights among supposed comrades almost as much as he suffered from the hatred and misrepresentation directed at him personally. His attitude was far removed from the Left's myth of an arrogant politician, who would make no move until assured of victory by the big trade union battalions, and who was driven by 'cold and methodical ambition for Party power'.[71]

Gaitskell was more convinced about his own judgment than Crossman supposed. As leader he did not entirely lose his inner doubts, but they had less and less effect on his actions as his self-confidence grew. The emphasis on his strong emotions was better justified, for he had deep feelings about people and the tears did flow easily. But on public affairs those emotions were not in the least vague, but precisely directed and singularly consistent over the years. He had no sympathy at all for those left-wing enthusiasts who regretted the past with its simple choices – when ordinary human beings were miserable and frightened, but some political activists could satisfy their hunger for emotional thrills. 'His nostalgic remarks about the 30s frankly shocked me,' Gaitskell wrote to his daughter about one such writer. 'It was a horrible period and you were lucky not to be alive then!'[8e] Nor had he much sympathy for those who thought emotional drive a substitute for serious intellectual effort. When his friend Dr Rita Hinden wrote that 'Socialists must be visionaries', Gaitskell asked what she meant: if idealists, he agreed; if utopians, he dissented. A Party 'either in power or on the verge of it' could not conduct itself like 'a pioneer hoping to convert people to a general point of view but not concerned with any immediate practical problem'.[72]

Gaitskell was passionately committed to working out in an intellectually respectable way the practical political means of realising his objectives, and then to persuading people to support them by means of rational discourse. His enemies called him an elitist; it was the very reverse of the truth. Ten years after his death, David Watt commented that his were the only parliamentary speeches of the period which still read well, because they were 'the product of a calm belief that people are quite capable of understanding sophisticated arguments and responding to them'.[73] As the country's prospective Prime Minister, he remained a dedicated teacher, determined to educate and not merely cajole, anxious that people should not only do the right thing but do it for the right reason. After an interminable discussion with a group of Durham miners, he replied sharply when a friend reproached him with taking so much trouble over people who were going to vote Labour anyway. 'It's not trouble, it's the whole point of our party, that we do try and see their point of view, that we do argue the toss, that we all go forward together.'[74]

iii   A civilised Populist at Home, a Liberal Realist Abroad

For Gaitskell, always an educator, the Party leadership provided (as Theodore Roosevelt said of the American Presidency) a 'bully pulpit'. Before his election, in the same Margate speech which impressed the delegates with the sincerity of his Socialism, he had already called for serious thought about Labour's fundamental aims, concluding: 'Let the clear fresh wind of hard and fearless thinking blow through our minds and hearts.'[75] Now he had the opportunity to try to make his followers face reality as he saw it. In private he insisted on analysing situations with intellectual rigour undistorted by political calculation.[76] In public he revealed the results of that analysis much more fully than most leaders, particularly in pressing for policies which did not merely reiterate old slogans but related to genuine contemporary needs. As a journalistic admirer wrote in 1959: 'He is an enormously persuasive speaker – a surgeon, not a butcher – and he inflicts no unnecessary pain. But the incisive surgery is there to let out stale political flatulence and let in the fresh air of thought.'[67]

The need to win democratic consent for Socialist policies was Gaitskell's fundamental premise. Since his ethical priorities were equality and freedom, he decisively rejected the revolutionary road – as a short cut not to the Socialism in which he believed, but to a society without equality or freedom and bearing no resemblance to it. But if only democratic means could attain his objectives, the implications were inescapable. Those who rejected the democratic road to power were deadly enemies; and he did not take very seriously those who accepted it but ignored the constraints it imposed. Opponents must be fought but not gratuitously outraged: their reasonable grievances should be heard, and essential changes made in a way that minimised hostility. Oppositions must resist the dangerous temptations of irresponsibility, and avoid making promises or advocating policies which could never be carried out. Above all, unconvinced voters must be persuaded of the relevance of Labour policies.

The need to win over ordinary voters made Gaitskell wary of anything hinting at a return to post-war austerity. That did not stop him keeping up, even in these golden years of affluence, his Cassandra warnings against subordinating British economic growth to deflationary international pressures or sacrificing long-term investment to immediate consumption. (Indeed, Harold Macmillan accused him of 'always entering horses for the Calamity Stakes, but they get scratched one after the other before the race starts':[41b] a gibe sounding better then than it does today.) Those warnings fell on the deaf ears of those who had never had it so good. But they reflected economic caution, not sympathy for the 'squeamish' attitude to material progress of some of his friends: 'People do want a higher standard of living, and I do not see why we should not accept this. Certainly if we fail to accept it there is precious little chance of getting ourselves accepted by the electorate.'[72]

That populist strand in his make-up helped Gaitskell in his relations with the unions, though like every Labour leader he had to make some unwelcome concessions. (He would have liked the National Executive to propose safeguards for the liberties of unpopular individuals and minorities; but, as he had feared, the unions proved very cautious and he did not press the point.)[77] He made a few courageous speeches[78] on the difficulties of reconciling free collective bargaining and full employment without inflation; but it was a long-term problem which could best be tackled in government, and he would not make it a major theme.[3a] On industrial matters he was always careful of trade union feelings, and once defended Frank Cousins at serious political cost.[79]

On the basic problems of policy expressing Labour's aspirations towards a classless society, Gaitskell's outlook emerges throughout this narrative. Rather than recapitulate at length here, this section concentrates instead on the other problems which the leader of a progressive party must face from time to time, where minor incidents often reveal significant attitudes. Gaitskell displayed an unusual combination of views, for he frequently showed strong populist sympathy with the values of working-class voters — as well as the familiar concern of the affluent middle-class progressive with humanitarian and libertarian causes, issues affecting the quality of life, and a liberal approach to problems of race and international affairs.

Public ownership had never been the central tenet of his Socialism, but it was quite false to infer that he was against it. Six months before his death he told the ETU that people who thought so 'couldn't be more wrong. I was responsible ... for nationalising three industries [and am] very proud of that. But you've got to have the political basis for doing it'. As leader, he sought new approaches to old objectives. Conventional nationalisation of entire (usually unprofitable) industries under a public corporation had been severely — if not constructively — criticised from both Left and Right. But the state might have to make up a deficiency of investment capital due to redistributive taxation, and it should then acquire corresponding control. This concept, the germ of the National Enterprise Board idea, briefly won the unanimous support of Labour's National Executive.[80]

Just after becoming leader, Gaitskell published an essay on 'The Ideological Development of Democratic Socialism in Great Britain'.[63] He explained how the British tradition differed from the Continental: Marxism much weaker, trade unionism much stronger, the ILP influenced by Christian Socialism, the Fabians by Henry George. But he concentrated on the issues of his own generation. The egalitarian goals expounded by Tawney, he wrote, could now be approached more directly by Dalton's fiscal plans than by nationalisation (which in a democracy entailed compensation). For planning the whole economy, Keynes's ideas and the experience of the Second World War had transformed Socialist views; though there must be limits — not yet resolved — to government control and redistributive taxation in a mixed economy. Discussing the Left, he showed little sympathy for pre-war writers like Harold Laski who were ambivalent about political democracy. The war and its aftermath, he concluded (rather optimistically) had confirmed Durbin's ideas, cleared up 'the old confusions', and established the democratic tradition in British Socialism far more solidly than in the 1930s.

He was much more sympathetic to G. D. H. Cole and to ideas of workers' control. As Minister of Fuel he had fought against Communist efforts to exploit syndicalist feeling, but out of office he was sympathetic to the 'influential minority [who] are undoubtedly keen about industrial democracy'; though participation could not be compulsory, he stressed 'the importance of providing the opportunity to participate for those who want it'.[81a] As Party leader he thought of starting a pilot scheme in the Post Office,[53] where the unions were traditionally favourable.[82] In 1961, he spoke of oligarchic control of industry as among the aspects of modern society crying out for reform.[83]

Throughout his life, however, equality rather than public ownership had always been the driving force of his Socialism: an emphasis which emerged in the choice of subjects for his floor speeches at the 1953 Party Conference — taxation and public schools — which surprised George Brown.[84] He chose them not to win votes but because he thought them important, trying persistently to persuade an unreceptive National Executive, and telling the editor of the *Guardian* in 1961: 'The public schools were a source of snobbery and social evil. He had believed that all his life ... gradually and with the maximum consent... in the end they must abolish the public schools.'[85]

Here he was responding not to the working-class majority who were quite indifferent, but to another audience to which he was sensitive: the younger university generation who would be the opinion leaders of the future.[86a] He was concerned at Labour's failure to develop a strong youth movement like some Continental Socialist Parties which he knew well, such as those in Germany or Austria; and in 1959 he set up a Party Youth Commission to find ways of improving its appeal.[87a b] He feared that as prosperity eroded class consciousness, young people were repelled by what they feel to be the fusty, old-fashioned working-class attitudes of the people who run the Labour Party. How can one meet the demands of these young people without seeming to betray all the ideals of the old people?[88]

The commission's brief was not mainly political (though it was the first to recommend votes at eighteen, which Gaitskell promised to support).[89] But he aimed much wider. It was to study the problems of the 15–25 age group, and how the government, local authorities or voluntary groups could encourage sport, drama and the arts. Anthony Greenwood was responsible on the Executive, but Gaitskell was active in recruiting members – preferring prominent sportsmen, writers, musicians, actors and artists of broadly Labour sympathies to Greenwood's politicians. Gaitskell's old pre-war opponent Ted Willis was a member, and commented that the leader appreciated, well before most people, the new outlook of a younger generation enjoying financial independence and personal mobility, understanding

that there was a new sound in the air, that old values were breaking up, and a new shape was coming to the world ... He said, 'It's never going to be the same again with young people, and I want this reflected in the Labour Party.' I was very impressed, I hadn't even myself thought of it that way before.[90]

Following that precedent, and with the same audience in mind, Gaitskell set up in 1962 a similar Advertising Commission. Again he tried to strengthen its authority and broaden its appeal by attracting well-known people who were sympathetic to Labour as well as publicly committed supporters.[91] He chose as chairman Lord Reith, creator of the BBC and high priest of the improving paternalism Gaitskell deplored in other contexts – though he did worry about repercussions on the current television controversy, making elaborate inquiries about Reith's political views and state of mind.[87a c] Some of his choices thought it a misdirection of effort.[92] But he had confessed a year earlier that there were

some aspects of the affluent society that I find rather unattractive ... something rather nauseating and humiliating about those [television] advertisements ... [where] people are regarded as sort of objects on which the ad. men can get to work.[86c]

The New Left, who were somewhat obsessed by that problem, had by then achieved intellectual prominence. Gaitskell fought them on foreign and defence policy, and had no sympathy with their more esoteric preoccupations. He thought some of their ideas

pretty lunatic – though I should not mind that if only they recognised a 'division of labour' and did not go on talking as if they were our main opponents. I suspect, however, that while some are genuine 'thinkers', however muddled, others are ex-communist & trotskyist politicians with more than their fair share of aggression.[8h]

But he willingly consented to speak to them privately, and shared the wider anxieties they reflected:

[T]he younger generation at the universities ... hate the growing influence and power of advertising and ... feel insulted and humiliated that their desires and wants are being dictated to them regardless of how real they are ... I understand and sympathise with them. But I have to point out the limits of what can be done, how most people do not yet seem to feel the way they do, how cheap newspapers have to depend on advertising, etc. Nevertheless, I am glad they are worried ... If this sort of worrying was not going on the Labour Party would lose something very vital to its character.[86a]

Gaitskell's concern for majority views was not just vote-catching. On many matters he shared the instincts of his working-class followers rather than those of the progressive intellectuals. Even when his own sympathies were with the latter, he was often made cautious by his awareness of popular feelings. So, when 'moral' issues came up in Parliament, he usually took a liberal but not a crusading stance. He always voted to abolish the death penalty, but was not passionate about it, gave it a low priority and would not have endangered Labour's programme for its sake.[93a b] He favoured reform of the homosexuality laws, and privately assured the government that if they acted Labour would make no Party capital out of it; but that was as far as he would go.[94] He was most reluctant to interfere with the pleasures of others. In 1949 he assured a Winchester contemporary, a keen huntsman, that on those grounds he would oppose a Private Member's Bill against blood sports.[95] Ten years later, defying the old Nonconformist temperance tradition so strong in the Labour Movement, he persuaded the Party to agree to revise the 'moth-eaten laws' on licensing.[96–7] A supporter of the police, he was shocked when younger friends once suggested attacking them in an election campaign.[93a]

As a politician he knew that independent television was popular, and he would never join the Establishment's cultural crusade against it.[98] As early as 1953 he told Crossman, who had asked if the next Labour government would reverse the newly proposed policy: 'No, and anyway it's a pity we didn't encourage the BBC to lease out time to commercial companies.'[99] A decade later he would not be bounced by Labour's broadcasting spokesman Christopher Mayhew (normally his staunch ally) into supporting the latter's proposals for separating the control of independent TV programmes entirely from the sale of advertising time.

Mayhew's plan had strong Labour support, and it was unanimously adopted by the Pilkington Committee on broadcasting, which reported in June 1962 praising the BBC and criticising the independent companies.[100] But while Gaitskell was quite willing for an experiment with the plan, he was among the experienced Labour broadcasters who were not sure that it would work; also he was not at all convinced that BBC programmes were always better.[101] The press had accused Pilkington of wanting to suppress the most popular programmes, and he wanted to shield the Labour Party from that charge — but 'electoral considerations [were] not dominant' in his mind, and he was quite willing to back Pilkington and lose votes on it if the Party so decided.[102a] But while he had no love for the advertisers at all, that did not convert him to Pilkington's specific proposals:

> For example, the Pilkington Committee do not want to cut down advertising; personally I would like to see less of it. The Pilkington Committee want the B.B.C. to raise all its money by licence fees; I am not at all sure about this. The Pilkington Committee on the whole defend [newspaper?] ownership of shares in Television Companies; I very much doubt that they are right ... I do not much like the idea of the fourth channel going to Commercial Television at all.[103]

He reacted strongly against the committee's 'very indifferent' arguments, and above all against its elitism:[104] 'I have seldom been more irritated. The priggish, arrogant, puritanical tone dominates the whole Report.'[103] He warned Mayhew that 'we must beware of imposing our own middle class and intellectual concepts on the workers'.[105]

That warning went much deeper than mere opportunism. Years earlier, he had had just the same private reaction to the draft of a philosophical book by his worthy 'do-gooding' friends in Socialist Union. They over-emphasised quality-of-life issues, he wrote, in a way

> terribly reminiscent of Fabian drawing-rooms. It is school-marmish in its flavour. It suggests the refeened middle-class lady holding her nose against the vulgarity that she sees round her. I had hoped we had got away from this kind of thing.[72]

When they exhorted ordinary people to perform civil duties, he demurred:

> I get impatient with those who think that everybody must continually be taking an active part in politics or community affairs! The vast majority find their happiness in their family or personal relations, and why on earth shouldn't they! There will always be a minority who are genuinely interested in social activity and social work. They can get on with the job.[72]

He reacted similarly to their unhappiness about affluence, and was anxious for people to enjoy more of its fruits. He pressed for the Labour programme to include setting up a consumer research organisation.[106] Among his first acts on the National Executive was to sponsor the consumers' back-bench champion, Elaine Burton, in her effort to make shoddy goods the theme of one of the earliest party political broadcasts. There was opposition from the other lady members of the NEC, and from Wilson and Crossman; as Miss Burton wrote later to Gaitskell, 'I know full well that it is only through you that we have the chance of putting this over to the public.'[107] The broadcast was a triumph, drawing the best response yet recorded.[108] Years later, Gaitskell remained an enemy of resale price maintenance;[102b] and one of his last business letters pressed Transport House for policy proposals, especially on hire purchase, as 'a pretty good vote-puller'.[109] But again the electoral impact was not his only concern, for he told his puritanical Socialist Union friends in 1955:

> I just cannot share this Gandhi outlook ... If people have more money to spend they may, it is true, gamble or smoke or drink it away. But a lot of them will also enjoy nicer holidays, which is a very good thing for them. We really must keep under control, and pretty strict control, the area within which 'the man in Whitehall knows best'.[72]

That outlook made him a libertarian, sympathetic to practical proposals for protecting the individual against bureaucratic abuses. He raised the problem at the 1959 Party Conference, and welcomed the remedy – the appointment of an Ombudsman – soon after the Whyatt Committee suggested it two years later.[110] Gaitskell also, despite the extreme caution of his chief adviser, supported the National Council for Civil Liberties' proposals for the treatment of civil servants who became suspect in security cases.[111]

Populism was not philistinism. Gaitskell was much more sensitive than most politicians – and much earlier – to quality-of-life issues. As Minister of Fuel he had shown an interest in environmental problems which was to persist, notably in his continued enthusiasm for town planning.[112] As Chancellor he had actively encouraged the arts, and he did the same in opposition, where Anthony Greenwood, the Front Bench spokesman, found him very sensitive on all aesthetic matters.[113] Far from having a vote-catching motive, he wrote that his main aim was 'to build up public opinion behind the idea of more State aid and support'.[114]

While Gaitskell opposed attempts by superior persons to impose their own tastes and preferences on the ordinary man, he firmly resisted popular prejudices against supposedly inferior people – whether over Suez, or coloured immigration, or colonial problems (to which both he and Bevan

gave a prominence which some trade union MPs resented).[115] In the electorate, Gaitskell's leadership on these questions both extended Labour's
appeal to the liberal middle class, and alienated some of its working-class
support.

When he became leader, foreign affairs replaced finance as his main single
preoccupation; for his accession to the leadership coincided approximately
with the Indian summer of the British economy, in which prosperity produced electoral complacency and the political waters were ruffled by fewer
of the economic squalls in which he had made his reputation, but by more
typhoons from distant oceans. Prime Ministers, prospective or actual, had
now to deal with the problems of the emergent Third World countries in
such crises as Rhodesia or Suez. Labour leaders faced special problems,
for different sections of their followers traditionally sympathised with
Zionism, regarding Israel as the progressive homeland of an oppressed
people; with the Soviet Union, still seen as a Socialist state; or with pacifism, given a new lease of life by the fearful prospect of nuclear war.

Gaitskell's international outlook showed his familiar fundamental values
and balanced appraisal. His approach was set out fully in the Godkin
Lectures at Harvard after a year as leader.[116] Welcoming Anglo-American
co-operation in defence of freedom, he warned in the friendliest tones
against many past and indeed future American mistakes. He rejoiced that
the Eastern European revolts of 1956 had shown that indoctrination and
terror could never produce 'a robot-like race in whom the desire for freedom itself had died'.[116a] But his suspicion of Communism gave force to
his rejection of the crude and strident anti-Communist crusaders; and,
while wanting NATO strengthened, he was most sceptical about similar
alliances elsewhere.[116b]

Even in Europe he opposed the Bonn and Washington hard line over
Germany; he was always sympathetic to Yugoslavia; and he favoured
demilitarising all central Europe. For the Polish and Hungarian risings of
1956 had shown, first the unpopularity of Communism there, so that disengagement was unlikely to mean Communist control of West Germany;
secondly the trouble the satellite countries were giving the Russians; and
thirdly the risk of a new East German eruption provoking West German
intervention. Contrary to the claims of the Labour Left,[117] Gaitskell had
not changed his mind about the dangers of a disarmed and neutral Germany
— and was under no pressures of party politics, for no one but Denis
Healey had ever suggested disengagement to him.[118] Instead he was thinking in a new international context, in which the Russian occupation of the
satellite states was bringing them less advantage. He hoped that demilitarising these countries — Poland, Czechoslovakia, Hungary, and both East
and West Germany — might change that context further, since without
Soviet troops their domestic balance of power would be transformed.[116c]

(Like most people, he expected international détente to bring relaxation within Communist countries, not tighter controls.)

In Asia, he doubted China's alleged aggressiveness, and favoured her admission to the UN despite strong American hostility.[116d] Denying that international Communism was monolithic, citing Ho Chi Minh as a Communist ruler likely to remain independent of his powerful neighbour, condemning Western military intervention in Asia, and warning that democracies would never fight long wars of repression, he demolished years beforehand the whole rationale for the Vietnam disaster:

> The Western powers suffer in these areas from the taint of 'colonialism' ... the technical and psychological problems associated with land fighting in Asia can hardly be exaggerated, if the local populations are indifferent or even hostile ... A great deal turns on the attitude of the local populations as well as their governments ... the political front is the really vital one and ... the value of a military alliance itself turns largely on its political consequences.

Critics of decolonisation

> gravely underestimate the immense force of nationalist feeling ... [and] the advantage which communist propaganda has if it is working together with such nationalist feeling. Finally ... [a] democracy cannot for long maintain a policy of complete repression in its colonies without the people of that democracy themselves deciding to abandon the struggle. And ... public opinion in the rest of the world ... will declare itself against policies of this kind.[116e]

He repudiated both the connection between economic *laissez-faire* and political freedom, proclaimed by the ideologues of the American Right;[119] and the view that all neutralism was immoral as the Secretary of State, John Foster Dulles, so often preached. The Third World countries, Gaitskell explained, were attracted to neutralism because of their colonial past, their remoteness from recent European experience with totalitarianism, their reluctance to spend heavily on defence instead of on urgent economic development, and their desire, which should appeal to Americans, to assert independence by breaking with 'wicked power politics'.[116g] They should be given economic aid 'without expecting a flood of appreciation or attaching to such help any military strings ... [solely so that] they can enjoy the same opportunities of economic progress as ... [us] on a stable and democratic basis.'[116h] Aid should enable these countries to raise their standard of living without such stringent restrictions on current consumption as to provoke revolt and destroy any hope of democracy (he was thinking no doubt of India).[116i] Mainly because of the impact on these countries, he was against Britain joining a European political union or the embryo Common Market unless one day the Commonwealth disintegrated, leaving Britain only an offshore island.[120]

He thus managed without wishful thinking to discuss foreign affairs in an idealistic and principled perspective and, without offending his American audience, to put to them a distinctive approach, which on most matters commanded very wide support in Britain. There were obvious exceptions: at home, among the nationalist Right (then vociferous because of Suez) and the fellow-travelling Left (then reticent because of Hungary); abroad, with respect to the Middle East and the United Nations. But on world affairs Gaitskell's outlook was generally welcomed far outside the Labour Party, as well as by most people within it.[121]

iv   *The Leader and His Approach to Power*

Gaitskell would not truckle to popular prejudice or abandon his own principles in order to extend support or seek consensus, either in external or domestic affairs. But his confidence in the rationality and decency of ordinary people assured him that they could be convinced by good aims and a good case, and his fundamental commitment to democratic methods required the Labour Party to convert a majority before it could come to power and start to carry out its objectives. He could become impatient with those who ignored that necessity and its implications. Forgetting his own inexperienced and passionate youth, he wrote in 1958 to his daughter at Oxford:

> [M]any of your friends do not understand about *democracy*! ... or the practical problems of achieving Socialist goals under democratic conditions. Yet it is the only thing really worth talking about ... The difficulty, if anything, is that [Labour's programme] is probably still too radical for the electorate.[8c e]

A few years later he told a trade union audience that most of the trouble in the Party came from those impatient with the need to convert marginal voters. Yet that need was 'basic', for 'without power we can do nothing; we can only win power when we have the confidence of our fellow-citizens'.[102c]

Far more introspective than most of his political colleagues, Gaitskell was fascinated by power, irresistibly attracted to it, yet always conscious of its fragility and elusiveness. He suggested more than once that friends should write a book about it, because real power did not exist.[122] In a television interview in 1961, Malcolm Muggeridge said that he himself looked on power as 'a dreadful thing, a dangerous thing', and asked, 'Do you feel frightened of this, uneasy about it or avid for it?' Gaitskell replied that power was far less freely exercised than most people believed:

Certainly not avid for it, but ... [your] whole conception ... is a wrong one ... from personal experience ... [it is] extraordinarily limited ... ... [As] a Minister, you can make certain appointments, and on the whole they rest with you, but you know the care you have to take ... that the right balance in a particular board or council is preserved, that the right sort of people are put on, that they are going to succeed, [so] that you don't think 'I am controlling a benefit' at all, indeed very often you're much more concerned as to whether the persons are going to accept the jobs ... you do not decide [policy] on your own, except to a very limited extent, you have to persuade people ... you've got to take [your officials] into account, you probably have to persuade your colleagues.

Not even the Prime Minister had

personal absolute power, he's got to think of all his colleagues, you can have a revolt after all [like Eden] ... In forming your Cabinet again you would have to take so many things into account, but above all the question of success, of whether you were going to succeed as a government ... [a] complex of personal relations to consider, the whole question of how you can keep the team working together, it may be a word you dislike but ... it does mean something ... the idea of I decide, a sort of dictatorial power, nobody questions my decision is complete nonsense in my experience.[123]

Of course Gaitskell was ambitious: men who are not rarely go into politics, let alone succeed there, and Gaitskell had never been concerned to preach the word without seeking the power to apply it.

[B]eing a practical politician and wanting to get results rather than satisfy emotions, he accepted the inevitability of working in a team ... he was interested in the winning of power in order to get things changed. He was contemptuous of those who seemed more concerned with the emotional satisfaction of expressing minority views.[124]

He saw nothing wrong with ambition in the service of principle. The Labour Party, he told his daughter, needed

people with integrity & ability & common sense plus the ordinary good qualities of loyalty, courage & honesty. It's better to ask whether people have these qualities rather than whether they are careerists. Ambition doesn't matter (& is to be expected anyhow) so long as people have the other things too.[8i]

But the object of getting into power was to put principles into practice, and he had no respect for colleagues or opponents who sought it as an end in itself, or simply as the culmination of a personal career. He hated the cynical view of politicians as men who subordinate self-respect and ordinary human decency to its obsessive pursuit, and when the behaviour of others appeared to fit that stereotype he found politics utterly distasteful.

Shortly after entering Parliament, he was asked on a BBC brains trust what he would like on his epitaph, and replied by specifying the qualities of character he most valued: kindness, courage, vitality, living a full life, integrity.[125] As a Minister he hoped to disprove the sad old comment that there is no friendship at the top.[126] Before his election to the leadership, he praised in a private letter the virtues he saw in his own circle of close political friends: intelligence, intellectual honesty, loyalty, judgment.[81b] And a couple of years later Arthur Allen, his trade unionist PPS, wrote to him:

Let me first wish you both a very Happy New Year ... You deserve happiness in that you work wholeheartedly for the good of others and have done so for many years even when there could not have been any reward in prospect for so doing ... [There was] a time when the ethical ideals of Socialism carried compulsion in the hearts and minds of sensitive people like yourselves; a time when not to serve those ideals would have been rank treachery to your innermost thoughts ... I still think hearts can be stirred to react against injustice and minds enlisted to promote the good. That is why I am so glad that you, Hugh, have become the leader of the Party ... You have qualities of heart and mind incomparably superior to so many of those with whom you of necessity must associate. That is the reason why it gives me so much pleasure to do the little I can to help you. We must make you Premier. It is so desperately important that guidance of our affairs should be taken out of the hands of cynics.

By the way, I didn't set out to write like this at all.[127]

O

TABLE 3 *Chronology, 1945–63*

	1945	1947–8	1949	1950–1	1951	1952–3	1954	1955
Prime Minister	Attlee				Churchill			Eden
Foreign Secretary	Bevin			Morrison	Eden			Macmillan
Chancellor of the Exchequer	Dalton	Cripps		Gaitskell	Butler			
Leader of the House of Commons	Morrison			Ede	Crookshank			
Labour Leader, Treasurer	(Attlee) (Greenwood)						Gaitskell	
Labour Deputy Leader	(Morrison)							
Shadow Foreign Secretary					Morrison			
Shadow Chancellor					Morrison Gaitskell			Robens
Labour Party events conferences				Bevan out		Morecambe	Bevan quits	
UK events political economic	US loan	Fuel crisis Convertibility	Lynskey Devaluation	Election £3600 m. arms £4700 m.	–£ crisis	Terms of trade+		Election
Foreign rulers	Truman		Mao Adenauer NATO			Eisenhower Stalin d.		
Foreign events		Cold war Prague, Berlin Marshall Plan		Korean war			Indo-China partition McCarthy falls	

	1955–6	1956	1957	1958	1959	1960	1961	1962	1963
Prime Minister			Macmillan						
Foreign Secretary	Lloyd					Home			
Chancellor of the Exchequer	Macmillan		Thorneycroft	Amory		Lloyd		Maudling	
Leader of the House of Commons	Butler						Macleod		
Labour Leader, Treasurer	Gaitskell	Bevan				Gaitskell / Nicholas	Gaitskell		Wilson
Labour Deputy Leader	Griffiths	Bevan			Bevan	Brown	Brown		
Shadow Foreign					Bevan	Gaitskell	Wilson		
Shadow Chancellor	Wilson						Callaghan		
Labour Party events conferences	Cousins T&G		Brighton	CND	Blackpool	Scarborough	Blackpool	Brighton	HG d.
UK events political					Election		EEC talks / Immigration / Pay pause	Orpington / Cabinet: 7 out	
UK events economic			Bank rate+	Bus strike		End of Blue Streak			
Foreign rulers	Khrushchev speech			De Gaulle		Kennedy			
Foreign events		Suez / Hungary		Cyprus / Lebanon	Kenya / Nyasaland	U.2 / Congo	Berlin / Cuba / Laos	Missile crisis / India/China	

PART FIVE

LEADERSHIP: THE YEARS OF RECONCILIATION

*'First of all his job is to keep the Party together ... second to listen to other
people ... thirdly ... to tell them what he thinks'*
(HG, 1957)
*'His ability to compromise is famous in the Labour Party. But Britain needs
leadership, not compromise'*
(INDEPENDENT JOURNALIST, 1958)

CHAPTER 14

BRIEF HONEYMOON 1956

'*We can perhaps count on Mr. Gaitskell to lean rather more to the Left than is strictly necessary for party purposes*'
(DAILY TELEGRAPH, 1956)
'*Our present leadership is not only more intelligent but also much more flexible than the Attlee regime*'
(IAN MIKARDO, 1958)

i *Healing the Wounds*

GAITSKELL was the youngest leader of a major Party for sixty years, chosen after the shortest period in Parliament. He was elated at winning by the most convincing majority in Labour's history. But his sudden transformation from factional spokesman to Party leader left many doubts about him, especially outside Westminster. Labour activists were accustomed to opposition not government, and so more disposed to criticism than construction. Often they were receptive to utopianism and wishful thinking, and uneasy with a leader who had only briefly been a backbencher and never a rebel. Always suspecting their own Front Bench of caution, compromise and careerism, they were liable to mistake the trumpetings of *Tribune* and the sneers of the *New Statesman* for the voice of Socialist purity.

In his twenty years of leadership, Clem Attlee had often been cautious and compromising in handling the Left. In office he had taken an unpopular stand occasionally, but in opposition he rarely risked his credit by standing up to dissidents. His successor was described by one commentator as 'Left-inclining with almost undignified speed'; another thought that he 'more than any alternative leader, may be able to hold them together';[1] a third expected him to 'attempt to do deliberately what Mr. Attlee appeared to do intuitively, that is, to lead the party from the centre'.[2]

During his first Parliament as leader Gaitskell met those expectations. He set out to reunite the Party in two ways: first by healing bruised personal relations, then by working out a new and broadly acceptable policy. In dealing with other politicians he was neither naive nor neurotically suspicious. He gave them the benefit of any doubt, though he was indignant when he felt his confidence betrayed. But he did not bear grudges, and was so unsectarian in choosing his colleagues that Leslie Hunter could write of him in 1958 heading 'a predominantly left wing team'.[3] During those early years, now quite forgotten, he was strikingly successful within the Party; outside it, critics felt he gave too little weight to the Opposition leader's role as a national as well as a Party spokesman. In 1958 a writer compared him to Attlee, adding:

> Gaitskell has within his own party drawn together many loose ends of discontent. But can he do the same for the country?
> His ability to compromise is famous in the Labour Party. But Britain needs leadership, not compromise.
> Too often Gaitskell has seemed the leader who follows.[4]

By those means he succeeded in carrying his followers with him even on most issues of foreign policy where differences had recently been so sharp. At home he had always thought the split unnecessary and artificial. He recognised that any radical Party needs a pioneering as well as a governing element;[5c] but why, he asked, was equality more Left than economic security, or nationalisation than higher death duties, or collective security than appeasement?[6] An old critic, now in the Shadow Cabinet, assessed his style at this time as 'efficient and conciliatory';[7] and he rightly saw that with mutual goodwill, it should not be hard to unite the Party on an agreed domestic programme.

Since he led a party not an army, its members had to be convinced not commanded. Before 1959, skill in accommodation was the aspect of his leadership most emphasised alike by himself and by his critics on Left and Right. After eighteen months, a BBC interviewer brought up 'the commonest criticism of your leadership ... that you don't really lead them – that you wait to hear what they want and then say it'. Gaitskell replied that a leader had several tasks:

> [F]irst of all it is his job to keep the Party together, to keep it united; second it's his job to listen to what other people say, he's not a dictator; but thirdly ... he's got to tell them what he thinks ... [not necessarily in public] ... but he's jolly well got to take into account what people's thoughts and views are; and frankly anything else would not be tolerated in the Labour Party.[8]

His willingness to do so delighted even his old critic Ian Mikardo:

> What is good is that our present leadership is not only more intelligent but also much more *flexible* than the Attlee regime. It is ready to give

way, and if need be to reverse its ideas, in deference to a clearly-expressed view of the back-benchers. And it does so with good grace.'[9a b]

Leadership of the Labour Party made Gaitskell, as Leader of the Opposition, the country's alternative Prime Minister: two inseparable yet distinct roles, not easy to reconcile. There was an electoral problem: as he wrote early on to a veteran ex-Minister, Lord Pethick-Lawrence, policy proposals must be both exciting enough for the activists and convincing enough for the floating voters.[10] There was also a problem of outlook. Conservative critics made exactly the same points as Mikardo from the other side. Before the attack on Suez the *Daily Mail* called Gaitskell 'The Rt. Hon. Jellyfish'; a year later Earl Winterton wrote that with him in Downing Street instead of Attlee, Labour's 'lunatic fringe would be un-hindered'.[11] One of the friendlier Tory journalists claimed:

At no time, since he became leader of the Labour Party, has Mr. Gaitskell given his party a personal lead, irrespective of the consequences.

He has united his party behind an agreed policy, certainly. But he has united it by following ... Never once, since he became leader, has he ever risen above party, or ever given a hint that he would be capable of rising above it.

He has brought to the Front Bench in the House of Commons the narrowest kind of backbench mind.[5a]

His reputation at the time was thus quite unlike that for which he is now remembered. Tory partisans had long seen him as a dangerous enemy trying to steal Bevan's clothes; as the *Daily Telegraph* wrote: 'We can perhaps count on Mr. Gaitskell to lean rather more to the Left than is strictly necessary for party purposes.'[12] Then, over Suez, he encountered real hatred from many Conservatives who mistakenly attributed his opposition to partisan calculation. In 1959 an old Beaverbrook-Bevanite confessed:

[F]rom the party point of view he has acquitted himself magnificently ... he has established an ascendancy that Attlee never accomplished ...
He does not have to rely, like poor Clem, on the tyrannical power of trade union bosses to prop him up and lay down policy.[13a]

He was seen as a brilliant Party leader, skilful at reconciling a quarrelsome following, unassailable since he led from left of centre;[5b] but prone to pay too high a price for unity, and too willing to yield to pressures from the ranks behind him. In Labour's official paper a warm supporter pointed the contrast. One article recorded:

For he has largely united the left and right in the Party, won the hard-working cooperation of dissident intellectuals such as Crossman, and persuaded the man who began as his most bitter rival and opponent, Bevan, to work in harmony with, and under him.

It is a staggering record.

The next asked: 'Can the Party chief lead the Nation?'[14]

The commentator was correct who described Gaitskell's early style of leadership as one deliberately chosen,[2] for his instinctive conception was quite different. He had hinted at it thirty years before, at the age of twenty-two, when in his youthful study of Chartism he condemned the men who gave no positive lead of their own:

> Tormented by fear of desertion, [the Convention] chose the weakest course. They must do what the people wanted, and the people must be asked what they wanted to do … A belief in democratic principles was doubtless behind the support of a few for this policy, but for many it was only a cloak under which they might escape for a time from their too responsible position.[15]

In the late 1950s – a time of general prosperity felt to be insecure – Party unity proved not to be enough: a necessary but not sufficient condition for electoral victory. In 1959 Gaitskell fought an impressive personal campaign, backed by much improved organisation and arousing immense enthusiasm among Party workers – but Labour was decisively beaten. That defeat had a great impact on both him and the Party, and it divided his leadership into two sharply contrasting periods.

Before his selection Gaitskell had been prominent in trying to revitalise the Opposition, supporting the major policy-making programme approved by the Margate Conference in October 1955. Twenty turbulent years had passed since the Party had last systematically formulated its policy. Attlee's government had enacted the pre-war programme, and reconstructed the post-war economy, but increasingly it was reduced to reacting to successive crises instead of trying to shape events. In opposition Labour was obsessed by its internal dispute, and baffled by the Tory exploitation of affluence. At elections the Party came together, but its recent manifestos had reflected no serious long-term thought, proposing to nationalise one group of industries in 1950, none in 1951, and a different list in 1955. Conference then agreed that a new policy should be worked out, approved by stages over three years. Gaitskell had favoured the conception, and was now to preside over the execution.

His enthusiasm for precise policy-making was in some ways surprising. He was well aware that the record of a government counts far more electorally than any Opposition proposals.[16] He realised that its first task is to govern; that its standing depends on its handling of the (probably unexpected) problems which it faces; and that if it fails over those, no one will notice that it had fulfilled two dozen minor and forgotten manifesto pledges. Those lessons were evident in 1951, much more so in later years. Yet it was under him that Labour in opposition went furthest in working out detailed policies for government – which made no impact on the electorate and some of which were irrelevant by 1964 when the Party regained office.[17] It was surprising, too, because usually the Labour Left, not the Labour Right, is keenest on laying down precise policies out of power. Gaitskell did so partly from mistrust of broad professions of principle unsupported by practical plans.[18] But he also respected and accepted the Party's policy-making machinery, and was anxious to work with its elected spokesmen on the National Executive in devising policies to go to Conference.

ii *Labour Harmony, Tory Disarray*

In January 1956, his first month as leader, Gaitskell consolidated his Front Bench team, improved his Transport House contacts, and established personal relations with the press and BBC. For several months he reverted to keeping a detailed diary, beginning dramatically with a call on the Prime Minister on New Year's Day to propose (unsuccessfully) the recall of Parliament to debate Egypt's acquisition of surplus British tanks. He spoke at half a dozen receptions and conferences, attended over a dozen Party committees and talked to twenty-five prominent colleagues. He also saw individually most members of the Shadow Cabinet, to urge on them the need for more teamwork and less back-stabbing and intrigue.* He had a dozen official engagements (largely diplomatic), saw several journalists, and had four sessions with photographers and three exhausting rehearsals for his first television appearance as leader. His one weekend at home was broken by a lunch with Dalton and a party at the Attlees' Chiltern home.

Day-to-day parliamentary opposition was already taking a new form. Attlee had made the main change immediately after the 1955 election, under pressure from Gaitskell and his new allies Wilson and Crossman, by introducing the modern Shadow Cabinet organisation with members responsible for (and confined to) specific departmental functions.[20] Specialisation was partly a reaction to Conservative jeers – inspired by Bevan's SEATO intervention a year earlier – at the Opposition leaders jostling to contradict one another at the dispatch box.[21a] The new arrange-

* He defended Harold Wilson as 'a cold fish [but] I thought he knew the need for loyalty ... [and] was not really dangerous because he would not have much support if he made trouble'.[19a]

ment had the grave drawback of limiting spontaneity and flexibility, and Harold Macmillan, Herbert Morrison and James Callaghan were among its many critics.[22] But it ensured quick and informed parliamentary and television replies to all ministerial statements, avoided clashes within the alternative government, and concentrated the front-benchers' minds on effective teamwork instead of intermittent freelance activities. While that style of opposition reflected Gaitskell's personality, all his successors have retained the system.

When the House of Commons met on 24 January 1956, the PLP had to choose a deputy leader to replace Morrison. The latter, like his chief supporter Shinwell in 1947, believed Gaitskell to have supplanted him and nursed his enmity for years. There was even talk of mobilising the older working-class leaders for a revolt which Bevan might join.[23] The Bevanites remained divided. Michael Foot, Ian Mikardo and Jennie Lee remained irreconcilable, but Gaitskell knew that Bevan himself was inclined to seek an accommodation as the moderates—Wilson, Crossman and Castle— wanted him to do.[24] (Gaitskell had just been reported as having said a year earlier that those three were the only ones he would have in a Cabinet.)[25]

Bevan disliked having to solicit the votes of his despised parliamentary colleagues, telling the Chief Whip: 'there ought to be no *election* to the Deputy Leadership. Gaitskell should *appoint* me as Deputy Leader. I am the Leader of the Party in the Country'.[26] Nevertheless, well before the House met he had decided to contest the election, in order to show his willingness to serve under Gaitskell. He lost by only thirty to James Griffiths—who had few personal enemies, was too old to become leader, and could compete with him for the votes of miners and Welshmen.[27] With 111 supporters, Bevan polled 30 more than he had against Morrison in the old House with its larger PLP, and only 7 fewer than for the Shadow Cabinet in the new House in June. Many MPs were again signalling their anxiety to end the quarrel—and many more did not do so only for fear that within a few months Bevan would again shatter the new unity.[5d]

They were nearly right. When the result was announced, wrote Dalton, Griffiths made a 'perfect' response. Then Gaitskell asked Bevan if he wanted to speak, but 'with a most ugly, contorted angry face ... [he] made a contemptuous, scowling gesture of refusal, seen by all, & remained seated.'[28a b] His good intentions forgotten, he reopened the wounds two days later at Manchester:

> If the Labour Party is not going to be a Socialist Party, I don't want to lead it ... When you join a team in the expectation that you are going to play rugger, you can't be expected to be enthusiastic if you are asked to play tiddly-winks.

It was 'retrograde' to propose (as Gaitskell had at Margate) investigating whether individual industries qualified for nationalisation. The PLP's private meetings upstairs were an undemocratic conspiracy. He knew, he concluded, that these words would get him into trouble.[29]

Bevan was clamouring for martyrdom, and the Conservative press urged Gaitskell to take up the challenge.[21b] To the disappointment of the journalists hungry for copy, he ignored it. He took the decision entirely on his own.[30] He told a friendly journalist[31] that he would not

> allow Mr. Bevan the luxury of becoming a storm-centre again. He can lower his head and charge, bull-necked, as often as he likes; he will not meet opposition, for his colleagues will just open their ranks and let him pass headlong through to his appointed destiny ... Mr. Bevan, is not going to prevent the PLP from getting on with a serious job of work.[5e g]

Gaitskell did not exploit his patronage, but used it for conciliation. He gave shadow posts to only thirty-four MPs (one fewer than Attlee)[32]; and Dalton noted with glee that, though Conservative MPs are generally younger than Labour, the average age (fifty-two) was below that of the Tory Ministers.[28a] At least a third were old Bevanites or Keep Calmers. In the Shadow Cabinet, the few changes were also designed to unify the PLP, for the posts vacated by the new leader and deputy leader went to Wilson, who took over from Gaitskell as Shadow Chancellor, and to Bevan himself.[33] Griffiths had shadowed the Colonial Office, a post which Bevan had long coveted. Griffiths and the Chief Whip both agreed, first that Gaitskell should make the offer to Bevan, and then that he should maintain it after Bevan's Manchester speech.[34] As the leader recorded:

> He came in, evidently expecting that we were going to put him on the mat about his weekend speech — swaggering in in a sort of defensive way. So I said very sweetly, 'Come along, Nye, come and sit down', and went on, 'Allocation of jobs'. He was quite startled, and quite obviously surprised at this development. Then I said, 'We would like you to take the Colonies'. He then proceeded to talk in a more sensible and rational manner than I have heard him for a long time. He said, 'I would have liked Foreign Affairs'. I ignored that, and then he went on, 'The only difficulty about the Colonies is that I really know so little about them'. This is a very rare admission from Mr. B! ... We are giving him every possible chance ... an interesting [job] with plenty of Parliamentary scope, with travelling ... that he can really get his teeth into. If, despite this, he refuses to work in the team, and goes on behaving as he has been doing recently, sooner or later he will simply get himself out of the Party. But whether he will do that, or whether after all he will settle down, we cannot yet say ... his pride

will always make it very difficult indeed for him to work in a team under my leadership, or indeed under anybody else's who is now on the scene.[19c]

For once party leadership seemed more of a problem for Conservatives than for Labour. Eden's apprenticeship had been as prolonged as Gaitskell's was brief, and in Downing Street he was always overshadowed by his famous predecessor. Nine months after Churchill retired at last, the new Labour leader remarked to the old one how far the Government's stock had fallen. Attlee replied with a characteristic cricketing metaphor: 'Yep. It's the heavy roller, you know. Doesn't let the grass grow under it.' He added that the new Prime Minister had no experience of running a team.[19a] Since 1951 domestic policy had been dominated by Butler, but he had had to leave the Exchequer after Gaitskell's assault; and it was an area in which Eden had never before had any responsibility. But even abroad he appeared to be losing grip. In a critical debate in March 1956, after the King of Jordan dismissed his British commander General Glubb, Gaitskell thought Eden made an 'almost pathetic' winding-up speech:[35] 'everyone was saying after it that he really could not last much longer ... He looked old and tired and ill and one could not help feeling really rather sorry for him.'[19d] Dalton wrote next day: 'I'm still purring over your performance ... on my rounds, a taxi driver, a banker and a nurse all took the initiative in praising you and dispraising Eden.'[36] Ian Waller predicted after this debate that by 1957 Harold Macmillan would replace Eden in Downing Street.[37]

Even earlier, at the New Year, Eden had been bitterly attacked editorially in the *Daily Telegraph* — a reflection, said society gossip, of an obscure vendetta against Lady Eden by Lady Pamela Berry, wife of the editor-in-chief (and daughter of F. E. Smith). Gaitskell was as curious as he was astonished when Lady Pamela, whom he had never met, tried very hard to get invited to a very small dancing party of his intimate friends at Frognal Gardens. Though she succeeded, she never appeared. But she met the Gaitskells next day at a fashion reception in the Fishmongers' Hall, where she cornered them to demand insistently:

'Tell me, Mr. Gaitskell, is it possible to get rid of a Prime Minister in peacetime?' I said, 'It is extremely difficult if he doesn't want to go. But you can, of course, make life so intolerable for him that he becomes ill and cannot carry on.' 'You aren't suggesting that I should murder him' she said. She continued to talk in this strain.[19e]

A month later Hugh and Dora dined with her, and she and her Macmillanite guests gossiped gloomily about the shocking state of the government and the economy. Gaitskell suggested quite wrongly that Labour's problem 'was not the top three in the Conservative Party, all of whom seemed to me to be pretty discredited, but the next crust, i.e. Selwyn Lloyd, Macleod, Reggie Maudling, and Duncan Sandys'.[19f] A little later the Gaitskells dined with Anne Fleming, 'one of the most entertaining and amusing hostesses in London ... [and] one of the few Tories who seems to be reasonably loyal to Eden'.[19g]

In his memoirs after Suez, Eden called Gaitskell's election as Labour leader 'a national misfortune', and claimed: 'We never seemed able to get on terms.'[38] But their early relations showed no such hostility. When Gaitskell first visited Downing Street, over the surplus tanks for Egypt and the Middle Eastern situation, 'The P.M. received us with great cordiality—Christian names and all ... The discussion was perfectly friendly'.[19a] The next week, after an official dinner at No. 10, to Gaitskell's surprise Eden chatted freely about the press campaign against him.[19i] Some months later Gaitskell remarked:

> he is a queer person; every now and then he treats me as though I were a member of the Government. For instance, he greeted me in the House the other day, 'Have you heard the good news? ... ' as though I were one of his closest colleagues. Very odd altogether.[19h]

Eden's personal unpopularity was not the government's only weakness, for the last instalment of Butler's economic legacy was now coming due. Macmillan, the reluctant new Chancellor, introduced the fourth deflationary package in twelve months and, as Gaitskell soon learned, had to threaten resignation to force it through.[39] It worked very rapidly. In February, Gaitskell told a leading bank chairman that there was an even chance of a really major crisis in 1956—and was accused of overoptimism.[19b] But in April, even before the Budget, he said to Crossman that after all the Conservatives might manage to deflate the economy without needing physical controls.[40a]

The new policy made an easy target for the Opposition. Gaitskell made his first big speech as leader celebrating the PLP's golden jubilee before a packed audience in Leeds town hall, with 110 enthusiastic Yorkshire pioneers, members for fifty years, on the platform. Strangely, it was his first successful speech in that hall in nearly twenty years in Leeds politics.[19j] He denounced once again the false prospectus of the recent election, the attack on growth and investment in order to reduce imports, and the new burdens on the poor—first pots and pans, and now lower bread and milk subsidies—after the big budgetary concessions to companies and to the better-off.[41] In the House Labour's vote of censure used the very words of the Chancellor's announcement. Gaitskell left the opening assault to his colleagues, commenting:

Harold [Wilson] and Douglas [Jay] both made outstanding speeches[42] ... Harold ... adopted a really responsible line. I am delighted ... because if he is to be Chancellor in the next Government, it is essential that he should build up a store of confidence in the country ... If we can only make the Party understand that they should attack on themes where the Party is most united and the Government most vulnerable, and not attack on the opposite occasions, then I think we shall continue to do fairly well.[19J]

That glimpse of the obvious speaks volumes for the tactical problems facing Labour leaders.

Gaitskell decided from the start to concentrate the PLP's energies by seeking fewer major debates. He quickly earned newspaper praise as 'the man who is putting most of the new zip into Parliament',[43] and for becoming 'the most effective Parliamentarian for many a long year'.[5e] Feeling themselves more useful, the mood of Labour MPs improved, and the friendlier atmosphere in the PLP percolated down to the constituency Parties.[44] Crossman no longer worried about opposition from the working-class veterans:

[A] new young leadership is actually taking over and the old men are actually moving to the sidelines. Even six weeks ago I had an uneasy query whether Hugh & Co. could really take over ... Now ... they are actually doing so, just at the moment when the Tory leadership is showing every sign of disintegration.[40b]

iii   'The Night of the Long Spoons' and the 'Mush of Unity'

The first attacks on Gaitskell's leadership arose from a visit of the Soviet leaders to Britain. Stalin had died in 1953. Malenkov, who had once seemed his likely successor but was now only a Deputy Premier, came over in March 1956. He charmed his hosts by his open-minded frankness, and was evidently impressed by his first contact with the West. Gaitskell spent five hours with him, presented him with Durbin's Politics of Democratic Socialism, and warned him that the local fellow-travellers only misled the Russians about British public opinion, while the Communist Party only impeded normal relations between the two countries. Malenkov asked questions most of the time, and Gaitskell felt 'that he was genuinely seeking information, that he even seemed prepared to believe what I was saying and that, in contrast to Mr. Malik and Mr. Gromyko, he scarcely ever made use of the stock Communist formulae when he spoke'.[45] Malenkov delighted his hearers by favouring a Soviet guarantee of Israel's frontiers, and by agreeing that a nuclear war would obliterate communism as well as capitalism—a view he had earlier expressed publicly and had to recant.[46] All his hosts found him very easy to talk to, and Khrushchev told Gaitskell later: 'You seem to have made a great impression on him.'[19k]

He was soon followed by the two men who had recently taken over his former posts: Khrushchev the new First Secretary, and Bulganin the new Prime Minister. With them, relations were very different. Not yet mellowed by experience, Khrushchev pursued intransigent policies in the crudest style, revelling in the destructive power of his nuclear weapons, which he insisted would wipe out capitalism while communism would survive. Gaitskell had forty minutes with him in private, and intended to seek the release of social democrats imprisoned in Eastern Europe. But the moment never came, for there was an earlier explosion at Gaitskell's warning that good relations could never be achieved through Communist front organisations or egregious fellow-travellers like the Dean of Canterbury. Unlike Malenkov, Khrushchev reacted furiously, denouncing British trade unionists who visited Russia and complained about conditions, attacking Labour's foreign policy and its anti-Communism, and saying he found Tories much more congenial.[19k]

A week later the Labour Party gave a dinner for the Russians. The guests had agreed to only two speeches, followed by questions in which they knew the imprisoned social democrats would come up.[47] Some sixty people were present in the Harcourt Room at the House (where acoustics are not perfect). It began well enough with brief speeches by the chairman Edwin Gooch, and by Bulganin—though George Brown's jocularity seems to have annoyed the Russians. Some Labour diners, who did not know the arrangements, then called for Khrushchev, who had not expected to speak. Gaitskell recorded:

> He spoke, including the translation, for an hour and it was, in places, extremely provocative. The verbatim report, which I have, shows what was said, but it does not show adequately the vehemence, almost brutality, with which it was said ... people began to feel gloomier and gloomier ... When he came to the Stalin-Ribbentrop pact and defended it, George [Brown] said 'God forgive him' ... I am sure that it was Stalin and not Khrushchev that George was referring to.[48] Nye Bevan also interrupted, but in a more moderate manner ... Two other aspects of the speech were pretty frightening. First, he definitely pooh-poohed the idea of [disarmament] controls ... and, secondly, he gave us a very plain threat that if we did not look out they would come to terms with Germany.

Other diners were appalled;[49] Crossman wrote eighteen months later: 'I will never forget ... [Khrushchev's] couldn't-care-less suggestion that we should join the Russians, because, if not, they would swat us off the face of the earth like a dirty old black beetle.'[40c]

Gaitskell decided he could not simply forget about Labour's questions, but was carefully conciliatory in wording his reply, stressing that he sought no immediate answer. But without being called, Khrushchev at once jumped up and told his listeners offensively: 'If you want to help the enemies of the working class, you must find another agent to do it.' Sam Watson and Nye Bevan also intervened quite mildly; and Khrushchev rushed out in a furious temper without shaking hands. Next day the papers indicated that there had been a row. At the Speaker's lunch, Bulganin was quite friendly, and Khrushchev shook hands with Gaitskell but not with Brown. When he again insisted that the Russians would do as they pleased in their own sphere, Bevan became exasperated and said loudly: 'He's impossible. It's time he grew up.'

Next morning at the NEC there was much criticism – though none from Bevan, and directed only at Brown.[50] Gaitskell and Griffiths went to say goodbye to the Russians, and Khrushchev said they would publish an account of the meeting in the USSR; Gaitskell politely replied that the Labour Party would correct any misleading summaries in the British press by publishing its own verbatim report.* After a frigid hour they thawed a little, and when Gaitskell boldly said that George Brown and Khrushchev were rather alike, the latter burst out laughing. At the very end, they invited Gaitskell to Moscow and departed 'with continual handshakes and general cordiality'.[51] It was superficial, for Khrushchev nursed his resentment for years.[52]

At the Party Meeting Shinwell and a handful of MPs wanted to apologise, but Gaitskell said Labour had done itself good by standing up for its principles, and won great applause.[53] Only the *Daily Express* and *Daily Worker* attacked Gaitskell; the latter abused Bevan equally, and *Tribune* did not join the critics – though a leading Beaverbrook-Bevanite said Gaitskell clearly could not negotiate with the Russians and Eden was 'a better bet for peace'.[13b] But Gaitskell never believed that self-deception about the Russians or concealment of differences was the way to lasting agreement. He thought it would have been shameful for Labour to behave any differently at the dinner, and was rightly sceptical about the permanence of the Soviet 'new look' policy.[54]

Incensed at the exploitation of the dinner incident by Eden and the Conservative Party, Gaitskell unwisely struck back over the strange affair of Commander Crabb, a naval frogman who had vanished after diving near the Soviet visitors' cruiser off Portsmouth – where evidence of his stay at a local hotel was removed by the police. Eden publicly announced that he had not known of Crabb's doings and was taking disciplinary

* The Russians never took the risk.

action. Gaitskell insisted on a debate, but muted his attack to avoid Tory charges of lack of patriotism, and both Morrison and Shinwell ostentatiously abstained from voting.[55] Roy Jenkins called it 'a typical Opposition leader's mare's nest';[56] a more experienced man would have left it alone.

The honeymoon had ended and some mutterings now began against Gaitskell's leadership.[57] There was a little sniping from the *Tribune* irreconcilables, aided by their Beaverbrook-Bevanite allies.[58] But the Party's policy statements and the leader's own Fabian pamphlet on nationalisation were quite well received. Even some critics admitted that he had made the parliamentary Opposition far more cohesive, purposeful and effective; and the *Daily Worker* lamented the 'curious hesitancy' of left-wing MPs to attack a leader whose policies they suspected but whose efficiency they conceded.[59]

In the autumn of 1956, Gaitskell attended his first Party Conference as leader, at which Bevan returned to the National Executive by winning election as treasurer at last — by 3,029,000 to 2,755,000 for George Brown and 644,000 for Charles Pannell of the AEU. (Bevan told a press conference that he now considered himself a calculating machine, but he hoped not yet desiccated.)[21c] Gaitskell had played no overt part in the contest. But though the feud was no longer public, the old suspicions persisted, and he had participated in early cabals with the big unions to find a strong candidate against Bevan — in which Frank Cousins, the new Transport Workers' secretary, insisted on Brown becoming their standard bearer.[60] Neither the Miners nor Municipal Workers were keen on Brown;[40d] but Gaitskell quietly helped promote his candidature.[61] As the leader had always expected, the NUR and USDAW votes were decisive, and Bevan won narrowly, to the delight of the CLP delegates. It helped maintain 'an atmosphere of unity such as the party has not known for years'.[62]

Cousins, appearing at his first Conference in his new post, promised he would maintain that unity and not tell the Labour Party how to do its job;[63a] and at his own union's dinner he gave Bevan a clear warning against disruption (they had already clashed in private). Gaitskell was not intellectually impressed with Cousins, whom he found 'profoundly ignorant of the real issues', much too prone to talk without thinking, and obviously hungry for power. But the leader saw the importance of keeping in close touch, and felt that would be easy since personally 'he and his wife were extremely friendly to us. And he several times went out of his way to show that he was entirely on my side'.[19l]

Gaitskell himself presented the new policy document *Towards Equality*. He told the delegates that it was the aspect of Socialism he had cared about most for thirty years;[63b] and a Tory critic felt that his 'obsession' with a classless society revealed the 'fanaticism' beneath his charm.[21d] (Tories hated egalitarian tax schemes far more than nationalisation.[40e]) His

'I SEE TWO DANGEROUS MEN IN YOUR LIFE..'

speech changed the minds of delegates previously convinced that the PLP had chosen the wrong man.[64] They gave him 'another ecstatic ovation',[21d] and he came beaming to the rostrum: 'Thank you, comrades. We take that as a pledge between us.'[63c] It was a moment of triumph not repeated until his final Conference six years later.

In the new mood, not even foreign policy and defence were obstacles to unity. In the spring of 1956, Labour had enjoyed 'the best Defence debate we have had for years';[19m] and though controversy continued over national service and the size of the defence budget, and Bevan still flirted privately with the idea of opposing NATO — he did nothing to provoke another conflict.[19h n] As part of the new mood Gaitskell recruited old left-wing sympathisers like Younger and Crossman to work with Healey and Robens in shaping foreign policy.[65] Bevan's irreconcilable friends were unhappy that the old battle lines between the rebellious Left and the leadership were dissolving into an agreed compromise amid what Jennie Lee called a 'mush of unity';[40f] but to Younger's great amusement Crossman 'firmly lectured her on the folly of proposing policies in opposition which you are not prepared to implement in office!'[66] In the last regular foreign affairs debate of the dying session, Gaitskell persuaded even his old *New Statesman* critics that 'the Labour leadership has moved far and fast in recent months ... his view of the world is a totally different one from that of the government'.[67]

That did not please everyone. To one Tory journalist, Gaitskell's 'outstanding ability to handle the party meeting' showed only that he was 'mastering the art of leading from behind'.[21e] But another noted that the Parliamentary Party now often reached a consensus without a vote.[5f] And Anthony Greenwood rejoiced that 'The differences between ourselves and our opponents, which have sometimes seemed blurred in recent years, are becoming more clearly defined. Consequently enthusiasm in the country is running high'.[68] Gaitskell's leadership thus seemed accepted, successful and secure when, on the very eve of the recess, there erupted his first major challenge: the Suez crisis.

CHAPTER 15

SUEZ 1956–7

i *Colonel Nasser's Rhineland?*

GAITSKELL'S very first act as leader had been his New Year call on the Prime Minister over the surplus tanks for Egypt. Giving the affair far more importance than it deserved, it was, as he privately recognised, an act of rashness.[1] In the House he astutely turned the debate to the Middle East as a whole, and delighted even a left-winger like Sydney Silverman: 'At last we have a leader who can speak for all sections of the party.'[2] Gaitskell told Crossman, 'I've been wanting to make that speech for two years, ever since I came back from Israel.'[3a] A few weeks later the King of Jordan suddenly dismissed General Glubb. Labour was divided into a pro-Israeli majority and a vociferous pro-Arab minority, but Gaitskell skilfully contrived to satisfy MPs from Julian Amery on the far Right of the House to Konni Zilliacus on the far Left. He insisted that Britain must abandon paternalism, allow Jordan to go neutralist if she chose, supply modern arms to Israel, and settle the oil quarrel with the Americans.[4] He had what he called 'a wonderful ovation' while the Government gave an 'appalling display'.[5a]

By the summer of 1956 the West was taking alarm at President Nasser's ambitions: his sponsorship of Arab nationalists from the Atlantic to the Persian Gulf, his subversion of traditionalist Arab regimes and his hostility to Israel (whose shipping, in defiance of both the 1888 convention and of a UN resolution, he barred from the Suez Canal). For Eden, the last straw was Glubb's dismissal; for Dulles, it was Nasser's big purchases of Czech arms. On 19 July the United States abruptly withdrew her promised support for building the Aswan High Dam to promote Egyptian economic development. A week later, without notice or negotiation, Nasser seized the Canal installations by night, announced that the dam would be paid for by much heavier Canal dues, and threatened to imprison foreigners who tried to leave their jobs. In manner even more than substance, it was a blatant challenge to the Western powers, as Bevan later remarked: 'if the sending of one's police and soldiers into the darkness of the night to seize somebody else's property is nationalisation, Ali Baba used the wrong terminology.'[6a]

Gaitskell heard the news in 10 Downing Street, of all places, at an official dinner for the King of Iraq. At 10.45 p.m. Eden came up as he was talking to the King, and told them of Nasser's speech:

> He said he was getting hold of the American Ambassador immediately. He thought perhaps they ought to take it to the Security Council ... I said 'Supposing Nasser doesn't take any notice?', whereupon Selwyn [Lloyd] said 'Well, I suppose in that case the old-fashioned ultimatum will be necessary'. I said that I thought they ought to act quickly, whatever they did, and that as far as Great Britain was concerned, public opinion would almost certainly be behind them. But I also added that they must get America into line.[5b]

That night Eden held a Cabinet meeting, attended by the French Ambassador and the American Chargé d'Affaires.

Gaitskell carefully ensured that his impromptu reactions to late-night news had not given a false impression. He knew that the fire-eaters of the right-wing Tory Suez Group had been critical ever since the decision to withdraw British troops from Egypt in 1954; and now he re-emphasised Labour's disagreement with them. First, he consulted his colleagues. Next morning Griffiths, Crossman, Strachey, Robens and the Chief Whip all 'agreed that I should complain about Nasser's high-handedness and also suggest blocking the sterling balances. This is pretty well what happened in the House[7a] itself'.[5b] On Monday afternoon, 30 July 1956, the Shadow Cabinet met and

> there was some anxiety about our going too far in a bellicose direction and it was felt important that we should stress exactly what our attitude was to nationalisation, as contrasted with the breaking of international agreements or concessions.

That evening

> Jim Griffiths and I went to see Eden at my request ... I was a little concerned lest he might suppose that we would back force as a Party in the same way as the [Tory] Suez rebels ... I said that this was not the case ... force would be appropriate [only] in self-defence or, at any rate, in circumstances which could be properly justified before the United Nations ... Eden said, rather contemptuously, 'Well, you

surely don't believe that we are going to pursue Hugh Fraser's policy'
... to my suggestion that we ought really to see that Israel got some
more arms, but privately, Eden appeared to agree ... He confirmed ...
[that he favoured] international control of the Canal under the United
Nations, I think, with the hope that Nasser will accept this. I said
'What happens if he doesn't? Do you then use force?' Eden said,
'Well, I don't want to take that hurdle yet.' I had already made it plain,
I may say, that I doubted whether we could support force merely on
those grounds.[5b]*

The Shadow Cabinet met again on 31 July:

I told them roughly what I proposed to say in the debate ... there was
no great disposition to argue with me. Bevan made a rather lengthy
speech saying that all waterways like the Suez Canal should come
under international control, and not only the Canal itself.

But they agreed with Gaitskell that it was unwise to attack the Government
when Labour could so easily be 'framed as unpatriotic and ... irresponsible'. He checked the legal position with Sir Frank Soskice, talked at
length next day with Healey, and then saw three MPs (Benn, John Hynd
and Warbey) whom he found much too pro-Nasser and equivocal about
Israel. He reassured them that he would

distinguish sharply between the act of nationalisation and the question
of controlling the Canal, that although I thought that action was
necessary against Nasser, force could not be used and should not be
used unless there was real justification for it ... that [control] ought to
come under the United Nations, and that Russia should be asked to
the [forthcoming] Conference.[5b c]**

Gaitskell's views did not shift. Britain had a major legitimate interest in
the Canal, for most of her oil came through it and nearly half the ships
using it were British. While nationalisation alone gave no justification for
imposing an international solution by force, the manner in which Nasser
had acted showed he had an ulterior aim: to score a prestige triumph over
the West and so promote the expansion of Arab nationalism – or the
aggrandisement of Egypt. Gaitskell never believed in the 'Third World'

* Griffiths's contemporary note confirms that they told Eden 'that we could not
and would not support force except in accordance with the Charter, while
agreeing that some precautionary measures were wise'.[8a] (Hugh Fraser was a
'Suez rebel' MP.)

** He added: 'Tony Benn ... talented in many ways, a good speaker and a man
of ideas has extraordinarily poor judgment. He is the last person in the world
I would go to for advice on policy.'[5b]

right or wrong, or approved of ambitious military dictators when their skins were dark; and his sympathy for the Israelis, felt by most Labour people since the 1930s, had been keen since his visit in 1953.[9-10a] But any action to block Nasser's expansionism needed American backing. So did the economic pressure which he hoped would bring Nasser to the negotiating table. That policy might have worked in 1956, when Britain and France enjoyed the goodwill of most other countries and particularly the United States; it had no chance in 1957 after the invasion had isolated them totally.

Uncertain of what might occur next—and Cairo had seen murderous riots with foreign victims only four years earlier—Gaitskell at first approved of Eden's military precautions, which he thought any Government would have taken. He soon became alarmed at their scale and at the bellicose official propaganda about them. But he thought an attack on Egypt, in defiance of the Commonwealth and the United States, would be inconceivably reckless—especially after the assurances he believed he had from a Prime Minister who had always seemed the incarnation of modern liberal Conservatism, devoted to an internationalist foreign policy backed by domestic bipartisanship. All Gaitskell's speeches during the crisis therefore put precisely the same point of view, but with an emphasis that changed with the situation. On 2 August he sought to prevent his own Party becoming Nasser's apologists, and so stimulating both antagonism at home and intransigence in Egypt. On 12 September he feared an immediate naval confrontation in the Canal, and concentrated on demanding a reference to the UN instead. On 4 November, after the British and French governments had sent Egypt an ultimatum and vetoed an American resolution in the UN, he denounced their 'criminal folly' which could lead only to catastrophe.

The first debate was on Thursday 2 August 1956. The day before, Kenneth Younger had come in while Gaitskell was preparing his speech to suggest 'exactly what I should say on the United Nations ... he has been very helpful recently'.[11] On Thursday morning Eden saw Gaitskell alone to warn that he would be inhibited in the debate by continuing international talks on the users' conference proposed by Britain, France and the United States. Gaitskell later came to feel that the Prime Minister misled him in this conversation:

I pressed him once more about the use of force. There was not disagreement on the military precautions but I said, 'What is your attitude to be if Nasser refuses to accept the conclusions of the further conference?' As I recollect and so implied in what I subsequently wrote to him, he said, 'I only want to keep open the possibility of force in case Nasser does something else'. I must add, in fairness, that he claimed later that he had said that he only wanted to keep open the possibility of force *or* if Nasser did something else.[12] But at any rate I certainly thought he said the first, because I went into the House of Commons and told John Strachey who was sitting beside me just before the debate began – having an interest in the War Office – that Eden had said that force was to be used only if Nasser did something else, and we agreed that that was satisfactory.[5d]

Twenty minutes later Gaitskell rose to make a speech quite consistent with all he said later, yet which was to lead to his being widely charged with trimming for partisan reasons.

He spoke for less than half an hour, with no surprises for his colleagues. He said that the seizure of the Canal was objectionable not as an act of nationalisation but for three other reasons: a single state (which already interfered with shipping, in defiance of the UN) should not have sole control of an international waterway; the manner of the seizure undermined all confidence in Egyptian assurances; and that deliberately brusque challenge was plainly 'part of the struggle for mastery in Middle East'. It was calculated to raise Nasser's prestige so that

> our friends desert us because they think we are lost, and go over to Egypt ... It is all very familiar. It is exactly the same that we encountered from Mussolini and Hitler in those years before the war ... the danger ... [in] the other Arab States ... is probably the most important immediate effect.

Iraq and perhaps Jordan were at risk at once, Israel later. Gaitskell urged a conference of the 1888 signatories, to include Russia and Egypt; a UN control commission; a ban on arms to Arab states, and perhaps a delivery to Israel; a pipeline laid at once from Aqaba to Haifa;[13] and help to shipowners to build big tankers to go round the Cape. Military precautions were justified, but it was settled British policy not to use force

> in breach of international law or, indeed, contrary to the public opinion of the world. We must not, therefore, allow ourselves to get into a position where we might be denounced in the Security Council as aggressors, or where the majority of the Assembly were against us.

Nasser's ban on Israeli ships might once have justified force, but it had not been used then. In his other actions

> it would, I think, be difficult to find ... any legal justification for the use of force. What he may do in the future is another matter ... While force cannot be excluded, we must be sure that the circumstances justify it and that it is, if used, consistent with our belief in, and our

pledges to, the Charter of the United Nations and not in conflict with them.[7b]

The reception gave no immediate hint of the coming storm. The passage on Nasser's expansionism, he wrote,

> was not popular with the Left-Wingers but apart from this the speech was reasonably well received ... presumably by chance, almost all of those called on our side belonged to the extreme right wing ... and ... were prepared to back the use of force now ... only Warbey from the Left was able to speak ... [so] they had a grievance owing to their enforced silence on this occasion.
>
> I was a little embarrassed by far too much praise from the Tories ... Presumably they did not listen to the last part of my speech ... Looking back on it now the criticisms of the speech made in the [Labour] Party owed more to my decision not to attack the Government than to anything I actually said, though the pro-Arab element did not like my attack on Nasser.[5d]

In underlining the provocative *fait accompli* which spectacularly humiliated the other side, as in the Rhineland occupation, Gaitskell compared neither Egypt to Germany nor Nasserism to Nazism. But he should have known that his analogy was far more memorable than the cautious unremarkable sentences at the end expressing his reservations about using force. No phrase-maker, he thought of his whole balanced argument and not of the selective reporting.[14a] 'It is extraordinary', he wrote later about this episode,

> how difficult one finds it to get across to the public exactly what one thinks. If you make a speech, then only part of it is reproduced ... [often] giving a totally false impression. If on the other hand you write an article ... no other newspaper ever dreams of referring to it.[5e]

Gaitskell's lapses in communication were a serious professional weakness. But this time he was walking a political tightrope, trying to discourage both British bellicosity and Egyptian intransigence:

> I would have spoken even more plainly in the debate had I not been so anxious to avoid any appearance of disunity ... I tried to make it as plain as I could that we could not support force, except as permitted by the U.N. Charter — without giving Nasser encouragement that he could disregard any idea of any international solution.[15]

Gaitskell did not know that the Cabinet — with no absentees — had already agreed to use force unless a negotiated solution was quickly found.[16] He later felt personally betrayed, believing that the Prime

Minister had deliberately misinformed him.[17] At the time of the debate, 'it never entered my head that the Government would do what they finally did'.[18] That same Thursday evening, however, Douglas Jay telephoned to say that the Foreign Office were telling journalists that Egypt would face an Anglo-French ultimatum after the conference and an invasion if it was rejected:

> I said to Douglas that I could hardly believe this because it did not fit in with what Eden had said to me. But the next morning, it was obvious that Douglas was right ... I sat down and wrote to Eden a letter in my own hand ... not [to] assume that the Labour Party would support the policy of force ... repeating what I had said to him in the two discussions ... much more emphatically in the letter. We then went off to Wales.[5d]

The letter, wrote Gaitskell, was 'a further word of friendly warning'. Written in the spirit of foreign policy bipartisanship, it was quite explicit:

> I deliberately refrained from putting the hypothetical question in public 'Was it proposed to use force to compel Nasser to accept the International Control Scheme?' For I felt that it might embarrass you to do so. Had I said in my reply to my own question that we could not support such action, it might, I felt, have gravely weakened your chances of achieving a settlement. Even to have said publicly that we were uncommitted on this issue would have done harm ... While one or two members of our Party indicated in the debate that they would support force now, this is, I am pretty sure, not the general view ... If Nasser were to do something which led to his condemnation by the United Nations as an aggressor, then there is no doubt, I am sure, that we would be entirely in favour of forceful resistance. But I must repeat, what I said in my speech yesterday, that up to the present, I cannot see that he has done anything which would justify this.[19]

Yet both the Conservative press and Gaitskell's Labour enemies propagated the myth that he had supported Eden's policy of using force, but changed his mind because of a Labour revolt.[20] Scholars who have studied the episode do not take that myth seriously.[21] Its persistence demonstrates only the capacity of some politicians for self-deception.

Gaitskell's policy, right or wrong, reflected his own judgment. He never hinted either that Labour might support seizing the Canal by force, or that he personally favoured doing so. Instead he said exactly the opposite in the House itself, and then, before any breath of Labour criticism reached him, gave Eden three separate private warnings. Nevertheless some Ministers ignored Gaitskell's words in the House, and convinced themselves for years that the myth was true.[22] They had a little excuse, for the Prime Minister may not have told them of Gaitskell's private warnings.[23a] Eden had none. Apart from Gaitskell's letter and visits, he was warned after the debate by both his Chief Whip and his own press officer that Labour would not support a policy of force.[24] But unhappily, at the time the sick Prime Minister chose to 'see only what he wanted to see';[25] and in retrospect he obliterated all reference to Gaitskell's public and private warnings from his memory — and from his memoirs.[26]

Bellicose briefings from No. 10 and the Foreign Office now filled the press, where Conservative papers claimed the full support of the Opposition. Labour anxiety spread quickly, and a dozen MPs sent Gaitskell friendly advice while he was on holiday. Most urged him to denounce the use of force, though the few who dissented were not all on the Right. With his encouragement Douglas Jay and Denis Healey wrote a strong letter in *The Times* of Tuesday 7 August;[27] he told Eden (and others) that it 'broadly coincides with my own view', though he had been cautious in public so as not to 'encourage Nasser's intransigence'.[28] Next day two dozen left-wing MPs sent to the press, and then to the NEC, a denunciation of the Government's provocative language and behaviour.[29] Gaitskell found nothing much wrong in it;[5d] but the Tory press called it a major challenge to his leadership.[30] Prominent Labour supporters outside the House were alarmed by the misleading press reports of Gaitskell's views, and on 9 August the Party's deputy leader and general secretary therefore circulated his speech — stressing the UN passages — to MPs, candidates, unions and local Parties.[31] When the House was recalled in September, Griffiths urged Gaitskell to wind up in the debate

> to strengthen my position in the Party. Both he and the Chief Whip then said in a kind of guilty way, which was rather charming, that they thought I ought to know now that there had in fact been a good deal of trouble about my speech on August 2nd in the Constituencies ... The decision ... to circulate my speech to the Constituency parties had undoubtedly done much to stop that ... I really do consider myself extraordinarily lucky in having such a wonderfully loyal and thoroughly decent person as the Deputy Leader.[5g]

Gaitskell shared the alarm at the government's sabre-rattling, for Eden's reply to his letter of 3 August was 'guarded and not very satisfactory'. It gave no assurance about force, and Gaitskell now suspected that the military preparations were not merely precautionary. From Wales, he asked Griffiths to go to Downing Street yet again on his behalf — and even 'to take someone with him (as a witness!)'[32] He sent the Prime Minister another letter, his fourth note of misgiving and anxiety:

> I could not regard an armed attack on Egypt by ourselves and the French as justified by anything which Nasser has done so far or as consistent with the Charter of the United Nations ... [or as] justified in order to impose a system of international control over the Canal — desirable though this is.[33]

On 10 August Griffiths and Robens saw Eden, who promised only that short of new Egyptian aggression he would not 'use force *until the Conference*'.[34] As Griffiths was going on holiday, Gaitskell cut his own vacation short and returned to London on Sunday 12 August. On Monday afternoon the Shadow Cabinet unanimously endorsed his speech of 2 August, reiterated his warnings against using force, proposed reference to the UN Assembly and supported a UN control scheme. 'Nye & Hugh saw exactly alike, Nye being if anything tougher against Nasser,' wrote Kenneth Younger.[14a] They shared another view. *Tribune* had twice carried pieces advocating internationalising all waterways like Suez: Bevan's first article on 3 August and, a week later, the statement of the twenty-four MPs. But on the same page as that was another Bevan article headlined 'It Must Not Be All "Take", Colonel Nasser'. This attacked Egypt's claim to a sovereign right of 'closure, obstruction or discrimination by one nation ... a stranglehold on the economic life of Europe'; but it no longer referred to other waterways (like Panama).[35] * At the Shadow Cabinet, wrote Gaitskell:

> To my particular astonishment Nye Bevan himself was very much in agreement with me ... He was in no doubt about Nasser being a thug ... [or] about the need for international control ... [He] opposed the proposal to put in a reference to the desirability of general internationalisation of waterways. He said, 'You will be surprised to hear this from me but I think it would be a great mistake to say anything at the moment which would embarrass the Americans' ... the meeting could not have been more harmonious or friendly.[5d]

After much hesitation (and against Bevan's wishes), Gaitskell, Griffiths and Robens again went to No. 10 next morning and talked for forty minutes with Eden, Lloyd and Salisbury, the Lord President. Gaitskell urged them to say that the military precautions were for self-defence only. 'We did not get very far with them ... [but] they certainly were left in no doubt about our views on the whole situation.'[5d] The Labour Party learned of the scale of the preparations from Mintoff the Prime Minister of Malta;[37] and Thorneycroft told Gaitskell (who knew it was the general ministerial line) that the government reserved the right to use force eventually. Gaitskell still did not believe they would do so, though he did

---

* Foot has over a page on these two articles, omitting Bevan's change of front.[36]

believe Pineau the French Foreign Minister, who claimed to want not that force should be used, but that Nasser should think it might be:

> I am sure that really is the basis of the Government's policy. Perhaps at the start they really did contemplate using it. But it was more a question of appeasing the [Tory rebel] Suez Group on the one hand, taking perfectly legitimate precautions on the other, in case Nasser did something silly, and finally the bluff, as well of course, as I have mentioned already, the desire to use force or to be free to use force.

He was sceptical of the power of the Suez Group: 'It is very rare in English politics for a minority to be able to dispose of a Party leader unless he is very weak indeed.'[5d]

On 24 August Gaitskell saw Dulles, congratulated him on proposing his international control scheme at the users' conference, and repeated that half the country would not support the use of force. (The Secretary of State then warned Eden that he was misjudging British public opinion, and Eden again rejected the warning.)[38] Gaitskell and Dulles agreed that in the event of Egyptian refusal to negotiate, the Canal users should 'continue to put financial and economic pressure on Nasser until he had become more reasonable':[39] building pipelines, organising alternative transport, and increasing American oil supplies to Europe. An appeal to the UN was not an automatic solution to the problem but part of a strategy, as Gaitskell argued to the French Ambassador:[40]

> [W]e had to so conduct ourselves to get world opinion more on our side ... First, if we did not do it somebody else would, India, America or Russia. Secondly, it provided a new forum for further negotiations with Nasser. Thirdly, obviously Nasser ... would be embarrassed at the U.N. partly because of the failure of Egypt to carry out the Security [Council] resolution on the Israeli ships. And finally I said that whatever we may have to do eventually it can only be an advantage to have been to the United Nations, whatever the exact outcome of that would be.[5f]

At the end of the month he still did not believe that Eden meant war, to the surprise of the *Manchester Guardian* staff and its dying editor A. P. Wadsworth. At Wadsworth's insistence Gaitskell gave the paper an interview which helped, he thought, to cool the Government's ardour.[41–2] As in *Reynolds* a few days before, he condemned both extremes: 'Nasser is an ambitious military dictator ... But, so far, what he has done does *not* justify armed retaliation.' If Nasser refused to negotiate on the users' conference proposals, the West should not use force but boycott the Canal and prepare for a long economic struggle.[43]

Gaitskell was glad the Gallup poll showed the UN line to be popular, for that would restrain the Tories.[59] Its popularity was not, as Crossman thought, his ground for adopting it; but he knew it helped avert a Labour split.[3b] For in early August the pacifist protests from the Party in the country had come in response to bellicose cries from Morrison and the PLP extreme Right in the debate. Eden consulted Morrison frequently;[44] and before the TUC met at the beginning of September he called its president, Charles Geddes, to Downing Street. Geddes mobilised a majority of the General Council's international committee behind the Government, and only a prolonged filibuster by Alan Birch of USDAW and other younger members dissuaded them from saying so.[45]

The General Council majority were not alone. Millions of trade unionists had served in Egypt during the war, coming into contact mainly with the parasitic hangers-on around the army camps, whom they despised more than the people of any other foreign land. Though Gaitskell so often stood with the working-class populists against the intellectual Left, he rejected the feelings of hate and contempt for Egyptians which tempted many Labour voters to approve of the invasion. Whatever the political consequences, he would not play to that gallery.

ii *Lull before the Storm*

The crucial issue was whether or not to use force to impose international control on Egypt. A scheme was agreed in August 1956 by the conference of eighteen user nations, mostly small and some from the 'Third World'. It was put to Nasser by a negotiating committee of five, led by Menzies the Australian Prime Minister. Dulles had declined the task, and when President Eisenhower publicly renounced the use of force, the Egyptian President felt he could safely break off the talks. The UN now became a field for tactical manoeuvre. The Labour Opposition, wanting to use it for serious negotiations, had urged on 13 August that the issue should go to a special UN Assembly – dominated by small countries though, in 1956, not yet by Afro-Asian ones. Instead the British and French Governments proposed to go to the Security Council, expecting a Soviet veto and intending then to attack Egypt.[46] Dulles feared that would oblige the United States to choose between her allies and the 'Third World' countries, and suggested instead a new Suez Canal Users Association (SCUA) to employ the pilots, control the navigation and collect the dues. With many misgivings, but hoping to commit the United States to oppose Egypt if SCUA's ships were obstructed, Eden persuaded his colleagues and the reluctant French to accept this plan. In presenting it to the recalled Parliament at the start of a two-day debate, he implied that escorting warships would force the convoys through if necessary.[47a]

Gaitskell, who had known nothing of the plan, at once protested at the

42 A Million Pounds Poorer. Leaders of the Transport Workers' Union Frank Cousins (*left*), Arthur Townsend the busmen's spokesman (*centre*), and Harry Nicholas call off the London Bus Strike, May 1958

43 After unveiling a plaque to Jack and Bessie Braddock in Liverpool, 1958

44 With European Socialist leaders, including Willi Brandt (*far left*) in Stockholm, 1959

45 Speaking to a rally sponsored by Sir Miles Thomas (*centre*), Chairman of the British Productivity Council in 1959. The platform is shared by Prime Minister Macmillan

threat; so that his speech on 12 September had quite a different emphasis from that of 2 August. He still reaffirmed all his old criticisms of Nasser's conduct. But while giving a clear warning in August against using force contrary to the UN Charter, he had not then stressed his opposition to a course which was not being proposed and which he then thought Eden had abjured. That course, from the very day after the August debate, had been repeatedly and publicly canvassed at the instigation of Ministers. A Leader of the Opposition, foreseeing catastrophe, had a plain duty to probe their aims and expose the dangers – both to the country and to the no longer united Cabinet.

Gaitskell warned that the talk of war rallied the Arab world to Nasser, alarmed the United States and India, and found no European support except in France. Joint Anglo-French action, opposed by the rest of the world, would mean disaster. If the threats were meant, the post-war international order was at risk; Asia and the Arab countries would be alienated; the Commonwealth might collapse; the danger to oil supplies would grow; and the Middle East would become a breeding-ground for Communism. If the threats were bluff, then Britain faced 'the greatest diplomatic climb-down in our history' and Nasser's prestige victory would be enormously magnified. The Government should state now that they would not use force against the Charter, and would take the dispute to the UN: 'I want to emphasise with all the strength that I can that ... [this] is not just to go through formalities so that we may thereafter resort to force. It is that there may be a further period of negotiation.' Similarly, the users' association seemed to be proposed as a device not for instituting talks, but for provoking Egypt to obstruct the ships – and if so, would the United States act with us?[47b] The Conservative benches became 'a howling mob'.[5g] But the Labour ones erupted in 'the loudest ovation ... for years'.[48a]

Eden still refused a pledge not to use force contrary to the Charter. A former Conservative Attorney-General, Sir Lionel Heald, pressed for it in a weighty speech, but at 6 p.m. the senior Ministers decided against giving it – Butler wanting to do so, Macmillan strongly objecting.[49a] Winding up the second day's debate, Gaitskell again called for the pledge. While on his feet, he was told of Dulles's press conference statement that the United States would not 'shoot our way through the Canal'. Yet again Eden had convinced himself of what he wanted to believe; and Gaitskell repeated the question in the words of the Secretary of State: 'Is he prepared to say on behalf of H.M.G. that they will not try to shoot their way through the Canal?' In a tumultuous and passionate House, Eden replied in the last five minutes of the debate, apparently giving the assurance demanded. 'I have never seen', wrote one level-headed Labour MP, 'a clearer or more outstanding victory of Opposition over Government.'[50] But instead of withdrawing the censure motion and consolidating his triumph like an

P

astute parliamentarian, Gaitskell wrote to *The Times* to point out that the Prime Minister had been interrupted and that the disavowal was not clear-cut.[51] He was more concerned with the policy outcome than with personal or party gain.

Before the debate Gaitskell had already lost all confidence in Eden, but still could not conceive that the government would perpetrate 'sheer lunacy'. After it, he believed that at least for the moment they had drawn back:[52] 'I may be too optimistic but my feeling is that we are probably over the hump now. Certainly the danger of immediate war provoked by trying to break through the Canal seems to have been averted.'[59] (So also thought Nasser, the French Chief of Staff, British MPs and newspapers on both sides, and Eden's own Minister of State, Anthony Nutting.)[53] Gaitskell knew that public opinion was uneasy, that the moderate Conservatives were mobilising, and that senior Ministers were struggling to restrain the fire-eaters.* Yet with many Conservative Ministers and MPs doubting parts of Eden's policy — including nine members of the Cabinet — Macmillan could persuade himself that Gaitskell was 'getting off the patriotic line ... on to the "party" line'.[49b c]**

Only invincible wishful thinking could have persuaded Eden that Labour, under any leader, might have supported his policy.[26] Gaitskell did not wish to do so; or to be pushed too far the other way. He had to try to influence the Cabinet against its reckless course, without seeming to criticise his own country. Just before his first Party Conference as leader, Crossman wrote:

> He has seen the dangers of getting ourselves tagged as simply a pro-Nasser, anti-British party. He has made great efforts to get the Left and the Right of the Party working together, with some success, and his own speeches have been really very good.[3d]

But when Conference debated Suez on its opening day, 1 October 1956, the speeches were so strongly pro-Nasser that it seemed Gaitskell must 'go with the tide or be overwhelmed by it'.[57a b] He rose 'to an extremely perfunctory welcome ... [but] seized upon the most tactful approach apparently by instinct, and thereby turned the political tables in a trice.'[58] He urged the delegates to concentrate on the central question, not play the Tory game by sounding unpatriotic. Reference to the UN must not be a formal prelude to an invasion, but an opportunity to negotiate and to bring economic pressure on Egypt. If it were handled like an industrial dispute, 'I think there is not much doubt that Colonel Nasser will agree to

---

* Monckton, Minister of Defence, so informed Gaitskell who urged him to stay and argue, not resign.[54–5a]

** The nine were Amory, Buchan-Hepburn, Butler, Eccles, Hailsham, Home, Lloyd, Macleod and Monckton.[56]

a negotiated settlement'.[59a] (If so, Gaitskell's reference to Hitler looked rather silly.)[60] He again condemned Nasser's past conduct, but insisted that it did not justify attacking Egypt: that was Labour's essential difference with the government.

> [W]hether Colonel Nasser was right or wrong, the rights of Canal users, the right of self-defence, and the question of precautionary measures, are issues thrown in to muddy the water and confuse ... *the* crucial issue of the use of force ... we have had no clear undertaking from the Government that they would only use force in accordance with the Charter ... I wish I could say even now that the danger is entirely over.[59b]

It was a triumphant handling of a most awkward situation,[61] reversing Attlee's usual reception: 'tumultuous applause at the beginning of his speech, and polite clapping from the faithful at the end'.[58] Crossman was impressed: 'It's a real test for a new, untried, suspect Leader to have to start by rebuking and educating the Party, and I thought he did it extraordinarily well.'[3e]

iii   Invasion: 'Criminal Folly'[62]

Gaitskell had turned a nasty political corner, but the real crisis lay ahead. The danger of war was not over, and the die was apparently cast in that very week.[63] Gaitskell did not discover that the Cabinet fire-eaters had regained their ascendancy. He was emotionally drained, and distracted from public affairs, by his mother's death on 14 October. Rationally, too, he was convinced and indeed insistent that no British Administration (as distinct from Cabinet) would embark on so crazy an adventure in 1956.[64] Official advisers, he clearly assumed from his own governmental experience, would oblige blind or self-deluded Ministers to face reality.

He was too orderly an administrator and too far-sighted a politician to conceive of a sick but stubborn Prime Minister rigorously excluding all unwelcome news or views. For Eden's colleagues 'were perplexed by decisions taken outside the Cabinet in the Suez Committee';[65-6a] naval plans were concealed from the First Lord of the Admiralty;[67] very few officials were kept informed; advisers seemed reluctant to report bad news;[68a] the Foreign Office and legal experts were deliberately not consulted;[69] the British ambassadors concerned were kept in the dark;[70] communications with Washington were cut;* the angry Commonwealth countries were told nothing.[72] Eden and Macmillan relied on intuition to

* The Embassy was kept vacant from 11 October to 8 November when the new incumbent arrived by sea.[71] His predecessor had become head of the Treasury — and learned of the ultimatum in the press.

predict the response in those capitals, wantonly closed off any means of testing their own wishful thinking, reassured their worried colleagues – and then, after the invasion, expressed pained surprise at the furious reactions they had inexcusably misjudged.[73]

The wounds were self-inflicted. Eden boasted of rejecting normal international consultations precisely because they would generate pressure against the project.[74] Astonishingly, he did not see that a long-drawn-out military operation would also generate such pressures (especially in a Washington irritated at the secrecy and enraged by the timing, on the very eve of the presidential election).[75] Whatever its morality or wisdom, the attack was sure to fail unless it presented the world with an instant *fait accompli*. But the military refused to use paratroops alone; and seaborne forces would take six days from Malta.[76] The shrewder soldiers knew these military constraints made political failure inevitable.[77] But, self-insulated from any unwelcome advice, the politicians crashed ahead.

Yet, though Eden would not rule out using force to impose international-isation, he had privately thought it impossible without a new forcible act by Nasser.[78] By 16 October, however, the French had persuaded him that after a pre-emptive strike by Israel against Egypt, French and British forces could 'separate the combatants' by seizing the Canal.[79] French and Israeli (but not British) leaders have testified that the Israeli intentions were known in London in advance – and depended on a written British promise to eliminate the Egyptian air force.[80] The 'hypocritical and dis-ingenuous ultimatum', as Randolph Churchill called it,[66b] was ostensibly to justify an emergency peace-keeping intervention. It deceived no one outside Britain, and finally hamstrung the military operation itself. For the British government, fearing exposure, had to reject Israeli offers of help;[66b] and when Israel and Egypt stopped fighting, it had to accept its own cease-fire proposal before it had attained its real objectives.[81]

Gaitskell was presenting a television award when he learned on the evening of Monday 29 October, that Israel was mobilising. His extreme tenseness made an abiding impression.[82] At 4.15 p.m. next day the Prime Minister – once the champion of internationalism and advocate of bi-partisanship – gave the Leader of the Opposition fifteen minutes' notice of the Anglo-French ultimatum.[83] (One experienced Labour front-bencher thought it as one-sided as the Austrian ultimatum to Serbia in 1914.)[14b] Gaitskell obtained a short debate that evening, in which Healey from the back benches made the first strongly critical Labour speech.[10b]

The leader's comments were too cautious for the anti-Suez zealots of the *Manchester Guardian*.[84] But they were impressive for moderates: two years later an anti-Suez Tory MP said to him: 'I don't think there is a single word you would wish to change in it. It is pretty remarkable because you had very little time to prepare it.'[85] Accepting the government's

version – a surprise Israeli attack on Egypt which must be halted at once –
he argued that Britain should propose in the Security Council, first an
Israeli withdrawal and then prompt redress of her grievances. He probed
how far the Commonwealth and the United States had been consulted;
and asked what the government would do if it proved (as it did) that the
Israeli forces were still too far from the Canal to threaten it.[23c] Receiving
no promise to delay military action until the Security Council met, and
assuming that the invasion would be immediate, Labour divided the
House.

Next day brought no assurances, no invasion, but an Anglo-French
veto of an American resolution in the Security Council – which Gaitskell
condemned as

> an act of disastrous folly whose tragic consequences we shall regret for
> years ... irreparable harm to [our] prestige and reputation ... a
> positive assault upon the three principles which have governed
> British foreign policy ... solidarity with the Commonwealth, the
> Anglo-American Alliance and adherence to the Charter of the United
> Nations.[47e]

The Security Council was paralysed by the veto, but in the Assembly the
invaders would face a hostile two-thirds majority, perhaps alone.[86] No
others would believe the 'transparent excuse' for a long-planned policy
of force, particularly ill-timed at a moment of hope in Warsaw and Budapest.[47f] Gaitskell called for a denial of collusion with Israel;[87] and
appealed to the Tory dissidents, particularly Butler, against this 'reckless
and foolish decision' which would arouse a wave of hatred against Britain,
and which Labour would oppose 'by every constitutional means at our
disposal'.[47g] A Conservative paper called it 'perhaps the most forceful
speech Mr. Gaitskell has ever made in the House of Commons ... amid
triumphant cheers from his own supporters. The Government back
benchers for the most part sat in thoughtful silence'.[88] The mood did not
last.

Next day, Thursday 1 November, the Prime Minister condemned the
Opposition for not supporting British soldiers going into action. But he
did not even know the rights of those soldiers if captured, for he was
unable to say whether the United Kingdom was at war.[89] Nor had Ministers any news of the many British civilians in Egypt whose lives were now
in jeopardy.[47i n] For the first time for over thirty years the Speaker had to
suspend the sitting for half an hour. Next day it became apparent that the
oil supplies and free passage through the Canal, which it was Eden's
stated aim to preserve, had both been lost before a single soldier landed.[66c]
Moreover, while world attention was centred on Egypt, the Russians
seized their opportunity and sent their tanks back to Budapest to destroy

the new national-communist government of Hungary which had hopefully proclaimed its neutrality.

Most exceptionally, Parliament met on Saturday morning, 3 November 1956. The Prime Minister was still claiming to have acted solely to stop the fighting. Gaitskell replied:

> The Canal is blocked, there has been no rescue operation for British ships, no British lives have been saved, and all that has happened is that the intervention of Her Majesty's Government on behalf—or, rather, against Egypt—has *no doubt prematurely* brought the operations in the Sinai Desert to a close.

Eden at once, like many Conservatives later, quoted the unwise adverb against Gaitskell, who then dismayed Israel's Labour friends by his riposte: 'The Prime Minister is perfectly right. What we did was to go in and help the burglar and shoot the householder.' These verbal lapses and debating points were trivial beside the gravity of his major theme. Hitherto he had hoped and believed that the government would abandon a disastrous course which shocked half the country, world opinion and the UN. They had not done so.

> [T]here is only one way out, and that is a change in the leadership of the Government. Only that now can save our reputation and re-open the possibility of maintaining the United Nations as a force for peace. We must have a new Government and a new Prime Minister.

Only the anti-Suez Conservatives could achieve that. 'I ask them to do their duty.'[47l]

Sir Anthony Eden broadcast that evening, and Gaitskell claimed the right to reply. The Prime Minister tried hard to deny it, and allegedly planned to take over the BBC by legal manoeuvres which the directors and staff successfully resisted.[90] The BBC, which then decided such disputed cases, accepted Gaitskell's claim to reply to Eden after a great row with Downing Street and some delay.[91] His broadcast on the Sunday was therefore prepared in utter chaos at very short notice.[92]

It attracted a record audience. He said the Government argued that Britain and France had to act because the UN was too slow; if so, that was due solely to their own veto. Otherwise it would have reached an early decision, which Britain could have offered to help enforce by providing part of a UN force. That would genuinely have separated the combatants—but would not have given Britain control of the Canal. Instead we had gone to war against Egypt, split the Commonwealth and the country, imperilled all that we claimed to protect, and forfeited our own moral standing in the world at the very moment of the Russians' savage aggres-

sion in Hungary. We should at once abandon the invasion, accept the
UN's cease-fire resolution and welcome its force on the Arab-Israeli
border. But that required a new Prime Minister.[62]

Orthodox Conservatives were enraged by such a broadcast, coming
when the troopships were approaching Port Said. To many officers
aboard—who alone were allowed to listen—it seemed virtually treason-
able.[93] But other people saw it as redeeming Britain's ruined reputation.
One Labour MP reported that view from British diplomats in the Middle
East; another, in India and Pakistan, was told everywhere that only the
broadcast had kept those countries in the Commonwealth.[94] Conor
Cruise O'Brien watched it on television in an Irish pub:

> A crowd accustomed to be cynical both about politicians and about
> Englishmen, was deeply moved by Gaitskell's controlled and genuine
> passion and by his power of argument. Most understood the political
> and moral courage which it took to make such a speech at such a time.
> A tram-driver lowered his pint. 'You can't beat an Englishman', he
> said, 'when he's straight'.[48e]

The broadcast delighted the government's opponents (and was cited for
years to justify political talks straight to camera, without tricks).[95] But it
was not directed to opponents, for Gaitskell concluded by appealing again
to Conservatives who were also 'shocked and troubled ... our purpose
too ... rises above party ... we undertake to support a new Prime Minister
in halting the invasion of Egypt, in ordering the cease-fire, and complying
with the decisions and recommendations of the United Nations'.[62] The
appeal was counter-productive, and rallied waverers to Eden.[96]* Gaitskell
seems genuinely to have misjudged the likely reaction of the dissident
Conservatives.[3f g] Yet if he had omitted his appeal, the outcome would
have been the same. Those unhappy men were alarmed by Eden's policy—
but also at the prospect of a general election or a Labour government, to
one or both of which the overthrow of Eden must, without Gaitskell's
pledge, inevitably have led. To most Conservatives that would have seemed
a betrayal of both party and country, and the dissidents naturally shrank
from it. They welcomed any excuse to give Eden another chance. Gaitskell
provided a pretext by making his appeal—and would have provided
another by not making it.

It might well have been otherwise if—as Gaitskell probably hoped—a
senior Minister had resigned to lead the revolt and offer troubled Conservatives an alternative leadership.[68b] But Monckton decided not to resign,
since he neither wanted the Opposition to come to power nor believed in
Labour's notion of 'a kind of rump of the Tory Government led by Butler,

* So did the assault on Downing Street a few hours earlier by a section of the
crowd following Labour's 'Law not War' meeting in Trafalgar Square.

which they would support. This could not last'.[55b] Butler too thought the appeal was specifically addressed to him, and Gaitskell apparently tried to reach him (whether successfully or not is unclear) through PPS channels.* Butler asked many friends soon afterwards whether he should have resigned;[66d] but did not do so.[98]

Plainly the Opposition would have benefited from any change of government in such circumstances—though most people on both sides expected Labour to gain anyway. But no one could have done more than Gaitskell to demonstrate that he opposed the invasion not from party or personal ambition, but from his clear obligation to speak for the horrified half of the British people. His denunciation expressed the political character of a lifetime. As a consistent internationalist, who had founded a schoolboy branch of the League of Nations Union and made his very first speech against Mussolini's attack on Corfu, he was appalled when his own country was rebuked as an aggressor threatening international order. As a militant democrat, he was furious that its government was helping the Russians escape any political penalty for their outrage in Hungary. As a mature politician who tried to foresee the consequences of his own acts, he was dismayed when others headed straight towards predictable disaster:[99] for Nasser's fall would not have enabled a viable but docile Egyptian Government to be formed, or the Canal problem to be solved, or Israel to be made secure, or French rule to be preserved in Algeria.

Suez was one of many episodes in Gaitskell's career showing his characteristic shift from cautious judgment to total, even reckless commitment. The invasion ended any need to discourage Nasser as well as Eden, and any hope of satisfying simultaneously both Labour's militant trade unionists and Jews, and the bulk of the Party. The act of 'criminal folly' imposed a new priority: no longer to warn against the folly but to condemn the crime. The warnings were in retrospect unquestionably justified, the condemnation still remains violently controversial. Gaitskell represented a long British tradition of pacific, often moralising internationalism, which repelled some normal Labour supporters but appealed to many people beyond Labour's ranks. In that tradition, Gladstone had denounced the Bulgarian atrocities and Lloyd George the Boer War;[100] in 1956 there were Conservatives too who took the same side.

Government supporters of course thought Gaitskell's vehement opposition ill-judged, but were silly and petty to assume it concealed party calculation or personal ambition. Yet so they did, the more virulent of them accusing him of time-serving, political cowardice and even

---

* Gaitskell's PPS was to tell Butler's: 'tell your boss that if he intends to strike he must strike now': interview, Arthur Allen. But neither Butler nor his PPS recalled any communication.[97]

treason.[101-3a] Many felt that a Leader of the Opposition, whatever his own doubts, had a duty to hold his peace and support the government when British troops were going into action. Gaitskell did not share their view, or expect their fury: another instance of weak antennae. But the government's case was so threadbare and unconvincing that all sections of the PLP, a few Jewish MPs apart, at first applauded his handling of the affair.[104] Still warmer tributes came from those outside the Labour Party for whom he had spoken. Three will suffice. 'Nothing aroused my own contempt more', wrote Sir Edward Boyle, 'than the personal attacks on yourself ... I don't see how the case against the Government could have been put better than you put it.'[105]* Commander King-Hall in his influential *Newsletter* praised the Labour leaders' fulfilment of 'their duty to speak and struggle for a cause greater than any political party issue'.[106] Lady Violet Bonham Carter, Asquith's formidable daughter, sent before the broadcast 'a line of passionate personal gratitude for your magnificent speeches during this week. It was not for your party only you were speaking — you "spoke for England" — for England's *real* & best self.'[107a b]

iv *National Humiliation and Tory Popularity*

The high drama intensified over the next few days. On Sunday 4 November 1956 at 2 a.m., the Canadian Foreign Minister Lester Pearson, trying desperately to forestall invasion, had steered through the General Assembly a resolution to send a UN force to Egypt. It was unopposed, for the British Ambassador for fear of worse connived at a vote before London could instruct him to reject it.[68c] Plans were ready by lunchtime. Eden, who later claimed credit for the UN action, considered accepting the force provided it included Anglo-French troops — which the Afro-Asians vetoed. By the end of the afternoon the British government, stiffened by the French, had decided to invade: yet when the paratroops were already on the tarmac with their harnesses on, London was still asking how late it could order a twenty-four-hour delay.[108]

At dawn on Monday 5 November, the troops at last landed. That afternoon the Prime Minister told the House incorrectly that Port Said had fallen, winning an ecstatic standing ovation from Tories eager to believe all Egyptian resistance was over — but not from Labour, who were bitterly attacked for not joining in. Rightly doubting whether the cease-fire was general, Gaitskell stressed that if so the government had achieved its ostensible objective of ending the fighting, and should at once withdraw.[47m]

---

* In a remarkable letter written explaining why he was rejoining the Government, in which some phrases could have done the writer serious political harm. It is an extraordinary tribute to Gaitskell that a rising Conservative MP should have written so frankly to a Labour leader whom he did not even know very well.

Israel, like Egypt, now agreed to stop hostilities, depriving Eden of his cherished fig-leaf. So the British Cabinet, to the dismay of the French, halted the operation at midnight on Tuesday—election day in the United States—with the troops still seventy-five miles from Suez. The pound was under pressure, and Washington, by preventing Britain borrowing from the IMF, drove Harold Macmillan—Chancellor of the Exchequer and Eden's strongest supporter—to insist on an immediate cease-fire.[109] The USSR exploited the capitulation, threatening to bomb London and Paris (which did not alarm Eden or Mollet*) and to send 'volunteers' to Egypt (which did).[110]

The new parliamentary session opened that day, and Gaitskell indignantly repudiated the charge of lack of patriotism:[111] 'they have different views from ours as to what constitutes the honour and interests of Great Britain'. Denouncing the Soviet repression in Hungary, he added: 'the law of the jungle has been invoked by the British Government and ... there are much more dangerous animals wandering about than Great Britain or France.'[112a] Before Eden announced the cease-fire, Gaitskell learned of it from Leslie Hunter. He was to speak that night at the Albert Hall, and felt at first that the rally had become pointless—an astonishing misjudgment for, as Hunter pointed out, the cease-fire was a triumph for the Opposition.[113] The packed audience thought so, giving Gaitskell 'an ovation such as few party leaders can expect even after a great election victory'.[48d] At the end the Pakistani High Commissioner came up to him to say: 'Thank God for your speech, you have saved the Commonwealth.'[114]

The next six months showed the humiliating cost of offending the rest of the world by a display of vanished power. In December the British and French troops were withdrawn, after Washington would not let them be used as a bargaining counter for a Canal settlement. Eden, who all his life had been used to warm bipartisan public approval, suddenly for the first time faced bitter attack and the ruin of his policy; his health finally broke under the strain, and after a brief escape to Jamaica he returned for a last sad speech in the Commons just before Christmas, denying collusion—Hugh Thomas just calls it a lie.[115a] At the New Year he resigned, and the Conservative kingmakers mysteriously concluded that while Butler's equivocations over Suez disqualified him from the succession, Macmillan had qualified by advocating with equal ardour first invasion, then cease-fire and withdrawal.

The thought-processes of the British public, as shown in the Gallup polls, were no less mysterious.[116] They did not share the government's open contempt for the UN, and most people opposed military action beforehand and even at the time; but a plurality, though never a majority,

* The French Prime Minister, and a Socialist.

approved of it afterwards. Few government supporters believed the official grounds for intervention. But Eden's popularity – like Kennedy's after the Bay of Pigs – grew as his policy visibly collapsed. His frustrated followers eagerly hunted scapegoats. 'The Americans come first with the Labour Party a close second,' wrote Gaitskell.[117a]

A Gallup poll on 14 November showed both the rallying to Eden, and Labour's loss of its six-point lead. The PLP met that morning, and some MPs, hitherto enthusiastic over Gaitskell's leadership, now began to criticise it.[118] But he would not alter a course which, he told the cynical Crossman, was morally right.[119] A confused public opinion, he believed, would change as it discovered the government's 'appalling blunder'.[117b] Probably he was wrong: politicians on both sides thought that three years later the memory of Suez brought more votes to the Conservatives than to Labour.

The crisis had stirred deep emotions at Westminster, where the House of Commons was more disorderly than for decades. Unrestrained Labour turbulence and fury were partly caused by the justified but unprovable suspicion that the government was successfully deceiving the country about its real aims. Gaitskell, like all political leaders who condemn the catastrophic military adventures of their governments, met the most virulent hostility. He was accused simultaneously (if inconsistently) both of hysterical revulsion against Eden's policy and of calculated exploitation of it. The first charge was false as well as the second. His feelings were passionate, and his phrasing once or twice infelicitous. But twenty years later the impression made by his speeches is not of hysteria but of an always courteous tone expressing forceful argument and acute prediction. The attacks on him reflected no objective view, but the passions of the critics themselves.[120-1]

Gaitskell never doubted the rightness of his conduct, but he was a sensitive man and by no means impervious to the hatred. In the House, the persistent and bitter interruptions whenever he spoke, well into 1957, even made him wonder whether his effectiveness as Leader of the Opposition had been permanently impaired.[122-3] In the country, Suez did his reputation some harm, though not where he could explain his case in person.* An early taste of angry hostility came at his old school, where he was to speak on 16 November on the role of the Opposition. The night before, he promised the alarmed headmaster to avoid controversy – and then was asked at immense length by a choleric retired housemaster to explain why he had behaved as a traitor. His reply completely won over the bulk of his audience.[124]

In the electorate at large, he held his own among his own supporters, for

* Notably in Leeds, where Solly Pearce arranged for him to speak to Poale Zion to allay criticism from the large Jewish community there.

two-thirds of Labour voters thought Gaitskell a good leader in both September and December (69 and 67 per cent) and only 12 per cent (on both
dates) thought him a bad one.[125] Overall he had 9 per cent fewer supporters,
because he had lost half his former Conservative admirers; and the number
thinking him a bad leader had nearly doubled, owing to Conservative,
Liberal and especially Don't Know voters who earlier had had no view of
him. Probably his new detractors were rather non-political people, liable
to unthinking patriotic reflexes, and influenced by the newspaper attacks
upon him.

For Suez had one strange by-product: an extraordinary press campaign
praising Bevan at Gaitskell's expense. The Beaverbrook press began it with
a denunciation of Gaitskell's 'contemptible leadership' and a warm
accolade for Bevan as 'incomparably the bigger man'.[102] Other newspapers
and politicians quickly took up the theme.[126-7a] Though Bevan's speeches
appealed to the UN just as frequently as Gaitskell's, and were no more
tender to the government, the Conservatives pretended that, unlike those
of his leader, they contained only temperate and good-humoured criticism.[128] Many Conservatives hated Gaitskell as a traitor to his class and
distrusted him as an intellectual and a 'preacher'; they sensed that his
feelings were more passionate and his instincts more internationalist than
those of Bevan (who was more sensitive to mass emotion, and was privately
suspicious of the UN); perhaps above all, Bevan's views and record
appealed to their new and violent anti-American mood.[129]

Yet far from reviving the conflict between the former rivals, the crisis
consolidated their rapprochement, for they agreed from the very start and
worked harmoniously together throughout.[130] Early in October Bevan
told Leslie Hunter (and later others) that an offer of the shadow foreign
secretaryship could lead to a reconciliation. It was not a public challenge
as in the past, but a private feeler giving Gaitskell six weeks to respond
without loss of face.[131]

Gaitskell knew that in both big foreign affairs rows — first the Russian
visit, then Suez — Bevan had supported rather than embarrassed him. He
knew too that Alf Robens, Attlee's choice for the post, who had family
troubles, was poor in the House (though good within the Party) and had
performed disastrously in the September debate. Gaitskell was reluctant
to demote him, but just before Conference Robens volunteered to resign
if the leader wished.[5h] In the last surviving entry in his Diary, Gaitskell
noted:[132]

[E]verybody is wondering whether we are going to offer [Bevan] foreign
affairs. If it were not for Alf's failure I wouldn't think of it, myself.
But we have to think of it. I don't know what we shall do and I am
inclined to wait a moment and see what opinion in the Party is like.[5h]

It was favourable, and Bevan was chosen to wind up – very successfully – the Suez censure debate on 1 November. He in turn did not stand again for deputy leader, but came third for the Shadow Cabinet – well behind Wilson but only one vote behind Robens, and with thirty more than in 1955. Robens had fortunately just made a good speech in another Suez debate, and could now repeat his resignation offer in better circumstances; so 1956 ended with Bevan as Labour's foreign affairs spokesman.

In the international arena Gaitskell led the Socialist International, meeting in Copenhagen in early December, to condemn the invasion of Egypt – provoking a walk-out by the pro-Mollet French delegation.[133] At the New Year he delivered his very successful Godkin Lectures at Harvard. He was still across the Atlantic when the American President put forward the 'Eisenhower Doctrine', which tried to detach the Middle Eastern countries from both Cairo and Moscow by promising them economic help and military protection against overt Communist aggression. While Bevan deplored it, Gaitskell welcomed it; but he played it down to prevent the Conservatives exploiting the rift.[134] (He might have acted less benevolently towards Washington if he had known at the time, as he was shocked to learn five years later, that in December 1956 the Eisenhower Administration had softened its policy on oil supplies to Britain solely in order to strengthen the Conservatives at the humiliating moment of announcing withdrawal from Suez.)[135a b]

Another Labour rift was threatened when Eden resigned and, in Gaitskell's absence, the Shadow Cabinet made a constitutional issue of the selection procedure for Prime Ministers, talking of a censure motion and a call for a general election. Gaitskell may not have smelt a Bevanite plot as Robens did;[136] but as soon as he returned to London he persuaded his colleagues (easily, to Crossman's surprise) to drop the censure.[137]

Harold Macmillan took over the leadership of an unhappy party at an unpopular moment, with the Conservatives in a violently anti-American and resentful mood, British foreign policy in ruins, and the economy hard hit – most visibly by petrol rationing. Washington had feared the old Cabinet would fall on announcing withdrawal;[135a] the new one seemed so precarious that Macmillan told the Queen it might last only six weeks.[138] In restoring Conservative unity and morale he displayed brilliant political leadership. Yet a government with a majority of sixty could have been brought down only if the Suez Group of Tory rebels had combined with the Labour Opposition – as he himself evidently feared, many foreigners expected, and some Labour men hoped.[139]

Gaitskell was always sceptical. The internationalist Conservatives, with whom he was quite friendly, had let the Suez adventure continue rather than overthrow Eden; and the Labour leader knew that the diehards who loathed him would never upset their own Government to bring him to power.[140] Their leader, Captain Charles Waterhouse, had even said that if their dissent might put Labour in, 'I should no more think of abstaining than I should think of singing a song instead of making a speech in this House'.[103f] After the final humiliation in May 1957, when the Government advised British shipping to return to the Canal on Nasser's terms, the Opposition carefully worded their motion to avoid alienating the Suez Group.[49f] Yet only fourteen Tories abstained.

Rather than give way to Nasser, the right-wing critics now wanted to insist on the ships still going round the Cape.[6e] But Selwyn Lloyd told them that was no longer practicable, since the user countries' governments could not impose their policy on shipowners and would not maintain their solidarity beyond the next day or two.[6f] At last the full folly of the fire-eaters was exposed. The show of military force had demonstrated Britain's political impotence, and in doing so had destroyed a negotiating position which had once been quite strong. Before the invasion Gaitskell had expected to settle the Canal dispute reasonably by talks, for he believed that Nasser's situation was weak. To boycott the Canal, build large tankers and lay new pipelines would be slow, but once Egypt came under economic pressure, time would be on the side of the West.[141]

That policy depended on solidarity among the users and goodwill in the United States: assets which the fire-eaters had dissipated by May 1957. But in the previous autumn it might have succeeded. Gaitskell was not making reliance on the UN a substitute for a British policy.[142] He always saw the UN as a useful forum for negotiations, but it was only after the invasion took place that he insisted on compliance with UN resolutions. By then Eden's folly had changed the problem, lost any chance of a satisfactory settlement, and destroyed British influence in the region as Nasser could never have done: in Kenneth Younger's words, 'No one wants her backing ... and no one asks her views.'[14c]

There was a postscript in March 1959, over the unsatisfactory compensation offered to British nationals owning sequestered property in Egypt.[143] Gaitskell mocked the Government's successive claims 'that it was vital to go into Egypt, vital to stay in Egypt, vital to get out of Egypt, vital we should not make terms with Egypt, now vital to make terms with Egypt'.[144b] That last claim, he stressed, reflected their belated discovery in the 1958 Iraq crisis that Nasserite Arab nationalism was a bulwark against Communism, not its agent as they had so long pretended.[144b] Macmillan thought it one of Gaitskell's very best speeches;[49g c] his own 'wholly irrelevant and very vulgar' reply[107c] violently berated the Labour leader, while teasing Bevan as 'a shorn Samson surrounded on the Front Bench by a bunch of prim and ageing Delilahs'.[144c]

Labour lost rather than gained politically by trying to expose the disastrous outcome of Suez: 'all old cabbage', wrote Crossman, about which nobody outside Westminister cared any more.[3h] Gaitskell agreed. When Crossman himself, volatile as ever, later kept trying to bring the cabbage back to life, Gaitskell was discouraging;[145] and was therefore denounced by his old enemies on the Left for 'the most amazing example of feeble Opposition leadership in modern times'.[146] But the Government would not concede an inquiry, and that last parliamentary debate in 1959 simply revived the old Tory smears.

Suez was Britain's last imperial fling, both displaying and accelerating her decline. In default of the military power she could no longer wield, Britain might still have exercised considerable political influence; Suez undermined it both in the Middle East and generally. The government's policy thus led swiftly to the total disaster Gaitskell had foreseen. But while the Conservatives had saved themselves by sacrificing their Prime Minister, it was the Labour leader who suffered politically from the false charge of equivocation and from the government's irrational popularity for 'having a go'. Suez had seemed a crime to many people in Britain; even among its initial defenders some, like Randolph Churchill, clearly saw that it had been a colossal blunder. Yet the blunder was advantageous to its perpetrators (Eden apart), and Gaitskell was wise not to keep harping on it. As Macmillan rightly judged after the debate of May 1957, his government was secure for the rest of that Parliament.[49h]

CHAPTER 16

INTO PARTNERSHIP WITH BEVAN 1956–7

'[His] *almost pathetic anxiety to lead the party in whatever direction it wishes to be led'*
(TORY JOURNALIST ON HG, 1957)

i *Attlee's Successor*

WHEN Harold Macmillan became Prime Minister in January 1957, the crisis within the Conservative Party was acute. He was brilliantly successful at keeping his followers loyal by paying formal homage to their prejudices, adopting a studied traditionalism of manner and rhetoric and ostentatiously facing in a direction opposite to the one in which he meant to go.[1] Before long, Harold Wilson was admiring his skill at holding up the banner of Suez while leading the retreat from it.[2] Gaitskell, in contrast, was 'disdainful of Macmillan's fondness for doing everything behind a smokescreen';[3] his contempt for his adversary's performance perhaps contributed to the sharp shift in his own political stance after his 1959 defeat. But in his first Parliament the style baffled as well as infuriated him, and he did not cope with it well.

During these early years of leadership, Gaitskell gave priority to conciliation within his own Party. He was active — perhaps too active — in the preparation of the three-year programme of policy statements, working through the National Executive. Where the Labour Party usually tears itself apart over plans for its next government — so reducing its chance of implementing them — these statements were endorsed in an atmosphere of concord quite unlike the turbulence of the early 1950s or early 1970s. But that unusual harmony did not suffice. In the House, Suez was not the only question to unite Labour MPs on the electorally unpopular side; and in the constituencies, affluence was the government's trump card. Sadly, Gaitskell wrote in 1961: 'If there is one thing that the 1959 General Election result shows, it is surely that unity is not enough.'[4] Political leaders are as vulnerable when they lose elections as they are dominant when they win, and that defeat was to put at risk all his patient efforts to reunite the Party.

At Westminster, Gaitskell dropped in to listen quietly at MPs' regional group meetings, and was alert to spot talent among young back-benchers, who were often neither ideological sympathisers nor personal friends.[5] Indeed his constant activity worried his colleagues.[6a b] Crossman observed pertinently that while he was nice, intellectually honest, and tactically skilful enough to surmount his right-wing instincts, he spent far too much effort on 'endless talks and visits', on secondary issues and on drafting details, and did not know how to remain 'indolent until the moment for intense activity'[7] But there was never enough time, and back-benchers who had not resented the unapproachable Attlee now grumbled that the new leader did not gossip in the tea-room. One journalist recorded 'the latest complaints I hear among his hard-to-please followers: 1. He is too inaccessible. "So aloof you can never see him without an appointment." 2. He is too accessible. "Always poking his nose in and asking what we're thinking".'[8] He was so far from imposing his personality that Henry Fairlie said no party since the Whigs after 1832 had so suffered from the 'lack of any commanding individual will'.[9a]

Gaitskell was not at his best in the House in the early months of 1957, and slipped back in standing within the Party.[6a] He had, wrote the same Tory journalist, unjustly incurred 'more public discredit more quickly than any other politician, at least since the war. No Labour leader is more bitterly hated by the Conservatives or more distrusted by the general public'.[9b] A former government whip told Dalton that the Party would surely have to change its leader.[10] Enjoying the psychological advantage of any Prime Minister over any Leader of the Opposition, Macmillan used mocking badinage or wounding disdain to provoke the derisive back-bench jeering which made Gaitskell wonder if he should continue.

As often in politics, a reverse for the man on the spot gave an unearned advantage to a fortunate absentee, and Bevan returned from a visit to India with a 'fantastic reputation'.[11] The Conservatives were indeed victims of their own propaganda, for Lord Hailsham said that 'almost every Tory leader' thought Gaitskell was losing control to him.[12] But Bevan's rising stature largely reflected Labour's hunger for unity and appreciation of his recent co-operative behaviour.[13]

Bevan had decided to settle for influence rather than status, to give priority to the common purpose of ousting the Tories, and to encourage his followers to work for progress in the right direction rather than wrangle about its pace. He made those priorities clear both before and at Labour's 1957 Conference, first in approving and lobbying for a compromise policy of nationalisation and then in dramatically repudiating his old supporters over unilateral nuclear disarmament. His decision that co-operation was both necessary and tolerable was indispensable to Gaitskell's success. The general expectation of an early election also reinforced the pressure for unity—for which both men called, using the same phrases.[14] Gaitskell's own skills helped too. An old friend praised his 'exceptional instinct for the predictable reactions of others' and his ability, essential to anyone trying to lead and educate the Labour Movement, 'to feel, and be felt to be, part of it—at once the class-mate and the invisible tutor'.[15]

The change of mood was crystallised at the Party Conference at Brighton. As it assembled, one Tory correspondent predicted that Bevan would soon supersede the inadequate Gaitskell, 'who cannot be faulted for industry and zeal, and an almost pathetic anxiety to lead the party in whatever direction it wishes to be led'. As it ended, another said that Gaitskell had in two years 'transformed Labour's policy in all essentials to Gaitskellism, a great personal achievement ... Brighton has left him with his personal authority at its peak'.[16–17a]

ii   Nationalisation: 'Industry and Society'

The arguments over domestic policy produced several disagreements, but only one that rekindled old passions. The issue was public ownership, the alignment unfamiliar: Frank Cousins and Aneurin Bevan stood with Gaitskell, who was opposed by Herbert Morrison and the right-wing intellectuals of *Socialist Commentary*.

The words 'public ownership', instead of nationalisation, struck the new note. Morrison's concept of the public corporation was originally devised for the public utilities and always had its critics. Gaitskell had favoured it as a Minister, and in 1957 he chaired a working party on the nationalised industries which, he claimed, 'rather thought we might be going to recommend quite striking and radical changes. But we were convinced by the evidence submitted to us by the Boards and the Unions and by outside experts and by ex-Ministers'.[18] The pamphlet that emerged, which he mainly drafted, therefore remained very orthodox and defensive.[19–21a] But he recognised the drawbacks of such large-scale organisation, which he thought set limits to further extension of that structure. He felt that the traditional arguments for it were weaker, since nationalisation was neither indispensable for achieving full employment or industrial democracy, nor certain to satisfy the demand for a transfer of economic power. His own ideas were worked out by 1953, and set out in *Socialism and Nationalisation* in 1956.[22] Very similar views were more thoroughly developed by Anthony Crosland.[23]

Gaitskell thought the main contemporary role for public ownership was to generate investment resources to replace those diminished by redistributive taxation: either by nationalisation, or by new competitive state enterprises, or by buying up particular firms, or expanding nationalised industries into new fields (e.g. chemical plants run by the Coal Board). It could also contribute to a more egalitarian society if the state acquired shares in lieu of death duties (as Dalton had suggested for land), or through a capital levy (if politically possible), or simply through purchase, to ensure a share for the community in the mounting capital gains.* All these ideas appeared in the Party's new policy statement, *Industry and Society*.

The Bevanites were no admirers of the old Morrison formula. Ian Mikardo[25a] in January 1950 had criticised it in a pamphlet which many future Bevanites signed:

> Most early Socialists ... identified socialism with public ownership, and believed that all the world's ills could be dispersed through the formula of nationalisation.
>
> In the last few years we have learned to distinguish the means of socialism from its ends ... We are approaching the end ... of the 'natural monopolies'; and we can therefore move beyond the technique of nationalising whole industries one at a time by one Act at a time.[26]

That method of announcing target industries later became known as the 'shopping list'; the pamphlet preferred the Party's 'new proposal of flexible, multi-purpose competitive public enterprise'.[26] At the 1950 Conference Bevan himself, not yet wholly disillusioned with Attlee's government, spoke in favour of an electoral programme not mentioning nationalisation. Although 'more nationalisation now' later became an intermittent Bevanite rallying cry, the 1953 Conference heavily defeated proposals for sweeping extensions of it; and in the 1955 election Wilson and Crossman were very impressed by its unpopularity.[21b] Bevan revived the issue, but only momentarily, in his 'tiddlywinks' challenge to Gaitskell just after the leadership election.[27]

Industry and Society was drafted by a very representative working party.[28] The chairman was Jim Griffiths, and among its members were Ian Mikardo, Barbara Castle and Aneurin Bevan (though the last two were often absent).[29] There was no serious division over the drafting;[30] and the National Executive accepted it unanimously.[31] Previously, the General Council representatives met those of the NEC and found that their unity was not 'face-saving or illusory ... Mr. Aneurin Bevan spoke enthusiastically and strongly in support of the policy document. He need not have done so; he was not the spokesman; Mr. Gaitskell was'.[32b] [c] In July, Michael Foot privately called it first-rate—until he was told that Bevan had changed his mind the day before and had said 'it was a lousy document

---

* Those gains, as Richard Titmuss later pointed out, frustrated the aims of redistributive taxation by allowing the rich to keep up their expenditure.[24]

but one can't spend all one's time fighting'.[33] But Bevan did not fight the policy in 'the last ditch — or even in the first'.[17b]

Attitudes were flexible because the policy was imprecise, facing in all directions and hoping to please all sides: precisely the kind of intellectually inglorious but politically convenient compromise of which Gaitskell was later supposed incapable. The document stressed the growth of large firms dominated by managers, financing their own expansion, and with function-less shareholders reaping very large capital gains. It advocated both taxing these, and diverting some of the benefits to the community through share-buying by the state or the new National Superannuation Fund;[34] and suggested state provision of investment capital, as organised years later in the National Enterprise Board.[35a c] It promised to renationalise steel and road haulage, and — perhaps by taking over specific firms — 'to extend public ownership in any industry or part of industry which, after thorough enquiry, is found to be seriously failing the nation'.

There were many ambiguities. Would the 'thorough enquiry' precede or follow the next Labour government? What constituted 'failing the nation'?[36*] How widely and rapidly would the powers be used?[38] What distinctions would be made or conditions imposed? For the state might intervene here to 'share in the fruits of industrial expansion' without control, there to supply investment capital, elsewhere to take over a monopolistic or inefficient industry or firm. *Tribune* commented justifiably: 'We do not say dogmatically that the words mean nothing. What we do say with absolute assurance is that no one can state for certain what they mean.'[25d e] On the opposite wing, *Socialist Commentary* agreed that 'everyone can find something which he likes' in a document which gave the Labour Party 'a mandate to do about public ownership whatever *it* may happen to like when it is returned to office: it may be a great deal or it may be precious little'.[39a] That was the idea:[40] Crossman called it 'a brilliant gimmick ... the drafts are all designed to avoid the issues'.[21d]

The left-wingers professed that anxiety to avoid a split had deterred them from calling for a vote before publication, even in the privacy of the NEC. Yet immediately afterwards they sought maximum publicity for articles stressing the ambiguities and underlining the differences.[25b] Their belated switch owed more to calculation than to cerebration. For, just as the NEC hurdle seemed to have been safely cleared, rumbles of dissent had begun among the unions which Bevan had so often dismissed as bastions of the Right. Ellis Smith, a disappointed ex-Minister, led thirty-two trade-union MPs who wrote a critical letter to *Reynolds*.** Unexpected champions

* Both Wilson and Gaitskell specified that efficiency was not the only criterion.[37]

** Charles Pannell mobilised a larger and more prestigious group to reply, and proudly showed his list of signatories to a grateful Gaitskell — who at once began trying to redraft their letter![41]

of red-blooded Socialism now emerged: Herbert Morrison attacked the document in *Forward*,[42] and *Socialist Commentary* strongly opposed it.[39b] The storm blew hard enough 'to make the *Tribune* change its mind and compel Ian Mikardo to write an article[25e] attacking Hugh Gaitskell, Harold Wilson and myself', wrote Crossman.[21c] With NEC elections due, Barbara Castle as well as Mikardo discovered that the policy they had approved was another betrayal of Socialism by the right-wing leadership. Gaitskell told Crossman that: 'if they can't stand by a document which they have helped to draft in the National Executive, he wouldn't trust them in a Cabinet.'[21d]

Understandably, the press began to wonder if Gaitskell had not been using his persuasive powers in the wrong quarter.[43] The unions were already cool to the sweeping pension plans proposed by Crossman; they may have felt that in accommodating his political colleagues Gaitskell was taking them too much for granted. (It was a lesson he should have recalled before launching his Clause Four campaign, when the unions were again not so much bent upon sweeping nationalisation as reluctant to abandon entrenched habits of mind.) Just before the TUC met, he was due in Blackpool for the jubilee dinner of his own union, the NUGMW. He did his best to lobby the TUC leadership, but they would not risk a row over political issues. After a brief debate in which no major union put its view, the General Council accepted both the main motion on public ownership — imprecise in wording but vaguely fundamentalist in tone — and a specific resolution for nationalising the machine-tool industry; and its spokesman gave an assurance that the new policy was more 'an adjunct to a nationalisation programme than a substitute for a nationalisation programme'.[32b] Gaitskell privately gave similar assurances to Cousins;[44a c] but he was upset by the general weakness of the union leadership:

> I had thought when I returned from Blackpool that everything was all right, but they seem to have behaved in a most confused and irresponsible manner yesterday, which is rather a bore. However, I think we can straighten things out before or at the Conference at Brighton.[44b c]

Inevitably, the Left assumed that Gaitskell's only aim was to bury public ownership. They were wrong. All his associates privately favoured nationalisation for one industry or another: Jay for aircraft;[44a] Wilson for chemicals; both of them probably, and Dalton and Crosland[23c] certainly, for machine tools.[45] Before becoming leader, Gaitskell had always loyally defended Party decisions on it; now, though cautious about going beyond the agreed line, he privately agreed over aircraft and chemicals,[44b] and publicly spoke of 'a pretty strong hunch' of his own for machine tools and perhaps aircraft production.[18] Another very old friend wrote later that, 'had he been then in power, his shopping list of industries and interests to be nationalised would have been far wider than that of many defenders of Clause 4.'[46]

In arguing that the statement was intended to stop any extension of public ownership, the Left were thus as wide of the mark as the Tories were in charging—highly effectively in the 1959 election—that its aim was the opposite, to carry out a vast extension by stealth.[47] Gaitskell's objective was much more immediate: to return a Labour Government, knowing that its policies must depend on the problems it faced on coming to power. One obstacle to a Labour victory was defeatism in the ranks: it had been rampant when he arrived in Blackpool, but his appeal was so effective that when he left, 'the trade unions are now in the forefront of the battle—a wonder that few of us had expected to see'.[17b] Another obstacle was an unconvincing and apparently doctrinaire outlook, illustrated by Labour's successive electoral shopping lists which had little in common beyond the inadequacy of the preparatory analysis and the supporting arguments. Instead, he sought to secure a reasonably free hand without provoking a split, to conceal the differences of purpose behind an acceptable formula, and to defuse a divisive issue. Dick Stokes, with Sir Hartley Shawcross, had been agitating against any major nationalisation; in reply Gaitskell argued (before the pamphlet was published) for 'keeping an open mind and deciding what to do when we get there'.[48a] After the policy was safely adopted he wrote:

> Candidly, I doubt whether the public ownership plan is a positive and saleable proposition. I look on the whole thing rather in a negative way. If we had gone wrong here we could have lost millions of votes. Our positive attraction to the electorate is going to be far more through superannuation, housing and education.[49a]

By 1959, Labour was increasingly and damagingly identified as the party of nationalisation.[50-1a] Business spent a lot of money to maximise that damage;[52] and Gaitskell did not mean to concentrate Labour's propaganda on its least popular theme.[21f, g] But he sought no change of policy. Privately he favoured nationalising steel, though without enthusiasm; the nearest he ever came to a backward step was once to hint at perhaps deferring it to the second parliamentary session rather than the first.[21f] He thought Tory denationalisation had merely given 'something for nothing' to functionless shareholders;[53] and he saw no way to get sufficient expansion of capacity except by public ownership,[49b] against which there was no strong practical case. The steelworkers had never been keen nationalisers like the miners or railwaymen, but would give adequate support;[54a] and the administrative takeover could be smooth, as it had not been in 1951 when Labour had only a tiny majority.[49b] His ideas about how to renationalise road haulage were rather cautious, but he would settle nothing until Labour was in office and could consult properly.[54a b] Then, too, there could be serious inquiry about further measures. In May 1959 Gaitskell wrote to Strachey, on a forthcoming book by the latter: 'I am glad that you have brought out the argument for the gradual extension of public ownership. So many people have misunderstood this part of Industry and Society that ... emphasising it ... would be no harm.'[55]

In 1957, however, the old factional lines were still thoroughly blurred. At the Party Conference at Brighton, flat rejection of the document was moved by Jim Campbell, general secretary of the NUR—a moderately left-wing union which voted for Gaitskell for Party treasurer in 1955.[56] Campbell explicitly wanted a return to 'shopping lists'. On the NEC, Bevan once voted in a minority of 6 against 22—but out of loyalty to his friends rather than agreement with the Left.[21h i] Publicly he undermined the critics by refusing to associate with them, and by conspicuously applauding Gaitskell's speech.[57] Privately, he told Gaitskell he did not want a shopping list;[21j] and he helped to persuade Cousins to argue about interpreting the policy, and not to oppose it on principle.[58]

Harold Wilson proposed the document from the platform, playing down differences among its supporters by claiming that all shared the same Socialist faith with differences of emphasis about the reasons for it.[59] Morrison's attack was backed by the equally disgruntled Shinwell. Gaitskell replied, reminding the delegates that inquiries were necessary because

> the millions of electors we have to convince, including many millions of Labour supporters ... want to know what the specific reasons are for nationalising ... We have to show to our fellow citizens that what we propose in the field of public ownership is not only related to some distant ideal but is relevant to the actual problems of today.[60a]

He reaffirmed that inefficiency was not the only criterion, and again underlined that the statement did not preclude further 'old-style' nationalisation —assurances which were explicit in the pamphlet,[35b] which he had already given privately to the trade union leaders at Blackpool,[44a] and which Wilson had repeated in the Brighton debate.[60b] Cousins told Crossman he was satisfied.[61] The same assurances won over the AEU and Post Office Workers, and the policy was carried by 5,309,000 to 1,276,000—with half the constituency Parties voting for it, and only one big union (the NUR) against.[62] Shopping list nationalisation had been buried for a long time.[63]

Dalton called it 'a great triumph. Old Believers routed'; and congratulated Gaitskell on becoming not only the unchallenged leader but 'a (surprisingly) successful maker of new Policy'.[64] Yet for all the compromises embodied in *Industry and Society*, Gaitskell's speech showed that it was not mere leadership from behind. The Executive, he concluded,

could have presented a document with a long list of future industries
to be nationalised without a new idea, and very probably you would
have received it with acclamation ... [But] we would have been putting
something to you which in our hearts we did not believe we could
carry out ... which in our hearts we believe the electorate was bound
to reject ... We do not believe in that sort of leadership; we believe in
leadership which ... does not flinch from making the Party and the
Movement face the facts of the day, both the economic and the
political facts.[60c]

Gaitskell's speech, wrote Crossman, 'undoubtedly did impress them by
his readiness to rebuke them ... [Conference] resents it the moment you
do more than they think you are entitled to. On this occasion Hugh showed
his leadership by proving he was entitled to a good deal'.[21k]

He had devised a policy which Wilson proposed, Bevan commended,
Tribune accepted then repudiated, Morrison and *Socialist Commentary*
denounced, and on which many years later Tony Benn founded his new
model Socialism. Its meaning depended on the political and economic
circumstances in which it was introduced; and just because everyone
could hope to deflect it in his own direction, all might have deferred their
quarrels over the wording so as not to hamper their chance of winning
power. Gaitskell did not despise such devices to keep his coalition together,
and could afford them when his leadership was secure. He was to discover
in the next election that the price paid for them was high, and after it that
the unity bought by them was short-lived.

iii   *The Bomb at Brighton: 'Naked into the Conference Chamber'*

For the Labour Party, defence had always been a topic provoking even
sharper disagreement than nationalisation: the more so, understandably,
in the nuclear age. But in April 1957 the Conservatives were no more
united on it. The Minister, Duncan Sandys, announced in a White Paper
a strategy of total reliance on the nuclear deterrent, sweetened by the
abolition of conscription; his claim that manpower needs could be met by
volunteers was promptly challenged by his predecessor, Brigadier Antony
Head. That was not the only dispute among Tories, for a very senior and
respected Minister, Lord Salisbury, had just resigned in protest at the
release of the Cypriot Archbishop Makarios from detention; and the
Prime Minister, worried about his party's reaction to the coming capitulation over Suez, wrote privately, 'What a blessing he went over
Makarios!'[65a d] But the vigilant press, as usual in those days, found the

divisions in the government ranks, which might have real consequences for policy, a less alluring topic than exposing ideological splits in the opposition. It was, for Macmillan, a most convenient conception of news values.

In 1955 Attlee had dodged the issue of the H-bomb by supporting the decision to make it while opposing testing it. The price of that absurd compromise had to be paid when, in March 1957, Britain announced a forthcoming series of H-bomb tests at Christmas Island. The health hazards were just becoming known, and the Labour Party was thrown into turmoil. Labour's defence specialists saw no point in making a bomb which could not be tested, but many others (not only old opponents of making the bomb) were appalled that Britain too should poison the atmosphere and perhaps spark off more tests by others. They protested at a PLP meeting one Thursday, 28 March, and Gaitskell proposed deciding the policy a week later and staying silent meanwhile.[21m] But over the weekend George Brown on television reaffirmed the existing policy of making the bomb, and supported the tests.

On Monday 1 April the House debated Macmillan's wide-ranging talks with President Eisenhower in Bermuda, intended to restore the relationship shattered by Suez. The Prime Minister skilfully diverted attention from Salisbury's resignation two days earlier (which he did not even mention) and from Suez (so contentious within his own party) to the nuclear issue.[65b] His long statement on the technicalities ingeniously minimised the health dangers; and he challenged Gaitskell to say whether in office Labour would stop the tests, abandon the bomb, and so accept both permanent conscription and military inferiority against Russia. Inhibited by the division in his own ranks, Gaitskell replied that only a government had the information to make such decisions, but that Labour would not unilaterally stop tests.[66] Privately he said next day that he could not commit the Party finally against them when he might suddenly find himself in office.[67] The Tory press pounced on him for equivocating;[68] many of his own followers were displeased, and a week later he wrote privately: 'I blame myself for not understanding sooner how strong the feeling in the Party was.'[69]

No Labour rivals used the issue against him. Bevan was abroad; and Morrison and Shinwell supported the official line.[70] But the PLP was deeply troubled, and Gaitskell, knowing that he could command only a small majority, persuaded the Thursday morning meeting to adjourn until the evening.[71a b] His friend Charles Pannell wrote to him: 'No more German rearmament narrow margins. What we want is confidence.'[72] Christopher Mayhew then proposed a compromise which the Shadow Cabinet recommended: to call for a temporary suspension of the British tests while appealing to the super-powers to cancel theirs.[73] Supported in the interests of unity by both Jennie Lee and George Brown, the plan – a precursor of the 'non-nuclear club' – was approved by acclamation.[74] Gaitskell wrote candidly to a friend:

> The H-Bomb is an almost impossible subject for us ... It is impossible to reach a real logical conclusion without splitting the Party. So I am afraid we just have to go on with compromises of the kind we had last week. It is perfectly clear that the Party much prefers this, even if they look rather silly, to a real split and a resumption of the trouble of a few years ago and I am sure that in this they are perfectly right.[49c]

Gaitskell was as conciliatory in 1957 as he was to be combative in 1960 on the same issue. But the sequel on the first occasion, when the problem was minor and quite temporary, shows that the later and far more serious conflict could not have been fudged with a formula. In 1957 all the political commentators for once agreed on the outcome: that Conservative morale revived and Labour's declined; that opposition MPs became more critical of their leader and government back-benchers more enthusiastic for theirs; and that the Bermuda debate, and Labour's compromise on tests, inaugurated Macmillan's ascendancy in the House.[75] Richard Crossman was a leading advocate of fudging in 1960; but in 1957 he wrote:

> That debate turned out to be the moment when he [Macmillan] consolidated his leadership and stopped the collapse of the Tory Government ... playing Gaitskell as an angler plays a young, inexperienced trout. That was the beginning of the turn of the tide for the Tories.[21m]

Outside the Westminster hothouse the Gallup poll found increased support for testing over that month, especially among Labour voters; and a 10 per cent jump in approval for Macmillan, which brought him his best rating of his first eighteen months in Downing Street.[76]

The Prime Minister was sensitive to public disquiet about the H-bomb. He feared its electoral impact, and thought Bevan would use it both as 'an electoral winner for the Socialists' and also to 'outmanoeuvre Gaitskell'.[77] Bevan had been in India during the argument over the British tests, and on his return he came closer than ever before to the unilateralist position. At Reading on 5 May 1957, he said he hoped that Britain would declare that though able to make the H-bomb, she would refrain from doing so, showing the courage and vision to lead the world. These speeches, Mr Foot asserts, reflected the public anxiety. 'Certainly they were influenced by the mood he discovered or helped to elicit among the great audiences ... it was his method of public speech and political activity.'[78a]

Yet the committed and consistent unilateralists knew that Bevan had never been one of them.[79a] He had served in the Cabinet which made the atomic bomb, had been aware of that decision and had actively supported it.[80] He had encouraged Crossman to write in favour of making the H-bomb in 1955, and had called on Attlee in the House to pledge only that Britain would never use it first.[81] A few weeks later in the election campaign he had changed his mind, saying that he was 'profoundly opposed to its manufacture'.[82] In June 1957 he and Gaitskell had both protested strongly at the second British test.[83] Late in July, when Sydney Silverman was denouncing nuclear weapons, 'Nye had smacked him down for wanting them abolished and said that such ideas were entirely obsolete'.[21i l]

Earlier that month the Socialist International met in Vienna, in an appalling heatwave. As rapporteur on the international situation, Gaitskell argued for disengagement, attention to the Third World, a disarmament agreement without prior political conditions, and an immediate test ban — recognising that 'an agreement on tests is bound to be dependent, eventually, for its permanence on whether we also get an agreement on the control of nuclear production'.[84] Bevan too was on the British delegation, which drafted the final resolution including these disarmament proposals;[60d] they differed from British Government policy, which in Bevan's eyes gave them 'special merit'.[78b] A week later Gaitskell, Bevan and Philip Noel-Baker (a disarmament specialist throughout his political life) put forward proposals, which the PLP accepted, for seeking multilateral disarmament by stages: first stop the bomb tests, then production, then destroy stocks — with international inspection and reductions in conventional forces at each stage.[85] Still looking for consensus, Gaitskell was writing hopefully just before the Party Conference to Konni Zilliacus — now back in the House, and later an implacable opponent of his: 'It is not easy to reach agreement on matters of this kind in the Party, but I think we did pretty well in the Spring and I hope we shall continue'.[86]

In September 1957, Bevan and his wife went to the Crimea. He had long talks with Khrushchev, who made it quite clear that British renunciation of the H-bomb would make not the slightest difference to the Russians.[87] He returned just in time for the Party Conference. On the Thursday before it opened, the National Executive met in London to discuss a draft statement on Labour's defence policy written by Morgan Phillips and revised by Crossman, which ignored the issue of the British bomb. Bevan objected that a stoppage of tests logically led to a stoppage of production, and suggested instead endorsing the Vienna resolution. 'Hugh Gaitskell immediately agreed with him and said we might well substitute that for our draft statement. But at this point Sydney Silverman and Barbara began to needle him [Bevan].'[21i] Bevan then said that unless the Party opposed manufacturing the bomb, he could not speak for the resolution from the platform. Barbara Castle, Mikardo and Silverman supported him. Gaitskell said it was not acceptable to oppose manufacture but not necessary to reaffirm support for it: 'we had agreed ... [to] make it clear that, on these great issues, the Party had not made final decisions.' Cross-man and Sam Watson said that defence policy could not be reversed overnight, and asked if Bevan advocated continuing conscription – for if not, what defences would we have? The discussion was adjourned.[88]

Bevan went to see Gaitskell that afternoon, seeming 'not in the least inclined for a row' over either *Industry and Society* or the bomb. He was worried over the absurdity – shown in April – of advocating stopping tests but not production also; and at his suggestion discussion was post-poned till Sunday.[21j h] At Brighton over the weekend Bevan tried to get the unilateralist motion modified, but its sponsor, 'the most militant Trotskyist in the Labour Party',[79b] refused.[89] Sam Watson 'gradually got him [Bevan] round to the mood of the next Foreign Secretary and the represen-tative of the world's mineworkers'.[90] For Bevan believed that if a Labour government came to power he could help to check the proliferation of nuclear weapons, and therefore wanted to avert a Party split.[91]

> Also, he was profoundly convinced that no party that appeared to be playing fast and loose with national security could hope to become the Government. It was one thing before Britain had the bomb to argue that we should not have it. It was another matter to go into an election advocating nuclear disarmament.[91]

At the crucial NEC meeting on the Sunday, therefore, Bevan favoured suspending tests, but condemned the resolution because of the diplomatic consequences of repudiating nuclear weapons without consulting the Commonwealth or the Americans. 'Surely,' he concluded, 'it would be a mistake to take all the cards out of the hand of Labour's next Foreign Secretary.' Crossman remarked drily that it was the first time most of his hearers

> had heard one of Nye's intellectual emotional somersaults ... Barbara Castle welcomed Nye's speech as a magnificent statement of policy ... Tony Greenwood, one of the great anti-H-bombers, remained absolu-tely silent. So did Ian Mikardo. Hugh Gaitskell then said he agreed with every word Nye had said and only wished he could have said it as well.[21h]

Despite his followers' dismay, Bevan's decision confirmed and did not contradict his general political stance (as well as his past attitude to horrific weapons). As a young rebel he had denounced Jennie Lee for seeking purity at the price of impotence. As a mature Minister, he had accomplished his domestic reforms by negotiation and compromise; while abroad he had favoured a Western guarantee to Yugoslavia, a tank convoy to relieve Berlin and a building-up of West Germany against Russia. After his resig-nation, he was always a 'cautious rebel';[92] apart from one single year, he had sided with his moderate rather than extreme associates. Now he had wearied of throwing stones through the window and wanted to go back into the shop.[93] Never content with moral poses, he always wanted to influence events. In the words of Peggy Duff, later secretary of CND:

> Nye believed in power ... for him the only instrument to achieve power was the Labour Party ... The possibilities of swinging the party behind himself and the Bevanites had faded by 1957. He thought there could be no progress at all if Labour remained in opposition. So he accepted, at last, the leadership of the man he disliked so bitterly in the interest of the party he loved.[79c]

His decision at Brighton entailed no renunciation of principle, as she knew. In opposing the unilateralists

> he was not reneging on the left. He merely stayed where he was, and maintained what had always been his position. Yet, in another sense, he deserted them, because, for the first time, the left in the Labour Party moved beyond him, leaving him behind.[79d]

But his former followers were not charitable folk. They were used to hearing him explain, not that unity required compromise with others, but that the others either had no principles at all or sacrificed them all too easily. Bevan now became a victim of bitter and furious reproaches from his old admirers; and his close associates, who had levelled such crude and malevolent charges against Gaitskell and the leadership, were now dismayed to find Bevan too suffering 'the vilest form of personal abuse' (some even suggesting that it contributed to his early death).[94]

During the Brighton debate, Cousins spoke in so unilateralist a tone that it was assumed that he would vote for the resolution. But in 1957 his union's mandate was clearly against unilateralism;[95] and when Cousins sat down, Harry Nicholas (the T&GWU member of the NEC) told Crossman that the speech was meant to leave its vote open until after Bevan had spoken.[96] In a famous reply to the debate, Bevan borrowed Sam Watson's phrase about sending the next Foreign Secretary 'naked into the conference chamber ... to preach sermons ... Do it now as a Labour Party Conference? You cannot do it now. It is not in your hands to do it. All you can do is pass a resolution.' That resolution would produce a 'diplomatic shambles', for it would mean withdrawal from all international commitments: 'And you call that statesmanship? I call it an emotional spasm ... What we have to discuss is what is the consequence of the action upon other nations with far more deadly weapons than we have.'[60f]

When he finished, Cousins at once sought an adjournment, and the T&GWU delegation voted narrowly to support the platform.[97] The Communist Party at this time opposed unilateral disarmament by Britain, and with the unions under its leadership voting for the Executive, the resolution was massively defeated by 5,836,000 to 781,000.[98] Crossman summed up:

> [F]rom Hugh's point of view and from the Party's point of view, [it] has been a monumentally successful Conference. In the first place, the Bevan-Gaitskell axis ... is now securely and publicly established ... In the second place, on two really critical issues – nationalisation and the H-bomb – the two big leaders, Gaitskell and Bevan, have strengthened their position with the electorate at large by curbing the Party extremists ... Seen from the inside, it has, of course, been a complete victory for Hugh ... every member of the Executive has watched this test of strength between him and Nye and knows from inside the qualities each man showed – Hugh firm, obstinate, not very adroit, but keeping his eye fixed on his long-term objectives: Nye immensely more powerful personally, tactically far more skilful but completely failing to achieve his long-term objectives because of the pendulum swing of his emotions.[21k]

Gaitskell himself wrote to a friend: 'Naturally, I am very happy about the whole thing ... it could scarcely have gone better.'[49a]

CHAPTER 17

MACMILLAN ASCENDANT
1957–9

*'The Labour Party needed a tranquilliser. He provided one. But ... now ... a
tonic is needed'*
(LABOUR JOURNALIST, 1957)
*'Mr. Gaitskell is ... going through all the motions of being a Government
when he isn't a Government. It is bad enough having to behave like a Government when one is a Government'*
(HAROLD MACMILLAN, 1959)

i   *Bank Rate and Bus Strike*

THE reconciliation flourished in late 1957. Gaitskell and Bevan each
invited the other to lunch – 'really decisive events', exaggerated Crossman,
'in the life of these two men, who have never had a drink with each other,
much less a meal, in their whole lives.'[1] Gaitskell went out of his way to
help with Bevan's tour of the United States.[2] Over there, his new ally
supported American military bases in Britain, championed NATO, and
denied ever having advocated a neutralist third force.[3] Bevan fully realised
that, as Gaitskell wrote to Crossman, 'in the field of foreign policy,
"unity" is such a delicate plant that a good deal of care is necessary.' It
was quite consistent to advocate both adequate Western defence and a
settlement with Russia, but not to try to combine influence in Washington
with open indifference to NATO.[4]

Gaitskell as leader also had to appease some prominent right-wing
Labour MPs like Reginald Paget, who had complained bitterly of a Crossman column as a 'lurch into neutralism'.[5] He incurred a similar charge
himself from Chancellor Adenauer – it was election year in West Germany
– because of his advocacy of disengagement.[6] But in reality the purposes
of these proposals, as he explained to an expert study group at Chatham
House, were

helping the States of Eastern Europe in their struggle for independence; to make possible the reunification of Germany; and to give
the West a degree of flexibility in policy, the lack of which was a
major disadvantage in its negotiations with the Soviet Union.[7]

Early in October 1957 the Russians scored a propaganda triumph by launching the first earth satellite Sputnik, and Khrushchev promptly asked several Socialist Parties to meet Soviet Party representatives to discuss the risk of a Middle Eastern war. Bevan and Gaitskell agreed that it would be 'unconstitutional' for an opposition party to negotiate with a foreign government, and on 13 October they jointly reported the approach to the Prime Minister[8] — who at once sought to exploit the gesture by making bad blood between them.[9a] Bevan called the Russians' proposal 'a United Front subterfuge', and Gaitskell feared that if suspected of negotiating with the Russians, Labour would 'lose a million votes'.[10a] When the NEC discussed the Party's reply, the 'extraordinary atmosphere of bonhomie between Nye and Hugh' completely convinced Crossman 'that Nye has decided, as irrevocably as he can, to work with Hugh, win the election and be Foreign Secretary'.[10a]

It is not foreign but domestic affairs that preoccupy most of the electorate. There, a Labour opposition leader's dilemma becomes acute when the government adopts a deflationary policy and resists wage claims in the public sector. If he defends the unions, he seems irresponsibly indifferent to inflation and risks his public support; if he opposes them he alienates many of his own followers. In 1957–8 Gaitskell's problem was personified in Frank Cousins, the new leader of the largest union in the country, who meant to take a different path from his predecessors. Cousins was eager to assert views on both domestic and foreign policy which differed substantially from Gaitskell's, but at first he was careful not to rock the Labour boat. Gaitskell took pains to foster their personal relations;[11] and was anxious not to alienate Cousins on political, still less on industrial, matters.

That was manageable while Macmillan was still happily telling people they had 'never had it so good'.[12a] Gaitskell always said that trade union leaders could not be expected, and their members would not allow them, to hold back while other groups improved their economic position.[12b] Anticipating the 'social contract' of twenty years later, he warned against decontrol of rents and other governmental actions provoking pressures for wage increases. 'If you refuse, in fact, to help them help you, you're in trouble.'[13a] When Cousins led the TUC in 1956 to repudiate wage restraint, Gaitskell was not surprised. Nor was he impressed by middle-class clamour at the unions' irresponsibility. Instead he entirely agreed with his friend John Murray (a successful industrial consultant of Labour sympathies) in preferring Cousins's industrial strategy to that of the cautious Tom Williamson, since they both thought only union pressure for higher wages — as in the United States — would make manufacturers use labour efficiently.[14a–16]

46 With Aneurin Bevan and Sam Watson at the Durham Miners' Gala, 1959

47 Visiting an anhydrite mine near Whitehaven, the town where his ancestors had lived, in 1959

48 In Moscow, 1959: with Khrushchev (*centre*), Bevan and Suslov

49 Welcome back. Returning from Moscow for the election, Gaitskell and Bevan are greeted by Barbara Castle, Chairman of the Party, Jim Griffiths, deputy leader (*left*), Ian Mikardo and Bert Bowden, chief whip (*behind*), and Alice Bacon (*right*)

However, Gaitskell's political problem became acute when on 19 September 1957 the Chancellor, Peter Thorneycroft, abruptly changed the economic signals to 'Stop'. Among his restrictive measures, bank rate was raised from 5 to 7 per cent – the highest since 1921, and the biggest peacetime increase for well over a century. For the only time in Gaitskell's parliamentary career, a Chancellor specifically subordinated full employment to price and currency stability as the primary economic objective, and chose as his method a strict limitation of the money supply.[17-18a]

The announcement provoked a political storm. The change of policy was widely rumoured to have leaked, and Thorneycroft's prior consultations seemed to the Opposition unusually and injudiciously extensive. Labour demanded an inquiry by a High Court judge. But the Government obstinately refused any information, or any external investigation, until Harold Wilson in a supplementary question was thought (though he denied it) to have imputed misconduct to the Conservative Party vice-chairman, Oliver Poole. The Prime Minister then invoked the formidable Act of 1921 to set up a Tribunal of Inquiry, like the Lynskey Tribunal which had so distressed Gaitskell nine years before. It found no leak and no misconduct, but its disclosures showed that ample *prima facie* grounds for an inquiry had been available to the Prime Minister; Ministers repeatedly refused to say whether the Lord Chancellor had been told of them before he reported that there was nothing to investigate. Gaitskell severely criticised the conduct of the Chancellor of the Exchequer before the event, and of the Prime Minister afterwards;[19] both their behaviour and Wilson's refusal to apologise damaged public respect for politicians and good relations between the parties. Wilson's reputation suffered most, especially in the City – with indirect repercussions on Gaitskell's fortunes later on. Macmillan's insouciance delighted his back-benchers;[20] but did nothing to check the sad slide in standards of British political conduct which began in his reign.[21a]

The September measures were caused by a sterling crisis, in which Gaitskell helped the Chancellor by condemning devaluation talk;[22a] and subsequently the Opposition was wary of letting Ministers accuse them of indifference to inflation. But Gaitskell disbelieved the official diagnosis, writing to a Tory expansionist, 'I *do* think that the Government are muddling up the internal and the external ... [though] they may ... [want] a really tough deflation for internal reasons ... If so, they could hardly have chosen a worse moment.[23-5] Later economic observers fully confirm his doubts, agreeing that the British economy was not overloaded, and that its healthy balance of payments was not endangered by inflationary pressures at home:[26-9] 'The pace of wage inflation was already beginning to decline when he [Thorneycroft] decided to hit the British economy on the head.'[28b]

The reserves fell so fast because of currency speculation arising from

Q

irrelevant external factors. In early 1957 alone £70 million went through the 'Kuwait Gap' in the exchange control[29c] – which (according to Thorneycroft) the Bank of England opposed closing.[28c] The September measures responded to a false diagnosis, and did grave damage. They halted the slow re-equipment of British industry,[27c] and missed the best chance of escaping from the straitjacket of a rigid parity for sterling.[28a] Old suspicions among the trade unions were revived, and exacerbated by governmental pressure on the machinery for industrial adjudication, notably for NHS employees.[30] Gaitskell himself spoke of 'a declaration of war by the Government on the Trade Union Movement', and called the measures 'the wrong cure for the wrong disease at the wrong time'.[31]

Gaitskell knew from experience that Chancellors could not seriously probe the advice from Threadneedle Street. A year later he gave evidence to the Radcliffe Committee on the monetary system, urging much closer relations between Bank and Treasury, and the Committee so recommended.[32] On this occasion Treasury officials were lukewarm or hostile to the September measures, and only the Bank was enthusiastically for them.[33] Though the Cabinet was unhappy, the threat to the reserves made the Chancellor unchallengeable for the moment.[28e] But Thorneycroft himself – inspired perhaps by his able, dominating and rigid junior Ministers, Nigel Birch and Enoch Powell – was a very recent though fervent convert to strict monetarism;[34] and at the New Year the Treasury trio discovered that they had not persuaded their colleagues. They opposed any increase in the civil estimates (which meant a cut in real terms), were overruled, and all resigned. Macmillan, off on a Commonwealth tour, dismissed 'these little local difficulties' and endeared himself to the press and, perhaps, to the public.[35] Gaitskell told a Labour MP who had been arguing with Powell about monetarism: 'I very much doubt if the three resigning Ministers, apart perhaps from Birch, have much understanding of Keynes.'[36]

The hard line on wage claims was not at once relaxed. Two nationalised transport enterprises faced claims that spring. The Minister of Labour, Iain Macleod, first approved but then unexpectedly rejected his own chief industrial commissioner's proposed inquiry limited to the case of London busmen, insisting on arbitration instead;* they reluctantly agreed, then refused to accept the award. Meanwhile the railwaymen's claim was turned down by the Railway Tribunal, but the Prime Minister, who thought the public shared his own sympathy with it, intervened to avert a strike. Despite the treatment of the NHS workers and the railwaymen, Macleod appealed to the sanctity of arbitration awards to justify resisting Cousins's busmen; and the Opposition rightly suspected that senior Ministers and Conservative back-benchers both welcomed a conflict which would

* He would have accepted an inquiry involving all busmen, not just Londoners.

exasperate the London travelling public. As Labour thought, Macleod had been overruled and obliged 'sadly but deliberately [to] let Frank Cousins down' over the inquiry.[37a] Beforehand, the Prime Minister privately thought that the strike might be 'salutary', for 'nothing could suit us better than to satisfy the desire for calling a halt over [this] issue'. Subsequently he saw it as a political turning point.[38]

Macmillan had as usual chosen his ground shrewdly. The busmen could not win alone, and after the railway settlement they had no likely ally. Cousins knew it, and was anxious to avoid a strike. But he was even more anxious to differentiate himself from Deakin or Bevin, who would have prevented an official strike that was sure to fail, and broken an unofficial one if necessary. Cousins, however, would not defy the busmen's leaders:[39a] a course that seemed democratic to him, but which the General Council – to whom his assertiveness had not endeared him – saw as an abdication of responsibility which cost him any hope of wider support.[40]

Gaitskell's position was now impossible. The strike would be most unpopular and he knew it was bound to fail when the General Council disapproved of it.[41] Yet he was critical of the government's general policy, and also rightly suspected that Cousins had and the Cabinet had not tried to avert the strike.[42] He himself wrote privately, 'the government and Cousins are, I think, equally to blame. But it will be a bad thing for us politically, though not serious.'[43a] The Transport Workers' secretary had loyally supported the Party leadership so far, and Gaitskell valued that goodwill – above all with an eye on the expansionist Gaitskell government of the future. He criticised the government's handling of the dispute at Glasgow on May Day weekend.[22b] The following Monday Macleod in the House was 'peremptory and provocative and hostile';[10b] the Speaker would not allow an immediate adjournment debate, and an indignant Shadow Cabinet suddenly decided upon a censure motion.[44]

That was imprudent, for Cousins was not a popular figure. Macleod saw an opportunity to repeat a youthful parliamentary triumph when he had virulently assaulted Aneurin Bevan. He had recently asked for more parliamentary debates on industrial relations;[18c] yet now he theatrically proclaimed his 'scorn and contempt' for Gaitskell both for calling for one at so delicate a moment, and for the Glasgow speech.[45] Gaitskell later replied effectively. But Tory back-benchers still loathed him; and he was vulnerable because of his current reputation as a leader too preoccupied with the Party's internal problems.

The ground thus lost in the House could not be regained in the country since the strike was doomed to failure.[46] When Cousins in desperation talked of calling out the petrol-tanker drivers contrary to existing agreements,[10b] the TUC leaders strongly opposed that;[39b] and Bevan spontaneously offered to accompany Gaitskell to tell Cousins that it would be politically disastrous.[10c] After seven weeks the strike collapsed, causing Gaitskell an unexpected worry: 'H.G. says that all G[eneral] C[ouncil] of T.U.C. now either hate or despise Cousins so much that the danger is that they will move too much to the right.'[47a] But he knew that he too had suffered:[48-9a] 'Of course, we lost a lot by supporting the strike and got no kudos within the TUC because they hate Cousins. I myself was more personally responsible than anyone else.'[10c] Macmillan indeed believed that his government's recovery in the country dated from the defeat of the strike.[9d]

Gaitskell was an unrepentant Keynesian, influenced by his experience in office, who remained confident that inflation need not be the price of economic expansion. In 1958 the stop-go cycle was new, and he believed that the Conservatives had repeatedly mismanaged the economy: in 1955 for short-term electioneering purposes, in 1957 from doctrinaire devotion to monetary measures, and generally by removing exchange controls out of excessive respect for the City. Labour's central attack was to criticise restrictionist economic policies keeping production far below capacity. Its 'key issue' would be 'how can we have expansion and stable prices? Under a Tory free-for-all philosophy I say that it is impossible and all the evidence of the past few years proves it'.[49b] Higher investment was essential; and to check inflation the Government must work closely with the unions, and must control industrial building and foreign currency transactions.[50a-51]

At the end of 1958, the European Payments Union was wound up and the pound made fully convertible. Gaitskell criticised the move.[52] The institution he had created[53] could no longer foster international liquidity or effectively encourage creditors to reduce their surpluses; it had already acquired a deflationary bias, and he recognised both that much damage had already been done and that the new step was irreversible.[54a] But he still feared convertibility:

> [W]e shall increase the risk of and the scope for speculation against the £ in time of trouble while ... throwing away ... one possible weapon to be used against that speculation ... [so] we shall be told that our internal policies have to be adjusted ... that we must delay expansion ...because of what might be thought by speculators ... 'it will restore the power enjoyed by a minority of rich men in the past to vote with their bank balances'.[54b]

Convertibility aroused no public interest. The political imperative was to convince voters that a Labour government could work constructively with the unions without becoming subservient to them. In January 1958 Gaitskell and Wilson were

appalled by the pressure of commitments for the first Labour Budget
…They realise that the whole of their planning depends on getting a
quick agreement with the Unions for a virtual wage freeze, and somehow avoiding an enormously inflationary Budget, full of social service
improvements. If they could do this, and have a huge below-the-line
surplus and give industry a fillip, then they believe they really could
get expansionism going.[10d]

Just before the bus strike, Gaitskell arranged to appear with Cousins (and
with Alan Birch, chairman of the TUC's economic committee) in a party
political broadcast intended to show that Labour and the unions could
agree on 'what you [Cousins] will call responsibility and what I frankly
would say was restraint', so that higher wages would match productivity
and not be eroded by inflation.[55]

Later that year at the Scarborough Conference, the major union
leaders—Alan Birch of USDAW, Ernest Jones of the NUM, Bill Carron
of the AEU—warmly commended the Party's economic policies. Cousins,
the principal critic of wage restraint, thanked Gaitskell handsomely for
his support in the bus strike, and obscurely blessed the policy. Gaitskell
wound up the debate, offering Cousins some rhetorical satisfaction:

We do not want, and we shall not attempt a wage-freeze, but we do
not want a wages spree either … we believe that through our policy
we can create a climate in which the unions would in their own interests
be prepared to work with the Labour Government so that wages and
productivity go up together—and by wages I mean real wages …
There is no dead end to Socialism. The Welfare State is only one stage
on the way.[49c]

ii   *Labour Policy-Making at Home*

A Leader of the Opposition has problems over policy-making which vary
with the man, the subject, and the political circumstances. Whatever his
party, he must reconcile the pressures of his own enthusiasts with the
doubts of the uncommitted. A Labour leader must also manage conflicts
among his own followers: middle-class progressives against bread-and-
butter-conscious trade unionists; moderates seeking broadly acceptable
reforms which would enter the consensus and become irreversible, against
utopians who would prefer no bread to half a loaf; MPs, sensitive to the
ordinary voter, against a National Executive chosen from the different
sections of the Labour Movement and so (even before its open war with
the leadership) responsive to a different set of demands.

Gaitskell's temperament did not always help. Where Attlee gave no
lead until the discussion in the National Executive had revealed the major-

ity view, Gaitskell risked his prestige by entering the fray at the start.[56] Twice at least in 1958–9, over public schools and municipalisation of housing, he found himself in a minority of one. These ventures did not endanger his leadership, but they did show how strict were the limits of his personal initiative. He also failed, as a prominent private individual acting at the request of its own leaders, to persuade the Co-operative Movement to modernise. But on the very sensitive issue of the House of Lords, where he had to guide Labour's responses to government proposals, Gaitskell proved skilful at keeping his fractious coalition together by judicious use of his authority as leader. He assessed the electorate better than his followers, knowing Labour's attractive plans were not those for nationalisation but for houses, pensions and schools.[57a]

On general educational policy Gaitskell was always a moderate. Privately as well as publicly, he vigorously defended comprehensive schools;[58] and he was eager for more to be built on an experimental basis.[59a b] He detested both selection at 'this frankly absurdly early age of 11 +', and the segregation of middle-class from working-class schoolchildren; but he was always against Labour becoming the open enemy of the grammar schools.[60] He thought that would both be unwise in itself and would 'lose some very useful support', and had therefore argued in 1954 for 'toning down the commitments'.[61a] That October, he thrust his head in the lion's den by putting the case for comprehensives at a Lake District conference of grammar school headmasters. He made a very favourable impression;[62] and concluded 'that if only our programme had been phrased a little more wisely we should not have had nearly so much hostility from ... the teaching profession, as well as some of our own Labour Education Committees'.[63a] He himself was careful to reassure audiences that Labour would not destroy the grammar schools or 'bully or bulldoze local councils'.[64]

As leader he maintained the same moderate stance.* He was insistent that 'You cannot pigeonhole human nature at the age of 11'.[66] But about positive proposals he was cautious:

> I can assure you that there is no question of our throwing away the tradition of the Grammar School ... We declared in favour of the *comprehensive system* of education, not just in favour of comprehensive schools. Even the latter I think have been unnecessarily criticised.[67a b]

He always emphasised that the 1958 policy statement allowed a very great

---

* He did so also on private pay-beds in NHS hospitals, a part of Bevan's compromise which he never liked. Two correspondents objected when the 1954 Conference was told they would be abolished; he replied that they would be replaced by cheaper but equally private amenity beds, and that of course no one (including MPs) should have priority in NHS beds.[65]

flexibility to fit local circumstances.[13b] But when a grammar school spokesman suggested that Labour was losing interest in comprehensives, he replied sharply that there was 'no question of our moving away from the comprehensive idea although, equally, we do not intend to be framed by the Tories as the murderers of the grammar school'.[68] That interpretation of 'comprehensive' as simply a rejection of 'permanent segregation' went entirely unchallenged at the Party Conference in 1958.[69a d]

On these public sector issues, Gaitskell was not far from Labour's centre of gravity at that period, and his personal contribution was mainly in presentation. On the role of the independent sector it was another story. He had at one time shared the common Labour view that the 'public schools could be left to wither as the state schools improved. He said so in an article on Labour policy in 1953,[21e] and provoked a correspondence with Lady Simon of Wythenshawe which may have changed his mind.[70] He was never happy that wealthy parents could buy privileged education for their children;[71a b c] and urged the NEC to include the abolition of fee-paying in Labour's new programme, but was beaten by an unlikely alliance of Crossman with Alice Bacon.[10e] At the Margate Conference that year he made one of his two speeches on that 'most improbable subject'.[72] Two years later he was again puzzled and irritated that 'the Executive always fights shy of tackling the private schools'.[73]

Speaking at his first Conference as leader, Gaitskell promised to 'have a go' at persuading the NEC of its importance.[49g] He failed lamentably.[74] As he told his old housemaster:

Unfortunately, within the Party most people are either in favour of 'abolition', which is administratively rather impossible and politically extremely difficult, or doing nothing ... because it is not for them an educational problem. Again, in terms of politics, I must confess the issue has no value. All our enquiries, gallup polls, etc., confirm that the ordinary man does not disapprove of the Public Schools and, on the whole, does not want much done about them.[67a]

Gaitskell had always favoured 'Fleming Plus' — requiring half the intake to be 'free places' for boys from the state system.[75] Both Right and Left of the Party opposed that, and he convinced neither the NEC's working party nor the Executive itself; indeed he would have been in a minority of one there but for his friends filibustering until he had to leave for another engagement.[76]

His policy was really more radical than the abolitionists', for the defeat of his proposals meant in practice that the public schools would survive intact, as he had warned they would.[59b] At the 1958 Conference, a motion to abolish them was fairly narrowly defeated.[77] Gaitskell wrote to his daughter:

There are real practical difficulties in the way of 'abolishing the public schools' which are explained in the pamphlet. I'm afraid I do take the view that to forbid parents under any circumstances to pay for the education of their children is to go too far in interfering with people's liberty.[78] If in taking this line we lose your radical intellectuals of 18–21 I can only say that if we did what they want we should lose literally millions of votes – from catholics and other denominations as well as some good solid Labour ones too. The truth, I'm afraid, is that even the working class is *not* against the public schools: they're mostly not interested in the problem. But they *are* interested in better State education.

Personally, as I expect you know, I wanted to throw open 'public' schools like Winchester to merit not wealth – but I could not carry the Party on this.[43b]

Housing policy presented some political problems not unlike those posed by comprehensive schools. One was the future of the rent restriction acts. Gaitskell may privately have wondered whether Labour could be committed for ever to provisions which had become 'not the protectors of the poor but of the fortunate';[79] but with Party and electoral opinion coinciding, he approved the Opposition's call to repeal the 1957 Rent Act.[57a c]

As a positive policy Labour wanted municipal ownership of all rented accommodation. That was an ambiguous formula, not specifying whether the takeover was to be simultaneous and nationwide, or decided upon over time by individual local authorities.[80] The first course was impracticable, at least in the near future, owing to a shortage of both qualified staff and (for improvements) of building labour;[81] the second was therefore indicated in the Party's popular summary pamphlet, *The Future Labour Offers YOU*. Without consultation, Anthony Greenwood as housing spokesman wrote to *The Times* in answer to a challenge, reaffirming the first course. Gaitskell rebuked him privately;[82] but on raising the issue at the Campaign Committee of the NEC, the leader met a harsh rebuff. 'I knew things were serious', remarked Crossman, 'when Harold Wilson sharply and unequivocally supported the opposition to Hugh'. Bevan moved that the policy statements must prevail over the new pamphlet:

Constitutionally, this was irrefutable, but of course it dished one of the main purposes of the new document ... and leaves open all the disputes about the interpretation of 170,000 words ... Tony Greenwood and I didn't vote and it was carried with one vote against – the leader's ... I doubt whether any of them considered the matter on its practical merits, and I believe the major motive in their minds was that they were not going to have the Party policy watered down by Gaitskell.

This was really a test of his power to impose his will, in which he abjectly and totally failed.[10f g]

Eventually Wilson found a solution—to issue no statement, since the pamphlet and the policy document were not contradictory.

Crossman wrote, as often before, that Gaitskell had been

> mistaken in constantly interfering and putting forward his views and getting defeated. I must add, however, that though that is what it looks like at very close range, one must admit that, by and large, he has got his way about Party policy. Certainly on this occasion he showed considerable intellectual bravery, insisting, extremely sensibly, on the absurdity of a position that one couldn't ever change a document written three years ago, particularly since the Rent Act had occurred afterwards ... he brought down on himself the rebukes of those who obviously thought he was betraying principle ... On the other hand, he does effectively control things.[10h]

Gaitskell did so enough to tell a journalist that it was merely a matter of timing, not of policy, and of freedom for local authorities, not for land-lords.[51] He was still the acknowledged spokesman in 1958, and his leader-ship was not yet challenged. But the limits to his authority were evident.[83]

Partly no doubt to strengthen his links with a neglected section of the Movement, Gaitskell took a keen interest in the Co-operatives. Their leaders asked him in 1955 to chair an independent Commission of Inquiry to advise on their future, and then pressed him to continue even after he became Leader of the Opposition; he agreed to do so with a limit of time and no pay.[84] He played an active part, going on some local visits and smoothing over many conflicts within the commission.[14b a] Its proposals, mainly drafted by its secretary Anthony Crosland, were individually familiar but together involved radical reform:[85] drastic amalgamations of local societies, concentration on fewer and better products, higher-paid officials, and chains of specialist shops. The Communists supported the reform, but the traditionalists were predominant among Co-operators and ensured that little of it was ever implemented. Gaitskell expressed 'intense personal disappointment that three years work should have had so trivial a result'.[86] There was also friction on the political front, over the number of parliamentary seats claimed by the Co-operators, which led to a difficult renegotiation of Labour's pact with them in 1957–8.[87] Later Gaitskell tried to enlist them on his side over Clause Four, advocating an extension of co-operative ownership as an alternative to either private business or traditional nationalisation.*

* E.g. in his Clause Four speech at Blackpool; and at Nottingham on 13 February 1960. (Over defence, they were always unilateralist.)

*   *   *

The House of Lords was a bastion of privilege like the public schools, which in theory Labour wanted to abolish but in practice cared little about (since as an upper house it was too anomalous to carry political weight, and so was not dangerous). The cases differed in that the Conservatives talked occasionally of modernising its composition to prepare the way for strengthening its powers. Gaitskell favoured reform, but not appeasement. He saw that there was a practical case for a second chamber;[88] and that in it Labour must have proper representation. But he did not mean to help the Tories rebuild a strong barrier against governments of the Left. Preferring a powerless revising chamber, he favoured a Norwegian-type reform, with party strengths in the upper house kept proportional to those in the lower:[89-91a] a plan simple, equitable, but unacceptable to Conservatives.

The hereditary peers wanted no change, and would not hear of the Norwegian scheme. Eden as Prime Minister had thought of giving them elected representatives to sit alongside a new category of life peers, and warned Gaitskell very early on that he might legislate even against Labour opposition.[92] In July 1956 the PLP set up a preparatory committee for which Gaitskell proposed Bevan: 'I was anxious to get Bevan heavily involved in this ... [instead of] making trouble in the Party, which is apt to be highly emotional about the whole business.'[63b]

He was wise. The life peerage bill was produced without consultation in the autumn of 1957. Bevan's wife Jennie (now Baroness) Lee led the die-hard abolitionists.[91b] Though very suspicious of the Government, Bevan would not go so far.[91c] Gaitskell spoke out against hereditary qualifications, sex discrimination, and power for the second chamber to obstruct the first; but he did not commit the Party to these reforming views, or rule out abolition.[93] The Bill passed, and in June 1958 without criticism or conflict the PLP agreed that Gaitskell should nominate life peers.[94] He had over 400 requests, took pains over his selections, and expected them to work twenty hours a week there.[95] He also warned them that apart from the Lord Chancellor, only one peer would sit in a Labour Cabinet.[96]

Early in 1961 when his leadership was under attack from the Left, Michael Foot (not an MP in 1958) attacked him for putting forward names; but the PLP reaffirmed its approval by 81 to 31.[22c] Yet, while wanting the system to work, Gaitskell too was suspicious of moves to create a more defensible House of Lords. The Conservatives hoped to use as a pretext the efforts of Anthony Wedgwood Benn, who had become Lord Stansgate, to renounce his inherited title. On Gaitskell's initiative the Labour Party refused to co-operate in that manoeuvre.[97-9a] Gaitskell had little enthusiasm for Benn's case (which had no appeal to the working-class voters)[10i] until Charlie Pannell convinced him that the principle mattered;[100] but then fought for it vigorously. Finally the Cabinet accepted Labour's terms for a committee on that issue only, convincing him that at last they wanted an agreed settlement. Then he recommended the PLP to participate: only Jennie Lee dissented as a (still) staunch abolitionist.[101] The law was duly changed, bestowing on the nation a fleeting glimpse of a reborn Mr Quintin Hogg;[102] the brief chance to be governed by that unnatural commoner Sir Alec Douglas-Home; and the prolonged drama of the downward social mobility of Mr Tony Benn.

Though Gaitskell was often unable to get his own way on important secondary matters, in 1958 his leadership was unquestioned in any large section of the Party and his general political approach almost unchallenged. There was no serious conflict over the new detailed policies so conscientiously hammered out during Gaitskell's first three years as leader. After the acrimonious quarrels of the recent past, that was an extraordinary transformation; and with Bevan's indispensable help he had accomplished it in a very short time. But the new unity was bought at a price, for in order to avoid alienating either Labour enthusiasts or floating voters, the policy statements too often reflected Gaitskell's 'painstaking compromises'.[103a] They were quite sensible, but made no more public impact than 'a jellyfish dropped from a fifth-floor window'[104a] or 'a Third Programme talk on needlework in the age of Diocletian'.[105a] Some were frankly designed to avoid embarrassment.[10j] Indeed, an independent Conservative journal attributed Labour's failure to attract the uncommitted to

> the shifty appearance given by the party's *persona*. In trying to bring the disparate elements of the Left into a coherent party, capable of offering a stable alternative government, Mr. Gaitskell can claim to have been surprisingly successful; but the end-result is unappetising ... in the process of trimming its sails to catch what few fitful breezes are now blowing it has lost its soul.
>
> This is not the fault of its leader. Mr. Gaitskell was appointed Lord Attlee's successor to do a job which, in the main, he has succeeded in doing: fusing the party's discordant elements.[106]

iii *The Party: Petty Friction, Precarious Unity*

In 1958 the Labour Party was enjoying an interlude of comparative peace, with Bevan reconciled and the 'Cousins war' — as Gaitskell was to call it — not yet begun. Commentators of different views agreed on his style of leadership though not on his personal role. Some thought him very skilful;[107a] 'more than in almost any other period in Labour's history ... what the leader says ... now usually goes'.[103b] He was seen as 'a clever politician, quick to detect changes in popular feeling';[108a] and he was acutely sensitive both to the still suspicious electorate and to the risk of jeopardising the Party's newly recovered unity. (So was Bevan.)[10d][k] But since Gaitskell's successes were obtained by persuasion, other critics continued to accuse him of giving no lead: 'Mr. Gaitskell regards political leadership as a series of exercises in intrigue ... his public reputation stands lower than ever before ... he may lose the next election by himself.'[109a] The charge of intrigue was a hostile phrase for Gaitskell's achievement in healing the factional feud. That Tory assessment was largely echoed, however (in substance if not tone), by a sympathetic Labour journalist. Some people wondered, wrote Francis Williams, if Gaitskell was 'no more than the passive instrument of an instinct for survival within the Labour movement — the reflection and symbol of a need to compromise ... the Labour Party needed a tranquilliser. He provided one. But ... now ... a tonic is needed'.[107a][b]

It was a familiar dilemma, for the Party worker's tonic might repel the uncommitted voter. In a time of prosperity, Labour was still blamed for post-war austerity, still seen as doctrinaire, still suspected of anti-British instincts.[110] It was not that the Conservatives were popular: since early 1946 they had never fallen below 35 per cent on the monthly Gallup poll, but in 1957 and the first half of 1958, they did so 10 times out of 16. But the Labour scores and Gaitskell's personal rating were both unimpressive, so that the Opposition owed its comfortable lead to defections of government supporters to the Liberals. Gaitskell thought that situation hard to change, and was not worried by it:

> Labour is a high taxation party, Labour is a trade union party, Labour is a nationalisation party, and Labour is not as sound as the Tories on the foreign issue ... there was a very limited amount one could do. He himself would play down the nationalisation of steel, but after all we are a trade union party with these views and, even with all this hostility, he was confident we should get in and would be content with a majority of 50 to 100 ... [which] 'would in certain ways be more convenient than 200 ... if one is to get to power, one may have to rely on non-Labour votes' ... we mustn't over-estimate the desire for self-sacrifice. This was a totally different situation from that which faced Cripps.[10l]

Gaitskell was therefore philosophical about short-term political swings. Labour took a record lead on the Gallup poll and became buoyantly confident in the autumn of 1957, just after the Brighton Conference and the rise of bank rate to 7 per cent (then a post-war peak). But the sudden gain disappeared again in December, following a poor by-election in a safe Tory seat at Leicester.[111] Then at another by-election at Rochdale in February 1958, the Conservatives fell badly behind the Liberals and lost the seat to Labour, and Gaitskell noted that government morale was 'frightfully low'.[112] Liberal progress continued with a victory at Torrington in April, provoking some disquiet with the leadership because Labour was not benefiting from the government's unpopularity.[113-14a] Dalton[47a] and Gaitskell both felt that such criticism reflected prolonged opposition, and would vanish with Labour's imminent return to power.[43a] Thus grumbling about Gaitskell's leadership was no longer on the old Left-Right lines, but reflected the volatile moods of politicians bored with opposition in a Parliament which, as Crossman kept complaining, was dull and listless. Bevan found that House of Commons the most wretched he had ever sat in;[115a] and Gaitskell felt much the same, saying of it later: 'In the last Parliament the situation was not satisfactory. The attendance was bad. People were not interested. The reputation of Parliament in the country was deteriorating.'[116] The Opposition's ability to affect that situation was small, as even Crossman (a political warfare specialist who often overestimated it) would now and then admit. Gaitskell lamented that half the Parliamentary Party were 'hopeless', and Wilson and Callaghan were equally pessimistic.[10m]

In the House, Gaitskell paid a price for his rapid rise. The Conservative whips noticed that on parliamentary business he was much less able than Attlee to commit his followers to decisions they would accept.[117] Moreover, the withdrawal or disaffection of many leading veterans proved a severe handicap. Because he lacked influential colleagues with solid backing in the Parliamentary Party, the weight of leadership fell very heavily on Gaitskell's own shoulders. In crises, therefore, he had neither time to consult nor powerful associates to deliver solid support. *The Times* political correspondent pointed out:

> Mr. Gaitskell cannot lead his party by economically winning over, or falling into line with, lieutenants who would bring their troops with them. More than any of his predecessors, he has to win over the party as a whole, and that is difficult and laborious work in a sudden crisis that sets the rank and file in turmoil.
>
> How often Mr. Gaitskell must pray for the boon of a second Ernest Bevin.[118]

Gaitskell's own speeches were usually effective, though they were a strain. During one series of major debates he wrote ruefully: 'if you do badly everybody notices it—though if you do well they forget it quickly enough. One keeps on running in order to stay still.'[43c] But in spite of Dalton's purge, the Shadow Cabinet was elderly and uninspiring, with more members over 65 than under 45, and only six of the fifteen under 50. Able men left politics in frustration, and few of those who stayed seemed to share the leader's undoubted will to win.[119a] In terms of parliamentary tactics (which affect morale at Westminster, if nowhere else) some Labour initiatives were unwise and, like the 'sticky labels' fiasco, damaged the Opposition more than the Government.[120] Gaitskell was not skilful at timing, and did not stop a debate being held on unemployment on the very day a sharp decline was announced.[10n] 'I cannot help it', taunted Iain Macleod, 'if every time the Opposition are asked to name their weapons they pick boomerangs.'[121] Three months later Macleod told a Tory rally: 'Mr. Gaitskell, leading his party with all the dedicated drive of a bumble bee, is a jewel beyond price for us.'[108b]

The Prime Minister was particularly effective at exploiting Gaitskell's difficulties, playing on his own followers' distaste for high-minded radicals, and for Gaitskell in particular, by offensive and wounding phrases.[122] In their weekly parliamentary duels Macmillan was soon to be sustained by favourable polls (and therefore Tory enthusiasm) as well as by the prestige of his office. Relations were bad between the two men, who seemed to typify the political 'bishop' and the political 'bookmaker', and who at this period had no mutual respect. Gaitskell thought that Macmillan 'cheated at politics';[123] and trusted the Prime Minister so little that he tried to avoid meeting except in the presence of the Liberal leader Jo Grimond.[124] Macmillan thought Gaitskell tiresomely stuffy and 'responsible':

> The trouble about Mr. Gaitskell is that he is going through all the motions of being a Government when he isn't a Government. It is bad enough having to behave like a Government when one is a Government. The whole point of being in opposition is that one can have fun and ... be colourful.[125]

Macmillan's tactical ascendancy at Westminster was bad for morale in the PLP.[10n] But that was far more directly dependent on the electoral outlook. As Gaitskell had written in 1955: 'As soon as the wicket changes, so does the attitude of our people. I very much doubt in fact if there is a deep-seated malaise.'[126] The wicket could change quickly. Trouble began with the sudden disappointment of the December 1957 poll, and fastened on the Labour leader's prolonged absences abroad. Crossman, whose *Mirror* column kept embarrassing his colleagues, touched it off with a protest at Gaitskell's absence from the debate on a NATO meeting.[127] He also attacked the Shadow Cabinet for losing the initiative in the House by its ineptitude.[128] Several young non-Oxbridge MPs—Bob Mellish, Denis Howell, Fred Peart and Charles Pannell, all future Ministers— formed a 'ginger group', not to challenge the leadership but to stimulate more vigorous parliamentary opposition.[129]

The ginger group was mainly composed of trade unionists; the other signs of frustration in the working-class wing of the Party were less healthy. Outside Westminster, the TUC leaders had been restive at the Blackpool Congress; they were unhappy about Crossman's pension plans, and disagreed with the PLP over the government's Maintenance Orders Bill.[130] In the House the younger trade unionists were full-time MPs, working hard in committees, who worried about their families because salaries were very low, and who bitterly resented resistance to raising these from the prosperous lawyers, journalists and company directors who were part-time and even absentee members. Their older colleagues of the Morrison-Shinwell generation were still more aggrieved at the university graduates taking over the positions of leadership, with George Brown and Alf Robens almost the only trade unionist newcomers.

The first worry was alleviated by a belated salary increase for MPs in July 1957, after a long campaign in which Gaitskell was very active.[131] The second caused an explosion when the 100-strong trade union group reported Crossman to the National Executive for saying Bevan, Brown, Griffiths and Robens were the only ones fit for high office.[132] That group, under Brown's leadership, was changing character and becoming an outlet for the less articulate MPs who felt frustrated both in PLP meetings and in the House.[133-4] Welcoming instead of shunning publicity, it was fastened on by Fleet Street's professional mischief-makers.[135]

It was the trade union group which first attacked Gaitskell for consorting with a 'Hampstead set' of Oxford-educated Labour intellectuals – later (though not at the time) a frequent ground of left-wing criticism. Because he invited these friends and neighbours to his home, they were supposed to exercise a nefarious political influence, and old myths about the XYZ Club were supplemented by a new one: that Crosland and Jenkins, Gordon Walker and Jay, Healey and Pakenham and Soskice settled Party policy over the white wine on Sunday evenings at Frognal Gardens.[136]

The falsity of that inference was never more obvious than the first time it was drawn; for when the trade union group met on 10 December 1957, Bill Blyton – a Durham miner MP – denounced the intellectuals for trying to foist a pro-Common Market policy on the Party without discussion.[137] (If so, they were to have precious little influence on its leader.) Two disgruntled ex-Ministers, Charlie Hobson and Ness Edwards, joined Blyton in sounding a note of virulent class feeling which the press lovingly recorded.[138] Gaitskell was not forgiven for insisting on his right to have a personal life and to choose his own friends; others grumbled that he did not invite them enough (though nobody ever criticised his predecessor who had no friendly personal relations with any colleague, or his successor who never asked any of them to his home). Dalton recorded a spate of gossip about who had the leader's ex-directory telephone number and other matters 'of almost unbelievable pettiness'[139] – all detailed and magnified by Lord Beaverbrook's favourite poison-pen columnist Crossbencher.[104b]

Fuelled by social jealousy not ideological passion, these complaints came from the Right rather than the Left of the Party: 'trade unionists, like George Brown and Bill Blyton', wrote Crossman, 'growl around the place that they are excluded from the secret confabs and generally give an extra stench to the moribund atmosphere.'[100] Brown had recently reproached Gaitskell for neglecting him, and warned that he would shift his own political stance rather than be isolated by the leader's search for a 'left-of-centre' consensus.[140] On Gaitskell's return from abroad, his loyal PPS Arthur Allen sent a friendly warning: 'And, my dear Hugh, you yourself have got to go a'courting.'[134] He did his best, keeping up regular visits to regional group meetings which, in Dalton's view,[47b] were a far more efficient way to keep in touch with back-benchers than gossiping in the tea-room.[109b] But it all added to his burdens, for he still probed conscientiously into detail and would not take enough time to relax.

Gaitskell had largely succeeded in reconciling the old factions, and most of the Left made no move to exploit the discontents. Bevan stayed completely loyal;[141] his response to the new mood was to develop close relations with Brown, as another working-class Labour leader untainted by universities.[10p] They worked closely together as Party spokesmen on foreign and defence policy respectively;[142] and Brown suggested (prematurely) that Bevan should become deputy leader, with a roving assignment not confined to one policy area.[143] Bevan's devoted friend Hugh Delargy (while also lamenting the lethargy of the PLP) defended both Gaitskell and even XYZ, saying the gossip was 80 per cent true and the conclusions drawn from it were 80 per cent false.[105b] Even Ian Mikardo warmly approved Bowden's management as Chief Whip and Gaitskell's tolerance and flexibility as leader.[105c]

Bevan's attitude must have disappointed Labour's shrewd opponent in Downing Street. For Macmillan knew he needed three million trade union votes to win an election, and founded his strategy on the hope of another left-wing revolt. At the trough of Conservative fortunes after Brighton, he wrote in his diary on 5 October 1957:

> At the moment the whole thing is swinging *away* from us. But has it swung to Labour? Gaitskell is trying to attract the middle vote. But will he lose the enthusiasm of the Left? (The H-bomb is perhaps the real test.) I think he will probably succeed — but he has made a tactical mistake in trying to get his troops rallied too early. If I can [postpone the] battle ... it is quite likely that they will quarrel again.[9e]

The Prime Minister had grounds for thinking so. In February 1958 Mikardo launched 'Victory for Socialism' (VFS) as an attempt to revive Bevanism without Bevan coinciding with a new agitation on nuclear weapons. VFS circularised all constituency Parties about meeting to organise local branches throughout the country, and offended the trade union hierarchy by talking of a one-day political protest strike.[144a b] Mikardo alienated even his former friends on the NEC and was in a minority of one. The trade unionist members swung back into anti-Left intransigence. Gaitskell was determined to stamp out any factional organisation in the constituencies, and wanted to warn local Parties that it would be unconstitutional to associate with VFS;[145] and the press wrote of a new Gaitskell who 'has never been seen quite like this before. His present mood is tough, ruthless, even merciless. Far from having to steel his courage to say Boo to a Labour goose, he now brandishes the chopper menacingly and with fell intent.'[144a c]

The VFS threat receded when its organisers abandoned any plan for local organisation and denied ever having meant it.[108c] But privately Foot and Mikardo were soon trying again to persuade Bevan to launch a new challenge for the leadership.[146] Publicly *Tribune* resumed its sniping at Gaitskell;[147] and was soon 'revelling' in a Tory press campaign against him (of the kind it had once claimed as proving Bevan's Socialist credentials).[14c] Bevan was irritated by Gaitskell's failures of tactics and timing and thought they showed a total lack of political flair.[148] But he did not say so in public, even when exasperated as he was over the VFS affair (and even there he was just as critical of Mikardo).[149] Nor was his new course appreciated by the old irreconcilables. Michael Foot denounced him for emphasising the need for Party unity, notably at a Trafalgar Square demonstration on nuclear weapons; and before long they had a violent quarrel.[150] Now that he was no longer a useful instrument to split the Labour Party, Bevan was also attacked by the Beaverbrook papers which had so often built him up in the past.[151]

The unity extended even to foreign policy, where Gaitskell's commitment to the American alliance did not mean unconditional support for Washington. Just as he thought the US Administration had rightly condemned Britain over Suez, he regarded 'obsequious silence' when we believed the Americans wrong as unhealthy, and indeed unhelpful to those of them who disapproved of their own Government's 'profoundly dangerous acts of folly'.[49d] So he unhesitatingly condemned them for apparently contemplating nuclear war with China over two offshore islands held by Chiang Kai-shek. First he issued a statement repudiating American brinkmanship, and urged Macmillan to make clear that Britain would not support such a war.[152] Macmillan too—though worried about Hong Kong, and determined not to criticise the United States—was privately unhappy about Dulles's intransigence, acutely aware of British opinion, and most relieved that Parliament was in recess.[9f] On the opening day of Labour's 1958 Conference at Scarborough, Gaitskell moved an emergency resolution — which was carried unanimously — to oppose any British support for a war over Quemoy (which Chiang ought to evacuate) and to urge the entry of Communist China into the UN (which should administer Taiwan pending self-determination). American policy changed that week, and the delegates implausibly claimed some of the credit.

Almost everyone in the Labour Party now agreed on most foreign policy issues: disengagement in Europe, non-intervention in the Middle East, and bringing Communist China into the UN. For as the cold war thawed, Labour policies had changed accordingly – while Selwyn Lloyd at the Foreign Office seemed frozen in the postures of the past. Denis Healey could therefore speak of 'a policy which unites our whole party from left to right ... [and] differs from the Conservative Government's policy on almost every major issue'. And Sydney Silverman, that symbol of the old pre-Bevanite Left, could respond: 'I agree with Denis Healey. I never thought I would live to say that at a Conference.'[49e]

Tribune apart, Labour's new unity was sealed at the 1958 Party Conference at Scarborough, with the series of domestic policy statements completed and with Healey and Silverman celebrating agreement on foreign policy. On Sunday at the pre-Conference rally, Bevan gave a famous pledge: 'The movement should realise that the leadership of the Party has been settled and the gossip should stop. Hugh Gaitskell is there, elected by the Party, and he commands the loyalty of us all.'[115b] Jennie Lee testified to the 'more comradely spirit' prevailing now that 'the rank and file' (an unusual synonym for 'my husband') were 'having more say'.[153a] In the economic debate, Gaitskell won a warm tribute from Frank Cousins and his biggest Conference ovation so far.[153b c]

That week transformed the mood. Beforehand, wrote Crossman,

People really had begun to believe the Tory press that Labour had no leaders and no policy and was utterly down and out ... Day by day the morale went up as the delegates were surprised to find their leaders weren't so bad and their policies made sense.[10q]

The delegates, as the *Observer* correspondent recorded, departed

in much better heart than even an optimist could reasonably have expected ... [they] left Scarborough believing they have something to talk about, something to sell. That was certainly not their attitude when they arrived. Most of them ... had not even read the policy statements ... [Hugh Gaitskell] has been almost unrecognisable here. In the old days he was often both diffident and hesitant ... Now ... [he] has entered into his kingdom; it could almost be said that the present policy is his and his alone.[154]

The writer concluded that the critics were of no importance – unless Labour lost the next election.

vi   *Policy-Making Abroad: Near East and Africa*

Despite what his Tory detractors said, Gaitskell as Leader of the Opposition tried hard to identify and support the long-term interests of his country without sacrificing the unity of his party. Macmillan was to find that difficult over Africa, and Suez had shown that it posed problems for Labour too. Gaitskell's freedom of action and decision was limited, and tactical adroitness was not his forte; so he was sometimes out-manoeuvred. Two Eastern Mediterranean crises in the summer of 1958 illustrate his outlook and his difficulties.

Since 1954 Cyprus had been in turmoil, precipitated by a foolish ministerial statement that Britain would 'never' relinquish her sovereignty. No Labour politician thought she could stay there indefinitely. Gaitskell argued succinctly, in a letter to the *Evening Standard* protesting against an anti-Labour leading article, that Britishers should be proud that our principles forbade us to repress a popular movement ruthlessly as a totalitarian government would – but that this very fact implied that our interests could be served only by a negotiated solution.[155] He was privately appalled at Eden's folly in exiling Archbishop Makarios, the Greek Cypriots' acknowledged leader, in March 1956.[156] Most Labour people sympathised with the Greeks on grounds of self-determination, but several were very suspicious of the Orthodox Church and its political prelates;[157] and many more were bitterly resentful at the killing of British soldiers by EOKA terrorists.[158]

The main obstacles to a solution were the mistrust between the Greek population, wanting *enosis* with Greece, and the 20 per cent Turkish minority whose mother country was only twelve miles away. The Greeks and many of their British friends never allowed for the Turks' military superiority and political determination.[159] But the local nationalists would settle their own course partly according to the expected policy of Britain's alternative government; so that one authority cites Cyprus as the classic case of an Opposition having a direct influence on events.[160a] Gaitskell scribbled a note to himself just before one critical debate:

1. What is our long term *national* interest? No more than a base if that.
2. At present both Greece & Turkey think that *we* are going to impose a solution which suits them – the Turks rely on the Tories the Greeks on Labour.
3. We should disillusion them about this – especially the Greeks. We can say we are for self-determination & against Partition. *But* we should add that we are not going to fight the Turks for this. Therefore they will have to face the choice – either compromise with Turkey *or* they may have to fight, and they may lose.[161]

From the start Gaitskell sought so to conduct the Opposition as to moderate Greek intransigence and avoid driving HMG into rigid commitments, and after his first month a Tory journalist commended him for 'leadership which deserves to be recognised as statesmanship' on this issue.[162] By the beginning of 1958 he believed the Conservatives were at last genuinely trying to reach a settlement, and was anxious to help them, not just from altruism but also to avert guerrilla warfare dragging on to plague a Labour government.[10l k] A new Governor, Sir Hugh Foot (now Lord Caradon), enjoyed Labour confidence, and feared like the Cabinet that his proposals were bound to fail if the Greeks thought they had only to wait for a Labour government to grant their full demands.[9g] So, on first taking office, Sir Hugh secretly met Gaitskell, Griffiths and Bevan to urge them not to oppose his proposals.[163] Later he sent his 'heartfelt gratitude', saying their 'invaluable' good will 'may well be decisive in the success of the operation.'[164a]

When his plan had to be put into force without Greek or Turkish consent, he renewed his private appeals.[164b] Bevan as well as Gaitskell was wary of making the Greeks overconfident, and insisted that Labour must not oppose the Governor's plan, though there was widespread scepticism about its prospects.[10k] Gaitskell's note, written on that occasion, concluded:

4. As *short term* it would still be foolish for us to *oppose* the plan. We should *not* vote on Thursday. If we did we should encourage the Greeks to stand out, wreck the plan & land ourselves with an implied commitment to Greece which we cannot carry out.[161]

Callaghan, opening for the Labour Party, followed closely the 'best line for debate' which Gaitskell had sketched.[165] Both at the time and later, the Prime Minister expressed almost fulsome gratitude for 'the firm and patriotic line which Gaitskell impressed upon his Party';[166] and soon took advantage of his opponent's restraint for his own party advantage.

As Gaitskell intended, Labour's attitude did put pressure on Makarios, and was the main reason for the Archbishop making 'his first important concession in the whole dispute' by renouncing immediate *enosis* in the autumn of 1958.[160b] That paved the way for an agreement between the Greek and Turkish governments, conditional on the British government at last abandoning its claim to sovereignty over the island. Macmillan did so, even inviting Makarios to the final conference. Gaitskell welcomed the news 'with great satisfaction and relief', congratulating Ministers on 'eating so many words ... at long last they have seen the light'. The criticism was well deserved but ill attuned to the mood of the House. Macmillan was anxious as always about his back-benchers;[167] and seized the chance to divert their wrath by a bitter attack on Gaitskell, saying: 'He never has been, and never will be, able to rise to the level of great events.'[168]

* * *

At the moment when Labour was making its contribution to the Cyprus settlement, another crisis was brewing nearby in another land of mixed population: the Lebanon. Gaitskell called it[169] 'a horrid mess where if we intervene we make things worse (& anyway there's little to justify it) & if we don't it may fall into Nasser's lap'.[43d] On 19 June 1958 the Prime Minister recorded:

> Gaitskell, Bevan and Griffiths came (at their request) to see the Foreign Secretary and me about Lebanon. Bevan was more robust than the others. I refused to give any pledge that we would *not* intervene in any circumstances. (They really accepted that such a *public* pledge would be a fatal encouragement to Nasser and his party in Lebanon.)[9i][p]

In fact Macmillan had already promised the Lebanese Premier to intervene if asked.[9d] Yet he gave the Labour leaders a very different impression. They understood him to give assurances against a new Suez by saying both that it was 'hardly conceivable' that either he or Eisenhower would land troops without a request from the UN, and also that the UN Secretary-General (who had been empowered to bring in an international police force) would not ask for American or British aid.[170] Three weeks later a brutal revolution in Iraq aroused fears for the other pro-Western Arab regimes, and American marines landed in Lebanon.

Gaitskell wrote privately:

> [W]e want ... the firmest possible guarantees against aggression across frontiers but we should leave the internal situation alone. It really is impossible to keep our puppet kings in power if they cannot even control their own armies. And the effort ... spoils everything else.[57b]

He advised both the Shadow Cabinet and the PLP meeting not instantly to condemn the United States, but to try to dissuade the British government from the far riskier adventure of going into Jordan whose King was now claiming the Iraqi crown.[22d][g] Bevan would have preferred to divide the House, but that would have openly split the Shadow Cabinet and, in a most obscure situation,[171a] the majority decided against doing so.[172a] Few back-benchers differed from their leaders on substance;[172a][b] though *Tribune* wrote hysterically: 'It took Mr. Gaitskell two months to grasp the real meaning of the Suez crisis. This time we can't wait – our very lives are at stake.'[105d]

Gaitskell described it as a week so 'strenuous & difficult politically' that he could think of nothing else, one in which he strove to

> (a) keep the Party united (b) stand by our principles (i.e. anti-gunboat diplomacy) (c) avoid getting quite out of touch with public opinion here. On the whole it could have been worse. I can see no way out for

the present Anglo-American line; it is too much in conflict with the dynamics of Arab Nationalism.[43e]

Crossman recorded that in the House, Gaitskell's speech was not taken as partisan even by opponents: 'by its moderate tone it did gain the attention of the Tories as the speech of someone trying to think about British national interests, and it got quite a good press.'[10r] A neutral journalist observed that the PLP

> were kept in check by Mr. Gaitskell on the understanding that there would be no support for a British landing ... As a party leader, he managed far more than anybody could have dared to predict, and he managed it almost single-handed.[22e]

He had steered his followers away from either violent anti-Americanism or another Suez-style campaign — both courses which would certainly have split the country and probably harmed the Party. But he had done so at a heavy tactical price.

Next day British troops entered Jordan, and the Shadow Cabinet agreed that Labour must vote against that, though more in sorrow than in anger as Gaitskell told the PLP.[10r] (George Brown objected, abstained, and offered his resignation from the Shadow Cabinet, which refused it.) Macmillan made a brilliantly moderate opening speech, and Crossman wrote:

> I really felt sorry for Hugh when he rose, and knew this was a job I just couldn't possibly have done ... Hugh managed to sound not partisan, not a stirring party demagogue, not an adroit party manager, but a sincere, thoughtful, highly intelligent man, who regretfully had to dismiss the Prime Minister's case.[10r]

One outside observer wrote that his performance had enhanced his stature and consolidated his leadership;[173] and Crossman confirmed that outcome (while noting that Bevan had made surprisingly little impact):

> [L]ooking back over the last eight days, he has achieved a tremendous step forward, since it was largely owing to his personal example that we did not relapse into Suez rowing, that we took a dignified line and that, on the whole it came off pretty well.[174]

But in refusing to exploit the situation for party ends Gaitskell had offered an opportunity to the Prime Minister, who was not so squeamish. In what he happily called 'a phrase that will stick', Macmillan said as his last words before the House divided: 'If it is not right to vote against America, why is it right to vote against Britain?'[171b] In his memoirs he appears as showing dignified Prime Ministerial restraint, but an eye-witness was nauseated by his 'almost incredible' display of unbridled partisan glee.[175]

*   *   *

Even in opposition, Labour had a direct influence on African events because, as in Cyprus, powerful local leaders chose their course of action with one eye on the policies of the alternative British government. Gaitskell was kept in touch with their views by an excellent private source, his brother Arthur. He was always anxious to preserve close links with these local spokesmen, seeing them as precious assets for a future Labour government, and regarding the Party as a trustee for the unrepresented black majority.

That became important early in 1959, when eleven Mau Mau prisoners were beaten to death by guards at Hola Camp in Kenya. Macmillan himself told the Queen that the Governor had 'by no means satisfactorily explained, or excused' the event.[9m] A few days later in March, the Governor of Nyasaland (now Malawi) declared a state of emergency, soon imposed also in Northern Rhodesia (now Zambia). Dr Banda, the Nyasa leader, was detained and the Commons were told that a massacre of Europeans had been planned. Gaitskell was alarmed, saying privately, 'Won't they ever learn?'[176a] The Africans became more suspicious than ever of the forthcoming constitutional negotiations over the Central African Federation.

The Federation—Southern Rhodesia, Northern Rhodesia and Nyasaland—had been proposed on (bad) economic grounds by the Attlee government, premised on African consent. The Africans feared it would mean rule by the white Rhodesian settlers, under whose pressure the Conservatives had abandoned the premise; Labour had therefore turned against the concept.[177a d] Arthur Gaitskell had warned his brother against it from the start;[178a b] and Hugh said he had been 'bamboozled' by the economic arguments.[176b] Macmillan wanted Labour to participate in the constitutional negotiations in order to influence the Africans, but he also needed to carry the settlers, led by the Federal Prime Minister Sir Roy Welensky. With the Tory right wing indignant over the Suez withdrawal and Cyprus, he had felt in 1958 that the progressive line he would most likely have preferred 'entailed too great a risk with the party'.[160d]

The Labour Opposition at Westminster and the Federal Government at Salisbury posed mutually incompatible conditions for joining Lord Monckton's proposed Commission of Inquiry on the constitution of the Federation. By giving them contradictory assurances, Macmillan tried to cajole both into joining and so earned the deep distrust of both. From the start Gaitskell feared that HMG would never defy Welensky.[176b] He therefore wrote to the Prime Minister that Labour would consider the government's proposals but he doubted if they would be acceptable;[179a] and on the same day he assured his brother:

You need not worry about our compromising with the Government.

As a matter of tactics it was necessary for us to try to agree on a bi-partisan policy but I would never be party to abandoning the principles in which we believe.

We saw the Government yesterday and I am afraid that your fears are amply justified. But we shall do our best before a final break is made to win them over to a wiser point of view.[180]

Opposition to the settler demands went far beyond Labour's Party ranks. Gaitskell feared that Welensky might not realise that;[176b] and if any such illusions existed in Salisbury they were unlikely to be discouraged in London, for Macmillan preposterously thought the African flames were being 'fanned by the Left here for purely political advantage', and also by the 'dangerous and subtle agitators' of the Scottish Kirk.[181] But Gaitskell would endorse no proposals which the Africans would see as a betrayal. Taken aback by his determination, Macmillan told Welensky on 6 June 1959 that he hoped public opinion would make the Labour Party accede, and refused any concession.[182a] Instead, on 18 June Gaitskell broke off the talks he had himself initiated, and — after three months of silence — called for a debate to reassure the Africans.[179b] He saw their assent as 'of paramount importance',[183a] and would not join the Commission without guarantees for them: representation of the coloured Commonwealth (e.g. Ghana); an immediate franchise reform in Nyasaland; and a recognised right of secession from the Federation.[176c]

On 6 July, Macmillan agreed both the composition and the terms of reference of the Commission with Welensky, who believed that Downing Street was firmly committed to appoint no Africans in detention, no members from the coloured Commonwealth, and no British MPs except Privy Councillors.[184] (All three points were still at issue in the Commons.) Above all Welensky had from Macmillan, as from previous Conservative governments, a secret pledge that secession would not be permitted.[177b e] He specified publicly that he accepted the Commission only provided secession was ruled out.[182c]

Gaitskell was suspicious of the Prime Minister (and said so publicly)[183b] for misrepresenting their talks and for hinting at concessions (for instance on Welensky's first two points) without ever promising anything.[176d] He rightly thought Macmillan was preoccupied with the electoral consequences in Britain of a breach with the settlers. But Gaitskell liked Welensky when they met on 10 July;[178a] and assessed him as an opportunist who might well, like many politicians in the American South a decade later, turn more liberal if he depended on black votes for election.* Welensky

---

* A new franchise ensuring that dependence would, Gaitskell thought, be a way to reassure the Africans.[183c] But Welensky could never accept that while the electorate was still white.

told him of Macmillan's commitments.[16ab] That convinced Gaitskell of the Prime Minister's trickery;[119b] but he did not yet realise that Welensky was the dupe. That became evident only in the next Parliament.

Labour's suspicions were not diminished by Macmillan's handling of the critical reports on Hola and Nyasaland, published together in July. For the government's own Nyasaland commission under Lord Devlin found no massacre plot, denied that Dr Banda was a man of violence, and said that the Nyasaland Africans were wholly against federation. The Colonial Secretary offered to resign. But its report was rejected and a reply, written by three Ministers, was published in the name of the Governor.[185] Macmillan was desperate to avoid resignations and a party crisis: he candidly says so in his memoirs,[9n] and Welensky was struck by his preoccupation with the electoral impact of these affairs.[182d] Academic critics all confirm that preoccupation,[186] which the then colonial correspondent of *The Times* recalled later as 'a shameful exercise in electoral expediency'.[177c]

v *Doldrums of Affluence*

The Scarborough Conference had revived Labour morale, and the Opposition had to be ready for a spring election. One weekend late in November 1958 a big propaganda campaign was launched, with meetings for trade union delegates, MPs and candidates, and party organisers. A very professional and successful propaganda pamphlet, *The Future Labour Offers YOU*, was published on the Monday to publicise the proposals in all those neglected policy statements.[22f] It was written by Crossman and Tom Driberg from the Executive, helped by Hugh Cudlipp and Sydney Jacobson from the *Daily Mirror* and, as Crossman testified, with

> Hugh Gaitskell, to do him credit, making all this possible. True, he was a nuisance, true, he interfered too much. But then, after all, he is the Leader, and ... it was his simple, passionate faith in this pamphlet and in our capacity to write the best piece of propaganda ever seen which contributed an essential element to the publicity build-up. If we had had Attlee leading and not believing in it, there would not have been this strange belief that something unique was occurring.[187]

Even the *New Statesman*, so often critical, grudgingly approved 'a reasonable programme ... and ... a carefully devised plan – more simple and effective than anything they have been given before by Transport House'.[188]

Publicising the Party also entailed publicising its leader. Gaitskell disliked what Bevan used to call 'leaderolatry', but he felt he could not simply opt out of it, and that it was part of the price of democratic responsibility: 'That is, after all, what they expect of me. That is what millions of people are hoping for. I cannot allow my own squeamishness to go too far or shut myself up in an ivory tower just before an election.'[43f] The occasion of that comment was his first favourable interview in the Beaverbrook press[51] – which his wife and daughter both hated, and indeed he himself found 'rather nauseating'.[43f] Six months earlier he had met the magnate for the first time, and wrote to his daughter:

> [L]ast night Mummy and I dined with Lord Beaverbrook. He has of course been persistently hostile to me ... We went with Anne Fleming (who is a great friend of his) ... the fire inside him has died down & he is less prejudiced & irresponsible & evil than he used to be; after all he is nearly 80. Mummy got on with him very well – as I expected she would. I am glad we went. I would have been sorry never to have met him. I doubt if he liked me (I'm too smooth and polite & Wykehamist for him) & I don't expect there will be any change in the papers![43g]

(Dora often got on better than Hugh with those who were not 'smooth & polite'.) Gaitskell's prediction about the papers proved wrong because – so he learned – the *Daily Express* decided that its circulation would benefit from a show of political impartiality.[43f]

Another part of the leader's exposure which Gaitskell at first found awkward was the Party's organised provincial tours. The first of these, in industrial Lancashire before Scarborough, was far from a success; it was poorly organised and Gaitskell himself seemed gauche and ill at ease.[189] (It did not matter: that was one of the few areas where Labour gained in 1959.) His technique greatly improved as time went on, though a year later he still struck one observer as rather like a polite hospital visitor in a foreign land.[114b] But, as his professional adviser commented:

> His manner with the rank and file eased enormously, became less aloof. There was a time when you couldn't imagine him with a pint of beer in his hands. And at the end ... we had done a round of clubs in Bolton ... and he had a pint in each of nine clubs. He adapted himself ... and got along with the grass roots increasingly well until the end ... and Dora blossomed.[190]

He was in Scotland in October 1958, and in Cornwall and Devon in November. After the New Year he visited Northern Ireland, North and South Wales, and the north-east coast – areas where unemployment was high, and he could see the human cost of governmental caution in delaying economic expansion. He insisted throughout that his object was to learn the local problems, not to advertise his wares: to listen rather than to be seen.[191] The impressions he formed were overwhelmingly economic, not political, and he did not foresee how soon the national problems of the three peripheral countries would be in the forefront of United Kingdom politics. He was aware of those problems, but wary also of offending the Labour Party in Scotland.[192] Some time later, at the request of its MPs, he opened a debate on Scottish affairs and underlined that the Scots were among the main sufferers whenever the government, because the economy was becoming overheated in southern England, applied the economic brake throughout the country.[193] Abnormal unemployment and appalling housing were indicators of the neglect which was soon to erode, first Scottish support for the Conservative Party, and then Scots acceptance of government from London. But in 1958 it was still unemployment, not devolution, which Gaitskell felt might have an impact in future nationalist heartlands such as North Wales and the Scottish Highlands and Islands.[194]

In the spring he moved on to the more prosperous regions with many marginal seats: to the East Midlands in March, and in May to East Anglia where Labour had just won a by-election in an idiosyncratic rural constituency, South-West Norfolk.[195] John Harris had dealt with the press there; he went with Gaitskell on the regional tour, and soon became the leader's public relations adviser.[196] In August Gaitskell returned to Kent, where he had begun his political career a quarter of a century before. The early sneers had died away, and press reports now referred to his charm and to their own previous failure to record it.[119c]

Even when some Conservative journalists were portraying Gaitskell to their readers as constantly ill at ease, other reporters discovered that 'He just likes meeting people – to the point of causing impatience among some of the managers'.[197] Certainly Gaitskell found the tours a refreshing escape from the Westminster hothouse, and welcomed contacts with the ordinary people who kept the constituency organisations going. These visits helped – though a more flamboyant man might have done more – to remedy his old problem that, while his personal leadership was secure in Parliament and in the Party, his personality had made little mark in the country.[198]

Television, though still a novelty, was already the principal medium for projecting a public personality. Gaitskell took endless trouble to master the technique; for one particularly important broadcast he took four hours over the script and did five rehearsals (to which Bevan never turned up). Crossman felt that those seven or eight hours were well spent, for 'Gaitskell did put himself across and prove that success in television is, quite literally, a capacity for taking pains'.[10s] Other commentators praised his 'warm, friendly understanding of what was in the other person's mind', and saw him as 'deeply sincere ... a man who was not prepared to conceal any awkward fact in order to placate the electorate'.[199] Once when he was described as 'characteristically agreeable' on the screen, his old enemy Emanuel Shinwell derided him in the PLP, where Gaitskell mildly but effectively replied that making a disagreeable impression on several million viewers would not do the Party much good.[200] He scored a triumph in April 1959 when he courageously answered spontaneous questions from people in the streets of Watford for a party political broadcast,[13c] which obtained one of the top ten ratings — an unheard-of event.[201]

He welcomed television exposure, which gave a chance to correct

the image people have of me [which] — rather because of Tory propaganda — has hitherto been pretty different from my real character. I long to say something — perhaps in a television interview — on how the Press always tries to make one either inhuman or too human whereas in fact one is merely human.[43f]

But he was not corrupted. Some people, worried that his personality made too little impact, wanted him to imitate what an adviser on broadcasting contemptuously called 'the "admass" selling of Macmillan'. Gaitskell would not hear of that:

Of course, I wholly agree with what you say both about my not changing my public personality (you need not worry about this — I would not tolerate anything of the kind) and also about the much more profound dangers in the techniques of public persuasion.[202]

The Prime Minister was not only a splendid performer on the screen, but also enjoyed the appurtenances of power and the sympathy of the press, which praised Macmillan (and later Wilson) for the skill in Party management for which Gaitskell was condemned; and gave the Prime Minister six times as many news stories as his adversary.[203a] Macmillan's first television success coincided with (and perhaps even caused) a rise in his popularity.[203b] After the middle of 1958, he was rated a good Prime Minister by over half those polled, and Gaitskell came far behind. Labour supporters stayed loyal to Gaitskell, with 70 per cent approving and only one in eight disagreeing.[204] But in the electorate as a whole, though not many were hostile, only 40 per cent thought him a good leader — even fewer in two disastrous polls in the late summer of 1958, when those approving of him were outnumbered by the Don't Knows.[205] Though that was a freak, a Tory paper could tell the public that Macmillan 'outshines Mr. Gaitskell as a lighthouse does a glow-worm';[104a] while Gaitskell felt Labour was 'fighting with bows and arrows'.[10c]

At the same time, the Labour Party had lost its long-standing lead. Crossman wrote that he and Gaitskell were unable to persuade their colleagues

that the Don't Knows could only be won for Labour by concentrating

on simple bread-and-butter home issues ... [failing] partly because
the Campaign Committee is dominated by people like Barbara
Castle, Ian Mikardo and Nye Bevan who don't believe in a strategy
of that kind.[10n]

Now, after Thorneycroft's austerities and well before the election, economic restraints were relaxed and affluence began to pay political dividends.
The Liberal defectors returned to the Conservative fold, and in autumn
1958, after prophesying defeat for over a year, Central Office regained
confidence.[206] There was a brief flurry in February and March 1959, when
Tory support slipped (without the Opposition's rising) and the Government
seemed to be falling behind again. Labour's volatile morale jumped at
once, only to drop back in the spring when the Conservatives recovered
after Macmillan's visit to Russia and a generous Budget.[207] In the whole
year from October 1958 to September 1959, the Conservatives scored at
least 38 per cent in nine polls out of twelve while Labour (which had never
dropped below that level from losing office in 1951 to the beginning of
1958) attained it only once.

Though publicly indifferent to the polls, Gaitskell privately expected a
small Labour majority until early in the spring;[208a] so did Bevan.[10t u]
Central Office too thought the Conservatives would only just win an
immediate election.[209] When the Tories regained their lead in May,
Gaitskell for the first time admitted to himself the possibility of defeat;[10v]
though by the summer he again thought the outcome uncertain[176a] and
'desperately close'.[208b] But he gave a simple answer to one common
complaint: that Labour's policies were not sufficiently distinct from those
of the Conservatives.

> I certainly would like a sharper differentiation in the public mind
> between ourselves and the Tories so long, of course, as this is to our
> electoral advantage and not to the contrary. The Tories undoubtedly
> try to blur the distinction whenever they think we produce proposals
> which are popular. Of course, it must be our job to avoid the blurring.
> On the other hand, they try to sharpen the distinction when they think
> our policy is unpopular as, for example, nationalisation. That is what
> I meant when I said that the sharpening must be to our advantage.[210]

That obvious qualification was often neglected on the Left, where
leaders may be attacked not just for failing to win votes, but even for
trying to.[211] Gaitskell repudiated that criticism too. He wrote to a university lecturer:

> Although it is our job to win the Election and the way we present our
> policy must be geared to the need to win over marginal voters (if we
> did not do this we should not be worthy of our jobs) I would certainly

not accept that we are just concerned with vote-catching ... an immense amount of thought and discussion has gone into the working
out of our programme.

I would not say that the Labour Party is any more or less respectable today than when I first joined it over thirty years ago. It is ... no
longer a pioneering minority. But it is still inspired by the same
ideals ... in which for my part I still whole-heartedly believe.[212]

Neither Macmillan nor his followers suffered from such inhibitions. The
Conservative leader enjoyed all the strategic assets of a Prime Minister:
the opportunity to make news, to take over attractive Opposition policies
at the moment of his choice, and sometimes to benefit from the favours of
foreign powers who preferred a familiar partner in Downing Street.
Gaitskell could never compete for publicity on equal terms, even if
another Prime Minister had had less flair for it than Macmillan. Adept at
using his advantages, in the spring of 1959 the Conservative leader underlined his chosen theme of 'Peace and Prosperity' by adroitly removing
Labour's most popular cards: economic expansionism, European disengagement, and Summit talks among the great powers.

At the beginning of the year Gaitskell had said he was confident that a
Labour government's policies would create a social climate in which it
could count on the unions' co-operation and goodwill.[213] He therefore
believed that higher productivity, rising by $3\frac{1}{2}$ per cent a year, could pay
both for increased wages and for Labour's social programme. 'He might
even hope to lower the standard rate of income tax.'[51] But in April 1959

the most cautious of Chancellors was responsible for the most generous Budget ever introduced in normal peace-time conditions ...
Macmillan himself ... was responsible for enlarging the income-tax
cut, which was to have been 6d., to 9d. ... Orthodox economists and
officials have ever since regarded the 1959 Budget as an object lesson
in the dangers of trying to go too fast.[28f]

There were respectable reasons for that decision;[28g] but time was to show
that 'the stimulus ... [of] another pre-election budget — was excessive'.[214]
As Gaitskell and many others at once said, all the respectable reasons for
expansion had applied much more strongly a year earlier — and were then
rejected.[215] An academic wrote later that many unofficial advisers were
pressing the Chancellor to expand, but: 'One cannot help wondering
whether he would have responded so fully in a non-election year'.[29f]

Symbolising a sudden new flexibility in British foreign policy, Macmillan visited Moscow in February 1959 wearing a white fur hat to delight
cartoonists. (Gaitskell wrote privately that the visit was certainly 'for
internal political reasons. All the diplomats think so'.)[216] The Prime

Minister went on to Bonn, Paris and Washington. No umbrage was taken there; instead, the Republican Administration itself helped to manipulate the news and assist Macmillan's re-election. Gaitskell protested indignantly at indiscreet publicity for their preference in an American newspaper;[217] he could not stop Eisenhower arranging his European tour to give his ally the maximum help and news coverage.[218]

An astute Prime Minister in a prosperous country thus began with every advantage in 1959. Then, in that election summer, Gaitskell's achievement in reuniting his quarrelsome followers began to fray, just as Macmillan had hoped, over the great issue of nuclear weapons. Rejection at the polls would not merely postpone Gaitskell's opportunity to inaugurate new policies from Downing Street; it might, as he knew all too well, end that hope permanently by jeopardising his leadership of the Party. For though he was unchallengeable in the pre-election period, colleagues from the unforgiving Left—and elsewhere—were 'all carefully preparing their positions to blame others for the defeat' if it came.[219]

CHAPTER 18

THE CAMPAIGN FOR NUCLEAR DISARMAMENT 1958–9

'Our party decisions are not dictated by one man — whether the leader ...
or the general secretary of the T&GWU'
(HG, 1959; CONDENSED)

i *A United Party Leadership*

THE H-bomb was an awesome problem which aroused passionate feelings, going far beyond the ordinary course of Labour politics yet soon to impinge sharply upon it. In 1957, after the Brighton Conference, Gaitskell had discouraged moves to specify Labour's attitude beyond the call for conditional suspension of British tests. He had told a colleague that while the Party was on record against unilateral renunciation, it was not committed to continued manufacture: 'My personal view is that we will do best to leave the matter there. It is really quite impossible in opposition, and on the limited information available, to work out a detailed defence policy.'[1] The situation was always changing; for instance, the United States might (as it soon did)[2] repeal the McMahon Act which forbade giving information on nuclear matters to other countries.[1]

Gaitskell's caution was reinforced by the need to keep his querulous flock together. He knew that the compromise was no substitute for a policy: 'I have never regarded the suspension of H-bomb tests as more than a starting point. Obviously, the main problem is getting an agreement on nuclear weapon production.'[3a b] But, both as a prospective Prime Minister who might soon be responsible for the country's defences, and as an Opposition leader anxious to maintain party unity, he hoped to avoid either firm commitments or bitter arguments over matters which might look quite different when serious decisions needed to be taken. That hope proved untenable when the bomb evoked the greatest and most sustained movement of public opinion in post-war Britain.

At New Year 1958, Anthony Greenwood wrote to Gaitskell that he had been invited to discuss nuclear questions with several prominent intellectuals; that if Gaitskell had no strong objection he would like to accept;

that he would propose they should concentrate on the problem of testing; that it was valuable for the Party for 'prominent and responsible members' to develop such associations, and that otherwise they would ask 'somebody like Tom Driberg or Ian Mikardo'. Gaitskell replied with warm encouragement and a warning:

> You will, I know, naturally bear in mind that as a prominent member of the Party you cannot be associated with proposals which conflict with Party policy. But so far as the idea is all-round disarmament there will be no difficulty [nor on tests] ... I agree very much ... that the Party should keep in touch with movement [sic] of this kind supported by what one might vaguely call liberal opinion.[4]

Greenwood went, and that meeting launched the Campaign for Nuclear Disarmament.[5a]

The issue of nuclear weapons revived left-wing opposition to the leadership. Mikardo's 'Victory for Socialism' (VFS) was credited, rightly or wrongly, with organising the sixty-five MPs who broke Labour's precarious truce on 25 February by calling publicly for a new Party policy on it.[6-7a] A day later the official Labour and TUC paper, the *Daily Herald*, threatened the compromise more dangerously and unexpectedly by calling on the front page for an end to manufacturing the bomb. That was not the policy of either organisation, and it infuriated the leaders of both.[8-10a] Far more serious pressure for a reformation of Labour policy came from the non-political anxiety in the country mobilised by CND, and fed by two new developments: the discovery that planes carrying H-bombs patrolled regularly from British bases; and the NATO decision to accept United States missile bases, threatening that Labour would split yet again over an emotional question which it could not affect. Like Bevan, Gaitskell saw no objection in principle to missile sites, once bomber bases had been accepted.[11] But he agreed with his colleagues – and with the government – that they must be under British control; and since the V-bombers would be operative for years, Labour saw no urgency about starting work on the sites. In the leader's absence before Christmas, Bevan and Brown formulated a policy: to stop the H-bomb patrols, and postpone physical work on the missile sites pending the proposed summit talks with the USSR.[12-13a 14a] Gaitskell endorsed it both privately[3a] and publicly.[15a b] When the TUC asked for fuller discussions, he welcomed a new political initiative – while Bevan stood pat on the previous policy.[7b]

At the first of these talks with the TUC, on 13 February 1958, the two leaders agreed on every issue: disengagement, missile bases, and an international agreement by stages on nuclear weapons – first a ban on testing them; then a pledge not to use them (linked to an agreement on conventional weapons); then an inspected stoppage of production; finally the

R

destruction of stocks.[16] The talk was reported to the NEC a fortnight later. Only three people voted for Mikardo's motion against either manufacture or use of the bomb; Bevan and Gaitskell both discouraged the precise statement of nuclear policy sought by Crossman.[7a c] In the House, the parties differed on deterrence: the Government relied on the H-bomb alone, Brown and Strachey on tactical atomic weapons—even against a conventional attack.[14b] Strachey cited Berlin as an instance, and Bevan warmly approved.[7d e] (Gaitskell, it later appeared, did not.)[9b]

At the resumed TUC talks on 6 March 1958, the argument shifted—as it so often did in the nuclear weapons debate—to another point: not testing them, or making them, or delivering them, but when they might be used. In March 1955 Bevan had challenged Attlee to declare that Britain would never be the first to drop the H-bomb; now he asked for the first (and last) time for that declaration to cover all nuclear weapons.[17] The TUC spokesmen split, Frank Cousins and Robert Willis supporting Bevan and the others opposing him. Gaitskell feared that a pledge not to use the H-bomb first would eliminate deterrence if believed (Bevan said it would not be). He pointed out that the subject was not current defence policy but future disarmament negotiations, linking a nuclear ban with an agreement on conventional weapons. Crossman said that though he disliked established Party policy on defence, it could not be reversed so casually; Barbara Castle asked why not; and James Griffiths reminded the negotiators that that would exceed their authority. The 'first use' question was therefore deferred, and the joint declaration was confined to the points agreed—on tests, patrols, missile sites, and a ban on nuclear weapons within an eventual disarmament treaty, which would at all stages maintain the military balance between Russia and the West.[18a]

The joint meeting had decided—Bevan dissenting—to mount a national campaign on the subject;[7a] for which the NEC authorised issuing a pamphlet by Strachey (*Scrap All the H-bombs*) with a foreword by Gaitskell.[19] Speaking with Gaitskell to 10,000 people in Trafalgar Square, Bevan concentrated—to Foot's annoyance—on the need for unity.[20] In the PLP, Gaitskell as chairman managed a surprisingly harmonious debate, selecting many pacifist speakers and ruling out of order a right-wing motion endorsing the joint statement.[21] Crossman felt the meeting and the whole episode showed 'the Party's furious determination to win the next election by avoiding disunity ... the extremely fluid situation behind the scenes in the leadership ... and the influence which two people, George Wigg and myself, can exert'.[22a c]

Crossman's assessment referred to a further set of talks, and contrasts sharply with Michael Foot's picture of Gaitskell as impatient and intransigent on the question. The Party leader did not just try to preserve unity by tact over the formalities once he had got his way on the substance. His clash with Bevan and Cousins on 6 March had leaked to the press;[23] so, to repair the damage and restore his compact with Bevan, Gaitskell convened three secret meetings of senior Parliamentarians concerned with defence in an effort to reach agreement on all the main aspects of the nuclear problem: tactical atomic weapons, conditions of possible British renunciation, and 'first use'. Besides the leader and his deputy, six MPs attended: Brown, Healey and Strachey from one wing; Bevan, Crossman and Ungoed-Thomas from the other. An unexpected alignment emerged, for Bevan gave up his brief flirtation with unilateralism before they met. At the end of the talks, Crossman complained to Gaitskell that 'one against five was a bit tough', and was told: 'I thought I had balanced it evenly, but Nye, to my surprise, was against you and Ungoed-Thomas and with George Brown.'[24]

Crossman suspected that Bevan would accept the use of tactical atomic weapons against a conventional attack, if the others agreed to repudiate first use of the H-bomb.[7f] He objected (on information from Wigg, contradicting what the rest thought) that very few tactical atomic weapons existed and that they were enormously costly.[25] Gaitskell conciliated him in the three-page memorandum which summarised the talks; it included a commitment not to renounce tactical atomic weapons but no mention of using them.[26-7a] Crossman told Gaitskell he was satisfied with that. In reply: ' "Yes, I've been pretty fair to you", he said, with quite a twinkle in his eye, and it was obvious he had had quite a time with Mr Bevan and quite an effort to break Mr Brown off from him.'[28]

Gaitskell's memorandum recorded unanimous opposition to British renunciation on political grounds of all nuclear weapons; to any general Western pledge not to use them first, while Russia remained dominant in conventional forces; and to instituting without international controls the 'non-nuclear club' advocated by the *Manchester Guardian* – i.e. British renunciation if everyone other than the Americans and Russians also renounced – because it would force all other countries to shelter behind a super-power, dangerously increasing polarisation.[29] (Gaitskell was always careful not to rule out the club in all circumstances.)[30a e] The memorandum noted a minority opinion (Crossman's) that Britain should concentrate on conventional forces, leaving nuclear weapons to the United States, and might give up both their use and manufacture if France and Germany did so too. There was no general view, and Gaitskell thought it foolish to decide in opposition, whether Britain should continue to make tactical weapons and missiles (as distinct from the H-bomb).[9b] Everyone wanted to limit conflicts, abhorred 'massive retaliation', and was deeply reluctant to contemplate using the H-bomb. But a firm pledge against its 'first use' might cause public misunderstanding between H-bombs and smaller nuclear weapons; and there were too few of the latter to deter a big conventional attack either in the near future, or if American protection failed. The memorandum carefully recorded dissents on other points, but none here; presumably Bevan did not insist — even as an individual — on repudiating first use of the H-bomb.[27b]

The talks had restored unity among the leadership.[31] At Scarborough in 1958 as at Brighton in 1957, Bevan joined Gaitskell in resisting the unilateralist pressure, arguing that no decision on manufacturing the bomb could be taken on the information available in opposition.[30b] Gaitskell crossed the platform to congratulate him and shake his hand. The leader maintained that a unilateral gesture by Britain would have no effect; to stay in NATO meant sheltering behind American bombs; to withdraw from it would endanger peace. For the United States would either revert to isolationism, leaving us defenceless against Russia, or — more likely — build up Germany. Any influence British opinion might just have had over Quemoy would never be repeated if we contracted out.[30c] The unilateralist motion was lost by over 6 to 1, winning very few votes apart from Labour's permanent small minority of pure pacifists.[32]

At the time of the Party-TUC talks, Gaitskell — like Winston Churchill under the Labour government — had declined the Prime Minister's invitation to confidential talks about defence, lest they compromise the independence of the Opposition.[33] He feared that the proposal was 'put forward by Macmillan for personal political ends ... and not to let [him] question the service and scientific experts'; and he knew that acceptance would provoke 'great suspicion on his own side of the House'.[9b] Again the press was being critical of him for concentrating on Labour's internal harmony over defence:

> The compromises for which he has been responsible, valuable though they have appeared to members of the party, have a tarnished look to the public. Within the party, for example, it must have been regarded as a triumph of diplomacy when Mr. Aneurin Bevan, Mr. George Brown and others were induced to thrash out their differences in private, and produce for public consumption a defence policy that it was possible for the party to defend ... but to the detached observer, it simply seemed ... a spurious unity between men whose views were fundamentally irreconcilable.[34]

More brutally: 'He has shown once again that he badly needs a backbone to attach his brave teeth to his needlessly flapping tail.'[35]

ii   The Non-Nuclear Club

At Easter 1959 Frank Cousins and Robert Willis, chairman of the TUC General Council, were spotted in Trafalgar Square at the end of CND's march from Aldermaston. A great political storm was brewing, which burst on 4 June when the annual conference of the most loyal and cautious of unions – Sir Tom Williamson's NUGMW, to which Gaitskell himself belonged – voted for a unilateral British ban on the manufacture or use of the H-bomb. The result was perhaps accidental, for many delegates were at tea; the majority was 150 to 126 (with 75 votes not cast), and on 22 August when Williamson unprecedentedly recalled the conference, the decision was reversed by 194 to 139 (with only 3 not cast).[36] But the sensational June vote, shortly before a general election was due, revived the public dispute over defence policy and set off or speeded up a flurry of political activity.

Changes in the international situation were affecting Gaitskell's attitude. After the new policy statement came out, he was to write privately:

> I tried to be as honest as I could about the timing of our declaration. I think it would be fair to say that I had always been aware of the gravity of the problem but the failure of the general disarmament negotiations on the one side, the more successful conference on tests on the other, together with more information from American scientists about the capacity of other countries for producing nuclear weapons, were the things which influenced me.[37]

In April 1959 the General Council, no doubt under pressure from Cousins, had sought clarification of the Party's nuclear policy;[38] the day before the NUGMW's vote, the National Executive was already considering the TUC request for further talks, and also representations from the Socialist International.[79] But the NUGMW resolution made agreement on a new policy far more urgent, and an element of moral initiative by Britain in that policy far more politically desirable. Technical and political developments both pointed to the 'non-nuclear club' idea, which had previously seemed to unilateralists a useful advance, and to Gaitskell a device not to be ruled out.

That idea was the germ of the future non-proliferation treaty. It was for Britain to promise to give up her own bombs if all other countries, excepting the two super-powers, agreed not to make or acquire nuclear weapons. It had sprung independently from two sources. Conor Cruise O'Brien (then an official in the Irish Foreign Office) suggested it to his Minister Frank Aiken, who sponsored a UN resolution in 1958, and reintroduced it with much more support in 1959.[39] Also, since February 1958 the *Manchester Guardian* had advocated it vigorously (recently joined by the *Observer*). Gaitskell was friendly with the editor, Alastair Hetherington, who wrote all the leaders on it (consulting Leonard Beaton and John Maddox). Hetherington kept in touch with the unilateralists through Lord Simon of Wythenshawe, a leading Manchester political figure of the past generation. Simon raised the subject in the Lords in February 1959. He was in close contact with Bertrand Russell, who warmly welcomed the proposal, which had temporary support from Michael Foot.[40]

Gaitskell had hitherto been sceptical. He thought the non-nuclear club would not work without effective controls, while with them Russia and the United States could be brought in, too. He told Hetherington in November 1958 that giving up British nuclear weapons would mean

> a loss of influence over the United States, a loss of insurance lest the United States backed out of its European commitments, a loss of the present double veto over use of weapons and a loss of the value of tactical atomic weapons in the defence of Europe. There would be a gain only if all probable third parties accepted the control system.[9b]

He was very doubtful whether France and China would ever agree;[9a] and thought that if they did, the super-powers would do so too.[41] But he had carefully avoided a public commitment against it, telling the Scarborough Conference: 'I recognise the force of the idea ... if we in government knew for certain that only our continuing to manufacture these weapons stopped this agreement ... my colleagues and I would regard that as a very powerful argument indeed.'[30a]

On 25 March 1959 Greenwood proposed something similar at the NEC,[10d] without Gaitskell's support.[5b] Its attractions multiplied that spring as the risk of new countries acquiring their own nuclear weapons grew rapidly: American scientists reported that 12 countries might do so within five years, and 8 more in ten.[42] Gaitskell insisted privately on these reasons for the new policy:

> It is not, of course a concession to the Left, nor is it intended to unite the Party on some wishy-washy compromise. On the contrary, I was determined that we should spell out our support for N.A.T.O. more clearly and definitely than before.[43]

But for many of his colleagues the proposal was a necessary tactical manoeuvre, and Crossman, who was for it on merits, had also seen it from the start 'as the one positive attitude which could unify the movement'.[7g] The French and Chinese obstacles had not diminished but to Gaitskell they came to seem less cogent. His reassessment may have been subconsciously affected by his political need for a new initiative.

Meanwhile de Gaulle was ejecting American bombers from France, and eighty Labour MPs signed a motion opposing their transfer to Britain. Gaitskell disapproved, arguing that a British refusal was impossible both militarily, since NATO needed the planes, and diplomatically, because the existing Anglo-American agreement did not limit their numbers (though forbidding their use in war without British consent). Vigorously supported by Morrison and Shinwell, he had 'a personal triumph':[44] nearly half the signatories eventually withdrew their names.[45a b]

At the NEC meeting on 3 June 1959, the General Council surprised Gaitskell by proposing talks on defence policy. Crossman recorded that, apparently under pressure from Cousins, they wanted a clearer statement on testing and also to discuss 'the non-nuclear club, a subject on which Gaitskell is quite open-minded, [but Bevan] said it was diplomatically impossible and raised every kind of objection.'[7g] A few days later Bevan was 'developing the idea as though he had just thought of it', and the NEC's international sub-committee decided to aim at early agreement on it with the TUC.[7h] Gaitskell, determined not to appear to have given way to pressure, was niggling and stubborn about phrasing the new statement. Bevan wanted a pledge to 'stop' not 'suspend' testing; they compromised on Crossman's phrase 'refrain from resuming'. Once Bevan protested. 'My dear Hugh,' Crossman reported him saying quietly,

'if you believe that I am going to cross every t and dot every i of the drafts you write you are sadly mistaken. I am just not going to.' After which he muttered to me *sotto voce*, 'Now you know how he broke up the Labour Government in 1951 digging his toes in for £11 million in a £3,000 million scheme.'[7i]

Gaitskell was adamantly against buying immediate political peace by commitments binding a future Labour government. While he thought it 100 to 1 against tests ever being resumed, he would not rule it out finally (it might prove possible to test underground without spreading radiation).[9c] He was privately sure that Britain should never use the H-bomb first, but almost obsessively opposed to a public commitment, lest confusion should weaken NATO's deterrent.[46a b] He told Hetherington that he sympathised with those who wanted such a statement but it must be most carefully considered, for the alliance as a whole probably could not afford to renounce first use of tactical atomic weapons; and a commitment from the United Kingdom alone would be meaningless.[9c]

When the negotiators met on 23 June 1959, Cousins had only Willis as an ally among his TUC colleagues; four were against him and the fifth, Sir Tom O'Brien, prevaricated. The politicians stood together, with Bevan as his leading opponent. Cousins wanted Labour to promise to end production and tests permanently, and not to use nuclear weapons first; he called the non-nuclear club only 'a tricky manoeuvre ... [as] China would refuse to join'. The last two points were well designed to split Bevan away from Gaitskell (who, like his colleagues, believed Barbara Castle had suggested them). But Bevan declined the bait, coolly calling them 'mere questions of nomenclature on which there was no serious controversy'.[47] He rejected Cousins's insistence on his own policy:

Nye, timing it nicely, burst out that trade unions have useful functions but were a poor place for making serious political decisions. He would rather get out than be told by trade unions what to do in the Foreign Office. Anyway the way union delegates voted at their conferences bore no relation to the way their members voted at elections ... We were just before an election, and if Frank Cousins carried this division further, he would make defeat certain.[7k]

A visible victory for Cousins would have exasperated the other unions – and infuriated many MPs even more. Great (though vain) efforts had been made to keep the draft statement secret. There was – perhaps inadvertently – no informal consultation in advance; the TUC representatives saw it barely an hour before agreeing it; NEC members (the international sub-committee apart) had no more notice; the PLP were not informed. After 23 June neither the National Executive nor the PLP could repudiate or modify it without a most damaging row. Both were furious at being pre-empted, especially those who disliked the concessions of substance that Gaitskell was making – who included such close allies of his as Alice Bacon and Sam Watson on the NEC and Desmond Donnelly and Charlie Pannell in the House, as well as MPs like Fred Peart, Chris Mayhew and Herbert Morrison.[48] A right-wing revolt in the PLP was expected, but did not occur;[49a] it might well have developed if the proposals had appeared as a capitulation to Cousins.

That same afternoon Bevan told the PLP that the policy needed revising, not because of union votes, but because the situation had changed. Gaitskell recalled Bevan's earlier warning that a mistaken decision (to accept unilateralism) would mean an election defeat like 1931.[45a] There was some grumbling on the Left, but 'the Gaitskell-Bevan policy on nuclear weapons united all but a rump of the Parliamentary party'.[18b]

Next day at the Executive the unilateralists pressed for Cousins's three points, especially a pledge against first use of nuclear weapons. Bevan, reported Crossman, came down

> to my great surprise, firmly against it ... what struck me again was his great buoyancy and good humour and the way he was standing by Gaitskell, even on points where he could well have extorted a concession from his Leader. I suppose he realised that he and Gaitskell must stand together, whatever happens, and take a simple, sensible position against Frank Cousins and the unilateralists.[50a]

Gaitskell was impressed and delighted at Bevan's loyalty. He emphasised to his friends 'how Nye had genuinely made unnecessary concessions to his point of view and expressed a worry lest Nye should have been upset by the hecklers over the weekend'.[50a b] But the T&GWU representatives (showing impressive discipline, for the union had made no decision) were all among the few opponents of the new policy — six on the General Council and four on the National Executive.[51] Once it was adopted, therefore, Gaitskell, Bevan and Brown[49b] [a] all spent hours with Cousins trying in vain to bring him round.[7l]

On 24 June Labour's support for the non-nuclear club was announced at a press conference. Just beforehand, Gaitskell lunched with two leading unilateralist supporters of the policy, Bertrand Russell and Lord Simon of Wythenshawe.[49a] The new document also reaffirmed Labour's commitment to disengagement in Central Europe, a summit conference, and multilateral disarmament by stages. The press enthusiastically greeted Gaitskell's 'great personal victory ... proof of his command over the Parliamentary party and the leaders of the trade unions'.[45a] Henry Fairlie called it 'one of the most daring, confident and successful manoeuvres of his career ... it is in tactics that Mr. Gaitskell excels ... daring timing ... iron nerve ... Mr. Gaitskell has not just won a battle, he has won a war.'[52a] Crossman summed up objectively:

> If leadership means reacting to opportunities for changing party policy rather than creating them, this has been quite good leadership. To do nothing would have split the movement. So would any surrender to abolitionists. We have seized the opportunity to introduce a new idea ... [though] the Labour Party never does like a new idea at first.[7k]

The disgruntled Left would become dangerous only if the election were lost. Their discontent was not confined to Westminster: Crossman thought that 70 per cent of active Party workers were against the policy, and that its supporters would be thrown off the Executive if the election were delayed and the Conference held.[53] Gaitskell, however, was sure that Macmillan would (as he did) call the election early enough to deny Labour a chance to show its unity at a Conference which, he was sure, would approve the new policy whatever Cousins did.[9c] Nor was he worried that as yet public opinion was not convinced.* He and Bevan both believed that the ordinary voter would recognise and respond to the imminent risk of proliferation (which had come so much earlier than the politicians themselves had expected) once France or China began testing bombs.[55]

Gaitskell and Cousins tried once more to agree, exchanging confidential letters shown to no one else. Cousins wrote to Gaitskell regretting that they had not talked before the negotiating meeting; denying as 'absolute nonsense' that he was campaigning against Gaitskell himself or the NATO

---

* Only 9 per cent of Labour voters supported the non-nuclear club, with 17 per cent unilateralist and 61 per cent wanting to keep the British bomb.[54]

commitment; resenting what he saw as moves to isolate and defeat his union and himself; promising not to make an issue of the non-nuclear club, though he thought it unreal and perhaps dishonest; but saying that he would go on calling for pledges against first use of nuclear weapons, resuming tests, or continuing production.[56a] Gaitskell replied on the same terms in fourteen tactful pages with no concession of substance; as Party leader, he said, he could not put any gloss on an agreed document, and as prospective Prime Minister 'I have to ask myself all the time when I am pressed to accept a certain form of words, "Am I quite sure I am not embarrassing a future Labour Government? ... " I know that if you were in my position you would behave in exactly the same way.' He stressed that the difficulties of bringing about the non-nuclear club were emphasised in the document, so that it was not dishonest; Bertrand Russell and Adlai Stevenson approved the plan. He thought Chinese reactions likely to depend on the Americans and Russians, and wrote:

> I would not deny for a moment that China is a tremendous problem. But ... in the case of France their desire for national prestige may be satisfied if they find themselves on the same level as ourselves. This was the impression I received when I saw de Gaulle in January and Gladwyn Jebb [Ambassador in Paris] confirmed to me that this was his opinion.[57]

Rightly arguing that Cousins had misunderstood Bevan's Brighton speech, he gave no ground over production. But on Cousins's two other specific points, his tone was no longer stubborn but conciliatory:

> [I]t is in the highest degree improbable that we should resume tests, and in the case of H-bomb tests which pollute the atmosphere, almost inconceivable ... We have gone to the limit in implying we should not resume tests, short of absolute commitment. That I really do not consider would be right ... If we come out with the declaration that we will never use these [tactical atomic weapons] first, we say in effect that we are prepared to accept ... defeat with superior conventional forces ... By saying it we run at least the faint risk of encouraging them [the Russians] to do so. That is the difficult [sic] about the pledge of the kind you want ... These objections do not apply in the same way to H bombs which I do not think we could or should ever use first ... As to whether, however, a declaration of this kind, limited to not using H bombs first, would be worthwhile, I am rather doubtful. I am afraid that it would lead to too much confusion.

He did not rule it out, but suggested the NEC's defence sub-committee should examine it. Disingenuously, he assured Cousins that he had never thought the latter was campaigning against him:

I know you far too well to suppose that you would do any such thing ...
I fully appreciate the deep emotion which motivates you ... do me the
justice of believing that I too have deep feelings on the subject. I
should be only too glad to talk with you further about it all.

Regretting their failure to meet sooner, he hoped Cousins would argue
his case without breaking Labour unity.[46a]

Cousins was not appeased. A few days later, the T&GWU's biennial
delegate conference in the Isle of Man opposed official policy on both
nationalisation and defence. Its complicated defence resolution, carried
after an intense debate with only 50 dissentients out of 760, fell short of
explicit and total unilateralism. Along with uncontroversial points—
multilateral disarmament, and political rather than military control of
destructive weapons—it demanded commitments against missile bases in
Britain; against aircraft patrolling with H-bombs; and against testing,
production or first use of nuclear weapons, or a policy based on the
threat of using them. It specifically rejected the non-nuclear club.[58a]

Gaitskell had not expected it to go so far, but he was not very surprised:

> [T]he wish for *power* was the key to Cousins's action. Cousins was a
> demagogue and ambitious. He was throwing his weight about so that
> he could make his power felt. Gaitskell did not believe that Cousins
> was really very deeply concerned about the details of policy ... but
> Cousins was anxious to show his strength.[9c e]

The union would follow its general secretary but the Labour Party would
not, though it would suffer from seeming to be at sixes and sevens.[9c]
Gaitskell knew that though the Left rejoiced to see a union leader seeking
to change the defence policy of the alternative government, the country
would resent it. To defy Cousins would therefore help Labour electorally;[59]
and Macmillan knew that too.[2b]

iii   *Workington: Return of Fire in the Cousins War*

Gaitskell replied on 11 July 1959 before a hundred people in a cold wind
at Workington.[7m o] He admitted that other countries might not join the
non-nuclear club, but said the best chance was now, before they had made
bombs and acquired stocks. The unilateralists argued that France and
China would not join an agreement with effective controls—yet assumed
that, if Britain renounced the bomb, other countries would follow even
without such an agreement. They must decide whether or not they intended
Britain to stay in NATO.[60-1a] If not, their policy was honest but 'escapist,
blind and positively dangerous to the peace of the world'. If so, then we
must play our part loyally. A declaration that we would never use nuclear

weapons first could imply continued conscription and might even encourage a Soviet conventional attack. However: 'Personally I think we could safely say we would never use the H-bomb first ... And I think the policy of being prepared to use even tactical atomic weapons first is to say the least questionable.' But any commitment must await discussions between a Labour Government and Britain's allies. A resumption of H-bomb tests was 'in the highest degree unlikely and indeed almost inconceivable'. But if underground tests did not poison the atmosphere, 'I cannot give an absolute pledge ... [which] might conceivably ... jeopardise the future security of our country and that I will not do under any circumstances.'

Gaitskell also met Cousins's challenge directly:

The problems of international relations ... will not be solved by slogans, however loudly declaimed, or by effervescent emotion, however genuine ... [but by] very hard, very clear, very calm and very honest thinking ... our Party decisions on these matters are not dictated by one man whether he be the Leader of the Party, our spokesman on Foreign Affairs, or the General Secretary of the Transport & General Workers' Union. They are made collectively ... we should argue out and settle ultimately in our Conference the great issues of policy. But it is not right that a future Labour Government should be committed by Conference decisions one way or the other on every matter of detail for all time – when the facts are not always available, when the situation is continually changing and where the problem has not always been fully and adequately thrashed out ... A Labour Government will take into account the views of the Conference ... but Annual Conference does not mandate a Government ... This has always been understood in the past, and it must be clearly understood again today.[62]

A week later he was asked on the BBC: 'suppose the Conference carried a resolution in favour of unilateral nuclear disarmament, a tremendous issue of policy, would not that bind a future Labour Government?' He replied: 'I think that would, yes.'[63] He was not asked whether he would lead a Labour Government so bound, and commentators assumed he would not.[64]

Four days after the T&GWU meeting, Williamson – without consulting Gaitskell[7n] – had reconvened the NUGMW's conference to vote on the new policy statement. When it decided in favour, reversing its unilateralist decision, Cousins was isolated and the Party Conference would plainly support the leadership. Gaitskell was now in militant mood, 'determined to smash Cousins'.[7n] Crossman called the Workington speech 'an immense success', and the Shadow Cabinet sent Gaitskell a congratulatory telegram in Hamburg.[65a b*] There had been some fear among MPs that Cousins had cost Labour the election, and some grumbling that Gaitskell should have acted earlier to forestall trouble – but after Workington they recovered their nerve, expecting his 'leadership to impress the waverers and the uncommitted'.[66]

George Brown was the PLP's defence spokesman but not a negotiator with the TUC leaders, as he was not on the NEC. He was also an old T&GWU official, in touch with the general secretary and always anxious to win him over. He had suggested that Cousins could be propitiated by a commitment not to use the H-bomb first – but told Crossman: 'Gaitskell turned it down flat ... "From the first, Hugh manoeuvred to isolate Cousins. He didn't want an agreement ... I warned Cousins he was going out on a limb and Hugh would lick him, but he wouldn't listen." '[7m p] Brown's interpretation was understandable, since Gaitskell not only thoroughly distrusted Cousins but was soon to make the commitment after all, though only as a personal assurance.

In refusing Brown's advice to avert the clash by accepting Cousins's main demands, Gaitskell took a great risk; Bevan too had once wanted to commit the Party both against ever resuming tests, and against first use of the H-bomb. Had he insisted again, both Crossman and Brown thought he 'could have overthrown Hugh ... quite easily'.[7m] Yet the differences were small. Gaitskell was willing for any promise on tests short of an absolute commitment; and after stubbornly refusing to have the bomb pledge in the joint statement, he privately assured Cousins, and then said publicly, that personally he agreed with it. The dispute seemed more suitable for splitting hairs than splitting a political party, and it was unreasonable – indeed a sign of profound mistrust – of Cousins to risk that by demanding ironclad official pledges. It was courageous, but was it not equally unreasonable of Gaitskell to risk it by refusing them?

Cousins was a decent, honest man with passionate convictions about the bomb, and an uncomplicated faith in traditional Socialist ideas. For two years he had gone slow on both issues in the interests of Party unity. In that time, the nationalisation compromise had not been changed; and on the bomb, Labour policy – and public opinion too – had moved the way he wanted, though not far or fast enough for him. Yet having for so long patiently agreed to differ with the leadership, he now dramatically broke with it on both questions. He did so a few weeks before a general election, using the familiar left-wing justification so welcome to Tories: 'I have never believed that the most important thing in our lives is to elect a Labour Government. The most important thing is to elect a Labour

* He was at the Socialist International, where the Germans favoured the non-nuclear club and only the French mildly opposed it.[9d]

Government that is determined to carry out Socialist policy.'[67a b] Gaitskell did not take a charitable view of his motives.

Some of Cousins's personal characteristics were peculiarly antipathetic to Gaitskell: a muddled mind, a tendency to self-deception, a reluctance to face the unwelcome implications of his own actions. Determined to behave differently from Arthur Deakin, he could still in the authoritarian tradition of their union deal ruthlessly with his senior subordinates;[68] and though he addressed its 1959 biennial conference a dozen times a day, often twice on the same subject, he was indignant at the suggestion that its decision on the bomb — for which he had been working for two years — was anything but the spontaneous wish of the rank and file.[69] He convinced himself, and told the delegates, that his own three main points had already been put forward as Labour Party policy.[56a b] (That was quite untrue.) He would not admit the consequences of his policy either for defence or for the Party. He denied that it entailed leaving a nuclear-armed NATO, and refused to say whether he would wish America to renounce nuclear weapons when Russia had not done so: 'These hypothetical questions are not going to lead us anywhere.'[70] He insisted that he was not splitting the Party;[71] and when reminded that he was challenging the leadership whatever his intentions, since Gaitskell and Bevan would resign if they lost at Conference, he replied confidently, 'That has nothing to do with the issue at all.'[70]

By the beginning of 1959 this powerful, awkward, insecure man was feeling isolated and harried. The London bus strike had been a disaster, costing his union a million pounds.[72a b] His General Council colleagues distrusted, feared and even hated him.[73a] One of them told a journalist: 'The H-bomb controversy has been a godsend to Frank. It diverted attention from the ghastly failure of his industrial policy ... there was no inquest on ... the million pounds.'[74] In this mood, Cousins at the beginning of the year was receptive to the influence of Michael Foot.[73a] He was irritated with Wilson for emphasising the defence of sterling, and with Gaitskell for seeing 'that tinpot dictator' President de Gaulle; and muttered privately that he might 'break with them for good and teach them a lesson'.[74] Later, he complained of Gaitskell advocating wage restraint at a National Council of Labour meeting.[73a b]

In the next few months, Cousins and especially his wife complained of not seeing enough of the Gaitskells.[75] He hinted at his resentment in his letter to Gaitskell, and poured it out for over an hour, in his hotel room in the Isle of Man, to Randolph Churchill who was covering the union conference as a journalist. But Gaitskell had offered Cousins much hospitality in the past: 'I do not suppose that any Trade Union leader has been invited more frequently to our home ... recently ... we have not been able to do much entertaining. But, in fact, Cousins dined with me alone a few weeks ago.'[76] And the unpredictable general secretary later complained that he felt quite out of place in that milieu.[73a]

In his new mood, Cousins accepted all the old suspicions of Gaitskell's motives – and not only over defence. The 1959 T&GWU conference now unanimously rejected the policy of *Industry and Society*, calling for old-fashioned nationalisation instead. 'You are a good Socialist,' Cousins was told in a telegram from Shinwell and even from Morrison, whose enthusiasm for nationalisation had waned when he was making Labour's policy but reappeared once Gaitskell was doing so.[77] Privately, Gaitskell commented sadly on 'the spite of two disappointed old men';[78] and he did not answer that challenge from Cousins.

Cousins's switch on nationalisation reflected his disillusionment over defence. He was already feeling aggrieved when he suddenly found himself presented with a new defence policy: he had not been consulted about it, and his cherished modifications were turned down. He disliked its verbal compromises (like 'refrain from resuming' tests rather than 'stop' them) and wanted plainer language (provided it was his own, however unacceptable to others).[79] Understandably resenting the way the policy had been formulated, he apparently saw it, like the suspicious Left, as a hypocritical device for clinging to the British bomb, relying on France to ensure that the non-nuclear club was never born.[65a]

While people who supported CND on moral grounds would naturally not modify their views merely to help a political party, some of them, like Russell and Simon of Wythenshawe, favoured the non-nuclear club. But for the irreconcilable Left in the Labour Party, Gaitskell's support was enough to condemn it. They did not vote against it in the PLP, feeling that it 'must be tolerated until the general election is over, but after that – then, we are assured, hell itself is going to break loose'.[45a] Some were not willing to wait. Zilliacus wrote in his pamphlet *This Way to Peace* that if Cousins's proposal was rejected,

> the dissenters on the H-bomb will take the line in the election campaign and after, that they feel to be morally right. And win or lose, the demand for total renunciation of nuclear weapons will become irresistibly strong at the 1960 conference. Why wait for unity? Why not forge it before the election instead of after?[18c]

As usual, the Left assumed that everyone but the hated leadership agreed with them. But when it moved to accommodate them, they quickly moved too to keep their distance. Crossman lamented that Michael Foot was now calling

> for a fight to the death and the campaign to go on throughout the election ... the nuclear disarmers a few weeks ago agreed that the non-

nuclear club was a first-rate idea, though not enough ... when Michael
Foot dined, only a fortnight ago, he too that week regarded the non-
nuclear club as a real advance. But, as so often happens, anything
which is accepted by the Establishment becomes unacceptable to the
opposition within the Labour par ty... young Left-wingers ... used to
think the non-nuclear club an excellent idea when it was put forward
by Bertie Russell and Nehru. But the moment we adopt it, they feel it
has been corrupted, because they don't trust us. What they are looking
for is an undefiled cause with undefiled leaders ... At least these two
[Gaitskell and Bevan] have faced the issue with intellectual honesty
and have worked out what is pretty well the best policy they can.
What is depressing is that they get no credit from their closest colleagues
or from the Left for doing so, although it is not denied that public
opinion would sweep away any Labour Party which conceded the
Left unilateralist position.[80]

For among the suspicious young men of the Left, Crossman found,
'there is a really deep malaise about the Party and the leadership, which is
finding a convenient expression in this nuclear controversy'.[7r] For some
years CND continued to crystallise that malaise;[81] it has since taken
much uglier forms. By the summer of 1959, Cousins had come to share it,
and Gaitskell to count him among the irreconcilables.

'Power is all he wants. It's as simple as that.'[7k s] Gaitskell would not be
budged from his conviction that Cousins was 'out to do me in', or even
be persuaded that the general secretary was above all concerned with the
union's interests as he saw them.[82] George Brown indeed thought hostility
to Cousins alone explained Gaitskell's stubbornness over both the substance and the wording of the new statement. But that view was too
simple. Gaitskell's temperament played a part, for he was always perfec-
tionist about the precise wording of drafts. He was also insistent on demonstrating his own integrity — so that he denied any suggestion of making a
political compromise, stressed the continuity between the old and the new
defence policies, and thus gave a defensive tone to both his own and the
Party's statements, which did not inspire the Left and the young idealists
with any sense of novelty or movement at the top.[65a c]

It was a special case of a Labour leader's perennial problem — how to
appeal to his own enthusiastic followers without alienating the rest of the
country, this time in tone rather than content. Gaitskell had been accused,
in venomous personal attacks which did great harm to the Party as well as
to himself, of giving way to pressure over Suez. He had to guard against
allowing that charge to be revived. Moreover, he knew that the Left
would accept no compromise for longer than a few months. He would pay
a high price elsewhere for conciliating them momentarily; but when they

revived the quarrel, it would be harder to defend the essential positions from which he would not shift. Above all, neither he nor Bevan would allow a powerful union leader to determine government policy.

Cousins now felt that his Socialist conscience required him to use his power as Deakin had, but for ends he saw as better ones. His duty was to prod the laggard leadership, and theirs was to attend to him. He told Douglas Houghton, an MP who was on the TUC General Council: 'if you have influence with your [sic] leader, you ought to advise him to take more notice of where power lies in the Party.' Houghton thought he was complaining both of not being consulted on the defence draft and of carrying less weight than Deakin.[83] But the earlier general secretary of the T&GWU had expected the leaders of the Party to lay down policy and had then offered his staunch support for it. His successor was trying to invoke his power as a trade unionist to insist on a change of defence policy by the politicians who might form the next government of the country.

Cousins would not have recognised any difference in principle. But to Gaitskell there was, and it was a crucial one. He too had strong convictions on the issue, which he would not abdicate to a man he (rightly) thought intellectually incapable of mastering the complexities of the subject.[84] * He too had other motives: he believed as in 1951 that he was in a struggle for power;[86] his leadership might be threatened or nullified by concessions interpreted as weakness; and appeasement of Cousins would shock public opinion and gravely damage the Party. But above all he thought appeasement wrong in principle. Gaitskell expected to work closely with trade union leaders, hoped to persuade them to co-operate with a Labour government's economic policy, but would never try to interfere with the way they ran their unions. Instead, he had gone much further than most of them thought wise in backing Cousins over the bus strike, to his own severe political loss. Therefore he expected that the union leaders should, as most of them did, leave the politicians to formulate policy:[87] especially when he believed the stakes were the security of the country, and perhaps the prospects of peace.

After three years of uniting the Party by conciliatory leadership, he now surprised many commentators and colleagues by demonstrating, on the very eve of the election, that there were concessions he would never make. It was a risky decision. The same Shadow Cabinet members who wired congratulations on the Workington speech were careful not to challenge Cousins themselves in case he won the battle.[7m] As Brown told Crossman, the open breach between the two men meant that, if the general election

* Some prominent unilateralists would have changed their minds if — as might well have happened — Nazi Germany had made the bomb. Cousins, however, could publicly maintain that the West did not need it since 'we defended ourselves very well in 1939 without these weapons'.[85]

were lost, the assault from the Left would be far more dangerous.[65a b] Often in the past Crossman had found Gaitskell complacent and even 'wet'. But now he saw 'a man who is rapidly growing up, growing tougher and growing stronger'.[7n] Henry Fairlie, an old admirer turned critical, was also impressed again: 'Mr. Gaitskell has grown in the past year. He is assured and confident and fit for power.'[52b]

CHAPTER 19

GAITSKELL ABROAD 1956–9

'He could be elected to anything in this country'
(THOMAS E. DEWEY ON HG, 1961)
'I know now that he's a really good man'
(LENINGRAD PARTY OFFICIAL AFTER HG'S VISIT, 1959)

i *The United States*

GAITSKELL was always fascinated by the problems of foreign countries, for their own sake as well as for the lessons they might carry for Britain. As he was also an enthusiastic sight-seer, he took every opportunity of foreign travel in all parts of the world; but he felt most at home and enjoyed himself most in the United States and Yugoslavia. He was more often in the former, which he had a special motive for visiting in the need to understand current developments which profoundly affected Britain's prospects, and to try to estimate future ones.

His first unofficial transatlantic visit was in 1952, during the Bevanite offensive. As always in speaking to American audiences, he both underlined his strong attachment to the United States and insisted upon unwelcome home truths. Thus he told a collection of Chicago businessmen that he rejoiced that the democracies were now working together, in contrast to the 1930s, and promised: 'I have fought and shall continue to fight those in my own country who seek to divide us.' But he went on to refute their favourite legends about Britain's poor economic performance, and warned tactfully that if Americans repudiated the creditor's responsibilities to invest and import from abroad, they must expect other countries to discriminate against their goods.[1]

On his next trip, a year later, he was much in demand among Americans who had met him in England; a right-wing journalist wrote that he had almost 'converted a party ... of hardshell Republicans into ardent Socialists', a liberal one was impressed by a politician whose intellectual integrity took precedence over his politics.[2] It was Dora's first visit there, and his longest. Much of it was spent at an international economic conference on Long Island, where Gaitskell took an active part in discussing sterling-dollar problems and the role of national reserves; there too, his colleagues were impressed that he talked as a highly competent economist rather than as the party politician they had expected.[3]

The Gaitskells thoroughly enjoyed themselves, though Hugh sprained his shoulder swimming on the very first day and, on finding out how expensive medical treatment was, wrote home that there was 'a lot to be said for the Health Service!'[4] As usual he was a great success, and that incident was recorded in verse; another participant wrote to him that the organisers 'were full of admiration for you and sang songs about it, literally as well as figuratively'.[5] They visited Harvard, Washington and Ottawa, missing the politicians who were away in August; went to another economic conference near Toronto, where Hugh again argued against sterling convertibility; and impressed the 'rock-ribbed conservative bankers' at the Council on Foreign Relations in New York.[6] They returned tourist class on a French liner, the *Liberté*, enjoying the gaiety as much as the food.

They were back in the United States five months after Hugh became leader, again travelling tourist, to the dismay of their prosperous hosts of the Garment Workers' Union. He spoke at its convention in Atlantic City, and was given 'a most staggering demonstration'.[7] He was gratified to discover that McCarthyism had disappeared since 1953, and attitudes towards the neutral countries had become more sympathetic. China was still a sore subject, about which he talked frankly on 'Meet the Press' to a television audience estimated at 10 million — feeling that the recent row at the dinner with the Russian leaders had eased his passage. He was also able to see the President and several senior advisers, finding Eisenhower 'more forthcoming on China trade than anybody else', Dulles much friendlier than at their previous frosty meeting in 1951, and the White House rather like an 'Eastern Potentate's court with a lot of people waiting to have their case heard'. The British Embassy felt he had 'created a *very* good impression' on his hosts.[8]

The preoccupation with the Far East persisted. Gaitskell attacked the reigning American orthodoxy about China in his Godkin Lectures in January 1957, severely condemned United States policy over Quemoy and Matsu late in 1958, and wrote privately after a TV debate in 1961 that his opponent, Congressman Judd of the China lobby, was 'an extraordinary character … I have seldom heard such nonsense but I suppose it was good for me to come up against somebody like this'.[9]

Those Godkin Lectures, delivered at Harvard just after Suez, made a great impression on American opinion. A friendly reviewer called them 'an astonishing achievement … three sermons of impeccable British patriotism which are as sound in their democratic socialism as they are acceptable to his American hosts … but one is never oppressed by the sense of tightrope walking'.[10] Gaitskell was delighted by his reception, 'a unique experience – quite one of the nicest we have had in our lives'.[11] His hosts appreciated it too. He was spectacularly successful everywhere, and one of them told him: 'You helped Anglo-American relations mightily in time of crisis and you certainly gave the Labour Party new stature in the eyes of the American people.'[12] * As usual Gaitskell would not simply tell his audience what they wanted to hear, and insisted (amid applause, too) that it was now high time United States and UN pressure over the Suez Canal was directed towards Egypt rather than the Western Powers.[14]

All his life he continued to have the same powerful appeal across the Atlantic. In 1952 one young professor compared him to Adlai Stevenson, then at the height of his popularity among liberals;[15] and ten years later a group of American academics in London, with long political experience, all thought that in office Gaitskell would become a standard-bearer for liberal opinion in the United States.[16] But though strongest in university circles, his appeal was not limited to them, and a prominent Republican wrote in 1961 that Gaitskell was 'acquiring Sir Winston's status: whether he won or lost in Britain, we were always sure he could be elected to anything in this country!'[17]

Gaitskell's own preferences in American politics were never in doubt. He found the Democrats far too inegalitarian in principle, and too suspicious of state intervention in practice, to satisfy any British Socialist.[18] But he always greatly preferred them to the Republicans, and not only because they were much more sympathetic to British interests; though he was careful to explain that the detested Senator Joe McCarthy and the Republican Right were powerful only because of lax party discipline and Eisenhower's reluctance to fight them. He hinted gently at the lessons for critics of disciplined parties in Britain.[19a]

On his visit in 1956 he had no official or academic commitments, and saw much more than before of the Democrats and the trade unions (as well as visiting the latest hit, *My Fair Lady*). He lunched with Governor Averell Harriman, was very put off by a New York dinner with anti- (and ex-) Communist intellectuals, and was attracted by Chester Bowles, the liberal former Ambassador to India: 'I ... found myself very much in agreement ... [he is] full of sound ideas ... about the handling of India and other neutral countries.' He was again impressed that labour and progressive attitudes were so similar to his own – over domestic social reform, aid to underdeveloped countries, the colonies (notably Cyprus) and the Middle East. Like other British party leaders before the 1970s, he was careful not to attack his own government when speaking abroad.**

* Six months later a visiting Labour MP wrote in almost the same words, saying that everyone was still talking about the visit.[13]

** *Tribune* therefore criticised him for saying that colonialism was dead without

In January 1960 he again made the rounds of friends in the trade union and liberal Democratic worlds. Right at the start of that election year he foresaw that Kennedy was the likely nominee;[21] and three months later he said wistfully that though primaries might exhaust the candidates they at least gave the Opposition leaders publicity which 'in Britain they got only ... [from] a big quarrel among themselves'.[22] (He also pointed out pertinently that the system made it hard for the party out of power to formulate a policy or give the voters a clear choice.) He found John Kennedy's Administration thoroughly congenial, and had seen by March 1962 that Robert Kennedy was—as most observers discovered only much later—a genuine and committed radical reformer.[23] It was not, as we have seen, that he was an uncritical admirer of that family.[24] But as he wrote home on the 1960 visit, it was 'quite remarkable how closely the attitude of the Democrats to the Republicans, and especially to Nixon, corresponds with our own attitude to the Tories and especially Macmillan'.[21]

ii   *Yugoslavia, the Third World and Western Europe*

Gaitskell's other favourite country was Yugoslavia. In August 1957 he went with his family to Venice at its humid worst, and they then took a Yugoslav boat down the Adriatic coast where he had gone with Bowra thirty years before. They visited shipyards at Rijeka, stayed with President Tito at Brioni—where his younger daughter Cressida entertained their hosts on the guitar—saw Diocletian's Palace at Split, and finished with a week at Dubrovnik. Twice in the next four years he returned to Dalmatia with his family. The first time was during Labour's defence crisis before the Scarborough Conference, when he went for three weeks' holiday and then on a week's official tour which began with talks in Ljubljana with Edvard Kardelj and others. Gaitskell's companions were Denis Healey, Sam Watson and David Ennals; they were accompanied by their wives, and Cressida went with him. After the talks they all went visiting industrial enterprises and beautiful sites in Slovenia and Croatia. The politicians recall a very happy and relaxed visit, though Hugh exhausted them thoroughly with his exuberance in the small hours and his insistence on finding a nightclub even on a hot July evening in Ljubljana (he succeeded, but the place was appalling).[25]

Gaitskell was very friendly with four successive Yugoslav Ambassadors in London, one of whom arranged not only for the 1960 tour, but also for the Gaitskells to stay—both then and in 1961—in a magnificent cliff villa at Dubrovnik, a town which had fascinated Hugh ever since his Oxford

referring to the surviving examples (which he had explicitly condemned without naming) and for not talking about socialism—the main theme of one of his speeches to a union audience.[20]

days, where the family could enjoy 'privacy (very precious to a politician on holiday)'.[26] He was always an energetic holidaymaker, enjoying walking or swimming or expeditions to the local sights rather than lazing in the sun, but was also capable of forgetting his problems and relaxing totally. There were plenty of spare rooms in the villa, with guests arriving and departing (his sister stayed there for a time). One of Julie's friends who was there recalled his amazement at the embattled politician whose only apparent worry was his missing schnorkel.[27]

The visits had a serious side too. Gaitskell was particularly interested in the functioning of the system of workers' control, checking on the details of its operation in the hotels where they stayed and the factories they visited, and coming to the conclusion that the bonuses and profit-sharing arrangements were quite effective but the theoretical structure of decision-making by the employees rarely was. Like so many other foreigners, the family were immensely attracted by the gaiety and light-heartedness of the Yugoslavs they met, official as well as unofficial, and felt no sense of living in an oppressive dictatorship. They argued constantly and strenuously against the imprisonment of Milovan Djilas. But at a period when the regime was relaxing controls rather than tightening them, Gaitskell – devoted as he was to democratic government and individual liberties – was reasonably optimistic about the way things were going in a country which had never known those advantages in the past.[28]

He was hopeful also, though not at all blindly, about the prospects for democracy in newly independent Ghana, where he set foot in Africa for the first time in May 1959. That was a sensitive moment in the settler territories of Rhodesia and Kenya, which he felt it 'impolitic' to visit; he went to Ghana instead, 'partly as a gesture to the Africans' that their point of view had sympathisers in Britain.[29] He thoroughly enjoyed himself, dancing in a 'suitably low-class "night-club" ... girls very pretty ... Ghana Chief Whip superb dancer'; being charmed by the people, who were 'gay, always laughing'; being impressed by the 'wonderful absence of colour prejudice';[30a] and finding it, as the first of many new countries, 'quite exciting ... a little like Israel'.[31] He dined at Nkrumah's Danish castle, which reminded him more of Othello's than of Elsinore from which it was supposed to have been copied.[30a] He met opposition spokesmen, one of whom had married Cripps's daughter;[32] and, though well aware of the risks, he was optimistic about the future and later dismayed at the speed with which his hopes were disappointed. 'It will be touch and go whether they maintain anything like democracy. The forces making for dictatorship in Africa are pretty powerful although I think Nkrumah himself will do what he can to resist them.'[33]

Apart from his delight in travel, Gaitskell was always concerned about relations with the New Commonwealth. In March 1954 he was the most prominent figure in the British delegation to a high-powered unofficial twelve-day Commonwealth Conference in Lahore. He got on splendidly with the Indian and black delegates (a bit less well with the Pakistanis);[34] and was gratified by the unanimous good will towards Britain and by the great popularity of the Colombo Plan. On racial problems there was no conflict on principle, except from a Nationalist South African; and on economic policy none except between the two British parties.[35] He spent three weeks in the sub-continent, sight-seeing in Lahore and at the Khyber Pass:

> At Agra where the Taj Mahal is there were lots of green parraqueets flying about and monkeys too beside the road. Apart from the Taj we visited a deserted half ruined palace built by the Emperor Akhbar about 1550, quite impressive with a wonderful tomb all covered in mother of pearl.[30b]

After becoming leader of the Labour Party he had, as a VIP, less fun but more opportunities, which he took up perhaps too eagerly. At the end of 1957 he was a delegate to another Commonwealth Parliamentary Conference in New Delhi, where red-coated servants 'keep on coming in & going out of my room & poking around to see if they can tidy anything up. There seems to be no idea that I am likely to want privacy!'[30c] There he defended neutralism for India and South-East Asia but repudiated it for Britain, and proposed – before it was fashionable – a British contribution of 1 per cent of GNP to underdeveloped countries.[36] He also caused a small sensation by meeting leaders of the Praja Socialists as well as of the Congress Party, and later said India badly needed a strong opposition.[19b] Then he went on to Burma where his family had lived for so long, but feared that he would be prevented from seeing the country by 'the usual round of – Press Conference – State Dinner – Talks with Ministers – Tea with M.P.s – lunch with Ambassador!'[30c] After a short visit to Malaya, where he was rather gloomy about the prospects of democracy, he returned by way of Ceylon and Pakistan. He visited Mount Lavinia where the snake-charmer had frightened him as a child, and at Karachi he went for a swim with the Prime Minister. 'I rode on a camel in bathing trunks behind P.M. – most uncomfortable but said to be good for liver.'[37a] On his return to Britain he faced some grumbling within the Party, and complaints that he should have curtailed his journey and returned for an important debate in the House. There was to be similar trouble in January 1960, when his critics had a field-day over Clause Four while he was off in the West Indies on a much-needed holiday; and in April that year when he was at the Socialist International's first Asiatic meeting at Haifa when the House was debating the end of Britain's truly independent deterrent.

* * *

His European travelling, apart from family holidays, was also mainly in connection with the Socialist International and its member parties, an area where he was much more active than any previous or subsequent Labour leader. In May 1953, when he was speaking in Germany on Britain's economic recovery and on the welfare state (how times change!) he made many contacts which later proved valuable: not only with the Federal and the Bavarian Socialist Parties, but also with Frau Lilo Milchsack of the Anglo-German Association. She became a good friend, and he went to many of its annual meetings at Koenigswinter. The following year he and Dora spent ten enjoyable days in Denmark and Sweden, talking on British politics (but carefully avoiding partisanship) to Socialist students and right-wing businessmen. He saw a couple of historic Danish boarding schools, now state-controlled, and attended the final torchlight rally and firework display in Gothenburg at the end of the Swedish election campaign. Besides seeing the local Socialist leaders, he made a point of seeking out a Danish family who had been hospitable to him in Copenhagen eight years before.

As Party leader he kept up these contacts conscientiously. Thus in December 1956 and July 1957 he was at Socialist International meetings in Copenhagen and Vienna, while in between he spoke to a Dutch Party congress, visited West Berlin, and twice was in Italy where the Labour Party was promoting the reunification of the rival Socialist Parties. In April he was in Rome seeing not only Socialist politicians but the heads of state, government and church, before escaping for a few days' holiday with Dora in Italy and Greece. In June 1958 Gaitskell and Bevan went to Brussels for a Socialist International meeting—and then to a kermesse at a village where Brueghel had lived, where after an address in old Flemish everybody had to dance in clogs.[30d] In April 1959 he was in Stockholm for the Swedish Social Democrats' seventieth anniversary, a visit without political consequences—which produced a most comic correspondence with a Swedish friend who tried to send Dora black wooden cats with whiskers instead of the white china ones with blue ribbons on which she had set her heart.[38]

The Italian Socialist dispute rumbled on, and in 1959 it got Gaitskell into hot water with the Labour Left. It had begun in 1947 when Nenni's followers allied with the Communists, and Saragat's supported Christian Democratic governments against them. Now Nenni (though not all his friends) meant to break with the Communists, and there was hope of reunification. Gaitskell's loyalty to Saragat had already so exasperated his own left-wing colleagues that Crossman had wondered if the row would 'split the Labour Party on ... how to unify the Italians!'[39a] Gaitskell felt let down by Nenni's associates reneging on past pledges;[40] and at one angry dinner told them that their intransigence gave him no chance of influencing Saragat towards unity.[41] Crossman disapproved, writing at the time: 'I have not seen him behave in this violent, irrational way on any other subject';[39b] and a decade later it still coloured Barbara Castle's recollections of him.[42]

He offended the Left also by his attitude to the fall of the French Fourth Republic. Yet there his own first reactions were similar to those of his critics, for late in May 1958 he wrote to a friend:

> Oh god isn't the news awful? de Gaulle doing his best to lose us the Cold War and Cousins doing his best to lose us the Election.[43] I feel very sad about France — worst of all is the hypocrisy — Army officers seizing power & trying to pretend it's all quite legal — People assuming that this old egotist of 67 can solve their Algerian problems ... when its all really just this bad temper induced by humiliation and inability to accept the facts of life.
>
> I'm afraid that what looks like being a military dictatorship in all but words will have a terrible effect on NATO & the West. The Communists will gain as the 'resisters' — neutralism will spread — and left wing parties everywhere will be driven further left — or at least become pacifist. It's bad enough having to back reactionary feudal regimes in the Middle East & I've never been very keen on Portugal as a nice representative Democratic State — but to have France like this![37b]

Two days later General de Gaulle was elected Prime Minister, with nearly half the Socialist deputies voting for him to escape the threat of a *coup d'état* mounted by the mutinous army in Algeria. Gaitskell had little sympathy either for Guy Mollet, the French Socialist leader[44] (whom the British Left loathed), or for French policy in Algeria for which — as for Suez — Mollet was largely responsible.[45] But he had already begun to feel less gloomy about de Gaulle; and now his old friend Jules Moch, a Socialist opponent of Mollet who had been Minister of the Interior in the government which had collapsed, convinced Gaitskell that the old regime had lost all support both in the state machine and in the wider public.[46] He therefore refused to support one half of the French Socialist Party against the other. Six months later he visited de Gaulle, now President, and returned fairly reassured about the prospects for French democracy. He was also pleasantly surprised by the man:[47] 'he was not only affable but even had a certain amount of charm and was also intelligent and interesting. It was a real discussion in which he listened to what I said as well as telling me what he thought.'[30e] The British Left — including Bevan and Cousins — were irritated; and Michael Foot, mistaking de Gaulle for a diehard who to cling to Algeria would destroy democracy in France, was 'furious' at Gaitskell for visiting a repressive dictator.[48]

iii *Poland and the Soviet Union*

Gaitskell's visits to Communist regimes occasioned quite a different kind of left-wing criticism. His only trip to the USSR was delayed until the very eve of the 1959 general election at home, so that he was unable as planned to go on to Poland. Instead he went there three years later, in August 1962, mainly to discuss foreign policy: he gave a talk on security in the region to the Warsaw Institute for International Affairs, and spent five and a half hours with the country's leaders discussing the Common Market, Germany, and the old plans for military disengagement in central Europe.

The Russian visit was a long-postponed sequel to the 1956 tour of Britain by Bulganin and Khrushchev, whose dinner with the Labour Party had left unhappy memories on both sides. Though those visitors had spoken at the time of a return invitation, it did not arrive until 1958. Gaitskell at once set about cultivating Soviet contacts.[49] He also, out of courtesy, informed the Prime Minister, who advised him not to go – advice he instantly rejected.[50] But then in June the Russians executed Imre Nagy and Pal Maleter, Prime Minister and military commander of the independent Communist government of Hungary, whom they had seized (dishonouring their own safe-conducts) in November 1956 when their tanks were occupying Budapest. The murders drew a protest from the Socialist International, which would – very conveniently for the executioners – have become a hypocritical mockery if the leader of the Labour Party had immediately accepted their hospitality. Worried that the 'loathsome executions' might show Russia to be 'lunging back to Stalinism',[30d] Gaitskell decided to postpone the visit.[51] Michael Foot, so censorious of him for meeting de Gaulle, later accused him of staying at home for fear of being accused of Communism and losing votes, and so allowing Macmillan to get there first.[52]

The falsehood found some credence since the consequence was undeniable. Gaitskell's visit was rearranged for March 1959, but – so he suspected – on hearing that news, Macmillan promptly contrived to get himself invited instead. Gaitskell wrote to a friend: 'It's all very chess like & unreal isn't it? That's the trouble when you have a super tactician like MacWonder.'[37c] Gaitskell hoped that his own journey in August would impress the electorate, but again he was unlucky, for President Eisenhower diverted all the publicity by arriving in London on the previous day to begin an official tour of the Western European capitals.

Labour's expedition was not very well organised, but the Gaitskells had never been before and looked forward to a fortnight in Eastern Europe. The party consisted of Hugh and Dora, Aneurin Bevan, Denis and Edna Healey, David Ennals the Party's international secretary, and a few journalists. The politicians' talks with the Russians were not fruitful. After their return, Gaitskell tactfully mentioned hopeful discussions on testing the bomb, the spread of nuclear weapons, controlled disarmament in central Europe, and Berlin.[53] But in Moscow he was 'extremely vigorous and terrier-like on all the issues, always pressing the Russians'.[54] Their replies were discouraging. Asked if unilateral nuclear disarmament by Britain would find any response, Krushchev answered: 'We do not want our grandchildren to call us fools.'[55a]

Bevan too warned the Russians against the risk of nuclear proliferation. Like Macmillan, but unlike his Labour colleagues, he was alarmed at the prospect of Khrushchev and Eisenhower exchanging visits;[56] and he told Khrushchev that neither the Soviet Union nor the United States would remain forever powerful and secure.[57] Gaitskell was pleased by Bevan's handling of the Russians. He told John Harris affectionately on their return that it had been hard to stop him getting into punch-ups with their hosts, and later recalled that Bevan's 'reactions to the regime were very similar ... [though] rather stronger than mine'.[58a b]

There was minor friction between the Gaitskells and Bevan. They were keen on the visit while he, having often been before, was reluctant.[59a] He was invariably late, and soon became thoroughly bored. Their tastes were quite different (Bevan had no time for dancing); and while none of them liked organised hospitality much, the Gaitskells concealed that feeling better. Two published accounts (from opposing political standpoints but both hostile to the Labour leadership) depict them as loathing one another;[60a d] others on the trip deny it.[61] None of those consulted corroborates (and Dora angrily denies) Michael Foot's bizarre story of her 'wild invective' against Bevan at a dinner in Leningrad.[62] Hugh, unlike Bevan, appreciated his rival's talents as much as his weaknesses and just at this time, according to Crossman, was 'getting really fond of Aneurin, whose loyalty and basic integrity he stresses, in sharp contrast to Harold'.[39c] All Gaitskell's comments after Bevan's death refer to his 'especially happy memories' of this visit and recall how 'Nye was in tremendous form ... Ebullient, gay, full of enthusiasm'.[63a] Dora found him excellent company and 'an enchanting conversationalist', and greatly regretted not having got to know him earlier. Denis Healey thought Bevan particularly mellow.

The visitors had not concealed their criticisms. Bevan was particularly adept at 'spicing with wit and humour which charmed them' his 'tremendous onslaught on what he regarded as [Soviet] bourgeois puritanism'.[63b] Gaitskell introduced the Russian public to a quaint Western practice by writing to *Pravda* in defence of the Red Army goalkeeper whom the journal had attacked. Everyone, especially Bevan, was infuriated by a Bolshoi ballet which presented the British — in admirable choreography — as grotesque Kiplingesque imperialists; Bevan harangued the Russians at length, listing the many countries and hundreds of millions of people in the ex-Empire now independent (and prematurely throwing in a few more).[64] Both he and Gaitskell appeared on Soviet television to repeat the point, and to reveal that Britain had changed since Dickens's day; to Bevan's particular dismay, the Russians were quite ignorant of the National Health Service.[65] But as elsewhere, Gaitskell's greatest impact was face to face. After their three days in Leningrad their escort (a local Party leader) said to Edna Healey:

> You know, I'd never seen Mr. Gaitskell or met him; I've read a lot about him; I know now that he's a really good man — that he wants the sort of things that I want. No matter what I read about him in the newspapers from this day on, I shall always remember him as he really was.[66]

On the last day they enjoyed themselves at the Gorki collective farm, where Bevan knowledgeably criticised the quality and treatment of the pigs.[67] Hospitality was lavish, with endless toasts. After nineteen glasses of vodka, followed by brandy, Gaitskell succumbed for the only time in his public career. Back in their Moscow hotel, he could not be roused to be told that Macmillan had announced the election for 8 October.[60c e] His companions stalled the clamour for a press conference for three hours, and he then mumbled a short prepared statement and left Bevan to take questions. Much against the leader's will, they abandoned the Polish visit and flew straight back to London, where Gaitskell had an electoral briefing in the VIP gents at Heathrow.[58a]

CHAPTER 20

UNITED WE FALL
THE 1959 ELECTION

'The 1959 election shows that ... unity is not enough'
(HG, 1961)

i *Triumphant Fortnight*

THE 1959 election gave the Conservatives their biggest victory since the war. It also began the break-up of the homogeneous two-party United Kingdom. For the first time for thirty years the Liberals gained votes. Labour made progress in Scotland and Lancashire while declining elsewhere, and won over middle-class voters repelled by Suez and colonial repression while its working-class supporters were falling away.

It was striking among post-war elections above all in the disjunction between the campaign and the results. Only twice, in 1959 and 1970, has an apparent trend been reversed at the very end. In several other ways conventional wisdom was upset. Normally the opening of the campaign benefits the party in office; only in 1959 did the opposition gain, as both sides and the pollsters agreed. Normally enthusiasm among Party workers is said to bring out stay-at-home voters; in 1959 when the enthusiasm was exceptional among Labour activists, the marginal electors defected. Normally the Conservative effort is the better organised and more professional of the two; only in 1959 was it clearly outclassed by the best campaign, technically, that Labour has ever waged.

Gaitskell was responsible both for the main blunder of that campaign, and for its general appeal. Normally, failure at the polls undermines the standing of even a hitherto successful Party leader—and he had as yet made little impact on the country. But his performance in 1959 was so universally acclaimed that, in spite of the blunder, he substantially enhanced his reputation even in defeat.

When Parliament rose on 30 July, he expected to open in six or seven weeks the election campaign which might carry him into Downing Street.[1a b] In August, after touring Kent and a week's holiday at home, he spent another week planning for it before leaving for the USSR, having to return precipitately when Macmillan announced the dissolution. Gaitskell showed both his old weakness for going into detail, and his ability to overcome it and to delegate authority. Crossman, who partly wrote the Labour manifesto, complained of the leader fussing over the economics and putting in qualifications over nationalisation;[2a] his co-author Driberg lamented that Gaitskell would not denounce the Establishment because Labour could not help being part of it.[3] But Macmillan called it 'a document in which Gaitskell's profound economic knowledge was displayed with force and persuasiveness'.[4a] And Crossman also testified that Labour's television team (Benn, Mayhew and Wyatt), like the group who wrote *The Future Labour Offers YOU* (himself, Cudlipp and Jacobson) had 'shown what can be done if you're not messed about and are allowed really to work out a good idea'.[2b] Gaitskell had 'very artfully' arranged for Crossman to chair the campaign committee, and then relied on him.[2a b] *

The Conservatives, who could pick the election date, were for six weeks before the announcement the largest press advertisers in the country, spending £113,000.[5a] But the campaign formally opened only when Parliament was officially dissolved nine days after Gaitskell's return, and he used those days well. He was just in time to appear on television on his first night back, rescuing a disastrous party political broadcast.[6] Next morning he spoke to the TUC at Blackpool, using the occasion — for the Party Conference was cancelled — as a springboard for his campaign.[7] Congress defeated Cousins on the bomb by over 2 million votes, but even that result was overshadowed by Gaitskell's 'virtuoso performance' and his reception which 'crowned a day of triumph'.[8] Yet as usual he made his impact by hard home truths:

> The Trade Union Movement has a choice here between either cooperation with a government which is determined to carry out industrial expansion in a planned way, without inflation, or it will be driven back to an inactive role, kept quiet by a certain amount of unemployment, and not wielding any serious influence in the community ... We are comrades together, but we have different jobs to do. You have your industrial job and we have our political job. We do not dictate to one another. I should get the brush off pretty quickly if I started trying to dictate to Bob Willis [TUC chairman]. And, believe me, any leader of the Labour Party would not be worth his salt if he allowed himself to be dictated to by the trade unions.[9]

Then Hugh, Dora and Nye Bevan appeared on ITV to chat about their Moscow visit in a 'cosy little family affair, midway between a lantern lecture and a discussion' — no party politics, but a useful chance to show

* Gaitskell cannot claim credit for another great success of the campaign, Morgan Phillips's daily press conferences.

Labour's harmony, and to report blunt talks with Khrushchev.[10a] 'This was the first step in the growth in his public stature, which was so marked a feature of the election.'[11a] A week later came Labour's first election broadcast, on foreign affairs and disarmament. (Gaitskell talked in all five.) The public commentaries were enthusiastic,[12] and his chief opponent wrote: 'The Socialists had a very successful TV last night – much better than ours. Gaitskell is becoming very expert.'[4b d] Even before his speaking tour began, Crossman recorded that his 'personality has so far completely dominated the campaign ... a television star, a political personality in his own right – confident, relaxed, a leader'.[2b]

Unlike Attlee, Gaitskell carefully prepared his major speeches for his gruelling campaign trip:[1b] fifty meetings in eleven days, moving from London up through Essex and East Anglia to the Midlands, then north through Yorkshire and the north-east coast to Edinburgh, and southward again from Glasgow through Lancashire to Yorkshire for a final brief appearance at home in South Leeds. Concentrating on marginal seats, he had nine meetings in East Anglia, ten in the Lancashire area, and eight in the West Riding. It was more exhausting than was wise;[13] but he drew enormous crowds and a passionate response. The accompanying journalists were as enthusiastic as the participants. A typical example:

> The 1950, 51 and 55 campaign produced nothing like this. These audiences, predominantly Labour, are mad keen on politics just now.
>
> Not since 1945 has there been such a will to win among Labour's rank and file. Nor so many active youngsters ...
>
> As for Gaitskell, this man forges ahead of the other Parliamentary leaders in what it takes to be successful on the hustings ... self-possessed, calm and charming. He tried none of Macmillan's folksey gimmicks. He had no need to.[14–15a]

At Labour headquarters the campaign committee chairman recorded:

> [T]he Gaitskell boom has been rapidly swelling. How strange political leadership is! ... I can watch the godhead emerging from the man ... The leader emerges from the husk of the ordinary politician ... Up till a week ago it was assumed that a Labour defeat would all be blamed on Gaitskell and the Labour propaganda. Now Gaitskell is superb in the public eye, and second only to Gaitskell is the brilliance of the Labour propaganda.[2d]

Transport House, who at first had doubted if Labour could reduce the Tory majority, began to believe they could win.[16] Among Conservatives who suddenly saw the election slipping from their grasp were the Prime Minister, the Chief Whip, and the previous and current party chairmen.[17a b]

50 Canvassing in South Leeds in the 1959 election

51 Dora Gaitskell   52 With daughter Cressida

53 Four Leeds Labour MPs: *from the left* — Denis Healey, Alice Bacon, Hugh Gaitskell and Charles Pannell — on the terrace of the House of Commons

The latter had appealed often and solemnly for a clean campaign without personal smears, then was panicked into an unprovoked attack on Gaitskell — disapproved even by the *Daily Telegraph* — for not having fought in the war.[18a]

Gaitskell's eight major speeches recalled all the issues on which he had constantly attacked the government. He emphasised world affairs in his opening speech at Bristol, giving three tests: the international rule of law which the Conservatives had shamefully flouted at Suez; disarmament and disengagement where they were slow and timid about Labour's practical proposals; and the underdeveloped world, where their disastrous actions in Africa outweighed any words of deathbed repentance. At Norwich he condemned their Cyprus record of taking up Labour policies 'four years and 400 lives too late', and of pretending falsely that the problem had merely been a quarrel between Greeks and Turks. He kept returning to Central Africa — especially in Scotland, where the crisis attracted most attention since the Church of Scotland had a long missionary tradition there. For Gaitskell was a highly professional politician, who saw it as his duty not only to sound a high-minded note of 'conscience and reform', but to win votes by doing so; just as at Bristol he had appealed specifically to Liberals with either a large or a small 'l'.

ii *Blunder and Concession*

Knowing that elections are rarely decided on foreign issues, he spoke mainly on domestic problems, and did not delude himself that a purely idealistic appeal was enough. Rightly, he saw higher pensions as Labour's best vote-winner — yet even that meant asking others to give priority to a needier group then themselves. Above all a sceptical electorate had to be convinced of the practicability of these policies. At Birmingham on 26 September 1959 Gaitskell made that his third major theme. Reminding his audience of all the past reforms which contemporary Tories had called too costly, he contrasted their present caution with Butler's boast before the last election of doubling the standard of living in twenty-five years. That, said Gaitskell, was quite a practicable aim if the economy expanded steadily — as it had after 1945, had not in the last few years, but could again under Labour rule. At the rate needed to achieve Butler's target (2·8 per cent per year) the Chancellor would in five years' time, with present taxes, have an extra £1,000 million a year. Past gains from expansion had been diverted by Tory dear money policies into higher interest payments on the national debt; Labour would tighten up on expense allowances and tax capital gains; its programme would cost far less than the Tories pretended, and so a Labour Chancellor could count on extra revenue for financing the Party's social programme and also 'for relieving

S

taxation where the shoe pinches most'.[19] The lines of the speech were prepared by Crossman, who was gratified at 'its excellent reception'.[2e]

That night Gaitskell told Roy Jenkins he expected to win.[20a] His sudden popular acclaim had come with no change of style; when Crossman suggested exploiting a current financial scandal (the Jasper affair)[11b] to wonder on television if money in building societies was really safe, Gaitskell would not 'think of using a most effective if slightly pitchy weapon'.[2d] 'He must', wrote one journalist, 'be the only economist in Britain to have a bobby-soxer following ... Mr. Gaitskell has won hearts not with emotional gestures and cries but with economics and figures ... he has captured the Labour voters. Nye Bevan ... has slipped behind.'[15a] But another, who found him strikingly thorough and intellectually honest, felt also: 'he was convincing. But, unlike Mr. Macmillan, he did not give the impression that he was certain he would convince.'[21] That uncertainty provoked his blunder.

Crossman's Birmingham brief reflected an accurate campaign committee forecast of four days earlier, that the Conservatives would counter-attack on the cost of Labour's programme:[22a] so far a theme of Lord Hailsham alone among leading Ministers.[23a b] Now Gaitskell learned – or thought he did – of a forthcoming massive Conservative scare that Labour would increase income tax by 2s. 6d. ($12\frac{1}{2}$p.) in the pound.[24] Over the weekend, John Harris warned him that he would have to go further, and should promise explicitly not to raise income tax.[25a] Gaitskell did not inform the campaign committee but he did consult his Shadow Chancellor, taking a pre-arranged telephone call at lunch at Northallerton on Monday 28 September.[26] At Newcastle that night Gaitskell promised that in normal peacetime conditions a Labour government would not increase the rates of income tax.[27]

The Conservatives pounced at once. Macmillan challenged Gaitskell to extend the pledge – 'queer for an ex-Chancellor' – to other taxes.[23a c] Then, at the daily Transport House press conference on 1 October, a journalist picked up a handout saying Labour would reduce purchase tax on essentials – as Wilson had often stated, both in the House and in the campaign (in his election address, on the air and in the press). Morgan Phillips had not expected the question, would never admit to an organisational fault at Transport House, and so said that it was indeed a Labour Party commitment.[28] Gaitskell was furious, and it gave him his one sleepless night of the campaign.[25a b] For though he had still thought the income-tax pledge politically advantageous, even after Macmillan's reply, he now realised instantly that the purchase-tax statement had transformed it into a liability, fuelling the raging fire of Tory criticism of Labour's and his own orgy of mass bribery.[25a b] Conservatives were more charitable in private, presuming that 'the machine' had persuaded Gaitskell to act out of character.[17b]

Not all Labour people were. Shinwell repeated the crudest Conservative charges;[29a b] while Crossman and the campaign committee felt the pledge to be 'foreign to his nature' and an appalling 'breach in [his] intellectual integrity ... The last thing I would have expected'.[2c f]

Gaitskell had taken no sudden decision to turn the election into an auction. The financial arguments, like the policies themselves, had been put forward for years and had never produced the slightest reaction. In the 1955 campaign Gaitskell already claimed that expansion would provide the extra revenue for domestic reforms.[30] In January 1959, before the Budget, he was publicly hoping both to carry out reforms and to reduce income tax.[31] After it was cut in the Budget, he again said publicly that over a full Parliament the programme could be paid for without putting taxes up again.[32] Now, thrown on the defensive in the final week, Gaitskell recalled the desiccated calculating machine, telling his constituents:

> They are representing me, not as the austere dry-as-dust character I used to be in their cartoons, but as a gay, reckless gambler, prepared to stake everything in the casino and without any sense of responsibility. I would not have been a party to the Labour programme unless I was sure we could carry it out.[18b]

He had calculated the costs with his usual thoroughness. His fault was naivety not cunning. He knew himself to be a man of integrity, and believed the public knew it too; so he thought he could enhance Labour's credibility by staking his own high financial reputation.[23a d] Stop-go was new, and politicians were not yet derided for thinking they could manage the economy better than their opponents; Gaitskell certainly believed what he said.[33] Indeed his failure to foresee the storm was partly because he had said the same so often before without trouble. But a pledge from the prospective Prime Minister at the height of an election was bound to have a vast resonance, and a politician of his experience should have foreseen how it could be exploited by his opponents.[34] His antennae had failed him badly.

Politicians on both sides instantly saw it as a big mistake. The dismay of Labour's campaign committee perhaps owed something to wounded *amour propre*;[2f] and Bevan's to his fear that a Labour government would have no room for manoeuvre.[2c] But the Transport House professionals also thought at once that the election was lost, and so did Jim Griffiths.[35] The pledge reinforced the theme of the Conservatives' counter-attack, which now concentrated on Gaitskell himself — for his performance in the campaign had finally convinced them that he not Bevan should be their target.[36]

Labour were now suffering for failing to publicise their policies before the campaign began. Far from being last-minute bribes to catch votes, the pensions increase, the redistribution of purchase tax and the argument that revenue would expand with the economy were all themes sounded for years.[5b] Yet the attacks on them revived many latent doubts and suspicions. Crossman drafted the campaign committee's report and, becoming critical of Gaitskell very soon after the election, 'sharpened it up a great deal' to stress that this was the turning-point.[2g] 'The Conservatives, who had not effectively challenged our policies, succeeded in blurring the image of the party's integrity. From then on all the Tories' anti-Labour propaganda was effective.'[22]

Most Labour candidates, according to the general secretary, felt that the tax pledge did harm.[37-8a] Gaitskell's critics were not alone in asserting that it had lost the election.[39] He himself came to think that, while the Conservatives would have won anyway, it had been 'a very grave mistake' and probably brought them their increased majority.[40] Others on both sides (including Lord Butler) thought it made no difference and prosperity was decisive.[41] The controversy was said to have had a great impact in the West Country, but not elsewhere.[11f] The polls showed when opinion moved but not why: as the campaign went on the Don't Knows went steadily up and the Conservative lead steadily down, until the final weekend.[11g] At the same time Labour window-bills were being taken down.[38b] One or both of the tax pledges may have done the damage, but quite likely the doubtfuls would never in a time of affluence have risked voting Labour, and the pledges merely gave them a pretext for playing safe.[42a b]

That damage was not known at once, for published polls reflect opinion a few days late. Gallup, the best known, showed the major parties neck and neck on the last Monday morning, and NOP too had Labour still catching up.[43] Gaitskell had begun the campaign expecting both gains and losses of seats, and thinking victory unlikely. Just before the income-tax pledge he was expecting to win; and on the final Sunday when he learned of the coming Gallup findings, he felt sure of it.[44] That night he wrote out his Cabinet list.[45] He returned to London on Monday for the final television programme (on the tax pledges), again showing himself 'a master of the art of chatting to the individual viewer ... with steadily greater assurance and authority'.[11h] He spent the last days in South Leeds where, in a three-cornered fight, he had a smaller share of a higher poll and a majority down by 500:

Hugh Gaitskell (Lab.)	24,442
John Addey (Cons.)	12,956
J. B. Meeks (Lib.)	4,340
Majority	11,486

The Conservative candidate sent charming congratulations on his 'impressive national campaign' and on his bearing in defeat, ending: 'Thank you for all your kindness – and your training!'[46]

Gaitskell was at the local count in Leeds town hall when John Harris gave him the gloomy news – that the Conservatives had won, and by a bigger majority.[25a] At 1 a.m. he conceded the election in an unprecedented gesture that infuriated Aneurin Bevan, who resented all the paraphernalia of polls and swings.[47] It was the worst disappointment of Gaitskell's public life, a profound shock very deeply felt.[48] Yet the grace with which he swallowed the bitter pill, first in Leeds and then in London, earned him immense credit from admirers and opponents alike. 'I can hardly convey strongly enough', said a BBC correspondent who was with him on election night, 'the dignified impression he made in those first-realised moments of defeat ... Sad, generous: he was worried lest his Liberal opponent should have gone away with the mistaken impression that he'd lost his deposit. But, above all, dignified and thoughtful.'[49a]

He travelled back on Friday on an early morning train, warmly cheered by the railwaymen along the way and at King's Cross.[50] That evening, after the galling experience of visiting Downing Street to see Harold Macmillan, he said on BBC television: 'the ideals on which [our] policies are based shine as brightly as ever ... our ranks are unbroken. We have attacked, and on this occasion we have been repulsed. We shall attack again and again until we win.'[51] (Unnoticed at the time, it became the most famous phrase he ever spoke when used in another context a year later.) The moment of defeat was when Gaitskell's personality most impressed the country and established his claim to national authority. 'It was the voice of a leader', wrote the British Ambassador in Moscow, 'whose day will inevitably come and who will be worthy of it when it rises.'[52] Leading civil servants in Whitehall expressed similar admiration;[53] and so did the letters that poured in from prominent Conservatives and Liberals as well as Labour people and foreign ambassadors and journalists, and men and women in the street – most of whom referred to the impact on others as well as themselves.[54] 'I don't believe in this business of promising the earth,' said one voter from a marginal seat. 'I think Mr. Gaitskell was much more noble and real in his defeat than ever before.'[55]

iii Inquest: 'Irreproachable aud Unassailable'

Gaitskell's political contacts immediately after polling day were later to provoke suspicion on the Left. On the Sunday morning, 11 October 1959, several political friends came to his home to bid farewell to Hugh Dalton, who had retired from the House of Commons, and to gossip about the election. On the Tuesday, Gaitskell visited two prominent colleagues at their farms, lunching bibulously with Bevan at Asheridge[47] to talk about the vacant Speakership and to arrange for him to take over the deputy leadership which Griffiths was giving up; and then spending that night with Crossman at Prescote (near Banbury) before snatching a few days of escape on the Berkshire Downs, staying at a Wantage pub.[2h] Back in London he found that the Prime Minister had been hunting him to discuss electing Sir Frank Soskice as the first Labour Speaker. But Soskice was known to be reluctant, and when he declined the Tories would accept no substitute; for the second time running they chose a serving member of the government, leaving Labour MPs more resentful than before, and the two Party leaders more suspicious of each other than ever.[56] Soon the row over the Monckton Commission was to exacerbate those feelings.[57]

To cheer up his disappointed followers, Gaitskell repeated just after the election that Labour had suffered only a minor setback not a disaster, for the Conservative swing was very small.[49b] That was most misleading, given Labour's poor showing in 1955. For the first time in a mass electorate, a political party had gained seats at four successive elections and won a majority in three successive normal Parliaments. The pendulum had stopped, and the uncommitted voter evidently recoiled from electing a Labour government. Worse: defections were greatest among the young. Between 1955 and 1959 Labour's share of the vote rose by 7 per cent among over-65s, was unchanged among the middle-aged, but fell by 6 per cent among the under-30s—where the Conservatives now led.[58] In one Birmingham seat—lost by twenty votes—24 per cent of the 'Y voters' stayed at home, 20 per cent voted Labour, and 56 per cent Conservative (nearly half of whom had two Labour parents).[59a] Labour had only 10 per cent of middle-class people aged 18–24, while 35 per cent of working-class youngsters preferred the Tories.[60] In private Gaitskell did not pretend it was a minor setback, but saw the causes as deep-rooted.[61] He had told Crossman before the election: 'If the Tories increased their majority, it would only prove that we were more out of touch with the electorate even than you or I now think we are and that our renovation of the Party hasn't gone far or fast enough.'[2l]

The income-tax pledge was one of several contingent excuses. Labour's superb election performance could not offset its earlier failure to make an impact, since so many voters made up their minds years before.[38c d] The long and expensive business advertising campaign might have affected the climate of opinion. Thanks to prosperity and his own skill, Macmillan enjoyed a tremendous advantage in publicity, and as Gaitskell wrote:

> [I]t is extremely hard to get the public interested in political causes except at Election times. I myself have made speech after speech in the last four years without being fully reported but since the Election started everything I said had news value.[34]

Gaitskell did not take much account of these contingent explanations. Indeed, everyone agreed on the principal reason: it had been a safety-first vote. The current prosperity might be dependent on favourable economic conditions in the short term, and would be endangered in the long run by low investment; but like Heath in 1966, Gaitskell found people unconvinced by that case as long as experience had not yet shaken them — though had he survived, he might have reaped a deferred electoral harvest as Heath did in 1970. Labour's gains were only in Scotland and industrial Lancashire, with their high unemployment, and *Tribune* bluntly said that 'the results can be correlated almost without exception with the prosperity (or lack of it) of various regions'.[62a] [b] Elsewhere the Conservatives still received credit for affluence. Crossman wrote that 'Tory voters are far more afraid of another Labour Government than Labour voters are afraid of another Tory Government.'[2j] In the prosperous South and Midlands, 'Don't let Labour ruin it' was a potent slogan.

Those alarms were reflected in scepticism about inflation and the costly Labour programme, crystallised by the tax pledges; and also in fear of back-door nationalisation of the '600 companies'.[11j] Bevan thought that fear had been very damaging. Of 200 candidates answering Morgan Phillips's questionnaire, 6 had found nationalisation a benefit and 97 a drawback. Other policy issues counted for less. Colonial and foreign policy were seen as assets, disarmament as an electoral bore, and disunity on defence as a liability.[38e] [a] *Tribune* claimed that Labour would have done worse without the conscience issues, and better with a stronger line against the bomb.[62a] But the campaign committee, confirming the harm done by divisions over defence, added that the anti-British label 'was terribly damaging' and that Suez, Cyprus, Hola and Nyasaland[63] had probably lost votes for Labour.[22] Yet only 6 of Phillips's 200 believed that the Party had suffered because of its policies.

Labour supporters themselves, indeed, were not just content but enthusiastic. A regional organiser wrote round his local Parties that it had been 'a wonderful campaign. We have witnessed nothing like it for very many years'.[64] Correspondents from Derbyshire and Dundee, from Gloucester and Leeds, from Rutherglen and Southampton, from Wandsworth and Wycombe, from Plymouth and Coventry and Blackburn, wrote of the numbers and the keenness of the Party workers in their own areas — greater, said many, than since 1945.[65] Morgan Phillips's report rejoiced at the 'magnificent response from our workers everywhere, sustained right to the end', adding: 'There was much praise for the campaign and the leadership. Such expressions as "brilliant", "the best campaign in history", and so on were frequent.'[38c]

Gaitskell's leadership, despite the income-tax pledge, was rated an asset by sixty-nine respondents, with no dissentients.[38c] He thus became the first and only leader of the Labour Party — perhaps of any party — to add to his reputation in a heavy election defeat. The point needs stressing, since the mistake he was about to make is otherwise incomprehensible. No one put forward the familiar excuses for Labour defeats — poor propaganda, decaying organisation, indifferent leadership, an impression of endless fratricidal strife; instead Barbara Castle publicly testified to Labour's 'good programme, better organisation than we have ever had and brilliant leadership by Hugh Gaitskell'.[59b] Privately she sent a warm tribute:

> You fought a magnificent fight and have enhanced your reputation greatly. The party workers, too, have never been in better spirits and the enthusiasm among our supporters was real and new ... please don't be discouraged. You have every reason to be proud of yourself. Affectionately, Barbara.[66]

Crossman underlined the contrast with the Party's customary 'hunt for the scapegoat ... blaming Transport House, or accusing the leadership of sacrificing Socialist principles. What has been noteworthy this week has been the complete absence of this odious search for an alibi'. Instead, he went on, every candidate he had met was 'inspired' by Gaitskell's leadership, which alone had 'prevented a catastrophic landslide' sweeping away up to 100 seats instead of 20, including everything south of the Trent.[67a c]

Trade union leaders were impressed too. Ernest Jones of the miners' union, an old ally, thought it the best leadership in Labour's history; Harry Knight, the unilateralist general secretary of ASSET (now ASTMS) and an old critic, wrote that it was 'as near ideal as any mortal could hope for, and if Labour is in the future to gain control, it can do so only with you at the helm'.[68] A most experienced agent wrote to Gaitskell of

> our great gain ... the respect and admiration the rank and file of the Party now feels for its leader ... the workers of the Party have never felt a greater sense of unity, nor of happiness in the conduct of a General Election, than under your leadership. I speak with some authority. I have been engaged, professionally, in every General Election since 1922.[69]

Tribune struck the one discordant note, putting an article praising the 'remarkable level of enthusiasm and efficiency among Labour campaign workers' next to a photograph of 'Mr. Gaitskell' captioned 'The impression was given that Labour did not believe in its own programme'.[62a c] At this time, however, as an experienced American journalist was to recall two months later,

> Hugh Gaitskell was receiving from his followers from Left to Right an acclaim and devotion and support which no Labour leader had been

given in decades. Whatever the proportions of the election defeat, Labour was unanimous that it had a leader, and that his handling of the campaign had been masterly and his inspiration superb.[70]

Gaitskell had expected to be vulnerable if the election was lost, but was reassured by his reception. The press were sure that whoever was blamed, it would not be he.[71] Henry Fairlie told his readers that within the Party he 'is now irreproachable and unassailable. He can, if he wishes, order the execution of either particular promises or particular personalities'.[72] J. P. W. Mallalieu, once a bitter Bevanite, wrote in his column that apart from the income-tax pledge, 'Gaitskell's leadership in the campaign not merely satisfied but inspired the party ... there is no possibility of a personal challenge to Gaitskell'.[67b] Privately Gaitskell was hearing much the same. One well-informed German friend wrote optimistically: 'You have established yourself most effectively once and for all as the leader of your party, which may make life easier for you in the future.'[73] In spite of the defeat he could therefore reasonably hope that his advice would be received as coming not from the suspect chief of a discredited faction, but from the trusted leader of a united movement. That mood was not to last.

PART SIX

LEADERSHIP: THE YEARS OF STRIFE

'The atmosphere is full of suppressed hysteria and neurosis – not so suppressed either'
(HG, 1960)
'A triumph won by fortitude and character'
(JAMES GRIFFITHS TO HG, 1961)

CHAPTER 21

CLAUSE FOUR 1959–60

'It is [not] prudent ... that all forms of private property should live under
perpetual threat'
(ANEURIN BEVAN, 1952; condensed)
'It was never an issue of principle; it was an issue of presentation'
(HG, 1960)

i *Enter the 'Hampstead Set', with Boomerangs*

GAITSKELL'S immediate reaction to the 1959 defeat fitted his past, not his
future style of leadership. He rejected appeals to present an analysis of the
defeat or to suggest remedies. Since the MPs were enthusiastic about his
performance in the campaign, Charlie Pannell urged him to make the most
of their support, tell them how his mind was working, and rely on them to
persuade the constituency Parties. It was excellent counsel. But Gaitskell
maintained that a major reappraisal of the Party's basic outlook and
strategy was properly a matter for Conference.[1a][b] Besides, he disliked
jumping to conclusions without time to reflect, he knew that his own impressions might have been distorted by his triumphal tour, he could not
quickly contact the trade union leaders, and he was reluctant to give unwelcome advice so soon to the disappointed Party workers.[2a] He meant to
use the established machinery to persuade his followers of the need for a
bold solution. Once he had decided against giving his own views immediately after the election, Conference would provide the best moment and the
best platform.[3a]

As usual it was a reasoned decision, but one which failed to foresee the
speedy and total disappearance of the goodwill towards himself and the
desire for a united Party which the campaign had generated. After a lost
election the rank and file often blame the leader; and his influential colleagues suddenly perceive, instead of a man about to appoint a Cabinet,
a vulnerable politician and a shaky balance of power, which might shift —
or be shifted — to open up new personal and ideological opportunities.
Gaitskell had known very well that a reaction against his leadership might
follow a defeat. But the general acclaim for his own electoral performance
had created a mood of false security.

He himself did a little, and his friends much more, to foster that reaction:

though not, as the Left assumed, by 'a *coup d'état* ... a deliberate design to alter the nature of the Labour Party ... [a] conspiracy'.[4] But paranoia on the Left, and mistrust of the leadership among some constituency activists, were such familiar features of Labour's psychological landscape that Gaitskell and his associates should have been far more wary. Instead, he was unwilling to let political calculation intrude upon his personal relationships, or to interfere with his friends' individual activities, or to stop the right wing of the Party contributing to the debate as freely as the Left.[5a b] He was to pay a high price for these inhibitions.

Gaitskell's farewell party for Dalton, barely forty-eight hours after the results were known, was an opportunity to exchange impressions about the dreary outcome. Crosland, Gordon Walker, Jay and Jenkins were old friends of the host and guest; John Harris came too, and so did Herbert Bowden the Chief Whip. While the wives chatted in another room, the men talked politics. It was neither a group of friends meeting at random nor the planning session for grand political strategy assumed by the Left — who, like the press, learned of it at once, and still suppose it orchestrated a 'bold initiative by the Right wing of the Party'.[6a]

The participants were far too punch-drunk by the campaign, far too close to the result, and far too individualistic in their reactions for that. They speak of 'desultory talk' among very tired men, which 'roamed over the whole field' in a 'rambling discussion' on an 'unbelievably superficial' level.[7] Everyone agreed, and assumed that others would too, that British society was changing fast and Labour must adapt to survive.[7a c] Everyone present — like everyone else — thought nationalisation had been an electoral liability.[7b d] Labour was said to have done well among owner-occupiers and badly on new council housing estates.[7b] There was no paper to discuss, no evidence to study, no agenda and no attempt to agree on a plan. Dalton's account shows Crosland almost and Harris completely silent:

> D.J. started off with a great oration on the moral of the election defeat. He wanted (1) to drop 'nationalisation', (2) drop the Trade Unions, (3) drop the name 'Labour Party' ... (4) drop the principle of political independence, & make agreements, even up to merger, with the Liberals[8] ... I said I thought this was rather wild, pouring out the baby with the bathwater & throwing the bath after them ... Others too were more cautious than D. J. G. Walker wanted a scientific enquiry ... He too thought the T.U. connection might be loosened ... Bowden was very practical, & H.G. said little in front of so many. He is ... resolutely, but cautiously revisionist ... Party Constitution might be revised, some new formula on public ownership substituted for 1918 text ... Party Const^n might also be changed by having Nat^l Exec elected by Unions (local parties represented regionally) ... and Parlia-

mentary Party, with shift of authority towards Parliamentary Leadership. But any such changes will take time & need most careful handling. H.G., very wisely, listens more than talks to groups like this.[5c]

Privately, Gaitskell was against most of the suggestions, especially Jay's: dropping steel nationalisation, breaking with the unions, a pact with the Liberals, changing the name. (That last idea, when an intermediary had put it to him in August at Jay's request, had made him angrier than she had ever seen him.)[9]

That Sunday morning, 11 October 1959, Jay said he might write an anonymous discussion piece in *Forward*, and John Harris (an old *Forward* journalist) told him a signed one would make more impact.[10] Jay's bugbear was the Party's working-class image, and he brought up nationalisation only as an afterthought (provoked by a telephone call from Eric Fletcher, MP, about its devastating impact on the doorstep), tentatively suggesting it might be dropped for steel.[10] Gaitskell did not suggest the article, or see the text, or agree with the content. All that he did beforehand was to encourage his friends to speak out like everyone else, and later to defend Jay for having the courage of his convictions.[11a b] But nothing can shake the Left's conviction, then and since, that here was proof of a Frognal Gardens plot.[6b] Crossman knew better:

> I now believe that he didn't discourage them and probably positively consented to their flying some kites about the need to drop nationalisation and to rewrite the constitution. On the other hand, I have no reason to doubt his word that the kind of kites flown in succession were not to his taste and that he himself does not agree with Douglas and Roy about dropping steel nationalisation.[12]

But the Left protested at those initiatives as though they were Gaitskell's, and so (in Crossman's view) prevented not the retreat from nationalisation, which had never been likely, but the chance of constitutional reforms:[13a] reforms favoured by himself, Morgan Phillips, Jim Griffiths and Aneurin Bevan.

On that first Sunday afternoon Anthony Wedgwood Benn called on Gaitskell. Already the leader was determined to listen to — rather than open — the debate within the Party; opposed to changing the name or weakening the trade union link; convinced that Labour must adapt to the new affluent society; and probably intending to question Clause Four.[14] In the evening, Gaitskell and Crosland both dined with Woodrow Wyatt. Clause Four was discussed; Crosland warned that revising it would cause far more trouble that it was worth, and Gaitskell insisted that the leader's duty was to try to 'shape' the Party — which must show that it was intellectually honest and was facing the present, not bound by nostalgia for the past.[15] Very probably they also discussed Wyatt's favourite remedy of an electoral pact with the Liberals (which both Jay and Gordon Walker were to criticise).[16a b] Privately, Gaitskell thought it might be possible to agree with the Liberals on policy, if they respected trade union feelings – but not electorally, for they could not deliver their vote. In Gaitskell's area, the West Riding, the Liberals were close to the Conservatives on economic and social questions and he seriously underestimated the penetration of youthful radicals into the Liberal Party elsewhere.[2a b] As the Labour debate developed, his distaste for the pact grew.[17]

The reappraisal was sweeping, covering also the Party's institutional structure, which all the leaders thought in need of reform, and the distribution of personal responsibilities, which was to arouse serious friction. On the night of Tuesday 13 October, Gaitskell stayed with Crossman and

> talked to me at length from 6 to 11 and then again in the morning when he could get a word in after our walk round the farm and discussion of cows. So he must have had six hours. First of all he made it clear that in his view we couldn't afford to lose the next election again ... 'Douglas Jay and Roy want to drop all nationalisation. I am not in favour of dropping iron and steel and road haulage. That is why I propose a complete rewrite of the constitution, defining our aims in modern terms and introducing a federal structure, with indirect election for all. This means the Parliamentary Party will elect its representatives as the trade unions do, and the constituency parties will elect rank-and-file members, as they will be forbidden to choose MPs.' I was at first very surprised by this constitutional reform, but he told me that Morgan [Phillips] had long ago recommended it and Jim Griffiths was keenly in favour. Nye Bevan also had concurred during lunch ... and had shown no signs whatsoever of wanting to lead a Left attack on moderate policies. I said ... any constitutional reform or moderation of our attitude to public ownership should not split the Party, and I would only support formulae to which Nye concurred. He must have the veto. Hugh looked a bit surprised but, on reflection, saw this was sensible.[18]

Gaitskell's mind was not settled, and he was far from sure he wanted the PLP represented on the NEC.[19] 'The danger was that it would leave the trade union leaders in a backwater. Already the National Executive of the Labour Party tended to get the second line trade union leaders. The first line people went to the T.U.C.'[2a *] Gaitskell also disputed Jay's view that the unions' power at Conference harmed the Party:

* NEC trade unionists sensed and resented that attitude.[20]

The leaders—with the exception of that megalomaniac Cousins—generally were among the few who had taken the trouble to inform themselves and to be well briefed on a subject before they made their minds up. They were often a much steadier element than the constituency section of the party.

He therefore feared that weakening the link with the unions might do more harm than good, and that strengthening the PLP might make Conference quite irresponsible.[2a b c]

At a meeting of the campaign committee at about this time, Bevan told Phillips that constitutional reform was necessary—'but mind you, Morgan, it's got to be handled with great finesse'.[21a b] When Gaitskell lunched with him, Bevan had revived his own old proposal that the Shadow Cabinet should be nominated by the leader, rather than elected by the PLP which he so distrusted.[22] Shinwell favoured that change, too;[5a d] and so did Crossman, who candidly admitted he did so because it would strengthen his personal position.[13b] He thought the back-benchers might be compensated for their lost votes by suspension of standing orders, to which at first Gaitskell demurred;[13c] indeed the leader was not at all keen on Bevan's proposal, 'since he somehow felt that he would get his way without it and that nomination would make him too open to be blamed for everything that went wrong'.[13b] Before long Bevan abandoned it.[13a] The Shadow Cabinet remained elective, though standing orders were suspended anyway.

Crossman always believed, as MPs often do, that parliamentary performance determines a party's standing in the country; and with his own power and influence very much in mind, he had further ambitious plans for creating new posts in the Shadow Cabinet. The leader would choose co-ordinators of publicity and research, linking the PLP with Transport House; Crossman proposed himself for the research post.[13b] Gaitskell was sceptical of Crossman's larger plans, but agreed with him that the Front Bench of elderly workhorses, loyally re-elected each year, was a heavy handicap. Already he had drastic changes there in mind.[23a] Suggesting Harold Wilson for Shadow Leader of the House of Commons, Crossman found Gaitskell 'very anti-Harold', and already inclined to shift him to another Shadow office. Before and during the election it was reported that Wilson knew he might not be Labour's Chancellor.[24] The Exchequer was indeed much discussed during Gaitskell's election tour, and the leader told Harris: 'It is a great mistake now to think a British Prime Minister has got to be his own Foreign Secretary; he's got to be his own Chancellor of the Exchequer.'[25]

Never a trusting man, Wilson called on Crossman on Thursday 15 October 1959,

furious and insecure and even more furious at the suggestion he should be promoted to Leader of the House. He regarded this as a conspiracy to chase him out of the Shadow Chancellorship and stood pat, with the only expression of anger and passion I've ever heard him use ... he was bound to regard me as a dangerous rival ... I told him it was his duty to go and see Gaitskell about it.[26]

The proposal to have a parliamentary and organisational chief of staff, as Morrison had been for Attlee, had been canvassed before and would be again;[27] and Crossman himself, suggesting combining it with the Shadow Leadership of the House, had put it to Wilson. The Gaitskells were sure of that;[28] and Dora still believes that it was done with malice.[29] It was not at all what Gaitskell intended. For to his wife's surprise, he talked freely to Crossman, who called at 18 Frognal Gardens the following Sunday evening, 18 October,[13b] about making Wilson Shadow Foreign Secretary:[30] because he was too unpopular in the City, was not a good enough economist, and 'wouldn't take the tough decisions'.[31] That was no demotion; but soon Crossman was blandly saying that indiscreet talk about moving Wilson had been 'Gaitskell's worst post-election blunder'.[32]

Wilson now thought that Gaitskell both meant to replace him by Roy Jenkins, and also had inspired another Henry Fairlie article saying that Wilson was being blamed for the defeat, might be 'slowly edged out during the next 12 months', and was far more likely than Bevan to lead a left-wing revolt.[23b c] Later, Wilson said that but for this affair he would not have agreed to stand for the leadership in 1960.[33a] Gaitskell told Alastair Hetherington that he had quite failed to reassure Wilson, and

> was finding it very difficult now to get on with him. Wilson was afraid that his succession to the deputy leadership – and so to the leadership 'say fifteen years hence' was in jeopardy ... even if he was not himself altogether conscious of his motives. It was this ... that had really upset him.

The editor had just suggested that Gaitskell could probably safely go abroad for a month at Christmas, since Harold Macmillan also would be out of the country. 'Yes,' was the reply, 'and Harold Wilson will be out of it too.'[2c]

Though no chief of staff was appointed at the time to the post Patrick Gordon Walker was eventually to fill, Gaitskell did reshape the Labour Front Bench. He kept the complete Shadow government organisation which Crossman disliked, but allowed the 'Shadows' to speak on subjects other than their own.[34] His list of forty-one was only two-thirds the size of his successor's, yet Gaitskell promoted talent without offending the older men. Of the twenty newcomers, five (all later in Wilson's Cabinets) were still in their thirties.[35] * It was again an unusually young team for a

* Benn, Jenkins, Mason, Prentice and Thomson.

Labour Opposition,[36] and Dalton was 'exceedingly delighted ... most judicious and skilful'.[37a] Gaitskell thought highly of them, telling his daughter in reply to press criticism of their ability that, given the chance, everyone in the Shadow Cabinet could have taken a good university degree.[38] He was careful not to favour his middle-class friends, omitting both Crosland and Wyatt, who had just returned to the House; some incorrigibly dissatisfied trade union members assumed that he did so owing to weakness.[13d]

A month earlier, on 21 October, Gaitskell met the PLP for the first time since the election and received a standing ovation.[39] Beforehand, Crossman had found him

> quite confident that he will have no difficulty on Wednesday morning at the Party Meeting and that the vote of confidence in him will be sufficiently fervent to prevent any Left-Right row. Maybe it will that morning but I'm pretty sure that already the hundred trade unionists are burning with anger against the intellectuals, not unreasonably, for having started this row within a few hours of polling day. As for the Party, I shall be very surprised if Hugh hasn't over-estimated the number of MPs who are prepared to throw nationalisation so gaily overboard in the full public eye.[13b]

The doubts were justified, and the prestige Gaitskell had acquired in the election was already more tarnished than he realised. As he had decided, he stayed in the background, appealed for a friendly hearing for everyone, and 'struck what was thought to be exactly the right note by making no excuses and frankly inviting criticism'.[40a] The debate was quite good-humoured and though Jay was denounced, he was also applauded when he answered the Left by quoting their own criticisms of nationalisation in 1950.[41] But 'the net effect of this morning's meeting was to show that the Jenkins–Jay line has no chance whatsoever of being accepted'.[13a]

In the two weeks since polling day, the unwonted fraternal harmony of the election campaign had been dissipated, and Gaitskell's friends had greatly harmed their own cause — not by secret intrigues but by ill-judged public statements. They had organised no conspiracy and agreed no objectives, but put up a cacophony of individual contributions (often condemning one another) which they naively supposed would be accepted as such. As Dalton wrote, Jay's 'article in Forward ... gave it all a bad start, and struck the tuning-fork for all the Gregorian Chants of the Old Believers'.[42a b] Ideas like reform of the Shadow Cabinet and even of the NEC, which might perhaps have been acceptable, were now discredited by association with those that were not. Gaitskell was blamed, and not only on the Left. There the old Bevanites reverted to factionalism, defensively as they felt; but Bevan, once he saw that moves to drop nationalisation would get nowhere, strongly opposed reviving the old organised group.[43] Far more dangerously for Gaitskell, Jay's article reawoke suspicions of the intellectuals among the trade union MPs, and affected (unfairly) their attitude to Gaitskell himself.[44]

By the time Gaitskell came to speak out at the Blackpool Conference, he had lost much of his room for manoeuvre. In stormier waters and a much worse climate, he was persisting with a familiar style of leadership which he soon had to abandon. The *Observer* noted:

> [H]e has become increasingly obsessed by one thing – the imperative need to keep the party united ... Like Clem, he would listen to the voices. Like Clem, he would be neither Left nor Right ... but, keeping resolutely to the middle way, show that he was the honest broker ... On October 8 ... it looked as if he could do anything he liked. Despite three defeats ... his prestige was so great that it seemed he could arbitrarily lay down the future party line ... the atmosphere is no longer quite the same. Mr. Gaitskell now has his critics ... He can hint, he can beckon and he can point; but the day seems to have passed when he could insist and command.[45]

The *Spectator* agreed: 'All he can hope to do is ... exercise his talent for restoring unity.'[46a] But at least he knew from those PLP meetings

> that the weight of opinion among Labour M.P.s is overwhelmingly against Mr. Jay and that [it] would invite disaster ... to steer the conference too fast and too far ... They made his task easy. He knows with certainty ... exactly what is expected of him and what his audience will bear. It will be surprising if he gets an emphasis, a gesture, or a tone of voice wrong.[46b]

If he provoked a storm, it was not for lack of warning.

ii   *Ends and Means*

Unlike many participants in Labour's debate in the autumn of 1959, Gaitskell saw the danger that refusing any change could lead the Party to disaster. Very shortly after polling day he told Crossman that another defeat would be final: 'Then there really would be a growth of the Liberal Party and a split. We must let the pendulum take us in and carry nothing which stops it swinging our way.'[13b] To Stephen Spender, he warned of 'very strong underlying forces working against us. The problem is how to deal with these without splitting the Party. It is not an easy matter'.[47]

Too many people would not face the danger. Left-wingers knew that any adaptation would be unwelcome to them, and had planned for months to shift the responsibility for defeat.[48] Many simply disliked change; more knew that change was necessary to hold Labour voters and attract new ones, but would not risk their popularity with the activists by discussing it openly. Gaitskell was dismayed at their 'political cowardice', saying half a dozen senior MPs had privately told Jay he was quite right but would not say so in public.* After Jay's experience, and having once decided not to give his own views immediately, the leader now had trouble 'getting people to speak up in the way he wanted them to on this issue'.[2b] That issue was the status of nationalisation, not in Labour's immediate policy but in the Party's conception of its own ultimate purpose.

Gaitskell never repudiated nationalisation where it could solve a real problem. 'One must argue for nationalisation instance by instance,' he told Hetherington privately, 'showing what had to be done, why it had to be done, how public ownership could help, and why it was necessary.'[2b] When the Conservatives denationalised Richard Thomas & Baldwin (the very successful publicly-owned steel concern in South Wales), Gaitskell denounced that doctrinaire decision as a 'squalid and disreputable' extension of an unjustified policy which had been bad for both the taxpayer and the economy.[49] A few months after this he called for public ownership of urban building land. But he wanted both to demonstrate that Labour reached such specific decisions on merits, not just for the sake of nationalising; and also to clarify its long-term aims.

In the shorter run he rejected no remedy as unpalatable, but many as either irrelevant or clearly unacceptable — for, as he told his old housemaster, to reduce the Opposition to chaos would help only the Conservatives.[50] He dismissed the Liberals as potential allies because he thought their voters would desert. He did not press for constitutional reforms within the Party, which would not influence the electorate and might have harmful side-effects. He defended the trade unions as an integral part of the Party, and trusted their leaders' judgment and responsibility. He envisaged no substantial revision of Labour policies, for he both believed in them, and knew that it would look like 'cynicism or opportunism' to jettison them because of the defeat.[51] But he thought it essential to improve the Party's image and modernise its appeal:

> I see no reason whatsoever [he said on the BBC] why we should have any doubts about the basic principles in which we believe. After all, one isn't in politics just for fun ... we still believe ... in equality and freedom at the same time, in equal opportunity, in a fair deal; in ... behaving decently and honourably to other nations. And these things are not temporary, not ephemeral, they're eternal things ... But how they should be attained, how they should be interpreted and expressed

* Characteristically Gaitskell, who thought Jay wrong, would not let his friends help him by revealing that publicly.[13e] [h]

to fit in with ... the approach of a modern generation, that always needs reappraisal, I think.[52]

The nationalisation question seemed to provide the opportunity.[53] The official election inquest reported that its unpopularity was due not to the steel proposal, but to 'general uncertainty as to the Party's intentions concerning nationalisation of other concerns. The Conservative claim that Labour would nationalise "by the backdoor" the "500 companies" [sic] was powerfully exploited at a local level.'[54a] [55] *Industry and Society* had talked imprecisely of measures to be taken against leading firms which 'failed the nation'. Its ambiguities had helped to win assent within the Party, since everyone could interpret it to his own taste; but now they permitted business and Conservative propaganda to exploit it. 'It wasn't iron and steel and road haulage, the specific pledges,' Gaitskell told Crossman at Prescote, 'but the general threat of the 600 firms which lost us votes this time'.[13b] Wilson said that was 'widely agreed';[56b] and Bevan thought so, too. Gaitskell knew that Bevan was critical of him on that point, but not how strongly.[57] Optimistically, he predicted:

> They would come to an agreement in the end – indeed they were not too far in disagreement even now. But Nye blamed him for the 'six hundred companies' and believed that had hurt Labour a lot. He blamed Gaitskell for having brought them up and thought that the fear that they would all be taken over in the end had been damaging.[2a]

In this context, Gaitskell fastened upon Clause Four, Section Four, of the Party constitution. Adopted in 1918 – before full employment, the welfare state, the growth of trade union power or widespread affluence – it proclaimed Labour's aim as

> To secure for the workers by hand or by brain the full fruits of their industry, and the most equitable distribution thereof that may be possible, upon the basis of the common ownership of the means of production, distribution and exchange, and the best obtainable system of popular administration and control of each industry and service.[58]

In principle, Gaitskell throughout his life thought of public ownership as not an end, but a means to the true Socialist objective of a just, egalitarian, classless society. In practice, he told a worried constituent in 1952: 'Some of my friends have also suggested that the clause you refer to is no longer appropriate, but for my part I do not think it is very important either way.'[59]* Just before becoming leader, he had referred to Clause Four which 'speaks

* In a conversation in 1950 or 1951 at Aidan Crawley's house, the host attacked Clause Four and thought Gaitskell rather agreed, but Douglas Jay and others defended it heatedly.[60]

of obtaining for the worker the full fruits of his labour on the basis of common ownership, the emphasis is really on equality'.[61] On his election six weeks later, commentators agreed he would emphasise the egalitarian element in Socialism, and Robert McKenzie suspected 'that he would dearly love to release the Labour party from the pledge' in Clause Four.[62a]

In 1956 Anthony Crosland published *The Future of Socialism*, emphasising *inter alia* the growing importance of managers as against owners. Gaitskell's PPS remembered his master often expressing serious doubts about the relevance of Clause Four.[63] But McKenzie tried in vain to get Gaitskell to repudiate it publicly: instead the leader told him: 'we do believe that public ownership, though we propose to do it gradually, nevertheless is necessary to achieve the ideals in which we believe.'[64] He did not change that view in 1959. The view he did change was the one he had put to his worried constituent seven years earlier: that nationalisation would be a long, slow process and so 'we can leave unanswered the question of what might be eventually left to the private sector'.[59] In the Labour Party of 1959, very few people envisaged nationalising the whole economy in their lifetime;* and now he wanted them to say so.

His decision astonished both friends and opponents, for Clause Four had played no part in the election.[66] Though it was (and is) on every Labour Party membership card, the Conservative *Speakers' Handbook* did not mention it; indeed it is said that Central Office, having no copy of Labour's constitution, had to go out and buy one after Blackpool.[67] But it did symbolise an approach to nationalisation (and even to politics generally) which had done great harm. Jim Griffiths, the retiring deputy leader, admired and disagreed with Gaitskell after their 'series of long talks' beforehand about Clause Four.

> Once he made up his mind there was no calculation of the consequences to himself ... Integrity, absolute integrity, this was the essential quality of Hugh Gaitskell's character ... He knew ... that Clause Four was an article of faith to me and my generation. When I reminded him of this he replied sternly: 'Maybe, but you know that we do not intend, any of us, to implement Clause Four fully, and I regard it as my duty to say so to the party and the country.' When he considered it was his duty to say or do something nothing could change him. The sharp edge of intellectual integrity would cut through all barriers.[68]

That verdict was more flattering morally than professionally. Gaitskell was

---

* Three years later a careful survey of CLP leaders found that fewer than half wanted Labour to move Left on 'nationalisation and national planning'; even among those who did, many no doubt still favoured a mixed economy.[65] That was in a new climate in which even Conservatives were calling for planning — in contrast to 1959.

a politician too, though a strikingly honest one, and before the inquest on the 1959 defeat he had felt no duty to decide about Clause Four or to share his conclusions with Party and country. When he did so, he presented them very cautiously: 'I do feel that it is necessary to remove what has undoubtedly been a great source of misrepresentation by our opponents and to show that ... our approach is essentially pragmatic and not doctrinaire. That is all that is at issue.'[69] But in reality Gaitskell sought more than a platitudinous negative with which no one disagreed. He thought the Party was confused between means and ends, and unclear about its real objectives:

> Gaitskell said it was important to state the basic aims of public ownership and of the Labour party in relation to the economy ... What kind of society did they want? ... How would they achieve it? These were the questions. They had never been properly defined of late and ... this should be done positively.[2a]

All his life he was an educator: a source of both weakness and strength. He spent far too long on precise drafting because he believed that people should say what they meant, even in politics, and would act more coherently if they knew why they were acting. The teacher and not the politician in him was passionate about getting the argument right, and insistent that his followers must tread the right road to the right destination – and for the right reasons. It would often have been far easier to cajole them into swallowing policies they did not understand and would not have approved if they had. Insisting on clarifying comfortable obscurities, and recognising unwelcome necessities, he created great and avoidable difficulties for himself. Many people saw it at the time as utter folly politically, even if admirable intellectually. But we now know that the astute management which buys politicians temporary tranquillity, and the deviousness with which they approach desirable objectives, may prove costly later when illusions can no longer be preserved and confidence is finally shattered.

Two experiences in 1959 thus transformed Gaitskell's attitude to party leadership: the triumphant campaign, establishing him at last as a popular leader appealing to the Party and people; and then the ghastly disappointment when sudden recognition and apparent success turned overnight into humiliating defeat. So far he had kept to Attlee's familiar role of tactfully balancing conflicting forces in the Party; now he feared that that would mean presiding comfortably over its inexorable decline. His personal reception convinced him that he could safely break out of that role to offer advice in good faith to serve the Party and its cause.

So believing, he made several misjudgments. He let his friends open the debate with their own individualistic, tactless, unco-ordinated – and counter-productive – initiatives. He did not foresee the instant revival of factional hostilities; or the hatred of his old enemies, concealed while he seemed about to become Prime Minister; or his opponents' skill in using the blunders of his allies to undermine confidence in himself. Above all he misjudged completely in hoping that a debate on Labour's vague long-term aspirations would minimise conflict. It was an over-rational view, as he quickly discovered.

> He said the majority of members had little capacity for real thinking. To them Nationalisation was an emotional issue. This had proved to be the case even more than he had expected. There was depressingly little readiness to think hard about ends and means. The discussion must be got on to that basis. It was not going that way now.[2b]

A little later he confessed publicly that he had not foreseen the reaction — and privately that if he had, he would never have raised the issue.[70] For that reaction was strongest in the trade union centre of the Party, so long the foundation of Gaitskell's political strength. The objective of public ownership was written into many union rule-books, and trade unionists, just because their daily activities concentrated their attention on hard practical realities, cherished the distant vision of a bright Socialist horizon. Gaitskell lost the Clause Four battle, and endangered his leadership, by driving most of the trade union centre for the first time into the arms of the Left.

It was a strange mistake. He had himself furiously rejected the very idea of changing the Party's name, with all its emotional links to the romantic attachments and moral commitments of his own youth. That response of his should have made him sensitive and sympathetic to the emotional freight carried by the concept of public ownership.

> Idols ... even when they are so quiescent as to seem almost lifeless, have a capacity for becoming suddenly and violently inflamed ... No politician can hope to prosper unless he has a weather-sense that warns him in good time what to expect ... [for] an idol whose worshippers have taken alarm, may threaten him with disaster.[71]

Gaitskell read that passage later, and regretted not having done so in time.[38]

iii   Blackpool: 'The Biggest Belly-ache'

Gaitskell often expected more from trade union leaders than they could deliver.[72a b] But over Clause Four in 1959 he was warned at the start — not only by leaders who had always supported him against the Left without having much affection for him, but also by staunch friends:[73] Sam Watson on the NEC, and Bill Webber (of the Railway Clerks) on the General Council, Griffiths and others among the trade union group of MPs, Charlie Pannell of the Engineers — a Leeds neighbour and loyal ally who found

Gaitskell 'as obstinate as only Hugh knew how'.[1] In the first back-bench speech in the PLP debate, Bill Blyton—a Durham miner who had supported Gaitskell in 1955, and denounced the 'Hampstead set' in 1957—told Douglas Jay to go and join the Liberal Party.[13a]

Yet the proposal to revise Clause Four was not concocted by the 'Hampstead set'. Jay had vigorously defended the clause in the past, had ignored it in his *Forward* article, and thought Gaitskell's Conference speech unwise.[11a] Crosland consistently advised against it.[74] Jenkins was abroad; he too had attacked nationalisation policies without mentioning the clause, and was gently ironical later about 'this philosopher's stone' discovered in his absence.[7f] Gordon Walker approved—but only when he saw the leader's draft speech a week before Conference.[75] When Gaitskell's press adviser said he thought it pointless to have a row over an anachronism, he found that Dora quite agreed.[76]

Gaitskell had taken very risky solitary decisions in the past, as over the 1951 Budget or the Stalybridge speech. This time, while listening to others he was already eyeing his target;[63] perhaps even before October, for Dalton wrote to him after Blackpool: 'you'll get the constitution revised sooner than I thought likely, when we first spoke of it, before, and then just after, the election.'[37b] That is not to say that his listening was hypocritical. For he modified his ideas of constitutional reform; he repudiated several unacceptable proposals; he defied no chorus of public support for Clause Four (since no one mentioned it); and if he hoped for constructive suggestions to arrest the Party's decline, he listened in vain. But, once he made up his mind, he would be deterred by neither pressures nor advice. To critics of Jay's article, he would invoke courage as a rare and precious political virtue—tactlessly citing his own Stalybridge speech as an example.[77]

Yet this time his behaviour was different. At Stalybridge he was a prominent front-bencher trying to fight a trend he thought disastrous; now he was leader, trying to persuade his followers. He told Alastair Hetherington that

at Blackpool he would have a three-fold task—the parts of which were incompatible:
1. To guide thinking on the right lines.
2. To keep the party together.
3. To cheer it up.[2b]

At Stalybridge he had consulted no one before blasting off. But at Blackpool his tone was conciliatory, and he had talked fairly widely in advance. At least once he tried out the idea on potential sympathisers in a provincial Labour Party.[78] He discussed it with friends like Crosland, Gordon Walker, Jay, Pannell and John Murray[79]—yet went ahead though four of them disapproved.

His old patron may have had some influence. Dalton, once an ardent nationaliser, was now a strong revisionist and happily sent material for Gaitskell's speech.* No election, wrote Dalton, had ever been fought plainly on Clause Four.** He advised Gaitskell to stress 'fair play for public enterprise' at Conference, against Tory doctrinaire prejudice, and to insist that no new industry would be nationalised unless its workers agreed:

> You liked this point this morning. It will protect you against excursions into steel, I.C.I., etc. But don't make this implication too clear. Put it over as a platitude in Democratic Socialist procedure, illustrating brotherly love between industrial and political wings.[42a]

Gaitskell's words at Conference showed little trace of Dalton's advice.

One very important colleague saw the speech beforehand: Aneurin Bevan.[82] Gaitskell had accepted Crossman's view that Bevan must have a veto on proposed changes. He agreed again when Pannell on the Thursday before Conference urged him to show Bevan the speech.[83] Gaitskell told Pannell later that Bevan had said he 'could not fault it in any way'.[82] John Harris recalled that

> he showed it to Nye the night before and Nye came into Hugh's bedroom while I was there, clutching the paper. He said 'that's all right' or words to that effect ... Maybe he agreed on that point, maybe he thought: 'he's going to say it anyway and it doesn't matter much'.[25]

Harris then showed it to Douglas Jay, who said it would cause trouble, and was told: 'But we've shown it to Nye and he didn't raise a single word of objection.'[11a]

Bevan's reaction was not quite as surprising as it seems. Years earlier in 1952, when to Gaitskell Clause Four was still unimportant, Bevan had explicitly rejected a wholly publicly-owned economy:

> It is clear to the serious student of modern politics that a mixed economy is what most people of the West would prefer. The victory of Socialism need not be universal to be decisive. I have no patience with those Socialists, so-called, who in practice would socialise nothing, whilst in theory they threaten the whole of private property. They are purists and therefore barren. It is neither prudent, nor does it accord with our conception of the future, that all forms of private property should live under perpetual threat.[84]

* He pointed out that Arthur Henderson, whose draft of the 1918 constitution included the clause, said nine years later that the crucial phrase needed reconsideration since it dated from 1892.[80]

** The space devoted to nationalisation was below 5 per cent in *Keeping Left*, the future Bevanites' 1950 pamphlet, and in every post-war manifesto but one (to 1962); and was above 10 per cent only in *Challenge to Britain* in 1953.[81]

That was precisely the message that Gaitskell intended by his Clause Four speech. But it was imprudent of him to rely on Bevan maintaining that view in 1959.

On Saturday morning, 28 November 1959, the leader rose in the Winter Gardens at Blackpool to address his followers in most unfavourable circumstances. The astonishing prestige which had suddenly flowed to him during the election campaign, reaching high tide at the moment of defeat, had ebbed in the intervening seven weeks. Feeling Conference to be the proper audience for his analysis of the defeat and the remedies, he had arranged no favourable build-up; while the unofficial discussions in the Party had done only harm. With charges of treachery so freely hurled about, many colleagues escaped criticism by prudent silence. A few loyal friends spoke out without guidance, often maladroitly, arousing resentment against the intellectuals. Recording that fact three days before Conference opened, Crossman added that

> the whole leadership of the Party is now stinking with intrigue and suspicion, since everybody knows that Bevan is now manoeuvring against Gaitskell and that Harold Wilson, who doesn't forgive easily, is going to take his vengeance for Gaitskell's vague plot to oust him from the Shadow Chancellorship.[13d]

In this sour mood, Gaitskell's decision to have no agreed lead from the platform was to prove a further handicap.[13f] He had told Hetherington that 'it would be an abnegation of democratic evolution of policy if he laid down the line himself at the outset'.[2b] He assumed that Conference could candidly examine where the Party had gone wrong before and in the election, acting as a discussion forum with Executive members putting their individual views. It was a trustful assumption.

In 'the most telling chairman's address ever delivered at a Party Conference', as Michael Foot called it,[6d] Barbara Castle set the tone with a frontal attack on the 'commercialised society' and the 'windfall state', eloquently proclaiming the indispensability of all Labour's traditional attitudes, especially on public ownership.[85a] Opening the debate after lunch, Gaitskell said there was no Executive view: 'this afternoon I speak for myself alone'.[85b] He had not seen the chairman's speech, nor she his (not even like Bevan at the last minute). Crossman noted that the three personal statements from the platform were

> deliberately uncorrelated and the first two highly competitive ... What was really fantastic was staging a conference without central direction or leadership and there's a very strong feeling in the Executive that this must never be allowed to happen again.[13f i]

* * *

Gaitskell maintained that an almost unprecedented third defeat, despite a better programme, better campaign, and better publicity and organisation, showed that 'more fundamental influences' were keeping the pendulum from swinging and checking the advance which Labour had always assumed to be inexorable. Great social changes had brought higher living standards and a welfare state. There were fewer and fewer unskilled workers, thanks to technological change.* Fear of unemployment declined now that governments were expected to avert future depressions by influencing the economy.[87] These changes did not justify the defeatism which preached permanent opposition, and would mean for Labour 'decay and decrepitude. The British people ... do not take kindly, in politics or war, to those who have given up the will to battle'. Three more 'rather desperate remedies' – the Lib-Lab pact, the change of name, the breach with the unions – should go 'out of the window right away'. But Labour must no longer count on old eroding loyalties. It must recognise the changes, continue to defend the underdog, and appeal to youthful idealism over 'Colonial freedom, the protection of the individual against ham-handed and arrogant bureaucracy, resistance to [the] squalid commercialism ...' It must seek to attract women and white-collar workers, and above all try 'to broaden our base, to be in touch always with ordinary people, to avoid becoming small cliques of isolated doctrine-ridden fanatics, out of touch with the main stream of social life in our time'. He spoke wistfully of unity: 'Is it a forlorn hope ... ?'

At last he turned to nationalisation, saying that most people agreed that it had lost votes; first, because some nationalised industries were unpopular, often on irrelevant grounds; secondly owing to fears that Labour meant 'to take over everything indiscriminately'. He presented his own view as a middle way, saying the existing boundary between the public and private sectors could not be permanent:

> We may not be far from the frontier of this kind of giant State monopoly. We may be more concerned in the future with ... public competitive enterprises, State factories in development areas, a greater share of the total trading going to the Co-operative movement. I would love to see that happen ... I cannot agree that we have reached the frontier of public ownership as a whole.
> At the same time I disagree equally with the other extreme view that

---

* A famous survey of affluent workers showed that most still voted Labour – but did not notice that support for Labour dropped by 4 per cent in their sample between 1955 and 1963–4: precisely when, in the rest of the electorate, Labour was gaining heavily.[86]

public ownership is the be all and end all, the ultimate first principle and aim of socialism ... [which is] a complete confusion about the fundamental meaning of socialism and, in particular, a misunderstanding about ends and means.

He set out again seven basic principles: concern for the worst-off; 'social justice, an equitable distribution of wealth and income'; a classless society without snobbery and privilege; equality of all races and peoples; belief in human relations 'based not on ruthless self-regarding rivalry but on fellowship and cooperation'; precedence for public over private interest; freedom and democratic self-government. Public ownership was 'not itself the ultimate objective; it is only a means to achieving the objective'. But it was necessary for a better distribution of wealth; for controlling 'the commanding heights of the economy' in order to plan; and for ensuring accountability to the people.

> I conclude that we should make two things clear to the country. First, that we have no intention of abandoning public ownership and accepting for all time the present frontiers of the public sector. Secondly, that we regard public ownership not as an end in itself but as a means – and not necessarily the only or the most important one to certain ends – such as full employment, greater equality and higher productivity. We do not aim to nationalise every private firm or to create an endless series of State monopolies. While we shall certainly wish to extend social ownership, in particular directions, as circumstances warrant, our goal is not 100% State ownership. Our goal is a society in which Socialist ideals are realised. Our job is to move towards this as fast as we can. The pace at which we can go depends on how quickly we can persuade our fellow citizens to back us. They will only do this if we pay proper attention to the kind of people they are and the kind of things they want.

The Party constitution set out Labour's fundamental aims, but it was forty years old and omitted 'colonial freedom, race relations, disarmament, full employment or planning'.[88] Only Clause Four specified domestic objectives and, 'standing as it does on its own', it was obviously inadequate. It confused ends and means, ignored other aims, and

> lays us open to continual misrepresentation ... It implies that we propose to nationalise everything, but do we? Everything? – the whole of light industry, the whole of agriculture, all the shops – every little pub and garage? Of course not. We have long ago come to accept ... a mixed economy ... [the] view ... of 90 per cent of the Labour Party – had we not better say so instead of going out of our way to court misrepresentation?[89]

Morgan Phillips foresaw bad trouble ahead when, for the first time in his experience, the leader here faced hostile interruptions.[72a] Gaitskell replied sharply that an uncontroversial, bromide-laden speech would have brought cheers:

> But I do not conceive that to be my duty today. I would rather forego the cheers now in the hope that we shall get more votes later on. I do not want deliberately to advise a course of action which could only involve me in leading the Party to another electoral defeat and I will not do so.

It was 'one of his few moments of passion'.[16c] The enthusiastic Labour workers in the election campaign, he insisted, 'wanted above all that we should win ... so that we could carry out the programme in which both we and they believe ... a supreme challenge ... to keep up the spirit of attack ... again and again and again, until we win.'[85c]

Many of his platform colleagues, not all of them left-wingers, conspicuously declined to join in the applause.[90] The friendliest report of all said that afterwards 'The dominant mood was one of cautious, if sometimes reluctant, agreement ... the best that Mr. Gaitskell could have hoped for.'[16c] That was not the tone of the floor speakers, the very first of whom praised doctrinaire politics, condemned the mixed economy as 'tripe', and pretended that Frank Allaun and Konni Zilliacus (both MPs from Lancashire, where unemployment was heavy) had increased their majorities because they were left-wingers.[85d] Then the chairman, blinded by the television lights, 'peered theatrically into the murk and cried "Michael!" whereupon Mr. Foot emerged coincidentally from the blackest and most invisible quarter'.[46b] Foot had just lost again at Devonport, suffering the third worst swing in the nation. He attacked Gaitskell for promoting disunity and enunciating principles to which Tories could subscribe.* He said the PLP had no will to battle; demanded sharper cleavages with the Tories; and called on the Party to question its leadership, and either follow the German Social Democrats who had just formally abandoned Marxism, or else seek victory by denouncing the 'evil and disgraceful and rotten society'.[91]

The ovation he received began 'an unbridled personal vendetta from the Left ... For several hours of acute tension nobody would have given much for Mr. Gaitskell's chances of survival.'[56a] A speaker from Tottenham even charged that the leadership 'did not come out forcefully in opposition to Suez until the General Election', and the candidate for Ormskirk preferred preaching Socialism in the wilderness to forming a government in the next quarter-century. On Sunday morning Frank Cousins defended

* Very few Tories did, then or since.

Clause Four, and called for mobilisation of the 'five or six million people who are Socialists in embryo waiting for us to go out and harness them to the power machine we want to drive'.[85f]

Then came a great change. First, the NEC election results were announced, and Ian Mikardo had lost his seat. Then Benn Levy was angrily booed from the rostrum for saying that Gaitskell seemed to have been addressing the conference of a different Party.[16c] Previous speakers had not, after all, spoken for the rank and file. Charlie Pannell, who came next, denounced them for making conference 'the biggest belly-ache I have ever come across'. He praised 'the best leadership I have ever fought under in my life', 'the best policy I have ever fought with in my life', and a PLP which had sometimes, as at Suez, been 'a magnificent opposition'.[85g] Denis Healey counter-attacked those who were content to

> luxuriate complacently in moral righteousness in Opposition ... who is going to pay the price for their complacency? ... In Britain it is the unemployed and the old-age pensioners ... You will have your T.V. set, your motor car and your summer holidays on the Continent and still keep your Socialist soul intact. The people who pay the price for your sense of moral satisfaction are the Africans.[85h]

Shirley Williams followed with a warning against the rancour which was a gift to the Conservatives, and against trying to split Bevan from Gaitskell.[85h] Ted Hill, the left-wing secretary of the Boilermakers, gave the leadership an amiable pat on the back. Crossman, noting the change of mood, attributed it to 'a strong tide of anti-split emotion' rather than support for Gaitskell's views.[13f] So, in the afternoon, Bevan wound up the debate in a new and better atmosphere.

iv   *Aneurin's Mantle*

Bevan's mood had changed too. Just before the 1959 Conference, his irritation with Gaitskell was well known;[13d] and though he had not objected on seeing the leader's speech on the Friday night, he was angry on hearing it on the Saturday afternoon. His journalist confidant Geoffrey Goodman told Harris so that evening. Harris was surprised, as Bevan had seen it in advance, but Goodman replied: 'He must have misunderstood or misinterpreted — he's absolutely livid.'[92] Bevan dined that night with Anthony Greenwood: 'He was still wondering whether to blow the whole thing wide open ... and he was not in much of a mood to be talked out of it.'[93] The irreconcilables were active again:

> Mr Bevan's own attitude was in doubt right up to the last minute. He was under extreme pressure from some of his old Bevanite friends to

54 James Cameron, Ritchie Calder, Michael Foot, Emrys Hughes and Sydney Silverman lead the CND's Aldermaston March

55 'Fight and fight again'. Gaitskell strongly opposes nuclear disarmament

56 In Glasgow, May 1961

57 With Glasgow schoolchildren, May 1961

go all out for a quick kill, and they tried to press the dagger into his hand. Mr Bevan could have had the leadership for the asking ... Messrs Wilson and Callaghan had a greater influence on Mr Bevan's line at Blackpool than Messrs Driberg and Mikardo.[56a]

Bevan decided against the latter at the last minute;[94] and told Gaitskell so.

Gaitskell said there was never any likelihood of Bevan leading a revolt at Blackpool or after. Gaitskell knew at Blackpool what Bevan was going to say in his winding-up speech: and he knew that Bevan couldn't bring himself publicly to follow all the Gaitskell line.[2c]

Bevan's speech was superb oratory, contributing nothing to Labour's long-term political education but much to preventing an immediate explosion. He talked of variety within unity, ingenuously pointing out that both the leader and the chairman had quoted his own phrase about the commanding heights of the economy: 'If Euclid's deduction is correct they are both equal to me and therefore must be equal to each other.' Skilfully he combined Foot's rhetoric with Gaitskell's realism:

The so-called affluent society is an ugly society ... in which priorities have gone all wrong ... but ... only by the possession of power can you get the priorities correct.

Therefore I agree with Barbara, I agree with Hugh and I agree with myself ... I am a Socialist: I believe in public ownership. But I agreed with Hugh Gaitskell yesterday ... I do not believe that public ownership should reach down into every piece of economic activity, because that would be asking for a monolithic society ... What I do insist upon is ... a planned economy.[85l]

Yet Bevan's only published comment on Blackpool struck a different note not easy to reconcile with his 1952 support for the mixed economy:

[I]f the Labour Party were to abandon its main thesis of public ownership it would not differ in any important respect from the Tory Party ... the overwhelming majority of the Labour Party will not acquiesce in the jettisoning of the concept of progressive public ownership.[6f]

Such ambivalence was not new to Bevan. His generalisations contained no commitments, and different observers attributed to him quite different intentions.

At Blackpool his friendly tones persuaded many people that Gaitskell had 'escaped total eclipse only by the oratorical brilliance of Mr. Bevan'.[56a] Gaitskell did not think so: had there been a vote, he was confident he would have won easily.[95] But he warned the absent but enthusiastic Dalton not to be too optimistic: 'it will be a rough crossing and we have only just begun it.'[3b] He felt the inevitable argument was best got out of the way well

T

before the next election;[96] and hopefully believed that Bevan would be on the same side of it, and that together they would have persuaded Conference to revise Clause Four.[2d] There were limits, he knew, to the help he could expect from Bevan; but also, he thought, to the trouble he had to fear. Bevan would not bid for the leadership, Gaitskell told Hetherington, recalling his split with the unilateralists since,

> the Brighton speech ... was a terrible experience for him. He can't now bring himself to go wholly against the left ... I said I thought Bevan was 'a spent force'. Gaitskell said no ... he was indolent. He couldn't bring himself to think seriously ... now about winning an election five years hence ...
>
> Bevan knew that if he [Gaitskell] had been dislodged he would have stayed on the National Executive ... and would have fought hard there. He would have made Bevan's life exceedingly uncomfortable. Gaitskell implied, indeed, that he had consulted with Morgan Phillips on this and was ready to put up a very big battle and that Bevan knew this.[97]

Others thought differently. At Blackpool, Bevan congratulated Foot;[6a] in the train back to London and afterwards, he told several people that he would overthrow Gaitskell and take over the leadership.[98a b] He fiercely denounced Gaitskell and Gaitskellism at a *Tribune* board meeting at the Café Royal, warning of 'great upheavals' coming in the Party.[6h] Harold Wilson was one who worked to dissuade Bevan from his threat of resigning from the Shadow Cabinet and fighting Gaitskell in the country;[98a] but does not believe he ever meant it.[33a b] Crossman concluded after long discussions that Bevan's real aim was to use his strengthened position to insist on greater influence within the leadership, rather than to seize it for himself:

> Aneurin Bevan ... now thinks at least that he won't repeat his sloppy behaviour during our discussion of the non-nuclear club. Never again will he let Hugh get away with insisting on his personal prejudices. This is felt even more strongly by Harold Wilson ... [who at Blackpool] expressed the bitterest criticism of Gaitskell's performance, though he never doubted that Nye would rescue him.[13f]

Years later, Michael Foot too became convinced that Bevan would have continued the partnership with Gaitskell.[99]

Had he lived, Bevan must have benefited from Gaitskell's difficulties.[100a b] It need not follow at all that he approved Gaitskell's speech deliberately in order to lure the Party leader into an exposed position. It is much more likely that Bevan, aggrieved at being consulted far too late to have any real say, felt that Gaitskell should lie in the bed he had made.[101] For himself, he would not (consciously) decide his course till he had to. He could not have overthrown Gaitskell without conciliating the unilateralists, and eating all his words since Brighton. That choice never confronted him, for in December 1959 he had an operation for cancer, and he died in July.

For just ten years his fortunes had been intertwined with Gaitskell's. Before 1950 they had been friendly though not intimate, with the younger man expecting his senior in time to accede to the leadership and the Premiership. Then they became bitterly antagonistic rivals over government policy, and Cabinet power, and the Party's development. To most people Bevan, with his glittering gifts of oratory to which Gaitskell could not aspire, with his roots in the Welsh mining valleys and his devoted following in the local Parties, seemed Labour's natural leader. Yet he dissipated his assets as though dominated by a death-wish. To some people the same affliction, over Clause Four and once or twice afterwards, seemed to grip Gaitskell too. For both men were moved by passionate emotion — in Bevan instantly visible, in Gaitskell seething deep beneath layers of Wykehamist schooling. So both sometimes chose bad ground to embark on great battles, and were then proudly determined not to retreat or compromise.

In utterly different ways both cared deeply for the Party they led and the country they hoped to lead. Their talents were completely contrasting, and splendidly complementary. Gaitskell thought through his positions with rigorous intellectual honesty, and then clung to them too inflexibly. Bevan derived his from intuition rather than reasoning, inhaling his inspiration from communion with the emotions of great meetings.[6i] (He was understandably jealous that the educational system had given his rival, whose mind he felt inferior to his own, a vastly better training.)[93] His Celtic fire excited mass audiences as Gaitskell's carefully argued speeches never yet had, though from 1959 onwards Gaitskell did develop a new force and passion. Their publics differed as well as their styles, for Bevan responded to the Party enthusiasts, Gaitskell to the ordinary Labour voters — and to the others whose confidence had yet to be won. He lacked Bevan's quickness and flexibility in parliamentary debate, and there too displayed real emotional force only in his last years.

Their reconciliation did not come easily in 1957. With their different temperaments, Gaitskell appreciated Bevan's qualities more than Bevan did his; and it was naturally harder for the loser to accept that the outcome was final. Bevan's co-operation was always on terms, and his impeccable public loyalty always concealed private reservations: not surprisingly, for an Opposition leader who has never led a government is always on trial until he wins a general election. It does not follow that the two men would have found it hard to work together in office. For the victory transforms the status and prestige of the new Prime Minister; it enhances his political power and assures his security; it mobilises all the loyal instincts of the Party behind its leaders; and it gives those leaders a common interest, since their reputations depend on the government's success.

Their past records do not suggest exceptional strains threatening their co-operation. Gaitskell as Prime Minister would have been much more radical and acceptable to the Party faithful than his detractors believed; he might occasionally have flouted their feelings, but Bevan would have restrained him from doing so too much. Both in office and as Shadow Foreign Secretary, Bevan had shown an acute sense of practical possibilities. Making out his abortive Cabinet list on the Sunday night before the 1959 election, Gaitskell gave a clue to their likely relationship when he told John Harris that a Prime Minister should not try to be his own Foreign Secretary. Bevan's policy preferences would have been closer to Gaitskell's than his admirers supposed, and his ability to win Party consent to them far greater than Gaitskell's without him. It was a sad deprivation for the Labour Party and the British people to lose the leadership of either man in facing the problems of the 1960s. To lose both was a major disaster.

v 'A Torment of Misrepresentation'

Whatever Bevan might have done, he helped Gaitskell by his last Conference speech. But though Gaitskell might have won on a vote, he emerged from Blackpool badly battered and his enemies on the Left at once began planning his downfall.[100b c] Most observers were astonished by the sudden collapse of his authority in late 1959, and even more by the issue on which he had risked it: for as *The Economist* argued in advance, failure in that struggle would endanger his position in the Party while success would do nothing to strengthen it.[102] His Conservative opponents were first puzzled, later mocking; Iain Macleod said Labour had 'provided us with a mine so inexhaustible but so rich that every Tory candidate can dig with profit in it for ever. I do not understand why they should load us with such golden gifts.'[103] Attlee thought the affair pointless, like attacking the 39 Articles (one of many religious references during this controversy).[104] So did George Brown.[105a] Denis Healey spoke courageously at Blackpool, yet thought the proposal Gaitskell's 'ghastliest mistake'.[106] Strachey (who was now a close friend) and Freeman (who was not) came formally to say that the ground was ill-chosen; Gaitskell was quite unmoved.[107]

Quite apart from the strategy, the leadership's tactics remained—in Jenkins's word—'appalling'.[108] Before Conference, Gaitskell had shown his respect for Labour's traditional policy-making procedures and his anxiety for Conference to decide, by neither giving a personal lead nor

SOMEONE ISN'T USING SOCIALISM

arranging for an Executive one. His reward was to see his critics exploit his restraint, attacking him vicariously through his friends, and questioning his motives and principles. He was so shocked by the bitterness — especially after his triumphant reception in the election – that he wondered if he could remain, or should ever have begun, in politics.[109]

The hostility had political as well as personal consequences. After Blackpool prudent colleagues, who privately agreed with him, would not risk similar vilification by speaking their minds; loyal friends feared they might again do him more harm than good; bitter opponents thought the time had come to strike. Yet Gaitskell chose that difficult moment for a long-deferred and desperately needed holiday abroad.

Like his other vacations, it was strenuous. On Monday 28 December 1959, 'Mr Thornton' flew to Toronto to appear on Canadian television. He spent four days in New York, then on 8 January flew on to the West Indies, seeing personal friends like the Flemings and the Walstons, attending a Cabinet meeting in Jamaica and visiting an industrial estate and local political leaders. He was to have rested completely with the Walstons off St Lucia, then visited the French West Indies and returned via Paris; but Bevan's illness brought him back early.[110] He and Dora went at once to the hospital, but they were not able to see the sick man.

During his absence the critics had kept up their campaign which, as Ian Mikardo explicitly said, was directed not at Gaitskell's actual proposal, but at the imaginary conspiracy which they sniffed behind it:

> If these members thought that the only purpose of this revision was to make it clear that we're not proposing to nationalise right down to the last street corner shop or the last boot-black, then nobody would be against it. As it is ... [they] see it as a first step towards the acceptance of a public sector which is very little different from the present one.[111]

Equally explicitly, Mikardo denounced efforts to fudge differences with a formula, as in *Industry and Society*: 'We have not suffered from the clash of opinion but from blanketing the clash of opinion under forms of words which each side could interpret to mean what it wanted them to mean.' It was the Left who now hoped to profit politically by dispelling ambiguities, so that Mikardo, hoping that the National Executive would propose no change in Clause Four, appealed 'that if they do propose an amendment it shall be in absolutely unshaded and unclouded terms, meaning one thing to all men'.[112a]

At the same moment a Conservative paper recalled 'the instinct of the Labour party ... to compromise rather than split. There is no one more skilled in the art of compromise than Mr. Gaitskell'.[62b] It was precisely that reputation which had suddenly become a liability, arousing unjustified suspicions not confined to nationalisation. Knowing it would be damaging to change policies immediately after an election defeat, he had not done so – but was charged with opportunism as if he had. Vicky caricatured him as a doorstep pollster asking a bewildered housewife, 'Which party would you like Labour to resemble?', and as the manager of 'Labour Stores' with notices in the window: 'Gigantic sell out', 'Socialist principles practically given away'. Challenged on this very point on TV just after Blackpool, he made himself unmistakably clear.

> [T]o try and clear it up, once and for all, if you were to say to me ' ... really we've got to accept the colour bar, because you'll never get into power if you don't' I should say, well, in not very polite language 'Go to hell ... that's absolutely against my principles'. If you were to say to me 'Don't bother about the old people ... you'll never get into power again unless you concentrate on the majority who are well off', I should say again 'It's no good talking like that to me'. But if you say to me 'I think that your argument for nationalising the machine tool industry ... is rather weak', I would say 'Well I'll discuss that with you' ...
>
> Kee: There are some principles (Yes) which you would stick to however many votes they were going to lose?

Gaitskell: Most certainly ... but don't misunderstand me, I do think ... public ownership, in various forms ... is necessary to achieve the other things that we want.[113]

The charges of opportunism were part of what *The Times* called 'a torment of misrepresentation by those who have ... [fought] him since at least 1951'.[40c] All Gaitskell's old enemies seized their chance to join in. Michael Foot produced his untruth about the cancelled Russian visit, and said everywhere that Gaitskell should not remain as leader unless he supported further nationalisation.[114] Shinwell, pursuing an old feud, added vocal support.[115] Bitter personal attacks were resumed, in 'a deliberate campaign to isolate Mr. Gaitskell ... Then we have Mr. Mikardo ... sneering about the "Crosland-Jay branch of the Bow Group". The pattern is clear. The Left feels it is now strong enough to win.'[116] At the annual conference of VFS, Mikardo condemned the leader as spokesman for 'a small and esoteric group rather than ... the party as a whole'.[62c]

When Gaitskell arrived back in Britain, his friends were alarmed. Hugh Dalton exploded:

Is this Labour Party worth leading? Are its diseases curable? This endless public quarrelling? This wide-open suicide club? This idiot loyalty to an undigested phrase! This built-in personal bitterness by a faction; these built-in sneers; this massive moral cowardice; these pseudo-diplomatic trimmers' silences.[37c]

Douglas Jay wrote saying that Michael Foot was 'capable of anything — obviously egged on by Beaverbrook'; hoping that a recovered Bevan might manage to restrain him; but warning that on Clause Four many friendly or uncommitted MPs could not be counted on, for instance James Callaghan, Anthony Greenwood and Fred Mulley.[117] A few unknown young politicians took the risk of speaking out. A new trade union MP, Richard Marsh, challenged the Left to have the courage of their convictions: anyone was entitled to seek a new leader, but until someone did Gaitskell was equally entitled to 'undivided support'; his critics should either give it, put up a rival, or get out.[62b] Fifteen defeated candidates under forty (including six who became Ministers under Wilson) offered Gaitskell public backing.[118] But more senior — and normally voluble — figures offered only 'calculated public silences';[40c] for half the Shadow Cabinet thought changing Clause Four either wrong or inexpedient.[119] At length Crossman urged Gaitskell to abandon a proposal that would lead only to a woolly compromise after eighteen bitter months disputing 'semantic abstractions'.[120] Harold Wilson concurred. Just after Blackpool he had made a personal statement to the PLP, indignantly denying press reports that he was leading a movement against Gaitskell, and he had repeated his denials to Crossman in terms 'which would fully justify anyone who overheard it concluding that he was leading a campaign'.[121] Two months later Crossman reported him 'pouring out his venom against Gaitskell and not concealing his desire to get rid of him'.[122] In public he was more cautious, as the press remarked. 'Mr. Wilson will not deny that his speech was most carefully calculated and timed ... like the crafty political general he is, he left himself ample lines of retreat.'[123] He deplored the prospect of a long argument about 'theology', saying that the Party could easily be united on specific nationalisation proposals which could be produced in ten minutes. But the leader was unconvinced.

> Gaitskell said that Wilson wanted to do things the wrong way round ... To change the policy now would be both a criticism of the lines on which the last election was fought — in itself damaging to Labour — and would try to tie Labour down in detail on matters which events in the next two or three years ought to affect. It would be much better to re-state a general aim now, and to leave detailed policy until they saw how the economy progressed.[2e]

In less than four months the Labour Party had thus moved from the unity and fervour of the general election into the worst mood of bitterness and suspicion since the war. But Gaitskell was a very stubborn man. On his return to England he had meant to put the issue immediately to the National Executive, but postponed doing so — partly because of Bevan's illness, but also because he might have lost.[124] But though Hetherington found him 'grim and dispirited', he was sure 'there could be no going back', since that 'would give a deplorable public impression' — whether of 'being run by the all out nationalisers or of funking a decision because of disagreement within the party'.[2e g] As he wrote to a friend on his return:

> the going is rough — very rough inside the Party ... I'm depressed at the whole dreary prospect ahead ... It's really been horrible the last fortnight — the most depressed for a long time and I have never been nearer to giving it all up in despair, unhappiness and lack of self-confidence.

But he still thought he would have been wrong to 'have done an Attlee & just doodled'. Anyway, 'it's too late now for regrets. The fight is on and I must see it through.'

vi   *The 'New Testament'*

In a major speech to 600 people at Nottingham on 13 February 1960 (largely written by Crosland), Gaitskell repeated that Clause Four was too narrow, in omitting many basic aims; too broad, in hinting at nationalising everything; and unsatisfactory, in not distinguishing public ownership from its least popular form, 'the huge State monopoly'.* He specifically commended co-operative ownership, a bid for support in that quarter for the new statement.[125] Once again he denied that he was against extending public ownership:

> I said precisely the opposite of this at Blackpool ... To me it is absurd to think ... that we can achieve the degree of equality we want without an extension of public ownership ... [or] overcome the present crisis in town and country planning without more public enterprise ... [in] the ownership of urban land ... [or] solve our housing problem without more municipal ownership, or create an adequate counter-weight to big business without an extension of cooperative ownership.
>
> Above all ... to plan successfully for full employment, more investment and higher productivity, we shall need to extend the public sector.

Harm was done not by specific proposals but by the 'vague threat to all private property'.

He hit out at all his enemies, beginning with

> the small professional anti-leadership group—the self-appointed opposition to those elected in the party to a responsible position ... sublimely indifferent to the views of the electorate ... little concerned with winning power ... looking back all the time ... more and more remote from ordinary people.

Crossman, Wilson and the silent front-benchers were not spared. The constitution, he said, should not be 'a collection of meaningless phrases ... mere theology'; and he was puzzled by talk of revising a policy which everyone had so recently approved, for that 'really would be cynical surrender for the sake of electoral considerations'.[126] The people who had stirred up all the internal controversies were now charging him with dividing the Party; those who said there should be no talk of change until everyone already agreed on it were preaching false unity and permanent stagnation; and those who knew the constitution was out of date, but feared to say so publicly, were 'neither very honest nor very sincere. It is not the kind of leadership that I should want to give.' It was extraordinary to suggest that only public ownership divided Socialists from Tories; natural to want to examine the new statement of aims before altering the old one; but absurd to reject any change without knowing what the new statement would say.[40c]

The audience was actively favourable; and now Labour's heavy guns at last began firing on Gaitskell's side. A dozen leading spokesmen in Lanca-

---

* Clause Four leaves the specific form open, and the Left justly claimed to have criticised huge state monopolies while Gaitskell was still defending them.[11b]

shire pledged support, including three members of the TUC General Council, the chairman of the Co-operative Party, the leader of Liverpool Council, and his formidable wife Bessie Braddock MP.[62d] Trade union MPs like Roy Mason and Charlie Pannell joined middle-class colleagues like Eric Fletcher.[62e] As most front-benchers (except Sir Frank Soskice and Hilary Marquand) continued to hold their peace, an unknown back-bencher condemned them for 'looking both ways cautiously ... sitting on the fence, waiting to see who comes out on top? ... accept[ing] ... his promotion, but ... [withholding] loyalty'.[127]

Tribune sensed the altered mood, abruptly abandoning frontal attack for thoroughly misleading assertions 'Mr. Gaitskell changes his tune'[128] (a banner headline) and 'Not for the first time ... has had the grace and wisdom to bow to the rising tide of feeling in the party'.[112b] Until a week before, canvassing of names to replace Gaitskell had been rife; suddenly it stopped altogether.[129] Soon Gaitskell was writing cheerfully to Sam Watson (who was not sure he could carry the NUM) that 'in the last week or two opinion, down here at least, has been swinging very heavily in our favour';[130a] and to Dalton that things were 'going better, and I have little doubt that we shall get a new statement of aims'.[3c]

So reassured, he willingly compromised by withdrawing from his maximum objective to his Blackpool view that Clause Four 'standing as it does on its own cannot possibly be regarded as adequate'.[85j] He had drafted the new statement of aims with much advice (including Dalton's 'let them hear some dear old echoes').[37d] To Watson he admitted: 'I would infinitely prefer that we should adopt it in replacement of Clause IV. This is the straight, honest thing to do ... [and] would give us the best political result in the country.'[130a] But he told his old PPS (who was delighted with it): 'it became clear to me a little time ago that this [replacement] was not going to get sufficient support from the unions.'[131a b] He expected to carry the Executive, but to lose the Miners, Railwaymen and Transport Workers; so he settled for unity, by adding the new statement while keeping the old one for its historical associations. He wrote to Watson:

> The problem is really to choose words which, while satisfying the more reasonable of the fundamentalists, nevertheless makes [sic] it unmistakably clear (*this is essential*) that the new Statement is in fact a definitive one so that the Tories can no longer go on misrepresenting us ... a certain amount of opposition does no harm ... if we are to have the embalming process, then the embalming must be done as thoroughly as possible.[130a b]

The idea of adopting both statements – instantly christened the Old and New Testaments – was pressed by George Brown and Charlie Pannell, the main leaders of the trade union group; and strongly backed by Edwin

Gooch MP, who had the highest vote for the NEC of any trade unionist.[132] With Gaitskell's acceptance of it, the air cleared and a majority of at least ten on the Executive was now expected. 'The political assassins who have been sharpening their long knives for Mr. Gaitskell have been frustrated by his greater tactical skill.'[56c] For no one objected to the new statement of aims — even though the draft itself contained 'no second thoughts ... [Gaitskell's] seven basic first principles ... now form the substance ... and several key phrases are used in both pronouncements'.[133] Even Foot approved it, wrote Crossman: 'I hear from Michael that Gaitskell has got a very good complete redraft of the whole Clause which, with a bit of amendment, should be perfectly O.K.'[13g] There was as yet no serious expectation that the leader could be overthrown; and so, as soon as the argument shifted from suspicion of his intentions to his actual proposals, the controversy died away.

Those proposals became known in a surprising way. Great efforts were made to keep the 'New Testament' secret until the Executive met on 16 March, but Foot's journal published it five days earlier. That outraged one young politician who had been feeling neglected, Anthony Benn: 'Reading your new statement of aims in Tribune *before* it reached me as a member of the NEC proved to me that I was wasting my time.'[134] Many others reacted quite differently:

> *Tribune* may have done Mr. Gaitskell a service, although no one would wish to embarrass Mr. Foot by assuming that this was his intention. Many ... [MPs] have found that there was never any real need for them to have been alarmed. Since *Tribune* appeared the fever within the Parliamentary Labour Party has notably cooled.[40d]

Already, at the previous NEC meeting on 24 February, Crossman saw that all the trade unionists believed

> that a conspiracy was taking place among the politicians against his [Gaitskell's] leadership and immediately all their suspicion of change and dislike of his violation of the rules had been switched into a passionate anti-politician agitation, in which he was also backed by all the women.[135]

Crossman was feeling sour about Gaitskell for reasons of his own;[136] he still claimed that no one wanted revision, that nothing significant could be agreed, that Gaitskell would still have a hard time on 16 March, and that Revisionism had been jettisoned.[137] Gaitskell on the contrary thought that 'even the fundamentalists' would judge on merits and accept the new statement.[138] He had been lobbying assiduously, sounding middle-of-the-road Executive members like Eirene White, and having very frank (and secret) meetings with left-wingers like Danny McGarvey of the

Boilermakers, and Tom Driberg — who sent him a long, friendly and constructive follow-up letter agreeing that the Party constitution unfortunately 'reads, and looks, like the rules of a provincial loan club in the 1880s'.[139]

On the night before the crucial NEC meeting, Harold Wilson convened a group to discuss tactics. Crossman recorded:

> When Harold had gone, Tom Driberg, Tony [Greenwood] and I revealed to each other that we would all prefer to keep Gaitskell rather than work for Harold Wilson. It was clear, however, that Barbara would work for Harold ... none of them really seemed concerned in the least with any kind of policy issue.[140]

At the Executive, Gaitskell instantly accepted — to the distress of his outright enemies — a series of verbal changes proposed by critics like the NUR member, Crossman, and Jennie Lee. (Hers was to insert her husband's phrase about the 'commanding heights' — which Dalton had already proposed,[37e] and which Gaitskell considered more cautious than his own draft [2f]) An amendment by Harry Nicholas of the T&GWU, to delete any reference to the place of private enterprise in the economy, was lost by 8 to 16.[141] But the atmosphere was entirely harmonious, and Nicholas cast the only vote against the new statement.[142]

The next day, Gaitskell's confidence seemed to have been entirely justified. Most of his friends were satisfied. Pannell wrote that 'you have got most of what you wanted ... [with] no loss of prestige', and Jay took it for granted that 'now Clause 4 is more or less finished with'.[143] Gaitskell told Hetherington that 'he had achieved both his objectives — getting away from 100 per cent nationalisation and the inclusion of other things in the s.atement of aims'.[2f] But privately he was not so sure, and sometimes thought his success

> very slight. The difficulty with the Party is to get the changes made without such a row in the Party as to vitiate the whole object of the exercise. Perhaps I should have chosen more subtle and roundabout methods. However, even with these one does not seem to make much progress.[144]

He carefully avoided claiming a victory, leaving the Left to celebrate the frustration of his imaginary conspiracy. At the very worst, the result looked like a draw, for as he had set out to do at Blackpool, Gaitskell had clarified and amplified the historic but inadequate clause. His campaign seemed to many strategically misconceived, and to many more, tactically mishandled; but on 16 March it had apparently attained its purpose with virtual unanimity on the National Executive.

vii   *One Step Forward, Two Steps Back*

The election had shown that even with a united Party and much improved propaganda and organisation, Labour support was slowly eroding and seemed likely to continue to do so. Gaitskell could have chosen to wait for something to turn up; and hindsight suggests that Britain's gradual economic decline, which he foresaw, might then have brought Labour back to power. But in 1959 that would have been a rash gamble, which he would have seen as an abdication of his duty to his followers for the sake of an easy life for himself. Alternatively, he could have suggested changes of structure not of doctrine. But he was against radical action, such as a formal breach with the unions. He might have carried out less drastic changes, strengthening the leadership against its perpetual critics by altering the composition of the NEC as Bevan and Phillips wished; but at the time the benefit of that would have accrued only to the leader and not to the whole Party, though in the long run Labour might have gained electorally from it. Instead, Gaitskell put forward an expanded version of the Party's long-term aims, assuming correctly that his new statement would be generally acceptable, and mistakenly that the old statement would not be missed.

The acceptability was obscured at the time by Gaitskell's poor tactics. In withholding his own views at the start, in having no lead given by the NEC, and in allowing his friends to make unpopular suggestions, he ensured that his personal impact came in the worst conditions and aroused the maximum suspicion, so that the debate centred on intentions wrongly foisted on him and not on his actual views. Yet though the suspicion of ideological divergence was much and sometimes maliciously exaggerated, it was not wholly unfounded. In 1959 everyone of importance in the Labour Party took it for granted that the mixed economy would last a long time and that the next Labour government would have to manage it. A decade or two later that was no longer true, and the extent and pace of major and irreversible change were again seriously discussed within the Party. In that debate, the survival of Clause Four gave the Left some leverage, and made it rather harder for the leadership to present Labour convincingly to the country simply as a reformist party – whereas in Germany the Social Democrats by their theoretical repudiation of Marxism (simultaneous with the British argument over Clause Four) were by the 1970s to leave their unreconstructed left wing stranded and politically impotent.

Gaitskell's final failure to change the Party constitution was not due to the intrinsic strength of the Labour Left. He failed because his approach was over-rational and took too little account of the emotional overtones. It was true that the reputation of wanting to nationalise everything was widespread and damaging to Labour; that, as Mikardo said, nobody wanted to do so in 1959; and that a new statement of aims certainly could be devised (as it was) to which everyone could assent. It was at least plausible to suppose that while changing the policy would have seemed a capitulation, changing the symbolic clause would demonstrate both to the electorate and to the Party itself what its real objectives were. But it was a serious error not to foresee that the emotional revulsion he himself experienced against altering the Party's name would be felt by many loyal trade unionists against taking down the signpost to the promised land. The controversy was studded with biblical terminology: Pannell warned him against tampering with the Tablets of Stone, John Murray against touching the Ark of the Covenant, Attlee and Griffiths against bothering about the 39 Articles. The two statements were christened the Old and the New Testaments, and the defenders of Clause Four were attacked as fundamentalists and idolators. Gaitskell himself once told an old friend that he wished he led a political party and not a religious movement.[145] Yet it was a strength as well as a weakness of the Labour Movement that it shared some of the characteristics of both. And it was a weakness as well as a strength that its leader's commitment to rational discourse sometimes blinded him to the likely emotional reactions of his followers.

Not all his opponents were zealots for whom the revisionist issue was fundamental and who felt that he was seeking to alter the very identity of the Party. They also included pragmatists, fewer but influential, who thought the opposite: that any squabble over 'theology' should have been avoided by silence in opposition until the same ends could be attained, still silently, in practice after coming into power. The leading pragmatists were soon able to put their views into practice, sweeping away a few babies of principle with the bath water of Clause Four nationalisation. When Labour reverted to opposition at the end of the decade, a price was paid for this adaptation by stealth. Never openly challenged, the old shibboleths remained intact and emotionally powerful, while the suspicion of the new leadership had become just as intense, and even more widespread, than in Gaitskell's day.

In March 1960 the pragmatic politicians seemed to have been wrong; but soon Gaitskell found that he could not achieve his ends in the way he sought. For within four months, four of the six major unions had refused to amend the constitution and, facing certain defeat at Conference, Gaitskell had to downgrade the 'New Testament' to a mere 'valuable expression of the aims of the Labour Party in the twentieth century', while leaving Clause Four intact. Even that face-saving phrase was challenged; it was carried in the NEC by 18 votes to 5.[146] Privately Gaitskell confessed 'rather sadly that if he had foreseen the kind of opposition ... he would never have raised the Clause 4 issue at all. He admitted that he had erred very much ... the best thing now was simply to cut his losses.' It would have done no good to win in the NEC but lose in both Conference and PLP.[147] Keeping the new statement of aims in the NEC's report, however, still

> had the advantage of dividing the idolators from the Left. The idola-
> tors would not go against Gaitskell on this. It would also leave him
> with support in the Parliamentary party ... [and] permit a debate at
> the conference on a mixed economy – a debate which Gaitskell himself
> believed he could win.[2d]

No one objected to the content of the new statement of aims but, as Gaitskell wrote, his enemies tried to refer it back mainly 'to damage me personally'.[130c] That was said openly in the debate; and Cousins supported the move so 'that on at least one issue we should know what it is we are voting about'. Gaitskell in reply protested that his Blackpool speech had been misrepresented: 'I do not think it was entirely my fault [people] were misled.' But he admitted not only that he had quite misjudged the mood but that he had retreated on Clause Four owing to the crisis over defence:

> [W]e in the National Executive felt bound to take note of the obvious
> feelings that existed.
>
> I do not think that we were wrong to do so ... it was never an issue
> of principle; it was an issue of presentation ...
>
> And we did so for another reason – I will be quite frank about it.
> It was quite clear that we were going to have a major division over
> defence, and we did not want to add to the divisions in the Party un-
> necessarily.
>
> So we are not discussing amending the constitution.

He went on to welcome Cousins's repudiation of wholesale nationalisation, to pay a warm tribute to the Yugoslavs and to stress that in a democratic system, 'We must think in terms always of a programme of extending public ownership which seems relevant to the electorate, for ... if it does not they will not elect you to power.' The reference back was defeated, and a resolution endorsing the new statement was carried, by nearly a two-thirds majority.[148] Though Gaitskell's face was saved, he had lost the battle over Clause Four after all, because of a sudden change in the dynamics of the political conflict. Before the 1959 election, his willingness to compromise was taken to show his concern for unity, and so strengthened him within the Party. But now his enemies on the Left were uttering cries of triumph, his big trade union battalions were wavering, and his compromise for the sake of unity looked to some like a retreat, encouraging to his enemies and demoralising to his friends – one of whom predicted 'a landslide of questioning which destroys your leadership'.[149] Many others were soon to draw that conclusion, notably Dalton: 'Perhaps Hugh had been wrong on Clause 4, too compliant. Perhaps, I added, wrong at Blackpool, to raise Clause 4.'[5e]

That spring, the Left launched a tremendous new assault against Labour's acceptance of nuclear weapons; and the 'landslide', threatening to sweep away his policy and his leadership together, obliged Gaitskell to abandon any attempt to revise the Party constitution.

Appendix

THE FOLLOWING statement adopted in 1960 reaffirms, amplifies and clarifies Party Objects in the light of post-war developments and the historic achievements of the first majority Labour Government.

The British Labour Party is a democratic socialist party. Its central ideal is the brotherhood of man. Its purpose is to make this ideal a reality everywhere.

Accordingly –

a   It rejects discrimination on grounds of race, colour or creed and holds that men should accord to one another equal consideration and status in recognition of the fundamental dignity of Man.

b   Believing that no nation, whatever its size or power, is justified in dictating to or ruling over other countries against their will, it stands for the right of all peoples to freedom, independence and self-government.

c   Recognising that international anarchy and the struggle for power between nations must lead to universal destruction, it seeks to build a world order within which all will live in peace. To this end it is pledged to respect the United Nations Charter, to renounce the use of armed force except in self-defence and to work unceasingly for world disarmament, the abolition of all nuclear weapons and the peaceful settlement of international disputes.

d   Rejecting the economic exploitation of one country by another it affirms the duty of richer nations to assist poorer nations and to do all in their power to abolish poverty throughout the world.

e   It stands for social justice, for a society in which the claims of those in hardship or distress come first; where the wealth produced by all is fairly shared among all; where differences in rewards depend not upon birth or inheritance but on the effort, skill and creative energy contributed to the common good; and where equal opportunities exist for all to live a full and varied life.

f   Regarding the pursuit of material wealth by and for itself as empty and barren, it rejects the selfish, acquisitive doctrines of capitalism, and strives to create instead a socialist community based on fellowship, co-operation and service in which all can share fully in our cultural heritage.

g   Its aim is a classless society from which all class barriers and false social values have been eliminated.

h   It holds that to ensure full employment, rising production, stable prices and steadily advancing living standards the nation's economy should be planned and all concentrations of power subordinated to the interests of the community as a whole.

i   It stands for democracy in industry, and for the right of the workers both in the public and private sectors to full consultation in all the vital decisions of management, especially those affecting conditions of work.

j   It is convinced that these social and economic objectives can be achieved only through an expansion of common ownership substantial enough to give the community power over the commanding heights of the economy. Common ownership takes varying forms, including state-owned industries and firms, producer and consumer co-operation, municipal ownership and public participation in private concerns. Recognising that both public and private enterprise have a place in the economy it believes that further extension of common ownership should be decided from time to time in the light of these objectives and according to circumstances, with due regard for the views of the workers and consumers concerned.

k   It stands for the happiness and freedom of the individual against the glorification of the state – for the protection of workers, consumers and all citizens against any exercise of arbitrary power, whether by the state, by private or by public authorities, and it will resist all forms of collective prejudice and intolerance.

l   As a democratic Party believing that there is no true Socialism without political freedom, it seeks to obtain and to hold power only through free democratic institutions whose existence it has resolved always to strengthen and defend against all threats from any quarter.

CHAPTER 22

'BAN THE BOMB!' 1960

'I never like evasions. But I suppose it is necessary this year'
(HG, JUNE 1960)
'He can't last long now'
(HAROLD WILSON, MAY 1960)

i *The End of Blue Streak*

LABOUR'S crisis in 1960 was more than a struggle over a doctrinal point like Clause Four, or over a policy issue like unilateral nuclear disarmament, or over a personality clash concerning Gaitskell's leadership, or even over the location of power within the Party. It was a conflict about its character: whether the Party was to be a protest movement or a prospective government of the country. For one wing, it was or should be controlled from below by its dedicated activists, who expected their parliamentary spokesmen normally to defer to Conference, and feared that the PLP's recognised discretion over tactics and timing might allow the Front Bench to assert the wrong priorities. For the other wing, Labour must not remain content to witness in the wilderness, impotent but pure: it must seek political power to put principles into practice. In between, a few of the power-seekers crossed the dividing line to form a tactical alliance with the purists.

Throughout Labour history that line has been sharpest over national defence. As a protest movement, the early Labour Party attracted many Christian pacifists who objected to all wars, many minority groups who hated British imperialism, many Socialist internationalists who loathed national rivalries, many ardent domestic reformers who resented money being freely spent on armaments but begrudged for social improvements at home. In the 1930s, the Opposition's call for resistance to Hitler went unheeded because of its votes against arms estimates; Labour as the alternative government was harmed by the ambivalence which reflected the heritage of Labour as a protest movement.

Whenever driven to decide, the Party had repudiated pacifism and accepted—sometimes reluctantly—the distasteful obligations of national defence. In 1960, however, the issue took a new form: whether Britain or her allies should retain a horrific type of weapon. Its abandonment would leave the country at the mercy of a potential enemy possessing it; its use would mean suicide; the threat of its use seemed, to young people particularly, profoundly immoral. The Campaign for Nuclear Disarmament aroused the largest spontaneous popular movement in post-war Britain. It won much support within the Labour Movement, and indeed attracted attention from many groups hoping to harness the fervour and enthusiasm to their own ends.[1] To the parliamentary leaders who were asking the electorate to entrust them with the government of the country, CND's pressure was doubly threatening. They were sure that renunciation of nuclear weapons by Britain alone would have no effect elsewhere, while her withdrawal from an alliance which retained them would have de-stabilising and dangerous consequences. But they thought such decisions would never be taken since Labour's leaders would be discredited in the electorate's eyes (and indeed in their own) if their defence policies could be settled in a Party Conference where votes were distributed irrationally, were often decided before the situation was known or the issue formulated, and above all were cast by people with no responsibility for the consequences.

CND had an explosive impact on the Labour Party. Early in 1960, forty-eight Labour MPs signed a unilateralist motion; and over the government's defence White Paper on 1 March, forty-three MPs—led by Crossman, Wigg and a new dissenter, Shinwell—abstained on an official Labour defence motion.[2a] Most of them came from the far Left, but those three reflected an anxiety about nuclear weapons spreading far outside the Labour Party. Other Left leaders voted with the Party from tactical calculation, giving priority to Clause Four—including Wilson, Greenwood and Barbara Castle.[3a] The alliance of Crossman and Shinwell with the extreme Left aroused 'seething resentment', hardening PLP opinion in Gaitskell's favour.[4a] [5] Nevertheless the next PLP meeting, where Gaitskell showed 'ultra-moderation',[6a] accepted the official policy with Wigg alone opposing;[7a] and the whips warned of stern measures against anyone voting to reject the defence estimates.[8]

Two years before, George Brown had quietly stayed away from the House rather than vote against the government after the Iraqi revolution, and Crossman had demanded his dismissal from the Shadow Cabinet;[6b] now Crossman was not merely abstaining but flaunting his dissidence, and proclaiming that he meant to continue doing so.[9a] [e] Brown, at the head of the trade union ranks, called loudly for discipline.[10] Gaitskell was not eager.[11] He 'couldn't have been more conciliatory or personally friendly,' wrote Crossman;[3b] but he made it clear that persistent revolt was incompatible with Front Bench status.[12a] As the NEC assembled for its crucial meeting on Clause Four, therefore, the breach between the two old schoolfellows again yawned widely. Crossman did not 'care a fig' about Clause Four, or disagree with Gaitskell on the merits of the issue;[13a] his opposition was a sign of reviving factionalism. No longer caring to influence policy from within, he felt delighted 'to be back ... in my natural habitat' trying to make life difficult for the leadership.[6e]

An external event now intervened. At the end of April the Government announced the abandonment of Blue Streak, the fixed land-based rocket which would have kept for Britain an independent nuclear deterrent wholly under her own control. That change came at a critical moment in the annual cycle of Labour politics. Party Conference decisions in the autumn are dominated by the big trade unions, each of which casts its vote as a block and may be bound by the mandate settled at its own conference months earlier (where it often had quite different motions before it). Frequently, as at the Party Conference itself, the activists on the floor try to impose binding commitments on the platform, which seeks a free hand in order to help the Party leadership the following October. In times of tension, the decision of one union conference may affect the mood of another; and since two large and unpredictable unions (AEU and USDAW) meet around Easter, that is often the moment when a trend begins.

Easter was also the season of the nuclear disarmers' Aldermaston march, which in 1960 had an exceptional impact on the unions. For, first, the Clause Four controversy had revived old trade union suspicions of Gaitskell as a middle-class intellectual, making it harder for him to convince the leaders and for them to hold their followers; Frank Cousins himself hinted later that but for Gaitskell's line on Clause Four, his own on defence would have been different.[14a] Secondly the Communist Party had belatedly but nimbly leapt on to the rolling CND bandwagon, hoping to upset the Labour leadership;[15] and in trade union policy-making, Communists often played an active part and wielded a substantial minority vote. Thirdly minds were changing, and in April 1960 pollsters found the highest support ever achieved by the unilateralists: 33 per cent.[16]

The abandonment of Blue Streak required a decision on whether Britain should try to retain her own strategic nuclear weapon. Labour's policy-making processes were singularly ill-suited for such a problem — which involved technical costs and consequences hard to assess in opposition, which gave rise to passionate emotional conflicts, and which might require premature pronouncements in a fast-changing situation. Gaitskell knew he risked provoking storms by announcing a change of policy without adequate consultation; he did not allow enough for the danger of seeming so to lag behind events that he lost all power to influence them.* In this crisis the man's personal stubbornness played a part, but so did the Party leader's

---

* The people who reproached Gaitskell for not moving quickly enough in the direction they wanted on his own responsibility, were precisely those who in principle insisted that policy changes must be exhaustively discussed and settled only at annual Conference.

awareness of internal differences. As in his respect for its traditional policy-making machinery over Clause Four, he denied himself flexibility and dangerously weakened his own position.

The consequences were sudden and drastic. At the end of March 1960 he seemed to have beaten off *Tribune*'s assault on his leadership and had won near-unanimous consent to a new statement of aims. But to all his enemies (and some of his friends) that compromise looked like a retreat; and now he was vulnerable on another flank. By the middle of July he was obliged to abandon any amendment of the Party constitution, and concentrate on resisting the Left's campaign to commit the Party to unilateral nuclear disarmament: a commitment which he would not accept, which would put his leadership in jeopardy, and which—owing to the big union votes already decided—seemed pretty certain to be carried easily at Conference in October.

ii *Gaitskell and the British Deterrent*

The decision to abandon Blue Streak was taken in principle by the Cabinet's Defence Committee on 26 February 1960, and ratified a month later by the Cabinet after the Americans had promised to supply an air-to-ground missile, Skybolt, pending later arrangements for a submarine-based one, Polaris.[17a] Rumours leaked out, to which Gaitskell referred in the House:

> [E]verybody is saying that this is just a quiet way of getting rid of Blue Streak altogether ... the carrier, whether it be a rocket or an aircraft, is not tied up by United States legislation ... There is no particular difficulty about buying the carrier if we want to. Therefore, the case for developing our own ballistic missile is surely enormously weaker.[18a]

He reiterated the views he had held for years.[19a d] Britain must stay in a nuclear-armed NATO as long as the Russians had the bomb; that was clear. But the argument for an independent national deterrent was finely balanced: it would avoid complete dependence on the United States, but at heavy cost which could not accurately be assessed in opposition.[18b] In the new situation Gaitskell would have been wise, while insisting on staying in NATO, to repudiate the independent British deterrent to which he had never given more than tentative support;[20] but Labour's parliamentary spokesmen on defence (George Brown and John Strachey) were committed to it, and he did not do so.

Gaitskell did not stand alone against a united movement as the left-wing weeklies pretended. On the contrary, many Labour people stood well to the Right of him on defence: Shadow Cabinet colleagues, union leaders and old Keep Calmers as well as the trade union Right in the PLP.[21] But while Gaitskell did not defend the British bomb out of personal obstinacy, he did fail for many months to realise the damage he was doing himself in the Party by refusing to repudiate it explicitly.[22] His public statements stressed how little Labour's policy had changed (which he thought, probably correctly, was what the ordinary voter wanted to hear) rather than how much (which would have appealed to his own Party workers).[7b] Opinion in the country was sharply polarised, with a substantial unilateralist minority and a larger number who still favoured a British bomb.*

The intermediate positions — including the non-nuclear club — had no emotional overtones, and little public support.[24] But it was those intermediate opinions that carried the most weight in informed circles, both in the serious press and in Parliament. There, the Liberal Party had for years opposed the independent British deterrent, and experienced Conservatives — including senior ex-Ministers — were already voicing doubts.[25-6a] Gaitskell's far Left opponents in the Labour Party were joined by some conscientious but not left-wing objectors to the nuclear strategy, like John Cronin and David Weitzman;[27] and by its critics on military grounds, like Crossman, Shinwell and Wigg. There were even signs that George Brown was worrying that the Government might renounce the independent deterrent policy while the Opposition still clung to it.[28]

Gaitskell missed those signs. His lieutenants were strongly resisting any change of policy; and Gaitskell was convinced that Brown concurred. He had said in the spring that a shift 'would cause trouble in the Parliamentary Committee and would probably cause George Brown to resign;'[29a] in early May, when reproached by Crosland for this misjudgment, he scribbled in the margin that Brown's change of mind 'cld not possibly be foreseen'.[29a b] In September he told George Wigg, who asked why he had not moved in advance of the inevitable cancellation of Blue Streak, 'I would have done what you suggest but George Brown was opposed and, as he was Defence spokesman, I could not overrule him.'[30]

Gaitskell was 'well aware'[29b] that opinion on the H-bomb was changing rapidly both at Westminster and in the country.[31] Crosland wrote reproachfully in May: 'at least a month ago ... Brown-Healey should have been instructed by you to start considering in detail what shift and when';[29a] Gaitskell commented 'he was & we did!'.[29b] The shift was cautious. Blue Streak was officially cancelled on 13 April — the very day on which Gaitskell told the PLP that the Shadow Cabinet would reassess Labour's nuclear policy, as the TUC had proposed.[32a 33] On the same day he sent a long memorandum on it to Sir Vincent Tewson, the TUC general secretary. But his covering letter showed both that he would maintain his stand on the wider issues of defence and the alliance, to which he attached supreme

* The unilateralists, however, became the smallest of the three groups (27 per cent) in June 1960 and much the smallest (22 per cent or fewer) from September onwards.[23]

importance; and that he did not see that he could do so more securely by abandoning the British bomb, to which he attached little importance. In both scope and timing the leadership moved too little and too late.

Gaitskell's letter to Tewson summed up the views put at their lunch on Wednesday 6 April:

> We neither of us feel that any significant arguments exist for revising our existing policy ... [of] multi-lateral disarmament ... ending of all nuclear tests ... our N.A.T.O. commitments ... We consider that Britain should only abandon her existing independent nuclear weapons in the event of the formation of the non-nuclear club ... or [for] some similar major compensating advantage.

The forthcoming conferences – on testing, disarmament and the Paris Summit – might require last year's statement to be updated but 'the process is not likely to involve any departure from the principles ... hitherto ... accepted'. As a new NEC statement was unlikely to involve substantial change, it could come out on the eve of Conference – or earlier if the TUC wanted, as they did, only 'a new document which in large part would be a reaffirmation of last year's statement'.[34] Delay was to prove unwise, reducing its chance of acceptance.

Gaitskell's memorandum, written for the Shadow Cabinet, set out his own attitude comprehensively.[35] Pending multilateral disarmament, Labour was committed to effective defence through a NATO alliance with adequate arms, nuclear and conventional, to deter or resist a Soviet attack. Unilateral nuclear disarmament (by Britain or the West) would not be followed by other countries – for had the requisite mutual confidence existed for that, multilateral disarmament would long ago have been agreed. Renunciation by Britain alone was

> often based on the desire to contract out ... associated with a vague though violent distaste for nuclear weapons. While ... supported by the high-minded through the doctrine of example, it is popular with others for purely escapist or beatnik reasons, and with others, again, because they are fellow-travellers, if not avowed Communists.

Neutralism would not lead to disarmament (Sweden and Switzerland were heavily armed). But it might well lead either to the break-up of NATO and Soviet ascendancy in Europe, or alternatively to the replacement of British influence by German – while Britain would be unable either to affect events, or to escape a war if it came. Neutralism was therefore an impossible policy for the Party and would, incidentally, condemn it 'to a further and far greater electoral defeat'.

Remaining in NATO meant sheltering under American nuclear weapons and sharing any guilt involved in that: so no new moral issue arose. Gaitskell summed up:

1. Our paramount aim is still comprehensive multilateral disarmament with effective international controls.
2. In the absence of this, we must play our part in N.A.T.O. which must possess the means of deterring a Soviet attack.
3. We should press that N.A.T.O. policy should rely more on conventional and less on nuclear arms; similarly we should urge that the balance in the British budget should be shifted in the same direction within the limits set by our policy of not reintroducing conscription.
4. We should be prepared to give up our *existing* nuclear weapons — as a means of forming the non-nuclear club and so stopping the spread of nuclear weapons.
5. As regards the future, we should not develop the *production* of our own missile, but consider the three alternatives:
(a) buying from the U.S.A. and adding our war heads,
(b) sharing in some sense with the European members of NATO,
(c) leaving it to the U.S.A. to supply and control all nuclear weapons — though reserving the veto on any to be used from our territory or by our forces.[36]

On May Day at Leeds, he was to repeat the same case publicly. Meanwhile he was out of the country, and the political scene shifted dramatically.

His experience at the New Year should have warned him of the dangers of going abroad at a critical time. But on Good Friday, 15 April 1960, the day the recess began, he and Dora flew off to the United States for a week. The following weekend he passed through London *en route* for Paris and Haifa to attend the annual meeting of the Socialist International. He arrived back in England late on Friday 29 April, to find his leadership under very heavy fire.[37]

Both at the Easter conferences and at Westminster, Labour's mood had changed. The Co-operative Party had always leant to pacifism and at the time also had a growing Communist influence; it voted unilateralist by 3 to 1.[38] USDAW, with its old ILP tradition, narrowly did so too.[39] Then, in the House, the second day after the recess was devoted to the debate on Labour's censure motion over Blue Streak, which Gaitskell unwisely did not attend because of his promise to the Socialist International.[40] On his brief stop in London during the previous weekend, Roy Jenkins tried hard but vainly on the telephone to persuade him to stay for it and 'switch our policy from the great deterrent'.[6f] In the leader's absence, George Brown made it clear that once the V-bombers became obsolescent, the failure of

Blue Streak would make it impossible to retain our own missiles and means of delivery, and must

> commit the future five or ten years ahead ... The argument for main-taining an independent British deterrent for basic political reasons is one thing when we have it. The argument for going back into the business once we are out of it is altogether different.[26b]

Winding up, Harold Wilson went further: 'From now on, there is no sense in any defence talk about independence.'[41]

Gaitskell heard the news in Haifa, and was very angry. Both before and after becoming leader he had scrupulously defended Party policy in public without additions, subtractions or glosses. Now his annoyance at this personal policy-making by his lieutenants prevented him from realising that they had done him a service. According to the Transport House official who accompanied him:

> He was furious when he first heard it ... extremely irritated to find that a new line had been taken in his absence ... he felt it's not how the team should behave ... not unless they had consulted the leader. He was an absolute stickler for sticking absolutely to the line, never fudging it, never putting his own interpretation on it – his admirable qualities which were at the same time his weaknesses.[42]

But his colleagues were loyally assuring the press that the new line came as no surprise to him. At the airport, Gaitskell kept up the front, claiming to have been 'fully aware of what Mr. Wilson and Mr. Brown would say', and to be unable to understand why the press was making such a fuss. Obviously, he said, the government decision had created a new situation. It would be necessary to choose between trying again to manufacture our own rocket (which he would oppose), or buying one from America, or seeking a col-lective European NATO deterrent, or leaving nuclear arms entirely to the United States.[4b] He repeated the same arguments the next Sunday, May Day, at a rally in Leeds. The Labour spokesmen, he insisted, had never suggested 'that they wanted us to disarm unilaterally, give up Nato and become neutralist. They were concerned solely with the future, of what Britain's position was to be in five years' time'.[4c] Then, when Crosland wrote a day or two later referring favourably to 'snap decisions ... by Brown and Wilson', Gaitskell wrote irritably in the margin, 'no decision taken'.[29a b]

Many of Gaitskell's associates, as well as his enemies, thought him – owing to his silence – still attached to the British bomb.[43] But his views in his private papers do not differ from those he stated in public. He told a union audience that the independent British deterrent was merely 'a matter of balance ... rapidly becoming an out-of-date issue';[44] its abandonment should have united the Labour Party by removing a source of internal dissension, and he did not understand why it seemed to be provoking 'the greatest argument we have ever had'.[45a d]

Gaitskell's listing of the long-term possibilities of remaining in the nuclear race shows that he was most unlikely to take up any of them. For, among his four choices, he at once ruled out efforts to build a British carrier. The purchase of an American vehicle would undermine his case for the British deterrent – that it avoided dependence on the United States. The European deterrent had far-reaching implications for Common Market relations, on which in 1960 Gaitskell was anxious to keep a free hand; and it meant German access to those weapons, which the Party would never tolerate and which he himself had recently opposed in the House.[46] * As soon as he thought it out, then, he rejected both a British-produced and a joint European missile, and he recognised that one purchased from the United States would give no independence – calling it 'a rather dishonest verbal trick' to pretend otherwise.[50] Yet he weakened his own position, and his ability to defend policies he cared about, by refusing to renounce explicitly the British bomb which he had never thought essential and now thought probably impracticable.

Gaitskell's thorough reappraisal in his memorandum to the Shadow Cabinet was written before Blue Streak was cancelled, though after cancellation looked likely. When it happened, he quietly redrafted the conclusions. He put much less weight on the advantages of purchase from the United States; and his presumption was no longer for keeping the British bomb, but for abandoning it as a contribution to non-proliferation.[51] In this shift of emphasis all his close friends concurred;[52-3a] though we have seen that many others in the Party did not. His reluctance to speak out in public, in contrast to his willingness to adapt in private, was probably partly because, once he committed himself finally against the British bomb, he would instantly come under pressure to scrap the (still operational) V-bomber force;[54] if he then did so he would abandon five years of still valid deterrence, give up any leverage to entice other countries into the non-nuclear club, and publicly change his defence policy under Party pressure. Some months later Crosland wrote to him, 'you would enormously strengthen your position against the Left if you made a forthright declaration that you were against the British H-Bomb now *and in the future*', and Gaitskell noted in the margin 'no popular support on this'.[29c]

* Some colleagues suspected that he supported the European deterrent:[47] suspicions based only on misleading press headlines to his speech at Newcastle on Saturday 21 May, which he corrected at once: 'to make it perfectly plain, I am not suggesting that there should be a European deterrent independent of the United States'.[48] A few days later he explicitly condemned it again as impracticable.[49]

In that comment he was clearly thinking – yet again – of the mood of the electorate as a whole not of the active Party workers.[55]

Another old inclination helps to explain his attitude: to think as a future Prime Minister rather than as a present Leader of the Opposition. Where many politicians would have cheerfully committed and then reversed themselves, saying circumstances had changed, Gaitskell took pledges seriously. As over stopping rather than suspending nuclear tests, or not using the H-bomb first, he hated making advance commitments even when they greatly eased his immediate political problem. That political problem, too, was less simple than his critics pretended, since most Labour voters, and many political and trade colleagues, were well to the Right of Gaitskell on this issue.

Such rational considerations account for his reticence, but not his intensity of feeling. Unlike many of his critics, he had weighed up the alternative courses and their likely results. Throughout the controversy he was determined not to let them make him feel guilty by, or confine the argument to, their endlessly repeated question, 'Would you press the button?'* Now, in the critical two weeks after he came back to Britain to face savage criticism, he shocked his closest friends by insisting on 'extreme and provocative clarity'.[57] His combative instincts, conscientiously suppressed for years, had been revived in full fury by the injustice, the pettiness, the virulence – and the success – of the attacks on him. He was acclaimed just after the election, reviled a few weeks later. He had given honest advice about the reasons for the defeat, without seeking to pre-empt the Party's decision, and was accused of conspiracy and treason for doing so. He had compromised over Clause Four for the sake of unity, and found the same enemies attacking him still more aggressively, hoping to drive him from the leadership as his union bastions crumbled. Now he was execrated as though he would welcome a nuclear war. So his blood was up, and publicly he would not recede an inch. A year later Denis Healey was to write of nuclear independence as 'the virility symbol of the atomic age ... Britain and France both clutched at it in the shock of having their military impotence exposed at Suez'.[58] For one brief moment in May 1960 perhaps Gaitskell too, fearing his political impotence might soon be exposed, was clutching at a symbol rather than defending a policy.

iii Crossman's First Compromise – Accepted in Vain

Gaitskell's rash absence from the Blue Streak debate provoked a furious personal assault from Michael Foot, who called it 'the bottom – a total

---

* That was why when CND was launched he wrote to his daughter that it was 'dangerous and nauseating and stupid. For it won't stop war and may indeed encourage it'.[56]

declaration of incapacity and unfitness to lead'.[59a] At Leeds on May Day 1960 Gaitskell hit back: the NEC had asked him to go to Haifa, he was the main speaker there, the date had been changed for his convenience, it was the first Socialist International meeting in Asia to concentrate on Third World problems – and, had he cancelled his visit, 'this little professional anti-leadership group, whose journal only survives on rows within the Party, would have attacked me just as bitterly ... [and] written up ... the rebuff to the Indians, the lost opportunities of giving a British lead, etc., etc.'[4c] Very likely they would, but they would have had far less impact; for there were 'angry growls in all wings of the Party', which felt 'deep shock and anger' at his absence.[60] The *Daily Herald* recorded growing uneasiness about his judgment and sense of tactics, and ominously mixed feelings about his absence from the censure debate: 'The view that as leader he ought to have been there was combined with a suspicion that if he had, the situation might not have been handled so well.[61]

That summer was the low point of Gaitskell's leadership. As Crosland wrote to him on his return from Israel:

> In the 7 months since the election we have suffered a major defeat over Clause 4; we are now fighting an unplanned defensive battle over the H-bomb; we have achieved not one single one of the positive reforms ... your own position is weaker, and you yourself more criticised, than at any time since you assumed the leadership; and the morale of the Right-wing of the Party is appallingly low.[62]

On the same day the national committee of the AEU, the second largest union, voted unilateralist by 38 to 14. Politically, recent by-elections had gone badly for Labour, and press speculation about Gaitskell's chances of remaining leader became general.[63-4] Grumbles resumed about his remoteness from his back-benchers; [63 65a] and were now endorsed by his friends, like Dalton:

> You've allowed yourself to walk much too much by yourself, when many others would have liked to walk with you ... there's no serious personal challenge for the Leadership but there's very little serious personal support for the Leader – outspoken, continuous and effectively articulated.[53b]

It was the only period when Gaitskell really was consorting with the 'Hampstead set'. For many prominent colleagues had concluded that in the interest of the Party – or of their own careers – they should detach themselves from a leader in decline; and Gaitskell was becoming correspondingly suspicious of the motives of those who disagreed with him.

George Brown was a key figure, both as official defence spokesman and as chairman of the trade union group of MPs. He was also an old T&GWU

official, an old friend of Frank Cousins, and a politician with ambitions of his own. He believed that a formula could be found to blur the issues, and meant to save Gaitskell from himself by working with the leader's critics to fix a compromise. At one of the many Shadow Cabinets early in May 1960 (probably on Monday 9 May) he and Gaitskell 'had a flaming row for a long time'.[66a] At another, on the afternoon of Thursday 12 May, Brown by his own account vetoed any immediate statement on defence, and afterwards Crossman found him 'extremely violent about the impossible, interfering Leader'.[66b] Later that evening, Gaitskell dined alone with Dalton, who had been Brown's first political mentor as well as his own. In departing, Gaitskell tried to enlist Dalton to persuade his former protégé 'not to concoct some humbugging resolution with Cousins. We wanted the issue clear cut'.[13b] But Brown went to hospital after a fall, and then dodged his old patron for a month.[53c]

The sudden sense of isolation momentarily affected Gaitskell's attitude even to his intimates. For a short time he behaved like the left-wingers whom he had despised for insisting on purity and principle at the price of political futility. On that same Thursday, 'a heavy, oppressive day', political disillusionment and pouring rain washed nearly 600 Labour municipal council seats down the drain all over the country.[69] After the House rose, Gordon Walker and Crosland went with Gaitskell to talk at Roy Jenkins's home, and Gaitskell told the others that

> he was very suspicious of Geo. Brown who was paying too much attention to winning Conference ... Then C[rosland] said it was essential to keep in step with Brown & Robens – otherwise we would be a powerless rump. I [Gordon Walker] strongly agreed & said G. must assume their good faith & not be suspicious.[57]

Thoroughly alarmed, Gordon Walker noted:

> I began to fear that G. has the seeds of self-destruction in him ... a death wish. He is becoming distrustful & angry with his best friends & wants to take up absolute & categorical positions that will alienate all but a handful ... G. said it was certain that a pacifist resolution wd. be carried at Conference. The alternatives would then be :– (a) to carry the parly. party into defiance of the Conference; (b) to go into opposition in the party ... with perhaps 100 supporters – & fight back from the back-benches.[67] 'It wd be a relief to be able to talk frankly & without compromise' ... G. was not prepared to 'fudge' principles ... He wanted to say specifically that we should retain & use nuclear weapons as loyal members of the NATO alliance. I said this was madness ... Crosland said that if G. took this line how many wd. he carry into opposition? He cd not hope for 100. 'Perhaps 10' said G. who became very angry & rounded on the other 2 sharply & implied that I was a

'fudger' of principle ... G. kept on coming back to his personal position. He was not going to falter on defence. He must spell things out. What shd he say on T.V. after a defeat in Conference? ... What about tactical nuclear weapons? Refuse to discuss them in detail, I said.[57]

Gaitskell's intransigence was untypical of him even in that embattled year, and it lasted less than a fortnight. A couple of days later he saw Brown in hospital, and found to his relief that the latter's ideas for a statement

were quite satisfactory to me ... The thing I most fear at the moment is being urged by those whom I still count as friends to compromise too much so that I am faced with the beastly choice of a break, even with them, or being driven down a slippery slope.[68]

At precisely that moment, too, the world situation changed dramatically for the worse.

The Summit meeting of four heads of state, which Harold Macmillan had spent years promoting in hopes of launching an annual series of consultations, was about to meet in Paris. At the very moment of assembly it was ruined by the Russians' capture of an American U–2 espionage plane, the inept and mendacious reactions from Washington, and the brutal re-rejoinder by a Khrushchev already under pressure from the Moscow hard-liners.[69] The Summit meeting had aroused great hopes both of a long-term reduction of tension and of a settlement over Berlin, still vulnerable to the Soviet pressure which Khrushchev had threatened in 1958; when it broke down amid bitter recriminations in the middle of May, the prospects for world peace seemed to have darkened catastrophically. Fears of the Soviet threat revived, and support for the American alliance with them. On 19 May Gaitskell wrote to a friend that the likelihood of his having to resign was 'receding fairly fast', since 'Mr. K is generally thought to have rescued the leader of the Labour Party'.[70]

No longer feeling so beleaguered, Gaitskell again sought an accommodation with his opponents; and the 'impossible interfering leader' denounced by Brown to Crossman on 12 May proposed twelve days later that the committee to draft the new defence statement should include both those two—the one so recently driven off the Front Bench, and the other who had insisted he should be.[69] That did not mean that they were all in agreement, but the difference was now much narrower. Gaitskell wanted to win the vote at Conference, as the others did, but he would rather lose it than sacrifice the substance of the argument:

If, for instance, the draft statement was generally taken to mean that we had conceded the case to the pacifists and unilateralists, this would, in my view, be much worse for the Party than the risk of being defeated at the Conference.[71b]

As a prospective Prime Minister he would not give way on what he saw as a fundamental question of national defence – and as a Party leader he could look back on past compromises turned sour: the equivocation over tests in 1957, the ambiguity over the 600 companies, his own acceptance of Clause Four alongside the 'New Testament'. Gaitskell felt sure that his critics on the Left would be implacable, so that further concessions would produce not unity, but only harm to his supporters' morale. The danger, he believed, came above all from the man who dominated nearly one-sixth of the vote at Conference: Frank Cousins.

Thus Gaitskell's brief mood of belligerence had passed by late May 1960, and his disagreement with the compromisers turned only on the possibility, the price and the propriety of appeasing Cousins. The argument over that continued intermittently over twelve months, repeatedly distorted by stories fed to the press to create the impression that, but for Gaitskell's individual obstinacy, agreement would be easy. That legend, plausible if he had persisted in his mood of early May, was quite false. In reality, large bodies of embattled opinion existed on both sides; neither Gaitskell nor Cousins was as intransigent as some of their allies, but neither would sacrifice points of real substance to reach agreement; Brown and Crossman hoped to conceal those real differences by ambiguities and omissions designed solely to satisfy Cousins; and they failed because opponents of unilateralism, quite apart from Gaitskell, would not agree.

Even in his difficult mood of early May, Gaitskell – by Crossman's own account – was much less adamant against concessions than some colleagues. At one Shadow Cabinet (probably on 9 May) Crossman learned from Wilson 'that Gaitskell was coming fast my way. But Soskice and Gordon Walker were holding out for the British deterrent'.[6h] Then on 11 and 16 May nearly one-third of the whole PLP attended its defence group;[72a b] and Crossman discovered

> that the serious opposition [to his own views] would come, surprisingly enough, from people who used to be the moderate centre of the Party – Michael Stewart, George Strauss, John Strachey – all still believing in the independent British deterrent ... it was clear, after I had argued the case for a non-nuclear NATO, what the Group's reaction would be. Up jumps Mayhew to ask whether we shall send British soldiers into battle without the very best weapons ... though this was the undoubted mood of the majority of those there, George Brown has committed himself to our side.[6h]

At the PLP itself on 24 May, a miner, Roy Mason,

> made a tremendous Right-wing attack on any sell-out of Britain's nuclear weapons and got a good deal of popular support, which was

repeated for Michael Stewart ... Emrys Hughes made a tremendous
personal attack on Gaitskell, whom he described as a jumping flea
and a Ramsay MacDonald. He got a rough reception ... Hugh
Gaitskell wound up, fairly all right.[69]

Far from taking the side of the right wing, Gaitskell said he 'thought the
Party was pretty much in agreement with George Brown' (whose opening
Crossman had called 'really admirable'). The vast majority were against
unilateral disarmament; we should stay in NATO but it needed reform,
to avoid 'too early reliance on nuclear weapons', to improve political
control, and to avoid proliferation. 'The Chairman was given an ovation
by the majority present.'[72a]

The minority felt differently. Apart from the outburst by Emrys Hughes,
an amiable pacifist eccentric, there were many signs that the Left scented
blood and had no intention of compromising. Victory for Socialism put
out a violent unilateralist statement before the first meeting of the defence
group;[73a] Sydney Silverman hinted that the leader was not far from being a
Fascist;[74] Michael Foot telephoned Crossman to say that the latter's latest
article on defence 'was OK, as long as no concessions were made to
Gaitskell'.[6h i] But those predictable reactions mattered only if Cousins
shared them.

The Labour Party Executive and the TUC General Council were to meet
on 31 May. Four days earlier, Crossman had persuaded George Brown
and Morgan Phillips 'to prepare our own draft secretly without consulting
Gaitskell ... going through the trade union conference resolutions and
noting the points which we would have to avoid if we were not to compel
the Union Secretaries to vote against us'.[6j] The outcome, he assured the
leader, was a carefully worded defence policy making military sense with
no sacrifice of substance, but so presented as to win maximum support.[71a]
Understandably, Gaitskell felt that Brown and Crossman could not be left
to decide alone whether the sacrifices were on points of substance: 'Neither
Sam Watson, nor the T.U.C. nor I could possibly accept such a proposi-
tion.'[71b c]

The NEC and the General Council each appointed drafting committees
of four. Determined to get his assent, Brown privately proposed adding
Cousins—though Crossman disagreed with that.[6g] However, Cousins was
kept fully briefed in advance;[75] and the draft withheld from Gaitskell was
shown to him.[76] He accepted it provided it was not amended.[77] But the
other side had become suspicious, and to Crossman's fury, when the two
committees met at Congress House on 1 June, Gaitskell was also present.[78]
'If the eight of us had met,' Crossman wrote,

we could have brought Frank Cousins over ... But Hugh ... wants to make sure we fight with him in Conference, win or lose ... Sydney Jacobson ... [said] Hugh ... had been very polite about George Brown and myself but expressed anxiety lest things were being cooked up behind his back.[6k]

At Congress House, the 'acrid bickering' lasted for four hours.[71a] The crucial dispute was over stating that the NATO alliance, in which Britain should remain, must retain nuclear weapons as long as the USSR had them. Brown and Crossman of course agreed with that policy themselves, and moreover claimed that Cousins too was prepared to tolerate it. But if so, his condition was that the draft must not say so;[79] and then, as Gaitskell pointed out, 'the argument which would follow on interpretation would tear the paper in shreds long before the Conference met'.[71b] Crossman's draft deliberately omitted the crucial statement; in drawing attention to the omission, the other TUC leaders exposed his semantic shams as hopelessly fragile. Yet someone falsely told the press that only Gaitskell's obstinacy had stood in the way of general agreement; that in return for the abandonment of the British bomb Cousins had agreed to support continued British membership of NATO with tactical atomic weapons; but that the deal had been wrecked by a 'flaming row' between him and Gaitskell at Congress House.[80] Cousins himself denied that;[81] and Gaitskell 'bitterly resented' the leak as 'both highly inaccurate and calculated to cause further trouble'.[71b]

Right at the start of the meeting, Crossman recorded 'a stupid row between Tom Williamson and Frank Cousins, about nuclear disarmament and all that, without any reference to the draft'.[6k] He blamed Gaitskell for wanting to discuss basic principles instead of Crossman's sacred text; Gaitskell protested that he had merely intervened in a confused dispute between Williamson and Crossman about NATO's nuclear weapons, to suggest that they must remain as long as Russia had them. That, the leader felt, was 'surely a point of principle on which there is no dispute ... Yet ... to my amazement you and George and Frank Cousins all became absolutely furious.'[71b] (He was amazed because he did not know about Cousins's conditional acceptance of the draft.) In Gaitskell's account:

Both George and Dick were appallingly prima-donna-ish about their draft and seemed to resent the slightest criticism either from the Trade Unions or from myself. They had clearly prepared their draft, which I had not seen beforehand, with the view to securing Frank Cousins' assent. I do not mean to suggest that there was much in it to which one could object, but the tone certainly was designed to give as little conceivable provocation to the Left Wing. Partly for this reason, I felt that the issues of principle were not so clearly stated as I should have wished, while the points of detail were too much emphasised.

U

In the event, it was quite useless. So far as Cousins was concerned, after a long interchange in which I myself took no part at all – chiefly between him and Bill Webber – he made it plain that, in his opinion, NATO should have no nuclear weapons at all. Indeed, I think he went so far as to say that we should not be in an alliance whose strategy was not [sic] based on the use of such weapons at all. This categorical statement from him obviously shook Dick Crossman and George Brown and the proceedings became rather quieter ...

Tewson and others ... are by no means satisfied with the draft because they think it goes too far in the direction of appeasement. Indeed,Tewson was half-minded to recommend rejection of the whole thing although I do not think in fact he would do that.[82a] [83]

Misunderstanding was all too easy between these two donnish Wykeham-ists, one pernickety about precision and the other vain about language, whose political objectives differed. Gaitskell did not seek a quarrel with Cousins but would give up nothing of substance to avoid one. Crossman, eager to blur the differences, saw Gaitskell's points of substance as mere matters of presentation, and interpreted optimistically the obscure phrases in which Cousins normally clothed his thoughts. Pursuing his own political ends, Crossman next day wrote Gaitskell a 'private and confidential' letter carefully drafted for later publication.[6k] In it he ignored Cousins's intransigence and blamed Gaitskell for the breach:[84] 'you seemed quite deliberately to pick a quarrel with Frank Cousins ... [as if] you felt you would be lacking in duty if you failed to have a row at Conference'.[71a] Gaitskell replied sharply: 'I certainly want our statements to be carried by Conference. I do not want to have unnecessary quarrels with Frank Cousins or anyone else.' But he would not sacrifice points of substance, or take refuge in futile ambiguity leading to immediate disputes over interpretation. The aim should be

not to *hide* but to *narrow* points of difference ... any narrowing will have to come from both sides and not from one side only ...

As for Frank Cousins, you are quite wrong in supposing that I deliberately picked a quarrel with him. On the contrary, sensing his personal antipathy to me, I kept, as you know, completely silent throughout the long exchange between Cousins on the one side and Bill Webber and the rest of you on the other which led to the ultimate declaration by Cousins that he was against NATO having any nuclear weapons at all.

As for your comment that I seem to regard the failure of Blue Streak as a bitter disappointment, I certainly do not recall giving that im- pression, though it is a line which George has taken personally on several occasions ...

At one point you speak of the desirability of not 'disturbing the convictions of a large number of active workers of the Party'. If you are thinking of unilateralists, pacifists and fellow-travellers, I do not see how we can avoid coming out in clear opposition to them. But, as for others, I see no reason to fear that we shall do anything of the kind [or] why we should not be able, without too much difficulty, to get a draft accepted first by the N.E.C. and later by the Conference, which is both clear cut on principles and also sensible from a technical, economic and military point of view.[71b]

Gaitskell meant what he said, and agreed to the Crossman draft without major changes, in a spirit of conciliation. Having thoroughly misconceived his attitude, Crossman and Brown were so astonished that by Crossman's own account they did not realise the leader had accepted it: 'Gaitskell, genuinely surprised: "But no new draft is required! We've agreed this one." And blow me, we had, with the tiniest modifications. All those four hours rowing, wrangling, for nothing, except to make sure Frank Cousins was against us.'[6k] But that opposition from Cousins was provoked by his own TUC colleagues—not by Gaitskell's nostalgia for a British bomb, or tiresome stubbornness over some pernickety phrase, or insistence on the 'provocative clarity' which had recently alarmed his friends. Besides the major point which offended Cousins, he and the TUC added phrases re-affirming the need to defend West Berlin, give loyal support to NATO, ensure better political control of nuclear weapons, and raise the 'threshold' at which these might be used. The non-nuclear club plan was recalled though not named (as a first step, Gaitskell wanted the British government to approach the French, suggesting joint proposals against proliferation).[85] He offered no amendments to the draft's pledges of no further British tests and no first use of the H-bomb (both commitments he had once opposed); nor to its rejection of a joint European deterrent; nor to its statements that Britain would in future contribute to 'the Western armoury ... in conventional terms', since she would soon have no 'truly independent strategic deterrent' and cease to be an independent nuclear power.[86-7a] He was happy with the content if not the emphasis, and agreed 'to accept the document ... for the sake of keeping the party together'.[9b] To Sam Watson he wrote:

The document is not ideal and, for my part, I never like evasions. But I suppose it is necessary this year, and there is a limit beyond which I cannot press George Brown. The most urgent thing in this field is, of course, to get the support of the miners and, if possible, the railwaymen too.[82b]

iv *Stampede of the Unions*

Gaitskell made several major speeches and broadcasts on defence, especially to a regional Labour conference at Newcastle on 21 May 1960 and to the NUGMW conference at Great Yarmouth two days later. (The latter speech was acclaimed as 'the best he had ever made outside Parliament', producing 'that delicious sensation of triumph when one can almost feel minds changing all over the hall'.)[88] Always he stressed the three issues of principle: support for national defence, for staying in NATO, and for NATO's retention of nuclear weapons while the Russians had them. He thought the USSR was not rashly aggressive like the Nazis, but would expand if it could without cost. A disarmed West would be vulnerable to Soviet threats as well as military action, while an armed alliance would not need to fight to maintain its freedom. NATO without Britain would either break up or fall under German domination. Compared with those crucial questions the British bomb was a minor issue.[89]

The Easter stampede to unilateralism was temporarily checked when the NUGMW, which had begun the slide a year before, voted so heavily against it (260 to 80) that the movers declined a card vote.[90] The leadership also held its own in several middle-sized unions. The Post Office Workers gave Gaitskell a victory on both defence and Clause Four;[91] the Building Workers joined the Boilermakers who were always on the Left, and the Electricians who followed the Communist line; but the Railway Clerks and Woodworkers supported the platform, giving it a majority of 80,000 from among these six unions. As the talks began at Congress House, Gaitskell was 'feeling more cheerful' — hoping to win, but thinking that Conference would probably accept the forthcoming new defence statement even if it carried a unilateralist motion too.[92] The content of the new statement became known late in June;[93] a couple of days later the Yorkshire miners voted decisively for it (by 75 to 19).[73b] Yorkshire usually determined the outcome in the divided NUM, and Gaitskell wrote optimistically: 'It looks as though there should not be any great difficulty with the Defence statement now.'[94]

Even after Easter, Gaitskell had stubbornly resisted advice from trade union friends to give up the Clause Four battle, where the Left were proving much stronger, in order to win the more crucial one on defence.[95] The 'New Testament' had been accepted by USDAW, but not as a constitutional amendment, and by the NUGMW, but only by 204 to 132 (a much smaller majority than on defence). Then the AEU and the Yorkshire miners both voted unanimously to retain Clause Four unchanged. Now Dalton wrote to urge retreat: 'We under-estimated the bone-headedness of large sections. Stick to Defence (two aspects) this year. Now relax and smile at (nearly) everybody.'[53c] [d] Reluctantly Gaitskell agreed, seeking only to save face by getting his 'New Testament' approved. He told Sam Watson: 'There is a great muddle about this ... Many resolutions ... seem to assume that the new proposals question the principle of public ownership. Of course they do nothing of the kind.'[82c] Early in July the last two big unions decided: among the Miners, Yorkshire duly foreshadowed the national verdict on both Clause Four and defence; among the Railwaymen, usually on the moderate Left, the leadership was defeated on both.* Both unions had, like the AEU, rejected their executives' advice on Clause Four; and among mandated votes there was now a majority of nearly 1,700,000 against amending the constitution.[97a] Many union leaders were giving priority to resisting the unilateralists, and abandoning any effort to persuade their members to vote for the new statement of aims.

The trade union movement has a strong tradition of loyalty to elected leaders and majority decisions, and had always been a reliable bastion. In April, Gaitskell reassured Dalton that the union leaders were not being neglected but 'pretty well taken care of subject to the amount of time *they* have as well as myself ... their relations with me are excellent'.[98] But now there were doubts. Gaitskell had badly misjudged their attitude over Clause Four; and he had handled them clumsily over the defence talks, annoying their NEC representatives by an ill-prepared effort to bring the Shadow Cabinet into the talks as well.[6h] In the inquest on the municipal election defeats, he irritated the NEC again by showing more concern over the average voter than over the disillusioned Party activists.[6g] The ferocity of his opponents, and his own tactical blunders, made even sympathetic trade unionists wonder whether Labour could ever regain its unity under his leadership.

Gaitskell had written in April that what the unions lacked was 'a really formidable figure, like Deakin, to give a lead on policy'.[98] Few general secretaries would risk trouble in their own unions to defend a political leader whose days seemed numbered; and trouble was certain now that the pacifists, neutralists and conscientious objectors to nuclear weapons were reinforced by the Communist Party, which was powerful in several important unions. Harold Wilson told Crossman that the trade union leaders a few weeks earlier had been wishing that there were an alternative to Gaitskell. 'Now they are saying they must get rid of him, whoever takes his place. He can't last long now.'[6l] Trade union reticence, and cautious trimming by most prominent politicians, obliged Gaitskell to fight almost alone – not because few agreed with him, but because few had the courage of their convictions. The Left were quite wrong about the division of

---

* NUR: by 66 to 11 and 39 to 38 respectively. NUM: for Clause Four by 354,000 to 326,000, anti-unilateralist by 479,000 to 201,000. At the Party Conference the NUR had 272,000 and the NUM 642,000 votes.[96]

opinion in the Party, much less wrong in thinking him personally the real obstacle to their victory.

Thinking their hour had come, they overplayed their hand. In mid-June VFS demanded Gaitskell's resignation – provoking three of the fifteen VFS MPs to resign.[2b] The leader's own ward party in Hampstead passed a well-timed vote of no confidence;[99] Mikardo and Foot made direct personal attacks on him, and Zilliacus too called him 'indistinguishable from a Liberal in home affairs and from a Conservative in foreign affairs'.[100] The left-wing weeklies trumpeted that 'the leader of the Party has made himself the spokesman ... of a small unrepresentative clique',[59b] and was 'manipulated by a small and much disliked group of anti-Socialist zealots'.[101a] Those unjust attacks were aimed at Crosland, Jay and Jenkins (who had not in fact advised Gaitskell to raise Clause Four, and had urged him to repudiate the British bomb). In his first public statement since the election, Dalton passionately protested against the charges, blaming the weeklies themselves for the 'persistent plague of public squabbling; an unending stream of personal attacks on individuals ... personal bitterness and malice unbounded ... distortion, spite and downright falsehood ... hatred, bile and jealousy.'[102] It was barely eight months since Crossman had earnestly warned the Party against the 'odious' temptations into which it, and he, so soon fell headlong: 'Too often our Socialist reaction to defeat is the hunt for a scapegoat, we exculpate ourselves by ... accusing the leadership of sacrificing Socialist principles ... this will lead first to tensions and then to splits.'[101b] Already it had led to a 40 per cent drop in Party membership subscriptions.[103]

The Left had gone too far, allowing Gaitskell's friends to mount a counter-attack. When the NEC met to ratify the new defence statement, Sam Watson expressed dismay at the feuding and called for a vote of confidence in the leader; the Executive unanimously gave it[19b] – after Wilson and Harry Nicholas had failed to substitute a general resolution condemning all personal attacks.[6m] The Shadow Cabinet then tabled a similar motion for the next meeting of the PLP. Shinwell moved that it be not put, but later withdrew, eliciting some splenetic expletives from his old enemy Dalton.[53c] The PLP passed it overwhelmingly, but only after the spokesmen of the trade union group had made their support depend on abandoning any revision of the Party constitution; the 'New Testament' was not to become part of holy writ.[104] At a special meeting on 13 July on the state of the Party, the Executive agreed to drop the constitutional revision and merely commend the 'New Testament' to Conference. Many of Gaitskell's allies agreed with the general secretary who 'was anxious that they should fight on only one issue – defence'.[9c]

The retreat was inevitable, but so were the headlines ('CLIMB DOWN BY GAITSKELL'). Again his position seemed in serious jeopardy. By late July, the settled union votes showed a unilateralist majority of almost a million;[105] which was generally expected — though not by Gaitskell[106a] — to be reinforced by most of the 1 million-odd CLP votes.[107] The press gave him only a fifty-fifty chance of surviving Conference;[106a] and many of his supporters were completely defeatist. In Lancashire, he was told, Labour leaders felt:

> It's a pity about old Hugh. He's quite right ... and it's tragic that the Party won't accept his lead. But it won't and there it is ... So Hugh had better go. God knows who'll follow him but the Party will survive — it always does.[108]

v Conference and Parliamentary Party

If Gaitskell's policies were defeated at Conference, his fate would depend on the loyalty of the Labour MPs. Their support for his views was not in doubt, but their willingness to defy Conference was far from certain; neither Gordon Walker[57] nor Dalton expected it.[13c] Bevan had once thought the PLP followed the leadership because too many prominent figures were place-seekers hoping for office; if so, Gaitskell found no help among them. The disputes over policy were indeed entangled with the struggle for political power, but not at all as Bevan had assumed. Before the general election, when Gaitskell was a prospective Premier who might soon be appointing Ministers, his future challengers like Greenwood, and his critics like Barbara Castle, had been carefully loyal or effusively friendly. All agreed that he had acquitted himself splendidly in the election; and no political commentator doubted that he was far superior as Party leader to any conceivable successor.[109] But when the storm broke, most senior figures relapsed into a silence of 'spineless expediency — the words are not harsh enough'.[110] Brown and Crossman shared Gaitskell's views over defence, and yet tried to impose on him a defence statement approved by Cousins behind his back. Harold Wilson foresaw the defection of the union leaders and hopefully predicted that Jonah would soon be thrown overboard.[111] George Brown told Dalton that 'ambitious young Parliamentarians were saying: "How long will H.G. last? I don't want to be dragged down with him, if he goes" '.[13b] [d] Crossman found Anthony Benn, who six months earlier had been promoted far ahead of his generation, 'full of gaiety and excitement and also pretty clear that Gaitskell couldn't last very long'.[6g] As the French Third and Fourth Republics showed, however shadowy the positions of power available, some politicians are excited by hopes of new combinations, new vacancies and new opportunities. Rationalisations are never hard to find for those who need them; not all do. In June, one journalist remarked that 'Mr. Gaitskell has suffered more

back-stabbing and personal disloyalty ... than any other political leader'
of recent times.[106b] Gaitskell himself wrote to a friend of how he loathed
'the treachery & disloyalty ... hysteria & neurosis'.[112]

Gaitskell owed his vote of confidence at the end of June 1960 to the
solid trade union back-benchers, numbering nearly 100 out of more than
250 Labour MPs. They had many complaints and grievances against him.
But they felt the need for loyalty to the elected leader; they had little hope
of office themselves, and no time for those who manoeuvred to acquire it;
and they kept in touch with their working-class constituencies and knew
how limited was support for the far Left.[113] At the PLP meeting itself,
Jim Griffiths defended Gaitskell as a leader of integrity who was not afraid
to say unwelcome things. Two more miners, Bill Blyton and David
Griffiths, and also Ray Gunter supported him, but complained again at
his raising Clause Four and not spending enough time in the tea-room.
Sydney Silverman, of VFS, faced 'impatient and angry interruptions'.[4d]

Gaitskell replied mildly. He saw less than he would like of the back-
benchers because of shortage of time, especially with the deputy leader
absent ill for months. (Bevan died the next week.) Answering the old myths
about XYZ and Jay's *Forward* article, Gaitskell said he had dined at XYZ
only three times in five years, and that he would not be bullied into attacking an old friend with whom he did not happen to agree.[73c] The vote of
confidence was passed by 179 to 7, with 12–18 abstainers.[114] Next day the
defence statement was approved by 97 to 15. The Prime Minister ironically
congratulated Gaitskell in the House,[115] adding privately: 'I was beginning
to get anxious – for on the whole Gaitskell suits us pretty well.' In contrast
to 1957, Macmillan now felt: 'I should be sorry if he went, for he has ability
without charm. He does not appeal to the electorate, but he has a sense of
patriotism and moderation.'[17b]

Gaitskell's opponents were demanding that he should promise in advance
to resign the leadership if he lost at Conference. In reply, a dozen prominent
MPs of the second rank – including several of the old Keep Calm leaders,
and seven future Cabinet Ministers – were recruited privately by G. R.
Strauss late in July to urge on him that resignation 'would be constitutionally wrong and politically unwise'.[116] Shortly before Conference on 22
September, Gaitskell sent for Strauss to say he would not resign;[117]
though at Scarborough itself he still showed signs of hesitation.

A Conference vote for unilateralism would at last face Labour MPs with
the dilemma inherent in what Crossman called the Party's 'completely
unworkable constitution'.[118] If, despite the Conference decision, they
backed the leader they had elected and the policies they supported, the
Labour Movement would face bitter strife and damage. They would out-

rage many active Labour workers who believed that great policy decisions should be made by Conference, not by MPs suspected of preferring office to principle. They would in theory risk expulsion by the NEC, in practice trouble from their own management committees. But the alternative was still less appealing. MPs were well known to believe that for Britain to repudiate nuclear weapons and leave NATO would be disastrous for the country's security and dangerous for the peace of the world; if they now said the opposite because Conference told them to, they would be discredited individually and collectively, and the Labour Party with them — less by their new views than by the blatant fact that those views were not their own.

The question of authority in the Party, evaded so long, so cunningly and so often, was at last inescapably posed. A conflict was inevitable because its constitution reflected the circumstances of a time when Labour was essentially an extra-parliamentary movement, part ideological crusade, part trade union pressure group, without serious claim to govern. That conflict could be postponed as long as the major union leaders wielded their voting power in agreement with the views of the ordinary Labour elector and in support of the parliamentary leadership. For Labour to win power, that leadership had to be seen to make up its own mind on the central issues of policy — subject to ordinary political pressures, but not to directions from industrial potentates or from militants without responsibility to the electorate.* Many politicians, conspicuous for prudence or ingenuity or ambition, sought desperately to find a way of escape. But others, notably James Callaghan, realised that on this issue accommodation to the pressures would be fatal, exposing the Party to Macmillan's deadly charge: 'as I understand it, the defence policy of the Party opposite depends on the chance vote of a delegate conference of the NUR'.[120]

The Left had hitherto violently criticised the power of the union leaders, but now claimed that the system represented the rank and file; the Right had previously excused it, but now Woodrow Wyatt attacked Cousins as 'the bully with the block vote'.[121] Those were the familiar inconsistencies of politics. The real change was that union spokesmen without responsibility, instead of endorsing the policies decided upon by elected politicians seeking approval from the voters, were now determined to impose on the prospective government major policies it believed wrong and disastrous. Gaitskell and the Parliamentary Party rightly rejected that imposition,

---

* Gallup polls in the 1970s found this repeatedly. Asked who *should* have most influence on Labour policy, 51 per cent of respondents in 1977 said the leader or Cabinet; 38 per cent said Labour voters or MPs; 10 per cent said Party workers or the NEC; 3 per cent said the unions. (Asked who *did*, the replies were 24, 7, 9 and 61 respectively. There were similar results in 1975 and 1976.)[119]

causing anguish and fury to many worthy Party workers who believed in the right of the 'rank and file' to decide.

Both sides now prepared for the clash. Resolutions were put down seeking to bind MPs to accept policies decided in Conference, while much of the press urged Gaitskell immediately to challenge its authority. That support did him only harm in the Party; and that course would, as he knew, risk alienating once more his natural allies in the trade union group.[122] He told an MP, who wanted him to make the PLP's stand clear, that it was 'wiser at the moment to keep rather quiet on the Constitution and leave Morgan Phillips to explain the position'.[123] Phillips had emphasised the PLP's autonomy, and Gaitskell thought it imprudent to say anything more as yet about the authority of Conference:

> Gaitskell said he couldn't breathe a word now about any change in the constitution, nor could any of his known friends ... eventually the constitutional position and the methods of policy making would have to be revised, but nothing could be done immediately.[9c]

In July Phillips produced a long report on the state of the Party and a draft on the constitutional position, and the NEC (at Gaitskell's suggestion) unanimously agreed to publish them over the secretary's signature and not as official statements.[87b c] 'The whole atmosphere', wrote Crossman, ' ... is now that of ... trying to get through the day's business without touching on any serious issue for fear it might blow up.'[6n] The constitutional statement satisfied Gaitskell, for it argued:

> The Parliamentary Party could not for long remain at loggerheads with Annual Conference without disrupting the Party ... On the other hand, the Parliamentary Party could not maintain its position in the country if it could be demonstrated that it was at any time or in any way subject to dictation from an outside body ...
>
> A satisfactory relationship between the several elements of the Party can only be based on mutual trust and confidence, not only between the elements but between individual members as well ...[124]
>
> Annual Conference does not instruct the Parliamentary Party; it does instruct the National Executive Committee ... The Election Manifesto ... on which its members are elected, is the one thing to which, under the constitution, the Parliamentary Party is bound.[125]

The press treated that as endorsing Gaitskell's view, and his NEC opponents—Castle, Crossman, Driberg, Greenwood and Nicholas—publicly disowned it.[126]

So, after four years of conciliation, Gaitskell had changed his whole style and challenged all his followers' central myths—over domestic policy, international affairs and the very structure of the Movement. In home affairs he saw that the great majority of Labour supporters and activists accepted the mixed economy in fact (as they did in 1959, though not necessarily a decade or two later); but he did not see that they were none the less (or all the more) reluctant to say so formally. Abroad, the Labour Movement had since the war grudgingly recognised the unwelcome reality of power in international affairs; but natural horror at the H-bomb had revived the pacifist tradition – and the invincible propensity for wishful thinking – which Labour had gradually discarded after 1933. In the former case, Gaitskell had hoped that intellectual honesty about the Party's long-run aims would reassure the uncommitted voter without alienating the faithful; that assumption proved false, but his retreat entailed no unacceptable commitments, though it cost him heavily in personal prestige. In the latter case there could be no retreat; the Party could not dodge or fudge on the main lines of defence policy, and while he strongly opposed a consistent policy of unilateral disarmament and neutralism, he was revolted by 'the basest hypocrisy' – that of renouncing nuclear weapons for Britain, and so claiming moral superiority over the guilty Americans, yet still relying on their bomb to preserve our independence: as he put it, ' "Yank go home, but don't forget us if there is any trouble" ... the thing I most dislike'.[45c]

His insistence obliged the party to face yet another hateful truth. Its constitutional arrangements, framed for a purely propagandist movement, were odd or unacceptable except to devoted traditionalists or left-wingers with an axe to grind. To Labour as a potential government, they were a grave handicap; for in the eyes of ordinary voters, the most important single quality of a good Prime Minister was the ability to provide strong leadership.[127-8] Labour's claim to govern conflicted with its revered traditions, and the Party's vocation was at stake.

In all parties, before and since, many a political leader has evaded or postponed such conflicts between myth and reality by putting up a rhetorical smokescreen to conceal his own preferred destination; the more successfully his followers were cajoled during the journey, the more thoroughly they were liable to be disillusioned on arrival. Such politicians open themselves to suspicions which may be quite unjustified but are not hard to understand. But when similar suspicions were directed against Gaitskell, whose passion for explaining in public exactly what he meant kept landing him in trouble, they told much more about the accusers than the accused. In the summer of 1960 his confident enemies were saying openly that the new policy statement was in itself acceptable, but would not do because the untrustworthy leader would interpret it so as to continue the policy – support for the British bomb – to which they wrongly thought him committed.[101c] Crossman himself feared (or said) that 'even if we adopt the Wigg-Crossman line, it would be voted down by Conference if Gaitskell were to move it, so great is the hatred and distrust of him'.[6h] (Whose fault?) Some people blamed the leader for treating his followers seriously by clarifying what their views would mean in practice, 'when all they needed was a soothing form of words'.[129] But there were unilateralist spokesmen who took a more detached view. A. J. P. Taylor wrote: 'Gaitskell does not try to cheat us. Those who put unity before principle do.'[101d]

vi *The Art of Manipulating Mandates*

Most Labour spokesmen were distracted by the furious internal Party debate from pressing the attack on the Conservatives. Gaitskell was not, for he felt strongly

> that the right can only win the struggle within the Party by being the most effective spokesmen against the Tories and for the Party ... And of course, we only do well for the Party by winning the battle within the Party. The two things are mixed up.[29e]

His domestic speeches in that summer of 1960 demonstrated once again his commitment to the principles his enemies accused him of betraying. Instead it was they who were now giving the Tories a welcome respite. In Crossman's view, 'if the Opposition hadn't ceased to exist, this Government would be getting into very rough weather at this moment'.[6n] Gaitskell wrote to his brother that the Conservatives were 'much less at ease' with 'troubles of their own inside the Party and ... much rougher economic weather'.[130] But the Prime Minister was for once unworried, recording complacently in his diary: 'The Labour row seems to grow in bitterness and intensity. One begins to wonder whether Gaitskell will be able to survive and ride the storm.'[17b]

In August Gaitskell escaped with the family to Yugoslavia for 'the best holiday we have had for years',[131] followed by a week's official tour and talks. At the end of the month he returned refreshed, to plunge back instantly into routine duties and friendly contacts—meeting his Party colleagues and journalists, seeing factories, schools and housing estates in and around London, looking after his own constituency, speaking in support of the Labour campaign on London rents, and visiting the West Indian community in North Kensington (where he delighted his hosts by dancing to a calypso on the minute carpet space in the crowded room). His diary includes a dozen separate appointments with different trade union leaders in nine days, reflecting the approaching battles at the two annual conferences: those of the TUC at Douglas, Isle of Man, and of the Labour Party at Scarborough.[132]

Again the views of a friend were erroneously imputed to Gaitskell.

Conference was expected to reject the joint statement agreed in July by the NEC and TUC. Anthony Crosland had welcomed the coming defeat, since the PLP by successfully defying Conference could *de facto* change the Party balance of power.[133] Gaitskell disagreed:[134]

> Our immediate object must surely be to win the battle against Cousins ... it looks as though the T.U.C. will be a draw—with the Statement and Cousins' resolution both being accepted. The same thing may well happen at Scarborough. This is thoroughly bad for the Party, because it makes the T.U.C. and the conference look ridiculous—BUT it probably gives us a better prospect of holding the P.L.P.[29e]

Houghton's report from the TUC reinforced his determination:

> Cousins' conversation on Thursday was an attempt to persuade me to intercede with you ... I reminded him that if it was compromise he was seeking, he had shown no disposition for it up till now. The Joint Statement had gone a long way to meet his point of view; how far had he gone to meet opposite views? He was vague except to say—'After all, I am the secretary of the largest union' ...
>
> Cousins would welcome a call from you to meet and discuss the situation. I fear that nothing would come out of it ... It is not agreement but submission he is after ... 'The Party leaders', he told me, 'have changed their minds before under pressure from the rank and file; they can change them again' ...
>
> Cousins I am sure sees himself as saving the soul of the Labour Party on this and other issues ... He would like to be granted a place in the counsels of the Party which would make him intolerable, quite apart from being bad for us in the country.[135a b]

The month of September 1960 was a festival of the Labour Movement's arcane art of interpreting and bargaining over Conference resolutions. The TUC had two defence proposals before it: the joint statement, and the resolution by which, a year earlier, the T&GWU's biennial conference had perturbed the Labour waters on the eve of the election. That motion rejected defence policies based on the threat of using nuclear weapons. It was opposed to production, testing or first use of those weapons, and to having bases in Britain either for missiles or for patrolling aircraft with H-bombs. It did not explicitly call for Britain to leave NATO; but many resolutions which did so had been withdrawn in its favour.[136] During the debate Houghton asked Cousins whether it was a unilateralist motion, getting no reply and expecting none, since he knew it had been put forward as not unilateralist in 1959. In a tea-break afterwards, Cousins told Houghton that he disliked the word unilateral and would not use it: ' "We want to have nothing to do with the bomb at all. That is our position." He added that if that wasn't clear to me I was the only man in Congress left in any doubt.'[135a]

Gaitskell and his supporters were not committed to Britain retaining a nuclear weapon of her own, but were committed to her remaining in an alliance possessing those weapons as long as the Russians did. Three groups opposed that position. The 'fudgers' like Wilson and Crossman agreed with the policy but not with Gaitskell's insistence on spelling out the implications. Unilateralists wanted Britain to renounce the weapons without always specifying that that implied renouncing protection from an alliance which retained them. Cousins agreed personally with the unilateralists, but his union would not say so explicitly though it supported most of their proposals.

The largest union which was explicitly unilateralist was the AEU. Its president Bill Carron was a Gaitskell loyalist, who at the TUC cast its 900,000 votes in favour of both the rival defence motions – drawing ridicule in the press, and saving the platform from defeat. Cousins took advantage of the AEU's vote to suggest that the General Council should support his own motion;[135a] but it ruled them incompatible, as indeed Cousins had himself agreed just before Congress opened.[137] It then voted by 28 to 6 to oppose the T&GWU resolution. Both motions were passed, however, thanks to the AEU: the joint statement by 4,150,000 to 3,460,000, and the T&GWU resolution by a bigger margin, 4,356,000 to 3,213,000.

Soon afterwards the Gaitskells met Carron and his wife at dinner at George Brown's home, where they normally found the atmosphere thoroughly congenial. But this time Brown grated on Hugh's sensitivity by shouting at Carron that the Party's whole future depended on his delivering the AEU vote again. The union's Labour Party delegation was thought more malleable than its unilateralist national committee, but Carron warned that he could not be sure of success; Dora said that on some matters one had to fight, win or lose; and their host told Hugh that she would ruin the Party and her husband's career.[138–9a]

Brown now revived the idea of an accommodation with Cousins. He and Crossman had in May proposed a form of words omitting everything to which Cousins might object, only to find it unacceptable when the two drafting committees met. In September Brown tried again, urging the NEC to follow Carron's example in supporting both resolutions. He wrote a memorandum for its international sub-committee arguing rather tortuously that the motions themselves were compatible if the T&G resolution was judged on its wording, not on Cousins's glosses intended – said Brown – 'to secure the support of all the unilateralists and pacifists for a motion which was neither unilateralist nor pacifist. By any unprejudiced judgment he was facing both ways to a far greater extent than was Bill Carron'. The NEC should therefore argue for its own motion, 'show the weaknesses of the T&GWU motion and the equivocal way in which it has been presented', but claim that it was 'not necessarily inconsistent with the joint statement'.[140]

The secretary of the sub-committee, David Ennals, asked Gaitskell if Brown should not be invited along to discuss his memorandum; instead Gaitskell, displaying real ruthlessness for the first time, instructed Ennals not to circulate it at all. He wrote to tell Sam Watson the chairman:

> George comes down in fact in favour of arguing that the resolution does not mean what Cousins says if means ... I cannot possibly accept this suggestion [of saying so at Scarborough] ... Of course we must tear it to pieces. Of course we must challenge Cousins on its meaning. Of course, we must point out the evasion and trickery which lie behind it. But, having said all this, it would be quite ridiculous to say that we do not mind if it is passed ... Whether or not you agree with me or him, nothing would be more foolish than for us to have an open argument about this matter in front of that particular Sub-Committee.[82d]

Gaitskell was quite right to be wary of that sub-committee, though wrong in thinking Crossman was already privy to Brown's operation.[139a c] But now Crossman as a member of the sub-committee was asked by Ennals (at Brown's suggestion) to present the paper; having carefully got the approval of Wilson and Barbara Castle, he agreed to do so.[141] Privately he hoped either that the Executive would be beaten 'so heavily and ignominiously that Gaitskell had to resign', or that, if the leader eventually stayed 'on ignominious terms', a Bevanite group would be revived to oppose him.[6r p] But misjudging again, Crossman had wrongly counted on the support of the NEC trade unionists, forgetting that the General Council had with Cousins's agreement ruled the two motions incompatible; at the meeting, wrote Crossman, he was 'annihilated' and obliged to withdraw his (or Brown's) memorandum without a vote.[142] Instead he issued a press statement which, as Gaitskell wrote acidly to Watson, was 'as you know ... by no means what he said in the Committee'.[82e] But to Crossman Gaitskell sent an 'extraordinarily friendly reply'.[143]

So strong was the opposition of the other unions to appeasing Cousins that George Brown later attributed Gaitskell's stubbornness not to personal temperament but to his reluctance to abandon his early backers – like Watson, Williamson and Webber—for a new trade union ally.[144] That a deal with Cousins might well have been so interpreted publicly is apparent from the comments on the Common Market debate two years later. But nobody doubted in 1962 that Gaitskell's decision was his own, whatever their reaction to it. In 1960, however, to accept Cousins's demands under the threat of a Conference defeat would have undermined the leader's authority—as 'peacemakers' like Crossman indeed hoped.

Gaitskell's letter to Crossman charitably assumed otherwise, suggesting that to adopt his proposal would have consequences 'very different to what you suppose'.[12b] He underlined the point to George Brown, who later recalled:

> I was, however, totally unprepared when he abruptly ended the argument about the merits and, walking up and down the room in his characteristic way, quietly and coldly gave me a personal tutorial on politics and the significance of power. He ended it with a comparison. The clash between himself and Bevan at the time of the 1951 Budget was about something much more vital than the issues involved, he told me. 'It was a battle between us for power – he knew it and so did I. And so is this.'[145]

Understandably aggrieved at the way his memorandum had been withheld, Brown sent Gaitskell a furious protest: 'I have stood more from you than from *anybody* else but there's a limit. It has now been passed ... The future will be much affected by your actions this past week.'[139b] On the eve of Conference he went public in the *New Statesman*, arguing that any explicit call for unilateral nuclear disarmament or leaving NATO must be defeated, but that the NEC could accept the T&GWU motion, and the T&GWU could accept the official policy as at least an improvement. Both sides should vote, as he would himself, for both motions; for the union's proposal was

> *not* a flat contradiction of the official statement ... rejection of a defence policy *based* on the threat to use nuclear weapons ... is fully in harmony with the official policy statement ... the only *effective* defence policy today is complete and general disarmament.[101e]

Another self-styled peacemaker now emerged. Anthony Benn was privately 'discussing quite openly how to get rid of Hugh because, with him as Leader, we can't get anything done';[6a] and telling his constituents that a 'contrived clash' between Conference and PLP might destroy the Party over 'this sterile defence question'.[73d] He bought 2,000 copies of the *New Statesman* with Brown's article and distributed them to delegates in the train to Scarborough and at Conference. Desperately, even frantically, he tried to build bridges between two determined men who had no time for him at all. Gaitskell wrathfully rejected any appeasement of the nuclear disarmers and, Benn felt, greatly exaggerated the influence among them of Communists and ex-Communists like Cousins's wife. Then Cousins denounced Benn as an emissary of Gaitskell, warning him that he was risking the end of his own budding political career.[146] At the pre-Conference NEC, Benn proposed a meeting with Cousins, was defeated, and resigned his own Executive seat twenty-four hours before he came up for re-election.[87d] That made a poor impression and he lost one-fifth of his 1959 vote and his seat.*

In the week preceding Conference, the Left triumphed when Ebbw Vale, Bevan's old constituency, selected Michael Foot; Gaitskell's message of support said he was sure the new member 'will prove as valuable a colleague as he was when he was in Parliament before'.[19c] His own counter-attack began with a speech to London Party workers in Battersea town hall. Except for religious pacifists, he said, the test of unilateralism was whether a British example would be imitated elsewhere:[147]

> If I believed that by giving up our defence we shall [sic] be followed by other nations, including Russia and the United States, I should say 'Let us do it'. But I do not believe that. There is not a shred of evidence to show that either Russia or the United States would do any such thing.[19c]

CND officially interpreted unilateral nuclear disarmament to entail 're-vision of, and if need be withdrawal from any alliance' relying on nuclear weapons. But if NATO gave them up while Russia did not, 'this is not going to preserve peace and freedom. It is simply handing over the west lock, stock and barrel to any kind of Soviet threat and pressure.'[19c] His supporters had at last found their tongues too. Press reports told of many local Parties switching sides, and estimated for the platform a much bigger share of their votes than they had before.[148]

As Conference convened, everyone knew that for the first time Labour's leaders faced a major defeat. They wanted no bogus compromise, and their jubilant opponents did so still less. On the Sunday afternoon 5,000 demonstrators led by CND's chairman Canon Collins marched outside the Royal Hotel chanting 'Gaitskell must go!'. (That outraged the trade union MPs and greatly helped the leader's friends.)[149] The same evening Alan Birch, USDAW's pro-Gaitskell general secretary, was shouted down as the pre-Conference demonstration became a near-riot: 'attitudes towards the Bomb have banished fraternal feelings ... [producing] complete absence of tolerance towards opposing views. The critics did not want to hear the official line.'[65b] Long before Gaitskell's speech that was said to cause offence, Hugh and Dora felt that 'hostility rang through the air – you felt a physical hostile atmosphere'.[138a] Inside the Royal Hotel neither camp would speak to the other; most people, except the leader's close friends, gleefully or gloomily gossiped about his successor. A Transport House sympathiser was struck by an 'overpowering sense of this man being

---

* It went to Mikardo, elected with fewer votes than when Benn had replaced him the year before.

shunned and isolated' by colleagues fearing association with inevitable defeat.[150 - 1a]

> It is the same scene on the promenade – Mr. and Mrs Gaitskell left by other Party leaders to walk alone ... not once have I seen other key Labour Parliamentary leaders talking to Mr. Gaitskell ... Never before has a party and its leader fallen apart in an atmosphere so devoid of compassion.[152]

Manoeuvring to the last over the defence resolutions, the rival union leaders that weekend still sought to deny Cousins his victory. Besides the two proposals voted at Douglas – the official policy and the T&GWU resolution – the Scarborough Conference had before it the AEU motion calling (after an innocuous preamble) for 'the unilateral renunciation of the testing, manufacture, stockpiling, and basing of all nuclear weapons in Great Britain'. Three of the big six unions were mandated to support unilateralism but the Transport Workers were not, having in 1959 most carefully denied any such commitment. But on Cousins's own resolution the three were not bound – and not friendly. The Railwaymen's executive had been on sour terms with the Transport Workers since the bus strike of 1958, and recommended a vote against it;[73e] USDAW's leaders took a similar line; and Carron as president urged the AEU delegation to abstain on it while voting (as at Douglas) for both its own motion and the official statement (which was silent about American bases). So the AEU's unilateralist motion, for which these three unions had to vote, might lose without T&GWU backing; and the T&GWU resolution might still be defeated owing to this reticence of the other unions.[153a]

To prevent that outcome Cousins was quite prepared to treat his mandate just as flexibly as Carron. First he vainly offered to withdraw his own motion and support the AEU's on condition they promised not to vote for the official statement:[154a b] demonstrating conclusively that he would not compromise as the 'fudgers' like Benn, Brown and Crossman had hoped. Gaitskell had already given his answer to that idea: 'a very simple one. If indeed there is no difference between the T&GWU resolution and the Statement, let the T&GWU support the Statement instead of opposing it.'[82e] Now Cousins had given his, and when Brown reached Scarborough on the Saturday, he went straight to Gaitskell to say he had abandoned his plan.[155a b]

Sunday 2 October 1960 was a decisive day. That morning Gaitskell, reading the Lesson at the traditional pre-Conference church service, pronounced words which the press found apposite: 'Then there arose a reasoning among them, which of them should be greatest'.[65b] In the afternoon the CND demonstrators condemned Gaitskell; and, at the NEC, the trade union members again surprised Crossman by adamantly rejecting any deal with Cousins. The Executive voted 17 to 4 to oppose the AEU unilateralist motion, 14 to 5 not to negotiate with the T&GWU, and then (after Benn's resignation) 13 to 7 to oppose the T&GWU motion.[156] Within the individual unions, the NUR followed their leadership and opposed the Transport Workers, but USDAW refused to do so. Meanwhile Cousins had ensured Gaitskell's defeat (though not his own victory) by persuading his union to vote, without a mandate, for unilateralism.[153a b] Everything now turned on the AEU.

That union's unilateralist motion was opposed not only by the regular leaders, but also by the 'fudgers' Benn, Brown and Crossman. It could not be withdrawn, for its seconder Ian Mikardo would certainly not consent. As a desperate expedient Carron conceived the idea of treating it as compatible with official policy by offering to remit its last nine words about bases for negotiation with the NEC and the General Council.[154a] But the AEU delegation were irritated at the press ridicule for their vote both ways at Douglas; on Tuesday night, 4 October, they decided after some assiduous lobbying to oppose the official statement and support both hostile motions, the T&GWU's and their own.[157] Carron was at Leeds at the annual dinner of the union's Yorkshire district committee, which protested unanimously; and he declined to move the union's motion.[158] But now the leadership was bound to be defeated on defence.

vii *Scarborough: Pyrrhic Defeat*

Gaitskell's leadership was challenged on two other fronts. One was the Party constitution, where he lost a preliminary skirmish but the position was unexpectedly retrieved on the floor. The other was the Left's effort to refer back his new statement of aims which was to supplement Clause Four.

Two motions asserted the supremacy of Conference over the PLP: an extreme one from Nottingham Central required MPs to 'carry out fully' its instructions; a milder one from Wednesbury said that as the final authority it should determine 'the policy of the Labour Party to be pursued nationally and in Parliament on questions of principle'. Its mover was the local MP John Stonehouse, who had pressed the issue all summer. In June the PLP had agreed to attach to its vote of confidence in the leader an addendum by Stonehouse which in that context was too ambiguous to be damaging;[73c] now he was trying again.[159]

On returning from Yugoslavia Gaitskell lunched with Sam Watson and Len Williams the national agent, who was to speak in the Conference debate because Morgan Phillips was ill.[82f] (They were seen by Harold Wilson, whose lively suspicions were at once aroused.) Next day Gaitskell met the Party officers and, supported by Williams, urged the Executive to take 'a clear, strong line' that Conference had no right to instruct the PLP. Crossman, present as vice-chairman, protested that the Executive speaker must also stress its right to expel defiant MPs (which Gaitskell called 'very theoretical'); and then arranged a conspiratorial dinner with Wilson and Barbara Castle to frustrate any attempt to use the PLP against Conference: 'I am quite sure he [Gaitskell] is not going to get away with this as soon as the NEC trade union members smell what is up.'[6r] Those three agreed to revive a Bevanite-style group, and after the dinner, 'miracle of miracles – he [Wilson] seized the bill ... and himself paid £6. This makes me think that he is really seriously out for the Leadership!'[6p]

Several members argued at the NEC that to oppose the Wednesbury resolution would raise the Conference temperature so that the Nottingham one might sweep through on angry protest votes.[153a] Gaitskell strenuously disagreed, but lost by 12 to 11, and the Executive then voted 15 to 8 to accept the one with qualifications while opposing the other.[87e] In the debate the Nottingham mover stressed that her motion was directed against Gaitskell and his friends, was meant 'to bind our Parliamentary Party hand and foot', and should lead every CLP with a Labour member to consider whether to 'get rid of him – sack him – kick him out'.[14b] That was felt to be going rather far. Christopher Mayhew pointed out that if the unilateralists won

> Conference will be asking me to vote in Parliament not only contrary to my strong personal convictions, but contrary to the views of my local Labour Party ... of the great majority of my constituents ... of the Parliamentary Labour Party ... and, above all, contrary to my election pledges.[14c]

To the delight of the Gaitskellites, Len Williams wound up with unexpected skill, recalling that Conference needed a two-thirds majority to include any item in the Party programme, and saying that the NEC accepted the Wednesbury resolution within the normal rule 'that nobody at all has the power to instruct, control or dictate to the Parliamentary Labour Party'. Stonehouse enraged his more intransigent supporters by agreeing to that interpretation, and his motion passed easily while Nottingham's was overwhelmingly lost.[160] Shadow Cabinet members were now showing a new sympathy for the leader as they saw his 'personal prestige rising steadily, hour by hour ... there were six other compliments to Mr. Gaitskell's leadership. And each burst of applause was warmer, louder and longer than the one before'.[65c]

The third front, the attack on the new statement of aims, was meant as a direct condemnation of Gaitskell personally; and here Cousins was joined by only one other big union, the NUR, supporting old-style nationalisation as it had in 1957. With over 4 million votes cast for the platform, there was plainly no general opposition majority at Scarborough. That made the defence debate on Wednesday 5 October the more dramatic. After all the weekend manoeuvres the leadership seemed doomed to heavy defeat on this issue at least, for the latest calculations of committed votes gave the critics a majority of nearly a million.[161]

Sam Watson opened, saying many unions had decided their votes before the official policy was worked out, and (while respecting Labour believers in unilateralism) denouncing the 'Communists, Trotskyists and fellow travellers' who were using it 'to weaken, disintegrate, and, if possible, destroy this great social democratic movement of ours'. (Gaitskell was later bitterly condemned for saying much less.) Watson twice asked opponents of the official policy whether NATO (as well as Britain) should give up nuclear weapons which Russia kept.[14e] The AEU motion was silent on that, though its mover was explicitly anti-NATO.[14f] But Cousins was as evasive or incomprehensible was ever: 'When people say to me, do I think the Western Alliance should have nuclear weapons whilst the Russians have them, I say that I am not talking for the Western Alliance, I am talking for Britain.' He concluded with a masterpiece of obscurity:

> When I am asked if it means getting out of N.A.T.O., if the question is posed to me as simply saying, am I prepared to go on remaining in an organisation over which I have no control, but which can destroy us instantly, my answer is Yes, if the choice is that. But it is not that.[14g]

On television that night Kenneth Harris at last extracted two intelligible phrases from the flood of words:

> HARRIS: Would it be fair to say, Mr. Cousins, that what you would like to see is a British Government in NATO, telling NATO to give up the H-bomb?
> COUSINS: Of course, of course ...
> HARRIS: Would you get out of NATO if necessary?
> COUSINS: If necessary, of course, yes.[162]

In the debate, Cousins alleged quite wrongly that the drafting committee had rejected an item included in both the T&GWU resolution and Labour's 1958 policy: opposition to aircraft carrying nuclear weapons patrolling from British bases. 'If they had agreed that, we could have been nearer agreement now than ever we have been before in our lives.'[14h] * He had indicated the previous day that his approach over defence would have been different if Gaitskell had never raised Clause Four; but now he claimed

---

* Gaitskell replied that as part of previous policy it was reaffirmed in the second paragraph of the official statement; and that no one had ever raised the point in any of the talks.[14i]

'very proudly' that he and his union had taken their stand against the bomb when the Communists were supporting it. (That was true of himself though not of the union.) He rebutted any suggestion of pacifism:

> Sam talks about our being repudiated if ever we were to tell the electorate in this country that we had surrendered the defence of these fair isles. Of course we would, and we would deserve it. But we regard ourselves as the real patriots ... this is an attempt to make you an expendable base for America.

Shortly before 3 p.m. Gaitskell rose in a tense and crowded hall to make the most important speech of his life. Neither he nor his wife had slept the previous night. He had written the peroration at 4 a.m., and—for the first time since his maiden speech in the House fifteen years before—told her most of what he intended to say. He told her, too, that probably he would lose, retire to the back benches, and carry on the struggle from there.[163]

Now, under the glare and heat of the television lights, he was 'white with tension ... [and] looked intensely tired'.[164a] He began by saying that the Party was united on so much that he had hoped that the official policy— with the give and take it involved, including 'the decision not to remain an independent nuclear power'—would have been accepted by the over- whelming majority. It had not: and as he turned to his unilateralist critics, the tiredness vanished.[164a] It was to CND's credit, he said, that they did not pretend to moral virtue by renouncing Britain's nuclear weapons while still sheltering for security behind America's; but neither Cousins nor Foot nor the AEU spokesman would say openly that Britain should leave NATO unless it gave up those weapons. Suppose NATO did so:

> Are we really so simple as to believe that the Soviet Union, whose belief in the ultimate triumph of communism is continually reiterated by their spokesmen, are not going to use the power you put into their hands? ... if the Japanese had had atomic weapons in 1945, do you think that President Truman would have authorised the dropping of the bomb? ... Mr. Kruschev himself ... believes that the possibility of retaliation deters the United States ... why should we not apply the theory the other way round?

So, since the other NATO countries would not give up nuclear weapons:

> You cannot escape it. If you are a unilateralist in principle, you are driven in to becoming a neutralist ... either they [the AEU] mean that they will follow the cowardly hypocritical course of saying: 'We do not want nuclear bombs, but for God's sake, Americans, protect us', or they are saying that we should get out of N.A.T.O. ...

if you give them [the USSR] an opportunity of advancing the cause they believe in without cost or serious risk to themselves, they will not reject the opportunity.

The AEU motion was mostly innocuous, but sixty resolutions calling for Britain to leave NATO had been withdrawn in its favour, and if he now pretended it was compatible with the official policy, Labour would become 'the laughing stock of the country'. He could not understand what the T&GWU motion implied about NATO, or what Cousins's explanation meant. 'I leave it to Conference to decide whether we had a clear answer.' Either the differences between it and the policy statement were serious and the Executive had to oppose it, or they were 'almost negligible, as some of my colleagues believe. But if that is the case, how can one explain [Cousins's] determined opposition to the policy statement?'[14J]

After speaking for forty-five minutes, 'he turned to the issue that everyone has been talking about ... [except] in the debate. THE LEADERSHIP'.[164b] That, he said, was a matter for the PLP:

> I would not wish for one day to remain a Leader who had lost the confidence of his colleagues in Parliament. It is perfectly reasonable to try to get rid of somebody ... who you think perhaps is not a good Leader ... What would be wrong ... and would not be forgiven, is if, in order to get rid of a man, you supported a policy in which you did not wholeheartedly believe.

Furious interruptions began, especially from the galleries packed with his implacable foes.[165a b] 'I have been subject to some criticism and attack,' he shouted back. 'I am entitled to reply.'[164b d] He took up the constitutional issue, no longer in the abstract but as it would soon face the PLP:

> It is not in dispute that the vast majority of Labour Members of Parliament are utterly opposed to unilateralism and neutralism. So what do you expect them to do? Change their minds overnight? ... Supposing all of us, like well-behaved sheep were to follow the policies of unilateralism and neutralism, what kind of an impression would that make upon the British people? ... I do not believe that the Labour Members of Parliament are prepared to act as time servers ... because they are men of conscience and honour ... honest men, loyal men, steadfast men, experienced men, with a lifetime of service to the Labour Movement.
>
> There are other people too, not in Parliament, in the Party who share our convictions. What sort of people do you think they are? What sort of people do you think we are? Do you think we can simply

accept a decision of this kind? Do you think that we can become over-night the pacifists, unilateralists and fellow travellers that other people are? How wrong can you be? As wrong as you are about the attitude of the British people.[14l]

The passage brought continuous boos and shouts, reaching a crescendo at the words 'fellow travellers'.[166] 'It was a fantastic scene, unprecedented as the Party leader's remarks were lost in the howls of protest.'[164b]

He suggested that the system by which most votes were predetermined before the Executive recommendations were known

is not really a very wise one ... the result may deal this Party a grave blow ... but ... There are some of us, Mr. Chairman, who will fight and fight and fight again to save the Party we love. We will fight and fight and fight again to bring back sanity and honesty and dignity, so that our Party with its great past may retain its glory and its greatness.

He appealed to 'delegates who are still free to decide' to support 'a policy ... which yet could so easily have united the great Party of ours, and to reject what I regard as the suicidal path of unilateral disarmament which will leave our country defenceless and alone.'[14l]

Gaitskell's speech did not create the division in the Labour Party. But it certainly made the split obviously, physically visible. As he finished exhausted, drenched in perspiration under the hot television lights like an actor after a major performance, he was greeted by cheers from nearly two-thirds of the delegates.[65d e] It was 'the biggest ovation of his life ... He sat down — but they would not let him go. Far more than half were on their feet again singing with great fervour that he was a Jolly Good Fellow.'[164c] On the platform where the NEC sat, several trade unionists joined in enthusiastically, while the middle-class MPs alongside them stayed ostentatiously seated like the glum minority in the hall:[167a b]

Never have so many matches been struck in such a short time on one small pipeful of tobacco as there were by Mr. Wilson during Mr. Gaitskell's speech. He remained seated in silent demonstration of protest during the standing ovation the leader received.[167a]

Then the votes were announced. The Executive had lost four times. The official policy went down by just under 300,000. Slightly bigger majorities carried the AEU's unilateralist motion and defeated a Woodworkers' resolution endorsing the official statement and supporting NATO. Cousins's ambiguous resolution squeaked through but, thanks to the opposition of the NUR, by only a tiny margin.

TABLE 4   *Defence Votes at Scarborough, 1960* (*in thousands*)

Motion:	NEC	ASW	AEU	T&GWU
For the leadership	3,042	2,999	2,896	3,239
For the opposition	3,339	3,331	3,303	3,282
Majority	− 297	− 332	+407	+ 43
Result	lost	lost	carried	carried

For the first time the Left had beaten the leadership on a major issue – and Dora was puzzled that they looked so glum at the results, while Hugh sat beaming.[138a] 'He smiled until he almost laughed ... This was none of the predicted humiliation and disaster for the Leader.'[164c] For instead of the million-odd votes expected, the majority against him was only a third of that: he had appealed successfully to those 'still free to decide'. One unilaterist later recalled the impact of 'the most telling speech any politician has made for a very, very long time'.[168] Two unions, not mandated, switched their votes while Gaitskell was on his feet.[164a] The secretary of the Campaign for Nuclear Disarmament herself testified: 'He was extraordinarily effective ... as he spoke you could feel the Constituency Party votes falling like heavy rain around you ... it was a hollow victory.'[169]

The figures showed roughly how the constituency Parties had voted. In 1960 the local Parties were much bigger, more vital and representative than they have since become, and their verdict was trebly significant. First, most of those who decided after hearing the debate were from CLPs; most other votes had been settled months before by people pronouncing on documents they had not seen. Secondly the CLPs, which could make and unmake MPs, would influence Gaitskell's next vital battle in the PLP. Thirdly they symbolised the Left's cherished myth: a democratic, struggling rank and file perpetually baffled by an elitist leadership.[170] The very people who had so long been trumpeted by *Tribune* and the Left as the authentic voice of the Movement had come down decisively in Gaitskell's favour – almost by the two-thirds majority he and others claimed at the time.[171] He won about 64 per cent of the CLP votes cast, with perhaps one-fifth abstaining.[172] 'It was', wrote one journalist,

> Gaitskell's finest hour. He turned what looked like an exultant triumph for his enemies into the hollowest of paper victories ... It was the greatest personal achievement I have ever seen in politics ... Everyone in the hall knew that if there had been a straight vote of the delegates Gaitskell would have won overwhelmingly.[164a]

People outside knew it too. Turning from the television screen a sixteen-year-old schoolboy said to his mother: 'I feel as if I had watched a great moment in history, a defeat turned to triumph before our very eyes.'[173] As another reporter put it: 'This was no old leader going down; it was a new man rising.[164c]

viii *A Necessary Struggle*

Only a year earlier, Gaitskell had been the unchallenged chief of a united army, acclaimed by his own forces even in defeat; now he was leading a sortie by half those troops against the other half who were besieging his own headquarters. His political style had changed dramatically. Over four years he had earned a reputation for conciliating all Labour factions; for ingenious ambiguity in papering over differences; for giving the highest priority to Party unity, and for skill in preserving it even at some cost to its (and his own) public standing. The doyen of industrial reporters wrote that critics as well as supporters saw him as 'more anxious to co-ordinate conflicting views than any previous leader'.[65b] But for six months he had been behaving quite differently, insisting on policies clear in substance and presentation which marked out the fault-lines within the Party instead of blurring them. In this new role he attracted passionate loyalties and aroused bitter resentments which long survived his death.

Two explanations were advanced for the change. One—held by both admirers and detractors—was that the clash was inherent in his commitments to intellectual honesty and clarity, to teaching his supporters that the right thing must be done for the right reasons even at the risk of a split. That half-truth seizes upon strife-torn and therefore dramatic episodes— the 1951 budget, the Stalybridge speech in 1952, the drive against Bevan in 1955, the crisis of 1960—and overlooks long years before, between and after: it does not explain why those characteristics predominated only for a few brief periods.

Gaitskell was a believer in political teamwork, not individualism. His loyalty to 'the Party we love' was old and deep and strong, and he never saw it as merely a vehicle to power. His attachment to the working-class movement had been firmly rooted since Nottingham; he was thoroughly at home in the slums and working men's clubs of South Leeds; he drew emotional sustenance from mixing with ordinary workers on his provincial tours; at the Durham Miners' Gala, 'he was at his most benign as he watched the banners pass—almost like a teddy bear in his warmth and spontaneity ... much loved by the Durham miners and their wives'.[174] He did not believe (as his opponents pretended) that the Movement had a left-wing rank and file which must be manipulated from above through discipline and intrigue by a handful of middle-class intellectuals and union bosses—but thought rather that he and not the Left represented the real rank and file: the ordinary Labour voter and trade unionist, and the election workers who had turned out in 1959 in greater numbers than ever. Those people, he was convinced, believed in his kind of Labour Party – out of instinctive loyalty, or to achieve practical reforms in an unsatisfactory society, and not at all for the ends sought by the dedicated ideologues of the far Left.

A second type of explanation for Gaitskell's new stance was cherished – or publicised – by his enemies in the Party. At the time of Clause Four it was fashionable on the Left to suggest that he was obsessed with winning power for its own sake and not for a purpose: a view he soon showed to be absurd by risking his own political survival with reckless courage. He had sought power before 1959 through Party unity, always trying to conciliate and compromise with the Left. In 1957 he had found a formula to conceal the differences about nuclear testing – and Macmillan's ascent to popularity began with a denunciation of him for that. He had repeated the miracle over nationalisation – and the Conservatives exploited the ambiguities two years later. He had incurred trade union criticisms, devastating rebuke from Macleod and electoral unpopularity by supporting Cousins in the bus strike; and the union leader promptly repaid the politician's costly sacrifice by a direct political challenge over defence on the eve of a general election. In that election Labour kept its unity despite Cousins, its spirits were better than ever, its prospects seemed good up to polling day; yet it found its popular support had quietly dwindled away.

Gaitskell therefore set out to make the Party adapt its appeal to new social conditions – as the Conservatives had so often done and the Liberals had failed to do. That attempt involved him in a battle on three fronts: Labour's domestic aims, its international stance and its own internal structure. The first front was opened up by his own choice, the second by developments elsewhere, and the third by the battle spilling over on to ground where in October 1959 he had deliberately – if probably unwisely – decided not to engage. He was eventually driven to humiliating withdrawal (short of total defeat) on the first front in order to protect his flank on the second. There, after an initial setback, his counter-attack brought for several years decisive victory on both second front and third. But the struggle left him an object of intense suspicion and even hatred to a large minority of the Party. How far was he responsible for inflicting these deep and lasting wounds? Could they have been avoided? If not, were they justified by the causes for which he fought?

To some extent the disputes arose from misunderstanding; as Gaitskell wrote to one Labour agent, 'The trouble is that people do not read or listen to what one says'.[175] Frequently, they heard only what they wanted to hear. When Gaitskell said he would 'fight and fight again', Anthony Benn whispered to Crossman: 'If only he had said that about the Tories'[176] – quite forgetting that he had, almost in the same phrase, just a year before.

Distrust of him fed on misinterpretation – and caused it too. In that Scarborough peroration, the words 'fellow-travellers' infuriated many people (especially those 'not quite certain whether they are fellow-travellers or not').[65f] Some of Gaitskell's own friends regretted the words.[177] Yet his phrase 'pacifists, unilateralists and fellow-travellers' plainly applied to three groups not one, for no true pacifist can be a fellow-traveller, or vice versa.[178] That night on television he reaffirmed explicitly that he was 'not for one moment suggesting, of course, that all the people who support Unilateral Nuclear Disarmament are fellow-travellers, but I think some of them are'.[162] So some of them were, and he was just as entitled to say so as they were to point out that the Tory press took his side.[179]

Besides the misunderstanding of words there was misconception – and misrepresentation – of what Gaitskell stood for. That was most marked over Clause Four, where he was ferociously attacked not for what he said but for what he was wrongly assumed to mean. His opponents were not totally wrong in reading a little more into his intentions than he said, for though his proposal was only to supplement Clause Four, his private preference was for replacing it. But they were totally wrong in inferring that he was temperamentally a Liberal, without emotional roots in the Labour Movement. George Wigg, who managed both Harold Wilson's leadership campaigns, claimed that the clash at Scarborough arose 'not from conflicts about defence, but from distrust about what Hugh Gaitskell and some of his Right Wing friends would do if they had the power'.[7c] Ironically in the light of events only four years ahead, Wilson himself publicly suggested that Gaitskell secretly hoped to resuscitate the independent British deterrent which Labour had officially pronounced to be dead.[32b] There was misrepresentation also over the structure of the Party, for it suited Gaitskell's opponents to attack him personally for policies which had emerged from long discussions within the leadership.[14m] Yet often the leadership was more willing to compromise than its supporters in the unions, the country or Parliament.[180]

Behind all the misunderstandings lay Gaitskell's sharp policy differences with the unilateralists (if not with all their political allies). Over Clause Four, to many of his followers he seemed to threaten the identity of the Labour Party as they understood it. Over defence, he and his supporters rightly or wrongly felt the same about the unilateralists, who were reverting to the pacifist stance which Labour had abandoned in the 1930s. While that wing were in a minority, said Gaitskell, they would always prefer Labour to the Tories; but if they became a majority the other wing could not defend the new policy and 'it would have been, frankly, the end of the Labour Party'.[181]

Vienna and Munich in the 1930s had shown Gaitskell what military defeat and occupation could mean to a working-class movement and a nation, and impressed on him for life the unpleasant realities of power in international affairs which men and women of good will are so prone to ignore. The Campaign for Nuclear Disarmament mobilised those people in force, expressing a natural moral revulsion at the horrors of a nuclear war rather than a coherent political argument about the best means of avoiding one. That revulsion harnessed more of the enthusiasm and idealism of the younger generation than any other post-war movement, but Gaitskell was unable to canalise or indeed, it sometimes appeared, to appreciate its achievement: not altogether surprisingly considering how he was vilified by CND spokesmen, and especially by some of their allies who had no place in a democratic movement.

CND sought a moral gesture by Britain in the hope, but not on the condition, that others would follow the example. On that condition, Gaitskell too would have made the gesture. Without it, he was exasperatingly but rightly emphatic that the gesture would be hypocritical, not moral, unless Britain further renounced the protection of the American bomb; but that if she did so, her own security and peace itself might be at risk. Unlike the CND rank and file, the Left politicians preferred to have these unwelcome implications clothed in discreet obscurity—rather as their pre-war predecessors had tried to embrace collective security without quite renouncing pacifism, thus paralysing Labour's opposition to Hitler and denying it either immediate influence or subsequent credit.

Gaitskell was therefore opposed, over defence as well as over Clause Four, by some who disagreed not with his policies but with his tactics— hoping to cover up substantial differences by ambiguous phrases, and to purchase unity by further Danegeld to the Left. They condemned his uncomfortable insistence on speaking out when he might have eased his— and their—political position in the short run by a judicious silence. As one commentator noted:

> Mr. Gaitskell's chief offence has been to demand a frank answer from his party ... some M.P.s would much have preferred to discuss other topics with their constituency officers.
>
> The more embarrassed they feel, the more they regard Mr. Gaitskell as the author of their unhappiness ... [Though] he is only sticking to the policy approved by the National Executive, the Parliamentary Labour Party, the General Council of the T.U.C. ... other colleagues on these bodies have found it unnecessary to stick so closely to the policy.[32c]

Sticking to the policy called for political courage; but when explained, it carried conviction. At Scarborough, Gaitskell's speech was so effective that Crossman, the arch-fudger, told a Fabian meeting next day of its 'enormous importance' since it 'showed overwhelmingly' that only pacifists

or absolute unilateralists need vote against the Executive. 'It offers a basis
for unity.'[165b]

Gaitskell found that basis by emphasising the choice between NATO and
neutralism: not a provocative side-issue but the real decision facing the
country. Some sympathisers have questioned that emphasis, and suggested
that the unilateralists could have been satisfied if Britain, like Norway, had
stayed in NATO without nuclear arms of her own (relying on those of the
USA).[97b] That course would have seemed evasive and hypocritical to
Gaitskell, and it was also dangerous for him. He would at once have come
under pressure to advocate destroying existing stocks and removing existing bases – pressure less easy to resist when the argument of principle had
been conceded and his own political authority undermined. In the past he
had often acceded – with mixed results – to the call to compromise for the
sake of unity. Now he knew it was a dangerous siren song.

His implacable enemies on the Left treated each concession as a sign of
weakness: not as a basis for uniting the Party but as a springboard for
demanding more. In March those enemies had sought to refer back the
new statement of aims, to which they had no objection at all, solely in
order to injure Gaitskell. In June Crossman testified that the new defence
statement included only 'the tiniest modifications' to his own compromise;
but those enemies rejected it, demanding further changes (which would not
have satisfied them either).[182] When Houghton put it to Cousins that the
leadership had made all the concessions so far, Cousins answered that
they should make more.[135a] Feeling the wind in their sails, the Left would
permit no unity in the Party except on their own terms. But those terms
would not have led to unity either, for the other wing would not have
accepted them; and even if it had, *Tribune*'s temporary allies from the far
Left would at once have broken away to resume the battle.

So if Gaitskell did not stand and fight, he faced ejection or humiliation.
Before Scarborough some of his calculating colleagues foresaw him surviving an adverse vote only after ignominious fixing – by a rescue operation
purporting to unite the Party, soon to be followed by the *coup de grâce*
delivered by a newly-elected deputy leader.[6r] Suspecting some such plans,
Gaitskell knew that concessions made to preserve his nominal leadership
would only render it futile, destroying the kind of Labour Party in which
he believed and finally alienating the voters.[183]

Of course he made mistakes of judgment. After the 1959 defeat, he had
enough personal standing and enough assent from his colleagues to seek
structural changes strengthening him for future battles: an appointed
parliamentary committee certainly, perhaps even a reconstituted NEC
representing directly both the Party in the country and that at Westminster.
Instead he chose to assault a cherished myth. 'We were wrong (*all* of us),'

wrote Anthony Crosland — tactfully, since he had discouraged the idea — 'to go for *doctrine*; we should have gone for *power*.'[29d] The upshot was a retreat, honourable enough since the issue was one of presentation not of principle, but still humiliating and damaging to Gaitskell's leadership.* He replied to Crosland: 'I agree ... that by going from [*sic*] doctrine we have lost a lot of power. We have to regain the power and use it more cautiously.'[29e]

Nobody had expected the nuclear disarmers' speedy capture of the unions, and Gaitskell admitted in the same candid confession: 'Our great mistake in the last year has been to underestimate the strength of the forces against us within the Party.'[29e] That error was not the result of listening too much to a small and unrepresentative clique (in raising Clause Four he listened to them too little). It came from two optimistic beliefs: first that he could once again reach a consensus among conflicting views on the line of adaptation to the new social configuration revealed by the election; and probably also that his former critics sought unity, too, and (especially after his triumphant reception in the campaign) would not seek to reopen the old wounds at the first opportunity.

That second assumption, he soon learned, was far too charitable, and instead he found prudent reticence in many quarters, and efforts to exploit his difficulties in some. The experience had a powerful effect in making him wary about his colleagues and dubious of their motives. For a short time he became dangerously isolated, and momentarily almost as over-suspicious as his successor was permanently. His old friend Frank Pakenham sent a worried warning:

> I am convinced that you are ... infinitely the best Leader available ... But ... your leadership is in real jeopardy ... I find a widespread conviction that you expect loyalty without providing the opportunity of consultation which your leading followers might reasonably expect ... particularly some who are younger rather than older than you and me and who are somewhere near the middle of the road.[184]

Gaitskell took that very seriously, telephoning Pakenham at once to arrange to meet that same afternoon. But he was cautious when others encouraged him to develop closer relations in the PLP. Eirene White, just such a representative figure of the Centre, wrote with sympathetic understanding:

> That you are by far our best player no one could doubt. But holding a team together is a different job from being a brilliant player and it is asking a great deal from one man to expect him to do both with equal

---

* The retreat caused further loss, but no retreat would have lost more: which is why raising the issue had been an error of judgment.

success, especially in the exceedingly difficult position of Opposition, with no real sanctions or benefits at one's disposal. The temptation to work with like-minded men who leave one in peace and don't intrigue must be almost overwhelming. But they are not a sufficient basis for leadership ... What worries me is the lukewarm loyalty ... [of] almost all the leading figures in the Parliamentary Party.[185a]

Gaitskell replied that he agreed to such co-operation if it did not endanger the line he thought indispensable for the Party's survival.[185b] To Anthony Crosland, who also wrote to urge him to consult more with Brown, Callaghan and Wilson, he was blunter:

> The timing ... is very important ... it would be a bad atmosphere, I think, if the election of deputy leader had not taken place.
> The three people cannot really be regarded as just rational human beings, each principally interested in winning the next Election. They are all able and talented, but they are *not* like that! ... I do not think any 'agreement' which might be supposed to emerge would really be worth anything, though I certainly would not rule it out at a rather later stage — when we are through the rapids.[29e]

In the Party as a whole, Gaitskell knew he was far stronger on defence than on Clause Four: with unprecedented support from the CLPs, the supposed fortress of his opponents; a strong majority in the TUC General Council; and almost solid backing from the trade union MPs who knew how working-class voters felt. Strong enough to stand firm as he had not been over Clause Four, he had far more compelling reasons to do so. Defence was not a matter of presentation for the long term but an immediate issue of major policy. It was a decision expressing the whole character of the Party, likely to decide whether Labour could ever regain the voters' confidence, or would rather languish in the impotent purity of perpetual opposition. Besides, Gaitskell's supporters were equally aware of the stakes. Even if he had himself been inclined to further compromise, their strong hostility to it would have driven him to think again.[186]

The Scarborough result brought the issue of power in the Party into the battle. Like Clause Four, defence policy was now entangled with the power struggle, and Gaitskell knew that every retreat and concession now gave momentum and enthusiasm to his enemies, demoralised his supporters, and set his allied chieftains wondering whether the time had come to desert. So, unlike his successor, Gaitskell did not seek to devalue Conference by ignoring the verdict, but to restore harmony between the different sectors by reversing it. Had Conference voted really heavily against him in 1960, he might have felt it wrong, or found it impossible, to organise the resistance as Party leader. But the narrow vote banished any thought of resignation from his mind, or of trimming from those of MPs. As one of his chief opponents had once written: 'Conference is ... wholly unrepresentative of public opinion and ... [if the leader] concedes to it too far, he will certainly lose the next Election.'[65] Scarborough made it both possible and necessary for Gaitskell to base himself on a representative body of the Movement which was responsible, and therefore responsive, to the mass of Labour supporters in the country: namely, the Labour Members of Parliament.

CHAPTER 23

'FIGHT AND FIGHT AGAIN'
1960-1

'The fire of wrangling was hurriedly quenched'
(CROSSMAN, 1961)

i Challenged for the Leadership

THE debate and vote at Scarborough transformed Gaitskell's position. Previously colleagues and outsiders had both written him off. At the worst moment, back in May 1960, he had himself doubted if the Labour MPs would follow him in defying Conference, and expected to have to conduct the battle from a back-bench with less than a hundred followers.[1a] Few senior advisers had believed the MPs' nerve would hold.[2] At Scarborough itself his friends were increasingly gloomy;[3a] and on the night before the debate the Chief Whip, thinking the PLP would break ranks after a defeat, told the BBC he would himself resign if Gaitskell lost.[4] Subsequently, both he and George Brown remained pessimistic;[5] Denis Healey wondered if the Party could ever be united under Gaitskell;[6] and most of the press still thought the leader would probably be out by Christmas.[7-8a]

Gaitskell, recovering from his earlier doubts, was now far quicker to see the significance of the narrow Conference vote. In May he had seemed indifferent to victory or defeat, concerned only not to appear to compromise his principles. That mood did not last long, and once the Executive statement had been agreed, he wanted and hoped to carry it at Conference even if a unilateralist motion also passed. That was still his view early in September 1960; however absurd, such a 'draw' would help to keep the PLP firm. Yet in the sleepless night just before the debate, he was still telling Dora he might lose, and have to go.[9]

The narrowness of the adverse majority instantly banished that idea, offering an unexpected second chance. That night he was sleepless again — planning to campaign throughout the country, particularly in union branches, to 'deal with Mr. Cousins'. Usually he was silent at breakfast, buried in a newspaper; but next morning he received John Harris in his dressing-gown, full of his plans, having already digested the wildly enthusiastic papers and found them 'not bad'.[10] From Scarborough he went on to a local Party's annual dinner-dance, then to a weekend in loyal South Leeds, staying with his agent George Murray. When Alice Bacon arrived to go round the working men's clubs with him, he was watching the end of a western on the Murrays' television, and only when the bad men had been rounded up would he turn his mind to doing the same at home. In bed that morning, he said, he had started planning operations at the grass roots to reverse the decision.[11] His sketchy note of his 'Objects' begins 'This year – To consolidate and capture power. Next year – To clean up ... This year desperately good organization needed. Next year completely ruthless decisions.'[12]

The excesses of Gaitskell's opponents made his task much easier. At the top the amenities were still observed, and Cousins infuriated his wife by inviting Gaitskell to the union's dinner.[13-14] But in private the critics displayed 'poisonous hatred',[15] and the public debate was conducted with such 'incredible venom' that many viewers were appalled and wrote to say so; one man, who had 'idolised' Bevan and disagreed with Gaitskell, called it 'a disgrace to ... British Socialism'.[16] Many unilateralists, being neither sectarian nor vicious, were also shocked by their colleagues who were. One of the former, an MP, wrote to Gaitskell deploring the attacks as 'most unfair, irresponsible and sometimes pathological'; another, a T&GWU member, broke with CND because of its tactics within the Party; a third, a Co-operative councillor, felt 'ashamed' at the Scarborough mood; a fourth, a Yorkshire teenager, who made the best-received speech at one Conference session, said that Young Socialists deplored the tone of the argument and the 'unfounded and baseless suspicions' of the leadership, and were 'sick to death of the petty bickering'.[17-18a] Among the many other Gaitskellite unilateralists who wrote were a trade union secretary, a big-city councillor, a secretary-agent of a large borough Party, a present and a future MP, and several ministers of religion.[19] In one local Party, where the MP was chairman of VFS, a careful academic survey found that a third of the members were unilateralists – among whom, half supported Gaitskell's leadership. His opponents never understood that many voters wisely judge a political leader not on policies (which may soon be out of date) but on character (which suggests his response to the unforeseen crisis).[20] To such people Gaitskell seemed 'a lion beset by jackals'.[21]

Those who agreed with Gaitskell's views naturally reacted still more strongly. Trade unionist MPs in particular, as James Griffiths testified, had many grumbles about Gaitskell but felt all their traditions of loyalty outraged by the 'bitter personal attacks'.[22] The most extreme was Zilliacus's call for the removal of 'this man, with his arrogance and fanaticism' in the name of 'the cause of human survival', since Gaitskell and the 'amateurs of genocide' were 'wrecking the party ... [and] making a burnt offering to Pentagon brinkmanship of the British people'.[23a d] The trade union group raised this as blatantly infringing the 1952 rule against personal attacks; those familiar with the Labour Movement and its double standards will at once appreciate, and no one else will ever understand, why it was Mr Gaitskell who felt obliged gently to explain that he felt no personal animosity towards Mr Zilliacus, at whose feet he had sat twenty-five years before.[24a] [25a] Zilliacus refused to discuss the matter with the PLP officers, and the Party Meeting decided by 114 votes to 2 to enforce the rule.[26-7a] A few weeks later he lost the whip when the National Executive suspended him from the Party for publishing an article in *World Marxist Review*, an official Communist journal in Prague.

The first test of the mood came about because of the death of Aneurin Bevan in the summer of 1960. That left two major posts vacant, for since 1959 Bevan had been both Party treasurer (re-elected that October by Conference) and deputy leader (chosen a month later by the PLP). Brown and Wilson both thought of contesting the treasurership; but the unions did not want another bitter political feud over it, and settled early on Harry Nicholas, Cousins's deputy and T&GWU representative on the NEC, who was elected unopposed at Scarborough.[28] At Westminster, where officers were chosen at the beginning of each new session, contests were normal for vacant posts but unheard-of against incumbents. But precedent was broken in 1960.

Already the absence of a deputy leader owing to Bevan's illness had made Gaitskell's task far more burdensome; and now the coming election of a new one greatly complicated it. Apart from Robens, who had just left the House to become chairman of the Coal Board, all his principal colleagues were calculating their chances as potential candidates.[29a b] Brown, already having a solid base as chairman of the trade union group, was reluctant to stand until persuaded by Sam Watson.[30] Callaghan saw an opportunity, and by October Gaitskell was wondering which of them he would prefer: 'Deputy Leadership   B or C?'.[12]

Harold Wilson was the third likely contender for the vacant deputy post.[31] Instead he stood against Gaitskell in an unprecedented challenge for the leadership itself. Knowing his prospects were far worse in the latter contest, he was reluctant to do so; but the Left wanted the strongest possible candidate to oppose Gaitskell.[32a c] Jennie Lee led a deputation to Wilson, who came under heavy private pressure;[33-4] but he resisted until Anthony Greenwood decided to quit the Shadow Cabinet to stand, not as a serious aspirant to the leadership, but as a champion of Conference decisions.[35] That put Wilson in a new and uncomfortable situation. For a leadership contest was now inevitable, and if Wilson refused to carry the Left's banner in the major fight, he risked losing their backing in the minor one — and afterwards.[36] He 'went badly off his sleep, and ... showed an unprecedented short temper' to his associates.[34] But he was still furious with Gaitskell for trying to move him out of the Shadow Chancellorship a year before; so after forty-eight hours, Wilson invited Greenwood to withdraw and leave the field clear.[37]

As usual, the Left were divided on tactics. VFS went furthest, publicly threatening that if the PLP defied Conference decisions, it would secede and set up its own organisation with its own whips.[38] Crossman, at the other end of the left-wing spectrum, had a scheme for preventing Gaitskell leading the counter-attack – by proposing to call a halt to the public argument on both sides while diverting attention from Scarborough by drawing up yet another defence statement; he thought his left-wing friends had consented to this, then at dinner on Wednesday 19 October found them all outraged at the idea, precisely because they suspected Gaitskell might agree to it too.[25b c] (Gaitskell might have done so, no doubt in a modified form.)[39] At the same dinner Crossman, supported by Barbara Castle, insisted that Wilson should stand – and should seek centre support by flatly repudiating unilateralism; but if Wilson did so, Greenwood – a strong unilateralist – saw no reason to stand down, and was encouraged in his intransigence by Michael Foot.[25b] Next day, Thursday 20 October 1960, Wilson announced that he was standing as an opponent of unilateralism who as leader could unite the Party.

Wilson did not confine himself to the issue of unity; perhaps to conciliate the unilateralists whom he had just rebuffed, he attacked Gaitskell on defence also – particularly over American bases in Britain. Optimistically he argued: 'It would be a tragedy to destroy this 60-year-old party on a problem which may not last two years.'[40a] The policy statement did not mention bases, which Gaitskell would not oppose in principle; and the leader was politically vulnerable on that subject, since he could not count on one of the two big unions friendly to him, the NUM.[18d]

Wilson also sought to revive old suspicions about Gaitskell and the British bomb. They were unjustified, as the leader's private correspondence shows. He had written just a week before to yet another friendly unilateralist, Commander Stephen King-Hall, saying again that the issue was

clear cut and straightforward – on the one side, unilateralism on principle equals neutralism; on the other, collective security with Britain ceasing to be an independent nuclear power but remaining an important and loyal member of the alliance.[41]

But he still would not commit himself publicly.[42] Wilson could thus say:

I believe the crisis of confidence arises from the feeling that some of our leaders do not unequivocally reject the idea of the independent British bomb, and that they are waiting for Skybolt or Polaris to come along, with the idea of returning to the notion of a separate British deterrent, with an American rocket to deliver it. I believe it is essential that the Leader of the party states beyond all doubt that, as the policy statement intended, he accepts that there will be no British H-bomb.[18e]

Wilson as leader of the Party certainly did put matters beyond all doubt, for the 1964–70 government kept the American Polaris submarines and built a few more of its own.

No commentator thought Gaitskell would be beaten, but his majority — out of over 250 Labour MPs — was generally expected to be only 30 to 40.[43] Few people realised how thoroughly the mood had changed on the back benches. Scarborough had influenced the MPs in several ways. The behaviour of the Left provoked resentment; the course of the debate strengthened members' convictions on the merits; the narrow vote made calculators reassess. Those who shrank from offending their local general management committees suddenly realised that most CLPs were not on the left after all.[44] Besides, support for CND was dwindling, from 33 per cent in April 1960 to 21 per cent in October and 19 per cent in April 1961;[45] so those concerned about the next election, and the immediate damage from a bitter internal struggle, had also to fear a commitment to unilateralism which would lead to a Labour holocaust at the polls.[46-7a] *

Above all, most Labour MPs were no longer trying to appease the unappeasable, but were feeling (like Harold Wilson on another occasion) that 'formal unity without a right sense of direction has been the prerogative not of statesmen but of Gadarene swine throughout the ages'.[48] They sensed that on the morrow of its first Conference victory, and seemingly on the eve of deposing the hated leader, the Left had no interest at all in conciliation except as a manoeuvre to undermine Gaitskell's position still further. The mood of the PLP rank and file had hardened against further concessions, as Crossman himself recognised at the critical meeting before the leadership vote.[49] A fortnight later, they voted 4 to 1 against Barbara Castle's complicated resolution on Polaris bases.[50a] Gaitskell and Crossman gave the same explanation: MPs knew that as soon as it was accepted, she would ask for more.

> Two or three years ago the Parliamentary party would have fallen for Barbara Castle's gambit. Gaitskell would have been under heavy pressure to give way — to unite the party and so on by acceding to a reasonable request. There had been no suggestion of that this time.[51]

The PLP reaction came not mainly from the placemen whom Bevan had so despised, but from the rank and file MPs without much hope of

---

* Gaitskell thought that commitment would cost the Party one or two million votes and leave it only 50 or 100 seats.[23b] So had Bevan, two years earlier.

office or flair for publicity. It was not orchestrated by old leaders of the parliamentary Right; for the first pressure on Gaitskell not to resign or concede any further had come from Strauss's group, mainly old Keep Calmers; and other respected and influential figures supporting Gaitskell included Jim Griffiths whose career was almost over, and Philip Noel-Baker whose life had been devoted to disarmament. But a few hopeful compromisers still thought it possible to conciliate the Left, and four of these sat in the outgoing Shadow Cabinet: George Brown; Wilson, preparing to launch his challenge; Fred Lee, his running-mate for deputy leader; and Crossman, who had been co-opted. Greenwood resigned. They had mistaken the mood, and James Callaghan took the lead there in insisting on fighting to reverse the Scarborough decisions.[25b]

In such conditions a universally-trusted peacemaker would have faced an uphill task, and Wilson and his friends did not qualify. At Scarborough itself *New Left Review* had cruelly commented in its daily bulletin: 'If the Labour party ends this week facing in two directions, it is certain that the figure of Mr. Wilson will be there, at the end of both of them.'[52] Gaitskell, attending an American election-night party just after the PLP's leadership vote, would not take sides by displaying either a Nixon or a Kennedy button—and when someone suggested wearing both, he replied, 'I can't, they would take me for Harold Wilson'.[53] The critical PLP meeting—held in Committee Room 14 with its large picture of 'The Death of Harold'— further sharpened lines that were clearly drawn. Perhaps disconcerted at having misjudged the mood, at getting a very bad press, and at meeting contempt from his colleagues, Wilson was unusually ineffective.[54a b] Brown returned to Gaitskell's side to affirm that no compromise was possible. 'You can't do it, Harold. I know—I've tried.'[55] He had done his best and failed, he said, to persuade Cousins not to insist on a strict unilateralist pledge from Conference. 'In other words Mr. Gaitskell was right, and I was wrong.'[50b]

Wilson's friends knew their committed supporters and hoped at best to poll 100, as some of his opponents feared.[56] But they counted on 20 abstentions to weaken Gaitskell's strength.[57] Instead, only 7 of the 254 Labour MPs (four being abroad) failed to vote.[58] Wilson had 81, and Gaitskell more than double: 166, nine more—thanks largely to the young newcomers—than when he was elected leader five years before.[59] Other results were as decisive. Fred Lee polled 73 for deputy leader, ahead of Callaghan's 55 but far behind the 118 for Brown, who won on the second ballot a week later by 146 to 83. To Gaitskell's regret but not surprise, Wilson and Lee survived in the Shadow Cabinet:[60–1a] each dropped more than 40 votes and they came ninth and twelfth (bottom) instead of top and fifth.[62] The trade union group threw all Wilson's supporters off its executive—sometimes humiliatingly.[63] Harold Macmillan foresaw that

Gaitskell's personal position would be stronger by the time of the next election: 'People admire tenacity and courage – and he has shown both.'[64] Hugh Dalton characteristically trumpeted: 'After a month as squalid, ignominious, faithless & ego-ridden as any I can remember in my long political journey, decisive victory at the end, & a strong wind blowing the sheep & goats apart.'[61b]

ii 'To Save the Party We Love'

The Labour Party machine felt the impact of public opinion less directly than the MPs, who both knew Gaitskell's qualities as a leader, and feared that the unpopularity of unilateralism might turn the reviving Liberals into dangerous competitors. For other power centres in the Movement, feelings (and votes) within the Party itself were more crucial. In Transport House, where views were divided, the Clause Four campaign had turned many officials against Gaitskell;[65] and the National Executive, although not yet having a left-wing majority, was properly conscious of its responsibility to Conference.[47a b]

The role of Conference soon became central to the controversy, partly because unilateralism was losing popular support not gaining it. Party members who had for years opposed Conference decisions naturally made the most of their unfamiliar majority status, but rarely sought to deny Gaitskell's right to dissent. Instead, through Appeal for Unity (later the Campaign for Labour Party Democracy), they maintained with heat that Gaitskell was entitled to campaign against the decisions of Conference only as an ordinary MP, not as leader of the Party, and therefore should not have stood for re-election: a view with much appeal to other, less hostile Party workers too.[66]

At Cardiff on 23 October 1960, just before the PLP voted on the leadership, Gaitskell devoted a major speech to the defence and constitutional issues. The argument against his contesting the leadership, he said, would require that no one else with his views should stand for leader, deputy, chief whip, or Shadow Cabinet; so that the MPs could elect only officers with whom most of them disagreed. Of course the situation of the PLP would become 'extremely difficult' if Conference repeatedly took up a unilateralist or pacifist position by

> substantial majorities which clearly reflected the views of the vast majority of members and supporters ... But ... what has happened is something else. The Labour Party Conference has, by a very narrow majority, at one Conference only, abandoned ... our traditional policies ... Of the four major unions [in that majority], two ... made their decision before even the policy statement had been produced.

He believed that Labour supporters in the country were against the decision and that the next Conference would reverse it, so individual MPs and the PLP would 'look a little silly if, when they have adjusted themselves to a conference decision, they have to re-adjust ... next year'.[67]

Privately Gaitskell knew that if the clash continued over a long period, his position would become untenable; he felt he should, and would have to, resign the leadership if Conference went against him again.[68] But he would not undermine his support by saying that publicly (though Pakenham urged him to do so in order to reduce bitterness within the Party).[69] Instead, he reacted to the mass movement's aberration in 1960 by working furiously to win it back in 1961. Symbolically, as his Cardiff audience began to disperse after singing 'Cwm Rhondda', he stopped them to lead them in singing 'The Red Flag'.[70]

Since Gaitskell's most visible asset was the support of the Labour MPs, his left-wing opponents at Westminster tried to weaken him there by ostentatious dissidence – a tactic which produced sharply diminishing returns after the end of 1960. Their first effort was a display of contempt for the PLP majority, as well as the leadership, on the issue shrewdly picked out in advance by Wilson: the new Polaris base in Holy Loch. Gaitskell's view, privately as well as officially, was that loyal membership of NATO ruled out refusing bases in principle but need not mean 'accept[ing] blindly whatever the U.S. want to put here'.[71] Labour therefore attacked the government for its inadequate provision for consultation and political control, and the PLP repeatedly endorsed that line without serious opposition. One week before the revolt, 150 MPs debated the policy for two hours, and only 12 voted against it.[72] The Left chose not to argue with their colleagues in the private Party Meeting but to emphasise the split on the floor of the House: 50 of the 70 abstainers sat on their benches during the division. Among them were the left-wingers, the dozen pacifists, Scotsmen under constituency pressure, and also Crossman, Shinwell and Wigg. (Wilson, like Fred Lee, shared collective responsibility and had to vote for the motion – though during the crisis he was absent from the Shadow Cabinet whenever hard decisions were taken.)[73] A second flurry followed three days later over Harold Davies's motion condemning these bases; against another three-line whip calling for abstention, 48 MPs voted for Davies – including tellers – and Crossman and Shinwell were again among them. It was the last parliamentary revolt of any size: instead of swelling, the rebel forces shrank as all but the irreconcilables recognised the changing mood in the Party.

The Left had been misled by their own propaganda. Energetic and articulate if not always appealing, they were strong among active Party workers (notably in middle-class parties in safe Tory seats)[44] and in the militant opposition within some unions. But even there they greatly exaggerated their predominance; and they never recognised that the more strident activists were out of touch with many other keen supporters of the Party and the great bulk of its voters. Gaitskell, far from creating a division in the ranks, gave voice and heart and leadership to a body of inarticulate but solid Labour and trade union loyalists, who found their views misrepresented by Foot's tirades and Cousins's block vote.[74] The activist minority, who dedicated their whole lives to politics, were themselves split between those who subordinated everything to the triumph of their ideological cause, and those who preferred compromise to discord within the Party. But far more numerous — though often less active — were those who resented the transformation in its character, and opposed further concessions to the Left. Crossman noted how exasperated Labour supporters were at the Party's obsession with its own civil war. But he admitted also that 'the overwhelming mass of the electorate are anti-neutralist and Gaitskell is more popular with them than ever before, and also with the rank-and-file workers'.[25f]

Gaitskell's own enormous postbag certainly showed those effects. Enthusiastic letters flowed in from all points of the geographic, social and political compasses. Outside the Labour Party, they ranged from the Archbishop of Canterbury to Young Liberal activists, while his old housemaster wrote from Devon: 'it's nice to have people ringing up to say ... "I've quite changed my mind about your friend Gaitskell".'[75] Woodrow Wyatt assured him: 'Your patriotism is now unquestioned by the public (Suez hangover has gone since Scarborough).'[47a] The reaction spread far beyond the Tory ranks. A baker's roundsman from Lancashire, a Labour voter until 1959, wrote:

> You pull it off sir my vote will come back with lots of others ... I and many other people are very thankful for what Labour has done ... *I like you*, but what the party stands for at present ... no thanks I'll stand a bit of hardship and vote Tory ... my vote will change when you are in control again.[76]

There were plenty of young Labour Gaitskellites, but the most indignant correspondents of all were the many veterans from the Party's early days who agreed with him that its aims were being perverted.[77]

The same notes kept recurring. Sympathisers from outside the Party stressed the need for an effective Opposition, and told Gaitskell that he was a bigger man than they had ever realised. Labour letter-writers appealed to him not to compromise and not to resign, for then (said many) they could no longer remain in the Party or vote for it. Trade union branch secretaries, especially from the T&GWU and the AEU, insisted that Cousins did not speak for his members; often they conducted their own little polls and won overwhelming majorities.[78] Gaitskell hoped that a big union would ballot its members and show the shallowness of unilateralist support: but the AEU executive of seven decided not to do so (one Gaitskellite was ill);[27b d] and Sam Watson could find no procedure allowing a ballot of the Durham miners.[79a] Scarborough was dramatic enough to inspire a lot of pub and factory talk, with people discovering that their own sense of outrage was so widely shared that the trend might be reversed.* Only a week after the Conference Gaitskell was telling Dalton of 'a new excitement in the air. The sensible right and centre is more enthusiastic and determined than it has been for years.'[81]

Gaitskell's friends mobilised his 'Praetorian Guard' through the Campaign for Multilateral Disarmament, which met weekly in the House. They tried — not altogether successfully — to organise the PLP elections by agreeing on a list, discouraging individualists who might split the vote, and canvassing doubtful MPs not to back Wilson and Lee, whose survival disappointed them. They also arranged public meetings and promoted CLP resolutions on defence.[82] They were helped outside the House by the Campaign for Democratic Socialism, which issued a manifesto on 19 October 1960 appealing for grass-roots organisation to resist the Leftward trend in the Party and reverse the Scarborough decisions.[83-4a]

CDS was originally conceived by some of the younger Labour candidates who had written to support Gaitskell over Clause Four in February, and by a number of local councillors and trade union officials who were dismayed at the influence of noise rather than numbers in swaying Labour decisions. Its sponsors were at first highly critical of the Labour MPs for their reticence, and of Gaitskell himself for compromising too far over Clause Four; it was only just before Conference that they decided to concentrate on supporting Gaitskell's defence policy and leadership, since defeat on those would mean losing the rest. Some members of the 'Hampstead set' — Jay, Jenkins and particularly Crosland — played quite an active though never dominant part at that stage, and later Gordon Walker kept up cautious and indirect communication with Gaitskell. But the leader was never personally involved and gave no official blessing; he even told the Chief Whip not to have any dealings with the campaign (though Bowden did nonetheless co-operate with it at times, notably over parliamentary candidatures). CDS won some following in the unions and local parties, and kept as active Party workers people who, if isolated, might well have lapsed into apathy and discouragement. It was endorsed by three prestigious figures, R. H. Tawney, Hugh Dalton, and Clem Attlee — who wrote quite unexpectedly without being lobbied. Herbert Morrison declined.[84b]

* There were even many pro-Gaitskell intellectuals — a fact the *New Statesman* did its best to conceal.[80]

Far from dominating the Movement as the Left had so often claimed, the trade union leaders were slow to take any initiative. Gaitskell kept contact with his friends on the General Council through monthly dinners — each at a different place — on the nights before it met.[85] But while willing to combine against Cousins in the General Council, and to fight their left-wing opponents in their own unions, few of them would act on a broad front. As Gaitskell had always known, 'They will expect us to do *all the thinking* and planning'.[29a c]

He was not over-optimistic. He and his close friends met on 29 December 1960 and assumed that they would lose again on defence policy at the next Conference. Most thought Gaitskell could then still be re-elected leader by a small majority — only 20 or 40. But he himself felt 'there wd be a big move for unity at any price — no leader cd be elected who resisted. He could not give way — nor did he want to be defeated. Perhaps we should go on to the back-benches. We all resisted this'.[86]

iii   *Crossman's Second Compromise: A House of Marked Cards*

Gaitskell had said at Cardiff that the parliamentary leaders would naturally discuss the situation with the NEC and the TUC General Council, but would not compromise on essential principles or seek to cover up differences by ambiguous forms of words, for that would invite wrangles over interpretation and public contempt. The NEC voted[87a] by 17 to 9 (with Harold Wilson in the majority) to 'present' — rather than 'advocate' — the Scarborough decisions in the coming discussions.[88] On 24 January 1961 the Shadow Cabinet, NEC and General Council — over 60 people — met at Congress House and set up a drafting committee of 4 from each of the three constituent bodies.[87c]

Including only two unilateralists, the Twelve were predominantly pro-Gaitskell. His PLP colleagues were Callaghan, Healey and — still a doubtful quantity — George Brown.[25h] The NEC sent a Gaitskellite, Sam Watson; a unilateralist, Tom Driberg; and two likely compromisers, Crossman and Walter Padley of USDAW.[89] The General Council flanked Cousins by three stout multilateralists: Fred Hayday, Bill Webber, and Sir Alfred Roberts the chairman of its international committee. Gaitskell was therefore confident that the statement would basically be acceptable to him, and hoped to win over Padley and even Crossman, who 'might very well be more interested as party chairman in keeping the party together than in playing with the unilateralists'.[27d e] After all the recent battles, Gaitskell's judgment was still far too charitable.

Crossman, the ingenious draftsman, tried again — as in the previous summer — to find a formula acceptable to Cousins. But this time his aim was not to win a Conference majority by the skilful blurring of differences but specifically to isolate and injure Gaitskell. In this endeavour he spread confusion about Gaitskell's attitude which only a detailed account of the talks can unravel. Having become Party chairman by rotation, he intended to use his new post to promote the interest of one faction while pretending to reconcile both.[90] In private he had called his own early speeches 'ostensibly the most bromidic appeals for unity ... universally and correctly diagnosed as attacks on the Gaitskell position'.[91] Now he planned to present Gaitskell as the sole obstacle to unity, who could first be discredited and then removed. The plan failed because he was too clever by half. Since the left-wingers were insatiable, Crossman forfeited their support whenever he minimised his differences with Gaitskell, and thus undermined his claim that his proposals would produce unity. But when he tried to win back the Left by maximising those differences, he undermined his other claim that Gaitskell alone was showing stubbornness. Either way, his own policy lost credibility as a unifying force.

Crossman thought Foot 'certainly more intransigent than Gaitskell' in public, but a useful potential ally in psychological warfare if he would join in exploiting the tripartite talks to destroy the leader:

> I had Michael to myself for forty minutes and discussed our tactics. I told him I wasn't going to draft a compromise motion for Gaitskell this time ... [but] I was anxious to get a document of the kind which we could say afterwards could have united the Party if Hugh had agreed it.[92a]

So Crossman asked Foot to help draft such a document 'in close confidence ... He greatly liked the idea'.[92a] Throughout these talks among the Twelve, Crossman concerted tactics with 'our gang' of old Bevanite friends, and showed each proposal in advance to Wilson and Cousins.[92b] When Cousins insisted on submitting his own draft demanding unilateral repudiation on moral grounds, Crossman urged him to ensure that 'on every other issue we are fairly close together'.[93] In short the chairman was not neutral but one of the anti-Gaitskell team, concealing his allegiance the better to serve its factional interest.

The Twelve considered three proposals successively: Healey's for the majority, Cousins's and Driberg's for the unilateralists, and Crossman's (in which Wilson later claimed a major hand). They offered a neat study in Labour semantics as each group tried to present its view in the most appealing phrases.[94] The general preamble about foreign policy was accepted by everyone, and so – with only rhetorical nuances – was the renunciation of the British bomb; after hesitating throughout 1960, Gaitskell assented to that commitment even before the talks began.[95] He told

Hetherington, 'The statement would say there should be no separate British deterrent'.[27d] The Healey draft was silent on tactical atomic weapons; the Cousins–Driberg draft rejected 'the threat to use nuclear weapons', to which Crossman's added the one word 'first'. Healey's other main difference from the others was over nuclear bases, which Cousins rejected on principle; Healey refused to do so, while Crossman made it a 'major objective' of NATO reform 'to end the need for them'. Gaitskell had argued at length with his friends against giving way on this issue,[96] on which he now expected his opponents to concentrate – for the miners' vote against bases made it, as Wilson had seen months before, politically his weakest point.[27d]

At the first meeting on 31 January Crossman felt that 'all was sweetness and light ... everybody genuinely contributing'.[97a b] Cousins did not insist on leaving NATO;[97a c] Crossman even thought he might sign a unanimous report – and, when Gaitskell found that incredible, at once concluded that the leader did not want unanimity.[97a d] A week later the Twelve argued over Healey's orthodox draft, then adjourned for Crossman to prepare his. Crossman's criterion was not to find a viable policy, but to appease the man with a million votes. As he put it, the majority were 'desperately anxious' to agree on his draft if only he would modify the policy – but then it 'would be of no value, because Cousins wouldn't support it'.[25e l]

Crossman's draft was rejected as a basis of discussion by 7 to 4. Cousins voted in the minority, but then exasperated Crossman by saying he would put in his own draft.[25e] On 15 February, an amended Healey version was finally approved by 8 to 1: Driberg voted against, Cousins was ill, Crossman went abroad (partly to avoid voting against Cousins),[25e] and Padley, after withdrawing his own amendments, abstained.[98 99c] The Healey draft then went to the three constituent bodies. The General Council accepted it by 26 to 6 (three of them from Cousins's union).[100] The PLP, after the longest meeting in memory, rejected Cousins's draft by 36 to 141, and Crossman's by 69 to 133; the majority statement went through by 133 to 61.[101] In the National Executive the unilateralists lost by 7 to 18, and the official policy carried by 16 to 10; but Crossman's draft was rejected very narrowly, 15 to 13.[102] Press comment predicted that the leadership would again lose at Conference.[103]

Many of Gaitskell's supporters feared so too. CDS stalwarts in the country, and some MPs like Crosland, thought Crossman's compromise preferable to another disastrous defeat for the leadership.[104] But Gaitskell disagreed (though he had been keen on a new document to get the argument away from Scarborough).[27b] He disliked the draft on grounds of tone, substance and tactics. He found its style 'demagogic' and its phrases 'ambiguous and bombastic'.[105] He was against both its concession about bases, and its pledge not to use nuclear weapons against a conventional

Soviet attack — which he called 'very irresponsible' when the West's conventional forces were so weak.[99c] He was far from confident that the new official policy would pass Conference, but thought Crossman's draft 'a very much worse document, far more exposed to Tory criticism, far more likely to have weakened some at least of our right-wing support without any guarantee whatever of getting more [Conference] votes for it'.[99c]

Gaitskell, with an aim different from Crossman's, showed sounder judgment. Crossman persistently misjudged the number of people who, like himself, opposed both Gaitskell and the unilateralists but were determined to find a formula acceptable to the latter so as to isolate the leader. Crossman confidently and quite wrongly assured the NEC that his policy would win an 80 per cent majority at Conference while Healey's 'would doom us to certain defeat'. Then he repeated the claim to the PLP, where the adverse vote greatly disappointed him.[25J k] But as the leader pointed out, Crossman himself had written the draft rejected at Scarborough; and Gaitskell doubted if the chairman's latest version would attract any more support at all in the unions — not even from USDAW, since Padley had disliked it enough to submit his own amendments.[96] (He was nearly right about USDAW, whose executive agreed only by 9 votes to 7 even to allow a debate on the compromise draft.)[106a]

Crossman had skilfully confused the issues, even in the minds of many of the Twelve.[107] But he himself knew perfectly well that the argument was not just semantic: 'to accept my draft as it stood was to make a very large concession ... George Brown and I found ourselves, time and again, in agreement that there really was a difference between us which others wouldn't admit.'[25k l] The other politicians knew it too, and both Gaitskell and Crossman recorded that the leader's objections to Crossman's draft were felt even more strongly by Healey, while Brown and Callaghan thought Healey's draft itself conceded too much.[108] Gaitskell revealed his private views in a candid letter to a friend:

[E]verybody is behaving pretty much as expected — Mr. Cousins impossible — Mr. Crossman petulant and treacherous — Mr. Driberg like a tired snake. On ... our side [there] has been more loyalty and firmness and successful planning than for a long time ... by the end of the month we should have scored a useful advance. It does *not* mean we have won the civil war.

In the talks, he left his colleagues to oppose the Crossman draft; its author himself describes the leader as 'silent' at one meeting of the Twelve, 'quiet throughout' most of another, saying 'very little at the beginning' of the NEC debate, and making only a 'very quiet' speech at the end. Only in the PLP did Gaitskell take a leading part, arguing that Crossman's policy of massive conventional rearmament could not be carried out in practice without conscription.[109]

Political acceptability, not a coherent defence policy, was Crossman's primary purpose. It was not achieved. The majority rejected his proposals independently of Gaitskell, who kept in the background. The unilateralists, especially Cousins whom it was Crossman's main aim to placate were no better satisfied. The T&GWU leader had made clear – and neither he nor Crossman ever denied it – that he had voted for the compromise draft only because he preferred it to Healey's as a basis for discussion; no sooner was it defeated than he said that he would submit his own. As Gaitskell wrote to Crosland: 'there was no suggestion during the proceedings that Cousins would support the Crossman draft ... For most of the time, he adopted a completely lone position without agreeing to anything.'[96] Later, at the PLP on 2 March, Brown challenged Crossman to deny that Cousins had voted for the compromise only when sure it would lose;[50d] and privately Cousins had indeed been delighted that the majority had by rejecting it enabled him to avoid doing so himself.[110]

Crossman's house of cards could not stand. He had persuaded a few people on the Right, but no important unilateralists. As his own account shows, Cousins had not turned into a docile compromiser on one side and Gaitskell had not isolated himself by individual intransigence on the other. Nevertheless, Crossman had for ten weeks been planning to manipulate the talks so as to present himself as the architect of conciliation, with Cousins as willing and Gaitskell as the obstacle;[25a l] and he did not intend to abandon his psychological warfare operation now:

> I have succeeded in my manoeuvre of demonstrating with proof what I asserted last summer, namely that a compromise was possible between Frank Cousins and the Executive ... [though] I have to be very careful not to ... make him fire off in the wrong direction.[25k]

The uncharacteristic note of hesitation shows he had not fully convinced himself. But in public he displayed no doubt, calling it at Cardiff on 25 February 1961 'an absolute tragedy that Hugh Gaitskell found it impossible to accept the compromise plan ... for which Frank Cousins voted in the committee ... [so that] there is a grave danger that the civil war in the Party will go on'.

He was taken aback by the response. As soon as the press had left, Callaghan – speaking at the same meeting – 'lambasted' him so hard for lying and disingenuousness that 'inside myself I was shaken'. Resilient as ever, Crossman persuaded himself that his carefully prepared statement had never been meant to isolate Gaitskell and attack him personally, but only to show regret at the obstinacy of the majority. He persuaded no one else. To his indignation, Healey and Brown told the PLP that the chairman was lying; and the members believed them. Crossman found it 'the ugliest meeting I have ever experienced'.[111]

Gaitskell and his colleagues were furious. To keep silent meant that everyone outside Westminster would believe Crossman, but to retort meant prolonging the backbiting; and that—as both sides knew—was doing terrible harm to the Party.[112] Sam Watson called it 'a despicable performance ... like Judas', and testified that nobody, 'least of all yourself', had behaved obstinately during the talks. Gaitskell replied that the manoeuvre was 'intended to frame me as responsible for all the disunity. You know how utterly untrue this is'.[79] When his daughter phoned from Oxford to say that people there believed Crossman, he wrote back: 'No one who knows him would'.[113] Gaitskell briefly considered moving a vote of censure on the chairman in the NEC, but Watson warned that forcing Crossman to resign would make him a martyr;[114] and even before receiving that advice, Gaitskell urged the PLP to let the whole matter drop.[8b]

Crossman's claim to have won over Cousins was so fragile that, before Cardiff, he had had to tell the PLP on 23 February that he did not know why the T&G leader voted for his draft—which 'the Whips felt ... deflated me a good deal'.[25j] Now, after Cardiff, neither he nor his unilateralist friends felt any confidence that Cousins would back him up.[25J m] But the latter could not resist the chance to strike a blow at Gaitskell; so he issued a statement—first cleared with Crossman—that he accepted the latter's draft as a basis of policy.[25J] He had never said so before. Gaitskell wrote in one private letter of 'a more than usually monstrous piece of dirty work' by Crossman and 'his accomplice' Cousins, and in another that 'the latest effort by Crossman & Cousins is shockingly dishonest ... another phase of Cousins' hysterical hatred for me'.[113] He told Crosland that even Padley might not have accepted the compromise draft and that 'I do not believe for one moment' that Cousins would.[96] To William Rodgers, secretary of CDS, he wrote the same:

> I can assure you that during the discussions there was not the slightest indication that Cousins would in fact put the T&GWU behind it. Indeed, I am convinced myself that had we accepted the Crossman draft, Cousins would have most definitely rejected it. It was only after our rejection of it ... that he changed his attitude.[99c]

The eight majority signatories agreed, publicly rejecting Crossman's charge that only Gaitskell's 'obstinacy ... prevented unanimous agreement' as 'totally untrue' and 'offensive to the rest of us'.[115] *

* Driberg supported Crossman, saying Gaitskell could surely have reversed the narrow executive majority of 15 to 13: a classic example of what the Left meant by 'uniting the Movement', in its complete disregard for the massive PLP and General Council votes.

Crossman had overreached himself.[116] Before Cardiff he was aware that his unneutral behaviour as chairman worried even left-wingers.[117] Two days after it, Rodgers was no longer warning Gaitskell of doubts within CDS, but reassuring him that the resentment against Crossman would now help carry the official policy.[99b] Alarmed by these reactions, Crossman beat a retreat:[25n o] only to find himself in trouble on his other flank. First Cousins let him down. In their statement, the majority had welcomed Cousins's belated conversion, regretted that he had not revealed it during the talks, and stressed 'particularly the abandonment of his opposition in principle to American bases in Britain which it involves'. It was too much for Cousins, who upset the house of cards by telling his executive a week later: 'I am still opposed completely to American bases in Britain.'[118]

The left-wing politicians were no more accommodating. Greenwood and Driberg had supported Crossman's draft in the NEC, but both had made clear throughout that they did so most unhappily.[25k] Michael Foot had given the plan half a blessing in *Tribune*;[119b] but now, when they dined together on 12 March, Crossman found him 'greatly disturbed at the new line that there is no difference between my draft and Gaitskell's and the apparent desire of Gaitskell to ... do something to compromise on this issue'. (The chairman promptly reassured Foot that 'there were considerable differences and when we spelt them out it seemed quite impressive'.)[25n] Next, Barbara Castle warned Crossman that her vote for the compromise had been purely tactical, to weaken Gaitskell.[25p] *Tribune* became grudging and non-committal.[120] Finally, the *New Statesman* confessed: 'The tragedy is that it was received so coldly and suspiciously by the left ... it was never clear how far Mr. Cousins was prepared to go, while most of the more significant unilateralist spokesmen condemned the compromise root and branch.'[121] Crossman himself wrote the last word on his clever device: 'The truth is that the Left disliked it even more than the Right.'[25q]

iv 'The Passion to Stop Wrangling'

The Crossman affair was the first of three manoeuvres mounted by the Left in their factional feud. They acted just when the Party was recovering the parliamentary initiative. The Conservatives were in disarray over the Central African Federation, and Opposition morale was much improved by the all-night sittings to fight Enoch Powell's greatly increased health charges.[122] Only the government gained from Labour rows diverting attention to defence; so Gaitskell, while resisting direct attacks on himself, did his best to meet genuine anxieties on that subject.

The second left-wing manoeuvre came in the NEC. On 7 March 1961 its international sub-committee debated Macmillan's agreement with the Americans on Polaris. Jennie Lee and Crossman suggested attacking the proposal because there was no commitment either against firing first, or to removing the dangerous first-strike Thor missiles which the Polaris submarines replaced. Gaitskell welcomed both suggestions and, wrote Crossman, showed himself 'extremely anxious to reach an agreed statement'.[25r] But the Left did not, moving in the NEC to reject the bases on principle in accordance with Scarborough. They lost by 14 to 8;[87e] for—to Crossman's surprise—the NEC majority now saw that only the leadership was interested in unity.[25s]

In the third incident, the maverick Left staged another defence demonstration in Parliament. Both sides avoided trouble over the government's White Paper, Michael Foot proposing and the PLP accepting simple opposition without a reasoned amendment; *Tribune*[119b] as well as Crossman[25j] appeared satisfied with Healey's speech in the debate. But trouble came nevertheless, over the defence estimates—always a sensitive subject because of the memory of the 1930s. Three times the PLP decided not to vote against them; yet on 8 March 1961 twenty-four unilateralists voted against the air estimates. It was not even a gesture required by the Scarborough decisions, and when the PLP reaffirmed the policy, the rebels were warned of disciplinary action if they did it again. A week later, on 15 March, five MPs divided against the army estimates: three old VFS rebels, S. O. Davies, Emrys Hughes and Sydney Silverman; a persistent Scottish dissident, William Baxter; and Michael Foot. Gaitskell (who had not been present) thought their behaviour 'outrageous', but he was far from keen to penalise them;[123] the very few he would have liked to be rid of were the fellow-travellers, not this group.[124] But the whips, and reportedly George Brown, threatened to resign if nothing was done.[125] Gaitskell said privately: 'whatever was done would be wrong. He himself had not been at all anxious to have drastic action ... It was, however, essential to back George Brown and the Parliamentary Committee had been unanimous (Wilson being absent).'[27f]

The Shadow Cabinet recommended withdrawing the whip, but the PLP agreed by only 90 votes to 63, and among the seventy-eight MPs who protested was Chuter Ede, a former Leader of the House. Yet this time the narrow majority did not weaken Gaitskell in the PLP, for the pressure on him from the Right was well known. Instead, wrote Crossman (citing Barbara Castle among others), 'there is, on the Left, quite a strong, growing feeling ... that Gaitskell must be supported against Brown'.[25t] The protest implied little sympathy for the rebels, In May the Left moved to restore the whip to them, and to require a two-thirds majority in the PLP for future withdrawals; the back-bench Right called for reimposing standing orders; Gaitskell advised against both. The Right withdrew their proposal, and the Left's attracted only eleven votes.[126]

The carefully cultivated idea that Gaitskell kept Labour MPs under stern discipline is false, for this was the only time sanctions were invoked in his seven years of leadership, and then contrary to his own inclinations. They could never be used against a big revolt, and he knew that they limited the size and frequency of little ones only at the cost of unpopularity outside the House. But renouncing what Michael Foot called 'tinpot totalitarianism' also has its price: namely that some MPs, who fear unpopularity with their local activists if they vote to keep a Labour Cabinet in office, first make absolutely certain that enough of their colleagues will bear that distasteful responsibility to make their gesture quite safe, and then register their ostentatious dissent: a display of fraudulent heroism for the gallery, while the loyalists on whose backs they ride take the heat for betraying the day's good cause.[127]

Outside Westminster, the Campaign for Nuclear Disarmament had lost ground since Scarborough, and Gaitskell's critics continued unerringly to present themselves in the least attractive light. At the moment of the Labour Conference, the CND leaders were embroiled in an acrimonious dispute over the decision of their president, Bertrand Russell, to support the new Committee of 100, which broke away to organise sit-down demonstrations and challenge the police.[128] The rhetoric escalated till Lord Russell was calling Kennedy and Macmillan — who were working hard for a test-ban treaty — 'much more wicked than Hitler ... the wickedest people in the story of man'.[129] The new type of publicity-seeking demonstration also tended to excite the fanatical but alienate the uncommitted sympathiser: for it easily degenerated into violence, inadvertent or provoked by the revolutionary fringe groups.[130] In April the Gallup poll found support for unilateralism down to its lowest level, 19 per cent of all voters and 28 per cent of Labour ones.[131]

The far Left also did themselves harm after Scarborough by organising the systematic disruption of Gaitskell's meetings and attempting to deny him a hearing — an activity almost unknown in British politics for a generation. It started just after the leadership election, led at Manchester by two sitting MPs, Will Griffiths and Frank Allaun, and at Liverpool by a future one, Councillor Eric Heffer. At Manchester, Gaitskell thought most of the disrupters were Trotskyists; when he told the audience that unilateralism meant either persuading our allies to give up the bomb or quitting the alliance, the first statement was greeted with cries of 'No!' and the second with great cheers and approval.[27c e] The hostile element numbered about one-third of the audience at Manchester, and about two-fifths at Liverpool.[132] This ugly phase continued regularly for months, notably at Derby in January, and intermittently for the rest of Gaitskell's life.[133]

He stood up to it both physically and psychologically — 'The row at Manchester and Liverpool did not bother me in the least ... I am sure it does us good and them harm'[134]—and after Derby he amazed the exhausted journalists by whirling energetically round the floor at a local Labour Party dance.[15] But it added to the heavy strain on a man who was already over-conscientious in carrying out his burdensome duties. He added the extra load of these bitter meetings because he thought it his duty, believed in the power of rational argument, and was sure he could persuade ordinary people both of the sincerity of his beliefs and of the cogency of his case. Some politicians positively revel in violent controversy, and rather relish the hatred of the misguided. Gaitskell did not. As Roy Jenkins put it, 'Morally he was in the bravest of all categories: he flinched, but he always went on.'[135a] But those months of physical exhaustion and mental strain must have taken a terrible toll.

Gaitskell knew he was gaining ground, telling Hetherington that he expected the next Conference to produce neither another Scarborough nor a victory for his own policy, but a 'messy' intermediate result accepting his two essentials—staying in NATO, which must keep nuclear weapons while Russia did—after which he could 'cope with the consequences'.[27f] He did not relish the prospect, thinking that 1959 had exposed the falsity of 'the smooth and unreal solution that unity is all that matters'. He feared that 'a meaningless so-called compromise on defence would be disastrous for the reputation of the Party with the electorate'.[136] But it might be the best he could get, and he told Hetherington again at the end of April that if Conference accepted the two essentials 'that would be enough for him'.[27g] Yet among his intimates he was far from sure that the change would come quickly or thoroughly enough. 'As the Easter union conferences approached Gaitskell suddenly began to foresee ... a second defeat, and ... that in six months' time he might have to go.'[135b] At one such moment of pessimism Gordon Walker, who through CDS kept in close touch with the shifting currents in the unions, surprised his gloomy leader and friends by saying, 'But I think we are going to win'.[137] Below the surface, the new mood in the Labour Movement was already showing itself in the diminishing scale of parliamentary revolt and in the indignation aroused by Crossman's manoeuvre. It was about to produce a sudden transformation in the political scene.

The five who rebelled on the estimates had staged their demonstration just before a crop of five by-elections, the last and most critical of which was in a Labour seat, Birmingham, Small Heath. Contradicting fears that the row would be damaging, 500 helpers came from afar to do a record canvass of the constituency;[25n s] and a CDS leader, Denis Howell, held it with (for the first time in any of the sixteen by-elections in that Parliament) both a bigger majority and an increased share of the poll. It was a tonic for morale at Westminster, and also a demonstration that ordinary Labour workers were anxious for the Party to win, and increasingly irritated with the rebellious left-wing politicians. Even the middle-class readership of the *New Statesman* shared that mood, for Kingsley Martin was removed after a generation as editor 'largely because that absurd anti-Gaitskell campaign caused a dangerous sag in circulation'.[138]

After their respective contacts with the rank and file, the reactions of Gaitskell and Crossman were significantly different. The leader wrote to his daughter that, when utterly weary of the enmity at the top of the Party, he was 'revived & encouraged and bound by the response & attitude' he met on his weekend tours.[113] The chairman found no similar support among the selfless Party workers—nowhere better segregated from the ambitious ones, as he himself pointed out, than in the Women's Advisory Council. Whatever their politics, Crossman found there that

> in most of them there was a great worry and a great plea of 'Can't you make it up with Gaitskell? Can't you stop it? Because otherwise we must give up collecting subs' ... The defence debate vote—3 to 1 in favour of Gaitskell—was a fairly true reflection of the women there. But then ... no woman chooses to go [there] who has any political ambitions, because it excludes you from going to the real conference.[139]

Suddenly, more politically powerful bodies began to reflect that exasperation of the inarticulate Labour supporters; and soon Crossman was recording much sharper impressions:

> [T]he Left is taking a terrible beating ... up and down the country in the conferences I address ... [because of] the passion to stop wrangling, combined with a really savage disillusionment against unilateralism. People are seeing more and more that what we need is not merely a protest but a will to power.'[25*P]

Six weeks after Gaitskell's gloomy comments to Hetherington, the campaign of 1961 had been decisively won as suddenly as that of 1960 had been lost, and he could record everything going 'extraordinarily well – much much better than we dared to hope'.[140]

Over the summer, the union conferences decided the outcome at the Party Conference as they had done the year before. The swing away from unilateralism was already under way, but those meetings determined that the verdict would go in favour of the leadership's policy and not of Crossman's alternative. Some left-wingers, then and since, have argued that Gaitskell, if he had so chosen, could have accepted a compromise which would both have preserved the fundamentals of his policy and united the Party; and that he deliberately rejected that possibility out of either unnecessary stubbornness on inessentials, or a political determination to crush his opponents. That is not only false about the talks among the Twelve, but very misleading about the later argument. Once or twice a few of the Left made purely temporary and tactical concessions, hoping to weaken Gaitskell's position. But Crossman's compromise plan was genuinely supported by only one major politician, Harold Wilson, and by important elements in only two of the big six unions. The Left critics were not satisfied with it, so that it could not have united the Party; and Gaitskell did not need it to defeat them, for it attracted little more support than his own. He was therefore right not to weaken his own position by adopting it.

Gaitskell understood better than his opponents that in most unions the many delegates who were not intensely political would decide simply to support either the leadership or the unilateralists (now clearly a declining and divisive force in the Party) without caring much about the differences between the official policy and Crossman's alternative. It was different in USDAW, the Union of Shop, Distributive and Allied Workers, whose conference came first (apart from the strongly unilateralist Co-operative Party). There many delegates did care. But being so unrepresentative, it started a bandwagon for Crossman which rolled for Gaitskell instead.

USDAW was a union with an old ILP tradition, little Communist influence, direct representation from the branches, and a respected president, Walter Padley, who had been one of the Twelve and was against unilateralism. He also opposed changing Clause Four, and in 1960 had chosen to speak on that. The union had then voted for the unilateralists and started their drive. Padley now wanted to reverse that decision, and so resuscitated the Crossman compromise policy which he had seconded in the Twelve — henceforth known as Crossman–Padley. Presenting it as 'the key to party unity', he made it clear that he did so only as a policy to unite the Party, not as one to be passed by a narrow majority; and that therefore it would be submitted to the Labour Party Conference at Blackpool only if other unions accepted it too.

When the USDAW conference met, it was expected to carry both his motion and the unilateralist one.[8c] Privately Padley hoped that his own would pass while both the others (orthodox and unilateralist) were defeated;[141-2a] and publicly, he said beforehand that if other unions did not back Crossman–Padley, then USDAW would vote at Blackpool according to its conference decisions on the other two motions.[106b] Those decisions were clear. In a total of nearly a quarter of a million, the unilateralists lost by 139,000 to 93,000, dropping nearly 20,000 over the year while their opponents added nearly 50,000; many of those floating votes reflected USDAW's old ILP element, bitterly anti-Communist but not friendly to Gaitskell. The official policy (whose mover had refused to withdraw on CDS advice) was narrowly approved by 104,000 to 99,000. Crossman–Padley sailed through triumphantly by 153,000 to 80,000; so that it carried all the floating votes — but only one unilateralist in seven.[143]

One more union joined USDAW: the second biggest, the AEU. (Even there the unilateralists had, as in USDAW, opposed putting Crossman–Padley on the agenda and, as in USDAW, had lost on that in the executive by only two votes.)[144] On the AEU national committee the Communists with their fellow-travellers normally had 15–20 seats out of 52.[145] That powerful presence weighed heavily on the non-Communist unilateralists in the AEU, the only ones who answered Padley's appeal; the mover of the 1960 unilateralist motion himself said he would vote against it this year and in favour of a unity resolution, and most of the others evidently did the same, for the 1960 unilateralist majority of 38 to 14 turned into a minority of 23 against 28.[146]

The committee had already voted 37 to 12, with 3 abstentions, to instruct the executive to seek a policy to unite the Party. The AEU's leaders were thus free to decide whether the official defence statement or Crossman–Padley could best achieve that unity; they knew that the delegates preferred the latter, but also that the political winds were blowing from a new quarter.[147] In that same week the NUR executive, which in December 1960 had unanimously upheld the Scarborough decisions, supported the official policy by 16 to 8.[148] Westminster felt the draught, and John Cole wrote that the politicians had a mandate to stop wrangling.[18*] Crossman sensed it before his left-wing friends:

> On Tuesday, at our lunch, it was obvious that our Left group is in the process of breaking up again, with most of them only concerned to be anti-Gaitskell and openly saying they are not prepared for unity if it strengthens him, while Harold and I, as in the old Bevanite days, say we must consider the Party and that, since they agree there is no chance of getting rid of Gaitskell, we must go ahead and do the best we can with him.[25u]

But a week later he reported: 'the fire of wrangling was hurriedly quenched when it was felt that the Movement was getting sick of all the leadership, irrespective of Left or Right.'[25v] Those colleagues who were less committed to the leader's overthrow drew more cheerful conclusions: 'At last it seems that the long, long quarrel about defence is about to end ... [soon] we shall at last have an effective Opposition ... Labour M.P.s are ... *dreaming once again of the fruits of office.*'[149]

Gaitskell now had less reason than ever to abandon the official policy. USDAW could no longer oppose it, so that he saw 'a fair hope' of Conference passing it intact—not just endorsing the two essential points.[27h] Besides, both Padley and the union had emphasised that the Crossman–Padley alternative was intended to snub the leader: Padley had urged delegates to 'unite, unite and unite again to save the party we love', in open condemnation of Gaitskell's Scarborough speech; while the union had carried unopposed a resolution declaring public attacks on Conference decisions incompatible with holding leadership positions in the Party.[8d] Crossman–Padley therefore was presented as restoring unity by knocking the rivals' heads together, as its main spokesman in the AEU said in so many words;[8e] it did so by rebuking Gaitskell for resisting the policies which it appealed to Cousins to renounce.

The ball was in Cousins's court. His own cause could no longer win. If he now cast the Transport Workers' million votes for the compromise, Crossman–Padley would seem to be the formula for restoring unity; if not, the official line would do so. In the first case, Gaitskell would come under strong pressure to match his concession; in the second, Crossman–Padley would not even have a majority. Cousins's support for the compromise had been disingenuously claimed by Crossman during the talks among the Twelve. His statement after the talks were over had affirmed that support – which Crossman's friends in the press took, equally disingenuously, as a commitment making any previous hesitation irrelevant.[150]

But Cousins was an honest man and a proud one. Contrary to Gaitskell's impression, he cared about the substance of the issue more than about getting rid of the Party leader, and he was all the less willing to retreat when his own ideas were doomed to defeat.[14] Gaitskell's deep suspicion of his motives had been strengthened by Cousins's statement supporting Crossman's version of his own views: a statement made when the issue still seemed open. That was no longer so. To try now to bring his union behind Crossman–Padley might avert a humiliating defeat at Gaitskell's hands, but it would entail a worse humiliation: that of visibly preferring tactics to principle, and sacrificing his own beliefs to clutch at USDAW's lifebelt. He would not do that.

So, to Padley's disappointment, there was no shift in the largest union of all, and no sign that USDAW's motion would satisfy the unilateralists. It was therefore the leadership and not the compromisers who went on piling up impressive support elsewhere. Gaitskell's old supporters – like the Textile Workers, the Dyers and the NUMGW – returned massive majorities for official policy;[151] the Tailors, Foundry Workers and Vehicle Builders switched to his side as revolts from below overruled their left-wing executives. On 8 June Gaitskell wrote to Sam Watson that 'Things are going fantastically well. If you can swing the NUM, I think we can even win on Polaris.'[152] Less than a week later, and with no one putting pressure on him, Padley concluded that without Cousins's vote the Crossman–Padley compromise, once designed to unite the Party, could no longer even be carried.[141a] Noting that only the AEU supported it and that it was not on the agenda of unions still to meet (i.e. the T&GWU), the USDAW executive withdrew it.[153] The parliamentary Left, which had disliked it, characteristically accused Padley of betraying them by doing exactly what he had promised. Crossman knew better:

> Walter, probably correctly, calculates that there isn't a majority for it and that therefore it can hardly be described as a compromise document ... No man has more pedantically insisted on accepting Conference as the final authority and obeying majority decisions ... and he is bound to accept Conference's support for Gaitskell when it takes place.[254]

v   *Principle, Power and Unity*

By May 1961 Gaitskell's opponents within the Party had given up hope of ousting him from the leadership;[254] and there was no further serious pressure for unilateralism.[154] * It was a stunning victory, justifying in its amplitude and consequences the crude over-simplifications of the press rather than some later, more qualified and critical (if mutually incompatible) academic interpretations. One of these later views maintains that Gaitskell's was only a partial victory for principle, since he conceded so much of his original position on nuclear weapons to his opponents; a second, that it was a struggle not for principle but power, since they conceded everything of substance to him, and yet to reassert his authority he refused even a token reconciliation; a third, that he won at too high a price, for he could never have reunited the Party or led it to power. These plausible explanations are all mistaken.

M. R. Gordon puts the first: 'If the unilateralists were defeated at Blackpool in 1961 it was largely because the Gaitskellites had already stolen most of their clothes and produced a policy very close to the original program of the Campaign for Nuclear Disarmament.'[155] Official Party policy had indeed shifted a long way since Bevan declined to go naked into the conference chamber. The leadership would not oppose bases on principle, but kept finding practical arguments against them. Gaitskell repeatedly accepted commitments he had previously refused: to stop all British tests, to promise no first use of the H-bomb, to abandon the separate national deterrent — at first if others did so too, later unconditionally. He refused at first as a prospective Prime Minister, trying to keep a free hand for unlikely but unforeseeable contingencies; he conceded later partly as an opposition leader realising that stubborn insistence on a free hand to deal with the improbable once in power might split his Party and prevent

---

* This meaning of 'unilateralism' — total nuclear disarmament by Britain whatever other countries did — was accepted by both sides at the time. It is a semantic quibble to call the leadership 'unilateralists' after they agreed to unilateral renunciation of the independent British deterrent.

him getting there. But Labour Party tactics were not the whole story, and there were good objective grounds for every major change; for prominent Conservatives, too, came to think the British bomb pointless and wasteful, and the health hazards of testing and the proliferation of the bomb worried many people in all parties.

Far from viewing the shifts mainly as political exercises, Gaitskell was slow to seize some tactical opportunities, notably after Blue Streak failed. For Labour's moral absolutists his hesitation was intolerable; for the political tacticians it was simply inept. Michael Foot had grounds for writing: 'Moreover, on the defence controversy itself he has shifted his ground year by year ... his rigid resistance to proposals he was later ready to concede powerfully contributed to divisions within the party.'[119c] But Foot's own journal contributed to that resistance, for Gaitskell was not just a stubborn man but also a politician, aware—especially after his Clause Four defeat—that his opponents would exploit any sign of weakness. As Gordon notes, 'with each concession that the right had made in an effort to accommodate them, [the left] had responded by upping their demands'.[156]

Where one critic suggests Gaitskell's victory was only partial because over four years his policy shifted, another stresses its rigidity over twelve months to argue that defence was only 'a means of reasserting his dominance over the Party ... a test-case for re-establishing his authority ... badly undermined by his recent defeat on Clause Four'.[142c] Frank Parkin rightly recognises that the battle was between politicians—men who cannot afford to think exclusively of the merits of a decision, but must also assess its repercussions on their own power. Different people, at different times, weigh these factors differently; but no one can simply ignore the second factor and survive in politics for long. Parkin rightly says that the tenure and influence of the Party leader was an important stake for both sides; and that the Polaris vote, and the circumstances in which three big unions changed sides, showed no massive and unqualified conversion to Gaitskell's defence policy. But he is wrong to add that Crossman–Padley was so pro-Gaitskell as to be hardly a compromise at all; or that the leading unilateralists in Party and unions were docile and willing compromisers; or that their desire for unity explains the turnover in the unions.[142d]

The Crossman–Padley policy (as distinct from its rhetoric) was far removed from Cousins's, but it was also far more different from Gaitskell's than Parkin maintains—apart from being, as Crossman had intended, a snub to weaken Gaitskell's standing. First, it included commitments both to NATO and against first use of tactical atomic weapons, which together implied a return to conscription: making the policy very vulnerable to the government's attack. Secondly, its meaningless formula on bases would have undermined the leadership's stand in the principal defence controversy of the next year or two.[157] Both these substantive differences seemed important not just to Gaitskell but to Crossman and Padley on the one side, and to Brown, Callaghan and Healey on the other.

Parkin points to the unilateralists' brief tactical offer to vote for Crossman–Padley, then wrongly infers their willingness to settle for the 'token satisfaction' of seeing the Party leader swallow a purely 'nominal compromise'.[142e] No politician — not Gaitskell, not the unilateralists, not Crossman and Padley — took that simple and limited view. All knew that the struggle over the form of the defence statement and over Gaitskell's power were not two struggles but one. Had the compromise been accepted in the name of unity, the Left would at once have reopened hostilities in the name of principle. Both Foot and Cousins made that perfectly plain. Cousins told his executive that Crossman–Padley would be 'a step forward' but no substitute for the union's policy.[23c] Foot told his readers it 'would only be a bad second best. We would still have the right and the duty to argue for our own policy'.[119c]

On the industrial side Parkin succeeds in showing that the 'swing' unions were by no means thoroughly Gaitskellite; but not that they were swung by unilateralists swallowing their convictions for the sake of unity, except (probably) in the AEU where Gaitskell's defeat meant a Communist victory. In USDAW, Padley won over very few unilateralists; in the NUR, votes hardly shifted; in the T&GWU, Cousins preferred defeat to the compromise. Many people in both Party and unions did prefer unity to any particular defence policy; had the unilateralists really done so, Crossman–Padley might have provided a solution. Gaitskell rightly thought that most of them did not — and that those who did would accept the official policy too. So, on grounds of both politics and principle, he stood by the draft he preferred.

His defeat on Polaris shows, as Parkin and Gordon argue, that the Blackpool Conference was not totally converted to Gaitskell's defence policy. But Parkin draws an unlikely inference in suggesting that those unions which rejected both unilateralism and Polaris did so in order deliberately to dissociate themselves from Gaitskell on defence without challenging his leadership.[142f] It is quite implausible that ordinary Labour voters made such a calculation; yet they too turned down both unilateralism, by a 2 to 1 majority, and Polaris by 4 to 3.[158] Just because Gaitskell did not commit his prestige on Polaris, as Parkin stresses, it was not seen to involve any vital principle of national defence; and so people — including trade unionists — felt free to express their natural loathing for ghastly weapons. But Gaitskell knew that if he won on the major question, the could ignore a defeat on the detail; and even if it were to be repeated next year, he told his trade union allies, 'Quite frankly, it does not matter a great deal'.[159] Technically the journalists oversimplified in saying that the

Blackpool Conference was a triumph for Gaitskell's defence policy; politically they were quite right, since no one cared enough about the Polaris defeat to worry when it was disregarded. That was soon to be proved by Harold Wilson. Contesting the leadership in November 1960, he had condemned Gaitskell for splitting the Party on the transitory issue of bases; elected to it in February 1963, he at once announced that he too would ignore the Conference resolution on Polaris.[8f]

Gaitskell's new freedom of manoeuvre reflected the political reality: that MPs and union secretaries must again reckon with him as the prospective tenant of 10 Downing Street. His position was the stronger because he had rejected the compromise policy. He had ended the acute civil war in the Party, since no one now thought he or his central policies could be overthrown; but he had not genuinely united it, since some of the disappointed losers remained bitterly hostile to him for the rest of his life and beyond.

The advocates of concession, who had mistakenly believed that he could not win, now felt that his success had been too dearly bought: 'the price of ultimate victory, in a conflict which could certainly have been averted if there had been any willingness to compromise, was so appallingly high that no subsequent Party leader is likely to seek a repetition.'[160] To doubt that the fight could easily have been avoided is not to deny the high price paid for winning in the resentment of the defeated. But it is to question whether, without capitulation, Gaitskell could have avoided that consequence. Many thought that he could: that he was insensitive to the unilateralists' anxieties, scornful of their character, unfair about their motives. That was untrue. Individual unilateralists often sent him reasoned but critical or reproachful letters, and always received long, patient replies (inconceivable from his predecessor). In private he soon established easy relations with them, notably at Young Socialist rallies, where he surprised many by proving a very popular and successful visitor; they rejected his policies and his leadership at conferences, but appreciated his long and candid question and answer sessions, his support for their representation on the NEC, and his enthusiastic mixing and jiving into the small hours.[161]

On the platform he was less successful. He assured one unilateralist that 'Although I have suffered a good deal from the most bitter and offensive comments ... I have always tried to keep a sense of proportion and my temper.'[162] But sometimes he inadvertently caused offence, as when he apologised for making a major statement on defence to an audience he wrongly assumed were interested in other things.[163] Sometimes he exasperated them by his logical exposure of well-intentioned muddle, or his passionate criticism of people who took their own moral superiority for granted. Denis Healey put it even more strongly: 'It was in Hugh's character really to sharpen issues ... he always felt that he was fighting for the right not only against people who were mistaken but who were immorally mistaken.'[164] Hitherto the good intentions of the Aldermaston marchers had protected them from rigorous scrutiny of their policy proposals—or of their dubious political allies. Gaitskell's Scarborough reference to 'fellow-travellers' aroused furious resentment and misinterpretation from critics eagerly seeking grievances to stoke their emotional dislike for the man. Week by week two hostile journals spread the poison, presenting everything Gaitskell said or did (and many things he did not do or say) in the worst possible light—and then pointing to their readers' opposition to him as proof that he could never unite the Party.

Apart from phrasing and tact, there was a problem of political style and approach. Just after Scarborough, Gaitskell did conclude from the Clause Four retreat that he undermined his own position by blurring the issues at stake, and needed to clarify rather than obscure his differences from the unilateralists.[165] In 1961 the sensitive issue was the acceptance of the American bases, and Gaitskell in opposition would not attack in principle a decision he knew he would maintain in office. Many people therefore felt that an advocate—or co-author—of the deliberately vague Crossman–Padley formula could, as leader of the Party, better retain confidence among the passionate Left. In the short run that was plainly true. But intentions which can be dissimulated in opposition have to be revealed in power, and we now know that lack of candour may produce a slower but more lasting loss of confidence.

Gaitskell was not needlessly divisive over the Crossman–Padley compromise, because it could not bring genuine harmony to the Labour Party. That was not the aim of its author, who conceived it as a device to make Gaitskell look intransigent and Cousins conciliatory. It was not for long the hope of its seconder, who revived it as a formula for compromise—which he soon abandoned since Cousins did not respond. It was not the object of the Left, who rallied to it at one moment as a tactical means to damage Gaitskell, but never as a satisfactory defence policy, only as a springboard for demanding more concessions. Crossman–Padley was neither essential to attract a decisive majority nor sufficient to reconcile the aggrieved minority. That genuine unity was not to be had, since the Left would accept it only on their own terms, to which others would never agree.

Gaitskell's victory did not ensure harmony either, because of the losers' resentment, yet it did end serious hostilities within the Party as a bogus compromise would not have done. That would have repelled the electorate by continuing civil war, compounding the bitterness due to fratricidal strife with that resulting from permanent opposition: a recipe for a Party much less harmonious and in much worse spirits than Labour after Blackpool.

vi *Victory at Blackpool*

By the summer of 1961 the factional strife was ending. Recognising that Gaitskell was unassailable and that the rank and file resented the feud, his moderate critics quickly accepted his victory; though a few recalcitrant opponents kept up occasional demonstrative protests, like the July vote of seven MPs against training German troops in Wales. No one was penalised for that revolt, but the majority demanded a return to standing orders, which had governed the conduct of all Labour MPs except in 1946–52 and 1959–61.[166] The five MPs who had lost the whip in March did not give the customary assurances and did not get it back.[167] This minor tightening of discipline by reverting to normal past practice was far less than either the Left had mistakenly predicted, or intolerant trade unionists on the Right desired.

Gaitskell was no disciplinary 'hawk'. A fortnight before the 1961 Conference Ian Mikardo confidently announced that the leadership's 'one and only concern is to break the unilateralists into pieces at Blackpool, and after Blackpool to get out their disciplinary broom and sweep the pieces out of the party and out of sight'.[119d] But Gaitskell had never intended such a purge, and none was ever attempted.[168] At the height of the unilateralist battle he had privately thought the hard core of VFS might end up in the wilderness, perhaps by their own choice, but had still hoped the line could be 'drawn so as to keep as many people as possible in the Party'.[169] At that time some of his friends would have welcomed an opportunity to expel half a dozen or more MPs—only the fellow-travellers, not the pacifists or the old Bevanite Left.[170] But as soon as his victory was assured and long before it was actually achieved, Gaitskell reverted to his former conciliatory style of leadership; and after he had won, he told Robin Day on television that of course pacifists were still welcome in the Party, though revolutionaries were not.[171]

His support was reinforced at the last round of union conferences early in July. The Miners voted heavily for the official defence policy. But the Railwaymen provided a surprise. In 1960 they had gone unilateralist by only a single vote, and Gaitskell had hoped they would swing back;[27f i] yet when everyone else was doing so, they rejected unilateralism only by 39 to 37, and tied 38–38 on the official policy.[172] The Miners backed that policy by 417,000 to 199,000;[173] though both these unions opposed the Polaris base. A month later the Transport Workers held their biennial delegate conference. 'Rebellion in T&GW' had been one of Gaitskell's initial 'Objects' after Scarborough; and CDS had made some attempts to organise it. George Brown too held a meeting outside the conference— since he was not allowed to address it—but seems only to have evoked support for the general secretary against external critics. The union re-affirmed its policy on a show of hands by a majority of about 3 to 1.[174a b] (In 1959 it had been 14 to 1.) Cousins refused on procedural grounds to hold a ballot, saying it would require a rules change which could be debated the following year.[175] Defiantly he told his members that he would continue the campaign until 'this [Party] conference or ... the next, or the next election'.[174a]

Labour's Blackpool Conference in October 1961 registered the pre-determined victory for the platform on defence, another success on public ownership, and a willingness among all but the irreconcilable Left to re-unite under Gaitskell's leadership. A month earlier, the TUC had carried the official defence policy and defeated the T&GWU's by almost 3 to 1;[176] now the Party Conference passed the first by 4,526,000 to 1,756,000, and rejected the second by 4,309,000 to 1,891,000. Three of the big six unions, and nearly a quarter of the union vote, had changed sides over the year. Frank Cousins declaimed: 'Be not dispirited by any vote that is taken here today. It will mean as much, or as little, as apparently, in some circles the vote did that was taken last year.'[177] His speech 'misjudged the mood ... disastrously' and led to 'the first really hostile demonstration' against him at a Party Conference, with heavy booing and even the slow handclap — new indignities for the leader of the biggest union.[178]

The majority supporting the Executive's new statement in 1961 was ten times larger than that which had defeated the old one in 1960. Needless to say, those who had claimed the narrow Scarborough verdict as rigidly binding regarded the massive Blackpool reversal as irrelevant, while emphasising Gaitskell's two setbacks on detail (on Polaris bases, where the AEU voted against the platform, and on German troops in Wales where the faithful NUGMW rebelled) and ignoring the rejection of an explicitly neutralist motion by nearly 7 to 1.* Among the constituency Parties, the vote for the leadership increased a bit (from about 501,000 to 528,000) in a reduced total.[179] ** CDS had certainly made less of a clean sweep than Gaitskell had hoped;[181] equally certainly he, unlike Attlee over German re-armament, retained a substantial CLP majority for his essential objectives. Blackpool brought the unions back into the same camp as the MPs and the CLPs, and reunited the mass of the Movement behind him.

* The votes were: Polaris 3,611,000 to 2,379,000; German troops, 3,519,000 to 2,733,000; neutralism, 846,000 to 5,476,000.

** It was 61 per cent of the CLP votes actually cast: slightly below the 64 per cent at Scarborough, when about one-fifth (208,000) had abstained — those CLP votes which the secretary of CND had felt 'falling like heavy rain' around her during Gaitskell's speech.[180] Before the 1960 Conference, some two-thirds of local Parties were apparently mandated or intending to vote unilateralist; before that of 1961, under half. In the NEC elections, too, supporters of the leadership did a little better than in 1960.

These heavy margins restored his authority as leader despite the defeats on the training of German troops in Wales and on the Polaris base. Gaitskell expected both, and was laconically reported as 'Not worried. Won't take much notice'.[27J] He had routed a direct attack on his leadership with no sacrifice of principle. In the Party the outcome left him unquestioned as leader, while in the wider electorate his popularity soared: in January 1961 only 37 per cent thought him a good leader, after Blackpool 57 per cent.[182] The struggle, as Macmillan had foreseen, at last impressed Gaitskell's personality on the country.

For the second time in his career Gaitskell owed a much enhanced political reputation largely to his opponents on the Left. Bevan's attacks had given him the stature to become leader of the Party, and now he had established himself as a national leader by beating off another bitter assault: not thanks to the plaudits of the press, or even to the issues at stake, but because adversity brought out his qualities of character and showed everyone that he would risk his career to fight for his principles. Old James Griffiths summed up: 'Well Done. Warmest Congratulations upon a triumph won by fortitude and character and laurels won with dignity ... You are now free to get on with the job of paving the way to victory.'[183]

Y

PART SEVEN

THE THRESHOLD OF DOWNING STREET

'To unify the party and carry the country'
(HG ON HIS AIMS, 1961)
'The leadership issue is once for all out of the way'
(CROSSMAN CLOSING THE 1961 CONFERENCE)

CHAPTER 24

MACMILLAN IN ECLIPSE
1961–2

'Gaitskell falling over backwards to be conciliatory'
(CROSSMAN, 1961)
'When the showman is shown up ... it is time for the players to depart'
(HG TO MACMILLAN, 1962)

i *The New Mood of the Party*

EARLY in 1961 Labour's spirits were improved by the course of domestic politics, for the government's reputation was in decline. Labour forced several all-night sittings on Enoch Powell's Bill for much higher health charges, which came at a time of much-advertised prosperity and repeated tax reductions for the better-off: very different from the circumstances of 1951 as Gaitskell pointed out. He added that the government had

(a) Made [his] temporary charges permanent; (b) Introduced and twice increased the prescription charge ... (c) Brought in charges for dental treatment for adults ... (d) Abolished the subsidy for welfare foods; (e) three times increased the Health Service contribution ... now four times higher than under Labour.[1a]

In February 1961 the Government Chief Whip provoked a major row by prematurely stopping one of these debates. Gaitskell moved to expunge the minutes, and to censure the chairman of Ways and Means for having accepted the closure.[2a] One move was very rare and the other unprecedented, and he wrote to a friend that it was 'rather fun' as well as 'very helpful to the poor old Labour Party and especially its leader'. The campaign helped him meet the old complaint that he saw too little of his backbenchers, and it did wonders for Party morale in the country too.[3]

Still more important for that purpose was Gaitskell's handling of the Party once his victory over defence was secure. As we have seen, the Left mistakenly took it for granted that he would purge his opponents by ruthless discipline. They were equally sure, equally wrongly, that he would promptly try to emasculate Labour's domestic policy. Crossman had suggested that the Executive concentrate on that when the defence battle was raging, in the hope that 'while Hugh is distracted by foreign affairs, we might be able to prepare it without his noticing'.[4a] But six months later Crossman was reiterating his constant complaint that his left-wing colleagues would do no serious work on policy and so had wasted 'a tremendous chance ... the Left on the Executive has done absolutely nothing.'[4b] So, *Signposts for the Sixties*, like its predecessors, was drafted by Gaitskell, Wilson and Crossman, with George Brown as the only newcomer.

They worked in unusual harmony, as Crossman noted repeatedly. In April he attributed it to the leader's tactics: 'Gaitskell falling over backwards to be conciliatory ... willing to go a long way in concessions on home policy, in order not to have to fight on two fronts.'[5] In May that tactical need no longer existed, but Gaitskell's mood did not change: 'I could feel Hugh was longing to have me stay on talking to him and be reconciled – but not I.' Next day: 'Hugh and George ... [are] obviously desperately anxious to get an agreed domestic policy for Conference and to get personal relations a little better.'[6] The following month at Frognal Gardens, 'all was sunshine and light as we worked steadily away'. The leader showed the same spirit in personal matters. Barbara Castle had just lost several libel actions, undertaken without NEC authority, and was trying to get the Party to help with her heavy costs. Crossman found Gaitskell 'surprisingly sympathetic, considering the viciousness with which Barbara hates and attacks him. It only shows you what the new mood of the Party is.'[4f]

That new mood was less evident among those on the Left for whom reconciliation always spelt betrayal. During Labour's second civil war they had resumed weekly lunches with Crossman and Wilson,[4e] at one of which Crossman found that 'Ian Mikardo was determined to produce a draft on nationalisation that Hugh couldn't accept. I told him he would find it difficult but he tried his best.'[4c] But – again as in the 1950s – the irreconcilables broke off the lunches when Crossman and Wilson returned to co-operation with Gaitskell, and in May Crossman was writing: 'on this domestic policy I am sure we shall find Foot and Mikardo will attack it, whatever it says.'[4e]

It did not say what the critics expected. Early on, the leader told Hetherington that the new policy would favour selective public ownership: 'They would use the acquisition of certain companies to ginger up industries that needed it ... [and], where subsidies were at present being paid by the Government, take over part of the share capital of companies.'[7a] Crossman's reports were explicit. When Peter Shore's Transport House draft was first discussed, 'all the part about public ownership etc. is undisputed'.[4d] At the NEC:

Here again, very scrupulously, there was no challenge to the policy by Hugh and George, but plenty of other people thought we were committing ourselves far too violently to control and extension of public ownership ... Gaitskell and Brown were so careful not to challenge the policy or to talk about watering it down.

When Crossman went to Frognal Gardens for the drafting,

> Throughout the day it was clear that Gaitskell was not going to try to go back on the policies we had agreed before his defence triumphs. Most of my Left-wing friends confidently predicted that this would happen ... But ... he was scrupulously careful to preserve all the policy decisions and merely to concentrate on presenting them in palatable and convincing form, convincing both to the Party and to the voter ... no mean thing.[4f]

Like all his colleagues, Gaitskell was determined this time to avoid excessive detail. (He also avoided electorally perilous subjects which he privately favoured, like reform of the homosexuality laws.)[4d] The final document had five sections. Gaitskell had little to do with the one on taxation, which again proposed to tax capital gains, or that on social security, which extended wage-related benefits and advocated redundancy pay, and which he saw as a vote-winner.[1b] But he was very active over education, where he found much more support than before for condemning the public schools as major obstacles to a classless society.[1b] The main priority of the Executive was still to improve the state sector, by smaller classes and by expanding university and technical education, though – in sharp contrast to 1958 – it now accepted Gaitskell's objective and his approach. But, deciding after serious inquiry that it was not practicable to turn the public schools into residential sixth-form colleges, the Party merely proposed a rather shadowy educational trust to manage the schools;[8] so that Labour came to office with no policy prepared.

In housing policy, municipalisation remained in the new programme but now – to the Left's dismay – explicitly as a goal towards which councils should move at their own pace.[9-10a] Gaitskell's main personal contribution to the new domestic policy was a radical proposal to nationalise all development land, which he later called 'a hobby of mine for a number of years'.[11a b] He first raised the subject at Nottingham on 13 February 1960 in his counter-attack against the defenders of Clause Four. During that year he returned to it repeatedly. Already he was denouncing in Parliament the 'sensational and shocking rise in the price of land ... I have always regarded the case for the public ownership of urban land, or land about to be built upon, as exceptionally strong.'[12]

The following year, when he had beaten off the attack on his leadership, he told Hetherington: 'he was on the left of the party on this. He thought that it was essential to do something about the inflation of site values'.[7a]

In the very first discussion of *Signposts*, he said that at least local authorities must be empowered to buy up all building land. Crossman objected that only a central purchasing agency could afford to do it. 'Gaitskell agreed to this straight away. So there we were, three-quarters of the way to nationalisation of most of the land, before I knew what.'[4c] When he prepared a scheme, Crossman noted: 'Hugh's chapter on building land gets stronger and more radical each time he redrafts it and gets greater interest.[4f] Here was the complete conception of the Land Commission, set up in 1967 to buy the freehold of all but the smallest sites as their use changed, and then to lease them to developers on commercial terms, retaining the development value for the public.[7b] Gaitskell kept up his interest to the end, pressing Transport House for detailed proposals, writing a paper himself for the working party on it, and appealing for ammunition: 'I am always looking for new illustrations of the land racket!'[11a c] The *New Statesman*, which condemned the municipalisation retreat, welcomed the Land Commission as an 'imaginative device' for keeping down house prices and avoiding urban sprawl.[13a 14a] Had it not been emasculated before enactment, it might have averted the property scandals and speculation of the early 1970s; if not, Gaitskell would certainly have taken more radical measures. As he predicted all too truly,[15a f] 'It might be said ... that the horse had bolted. There were, however, many horses still to come.'[7a]

The section on economic planning incorporated nationalisation policy, where some of the ambiguous approach of *Industry and Society* remained: with similar drawbacks, like the vague reference to channelling insurance company investments which made no commitment yet invited hostility.[4g q] Within the Party, the meaning of the policy was far from clear. To Crossman, it seemed to show that Gaitskell had given way completely to the Left;[4g] to Crosland, that nationalisation might eventually be forgotten (like Swedish republicanism).[16a] To Gaitskell himself it called for whatever specific extensions of public ownership were strictly relevant – the criterion he had always favoured both on merits and to convince the public.[17a]

Signposts went much further on public ownership than the press had expected. 'It takes the party's domestic policy several paces to the Left', wrote *The Times*, 'and puts Labour on the offensive once again'.[18c] Far from being alarmed by that, Gaitskell's friends were enthusiastic. Jenkins called it the best home policy statement since the war.[19] Crosland much preferred it to the previous one:

[T]he issues chosen are of a radical and contemporary character calculated to appeal (far more than our 1959 programme) not only to the older working class, but also to the young, the liberal middle class (where we lost dramatically in 1959) and the new cross-pressured marginal voter.[16a]

In the Executive the Left were surprised and did not seriously oppose; only Mikardo voted against it, and in the PLP their role was not heroic:

> It is characteristic that Barbara [Castle], Tony [Greenwood], Tom [Driberg] are all notably absent when a document they have shared in producing, but on which they have agreed with Gaitskell, is being put to the Party. Each is busily preparing a position from which he can say that he did his best valiantly, month after month, but was defeated.[4g]

Introducing *Signposts* on television on 12 July 1961, Gaitskell (who had been very wary of including in it any phrases recalling post-war austerity) delivered a prescient warning that current prosperity was precarious and illusory.[4g h] He had insisted on having Crossman also on the programme, to demonstrate unity,[4i] and pro-Labour viewers responded favourably both to that impression and to Gaitskell's own sincerity.[20] To one Conservative paper the whole broadcast was 'a gradual build-up towards Mr. Gaitskell, now acknowledged as Labour's dominating personality'.[21a]

At Blackpool, Cousins opposed the policy, which Conference accepted more readily in 1961 than its predecessor for which he had voted in 1957. In the debate he denounced the politicians—who in the drafting, in the NEC and in the PLP had been unanimous in avoiding detail—for 'substituting Government by Conference with Government by Committee'. He called for assurances from the Party leader on public ownership, and explicitly attributed his 'suspicions' to Gaitskell's Clause Four speech. His electoral strategy was simple. 'Are we trying to get the Tories to vote for us? I thought that we were trying to get the Labour people, the people who are justified in saying that we are the political Party of their faith.'[22a]

Gaitskell replied 'almost contemptuously' to the demand for assurances:[23a] 'We have been challenged this afternoon to say whether the document involves an extension of public ownership. Frankly, I cannot imagine anybody who had read the document supposing that it did not.' More mildly, but enthusiastically applauded, he said that Cousins

> seemed to assume that all the voters who support us now and the marginal voters who we hope will support us were all convinced socialists. I would ask him ... is he sure that every member of the Transport and General Workers Union votes Labour? ... 3 out of 10 male trade unionists and 4 out of 10 of their wives vote Tory. We had better start by trying to convert them to Labour.[22b]

Cousins put out a furious press statement to rebut comments Gaitskell had never made.[24] Later, in private session, he denied reports that he was threatening to retaliate by a 30 per cent cut in the union's financial contribution to the Party;[25a b] but he was still wrathful ten days later on television, when he contradicted his own comments in 1958 by saying that the Party leaders had been lukewarm over that year's bus strike.[26]

The public-ownership proposals of *Signposts* were challenged by two resolutions: one from Ormskirk with a long 'shopping list' for nationalisation, defeated by nearly 3 to 1; and a moderate proposal for the NEC to report on monopolies, lost by over 3 to 2.[27] *Signposts for the Sixties* was then adopted by acclamation. Gaitskell had commended it to Conference in a major speech developing his own economic approach and touching briefly on the Common Market (both topics to be discussed below). He delivered 'an awesome prophecy' about Britain's economic future:[23a]

> [T]his is not just an economic crisis ... It is rather a crisis of outlook, of temperament, of spirit, a crisis deep in British society today.
>
> Now we could go on as before ... 'the sick man of Europe' today, we shall become the poor relation tomorrow ... the whole trend of the past ten years has been in this direction ... Never has a nation so urgently needed a change of government ... [to] get out of the valley of sluggishness into which the Tories have led us.[22c]

Both that speech, and the one next day on defence, were successful performances showing his complete mastery over Conference,[28] as 'the most effective and at times the most moving orator British politics have had since television made oratory once again important'.[14b] They went far to satisfy those like John Cole, who had wondered before Conference whether Gaitskell would 'bend enough to take all but the incorrigible Left with him' and so reunite the Party.[23d]

At Blackpool Gaitskell made a major effort to restore confidence as well as to win majorities. Though so often accused of being aloof, and so recently shunned by his time-serving colleagues, he was now endlessly in demand, apologising to one journalist friend who had missed him: 'Just to give you an idea – on Wednesday evening after making a major speech at the Conference I had nine engagements before going to bed!'[29] In one gesture of reconciliation, winding up the *Signposts* debate, he referred approvingly five times to Harold Wilson's speech opening it; in another, he said that in the last two years

> We have most of us both given and taken some hard knocks and we have learned some lessons, and I believe that in consequence today we are more in tune with the people and better equipped to serve them than ever before – I say 'serve them', because it is well to approach

this problem with a certain humility. There is something which should be awe-inspiring in asking our fellow citizens to entrust us with the duty of government.[22d]

Cole (no Gaitskellite) thought he had 'seized with both hands the chance to turn the Labour Party's face away from its internal wrangles', had aroused 'the vast majority of the delegates' to real enthusiasm at last, and 'would make a deep impression on the centre' – though not on Cousins and the Left.[23a]

Cole was quite right. Crossman, in his closing speech as chairman, congratulated delegates on the spirit of the debates: 'the personal rancour ... has quite disappeared ... We know the policy, and we know the leaders who are going to lead us into action. That leadership issue is once for all out of the way.'[22e] It was an impromptu phrase. He found at lunch that his *Tribune* friends had gone without saying goodbye, and ten days later 'I discovered that this sentence had been regarded as the great betrayal'.[4j]

Some of Gaitskell's old enemies did respond. The *New Statesman* felt that 'the tone and content of his speeches carried conviction in some unexpectedly left-wing quarters', and called the one on *Signposts* 'considerate towards those who do not share his views and ... appropriate to a leader who had assumed [Attlee's] traditional centre position'.[13b] The defence speech struck Tom Driberg as 'particularly welcome ... notably conciliatory in tone [to] those who disagreed ... and their sincerity was emphatically accepted'.[30] This image of a new, suddenly tolerant Gaitskell owed a little to his words, for a party leader no longer fighting for his political life could afford gestures now they would not be exploited against him. But mainly it reflected the critics' changed perceptions. In 1960 they had magnified or invented grievances against a leader they hoped to depose; having failed, they now sought – and therefore found – what matter for consolation they could. Both the dwindling of the irreconcilable Left and the reconciliation of the Centre contributed to the unity for which the Party yearned.

Labour therefore emerged after Blackpool 'more hopeful and more determined to throw out the Tories than at any time for the past ten years',[25a] as the reports agreed.[31a] Gaitskell could rightly point to

a tremendously widespread desire on the part of our members everywhere to accept the policy decisions ... made this week ... naturally, those who lost this year were bound to say that they would continue the fight ... But I don't think it will be a very serious attempt ... the large majority now want to say: ... We've settled our argument ... now let's get on with the job of ... getting the policies across to the public,

In the same interview, the journalist asked his opinion of Attlee's view that a Labour leader should place himself left of centre in the Party. Gaitskell replied (correctly): 'No, I don't think he did say that.'[32] He added that it was the wrong question: 'The question is ... what will both unify the Party and carry the country. I will endeavour to do both.'[33a]

ii   *Labour: The Politicians, and the Media*

That prospect looked much closer after Blackpool, though Gaitskell was too old a hand to be caught out by Robin Day asking if he now felt confident of becoming Prime Minister: 'Well ... if I say yes everybody will say how boastful he is, and if I say no they will say how defeatist he is.'[17a] *The Economist* hinted in the summer of 1961 that the floating voters would soon follow the Labour loyalists, among whom 'Mr. Gaitskell's personal prestige ... is mounting skyward like a Russian rocket, although this has not yet been reflected in the public opinion polls.'[14c] In October, with the Conference publicity, he had his best Gallup poll rating as leader, with 57 per cent of the whole sample (and 72 per cent of Labour voters) thinking him a good one. Though he did not maintain that figure, from the autumn of 1961 he never fell far below 50 per cent, which he had very rarely approached before.[34] In time that success was to be reflected in the Party's standing too.

Blackpool thus transformed Gaitskell's position both in the Labour Party and beyond. According to one quite critical journalist: 'He starts with the immense advantage that his leadership has never looked more firmly based and his prestige with the majority of the party higher.'[23d] For the moment the Left remained irreconcilable, as they had when Gaitskell was first elected. Then they had come round in time, partly because of the pressure for unity whenever Labour seemed capable of winning an election, partly through the influence of Aneurin Bevan, and partly thanks to the new leader's successful efforts to conciliate those critics who were concerned for the success of the whole Party rather than of a faction. In 1961 as in 1956, the hard-fought campaign was promptly followed by moves to settle the quarrel. Well before Blackpool, journalists observed 'a noticeable change in Mr. Gaitskell's attitude ... indications that he is broadening the range of his advisers in the Party and adopting a more conciliatory attitude to the moderates in the centre'.[35]

The analogy with 1956 was not complete. Before the storm, Gaitskell had often seemed to his friends too trustful about his critics, too willing to make allowances for them, too charitable in assessing their characters. During it, he had found many illusions shattered and had fallen back on the few people upon whom he could absolutely rely. After it, he seemed to some friends harder and tougher, rather more testy and less tolerant –

perhaps more effective as a politician, but not quite so agreeable as a companion.[36] His cruder critics were wrong to expect a purge of the Left, or a spectacular policy shift to the Right, or continuing dependence on a clique of friends for political advice. But relations were never fully restored with those associates of 1956–9 who had defected in 1960–1.

With Harold Wilson those relations had never been close, but his debating skill and his prominence in the Shadow Cabinet and NEC obliged the two men to work together. Wilson's biographers confirm Gaitskell's anxiety to resume co-operation, which the leader so carefully emphasised at Blackpool.[37] But some like Benn and Greenwood, who had had friendly dealings with him in the past, now felt – resentfully – entirely excluded from his confidence.[38] In particular, Crossman never recovered the place in the inner circle which, much to the wrath of his numerous enemies, he had enjoyed up to 1959. Like Wilson, he again took a big part in planning the new domestic policies, both in substance and in presentation. But he did not become, as he proposed, either chairman of publicity on the NEC, or general secretary of the Party after Morgan Phillips had to retire, or an active (i.e. Front Bench) parliamentary spokesman in the House of Commons; the first would have meant displacing Gaitskell's loyal colleague Alice Bacon, and the second and third would have aroused deep antagonisms elsewhere.[4j]

A more substantial reason was put by Crossman himself. 'You certainly can't have the party legislature working well, with our division of powers, unless the Executive is in the hands of a strong leader, with the confidence of the rank and file,' he wrote in the early summer of 1961.

> Compared to a year ago, I am seriously sceptical now about the limits of policy formation by party democracy. Certainly the committee machinery of the Executive is becoming completely unworkable ... [and] is made intolerable by the leaks from Left, Right and Centre of everyone concerned. Compared with this, a coherent Parliamentary leadership, grouped round a Leader, is a much more feasible centre of power.[4e]

But a 'coherent centre of power' was not, as he had himself remarked, Crossman's 'natural habitat'.[4k] By disciplining himself to work under those conditions he had won Gaitskell's confidence before 1959, only to spend his time since the election trying to outwit, defeat or depose the leader; then, realising early on that that had failed, he had abandoned the opposition camp as suddenly as he had joined it. Finding Gaitskell disinclined to trust him again, Crossman wrote a last resentful entry before abandoning his diary until the leader's death:[39]

> Hugh had quite deliberately pushed aside the idea of forming a Centre ... he was allowing Harold to work with him because he was indispen-

sable on the front bench and I could work on the same kind of terms in Transport House. But, as allies, he didn't want us ... We have tried our level best to create a situation where Hugh can be in the Centre, working with people on the Left as well as on the Right. Our overtures have been refused.[4j]

The end of active hostilities within the Party therefore did not radically change the composition of the leadership group. George Brown was now working cordially with Gaitskell, persuading him to adopt a less 'governmental' political style, and 'to find fun in his work, to let his instinct go in a Parliamentary fling, to give a knock with more force and to take a knock with less feeling'.[18b] When the House met, Greenwood contested the leadership as a signal that the Left opposition had not given up the fight, rather than as a serious bid. Gaitskell won by 171 to 59, drawing 5 extra votes while Greenwood had 22 fewer than Wilson.* For deputy leader, Barbara Castle did much worse than Fred Lee, and Brown polled far better than in 1960, winning by 169 to 56.

The recent minor tightening of discipline provoked the Left to put up a challenger (Ben Parkin) for Chief Whip, where there was no contest in 1960. At least a quarter of Gaitskell's opponents, as well as all his friends, voted for Bowden who won by 185 to only 44: evidently few Labour MPs in 1961 felt that dissidents should be wholly free to parade their private views without regard to the Party's reputation. Similarly, in two PLP meetings on reimposing standing orders, the Left never exceeded 36 votes and finally lost by 70 to 18.[40a] Ten Labour whips then sent Gaitskell a letter:

> These were extremely difficult meetings which without a firm, yet obviously scrupulously fair, chairmanship could so easily have become a bear garden to the serious detriment of the Party.
>
> As it is, we feel that the Party has been strengthened ... by ... superb Chairmanship, [and] we would like you to know of our appreciation.[41]

In the Shadow Cabinet elections of that autumn the same impression was reinforced, the outgoing members all returning with much bigger scores.[42] Wilson regained his lost forty votes and returned to the top, though Lee again barely scraped back in bottom place.

Gaitskell promptly reshuffled his shadows. Wilson now welcomed the move he had resisted in 1959, and gave up the Shadow Chancellorship to Callaghan, becoming spokesman on foreign affairs. (Gaitskell had said[43]

---

* Thus Wilson, in 1960, had gained only two dozen supporters apart from dedicated unilateralists, for whom the leadership contest was not the choice of a prospective Prime Minister but only one more opportunity for symbolic protest.

that in office 'he would prefer to have Wilson as Foreign Minister where he could keep a close eye on him. He'd have less independence of action there'.)[7c] Denis Healey took over the colonies at his own request, for Gaitskell would have preferred to broaden his experience by giving him a domestic job.[7d] George Brown became Shadow Home Secretary, and Gordon Walker took on defence along with Morrison's long-lapsed chief-of-staff functions.

Privately, Gaitskell said that an inner group of these five and himself played the main part in policy-making.[7d] The rest of the Shadow Cabinet were an elderly team; none of the other eight elected members was under 50 and one was over 70. Robens and several others left politics, and the Front Bench reflected the loss of talent.[44] If power corrupts, prolonged opposition can demoralise, causing bitter recriminations that poison the atmosphere, and frustrating any politician concerned to achieve results. Gaitskell felt that frustration deeply. When an old friend said of Robens, 'Alf has got out when the going was good', he provoked the only bitter moment in a long relationship: 'Don't talk like that, Ronnie. You have been fortunate; you have had jobs you wanted; you haven't had to wait for something useful to do, as some of us have had to.'[45]

During the long period of waiting, publicity resources were both indispensable and embarrassing. Though having an official Party newspaper might have seemed a major asset for a Labour leader, the *Daily Herald* was a constant worry to Gaitskell, and a source of controversy in which he was rarely at his best.

He showed the importance he attached to it in the *News Chronicle* affair. That daily fell between the qualities and the populars in style, and between the major parties in politics. With a circulation of well over a million, it clearly met a demand among readers – but not among advertisers. On 17 October 1960 the proprietors sold it (with its evening sister the *Star*) to the publishers of the *Daily Mail* – seeking no alternatives, and telling the staffs only at 5 p.m. on the last day.[46a] It was two weeks after Scarborough, and understandably (if not creditably) Gaitskell reacted as a professional politician, not as a radical critic of social abuses. He feared that a sharp, immediate protest 'would upset the Daily Herald, who are delighted ... and hoping to get the readers ... it was a bad paper, badly managed. That's all there is to it';[4l] and he was really sensitive only to the swallowing up of a Liberal paper by a Tory one, which reinforced his old concern about the political allegiance of the press.[47]

The *Daily Herald*'s own life was always precarious. Three years earlier it might itself have merged with the *News Chronicle*;[48] three months later it was to be fought over by rival tycoons. It was owned 49 per cent by the TUC, which controlled policy, and 51 per cent by Odhams, for whom it was a financial headache. Gaitskell was a friend of Odhams's new chairman, Sir Christopher Chancellor, and instigated talks about the *Herald* between Odhams and the Canadian newspaper magnate Roy Thomson.[49a][b] Meanwhile Cecil King, chairman of the *Daily Mirror* group, approached Chancellor at Christmas 1960, first to suggest rationalisation in the sector of women's magazines, where Odhams were his main competitors, but very soon to propose a full merger.[50a] Odhams preferred a merger with Thomson, and a spectacular Stock Exchange battle developed.

Labour MPs were alarmed. On Saturday 28 January 1961 Gaitskell, with Brown and George Woodcock of the TUC, met Thomson, Chancellor and the Odhams directors and editors over lunch at the Garrick Club. Brown[51] (like Cousins) favoured the *Mirror*'s bid;[50b] Gaitskell did not. As leader he was concerned with the strong feeling in the PLP, especially on the Right; he was alarmed – like the NUJ – at the prospect of a magazine monopoly;[52] and he believed that women's magazines subtly influenced politics by affecting the climate of opinion.[53] Privately he distrusted the *Mirror* magnates, and felt Labour's interests far safer with a millionaire uninterested in policy than with a dominating and unpredictable friend like King.[54a][b] Cudlipp, the *Mirror*'s joint managing director, was shocked by that –[55a] but before long was to see his point.[56]

The Labour leaders called for a public inquiry and a stronger law against monopolies.[18c] But, being unable to stop King winning the battle, Gaitskell preferred to get all possible assurances rather than 'bitch up our relations with him too badly'.[57a] When even George Brown became alarmed at King's reticence about the future of the *Herald*, Cudlipp reluctantly promised to keep the paper alive for seven years[50d] – while privately telling King he was a 'blithering idiot' for taking on 'the rag' at all.[4m] At the end of 1961 Gaitskell allowed Cudlipp to record formally that his anxieties were unjustified;[55a] two years later the *Herald* was replaced by the *Sun*; and when the seven years were up, it was sold at once.

Long before the takeover, Gaitskell had been extremely sensitive about the paper's political loyalty, protesting at articles which he disliked.[58] When Douglas Machray as editor backed the unilateralists, relationships became 'dreadfully bad'.[49a] Then John Beavan switched back to support the official Party policy. But early in 1962 Beavan wrote a front-page unsigned editorial, 'A Nation in Search of a Party', which criticised Gaitskell for not exploiting disillusionment with the Tory government. 'But the Party is stuck in the mud ... Hugh Gaitskell muffed his chance by attacking Clause Four ... What [Labour] needs now from him is another act of moral courage.' It called on him to convince the electorate that a Labour government would be 'dynamic and efficient' – by accepting entry into the Common Market, rejecting 'a punitive attitude to great businesses', and proposing a wages policy.[59a]

Next day's front page contained Gaitskell's vigorous counter-attack headed 'A Party in Search of a Newspaper?'. He said that those who tried to win over uncommitted voters, in Parliament during the week and in the country at weekends, 'find it an uphill job at times because the *Daily Herald* so seldom reports our efforts'; it had not mentioned his own speech on wages policy the previous Saturday. The three issues on which the leader should decide were 'funny little mice'. Wages policy required agreements which could not be negotiated till Labour was in power; the *Herald* had warmly supported the Party's anti-monopoly policy but perhaps 'since the Odhams-Mirror merger you just feel that all mergers are good?'; and entry into the Market must depend on the conditions.[59b]

The attack united the whole Party against the paper;[18d] and the reply drove it to expand its coverage of Labour's activities.[60-1a] Gaitskell's old friend Sydney Jacobson became editor in June 1962, and promptly offended the London Labour Party over the government Bill abolishing the old London County Council (wrongly expected to make a Labour majority on the new council unattainable). Gaitskell blocked a move to summon Jacobson before the National Executive to explain his attitude.[46b] But at a moment of unusual harmony in the Party, with the London MPe quite unanimous, it was politically impossible for him not to denounce ths Bill himself.[62a] *

There was a far worse row over the *Herald*'s long-standing support for British entry into the Common Market. Moving towards opposition, Gaitskell told Jacobson on 13 September 1962 that he did not expect a new editorial line but did hope the paper would refrain from open attacks on the Party. His hope was disappointed, and just a week later he testily warned the editor at a 'very cold' meeting that he might denounce the *Herald* from the platform at the coming Party Conference; Jacobson replied that nothing could be better for its circulation.[46b] It was an insoluble problem. With a subservient editor the paper was worthless, while with an independent one the Party leader had almost as many tribulations with his nominal Fleet Street mouthpiece as he would have had without one.

Labour hoped to use television to offset the ill-will of most of the press.[15a] Matters were complicated by the newspapers' financial interests in commercial television, which added another dimension, besides the cultural and populist aspects, to the debate on the Pilkington Committee's attack on the television companies in the summer of 1962. Of all political issues,

---

* He did so whole-heartedly, and from hospital in December he phoned to talk parliamentary tactics with Labour's Front Bench spokesman, Michael Stewart. But some local government experts thought he was rather embarrassed about doing so.[63]

commercial television was probably the one on which pressure groups had most direct influence on Tory politicians;[64] and now that the *Mirror* group owned every left-wing national newspaper except *Reynolds*, and had a big financial stake in television, many people feared that it would have a corresponding influence on the Opposition. Christopher Mayhew, Labour spokesman on broadcasting, had told Gaitskell in 1959 that Cecil King had personally threatened him with a 'Mayhew must go' newspaper campaign if his policies were ever adopted, but had added: 'the Party leaders would never accept my views on I.T.V. because they knew that the Mirror would then turn against the Party and we should lose the Election'.[65a] Now those leaders were showing reluctance to support Mayhew's plans, and he found George Brown so hostile that he told Gaitskell jovially it had been like 'listening to the voice of Cecil King himself'.[65d e] *

On 4 July 1962, a week after Pilkington came out, Mayhew came to the Shadow Cabinet to argue for an immediate commitment. To his disappointment Gaitskell shunned the potentially divisive and unpopular Pilkington policy, and the Shadow Cabinet would make no commitment or effort to persuade the PLP.[65b] George Brown as deputy leader led the opposition to Mayhew, whom Harold Wilson (who was about to challenge Brown for the post) strongly supported. Next day Mayhew found his new ally coming up to offer commiseration and also information:[66] namely that Brown, Mayhew's chief opponent within the Labour Party, drew a retainer from King, his leading antagonist outside it.[67] Brown had gone to Washington, and Mayhew at once cabled asking for a denial.[65d f] Within a day or two Brown wrote to tell Gaitskell about the row and ask his advice.[68a b e] As the explosion reverberated around him, the leader shrewdly guessed how the fuse had been lit, saying to Mayhew: 'I know who put you up to this.'[67] Brown returned to a furious confrontation with Mayhew, then made a personal statement to the trade union group of MPs (whose chairman he was) on his nine-year-old link with the *Daily Mirror*; 'it went without a murmur'.[68c] Since he still enjoyed much personal goodwill, prospective challengers for the deputy leadership were suddenly coy;[13c] and in November he was safely re-elected. But the fall-out poisoned the Westminster atmosphere and gave Gaitskell a difficult time in the PLP.[69]

Gaitskell's hesitation over the Pilkington Report reflected no indifference to cultural values. He often criticised the Macmillan era for its unhealthy stress on material satisfactions; he had no tenderness for the advertisers (to whom he felt the Pilkington Report had been far too kind) and has just organised the Labour Party Advertising Commission; only a few weeks earlier the Festival of Labour had shown his continuing interest in the arts.

* For Mayhew's and Pilkington's proposals, see above, pp. 390–1.

The Festival was the brainchild of Morgan Phillips, devised to raise morale in the Movement — though because of Phillips's illness it was organised by Merlyn Rees. It was 'a party for the Party' in Battersea Park one June weekend in 1962, with sporting and athletic activities, country dancing, concerts, exhibitions, a variety show, dancing, a firework display, a Young Socialist public speaking contest and a political demonstration.[70a]

Gaitskell helped a good deal with recruitment, proposing and arranging for an exhibition of paintings by young modern artists (suggested by his Leeds friends the Gillinsons).[71a] Through Jack Donaldson, a director of Covent Garden and Sadler's Wells, he attracted Rubinstein and Giulini, and even persuaded them to come to a party beforehand. (He also insisted on twice redrafting the Donaldsons' introductory leaflet.)[70b] * He took a lively interest in the Festival's artistic aspects: 'It was ... with the music and open-air stuff at Battersea Park, the concerts and jazz concerts that I really met Hugh. This was really him.'[71b] He even contributed himself, mimicking a Macmillan speech.

The Festival was a great success, and Gaitskell hoped to organise an annual event on a smaller scale.[70a b] It had one macabre sequel. Gaitskell told several people that its organiser Merlyn Rees should be found a seat at the first convenient by-election; Rees just a year later succeeded the leader as MP for South Leeds.[71]

iii *The Shadow of Economic Decline*

No politician could have been more conscious than Gaitskell that with electoral victory his real problems would begin. He was acutely aware of the long-term precariousness of Britain's economy and the risk of a sudden slide downhill. In his TV broadcast introducing *Signposts for the Sixties*, he drew a chilling but painfully realistic picture of the future.

> [W]e really are at the crossroads in Britain today. We can go on as we have done for the last ten years, and ... the standard of living will go up a little, but ... much less ... than in other countries ... People will say: oh, the British, of course they're nice people, they're friendly, they're tolerant, kindly, they're a bit perhaps sunk in the past ... But when it comes to producing and selling, well somehow or other they haven't got it in them. Now this is a very real possibility ... [if] we go on as we're doing now for another ten or twenty years ... We've got to get out of the really dangerous complacency in which we've been sunk these last few years. You've never had it so good is an attractive slogan, but it just doesn't match with what is needed today ... we've got to be, I think, rather less self-regarding than we tend to be these

---

* They did not think he improved the draft.

days ... we shan't solve this problem if the average wage earner or salary earner simply is concerned with getting his rise and never mind about the rest. Or the manufacturer with passing it on in higher prices to consumers, or all of us ... wondering how best we can dodge the tax collector.[72]

In 1959 (as in 1966) such Opposition warnings had attracted little attention. But a fortnight after Gaitskell's broadcast, on 25 July 1961, they were suddenly brought home when the Chancellor, Selwyn Lloyd, announced another all too familiar set of restrictive economic measures: a 'pay pause' in the public sector, public expenditure cuts, a credit squeeze, a 2 per cent rise in bank rate, and a surcharge on indirect taxation. The Prime Minister was already faltering, probably affected by the illness which led to his operation in 1963; but the Government could ill afford to lose his tactical skills, for Lloyd was an inept communicator. Unconvincingly explained, the proposals were resented as unfair in both content (penalising badly-paid workers) and context (since Lloyd would not withdraw his promise of benefits for surtax payers).

Gaitskell attacked the government's policies repeatedly: in January, on hearing the Chancellor's first note of alarm (which preceded the surtax concessions); in July when Lloyd's forthcoming statement was announced; in the later debate on it; at the Blackpool Conference; and on the Address when Parliament resumed. Always he stressed (as he had so often) the deep-seated nature of the problem; called for constructive policies to tackle it instead of short-term expedients which did long-run harm; and condemned the government's incomprehension in expecting co-operation from people who felt unfairly treated. He predicted gradual economic decline which could be averted only by a great change of psychological climate — inconceivable under Macmillan, 'the great architect of complacency and the materialist outlook'.[73a]

Gaitskell did not disagree fundamentally with the objectives of the pay pause:[74] 'on the basic issue of the need for relating incomes to productivity and production there is no dispute between us.'[75a] But he thought it crudely conceived and ineptly handled (as a senior Treasury official of the time was to confirm a decade later in comparing many phases of incomes policy).[76-7a] He called 2·5 per cent growth 'a miserable target' and 4 per cent (as proposed four months later by the National Economic Development Council) 'well within our grasp'.[78] He condemned official restrictionism, citing the NEDC's report that production had risen only 2 per cent, and productivity not at all, over the previous two years. He had always argued that it was a fundamental mistake to concentrate on keeping pay down instead of output up, so that unit costs rose as production stagnated or fell.[79] As he told the House once again, increasing productivity was the highest priority, but it required agreement with the unions – unattainable by a government whose policies seemed 'unfair and arbitrary'.[75b]

The pay pause was so resented because it came when 'Conservative policies have quite deliberately made the distribution of income more unequal': the previous year wages and salaries had risen 7.5 per cent, dividends 24·5 per cent – which the Chancellor lamented while rejecting a capital gains tax and promising surtax reductions.[80-1a] Even between wage-earners there was arbitrary discrimination, freezing the public sector but not the private, ensuring trouble when the restrictions were relaxed: for public sector workers would seek to recoup their losses, and the wanton destruction of established arbitration machinery might provoke serious industrial trouble.[82-4a]

Remembering the 1958 bus strike, Gaitskell suspected Ministers of being more machiavellian than inept, and hoping that a mining or railway strike might turn to their political advantage.[7d] When an interviewer suggested that talk of strikes might be taken as a political threat, Gaitskell heatedly denounced 'the extraordinary behaviour of the government in tearing up the normal procedure of settling industrial disputes in the public service, for the first time, I think, for forty years'. The 'fine tradition' of settling those disputes without strikes, he added, would be lost unless the government could 'restore what they have done their best to destroy'.[17a] By the summer, the Chancellor's policy was merely 'an ugly piece of shabby discrimination' against those with enough responsibility not to exploit their power: 'a penalty imposed on virtue'. The audience for that speech was the Confederation of Health Service Employees.[85] We reap what we sow.

With his personal background and his interest in young people, Gaitskell not surprisingly took up vigorously the cause of university staff, who (like nurses, teachers and others in the public sector) suffered from Selwyn Lloyd's crude application of the pay pause. Macmillan's government began the policy of allowing them to fall increasingly behind the civil servants, hitherto considered comparable, and behind technical college teachers too. That government was the first ever to reject the proposals of the University Grants Committee, and the victims, seeing a threat to the future of their institutions, sent Gaitskell more protests than he had ever received in recent years.[86] Broadening his attack to criticise the small numbers going to university and to call for large-scale expansion before the Robbins Committee did so, he condemned the government's policy as 'discreditable in substance, dishonourable in presentation, and deplorable in its consequences ... A formula for national decline'.[75d]

Gaitskell thought Lloyd had been astonishingly obtuse; his White Paper on incomes was 'an appalling document',[77b] and efforts to bludgeon the TUC were quite unnecessary:[7f]

Lloyd could very easily have put the T.U.C. on the spot ... said to them that the pause was a temporary measure ... to get effective means of planning and ... probably ... would end fairly soon when sensible measures had been agreed. He could have admitted that at the beginning the pay pause wasn't too well thought out. If he'd taken that line the T.U.C. really wouldn't have had any way of staying out [of NEDC].[7d]

But Gaitskell knew very well that a Labour Government would face similar problems and, since its policies would be too costly without faster growth, would be even more dependent on an understanding with the unions. He knew also that traditional collective bargaining was always liable to produce situations electorally damaging to Labour;[7f] though, with Cousins so suspicious of him, he prudently resisted appeals to say that bluntly in public. He mentioned it cautiously at Nottingham in January 1962, and told his old PPS 'it is not very easy in opposition and without proper negotiations with the unions to carry the matter much further'.[61a b] However, he was now using for this constructive purpose those monthly dinners with his allies on the TUC General Council which had begun during the Labour Party's internal crisis.[7e]

He also kept pressing Callaghan, the Shadow Chancellor, to use his economic advisers on the most urgent problems – productivity, exports and especially cost inflation: 'what I have in mind, of course, is the whole question of incomes policy. Somebody ought to be studying pretty seriously the Swedish and Dutch systems and considering the possibilities of applying them here.'[87a] Callaghan replied that they had been studied, and he often reminded Gaitskell that negotiations could not get far until Labour was in office with real authority. He did begin talks on incomes policy with Cousins and Nicholas of the T&GWU; later George Brown took over the task.[87b c] A few weeks afterwards Gaitskell was again asked on television about 'the fear ... that your Party with its heavy dependence on the Trade Unions would be less effective in getting any kind of wages policy'. He replied:

I ... always have said, as you know, that we must have some way by which incomes do not go faster than the output of goods. Indeed, we were the people who first, after all, tried to tackle this problem ... [T]he Trade Unions ... must see that it's fair because ... [we are] saying – look, we wish you not to exercise the power you have ... I, person-ally, believe that we can ... because the kind of social policies and taxation policies that we would pursue, would be much fairer than those pursued by the Tories. I mean, if you give away eighty millions to the surtax payers at one moment and then demand a wage freeze the next, if you do not consult the T.U.C. at all about it ... and if you then proceed to use your arbitrary power over public employees, disregarding everybody else, of course ... you get no response.[88]

Repeatedly he stressed the essential problem: that only in Britain did expansion immediately lead to a balance of payments crisis. He did not pretend to be sure of the cause or cure (though he had plenty of ideas);[79] he did insist that it was a long-term disease which the government was neither explaining nor tackling:

> The only people who can afford to be complacent are those who are content to see Britain in the 1970's enjoying a lower standard of living than most other industrial nations. This is not a panicky prophecy but a cold appraisal of the prospects.[89]

The country was still playing a world banking role with quite inadequate reserves, making the economy very vulnerable to short-run fluctuations. In the last six years Britain had borrowed a billion pounds abroad at short-term to lend the same amount long.[81b] She had had to borrow because the balance of payments was now in deficit (£344 m. in 1960). The exports of France, Germany, Italy, Belgium, Sweden, Japan and the United States had all increased more than twice as much as Britain's over the last year — or the last five years, or the last ten; so that in 1960 Britain had only 16 per cent of the world market in manufactures as against 25·5 per cent in 1950.[81b] * Only one other industrial country had expanded production less, or had a faster rise in prices; interest rates were lower everywhere else — and all 'when external trading conditions have been exceptionally favourable'.[22f]

Conservatives had promised that lowering taxes on the rich, and taking controls off private enterprise, would generate expansion, price stability and an export surplus; instead their policy had 'produced industrial stagnation, rising prices and trade deficits'.[91] Now the Chancellor was doing positive harm: 'he has treated a long-run problem as ... a short-run problem [which] he has tackled ... in the most foolish way imaginable'. Any long-term solution must concentrate on raising productivity, not on limiting incomes and massively deflating an economy already moving that way: 'it is not good enough to rescue the balance of payments at the expense of cutting back industrial production.' The price of the world banking role was an 'absurd' rate of interest to attract short-term borrowings to protect the exchange rate.[73d]

Gaitskell kept saying that the national lethargy must be shaken. Without the right psychological mood short-term incomes policy could not work — as it had worked under Cripps when people felt fairly treated,

---

* Down to 12 per cent in 1967 and 9 per cent in 1976 (below 9 per cent in the two previous years).[90]

which they did not feel now.[83b] To tackle the long-term problem required 'the hardest thing of all – to create a change in the whole climate of opinion in this country. A great attack has to be made on the soggy complacency of some managements, and the appalling indifference of some workers.'[81c] Characteristically, he spoke more bluntly to the unions at the Labour Party Conference than in the House of Commons: 'it is no use preaching the virtues of planning and when you get it ... practising anarchy. That way lies disaster, economic disaster and political disaster, both for ourselves and for our country.'[22c] People had been 'lulled into a false sense of security by the constant stream of cosy, complacent, Conservative propaganda before, during and since the last Election'. Waking them up would be a tremendous challenge to political leadership. That leadership could not come from the Chancellor, who lacked all inspiration and dynamism and had not even identified the problem;[89] or from a government which had 'not only misled the people ... [but] also, by their financial and fiscal policies, sacrificed the long term strength of Britain for their own short term party political gains';[91] or, least of all, from the Prime Minister whom Gaitskell had always thought a fraud.

Privately, Macmillan reacted to Labour's claim to be able to encourage responsibility in the unions by a disreputable effort to use that encouragement for Party advantage. For Labour calls for restraint were condemned on the extreme Left; and the Prime Minister later boasted of urging his colleagues to comb the Communist press for material inciting working-class hostility to the Labour leadership, who were trying to use their influence in the long-term interests of the country and its people.[92] Not knowing that, Gaitskell could still persuasively argue that Macmillan's past doomed his present appeals. His persistent encouragement of selfish materialism disqualified him from arousing the nation; his sudden repentance was nauseating hypocrisy. 'Having gulled [the people] into complacency, you cannot galvanise them into action.'[73a]

iv   *Commonwealth Immigration*

Ever since Attlee's day the Labour Party had taken a proprietary pride in the new multi-racial Commonwealth, which it felt a duty to maintain as a bridge between developed and undeveloped countries, white men and coloured, 'North' and 'South'. Labour's eager championship always had a slightly protective tone, and Gaitskell, influenced by his brother or his background, felt the responsibility strongly. In the autumn of 1961 that largely determined his and the Party's attitude to another political problem: the increasingly controversial issue of coloured immigration.[93]

The government had held what Macmillan called 'rather desultory discussions in the Cabinet' about it as early as 1954 and 1955, when the influx temporarily increased, and again in 1958 after the Notting Hill riots (which Gaitskell was one of the very few public figures to denounce promptly and severely).[40b] In 1961, numbers were rising again. On 30 May Ministers expected to legislate in the autumn, but it became clear much earlier that 'the Conservative Party ... was seriously alarmed ... The political pressure was renewed at the Party Conference in October'.[94b] As Gaitskell suspected at the time, that partly explained the government's 'indecent haste'.[95a]

Many signs betrayed that haste. Butler as Home Secretary justified the Bill by saying that 113,000 people had entered from the Indian sub-continent and the Colonies in the previous ten months — without knowing if the figures were gross or net.[95b][c][96a] Other official statistics contradicted them;[97] and they were plainly swollen by a rush to beat the ban. Again, there was a great muddle over Irish immigrants, originally included in the Bill as a 'fig leaf' enabling its numerous Tory critics to deny that it was based on colour.[98-9] Gaitskell suggested that the Irish should require passes issued in Northern Ireland,[7h] but the Conservative Cabinet was too tender to the Ulster Unionists.[100] So, as he quite accurately put it:

> First, they [the Irish] were in the Bill ... subject to control. Then, in the Second Reading debate, the Home Secretary said that we could not keep them out [of the country] ... Then ... the Minister of Labour, when winding up, said the Government would have another look and see whether they could pop them in again.[101]

That, it is said, was because the back-bench critics warned Macleod, Leader of the House, of defections on the second reading if the Irish were excluded from controls.[102a] (But, in the end, they were.) Thirdly, the Commonwealth countries were treated shabbily, HMG notifying the West Indian governments of its intentions too late for them to comment usefully.[103] First the Prime Minister prevaricated about this in the House;[95i] then, when Gaitskell published a protest from Sir Grantley Adams, the West Indian Federal Premier, Macmillan's sole concern was to get an instant reply into the press.[94c]

Gaitskell denounced the Bill as well as the Government's conduct, but he was not blind to the conflicts which might arise. Indeed, he was probably the only British politician to have discussed them in a West Indian Cabinet meeting, to which he was invited when visiting Jamaica in January 1960. He told his hosts then that any difficulties were caused by 'the concentration of coloured communities. No problems would arise if the immigrants were dispersed throughout the country'.[104] He thought inadequate housing the root of the difficulties, which could be solved by a bigger building programme.[7h] Exclusion of immigrants was, he believed, a crude and cowardly evasion of the real domestic issues, and unnecessary because they came only at times when Britain needed them. The Bill excluded entrants with no assured job — a provision either pointless or hypocritical, for 95 per cent of arrivals found jobs quickly but few could arrange them from overseas. If unemployment rose, Gaitskell thought the situation would correct itself, for the quarterly numbers of migrants and of vacant jobs had always moved up and down together.[105] But a Bill which was unnecessary in Britain would do great harm in the West Indies, where the economy had been shaped to suit British convenience and the unemployment problem would be desperate when the British outlet was closed as well as the American; the political consequences in the Caribbean might be explosive.[95k]

The Indian sub-continent was a different matter. Gaitskell recognised that Britain could not keep an open door in the event of a mass migration, which he thought 'an utter and complete myth' though it worried the government.[106a] There had been no legal bar to it earlier in the century, yet no practical problem arose, because immigrants had not come unless there were jobs for them. It was just as 'unreal and irrelevant' for the Right to ask whether he would let them all come in all circumstances as for the Left to ask if he would stay in NATO in all circumstances — both seeking a negative answer to justify rejection now. 'That is the exact parallel. The question is not whether if 50 million Indians came here we should be able to maintain the open door; the question now is whether this Bill should be passed into law or not.' The government had not investigated: they did not know the figures. They had not shown that the current rate of entry would continue: it had fallen sharply once before. Their 'extraordinary haste' demonstrated disgraceful discourtesy to the West Indian governments, and 'with the Irish out all pretence has gone. It is a plain anti-Commonwealth Measure in theory and it is a plain anti-colour Measure in practice.'

If the Bill would have kept out those who had come and found work the year before, it would 'stop people coming in even when we want them ... the most crazy kind of Conservative economic planning'; if not (as in the government's view) it would damage the Commonwealth without touching the problem. Racial disorder was a real danger, to be met by building houses, enforcing overcrowding laws, teaching tolerance and explaining why the immigrants were valuable to Britain; instead the government had 'yielded to the crudest clamour'. Butler, Sandys and especially Macleod should be ashamed of their failure to stop 'this miserable, shameful, shabby bill' by threatening to resign.[95l] The speech, which Gaitskell himself thought one of the most important he had ever given in the House,[107a] won the highest praise, from The Times to Tribune;[108a] one experienced American visitor thought it among the finest he had ever heard, and the occasion 'one of the most dramatic I ever saw'.[109]

It was devastingly effective because many liberal Conservatives and indeed Tory imperialists were thoroughly unhappy about the Bill. Some trade unionists and Labour members (led by Mayhew and mostly but not all from the right wing) equally disliked such strenuous opposition to it, wanting to repudiate the open door as well as the Bill. But in the PLP only a dozen members voted against Gaitskell, who insisted that the Bill, like Suez, cut at the roots of the Socialist faith and of belief in the brotherhood of man.[110] The committee stage was taken on the floor of the House, and progress was so slow that in January the guillotine was imposed.[111-12a] The Bill was drastically amended and – by common consent – substantially improved. But even in Gaitskell's lifetime Denis Healey's final speech for the Opposition said that, if controls really proved necessary, a Labour Administration would consult the Commonwealth governments about them;[99f] and Healey did not repeat in the House his previous demand to repeal the Act.[102c] Refusal of all control was not tenable in the long run, and Labour policy was to shift much further after Gaitskell's death.[113]

v *Central and Southern Africa*

Like Suez, the immigration dispute produced an unusual political align-ment, in which Labour won much support from liberal-minded opinion outside its own ranks while suffering from some division within them. That was also the case over many colonial problems, but not at first over the Central African Federation, for in the early days middle opinion still saw that as offering a prospect of settling the Rhodesian question. Gaitskell had to take care that his commitment to defending African interests could not be presented as an effort to wreck a promising solution for his own political purposes.

His own view of the conflict was simple. The settlers in Southern Rhodesia must not be allowed to enforce their own rule on the Africans in the neighbouring territories. Britain had the responsibility, would have intervened against a black revolt, and must not treat a white one differ-ently. Had he won the 1959 election he had intended, unless it proved logistically impossible, instantly to move overwhelming forces into the northern territories.[114a c] He had the same intention in mind for the next election also;[114b] and he was already thinking of buying out the settlers as the long-run solution.[115]

In his first speech in the new House in October 1959, he had warned that the constitutional negotiations would fail without African confidence. That required prior franchise reforms in Nyasaland and Northern Rhodesia; admitting their right to secede; and appointing to the coming Monckton Commission members whom the Africans trusted.[116] Both he and Bevan knew the danger of appearing to be wreckers, and Labour would certainly have joined the Commission if given any real sign of good faith.[117] None was forthcoming, and Gaitskell would not give the impression of betraying the Africans. He thought of setting up an unofficial Labour Commission of Inquiry, but found that the Party could not afford it.[7j]

The Monckton Commission was to include few (and those not outstanding) Africans;[7j] no one from the coloured Commonwealth; and only Privy Councillors from the United Kingdom. Gaitskell sought changes on all those points, and assurances on witnesses (it should hear Africans in detention) and especially on the terms of reference, which must not preclude any right of secession.[118-120a] The one obstacle was Sir Roy Welensky the Federal Prime Minister. Macmillan himself wanted to appoint a Malayan, and would have dropped the restriction to Privy Councillors (which caught Callaghan, as well as Stonehouse and Barbara Castle at whom it was aimed); but Welensky flatly refused.[121a] So in private Macmillan gave Gaitskell encouraging but ambiguous hints on the African nominees, the detainees' evidence and the terms of reference.[119b] In the House on 24 November 1959 he was firm on the Privy Councillors, but vague on the terms of reference.[120b] But to Welensky he wrote specifically but confidentially next day that *'he had not yielded and would not yield an inch'* on the latter point.[121b] Welensky protested at not being allowed to publish the promise, Macmillan reiterated it, and on 26 November Welensky, to his later regret, publicly accepted the Commission on those terms.[121c]

Those terms ensured that the Africans would not co-operate. When their prominent supporter Sir John Moffat appealed for Labour to join the Commission since otherwise no African would give evidence, Gaitskell sadly replied that they would not do so anyway, so that by joining Labour would 'have lost all the influence we have with them without achieving anything'.[122] On 1 December Gaitskell saw the Prime Minister, who rejected any amendments to the terms of reference and pressed him to appoint his three representatives forthwith. Macmillan recorded that he 'tried to "negotiate" – but I would not allow this'.[123a b] Two days later, after consulting the Shadow Cabinet, Gaitskell wrote formally that Labour could not join without concessions on the restriction to Privy Councillors, the release of detainees, reforms in Nyasaland, and the terms of reference. Macmillan sent his refusal the same day.[119c]

Lord Home, the Commonwealth Secretary, thought Labour's 'crippling decision' so disastrous that he later regretted not having abandoned the whole enterprise.[124a] But the Prime Minister as usual assumed that the Opposition were simply playing politics.[125] He at once exploited their refusal in a way which Gaitskell thought 'in wonderfully bad taste', 'very foolish', and solely designed to injure the Labour Party.[126] For Macmillan tried to recruit Labour malcontents, failing with Herbert Morrison but succeeding with Sir Hartley Shawcross;[123b] and appointed to the other two vacancies a former Labour – and future Tory – MP, Aiden Crawley, and the former Governor General of Ghana, Sir Charles Arden-Clarke. (Neither was a Privy Councillor.) Welensky, resentful of Whitehall pressure, then publicly reasserted his own rigid interpretation of the terms of reference. Gaitskell raised it in the House, but Macmillan would neither confirm nor repudiate it,[127] and admitted privately that their clash was a draw, 'rather in his favour'.[123a b] Within weeks of his electoral triumph, Macmillan's parliamentary ascendancy had vanished for good.

Formally, Labour had failed over the terms of reference. In fact they had won their point; for it was their refusal to join that led Shawcross, with Monckton's approval, to announce publicly that if the Commission found a case for secession he would not hesitate to say so.[124a b] Welensky wanted Shawcross debarred from the Commission. But Crawley agreed with Shawcross, and so did the Tory members Heald and Molson; if forbidden to discuss secession they would not have served. The Commonwealth Secretary knew that, and had assured Molson that it was not excluded.[124b] At the same time, the Prime Minister was telling Welensky that all the members had approved the terms of reference, which he would not change: leading both the Labour Party and Welensky to believe that secession was ruled out.

Buffeted by the 'winds of change' on his African tour, Macmillan walked his diplomatic tightrope from Lagos to Salisbury.[123d] But in March 1960, when Monckton came home from Africa to say that secession could not be excluded, he found that the Prime Minister agreed.[124c] In October the Commission reported, endorsing most of Labour's case. Dr Banda was already free; franchise reform in the Northern Territories was essential; and the right of secession was the best hope of averting the reality (for the Africans were thought likelier to accept Federation if a way of escape was left open).

Welensky and Gaitskell now distrusted the Prime Minister equally, but it was the former who had been misled.[128] He began to use overt pressure over Northern Rhodesia, and was vigorously supported from the Tory Right – notably by Lord Salisbury, who bitterly denounced Iain Macleod the Colonial Secretary. Gaitskell criticised Welensky's provocations, and urged Macleod not to be 'brow-beaten' by either Sir Roy or the revolting peers.[129] But the Prime Minister was alarmed as usual about Cabinet resignations and a party split.[94a f] Macleod was replaced, and Butler put in charge with co-ordinating authority which he announced to the House in what Gaitskell called an extraordinary statement, nonsensical and destructive of Cabinet responsibility.[130a] Gaitskell was surprised at the change, for he had come to expect the government to stand firm against the Tory rebels, whom he called 'a poor lot. They wouldn't do anything against Macmillan'.[7k]

The political pressures did not get Macleod's policy scrapped, but they did succeed in delaying its application. That made the break-up of the Federation inevitable.[106b] Its prospects of survival, always slim, had been doomed by intransigence in Salisbury, pusillanimity in London, and successive eruptions all round its borders.

Those eruptions drove South Africa out of the Commonwealth, opened the long struggle to expel the Portuguese from the continent, and brought UN intervention to the Congo, where anarchy was stiffening settler resistance in the rest of Africa.

The first crisis broke in South Africa itself. On 28 February 1960 Gaitskell spoke at a Trafalgar Square rally to launch the boycott of South African goods in — he said — 'passionate protest against a repulsive doctrine ... that a man's legal status, political rights, economic opportunities and social position shall be determined merely by the colour of his skin'.[131] He promised to consider seriously a boycott of the coming cricket tour.[40c] Soon afterwards the *Daily Express* sought to embarrass him by claiming that he held shares in a South African brewery;[132b] in fact he had recently sold those shares (inherited before the war), precisely in order to rid himself of any property there — and had contributed from the £400 proceeds to the Defence and Aid Fund for victims of the repression.

That repression reached a peak in the Sharpeville massacre on 21 March 1960. It was no British responsibility, but Gaitskell sought a debate in the House, contrived to raise several cases of individual prisoners, and warned against 'the dangerous and cowardly doctrine' that HMG should keep silent so as to retain South Africa in the Commonwealth.[133] That course would drive out its coloured members; for once it had expanded beyond the old white dominions, he did not believe the association could survive without minimal common principles, which South Africa was determined to flout. Next year, when she became a republic, the new members (and Canada) made it clear that he was right.[134] Gaitskell hoped that one day she might change and rejoin, and so was not keen on ending preferential trade or legislating on citizenship;[135a][136] and, formally at least, the British government shared his views.[135b]

All the problems of southern Africa were compounded by the whites' reaction to the violence near by. In Angola the first rising against the Portuguese brought the usual gruesome story: rebel killings followed by equally brutal and quite disproportionate reprisals. British Ministers showed ostentatious sympathy for Portugal their valued NATO ally — yet pretended in the House that their gestures to her had no significance. Gaitskell dissented,[137] reminding MPs:

I have always believed that it is impossible for a democracy, over a period, to maintain ... [a] colonialist position ... If we have to choose between standing by the principles of the alliance, or ... an ally which betrays these principles ... we must choose the former course.[138a]

Other allies agreed with Gaitskell's view. He was in Washington when President Kennedy was inaugurated, and heard welcome opinions there:

I found Stevenson openly critical of the British Government for not supporting anti-colonial resolutions in the United Nations ... They will not allow the West to be framed with the charge of anti-colonialism for the sake of Belgian or Portuguese sensitivity.[59c] *

Stevenson was still a hero to American liberals; Gaitskell encouraged him privately, writing to a friend: 'I had tea with Adlai ... and told him to stand firm on anti-colonial issues & not be bulldozed by MacWonder (as Ike used to be) into being associated with the Belgians and the Portuguese all the time.'[57b] The United States, Gaitskell pointed out in the House, voted for five UN resolutions on Angola on which Britain abstained; while Norway, because of British missionary reports, stopped sending arms to Portugal while Britain continued to do so. He felt the government were 'rather shaken and rather shaky' on the subject;[7b] not for long, for the problem roused no interest either in the Conservative Party or in Downing Street.[139]

In the Congo, however, Macmillan was under pressure from the right-wing back-bench friends of the Katanga secessionists, who briefly managed to rally the Tory centre for a revolt which at one point threatened to destroy the Government.[123f g] With his opponents in 'the tightest corner ... since Suez', Gaitskell showed — according to a Conservative paper — the 'immense ... gap between his own Parliamentary abilities and those of the ablest of his colleagues',[21c] by one question skilfully inducing the government spokesman to reaffirm the policy (acceding to a UN request for bombs) which so distressed its supporters.[140a] In the debate three days later, Macmillan reassured the worried Tories by rejecting the request.[140b] He thought Gaitskell highly effective in attacking the government's vacillation, its capitulation to its back-benchers, and its support of the colonialist powers, which alienated the United States and the Commonwealth.[140-1] But to his immense relief Harold Wilson rescued him by a violent denunciation of the Prime Minister's bitter enemies on the extreme Right, so discouraging them from helping the Opposition to overthrow him.[123h]

The British government had become more vulnerable to Gaitskell's

* Macmillan was less pleased, writing contemptuously of 'the Adlai Stevensons and other half-baked "liberals" whom [Presidents] commonly employ (for internal political reasons) at United Nations'.[123a g]

criticisms since 1960 when Selwyn Lloyd was succeeded at the Foreign Office by the Earl of Home. Though their personal relations were always friendly, Gaitskell thought Home generally reactionary and obsessive about Communism.[142] Citing Home's eloquent rhetoric to the Conservative Party Conference on the indivisibility of freedom, Gaitskell pointed his usual moral: 'I agree with that. I have already said it. But ... if we believe in freedom in Hungary and in East Germany, then we must believe in it in Angola or Rhodesia.'[143a] A few weeks later the Foreign Secretary endeared himself to his party by a diatribe against the new nations in the UN.[144] Gaitskell demonstrated – and no government spokesman tried to refute him – how completely Home had misrepresented the behaviour of those nations; and claimed that it revealed the permanent Tory suspicions of internationalism and anti-colonialism which shocked young Britons, and abroad 'have done our country grave harm over the years'.[145a] A decade or two later Gaitskell's hopes for African liberty look very optimistic – but the professed realists on the government benches now appear as victims of wishful thinking too. Their stubborn defence of the lost colonialist cause may put at risk their own successes in places like Tanzania and Zambia, once the neighbouring countries are ruled by the more extreme products of years of prolonged, bitter and futile White resistance.

With the Democrats back in power in Washington, Gaitskell now linked his two lines of attack on the government: 'We stand for freedom, it is said. We stand firm with our allies. We work together for peace with America. But ... in the United Nations on issues that are of great importance in Africa and Asia we then see a very different scene.' Resolutions on Portuguese colonialism and on South Africa were always supported by the United States, never by Britain.[143a] In reply to Home, Gaitskell insisted that 'it would be a disastrous error to try and eliminate the moral and ideological element in the alliance' by neglecting the democratic principles enshrined in the preamble to the NATO Treaty.[138b] Without those principles, he said, the Western cause would have no appeal in Africa and Asia; flouting those principles, he knew, multiplied his difficulties within his own Party; believing in those principles, he had no sympathy whatever for the defenders of colonialism on the far Right, for the apologists of Communism on the far Left, or for the anti-Americanism characteristic of both.

vi *New Men in Washington*

Gaitskell's old American sympathies were generally reinforced in January 1961, when he spent five days in Washington in the midst of his own troubles in the Labour Party. He enjoyed himself immensely (in spite of being marooned for five hours in a car one evening by a snowstorm). He

58 With Anthony Crosland in Grimsby, January 1961

59 With Richard Crossman, Party Chairman, at the 1961 Blackpool Conference

60 Roy Jenkins with Earl Attlee, to whom his father had been PPS and about whom Roy had (in 1948) written his first book

61 Unity? With Harold Wilson (apparently praying) and John Harris at a press conference on the Common Market, Brighton 1962

would not criticise the old Administration on his return, but was 'glowing' about the realism, grasp and understanding of their successors.[18f] On issues other than China, he found the newcomers thoroughly sympathetic. He attended the inaugural ball and met the new heads of the State Department: Dean Rusk the Secretary, and old friends like Chester Bowles (Under-Secretary) and Adlai Stevenson (Ambassador to the UN); he told Hetherington that the chief change 'was that there would now be twenty very able men [there] instead of only about two'.[7m] Over lunch at Averell Harriman's house, he spent two hours with the new President, whom he praised highly in private as well as public: 'cold and hard, but friendly ... a most competent person and interested in the kind of things we were interested in'.[7m]

Feeling this kinship with the new Administration, Gaitskell was acutely embarrassed by the bungled invasion of Cuba which failed at the Bay of Pigs. 'It was a great blow,' he told his old friend Arthur Schlesinger, Jr, in London as Kennedy's emissary:

> The right wing of the Labour Party has been basing a good deal of its argument on the claim that things had changed in America. Cuba has made great trouble for us. We shall now have to move to the left for a bit to maintain our position within the party.[146a]

But Gaitskell suspected the CIA of misleading the President, whose problems with American public opinion he understood.[7n] He would not join the clamour from Labour's back benches, and may have discouraged any NEC protest.[4p] In legitimately emphasising the leadership's embarrassment, *Tribune* characteristically insinuated also that an unnamed 'Labour spokesman' approved both of the invasion that had failed—and of a repetition.[108b]

That was false. When Castro first came to power in 1959, Gaitskell knew little of him (calling him 'Del Castro') but was decidedly sympathetic, excusing the early executions which his Washington enemies were using to discredit him.[57c] By 1961, however, Gaitskell rightly called Castro 'an avowed dictator who has exiled, imprisoned or executed most of those who made the Revolution with him'; and he would not condemn on principle any help to rebels against dictatorships, because of South Africa and Spain. But he deplored Kennedy's failure to 'stop the disastrous and futile escapade' at the Bay of Pigs, and warned emphatically that any further American attack on the island would have very dangerous world-wide repercussions.[147] (The speech went almost unreported in the press;[7a] *Tribune* condemned him for not making it sooner.)[108c]

A graver crisis arose that summer over Berlin, where the Western powers were locally weak yet feared that a retreat might spread defeatism everywhere. Khrushchev met Kennedy in Vienna, and set out to test the

z

new President's nerve by threatening to sign a peace treaty with East Germany that year, cancelling all existing Western rights in Berlin. On 13 August 1961 the East Germans walled off their sector of the city to block the escape route by which three million people had fled. On 26 August Macmillan told journalists on Gleneagles golf course that the crisis was 'all got up by the press'.[123i] But the Labour leaders knew that some Ministers were concerned enough to want to call up reservists.[68d]

As usual, Gaitskell was neither a pacifist nor an extreme cold warrior. He was worried by Americans like Acheson who demanded a show of force, he recognised the Russians' real anxieties about Germany, and he urged negotiations — though in public he spoke with caution for fear of 'weakening our bargaining position or making Khrushchev think he can do just what he likes'.[148] Knowing the West's local weakness, he was against leaving the Russians with the diplomatic initiative: a policy wholly opposed to that of Adenauer and de Gaulle, and exactly that of the British government. Macmillan met the Leader of the Opposition in September, and wrote: 'he seemed (as always) very understanding of all our difficulties. What he will say is quite another thing, when he speaks in public!'[123a J]

In private the Prime Minister was urging the same line on President Kennedy,[123k] as Gaitskell guessed and often hinted.[143c] Gaitskell wanted the West to bargain physical control of an access route against partial *de facto* recognition of East Germany (and of the Oder-Neisse boundary): still aiming eventually at a 'zone of controlled disarmament' in Central Europe.[149b] He favoured moving some UN agencies to West Berlin — to keep the city viable, discourage interference with access, and expose the 'concentration camp aspect' of East Germany to representatives of all nations.[150] But he insisted repeatedly that the West must not abandon Berlin; to do so would undermine the alliance, and to leave the Russians in any doubt would encourage them to run dangerous risks.[151] In the House, Macmillan noted, half the Labour members 'loudly applauded', the rest 'sat in stony silence. His speech was good and very helpful'.[123a l] At the Blackpool Conference Gaitskell was forthright, recalling Chamberlain's dismissal of a 'far off country of which we know nothing' as the prelude to world war. The Left 'squirmed' but did not protest[28] when he bluntly asserted that apart from Cuba and China 'the policies now being pursued by the American Administration closely resemble those of the Labour Party'.[152] A fortnight later, Khrushchev withdrew the threat to cut off Berlin in 1961. The Russians had been bluffing again, and the crisis was over.[153]

At New Year 1962 Gaitskell visited West Berlin as the guest of its mayor Willy Brandt,[154] and called the Wall a 'hideous and repulsive shop window'.[21d] Under questioning at a press conference, he expressed more explicitly than he had intended his willingness to bargain access rights against recognition, and was denounced by both the East Germans and Chancellor Adenauer. But Gaitskell thought it just as well to discourage West German intransigence publicly, and believed that Brandt privately knew he was right.[7p]

In South-east Asia the United States, a few years later, was to become involved militarily in just the way against which Gaitskell had warned in his 1957 Godkin Lectures. But in 1962 Kennedy was anxious to avoid being entrapped by his local officials and clients in the tangled politics of Laos.[155a c] The Thai government requested American military support in Thailand itself, which was given; the other SEATO powers then agreed to send token forces if asked.[94i] Gaitskell, who suspected the Thais of wanting to drag the Americans into the Laos fighting, disliked the British Government's decision but thought it inevitable.

> The danger was of a collapse of Thai morale if the Americans said no ... the Americans thought that a demonstration now of support for Thailand would prevent a collapse of the whole position in that area. They were ... determined not to involve their troops on the Laotian side of the border ... troubling though it was, we ought to back up the alliance ... [despite] the difficulty of getting out once one was in ... the Government genuinely didn't want to let our troops become involved anywhere other than in Siam itself.[7q]

The Labour Left sought an emergency debate in the House, which was refused by 173 votes to 36 – who included one or two orthodox Labour members like Chuter Ede, three Liberals and a maverick Tory, William Yates.

The Prime Minister promised that British forces were confined to defending Thailand, not Laos; and Gaitskell, with four followers,[156] went so far as to vote in the government lobby.[157a] (Yates then moved to cut his salary.)[21e] He was attacked that night at the PLP, and his later justification hinted at a domino theory: if Laos went Communist, Thailand might follow, causing consternation in Malaya. The Americans 'had decided to draw the line in Siam and to do what they could to prevent Laos going communist. He thought we ought to support them'; though dangerous elsewhere, that might work in Thailand where there was no strong hostility to American troops.[7r] As in the Godkin Lectures, he foresaw the risks of entanglement. 'Western forces involved on mainland also most unwise and dangerous,' he now wrote. 'Probably have to draw a line & Thailand may be best one'; but in Laos, 'intervention ... would be highly dangerous and possibly disastrous'.[156b] To Sydney Silverman, Gaitskell had shown 'arrogant, dictatorial self-satisfied leadership, purblind, unimaginative and unconstructive', in helping stop a debate on 'a matter pregnant with the direst perils for the peace of the world ... [and] the survival of mankind'.[108d] For once the hysteria was quickly exposed. Kennedy and Macmillan had sought in vain for a year to set up a coalition government for Laos. It was agreed upon within a month of the Western intervention; the Thais caused no further border trouble; and six months later the allied forces were withdrawn without incident.[94g]

In the international gloom following the meeting of Kennedy and Khrushchev in Vienna in June 1961, the problem of testing nuclear weapons arose again. The desultory Geneva talks about banning them had merely shown the Russians that they were far behind. In response they rejected any form of inspection, even occasional visits by verification teams from neutral countries, and quietly began the prolonged preparations necessary to restart the ghastly race.[158-9a] Kennedy had gone to Vienna in June with a test-ban treaty in his pocket; instead, the Russians resumed testing in August, exploding a gigantic (50-megaton) H-bomb in the atmosphere, and working towards an anti-missile missile designed to eliminate the West's deterrent.[160a c]

Testing the bomb, with all its unknown health hazards, had originally provoked the growth of CND; and the Soviet breach of the three-year-old moratorium revived the issue within the Labour Party. The Russian decision dismayed the Left at the Blackpool Conference, and the nuclear disarmers duly protested – but their real indignation was reserved for the Western response and the Labour leadership's reluctance to condemn it.[161] On 8 February the Prime Minister told the House that if the Russians again rejected a ban, Britain would carry out a small underground test of her own in Nevada, and in return would allow the Americans to test in the atmosphere over Christmas Island.[145d]

Behind the scenes Macmillan was tireless in seeking a test-ban treaty, and his approach and Gaitskell's were almost identical. Suspicious of the strong pressures on Kennedy to resume testing, both satisfied themselves that the President would accede only if he reluctantly concluded it was indispensable to retaining the Western deterrent.[162] Both sought to preserve cordial relations with the Americans without giving them complete *carte blanche* to do as they pleased on British territory.[163] Both felt that, as Gaitskell put it, 'there's only one thing worse than an arms race and that's losing the arms race';[17b] but that the public must be satisfied that the West had done all it could to attain an agreement to stop testing. Both feared sinister motives for Soviet intransigence about inspection, yet wanted the West to go to the limit of safety in meeting any genuine anxieties.[164] When Gaitskell suggested that Russian good faith could be measured by their willingness to accept international checks on disarmament, Macmillan agreed: 'I think that that puts it very fairly.'[159c]

They parted company over the British test in Nevada. As usual the Left assumed that the Labour leadership wanted to reverse the agreed Party policy, condone the test and resume support of the British independent deterrent.[13d] [i] As usual they were wrong. Gaitskell (who mistakenly thought the test unlikely to take place) condemned it publicly and privately from the first.[165] The United States resumption promised more serious trouble. The tendency to condemn the Americans and Russians equally was strong within the Labour Party (and in Transport House), and Sam Watson had protested furiously at it even before Christmas.[166] Its effect on Gaitskell was the opposite of that intended, for he was not yet convinced that the tests were necessary, but was privately concerned that to oppose them would 'look too like surrender to neutralists again'.[57d] He told the Party Meeting after Macmillan's announcement that in four days he was to see Kennedy in Washington, and it would be 'pure folly' to say to the President that Labour would denounce any United States tests even if the Russian breach of the moratorium had enabled them to progress towards the anti-missile missile. Opposed by Shinwell, but supported by Philip Noel-Baker and Dingle Foot as well as George Brown, Gaitskell won by 95 to 26.[14d]

Gaitskell described Kennedy, with whom he lunched at the White House on 19 February 1962, as 'highly intelligent, well-informed, vital, direct, no small talk, no postures, rational, above all rational'.[31b] (His colleagues thought it a self-portrait—though Gaitskell rather enjoyed small-talk.) George Brown, meeting Kennedy a little later, called it 'a sister Administration'.[68b] The President 'mobilised half the Cabinet to tell [Gaitskell] that Britain must plunge into Europe'.[146e] They discussed other issues, like Berlin, but concentrated above all on nuclear weapons, where their views were nearly identical.[18g]

The Americans, like the Labour Party, wanted a NATO strategy less dependent on nuclear weapons, were concerned about proliferation (especially to Germany) and saw no advantage in a British bomb; like Gaitskell they thought a European deterrent 'a non-starter'.[31b] [c] They convinced him that they had decided to test with the utmost reluctance, solely to preserve the Western deterrent – not to keep soldiers, scientists, politicians or voters happy. Learning from Dean Rusk that the tests were to begin at the end of March, before the Geneva talks could possibly produce any result, he both protested in Washington and sent Kennedy a long letter from New York urging a deferment till after Geneva.[167] When the tests were delayed, Gaitskell wondered if his letter had had any effect;[7t] in fact it had, greatly stiffening Kennedy's prior inclination.[168]

On Gaitskell's return Labour officially condemned the British but not the American tests, and he obtained comfortable majorities in both the NEC (18 to 5 and 18 to 4) and the PLP (74 to 22 and 72 to 21).[169] A few days later Macmillan spoke in the House of the Christmas Island United States test and the Western proposals for Geneva talks, which Khrushchev had now accepted; the Liberal leader, to unilateralist cheers, wanted all testing deferred until after Geneva — but Gaitskell disagreed[130c] and as Macmillan privately recorded, 'was very helpful and even shot down Grimond for me'.[94a p] Gaitskell did not find that role congenial, and the Government's obsessive secrecy exasperated him. A couple of months later he told Hetherington: 'He was getting a bit tired of doing the Government's work. All his information was that the radiation from the high level explosions would not be dangerous ... we ought to reassure people ... but [the Government] were being obtuse.'[170] But while defending the need for the coming tests, he was eager to stop any more, and reasonably hopeful that a ban might be agreed.[155a d] So were Kennedy and Macmillan.[94q] But those hopes were not fulfilled in Gaitskell's lifetime.

The resumption of tests in 1962 rekindled the alarm and indignation of the nuclear disarmers. Gaitskell always replied courteously and sympathetically to individual unilateralists,[171] with none of the 'barely concealed contempt' of which the *New Statesman* accused him.[13d] But he was still very wary of the CND leadership. When Canon Collins wrote asking the Labour Party to join a demonstration against tests, he passed the letter to George Brown with the comment: 'Please see attached trap. We must clearly not fall into it';[172] and both the NEC and the General Council declined.[21g] After their Blackpool defeat, the CND leaders lost ground to their intransigent followers who advocated either independent parliamentary candidatures, or active civil disobedience.[13e] The former faced expulsion from the Party, like anyone who opposed an official Labour candidate, and those nuclear disarmers who favoured that course were so reminded by the NEC.[10d]

In the next disciplinary incident, the Party was on weaker ground. Plagued for years by Communist front movements, the Labour Party hindered infiltration by keeping a list of organisations to which members were forbidden to belong. One was the World Peace Council, which sponsored in Moscow a disarmament congress attended by several leading unilateralists, headed by the rival chieftains Lord Russell and Canon Collins. They went intending to put an independent point of view, with the promise of publicity in the Soviet press (on which of course the Russians cheated).[173] Facing an awkward choice between disciplining the famous or giving them special treatment, the NEC's organisation sub-committee made the clumsy worst of it: first threatening Russell and Collins with expulsion, for which they had no legal case, then claiming that Russell's subscription had lapsed, and finally retreating amid ridicule.[174]

In the spring of 1962 CND's extreme-Left hangers-on resumed their efforts to break up Labour meetings, notably Willy Brandt's in London at the end of March, and two May Day rallies at which Gaitskell was howled down in Glasgow and Brown in London. Gaitskell was speaking quite unprovocatively on Scottish unemployment and pit closures, but 'for 45 minutes there was not one second when there wasn't an uproar ... nothing but yelling to break the whole thing up'.[15c] The secretary of Glasgow Youth CND resigned in protest, saying 80 or 90 per cent of the demonstrators were Communists.[40e] Gaitskell shouted to the 300 disrupters, 'Go to the Kremlin and put up your placards there,' and told the crowd of 5,000: 'When it comes to the ballot and the vote in an election these people are not worth a tinker's cuss. They are peanuts. They don't count. All they can do is make a noise.'[175] Once again his journalistic traducers used his contemptuous reply to a few deliberate wreckers to pretend that he had scorned all nuclear disarmers;[108e] once again they misled some worthy people, to whom Gaitskell had patiently to explain the obvious: 'It is a mystery to me why other members of C.N.D. should wear the cap that was not intended to fit them at all.'[176] But he wrote unrepentantly to a friendly Labour MP that, though people genuinely concerned about tests must be taken very seriously, at Glasgow 'there was very little option. If I had not hit back both the morale of our supporters would have collapsed and the meeting would have been a complete victory for the Communists'.[177] To one friend he went much further, linking that affair with his long struggle against neutralism and extending it back to before the war: 'if I were to die tomorrow, the one thing I would be remembered for is this particular battle that I have been fighting ... sometimes rather alone ... perhaps the thing of which I am most proud in my life.'

vii *NATO Strategy, and the Missile Crisis*

The affair of the nuclear tests illustrates in a minor way the influence a Gaitskell government might have had. His close relations with President Kennedy brought him under fire from the anti-Americans on both Right and Left. The Beaverbrook press attacked him for 'tail-wagging servility' in holding confidential talks on defence with a foreign leader after refusing Downing Street briefings.[178a c] The *New Statesman* suggested that he valued the link solely for electoral purposes.[13d h] Such sniping was a small price to pay for mutual confidence with the Kennedy Administration. He believed, as they did, that only countervailing power would dissuade the Soviet Union from misusing its strength to spread its influence; but also that the West had to demonstrate restraint to the Kremlin, and good will to public opinion in both the democracies and the uncommitted countries. Sharing the Administration's approach to nuclear weapons, and its distrust of both hard-line cold warriors and wishful-thinking neutralists, he still brought a rather different perspective to the assessment of public opinion, of the military and political risks that might have to be taken in a crisis, and of the need for Western initiatives (before the days of *Ostpolitik*). The voice of such a loyal but candid ally was welcome in the White House to counteract right-wing pressures, both domestic and European. Heard even from the Opposition Front Bench, it would have carried much further from Downing Street.

The new men in Washington shared Labour's long-standing worries about official attitudes in the Pentagon, in Whitehall and at NATO headquarters. The previous US Administration had relied on 'massive retaliation', a prospect so appalling as to render its willingness to wield the deterrent dubiously credible; the British government's emphasis on its own independent nuclear force made nuclear proliferation harder to check; the soldiers assumed that tactical atomic weapons were just a modern kind of artillery. Crossman and Wigg had done much to educate the Labour Party, and early in 1962 officialdom itself sounded the alarm when Sir Solly Zuckerman, Chief Scientific Adviser to the Ministry of Defence, warned in a powerful article that the military machine was terrifyingly liable to escape from human judgment and control.[179] Gaitskell had been a friend of Zuckerman's for over thirty years, had once tried to bring him into the Ministry of Fuel and Power, and had intended in 1959 to recruit him to Downing Street as full-time defence adviser.[180] The article reinforced Opposition criticisms of NATO strategy while giving reassurance that these doubts were understood in high places at NATO and in Whitehall; both General Norstad, Allied Supreme Commander, and Harold Watkinson, Minister of Defence, had authorised it. But Macmillan would not anticipate the defence debate by telling Gaitskell whether he agreed with it;[181b] and Watkinson (who both opened and closed the debate, very ineptly) resolutely ignored it in spite of challenges from his own benches as well as Labour's.[130d]

The government was still more embarrassed by the American Secretary of Defense Robert McNamara, in his speech at Ann Arbor, Michigan in June 1962. Gaitskell had first met him in February, found him 'most impressive',[31b c] and liked his intellectual puritanism.[54a] At Ann Arbor, McNamara stressed the dangers of reliance on battlefield atomic weapons, urged the importance of building up conventional forces, warned against the risks of proliferation, and regretted the existence of independently operated national nuclear deterrents.* The affinity between Kennedy's policies and Labour's non-nuclear club proposals of 1959 had been re-

* The British deterrent was not independently operated; but Kennedy had privately warned Macmillan that it risked encouraging not only French but German nuclear appetites.[182]

marked on long before;[23c] and Gaitskell warmly welcomed the speech,[183] though – knowing the Administration's views – he had not, despite some Conservative reports, discussed the British bomb in Washington.[7t]

Macmillan's considered reaction was mellow though critical: 'The trouble with American Cabinet Ministers is that ... neither tycoons nor academics are very skilful or sensitive in politics, particularly the politics of other countries.' But at the time it was petulant, mainly because the speech upset his delicate negotiations over British entry into the Common Market with a reluctant President de Gaulle, who was determined to have his own nuclear force. 'McNamara's foolish speech ... has enraged the French ... It's a racket of the American industry.'[94a r] At home he evaded persistent questioning from Gaitskell and others on proliferation by debating references to the latter's defence of the British bomb two years earlier.[184]

Late in 1962 the crisis over the Soviet missile sites in Cuba alarmed the world with the sudden imminent risk of nuclear war. At the same time hostilities broke out on the Himalayan border between China and India, which Gaitskell saw as a straightforward case of Chinese aggression. Publicly he urged the West to give India economic aid, privately he believed she should have arms too if she asked.[185a b] India was also a favourite country of the parliamentary Left, and Jennie Lee took the lead in calling for a statement from the Executive on it; indeed Gaitskell thought that their inhibitions about the Asian war partly explained why they caused little trouble about the missile crisis.[7v]

That crisis posed a terrifying threat. It seems likely now that such a confrontation was inevitable and only the combination of firmness with restraint then shown by Kennedy has so far spared the world a repetition. But at the time it evoked the horrifying prospect of nuclear annihilation – in a cause which Gaitskell's critics claimed to be foreign, and over a country towards which the United States had recently put itself in the wrong.

Kennedy broadcast announcing the missile crisis at midnight (British time) on 22 October. Gaitskell was at a Downing Street dinner for General Norstad, where Macmillan, forewarned, took him aside and showed him the President's messages and speech. 'He did *not* take a very robust attitude. He thought his party "would not like it". I doubt if they would like any decision – firm decision – on any subject.'[94a s] But as he rightly thought that 'There was really no difference between them on their views',[7w] Gaitskell pressed the Prime Minister to fly to Washington. He and Dora stayed that night with Sir Isaiah Berlin and his wife, and listening to the broadcast on her radio Hugh was alarmed that if the Americans invaded Cuba the Russians would retaliate against Berlin or the United States missile bases in Turkey.[186b] Next day he went to see Macmillan again, believing that the Russians were planning to act in Berlin and 'we must try to use any opportunity for negotiation and must press the Americans very hard not to go too far'.[187] Brown and Wilson accompanied him to Downing Street: 'They hadn't much to say. Brown was more robust than G. ... Fortunately, they all distrust each other profoundly.'[9a t]

Gaitskell's instincts were as pro-American as ever, and he shocked Denis Healey, who doubted if the United States had adequate evidence, by saying that they were entitled to prevent a Soviet missile base in Cuba by invasion just as Britain would be in Ireland.[188] In public he was cautious, and his phrase about 'alleged' missile sites annoyed the White House[186b] (though it helped persuade the Administration to publish their photographs).[189] He suggested publicly that an attack on Cuba might be met by Soviet retaliation in Turkey;[185a] privately he thought it would be 'a pretty good exchange' to get rid of both.[190] Not knowing how thoroughly Kennedy kept Macmillan informed, Gaitskell and subsequently Wilson complained later on of inadequate American consultation;[62c] so that the Prime Minister worried that 'our secrets were almost too well kept ... We are doing something to let the truth be known. It will gradually seep through from Whitehall to London society and then pretty generally'.[94a v]

Gaitskell received a large anti-American mail, some concerned and reasonable, some hysterical and virulent ('American piracy on the high seas').[191a] Many people in the Party thought him far too sympathetic to Washington, and called him mealy-mouthed for saying that the blockade was of 'doubtful legality' — a comment which irritated the Americans too but was, he maintained, 'exactly the correct phrase to use according to the international lawyers'.[191b] During the crisis he told a correspondent who was anxious about the consequences of an American invasion that he agreed and was trying 'behind the scenes to prevent this happening'.[191c] He did not believe that the Russians had been planning anything so dangerous (and militarily ineffective) as a first-strike force in Cuba;[7v] and full support for Washington would have reopened all the old Party wounds just as they were beginning to heal — a great deal to ask of an Opposition leader whose words could not affect events.

After the crisis was over, Gaitskell looked to the future, stressing again the dangers of proliferation, and warning against treating the outcome as an American triumph justifying mere 'toughness' in dealing with the Russians: 'Not the least of President Kennedy's achievements has been his absolute refusal to proclaim this as a victory for himself and a defeat for Mr. Krushchev.'[62d] Kennedy felt 'rather bitter about the lack of support from Gaitskell, as he saw it';[186a c] but that did not last, for his reaction to Gaitskell's death was to regret 'the vanished opportunity of their working together'.[146j]

In the parochial sphere of British party politics, the crisis had another significance. If anything could have revived the fears that gave rise to

CND, the Cuban missile crisis should have done so. They did not revive. The Labour Left abandoned the cause, and soon their leaders were serving without visible discomfort in a Cabinet which made no move to renounce the bomb. A chapter in Labour's history was over.

viii *Liberals and Tories: Dead Duck and Gilded Albatross*

From the summer of 1961 Gaitskell began to run ahead of Macmillan in the opinion polls.[192] As his reputation soared ahead of his Party's, Macmillan's slumped with that of his government. The duel between Gaitskell and the Prime Minister was fought on very different terms now, with Tory voters defecting to the Liberals in droves, Macmillan's health impaired, and the benches behind him no longer worshipping success. Gaitskell, moreover, was much more skilful in his assaults. For example, in denouncing the appointment of Lord Home to the foreign secretaryship (which had very rarely been held by a peer since Labour became the official Opposition) Gaitskell pointed out[193] — in what the Prime Minister privately called 'the cleverest and most effective speech I have heard him make'[123m] — that Macmillan had owed his own tenure of that office to the reluctant decision of Sir Anthony Eden that Lord Salisbury was debarred by his peerage.[194] Macmillan was said to have endorsed that decision warmly at the time. Yet in Downing Street he showed a predilection for Ministers from the aristocracy (and from his own family) of which Gaitskell made constant fun. The Duke of Devonshire, a nephew of both Lady Dorothy Macmillan and Lord Salisbury, held minor office; and when his uncle ferociously attacked Macleod over Rhodesia, and was rebuked for it by Hailsham and Kilmuir in the Lords, Gaitskell teasingly remarked how Trollope, the Prime Minister's favourite novelist, would have relished the Duke's embarrassment: 'Which of these will he follow? Will the ties of the direct blood relationship prove the stronger? Or is the prestige of the First Lord of the Treasury strong enough to outweigh the drawback of only being uncle by marriage?' Mocking the 'feuds between our modern Montagues and Capulets', he told the Cambridge University Labour Club: 'I should expect in the ordinary way that the Labour Party would win any prize for intra Party invective. But when the Tory Marquises and Viscounts really get to work on each other the ferocity ... puts us in the shade.'[195]

Once Macmillan had exploited the prestige of a successful Premiership to score off his antagonist; now the contemptuous retorts went the other way. In the period of the pay pause, Gaitskell made a critical reference to 'the stop-go-stop procedure ... with a devaluation every decade or so'. Macmillan interrupted to observe that he had not devalued the pound; and Gaitskell answered that he had 'devalued our moral standards' instead.[81d] Less bitterly, Gaitskell summed up his attitudes towards his rival in a metaphor worthy of Butler at his most rococo:

> The gilded dolphin on which [Macmillan] rode in triumph through the election has become a dead albatross and is hanging round his neck ... The Edwardian pose, the languid condescension ... are ... inappropriate today.
>
> The Prime Minister is a fine actor ... a splendid showman, but when the showman is shown up the play is over, illusion is shattered, and it is time for the players to depart.[83c]

From that summer, Gaitskell's personal popularity was securely established while Macmillan's was threatened. Their parties slowly felt the effects. In July 1961 Conservative losses at last gave Labour the lead, but still with less support than it had had up to 1959 (40 per cent when the Don't Knows were counted, 43 per cent when they were not). That sluggish progress at a time of Liberal upsurge provoked press speculation about an electoral pact, which Labour pessimists like Woodrow Wyatt began to advocate. When parliamentary co-operation against the Immigration Bill was at its peak that autumn, the Liberal leader Jo Grimond sent Gaitskell a note: 'The Lib-Lab pact seems even closer than Woodrow envisaged.' Gaitskell's reply was personally very friendly but politically not at all forthcoming.[196] Two days later he rejected any deal requiring Labour candidates to stand down. Privately he recalled that local resistance to doing so had blocked Morrison's efforts just after the war to arrange pacts in the south-west;[197a c] publicly he said: 'I will never be a party to that'.[198]

He had toyed with the idea for a couple of weeks just after the general election, but decided that the Liberals could not deliver their vote – so that a pact would be unnecessary to win over their progressive followers, and ineffective in winning the others.[7x J] Grimond thought, probably rightly, that Gaitskell underestimated the importance of the younger and more radical element among them; as was natural, since Liberals in Gaitskell's own West Riding were the most favourable of all to *laissez-faire* economics and, especially in local government, to alliances with Conservatives against Labour.[7x] Though very friendly with the leading Liberal MPs, he dismissed their supporters as 'far to the right of [Grimond and Bonham Carter] in their policies', and their candidates as taking more Conservative than Labour votes, concluding that 'an electoral pact is likely to do more harm than good to us'[199a c] since it 'positively pays us to have Liberal intervention in the marginal seats'.[197a b] These propositions were supported by Labour's regional organisers, but not by Gaitskell's usual thorough dissection of evidence.[200]

Probably these were not his real reasons. On many policy issues dear to progressive middle-class intellectuals, his views showed a strong populist streak. But his deepest differences with the Liberals were not electoral, reflecting calculations of their prospects of success; not cerebral, reflecting disagreements over policy: they were visceral. He wrote contemptuously to his daughter about some of the Liberal intellectuals at the BBC, where she was working:

> I recognise very well the description ... being essentially dilettante politically, they regard it as rather non U to be *really committed.* Non U to be Labour because we are supposed to be 'old-fashioned' and 'dreary' — which is double talk for 'working class' and 'uneducated' — Non U to be Tory because they are 'bourgeois' and 'stupid'. I used to get unreasonably annoyed with them before the war when the same sort of people were ... just vaguely left wing.[201]

He suspected Liberal voters of similar vices, and at Scarborough he told a Fabian meeting that he could not stand them because of the snobbery that kept them out of the working-class movement.[23g]

At his most favourable, in 1959, he told Hetherington that 'it was impossible for him to do anything openly at present';[7x] within a fortnight he was 'cooling off a good deal, especially under the impact of reactions in his own party'.[7j] In 1962 he clearly recalled Clause Four when his enemies had used Jay's *Forward* article as a weapon against him, and stressed 'strictly privately — that he personally could not move in this. He was very much under suspicion on the left of the party. He must not do anything to divide the party again'.[7t] Gaitskell was therefore furious when Wyatt called for a pact in the *New Statesman* on the very day (26 January 1962) when the leader was to speak in his Bosworth constituency. He had shown proofs to Gaitskell, who wrote to a friend that the proposal 'irritates the *whole* of the Labour Party'; and to its author that it was 'certain to utterly divide the party' and had no chance of being accepted — while if he were to sponsor it himself he would only 'get myself heavily defeated in the Parliamentary Labour Party and Executive and be obliged to resign'.[199a] He was particularly worried about Labour morale in the seats allotted to the Liberals. He concluded by peevishly appealing to Wyatt to cancel the article as 'gravely embarrassing'.[199a] Wyatt said it was too late, and incurred a stinging public rebuke at his own constituency Party's dinner, where his leader derided his plan as 'a dead duck'.[202] When he continued to advocate it, Gaitskell's tone changed from admonitory to threatening: 'I do hope you realise the dangerous position in which you are putting yourself ... you are positively discouraging members of the Party from voting Labour. That really cannot be tolerated.'[199b]

Wyatt's insistence reflected his persistent pessimism. Just after Scarborough he wrote that Labour's best hope at the next election was only to do well enough 'to encourage the belief that it could win a subsequent

General Election'.[203] He had also doubted whether Gaitskell could survive for long as leader. Gaitskell thought he still underestimated Labour's chances for 1964.[199a] Though the Liberals nearly halved Labour's vote in March 1962 at the Orpington by-election, the Labour vote held up in the other six by-elections of that month and the next.[204] Gaitskell was therefore sceptical of the Liberal revival, seeing it as just 'a revolt by disgruntled Tories'.[205] They were too snobbish to support Labour, he claimed: 'it's all right if you've been voting Tory to vote Liberal because it's somehow or other respectable, [but] to vote Labour is going down in the social scale ... [because] the Labour Party is associated with the trade unions.'[206]

He recognised that the Liberals might become a threat to Labour, or even hold the balance at Westminster. If so, he said to Hetherington that he was not sure what he would do; and to a persistent television interviewer in the summer of 1962 that probably Labour should try to form a government.[88] But if the disgruntled Tories helped Labour win seats on a minority vote, and brought him to power with a clear majority of seats, he would cheerfully

> profit by the opportunity that the Liberals might be making ... although of course he'd prefer to be in with a majority of the popular vote. He thought they'd now gone a long way towards getting the image of the party right. But they could really get it right only by being in office. People would find, when Labour was actually governing, that a lot of things they thought wrong with Labour were all right.[7s]

By January 1962 Gaitskell found that the Tories at Westminster, though not yet in the country, were 'somewhat depressed and quiescent'.[207] The Prime Minister still saw only a natural swing away from a government so long in power, while the Opposition had 'no glamour and no theme'. But his philosophical detachment collapsed next month when the Liberals spectacularly won Orpington, for Macmillan feared that they might drive the Conservatives into third place at the next general election.[94a w]

Gaitskell had written in January that Labour's prospects were vastly improved but that the Party had not yet managed to broaden its appeal in a society with fewer and fewer manual workers.[208] In the spring Macmillan's own old seat at Stockton, now safely Labour, was duly held: a result which Gaitskell tactlessly treated as just a prelude to a more important contest across the river at West Middlesbrough, where he hoped for a victory to rebuild Labour morale.[209] In 1955, when the nationalisation 'shopping list' had included chemicals, Labour had done disastrously in the Teesside (and other) constituencies where ICI workers voted. In 1962 Labour had no plans to nationalise ICI, but the Liberals suggested they had; so on the Saturday before the Middlesbrough poll Gaitskell got Transport House to deny that, and then, when the entire press ignored it, repeated it himself and told the reporters to ginger up their news editors.[7r] Labour duly won the by-election with an increased share of the poll: the first gain, and first increase in a marginal seat, since Birmingham Small Heath, fifteen months before.

> He was almost extravagantly pleased[15e] ... said it showed what the pendulum would do – if only some of Labour's own people wouldn't stop [it] swinging ... the sequence of by-elections was bringing in ... altogether seven good people ... creating an impression of good sense and reliability in the party.[7e]

Gaitskell's caution over ICI was simple electioneering; he had no great esteem for the company, and had recently denounced its Courtaulds negotiation as a takeover bid made 'without any consideration for the interests of the consumers, the workers or the nation generally. You cannot impose order on the wages front and allow industrial anarchy everywhere else.'[210] In an unexpected way, his old critics were also influenced by political expediency; for when a group of left-wing MPs put down a pro-nationalisation motion, they deleted chemicals from it so as not to challenge Gaitskell.[14e f] Times had indeed changed.

Six weeks later, the day after yet another humiliating by-election (at Leicester) any impression of good sense and reliability on the Treasury bench vanished when the 'unflappable' Prime Minister dismissed one-third of his Cabinet in what Lord Butler called 'the Massacre of Glencoe'.[112b] Many Tories saw the fall of Selwyn Lloyd, who was widely regarded as executing rather than making policy, as a crude sacrifice of a scapegoat by a Prime Minister fearing for his own leadership. Most of the other victims were past their prime, but shared the suspicion of panic in Downing Street. One wrote:

> I got the impression that he [Macmillan] was extremely alarmed about his own position, and was determined to eliminate any risk for himself by a massive change of Government. It astonished me that ... [he] should lose both nerve and judgement in this way.[211]

Macmillan justly replied that he had long been reproached for defending colleagues who merited dismissal; and, supported by Butler, contended later that Lloyd had exhausted their patience by his total lack of imagination, adaptability or constructive ideas.[212] But Gaitskell gained by either interpretation, since the attack discredited the head of the Government and the defence accredited Opposition criticisms of its policies. He heard the news at the Gillinsons' in Leeds, and they played with various bright ideas to catch the headlines; he discarded them all, simply commented 'They were all responsible so they should all have been sacked', and went to bed.[213]

He knew that any serious move against Macmillan would occur behind the scenes, not in public, and after his Suez experience he was wary of again attacking the Prime Minister personally. To do nothing – to 'let the wound remain open and the trouble rankle' – would have been the best parliamentary tactics;[214] but it would not have been understood outside Westminster. 'There would have been a lot of questions in the party and in the country and people would have wanted to know what was up.'[7y] The Shadow Cabinet therefore tabled a motion of no confidence in the government, calling for a general election. Though they could not win in the division lobby, Gaitskell felt 'Macmillan could hardly re-establish his authority now'; and he made immense preparations for a frontal assault. He told Hetherington: 'He wasn't putting any "moral uplift" into it. You couldn't call people scoundrels for three-quarters of a speech and then try to move on to a higher plane at the end.'[7y]

Gaitskell's followers were delighted with his speech.[215] Recalling the choice of Macmillan by the 1957 Cabinet, he asked: 'How many of the old comrades who voted him into power now remain? Six out of nineteen. Not since Stalin liquidated the old Bolsheviks has there been such a successful process of elimination.' He wound up with a scathing attack on a style of political leadership which he despised irrespective of party:

> Prime Ministers who have lived in history have set more store by their policy objectives than by the time they remained in office ... Peel, Gladstone, Churchill, Attlee, [Eden] ... It is not true of the ... [present] Prime Minister. His Government will be remembered not for the leadership they gave the nation but as a conspiracy to retain power. Men and measures have been equally sacrificed for this ... we cannot solve our problems as a nation without a deeper sense of national purpose. Such a purpose is not created when evasion is regarded as a virtue and double talk is regarded as a duty.[84e]

But though the occasion attracted enormous advance publicity, and seemed invented for a born Leader of the Opposition, Gaitskell was not one. He knew that his performance was by no means among his best;[107a b] Macmillan indeed called it 'a very *bad* speech, quite unworthy of the occasion or of himself'.[94a y]

Nevertheless, relations between the two antagonists improved somewhat at the end, and after one business meeting Gaitskell was astonished to be kept chatting for an hour by an apparently lonely Prime Minister.[216] That change came about largely because of their frequent dealings on questions of security: always a difficult test for a Leader of the Opposition who has both responsibilities as a potential Prime Minister and a duty to expose and criticise governmental laxity. The Prime Minister was conspicuously grateful for his adversary's balance and consideration on these delicate matters.[75g] But Gaitskell did not neglect his other duty, and when a serious spy case at Portland was soon followed by the George Blake affair, he warned Edward Heath that the Opposition must be properly consulted or they would force a debate and make 'an Almighty row'.[217] He felt that the Opposition were largely responsible for getting the Radcliffe Committee set up.[218]

His last major speech in the House was on yet another Admiralty security scandal, the Vassall case, where the Prime Minister had treated the matter unduly lightly and Thorneycroft, the Minister of Defence, had made things much worse by an unseemly and flippant debating speech. Some newspapers unleashed a scurrilous campaign against the Admiralty Ministers, and the Labour Front Bench (particularly George Brown) pursued the case hard.[62e] Macmillan, justifiably enraged at the slanders, then set up a Tribunal under the 1921 Act, mainly to harry the journalistic accusers but also to try to damage the Opposition as over the bank rate affair five years before.[219–20a]

It was a dangerous attack. Gaitskell neatly foiled any attempt to use the Tribunal against the Labour Party; as Leader of the Opposition he applied for legal representation before it, and its members, by refusing, in effect debarred themselves from that area of inquiry.[221] In the House, he argued that Labour had raised the matter publicly only because the government had rejected either an independent inquiry which the opposition proposed, or any confidential consultations whatever. He predicted a tremendous row with Fleet Street if the Tribunal sought (as it did) to imprison journalists who refused to reveal their sources – and asked if those writing pro-government stories would be required to give theirs also. Macmillan, he said, had ignored the spying to denounce only the rumours – which grew from the apparent cover-up frivolously justified by Thorneycroft.[22a b] 'Macmillan was pretty frightening and devastating,' said one Labour MP, 'and Hugh batted on this wicket absolutely brilliantly ... did his national duty *and* turned the issue away from the Opposition.'[222] After the debate and after meeting Macmillan, Gaitskell felt confident that the Tribunal would concentrate on the spying rather than the rumours, that relations would be resumed between the Front Benches, and that the Opposition would be properly consulted again.[7u] He had united his own followers and won some Tory sympathisers too; the days when the Prime Minister used to score off him in the House had vanished. 'Nowadays ... he is not simply Mr. Macmillan's equal. More often he is the master.'[178b] Yet while protecting his own side, he conducted himself with restraint and dignity and actually improved his personal relations with Macmillan.[223] It was an extraordinary political performance.

CHAPTER 25

THE COMMON MARKET
1961–2

i *Consistency and Evolution*

GAITSKELL claimed with justice that his attitude to the Common Market was consistent throughout. He never saw it as a great issue of principle and was irritated with those who did – whether strong opponents like Denis Healey or ardent advocates like Roy Jenkins.[1] He never felt himself primarily a European,[2a b] and thought that in a world perspective the EEC enthusiasts overemphasised a 'parochial' problem.[3a 4] The Common Market could not be ignored; that was a fact but no cause for rejoicing. In July 1962 he told a Commonwealth audience: 'Whether you and I like it or not the thing is there. In many ways I cannot help regretting it has been created although I see the advantage of Franco-German understanding is very important.'[5a] Where some saw a shining opportunity and others a sinister threat, Gaitskell at the height of the controversy told some disappointed supporters of entry that the subject was 'a bore and a nuisance and it had always been so'.[2] Like Pierre Mendès-France during the same debate in France five years earlier, Gaitskell thought his country's economic future would be determined by decisions made at home, not by joining or staying out;[6a] and time has shown he was right.

In the early years of the development of the European Communities, the Labour leaders were divided in their attitude. In 1953 Gaitskell told an American diplomat that they were at odds over the move to incorporate Germany into a European Defence Community: Morrison 'looked with favour on Continental efforts at integration' and would have welcomed British links with the EDC, while Attlee 'had a deep distrust' of such an association, owing to memories of 1940 which Gaitskell thought irrelevant.[7a] Then, soon after becoming leader, when the European Economic Community was just coming into being, Gaitskell told a group of State

Department and other policy-makers in Washington that British policy was determined by her being 'primarily an Atlantic rather than a Continental European power ... there was no possibility of the United Kingdom joining a kind of federal union ... but ... there should be close relations'.[7b] A few months later he said so publicly in his Godkin Lectures at Harvard, summing up on his return home:

> I said that most of us felt ourselves not only European but the centre of the Commonwealth, a Commonwealth including very important Asian and African countries, and that we would not want to go in closer with Europe if this meant weakening the Atlantic alliance ... going into a Federation of Europe was absolutely out of the question ... [unless] we were somehow cut off from the Commonwealth and left out on our own.[8a]

In 1962 he cited these lectures to show that he had not changed his views.[9-10a]

The PLP, without dissent for once, gave cautious approval to the idea of a European Free Trade Area late in 1956; and the TUC agreed. The Shadow Cabinet therefore discouraged a move to raise the subject again after *Socialist Commentary*, in September 1957, published a pro-EEC article.[11] When the trade union MPs met on 10 December 1957, Bill Blyton – a Durham miner, violently anti-Market – denounced the Labour intellectuals who supported it: the first attack on the 'Hampstead set'. A year later Gaitskell welcomed the government's effort to set up an industrial free trade area. He wanted both to put pressure on France (without saying so publicly) by bringing the future EFTA countries into a 'rival bloc'; and also not to preclude merging the two groups, if ever the Six agreed, into a wider free trade or low-tariff area.[12a] He criticised the government later, however, for having gone 'on and on and on with those negotiations' long after it was clear that the two groups could not agree, and so delaying talks with the EEC which were now to be begun in an unnecessarily weak position.[13a] But whenever in the late 1950s the topic came up at his weekly meetings with the lobby correspondents, 'he never deviated ... neutral, vaguely uninterested ... bored by it, he couldn't see what all the fuss was about'.[14a b]

During 1960 the first serious Shadow Cabinet studies were undertaken by Wilson and Healey.[15] Opinion in the Party was slowly moving against entry, mainly on political grounds.[16] Gaitskell did not concur, but he foresaw all the difficulties of entry.[12b] He warned a *Socialist Commentary* meeting at Scarborough that public opinion would insist on no federation and on fair treatment for the Commonwealth.[8b]

Commentators and colleagues all believed that he was privately a cautious supporter of entry.[17-19a] But he resolutely opposed any public declaration, thinking it unlikely to become an electoral issue, and fearing that any strong line either way would mean another Labour split.[20]

> Macmillan ... is a very crafty man. This is one reason why I am determined not to let the Party get committed on the Common Market. If we try to reach a decision ourselves I am pretty certain we would remain hopelessly divided while the Tories reluctantly decide to unite behind whatever Macmillan decides to do.[21]

The question became central just as he was winning Labour's defence battle; the wounds had not healed, and internal strife could easily have resumed. On both sides of that quarrel, the leading parliamentarians agreed with Crossman:

> Here, for once, the Labour Party is being canny ... Hugh Gaitskell and Harold Wilson are firmly determined to avoid making the mistake ... we made on nuclear weapons by trying to work out a detailed policy, that only splits us. On this occasion we are letting the Government make all the running.[19b c]

But that agreement was on tactics, not objectives. Wilson and Crossman were both quite hostile to entry, while Gaitskell as always took time to make up his mind—and rejected their efforts to commit the Party to specific terms: 'He was as determined as ever to say absolutely nothing either way, any kind of attempt to lay down detailed conditions would either be platitudinous or too detailed to carry conviction before we knew what Macmillan was up to.'[19a d]

Once the British government opened negotiations for entry in July 1961, the subject came to the front of the political stage and became fraught with risks for Labour's fragile unity. To most of the Left it meant, said Gaitskell, 'the end ... [of] an independent Britain ... sucked up in a kind of giant capitalist, catholic conspiracy, our lives dominated by Adenauer and de Gaulle, unable to conduct any independent foreign policy at all'.[22a] To some Marketeers it was a great venture in internationalism which Britain had earlier spurned, but which now gave her a last chance to join a partnership which alone could ensure her economic survival. Gaitskell called the first view 'rubbish' and the second 'nonsense'.[22a] In December 1962 he described his motives and aims very candidly in a long memorandum to President Kennedy:

> [F]rom the start not only the Opposition but the Government as well were *not* in favour of '*going in and trying to get the best possible terms*' but only for '*going in if certain conditions were fulfilled*' ...
>
> It may be said that in reality the Government had decided to go in whatever the terms and that they only laid down conditions in order

to make their new policy acceptable to their Party. I do not know whether this is the case ... As for the Opposition, we certainly took the conditions very seriously and always meant to stand by them. There were two reasons for this attitude. First, I myself and my leading colleagues all happened to believe and still believe that the arguments of principle were fairly evenly balanced for and against and that the balance would be tipped in favour of our entry only if our conditions were fulfilled. Secondly, this policy of making our final judgment depend on the conditions was the only one which could have been accepted by the Party as a whole. If I had urged unconditional entry (thus going even further than the Government) there would have been bitter opposition from a large minority which was basically hostile to our entry. If I had urged outright opposition whatever the terms, this would also have been bitterly opposed by another, though smaller, minority, who were basically enthusiastic about our entry. In either case, there would have been a major split in the Party, which, following the great dispute on defence which had only recently been successfully concluded, would have been fatal to our prospects. Both minorities, however, were willing to accept that the issue must be allowed to depend on the terms, nor was there any real disagreement about what the terms must be.[10b]

Gaitskell thought that the Six might develop either in the way the Marketeers hoped or in that feared by their opponents, and that the best case for going in was that British entry on the right terms might tip that delicate balance:

If we stay out and the EFTA countries stay out, as they will ... there would be a greater danger of this State being inward-looking ... not interested in the rest of the world, nationalistic in outlook, a third force wanting its own nuclear weapons and wanting to break away. The effect of this on the Western Alliance could be serious.

As things are, if we went in we could probably stop that happening, but on the one condition only, that as we go in we maintain our links with the Commonwealth. That is essential.[23a]

But he never believed that the 1961–2 negotiations were the last chance, for he felt sure that de Gaulle would prevent any irrevocable federal development. He also privately believed that if the worst came to the worst after entry, no legal text could prevent a country seceding:

It would be a tremendous upheaval and one would hope if we were to go in it would never happen. But ... supposing the worst fears of people are realised and we become a depressed area off Europe there would be a tremendous urge to get out of it. I do not think that is likely to happen but to avoid that I think the other countries would lean over backwards, and the spirit is likely to be just as important as the letter.[5b]

The fullest account sums up Gaitskell's concept of a Europe differing from that of either de Gaulle or the federalists:

A Europe based essentially on cooperation among states ... whose outer edges were fuzzy ... loosely joined together in a customs union ... which was low-tariff and liberal in its external policies ... [which] made no attempt to plan ... common resources ... [or to] act as a unit in its relations with third countries ... [or as] a political or military bloc ... Mr. Gaitskell's Europe was fairly close to the Europe favoured by much of the Conservative Party as well as by most of the Labour Party.[24a]

With these aims in his mind, substantive policy and party tactics both led Gaitskell to play a waiting game. He thought that the prospects of a Europe developing in the way he wanted depended on the terms. If those proved unsatisfactory, the loss would not be very grave; moreover, the Conservative uncertainty would be too great for the Prime Minister to proceed. Terms good enough to enable Macmillan to carry his own party would also allow Gaitskell to carry his; and without such terms the talks would collapse and Labour could only benefit.

On 22 July 1961 the Cabinet decided to apply, and the House debated it on 2 and 3 August. The committed back-benchers split right across party lines in a way which later became familiar. But Gaitskell's careful opening speech was as Duncan Sandys said, winding up,[13b] 'a notable balancing act, ably stat[ing] the case on both sides'.[25] To a pro-Market Labour MP who felt it strained his loyalty, Gaitskell replied that he had meant to keep to the compromise line agreed by the Party Meeting.[26a] Harold Wilson put forward obviously unobtainable conditions (provoking Roy Jenkins to resign as a Front Bench spokesman) – but that was without Gaitskell's approval.[27]

At the Blackpool Conference this official line was accepted without a card vote; a pro-Market resolution was rejected overwhelmingly, and the anti-Marketeers then prudently agreed to remit their motion to the NEC.[28a] Gaitskell did not speak in the debate, and on the air he kept carefully to the agreed compromise. Unconditional support for entry might destroy the Commonwealth, while refusal underestimated both the 'immense economic importance' of the Market[29] and the 'economic dangers and difficulties for us' of staying out.[30a] His 'absolutely essential conditions' were the same as the government's: British agriculture, the Commonwealth and Britain's neutral partners in EFTA 'must be taken care of'.[31]

At the Conservative Conference Macmillan mocked his caution with the music-hall song, 'She wouldn't say yes—she wouldn't say no'. Unmoved, Gaitskell told a Labour policy conference at Blackburn in December that the Commonwealth was the main worry, that the waiting attitude was 'right and commonsense', and that 'I do not want another internal party row about this'.[32a] He sought to reduce the temperature at Westminster by discouraging the rival groups from putting down motions, and by persuading the PLP that a vote on the issue might put him at a disadvantage against the 'master of political manoeuvre' in Downing Street.[33]

From his bitter experiences over Clause Four and the bomb, Gaitskell had learned to time his moves cautiously. To take sides in the abstract for or against British entry seemed to him pointless for the country, for it was a matter of balanced arguments and difficult judgments which need not be final; and dangerous for the Party, which was certain to split over the principle without even knowing what either decision would entail. 'His strategy at this stage', he told Hetherington,

> must be to get a full discussion ... He had to start from the fact that quite a lot of people in the party were hostile to the Common Market; and he must not on any account cause another open division ... The trend in other big unions might be similarly [to the AEU] against the Common Market. Therefore he had to move cautiously in bringing about a full and rational discussion of the issues within the party.[12c]

To an anti-Market Labour agent who condemned fence-sitting, Gaitskell stressed the

> great importance of the Party not becoming divided on this issue. Nothing could be more fatal to our prospects of winning the next Election. But if we are not to be divided ... we should avoid taking up firm positions before we know ... precise terms.[34]

From the other side Roy Jenkins protested that to meet the anti-Market campaign Gaitskell would have to give a lead, emphasise the advantages as well as the conditions of entry, and show some emotional sympathy.[35a] To that complaint he replied in a different tone. Gaitskell too thought it best for Labour that entry should not become an electoral issue at all, and he denied being opposed to it. But

> it is not really a matter of what I think; it is a question of carrying the Party ... [and] calls for the most careful tactical handling. I suspect that if I were to do what you want, we should be more likely to lose control altogether. Certainly the Union Conferences have only gone

the way they have because of these conditions which, you say, I am
continually stressing.[35b]

The lessons of 1960 had left their mark.

ii *Friendly on the Fence*

Twice in early 1962 he himself appeared to be taking a critical line. One
occasion was public, talking in the United States, where opinion was un-
critically favourable to British entry and he characteristically put the other
side. He told the New York Liberals (a largely trade union party not
unlike British Labour) that a federal Europe with nuclear weapons might
not be a force for peace; and that an inward-looking Community with a
high external tariff might harm the NATO alliance—both in its own
cohesion and in its relations with the 'Third World'. Britain must seek for
her former African Colonies treatment as good as the French ones had
got—but other underdeveloped countries might then suffer, and Africans
might suspect a plot to block pan-Africanism and maintain European
hegemony.[32b] He mentioned Labour's five conditions for supporting
membership: the government's three, and safeguards for an independent
foreign policy and economic planning.[36] But American officials still
believed him to be 'moderately in favor' of entry.[7c]

The second occasion was private, a meeting on 4 April 1962 of XYZ,
the group of Labour political economists and financial experts to which
Gaitskell had belonged for thirty years. Roy Jenkins had arranged an
invitation to Jean Monnet—the begetter of the original Franco-German
Coal and Steel Community back in 1950, whom de Gaulle called (not as a
compliment) the 'inspirer' of the supra-national European idea. If the aim
was to turn Gaitskell into a 'European', the outcome was catastrophic.
Monnet wanted to explain the broad philosophy of the EEC, while
Gaitskell tried impatiently to press him over attitudes to the 'Third World'
and problems of British entry. It was a characteristic difference between
the French and British styles, but in addition Monnet—like Jenkins—
thought that the will to solve the subsidiary disputes required precisely
that emotional commitment to the principle which Gaitskell would not
make. On his side Gaitskell felt that the visitor kept evading his questions
about the impact on one or another underdeveloped country; thinking the
questions beside the point, Monnet finally protested: 'You must have
faith'. Gaitskell was not conciliatory: 'I don't believe in faith. I believe in
reason and you have not shown me any.'[37a b] He said afterwards only that
Monnet 'hadn't been very good' and was evasive.[12c d] But he worried his
friends (including Jenkins) by his insistence; one called it 'a tremendous
clash which left me rather sad'.[38] Some of them decided (at once or in

retrospect) that Gaitskell was showing his hostility to the whole idea; others thought only that he personally felt the case unprov n and wanted stronger grounds than he got for dispelling his own doubts or – perhaps especially – those of his followers.[39]

That affair, and his own strong convictions, may explain why Jenkins thought Gaitskell was already moving towards opposition in principle.[40] He was not alone, for Peter Shore in the other camp believed the same.[41] But Gaitskell himself denied it vehemently;[35b] and within a week of the Monnet dinner he told Hetherington, who had suggested Labour was hardening against the Market, that 'on the contrary he thought it was moving rather towards support'.[12d] He often said later that he shifted only in the autumn of 1962;[42-4] and that was the view of many observers just as qualified as Jenkins and Shore and sometimes more detached: among them Harold Macmillan, George Brown, Herbert Bowden, Anthony Crosland, Denis Healey, Harold Wilson, Lord Gladwyn and Nicholas Kaldor.[45-8]

If Gaitskell had really become opposed to entry by the spring, he would have been strongly tempted to begin campaigning openly against it as much of his own Party demanded; for he was sceptical about the visionaries' conception of Europe, suspicious of the Prime Minister's cunning, certain that the Conservatives were desperately seeking an electoral lifebelt, and aware that Ministers would probably support entry on the best terms they could get, though they would not yet weaken their bargaining position by saying so.[49-50a] Gaitskell's closest pro-European friends feared that he might come out in open opposition;[35a] and Macmillan was privately astonished (and relieved) that he did not.[51]

Instead, he kept faithfully to his line in private as well as in public, giving no commitments but contriving to sound sympathetic to the very different views of each correspondent.[52a b] He wrote to his younger daughter at Oxford that the question was 'tricky and complicated' and it would be 'absurd' for the opposition to decide until the terms and the government's view were known – adding significantly that he did not share her worry that public opinion was hostile to entry, for 'Provided the terms are reasonable, I doubt if the country is going to be very anti'.[53a] But the intellectual fastidiousness which was later to make him exasperated with shoddy economic arguments for entry, at this stage led him rather to recoil from the exaggerations of the other side. In the summer of 1961 he was furiously critical of a Transport House paper on the political drawbacks;[54] that July he (rightly) attacked an anti-Market speech by Crossman as 'foolish and irresponsible';[19a d] late in May 1962 he was unhappy about another Transport House paper by Peter Shore;[54a b] and at the same time he dismissed a pamphlet on the dangerous political implications as being based on no real evidence.[56]

His concern for practical details rather than abstract principles was a familiar feature of his political personality. Just at the time of the Monnet dinner, the Labour Party was thoroughly examining the political and economic consequences of entry for both Britain and the Commonwealth, and in March 1962 the half-dozen senior leaders began privately working out minimum terms. They started from a paper by Gaitskell's old Oxford friend Professor James Meade, who favoured joining a liberal-minded and outward-looking Community but not a narrow protectionist one, and thought its terms for the Commonwealth would give a pointer to its likely development. Another economist, Robert Neild, did a full note for the Shadow Chancellor on the implications for controlling capital flight.[57]

On Thursday 12 April 1962, Gaitskell told Labour MPs that the Shadow Cabinet committee was studying the question intensively, and that after Easter three PLP meetings would be devoted to it.[58a] That Saturday at Fulham, he condemned the government for preparing a *fait accompli* after months of secrecy, and asked whether they would enter whatever the terms – the challenge he had so often put to pro-Market critics, as Macmillan had put it to the Liberals.[59] At that time:

> He thought the economic case ... about fifty-fifty ... possibly, however, the political argument was decisive. If we left the Six as a close knit unit of their own that would be less satisfactory than broadening, loosening, and leavening it – both with Britain and with the neutrals.[12d]

In October 1961 he had expressed his distaste for the strange anti-Market coalition of a Little-Englander Right with a frequently pro-Russian Left.[30a] That distaste emerged strongly from a memorandum he wrote in May 1962 for a group of friendly trade union leaders seeking his advice on dealing with anti-Market resolutions coming up at their conferences. In opposing any commitments on principle, he formally kept to the official line of reiterating the five conditions and making the decision depend on the terms – as, formally, he still did at Brighton five months later. But the emotional overtones of the May memorandum were at least as favourable to entry as those of the Conference speech were hostile. He dismissed as wholly unfounded many bogeys which might raise trade union hackles: there was no threat of cheap foreign labour, or of lower social benefits, or of losing the freedom to nationalise or conduct our own economic policies (except over foreign trade). Federation was as unlikely as it was unacceptable, so that French or German votes could not decide Britain's foreign policy. He emphasised '*that by not going in we do not prevent the Common Market from coming into existence* ... If we stay out of it, we run the risk of becoming nothing more than a little island off Europe. We shall be dwarfed politically by the Six.' Without Britain the EEC might fall under

German domination (a bogey of his own to make a Labour audience gibber) and might raise tariffs against our engineering goods (another, with which Bill Carron could make flesh creep in the AEU).

Another passage shows that in May he cannot yet have realised he would emerge as a hero of the anti-Marketeers:

> Most of the resolutions are very wide of the mark and almost certainly inspired by Communists. The Communists naturally oppose our going into the Common Market because they believe it would strengthen the democratic forces of the West. They are right in ... that if we do not go in ... there could be rather grave political consequences. By going in, on the other hand, we could prevent the formation of a tight, inward-looking federation.

(It was a familiar if not an endearing characteristic of Gaitskell to spy Communists among his opponents, where they were indeed busily active; had he already imagined that they would end up on his side, he would never have drawn attention to the fact.) He ended, as he later did at Conference, with an emotional appeal. But whereas in October he was to speak of Vimy Ridge and a thousand years of history, in May he invoked Labour's European Socialist friends who

> are very, very anxious indeed that we should join. They do not share any of the fears expressed in these resolutions. On the contrary, they believe ... [it] is a step in the right direction, internationalistic in its approach, and getting away from the narrow nationalism of the past.

He summed up: 'although there are undoubtedly circumstances in which we should not go in if our conditions are not fulfilled, nevertheless, if they are fulfilled, there is little or nothing to fear and great benefits may well result'.[60]

To some leaders such a great historic decision, about which alarm and enthusiasm both cut across party lines, might have seemed appropriate for an effort at bipartisanship. Macmillan never made the smallest gesture in that direction, and rebuffed at least one from the Labour side during the talks.[50b] Instead the Prime Minister managed the affair slowly and circumspectly, taking time to bring his recalcitrant colleagues round and taking pains to play down the political implications of entry.[24b] When fending off Liberal enthusiasts, his language was thoroughly Gaitskellite:

> And they would have us join right away — like that, without conditions and apparently negotiations. They do not care at all what is to happen to the interests of the Commonwealth ... [or] to British agriculture ...

we have entered into negotiations to see whether we can join ... with proper safeguards for all those to whom we have responsibility ... the only course which is at once prudent and honourable.[46c]

Yet within a few weeks he was planning a crusade to carry the great decision into history – and the Conservative Party back to power. In his diary on 21 April, he took it completely for granted that at the end of the negotiations Britain would go in: 'This will be the most exciting political issue since 1845. All Party allegiances and formations may be radically changed.' Yet, as the very next words show, he had no idea whether his public conditions would be met:[46a d] 'we don't know at all what are the chances of a reasonable offer by the Six. Will France refuse all concessions ... ? Will de Gaulle ... betray us after all? No one knows.'[61]

Macmillan's shift took Gaitskell by surprise; as he wrote to an old friend, 'I never expected the government would have the gall to propose to go in on such bad terms, which we were bound to oppose.'[42a] He told his old CDS supporters: 'As late as July he anticipated having to deal with the Left in the Party and bring the Party round to support for entry.'[2a c *] And he assured President Kennedy:

> [R]ight up to mid-summer 1962 we remained reasonably hopeful. I myself expected that the terms would be such as to prove acceptable to the Commonwealth Prime Ministers and that my task would be to persuade my Party to accept them because they were by and large in accordance with our own conditions. I did not think it would be easy to handle the extreme anti-Marketeers, but I was prepared to do it as being the only course consistent with the line we had followed ...
>
> We were, therefore, bitterly disappointed and indeed astonished at the provisional agreements reached at the beginning of August.[10c e]

That reaction affected his immediate decision, not his fundamental attitude. At his most hostile, he always distinguished opposition to entry on the proposed terms from opposition on any terms, and tried hard to avoid the former being exploited by the advocates of the latter. But closer contacts with Continental leaders convinced him that their political intentions were unacceptable and their economic outlook selfish; he told a trade union MP that they had disappointed him by their protectionism, rejecting the terms needed to 'carry the Commonwealth ... [and] convince the world that the E.E.C. was anxious to help the poorer, underdeveloped countries'.[63] While he was never utopian about the Commonwealth, its critical reactions had a profound effect in finally making up his mind. Domestic developments propelled him the same way, as soon as it became clear that the government was determined to enter on the best terms it

* He said so to Fred Mulley after the Executive on 25 July 1962.[62]

could obtain. Gaitskell was shocked by what he saw as Macmillan's exploitation of the issue for party purposes, contemptuous of the economic arguments advanced in favour of entry, and exasperated by the overwhelming pressure of the media. His astonishment and resentment were among the reasons for his abandonment of a precise cold-blooded calculating style for opposition with an emotional force and fire which astonished friends and opponents alike.

iii *The Issues: Politics before Economics*

It was always Gaitskell's view—and indeed the private opinion of all leading Marketeers—that the case for entry rested on political advantage not economic necessity. Much as he stressed the terms, he knew they must be assessed in context, writing to Kennedy:

> It is obvious that how one judges the terms is bound to be affected by how one evaluates the basic arguments for and against Britain's entry. The more enthusiastic one is, the worse the terms which would be acceptable. The more hostile one is, the more one would be inclined to reject any terms—even quite good ones. I have tried on this to take the middle road.[10f]

In deciding that the economic arguments were only 50–50, he followed the experts for whom he had most respect—'trying to find out what the best theologians thought ... a sort of "what do they say in Rome?" '[64] He was particularly influenced by James Meade, Sir Donald MacDougall and Sir Robert Hall.[65] (But when the latter came to favour entry on grounds of its possible dynamic effects on the British economy, Gaitskell dismissed these as only hunch.)[66b] He was not at all convinced that the Continental economic expansion—in which Belgium did not share—could be explained as a consequence of the Community arrangements.[13c] The government were rash to take for granted that that expansion would continue after Britain's entry, or would benefit Britain: 'We might find that we got in ... with all the economic disadvantages and adjustments that were entailed; that there was no expansion after all; and that we were then in the middle of a hideous balance of payments crisis.'[12c] But in April 1962 he was reluctant to discuss those economic dangers in public for fear of starting an anti-Market reaction;[12c] by October he concentrated on them exclusively.

Gaitskell did not share the Left's fear (and the Right's hope) that entry would prevent a Labour government from planning the economy: 'I don't, in fact, think there are going to be great difficulties here, but there are one or two problems which need sorting out.'[22a] In July he told the

Commonwealth Parliamentary Association that the treaty imposed no restraints on public ownership, or on controls not affecting foreign trade (where they were to Britain's advantage), or on measures to steer industry to areas of high unemployment, or on restricting capital movements in a balance of payments crisis;[67a b] even in the event of a flight of capital 'In practice I do not believe this is going to matter a great deal'.[5c] The Common Agricultural Policy was 'intolerable';[68] they might compromise, perhaps on a long transition period, but the issue was 'troubling'.[12c g] Publicly, he asked if Britain would be required to abandon agricultural subsidies for tariffs so as to encourage dearer food from the Continent against cheap food from the Commonwealth.[59] In June he said in the House that the CAP was

> pretty intolerable ... Let us have no nonsense about the moral idealism involved in this. This is strict protectionism for European agriculture ... I hope, therefore, that the Government are not contemplating, even in the long run, agreeing to anything of this sort ... We cannot keep the Commonwealth together on that basis.[23c]

Indeed he saw temperate-zone foodstuffs as 'the nub of the problem', for Britain could not accept grave damage to Australia and the ruin of New Zealand.[23d] He hoped the Commonwealth could propose permanent compromise arrangements;[5d] and in June he even envisaged Britain contributing to a solution, by paying higher prices for a smaller volume of imports.[69a]

Gaitskell was anxious to protect the products of these countries as far as possible, but knew it would be difficult, and assumed that Wilson, who demanded assurances that the volume of those exports would not decline, was consciously 'playing up to our left wing' by asking for the impossible.[70] Gaitskell's priorities were very different from Macmillan's, for whom it was 'the old Commonwealth' – a polite euphemism for the white dominions – that mattered.[46a f] The Labour leader said the Six must treat the Commonwealth as favourably as the former French colonies.[23d] Privately, he thought Britain could insist on free entry for tropical produce but not for Australian and New Zealand foodstuffs, and could do nothing to help Canadian manufacturers but must protect those of the Asians: that last item would be a 'test case' of how outward-looking the EEC was.[12c]

He held these views out of a sense of duty to poor countries towards which Britain had incurred responsibilities;[71] and also because he thought the attitude of the Six would signal whether they were developing into or away from the kind of Community he wanted to see and to join. But he knew quite well that the Commonwealth could not become 'a sort of alternative Common Market, because that is just not possible'.[23b] He did not take its political survival for granted either.[72] Characteristically, his strongest challenge was to the Commonwealth MPs themselves in July:

> supposing the Commonwealth is really gradually going to fall apart
> — if the ties are going to get weaker, if the African members of the
> Commonwealth are coming closer together, if India is drifting apart
> from us and if Australia and New Zealand are perhaps going to look
> more and more towards the United States, and that applies to Canada,
> too — so that we in ten or twenty years' time are just a little island off
> Europe and nothing more, we are bound to say, 'We had better be
> in this, too' ... it is very much a matter of judgment what is going to
> happen in the next ten years or so ... do not let us get illusions about
> it [the Commonwealth]. It is not a customs union, or a military
> alliance, and it is not now, I regret, entirely a community of demo-
> cracies ... It is not the same thing as a new state ... I only raise the
> issue, are you so sure that in ten or twenty years' time the Common-
> wealth will be there? Any fair-minded person must ask himself that
> question.[5e]

On the European side, Gaitskell distrusted the conservative Continental regimes for many reasons. Ever since his time at the Treasury he had loathed their banker-dominated economic policies (perhaps with better reason then than later).[73-4] He was worried about their strong protectionist lobbies, which Lady Rhys-Williams, President of the European Movement, compared to the old French nobles before the revolution.[75] He wrote to one Labour Marketeer: 'the vested interests, both in agriculture and manufacturing, in Europe seem determined to keep out for their own benefit goods produced more cheaply elsewhere in the world. I can see nothing idealistic in this and nothing stimulating either.'[76] He strongly opposed any idea of a European nuclear deterrent, which would make checking proliferation impossible;[77] and he warned Kennedy and his Cabinet early in 1962 that a European state might well develop in ways damaging to the Western alliance.[78] Those dangers were not just a figment of alarmist left-wing imaginations, for they worried the architect of the whole European idea, Jean Monnet himself.[50c]

One guarantee of the liberal intentions of the EEC would be its willingness to admit the neutrals as associates. In June 1962 Gaitskell went to Oslo for a Socialist International meeting, where he tried to mobilise support for the British case among the Continental parties, but warned that Britain would not break with the Commonwealth. The Swedish Socialist government spent many hours briefing him;[79] later he told the House that EFTA was an export market nearly as large as the EEC, and that if economic association were refused, Norway and Denmark might not join, being unwilling to erect tariffs against their neighbour.[23e]

The Americans opposed association for the neutrals, which Gaitskell thought 'idiotic';[80] so did some of the Six, which he thought sinister. He was irritated to find that the opponents included Paul-Henri Spaak the former Belgian Socialist Premier,[2a] and Joseph Luns the Dutch Foreign Minister (and future NATO Secretary-General).[1] Much more dangerous, the German Chancellor was also among them, and the prospect of a Community transformed by the entry of 'a whole block of socialists and neutralists' in Britain's wake was later to be a factor alarming Adenauer into undermining the resistance of the Five to de Gaulle's high-handed veto.[50d] Gaitskell was afraid that the Community those two leaders wanted would 'freeze the division of the continent' and make a clash over Germany likelier.[81] When Arthur Gaitskell told his brother of Dutch friends who wanted Britain in to liberalise the EEC, Hugh replied that that was hopeless while de Gaulle and Adenauer remained.[82] But that outlook was emotional as well as rational, for Gaitskell strongly (though vainly) urged James Meade, to keep the start of his pamphlet, which referred disobligingly to what the Continentals (and the United States), in contrast to the white dominions, were doing in 1940.[83]

Those suspicions of the Continental Europeans did not apply to the Socialist parties of the Six, with whom on many substantive policies co-operation was easy. It was hampered nevertheless because these parties were strongly federalist, while Gaitskell was clear that Britain was unready to enter a federation for at least a generation:

> [T]here is no question of Britain entering into a federal Europe now. British opinion simply is not ripe for this ... I am not saying that we have to commit ourselves for all time, for twenty, fifty or a hundred years hence. There is no reason to do that.[13f]

The Continental Socialists wanted British entry in order to tilt the political balance, but feared it might block all progress towards political unity, and they would not endanger harmony among the Six for the sake of satisfying the new applicants and their clients. That attitude gave Gaitskell another reason for wanting Norway and Denmark in and the neutral EFTA countries 'appropriately associated':[84] for the Scandinavians were Britain's most likely allies in the Council of Ministers.[23e] They like other Socialist Parties would help resist undesirable right-wing tendencies, and unlike the others they were not federalist. Gaitskell therefore counted on them to give Britain an effective veto. With the economic arguments evenly balanced, the shape of the Community's political institutions became crucial.

> The Commission was not a satisfactory body. We could not have bureaucrats governing the community. Equally, we could not have

62 Morale is high on the Party Conference platform, 1962

63 Catastrophe? With George Brown and Harold Wilson, visiting the
Prime Minister during the Cuban Missile crisis in 1962

64 With his wife in their garden

parliamentary sovereignty with a European parliament ... The British would not stand for this ... a Council of Ministers ... was the correct solution ... for major political decisions there must be a veto.[12c]

He was determined that the weighted votes must maintain for Britain plus one Scandinavian ally the blocking power already enjoyed by France plus Belgium, and he called this 'a point which I think we must be very tough about'.[55a c] He raised the question in his first speech in the House in August 1961, reverted to it at Fulham on 14 April 1962, again stressed it in Parliament in June 1962, and exasperated people on both wings of the Labour Party by his insistence.[85] Privately, however, he was less intransigent than he sounded.[86]

He was also well aware that Britain's position in the world might change radically. In June 1962 he said in the House:

After ten or twenty years we may find that the Commonwealth as we know it today, not through any fault of our own, changes, declines, and does not count ... we might find ourselves excluded from a tough, strong, European State, a little island off Europe with nothing else.[23g]

He told the Commonwealth MPs in July:

This powerful thing is growing up next door to us. After all, something like 200 million people have formed themselves into a State which could be decidedly awkward in all sorts of ways if we were outside it. What is the impact going to be on our relations with America if we do not go in? Are they going to squeeze us out and deal with these people alone? You cannot ignore the possibility of this. So it is not fair to denounce the Government as though it was a plain act of treachery.[5g]

In private he made it clear that even his hostility to federation was contingent and temporary, not absolute and permanent:

We could not now accept a Federal solution. Ten years hence, perhaps we might—especially if the Commonwealth had by then broken itself up (but we must on no account do anything to break it up) ... on the whole Heath could be trusted on this.[12g]

He even dropped a cautious public hint: 'There might come a time when, if the alternative was to be just a small island off Europe, it would be better to be in a European federated state, but that point would not arise unless the Commonwealth disintegrated.'[87]

Thus, throughout the first year of negotiations, Gaitskell refused to

2A

commit himself in principle until he knew the final outcome. He saw the way the Six treated the European neutrals (who were mostly Britain's EFTA associates) as a test of their political outlook, and the way they treated the Commonwealth as a test of their economic intentions. Moreover, he thought the Commonwealth's reaction to that treatment might well determine the verdict in British politics. He told the House of Commons when the talks began that the Prime Minister probably could not carry any terms opposed by the Commonwealth, and so had nothing to lose by promising a Commonwealth Conference before the final decision.[13h] Gaitskell hoped that in deciding whether the terms were acceptable to it, and therefore to both British parties or to neither, the Commonwealth would resolve his tactical problem for him:

> He didn't think Macmillan would sign an agreement that was contrary to the interests of the Commonwealth — the Conservative party would give him so much trouble if he did. If Macmillan signed an agreement that took proper care of Commonwealth interests then Labour would probably assent.[12h]

iv   *Summer Hesitation, Autumn Decision*

In the summer of 1962 Gaitskell's tactical analysis had not changed. Privately he still thought the government would probably obtain terms which Labour could support. He wrote a little later:

> Had the negotiations in Brussels, as I personally expected three or four months ago, gone the other way and the Six had conceded terms which by and large met our conditions, I should certainly have urged the Party not to oppose. In doing so, I should have been confronted with a great deal of opposition from other friends of mine (for this is not a straightforward left/right issue).[43]

Alternatively, he calculated that his own political difficulties would be less 'if the Government makes such a bad agreement that there is a tremendous outcry from the Commonwealth, the farmers and the Tory Party itself. But I don't think this is very likely'.[35b] He did not make enough allowance for Macmillan's eagerness to settle. 'He had never thought that the Government would give way so much. Indeed, they had not done so until they had collapsed at the end of July.'[12e p]

With those expectations, his objections in the spring were not obstructive ones. His Fulham speech on 14 April 1962, he told Hetherington, raised questions on which we had to decide — but certainly did not lay down final conditions.[88] He was worried that his careful criticisms on detail might be exploited by those who were opposed on principle, and when privately warning that European economic expansion might not continue, or benefit Britain, he added: 'possibly this was an issue that ought to be raised in public now. But it was difficult because it might stampede some of the unions and others into outright opposition to the Common Market.'[12c]

His major statement, a party political broadcast on television on 8 May 1962, held the balance fairly even. It began by emphasising the obvious:

> [Y]ou still hear some people speaking as though we could decide whether the Common Market existed or not. Now this, of course, is quite untrue ... what we have to ask ourselves, looking ahead, is whether ... we would be better outside it, or ... inside it.

He justified Labour's having 'resisted the shrill demand to declare ourselves now ... If the conditions are good, satisfactory – right, we approve and we'll go in cheerfully. But if they're wrong, then we shall feel bound to oppose it'. The government were foolish to give the impression that we were going in anyway:

> There's no need for us to be suppliants ... To go in on good terms would, I believe, be the best solution ... Not to go in would be a pity, but it would not be a catastrophe. To go in on bad terms which really meant the end of the Commonwealth would be a step which I think we would regret all our lives, and for which history would not forgive us.[22a]

The broadcast was a great success, praised by the press for its 'objective assessment and balanced judgment' and for 'his obvious devotion to truth and principle'.[89] But the balance was not quite even, for he did, as he had told Jenkins in advance he would, 'get rid of any idea that I am deliberately building up a position in which, whatever the terms, we should be opposed to them'.[35b] The Labour Common Market Committee hailed 'his best television appearance yet ... This is indeed a great advance'.[90] The Conservative press also concluded that he was approving of entry:

> Mr. Gaitskell tipped a finely balanced scale in favour ... His declaration ... will delight the 40 to 50 Labour M.P.s who enthusiastically support Britain's entry. It will incur the wrath of those almost as numerous who are violently opposed. Most important, it will help to sway the opinions of anything up to 150 [floaters] ... he is obviously determined not to let [Labour] be branded as the anti-Common Market party.[58b]

That, too, was the effect in the union conferences which might sway Labour's Conference vote in the autumn. One pro-Market MP, Fred Mulley, wrote that the Foundry Workers ... although they are practically C.P. controlled at Executive level, resisted a motion of outright opposition to the Common Market and approved a 'wait and see' formula.

It was clear from the discussion that your T.V. programme has had an immense effect on the rank and file delegates.[91]

The following month, Gaitskell used the parliamentary debate to put pressure on the government not to give too much away in their anxiety to settle by July.[92] He was worried that his speech might therefore have sounded much more negative than he wished, though it was not so interpreted.[93-4b] He was irritated but did not deviate when other Labour leaders shifted towards opposition – so rapidly that one journalist thought Gaitskell had already lost all room for manoeuvre. Brown and Strachey were for entry, but the Left were reinforced by Shadow Cabinet figures like Gordon Walker, Healey and Stewart; 'and now that Mr. James Callaghan has veered, perhaps decisively, away from Europe it is plainly all over bar the shouting of the disappointed [pro-Marketeers]'.[95b] The Prime Minister noted privately: 'The Labour Party is uncertain – a new battle *against* Gaitskell, who has been deserted by Healey and (probably) Harold Wilson.'[46a b] But others thought Gaitskell's position not just secure but dominant, counting 75 pro-entry Labour MPs, 80 anti-, and 100 who would follow their leader's line.[94c] As late as July Gaitskell was still determined to keep a free hand, telling Hetherington that while there might be no agreement to put to the Party, if there were one he

wanted to be sure that if Labour had to take a decision it would be taken by the Parliamentary party and not by the conference. It was a matter that the conference couldn't be left to decide ... he might find it necessary to recall the Parliamentary Labour party, even if there wasn't a general recall of Parliament.[96]

By then, however, his shift was already beginning, for Gaitskell was talking for the first time of making the Market an election issue – which in May he had hoped it would not become.[35b] On television on 19 July he denied the interviewer's assumption that Labour was sure to oppose entry, but said that if the terms proved

thoroughly unsatisfactory, if there's a great row from the Commonwealth Prime Ministers' Conference, we have betrayed the neutral countries [in EFTA] ... and possibly there is some further political commitment, we should then oppose it and ... I should certainly expect a General Election to test the issue.[97]

That was not from choice, but because he began to fear that the Government would make it a party matter. Asked by a West Indian MP whether it could not be put to a free vote of the House, he replied that he would not object to that 'if the Conservative Party were prepared to accept it but I do not think there is the slightest chance they will do so'. He still hoped the Tories would be constrained by the circumstances, telling the Commonwealth MPs that if there were a row with them and an attack by the Opposition, 'the Government has to carry with it the support of its own backbenchers; it can afford a minor but not a major revolt …the influence of Members is probably a great deal greater than appears'.[5g] *

For much the same reasons, he hoped to escape putting the issue to the Labour Party, and believed that might be possible since Commonwealth resistance might prevent any acceptable agreement emerging.[98]

> If, however … there is a hell of a row and if Mr. Menzies and Mr. Nehru — who do not always work together in harmony — both say, 'This is intolerable … and it means the end of the Commonwealth … ' then I am certain we [Labour] would come out against it and I do not think any British Government would dare to go ahead … the Commonwealth Governments should know the power they have to influence British opinion … is very great indeed … We are overshadowed by the fear of a breakdown in these negotiations but … There is just as much pressure in Europe for our going in as there is on our side, and I think, therefore, it is up to us to stand out for the terms which will make our entry tolerable.[5h]

To Arthur Calwell, the leader of the Australian Labour Opposition, he went further, writing in early August 1962 that in the British electorate only 15–20 per cent were committed on each side (perhaps slightly more against entry) and that among the others were

> probably a very large number who are quite likely to change in either direction … [so] the Prime Ministers' Conference in September will be of decisive importance … if [they] say firmly … that they will not accept the conditions proposed, then the Labour Party would come out in strong opposition to our entry. If the Prime Ministers declare that they are satisfied with the terms, then I think it probably [sic] that we should support entry …
>
> It certainly is within the power of the leading Prime Ministers to stop the whole thing if they want to do so. Whatever the British Government may say, I do not think they could proceed in the teeth of strong opposition from the Commonwealth and from the country at home.

* Yet he doubted if 'many more than a dozen' Tory MPs would vote against it — though others would be unhappy and worried, and there might be defections at an election.[52c]

Again, it seems to follow from this that you could more or less make your terms.[99a]

In May, the Commonwealth had been 'really the nub of the whole question' since its treatment would determine Britain's and the EEC's future roles in the world.

> [I]f we stay out, you might get a very tightly formed state in Europe with high tariffs, inward-looking, rather reactionary, and conservative and nationalistic in its attitude. If we can prevent that by going in, then I think we've certainly done a very good job. But we couldn't do that if, in going in, our links with the Commonwealth were to be broken

— by accepting either a European federal structure or a disastrous economic settlement.[22a] By July that emphasis had changed significantly.

> If in the process of going in there was to be a dreadful row and the Commonwealth countries felt they were being betrayed by us ... that would weaken our capacity for influencing Europe in the way we want to influence it ... I do not think any of us ... would say that the system of Imperial preferences is entirely sacrosanct ... It is the political implications or the political consequences of economic decisions I would worry about ... the danger that an agreement will be ... thought in the Commonwealth to imply ... that the British are abandoning the Commonwealth. This, I think, would be disastrous.[5e g]

Thus he was now worried about anti-Market, anti-British reactions in the Commonwealth which would break it up and so leave Britain too weak to have any real influence in the Community.

Yet when the House rose that summer Gaitskell was still uncommitted in his own mind, and still left different impressions in the minds of others. On 25 July 1962, he gave Fred Mulley a lift back to the House after an NEC meeting, and said he did not expect much bother in handling the intransigent anti-Marketeers;[62] but about the same time Bill Blyton understood that he meant to oppose entry at Conference because of Spaak's insistence on a commitment to federalism.[100] Unlike the zealots on both sides, he thought the coming decision — however important — was neither vital nor final. Even if Britain went in, a desperate country could not in the end be prevented from withdrawing. Even if Britain stayed out, that choice could be reversed later — in a year or so if the terms offered were improved, in a decade or so if the Commonwealth disintegrated. In the first case Britain's negotiating position would be weaker because EEC policies would have evolved without her — but it was being weakened still more by the government's rush to settle. In the second case he himself thought that Britain would urgently need to go in; but that it would be worse still for Britain now to initiate a perhaps avoidable break-up of the Commonwealth by accepting terms intolerable to it.

The political balance depended on how the Community and the Commonwealth each evolved over the next decade or two, and how each would be influenced by Britain's eventual decision: a very difficult judgment, which moreover might be altered when the terms for Britain's associates were known. Economically, the balance sheet for Britain herself was also obscure, for the long-term advantages would be outweighed if bad terms made the short-term drawbacks ruinous. Gaitskell may well have subconsciously exaggerated the difference which the terms could bring about, for the last two years had taught him to worry about tactics and timing, and the wait-and-see attitude was tactically advantageous for the Opposition. But he had never believed that Britain had to enter the EEC at any price, and he still thought the price must be known and reasonable first. Macmillan's mockery was not wholly wide of the mark in comparing him to a Frenchman who had recently stood or sat on a tightrope for 174 hours and then given up—'Poor deluded man, he thought he had set up a world record.'[101]

Gaitskell was well aware that the party advantage which the Conservatives counted on obtaining from entry would accrue to Labour instead if the talks failed. He said so in early August to his Australian opposite number when emphasising the strength of the Commonwealth's position, telling Calwell that British Labour was afraid of the government producing 'some kind of fancy formula' which meant either nothing or different things in Brussels and Canberra.

> [T]hey should not be allowed to get away with this. The Commonwealth should demand precision ... insisting that the British Government must try again and take its time about it ...
>
> Looking at it from the narrow angle of our own Party political advantage over here, we should, of course, gain rather than lose if the Government fail to get agreement ... [or] got involved in a major conflict with the Commonwealth. Our line would then be almost certainly that they have mishandled the negotiations and that ... [we] should take over the job ...
>
> I thought it best to be quite frank with you ... I am assuming that ... you would regard it as your job to see to it that [Menzies] does not sacrifice Australian interests. This attitude also suits us very well.[99a]

That is the first letter in Gaitskell's correspondence to hint that a breakdown might not be unwelcome, or to propose a course of action which might promote one; and it came two weeks after his first call for a general election on the issue if in the end the price of entry proved too high.

The price was known in August. Gaitskell later wrote to Kennedy:

> We were bitterly disappointed and indeed astonished ...
>
> I do not see how it can be seriously argued that these agreements in any way fulfilled either the Government's pledges or the Labour Party's conditions. Nor, indeed, have even the strongest pro-Market people in our Party ever suggested this. Had such terms been announced at the beginning of the negotiations, they would have been rejected out of hand by the British people ...
>
> It was perfectly clear that if these were indeed the final terms there was no change [sic] whatever that the Labour Party would accept them. I pointed this out early in August to Roy Jenkins ... He did not demur. My deputy, George Brown, also agreed.[102]
>
> There remained, however, the possibility ... that the Government would not regard the terms as in any way binding and would simply report them to the Commonwealth Prime Ministers' Conference in September without commendation or commitment.[10d]

Gaitskell was thus already tentatively considering opposing entry when he left England on 16 August for a fortnight's family holiday in Italy: 'a lovely time in Portofino – underwater swimming and highly intellectual conversation, plus a few walks and just a little dancing'.[103] The intellectual stimulus came from several non-political acquaintances who were staying nearby, including Isaiah Berlin, Maurice Bowra, Anne Fleming, Stuart Hampshire, and Victor Rothschild. (When Michael Foot and his wife turned up in the local bar, Bowra – who was the head of Foot's Oxford college – went over to greet them; but Hugh would not speak to the man who had persistently portrayed him as a betrayer of Labour's principles.)[104a b] Gaitskell talked a great deal about the Common Market, taking the same line as he did in public. His friends knew he was no EEC enthusiast but had no inkling of the vehement emotional revulsion which so soon emerged. Unlike strong opponents such as Jay, Shore and Wilson, he was afraid that Britain permanently outside might become a twentieth-century Spain. But, though impressed by the political case for entry, he still saw no need for an immediate decision to join.[105a-6]

Gaitskell finally decided on his course between mid-July and mid-September 1962. He had many reasons: his deteriorating relations with the spokesmen of the Six, his shock at the terms, his exposure to the Commonwealth reactions to them, his angry resentment at the government's conduct and at the pressure of the media in favour of entry. In mid-July the private clash with Jean Monnet had had a public echo in a bitter argument with Paul-Henri Spaak at a Socialist International meeting in

Brussels. Like many Continental Socialists, Spaak shared Monnet's federalist vision, and was torn between feeling that Europe would be incomplete without Britain and fearing that with her it could never progress towards political unity. Gaitskell had often said that nobody in Britain was advocating moves towards early federation; he said it again, and provoked an explosion from the Belgian. He was thoroughly unrepentant. Next day Harold Wilson produced an emollient formula to satisfy Spaak, but Gaitskell insisted on repeating that the Six would have to relax their tight organisation if they expanded to Ten.[107]

After his return from Brussels he again expressed surprise at Spaak's outburst, writing privately to Roy Jenkins: 'honestly I regard him as wholly responsible. What he was up to I do not know ... I have said [it] several times over here. Others, for example Marjolin, seemed to be perfectly happy.'[35c] He surprised Hetherington by agreeing that Britain should show both enthusiasm for the European idea and determination to make a success of the economic community – but stopping well short of any commitment pointing towards federalism.[12i] As Gaitskell told one of the little band of pro-European left-wingers, 'He [Spaak] wanted some definite commitment now whereas I ... was not prepared to go further than the Treaty of Rome at present.'[108] But that was not all, for Spaak was also unsympathetic to the Commonwealth, the neutrals and the Scandinavians.[95a] Gaitskell told the CDS group in October that

> His own feeling had been matured partly by his meeting with Spaak in Brussels. The contempt of Spaak towards the neutrals and his general arrogance had been very irritating. The whole occasion had been contrived to put him, HG, at a disadvantage. Spaak's attitude was that Britain had applied to go in – 'we didn't ask you'.[2a]

Though Gaitskell had said nothing new, Spaak rightly sensed a deep psychological gulf between the Continentals, for whom their historic reconciliation was the world's most important political development, and Gaitskell for whom it was 'parochial'.[4] The Englishman had no emotional sense of belonging to Europe, and told one old friend that on the contrary 'I ... probably feel that I have more in common with North Americans than with Europeans'.[109] Indeed his main case for British entry implied little confidence in the Continental partners, since he thought it would divert them from the undesirable courses they might adopt on their own. Though 'he had not simply adopted a preconceived position ... he obviously felt a deep distrust and even distaste for the negotiators for the Six and for the forces behind them.'[12j e]

A more serious and equally unsatisfactory encounter with the Continentals came in early September. The Commonwealth Prime Ministers were about to meet, and Gaitskell had arranged for representatives of both

Commonwealth and European Socialists to come to London also to try to resolve their differences.[12j] * It was towards the end of three days of talks with his overseas partners that Gaitskell made up his mind. He was impressed by their hostility to the terms;[110-11] Britain was to give up imperial preferences by 1970, in return for vague offers to discuss world commodity agreements at some future date. (Jean Monnet had aroused Gaitskell's suspicions months earlier by his evasiveness on precisely this point.)[12c] The most influential voices were those of K. B. Lall the Indian Ambassador to the EEC, Gaitskell's old friend Walter Nash the leader of the New Zealand Labour opposition, and Lee Kuan Yew the Prime Minister of Singapore.[112]

A special meeting of the Socialist International followed at once, but to Gaitskell's distress the European mystique of the Continental parties took priority over protecting the interests of underdeveloped countries. The spokesmen for those countries, he said,

> had been very bitter about ... the present terms. They had raised a whole series of specific points ... the European Socialists had mainly sat silent. They had hardly a single answer ... Roy Jenkins, Tony Crosland and one or two other friends [also] had no specific replies to these points. He had rather hoped that they would have, but they didn't.[12j]

Gaitskell felt that the government had played into French hands by their 'indecent haste', and had failed disgracefully to insist on safeguards for the Commonwealth and EFTA countries; the latter were now unlikely to join. Any protection for the Africans would require them to accept associated status, a condition they considered humiliating; Macmillan[46a l] and Home[12e] treated their objections to it with contempt, Gaitskell with sympathy.[12j] He kept reverting to the effects on India, but was concerned about New Zealand too.[113a c]

The first sign that Labour would oppose entry was a critical communiqué by the Commonwealth Labour leaders, fully reported in the *Observer* of Sunday 9 September. Harold Wilson had prepared a carefully balanced draft, but on the Saturday afternoon at Transport House Gaitskell insisted on rewriting it much more critically. (Characteristically he worried over its wording until Wilson, equally characteristically, warned him that he would miss the *Observer*'s deadline.)[114a b] He strongly maintained that Labour had not changed its attitude, but had simply decided, as it always intended to, once the general terms were known. But the shift into opposi-

* It did not suit Macmillan at all that the Commonwealth Opposition leaders were arriving as well as the Prime Ministers and likely to stiffen them.[46g h]

tion had its own momentum. He still claimed that a Labour government would re-open negotiations in 1963 or 1964; he had always expected that at least one breakdown must precede a satisfactory agreement.[12J k] He told a Labour Marketeer that better, more precise terms could be obtained only by serious British pressure; without that

> we are, in my view, bound to oppose Britain's entry ... [and] demand a General Election ... inevitably this is all quite hypothetical ... I bitterly regret that both the Government and the Six have failed to produce terms so far which we could with a good conscience recommend the Party to expect [sic].[115]

The Commonwealth Prime Ministers' Conference met on 10 September. At the opening Lancaster House dinner and reception, Macmillan sourly observed: 'A very tense atmosphere everywhere. Gaitskell going about smiling ... as if he had just kissed hands ... '[46a j] It lasted for a full week, and the Prime Minister himself saw his success not in having negotiated terms which satisfied the Commonwealth countries but in persuading them to gloss over their discontent in the final communiqué.[116] Gaitskell knew their real feelings, and he told his CDS friends a few weeks later that the government's handling of that Conference 'had convinced him that the aim was to enter Europe whatever the terms and ... despite all the undertakings'.[2a]

To his Australian ally he complained at the time that the Fleet Street dailies (apart from the *Express*) 'simply swallowed whole everything the Government told them'; and that the public relations efforts of Duncan Sandys the Commonwealth Secretary

> infuriated the Prime Ministers when each day in the British Press they saw the Government's views reflected ... The communique, frankly, was a disappointment. It ought to have been much tougher. I expect Macmillan managed to persuade Menzies and Holyoake [from New Zealand], as good Conservatives, not to make things difficult for him. It is a great pity ... you could mount quite an attack on Menzies for failing to sustain the Australian case right to the end ... the British Government made an attempt to bulldoze everybody into submission when they were determined to go in on pretty well the present terms. The only concession I believe they will try to get is something for New Zealand ...
> Of course ... [if] after all the Six will make the kind of concessions for which we have asked ... we should not oppose entry. But ... much more likely, any further concessions ... [will be] almost insignificant.[99b]

He was furious at the Prime Minister and Government 'whose double-talk in this matter has been, in my view, quite disgraceful'.[117-18a] Referring to Australia, he spoke bitterly in private of 'another example of Macmillan's smashing our relations with these people for personal political advantage in this country'.[119a b] To his CDS friends 'he implied that as leader of the opposition he would have been bound constitutionally to adopt the position he had done if only because of the shabby way the Government had behaved.'[2a]

In mid-September Gaitskell told Desmond Donnelly that he thought Britain would fail to get in anyway—which would be the best possible outcome on purely party grounds.[48a] Close advisers like Denis Healey predicted the French veto;[114b] and in retrospect Gaitskell's widow thought that his decision had been crucially influenced by the expectation that there was no chance of Britain entering—though that outcome was still speculative when he made his speech at Conference.[120] Even at that late stage, however, he was concerned to distinguish his conditional opposition from that of the intransigent anti-Marketeers, whose ultimate aims were quite different from his, and who would try to use him for their own purposes. After his first broadcast to take a distinctly anti-Market line, on 21 September, he told Hetherington that it had had to be stronger than he wanted, and so would his reply to any campaign by Macmillan for entry on the present terms:

> In the process of getting his point over to the public he would have to put things more simply than he would have liked. As a result, he might have the effect of strengthening opposition to the Common Market as a whole rather than just ... on the present terms.[12e]

He was walking a tightrope, for an attack on the government had to be wholehearted to be effective. He did not want to 'be pushed into crude opposition for inadequate reasons';[121] yet he felt that he could not afford to take a cautious muted line to satisfy the Labour Marketeers. One of his CDS correspondents wrote agreeing with Gaitskell as against CDS: 'I think it completely impossible to argue as a political party in favour of the Common Market in principle and, at the same time, mount a campaign against the present terms.'

The leader replied:

> What you say ... about the relationship between intellectual ideas and political practice is exceedingly shrewd. The problem really has been how to maintain our position against going in on the present terms and yet reply effectively to the Government's obvious intention to take us in on any terms.[122]

Between July and September, his assessment of that problem had changed. Before the recess he was talking of recalling the Labour MPs rather than putting the question to Conference;[123-4a] later he accepted the risk of stimulating its all-out hostility in order to take full advantage of its mood for his own ends. When Gaitskell committed himself, he did not do so half way.

v *Brighton: The Crunch at Conference*

On 21 September 1962 Gaitskell replied on television to Macmillan's broadcast of the night before, using the old arguments but now drawing negative conclusions. Britain was to abandon the existing trading system, but the Six offered only 'promises, vague assurances and nothing more'. For New Zealand, 'Special consideration, but nobody knows what it will be'; for Canada and Australia, 'world commodity agreements – but nobody knows when they will be made'; for India and Pakistan, 'A trade agreement by 1966 – but nobody knows what [it] will contain'. In return for dismantling imperial preferences the EEC should accept precise agreements:[125a] 'if the Six mean what they say ... it oughtn't to be difficult ... But ... after we enter ... we could not any longer help our friends in the Commonwealth ... this is the acid test of what the Common Market is going to become.' The government would not insist, since they wanted everything settled before the next election;[24e] and that was 'utterly wrong' when the terms were so contentious. He asked if the Prime Minister's claim that Britain should join a larger group of nations implied entering a European federation.[126] If so, it

> means the end of Britain as an independent nation; we become no more than 'Texas' or 'California' in the United States of Europe.[127] It means the end of a thousand years of history; it means the end of the Commonwealth ... [to become] just a province of Europe.[125b]

Gaitskell said again that the political case for entry was the hope of influencing the EEC's future by

> building a bridge between the Commonwealth and Europe; and we cannot do that if we destroy the Commonwealth ... I don't want to see a choice between ... [them] and I don't think it's inevitable ... But the present terms do confront us with this choice ... I have no doubt about what the answer should be. And ... I don't think the British people ... will in a moment of folly, throw away the tremendous heritage of history.[22b]

The Labour Marketeers found the broadcast 'demagogic & with no forward vision. But not closing the door'; Gaitskell, unlike the Left, was not opposing on principle but might be 'isolating himself'.[124b] Jo Grimond, the Liberal leader, gave it mocking praise: 'It would have been a credit to any Conservative Prime Minister—well spoken, pessimistic, with a proper suspicion of all foreigners, and considerable distrust of all change.'[128a] It struck a chord among Conservative listeners, for Gaitskell's postbag bulged with promises of support from serious and thoughtful anti-Market Tories as well as from shrill elderly ladies and rabid Protestant sectarians.[129] Apart from Beaverbrook's papers, the press—including the *Mirror* and *Herald*—were, like the Government, so convinced of the need for entry that they regarded the detailed terms as a minor matter.[130] They were therefore so critical of Gaitskell's views and motives that Macmillan called the broadcast 'a completely damp squib'.[46l] Crossman compared the furious Establishment and Fleet Street reaction to a famous occasion six years before:

> Not since the Suez crisis has Hugh Gaitskell been so hated outside the Labour Party and so popular inside it as he is today. And the reason is the same as in 1956. At a critical moment, when the Government was reckoning on his tacit support, he has attacked it ... It was Mr. Gaitskell's unforgivable sin to remind the Commonwealth Prime Ministers on their arrival that, whereas both Government and Opposition had made them clear and explicit promises, it is only the Opposition that intends to keep its word.[8c]

Contrary to the Left's view of him, Gaitskell was fortified in his determination by that solid hostility of the Establishment; perhaps it recalled the hated pressure for conformity at school. He had always been exasperated by the bogus economic arguments of those who really wanted to enter on political grounds which they preferred not to stress publicly;[131] now he was equally enraged by 'what I call the hush and mush technique' of the Government publicity machine.[132] He explained his (correct) political conclusions frankly to Kennedy: 'it seemed pretty certain that they were shortly to launch a major propaganda campaign in favour of Britain's entry on broadly any terms—leading up to the General Election.'[10g] * He denied that his Conference speech was anti-European: 'But, of course, I was spelling out the case against unconditional entry and deliberately rousing the Party against what the Government had done and issuing what might be called a "mobilisation" warning.'[10h] But it was 'utterly false' to suggest that this was simply electoral tactics:

> On the contrary, until August I had always assumed and said that we should not have an election on the Common Market. I took the view that either the Government would obtain sufficiently good terms to justify us in supporting them or that the terms would be too bad for them to proceed at all. On this I was wrong—and it is this—their

* So they were, as Macmillan makes clear.[46m]

decision to go ahead despite the fact that the terms were in flagrant breach of their pledges and therefore quite unacceptable to us — which has brought this whole matter into the arena of party politics in Britain.[10i]

Once he had decided to prepare for a clash with the government, he had to deal both with his old friends who were still in favour of entry, and his new allies who would always be against it. The Labour Marketeers would have fought harder for better terms than the government did (if only for party reasons). But their earlier acceptance of the conditional policy weakened their position when the conditions were not met, and Gaitskell could rightly tell his most powerful trade union ally, 'I think really everything else springs from this'.[133a] When the terms were known, the Labour Marketeers naturally recoiled from voting against entry and so missing what they saw as an opportunity that might not recur. Gaitskell, however, had no alternative; apart from his strong feelings on the merits, Labour unity was at risk: 'anything else can only result in a completely disastrous division in the Party as well as being quite inconsistent with all the things we have sought.'[44] Himself against entry on the terms offered, he thought the Party certain to reject it, and claimed that the leading Labour Marketeers agreed with that estimate.[134]

Those old friends and allies were distressed by his attitude, but not all were surprised, for after a long talk on 13 September Roy Jenkins had told them that Gaitskell, 'always hostile to Britain's entry', was 'determined to continue strongly this line in autumn'. On Tuesday 18 September, half a dozen of their leaders met at Jenkins's house and, as Albu recorded:

> Agreed best bring pressure on H.G.; preferably by T.U. leaders but also by new M.P.s who are his general supporters; to return to his 'neutral' line. Roy privately not optimistic — nor I ... Some discussion of H.G. as leader — agreed no one else in sight ... Roy and Strachey said at present Macmillan better P.M. than H.G.[124a c]

Some of their MPs were wavering, few would refuse to vote against the government, and all were worried about fighting an election before the legislation was through.[135] The day before Gaitskell's broadcast, they put out a careful statement underlining their points of agreement with him while reaffirming support for entry. They said, like him, that the government could get better terms, especially for New Zealand and for Asian manufacturers, while arguing — unlike him — that Britain's bargaining position would be stronger inside, and warning, as he had done earlier, that without Britain the Community might develop badly.[8d] But old personal ties with him, political calculation and a long habit of loyalty to the leadership inhibited them from violent resistance.

Gaitskell made a gesture, meeting them privately at the House on 27 September:

> [H]e was very relaxed, but serious. He ... was sure Heath had been accepting anything to get in quickly ... he said that he had not changed, but the terms known and the Labour C[ommon] W[ealth] meeting which had obviously impressed him very much, had forced him to say the terms were not acceptable.[124d]

There were different impressions from that meeting of how the leader's mind was moving. He staunchly denied that he was shifting towards hostility in principle, but many feared that he would unintentionally stimulate 'demagogic, xenophobic opposition'.[124d] Gaitskell knew that risk; but he also saw an opportunity for reconciliation with some of those in the Party who had fought him for so long. He told his deputy, 'do remember, George, that there's six million votes' to win at Conference;[14a c] and felt he could safely write off the

> small group of [Labour] right-wingers, many of them personal friends of mine, who ... have been making a little trouble ... But I am quite convinced that at next week's Party Conference there will be an absolutely overwhelming vote in favour of the official line.[99b]

They suspected him of counting on their old loyalty, and they resented it.

His new determination became evident in the week before Conference. At the Shadow Cabinet on 25 September, Gaitskell was 'tough and angry' with his old allies who unsuccessfully opposed his line: George Brown, Frank Soskice, Douglas Houghton and, less predictably, Fred Willey and Ray Gunter.[136] Bill Webber and Fred Hayday, two of Gaitskell's principal union friends, went to see him to protest.[124d] Before the NEC met at Brighton to approve the policy statement for Conference, Peter Shore wrote a strongly anti-Market office draft.[137] George Brown's criticisms of it were backed by the trade unionists on the Executive: right-wingers like Sam Watson, Fred Mulley and John Boyd of the AEU, the middle-of-the-road Ray Gunter, and Walter Padley who (like many old ILPers) was a left-wing Marketeer.[138] The NEC Left for once supported Gaitskell, whose allies from past battles were furious when Anthony Greenwood appealed for the 'loyalty to the leader' of which he had not lately been a shining exponent.[139a b] As in 1960–1, Gaitskell, Brown, Crossman and Watson were appointed as a drafting sub-committee;[140–1a] but this time Crossman was Gaitskell's ally against Watson and Brown. When they finished in the small hours, a journalist friend lurking outside saw Brown, 'black as thunder', head for the beach. 'I thought he was going to drown himself.'[14a]

They agreed a draft which, with the Left abstaining, was approved '*nem con*, but not unanimously'.[142] It did not mention the demand for a general election, very embarrassing for the Labour Marketeers, which was left for Gaitskell to raise at his press conference.[141b] The statement reiterated Labour's conditions, stressed the dangerous federalist intentions of the Six, rejected entry on the proposed terms, and demanded precise agreements protecting the Commonwealth countries.[28b] It gave no hint that a Labour government would withdraw if it were returned after British entry, saying instead: 'we do not rule out the possibility ... [of] new and more successful negotiations at a later stage.'[143] For the Marketeers, Albu summed up: 'Final document more balanced, but still hostile'.[124e] As one journalist reported after the NEC statement, his friends wanted 'to know whether the first draft ... prepared under the general supervision of Mr. Gaitskell, or the amended second draft really represents his position'.[58e] But Saturday's papers reported, and the Prime Minister at least believed, that Labour was 'back on the European fence' – united for Conference purposes by 'a pretty clever document' to the detriment of Gaitskell's prestige.[46a n] From the other side 'a senior member of the NEC and PLP' (Crossman?) told a Beaverbrook journalist that despite Brown and Watson 'The plot has been foiled'.[144] Lobbied hard by Watson, the Marketeers prudently accepted the compromise.[145]

On the Tuesday afternoon Gaitskell attended a *Socialist Commentary* tea, and said it was a question of means which should not generate emotional heat or disturb political friendships.[3d] George Brown, who was to wind up the debate, wanted to see the text of Gaitskell's opening speech – for recently he had made a pro-Market speech at Strasbourg after clearing with the leader, but had then apparently been disavowed by the communiqué of the Commonwealth Labour Parties. Now Gaitskell kept putting him off. His suspicions aroused, he went to the latter's hotel room at midnight for a last try; Gaitskell covered up the text, but assured his mistrustful deputy that he was not changing the agreed line.[47b c] Later, Brown's furious sense of betrayal[146] was shared by less explosive characters; an old opponent, Walter Padley, felt it was the only time Gaitskell ever showed 'duplicity'.[147a b c] Some less committed officials and NEC members also thought that the leader's speech followed the lines of Shore's office draft rather than the agreed compromise.[148] Yet not all the Marketeers felt the same. Eirene White (a mildly sympathetic NEC member) had no sense of having been betrayed; Desmond Donnelly heard on reaching Brighton that Gaitskell was 'adamant'; Sam Watson could not budge Gaitskell an inch during a night-long argument.[149]

Shortly before 10 a.m. on Wednesday 3 October 1962, Gaitskell mounted the platform in the overheated hall of the Brighton ice rink to address a

Labour Conference for—though no one imagined it—the last time. He had not slept at all the night before;[18e] but there was no weariness in his long, carefully structured, highly emotional performance. He began with a quiet plea for tolerance; and he was careful to say he opposed entry into the EEC only on the proposed terms, not on principle. He rejected 'unsound arguments' that economic planning would be hampered; praised the Continental Socialists; and stressed that the Community would continue in any case whatever Britain did. Otherwise balanced judgment gave way to a passionate repudiation of the government's policy; the emotional overtones were entirely hostile, and Crossman said he had never seen anyone so enjoy his own rhetoric.[150] Even the economic exposition was now entirely one way:

> We would gain in markets where we sell less than one-fifth of our exports and lose in markets where we sell about half our exports ... we are to be obliged to import expensive food from the Continent of Europe in place of cheap food from the Commonwealth ... You cannot have it both ways. It is either better for industry to have tougher competition—which it will certainly get at home, or better for it to have easier conditions which it will get in the markets of the Six. Both arguments cannot be true ... it is not mainly because of the Common Market that Europe has had this remarkable growth recently ... The truth is that our faults lie not in our markets or in the tariffs against us but in ourselves.

Here Christopher Mayhew turned to his neighbour Lord Longford: 'Now we shall have fifteen minutes of the arguments in favour.'[3e] Instead, Gaitskell summed up by reiterating that the balance was even—justifying his one-sided approach later by saying he was 'sick and tired of the nonsense ... on this subject'.[151]

Politically, Western European unity was not an 'outstanding' problem like those of world peace and world poverty: the East-West division and what is now called the 'North-South' one. He admitted 'the force of the argument' (so recently his own) that Britain could best influence the development of the Community from within; it 'must be brought into the balance, but the balancing has not been completed'. For 'there have been evil features in European history too ... it has its two faces and we do not know as yet which is the one which will dominate.' A European state might develop, seeking its own nuclear weapons. The creators of the Community openly sought federation. 'That is what they mean, that is what they are after'; but even if that was right for them, should Britain become only a Texas or California in the United States of Europe and accept 'the end of Britain as an independent nation state ... the end of a thousand years of history'? Becoming 'a province of Europe, which is what federation means', must wreck the Commonwealth. A transformed Community, keeping those links intact, would indeed be 'a fine ideal ... the building of a bridge between the Commonwealth and Europe. But you cannot do that if at the beginning you sell the Commonwealth down the river'.

Having set the stage for rejection, he repeated that 'the arguments ... are evenly balanced; and whether or not it is worth going in depends on the conditions of our entry'. He protested that the treatment of the neutrals sought 'to convert the Treaty of Rome into a military alliance'. On planning and agriculture, his presentation had become negative. Having stressed in May that nothing in the Treaty threatened Britain's independent foreign policy, he now said: 'The right of veto ... is imperative and must be maintained.' At last he came to the Commonwealth, citing the military help from the old dominions at Vimy Ridge and Gallipoli, and (less noticed) their economic contribution to Britain's recovery after 1945; and invoking 'this remarkable multi-racial association, of independent nations, stretching across five continents, covering every race ... potentially of immense value to the world'. He swept aside the government's terms. The Common Agricultural Policy was 'one of the most devastating pieces of protectionism ever invented'; the abandonment of imperial preferences meant they had 'given away our strongest cards'; the arrangements on Indian tea were scorned. 'It is true we are not obliged—it is very kind of them!—to impose a customs duty on tea over here. We are allowed to drink our national beverage as we like. Very handsome!' The Prime Minister had claimed that the Africans' terms were 'wonderful', ignoring their unhappiness at the political price demanded. 'What a patronising attitude!'

Worst of all was the 'astonishing' and 'odious' contrast with the government's pledges to the Commonwealth. Duncan Sandys had repeated those pledges in that very hall a year ago; now, in 'a desperate attempt to bulldoze the Commonwealth into accepting what had been done', he warned that Britain was going in anyhow. The government should instead go back and demand precise agreements before we began the 'irrevocable course' of dismantling preferences and subjecting ourselves to majority rules: 'Let us not underestimate the power of the vested interests in the Community. There are good features of Europe, but there is a very powerful protectionist lobby, and most of the Governments of the Six depend upon it.' No one had said the year before that Britain could not maintain an independent foreign policy or retain reserve powers to protect full employment— and 'Our other three conditions are all Government pledges! ... Surely they cannot be impossible to meet? ... The Government have made their pledges; we have made ours. But there is a difference between us. We mean to keep ours.'

Today, Britain's bargaining position had been destroyed by the government's open eagerness to go in. Tomorrow, we would not 'miss the political boat', for General de Gaulle would protect us against that risk. The government's haste had been due solely to its determination to enter without an election, which he berated in terms 'as furiously angry as anything [he] has ever said about the Communists and fellow-travellers'.[8e] His populist streak emerged in his rage at the respectable press which was denouncing him in chorus:

> We are now being told that the British people are not capable of judging this issue – the Government knows best; the top people are the only people who can understand it; it is too difficult for the rest ... what an odious piece of hypocritical supercilious arrogant rubbish is this!

Idealist causes in the wider world could be served only in a broad and outward-looking Europe, and that prospect depended on the terms. Those could be improved in a new negotiation later; the conditions could be met; final judgment should await final proposals:

> I still hope profoundly that there may be such a change of heart in Europe as will make this possible ... But ... if the Six will not give it to us; if the British Government will not even ask for it, then ... we shall not flinch from our duty if that moment comes.[28c]

vi *Strange Bedfellows*

'No other living British politician', said a friend and temporary opponent, could have so 'dominated a mass conference by the sheer force of intelligence and personality'.[152] During the whole of the long speech 'nobody coughed or stirred. I think nobody smoked'.[153] When Gaitskell sat down the wild applause of the delighted Left rolled on and on for an 'unparalleled' eighty-eight seconds.[58h] Standing ovations at Labour Conferences were not yet merely ritual,[154] and the Scarborough roles were now reversed as the cheers were led by those NEC members on the platform who had then been so reticent, while George Brown and Sam Watson now hardly pretended to applaud. Roy Jenkins prudently stood up, but other Marketeers – Jack Diamond, Bill Rodgers, Ray Gunter – would not do so. A trade union loyalist, very close to the Gaitskells, found Hugh 'radiant ... with the flowing tide' but Dora worried: 'Charlie, all the wrong people are cheering'.[155a b] Harold Wilson from the chair said 'this historic speech' should be printed and sent to every member of the Party, and Frank Cousins promised that the T&GWU would pay. Winding up from the impossible position in which he had been placed, George Brown dexterously contrived without actually contradicting the leader to support the same document from an opposite policy standpoint, and somewhat saved the faces of the Labour Marketeers.

Before Conference met, Gaitskell had hoped that an 'all-out anti-Common Market resolution' would be put and 'resoundingly defeated';[12e] one was duly moved, and rejected on a show of hands like the pro-Market one the year before. The Left had a more promising weapon in the demand for a general election before any decision was taken. That was an obvious move to foil the government, since it would make the Six wary of British entry; and it would also blow the Labour Marketeers out of their positions of influence or even right out of the Party. Gaitskell saw that consequence, and carefully made his pressure for an election conditional upon a difference between the parties when the final terms were known – a device to gain time and keep an escape route open in case either the Six or the government changed their mind.*

ASSET (now ASTMS) proposed the Left's motion for an unequivocal commitment to an election, which by 17 to 7 the NEC opposed.[58i] The union demanded a card vote, losing by well over two to one, 1,943,000 to 4,482,000;[28d] so that thanks to 'the tactical ineptitude of Mr. Clive Jenkins'[95d] the intransigent anti-Marketeers were 'resoundingly defeated' as Gaitskell had hoped.

The defeat of Gaitskell's friends was far more resounding. They felt his speech had shown no understanding of their views and no sympathy for their difficulties. They particularly resented an attack by name on a harmless backbench loyalist, Alan Fitch, for letting down his mining constituents in Wigan by supporting the Market. Learning of that, Gaitskell made amends by a generous apology and by deleting Fitch from the printed record;[157] but once again he had shown his occasional total insensitivity. He kept telling his old friends that he greatly regretted clashing with them – but that it was unavoidable, since he had friends committed on both sides.[158] For Gaitskell personal friendships always took precedence over political differences, and they resumed after a brief period of coolness.[159] But he pulled no political punches, for in order to show the Party united he had to isolate and weaken the awkward minority whose dissent could so easily be magnified in the overwhelmingly pro-Market press into another big Labour split.

His successful appeal to the Conference majority aroused varying reactions among Marketeers. To one old and very charitable personal friend Gaitskell was revealing his 'latent genius for human communication';[3g] to one or two zealous journalists, he was lurching towards neutralism and abandoning all he had fought for;[50f] to others, especially

---

* At Brighton, he seemed almost alone in thinking the Six might make real concessions;[156] though three weeks later he told his CDS friends that he feared that was 'crying for the moon'.[2a]

in the unions, he was unfairly exploiting their loyalty, knowing they would not retaliate.[160] Sam Watson feared that Gaitskell had destroyed his own coalition within the Party.[48d] But once the Conference debate was over, the leader had no wish to weaken or humiliate his old allies. He wrote at once – before they left Brighton – to Bill Carron of the AEU, Jack Cooper of the NUGMW and Bill Webber of the TSSA, to propose early meetings to clear up differences;[161] and after these talks he claimed that their 'objections were being, in some measure, met'.[12l] He told his CDS friends to reply as vigorously as they liked to the extreme opponents of entry, but urged them to concentrate on pressing the government for better terms.[162] It was excellent counsel which they could honourably follow, both to keep the Party from going overboard against the Market, and to defend themselves against the Left which was eagerly hoping to drive them into the wilderness. Yet at the same time the Labour Marketeers by emphasising the conditions now, as previously by accepting them, would weaken their own case for rebelling when the real clash came. Gaitskell's advice would protect them now but neutralise them later – both to his own advantage.

On the other side of the Market fence, he busily looked for allies outside the Labour Party. Before talking to a group of Cambridge economists, he wrote: 'we shall need to mobilise for action those who are definitely anti'.[69b] He maintained friendly contact with his old enemy Lord Beaverbrook – each of course hoping to use the other, for Gaitskell was without Fleet Street support since both the *Mirror* and *Herald* were now on the other side – and suggested a number of prominent people (including Attlee and Montgomery) who might sign advertisements against entry.[163] He admitted some discomfort with such an ally, but thought he could escape being dominated.[12e]

Within the Labour Party, Gaitskell exploited the opportunity to consolidate its unity and his own leadership by appealing to the constituency activists. Systematically misled about him by the left-wing weeklies, many of them had opposed him for years but were now – as his postbag showed – delighted to cheer a Party leader who was sounding notes they wanted to hear. Above all he achieved a genuine reconciliation with his one powerful antagonist, Frank Cousins, without whom the Parliamentary and NEC Left would have been a nuisance but no threat. Reached by a different route, Cousins's attitude to the Market was very close to Gaitskell's. The Transport Workers' leader had once favoured British entry, and though disliking the way the Community had developed, he was not irreconcilable on the subject like his political friends. By supporting conditional entry, the T&GWU had enabled the platform to defeat those who opposed entry on principle;[164] and unlike the left-wing MPs, its NEC representative apparently did not abstain on the policy statement.

Cousins, contrary to the suspicions of his General Council rivals, had made no deal and had expected Gaitskell to take a much milder anti-Market line.[165] His offer to pay for printing the speech was a gesture of reconciliation, surprise and pleasure. Then to appease the Marketeers the NEC decided to print the policy statement and George Brown's ingenious closing speech as well, and asked him to pay for those too — which he did, though he was 'far from enthusiastic'[166] * On 12 November 1962, a month after Brighton, the hatchet was finally buried. Cousins and his wife dined alone with Hugh and Dora at 18 Frognal Gardens, and the evening was a great success. There was no firm offer or commitment, but Cousins would probably have become Minister of Transport in a Gaitskell Cabinet.[167]

It was of great advantage to the Labour Party to heal the breach between the parliamentary leader and the most powerful man in the trade union movement. But other union leaders, who had taken big risks to support Gaitskell's policies against Cousins in the past, were understandably alarmed and anxious:

> [T]he Praetorian Guard of the General Council ... complain bitterly that Mr. Gaitskell gave a decisive anti-Market tilt to the agreed policy ... These were the men who ... put him in power and kept him there when his leadership was endangered ... they feel shocked and very angry.[139c d]

Some feared he was changing sides: 'some senior union men who have been the leader's personal bodyguard ... are deeply distressed by the tone of his speech. Most, but not all, are too loyal to use the word "betrayal".[8e f] The 'almost incredulous glee' of the 'ecstatic' political Left was indeed due to that breach with his old supporters even more than to Gaitskell's adoption of their preferred policy.[3g h] Barbara Castle underlined the point with relish:

> But for the Left its importance ... [was that] he slapped down some of his closest friends as ruthlessly as he had previously slapped down his left-wing critics ... by reaching his decision on the Common Market in defiance of the cabal which had created him, Mr. Gaitskell has healed the breach between him and conference.[95e]

Some Westminster politicians of the Left, delighted at the chance to separate Gaitskell from many of his former allies, affected an effusive and unconvincing new enthusiasm for the leader; his old enemy John Stonehouse drew hoots of derision from the Brighton delegates[124e] by calling him 'this great man with ice-cold intellect but human, sincere emotions'.[28e]

* 'Of course [recalled Tony Benn] being the Labour Party, the million copies ended up in packets of a thousand in a thousand committee rooms — my agent kept them all and we distributed them at the [1975] Referendum.'

But others continued to display 'an unloving and unlovable spite', and 'talked about him in private as ungenerously and viciously as ever before'.[118b c]

His old friends at Westminster were understandably worried. Before Brighton Charlie Pannell warned Gaitskell: 'They would shoot you again tomorrow.'[168] Three weeks after Conference Christopher Mayhew wrote to argue that Labour divisions would still follow Left-Right lines rather than views on the Market, and to warn him that by stressing the sacrifice of sovereignty rather than the terms of entry he would alienate his 'reliable, natural supporters' and isolate himself in the PLP. In his reply, Gaitskell agreed on policy (sending a copy of his Paris speech on world government[4] to show his internationalist credentials) and on the character of Party divisions – but disputed Mayhew's 'assumption that my Brighton speech involved some tremendous change of attitude and judgement on my part about the various individuals and groups of the P.L.P. I can assure you that this was in no way the case'.[169] A few days earlier he had indicated (though not explicitly) to his CDS friends that he would still prefer a new Labour MP who was pro-Market but a supporter on defence to an anti-Market unilateralist.[2a]

In the PLP at the end of the month Gaitskell was 'obviously unhappy' (the latest Gallup poll showed growing support for entry) and kept strictly to the policy statement. Herbert Morrison in 'his best speech for years' urged a free vote; George Brown appealed to the Marketeers to support the statement; and they rated it a 'very successful meeting & some progress'.[124g] Wilson had just challenged Brown for the deputy leadership; Gaitskell regretted that and had tried to stop the contest. Preserving scrupulous public neutrality, he told his daughter to say nothing – but 'you can probably guess that I do not want any change';[53a b] and he said to Hetherington that Brown should win by 10 or 20.

> It was a question of personalities. Wilson was not trusted. That wasn't only his feeling (though it *was* his feeling). It was also quite commonly shared in the Party.[170]
>
> With Wilson, you couldn't talk about any confidential matter and be sure that he wouldn't go and talk to the very people concerned immediately. Brown, when he'd had too much to drink, could be very disloyal to Gaitskell personally and he could be very offensive and aggressive with everyone. But it was a different thing to the kind of disloyalty encountered in Harold Wilson.[12m]

Brown had been tipped to lose,[171] but won by 133 votes to 103.

At the Conservative Conference at Llandudno, Macmillan had swept aside his own dissidents and carried a total commitment to entry. But in Brussels that only stiffened the Six against making concessions.[172–3b]

This in turn eased the situation inside the Labour Party, enabling the Opposition to concentrate on attacking the terms and tactics of entry rather than the principle, so that some Labour Marketeers were persuaded that Gaitskell was modifying his stance.[174] The government would not reopen the Commonwealth talks, and the treatment of the EFTA countries became, for Gaitskell, the crucial issue.[2a][d] 'At the moment, I should think it quite certain that the Tories will ditch them just as they ditched the Commonwealth,' he wrote late in October.[175] A week later he wondered 'why the Government had made such a fuss about agriculture';[12m] and thought it was because of four pending by-elections in county seats (where on 22 November Labour spectacularly won South Dorset). In his last parliamentary debate on the Market, he made effective use of Heath's original speech in Paris when the negotiations began, to show how little the Six had conceded.[176] He denounced the new suggestion of keeping the Scandinavians out, repeated that Ministers' press briefings at Brussels and during the Commonwealth Prime Ministers' Conference had 'deeply shocked' him, and repudiated any suggestion that he was turning neutralist.[173c] But as he told Hetherington, 'he hadn't got a great deal more to say.'[12m]

Gaitskell had no intention at all of reversing his alliances within the Party, and carefully avoided the trap into which his successor fell headlong ten years later, when the Labour Left were allowed to exploit the Market issue to extend their power in the Party at the expense, initially of their opponents on the pro-Market Right, but eventually of their temporary allies in the leadership. His awareness of the danger made him cautious about the demand for a general election on the EEC issue, although it seemed a logical consequence of his stand.[177] Whether he welcomed the prospect is not clear: his daughter thought so, his personal assistant not.* Certainly he was careful to make his call for an election conditional. On BBC television as the Conference closed, Hardiman Scott asked Gaitskell if he was gambling on an early election or saying 'that the Labour Party will fight an election against the Common Market?' 'No,' said Gaitskell, 'I was very clear, I think, about that, and you will recall that the Conference rejected by a very large majority a motion which would have committed us to a General Election on this in any event.'[30b]

He was cautious about it in order to avoid committing himself on the next and crucial problem: if he came to power after Macmillan had taken the country into the EEC, would he repudiate the treaty and take her out?

* Lord Harris thought he felt that an election might become inevitable and that he would win it, but that 'it would be highly disagreeable and he would have no enjoyment in it'. Mrs McNeal recalled him already inventing slogans and rather relishing the prospect.

That would do the maximum damage to Britain's relationship with her allies — but the threat of it would probably force an election, for the Six might well insist on one before letting Britain join. So the Left sought a pledge to repudiate, and commentators on Brighton treated that as the concealed object of the struggle in the Party.[139a e] (*The Economist* — consistently cynical and consistently wrong about Gaitskell throughout this controversy — accused the leader of himself working towards it, and therefore of deliberately trying in his speech to undermine George Brown's chances of re-election as deputy leader.[94d f] Though Gaitskell had treated Brown badly, that charge was quite false, and he protested furiously to the editor, his old UCL colleague Donald Tyerman, at the journal's 'filth' and 'personal slander' in questioning his honour.)[178] On television back in July, he would not reserve the right to repudiate, calling it a 'tremendously hypothetical question'.[97] Meeting the pro-Market Labour MPs on 27 September, 'H.G. did not foresee an early election & said he had no intention of saying anything that would imply a threat to take us out if we were already in. He did not think C[ommon] M[arket] would play the only role in an election.'[179] Again in October he flatly refused — four times — to answer a persistent questioner on the same point.[180] But while he would not commit himself, or let the Left bounce him into a pledge, he privately thought that he must reserve the threat in case Parliament jibbed at entry but still 'the Government tried to get through impossible terms by the use of the guillotine'.[2a] So Bill Carron's call for a promise not to repudiate was also met with silence.[28f] Two months later Gaitskell was still privately stressing his reluctance to Kennedy:

> If the final terms are as bad as now seems likely, then it is inevitable that we shall oppose them. This does not mean, of course, that the General Election when it comes will necessarily be fought exclusively on them. This is probably unlikely ... Nor does it mean that I should threaten to repudiate any agreement reached. I have been very careful to say nothing on that. There are circumstances in which I might feel obliged to do so — that is true — but obviously one would not dream of taking such a grave step without the most careful weighing up of all the possible consequences.[10j]

He was reserving his heavy weapons to dissuade the government from behaviour he saw as illegitimate. But he also replied candidly to an anxious CDS questioner at that private meeting: 'I won't play that card unless it will win.'*

---

* The author was present and vividly recalls this remark. Rodgers's note records: 'He would judge the issue when it arose by the approach which would ensure the maximum electoral advantage.'[2a]

Even before Brighton Gaitskell was said to have 'set off a new complex of pressures inside the party, and moved the point of leadership substantially further Left than he has ever done before'.[139a] The Conference was described as

> the revolution Mr. Gaitskell has carried out with ruthless determination ... a drastic reconstruction of the balance of power in the Labour Party ... the most assertive display of dynamic leadership he has ever presented ... What surprised his friends and his critics alike at Brighton was his self-confident toughness. Previously circumstances compelled him to act as the head of a coalition, preserving a precarious balance; but at Brighton, instead of soothing the Left and cosseting the Right, he moved in with utter ruthlessness.[139c f]

He knew quite well that the Left naturally hoped to make him dependent upon them and then impose their own policies on him. As Barbara Castle frankly put it:

> it would indeed be ironical if, after demanding the freedom to pursue an independent foreign policy as one of Britain's conditions for joining the Six, the Labour party were to behave as if it had no fundamental foreign policy differences with British Tories.[95e]

Underestimating Gaitskell's political skill, some commentators thought he was flirting with neutralism: a charge which he rejected as 'utter nonsense' and which its originator soon retracted, though the Prime Minister was not above hinting at it.[181]

Whatever Gaitskell's intentions, the Left hoped and the Right feared that a successful election campaign alongside the outright anti-Marketeers would so strengthen their influence and his need for their support that a breach with Washington would follow. Either he would have converted Kennedy, wrote Michael Foot, or the Anglo-American 'relationship would be impaired and great transformations would follow'.[182] *The Economist* thought he would have faced not merely resentment from the Europeans but 'cold fury in the Kennedy Administration'.[94d] Yet on two crucial points Kennedy agreed with Gaitskell. He saw no urgency for an immediate settlement, and had no sympathy for the intransigence of the Six, telling Hetherington privately that the Europeans must be made to show more generosity to Britain:

> He believed this could be done. They must succeed in this. It might take four or five years, but Europe must be argued out of its protectionist attitude. The U.S. ... would lose even more if Europe became restrictive and protectionist. He thought that if the Americans, British

and others kept up the pressure, the Europeans could be shamed into giving Britain proper terms.[183]

The President was as usual more enlightened than American opinion, and some crude press attacks on Gaitskell justified the victim's sour comment about their unthinking enthusiasm for 'anything with the words "U.S." in it'.[184] Gaitskell wrote to Kennedy very frankly, describing Dean Acheson's view that Britain should join the Community because she was no good to America outside it as 'a real bomb under the alliance, well calculated to break it, not cement it';[185] and the assumption (once his own) that Britain ought to enter to keep the Europeans straight as one arousing resentment both in London and on the Continent. He protested at the suggestion (in British press reports which he suspected the British government of planting) that the United States might help Macmillan win the election. He felt he had taken enough risks fighting neutralism and anti-Americanism to tell Kennedy: 'nothing is more calculated to stimulate them than [this] kind of attitude in Washington ... friendship and alliance cannot survive on the basis of threats and pressures.'[10k] Indeed he thought some members of Kennedy's Administration much too prone to use such means, and warned his American friends against George Ball 'who has always been a passionate European federalist'.[186] He was delighted,[12o] though, when the Secretary of Agriculture exasperated the French by vigorously criticising the Common Agricultural Policy.[50g]

Towards the French themselves, Gaitskell was ambivalent. They were very useful as enemies of federalism but very difficult on all matters of substance; so they made it much harder for Macmillan to get acceptable terms, and might help to weaken his position if the whole enterprise failed on that account. De Gaulle's preference for excluding Britain was in little doubt: the British Embassy had reported it in May 1962, though Ministers were reluctant to believe the bad news.[187] Gaitskell took such warnings seriously, telling Donnelly in September that he thought the talks would fail.[48e] But de Gaulle's ability to keep Britain out was not so clear. His usefulness to the French party politicians had vanished with the end of the Algerian War, and his hands were not free until he had routed them in the October referendum and November election.[24f]

Gaitskell learned in October 1962 that the Elysée was confident that, unless de Gaulle lost at the polls, Heath could not fulfil his timetable and get Britain in before her next election.[188] Kennedy and Macmillan met at Nassau in December — and de Gaulle acquired his pretext. A few days earlier Gaitskell went to Paris, deliberately avoiding seeing de Gaulle for fear that Macmillan would make him the scapegoat if the President did keep Britain out.[189] Instead he saw the Prime Minister and Foreign Minister (MM. Pompidou and Couve de Murville), who told him that a federal Europe was unthinkable for (respectively) twenty or fifty years.[190] He also saw Guy Mollet, the Socialist leader, and sources close to his French political contacts on both sides promptly began hinting that Britain might become an associate rather than a full member of the EEC.[191]

Back in London, Gaitskell suspected that de Gaulle might concede better terms in return for access to British nuclear technology, though American opposition under the McMahon Act would probably stop any such deal.[192] He told the Australian Labour leader that the talks seemed increasingly likely to fail, obliging Britain to seek an alternative.[193] 'The French are being very tough and are likely to make as many difficulties for us as they can.'[99c] On 11 January 1963, Macmillan was still hoping the negotiations would succeed, when 'we can let loose a great pro-European propaganda ... [so far] restrained, but ready to unleash'.[46a p] De Gaulle pronounced his veto three days later – and four days before Gaitskell's death.

vii *Community, Commonwealth and Offshore Island*

One American journalist friend of Gaitskell's wrote in his obituary of their last long talk:

> I went to see him at the House of Commons, wondering genuinely how I would feel about him when I left.
>
> For more than an hour we argued it all over again, but in a matter of minutes all suspicion of playing politics with the issue were [*sic*] swept away.[105]

But while not simply 'playing politics', Gaitskell was a Party leader who had twice fought battles against many of his own followers and was prudently – and rightly – trying to avoid another. He never concealed that his original 'fence-sitting' policy was adopted partly to keep the Party together. Political advantage and political principle were not in conflict, for that policy was tactically attractive precisely because it corresponded to what he, and most Labour people, felt about the substance. Few were narrow Little England nationalists, but many were suspicious of de Gaulle and Adenauer and concerned about the 'new Commonwealth'; so that, as Gaitskell told Kennedy, the conditions did outline the kind of Europe they wanted to join.

Until the summer of 1962, Gaitskell assumed that if he could avoid a premature clash within the Party, events would settle his main political problem – and that he would probably find himself leading and winning another battle against the all-out opponents of entry. Later he said so to everybody – the House of Commons, the President of the United States, close colleagues and unknown correspondents; and those subsequent assertions are confirmed by the tone of his comments before the event. But his assessment had misjudged both the Six and the British Prime Minister. He overestimated the chances of the conditions being accepted, not through having illusions about the French, but because he hoped for too much from the other negotiating partners putting pressure on Paris. Never really appreciating the emotional drive behind the European movement, he expected them to go further than was ever likely both in making concessions to the Commonwealth and in transforming the Community itself. Spaak apparently said in their clash at Brussels that Gaitskell was asking the Six to join the Commonwealth.[95a] Their row was due less to what Gaitskell said than to the way he said it:[194] not to a conflict of interests open to bargaining, but to his refusal to see Britain become 'a province of Europe'. Yet he knew that the Six themselves disagreed about the shape of the future Community. Socialists like Spaak differed from the European Right and shared many of Labour's objectives, but were keen federalists; the Gaullists and the British agreed in opposing federalism, but on very little else; the new military power of which Adenauer and de Gaulle dreamed was a nightmare to both the federalists and the British.

At home Gaitskell, being so wary of Harold Macmillan, suspected the Prime Minister's plan to change the domestic political agenda and so revive flagging Conservative fortunes. But he assumed that the terms would either be good enough for the Opposition to accept, or not good enough for the Government to propose, so that a party clash on the issue was unlikely.[195] Macmillan proved very successful in beating down the Tory rebels, as Gaitskell had come to expect; he also became committed to entry not on party grounds, but as a major historic decision for which he ran great political risks. He never forgot how Disraeli had overthrown Peel, and up to 21 August 1962 he feared a revolt led by his most influential colleague, R. A. Butler—which would almost certainly have destroyed either the policy or its architect or both.[46a] Once reassured about Butler, Macmillan took a bigger gamble than Gaitskell had expected to achieve the historic objective; for Gaitskell so mistrusted him as to attribute his haste essentially to party political motives, although recognising that he might have broader ones too.[196]

Gaitskell began to suspect in August, and became convinced in September, that the British government was abandoning many of the original conditions and preparing to enter a substantially unchanged Community. That discovery transformed his whole bearing. From being cool, rational and calculating, he became heated, emotional and passionate. The change was crystallised in his meetings with the Commonwealth Socialist parties: from indignation at the treatment of the Commonwealth, shock at getting no support from the European Socialists, suspicion of imprecise promises by the Six, and anger at Macmillan's determination to bring Britain into the Community on any terms before the next election – so that Labour would have to reverse a decision already in force instead of questioning a leap in the dark. As Leader of the Opposition Gaitskell felt a political obligation to the British peoples of the old Commonwealth and a moral obligation to the poor nations of the new. He had never believed that international economic co-operation and political union necessarily went together, as he had shown over Atlantic Union years before.[197] Now, 'nothing annoyed him so much as the question, "But what is the alternative?" '[1a] Perhaps the passion of Brighton came most of all from his repugnance at defeatism – the claim by some Marketeers that Britain had no future outside the EEC.[198a b] He saw that not as an economic miscalculation, but as a confession of political bankruptcy; for, in or out, Britain's future would depend on herself, and he loathed the suggestion that she could not get to her feet unless hauled up by foreigners.

His fence-sitting attitude during the EEC talks was therefore transformed by their outcome into furious opposition; and he set about preparing for a campaign which never took place, and which he would not have survived to lead. In doing so he reconciled many left-wing activists within the Labour Party – if not their national spokesmen – to his leadership. That was an intended consequence, but not his motive.[199] Some close friends suspected that he unconsciously recoiled from yet another battle on the old lines;[200] others more plausibly thought that he felt that a Party leader should not perpetually fight his own followers.[201] Certainly he made the most of his political opportunity, and certainly he was delighted to find the tide flowing his own way at last. But his course was no tactical necessity, for opponents as well as supporters of entry recognised that Conference would happily have accepted a more balanced line;[202] and by alienating old friends, he risked becoming needlessly dependent on old enemies.

He spoke at Brighton out of conviction not calculation. A fortnight later he told some pro-EEC friends: 'I suppose that I have been all along more emotionally against the Common Market than I realised.'[203] From opposite sides, Roy Jenkins and Peter Shore both felt that he had been moving steadily into opposition – contrary to his own well-supported statements that until the summer he still expected to end up advocating entry. Those committed and mutually hostile partisans at least agreed with one another, as against Gaitskell, that the terms mattered far less than the principle – and so may have been more realistic about what the conditions were likely to be. Besides, the prospect of bad terms and a collapse of the talks left Gaitskell indifferent, even in the summer; the passionate on either side might well have mistaken his equanimity for dislike of the whole enterprise.

His basic indifference was not, as with most uncommitted Labour people, a sign of puzzled indecision. He had thought through the alternatives and found them evenly balanced. Even at Brighton, his views did not coincide with those of the delegates who cheered them vociferously. Strong anti-Marketeers suspected the Europeans mainly as militaristic cold warriors; Gaitskell had some similar doubts, but he was more worried about their colonialist attitude in Africa and the UN, and about their quarrelling with the United States and weakening the Western alliance.[10m] He was rather less concerned than the Left with foreign policy, and more with the economic policies of the Six – especially with their consequences for the Commonwealth. To it, he gave higher priority than any leading colleague (except perhaps Gordon Walker, a former Commonwealth Secretary) or most Labour anti-Marketeers in the Party.* Gaitskell had no wild hopes of organising it as a long-term alternative to the EEC, but he did insist that Britain had a duty not to provoke its disintegration.

He shared neither the Commonwealth illusion of a few anti-Marketeers, nor their opponents' worry that the great opportunity, once missed, might never return. He always thought that a negative in 1962 might have to be reconsidered if circumstances changed, and never believed those changes would make reconsideration impossible. Some Marketeers feared that Britain would never again want to join because the Community would have moved so fast towards unification that Britain could never catch up; but Gaitskell saw that de Gaulle would prevent that development (enabling many other unenthusiastic Europeans to escape the blame for obstructing it). Other Marketeers feared that Britain would decline economically outside the Community, who therefore would not welcome her in; but Gaitskell never attributed European economic growth to the Market, and always believed that domestic developments would depend on domestic decisions – notably the quality of British political leadership, and the response to it of the British people.

He would certainly have looked afresh at the new balance of arguments when the Commonwealth lost its cohesion, Britain became a small offshore island with waning influence, and the mirage of a federal Europe receded. His close friends disagree about his likely conclusions. There is one pointer In opposing entry in 1962, Gaitskell had on his side not only the ideologues. of the Left, but also many Labour leaders who were men of government, as he was. With the sole exception of Douglas Jay, those colleagues – and his own widow – all changed their minds about the EEC in the next few years: Wilson, Callaghan, Healey, Stewart, Gordon Walker. But whatever his final decision, his approach would not have changed: a cool appraisal of the advantages and drawbacks, quite different from the uncompromising hostility or enthusiastic vision of the zealots on either side. Five years after Britain's entry, and fifteen years after Gaitskell's death, both

* Of the 19 anti-Market floor speeches at Brighton, only two said much about the Commonwealth; one mentioned it briefly, six perfunctorily and ten not at all.

front-benchers and back-benchers in both major parties by 'tacit consensus' saw the Community developing as 'a union of consenting national
governments ... working together for limited ends under arrangements
many of which should be altered drastically in Britain's interest'.[204] Had
he survived, Gaitskell might have found himself close to the centre of
gravity of British opinion about the EEC.

CHAPTER 26

IN SIGHT OF THE PROMISED LAND 1962–3

'He looked, sounded and was set to be the Prime Minister of England'
(OBITUARY OF HG BY A TORY JOURNALIST AND MP)

i *Gaitskell at Fifty-Six*

THOUGH Gaitskell's political personality was set before he became leader, his last three dramatic years influenced his attitude to other people and led him to reassess his own mistakes.[1] If all politicians are either bishops or bookmakers, Gaitskell the public man sat firmly on the episcopal bench. Yet his seriousness of purpose was tempered with gaiety, even frivolity, so that Malcolm Muggeridge could write: 'Earnestness, [that] disease of the Left in politics ... only afflicted Gaitskell as a rash, never as a fever.'[2] He emerged from the traumas of 1960–1 fully confident of his capacity to lead the Party back to power, put his principles into practice, and change the course of British politics. 'Last year', he told the 1961 Blackpool Conference, 'our task was to save the Party. This year it is to save the nation.'[3]

During that stormy period he suffered as much violent abuse as any British politician has ever faced, and was more bitterly reviled by his own followers than most Party leaders have ever been. There were moments when he wondered if he had made a mistake in ever going into politics.[2] The violence of that conflict turned him into a harder man, and chipped away at some of the amiable traits which made him so attractive as a person but sometimes handicapped him in the political struggle. He wrote to a friend at the worst period of all, early in 1960:

> Sometimes I hate it very much — most of all the treachery & disloyalty. I like things that are more straightforward. You sit round a table & discuss a problem calmly & rationally. You reach your conclusions. You act accordingly. But it's not like that at all — at the moment. People seem to be unable or unwilling to do that — except for the few friends you know. Everything is spiced & barbed & the atmosphere is full of suppressed hysteria & neurosis — not so suppressed either! It would be nice like you to treat it as chess. I find that hard.

More than ever he prized courage and loyalty. The courage to take an unpopular line in public, he once said, was the first qualification for political office; and when Roy Jenkins promised to support him whenever he was right, he replied like Disraeli: 'Anybody can do that. I want people who'll support me when I'm wrong.'[4]

In the heat of a bitter struggle, he could judge his opponents harshly — especially the moralisers.[5] Stimulated by a lively conversation among friends, he could become emotional about both people and issues. He assessed his close but not always loyal associates quite without illusions. He rejected a warning that one of them might try to stab him in the back: 'He's a shit and he knows that everybody knows he's a shit. If he stabs he'll stab from in front.' The same man's perpetual pursuit of his own self-interest was, he said, easier to cope with than the unpredictable vagaries of another colleague in search of his.[6] To a friend who wondered in the summer of 1962 how far he could trust a third prominent associate, he replied that he trusted nobody.[7] After so many desertions at critical moments, such resentments were not surprising, however sadly different from his early ambition to prove that there could be friendship at the top after all. But some of his own side also thought him tougher, less free and easy, more often testy and irritable when opposed or criticised. Refractory members summoned to his room in the House sometimes felt it was like going to the Headmaster's study. To his loyal secretary, whatever the strain, 'he never lost his temper, ever — goodness knows he had reason to, but never'.[8] But he 'sweated blood in controversies';[9] and it showed.

Gaitskell knew very well that such emotions were professionally dangerous. He gave a long, candid television interview to Malcolm Muggeridge in the summer of 1961 about his personal outlook, not his views. He told the interviewer that back-stabbing was no less common in journalism than in politics — though less noticed in the press, which loving-ly recorded all conflicts but no constructive activities. Muggeridge asked directly whether he felt too bitter to work with those individuals who had led the attacks on him. 'Well,' he replied,

> I think it's very important to avoid that if you possibly can, because in politics the situation changes a great deal, and very often you don't understand somebody else's motives, and if you were to sort of be a tremendously unforgiving, ruthless type I don't think again you could do your job properly. I am human and of course one doesn't like it when people, whom you perhaps hoped were on your side, turn against you. But, well, one must just try and get over it, that's all ... Politics is a very tense sort of existence, people are emotionally excited and roused ... that is part of the price you pay for a very interesting life.[10]

Nearly all the old friends who found him more difficult in later years were reflecting their first sharp political disagreement with him over the

Common Market. They were also reflecting Gaitskell's exceptional earlier standards of patience, tolerance and good humour to both supporters and opponents. At his worst moment at Scarborough, he sought out a left-wing journalist whose father had just died, to express his regrets.[11] After Labour's vote was halved in the Liberal triumph at Orpington in 1962, he asked the humiliated young Labour candidate to lunch at the House to be congratulated on the campaign. A future Conservative Cabinet Minister recalled fifteen years later his astonished delight at receiving a friendly letter of congratulations from the Leader of the Opposition praising his maiden speech – and added wistfully, 'it would never happen now'.[12]

Gaitskell was still concerned about his friends, whether valued henchmen or unknown comrades from his years of obscurity. When his staunch ally Alice Bacon was suddenly taken desperately ill in Yorkshire, he cancelled everything in London to go straight to her bedside.[13] He left early from a PLP discussion on the Common Market to attend the mayor-making ceremony in Chatham of his pre-war friend Mrs Grieveson.[14-15a] Strangers who appealed to him had the same attention; one, not a constituent and with no introduction, wrote to thank him for helping to settle a family problem overseas: 'I am still amazed that a member of the ordinary public such as myself ... should be able so easily to reach somebody as prominent as yourself in order to bring assistance to a needy relative so far away.'[16]

From goodwill and meticulousness, he accepted far too many commitments. He still prepared elaborately for every speech, and delved thoroughly into quite unexpected subjects: the assistant national agent was understandably amazed at the Party leader's concern with bands and styles of jazz for youth concerts.[17] Usually the pressures came the other way, with the machine demanding endless provincial tours to encourage the rank and file. Gaitskell did not resist enough, and took far more interest than Attlee ever had.[17] But when he was worn down by other work, he found it hard to pretend. In Leeds, he was not at home in university circles;[18] often he was obviously weary at the endless arguments with self-righteous critics who would not accept his good faith. Some mistook that mood for elitist indifference to the views of ordinary folk. But Gaitskell always found the workingmen's clubs exhilarating, and wrote to his daughter in 1959:

> I'm glad you went canvassing and liked it. There's a lot that's very tiresome and distasteful in politics but I absolutely agree that working with people for the Party is very satisfying: that's one reason why I like the tours. One meets so many of the *best* party workers – just *good* people.[19a]

Later an American, with long political experience at home, watched

Gaitskell mixing easily and naturally with the drinkers at the Belper Labour Club:

> This dignified, elegant, impressive man – I wondered whether he'll just look uncomfortable or will he try to become one of the lads which will embarrass me. He didn't do either. He was friendly, good humoured, exchanged jokes with them – but remained himself.

He was so kind to that visitor that from being 'a convinced Gaitskellite at the start of the tour I became a devoted one at the end'.[20]

With his parliamentary duties, weekend speeches and tours in the recess, he had little time for his family. Dora waited up for him to get back late from the House, and they met – silently – over breakfast. She looked forward eagerly to Labour's return to office, when she could see him at lunch as Molly Butler saw Rab. She went often to South Leeds, and with him at weekends and on tour: 'That's the point of going round the country with my husband. It's a chance to answer back, to argue. And to be together.'[15b] Sometimes they were able to take a break for a few hours, as when they went off hunting for antiques during the tour of East Anglia. In one interview on 'turning-points in one's life' Hugh said, moderately as usual: 'More than most jobs, politics imposes stresses and strains which are hard to take without the understanding and companionship of somebody who shares your own fundamental attitudes and interests.'[21]

Otherwise holidays were Gaitskell's main opportunities to see his family. After the children grew up, these were often abroad, especially in Italy and Yugoslavia. Even official foreign trips usually provided an opportunity for non-political relaxation. After the Socialist International met in Oslo, he and his old NEC antagonist Tom Driberg went looking at statues and sculpture, and then gossiped about jazz and ballet over a leisurely dinner: 'one of the most agreeable evenings I've spent with anybody – he was personally so charming, very courteous always and considerate.'[22] Always he detested pomposity, refusing VIP treatment when he took the family to Italy. 'Here is one politician', wrote a normally unfriendly newspaper, 'who does not have an inflated idea of his own position.'[15c]

At 18 Frognal Gardens they kept up a comfortable establishment, quite unaltered by Gaitskell's improved financial fortunes. During the booming later 1950s his investments flourished, thanks to skilful friends in the banking world to whom he had committed them. At his death he left £75,000 net;[23] death duties took well over one-third, for he had neglected to take some legitimate precautions. Quite likely he did not know how very well his investments were doing; certainly he did not tell his wife.[24] They wined and dined rather better but made little change in their style of life;

they considered having someone living in to run the household, but Dora disliked the idea and they never did.[24a] Hugh enjoyed his comforts, but always despised luxury and ostentatious spending.

However, he added a lively round of social engagements to his time-consuming political duties. In 1962 Anthony Sampson called him

> relaxed and gregarious, with an extraordinary capacity for enjoyment and no political pomp ... [and with] a talent for listening which is almost unknown among politicians ... His circle is large and surprising: he can be seen at Belgravia lunch-parties, at night-clubs, at the celebrations of café society and – more rarely – at trade union socials: he has never found it easy to adapt his social pleasures to political expediency ... He entertains widely and well, with cosmopolitan scope ... He talks about almost everything, travels widely and forgets nothing.[25]

The Gaitskells found their relaxation in parties, dinners and dances. He had never been one for what Dora called 'the Great Plains of domestic life' and his friends thought that in his methodical way, he allocated periods off-duty to enjoy himself as he pleased without caring what anyone thought. Never rigidly abstemious, he drank a fair amount; but he knew that alcohol can be dangerous for politicians under strain – from the weight of their responsibilities or the frustration of having none – and he ran no risk of overdoing it.

At home at Frognal Gardens, his guests were mostly progressive and few were actively Tory. But he kept up a few personal friendships across the political divide, largely through Anne Fleming and her circle. Crosland chided him about it;[26] but, with his Wykehamist sense of rectitude and distaste for the idle rich, Gaitskell was not in the least worried that he might yield to the embrace of the social Establishment, or might be sourly suspected of doing so. He appreciated its comforts, and its intellectual stimulus still more. But even his taste for that had limits. 'We see a great deal of the Berlins, Stuart Hampshire, Maurice B[owra] and Anne F[leming],' he wrote on one holiday. 'We liked the conversation very much at first but have begun to find it a trifle exhausting ... you can sit in silence if you are two or even three but not if you are seven or eight. So there is a certain atmosphere of effort.'[19b]

His friends, apart from Crosland, were convinced that his active social life had no effect at all on his political views. Indeed, when one Conservative friend wrote rather hectoringly about egalitarianism that it was bad for people to get something for nothing, he referred to her own inherited wealth and rebuked her: 'I don't take your ravings on politics seriously. There's a sort of Bournemouth bellow that comes through – something from a former non-rational existence which you once led.' Occasionally he himself feared that some of his political friends might be unduly attracted by that world, but he never doubted his own immunity to temptation; in an obituary of his old patron Hugh Dalton, he wrote: 'At no time was there the faintest chance that he would be seduced by "society" and for those who showed signs of succumbing to it he had nothing but contempt.'[27] Such complete indifference to the reactions of others was imprudent. But his social life did him less political harm than might have been expected.

Of course his present and prospective status partly explained why he was so much in demand socially; but only partly, for he was still a very pleasant and stimulating companion.

> He was never pompous or self-important, as are most politicians, even the best of them. He tried always to say what he meant and to mean something; likewise an unusual trait among politicians ... Gaitskell and Aneurin Bevan were ... the least boring politicians to spend time with.[2]

On first meeting him people felt his charm, notably because each conversational companion of the moment could always count on his undisturbed attention.

Some dedicated political opponents thought that he never understood young people. He did not think youth (or age) made prejudice or irrationality any more attractive; and he once confessed that there was 'nothing I like better than being flattered by the young — very soothing to the bruised ego'.[28] But it was not just political agreement or difference; he would happily argue into the small hours with students who discussed seriously, without slogans or rancour.[29] In March 1962 he spoke — surprisingly — in a funny debate at the Oxford Union, on a motion regretting that no one had succeeded where Guy Fawkes failed. Even for this he prepared elaborately, with material from the House of Commons library on the Gunpowder Plot and its successors. Yet on the night,

> his entire speech was composed of refutations of those who had spoken before. His style was ... dry (even desiccated) but the wit took everyone by surprise. He analysed one by one the political positions being taken by the factions of the day, including (perhaps particularly) those in the Labour party who opposed him. Each section of his speech ended with the conclusion, which became a refrain, greeted with rising gales of laughter, 'So you see, Guy Fawkes was not the man for *you*'.

He showed 'obvious and genuine delight' at the party afterwards, and was one of the last to leave.[30]

Next evening he dined with a college graduate society.

Conversation was relatively lighthearted and spontaneous ... [his] lack of any pomposity ... quickly put everyone at ease. Unlike so many politicians Gaitskell was neither a monologuist nor one of those who sit abstracted from mere mortals with weighty matters of state on their minds ... [he] was a remarkably good listener so one felt there was a real give and take in the conversation. I remember too a wry self-deprecatory humour and a style absolutely lacking in any 'side' ... some good-natured banter about Hampstead socialism, a couple of funny, slightly malicious anecdotes about Nye Bevan and the temptations of upper bourgeois life.

It was the largest and most enthusiastic meeting for a visitor at the college for at least five years—and the competition included Enoch Powell, Kingsley Martin, Angus Wilson and Stephen Spender. Gaitskell talked for an hour on the intellectual foundations of democratic socialism—with a moving reference to Evan Durbin—and then, in a stiflingly hot room, patiently answered questions for well over another hour, meeting a little mild criticism from nuclear disarmers and more from enthusiastic foreigners wanting Britain in the EEC: 'He received a standing ovation ... more like a party meeting than a society gathering ... [he seemed] a warm and likeable man, who had thoroughly enjoyed the evening and who was faintly surprised by the enthusiasm aroused.'[31] That autumn he dined in a Cambridge college where his host had banned any talk of politics, and Gaitskell greatly impressed a Harvard visitor by talking comfortably and knowledgeably about art and Russian literature.[32]

His friends often wondered how he could stand the pace. Worry about his stamina in office was almost certainly misplaced, for he would have been far better staffed, and would not have felt he had to do so much himself; besides, power is an elixir for frustrated politicians. But the physical strain of the life he led, defying all warnings, must have overtaxed even his robust constitution and lowered his resistance to illness. The mental strain told on him surprisingly little, for even at the nadir of his political fortunes he was always able to forget his troubles and relax completely. In the last year those worries were over; he was thought to be, and thought himself, on the threshold of Downing Street. Yet the strain was there, for he was a sensitive man, and beneath the courtesy, good temper and patience was much repressed disgust at the intrigue and the pettiness. At least once those emotions broke surface; in the early summer of 1962, when things were going well politically, a perfectly trivial incident with George Brown suddenly made him feel he had had enough of it, and he alarmed Alice

Bacon by hinting that he would resign and quit politics.[13a] The mood did not last long, but it revealed the tensions below.

Gaitskell was no more spoiled by the approach of power than distraught by the proximity of disaster. Malcolm Muggeridge, in his Granada Television interview, interrogated him about ambition, power and the motives and dilemmas of politicians. A couple of years earlier Gaitskell had written to his daughter that there was nothing wrong with ambition in a young man: 'The question is really how far he is a genuine Socialist — i.e. has thought deeply about politics & morals & knows where his sympathies lie ... if yes I'm not too worried about careerism.'[19c] Now in 1961 he was rather pleased to learn that Aneurin Bevan had once privately said that he was not ambitious enough. At once determined to be honest and afraid of sounding priggish, he confessed that

> of course I want to be Prime Minister, because being leader of the Labour Party that means a Labour government, but it's not a sort of personal overwhelming desire to be a Prime Minister of Britain ... there's nothing wrong with ambition, so long as it isn't sort of overriding, I think then it becomes intolerable.

He went on to stress 'one of the great drawbacks of politics ... the encroachment it makes on your private life, on your privacy ... it's been almost entirely a public life, and that, I think, is a bore.' He honestly admitted at once that he did not find the limelight altogether unattractive: 'I suppose one would miss it, sometimes one longs to be out of it but ... in time I think you'd feel you'd had your ration, and would be glad to go back to a quieter life.'[10]

ii Poised for Power

When the House rose for the Christmas recess, Gaitskell was at the height of his powers. In Parliament he had attained a new stature, and Macmillan's ascendancy was over. In the Party, he had demonstrated that the Left could neither overthrow nor intimidate him — and that he was quite independent of the Right. Now clearly his own man, he was also at last genuinely the leader of his followers, and he had behind him, as a prominent Labour Marketeer put it, 'a Party more united than at any time since 1945-7, poised and prepared for victory, a Moses on the verge of the promised land'.[33a] Even before Brighton the doyen of labour correspondents had written: 'Gaitskell stands out like an Everest on the plains against all others.'[15d] After Conference another well-known commentator wrote: 'Mr. Gaitskell is now at the peak of his command of the Labour movement ... Labour ... for the first time for years seemed to have overcome its obsessional complex about its inner self, appearing more outward-looking and healthy.'[34-5a]

His rising reputation attracted almost as much comment before his death as in the obituary columns.[36] In the opinion polls, those thinking Gaitskell a good leader had been close to 50 per cent ever since the summer of 1961 and went above it (thus outnumbering dissenters and Don't Knows together) in the autumn of 1962.* As Macmillan's ratings were slumping, Gaitskell soared ahead. From the election until the summer of 1961 voters had been far less satisfied with him than with the Prime Minister, whose average lead was no less than 20 per cent. In the next year the two men were running neck and neck. But in the last four months the advantage was Gaitskell's, by a comfortable average of 7 per cent.[37]

The Labour Party shared the benefit, winning two of the five by-elections fought on 22 November 1962. At Glasgow Woodside, a new Liberal and new Nationalist each took some votes from both big parties, but so many more from the Conservatives that Labour won the seat. All the other four constituencies had been Tory in 1945. Labour came within 1,000 votes in one, within 220 in another, and won a third, South Dorset, where a strong anti-Market Conservative split the Tory vote;[38] and Labour's share of the poll held up much better than in the times of internal strife and Liberal upsurge.** On the Gallup poll, Labour now had a comfortable lead, no longer just due to Conservative weakness: in December it at last began to climb above 40 per cent.† From March it had led on the 'casting vote' question (how would you vote in a general election when your vote might decide between five years of a Conservative government under Macmillan or of a Labour government under Gaitskell?). By December that lead was 49½ per cent to 42½ per cent†† Gaitskell's principal Labour critics did not doubt that he would lead the Party to victory at the next election.[39a b] As Crossman wrote:

> one of the most fascinating developments of 1962 was the almost invisible transfer of the nation's confidence, from the man with real power in Downing Street to the man with Shadow power in the

---

* In previous Gallup polls he had exceeded 50 per cent only six times out of 55, three of the six coming since Blackpool. From September he was over 50 per cent in four polls out of five (and at 49 per cent in the fifth).

** The median Labour drop in the by-elections of 1960 was 7·6 per cent, in 1961 3·7 per cent, at the Liberal peak earlier in 1962 5·3 per cent, in November 1962 1·9 per cent.

† With don't knows included; 45 per cent without them.

†† With 7 per cent of determined Liberals. Including the 16 per cent of don't knows, the lead was 41 to 36.

Opposition. This has made Hugh Gaitskell one of Labour's main electoral assets.
But should a Labour Party be so dependent on a single man?[40]

On the other side of the political fence the same note was sounded. In his huge postbag before Brighton was a letter from a Hertfordshire couple:

> We have agreed with your policies, cheered your speeches, admired your fighting spirit, your integrity & courage, your 100% British sanity & common sense.
>
> For two years we have been studying you & after a lifetime of voting Tory my husband & I decide you are the leader for us. You have our trust & vote of confidence as long as you & your policies lead the Labour Party.
>
> Keep us out of the Common Market & you will also earn our deep & abiding love, loyalty & gratitude.[41]

Four months later, in an obituary, a Conservative journalist and MP wrote of Gaitskell's new authority within the Labour Party – and beyond:

> His ascendancy was complete and overwhelming. Probably no Party leader since Parnell has enjoyed [such] unquestioning dominance ...
>
> It was [his] readiness to look at England's difficulties from the viewpoint of what should be done, rather than the viewpoint of 'How can we cash in on them' that has lifted him to the level of Downing Street.
>
> For this fact about his personality has gradually become plainer and plainer to the British people ...
>
> Over the last year or two his House of Commons stature has grown month by month. He never talked clap-trap ... [He] looked, sounded and was set to be the Prime Minister of England.[42]

But that was not to be.

iii 'The Abominable Virus'

When Gaitskell became leader, Dalton urged him to limit his engagements ('the comrades will kill you if they can');[43] and others kept repeating that advice. Gaitskell ignored it, telling everyone that he had the constitution of an ox.[44] To his frenetic pace of work he added an active social life. Then, when his leadership was challenged, he found that in personal contact with an audience he could dispel the hostile picture spread by his enemies and so make a major impact.[9b] But in 1962, after the challenge was over, he did not relax his pace.

Some time before, Gaitskell had suffered from rheumatic pains in his shoulder, supposedly strained while playing tennis. He had physiotherapy at Manor House, the trade union hospital at Golders Green, and seemed to respond; his electrocardiogram was remarkably normal for a man who had once suffered a coronary.[45] But the symptoms now returned; he took to wearing a bangle about which his colleagues teased him, and he became cautious about digging in the garden.[46] On 13 June 1962 he went to Battersea Park to record for the film cameras his opening of the Festival of Labour. When his remarks were played back to him, he protested that that was not what he had recorded and—though everyone else assured him it was—he insisted on a retake. Feeling ill, he sat in his car for some time, and eventually alarmed his companions by driving himself back to Westminster. He had momentarily blacked out, without losing his vision. He would allow no one at all to be told, least of all his wife. His colleagues worried at the strain it showed, though it was six months before they guessed its seriousness.[47]

Very few people knew of that episode, but his weariness that summer was obvious to his friends.[48] After one poor speech in the House, Alice Bacon took his diary and crossed out all the trivial engagements.[13a] At last, too late, he made a real effort—itself a sign that he was feeling the strain—to reduce his load. He apologised to an MP for not attending an annual constituency dinner: 'I feel not only that I get hardly any rest at all but that there is so little time to do serious reading and thinking.'[49] Even so, during 1962 he worked on two weekends out of three.[50]

By the autumn the shoulder pains were bad enough to make him try to avoid driving his car; and by the end of the session, policemen and secretaries around the House—as well as political friends—were saying that he was looking unwell.[51] At his last dinner party at home on 7 December, he said that he had 'to be careful with his diet that evening as he had picked up something in Paris'.[33b] But no one imagined it was anything serious. Dora kept pressing him to see a doctor, which he had not done for years (he had no regular GP). But he refused until the House rose on 14 December.

The following day, feeling quite ill with some tiresome kind of flu, he went into Manor House hospital—partly out of loyalty, partly because, knowing its head Sir John Nicholson, he expected to get much of his own way. Colleagues and friends came in such a steady stream that he might as well have been in his room in the House.[52] He asked Alice Bacon to take some Christmas presents to the Murrays and Gillinsons and Goodwills in Leeds—particularly asking her to visit each house and tell them how he was. Afterwards she thought that he must have been worried about himself, but only George Brown already suspected something seriously wrong.[13a b] 'They treat me like a piece of ancient porcelain,' Gaitskell wrote to Sir Tom Williamson;[53] and he told Alice Bacon: 'You know, I'm an interesting case. They are quite puzzled about me.'[13a] After a few days' rest he felt much better and became an impatient patient, insisting on spending

Christmas at home. On 21 December he was writing to friends that he would go to Russia as planned on New Year's Day.[54]

The doctors were not happy about his blood tests but had no adequate grounds to keep him in hospital, though he was told he must rest at home.[55] On 23 December he was discharged, and phoned friends saying he was fine and sounding it;[7] but Percy Clark, the Transport House publicity officer, was very worried by his appearance, and once home he felt ill again. A few days later he very apologetically phoned John Harris, who was to have come on the Moscow visit, to postpone it and cancel plans to tour Lancashire in January.[52] On new year's eve, feeling better, he wrote several more cheerful letters: 'I am now recovering very well from the second go, although everybody says I have to be rather careful for some time yet.'[56] Already he was thinking of rearranging the Russian trip. But visitors to Frognal Gardens were shocked to see how he looked and how hard he found it even to cross the room.[8] Four days later the illness was back in full force, and he entered the Middlesex Hospital – which the Manor House doctors felt would be quieter – in a room recently occupied by Sir Winston Churchill.

Though he had quite acute symptoms of both pleurisy and pericarditis, there was as yet no public anxiety. The catastrophe came suddenly, and the doctors, especially at Manor House, were much criticised later. But among those taking the early decisions were consultants equally involved later on, and the rare disease Gaitskell had was at that time very obscure indeed, though more has become known about it since.[57]

Lupus erythematosus is an immunological disease, in which a variety of tissues may be damaged by antibodies circulating in the blood. It can follow a mild and relatively minor course, but the systemic form which Gaitskell suffered was then incurable, though it does not often spread so rapidly. Its cause is unknown, and he could not have 'picked it up', as friends believed, in India or Warsaw or Paris.* But there is some recent evidence of a possible association with viral infection;[59] and it might have been activated by bringing home some other infectious disease. Lupus is not hereditary, though it sometimes affects siblings. It was so little known then that GPs and even hospital doctors might have dealt with only two or three cases in a lifetime. Moreover, Gaitskell was a most unlikely victim, for it is even more unusual among males, and in his age group: at

* Nor could it have been induced, as the security services suspected at one point, by his being given a drug while he was in Poland. Almost a year after Hugh's death, they inquired of his brother Arthur and of Dr Walter Somerville, who soon convinced them that there was no question of it. The source of the suspicion was presumably a defector's claim in 1961 that the KGB were planning to kill an opposition leader in the West, later supposed by some CIA officials to have been Gaitskell.[58]

least five-sixths of the known sufferers have been women, and the great majority are under forty. It can lie dormant for years, emerging from time to time in a different organ, or suddenly erupting everywhere as it did with Gaitskell. Since it 'mimics' the characteristic disorders of the particular organ attacked, it is very hard to diagnose in the early stages; the principal study at the time, among patients in New York, found many who had had it for four years – and half a dozen for twenty years – before it was identified.[60] Moreover, pleurisy, pericarditis and unknown fevers appear rarely as the first signs of the disease: only ten times between them out of 200 cases in the New York study.[61] A further complication in Gaitskell's case was the failure of a characteristic laboratory test to detect the 'anti-nuclear factor' – so that even though the doctors quite early suspected systemic lupus erythematosus or something similar, even the post mortem did not clearly establish it.[62] The evidence from the histology a week later convinced most of them, but the absence of that factor still left some minds in doubt.

As soon as he was in the Middlesex, they saw that both his heart and lungs were affected, apparently by a severe virus infection. Dr Somerville called in appropriate specialists, and four senior doctors saw him twice daily over the weekend. For several days there was no significant change and no real anxiety, though there were disturbing signs in the blood. The doctors were still unsure exactly what was wrong; though correctly suspecting a collagen disease, they dared not risk the normal treatment with steroids, fearing that a virus infection would be made worse by such an approach. As medical knowledge then was, probably at best it could only have delayed the inevitable. Gaitskell was already too ill to see anyone but his brother once or twice, and Dora who sat with him constantly. During the next week he became much worse, developing painful ulcers on the tongue and in the bowel, and the doctors tried heavy doses of one antibiotic after another, vainly hoping that one would produce a response.

Gaitskell faced his condition with the greatest courage, mentally coming to attention the moment he was roused, organising his thoughts clearly, asking sensible questions and firmly telling the doctors to do whatever they thought best – provided they let him know why. But he suffered from insomnia, and he was generally listless and rambling; he recalled popular songs of his childhood, had dreams and saw quite agreeable 'apparitions' (such as a Canaletto on the opposite wall);[63] and regretted a missed opportunity to meet Conor Cruise O'Brien whom he felt he had badly misjudged. By Wednesday 16 January, the doctors' anxiety was acute. The bulletins spoke of installing an artificial kidney; twenty people offered their own, including constituents grateful for past help.[64] The surgery was done next day, but the disease was now rampant, attacking every critical organ at once. On the Friday evening he collapsed, suffering from extreme pulmonary congestion. He died at 9.10 p.m.

The sense of shock was profound. He was only fifty-six. Within the previous year he had become accepted by the public as the right and inevitable next Prime Minister—and, more recently, as indispensable to a Labour Treasury bench which was being called 'a one-man band'. Only for a month had they had any idea that he was unwell; and for less than a week that it was serious. The grief was deep and general and lasting. The tributes poured in from all over the world, from the unknown as well as the famous. An unemotional political colleague reported Labour Party workers weeping that night in a West Country committee room; a young left-wing student was surprised and impressed to see tears flowing in the West Riding working-class pub where he heard the news.[65] In the constituency, Holbeck parish church was packed for the memorial service on a very bleak January evening, but the reporter at the door soon stopped taking names like 'Mr Jones, he were a right good friend to me', or 'Mrs Smith, he helped me through a bit of trouble'. They had no news value, for they were not public men paying formal respects, but obscure neighbours saying goodbye to a friend.[66]

To those who had worked closely with Gaitskell the loss went deep, like the unexpected and premature death of a parent. For a generation of politically-minded progressive people, most of whom had not known him personally—teachers, journalists, trade unionists, civil servants—an inspiration went out of public life which has yet to be renewed. That feeling was not confined to Britain. Some American liberals felt the loss more than the death of any public figure since Roosevelt. Barbara Castle, in Cairo, found every bazaar-keeper next morning wanting to commiserate, not formally but with genuine grief.[67] At home, opponents sensed it too. At Bristol, Iain Macleod stopped a dispersing Conservative audience to be told the news, hear a brief tribute and stand in silence: 'I was surprised to find … later how moved I had been.'[35b] In a generous gesture, Harold Macmillan moved the adjournment of the House of Commons—for the first and only time for an Opposition leader who had never been Prime Minister. It expressed the feeling of the country at the time. For many people years afterwards, the sense of loss has not diminished.

EPILOGUE

'No man is irreplaceable, but some men are unforgettable'
(SENATOR HUBERT HUMPHREY ON HG)

CHAPTER 27

THE LAST IRONY

'He was potentially a world statesman, he had that quality of leadership ... a man of total honesty, dogged bravery and iron will'
(ANTHONY CROSLAND'S BROADCAST OBITUARY)

THE poignancy was sharp. At fifty-six neither Churchill nor Attlee, neither Gladstone nor Disraeli had yet been Prime Minister. Gaitskell had served only a year in a prominent Government post, far less than Aneurin Bevan or Iain Macleod, John or Robert Kennedy. He was best known as Leader of the Opposition, a role in which he was not altogether at home. In the immediate outpouring of grief at his death, a Tory journalist wrote of it as Britain's 'most grievous loss of an individual – statesman, scientist, artist or administrator – since the end of World war II'.[1] Labour colleagues like Denis Healey and Anthony Crosland saw their leader developing into 'one of the half dozen greatest statesmen of the world this century'.[2a b] The sense of loss was lasting. Among his immediate political followers Gaitskell has remained an inspiration for over fifteen years, longer than almost any other politician this century. Beyond their ranks he is still admired and missed by people of different views and backgrounds, not only in Britain. Even before he had led a government, said Senator Hubert Humphrey, Gaitskell 'became the conscience of the Western world'.[3a b]

i   Retrospect: The Road to Leadership

Gaitskell represented a fairly new type of Labour politician: neither a carrier of the aspirations and frustrations of the working-class majority of the Movement, nor a resentful bourgeois in revolt against class or family. In early life he saw little of his parents, but was neither an unhappy child nor an adolescent rebel. As a young man he repudiated the pressures for external conformity that Winchester imposed, but its basic values had marked his character. His personality flowered at Oxford, but his emancipation was slow to take a political turn. In the General Strike he chose his side out of compassion for the underdog; and then went to teach unemployed miners at Nottingham, whose sufferings he never forgot. Those emotional sympathies were underpinned by intellectual exasperation at needless waste, making him as keen to find effective remedies for real social evils, and as impatient with gestures of impotent protest, as the most hard-headed trade unionist.

Gaitskell was immunised early on against the temptations of purism and irresponsibility which beset inexperienced movements of revolt. The General Strike and then the brutal Viennese repression showed him the danger of playing with revolutionary fire. For the syndicalist myth and the Austro-Marxist tradition had inspired no plans to organise revolution (if they had, the attempts would have failed disastrously). But they had inhibited believers from a realistic appraisal of their own circumstances; and Gaitskell never forgot the terrible consequences for innocent human beings as well as cherished causes. He also learned from Vienna and Munich the price of leaving thugs to monopolise the use of force, and became for life a staunch defender of collective security who could never escape into pacifism. Though never so alarmist as to equate the Russian rulers with the Nazis, and always alert to signs of change in the Communist world, he remained deeply suspicious of Soviet intentions.

The 1930s gave him also his horror of mass unemployment, his commitment to full employment as the primary economic objective, and his faith in Keynesian solutions. (But while he did not question them intellectually, politically he was among the few men of the Left who consistently warned that uncontrolled inflation could undermine prosperity.) His banner was Conscience and Reform, not class struggle. He saw collective action as a means to redress social injustices and to secure for all the opportunities already enjoyed by a minority. He appealed to feelings of equity and compassion, not militancy and greed; like Aneurin Bevan, he would have seen nothing socialist about working-class taxpayers who resented people on social security, or publicity-seeking leaders of middle-class trade unions who aggressively demanded more for their prosperous membership.

A believer in the primacy of private life and personal relations, he looked forward to no collectivist utopia. He gave high priority to securing effective government management of the economy, and regarded public ownership as an instrument not a goal. Where it was relevant, he was keen to use it and believed the voters could readily be persuaded: not elsewhere. A democratic Socialist, convinced that revolutionary dictatorships corrupt Socialist aims, he accepted the constraints upon the pace and scope of change required to convince the electorate — and keep it convinced.

Munich taught him another lesson. Some of his closest friends supported it out of hatred of war, and many right-wing Tories — whom he had deeply distrusted — detested it as much as he did. Opponents, he concluded, were sometimes right and colleagues wrong. Never a good hater, always enjoying social life, he later made a few good friends across the party divide. That had no political importance. He began his leadership of the Opposition by outraging upper-class feelings over foreign policy at Suez, and ended it by defying the consensus over the Common Market. His approach to domestic problems had long been firmly set; and though occasionally he might seem to belong to the conspiracy of gentlemen to keep the country on sound lines, his strong streak of populism separated him from the liberal intellectual Establishment as well as from the conservative social one.

Fitting uneasily into any familiar pattern, he seemed unlikely to enjoy a meteoric rise to leadership. In British politics high intelligence has often caused a man to be shunned, not chosen. By 1955 Gaitskell was known as an excellent administrator who had spent less than a year on the back benches, as a Chancellor controversial within his own Party, and as a Front Bench spokesman with no record as a rebel and no evident appeal to the ordinary voter: strange qualifications to attract Labour MPs in opposition, seeking a Moses to regain the Promised Land. Gaitskell's success owed much to luck and more to his rivals. The exhaustion of the previous generation of leaders, after eleven exceptionally gruelling years in office, had opened the way for a younger man. The union potentates, seeking a champion to back against Bevan, welcomed an alternative to Morrison whom they had never trusted on union issues. But it was not just accident that the beneficiary was Gaitskell: his decisiveness over the 1949 devaluation had made him the choice of all his seniors for the Exchequer, and his reckless risking of his career at Stalybridge had brought him the backing of the unions and the leadership of the moderate wing.

Even so, the idea of his supplanting Morrison or Bevan would have seemed ludicrous five years before it happened, and improbable two years before. Both were more experienced and far better known. Neither had as well-trained a mind, but Morrison had great shrewdness, and Bevan a streak of imaginative genius. A party based on the working class might naturally have felt that after twenty years of a public-school leader, his successor should come from a different background. Gaitskell overcame those handicaps because his competitors destroyed themselves. Morrison had made enemies both by ruthless pursuit of narrow objectives and by single-minded ambition; he had failed badly in foreign affairs, and he aged rapidly once out of power. Bevan had convinced his Cabinet colleagues that he was difficult to work with and would be intolerable to serve under. Mistakenly judging the unions to be the decisive arena, he had mortally affronted their leaders without being able to get them replaced. He had neglected and alienated the Labour MPs with whom the choice lay, who feared that he would endanger Labour's chances at the polls, and were convinced by his supreme contempt for them that, should he win, he would ignore the lobby-fodder behind him.

So Gaitskell owed much — including Clem Attlee's somewhat grudging blessing — to good fortune and the blunders of others. But those alone cannot account for the scale of his victory as the only Labour leader ever comfortably elected on the first ballot, with the votes of many former factional opponents. There were also the justified feeling that unlike his rivals Gaitskell learned from his mistakes, and the unfulfilled hope that choosing the youngest man would settle the succession for twenty years and so ensure Party unity.

ii *A Man of Government Frustrated*

At first, both the feeling and the hope seemed to be justified. From 1951 to 1955, while by no means engaged in continuous warfare within the Party, Gaitskell always assumed that the Left must be defeated if Labour were to regain power: the battles were intermittent — the Budget, Stalybridge, German rearmament, the foolish attempt to expel Bevan — but the priority was constant. In 1955 he revised it. Beginning as a tactical move to benefit from Bevanite divisions, his rapprochement with Wilson and Crossman was quickly extended in 1956 to Bevan himself. Elected as a conciliator, throughout his first Parliament as leader Gaitskell sought not confrontations but Party unity, and came as close to attaining it as Labour ever can.

He found that it was not enough. In 1959 a united Party went down to its heaviest post-war defeat, and its leader concluded that if Labour was to survive as a potential government it must adapt to uncomfortable realities. At once the hope of a generation of unity under an accepted leadership was dissipated as Gaitskell's few perpetual enemies were reinforced by those who turned against the policies when the opportunity arose to upset the man. But no sooner had the ensuing battles brought the Party back to the threshold of power than Gaitskell promptly resumed his efforts to come to terms with his critics.

The perspective of history does more than his foibles of personality to explain why his career was stormy. Like most men who have reached the top rank in British politics, and like almost all who have left a memorable reputation, he was both a conciliator and a confronter at different stages of his life. After four years of successfully playing Attlee's role, he seemed in 1959 to resume the combative stance which is usually thought to characterise him. Yet neither his past nor his future conduct was provocative by normal political standards. In 1951 he had underestimated the disruption which a difficult Minister could cause once out of office; but so had Bevan's other exasperated colleagues, like those of Joseph Chamberlain and Lloyd George before them. If overruled then, Gaitskell would have resigned (though without trying to split the Party); but most future Prime Ministers have taken such a stand at some point — all but three out

of the eleven in the last half-century.*In his factional battles over the next
four years Gaitskell also had many predecessors among ex-Ministers who,
once out of office, found their commitments and assumptions challenged
by more partisan colleagues.**

Once chosen as Labour's leader, and therefore Britain's alternative
Prime Minister, Gaitskell was on approval before both party and country;
alone among Labour leaders, he remained so to the end of his life.†
Each of the rest served eventually in Downing Street, and spent his tenure
of the leadership mainly as Premier, ex-Premier or Deputy Premier;††
so did every Conservative leader in the forty years before Gaitskell's
death. Alone among his peers, Gaitskell never won gratitude in his Party
by bringing it to power, earned prestige in the country by identifying its
rule with his personality, or based his reputation on his achievements in
government. Alone, he is judged entirely on his performance in a different
role, and not the one for which he was best fitted.

After Labour lost in 1959, Gaitskell like any defeated Party leader had
to struggle for survival against his own followers – and from a uniquely
weak position as the only Labour leader (and almost the only leader of
any Party) to lose his first election while still on approval in the
post.§ That occupational hazard operates differently in the major parties,
like the contrast drawn in Fisher Ames's eighteenth-century simile:
'Monarchy is like a splendid ship, with all sails set; it moves majestically on,
then hits a rock and sinks for ever. Democracy is like a raft; it never sinks,
but damn it, your feet are always in the water.' The leaders driven out
have all been Conservatives – in 1911, 1965 and 1975.§§ But Labour
ex-Premiers in defeat have also had a very uncomfortable time.¶ Without

* Neville Chamberlain, Attlee and Home. MacDonald resigned from the
Party leadership, Eden and Wilson from the Cabinet; Baldwin rebelled in 1922,
Churchill and Macmillan throughout the 1930s; Heath offended his followers
over resale price maintenance (and might have ruined himself over the Market);
Callaghan courted dismissal over trade union legislation. (Written in 1978.)

** Liberal Imperialists before 1906, Coalition Unionists after 1922, Dalton and
Morrison after 1931, Heathmen after 1974.

† Leaders before 1922, and from 1931 to 1935, were not alternative Prime
Ministers.

†† MacDonald 7 years out of 9, Attlee 15 out of 20, Wilson 11 out of 13,
Callaghan the whole.

§ The only Tory to do so since 1922 was Heath, whose defeat after only
seven months as leader was not held against him.

§§ But for Joseph Chamberlain's stroke Balfour might well have gone five
years before 1911; and Baldwin almost fell in 1930.

¶ MacDonald was irreplaceable but most unpopular after 1924; Attlee gave
no lead, yet almost had to resign in 1954; Wilson escaped challenge after 1970
by abandoning his major policies.

enjoying their prestige, Gaitskell nevertheless survived more nearly on his own terms than they were able to do.

The cost for the Party was heavy, but in the long run unavoidable. Most British party leaders have had trouble trying to reconcile the demands of the faithful with the need to adapt their party to social change. Peel succeeded after 1832 and failed in 1846; Disraeli overthrew him then but emulated him later, after twenty years of purity in the wilderness had given the Tories a lasting preference for office even at the price of compromise. Only Lloyd George repudiated party blatantly and never recovered; even Churchill learned that lesson and returned in the end to the Tory communion—and, in 1951, to office. But that success was due to R. A. Butler modernising a party desperate to regain and retain power.

It was Butler's and not Churchill's style of Conservatism which characterised their rule, presenting Labour with a difficult problem instead of the easy target many of its leaders had expected. Gaitskell never had. He applied himself to the harder task, circumspectly up to the 1959 defeat, rashly afterwards. In riding the storm which then buffeted him as defeated Opposition leader, he acquired for himself and bequeathed to his successor a new freedom of action. But even that successor, with his strong inherited position and his innate preference for compromise, was before long to find himself in disagreement with most of his followers, and preserved his position only by bending before the storm—with long-term consequences which are still developing.

In response to Macmillan's 1959 triumph, Gaitskell made a different choice—and badly mishandled it. Labour will ultimately have to decide whether it stands for democratic Socialism and the mixed economy, or for total nationalisation as its overriding priority. But in posing the question in that way at that moment, Gaitskell misjudged the mood—failing for understandable reasons to realise that his own influence would be impaired by the 1959 defeat. He misjudged the target, underestimating both the resistance to revising formal doctrine and the damage to his own position if he failed. And he misjudged the timing, twice leaving his critics to make all the running. Driven into a confrontation he had not sought but ought to have foreseen, he soon found he had weakened himself against a really dangerous attack.

Though powerful voices claimed it too was unnecessary, Gaitskell was justified in feeling that the unilateralist controversy had to be fought out. Early in 1960 he was insensitive to changing moods and inflexible over minor details; but when the conflict reached its height in the summer, he rightly saw that further concession would not only lead to a vulnerable defence policy, but would also weaken the morale of his supporters, the standing of the Party and the authority of its leader. As soon as the foundation for Labour's recovery had been laid by restoring that authority,

Gaitskell reverted at once to conciliation. He worked again with the colleagues who had been trying to supplant him, though he never trusted them as he had before 1959.

With his followers the change was more striking. He had always treated them seriously, never regarding Conference as a mere nuisance to be flattered, by-passed and ignored; not even as a curious anomaly to be kept in line by manipulating the block vote (though like his critics he did his share of that); but mainly as an awkward yet adult body to be persuaded by serious argument on real issues. Now at Brighton in 1962, he was at last discovering also how to evoke from it an enthusiastic emotional response.

Although he became impressive at leading the Opposition, it was never Gaitskell's metier. Loathing instant politics and quick decisions based on inadequate information, he was not adroit at seizing tactical opportunities. That weakness was compounded by his reluctance to change his mind and by his concern for consistency. He would not propose in opposition policies he could not carry out in government. He was hampered as a critic by temperamental sympathy for the men in power; thinking always how he would handle their problem, he was quicker to sympathise with their difficulties than to exploit these for his own advantage. Macmillan in a parliamentary obituary of him spoke of the opposition leader as 'a partner and even a buttress' to the government in times of national crisis; earlier, he had mocked Gaitskell as missing the fun of opposition by trying to behave like a government when he wasn't one.[4] (When Attlee was Premier, nobody could have accused Macmillan of that.) But as an educated electorate becomes bored with the party dogfight, an opposition leader who tries to act responsibly may hope to reap a reward later on. Gaitskell showed that a restrained and sober style can do more than virulent polemic to earn the reputation of a potential leader of the nation.

By the time of his death Gaitskell had acquired that reputation. In his first Parliament as Labour leader, he was generally seen as a mere party man – and by Suez enthusiasts as an unprincipled and dangerous one. His public breakthrough began with the 1959 campaign and particularly his dignified concession at the end; it was achieved by his fight to reverse the Scarborough decision on defence. That was not because the Establishment applauded his struggle – for with equal unanimity they condemned his attitude to the Common Market. It was partly because national defence is a sensitive subject, on which the average voter feels that leaders who seek to govern should resist pressure from people without responsibility. Above all it was because Gaitskell put the national interest as he saw it before his own career or the demands of political convenience. By winning that battle he proved himself a strong leader; by engaging in it at all, he demonstrated that he would show in a crisis both high courage and a sense of national duty. The political activist, especially on the Left, often judges leaders by their professed ideology and falls easy prey to calculated rhetoric. But the ordinary voter, less concerned about their views on specific issues, judges on character instead: very wisely, for Ministers must govern and not just legislate, and character is the only guide to how a man will deal with the unpredictable situations which will face him in power.

Within the Party Gaitskell's opponents remained resentful and suspicious. But he was glad to seize the opportunity of reconciliation with them afforded by Macmillan's handling of the Common Market issue. He adopted his policy because of his own convictions and commitments, but in his presentation of it he sought both to underline his independence as leader, and to win over those critics who were willing to bury the hatchet. A few months earlier he had described the need to satisfy the demands of both the activists and the unpolitical voters as 'the greatest challenge to leadership ... because the enthusiasm is no good without the votes and the votes are not much good without the enthusiasm'.[5a] Now in late 1962, as *The Times* political correspondent put it, he was coming to terms with the Labour Party.[6] At that very moment the opinion polls showed him coming to terms with the wider electorate also. By a tragic irony, the rare and mysterious disease struck precisely when he was at last resolving his central political dilemma as leader of the Party.

iii   *A Controversial Personality*

Gaitskell was resolving his personal dilemmas, too. His personality was full of apparent contradictions. In private life he was gregarious and warm-hearted, impressing those he met with his modesty and his interest in other people; but it was not until late in life that he shook off the absurd carica-ture of the desiccated calculating machine. He was an excellent listener in a profession where they do not abound; but once he had made up his mind he could be infuriatingly stubborn over petty details. For one observer he would analyse appreciatively the strengths and qualities of a bitter political opponent, and explain the conduct of another most charitably; but other people found him touchy, quick to take criticism as a personal affront, and without much understanding for young idealists as inexperienced as he had once been. In his early revolt against the inhibitions of the public-school regime, he was ardent in praise of spontaneity; but in his later years his friends sometimes found him both wary and testy (and once, though only once, felt he had seriously misled them). Thorough, cautious and slow to form his opinions, he was bold and even reckless in advocating them; judicious in weighing the balance of opposing arguments, he committed himself totally to the side he finally espoused; skilful and conciliatory in seeking consensus, he was so combative in a corner that he won the reputation of provoking confrontations; a devotee of reason and enemy of extremism, he defended moderate views with intense passion.

These contrasts led to his being misrepresented by his opponents, misunderstood by the public, and sometimes misjudged by his colleagues. Kenneth Younger, an old critic who by 1955 felt that Gaitskell was the only possible Labour leader, saw his contest with Bevan as a clash of Roundhead and Cavalier. For Gaitskell was, in his daughter's phrase, 'a conscious puritan of the intellect'; and his political style relied upon meticulous preparation and disciplined teamwork where Bevan displayed a Rupert-like impetuosity. But Younger's summary interpretation missed Gaitskell's own Cavalier qualities: the hedonism and libertarianism of the private man, the gambler's streak shown both in some everyday matters and at moments of crisis in the life of the public figure. Indeed he displayed both sets of qualities. He was dedicated to intellectual consistency and integrity, and stubborn about his own point of view. Yet he also saw politics as an activity requiring organisation, co-operation, and mutual accommodation, calling for both loyalty in individuals and solidarity in a team.

Those conflicting commitments were reflected in his own behaviour. Convinced that effective political action required strong, disciplined parties, he was normally punctilious about consulting the appropriate colleagues over policy. Yet at several turning points in his life he acted entirely alone, without support from his closest friends and sometimes defying their advice: over the 1951 Budget, the Stalybridge speech, Clause Four, the Common Market. In his obituary on R. H. Tawney, whom he so greatly admired, Gaitskell wrote of his friend's combination of strength and humility in terms which applied equally to his own character: 'He never hesitated to lay down the law ... [but] he never thought of himself in his heart as above or better than other people.'[7] For the genuine modesty of manner co-existed with an extraordinary self-assurance;[8] and in a crisis Gaitskell would suddenly demonstrate boundless confidence in his own judgment and his own star.

That strength of will and self-assurance reinforced a highly intelligent and reasoned outlook on public affairs. In 1959 he told Henry Fairlie: 'I am a rationalist ... I do not like to think that [people] vote as they do because something appeals to their subconscious.'[9] That approach was basic to his political style almost throughout his life, and was both his principal strength and his principal weakness in projecting his own appeal and that of his Party. In some quarters it won solid support founded on understanding, but it quite failed to arouse or excite others, and it left some potent weapons in the political armoury to his opponents—Labour ones as well as Conservatives. It attracted the loyalty and enthusiasm of people who shared his own cast of mind, but it seemed cold to more emotional and passionate types, and even unfeeling to the unperceptive or the prejudiced. Notable among twentieth-century politicians for his lucid and candid public statements, Gaitskell was equally notable for the frequency with which he was misunderstood, especially but not only on the Left — for whom he was neither protected by the prestige attaching to the leaders of 1945, nor recognised as the emotional man he was because he and they were often emotional about different objects.

Gaitskell was a communicator by profession whose meaning was repeatedly mistaken — over his first Suez speech, Clause Four, the British bomb, the Scarborough peroration. Yet far from being to blame for carelessness of expression, he exasperated all his associates by constantly polishing every draft and speech. Much of the confusion was due to unconscious or deliberate misrepresentation by his various enemies, and more to journalistic over-simplification which afforded opportunities for misunderstanding that his detractors eagerly grasped; for, being no phrase-maker, he saw his utterances as a whole, whereas the audience tended to fasten on a headline comparing Nasser to Hitler, or a reference to fellow-travellers in CND, and to forget everything else.

His speeches relied on logical organisation of the argument rather than on colourful wording to tickle the emotional palate. They were based on carefully gathered information, thorough analysis and a persuasive deployment of his case. There is rarely anything in them to haunt the memory, but read in retrospect they show an impressively detailed and realistic grasp of a wide variety of subjects, with little mere point-scoring. They meet in advance many common objections to his views: his Suez policy did not rest on a naive confidence in the United Nations, or his opposition to joining the EEC on seeing the Commonwealth as a permanent alternative, or his criticism of immigration controls on any commitment to the open door for ever. Yet in the rough and tumble of controversy, even attentive observers easily missed far-sighted qualifications about possible future changes modifying his position. Clarity and foresight and candour did not always ensure even that his meaning was fully grasped; and it was only towards the end that he appealed to the emotions as well as the intelligence. For most of his life he was a teacher not an orator, strong on rational argument rather than moralising fervour, speaking to the mind rather than to the heart.

His private warmth was not always appreciated. He was genuinely interested in the feelings of others. But he took on far too much and left himself too little time to reflect and relax; and he could occasionally behave as insensitively as Attlee did habitually. (Being unexpected, it was held against Gaitskell — whereas in his predecessor it was taken for granted and not resented.) More seriously, he was often misunderstood because his own rationalism made him misjudge the irrational responses of others. Far better equipped for national leadership than most men in the front rank of recent British politics, he was not an ideal Party leader in opposition, since his antennae were not finely tuned. He was generally shrewd about the long-term preferences of the British people, but less clear-sighted about their spontaneous outbursts of emotion. He failed to foresee the patriotic reflex when the troops went ashore at Port Said. He knew that elderly trade unionists no longer believed in nationalising all the means of production, distribution and exchange – and so was taken aback when they clung to Clause Four which symbolised the dreams of their radical youth. He was irritated by the emotionalism, born of desperate worry about nuclear war, which channelled all the fears and frustrations of a generation into CND. He recognised but never comprehended the distant vision of the enthusiastic Europeans, who believed they must seize a unique opportunity for practical internationalism.

That approach, and those failures, help to explain why for so long his personality was not easily projected. They were failures of imagination, not of conviction. Contrary to the legend spread by his opponents late in 1959, Gaitskell was no trimmer. The middle of the road appealed to his reason, but half-measures were alien to his temperament: over Munich, the blockade, nationalisation, devaluation, 'responsible finance', rearmament, Suez, the American alliance, the Commonwealth Immigration Act, the Common Market. Especially in his last few years, his appeals were delivered with a force and passion which bred misunderstanding. For with Labour in opposition the impact of the wholehearted final commitment led commentators to look only at the direction in which he was leading his followers. Had he been in office they would have had to attend also to the careful, balanced assessment which preceded decision, and on which the policy would depend. But the capacity to evoke so stirring an emotional response developed too late in Gaitskell's short life to help propel him and his cause to power.

Part of his problem was that many of his followers were ambivalent about power. Comfortable middle-class idealists without responsibility find it easy to keep their consciences spotless, preaching principle in the wilderness, while the price is paid by poorer people whose grievances go unheard by the men in government; yet the professional politician who rationalises his conduct by that legitimate argument, comes easily to pursue power so single-mindedly that he forgets or compromises away his original aims. Gaitskell never did that. But many Labour people were misled by their historic suspicion that insistence on workable policies, and on getting into government so as to apply them, is only a convenient screen behind which careerists without principles can manoeuvre. The brilliant cartoonist Vicky shared and spread a grotesque illusion in portraying Gaitskell as a politician eager to win votes by any means, and power without caring how to use it. But few of those who met him or heard him speak were deceived by that caricature. For while he was not a man to keep digging up his philosophy to investigate its roots, his principles were firmly fixed; and he was as determined not to betray them as he was willing to adjust the means of achieving them. He was untainted by the temptations of careerism – and by those of self-righteous and impotent purity.

Where Gaitskell's conduct was ruled by Max Weber's 'ethic of responsibility', many of his followers acted on the alternative 'ethic of ultimate ends'. Often, too, they had a strong propensity to wishful thinking with which he was impatient and scornful. Mutual suspicion and misunderstanding thus grew all too easily. When Clause Four was a sleeping idol, Gaitskell did not anticipate the fury he would arouse by disturbing it. When CND was in full flood, he seemed to its adherents to show scorn for their deep feelings. His own commitments reflected his temperament and preference for clear-cut solutions, together with his strong Wykehamist sense of public duty and of the need for leadership; they earned him at times the bitter dislike of people who violently differed from him or felt misjudged by him. Many Conservatives over Suez, many unilateralists after Scarborough detested him cordially and would never forgive him.

In part, that was simply because people became indignant when he broke the rules by which they had conveniently chosen to assume the game should be played. For Tories, Labour's middle-class moderates were supposed to support the government when it unilaterally proclaimed a national crisis. For the Left, a Labour leader was expected to genuflect before the noble motives of his attackers – not to refer contemptuously to their own calculations and manoeuvres. So on the Right Gaitskell's enemies reviled him for betraying his class and even his country, and on the Left for deserting Socialism and ignoring the horrors of nuclear war. Both sets of bitter critics, hot for action and scornful of compromise, had been led by passionate emotion to clamour for policies whose consequences they did not thoroughly examine. Both were quite annoyed at the cool and critical dissection of those consequences, but absolutely furious at the challenge to their claim to a moral superiority which they took for granted. Their resentments did not vanish when the crisis was past. Instead, wounded self-esteem made people whom he had criticised prone to adopt discreditable interpretations of his words and actions.

In fact Gaitskell was himself a man of powerful passions, but harnessed to realistic objectives. He felt keenly about translating the demands of 'conscience and reform' into practical measures; he had little time for dramatic protests which assuaged the indignation of the demonstrator not the condition of the sufferer. So he looked to a limited horizon, stretching beyond the present but not into the indefinite distance. Never obsessed by the next week's tactical problem (perhaps not enough so), he always sought policies valid for the foreseeable future. But, rightly thinking it unreal to look more than a decade ahead, he did not bother much about what might lie beyond.

That did not make him indifferent to new ideas: for a practising politician he was quite far-sighted in spotting future issues like consumer grievances, environmental problems, changes in youth culture, and even (despite his early disillusionment with syndicalism) looking for practical plans for workers' control. It did not make him a tame devotee of the reigning orthodoxy: he fought the Establishment over Europe as he had fought the predominant views of the 1930s or the Treasury's liberal doctrines in the 1940s. But he was a man of his time and his time was not ours. He was the standard-bearer of Attlee's post-war consensus, labelled and misinterpreted as Butskellism:[10] the mixed economy, the Keynesian strategy, full employment, strong but not overweening trade unions, the welfare state, the Atlantic alliance, decolonisation, and a tacit understanding that governments, whether moderate Conservative or democratic Socialist, would not strain the tolerance of the other side too violently. That legacy makes him a natural hero for social democrats.

When economic decline sapped the foundations of that consensus, Gaitskell the realist would have adjusted accordingly; but like everyone else he failed to foresee its imminence. He was no seer, and he lacked the broad imaginative sweep of General de Gaulle or even Aneurin Bevan. He was a man to handle issues as they arose, to look ahead for forces modifying the existing scene, rather than to try like a Joseph Chamberlain or even a Lloyd George to transform the whole political landscape. But he knew that the politician must work with the materials available and deal as best he can with the current tensions threatening the fabric of society. He would have done so, in office, in a manner to command public confidence: for the qualities in which he excelled were far better deployed in government than in opposition.

Being a man of high moral courage, who chose his course only after careful thought, Gaitskell was most reluctant to change it under pressure. During the bitter quarrel with many of his own side in 1960, a Conservative MP whom he had known since boyhood asked how he could stand the hatred of his assailants; he replied that when he had decided on the right thing to do, he just went ahead and did it without worrying about the criticisms.[11] He would have been a poor politician if he had really worked by that rule all the time, and we have seen that he did not; but he did try harder than most to apply it on matters of major principle, demanding to be convinced by arguments from reason, not expediency.[12] To Gaitskell, that outlook was frequently a short-term handicap. Since his death,

British public life has often shown how in the long run its absence corrodes public respect for politics and trust in politicians.

Partly because of that outlook, even more because of his style of express- ing it, Gaitskell had rarely aroused enthusiasm among the utopians and visionaries who naturally find their home in a party of the Left. Intellectu- ally he knew they were necessary to it, but emotionally he never really appreciated them – still less they him. But in his last few months he was overcoming that weakness too. In 1962, more than ever before, he aroused the enthusiasm of Conference by appealing to its emotions as well as its reason. It was not a political skill which he had previously exhibited. Once he had written, revealingly, that revulsion against exploiting it had inhibited his old mentor Douglas Cole from ever entering electoral politics.[13] Gaitskell's temperament and his whole career suggest that he too felt that distaste, and overcame it only at the end of his life. He was developing to the last: not merely resolving his political problem by finding how to appeal at once to his active followers and to the wider electorate, but also integrating the intellectual and emotional sides of his own character. Only close colleagues, said one of them, fully appreciated 'his extraordinary capacity to learn. He was always widening and deepening his personality as a politician'.[14]

iv   *Prospect: The Government that Never Was*

Friendly or hostile, no one who knew him doubts that Gaitskell was a natural Prime Minister rather than a natural Leader of the Opposition. He would not have continued long in the latter role. Had he lived and lost again in 1964, he would probably have felt obliged to resign the leader- ship without waiting to be repudiated.[15] Had he won with the same tiny majority as Wilson, he would doubtless have handled that difficult situ- ation less well, for day-to-day tactics were not his forte. But probably he would have won that election by a bigger margin. At the time of his death, Labour was at last beginning to run ahead of the Conservatives by attract- ing support on its own account, not just because Tories were defecting to the Liberals. For when the Liberals fell back again in the polls, it was now Labour which sharply improved its position.[16] Gaitskell's personal rating was comfortably ahead of his Party's, and like Harold Wilson he would assuredly have soared much further ahead in 1963. He too would have profited from the collapse of the government's reputation, and would, for the first time against the Prime Minister, have enjoyed extraordinary favour from a Fleet Street furious with Macmillan for having two journal- ists imprisoned over the Vassall case. Wilson was a new face as opposition leader, welcomed by the opinion-makers as the next tenant of No. 10; but

Gaitskell was accepted already in that role, which the good publicity would have consolidated in the public mind. Labour's lead might have slipped in 1964 as the approach of the election drew disillusioned Tories reluctantly back to the fold: but very likely by less than it did, since his reputation as fit for the Premiership was firmly founded at last.

In the 1959 campaign Gaitskell had proved far more formidable than anybody expected; and in 1964 he (like Heath in 1970) would have reaped the benefit of vainly exposing at the previous election the hollowness of the government's boasts of prosperity. Facing Sir Alec Douglas-Home, Gaitskell like Wilson would have been obviously superior on the domestic front; while because of the recent past he would have enjoyed much more confidence than Wilson on the very foreign and defence issues where the new Prime Minister was most credible.*

It is fruitless to imagine how Gaitskell might have acted in a radically different political world; but not absurd to speculate on his handling of problems he already foresaw. Any incoming Prime Minister enjoys good will (and patronage) at Westminster, and a new prestige among his followers in the country. If, as seems likely, he had had a majority of 25 or 40, he would have been able to think strategically, which was both his inclination and his strength.

A Gaitskell government in October 1964 might well have looked quite similar to Wilson's. The latter had inherited and then gave office to the old Shadow Cabinet, few of whom had supported him for the leadership; they were elected by the PLP, and Gaitskell would have selected much the same people, for he thought highly of almost all.[18] Wilson was generous in appointing and later promoting talented Gaitskellites; Gaitskell might have moved them up faster, though in the past he had often treated his friends less well than merit would have dictated.[19] Without sharing Wilson's obsession with the factional balance of his appointments, he would have tried as he did with Cousins to reconcile old opponents – and would have succeeded, for no left-winger but Cousins ever resigned over an act or omission of Wilson's government. Some who stood high in Wilson's confidence thought that they would have had very inferior offers from his predecessor; but those who earned preferment would doubtless not have been denied it on account of the past. Some Ministers who were appointed or survived because of their personal loyalty to the new leader might not have been chosen, and would not have been retained, by the

---

* The electoral conclusions, if not necessarily the arguments, were shared by most politicians of the Labour mainstream, though with several don't knows; and by nearly every Liberal and Conservative asked. Dissenters were almost all from the Labour Left, though a couple of distinguished spokesmen in each of the last two groups disagreed with their fellows.[17]

2C

old one. For Gaitskell would have been as relentless as Attlee in removing dead wood; he could justly claim that fear of having able men around him was not among his faults.[5b]

After thirteen years in opposition few members of the incoming government were familiar with the official machine. Half Wilson's Ministers had never held office; only two – Griffiths and Gordon Walker – had served in a Cabinet.* That situation would have obliged any Prime Minister to play a dominant role, and tempted Gaitskell to intervene too much. Some of his intimate friends doubt whether he would have delegated enough, but his record does not bear them out. Both at Fuel and Power and at the Exchequer he had given responsibility to his juniors; and the love of detail which appalled his civil servants and irritated his opposition colleagues had good reasons then (different in the two cases) which would not have applied in Downing Street. There he would have been both in unquestioned command of an efficient advisory machine which he knew how to use and how to control; and the central figure in a political team where individual reputations depend largely on collective success. Able to delegate more confidently, politically strong and personally secure, he would neither have needed nor hungered for constant public interventions to establish his authority. In one retirement tribute to Attlee, Gaitskell said: 'One of his great qualities was his capacity for devolving work and for trusting his colleagues to get on with the job on their own. This is nowadays almost a "must" for a Prime Minister.' In another, he praised Attlee as a Prime Minister who never tried 'to cut a dash or to make an impression himself. What he was concerned with from start to finish was the success of the team'.[20]

In 1961 and 1962, Gaitskell was looking ahead to the problems of taking office. Conscious of his own limited experience when he became a Minister, he took much trouble to ensure that the leading Shadow Ministers were better prepared.[21] There may have been a 'power book', perhaps similar to the 'war book' in which, before 1914, Whitehall tried to anticipate impending problems.[22] Gaitskell persistently pressed his Shadow Chancellor for studies on the central problems of the economy; and with the help of Desmond Hirshfield and others, he very discreetly compiled a panel of friendly industrialists from whom a Labour government could seek experienced business advice.[23] He had always been keen on relating science to public policy and, on becoming leader in 1956, he had set up an advisory group of quite senior scientists.[24] But he was never at ease with them, and did not trust their political judgment, partly no doubt because so many of them were left-wing unilateralists.[25] They felt (correctly) that he looked to them for specialist advice, not to run the country; and in November

* In the Cabinet of 23, nine had been junior ministers, one a whip, and two PPS.

1962 they protested by collectively threatening to resign.[26] But scientists in whom Gaitskell had confidence, like Zuckerman, would certainly have played a major role.[27]

Gaitskell's main priority as Prime Minister would have been to tackle Britain's long-term economic difficulties: partly because the viability of Labour's programme and the credibility of the government depended upon doing so, mainly because of his long-standing alarm at the gradual decline. He was better equipped to analyse its causes than any post-war Prime Minister, and his solutions would have been radical. Very likely, too, he would have taken early steps to phase out the sterling area as Roy Jenkins, a close friend and probable financial adviser, had long advocated;[28] he was himself an expert on the subject, unsentimental, self-confident, and sceptical of bankers' advice.

To secure a breathing space before slow-acting measures could affect the major problems of insufficient investment, low productivity and a precarious external balance, he would probably have devalued early.[29] He had been accused a few years earlier of having a penchant for devaluation;[30] and he would no more have seen it as morally iniquitous like Heath, or as politically fatal like Wilson, than as a remedy in itself. Such a decision might have avoided the deep disillusionment of both Labour and uncommitted voters at the mounting unemployment figures. Even the mood of militancy and revolt within the unions might not have developed so fast or so far in a better economic climate, making it easier to act on the long-term problems while they were still relatively manageable.

Gaitskell would have sought the co-operation of the unions through some kind of social contract, while tolerating neither the reality nor the appearance of union dictation. His legendary stubbornness would have been very valuable — perhaps even indispensable — in dealing with the Civil Service; for instance in arguing with the Inland Revenue over tax reform, and in tackling the problem of urban land against the resistance of a formidable Permanent Secretary.

In education, Gaitskell foresaw the danger, which Labour's Secretary of State had himself predicted,[31] that to attack selection for the grammar schools while leaving the public schools alone would end by narrowing the educational ladder and widening the gap between classes. There can be few more striking cases of a policy frustrating its original purposes than that by which the educational egalitarians drove the direct grant schools *en bloc* into the independent sector. Gaitskell would have sought to avoid that by a policy on public schools which might have been contentious. But for the education of the vast majority of schoolchildren his approach could well have proved acceptable to the moderate Conservatives who were then in the ascendant, and might have pointed the way to a stable bipartisan consensus instead of the now familiar sharp lurches in policy and disruption of young lives.[32]

He would probably have retreated on one major domestic issue: coloured immigration. Had Labour continued to oppose all controls, it seems unlikely that it could have won in 1964. Being a very stubborn man, especially where he saw a principle at stake, Gaitskell would have been reluctant and slow to move. But his principle was not unconditional free entry, which he had never endorsed and for which he would not have been likely to risk all his other aims. He would have preferred defeat to accepting a colour bar;* but he probably would have accepted controls on entry, compensating by early and effective measures to require equal treatment for coloured people already here, and by special treatment in housing for the areas most affected.

In the defence field he would not have evaded a difficult choice by trying to preserve both a frontier on the Himalayas and an expenditure ceiling incompatible with it.** Having in 1957 presciently condemned Western military intervention against popular left-wing movements in Asia, and reaffirmed that view over Laos in the spring of 1962, it is plain that he would have disapproved of American policy in Vietnam. If any foreign advice could get a hearing in Washington, or among the American public, Gaitskell's—coming from a proven friend who had risked his political life for the Atlantic alliance—had the best chance; a number of politically experienced Americans even thought that President Johnson would have listened to him.[3b] But he would never have reaped an easy harvest of left-wing cheers by strident denunciation of US imperialism (as General de Gaulle did, while escaping all publicity or opprobrium for his own imperialist activities in sub-Saharan Africa). In this area the Left would have been less tolerant of Gaitskell than of Wilson, with his odd reputation as one of themselves.

The most speculative question of all is the Common Market. Gaitskell would have been reluctant to change his mind, but he would have followed carefully all new developments in Britain and throughout the world. With his cosmopolitan tastes and sympathies—so different from many of his friends and early mentors—he was not in the least vulnerable to the charge of Little Englander insularity. In time, all but one of the other pragmatists of Labour's Right and Centre came round to support entry; perhaps he

* His widow in the Lords, and some of his prominent back-bench admirers in the Commons, voted against excluding the Kenya Asians in 1968.

** For a strong British presence east of Suez were the Malayan and Singapore governments (and the United States); for withdrawal, Woodrow Wyatt, a likely Gaitskell defence Minister; for decision one way or the other, Christopher Mayhew, a Wilson Minister who resigned over it.

would have done so too. If so, he would not have switched back in opposition.

Curiously, the Left would have preferred Gaitskell on the point of external policy where he would most certainly have differed from Wilson. He never thought that the Rhodesian settlers would be amenable to mere persuasion. Long before David Owen and Andrew Young, he talked of buying them out as the likeliest solution. But he also thought pressure would be needed, and said twice – once just before the 1959 election and again late in 1962 – that his very first act on arriving in Downing Street would be to move troops to Lusaka.[33] His policy might have led to early violence and a 'left-wing Suez'; it might have avoided a bloodier confrontation later on; it would unquestionably have changed the history of Southern Africa for good or ill.

There may be some exaggeration in the common assumption that a Gaitskell Government would have faced endless harassment from the Left. First, any Labour Prime Minister before the 1970s could – patronage apart – count on intense loyalty from the rank and file both in and out of Parliament. Secondly, Gaitskell was acutely conscious that back-bench opinion could be 'extremely powerful' and that if Ministers took its unconditional support for granted, the results could be disastrous.[5c] Finally, office transforms political attitudes both to men and to issues. In opposition, Labour leaders are assessed by their rhetoric; the Left is very credulous about those who strike its cherished emotional notes and very suspicious of those who do not. Within six weeks of Gaitskell's death his successor was making speeches which 'religiously copied out the Party policy' but, as Wilson's ally Crossman wrote, 'sounded astonishingly left wing ... no one had any idea until that weekend that the Labour Party had quite radical policies on every subject under the sun'.[34] Similarly, an American academic interviewer found that just before Gaitskell's death Labour activists were critical of the presentation of policies rather than the content, and that just after it they would say: 'Now that Wilson is leader, I'm satisfied with the policies as they are.'[35]

In government, those people would have worried less about how policies were advertised and more about whether they were implemented. They would have recognised the importance of problems like the exchange rate, which had no ideological significance and so were wholly ignored in opposition. Thus Wilson's government went through many crises, but they rarely aligned Left against Right and frequently found Gaitskellites and left-wingers combining against the pragmatists of the Centre. Wilson's past had given him a left-wing reputation (though not among Gaitskellites) which enabled him to pursue unexpectedly cautious policies with relative impunity; conversely Gaitskell might have benefited from taking action much more radical than the critics had anticipated. In that wholly different climate, the man who had aroused less sweeping hopes might well have fulfilled more of them, and left much less disillusionment behind.

v *The Promise Unfulfilled*

Outside Labour's ranks, Gaitskell on taking office would have been recognised as a potential leader of the nation. Some Conservative good will would have vanished as they found him more of a Socialist than their own myth had painted him; Rhodesia would have brought him real hatred from the far Right (incidentally helping him with his own back-benchers). But moderate Conservatives would have opposed in the same spirit as Gaitskell himself had done. To Liberals, he would have appealed more than most other Labour leaders: more than Attlee because there were few radical Liberals in 1945-51, more than Wilson because of his record and his less partisan style.* Had his economic management proved successful, he would have attracted uncommitted voters too, and changed the face of British politics. For the kind of practical undoctrinaire Socialism which Gaitskell proposed – the tradition of 'conscience and reform' – has a strong appeal in a country which has hardly ever given a majority of votes to a Conservative Party undisguised. He believed that a Labour Party which followed that tradition, seeking real solutions to real problems, would by adhering to its own principles and not by compromising them establish itself as Britain's natural party of government.

Harold Wilson also wanted to make Labour the natural party of government, and also believed it could be done only in office. Many of their policies might have been similar, but their style was quite different. In 1957 Wilson is said to have told a Tory editor that Macmillan was 'a genius ... holding up the banner of Suez ... [while] leading the Party away from Suez. That's what I'd like to do with the Labour Party over nationalisation'.[37] Gaitskell, however, wrote to a friend in January 1960, about Macmillan's skill at dissembling and his own incapacity for it: 'no doubt in politics the corkscrew is really what you need. It's no use being superior & goody goody about this, when it's really just that you can't do it that way'. If he was sometimes too careless of political constraints, of tactics and timing, yet he was always learning from those mistakes; while the proven commitment to principle convinced opponents as well as friends in the last year or two that he was not just another party politician but a genuine national leader, and led the spokesman of American liberalism to say of him: 'No man is irreplaceable, but some men are unforgettable'.[3a]

A recent American scholar has identified seven qualities of the successful political executive: willingness to take responsibility for hard decisions,

* As a student, the future Liberal leader David Steel was ready to join a Gaitskellite Labour Party at the end of the 1950s.[36]

audacity and zest for combat, sense of proportion and perspective, capacity to withstand unfair criticism, skill in judging men, ability to inspire confidence and loyalty, political sensitivity and timing.[38] With minor qualifications Gaitskell excelled on the first four characteristics. He was competent on the next count; on the sixth, he evoked hostility as well as devotion; he fell below average only on the last. No leader is perfect, and few have combined so many qualities so superbly, or developed hidden new capabilities so regularly.

A Gaitskell Premiership would not have been without risk. There was a streak of recklessness in his make-up, and sometimes a dangerous self-confidence. The increased prestige and power of the highest office, making it easier for him to win acceptance for his policies, might also have tempted him to plunge into hazardous enterprises. As Leader of the Opposition he was always conscious (as his opponents never understood) of his duty to his Party as he saw it; as Prime Minister he would unquestionably, in case of a clash, have subordinated that duty to his duty to the whole nation. There can be no certainty that a Gaitskell government would have accomplished its ends: only that he would have pursued them boldly and openly, and that even his failures would have marked British politics profoundly.

Always a 'do-er not a be-er', Gaitskell would have used the Premiership as an opportunity for teaching and for leadership, for which there was far wider scope before a deteriorating economic and political situation undermined governmental authority and trust in politicians. He would not have shown great creative imagination, and might have been slow to adapt to the changes of the 1970s in British society and particularly in the Labour Movement. But he combined a wider range, a deeper understanding and a more straightforward approach than any post-war Prime Minister. He identified major issues, faced difficult decisions, and built public confidence by explaining what he was doing and why. He attracted able followers and made them proud to work with him. He appealed to the best in others, not the worst. He sought the consent of ordinary people – both in the Labour Movement and in the country – by treating them as adults capable of intelligent judgment, and by arguing a serious case on great controversial issues. His style of leadership would have raised the tone of public debate and respect for public men, and the country would have been the richer for it. Many men of less promise, in Britain and elsewhere, have performed unexpectedly well in the highest office. Gaitskell, whose capacities had expanded and whose reputation had grown with every broadening of his responsibilities, might have been the great peacetime leader that twentieth-century Britain has badly needed, and sadly failed to find.

APPENDIX: INTERVIEWS

THE following list of people whom I interviewed excludes those who knew HG only in Vienna in 1933–4, in South Leeds, or in his last illness, who are named respectively in Chapter 2, nn. 100, 105, 107; Chapter 7, n. 90; and Chapter 26, n. 55. Relationships specified ('sister' etc.) are to HG.

1 From pre-1939

Sir Walter Adams, Mr and Mrs C. Allchild, Sir Hubert and Lady Ashton (sister), W. H. Auden, David Ayerst; Lord Balogh, Harold Barger, Sir Vaughan Berry, Sir John Betjeman, Dr John Bowlby, Sir Maurice Bowra, J. B. Brown; Sir George Catlin, Cecil Clarabut, Colin Clark, Dame Margaret Cole, Lady Cory-Wright, Christopher Cox, Rt Hon. Richard Crossman; Nicholas Davenport, Harry Dawes, J. C. R. Dow, Mrs Durbin; Sir Ronald Edwards, Kay Elliott, Rt Hon. Lord Elwyn-Jones; Sir Robert Fraser, Dr D. I. Frost, Raymond Frost (stepson); Sir Arthur Gaitskell, Baroness Gaitskell, Charles Gray, Mrs Grieveson; Sir Noel Hall, Frank Hardie, Mrs Hemming, Rupert Horsley; Norah C. James, Sir Jack James, Rt Hon. Douglas Jay; Lord Kaldor, G. V. Keeling; J. H. Lawrie, Rt Hon. Earl and Countess of Longford; Mr and Mrs J. Macmurray, E. L. Mallalieu, George Martelli, Rt Hon. Christopher Mayhew, James Meade, Mrs Middleton, Lady Mitchison, Oskar Morgenstern; Roger Nickalls; Redvers Opie, J. B. Orrick; John Parker, E. A. Pascall, Sir Henry Phelps Brown, Mr and Mrs A. Phillips, Charles Plumb, M. M. Postan; E. A. Radice, Lord Robbins, Cyril Robinson, W. A. Robson, P. Rosenstein-Rodan, Mrs Ross; W. H. Sales, A. J. P. Sellar, F. B. Semple, Sir Arthur Snelling, A. W. Stonier; Herbert Tout; George Wansbrough, Rt Hon. Lord Wigg, Lord Willis, Baroness Wootton; Lord Zuckerman.

2 Civil servants, etc., from 1939–51

Frank Allen, G. C. Allen, Sir Herbert Andrew, Rt Hon. Lord Armstrong; J. A. Beckett, Mr and Mrs G. Bell, Sir Robin and Lady Brook; Sir Alec Cairncross, Philip Chantler, Richard Cleaver, H. A. Copeman, Lord

Croham; Sir Goronwy Daniel, C. de Peyer; Sir Hugh Ellis-Rees; J. W. Farrell, Sir Frank Figgures, Lord Fulton; Lord Gladwyn, L. R. Goss, B. Gottlieb; Sir Patrick Hancock, Sir Alan Hitchman; J. R. Jenkins, D. le B. Jones; R. Kelf-Cohen, Lord Kings Norton; S. C. Leslie, J. G. Liverman, Muriel Loosemore, C. C. Lucas, Mrs. McNeal (daughter), Sir Leslie Murphy; Solly Pearce, Lord Plowden, A. B. Powell; S. G. Raybould, Sir Denis Rickett, Cressida Ridley, Lord Roberthall, Lord Roll, O. W. Roskill; H. Scholes, R. L. Sharp, J. J. S. Shaw, Sir Raymond Streat; Rt Hon. Lord Trend; Sir Geoffrey Vickers; Nita Watts, P. E. Watts, Mrs Wasserman (daughter), Sir Laurence Watkinson, Sir Henry Wilson-Smith.

3 *Politicians and post-1951*

Austen Albu, Arthur Allen, J. R. L. Anderson, Mark Arnold-Forster, Rt Hon. Lord Aylestone; Rt Hon. Baroness Bacon, Rt Hon. Anthony Benn, Sir Isaiah and Lady Berlin, Fred Blackburn, Lord Blyton, Mark Bonham Carter, Lord Boothby, Rt Hon. Lord Boyle, Lord Briggs, Rt Hon. Lord George-Brown, Baroness Burton, Rt Hon. Lord Butler, Michael Butler; Rt Hon. James Callaghan, Rt Hon. Barbara Castle, Rt Hon. Lord Citrine, Percy Clark, Lord Cooper, Rt Hon. Frank Cousins, Mrs Crane, Aidan Crawley, Rt Hon. Anthony Crosland; Rt Hon. Lord Diamond, Lord and Lady Donaldson, Tom Driberg; Norman Ellis, Rt Hon. David Ennals, Sir Trevor Evans; Mrs Fleming, Rt Hon. Michael Foot, Sir John Foster, Rt Hon. John Freeman; Mr and Mrs B. Gillinson, Rt Hon. Sir Ian Gilmour, David Ginsburg, Mrs Wyndham Goldie, Geoffrey Goodman, Rt. Hon. Lord Gordon Walker, Rt Hon. Lord Greenwood, Rt Hon. James Griffiths, Rt Hon. Jo Grimond, Rt Hon. Ray Gunter; Léo Hamon, Lord Harris, Rt Hon. Denis Healey, Rt Hon. Edward Heath, Alastair Hetherington, Lord Hirshfield, Rt Hon. Lord Houghton, Harold Hutchinson; Tom Jackson, Lord Jacobson, Rt Hon. Roy Jenkins, Carol Johnson; Nigel Lawson, Sir Will Lawther, Marcus Lower; Norman Mackenzie, Rt Hon. Harold Macmillan, A. J. McWhinnie, Ian Mikardo, Jules Moch, Peter Morris, Lord Morris, Lord Moyle, Rt Hon. Fred Mulley; Sir Harry Nicholas, Rt Hon. Lord Noel-Baker, Lord Northfield; C. C. O'Brien, Ron Owen; Walter Padley, Rt Hon. Lord Pannell, Baroness Phillips, Rt Hon. Reginald Prentice; Austin Ranney, Rt Hon. Merlyn Rees, Lord Rhodes, Rt Hon. Lord Robens, Rt Hon. Kenneth Robinson, Rt Hon. William Rodgers, Saul Rose; Rt Hon. Lord Shackleton, Rt Hon. Lord Shawcross, Rt Hon. Lord Shinwell, Rt Hon. Peter Shore, Mrs Skelly, John Sparrow, Sir Alec Spearman, Margaret Stewart (Lady Wilson), Rt Hon. Michael and Mrs Stewart, Rt Hon. Lord Stow Hill, Rt Hon.

George Strauss, Rt Hon. Baroness Summerskill; Sir Vincent Tewson; Reg Underhill; Lord Walston, Mrs Watson, Sir William Webber, Baroness White, Rt Hon. Shirley Williams, Lord Williamson, Rt Hon. Sir Harold Wilson, David Wood, George Woodcock, Brenda Woolgar, Woodrow Wyatt, Rt Hon. Sir Kenneth Younger.

SOURCE ABBREVIATIONS

WHEN reference is made to the Gaitskell Papers in the Notes that follow, only the letter and number of the file are given (e.g. P.35, F.16, U.83). Where there is no file reference, the material has been supplied by the relevant correspondents, a few of whom, as mentioned in the Preface, have asked to remain anonymous.

In addition to the abbreviations listed on pp. xv–xvi, the following are also used in the Notes:

Diary	Hugh Gaitskell's diary
AHD	Alastair Hetherington's diary (memoranda of conversations with Gaitskell)
GWD	Patrick Gordon Walker's diary
HDD; HDP	Hugh Dalton's diary; and papers (both at the LSE)
KYD	Kenneth Younger's diary
RCD	Richard Crossman's back-bench diary
ATV	Associated Television
BBC	British Broadcasting Corporation written archives, Caversham
BDG	Biennial Delegate Conference of the T&GWU
BRS	British Road Services
CBS	Columbia Broadcasting Service
DE	*Daily Express*
DH	*Daily Herald*
DMA	Durham Miners Association
DT	*Daily Telegraph*
ETU transcript	Gaitskell's talk and replies to questions at the ETU Training College, Esher, on 28 June 1962
FT	*Financial Times*
H.C. Deb.	*House of Commons Debates* (Hansard)
H.L. Deb.	*House of Lords Debates* (Hansard)
LPCR	*Labour Party Conference Reports*
MG	*Manchester Guardian*
NC	*News Chronicle*

NEC-M	National Executive Committee Minutes
NUAW	National Union of Agricultural Workers
PRO	Public Record Office
RACS	Royal Arsenal Co-operative Society
SE	*Sunday Express*
ST	*Sunday Times*

NOTES

WITHIN each chapter the books or diaries which constitute the main sources are each given a single footnote number and subdivided by letter references specifying the page or date in question (3^a, $15^{b\ c}$, 8^k, etc.); letters may also occasionally indicate a cross-reference. Publication details for books are given at the first mention within each chapter unless the book is quoted throughout the text or in widely separated chapters; in that case publication details are given in full in the bibliography, and references within these Notes are limited to the author's or editor's surname and the date of publication: see e.g. Rodgers (1964).

Chapter 1   *'Seeking Something to Fight for'*

1 It is now a farmhouse, which Hugh's father visited in 1902 and he himself (as a Minister) in 1949. This section is based on interviews with Gaitskell's family, and on the careful comments he sent to writers of profiles on him: to Alan Wood, 2 February 1951, for *Picture Post* (P.35-P); to J. P. O'Donnell, 5 November 1958, for *Saturday Evening Post* (F.1); to George Martelli, 29 June 1959 and 23 July 1959, unpublished (F.1); talking to Ivan Yates for an *Observer* profile, 20 January 1963.

2 So a Burmese judge told Hugh's sister in 1923. Hugh first heard it from a private secretary at the Treasury, and 'purred a bit': interview, R. L. Sharp.

3 Sir Maurice Bowra: *a.* in Rodgers (1964), p. 20; *b.* p. 23; *c.* p. 25; *d.* p. 28; *e.* p. 26; *f.* and in *Memories* (Weidenfeld & Nicolson, 1966), p. 177; *g. ibid.*, p. 179; *h.* and interview.

4 See Lucille Iremonger's work of amateur psychology *The Fiery Chariot* (Secker & Warburg, 1970); the careful review of it by Hugh Berrington in *British Journal of Political Science*, IV, pp. 345-69; and a Swiss medical article by Dr Pierre Rentchnick on 300 world leaders, quoted in *The Times*, 3 December 1975. Hugh Gaitskell shared about two-thirds of the dozen character traits tabulated by Mrs Iremonger (pp. 36-7, cf. pp. 308-9); though many other people share them too.

5 Diary, 1 October 1948. He kept this diary fairly regularly from 1945

to 1949, intermittently till 1955 with one long gap, regularly again in 1956.

6 Notes for speech to the Royal Scottish Academy, 27 April 1951: U.1.

7 For this and the next two paragraphs: interviews, Sir John Betjeman, J. B. Brown, C. Clark, R. Horsley, E. L. Mallalieu, C. Plumb, and the family.

8 HG to J. P. O'Donnell (see n. 1).

9 Interview, E. L. Mallalieu.

10 Interview, George Martelli (his cousin); Sir John Betjeman in Rodgers (1964) pp. 15–16.

11 The father, Fawcett, was a Liberal clergyman: his son's letter in the *Observer*, 27 January 1963.

12 Rodgers (1964), pp. 15–16 (Betjeman), 23–4 (Bowra), 35–6 (M. I. Cole). Interviews, C. Clarabut, Lady Gaitskell.

13 HG to George Martelli (F.1): *a.* 23 July 1959; *b.* 29 June 1959.

14 To HG, 22 October 1950: F.16. For this paragraph, interviews with his family and Lady Cory-Wright, and a few letters to his sister.

15 A. J. P. Taylor on HG: *SE*, 25 September 1960.

16 J. B. Orrick: *a.* to author; *b.* interview.

17 For this section, interviews with Cyril Robinson, Sir Arthur Gaitskell, Sir Kenneth Younger, R. H. S. Crossman and contemporaries at Hugh's house (A. P. Blair, C. Clarabut, R. Horsley, and A. J. P. Sellar, who also kindly collected letters from twenty others).

18 Interview, A. P. Blair, who in 1922 stood in a mock election as the school's first Labour candidate, and thought one of his handful of votes had come from Hugh.

19 Quoted in his obituary in *The Draconian*, no. 226 (Easter 1963), kindly supplied by the author, Mr J. B. Brown. HG to his sister, 27 September 1922 and 4 October 1922.

20 Once when a prefect he was 'imprisoned' in the dormitory, with crockery placed to deter him from climbing out; he made his besiegers pay for the breakages. His fag is said to have called him brutal, and he is once reported as having put the boot in during a dormitory fight.

21 Among twenty surviving contemporaries from his house, only one disliked him.

22 To Alan Wood, *Picture Post*, 7 April 1951 from: *a.* Cyril Robinson; *b.* George Keeling; *c.* a miner.

23 Rupert Wilkinson, *The Prefects* (Oxford University Press, 1964) p. 39. Interview, A. P. Blair.

24 C. Dilke, *Dr Moberly's Mint-Mark: A Study of Winchester College* (Heinemann, 1965): *a.* p. 141; *b.* p. 151.

25 Interview, Sir Arthur Gaitskell, confirmed by his sister Lady Ashton; also by Cyril Robinson and by comments in *The Draconian*.

26 Extracts from the records kindly supplied by Cyril Robinson; *The Wykehamist*, nos 633, 639, 643.

27 HG to Alan Wood (n. 1); to Ivan Yates (n. 1); cf. E. Estorick, *Stafford Cripps* (Heinemann, 1949), pp. 64–70.

28 Interview and letter, C. Clarabut.

29 Wilkinson, pp. 14, 177–8, 182–3 on the social (as distinct from the coercive) pressures at Winchester.

30 This paragraph is mainly based on an interview with Rupert Horsley.

31 Dilke, p. 150; Brian Gardner, *The Public Schools* (Hamish Hamilton, 1973), p. 21; Sampson (1962), p. 178.

32 HG in 'At Oxford in the Twenties', in Briggs and Saville (1967): *a.* p. 7; *b.* pp. 6–7; *c.* p. 9; *d.* p. 10; *e.* p. 15; *f.* p. 11; *g.* p. 14; *h.* p. 12; *i.* p. 16.

33 M. M. Postan: *a.* in interview; *b.* in Rodgers (1964) p. 62.

34 This group began adult life as Socialists, unlike their only predecessors, Sir Stafford Cripps and Sir Oswald Mosley.

35 HG to Arthur Gaitskell: *a.* 4 June 1932; *b.* 18 November 1928; *c.* 9 December 1927; *d.* 8 May 1928; *e.* his italics.

36 Interview, A. P. Blair.

37 This section is based on his own accounts (to profile-writers, in letters to his daughters and in n. 32); on those of Sir Maurice Bowra and Dame Margaret Cole; and on interviews with them and with Sir John Betjeman, C. Clarabut, R. Horsley, Sir Jack James, Lord Longford, R. Nickalls, J. B. Orrick, C. Plumb, Lord Robbins.

38 HG to his daughter Julie: *a.* 7 June 1959; *b. ibid.*, his italics; *c.* about 16 February 1958.

39 J. B. Orrick's diary, 1924–5 (kindly supplied by him): *a.* 3 and 4 December 1924.

40 To Alan Wood (see n. 1).

41 HG to his daughter Cressida, 5 November 1962.

42 Interview, Lord Robbins.

43 Interview, Sir Arthur Gaitskell.

44 Interview, Lord Longford (who clearly recalled the date but not the substance).

45 Tom Jones, *Whitehall Diary*, II (Oxford Unviersity Press, 1969), pp. 76, 85–90.

46 Sources as in n. 37, and interviews, C. Clark, C. Cox, Lady Longford, J. Parker, E. A. Radice, Michael Stewart MP.

47 Interviews, Sir Jack James, J. B. Orrick; Dalton (1953), p. 164.

48 HG at the Cambridge Union on 12 October 1954; HG to Julian Symons, 28 November 1955 (P. 99).

49 Article by HG in *Socialist International Information*, vol. V, no. 52–3, 24 November 1955, pp. 930–1; reproduced in *Forward*, 25 February 1956.

50 Interview, George Martelli.

51 HG to his sister: *a.* 11 January 1927; *b.* 16 July 1926.

52 Interviews, Mrs McNeal (née Julia Gaitskell), J. B. Orrick, C. Plumb; cf. n. 8. He himself dated the change from the strike: n. 32*e.*

53 Below, pp. 42–3.

54 Interview, Dame Margaret Cole.

55 Cole to HG, who was about to begin his first job: n.d. (F.42).

56 G. D. H. Cole, *The Next Ten Years in British Social and Economic Policy* (Macmillan, 1929), pp. vii–ix.

57 Clark's Memoir of Cole in *The Tablet*, 24 January 1959. Cf. M. I. Cole, *Life of G. D. H. Cole* (Macmillan, 1972), pp. 169–70. Ill health and post-1931 disillusionment soon put an end to Cole's parliamentary interest.

58 Interviews, Lady Longford, Rupert Horsley (who arranged the dinner).

59 HG to Margaret Cole, 12 March 1962 (U.1).

60 HG shared the southern preference also: interviews, Lady Bacon, Mrs Jenny Watson.

61 Interview, R. Nickalls; others too recall that as his characteristic phrase.

62 Interview, Christopher Cox. The other New College PPE men took 1 Second and 4 Thirds; there were 5 other Firsts in the University among 61 candidates.

63 H. W. B. Joseph (his well-known philosophy tutor) to HG, 20 July 1927, with his marks (F.42).

64 Interview, Sir Noel Hall (see below, pp. 28–9).

65 Interview, Sir Hubert Ashton (in whose car mother and son had a furious argument).

66 For this section, interviews: *a.* G. V. Keeling, H. Dawes, W. H. Sales; *b.* Sir Jack James, and visitors from Oxford; *c.* HG's comments to profile-writers.

67 Interview, W. H. Sales.

68 'The Battle of the Unions', *MG*, 16 April 1928. The Spencer Union lasted ten years.

69 Interview, G. V. Keeling.

70 Interviews, Sir Maurice Bowra, Sir Jack James, J. B. Orrick.

71 Interview, G. V. Keeling; cf. interview, H. Dawes, and H. L. Featherstone to author.

72 Interview, Lady Longford.

73 He told Alan Wood (n. 1) in 1951 that the classes were 'a great

ordeal', and Ivan Yates (n. 1) in 1963 that they were a 'terrifying experience'.

74 From a lecture on the same subject in Minnesota in 1952 (U.83).
75 HG to Arthur Gaitskell, 9 December 1927; to Ivan Yates (n. 1); M. I. Cole in Rodgers (1964) p. 41.
76 Interview, G. V. Keeling. Cf. interviews, W. H. Sales, Sir Jack James; Mrs A. Buck to author.
77 M. M. Postan in Rodgers (1964) p. 55. Cf. M. I. Cole in *ibid.*, p. 44; interviews with both, and with G. Martelli.
78 Interview, Lady Longford. On the Continent he went third class (HG to his sister, 16 July 1926) and his cousin used to tease him about his taste for squalid travel (interview, Lady Gaitskell).
79 Interviews, *a.* G. Martelli; *b.* Sir Jack James.
80 423 *H.C. Deb.*, col. 57, 20 May 1946.
81 Interview, Sir Jack James.
82 W. L. Ellis to HG, several letters 1928–30, F.42; and interviews.
83 Alderman Bill Mee to HG, 16 October 1955 (P.98).
84 HG to Seymour Cocks MP, 28 October 1950 (F.15).
85 HG at Workingmen's Club London Old Students' Club supper, December 1958.
86 Dalton (1962) pp. 426–7.
87 Interview, Lady Longford. Cf. Ivan Yates (n. 1).
88 Interview, G. Martelli (on Fisher); Yates (n. 1) on Robbins.

Chapter 2   Aiming at a Classless Society

1 For Gaitskell's early days in London, interviews, Lady Gaitskell, Sir John Betjeman, Dr J. Bowlby, Mrs M. Durbin, G. Martelli, Professor M. M. Postan. For UCL, also (sometimes for the later years), Sir Walter Adams, Miss Kay Elliott, Sir Ronald Edwards, Sir Noel Hall, Sir Arthur Snelling, Lord Robbins, and Professors G. C. Allen, H. Barger, J. C. R. Dow, J. Macmurray and his wife, W. A. Robson, P. Rosenstein-Rodan, A. W. Stonier, H. Tout.
2 Noel Hall to HG, 20 June 1928: F.43.
3 D. N. Winch, *Economics and Policy* (Hodder & Stoughton, 1969), pp. 148–50, 190–5. Interviews, Mrs M. Durbin, Professors J. E. Meade, M. M. Postan, P. Rosenstein-Rodan. Cf. J. Harris, *William Beveridge* (OUP, 1977), Chapter 12, especially pp. 296–7, 303.
4 Professor B. Crick (the student chairman) to author.
5 Interview, Mrs M. Durbin.
6 Richard Cranford, 'Gaitskell at University College', *East Anglian Daily Times*, 14 January 1956.

7 Noel Hall to HG, 26 January 1928, 7 and 15 May 1928, 7 and 20 June 1928: F.43. HG to G. D. H. Cole, 17 September 1928; to Arthur Gaitskell, 13 November 1928.

8 J. Macmurray, 'The Early Development of Marx's Thought', in J. Lewis, K. Polanyi and D. K. Kitchin (eds), *Christianity and the Social Revolution* (Gollancz, 1935).

9 HG's preface to Durbin (1954), p. 10.

10 Durbin's outlook was very different from that of Cole, who much preferred Tories to Liberals: n. 11*a*.

11 HG in Briggs and Saville (1967): *a*. pp. 12–13; *b*. p. 16, his omission marks; *c*. p. 14; *d*. p. 18.

12 Interview, M. M. Postan.

13 From Egypt: n.d., but about June 1945: F.8.

14 HG to Arthur: *a*. 6 May 1932; *b*. 13 November 1928; *c*. 27 December 1928, his emphasis; *d*. 17 July 1930; *e*. 4 June 1932; *f*. 3 December 1933; *g*. December 1927.

15 His chief said he was thought a very weak man at first; but there was some friction between them, and most others were surprised by this view.

16 Interview with George Gale in *DE*, 12 and 13 December 1955.

17 These works of popularisation were usually chapters in collections. The main ones are mentioned in their place; others included chapters on economics in books ranging from Naomi Mitchison (ed.), *An Outline for Boys & Girls and their Parents* (Gollancz, 1932) to J. I. Cohen and R. M. W. Travers (eds), *Educating for Democracy* (Macmillan, 1939).

18 On these, interviews, Dr J. Bowlby; Sir Walter Adams, Professor M. M. Postan (social history); Lord Zuckerman, M. M. Postan, R. H. S. Crossman (Tots and Quots). On the latter, also Mitchell Wilson, *The Passion to Know* (Weidenfeld & Nicolson, 1972), pp. 84–6; M. M. Postan in Rodgers (1964), p. 53; Zuckerman (1978), p. 60, Appendix 1.

19 Diary of a relative, November 1928.

20 HG to his sister, 26 December 1928; to Arthur, n. 14 *b c*.

21 Interviews, Professor H. Barger, Dr D. Frost, Lady Gaitskell, C. Gray, Norah James, Mr and Mrs Arthur Phillips, Professor M. M. Postan, Mrs M. Ross. Also Sir Francis Meynell, *My Lives* (Bodley Head, 1971), p. 236.

22 Interview, Lord Zuckerman.

23 On this paragraph: interviews, Mr and Mrs C. Allchild (the proprietors), Dr D. Frost, C. Gray, Norah James, Mrs Ross; cf. Hunter (1959), p. 217; Zuckerman (1978), p. 22.

24 Interview, Dr J. Bowlby.

25 Interviews, Dr J. Bowlby, Norah James, Lord Elwyn-Jones, E. A. Radice.
26 M. I. Cole in Rodgers (1964): *a.* p. 42; *b.* p. 41.
27 He was briefly introduced as 'Pussy' in *We Have Been Warned.*
28 Interviews, Lady Gaitskell, C. Gray, Mrs Ross; and n. 26*b.*
29 V. Gollancz, *More for Timothy* (Gollancz, 1953).
30 Interview, Sir Maurice Bowra.
31 HG to Cole, 17 September 1928.
32 Interview, Dame Margaret Cole.
33 Interview, Sir Noel Hall.
34 Mrs Pauline Hayward to HG, 28 March 1952: F.28. Also HG to Arthur, 17 July 1930, 4 June 1932, 3 December 1933; and interview, Mrs Ross.
35 He told the story often: in *DE*, 28 September 1961, and interviews, Lady Gaitskell, G. Martelli. Other open-air meetings went less well: at one, he had two policemen and eleven children: *Yorkshire Post*, 6 January 1947: P.12.
36 Interview, Sir Jack James.
37 HG to O'Donnell (Chapter 1, n. 1).
38 Fabian Society Papers, Box N.24, C/10/A. The note was by E. A. Radice, the secretary of SSIP (below, p. 45), which organised the meeting.
39 Interview, E. L. Mallalieu.
40 Interview, H. Barger: *a.* and n. 12.
41 *Chatham News*, 18 November 1932; cf. *Chatham Observer*, 18 November ('he is a firm believer in out and out Socialism'); and Dexter to HG, 14 November: P.2.
42 *North East Kent Times, Chatham News: a.* 23 and 25 November 1932; *b.* 18 and 20 January 1933, at a meeting of the unemployed; *c.* 4 and 6 October 1933.
43 *Chatham News: a.* 30 June 1933; *b.* 14 July 1933; *c.* 18 August 1933; *d.* 28 December 1934; the second was the Nazi *putsch* and murder of Dollfuss in July.
44 Keynes wrote two *Times* articles in March 1933 on 'The Means to Prosperity'. (I owe this reference to Professor Skidelsky.)
45 'Socialism and Wage Policy'; B.3/5/F, Cole Papers, Box 12 (Fabians). His copy identifies the opening pages as his own work.
46 E. A. Radice to author.
47 *Chartism* (1929), pp. 85–7 (cf. p. 64).
48 M. M. Postan in Rodgers (1964): *a.* pp. 56–8; *b.* pp. 55–6; *c.* p. 59.
49 In his 1955 essay on the ideology of British democratic socialism (Chapter 1, n. 49).
50 R. Skidelsky, *Oswald Mosley* (Macmillan, 1975), Chapters X and XII.

51 Interviews, Sir Noel Hall, W. A. Robson, M. M. Postan (who was on the platform at the New Party's inaugural meeting, to HG's lasting wrath).

52 At Easton Lodge, 8 May 1931: Fabian Society Papers, Box 15 (SSIP), C/9/C.

53 Interviews, Lady Gaitskell, M. M. Postan, Dr J. Bowlby, Sir Robert Fraser; Rodgers (1964) pp. 45-6 (M. I. Cole), pp. 50, 55, 60-1 (Postan).

54 MS notes in file E.6: his italics.

55 Interviews, M. M. Postan, Lord Zuckerman, Dr Frost; and n. 48 c.

56 For this section I am particularly indebted to the work and help of Professor Elizabeth Durbin.

57 C. M. Lloyd to Beatrice Webb, 10 December 1930: from her diary at the LSE (vol. 44).

58 *DH*, 7 November 1932, and n. 38.

59 M. I. Cole, *The Story of Fabian Socialism* (Heinemann, 1961), p. 227.

60 He thought so; HG to M. I. Cole (who attributed the rule to her husband), 21 April 1959 (P.135).

61 His memorandum was discussed on 12 June 1931: NFRB Minutes, Box J.7.

62 Interviews, Sir Ronald Edwards, Professor Macmurray; M. M. Postan in Rodgers (1964) p. 52. Lord Piercy became chairman of ICFC; Austen Albu succeeded Durbin as MP for Edmonton; Sir Anthony Bowlby became managing director of Guest Keen & Nettlefold.

63 Gollancz, 1933.

64 *LPCR* (1935), pp. 225-30. There is a verbatim transcript of a long discussion with Social Credit representatives in the J. S. Middleton Papers (Box 9) in the Labour Party Archives.

65 Lovat Dickson & Thompson, 1935.

66 Williams (1970), p. 112.

67 H. V. Berry, Memorandum on the origins of XYZ, unpublished.

68 Williams (1970), pp. 112-13. Cf. Davenport, another founder (1974), pp. 75-7. Also interviews, Sir Vaughan Berry, N. Davenport, J. H. Lawrie on its early days.

69 Geoffrey Faber to HG, 28 November 1932 (F.42). Durbin to HG, 15 April 1933 (F.43). Cole to Durbin, 6 November 1933 (F.42).

70 HG to James Meade, 20 June 1932 (also Cole to Meade, 11 July 1932), Meade Papers, LSE (Folder 124).

71 Winch, p. 207. *The Times*, 10 March 1933; 277 *H.C. Deb.*, cols 60-1: 25 March 1933.

72 Noel Hall to HG, 20 February 1928 (F.43); the Provost of UCL was also chairman of its extra-mural committee.

73 As E. A. Radice reminded him: to HG, 28 October 1950 (F.1). But

after the war WEA leaders found him less enthusiastic on their behalf than they had hoped: interview, Lord Briggs.

74 James Haworth to author; interviews, A. Allen (trade unions), Mrs Callaghan (Eltham), R. H. S. Crossman (Oxbridge), E. A. Radice (Shoreditch), Lady Wootton and Lord Wigg (colleagues); John Ramage to author (Gravesend).

75 Les Ellis to HG, 2 April 1929, 16 June 1929: F.42.

76 King's Norton was the seat from which ill health had made Cole withdraw.

77 Diary, 14 October 1947, p. 9. Left-wing: HG to Yates (Chapter 1, n. 1).

78 Provost Mawr to HG, 7 November 1932 (F.42); interviews, H. Barger, C. Dow, Miss K. Elliott; contrast very friendly letter from Noel Hall, n.d., 1935 (F.43). There was also some concern at UCL about his political links in Vienna: interview, P. Rosenstein-Rodan.

79 On Chatham generally, interviews: *a.* Mrs B. Grieveson; *b.* E. A. Pascall; *c.* Alderman F. B. Semple.

80 Dexter to HG, 12 October 1932: P.2. (In the end, he resigned for other reasons.)

81 Eric Cash the secretary to HG, 18 September 1932. *Chatham News*, 18 November 1932 (after Transport House apparently required a formal selection conference).

82 H. C. Macey to HG: *a.* 14 March 1933; *b.* 5 May 1933; *c.* 8 May 1933.

83 Interview, Lord Willis.

84 Cash to HG, 20 July 1933.

85 Provost Mawr to HG, 27 November 1932 (when the fellowship was already mooted). But for Hitler, he might have gone to Germany as well, or instead: T. B. Kittredge of the Rockefeller Foundation to HG, 22 July 1933 (F.42).

86 On the economists in Vienna, interviews, Mrs Hemming, Mrs Schicker, Professors A. W. Stonier and O. Morgenstern — who recalled seeing HG at occasional philosophical discussions also.

87 HG to Harold Barger, 1 December 1933.

88 Professor Howard S. Ellis to author. He was critical of HG's German.

89 Interview, Lord Kaldor.

90 HG to J. P. O'Donnell (Chapter 1, n. 1); to O. Morgenstern, 22 December 1950 (P.31–Y) and interview. 'Notes on the Period of Production' in *Zeitschrift für Nationalökonomie*, VII.5 (1936) and IX.2 (1938). It was the first case of triangulation of a matrix: R. Dorfman, P. A. Samuelson and R. M. Solow, *Linear Programming and Economic Analysis* (McGraw-Hill, 1958), pp. 234n., 253–4, 262–4.

91 M. Blaug, *Economic Theory in Retrospect* (Heinemann, 2nd ed., 1968),

pp. 517, 521–2, 569–70; C. E. Ferguson, *The Neoclassical Theory of Production and Distribution* (Cambridge University Press, 1969), p. 252n.

92 Published by William Hodge, 1936.

93 John Gunther, *Inside Europe* (Hamish Hamilton, 2nd ed., 1936), p. 314.

94 Interview, Lord Elwyn-Jones.

95 The fullest account is C. A. Gulick, *Austria from Habsburg to Hitler* (University of California Press, Berkeley, 1948), 2 vols. See also G. E. R. Gedye (a friend of HG), *Fallen Bastions* (Gollancz, 1939); Ernest Fischer (later the Austrian Communist leader), *An Opposing Man* (Allen Lane, 1974).

96 Gulick, I, pp. 762, 770; II. pp. 1214–6, 1389–90. Fischer, p. 166, writes of 'the discrepancy between word and deed that was inherent in Austro-Marxism'.

97 Quoted from a (Socialist) writer in the *Times Literary Supplement*, 24 August 1973.

98 Respectively Gulick, II, pp. 1266–8, and Fischer, p. 226 (reporting Otto Bauer); Gedye, pp. 99–100 (reporting Oskar Pollak); Gulick, II, pp. 1349, 1353.

99 Mrs I. Polanyi to author. (He wrote no thesis.)

100 Interviews, Dr Gertrud Wagner, Mrs Anne Weisselberg; also for general impressions of his political views in Vienna, O. Morgenstern, P. Rosenstein-Rodan, F. Scheu, A. W. Stonier, and Professor W. Ebenstein to author.

101 Naomi Mitchison, *Vienna Diary* (Gollancz, 1934), p. 31. HG is 'Sam' in this book, which he did not much like.

102 Interview, Mrs Schicker.

103 Official figures were one-twelfth of theirs: Gedye, p. 123.

104 From HG's own reports ('Notes for R.G.') kindly supplied by Mrs Grant.

105 Interviews, Mrs Grant, Mrs Hirsch, Mrs Macmurray, Mrs Schicker, Professor Stonier, Mrs Weisselberg.

106 F. S.[cheu] in the *Arbeiter Zeitung*, Vienna, 16 December 1955.

107 Interviews, Dr Oskar Bock, Mrs Hirsch, Lord Elwyn-Jones, Lady Gaitskell, Professors Postan, Rosenstein-Rodan, and Stonier, F. Scheu, Mrs Schicker, Dr J. Simon, Mrs Wagner, Mrs Weisselberg; HG to Yates (Chapter 1, n. 1); P. Seale and M. McConville, *Philby, the Long Road to Moscow* (Hamish Hamilton, 1973), p. 64.

108 Interview, Sir Walter Adams.

109 Interview, Mrs Irene Grant.

110 Interviews, Dr Oskar Bock, Dr Josef Simon, Naomi Mitchison; Professor John Mars to author. (The harsh repression turned another

Englishman there to Communism—Kim Philby, whom HG once called 'that silly young man': Seale and McConville, pp. 60–1, 64.)

111 Interviews F. B. Semple, Miss B. Woolgar (reporting Dexter).

112 His report (2 October 1935) on Labour's foreign policy summer school in Geneva (below, pp. 63–4).

Chapter 3   'A Proper Social Democrat'

1 Sir Noel Hall: *a.* interview; *b.* quoted by E. A. Radice to author.

2 Socialist strategy group memoranda (in U.3): *a.* 22 November 1934; *b.* 25 February 1935; *c.* 7 December 1934 ('social justice' inserted in HG's writing); *d.* there is no record of discussion of the third problem, which was probably the personal concern of Durbin who as chairman wrote these notes.

3 Most of the group were academics (among them H. R. G. Greaves, Postan and his wife, Tawney, Barbara Wootton and Leonard Woolf) but a few were politicians (John Parker, Creech Jones a future Minister, and apparently Lees Smith an ex-Minister); memorandum of 25 February 1935, and HG's pencil note on it.

4 Interviews, Lord Willis, Alderman F. S. Semple; Ernest Fischer, *An Opposing Man* (Allen Lane, 1974), pp. 207–9.

5 Interview, M. M. Postan.

6 Naomi Mitchison, *Vienna Diary* (Gollancz, 1934), p. 212.

7 M. M. Postan in Rodgers (1964): *a.* p. 60; *b.* p. 51; *c.* p. 63; *d.* p. 61.

8 Interviews, D. Jay, Norah C. James, E. A. Radice, W. A. Robson; Wigg (1972), p. 82.

9 Beatrice Webb's diary: Passfield Papers: *a.* vol. 51, pp. 13, 18–19 (15 February 1936); *b.* cf. *ibid.*, vol. 54, 18 April 1940.

10 So he claimed to Alan Wood in 1951, to Yates in 1962 (Ch. 1 n. 1) and in *DE*, 28 September 1961. Many friends—but not all—remember his views on rearmament dating from this early period: John Bowlby, M. I. Cole, Mrs Martelli, John Parker, M. M. Postan, Paul Rosenstein-Rodan.

11 HG to Arthur, 3 December 1933.

12 MS notes for a lecture on 'The Next Ten Years in Britain', 3 February 1935 (E.6).

13 *LPCR*, 1935, p. 158.

14 *Plebs*, May, July and August 1935, pp. 127–9, 155–6, 180–3.

15 Dalton to HG, 26 April 1935, F.43, and 4 August 1935, F.42; interviews, Lady Bacon, Lady Fraser, Lord Greenwood, John Parker; J. Ramage to author.

16 Paper of 2 October 1935, initialled H.T.N.G.: U.3–1.

17 Interview, Lord Willis.
18 Interview, John Parker.
19 Interview, J. B. Orrick.
20 *Chatham News*: *a.* 20 December 1955; *b.* 28 December 1934 (New Year Message); *c.* 15 November 1935.
21 Fabian Society Papers, Box N.29 (SSIP): report of NFRB conferences: *a.* Labour's Foreign Policy, 27/28 June 1936, pp. 10–11; *b.* Banking, Maidstone 18/19 May 1935, pp. 4–5; *c. ibid.*, p. 8; *d.* Winning the Election, Maidstone 18/19 January 1936, pp. 4–5, 15; *e.* Defence, Old Jordans 18/19 February 1939.
22 *a.* interview, P. Rosenstein-Rodan; *b.* on the Swedish influence, cf. Lord Vaizey in *Encounter*, 49.2 (August 1977), p. 86; *c.* M. M. Postan to author.
23 Research paper 311, June 1936. From Colin Clark's Papers at Brasenose College, Oxford; and interview.
24 Williams (1970), p. 111.
25 Discussion in Middleton Papers (Chapter 2, n. 64).
26 Durbin to Dalton, 26 December 1936: Dalton (1957) p. 124n. Durbin wrote to HG on 31 January 1939 (F.43) that Munich was their only major disagreement since 1934.
27 R. Skidelsky in the *Spectator*, 7 August 1976. Cf. D. N. Winch, *Economics and Policy* (Hodder & Stoughton, 1969), p. 215–8 and his Appendix on Keynes and the British Left, especially p. 348; and B. Pimlott, *Labour and the Left in the 1930s* (Cambridge University Press, 1977), pp. 36–40, 63–7, 200–1.
28 A survey of official and unofficial material by C. Mayhew for NFRB (probably 1939: Fabian Society Papers J 26/7, item 1) discusses the arguments at pp. 4–5, 15–19.
29 On the first two alone, fifteen single-space foolscap pages, dated 11 November 1938, are in HDP, II.A, section 2/3. Mayhew's survey (p. 14) indicates that the 'panic policy' draft was complete, thorough and by HG. I am again much indebted on this topic to Professor Elizabeth Durbin.
30 *DH*, 11 August 1939.
31 In Chapter 7 of M. Cole and C. Smith (eds) *Democratic Sweden* (Routledge, 1938), especially pp. 96, 106.
32 HG, 'Why I Am a Socialist', *South Leeds Worker*, December 1937.
33 'Notes for Lecturers to the LLY [Labour League of Youth]', 1938: F.6.
34 Privately he was more eclectic, arguing also against monopoly, or for reducing inequality by bringing down the supply price of managerial talent: interview, H. Barger.
35 Lecture on 'Forms of Socialisation', Hoddesdon, Herts, 9 December 1935: E.6.

36 MS notes for lecture, 'Government and the Man in the Street', n.d. probably 1935: E.6.

37 Around the central core were different associates for different subjects, embracing for instance the Socialist strategy group, and the economists led by Dalton (above, pp. 60–1, 66). Interviews, R. H. S. Crossman, Sir Robert Fraser, D. Jay, P. Rosenstein-Rodan, G. Wansbrough.

38 HG to M. I. Cole, 12 March 1962: U.1.

39 To E. A. Radice in New York: interview. In Vienna the Austrians thought so too: interview, Professor O. Morgenstern.

40 Dalton, (1962) pp. 426–7.

41 Dalton to HG: *a*. 31 December 1957 (P.115–16); *b*. 26 September 1938 (F.43).

42 Donoughue and Jones (1973), pp. 237, 243 (from Douglas Jay).

43 First and last paragraphs from HG's preface to Durbin (1954), p. 9. Remainder from HG to Alan Wood (Chapter 1, n. 1). They cover the same ground.

44 *North East Kent Times*, 2 May 1934.

45 Interview, Mrs Grieveson.

46 *Chatham Observer*: *a*. 14 December 1934; *b*. 1 November 1935.

47 Meetings: in *Chatham News*, 16 November 1934 (arms); *North East Kent Times*, 30 October 1935 (yards); *Chatham Observer*, 1 and 8 November 1935 (both). Letters to *Chatham News*, 11 January 1935, 3 and 10 May 1935 (arms); 22 March 1935, 12 April 1935 (both).

48 She later joined. HG to George Martelli, 23 July 1959 (F.1); and interviews.

49 Friends recalled long afterwards his astonishingly rapid improvement as a speaker: interview, Sir Arthur Gaitskell; John Ramage to author.

50 Interviews, Dr John Bowlby, J. C. R. Dow, Miss K. Elliott, Alderman F. B. Semple.

51 Interviews: *a*. Miss K. Elliott; *b*. Professor A. W. Stonier.

52 The swing against Labour (10 per cent since 1929) was the same both in Chatham and in comparable seats – i.e. those boroughs south of Yorkshire which Labour had won in 1929 in a three-cornered fight, and fought in 1935 in a straight fight (Birmingham and Greater London excluded).

53 Leopold Kulczar to HG, 31 November 1935 from Brno (U.3–1) implies that HG's previous letter had said so.

54 *The Times*, 28 September 1935, 12 and 19 October 1936; John Parker MP to the South Leeds agent: letter to Rodgers (1964) p. 68. (But the *Derbyshire Times*, 16 October 1936, says a local man was runner-up.)

55 Nina Beale, Assistant Secretary, officially to HG, 16 November 1936 (F.42), replying to his letter of 9 November 1936.

56 John Parker MP to HG, 17 April 1937.

57 HG to Alan Wood (Chapter 1, n. 1).

58 *The Uses of Literacy* (Chatto & Windus and Penguin, 1957).

59 Marjorie Brett in Rodgers (1964), pp. 68–9, who quotes his letter in full.

60 *Ibid.*; interview, Marjorie Brett; George Brett to HG, 1 September 1937. (Hyman is not recorded in the weekly *Citizen* as speaking, but some local people remember him.)

61 Brett to HG: *a*. 20 October 1950; *b*. 1 September 1937; *c*. 30 October 1937; *d*. 7 December 1937.

62 HG's notes, and HG to Brett, 8 September 1937.

63 Interview, Mrs Lucy Middleton (widow of the then general secretary of the Party). Brett wrote to HG on 29 November 1937: 'I note with interest your reference to NUR and NEC and am glad to hear that Shepherd [the National Agent] defended us there.' HG's letter has not survived.

64 Charleton's only (and slim) chance would have been a 1937 election, and the restoration of his NUR sponsorship: n. 61*d*.

65 Brett to HG, 15 November 1937, 7 and 14 December 1937; HG to Brett, n.d. but 6 and 7 December 1937.

66 Interview, Marjorie Brett. The writer later became Sir Donald Kaberry, MP for Leeds North West.

67 Brett, Watson and Murray were secretary-agents; Goodwill, who as the youngest delegate had nominated HG, became chairman after the war.

68 366 *H.L. Deb.*, col. 1617, 18 December 1975: 'at least three or four years earlier' than they did.

69 HG to Harold Barger, 7 July 1937.

70 HG to Raymond Frost, 30 August 1958.

71 HDD, 24 April 1945.

72 Interview, George Wansbrough.

73 Gordon Petter in *Victoria Times* (Vancouver Island, Canada), 6 December 1955.

74 Interview, P. Rosenstein-Rodan. Cf. interview, Professor J. Macmurray; Professor S. T. Bindoff to author.

75 HG to Yates (Chapter 1, n. 1); Provost of UCL in *The Times*, 22 January 1963; interviews, Lady Gaitskell, Professor H. Tout (to whom he told this).

76 It is strongly hinted in Provost Pye's letter to HG of 18 July 1944: F.42.

77 Interview, Lady Gaitskell.

78 Interview, Professor W. A. Robson.

79 Diary, 6 April 1949.

80 Interview, Lord Roll.

81 Interview, Lady Brook.

82 Interviews, F. Hardie, Lord Willis (above, p. 64).
83 Interview, Mrs M. Durbin. Cf. interviews, Lady Brook, Mrs Macmurray, Professor M. M. Postan.
84 'Watchman' (1939), p. 215; quoted Fairlie (1968), p. 60.
85 Interview, Mrs McNeal (née Julia Gaitskell).
86 HG to Julie: *a*. 21 January 1959; *b*. 17 November 1958 (below, p. 385).
87 Interview, Professor H. Barger.
88 NFRB Minute Book, pp. 176, 190; 13 December 1937 and 15 March 1938. L. Woolf to HG, 27 December 1937; S. H. Bailey to HG, 31 January 1938: F.42.
89 Quoted in Leonard Woolf, *Downhill all the Way* (Hogarth Press, 1968), p. 248.
90 HG to Harold Beale, 1 July 1938 (quoted in Beale's reply, 19 August 1938 from Singapore: F.6).
91 Notes (of Feb. 1938 or later): E.6.
92 HG to Dalton, 21 May 1957: U.1.
93 HG's pencil notes, n.d. but October 1938.
94 His memorandum of 13 October 1938, among documents kindly supplied by Mrs M. Durbin.
95 HG to Durbin: *a*. 6 October 1938; *b*. n.d. but 25 October 1938 (his italics).
96 HG's memorandum, 5 October 1938.
97 Durbin to HG, 3 January 1939: F.43.
98 Jay in Rodgers (1964): *a*. p. 83; *b*. pp. 84–5; *c*. pp. 83–4.
99 HDD, 19 October 1938.
100 Durbin sent the correspondence to Reg Bassett on 27 October 1938 with a covering note saying HG's letter seemed 'out of touch with reality'.
101 Interviews, Sir Noel Hall, G. Martelli.
102 HG to Strachey, 6 January 1956 (his italics): P.114–1. On the debate in 1936, above, p. 65.
103 Cripps's diary for 30 September 1938 – quoted in C. Cooke's *Life* (Hodder & Stoughton, 1957) p. 227 – says the same; Pimlott, Chapters 17 and 18, on Labour and Cripps. Also interviews, Mrs M. Durbin on the Cambridge meeting, Sir Jack James on HG's criticisms of Cripps in 1938.
104 *The Beeston Democrat*, November 1938: C-1.
105 Memorandum, 'The Conscription of Wealth', 24 April 1939 (F.6). The tax would rise from 0·5 per cent at £10,000 up to 5 per cent. It was HG's main theme at the Leeds May Day rally on 7 May 1939 (C-1); and he defended it in a lengthy letter to *The Economist* on 3 June 1939. Had there been a 1939 election it would probably have been the basis of Labour's policy.

106 For later proposals on wartime finance, see Durbin's *How to Pay For the War* (Routledge, 1939) and HG's appendix on 'New Forms of Taxation'.
107 HG to Brett from Milland, 13 April 1939.

Chapter 4   Coalition Politics: serving Doctor Dalton

1 Interview, Lady Gaitskell.
2 Jenkins (1974), p. 167.
3 HG to George Martelli, 23 July 1959: F.1a.
4 HG to George Brett: *a.* 14 September 1939; *b.* 8 September 1939; c. 19 October 1939; *d.* 23 September 1940; *e.* 30 December 1941; *f.* 30 April 1942. HG's side of this correspondence was kindly supplied by Miss Marjorie Brett.
5 Below, Chapter 5, section ii.
6 The Ministry moved to Berkeley Square in March 1940.
7 HG's review in the *Listener*, 20 March 1952, of W. N. Medlicott, *History of the Second World War: The Economic Blockade*, vols I, II (HMSO and Longmans, 1952, 1959).
8 Medlicott: *a.* I, p. 66; *b.* I, p. 17; *c.* II, p. 2; *d.* I, p. 62.
9 D. Jay in Rodgers (1964): *a.* p. 75; *b.* p. 85; *c.* pp. 86–7.
10 HG to Alan Wood in 1951 (Chapter 1, n. 1).
11 Dalton (1957): *a.* p. 296; *b.* p. 305; *c.* p. 318 (cf. p. 381); *d.* p. 328; *e.* p. 334; *f.* pp. 348, 367; *g.* p. 378ff., *h.* p. 381; *i.* p. 384; *j.* pp. 384–6; *k.* p. 397; *l.* p. 396; *m.* p. 399; *n.* p. 391; *o.* p. 402.
12 As he wrote in November, saying he could not rejoin Tots and Quots which was being revived: Zuckerman (1978), p. 110.
13 HDD, 7 October 1939; Medlicott, I, p. 250 ff.
14 Dalton (1957) p. 280. HG thought Cross able and amiable but too deferential to that arch-appeaser Sir John Simon, Chancellor of the Exchequer (whom Cross called 'Sir'): HDD, 17 March 1940, 10 October 1940, 27 May 1940.
15 HDD: *a.* 10 April 1940; *b.* 17 March 1940; *c.* 30 October 1941; *d.* 14 April 1940; *e.* 18 May 1940; *f.* 15 September 1940; *g.* 27 December 1941; *h.* 18 August 1940; *i.* 15 September 1941; *j.* cf. 10 September 1941; *k.* 25 September 1941; *l.* 12 November 1940; *m.* 13 November 1941; *n.* 29 August 1940; *o.* 24 October 1940; *p.* 5 August 1942; *q.* 5 March 1942; *r.* 27 April 1942 and 1 May 1942; *s.* 6 May 1942; *t.* 12 May 1942; *u.* 12 June 1942; *v.* 9 May 1942 and 1 June 1942; *w.* 9 June 1942; *x.* 28 May 1942; *y.* 11 June 1942 (quoting HG); *z.* 18 February 1943 and 24 March 1943.
16 Dalton (1957), p. 296; fuller, HDD, 17 March 1940. Interview, Professor M. M. Postan.

17 Interview, E. A. Radice.
18 Longford (1953), p. 151.
19 Partly perhaps HG's fault: HDD, 16 May 1940. Cf. Dalton (1957) pp. 327–8; and interview, Sir Noel Hall.
20 As HG feelingly wrote in a eulogistic report on Hancock (later Ambassador to Italy) to the Foreign Office: HG to W. I. Mallet, 16 January 1942 (HDP, III, 1942–3).
21 For the new system and its problems, see Medlicott (1952), pp. 422–4. The Intelligence Department of MEW had already, with some success, made a great row against the legal restrictions on the blockade.
22 Interviews: *a.* Sir Dingle Foot; *b.* Sir Patrick Hancock; *c.* Sir Herbert Andrew.
23 Apparently from Brendan Bracken, a crony of Churchill and Beaverbrook: Dalton (1957), p. 379.
24 HDD, 17, 19 and 22 May 1940 (Cripps); 23 May 1940 (warnings); 18 December 1940 (abusive letter to Sir John Anderson).
25 HG's draft obituary of Dalton (U.1–4); cf. *MG*, 14 February 1962.
26 Interview, G. Martelli.
27 Interview, Mrs M. Durbin, whose husband was present. Generally, cf. interview, Sir Patrick Hancock; D. Jay in Rodgers (1964) p. 86; HDD, 12 December 1941.
28 Interview, Miss K. M. Elliott. Another UCL and MEW colleague confirms: 'a different man, a stronger man than I'd remembered or even sensed': interview, Sir Walter Adams. Also interview, Sir Patrick Hancock.
29 M. M. Postan in Rodgers (1964), p. 74.
30 Visiting Leeds, both Wilmot and Dalton mentioned it: Brett to HG, 13 January 1941 and ? August 1942.
31 His sister, Lady Ashton, to author.
32 Interview, Professor Chick.
33 Despite the impression given by an official historian: M. R. D. Foot, *SOE in France* (HMSO, 1966), p. 15.
34 For contrasting explanations see *ibid.*, p. 18; B. Sweet-Escott, *Baker Street Irregular* (Methuen, 1965), pp. 40–1.
35 See Sir Campbell Stuart, *Opportunity Knocks Once* (Collins, 1952), Chapter 15; R. H. Bruce Lockhart, *Comes the Reckoning* (Putnam, 1947); C. Cruickshank, *The Fourth Arm* (Davis-Poynter, 1977), based on the official records.
36 Lockhart: *a.* pp. 155–6; *b.* cf. pp. 156, 160–1.
37 Cruickshank: *a.* pp. 17–21; *b.* p. 184; *c.* pp. 24–6, 180, 184.
38 *Ibid.*, pp. 20, 47–8, 182. Cruickshank thought Dalton weakly threw away his case.
39 Kim Philby, *My Silent War* (MacGibbon & Kee, 1968), p. 18. Cf.

Cruickshank, pp. 48, 56. Dalton's political concern was exclusively with the propaganda side of SOE: M. R. D. Foot, pp. 13–14, 16, 178.

40 A. Boyle, *'Poor, Dear Brendan'* (Hutchinson, 1974), pp. 267–8, 271–3, 281; Lockhart, p. 152; Dilks (1971), pp. 356–7; A. Briggs, *The War of Words* (OUP, 1970), p. 339.

41 Briggs, p. 36; Lockhart, pp. 117, 126.

42 His memorandum is in HDP, III, 1941–42. Cf. Lockhart, p. 134; interview, G. Martelli.

43 Dalton to Attlee, 25 September 1941: HDP III, 1941–2.

44 *Ibid.*, 26 February 1942. Strangely, Bracken too suggested handing over to Cripps: Lockhart, p. 153.

45 Cruickshank, pp. 31–2, 34, 48; Briggs, p. 417; Dalton (1957), pp. 381–2; Lockhart, pp. 143, 166.

46 HDP 1941–2, contain a memorable 'minute' – marked 'Destroy when Read' – of an imaginary committee to co-ordinate PWE and SO2, seen as a wrangling office committee on fire precautions which finally is 'very properly precipitated into the flames below'.

47 Respectively from HDD, 10 March 1941; interview, Sir Walter Adams; and HDD, 17 September 1941, reporting Crossman.

48 *a.* Interview, Sir Patrick Hancock; *b.* and HDD, 16 September 1940 (contrast 17 August 1940), 26 November 1941.

49 Cf. Dalton (1957), pp. 325–6; and Medlicott, I, pp. 423–4, 558.

50 HDD, 7, 8, 12 and 22 January 1942; Medlicott, II, pp. 267–73. It was the only such breach in the blockade in Dalton's time.

51 Interviews, Sir Walter Adams, Miss K. M. Elliott, Sir Dingle Foot, Sir Patrick Hancock.

52 HDD, 10 and 12 December 1941; cf. 9 and 27 January 1942.

53 The rank of P.A.S. corresponded roughly to the modern Under-Secretary.

54 To George Gale, 1955 (see Chapter 2, n. 16). Cf. HG to Ivan Yates (Chapter 1, n. 1).

55 *a.* The Board of Trade memo refers to a civil servant (born like HG in 1906) who 'was at New College with me'; *b.* the Mines memo, dated 28 February 1942, is initialled H.G.: HDP, II.30.

56 His own autobiographical note, given to the Department's public relations officer when he became Minister of Fuel and Power in 1947 (kindly supplied by Sir Leslie Murphy).

57 W. H. B. Court, *Coal* (HMSO and Longmans, 1951): *a.* p. 176; *b.* esp. pp. 22, 26, 48, 176; *c.* pp. 30, 115–18; *d.* pp. 27–8, 164; *e.* pp. 165–6; *f.* pp. 160–1.

58 HG had suggested that Hyndley might succeed either Hurst or Grenfell.

59 G. Baldwin, *Beyond Nationalisation* (Harvard University Press, 1955)

pp. 181, 202. On manpower, also A. Bullock, *The Life and Times of Ernest Bevin*, II (Heinemann, 1967), pp. 161–6.

60 380 *H.C. Deb.*, 10 and 11 June 1942: *a.* col. 1184 (Ness Edwards); *b.* col. 1198; *c.* cols 1196 (M. Hely-Hutchinson), 1329 (Gordon Macdonald); *d.* col. 1298–9; *e.* col. 1088 (Sir John Anderson); *f.* cols 1294, 1299.

61 HDD, 20 March 1942, 17 April 1942. The dissenter was Sir Andrew Duncan.

62 HDD, 20 March 1942; 3, 10 and 20 April 1942; 16 October 1942.

63 Dalton (1957), pp. 389–91; HDD, 11 and 19 March 1942, 30 April 1942. The deputation was led by Sir Evan Williams, the owners' leader since 1919.

64 HDD, 12 March 1942; 7 April 1942; 22, 28 and 29 May 1942.

65 Mass Observation survey cited by H. M. Pelling, *Britain and the Second World War* (Fontana, 1970), pp. 157–8; and A. Calder, *The People's War* (Panther, 1971), p. 327; but cf. p. 329. Also Court, p. 157.

66 Court, pp. 161–2, 215; W. K. Hancock and M. M. Gowing, *The British War Economy* (HMSO, 1949), pp. 472, 473.

67 Generally: Court, Chapter VIII sec. iv; Dalton (1957), pp. 392–402; Bullock, pp. 167–8; Lord Beveridge, *Power and Influence* (Hodder & Stoughton, 1953), p. 288; J. Harris, *William Beveridge* (OUP, 1977), p. 377.

68 Dalton (1957), p. 393; HDD, 21 April 1942; 379 *H.C. Deb.*, col. 491.

69 HDD, 6 May 1942; cf. Hancock and Gowing, p. 472. M. R. Hely-Hutchinson, MP (who had once advocated disfranchising the unemployed) admitted in the House that he was currently consuming six times his proposed ration: see n. 60*b*.

70 Dalton (1957), p. 400; HDD, 15 May 1942. (The MP was Godfrey Nicholson.) Cf. n. 60*c*.

71 The political factors are stressed by Calder, pp. 327–8 and Bullock, pp. 167–8.

72 Foot (1966): *a.* p. 312; *b.* pp. 310–12.

73 Brett to HG, 21 May 1942.

74 HDD, 1, 2, 12, 28 and 29 May 1942.

75 HDD, 12 May 1942, 9 July 1942. Food: Pelling, p. 57 (from Cabinet minutes 28 October 1939). Clothing: *The Memoirs of Lord Chandos* (Bodley Head, 1962), p. 205.

76 HDD, 1, 7, 8, 9, 11 and 21 May 1942. P. Goodhart, *The 1922* (Macmillan, 1973), pp. 114–19.

77 HDD, 14, 26, 27 and 31 May 1942; 1 June 1942.

78 Hancock & Gowing, p. 473 and n.

79 *Ibid.*; Court, p. 203, cf. p. 163. Contrast the complacency of Good-hart, p. 119.
80 Calder, p. 497.
81 Sir Frederick Leith-Ross, *Money Talks* (Hutchinson, 1968), p. 281.
82 Dalton (1957) p. 391. Also *ibid.*, pp. 399–403; Bullock, pp. 169–72; Court, Chapter IX section ii.
83 Interview, Sir Harold Wilson. P. Foot (1968), p. 52.
84 Court, p. 266; cf. Bullock, p. 171.
85 *LPCR* (1943), p. 124.
86 Court, Chapter XIII, particularly pp. 242, 248; 403 *H.C. Deb.*, col. 924, 13 October 1943; Bullock, p. 259.
87 *Ibid.*; Court, p. 248; Addison (1975), p. 253.

Chapter 5   From Whitehall to Westminster

1 Dalton (1957): *a.* p. 394; *b.* pp. 466–7.
2 HDD, 18 August 1942; HG to Durbin, 31 August 1942 (kindly supplied by Professor Elizabeth Durbin); interview, J. E. Meade. Meade's original paper is in the PRO (ref. B.T. 11/2000) and the final revised draft dated 5 November 1942 is in HDP, III, 1942–3: envelope Dalton 1942).
3 HDD: *a.* 18 August 1942, 15 October 1942; *b.* 28 August 1942; *c.* 12 October 1943; *d.* 6 January 1943, 7 April 1943; *e.* 21 September 1943, cf. 12 July 1943; *f.* 14/17 February 1944; *g.* 13 April 1944; *h.* 11 December 1944, agreeing with HG; *i.* 3 April 1943, 9 November 1944; *j.* but 4 November 1943 reports a critical view; *k.* 10 February 1947.
4 R. N. Gardner, *Sterling-Dollar Diplomacy* (McGraw Hill, 1969 edn), Chapters 8, 14 and 16.
5 Interview, Professor W. A. Robson.
6 *a.* interview, Sir Raymond Streat; *b.* Dalton's embarrassed emissary, who agreed with HG.
7 Interview, Professor H. Tout.
8 For the rest of this section, interviews, Professor G. C. Allen, Sir Herbert Andrew, Professor H. Tout, Sir Laurence Watkinson; John Ramage to author.
9 E. L. Hargreaves and M. M. Gowing, *Civil Industry and Trade* (HMSO & Longmans, 1952): *a.* Chapter 22 for its problems; *b.* Chapter 12, esp. pp. 272–3; *c.* pp. 280, 636.
10 See his comment in an interdepartmental committee on 20 November 1942 (PRO ref. CAB 87 55 6306) and his back-bench speech on 19 October 1945 (414 *H.C. Deb.*, cols 1592–5).

11 HDD, 7 September 1942; 2 October 1942; 15 and 16 October 1942; 13 and 15 December 1942. 383 *H.C. Deb.*, col. 1480: 13 October 1942.

12 D. Jay in Rodgers (1964), p. 88.

13 HG to Christopher Mayhew in the army, 22 September 1943 (his italics); kindly supplied by Mr Mayhew.

14 Eady's memorandum to Sir Richard Hopkins, 12 October 1943: PRO ref. T.161 1168/52098 ERD/7624.

15 Diary: *a.* 6 August 1945; *b.* 11–30 September 1945; *c.* 8 August 1945; *d.* 13–24 August 1945; *e.* 12 August 1948; *f.* 12 August 1947, covering his first fifteen months in office; *g.* 14 October 1947. The Diary was transcribed from tapes; spelling mistakes, etc., have been corrected.

16 On 25 June 1943: PRO ref. CAB 87 57 6568.

17 HDD, 16 September 1943, 18 October 1943, 6 December 1943.

18 Interview, Professor G. C. Allen.

19 W. O'Dea to HG, 8 October 1947: F.12. Cf *DT*, 18 September 1943.

20 Arthur Gaitskell to HG: *a.* 1 January 1945, P.60b; *b.* 15 June 1944, P.7 (HG's phrase); *c.* 11 July 1945, F.8.

21 Drogheda to HG, 16 June 1945: F.8. Cf. HDD, 16 April 1945.

22 HG to Rank (F.9): *a.* 24 September 1945; *b.* 30 November 1945.

23 HG to Brett: *a.* 30 December 1941; *b.* 16 January 1944; *c.* 19 February 1944, 16 November 1944; *d.* 14 September 1939; *e.* 18 October 1939; *f.* 19 February 1944 (average ages were an obsession of Dalton's); *g.* 23 December 1943; *h.* 11 June 1945; *i.* 12 July 1945; *j.* 29 July 1945; *k.* 14 July 1945.

24 HDD, 22 May 1942, 24 February 1943, 20 October 1943, 11 January 1944.

25 *Ibid.*, 4 November 1943 (mentioning little dissension); interview, Sir Kenneth Younger. Dalton's papers have no note of this discussion, but a memorandum by Durbin warning of Russia's post-war ambitions is in HDP, III, 1942–3. Ten years later (in his preface to Durbin, 1954, p. 12) HG called this 'astonishingly prescient'; so he probably did not agree with it at the time.

26 *a.* Ivan Yates (Chapter 1, n. 1); *b.* and interviews, Sir Noel Hall, Lady Longford, Sir Laurence Watkinson.

27 Interview, Sir Herbert Andrew.

28 Mary Warner to HG, 24 May 1945: F.8.

29 John Ramage to author.

30 Sir Arnold Overton to HG, 6 May 1945: HG to Michael Wallach, 1 July 1943.

31 Interviews, Lady Gaitskell, Professor G. C. Allen, Professor H. Tout.

32 As the friend reminded him: Harold Cowen to HG, 25 October 1950 (F.15).

33 Lunchtime talk in 1945, recalled by P. Lamartine Yates to HG, 23 October 1950 (F.15).

34 Marjorie Brett published several of his letters in Rodgers (1964): *a.* p. 72; *b.* p. 74; *c.* p. 76.

35 Brett to HG (F.43): *a.* 13 November 1939; *b.* 30 September 1940, cf. n. 36; *c.* 17, 20, 24 June 1942; *d.* 13 January 1941 and ? August 1942; *e.* 12 April 1945; *f.* 15 July 1945; *g.* 9 July 1945.

36 On two Communist sympathisers (at this time opposed to the war) being expelled from the city Party: Brett to HG (F.43), 1 December 1940.

37 Brett to HG, 10 February 1941, 24 May 1941, December 1941; HG to Brett, 30 December 1941; Charleton to Brett, 16 December 1941.

38 HG to Brett, 23 December 1943, 16 January 1944, 6 September 1944, 16 and 28 November 1944.

39 Dora to Brett, 21 April 1945.

40 HG to Brett, 9 April 1945. His brother and Evan Durbin both pressed him to stand – and then felt guilty about doing so.

41 Brett to Dora, 2 and 12 May 1945.

42 Brett to Dalton, 12 May 1945; Dalton to Brett, 15 and 26 May 1945; Horder to Dalton, 25 May 1945 (all P.7).

43 HG to Brett, 25 and 28 May 1945; Brett to HG, 24 May 1945, 'Sunday' (27 May 1945) and 30 May 1945.

44 On 30 May 1945: quoting *John Bull* predicting HG and Durbin as future Labour Chancellors.

45 HG to Brett, 9 June 1945 and 'Monday night' (11 June 1945); his italics. In fact Brett spent £424 with an income of £444: Brett to HG, 9 July 1945; also 31 May 1945, 7 and 9 June 1945.

46 *a.* Canon Beloe to C. E. Robinson, 3 December 1970; *b.* 'He did not expect to get in.'

47 Interview, Lady Bacon.

48 As his sister later recalled his telling her at the time: Mrs Ashton to HG, 4 February 1948 (P.60b).

49 E.g. Ramsden to HG, 19 November 1950: 'The wisdom of the electors of S. Leeds in 1945 is becoming more and more apparent as the years go on'. HG replied (27 November 1950) hoping Ramsden would find a safe seat, 'which would ... give me much personal pleasure' (both F.15).

50 'Richly deserved', wrote Dennis [Procter?] from the Treasury, criticising the honours list in general: 23 June 1945. Cf. Dalton to HG, 14 June 1945 (both F.43).

51 Laski to HG, 3 and 13 June 1945: P.7.

52 *a.* HG to H. Morrison, 15 September 1953 (kindly supplied by Sir Norman Chester); *b.* to Pannell and to W. Blyton MP, 18 November 1954 (P.80).

53 HG's presidential address to the Leeds Fabian Society, 6 October 1945 (*Leeds Weekly Citizen*, 12 October 1945); and 416 *H.C. Deb.*, col. 2362: 5 December 1945.

54 On the end of Lend-Lease: Williams (1961), pp. 127–34; Dalton (1962), pp. 68–72; Truman (1955), Chapter 10; Gardner, Chapter 9.

55 For his minute of the discussion: n. 15a. For the diners' names, n. 1b.

56 Diary, 6 August 1945; HDD, 28 July 1945; HG to G. Gale, 1955 (Chapter 2, n. 16).

57 Interview. Roth (1977), p. 92.

58 Interviews, Lord Stow Hill, J. Callaghan, A. Crawley; Alfred Edwards MP in *DH*, 30 August 1945; John Lewis (a 1945 MP) to HG, 15 December 1955; cf. *The Economist, New Statesman*, 25 August 1945.

59 John Dowler the auctioneer to HG, 16 December 1955: P.101b.

60 Interview, F. Hardie.

61 *Citizen*, 8 March 1946, 5 April 1946, 10 May 1946.

62 415–422 *H.C. Deb.*, 19 October 1945, 29 October 1945, 5 December 1945, 12 February 1946, 10 April 1946; Select Committee minutes, 20 November 1945. His last speech ever as a back-bencher was on 7 May 1946.

63 PPS: Dalton to HG, 8 November 1959: U.1.

64 For interviews on the rest of this Chapter see Chapter 6, n. 1.

65 Diary, 12 August 1947, p. 7. Shinwell said he never knew Wilson had been suggested: letter to author. Wilson confirmed that he was: interview, and cf. Roth (1977), p. 100.

66 PM: interview, Lord Moyle (Attlee's PPS). Miners: N.C., 12 May 1946; Ernest Thurtle in *SE*, 19 May 1946.

67 Shinwell to author; interview, J. W. Farrell. Attlee indeed thought HG would 'supplement the Minister's deficiencies in some directions': Williams (1961), p. 222.

68 Letter to George Martelli (quoted in the latter's reply, 17 May 1946, F.9).

69 Interview, G. Keeling. Notes for 'my first Front Bench speech': F.7. 423 *H.C. Deb.*, col. 57: 20 May 1946. All the main Tory speakers, who included Harold Macmillan, went out of their way to congratulate him.

70 William Pickles, European Service, 9 October 1947: BBC.

71 Donoughue and Jones (1973), p. 413; E. Shinwell, *Conflict without Malice* (Odhams, 1955), p. 185.

72 Speeches: in London, 16 October 1946 (housing); 3 August 1946 at Sheffield (pilots); 25 October 1946 (snobbery); 17 November 1946 at Chesterfield (Ascot).

73 Dalton (1962): a. p. 205, also interview, D. Jay; b. p. 203, my italics; c. p. 199.

74 Quoted *The Economist*, 18 October 1947.

75 Shinwell, p. 182; Wigg (1972), pp. 127-8; Dalton (1962), p. 205; and jnterviews.

76 Interviews, J. A. Beckett, Sir Robin and Lady Brook, D. Jay, Sir Leslie Murphy.

77 One official, who did contradict, never forgave Gaitskell (whom he detested) for not speaking up, too.

78 Interview, Sir Leslie Murphy.

79 'Industrial suicide', thundered *The Economist* on 18 October 1947 after a panicky Ministry proposed to give industry only two-thirds of its normal coal requirement for the post-crisis summer. Also L. Hannah, *Electricity before Nationalisation* (Macmillan, 1978, the official history), discussing the gamble which the Central Electricity Board officially criticised at the time: pp. 315, 318-19.

80 Hannah, p. 318 and nn, with the official references. Shinwell, p. 181.

81 Interviews, Mrs M. Hemming, Sir Raymond Streat.

82 *DT*, 3 January 1947; *Sheffield Telegraph*, 4 January 1947.

83 Wigg, p. 128. On the committee: HDD, 12 October 1947.

84 The measures were those demanded by the Central Electricity Board: Hannah, p. 316.

85 The miners' general secretary, Arthur Horner, was summoned on the Sunday night to be told this: A. Horner, *Incorrigible Rebel* (Mac-Gibbon & Kee, 1960), pp. 179-80. He saw Shinwell with HG, Harold Wilson, and senior officials.

86 R. Cleaver to author; interviews, R. Frost, Miss M. Loosemore, Sir Leslie Murphy. At this time Dalton gave HG his one and only hint that he might replace Shinwell: Diary, 12 August 1947.

87 On this paragraph: interviews, and letter from the secretary to author. Milk bottles: HG's brief for a statement by Cripps in the House. Wigg, p. 129.

88 It superseded Dalton's committee on 12 February 1947: Sir Norman Chester, *The Nationalisation of British Industry 1945-51* (HMSO, 1975), p. 808.

89 P. J. Gorner to author (and interviews).

90 Interview, J. R. Jenkins.

91 Dr F. E. Budd to author, on which this paragraph is based.

92 Russell Latham to HG, 24 October 1950; cf. Edward Monkhouse to HG, 20 October 1950; Sir Frank Lee, later head of the Treasury, with whom HG worked closely over steel: to HG, 20 October 1950 (all F.15).

93 *ST*, 17 March 1947.

94 Lord Shinwell denied this, but it was confirmed by Lord Wigg, and by most of the civil servants.

95 Diary, 12 August 1947, mentioning Dalton's hint (n. 86 above). Both he and Dalton wanted him to go to the Treasury: *ibid.*, and HDD, 12 October 1947.

96 Shinwell in 455 *H.C. Deb.*, cols 2064–6, 2 April 1947.

97 Cf. 436 *H.C. Deb.*, cols 2222–34, 1 May 1947.

98 *Star*, 5 February 1947.

99 Interview, F. Allen, a new clerk at the Table.

100 Draft in HG papers, F.11; quoted by Shinwell in *SE*, 12 March 1970, in letter to author, and in interview.

101 *The Times*, 4, 5 and 9 September 1947; and interviews.

102 He particularly blamed Sir Wilfred Eady—one of the three Treasury mandarins against whom he had warned Dalton just after the 1945 election: Diary, 6 August 1945. Dalton apparently blamed Cobbold of the Bank: Davenport (1974), p. 169.

103 Donoughue and Jones (1973), Chapters 30, 31; Dalton (1962), Chapters 29–31; Foot (1973), pp. 219–26.

104 Interviews, R. Frost, G. Keeling, G. Martelli, C. Plumb.

105 Harold Albert, their next-door neighbour, in the *People*, 28 December 1947.

106 HG in *Daily Mail*, 11 June 1955 (F.4).

107 HG to James Langham, 7 March 1946 (BBC: his personal file N.41).

108 Interviews, Mrs B. Grieveson, E. Pascall, Margaret Stewart.

109 Another long-lost contact of that tour was Tom Baxter, who had first persuaded him to stand for Parliament: Diary, 14 October 1947.

110 Autobiographical note (Chapter 4, n. 56).

Chapter 6   Minister of Fuel and Power

1 Diary: *a.* 14 October 1947; *b.* 22 October 1947; *c.* 18 June 1948; *d.* 15 November 1947; *e.* 30 January 1948; *f.* 16 February 1948; *g.* 23 April 1948; *h.* 28 October 1948; *i.* 23 April 1948; *j.* 7 May 1948; *k.* 1 June 1948; *l.* 29 June 1948; *m.* 3 December 1948; *n.* 6 April 1949; *o.* 8 October 1948; *p.* 5 May 1949; *q.* 20 September 1948; *r.* 26 October 1949; *s.* 12 July 1948; *t.* 5 August 1948; *u.* 4 December 1947; *v.* 29 July 1949; *w.* 21 June 1949; *x.* 17 March 1949; *y.* 27 January 1950; *z.* oil: see Section vii.

2 So would Wilson and Shinwell: HDD, 5 September 1947.

3 This chapter was assisted by interviews with Lord Citrine, Sir Ronald Edwards, G. V. Keeling, Lord Kings Norton, Sir Will Lawther, Lord Noel-Baker, Lord Robens, W. H. Sales, Sir Geoffrey Vickers, and twenty-two civil servants, six of whom served in HG's private office.

4 Wigg (1972), pp. 129–30; cf. HDD, 12 October 1947.

5 Interviews, Lord Robens, Michael Stewart (Shinwell's new under-secretary) and many civil servants.

6 To author, in interview, and in *SE*, 15 March 1970.

7 Interview, G. V. Keeling; cf. n. 1*b*.

8 Wilson was President of the Board of Trade, and Strauss Minister of Supply.

9 Congratulations flooded in from, among others, Alderman Bill Mee (a former Notts miner); Charles Waterhouse and W. S. Duffy (Tory MPs); Mrs Firth (wife of a Winchester master); R. S. Courtney (a WEA student); Sir Frank Lee and Sir John Maud (senior civil servants); Giles Romilly (Churchill's nephew who had revolted against the Establishment); Sir Frederick Bain (President of the Federation of British Industries); and Edgar P. Harries (the second man on the TUC staff). All F.12.

10 *Yorkshire Post*: *a*. 8 October 1947; *b*. 6 October 1947 (HG at Rossington).

11 *New Statesman*: *a*. 11 October 1947; *b*. 19 November 1949.

12 Above, pp. 113–14, on the dual control.

13 Fergusson to HG: *a*. 8 October 1947 (with Diary); *b*. 26 December 1947 (F.11); *c*. 11 October 1948 (F.10); *d*. 3 March 1950 (F.13). Cf. interviews, Sir Leslie Murphy, Lord Kings Norton.

14 Tactlessly he added that the Ministry of Labour, who 'have the expertise', would take over conciliation services in coal.

15 Interview, Sir Arthur Gaitskell. Diary, 28 October 1948, 21 June 1949.

16 It evidently crossed with one from HG, which has not survived, asking for two named officials to be replaced; but apparently Fergusson objected and they were reinforced instead.

17 HG to Molly Bolton, 21 November 1949. Murphy, who knew him best, wrote of the 'tremendous wrench' of parting, of 'all the kindness you have showered upon me', of his enjoyment of the job and appreciation of its opportunities and 'most of all ... finding a new friend': 23 December 1949 (F.11).

18 Interview, Sir Goronwy Daniel.

19 Interview, Sir Leslie Murphy.

20 Interviews, Sir Goronwy Daniel, D. le B. Jones, Lord Kings Norton, Lord Robens.

21 D. Jay in Rodgers (1964): *a*. 92, quoting Fergusson; *b*. 91 (& interview); *c*. 93 *d*. 92–3 (cf. n. 27*m*).

22 From a notebook (dated by internal evidence just before his appointment was announced) and an undated memorandum in his papers (P.19).

23 *DT*: *a*. 27 November 1947; *b*. editorials, 18 December 1947, 27 Febru-

ary 1948; *c.* 27 October 1947; *d.* 9 March 1949; *e.* 5 November 1947, 1 December 1947.

24 J. Latham, Deputy Chairman, to the Select Committee on Nationalised Industries, 18 July 1957: its report of 28 July 1957, p. 143. Cf. Hannah, p. 315.

25 National Coal Board, *Plan for Coal* (October 1950), p. 19.

26 *a.* at Sheffield: *DT*, 10 January 1948; *b.* at Leeds: *DT*, 3 May 1948; *c.* at Barnsley: *DT, MG*, 20 February 1950; *d.* to Rotary Club, *DT*, 14 October 1948.

27 Sir Norman Chester, *The Nationalisation of British Industry 1945–51* (HMSO, 1975): *a.* pp 799–804; *b.* pp. 804–7; *c.* p. 60; *d.* pp. 34–8; *e.* pp. 550–8; *f.* p. 556; *g.* pp. 767–70; *h.* p. 982; *i.* p. 709–13; *j.* p. 986; *k.* p. 710; *l.* pp. 712, 1036; *m.* pp. 985–6.

28 To the Leeds Fabians, 3 May 1947: *Leeds Weekly Citizen*, 16 May.

29 HG himself persuaded his old Nottingham area comrades to ratify the agreement, at a bibulous dinner which made a permanent impression upon his young teetotal private secretary.

30 G. Baldwin, *Beyond Nationalisation* (Harvard University Press, 1955): *a.* p. 217; *b.* p. 24; *c.* p. 185; *d.* p. 234 (cf. n. 7).

31 Diary, 22 October 1947, on Bevin's letter to the Chancellor: 'truly remarkable for something thrown off by the Foreign Secretary in his spare time'. HG later instigated an inquiry by the Board, but it failed to prove his point about the effect of income tax: 469 *H.C. Deb.*, col. 1432, 10 November 1949.

32 Dalton, (1962): *a.* p. 268; *b.* p. 199 (on Bevan).

33 *The Economist*: *a.* 18 October 1947; *b.* 24 January 1948, cf. 8 November 1947; *c.* 14 February 1948.

34 At Cinderford, 8 December 1947.

35 443 *H.C. Deb.*, col. 709: 28 October 1947.

36 His sad and warm letter of condolence is in HDP, IIA, folder 10/7.

37 Interviews, Sir Laurence Watkinson, J. W. Farrell; W. Plowden, *The Motor Car and Politics in Britain* (Penguin edn, 1973), p. 326.

38 Interview, J. R. Jenkins.

39 *FT*, 9 April 1948; Plowden, p. 328; Miss Dorothy Hodgson of Hampstead and Mrs E. Waddington of Wigan, both December 1955: P.101b.

40 The Prime Minister had been most reluctant to let him broadcast: Diary, 30 January 1948.

41 *The Times*, 4 May 1948; *DT*, 18 March 1948.

42 *FT, NC*, 9 April 1948.

43 *DT, Times*, 20 October 1948; Diary, 21 November 1949. He gradually restored the full standard ration to those drawing a supplementary, and gave a three-month extra bonus in the summer of 1949.

44 Cabinet Committee on Socialised Industries: HG's memoranda (summarised in Chester, *op. cit.*): *a.* S.I.(M) (48) 1 of 1 January 1948 (pp. 433–5); *b.* 'Taking Stock', S.I.(M) (47) 43 of 13 November 1947, paragraphs 2 and 5 (pp. 531–2); *c. ibid.* (quoted pp. 556–7); *d.* S.I.(M) (49) 38 of June 1949, paragraphs 3 and 11; *e. ibid.*, paragraph 9; *f. ibid.* (quoted pp. 548–9, cf. 506–29); *g. ibid.*, paragraph 10; *h.* S.I. (M) (49) 33 of 30 May 1949 (pp. 995–8) *i. ibid.*, para. 11 (p. 997) *j.* S.I.(M) (48) 2 of 8 January 1948 (pp. 689–90).

45 452 *H.C. Deb.*, 16 June 1948: *a.* col. 436, figures given by Robens; *b.* cols 534, 537.

46 Standing Committee, 1947–8, vol. 2, cols 465–9: 8 April 1948.

47 Interviews, Lord Diamond (the Labour chairman), Sir John Foster (an active obstructionist).

48 HG in 636 *H.C. Deb.*, col. 60, 6 March 1961.

49 HG to Dalton, 1 June 1948; HDP.

50 Diary, 4 December 1947; interview, Lord Robens.

51 HG to D.N. Chester, 1 February 1954 (kindly supplied by Sir Norman Chester).

52 Trevor Evans, *DE*: *a.* 17 May 1948; *b.* HG's Diary shows he did not inspire Callaghan; *c.* 25 May 1949 (also *The Times*, *DT*, 25 May 1949); *d.* 7 July 1949.

53 458 *H.C. Deb.*, 29 November 1948: *a.* col. 1756; *b.* col. 1758.

54 Letters in *DT*, 14 and 16 February 1951. He blamed the old owners for neglecting cleaning machinery: at Cardiff, *DT*, 9 December 1949; in *DH*, 27 January 1950.

55 On 2 November 1950 at its York Conference: Report, p. 7; quoted Baldwin, p. 138, and Chester, p. 822n. Cf. A. Horner, *Incorrigible Rebel* (MacGibbon & Kee, 1960), p. 188.

56 Diary, 6 January 1948. HG's own agenda on his appointment, scribbled in a notebook filed with his diary, includes the words 'Robin, MI 5 and the Party line'. (A close friend named Robin had helped to run SOE.)

57 Diary, 20 September 1948, 17 March 1949, 5 May 1949; he noted with his usual realism that West Durham was losing a lot of money, and that good relations did not always give a lot of coal. The Scots president was Abe Moffat.

58 Interview, J. Griffiths.

59 Williams (1961), p. 221.

60 In a meeting at Tunbridge Wells: interview, E. Pascall. Cf. Diary, 21 June 1949.

61 Diary, 17 March 1949; *Sunday Pictorial*, 13 March 1949. Cf. 426 *H.C. Deb.*, col. 158: 24 June 1946. (Indeed some lodge officials thought him too tolerant of it: n. 62*a*.)

62 HG to NUM at Porthcawl, 6 July 1949 (official text, P.15): *a.* p. 13.

63 *DT*, 8 December 1949; *DH*, 15 December 1949.

64 *The Miners and the Board*, pp. 10–11; HG's red-ink note to paragraph 14 of draft sent by Michael Young, 27 January 1949 (P.21b–1).

65 HG to John Thomas, 13 June 1949 (P.20x; his italics). Interviews, P. Clark, Lady White.

66 M. Foot (1973): *a.* p. 263; *b.* pp. 229–30, 306, 311, 345, 593; *c.* p. 230.

67 Shinwell at Bradford, 10 April 1948; Dalton (1962), p. 66; Chester, pp. 508–9.

68 Diary, 21 November 1949; *DT*, *Daily Mail*, 11 November 1949 (but cf. *New Statesman*, 19 November 1949).

69 *DT*, *FT*, 9 July 1948. Cf. his speeches to the NUM at Porthcawl on 6 July 1949 and to the ETU on 24 May 1949.

70 Figures from HG's article in *Labour Press Service* (MS in his papers, file P.20–1, early November 1949); his interview in *DH*, 27 January 1950; and his speech in 469 *H.C. Deb.*, cols 1423–35: 10 November 1949.

71 Durbin to HG, 5 May 1948: F.11.

72 Thomas (1973), p. 123. HG and Strachey became friendly later.

73 He cheerfully mentioned Bevan as an obvious future Prime Minister to others, e.g. George Wansbrough (as early as 1946) and Lord Citrine: interviews.

74 Foot to HG, 16 March 1949: P.17. HG to John Moore, 22 December 1947: F.12.

75 See Chapter 7, sections i and iv.

76 Diary, 28 October 1948. HG was also urging Pakenham not to resign over a departmental issue: Longford (1953), p. 218. Pakenham's long and far-sighted letters to Attlee, on 24 November 1948 and 30 December 1948, are in P.37.

77 HDD, vol. 36, 'end of 1948'. Addison was with Dalton, Jowitt against him and 'Tom Williams flared up'. (Foot uses HDD extensively, but not this entry.)

78 Diary, 17 January 1949, 2 February 1949. Crossman, the leading Palestine rebel, knew of HG's sympathies: interview.

79 Interview, Sir Ronald Edwards.

80 He said later that he 'wept for days' afterwards: to G. Gale, 1955 (Chapter 2 n. 16).

81 To Dr John Bowlby, 28 October 1950: F.15.

82 *Oxford Mail*, 19 October 1945.

83 To a conference of the National Assocation of Labour Student Organisations at Dorking on 13 April 1949 (P.24); based on Durbin's notes for a book on the Economics of Democratic Socialism (P.55).

84 G. L. Watkinson: *a.* to HG, 24 December 1948 (F.11); *b. ibid.*, 11 June 1949; *c.* to Dalton, 17 June 1949 (HDP, III.6 Misc.)

85 See Appendix on pp. 191–2.

86 He had later doubts about Mountbatten too: Diary, 10 August 1951.

87 HG to Morrison: *a.* January 1949 (P.19); *b.* 15 May 1950 (P.21a); *c.* reply 19 May 1950 (P.21a).

88 HG to Michael Young, 21 January 1949, commenting on the draft report of the NEC's sub-committee on nationalised industries: P.21b.

89 *a.* HG to Alderman Ed. Porter MP, 7 January 1949 (P.20x); *b.* cf. HG to Morgan Phillips, 30 June 1949 (P.15); *c.* Porter to HG, 3 March 1950 (F. 13).

90 Sir Hubert Houldsworth (Bowman's predecessor) to HG, 16 & 30 June 1953: P.60b.

91 See below, p. 388.

92 Lord Citrine, *Two Careers* (Hutchinson, 1967), pp. 283–4, does not confirm his suspicions of the ETU leaders; but there is reason to think them justified none the less.

93 This was precisely Fergusson's approach too: Chester, pp. 415–16 (and n. 13*a*).

94 See below, p. 188.

95 HG's interview in *Reynolds News*, 30 November 1947.

96 The Central Electricity Board was worried about the sale of fires: Hannah, p. 313 and n. 103.

97 ETU transcript (kindly supplied by Lady Cannon), p. 15.

98 Citrine, pp. 296–7.

99 *Report of the Committee on National Policy for the Use of Fuel and Power Resources*, the Ridley Report, Cmd 8647 (HMSO, 1952): paragraphs 13 and 14.

100 I.M.D. Little, *The Price of Fuel* (OUP, 1953), p. 154. Cf. W. G. Shepherd, *Economic Performance under Public Ownership: British Fuel and Power* (Yale University Press, 1965), pp. 14, 81.

101 Interviews, P. Chantler, Sir Leslie Murphy. Cf. Hannah, p. 325.

102 Interview, G. Wansbrough (his first choice as chairman).

103 Diary: *a.* 12 August 1948; *b.* 15 December 1948; *c.* 17 January 1949; *d.* 2 February 1949; *e.* 11 April 1949; *f.* 3 August 1949; *g.* 1 February 1950; *h.* 26 May 1950.

104 Ridley Report, paragraphs 241–8, 288–9; Little, pp. 65, 99–102, 107–9, 127–8, 151–2; Shepherd, p. 26; W. F. Coxon in *The Times*, 9 December 1975; Hannah, pp. 327–8.

105 He had also wanted to intervene with the Coal Board over pensions and redundancy: Diary, 12 July 1948.

106 On this paragraph, Chester, pp. 959–67, 972–9, 1048–9.

107 Research Department paper RD 160, paragraph 3 (September); sub-committee minutes RD 207, paragraph 4 (November); P.21a.

108 Vickers to HG, 7 March 1950: F.15.

109 Above, p. 159.
110 Notes in P.37–3; 26 July 1949.
111 HDD: *a*. 22 August 1948; *b*. 27 January 1950.
112 James Margach, *The Abuse of Power* (W. H. Allen, 1978), p. 86; *ST*, 5 February 1978.
113 Interviews, Lord Hirshfield, Sir Leslie Murphy, on this affair. He did not speak.
114 See Stanley Baron, *The Contact Man* (Secker & Warburg, 1966); and John Gross, in M. Sissons and Philip French, *The Age of Austerity 1945–1951* (Penguin, 1964), pp. 266–86.
115 Adrian Brunel, FRGS, to the BBC, 9 October 1948, with a copy to HG suggesting he sue: F.10.
116 HG to Arthur Gaitskell, 21 June 1949: P.20x.
117 Lord Chancellor's minute, Morrison's minute, 11 October 1948: F.10.
118 *a*. HG to L. Cadbury, draft letter 26 May 1949: F.11, protesting against a comment in the *NC*; *b*. reply, 1 June 1949, P.21a.
119 Kingsley Martin quoted their letter of thanks in *NC*, 27 May 1949 (cutting with n. 118*b*).
120 Interview, J. B. Orrick.
121 Interview, Miss N. C. James.
122 Interview, G. Keeling. Cripps to Dalton, 16 March 1949, 5 October 1949: HDP, III.6 (Misc.), III.5 (Misc.).
123 Interviews, J. R. L. Anderson, J. H. Lawrie.
124 Leslie Randall, *Daily Mail*, 7 July 1949.
125 *Sunday Chronicle*, 10 July 1949. For favourable comments: Garth Lean to HG, 11 July 1949 (P.20x); interviews, J. R. L. Anderson, Margaret Stewart.
126 C.P. (47) 330 of 16 December 1947, jointly with the Minister of Transport. The list of ninety-seven memoranda to Cabinet and its committees is in his papers (P.21b); those on domestic petrol consumption are not counted among the sixteen.
127 Diary, 23 April 1948, p. 52; L. M. Fanning, *Foreign Oil and the Free World* (McGraw Hill, 1955), pp. 194–9; and interviews.
128 Fergusson to HG (n.d., F.11) fearing he had not yet convinced his Minister that wrong decisions on oil policy might gravely harm the European Recovery Programme.
129 Even his fussy draftsman's eye missed the title of the paper, 'De-merging of the Petroleum Board', and a note came back from No. 10: ' "De-merging"? Is this the best Winchester and New College can do? C.R.A.' Interview, Sir Leslie Murphy.
130 Michael Young to HG, 1 and 11 December 1948. It asked also about tar distilling – where 95 per cent of the raw material was, however, already controlled by nationalised industries (March 1949 memo in P.21b).

131 HG to Young, 6 December 1948; Fergusson's minute attached: P.21b–4. Shinwell supported HG's objections, and the proposal was dropped.
132 Sir George Legh-Jones—a director of thirty oil companies including Shell—to HG, 12 June 1950: F.14.
133 *U.K. Balance of Payments 1946–53*, Cmd 8976 and 9119. This share— temporarily increased in 1951 by the loss of Abadan—includes all operations of United States companies. £150 million by 1952: Fanning, p. 198.
134 His successor Philip Noel-Baker paid tribute to HG's conduct of the negotiations, which the Conservatives attacked: 475 *H.C. Deb.*, cols 2386–8; 26 May 1950.
135 Interview, P. E. Watts.
136 Interview, B. Gottlieb.
137 Interviews, including Lord Kings Norton and Lord Zuckerman, whom HG twice proposed as Chief Scientific Adviser. Campbell Secord (one of the scientists) to HG, 1 March 1950: F.13.
138 Interview, C. Plumb (who was in the car).
139 Diary, 1 October 1948; Dr R. Lessing to HG, 9 July 1953. Interview, P. Chantler; Lt-Col. Cowell to HG, 12 October 1953; HG to Dr J. Bronowski, 19 October 1953 (all letters in P.60b). King (1972), p. 30.
140 Interview, G. Keeling, who took him to this Café Royal dinner of the Square Mile Club.
141 The phrases quoted are from Philip Chantler, Lord Robens and Sir Leslie Murphy.
142 Interview, Sir Raymond Streat.
143 Interview, Sir Geoffrey Vickers.
144 HG to Alan Wood (Chapter 1 n. 1).
145 Michael Milne-Watson (chairman of the North Thames Gas Board, 1949–64) to HG, 9 March 1950: F.13. Cf. Henry Nimmo to HG, 6 June 1953: P.60b.
146 Interview, Lord Williamson (on the NUGMW).
147 Two dozen civil servants from HG's days at MFP were interviewed, and the generalisation applies to all but one.
148 Interviews, A. Allen, Lord Robens.
149 Interviews, K. Robinson, P. Chantler, F. Allen.

Chapter 7 The Treasury: substituting for Stafford Cripps

1 466 *H.C. Deb.* (Cripps, 6 July 1949): *a.* col. 2151; *b.* col. 2150.
2 HG at Wakefield, 18 June 1949.
3 468 *H.C. Deb.*, col. 17 (Cripps, 27 September 1949).

4 Jay's paper of 5 July 1949 to Cripps's group of Ministers: file P.22. On the issue see, e.g. R. Triffin, *Europe and the Money Muddle* (Yale University Press, and OUP, 1957), Chapter 1.

5 D. Jay in Rodgers (1964): *a.* p. 95; *b.* p. 96.

6 Diary: *a.* 30 May 1949; *b.* 21 June 1949; *c.* 29 June 1949; *d.* 3 August 1949, entry covers several weeks; *e.* 21 September 1949, covers several weeks; *f.* 26 October 1949; *g.* 21 November 1949; *h.* 1 February 1950; *i.* 27 January 1950; *j.* 26 May 1950; *k.* 21 March 1950; *l.* HG's phrase; *m.* 11 August 1950, covers several weeks; *n.* 3 November 1950.

7 Interviews, Lord Plowden, Lord Roberthall, and D. Jay—who was the main source for Paul Foot's similar account in Foot (1968), pp. 83–7. Cf. Roth (1977), pp. 121–3.

8 HDD: *a.* 1 July 1949; *b.* on the first of these meetings; *c.* on Cripps and Bevin; *d.* 'end of July 1949'; *e.* 12 September 1949, his italics; *f.* 11 October 1949; *g.* 12 October 1949; *h.* 21 October 1949; *i.* 13 October 1949; *j.* 27 February 1950; *k.* 'end September—early October' 1949; *l.* 30 October 1950; *m.* 24 January 1950; *n.* 27 January 1950.

9 Quoted (including the *sic*) in Diary, 3 August 1949.

10 *Ibid.*; HG himself scotched Strachey's proposal that he should be seconded from Fuel and Power to the Treasury. HDD, 19 July 1949 and 12 September 1949.

11 Over the six quarters of 1948 and early 1949 it was (£ million): 147, 107, 76, 93, 82, 157. Cripps in 466 *H.C. Deb.*, col. 2150: 6 July 1949.

12 Jay decided on the Sunday (17 July), told HG early Monday morning and found he had decided too: interview.

13 Diary, 3 August 1949; but see P. Foot (1968), pp. 85–6 on the officials' and Wilson's doubts.

14 That was the only way, without risking leaks and lost reserves, to keep Britain's commitment to inform the IMF: Lord Roberthall to author.

15 Some of the less senior Ministers also wanted it early to facilitate an early election: Diary, 3 August 1949.

16 Jay's draft, of which four-fifths is on the date, is in file P.22.

17 A (presumably late) draft amended in HG's writing is in file P.22.

18 Dow (1970): *a.* pp. 43–5; *b.* p. 52.

19 *a.* interview, Sir Leslie Murphy; *b.* and n. 41.

20 Davenport (1974), p. 176; cf. D. Jay in Rodgers (1964), pp. 94–5.

21 W. Wyatt, *Turn Again Westminster* (Deutsch, 1973): *a.* pp. 179–82; reporting Cripps; *b.* p. 148n.

22 Not £700 million as Donoughue and Jones (1973), p. 447 (a printer's error).

23 Dalton (1962): *a.* p. 350n; *b.* cf. p. 350, attributing this advice to Morrison; *c.* p. 330.

24 Donoughue and Jones, p. 447.

25 Jay thought that regressive, much worse than prescription charges: HDD, 12 October 1949. It came up again in 1951: see below, p. 256.

26 Bevan in 495 *H.C. Deb.*, col. 401 30 January 1952.

27 His note of 13 December 1949 is in file P.20x.

28 McCarran was a reactionary Democrat and, as a powerful member of the Appropriations Committee, important for Marshall Aid.

29 HDD, 19 July 1949. Attlee and Bevin preferred 1950. Morrison, Dalton and the Chief Whip wanted to wait and see.

30 Among these were Dalton and (so Attlee told him) Addison, Ede, Shinwell and Tomlinson. Jay was his source for the dinner. HDD, vol. 37, entries of 'end September', 'early October', and 5 October 1949.

31 Cf. James Margach's scathing comment on the press at this period: above, p. 180.

32 HDD, 7 December 1949, with a postscript after the election: 'we were wrong and should have gone on till June'. Cf. Donoughue and Jones (1973), p. 449; and on HG's reasons, his Diary, 27 January 1950.

33 Diary, 27 January 1950; Jay expected to lose by thirty. Dalton was one of the optimists; Attlee thought it 'might be tight': HDD, 27 January 1950.

34 Charles Pannell in *Leeds Weekly Citizen*, 10 March 1950.

35 HG at Harrogate, Churchill at Edinburgh, HG at Cleckheaton: *DT*, 11, 15, 16 February 1950; also his correspondence in *The Times* with Lord Cherwell, 18, 21, 23 February 1950 and 2 March 1950, and H. G. Nicholas, *The British General Election of 1950* (Macmillan, 1951), pp. 95–6, 191–3. In May, when the Washington talks succeeded and rationing was abolished, HG recalled his statement to show that this was not Churchill's doing: Diary, 26 May 1950. (On his promotion of home refining, above, p. 185.)

36 M. Foot (1973): *a.* pp. 238–44; *b.* p. 294; *c.* p. 292; *d.* quoted pp. 293–4, last two sentences omitted; *e.* p. 294, reporting Jennie Lee; *f.* p. 308.

37 D. E. Butler in Nicholas p. 331. In 1951 the Conservatives, with fewer votes than Labour, won by seventeen seats.

38 HDD, 27 January 1950. 'Comfortable': HG to Campbell Secord, 6 March 1950 (F.13).

39 Granada TV interview, 28 July 1961.

40 Dalton to HG (F.17–7): *a.* 5 March 1950 (HG agreed n. 6*h*); *b.* 2 September 1950, his italics.

41 Fergusson to HG, 3 March 1950: F.13.

42 HG to Evelyn Hewitt, 8 March 1950.

43 HG to Leslie Murphy: *a.* 8 March 1950; *b.* 30 October 1950; HG was still trying to recruit him to the Treasury.

44 *Observer*: *a*. Sebastian Haffner, 22 October 1950, reprinted in *Observer Profiles* (1954), p. 68; *b*. 1 October 1950; *c*. Kenneth Harris, 8 October 1950; *d*. 22 October 1950.

45 Interviews, Sir Denis Rickett, R. L. Sharp, J. J. S. Shaw, Lord Roberthall.

46 D. Jay in Rodgers (1964), p. 96, and interview. (Ignored by M. Foot (1973), pp. 276–7, 291.)

47 The Estimates Committee recognised the difficulties, but unanimously pointed to some inexcusable elements in the underestimating: Seventh Report, paragraphs 30 (dental), 34–8 and 56(8) (ophthalmic).

48 Final estimate for nine months of 1948/9: £208 million. Original estimate for 1949/50: £260 million. *The Economist* (5 March 1949) queried it at once.

49 Cripps in 463 *H.C. Deb.*, cols 2084, 2093 6 April 1949.

50 Seventh Report, paragraphs 45 and 56 (1) – unanimous; paragraphs 44 and 56(2), carried 6 to 5 by 3 Labour and 3 Conservatives against 5 Labour.

51 P. Foot (1968), p. 87, dates this Bill in the wrong year and says it was introduced by HG (who was in no way involved) and 'violently attacked' by Bevan (who piloted it).

52 470 *H.C. Deb.*, col. 2263: 9 December 1949.

53 Seventh Report, paragraph 56(2).

54 Committee of Public Accounts, minutes, paragraphs 5202, 5204, 5218 (Minister's decision); generally, pp. 419–23, paragraphs 5167–226, 10 May 1951; and Fourth Report, 1950–1, paragraph 55.

55 Cf. H. Eckstein's study of the early Health Service: *Pressure Group Politics* (Stanford University Press, 1960), pp. 136, 138. 'Pyrotechnics': M. Foot (1973), pp. 291–2 (quoting *The Times*). Nearly half the increase (£45 million) was for the dental, pharmaceutical and supplementary ophthalmic services.

56 Foot (1973), p. 293; Roth (1977), p. 127; Smith (1964, based largely on conversations with Sir Harold Wilson), p. 150.

57 472 *H.C. Deb.*, cols 937–8: 14 March 1950.

58 474 *H.C. Deb.*: *a*. cols 59–60 (Cripps, 18 April 1950); *b*. cols 631–2 (HG, 24 April 1950).

59 Foot (1973), pp. 294–5; Roth (1977), p. 127.

60 Bevan to Cripps, n.d., about 2 July 1950, quoted in full by Foot (1973), pp. 296–7. Foot assumes that HG kept nagging about the charges at the dinners; but Bevan's letter implies the contrary and so does Strachey's account in the text. Jay was sure he never raised them there, and Wilson did not say he did: interviews.

61 Strachey's obituary of HG in the *ST Weekly Review*, 20 January 1963. He there put the (unexplained) clash in 1949. Foot (1973)

reasonably attributes Bevan's anger to the health charges issue: p. 295.

62 David Marquand in M. Sissons and P. French, *Age of Austerity: 1945–1951* (Penguin, 1964), especially pp. 182–5.

63 HG's obituary of him on the BBC North American Service, 22 April 1952: F.17–6.

64 In *DH*, 13 December 1945; his italics.

65 HG in 594 *H.C. Deb.*, col. 887: 4 November 1958. For the American Employment Act of 1946, the original version of which would have met British hopes, see O. L. Graham, Jr, *Towards a Planned Society* (Oxford University Press, 1966), pp. 86–90; R. Lekachman, *The Age of Keynes* (Penguin, 1969), pp. 140–8. A similar Bill sponsored by Senator Humphrey and Congressman Hawkins became the Democrats' main issue in 1976.

66 *The Times, DT*, 18 July 1950; *The Economist*, 18 August 1950.

67 HG to Dalton, 5 September 1950 (HDP, 1950 B). *a.* his italics.

68 485 *H.C. Deb.*, col. 319: written answer, 22 March 1951. He was later reproached for it, as he said in the House in 1958 (n. 65).

69 Lord Roberthall to author; interview, Sir Henry Wilson-Smith. Very brief reference in Diary, 26 May 1950. HG expected the Americans to raise the subject when he visited Washington in October, but no one did: n. 70.

70 HG's memorandum on the talks, 8–12 October 1950 (with his Diary).

71 For EPU see Triffin, Chapter 5; W. Diebold, *Trade and Payments in Western Europe* (Harper & Row, 1952), Chapter 5; Rees (1963), Chapter 5; Worswick and Ady (1952), Chapter 23 (by J. R. Sargent); A. O. Hirschman, 'The EPU...', *Review of Economics and Statistics*, vol. 33 (1951), pp. 49–55; N. Kaldor, *Essays on Economic Policy* (Duckworth, 1964), II, pp. 54–9.

72 Dalton's phrase when pressing a reluctant Bevan and Strachey to cut dollar imports: HDD, 20–23 October 1947.

73 Sir Denis Rickett's memorandum of 14 March 1950, initiating HG into the subject: P.30.

74 HG's memorandum of 27 March 1950 on his Paris talks (with Diary).

75 Cf. his correspondence with Sir Hartley Shawcross about the sterling area, 23 February 1953 and 10 March 1953 (A.6b): below, Ch. 10 n. 148.

76 Triffin, p. 153.

77 Rickett memorandum; cf. Rees, pp. 64–5.

78 HG to Cripps, 15 March 1950 (adding that Jay agreed); P.30.

79 Diebold, p. 105; Rees (1963), p. 97; interview, Sir Denis Rickett.

80 Lord Roberthall to author; interview, Sir Denis Rickett. The Americans believed Britain was alarmed at their moves to create a little EPU

without her: Triffin, pp. 166, 279; cf. Diebold, p. 91, Rees (1963), p. 105n. But that left no trace in HG's papers or in official memories, and was probably an empty threat: Diebold, pp. 141–3.

81 On Canadian television: reported in the *Evening Standard*, 27 November 1961.

82 Lord Roberthall to author.

83 Earlier, Cripps had been 'fed up with Harriman' over EPU: Diary, 21 June 1949.

84 HG to T. Balogh, 11 December 1953, his italics (P.21a). Among these Ministers were Strachey (food) and Bevan (housing): HDD, 20 and 23 October 1957, and Dalton (1962), p. 270. On Australia see above, p. 187.

85 Harriman to HG, 19 June 1950: P.30. Harriman wrote similarly to Cripps: Diary, 11 August 1950.

86 Interviews: *a.* Sir Hugh Ellis-Rees; *b.* Lord Roll; *c.* R. L. Sharp; *d.* Miss N. Watts.

87 Hirschman, p. 53.

88 HG to R. R. Stokes, 22 May 1953: P.60b.

89 D. Jay to author; interviews, Lord Armstrong, Sir Henry Wilson-Smith. Cf. Dow (1970), p. 52.

90 David Eccles warmly 'praised HG: 477 *H.C. Deb.,* col. 2373, 19 July 1950.

91 Rees (1963), p. 255.

92 HG to Averell Harriman, 24 June 1950 P.30.

93 HG at the annual Mansion House dinner on 3 October 1950, where he was the first person other than the Chancellor to give the main speech in over fifty years.

94 US Objectives and Programs for National Security: NSC 68, 14 April 1950.

95 D. Rees, *Korea: the Limited War* (Macmillan, 1964), pp. 19–20, 245n. Nikita Khrushchev said in *Khrushchev Remembers* (Deutsch, 1971), pp. 333–5, that Stalin approved the invasion but did not instigate it.

96 United States: Truman (1956), pp. 359, 446. Bevan on Yugoslavia: Foot (1973), pp. 306, 311. Crossman on Iran and W. Germany: n. 97a. Yugoslavs on themselves and Scandinavia: Macmillan (1969), p. 337, from Embassy information. The Hungarian commander-designate of the Yugoslav invasion force claimed after emigrating to the United States that Stalin cancelled it owing to American resistance in Korea: *New Republic*, 21 January 1978.

97 478 *H.C. Deb.*, 12–14 September 1950: *a.* Crossman, col. 1263; *b.* and cols 1269–70; *c.* Attlee, cols 959, 965; *d.* HG, cols 1129, 1135–6, 1145, 1150; *e.* cols 1011–16; *f.* cols 1561–81, 1669–76 (18 September 1950).

98 HG's 'Note on US Aid and Rearmament' for the Shadow Cabinet, 23 November 1951 (U.156): *a.* paragraph 3.

99 Figures (1950 prices) taken or inferred from Diary, 11 August 1950, and from n. 98*a.*

100 Shinwell's account is in *Conflict Without Malice* (Odhams, 1955), pp. 212–13.

101 HG also regretted Cripps's agreement to increase higher civil service salaries, as 'bound to make the wage situation far more difficult': Diary, 11 August 1950.

102 *DT*, 15, 17, 21 and 23 August 1950 and 20 October 1950.

103 480 *H.C. Deb.*, cols 334–5 (HG, 2 November 1950).

104 *Yorkshire Post*, 14 September 1950. Also Hannen Swaffer in the *People*, 17 September 1950; Dudley Barker in *DH*, 20 October 1950; cf. *DT*, 14 September 1950; *The Economist*, 23 September 1950.

105 *Tribune*, 15 September 1950; the *Tribune* pamphlet 'Full Speed Ahead' (October); Gordon (1969), pp. 229–30; E. J. Meehan, *The British Left Wing and Foreign Policy* (Rutgers University Press, 1960), pp. 161–5.

106 Rubber prices had trebled and tin prices risen 230 per cent in eight months. Diary, 10 January 1951, for the small countries; generally, Joan Mitchell, *Crisis in Britain 1951* (Secker & Warburg, 1963), Chapter 2.

107 On this paragraph see nn. 70, 98. Also *DT*, 11 September 1950 and 10 October 1950; *FT*, 13 and 14 October 1950; *NC*, 7 October 1950, *The Times*, 10 October 1950, *Observer*, 8 and 22 October 1950.

108 Interviews: *a.* Lord Armstrong; *b.* Lord Plowden.

109 Interviews, J. B. Orrick, Sir Henry Wilson-Smith.

Chapter 8   Chancellor of the Exchequer: Bevan and the Budget

1 HDD, 27 January 1950, 18 and 19 October 1950. Dalton to HG, 2 September 1950: P.17–7.

2 According to Attlee: in a profile of HG on 'Panorama', 1 October 1962 (BBC), and nn. 3*a*, 4*a.*

3 Williams (1961): *a.* p. 245; *b.* p. 246; *c.* p. 248, quoting Attlee to Bevan, 21 April 1951.

4 Hunter (1959): *a.* p. 26; *b.* p. 27; *c.* p. 32; *d.* p. 34; *e.* p. 158.

5 Interview, J. J. S. Shaw, one of the Chancellor's private secretaries — who still shudder to recall it.

6 Henry Coase wrote to HG (11 December 1955, P.101) that Bevin, 'my oldest personal friend' with whom he spent every Christmas, had spoken to him of HG as 'young, virile and full of brain'.

7 Hunter, p. 27, for their reactions when Attlee suggested Bevan. Shinwell however thought both Morrison and Bevan wanted the job, and had more claim than HG: n. 8*a f.*

8 Shinwell: *a. SE*, 15 March 1970; *b. Sunday Telegraph*, 30 July 1961; *c.* in his book: Shinwell (1963), p. 189; and *d.* p. 190; *e.* interview; *f.* interview quoted 9*a.*

9 Donoughue and Jones (1973): *a.* pp. 465–6; *b.* Chapter 34, n. 38; *c.* p. 468; *d.* p. 487 (fullest); *e.* p. 490.

10 *DT*, 21 October 1950 (Morrison); *MG*, 21 October 1950 (Bevan). But the American Embassy had expected HG: W. J. McWilliams to Secretary of State, 9 October 1950, State Dept. file 741.13/10.1950.

11 Callaghan to HG: *a.* 14 November 1950 (F.16); *b.* 10 April 1951 (F.17–9). Also cf. Stanley Evans MP to HG, 20 October 1950 (F.15).

12 *FT*, 26 October 1950; Crossman, in *Sunday Pictorial*, 22 October 1950.

13 Guy Eden, *DE*, 21 October 1950, specifying Bevan, Dalton, Ede, Shinwell and Wilson as particularly resentful. Yet Dalton recorded privately that HG's success had made his own political life worth living: on 30 October 1950, HDP, 1950B. Wilson wrote to congratulate HG: 'There is no doubt in the minds of any of us that you were the right man for the job ... You know you can rely on me': to HG, 20 October 1950 (F.16).

14 Treasury: also *DT*, 20 October 1950.

15 HG to Strachey, 29 October 1950: letter in Thomas (1973), p. 266.

16 Diary: *a.* 5 January 1951; *b.* 3 November 1950; *c.* 10 January 1951; *d.* 2 February 1951; *e.* 24 January 1951; *f.* 16 February 1951; *g.* 30 April 1951; *h.* 4 May 1951; *i.* describing his own arguments to Lord Addison; *j.* 11 May 1951; *k.* 10 August 1951; *l.* his italics.

17 Wilfred Sendall in *DT*, 2 October 1950: a most perceptive forecast.

18 *Ibid.* For his rosy view of the consequences of defeat a year before, HDD, 11 October 1949 (above, p. 209).

19 Dalton in HDD, 18 and 19 April 1951, reporting Will Hall and Douglas Jay; and in Dalton (1962), p. 358. In the summer of 1950 Cripps told John Freeman that HG would now have to succeed him as Bevan was on such bad terms with other Ministers, and did not now want it: n. 20*a.*

20 KYD: *a.* 6 December 1952, reporting a recent talk with Freeman; *b.* 13 May 1951; *c.* interview; *d.* quoting Douglas Dodds-Parker MP.

21 W. Wyatt, who had been one of the Keep Left group and was then very close to Cripps and a friend of Bevan: *a.* interview; *b.* cf. his *Turn Again Westminster* (Deutsch, 1973), p. 147; *c. ibid.*, p. 148.

22 D. Jay: *a.* interview; *b.* in Rodgers (1964), p. 100.

23 Strongly hinted at in Sendall's article (n. 17).

24 HDD: *a.* 11 September 1950, reporting HG; *b.* 18 January 1951, reporting Bevan; *c.* 30 October 1950; *d.* 26 June 1951; *e.* 8 February 1951; *f.* 4 February 1951; *g.* 11 April 1951; *h.* 19 February 1951; *i.* 5 April 1951; *j.* 9 April 1951; *k.* 10 April 1951; *l.* 12 April 1951; *m.* 19 April 1951; *n.* 20 April 1951; *o.* 6 April 1951; *p.* 24 April 1951.

25 Foot (1973): *a.* pp. 300–1, with Attlee's characteristic reply; *b.* p. 324; *c.* cf. p. 323; *d.* p. 330; *e.* p. 331; *f.* pp. 333–4; *g.* pp. 334–6; *h.* cf. pp. 317–18; *i.* p. 340.

26 Murphy to HG, 20 October 1950; Fergusson to HG, 22 October 1950 (both F.16).

27 A young American friend later recalled HG's dismay at their ignorance of economics: P. Ylvisaker to HG, 9 April 1952 (V.4).

28 HDD, 4 January 1951; adding that Edwards did feel overworked!

29 But he redrafted far fewer than he had as Minister of State: interview, Miss N. Watts.

30 Impressions of the attitude of his Treasury civil servants are based on interviews with: Sir Douglas Allen (now Lord Croham), Lord Armstrong, H. A. Copeman, Professor J. C. R. Dow, Sir Hugh Ellis-Rees, Sir Francis Figgures, Sir Alan Hitchman, Professor J. E. Meade, Lord Plowden, Sir Denis Rickett, Lord Roberthall, R. L. Sharp, J. J. S. Shaw, Miss Nita Watts, Sir Henry Wilson-Smith.

31 Brittan (1964), p. 155; cf. Brittan (1971), pp. 180–1; also Dow (1970), p. 65.

32 Lord Armstrong: *a.* interview; *b.* to author; *c.* confirmed by HG's Diary, 4 May 1951; *d.* on HG's changing view of the US parties see below, pp. 513–14.

33 *Tribune*: *a.* 4 May 1951 (A. Crosland); *b.* 6 April 1951; *c.* 20 April 1951.

34 HG to Morrison and to Wilfred Fienburgh (about the next election manifesto), both 25 June 1951 (P.133); to the 1951 TUC: Report, p. 368. HDD, 30 October 1951.

35 480 *H.C. Deb.*: *a.* HG, cols 350–2, 2 November 1950; *b.* col. 1906, 16 November 1950; *c.* cols 1727–9, 15 November 1950.

36 He wrote a long official paper on methods of credit control on 2 June 1951, initialled HG: in U.156.

37 Dalton to HG: *a.* 3 November 1950 (F.16); *b.* 31 December 1950 (P.60b).

38 Dalton to HG, 17 May 1950 (HDP, A) and 31 December 1950 (P.60b); Dalton to Attlee, 27 July 1950 (in HDD) and his marginalia; HDD, 9 November 1950, 20 December 1950, 4 January 1951, 4 April 1951, 30 May 1951, 5 June 1951. For HG's attitude, particularly 27 July 1950, 9 November 1950, 4 January 1951, 5 June 1951; for Wilson's, also 27 July 1950, 20 December 1950, 4 January 1951; for Bevan's (strongly in favour of action against monopolies), Foot (1973), pp.

262-3. HG was still for abolishing RPM in 1962: ETU transcript, 28 June 1962, p. 15.

39 Diary, 16 February 1951; cf. HDD, 4 February 1951. He feared the Opposition attacks would further weaken Britain's position.

40 Interview, Lady Gaitskell.

41 482 *H.C. Deb.*, cols 542-4: 7 December 1950.

42 485 *H.C. Deb.*, cols 2375-86: 20 March 1951. In office, the Conservatives increased the rate of repayment: HG at Halifax, 20 February 1953 (U.153).

43 Broadcast text in U.21. William Batt, the new ECA representative in London, confirmed it at their joint press conference: *The Times*, 14 December 1950.

44 J. W. Spanier, *The Truman-MacArthur Controversy and the Korean War* (Harvard University Press, 1959): *a.* pp. 51-5, 96-9, 168-9; *b.* pp. 180-6.

45 As Acheson told Attlee in Washington: Truman (1956), p. 427; and n. 46*a*.

46 Acheson (1970): *a.* p. 482; *b.* p. 513; *c.* pp. 437-42; *d.* p. 436; *e.* p. 483.

47 L. M. Goodrich, *Korea ... in the U.N.* (Council on Foreign Relations, New York, 1956), pp. 158-67; and nn. 44*b*, 46*b*.

48 L. Pearson, *Memoirs II* (Gollancz, 1974), pp. 305-10, esp. p. 309; HDD, 9 February 1951; KYD, 28 January 1951 and 4 February 1951, cf. interview, Sir Kenneth Younger. Jebb's speech followed full Cabinet instructions: HDD, mid-February 1951.

49 Bevan, Dalton, Griffiths and (doubtfully) Ede: Diary, 2 February 1951.

50 Foot (1973), pp. 314-15; Roth (1977), pp. 131-2; my article in *Political Studies*, 27, 1 (March, 1979).

51 Truman (1956), p. 400. Churchill: nn. 35*b*, 52*a*.

52 481 *H.C. Deb.*, *a.* cols 1335-6 (30 November 1950); *b.* cols 780-1 (Attlee, 27 November 1950).

53 The new Secretary of Defense, General Marshall, proved less adamant about Germany: Shinwell in n. 35*c*.

54 Acheson (1970), p. 443. C. E. Bohlen, *Witness to History* (Weidenfeld, 1973), pp. 292, 303. (Allegedly Stalin sent only arms, no men, for fear of involving Russia: N. Khrushchev, *Khrushchev Remembers* (Deutsch, 1971) pp. 333-5.) On the NSC, see Chapter 7 n. 94.

55 D. Rees, *Korea: the Limited War* (Macmillan, 1964), p. 145.

56 *The Times, Le Monde*, 6 May 1977.

57 Cf. HDD, 9 February 1951, on HG's anxiety about such a 'false deal'.

58 Bevin's argument to the Cabinet: interview, Lord Gordon Walker. HG's later defence: *Birmingham Post*, 25 September 1952. Acheson, p. 483.

59 Interview, Lord Croham.

60 Shinwell (1963), n. 8c e. Also D. Rees, *Korea*, p. 234; Foot (1973), p. 312; Hunter (1959), p. 39.

61 HG's later 'Note on US Aid' (Chapter 7 n. 98) said Shinwell accepted it as an ultimate (not immediate) aim. Also interviews, D. Jay, Lord Roberthall. Lord Shinwell claimed credit for reducing it, and for putting it on a three-year basis: interview.

62 483 *H.C. Deb.*, 29 January 1951: *a.* cols 579–87; *b.* col. 582; *c.* col. 583.

63 G. R. Strauss: *a.* interview, 10 July 1972; *b.* fuller in his Oral History interview, 19 January 1962, pp. 25–6 (in Nuffield College, Oxford); *c. ibid.*, p. 27; *d.* p. 30.

64 HDD, 6 April 1951. Interview, J. Freeman; cf. his letter of resignation (in Joan Mitchell, *Crisis in Britain 1951*, Secker & Warburg, 1963, p. 186).

65 Smith (1964), p. 155; Roth (1977), p. 131; Strauss reported in n. 20*b*. I have found no corroboration for Foot's unsupported assertion (Foot, 1973, p. 313) that Bevan and Wilson fought a long rearguard action and opposed any commitment to a figure.

66 Sir George Mallaby (a Cabinet secretary who was present), *From My Level* (Hutchinson, 1965), p. 55. The Chief of the Air Staff took him off afterwards to continue the argument over a drink – at White's Club, where Bevan was assaulted on the steps.

67 GWD: *a.* for 9 April 1951; *b.* quoted in his *The Cabinet* (Cape, 1970), p. 135, my italics; *c.* 12 April 1951; *d.* 16 March 1951.

68 Interviews, Lord Armstrong, J. Freeman, Lord Gordon Walker, Sir Denis Rickett, Sir Harold Wilson, Sir Henry Wilson-Smith, Sir Kenneth Younger. On Attlee: n. 3*b c.*

69 *DT*, 21 November 1950; *The Economist*, 2 December 1950; **and** nn. 9*b*, 17, 52*b*.

70 The Cabinet even discussed – but deferred – conscription of labour, bitterly opposed by Bevan during the war: G. R. Strauss, n. 63*a, c.*

71 484 *H.C. Deb.*, 15 February 1951: *a.* HG, col. 644; *b.* Bevan, cols 739–40.

72 504 *H.C. Deb.*, 30–31 July 1952: *a.* cols 1523–4; *b.* but cf. Attlee, col. 1692.

73 Other serious candidates were James Griffiths (Colonial Secretary), Sir Hartley Shawcross (Attorney-General) and Hector McNeil (Secretary for Scotland). HG favoured Morrison: Diary, 16 February 1951, 30 April 1951; cf. HDD, 19 and 20 February 1951.

74 His appointment would have weakened Britain's influence in Washington, and the Administration's in Congress; and Attlee felt he was 'out of the running' because he had made so many 'stupid remarks

about the Americans': Attlee in *Evening Standard*, 12 February 1962, quoted D. Rees, *Korea*, p. 238n. Morrison accepted partly to keep Bevan out: n. 9*a*. Shinwell says Bevan expected it but his 'name did not arise': n. 8*b*.

75 Addison (a close confidant of Attlee) 'told me that Bevan had tried to have himself made both Chancellor and Foreign Secretary': GWD, 12 April 1951.

76 Interview, J. Freeman; G. R. Strauss also thought he was already seeking an issue; cf. Smith (1964), p. 153.

77 Gordon (1969), p. 235. Strauss agreed (n. 63*d*).

78 Addison (HDD, 6 April 1951); Ede and Whiteley (Diary, 30 April 1951); Strauss and (perhaps) Gordon Walker (interviews). But cf. below, p. 266.

79 Dalton (1962), p. 362; Shinwell in n. 8*a, e*, cf. 8*b*; interviews, J. Griffiths, Lord Greenwood, W. Wyatt; cf. D. Jay in Rodgers (1964), pp. 99–100.

80 Smith (1964), pp. 157–8. This account, based on long conversations with Sir Harold, is accepted by Mr Freeman as authoritative on this topic. Both he and Sir Harold confirm the persuasion: interviews. Cf. below, at n. 116.

81 But he agreed to a vote on account of £398 million, foreshadowing compromise later.

82 Bevin was ambivalent to the end. He praised both HG and the Budget speech to the Chancellor and other colleagues: Diary, 4 May 1951; interview, Lord Noel-Baker. Yet Bevan and Wilson thought he was with them: interview, Sir Harold Wilson; cf. Smith (1964), p. 154. Bevin died just after the Budget.

83 GWD, 6 March 1951. Gordon Walker later promised to do so too, writing to HG on 11 April (F. 17–19), 'You were right and I was wrong'.

84 Diary; GWD, 12 April 1951; and HG's account to Dalton at the time (HDD, 22 March 1951). Foot, in a whole page summarising that last account, omits Bevin's compromise: Foot (1973), pp. 319–20.

85 Confirmed by Dalton (n. 24*j*), Morrison (n. 9*d*) and Gordon Walker (n. 67*b*).

86 Interview, Lord Gordon Walker.

87 Confirmed by interviews, Lords Armstrong and Plowden.

88 *Glasgow Herald*, 11 April 1951. Cf. *The Times*, 11 April 1951; *Spectator*, 13 April 1951; *People*, 15 April 1951.

89 486 *H.C. Deb.*, 10–12 April 1951: *a.* cols 879–82, 1059; *b.* col. 1145; *c.* col. 842; *d.* col. 1109; *e.* col. 918; *f.* col. 1283 (John Baird); *g.* col. 1122, cf. R. A. Butler, col. 1573, 16 April 1951.

90 Memorandum kindly supplied by Lord Boyle.

91 Mitchell: *a.* p. 100; *b.* p. 174.

92 £105 million on them; £23 million on middle groups or on all alike; £8–10 million on the worse off: A. Crosland, n. 89*b*.

93 *Economic Survey for 1951* (Cmd. 8195): respectively £325, £50 and £25 million (the excess of new imports over new exports), totalling £400 million, all at 1950 prices. (The £500 million in the Budget speech was at current prices – rising fast – and contrasted financial instead of calendar years.)

94 In a full year the new taxes would bring in £387 million: Worswick and Ady (1962), p. 12.

95 Inadequate statistics misled Labour Ministers into overestimating the proportion of national income going into investment, and so believing it could safely be cut back for a time: Shonfield (1959), p. 176.

96 Of Dalton's five suggestions (in n. 37*b*), only one was accepted.

97 Diary of Sir Henry ('Chips') Channon MP: R. Rhodes James (ed.), *Chips* (Weidenfeld & Nicolson, 1967), p. 458.

98 Freeman to Bevan before resigning: quoted Foot (1973), p. 326.

99 *The Times, DT, MG, Scotsman, Birmingham Post*, 11 April 1951. Cf. Younger, in n. 20*b*.

100 *The Economist*, 21 April 1951, p. 905.

101 *DT, NC, Daily Mail*, 11 April 1951; cf. *The Times, Scotsman, Birmingham Post, Birmingham Gazette*; Hunter (1959), pp. 32–3.

102 Diary, 4 May 1951; HDD, 11 April 1951; Foot (1973), p. 327; cf. Hunter (1959), p. 33.

103 HDD, 19 April 1951; GWD, 12 April 1951.

104 Interview, J. Griffiths; cf. Bevan in Foot (1973), p. 394.

105 Chuter Ede saw it: HDD, 19 and 20 April 1951.

106 He wanted a year's time limit: *ibid.*

107 Ede and Whiteley (reported *ibid.*), Shinwell (n. 8*b*) and Jay (n. 22*b*) all confirm this account by HG (from his Diary, 4 May 1951), except that they omit defence.

108 *Evening Standard*, 17 May 1951; cf. *The Economist*, 21 April 1951, p. 904; *Observer*, 6 May 1951. Diary, 4 May 1951.

109 Peggy Duff (then its business manager, later secretary of CND) in Duff (1971): *a*. pp. 29, 48, 76; *b*. p. 32.

110 Taylor (1974), p. 764, who adds: 'anyone who studies the names of the prominent writers on Beaverbrook newspapers will know what he meant.' Cf. *Observer* profile of Michael Foot, 10 March 1974. HG had commented before the war on Beaverbrook's fondness for hiring Marxists: in *Plebs*, July 1935, p. 155.

111 Press of 11 April 1951; cf. n. 92.

112 Bevan had himself used the analogy in private: HDD, 6 April 1951; Hunter (1959), p. 33. He later denied any bad faith by his old col-

leagues: at Ebbw Vale and at Glasgow, *DT*, 8 May 1951. But he implied it at Huyton on 21 July.

113 Bevan: 495 *H.C. Deb.*, col. 401: 31 January 1952.

114 Cripps to HG, 31 March 1951, Lady Cripps to HG, 24 April 1951: F.17–6.

115 Both letters in Foot (1973), pp. 332–3, and in Williams (1961), pp. 247–8.

116 As both separately told Dalton before the Budget: HDD, 4 and 6 April 1951.

117 Interview, J. Freeman.

118 HDD, 17 and 20 April 1951, reporting Freeman and Callaghan.

119 He was not in touch with Strauss (KYD, 13 May 1951). Strachey came close to resignation (Thomas, 1973, pp. 265–7; Foot, 1973, p. 329). Shawcross is said to have toyed with it (HDD, 29 May 1952).

120 *a*. Foot (1973), p. 331; Smith (1964), pp. 157–8; interview, Sir Harold Wilson; *b*. P. Foot (1968), pp. 91–4, casts some doubt, as do some officials.

121 487 *H.C. Deb.*, 23–26 April 1951 and 7 May 1951: *a*. cols 35–7; *b*. col. 632; *c*. cols 228–31; *d*. col. 230; *e*. col. 1619; *f*. cols 1348, 1351, 1658; *g*. col. 42; *h*. Will Griffiths (Bevan's PPS), col. 287; *i*. col. 1661; *j*. Mrs Mann, cols 1694–5; *k*. Sidney Dye, col. 1696.

122 *Ibid*. col. 40. Douglas Houghton, Labour's expert, denied that HG's proposal meant £100 million a year would either be stolen, or would come out of the contributions of the workers, or would go to pay for rearmament: n. 121*b*. Years later Bevan himself told a Party Conference that talk of keeping the fund on an actuarial basis was 'a lot of nonsense. There ain't no fund': Foot (1973), pp. 493–4. On these charges cf. 535 *H.C. Deb.*, col. 993 (Edith Summerskill) and cols 1126–7 (Douglas Jay), 8 and 9 December 1954; and vol. 655, cols 1243–4 (HG), 13 March 1962.

123 Col. 43. HG had helped restore the housing cut: above, p. 211.

124 *Spectator*, 27 April 1951.

125 Mitchell (who was present), p. 183. Also Macmillan (1969), p. 240 (from his diary, 23 April 1951), HDD, 23 April 1951; interviews, Lord Armstrong, D. Jay, R. Jenkins.

126 *DT*, 25 April 1951.

127 Freeman to HG, 12 April 1951, F.17–9; and 23 April 1951, F.17–12. His resignation letter to Attlee is quoted in Mitchell, p. 186; Wilson's was never published.

128 Diary, 4 May 1951. HDD, 24 April 1951.

129 His letter in *Tribune*, 11 January 1952 (MS in file A.4), quoted below, p. 297, n. 18*a*.

130 HDD, 24 April 1951; Donoughue and Jones (1973), p. 490.

131 He blames Ede's comment specifically for the tone of the meeting which preceded it, and inferentially for Bevan's outburst which it rebuked; omits HG; and says there was no effective reply to Bevan: Foot (1973), pp. 340–1.

132 Bevan's lack of self-discipline in the PLP was often noted; e.g. in a very sympathetic article by Henry Fairlie in the *Spectator*, 11 March 1955; and as early as 1939 by 'Watchman' (see Chapter 3, n. 84), quoted Fairlie, 1968, p. 60.

133 Interview, J. Callaghan.

134 Diary, 11 May 1951. The resolution could extend it for only a year at a time: n. 121*e*.

135 HG on his own meetings in Diary, 11 May 1951; confirmed in the House by McNeil, Mellish, and Stross who was against the charges: n. 121*f*.

136 But by September, the TUC defeated only narrowly a motion condemning the charges. So quickly can new symbols be created.

137 Cmd. 9663. Bevan had assumed that the committee was a Tory plot to discredit the Service: Foot (1973), p. 215.

138 McNeil to HG, 10 April 1951, P.31y.

139 Dentures: paragraphs 576–7; they condemned the Conservative charge for dental treatment. By 1953 95 per cent of those applying for tests already had spectacles: A. Lindsay, *Socialised Medicine in England and Wales* (Oxford University Press, 1962), pp. 110–11.

140 Peggy Herbison for the NEC *after* the Conservatives had imposed other, much heavier charges: *LPCR*, 1954, p. 164. Cf. the TUC's evidence to the Guillebaud Committee (SIIWC 12/2 of 14 April 1954, paragraphs 7 and 9) on these and other charges authorised in Bevan's time (copy in P.87); and n. 121*j k*.

141 Bevan in 470 *H.C. Deb.*, col. 2264 (9 December 1949); and at Huyton on 21 July 1951.

142 Hilary Marquand in *Tribune*, 25 January 1952; HG at Glasgow, 28 April 1951.

143 Morrison's phrase for their views in his autobiography: Morrison (1960), p. 267. Interview, Lord Gordon Walker.

144 Foot (1973), pp. 318, 321; another myth repeated by Roth (1977), pp. 133–6. Cf. J. P. W. Mallalieu in *Tribune*, 20 April 1951; Ian Mikardo in *New Statesman*, 28 April 1951.

145 GWD, 16 March 1951, for HG, McNeil and Gordon Walker himself. HDD, 22 March 1951, for Dalton.

146 Interview, Lord George-Brown.

147 Of nineteen interviewed, only one in each category did; neither was close to HG at the time. His private secretaries denied it most emphatically.

148 At the start he told Gordon Walker that 'the P.M. ... was wobbling': n. 67*d*. Cautious advice came from Jay (n. 22*a*, *b*), and from Gordon Walker and Dalton who later changed their minds (n. 83; p. 256); cf. George Brown to HG, 11 April 1951: F.17–9.

149 HG to Evelyn Hewitt, now Councillor Mrs. Haughton, 7 May 1951; in her possession. (His italics.)

150 Above, pp. 236–7. Mitchell, p. 174; and interviews.

151 Brown in *Spectator*, 24 January 1964 – specifying the Budget dispute not (as in Foot, 1973, p. 316) the 'brand China' one.

152 Interviews, J. Freeman, W. Wyatt; and Wyatt, pp. 147–8.

153 As he told first Dalton, and then the whole Cabinet: nn. 24*l*, 67*a*, *b*.

154 Bevan phrases in this paragraph from HDD, 22 May 1951; 6, 9 and 24 April 1951. Foot quotes from all these entries, omitting these passages which explain Dalton's view of Bevan which he rejects.

155 Perhaps a joke, like MacDonald in 1931 saying duchesses would want to kiss him. Confirmed by Shinwell, n. 8*b*.

156 HDD, 12 April 1951; Dalton to Attlee, 15 April 1951 (copy in HDP).

157 Dalton (1962), p. 365. Attacked by Foot (1973), p. 312.

158 Thought likely by both their private secretaries: interviews, Lord Armstrong, Sir Denis Rickett.

159 See nn. 3*a*, 4*e*, 9*e*.

Chapter 9 Chancellor of the Exchequer: The Economy

1 His advisers convinced him it was unnecessary; but his instincts may have been wise, for the Budget estimates of production and investment were optimistic: Joan Mitchell, *Crisis in Britain 1951* (Secker & Warburg, 1963), pp. 101–7. But there was no point in restricting consumption to release resources which would be wasted, not used for defence, because of the shortage of steel.

2 He would have agreed to a limited increase that brought stability on the wages front. But it probably would not have done so, for though prices were soon to fall sharply, trade unionists (and politicians) had not expected that: Mitchell, p. 225, cf. pp. 149, 285–6; and n. 3*a b*.

3 491 *H.C. Deb.*, 26 July 1951: *a*. cols 661, 663 (HG); *b*. col. 705 (Roy Jenkins – pro-subsidies); *c*. cols 656, 665–74; *d*. cols 653–4.

4 Interview, Sir Norman Chester.

5 486 *H.C. Deb.*, 10 April 1951 (HG): *a*. cols 830–1; *b*. col. 855.

6 Mitchell: *a*. p. 158; *b*. p. 132; *c*. pp. 115–24; *d*. pp. 124–30; *e*. pp. 130–2; *f*. p. 176; *g*. pp. 71–82; *h*. p. 244; *i*. pp. 284–5.

7 Diary: *a*. 10 August 1951; *b*. 9 November 1951; *c*. 11 May 1951; *d*. 9 August 1951; *e*. 16 November 1951; *f*. 23 November 1951.

8 HG had always been dubious about 'the mad rush towards liberalisation begun by Harold Wilson & al', wrote T. Balogh to HG, 6 June 1951 (F.17–12).

9 HDD: *a*. 26 June 1951; *b*. 27 September 1951; *c*. 24 September 1951 (his italics); *d*. 1 and 26 June 1951.

10 HG to Morrison, 25 June 1951, P.33.

11 See Roth (1977), p. 143. Earlier they had attacked HG for pleasing the City and dismaying the TUC by his 'downright rejection of compulsory dividend limitation' in the Budget: R. J. Edwards in *Tribune*, 20 April 1951. But, first, that was never his policy (486 *H.C. Deb.*, col. 855: 10 April 1951); secondly, the TUC had favoured voluntary limitation of profits throughout Cripps's wage restraint and still did (preferring control by taxation to control by statute: *The Times*, 12 April 1951; and thirdly, the City's hatred for HG did nothing to diminish that of the Left.

12 Astonishingly, he was surprised that he had to, having thought he could just invite himself: interview, Lord Roberthall.

13 So he told James Haworth of the General Council: Haworth to author.

14 He surprised his audience by his possible remedy – bonus shares for workers – suggested and perhaps inspired by Frank Hardie.

15 TUC Reports: *a*. 1951, pp. 363–71; *b*. 1952, p. 321.

16 Trevor Evans in *DE*, 5 September 1951; Harold Hutchinson in *DH*, 22 September 1959.

17 'Nobody can remember a precedent': William Pickles on 4 September 1951: BBC.

18 For the US view, Acheson (1970), pp. 503, 506–7, 509, 511. Cf. KYD, 28 August 1951, 3 October 1951; and for Younger's scathing memorandum to Morrison about Anglo-Iranian see Anthony Sampson, *The Seven Sisters* (Hodder & Stoughton, 1975: Coronet edn, 1976), pp. 134–5.

19 Acheson (1970): *a*. p. 597; *b*. p. 509; *c*. pp. 559–60.

20 Interview, Lord Gordon Walker; HG to Harlan Cleveland of *The Reporter*, 17 November 1953, U.154; at Leeds, *DT*, 24 October 1951. Cf. KYD, 3 October 1951.

21 Diary, 10 August 1951. He claimed he wanted to offer Mossadeq a £20 million bribe, but that HG was too straitlaced: interview.

22 HDD, 2 July 1951; KYD, 24 June 1951, 5 October 1951; n. 23*a, b*.

23 Donoughue and Jones (1973): *a*. pp. 407–9; *b*. pp. 503–4; *c*. pp. 501–3; *d*. p. 502.

24 Diary, 9 August 1951; Stokes to Attlee, 14 September 1951, in Williams (1961), pp. 249–54.

25 HDD, 27 September 1951: briefly in n. 23*b*.

26 At Edinburgh, Rutherglen, Kettering and Lewisham, 8, 9 and 10

October 1951; his notes (in P.34) repudiate Tory jingoism but admit 'we all have a bit of this in us'.

27 490 *H.C. Deb.*, col. *15* (written answer, 10 July 1951); excluding lost sterling once earned from non-UK sales.

28 *a*. Jay in Rodgers (1964), p. 98; *b*. HG's memorandum of 18 November 1954 (P.80).

29 Worswick and Ady (1962): *a*. p. 216 (M.FG. Scott); *b*. and Dow (1970), p. 62; *c*. p. 258; *d*. p. 22.

30 *DT*: *a*. 17 July 1951; *b*. 7, 13 and 14 September 1951; *c*. 19 September 1951.

31 Diary, 9 and 10 August 1951, referring to meetings in June.

32 540 *H.C. Deb.*, 20–22 April 1955: *a*. col. 560 (Jay); *b*. col. 353 (HG); *c*. and n. 28*a*.

33 HG to Strachey, 15 February 1954 (P.100). Same verdict by Scott in n. 29*a*.

34 *a*. Interview, Lord Croham; *b*. and n. 35*a*.

35 *a*. ECA position paper for meeting with HG on 6 September 1951: file no. 741. 13/8–3151 SF, dated 31 August 1951; *b*. and n. 37.

36 Diary, 9 November 1951; and n. 37.

37 HG's 'Note on US Aid', 23 November 1951 (Chapter 7 n. 98) paragraphs 7 & 8.

38 *The Economist*, 22 September 1951, p. 681. Cf. *MG*, 1 September 1951; *DT*, 10 and 14 September 1951.

39 *DT*, 31 October 1951, 14 January 1952. But HG thought also that the press were badly briefed, and Congress irritated, by Charles Wilson, Director of Defense Mobilisation: Diary, 9 November 1951, p. 5.

40 State Department memos: Linder to Secretary of State, 22 August 1951; Linder to Webb, Under-Secretary of State, 24 August 1951; phone conversation, Secretaries Snyder and Acheson, 28 August 1951: 741.13/8–2851RF.

41 In 1952 and later, rearmament on balance actually benefited Britain's balance of payments: W. P. Snyder, *The Politics of British Defence Policy 1945–62* (Benn, 1964), p. 214.

42 Press conference, Caxton Hall, 25 September 1951: BBC.

43 *The Economist*, 29 September 1951, p. 732.

44 *DT*, 19 September 1951, *Daily Mail*, 19 September 1951, *FT*, 20 September 1951; S. Haffner in *Observer*, 23 September 1951; *The Economist*, 29 September 1951.

45 Plowden found the job 'quite the most tiresome and exhausting that I have ever done': to HG, 5 December 1951, F.17–8.

46 Jay to HG, 26 September 1951 (P.34) summarising HG's Cabinet paper.

47 Mitchell, pp. 106–7, 133–7; I. M. D. Little in n. 29*c*; HG to T. Balogh,

28 October 1953 and 4 November 1953 (P.60b) and memorandum to W. Blyton and C. Pannell, n. 28b. Some stockpiling was for defence.

48 *Economic Survey*, 1952, pp. 10–11; C. A. R. Crosland, *Britain's Economic Problem* (Cape, 1953), p. 65; cf. Mitchell, pp. 131–45; Dow (1970), p. 63.

49 P. W. Bell, *The Sterling Area in the Postwar World* (Oxford University Press, 1956), p. 376. HG to W. Robertson, 9 December 1952 (P.53); to T. Balogh, 12 March 1953 (P.60b) and 11 December 1953 (P.21a, comment on a Balogh MS); and to Roy Jenkins, 14 March 1955 (P.98, commenting on a draft pamphlet). There he analysed developments in 1950 and 1951 as:

> the rise in the reserves and balances here, following on the high dollar earnings of the R.S.A., which in turn were due to the inflation of commodity prices; the coincidence of the collapse in commodity prices [which] affected the U.K. terms of trade with the increased spending of the R.S.A. out of the previous boom, and on top of all that the sharp increase in the volume of imports into the U.K., coincident with a large rise in stocks and work in progress.

50 Interview, J. J. S. Shaw.

51 493 *H.C. Deb.*, 7 November 1951: a. col. 192; b. cols 222, 226, 231.

52 The Treasury then expected a UK balance of payments deficit in 1951 of £400–£450 million. Its estimates were later revised upwards, but after many revisions it was put at £420 million: Dow (1970), p. 62n. (cf. Mitchell, p. 139).

53 Diary, 23 November 1951. Stokes ticked off each item in Butler's speech to his neighbour Crossman: RCD, 7 November 1951. Also HG in replying to it (n. 51b) and later (*LPCR* 1952, p. 149; 507 *H.C. Deb.*, col. 786, 11 November 1952; nn. 32a, b, 28a (HG, Jay); interview, Lord Armstrong.

54 Among the officials interviewed a small majority took that view.

55 KYD, 22 July 1951, dissects this shift of view.

56 484 *H.C. Deb.*, col. 733: 15 February 1951.

57 Probably crucial to his thinking: interviews, D. Jay, Lords Plowden and Roberthall. (In contrast, Bevan had strongly opposed British rearmament before the war.) Above, p. 245 on this paragraph.

58 On 23 April 1951; already on 15 February he had warned that it had led to hate and hysteria elsewhere. (But Senator Joe McCarthy's campaign preceded rearmament, and was fed not by that, but by Korean casualty lists.)

59 Except only for McCloy's wish to relieve Berlin in 1948 by tank convoy instead of airlift – with which Bevan agreed: Foot (1973), p. 230.

60 Gordon (1969), p. 233, draws striking analogies between Bevan and Taft; cf. J. W. Spanier, *The Truman–MacArthur Controversy and the Korean War* (Harvard University Press, 1959, p. 159).

61 Interviews: Sir Kenneth Younger (on Attlee), J. Callaghan (on HG), Lord Plowden (more tentatively, on Morrison); generally, Lord Croham, Sir Alan Hitchman, D. Jay, Lord Roberthall, G. R. Strauss, Sir Henry Wilson-Smith.

62 Hunter (1959), p. 40.

63 Attlee's phrase; my italics.

64 Freeman (a Supply Minister) said in his resignation letter that they had not accepted it. Bevan on 19 April told the Cabinet it was impracticable, apparently having just got that impression at a Defence Production Committee meeting: Diary, 4 May 1951. Callaghan always had doubts: HDD, vol. 41, 2 May 1951. Wilson gave some reasons on 16 April in his last gloomy speech as a Minister.

65 HG in *Tribune*, 28 December 1951; and to F. C. Evennett, 10 November 1952, P.53. The Minister of Supply repeated that as late as 23 July: 491 *H.C. Deb.*, cols 60–2.

66 See HG in *Tribune*, 28 December 1951. Michael Foot's shifty reply suggested it was illegitimate hindsight, but HG had used it in the PLP (HDD, 24 April 1951) and at Glasgow (28 April 1951, U.2), and Crosland in *Tribune* itself, 4 May 1951.

67 Churchill in 504 *H.C. Deb.*, col. 1496 (30 July 1952); cf. R. N. Rosecrance, *Defense of the Realm* (Columbia University Press, 1968), p. 156.

68 In *One Way Only* (July 1951). (The total European shortfall was put at $25 billion: Acheson, 1970, p. 559.)

69 487 *H.C. Deb.*, col. 37 (Bevan, 23 April 1951); HG in n. 70*a*. Its peak of 2·3 per cent in April 1952 'was short-lived, and by pre-war standards, barely noticeable': G. D. N. Worswick in n. 29*d*.

70 491 *H.C. Deb.*, 26 July 1951: *a.* HG, col. 653; *b.* Wilson, cols 737–8.

71 Cf. *Economic Survey for 1953* (on 1952), paragraphs 23, 53, 124, and Cmd. 8475, p. 9, and Cmd. 8768, p. 4 (Defence White Papers, 1952 and 1953); Churchill in n. 72*a*; Dow (1970), p. 64 and n.; Shonfield (1959), pp. 56–8, 91–8; Brittan (1964), p. 159 and (1971), p. 184. Cf. interviews, Sir Francis Figgures, Lords Croham, Kaldor and Plowden.

72 508 *H.C. Deb.*, 4 December 1952: *a.* col. 1776; *b.* col. 1780.

73 Cf. Roth (1977), p. 145. The target was £2,750 million, the final official figure £2,748 million: Mitchell, pp. 133, 139, 249, 299.

74 The Treasury forecast the higher prices of imports (which were due to world rearmament) but not their volume (which largely was not): Mitchell, pp. 132–7.

75 In theory the crisis might have been met by a bigger export drive and

2E

a reduced defence programme to divert engineering goods to that drive. In practice, extra exports could not have been produced quickly owing to steel shortages; and the crisis soon ended when import prices fell.

76 *DT*, 19 September 1951; *Tribune*, 20 September 1951; cf. S. Haffner in *Observer*, 23 September 1951.

77 Compare HG's Ottawa speech with Wilson in n. 70*b*.

78 As HG told the Labour Party Conference in 1952: *LPCR*, p. 149.

79 Rosecrance, p. 131.

80 'on the whole, we do not think that the worst emergencies with which we might be faced have approached any nearer to us': n. 72*b*.

81 Memorandum on anti-Americanism in Britain (below, Chapter 11, n.6).

82 Interview, Lord Armstrong; confirmed by all his other advisers there – Lord Croham, S. C. Leslie, Lord Roll.

83 HDD, 4 September 1951 (on Korea and Iran, cf. n. 23*d*; KYD, 22 July 1951). Also on his disapproving the date: interview D. Jay.

84 Interviews, Lords Croham, Roberthall, Roll and Shinwell; the hint in Shinwell (1963), p. 192. None of them vouch for the story, but his autobiography suggests Morrison believed it: Morrison (1960), p. 283. Lord Butler contradicted it: *Listener*, 28 July 1966, p. 114.

85 Dalton knew of it (HDD, 4 September 1951, MS addition), as did Gordon Walker. He and Lord Moyle (Attlee's PPS) agree HG did not influence the date: interviews. (Attlee later said – obscurely – that he dissolved then partly because he thought Morrison mishandled the Washington talks: Hunter, 1959, p. 124.)

86 *Daily Mirror*, 18 September 1951.

87 Another was 'struck by the way in which you always made a point of acknowledging any help ... it isn't a very common trait': S. C. Leslie to HG, 1 November 1951 (F.17–10).

88 Probably from Dalton (see HDD, 4 October 1951, pp. 1 and 5; 30 October 1951).

89 Only in 1951 has a major party controlled the House with fewer votes than its rival: Conservatives: 13,717,538 votes, 321 seats; Labour: 13,948,605 votes, 295 seats.

90 William Armstrong, Marjorie Caplan, S. C. Leslie, J. J. S. Shaw, 1 and 2 November 1951 (F.17–8 to 17–11); interviews, S. C. Leslie, J. J. S. Shaw.

91 Douglas Abbott to HG, 27 October 1951, F.28; William Armstrong, 1 November 1951, F.17–11; Sir Edward Bridges, reporting Churchill's message, 27 October 1951, F.17–8.

92 David Duffield, reported by his mother, Mrs Sadie Duffield.

93 Mrs Searle to HG, 11 December 1955 (wishing him luck for the leadership): P.101*b*.

94 Clark to HG, 5 October 1954: P.82.
95 Speech on 27 April 1951: notes in U.21.
96 Interview, Sir Arthur Snelling.
97 Lord Roberthall to author.
98 Interviews, Lord Roberthall, J. J. S. Shaw. One sign of his frustration, minor except for his biographer, is that he broke off his diary for two years.
99 Attlee to HG, 3 November 1951: F.17–8:

Chapter 10 Opposition Front Bench

1 With 3,159,000 votes to 1,855,000 for the other 74 unions, 985,000 for the CLPs and 61,000 for the Socialist societies (including the Royal Arsenal Cooperative Society).
2 Jennie Lee, *This Great Journey* (MacGibbon & Kee, 1963), p. 116.
3 In *New York Times Magazine*, 5 October 1952.
4 At Newcastle, 23 March 1952.
5 In *Daily Mirror*, 26 February 1952; this passage heavily emphasised.
6 Diary: *a.* 23 November 1951; *b.* 21 March 1952, his first entry for four months and his last for two and a half years; *c.* 6 October 1954.
7 RCD, 29 January 1952; cf. KYD, 8 February 1952; *DT*, 30 January 1952.
8 HDD: *a.* 29 January 1952; *b.* 11 December 1951, 3 January 1952, 1 July 1952; *c.* 3 March 1952; *d.* 4 August 1952; *e.* 'Morecambe' (September 1952); *f.* 24–28 October 1952; *g.* 12 May 1960; *h.* 25 September 1952; *i.* 3 January 1952; *j.* 17 November 1953; *k.* reporting Donnelly; *l.* 20 February 1954; *m.* 6 and 12 May 1954, citing Callaghan, Brown and Robens.
9 495 *H.C. Deb.*, cols 212, 231–2; 30 January 1952.
10 To NUGMW Conference at Whitley Bay, 16 June 1952: Report, pp. 313–14.
11 HG's memorandum on US aid, 23 November 1951: Chapter 7, n. 98.
12 Diary, 21 March 1952; cf. *DT*, 28 November 1951.
13 M. Merle in *Revue française de science politique* III. 4 (October 1953), p. 777.
14 HG to Wallace Phillips, 22 November 1951, F.28. Churchill in the House: nn. 15*a*, 16, 17*a*.
15 494 *H.C. Deb.*: *a.* cols 2601–2, 6 December 1951; *b.* cols 431–46, 1674–9, 1966–8: 21, 28 and 30 November 1951; *c.* cols 1970–3.
16 497 *H.C. Deb.*, cols 446–7, 5 March 1952.
17 504 *H.C. Deb.*, 29–30 July 1952: *a.* cols 1495–6, cf. 1309; *b.* cols 1299–1300.

18 *Tribune*: *a.* HG, 11 January 1952; cf. 14 and 28 December 1951; *b.* 31 October 1952, official Bevanite statement; *c.* 20 April 1952, 16 May 1952; *d.* its one attack on the Budget (31 March 1952) used HG's arguments but gave him no credit.

19 At Daventry: *DE*, 14 October 1951.

20 RCD: *a.* 21 January 1952; *b.* 1 August 1952; *c.* 6 May 1954; *d.* 30 September 1952; *e.* 12 February 1955; *f.* 10 November 1952; *g.* 23 October 1952; *h.* 15 October 1952; *i.* 14 October 1952; *j.* 27 October 1952; *k.* 2 and 3 December 1952; *l.* 23 and 30 October 1959; *m.* 11 July 1958; *n.* 23 November 1951; *o.* 6 June 1955; *p.* 2 October 1953; *q.* 18 December 1953; *r.* 12 November 1953; *s.* 5 March 1952; *t.* 3 December 1953, reporting Roy Jenkins.

21 Roth (1977): *a.* pp. 150–1; *b.* p. 174.

22 RCD, 26 November 1951, 21 and 28 January 1952, cf. 23 July 1952. KYD, 10 December 1951. HDD, 7 February 1952.

23 Hunter (1959), pp. 42–3; Roth (1977), pp. 139–40.

24 HDD, 30 October 1951, 15 November 1951; RCD, 4 December 1951. Roth (1977), pp. 140–1, 150–2, 160–6. Foot (1973), pp. 358–9, compares the Bevanites to the XYZ Club—but mistakes its origins (by a decade), its founders and its purpose.

25 For a Tory view, see Nicolson (1971), p. 205.

26 HDD, 4 March 1952; Diary, 21 March 1952. Younger thought their amendment showed a new and deliberate wish for a split: KYD, 9 March 1952.

27 Only Ede and Tony Greenwood dissented.

28 Hunter (1959): *a.* pp. 46–50; *b.* p. 123; *c.* p. 59; *d.* p. 63.

29 Contrast Foot (1973), p. 366n, and Roth (1977), p. 159, quoting Crossman on Attlee's middle-class support. Younger contradicts them both about the crucial vote, and generally: KYD, 10 December 1951, 14 March 1952.

30 Yet he was reported to be privately very bitter against the rebels: n. 31*a*.

31 KYD: *a.* 14 March 1952; *b.* 28 October 1952; *c.* 30 November 1952, 6 December 1952; *d.* 21 March 1954.

32 HDD, 11 March 1952; cf. Diary, 21 March 1952 and (milder) n. 31*a*. Same sources for this whole paragraph.

33 So were Dalton and Callaghan—the former always, and the latter normally, a bridge-builder in the earlier period. (McNeil had died in 1955. Benn and Greenwood were Keep Calmers who did support Wilson in 1960.)

34 Diary, 21 March 1952, 6 October 1954; HDD, 1 May 1952; KYD, 6 December 1952 (on Attlee).

35 GWD: *a.* 22 June 1952; *b.* 2, 24 and 30 July 1952 on this paragraph.

36 GWD, 22 June 1952, 2 and 16 July 1952. HG, Griffiths and Robens wanted delay; Soskice, Stokes and Gordon Walker did not. The group, which met several times, also included McNeil and Shawcross, Morrison (once), and Whiteley (later).

37 Interview, Lord Robens; and n. 38*a*.

38 Donoughue and Jones (1973): *a*. pp. 535–6; *b*. p. 520; *c*. p. 521.

39 HDD, 17 and 24 July 1952. George Brown was another who thought so.

40 RCD, 6 August 1952; HDD, 4 August 1952, p. 5. Contrast Foot (1973), p. 376; but cf. KYD, 4 August 1952; *DT*, 25 July 1952 on the PLP reactions.

41 The advisers were thought to be his PPS Arthur Moyle, and perhaps Griffiths and the Party's general secretary Morgan Phillips: GWD, 30 July 1952.

42 E.g. *DT*, 8 March 1952; *Spectator*, 28 March 1952.

43 In September Crossman lamented that the Bevanite 'army of innocents' had planned no Conference strategy, though 'This should not do us any harm in the actual voting ... since most ... [had already] mandated their delegates': RCD, 24 September 1952. (Foot 1973, p. 378, quotes the first phrase but not the second.) There was a feeble counter-effort by anti-Bevanite MPs: GWD, 24 July 1952.

44 HDD, 1 May 1952; Hector McNeil to HG, 13 July 1952 and reply 14 July 1952 (P.49); and n. 45*a*.

45 *Leeds Weekly Citizen*: *a*. 17 October 1952, Charles Pannell; *b*. 10 October 1952; *c*. Councillor Dennis Matthews; *d*. 24 April 1953, Pannell.

46 Solly Pearce, editor of the *Citizen*, to HG, 15 September 1952; Robens to HG, 22 September 1952, both P.50; HDD, 25 September 1952 and 'Sept. 1952'.

47 HDD, 1, 13 and 31 May 1952, 10 September 1952. Transport House thought both HG and Shinwell would win: *DT*, 23 and 27 September 1952.

48 They did not yet realise that: RCD, 27 October 1952, 28 April 1953, 30 June 1953.

49 Foot (1973): *a*. p. 379; *b*. p. 381; *c*. as p. 383; *d*. p. 388.

50 Interviews, H. Hutchinson, D. Jay, S. Pearce; and nn. 51, 52*a*.

51 Interview, M. Arnold-Forster.

52 Roy Jenkins in Rodgers (1964): *a*. p. 119; *b*. p. 120.

53 Interview, Sir Harold Wilson.

54 HG at Sunderland, *DH*, 13 October 1952; HG to Mrs Myers of Warrington, 28 October 1952 (P.44).

55 HG to Tom Reid MP, 7 October 1952; to Cornelius Dwyer, 8 October 1952 (both P.50); and n. 56.

56 HG to Marquand, 7 October 1952 (A.3).

57 Tom Reid to HG, n.d. (early October 1952), P.50, reporting Crossman.

58 Roy Jenkins to HG, 3 October 1952, P.50. Cf. interview, D. Healey; and n. 51.

59 Gallup poll figures. Proportionately, more than twice as many middle-class as working-class members were Bevanites.

60 HG to Lord Lucas of Chilworth, 11 October 1952: P.44.

61 As Henry Fairlie, the journalist, recalled in the *Spectator*, 11 December 1955, and *Daily Mail*, 10 May 1957.

62 George Murray, his agent, to HG, 5 July 1952: A.3. HG to Solly Pearce, 12 September 1952: P.50.

63 Letter to a friend in 1962 just after the driver died. Interviews, Mr and Mrs B. Gillinson, S. Pearce, M. Rees.

64 He did not talk to Morrison (RCD, 10 October 1952, reporting Morrison's PPS); or to personal friends, or Leeds neighbours, or weekend hosts, or to his Transport House ally: interviews, Lady Bacon; Lords Gordon Walker, Pannell and Rhodes; F. Blackburn, A Crosland, D. Ginsburg, D. Healey, D. Jay, R. Jenkins.

65 Interview, S. Pearce; also D. Healey, C. Pannell.

66 As Mrs Braddock MP, herself an ex-Communist, had remarked when the agenda appeared: GWD, 30 July 1952.

67 The figure of one-sixth came from Ian Mackay of the *NC*. HG's private estimate was 5 per cent: n. 68.

68 HG to Donnelly, 10 October 1952: P.44.

69 Interview, D. Jay. HG wrote of 'irresponsible exploitation of prejudice' as the hallmark of 'demagogy – or mob rule': in n. 70*a*.

70 *DH*: *a*. 14 October 1952; *b*. 15 October 1952; *c*. 13 October 1952; *d*. e.g. HG, 7 April 1953.

71 Hunter (1959), p. 59. It was constantly talked of at Morecambe: HG to all his correspondents, P.44, *passim*; interview, S. Pearce; *DT*, 6 October 1952.

72 J. R. Campbell in *Daily Worker*, 4 October 1952; his emphasis. Cf. James Callaghan, *LPCR* 1952, p. 132; and Crossman in RCD, 22 February 1955, p. 627: 'Nye and I have never had a defence policy which satisfied the cravings of most of our Bevanite supporters in the country.'

73 NEC Minute 26, 28 October 1952; RCD, 28 October 1952. Morgan Phillips denied there was serious infiltration.

74 File P.45. Omitted in both C. H. Rolph's *Kingsley* (Gollancz, 1973) and Edward Hyams's *The New Statesman* (Longmans, 1963).

75 Strachey at Ipswich: *Times*, 13 October 1952. HG to Frank Beswick: 11 October 1952, P.44.

76 *a*. H. Heslop, secretary of Taunton CLP, to HG, 7 and 16 October 1952, P.44 and P.72; *b*. similar correspondence with W. J. Molson of Grimsby (HG, 18 October 1952) and *c*. S. G. Grant of Cardiff.

77 Also in the *Spectator*, 17 October 1952.

78 RCD, 6 and 10 October 1952. Cf. Jenkins, n. 52*b*.

79 Dalton (1962): *a*. p. 386 (he would vote for neither Morrison nor Bevan for deputy leader); *b*. p. 395.

80 At the Festival Hall on 11 October 1952: *The Times*, 13th.

81 He would not hear either of Griffiths, or of serving himself as deputy to Morrison: interviews, Sir Harold Wilson, J. Freeman; *MG*, 3 October 1952; RCD, 4 December 1951, 21 January 1952; Smith (1964), p. 176; cf. n. 38*c*.

82 RCD, 14 and 15 October 1952. Roth (1977), pp. 169–70.

83 RCD, 23 October 1952; Crossman had expected to blur the issue by 100 votes for postponement. (KYD, 28 October 1952, suggests two dozen abstained.)

84 At Burnley on 25 October 1952; at Rock Ferry the following day.

85 *Reynolds News*: *a*. 19 October 1952; *b*. HG, 15 February 1953, his italics.

86 RCD, 14 October 1952 (contrary to Foot, 1973, p. 385). Crossman himself had recently felt like Bevan: RCD, 23 July 1952, cf. 1 August 1952.

87 RCD, 26 November 1952. Only two of them, and four Keep Calmers, reached 50: *DT*, 20 November 1952. The Bevanites had rejected an alliance: HDD, 13 November 1952, cf. Hunter (1959), pp. 59–60.

88 HG to Wyatt, 16 October 1952 (P.50); S. Pearce, 28 October 1952 (C.6); and nn. 68, 76*b*.

89 Hunter (1959), pp. 63–4; interview, Sir Harry Nicholas; cf. nn. 49*c*, 52*a*.

90 Interviews, Mrs S. Duffield, N. Ellis, Mr and Mrs B. Gillinson; and generally for Section iv, Lady Bacon, Alderman St J. Binns, Councillor H. Booth, W. H. Goodwill, Councillor Mrs Haughton, T. Jackson, D. and H. Kennally, S. Pearce, W. Preston, M. Rees MP, Alderman and Mrs A. Tallant, Councillor H. Watson, Miss F. Woolhouse.

91 Archdeacon W. H. S. Purcell at a memorial service on 23 January 1963 (address kindly supplied by him).

92 Interview, Miss B. Woolgar.

93 South Leeds CLP minute books: *a*. General Committee, 27 July 1952, p. 132; 19 October 1952, p. 153; 20 June 1954, p. 252; 4 November 1956, p. 72; *b*. AGM, 7 February 1960; *c*. in 1960, by 10 to 2 in the Executive (16 October 1960) and 22 to 7 in the General Committee (22 November 1960); in 1961 with no vote against (16 April 1961, 14 May 1961).

94 On CDS, see below, p. 631.

95 HG to George Murray, 7 October 1953: A.8.

96 Castle and Greenwood always; Benn from 1957; Wilson failed once,

Crossman twice. Driberg was selected if nominated, which he often was not. Silverman was chosen once.

97 Interview, Alderman St John Binns.

98 Interview, Mrs Tallant.

99 *Evening News* parliamentary correspondent, 17 April 1953.

100 Iain Macleod, *Sunday Telegraph*, 19 January 1964 (reviewing Rodgers, 1964).

101 Lord Butler (1973): *a.* p. 162; *b.* pp. 160–2.

102 Sir John Wheeler-Bennett, *John Anderson, Viscount Waverley* (Macmillan, 1962): *a.* pp. 279–89; *b.* p. 352.

103 Letter in *The Times*, 28 November 1951; at Sheffield, 4 May 1952 (MS notes, P.48); at Ipswich, 4 July 1953 (P.63); and in the House, n. 15*b*.

104 HG's interview, *US News and World Report*, 11 November 1955.

105 In his credit control memorandum of 2 June 1951 (Chapter 8, n. 36); to Nicholas Davenport, 6 March 1962, quoted Davenport, *The Split Society* (Gollancz, 1964) pp. 148–9; in 491 *H.C. Deb.*, cols 668–70 (26 July 1951), and n. 15*c*.

106 *The Economist*, 8 December 1951.

107 He thought Israel needed it to check inflation, since controls would not work there: n. 108.

108 HG in the *Observer*, 1 February 1953, after visiting Israel.

109 HG to Rita Hinden, 14 October 1955 (P.107–4); and on unemployment to Alec Spearman, MP (Conservative), 25 April 1955.

110 Arthur Allen (his PPS) to author; Lord Roberthall to author.

111 Lord Boyle's Memorandum.

112 Interview, Sir Alexander Spearman, reporting Lords Thorneycroft and Amory and Reginald Maudling.

113 *DT*, 13 March 1952.

114 HG in 502 *H.C. Deb.*, col. 2453: 26 June 1952. He was 'Very pleased with way Finance Bill is going. No Bevanite trouble here': HDD, 1 May 1952.

115 Interview, Lord Armstrong.

116 *New Statesman*: *a.* 31 May 1952; *b.* typically, it then blamed them because only experts attended — as always, cf. 7 June 1952 protest letter; *c.* 13 February 1954; *d.* 20 February 1954.

117 Interview, D. Jay. Also on to a new NEC sub-committee: interview, D. Ginsburg.

118 *MG*, 17 April 1953, on the public friendliness of HG, Bevan and Wilson. Also nn. 45*d*, 99. The speech stung Churchill into calling HG 'this old-school-tie left-wing careerist': 514 *H.C. Deb.*, col. 651, 20 April 1953.

119 *DH*, 6 April 1954; *Sunday Pictorial*, 7 April 1954; *Star*, 9 April 1954; and n. 120*a*.

120 526 *H.C. Deb.*, 7 April 1954: *a.* cols 373–5, 378–9, 381–3; *b.* cols 367–73.
121 See n. 123*a*; cf. n. 122*a*; and n. 124*a* for his effective attack, with Roy Jenkins, on takeover bids which were then new.
122 520 *H.C. Deb.*, 6 November 1953: *a.* cols 474–5; *b.* cols 468–76; *c.* cols 462–7.
123 524 *H.C. Deb.*, 3 March 1954: *a.* cols. 1202–19; *b.* cols 1204–7.
124 523 *H.C. Deb.*, 4 and 11 February 1954: *a.* cols 1436–8; *b.* cols 594–612.
125 See nn. 122*b*, 123*b*, 120*b*.
126 612 *H.C. Deb.*, cols 862–5, 3 November 1959; Foot (1973), p. 635.
127 Conclusion of his lecture to the Anglo-Israeli Association, 6 March 1953: V.2. He also encouraged Beveridge's proposed independent committee on wages and prices, while insisting it would not work without trade union good will: Beveridge to HG, 26 May 1953, and reply, 4 June 1953, F.39.
128 *Socialist Commentary*, September 1953.
129 HG to Morrison, 29 January 1954: P.100A.
130 Sub-committee, sixth meeting, 6 July 1954, Minute 3; Transport House paper R.394; NEC, 28 July 1954, M.240.
131 So at the time he told Henry Fairlie, who recalled it in *Spectator*, 16 December 1955.
132 In *The Reporter*, 1 September 1953.
133 As Durbin had already argued in 1940: Durbin (1954 edn.) pp. 293–4, 299–300.
134 Article in *Star*, 22 April 1953; speech at Exeter, *The Times*, 11 May 1953.
135 His two themes at the 1953 Party Conference; and n. 85*b*.
136 *Political Quarterly*, January 1953, on a gift tax; and n. 85*b*.
137 512 *H.C. Deb.*, cols 2044–6, 17 March 1953; cf. vol. 513, col. 1446, 2 April 1953.
138 David Howell MP, *The Times*, 12 February 1975.
139 *a.* HG to Dalton, 13 January 1955 (P. 97); *b.* on XYZ above, p. 47.
140 Lord Birkenhead, *The Prof. in Two Worlds* (Collins, 1961), pp. 284–94; Dow (1970), pp. 80–4; Brittan (1971), pp. 195–8; Shonfield (1959), pp. 217–19; Rees (1963), pp. 153–4; and n. 101*b*. Cherwell's role in stopping it earned a surprised tribute from HG: n. 141*a*. Also see Diary, 9 November 1954.
141 507 *H.C. Deb.*, 11 November 1952: *a.* cols 797–8; *b.* cols 783–800.
142 Letter to *The Economist*, 6 December 1952; and in the House, nn. 17*b*, 141*a*.
143 Dow (1970), p. 72 and n.
144 See 497 *H.C. Deb.*, cols 1592–7, 1960–2, 2035, 2055; vol. 498, cols. 2415–7, 2427 (13 and 17 March 1952; 7 April 1952).

145 HG in n. 141*b*, and in 510 *H.C. Deb.*, cols. 1697–1716, 3 February 1953; Boothby and Amery in that debate. HG put many questions on the Conference, wrote articles on it in *DH*, 27, 28 and 29 November 1952, and made many speeches on convertibility.

146 HG in *New Commonwealth*, 4 January 1954, referring back to the December 1952 Conference.

147 *Ibid.*; *Observer*, 24 January 1954; and in the House, nn. 122*c*, 124*b*.

148 HG (defending Robert Boothby against a rebuke in *The Times*) to Sir Hartley Shawcross, 23 February 1953, 10 March 1953: A6b.

149 HG to Sir Richard Acland MP, 7 October 1952 (P.50); to W. Mitchell of Newcastle, 11 October 1952; to T. J. Morgan of Greenford, 10 October 1952, suggesting taking over two or three new industries in the next Parliament (both P.44); and n. 70*a*.

150 By Professor Sam Beer, *Observer*, 7 October 1973.

151 He favoured higher death duties and taxes on gifts and dis-saving, but not bank nationalisation. On education see below, pp. 388, 466–8, 659.

152 Interview, Lord Douglass.

153 Planned as soon as Morrison withdrew: *DT*, 29 September 1953; HDD, 29 October 1953, reporting HG, and n. 154.

154 Interview, G. Goodman.

155 Down by 13 and 6 respectively; Dalton now 'voted gloomily for H.M., because A.B. has been so impossible in Parl. Ctee, in particular so rude to H.G.': HDD, 29 October 1953.

156 The second ballot had been abolished but the no-plumping rule retained. That led Bevan, 'full of egoism & bile & getting worse', to explode – mainly at HG: HDD, 23 June 1953.

157 A. Albu MP to HG, 18 August 1953: P.71.

158 RCD, 26 February 1953, 18 June 1953, 1 November 1954. Younger privately saw *Tribune* as 'a rag of no value', always making trouble by attacking colleagues, and thought the Bevanites 'quite unconstructive': KYD, 24 September 1953, 26 December 1953.

159 *Tribune*, 13 November 1953; HDD, 17 November 1953; Roth (1977), pp. 177–8.

160 Will Lawther, writing to deny that HG at Fuel and Power appealed to planners not miners, prudently insisted on a receipt for his letter, fearing it would otherwise remain unpublished – like Tawney's and Pannell's.

161 On HG and the BBC, cf. Grisewood (1968), pp. 188–9.

162 *Forward*, 25 October 1952; *Tribune*, 31 October 1952, where he said of course Foot was entitled to turn him down (contrast Foot, 1973, p. 384).

163 Correspondence in F.1b.

164 S. Pearce to HG, 30 June 1954 and his reply, 5 July 1954, P.88. HG to George Dallas, 21 March 1955, P.97; to John Murray, 2 November 1955, P.99. Rita Hinden to HG, 26 January 1955 and 31 March 1955, Rene Saran to HG, 11 February 1955, and his replies 28 January 1955, 11 February 1955, 2 March 1955, 1 April 1955; by then four big unions were taking over 1,500 copies (all P.90). There were somewhat conspiratorial meetings with the unions in December 1952 (P.53 and P.68), December 1953 (P.60b) and June 1954 (P.87).

165 HG to Tom Williamson, 19 January 1954, P.100A; to Tewson, Deakin and Williamson on 28 July 1954, P.97. Both enclose memoranda with examples of his complaints; the quotation is from the last letter. Cf. below, pp. 493, 668, Ch. 11 n. 68, Ch. 24 n. 58.

166 His secretary attached a note to the letters of 28 July 1954: 'Mr. Williamson 10.30. – has your letter and has destroyed it. Has your document and will deal with it. Will treat it as confidential – don't worry. He's going for a holiday.'

167 He had spoken in the general election for Ron Chamberlain at Norwood – one of the only three Labour MPs to vote against the Atlantic Pact, who wrote for the Communist *Daily Worker*.

168 RCD, 2 October 1953, reporting Henry Fairlie. But at another dinner Younger had found HG 'violent' and feared he was 'succumbing to sectarianism': KYD, 24 September 1953.

169 A. J. Cummings in *NC*, 9 February 1954.

170 Interview, J. B. Orrick; Orrick to HG, 6 August 1953, F.17–13.

171 HDD, 25 November 1953, and Dalton (1962), pp. 394–6. (Foot, 1973, p. 412 quotes that sentence, but not the next on HG's twenty-seven years in the Movement.)

172 HDD, 19 June 1954, reporting Geoffrey Bing. Bevan said much the same to Dalton in July: HDP, 1950(A), 'material for memoirs' 1954.

173 Foot (1973), p. 483; RCD, 21 and 28 April 1954, 3 May 1954; cf. KYD, 27 April 1954.

Chapter 11   Foreign Affairs, and the Disintegration of Bevanism

1 At Newcastle: *The Times*, 24 March 1952.

2 To the NUGMW Conference at Whitley Bay, 16 June 1952: Report, p. 317.

3 At York, 6 April 1952.

4 At Jarrow: *The Times*, 17 March 1952. Crossman was horrified: RCD, 17 March 1952.

5 In *DH*, 14 October 1952.

6 Unsigned 1952 memorandum (with insertion in HG's writing): P.68.

7 HG in *The Reporter*, 1 September 1953.

8 HG on 'In the News', 7 November 1952: BBC (Typically, Crossman thought HG's policies would be justified if the Democrats won, while Bevan, who took their victory for granted, was outraged by that idea: RCD, 5 and 7 November 1952.)

9 HG in the Labour Party publication *Fact*: October 1953.

10 HG to Sir Roger Makins, 4 September 1953: V.5.

11 HG at the Anglo-German conference at Koenigswinter, *DT*, 26 April 1954; and in n. 12.

12 HG in *Daily Mirror*, 5 May 1954.

13 526 *H.C. Deb.*, cols 969–72 (13 April 1954); Foot (1973), pp. 430–2; RCD, 21 April 1954.

14 *The Times*, 17 February 1953. J. B. Orrick to HG, 11 July 1954: P.82.

15 Obscured by Foot (1973), pp. 430–2, though clear from his source (Eden, 1960, n. 16).

16 Eden (1960), pp. 89–106.

17 Pierre Mendès-France represented France there as her latest Premier and her best, in HG's view: n. 18a.

18 533 *H.C. Deb.*, 17–18 November 1954: *a.* col. 588; *b.* cols 586–8; *c.* col. 606; *d.* cols 572–91; *e.* col. 477; *f.* col. 533.

19 RCD: *a.* 3 May 1954; *b.* 21 April 1954; *c.* 3 May 1954, re Walter Monslow; *d.* 28 April 1954; *e.* 6 May 1954; *f.* 19 July 1954; *g.* 8 July 1954; *h.* 26 December 1954; *i.* 22 February 1955; *j.* 28 February 1955; *k.* 3 March 1955; *l.* 8 March 1955; *m.* 16 March 1955; *n.* 24 March 1955; *o.* 31 March 1955; *p.* 21 March 1955; *q.* ignored by Foot, who used these diaries extensively.

20 Foot (1973): *a.* p. 432; *b.* p. 433, on the change; *c.* p. 439; *d.* p. 438; *e.* p. 450; *f.* printed p. 477n.

21 HG resumed his Diary by recalling the affair: 6 October 1954. Others confirm that Bevan 'clearly repudiated Clem': KYD, 27 April 1954, also n. 19b.

22 Diary: *a.* 6 October 1954; *b.* 14 December 1954; *c.* 9 November 1954; *d.* 19 March 1955; *e.* 2 April 1955; *f.* 25 March 1955.

23 HDD, 13 April 1954 (his emphasis). Writing six months later HG merely recalled that Bevan 'rather adroitly turned the discussion on to the policy issue'.

24 Diary, 8 October 1954; and n. 19b.

25 HDD: *a.* 14 April 1954; *b.* 9/12 July 1954; *c.* 17 July 1952; *d.* 7 March 1955; *e.* 28 February 1955; *f.* 8 and 12 March 1955.

26 Foot (1973), pp. 431–2; cf. Hunter (1959), pp. 74–5; RCD, 21 April 1954; KYD, 27 April 1954.

27 All Crossman's young left-wingers in Coventry 'found it impossible to explain in the factories': RCD, 3 May 1954. Also KYD, 28 May 1954.

28 Foot (1973), p. 431. Roth (1977) p. 180.

29 Donoughue and Jones (1973), pp. 530–1. (HG was enlisted to persuade Morrison to apologise: HDD, 5 and 6 May 1954.)

30 Hunter (1959), pp. 78–9, quoting Crossman; Foot (1973), p. 433; cf. report in Diary, 6 October 1954.

31 RCD, 28 April 1954, 3 May 1954 ('harm'). P. Foot (1968), p. 117; M. Foot (1973), pp. 433–4; Roth (1977), pp. 180–1.

32 Dalton (1962), p. 396.

33 Duff (1971), pp. 46–7, 49. By 1955 they were little more than a machine to get themselves selected: RCD, 13 October 1955.

34 RCD, 6 May 1954. Also to Dalton in July, at Sam Watson's house in Durham: (HDP – 'material for memoirs'). Cf. Foot (1973), pp. 439–40.

35 The view of Sam Watson, a shrewd friend of both men, in Rodgers (1964), p. 111. HG advised his supporters to use this argument: n. 36a.

36 HG to Solly Pearce, P.89: a. 20 July 1954; b. 5 July 1954.

37 HG to George Murray, P.89: a. 25 June 1954; b. 5 October 1954.

38 Harrison (1960), p. 311, suggests the AEU may have made the same deal with Deakin again in 1955.

39 Ibid., pp. 147–8 (for the wrangle), 180 (for the quotation), 318.

40 DT, 28 September 1954, reporting the president's reply to objections from nearly half their conference delegation.

41 HDD, 18 July 1954, reporting Watson who wrote wrongly nine years later that he had told Bevan that the NUM – rather than the DMA – had decided for HG. The latter had (Watson to HG, 4 May 1954, P.89); the former had not. Cf. Foot (1973), pp. 438–9.

42 Watson in Rodgers (1964), p. 110.

43 DT, 30 August 1954; letters to HG from the RACS MP and chairman 21 and 28 September 1954, P.89.

44 On this 'one package' policy see Acheson (1970), pp. 434–42.

45 HDD, 4 September 1951; cf. 9 February 1951, on HG's views on Germany; end August 1951, seven pages on the Cabinet debate. Morrison was backed by Shinwell (hesitantly), Jowitt and Pakenham; Dalton by Griffiths, Ede, Robens, McNeil, Alexander and Strachey. On the issue, L. D. Epstein, *Britain – Uneasy Ally* (Chicago University Press, 1954), pp. 245–51.

46 So Dalton told Bevan, who was 'disappointed, I think, and slightly incredulous': HDD, 15, 28 and 29 July 1952.

47 On Labour attitudes to it see below, p. 702.

48 *The Times*, 25 February 1954; Donoughue and Jones (1973), p. 530; Foot (1973), p. 427. The votes in the NEC were 14 to 10; in the PLP, 111 to 109 against Harold Wilson's amendment and 113 to 104 for the official motion.

49 HG to Wilfred Fienburgh MP, 22 November 1954: P.80.

50 HG to Solly Pearce, 23 July 1954 (re Leeds); Tom Reid MP to HG, 21 September 1954 (re Swindon): P.89. *DT*, 29 June 1954, on the conferences.

51 Speech at Saltburn-on-Sea, 27 June 1954 (U.182–1). Also at Greenford, 4 March 1954; at Mexborough 9 May 1954; in n. 52.

52 HG in *Socialist Commentary*, July 1954.

53 HG to Mrs Reeves of Ilford, 19 July 1954 (P.80) – answering hers of 14 July 1954 after one regional conference at which he spoke.

54 HG in *News of the World*, 26 September 1954; in Copenhagen, 14 September 1954 (A.8); in the House, n. 18*b*.

55 Correspondence, September and October 1954 (P.82) with Bjarne Braatoy, his contact with Ollenhauer the German Socialist leader. HG to Saul Rose, international secretary of the Labour Party (n.d. but about 17 September 1954), published by Rose in *Political Studies*, 14.2 (June 1966): a full account of Labour deliberations on German rearmament.

56 HG to Saul Rose, 7 September 1954 (P.82) refers three times to their reluctance. Crossman confirms: RCD, 26 December 1954.

57 *LPCR*, 1954, p. 92.

58 The CLP vote was probably 3 to 1 against it: Harrison (1960), pp. 228–30.

59 So said both his agent George Murray and Hugh Dalton in their letters of congratulation (P.89) and Crossman in his diary, 1 October 1954.

60 Half: *The Times*, 29 September 1954; RCD, 1 October 1954. A 'leading Bevanite source' made 'an unofficial examination of the ballot' and estimated 45 per cent; but Harrison (1960, p. 316 and n.) thought one-third likelier. No one can know, for unions do not publish their votes, and a bad guess about a small union would distort the CLP figure.

61 H. B. Boyne in *DT*, 10 April 1961. Also interview, G. Goodman (on Deakin).

62 Interview, Sir Harold Wilson; Wigg (1972), p. 177.

63 RCD, 1 October 1954; cf. 2 October 1953, on Mikardo suffering from his sectarian reputation – 'exactly the opposite of what Nye believes'.

64 Foot (1973), p. 452 (Bevan); Roth (1977), p. 191 (Wilson). Interviews, T. Driberg (Wilson), Lord Jacobson (Castle).

65 'By the way, we do need arithmetic for social progress', he wrote a day or two later (in n. 66). But privately he commented in 1958 that it was 'just as likely to have been said about Attlee as me' (to J. P. O'Donnell, Chapter 1, n. 1); and publicly he said in 1961 that Attlee was meant (in a programme on Bevan, 3 October 1961, BBC: p. 19).

66 In *Sunday Pictorial*, 3 October 1954.

67 *DT*, 30 September 1954 and 4 October 1954; RCD, 1 October 1954; and reported by HG, n. 37*b*.

68 He was furious when the *Herald* fanned the dying flame with Basil Davidson's articles on Germany: HG to the chairman Surrey Dane, 15 December 1954, 5 January 1955, 2 March 1955; to Tom Williamson, 24 February 1955 (all P.97).

69 At a dinner for eight German editors: RCD, 1 February 1957.

70 By 124 to 72: Hunter (1959), p. 84; HDD, 14 November 1954.

71 RCD, 22 November 1954, reporting Callaghan. On the Shadow Cabinet see Diary, 12 November 1954; on the PLP, *ibid.*, and RCD, 11, 15 and 22 November 1954.

72 Diary, 19 March 1955; cf. RCD, 22 November 1954.

73 HG to William Connor ('Cassandra' of the *Daily Mirror*), 26 November 1954, P.80.

74 Crossman in RCD, 22 November 1954, and n. 18*e*; Foot (1973), p. 451.

75 HG to Geoffrey Crowther, 22 November 1954, P.80. The 'seven brave spirits' (Foot, 1973, p. 451) were three old rebels (S. O. Davies, Emrys Hughes and Sydney Silverman), three pacifists (George Craddock, Ernest Fernyhough and Victor Yates), and John McGovern, an ex-ILPer and vehement anti-Communist, who by insisting on voting with the government earned newspaper praise for 'having the courage of Mr. Attlee's convictions'.

76 On that Party Meeting, RCD, 29 November 1954.

77 HG to Crowther, 22 and 27 November 1954; to Solly Pearce, 24 November 1954; to a constituent, Ernest Spencer, 24 November 1954; to E. C. Marshall, 25 November 1954: all P.80. Also Diary, 14 December 1954; and n. 73.

78 The Birkbeck Foundation Oration, 2 December 1954.

79 *Tribune*, 11 March 1955. Also Crossman in *New Statesman*, 2 April 1955; HG's papers include a typed reply (unpublished) apparently by him.

80 Diary, 9 November 1954, reporting Sir Vincent Tewson. On the negotiations see below, pp. 349–50.

81 RCD, 15 November 1954. Dalton wrote of his 'slow suicide': HDD, Christmas 1954; to HG, 27 December 1954, P.97.

82 On *Tribune's* attack: Hunter (1959), pp. 85–6; Duff (1971), pp. 64–8.

83 RCD, 27 October 1954, 1 November 1954 (misquoted by Foot, 1973, p. 454, as 'Bevanism ... could do without *Tribune*').

84 RCD, 26 December 1954; Crossman got them to change the title to 'The Query of the Year'.

85 Diary, 19 March 1955; Hunter (1959), pp. 86–9; Foot (1973), pp. 453, 455–6; Jackson (1968), p. 126; RCD, 22 February 1955; and n. 86.

86 Unsigned official PLP memorandum for Attlee on Bevan's conduct, drawn up for the Party Meeting on 16 March 1955: P.97.

87 Cf. Crossman to Foot, 4 March 1955 (in RCD); ignored in Foot's account.

88 537 *H.C. Deb.*, 1–2 March 1955: *a.* col. 2120; *b.* cols 1924, 2074–5; *c.* cols 2117–18, 2122; *d.* col. 2176.

89 *New Statesman*, 25 February 1955. Roth (1977), p. 186. RCD, 3 March 1955.

90 Diary, 19 March 1955. There was prior notice (nn. 91, 92*a*) contrary to Foot (1973), p. 458n. Dissenters were from 8 (n. 91) to 20 (n. 19*j*), mostly pacifists; cf. n. 86.

91 KYD, 21 March 1955.

92 Hunter (1959): *a.* p. 90; *b.* p. 91; *c.* pp. 104–5; *d.* p. 101.

93 Foot omits the first attack, briefly defends and subsequently ignores the third, and concentrates on the second, claiming (see next note) it was not aimed at Attlee. It was not HG's main charge against Bevan: Diary, 19 March 1955.

94 In n. 88*c.* Foot (1973), p. 463, explains that Bevan's gestures, invisible to colleagues sitting in front of him, indicated that between the first and second halves of that sentence 'they' and 'us' changed from meaning Labour's front and back benches to meaning the Government and the Opposition; and that 'recklessness' equally curiously 'signified the whole mixture of diplomatic immobility and nuclear dependence'. Relying on the *DH* report, he ignores Crossman's evidence of Bevan's mood.

95 Crossman to Ted Davies of Coventry, 7 March 1955 (in RCD).

96 HDD, 28 February 1955; they stipulated 'tolerable' behaviour by the Bevanites, and HG said Bevan 'was always in the hands of his officials'.

97 This account is from Diary, 19 and 25 March 1955. He stressed to worried friends the need to keep in step with these two: interview, D. Ginsburg.

98 This view of HG's (from his Diary) was shared by Morrison who said so to Attlee: Jackson (1968), p. 128.

99 Contrast Roth (1977), p. 188, who suggests HG was 'fanatical' for expulsion.

100 Also HDD, 7 March 1955. The doubters were Griffiths and (on tactics only) Dalton, Robens and Wilson.

101 RCD, 8, 15 and 16 March 1955. The Yorkshire miners heard a recording of Bevan's Scarborough attack on their leader Ernest Jones, then voted for disciplinary action by 141 to 124: *DT*, 16 and 17 March 1955; Hunter (1959), p. 104. Canvassers: Diary, 19 March 1955.

102 RCD, 16 March 1955, on their lunch the previous day (cf. HDD, 14 March 1955).

103 Diary, 19 March 1955; HDD, 12 March 1955, confirms that he said he had not meant to do so until Bevan's statement.

104 Press handout in HG's Diary. Foot (1973, p. 471n.) solemnly rebukes HG for 'not troubl[ing] to check what happened' in Bevan's second (disputed) attack on Attlee; he ignores the first and third attacks.

105 Diary, 19 March 1955; also HG to John Murray, 17 March 1955, P.99. Confirmed by *DT*, 14 March 1955.

106 The two were Griffiths (to whom the note was not shown) and Harold Wilson, who 'had carefully arranged to be in Paris': RCD, 16 March 1955; HDD, 16 March 1955. This account is based on HG's Diary, 19 March 1955 (which has the note with the signatures); HDD, 7–16 March 1955; Hunter (1959), pp. 97, 100.

107 Foot (1973), p. 471; RCD, 16 March 1955.

108 HDD, 16 March 1955. Foot (1973), pp. 469–72, and Roth (1977), p. 188, both report Bevan's charge but not the reply.

109 Diary, 19 March 1955. Hunter (1959), p. 100 and Crossman (n. 19*m*) thought Bevan more moderate than usual.

110 Diary, 19 March 1955; HDD, 16 March 1955; Hunter (1959), p. 101; Foot (1973), p. 471 ('the muffled answer seemed to be "Yes" '). Cf. RCD, 16 March 1955.

111 The friends were Sam Watson and Tiffin, the T&GWU man on the NEC.

112 Diary, 19 March 1955; Hunter (1959), p. 98. Both Foot (1973), p. 468, and Roth (1977), p. 199, cite from Hunter Attlee's attack on HG but omit Hunter's (and HG's) rebuttal of it.

113 Morgan Phillips's view. If Bevan was not expelled, Alice Bacon meant to move to restore the whip at once.

114 E.g. Ian Winterbottom MP to HG, 17 March 1955, and reply 21 March 1955: P.99.

115 Letter in P.97. Albu and Jay agreed (HDD, 18 March 1955 and 7 April 1955); so did Mulley (to HG, 12 March 1955, P.98), David Ginsburg at Transport House, and Dora (interviews).

116 Interviews, Sir Harry Nicholas, Lord Williamson.

117 Interviews, Lady Bacon, D. Ginsburg, G. Goodman, R. Gunter, Sir Vincent Tewson, Sir William Webber, Lord Williamson, W. Wyatt.

118 These were the ETU which was, and the NUR which was not (though it was mildly left-wing).

119 Foot (1973, pp. 473–4n.) quotes it at length; and himself compares Labour leaders and practices to McCarthyism, totalitarianism, near-Stalinism and the Spanish Inquisition: Foot (1973), pp. 383, 509, 598, 602, 636. It was in HG's mind: above, p. 332.

120 Interview, Lady Brook.

121 Contrary to Foot (1973), p. 475.

122 Diary, 25 March 1955 and Hunter (1959), pp. 105–6. The heaviest

pressure was on Tiffin of the T&GWU (from Deakin), on the right-wing representative of USDAW, and on Brinham of the Woodworkers.

123 Respectively Cooper, Gaitskell and Knight; Attlee, Castle, Griffiths and Haworth; Dr Edith Summerskill the anti-Bevanite chairman, and Morgan Phillips without a vote.

124 Foot (1973), p. 478. James Haworth to author; Lord Cooper to author, interview. Barbara Castle had forgotten that HG was on the sub-committee. Griffiths had forgotten what happened, and Lady Summerskill did not reply. The official minute, as Foot says, is 'sketchy'.

125 *Tribune*, 11 March 1955; 'Mr. Bevan behaved badly in the debate'.

126 F. Beswick to Attlee, 7 March 1955; J. Strachey to Attlee, 10 March 1955; KYD, 12 June 1955.

127 By 53 per cent to 24 per cent: Gallup poll in *NC*, 15 March 1955.

128 Wilson and Bevan both put it to Attlee: RCD, 8 March 1955; Foot (1973), p. 472. Cf. *Tribune*, 18 March 1955. Similarly, Greenwood is said to have charged HG in the NEC with prematurely trying on the crown; they certainly clashed violently (interview, Lord Greenwood).

129 Crossman to Bevan, 31 March 1955 (with RCD): quoted Foot (1973), pp. 482-3.

130 D. N. Pritt, Lester Hutchinson, John Platts-Mills and Leslie Solley: Jackson (1968), pp. 202-12. Konni Zilliacus was expelled in 1948 but soon returned; Platts-Mills and Solley did so years later.

131 When Crossman told HG that Bevan's expulsion would only widen the gulf, HG replied that after Conference it would soon be forgotten — and Crossman admitted that 'If there was any real leadership in the Party that might be true': RCD, 24 March 1955.

132 Hunter (1959), pp. 110-11; KYD, 4 May 1955. On 21 March *The Times* had predicted Churchill's retirement within three weeks; Eden succeeded on 6 April and promptly dissolved Parliament as expected.

133 Krug (1961), pp. 223-4; *Socialist Commentary*, April 1955, p. 105. (Such tributes aroused *Tribune*'s suspicions only when addressed to Labour leaders it disliked.)

134 Reproduced in D. E. Butler (1955), pp. 78-9.

135 For the third time in his case: besides 1939, he had recanted to avoid expulsion in 1944.

Chapter 12   Leader by a Landslide

1 Full-time agents were 291 at the 1951 election, only 227 in 1955: n. 2*a*.

2 D. E. Butler (1955): *a*. p. 107; *b*. p. 77; *c*. p. 61; *d*. p. 74; *e*. p. 205; *f*. p. 184.

3 Hirshfield's appointment was approved by the Finance and General

Purposes Sub-committee on 25 January 1955 and he reported to it on 27 September 1955. On this paragraph, NEC-M, vol. 116–9: 25 January 1955, M. 15, 17; 23 February 1955; 22 March 1955; 25 July 1955; and 27 September 1955, M. 49, 60. Also interviews: Sir Harry Nicholas, and nn. 4, 5.

4 Interview, Lord Hirshfield.

5 Interview, P. Clark.

6 Diary: *a.* 14 October 1954; *b.* 9 November 1954; *c.* 6 October 1954.

7 For this and the next two paragraphs, n. 6*a*, *b.*

8 Raising the T&GWU affiliation to 1,000,000 and the NUGMW to 650,000. Union contributions to the Party are paid (since 1913) from a separate political fund, financed by a political levy which individual members can 'contract out' of paying. Each union decides when, how much and to whom to contribute.

9 *a.* HG to Morgan Phillips, 20 January 1955; *b.* reply 21 January 1955 (P.99); *c.* and n. 10.

10 HG to David Ginsburg, 29 December 1954: P.82.

11 *DT: a.* 5 September 1955, Hugh Chevins; *b.* 14 October 1955; HG again had a sympathetic hearing for it in the private session at Margate; *c* 27 October 1955.

12 HG's interview with Percy Cudlipp in *NC*, 15 June 1955.

13 *a.* Interview, D. Ginsburg; *b.* RCD, 22 June 1955.

14 *a.* Interview, Lord Cooper; *b.* a member, and HG's preferred chairman: GWD, 16 October 1955.

15 *The Economist*, 10 September 1955.

16 Interviews, Lady Phillips (quoting her son); Mrs P. Crane.

17 John Murray to HG, P.99: *a.* 6 March 1955; *b.* 30 October 1955, reporting Benn and Shore; *c.* reply 2 November 1955; *d.* 18 September 1955; *e.* reporting Barbara Castle; *f.* reporting George Brown, cf. reply 9 March 1955.

18 Policy and Publicity Sub-committee, 17 January 1955, M.6 (from NEC-M for 26 January 1955, vol. 116). HG to Wilfrid Cave, 3 February 1955, P. 97 (a farmer and candidate, who had warned HG of the bad effect in rural seats); and to Phillips and Dalton, nn. 9*a*, 19.

19 HG to Dalton, 13 January 1955: P.97.

20 HG to George Springall at Transport House, 17 January 1955, P.99. Innocent bystanders recalled the recriminations twenty years later: n. 13*a*.

21 When the unions increased fees at Southport they demanded 'a fair crack of the whip' for their candidates against the intellectuals: n. 11*a*.

22 Interviews, *a.* R. Gunter; *b.* Sir William Webber.

23 HG to Len Williams: *a.* 7 June 1955, P.96; *b.* 19 October 1955, P.99; *c.* on King's Lynn, Darlington and Greenock.

24 *Tribune*: *a*. 8 October 1954; *b*. 3 June 1955; *c*. 14 October 1955.

25 *Socialist Commentary*: *a*. editorial, April 1955; *b*. HG, July 1955, his italics.

26 RCD: *a*. 6 June 1955; *b*. 26 December 1954; *c*. 28 January 1955; *d*. 22 February 1955; *e*. 19 and 26 April 1955, 3 May 1955; *f*. 15 October 1955; *g*. 28 February 1955; *h*. 2 December 1955; *i*. 7 June 1955; *j*. 16 December 1955; *k*. 16 November 1955.

27 Diary, 14 December 1954; cf. RCD, 9 December 1954.

28 Above, p. 337, for the same day's angry clash on foreign policy.

29 He blamed the Tory 'preference for economic anarchy' without referring to rearmament: n. 30*a*.

30 540 *H.C. Deb.*, 20–22 April 1955: *a*. HG, cols 185–204; *b*. reported R. A. Butler, cols 376, 566; *c*. cols 349, 526; *d*. cols 244, 350, 398, 526; *e*. HG col. 197, Crosland cols 237–40, Dalton col. 369, Butler cols 574–5; *f*. Jay col. 556.

31 *FT*, 24 April 1955. Contrast generous praise from Maudling and Spearman: to HG, n.d., P.99; and n. 30*c*.

32 *MG*, cf. *The Times*, *DT*, all 21 April 1955. For Tory MPs on Labour's enthusiasm, n. 30*d*.

33 Editorial, 21 April 1955.

34 HDD: *a*. 30 March 1955; *b*. 25 June 1953; *c*. 28 April 1955.

35 HG to George and Barbara (Cadbury), 31 May 1955, P.96. Like Dalton he expected a Tory majority of 40 to 100: Dalton to HG, 7 May 1955, and reply 9 May 1955 (both P.97); cf. Michael Straight to HG, 1 July 1955, 'still overcome with admiration at the accuracy of your predictions on the election' (P.99).

36 Privately at the time, HG put the Tory record first, the Bevan crisis second, and poor organisation third: n. 37*a*, *b*.

37 D. E. Butler's diary: *a*. 2 July 1955; *b*. 4 August 1955.

38 Donald Alger to HG, 28 April 1955: P.96.

39 *NC*, cf. *The Times*, 21 May 1955; cf. n. 2*c*.

40 *DH*, 11 May 1955; *Observer*, 22 May 1955.

41 Noel-Baker to HG, 25 May 1955; cf. Douglas Young to HG, 29 May 1955; Alma Birk to HG, 27 June 1955 (all P.96); *The Times*, *DT*, 21 April 1955; C. Pannell in *Leeds Weekly Citizen*, 29 April 1955; interview, F. Blackburn.

42 HG spoke against that: 536 *H.C. Deb.*, cols 335–7, 26 January 1955.

43 Agent's report in South Leeds CLP minute book, 10 July 1955, pp. 25–6.

44 Interview, Alderman A. Tallant.

45 RCD, 26 April 1955, 3 May 1955; Crossman to Gilbert Baker, 2 June 1955; cf. n. 2*d*.

46 HG to Brenda Woolgar, 7 June 1955: P.96.

47 The former's 1955 diary, quoted in Griffiths (1969), p. 141. Wilson: Smith (1964), p. 173. Morgan Phillips's official report to the NEC blamed prosperity first, the Party split second: P.96.

48 Taken in September 1954; copy in P.88.

49 In Gorton, Zilliacus won nomination against Soskice by 3 votes, then saved the seat by only 300; in Salford East, Allaun did far worse than his neighbours.

50 RCD, 31 May 1955; Crossman to Reg Underhill 2 June 1955, to David Butler 7 June 1955. Elaine Burton MP to HG, 31 May 1955, P.96.

51 HG to Dalton, 13 January 1955, 1 June 1955, P.96 ('we now face some very nasty water'). Crossman was surprised too: RCD, 3 May 1955.

52 HG at the Woodworkers' conference at Blackpool (U.184, and MG, 3 June 1955); to Percy Cudlipp (n. 12); and at Sheffield, 25 June 1955, U.184.

53 HG sent several Party officials copies of a letter about young workers' views from a Labour League of Youth member in Manchester: P. Donoghue to HG, 4 June 1955: P.96.

54 HG to Alma Birk, 3 June 1955, P.96.

55 Dalton (1962), pp. 413–21; Hunter (1959), pp. 115–17, 120–1.

56 Hunter (1959), pp. 114–15, 117–20, 125–8; Dalton (1962), pp. 417–22; Foot (1973), pp. 488–9; Donoughue and Jones (1973), pp. 536–7; RCD, 9 and 13 June 1955; DT, 9 and 10 June 1955. According to Wilson, Attlee told the Shadow Cabinet on 6 June that he meant to go in October: RCD, 7 June 1955.

57 RCD, 6, 7, 9 and 13 June 1955; 22 June 1955 ('a real melting of the Bevanite and anti-Bevanite blocks'); 15 July 1955 ('So now we are right back before Nye's resignation in 1951'). Cf. KYD, 12 June 1955; Foot (1973), pp. 676, 681.

58 He was already confident by January: n. 19.

59 Harrison (1960), pp. 133, 147–8, 318; DT, 15 July 1955 (Tiffin made it a vote of confidence).

60 DT, 6 July 1955. The minority were Scotland, South Wales, Kent and the (West) Midlands: Yorkshire Post, 28 June 1955. The Yorkshire under a third of their votes: DT, 12 and 15 March 1955, NC, 15 March 1955. His friends blamed the unrepresentative branch meetings usually championed by the trade union Left: DT, 15 March 1955. (The Telegraph then had very good industrial news.)

61 The NUR general secretary voted for HG to continue 'the splendid work he has begun': Railway Review, 7 October 1955. At its next AGM a censure motion was lost by one vote: DT, 4 July 1956; cf. Harrison (1960), p. 158.

62 Harrison (1960), pp. 316–17. That was a personal tribute to HG, for Bevan regained all but 100,000 CLP votes against other rivals the following year.

63 He lost 800,000. The increased affiliation by the general unions explains 37 per cent of the increase in HG's vote, not 75 per cent as a careless reader would infer from Foot (1973), p. 492n.

64 Hunter (1959): *a.* pp. 133–5; *b.* pp. 143–4; *c.* pp. 141–3; *d.* p. 150; *e.* pp. 137–8, 144; *f.* p. 135; *g.* pp. 144–8; *h.* pp. 152, 156–61; *i.* p. 167; *j.* pp. 173–4.

65 *New Statesman*, 22 October 1955. Cf. *ST*, 16 October 1955; Haseler (1969), p. 40.

66 Hunter and his wife, both experienced journalists, felt sure HG meant what he said: n. 64*b*.

67 Hunter (1959), p. 139; RCD, 15 October 1955.

68 *Observer*, 16 October 1955.

69 RCD, 15 October 1955 (he and Wilson nearly boycotted the meeting in protest against Bevan's earlier speech). Also *DT*, 12 and 13 October 1955; Hunter (1959), pp. 140–1; cf. Foot (1973), p. 492 (notable for his omissions).

70 *LPCR*, 1955, p. 175.

71 Interview, J. P. Morris who timed it; cf. *DT*, 13 October 1955, and n. 68.

72 Irving Kristol in *New Leader*, 16 October 1955.

73 *Observer*, 16 October 1955; RCD, 15 October 1955; on HG's role, Howard Smallwood (a senior T&GWU branch secretary at his first Conference) to HG, 27 October 1955, P.99.

74 A little later, 'according to an exception which is now becoming a norm, I found my ideas supported by Gaitskell': RCD, 16 November 1955.

75 HG in *DH*, 28 February 1955.

76 To Crossman in a broadcast on intellectuals in politics: *Listener*, 14 March 1974.

77 From June, higher national insurance contributions of £100 million would offset the tax cuts and leave a family on the average wage worse off: HG's Budget broadcast, *Listener*, 28 April 1955; and n. 30*f*.

78 Brittan (1971), pp. 201–3; Dow (1970), pp. 78–80; Worswick and Ady (1962), pp. 34, 262–4, 308.

79 *DT*, 17 June 1955.

80 542 *H.C. Deb.*, col. 162, 10 June 1955 (Thorneycroft); cols 762–84 (HG, quotation from col. 783); cols 784–801, 16 June 1955 (Butler).

81 544 *H.C. Deb.*, col. 1016: 26 July 1955.

82 *a.* In *DH*, 7 October 1955; *b.* at the pre-Conference rally at Margate: *DT*, 10 October 1955. His memory about Baldwin was faulty.

83 545 *H.C. Deb.,* 27–31 October 1955: *a.* HG, col. 406; *b.* Roy Jenkins, col. 609; *c.* and col. 615; *d.* HG, cols 390–408; *e.* cols 756–7; *f.* col. 701.

84 Rents also went up. Butler would have preferred harsher economies to new taxes, but was overruled by his colleagues: Lord Butler (1973), pp. 181–2; RCD, 28 October 1955 (reporting Maudling).

85 RCD, 28 October 1955; interview, J. Callaghan (also referring to his Margate speech).

86 *Observer,* 30 October 1955; HG to Dryden Brook, 9 November 1955, P.94–5; Percy Daines, n. 83*e.*

87 Interview, Sir Harold Wilson; Smith (1964), p. 175. Hunter (1959), p. 150, thought it was an Attlee manoeuvre against Morrison.

88 HDD, 31 October 1955 ('almost inconceivably bad'); interview, Lord Pannell; *DT,* 1 November 1955; nn. 64*d,* 89*a.*

89 Donoughue and Jones (1973): *a.* pp. 537–8; *b.* p. 536; *c.* p. 537; *d.* p. 539; *e.* p. 540; *f.* p. 541n.

90 *DT,* diary, 1 November 1955.

91 Shown in many private letters to HG in files P.44, P.52, P.93–4, P.103.

92 Henry Fairlie in *Spectator: a.* 4 November 1955; *b.* 9 December 1955; *c.* 16 December 1955.

93 HG to Jay, 2 November 1955, P.98; also to John Murray, 2 November 1955, P.99. However, he told the present Lady Butler at the time that he had just come from a memorial service (for Hector McNeil), was in an emotional mood, and later regretted some of his words: interview.

94 Hunter (1959), p. 150. RCD, 2 December 1955 called it 'the first effective fighting Opposition we've known for a long time'. Also Smith (1964), p. 175; KYD, 23 December 1955. Left-wingers too were enthusiastic: cf. Frank Allaun to HG, 20 November 1955, P.94–4; and below, p. 370 and n. 168.

95 Interview, Lord Aylestone (formerly Herbert Bowden, the Chief Whip); who told Wilson so at the time: n. 96*a.* Bowden also told Wilson the Party wanted him as deputy leader to HG: n. 96*b.*

96 *a.* Interview, Sir Harold Wilson; *b.* Smith (1964), pp. 174–6.

97 GWD, 16 October 1955.

98 E.g. *The Economist,* 4 September 1954.

99 *DT,* 27 December 1958, quoting Evans. Morrison (1960), p. 292, has the wrong venue and date (on which his biographers follow him): n. 89*b.*

100 Percy Cudlipp, *NC,* 15 June 1955; Wilfred Sendall, *DT,* 29 July 1955; Tom Reid to HG, 7 September 1955, P.99. (But cf. Dalton, 1962, p. 422.) Among MPs suggesting him were Bellenger (Diary, 14 December 1954); Callaghan, Chetwynd and Donnelly (Dalton to HG, 27 December 1954, P.97); Crosland, Jenkins and Wyatt, 21

March 1955; Dr A. D. D. Broughton to HG, 27 May 1955, P.96. Also Sir H. V. Berry of XYZ to HG, 17 March 1955, P.97.

101 Interviews, Roy Jenkins, David Ginsburg—who recalled HG's irritation and Jenkins's insistence. Also n. 102*a*.

102 Roy Jenkins: *a*. in Rodgers (1964), p. 122; *b*. also Jenkins (1974), p. 172.

103 As he told Gordon Walker in October: GWD, 16 October 1955.

104 Of all voters, 2 per cent (net) would be more likely to vote Labour under Morrison, 3 per cent fewer under HG and 33 per cent fewer under Bevan; of Labour voters, 4 per cent more, 1 per cent more and $17\frac{1}{2}$ per cent fewer (P.88).

105 Interview, Lord Aylestone, who said in a television obituary on 18 January 1963 that HG took a good deal of persuading to stand: BBC transcript.

106 Trevor Evans, *DE*, 11 March 1955.

107 RCD, 7 and 15 October 1955, 16 November 1955, 2 December 1955. *Observer*, 16 October 1955; *New Statesman*, 22 October 1955.

108 RCD, 16 March 1955 (quoted Foot, 1973, p. 484). Attlee had said much the same to Wilson: RCD, 8 March 1955. Cf. KYD, 30 October 1955; Hunter (1959), pp. 123, 159; interviews, Lord Greenwood, Sir Kenneth Younger.

109 Hunter (1959), p. 138. She hoped Bevan would become his deputy: *ibid.*, p. 135, and n. 17*d, e*.

110 E.g. *DT*, 12 and 15 October 1955; *ST*, 16 October 1955. Cf. Hunter (1959), p. 144; n. 89*c*.

111 Interview, Lord Aylestone, who thought this determined HG's decision.

112 GWD, 16 October 1955. On Robens v. Griffiths, cf. HDD, 3 November 1955; Crosland to HG, n.d. but 9 December 1955, P.101.

113 Reginald Paget to HG, 17 October 1955, saying he spoke for Elaine Burton, John Edwards, Roy Jenkins, Dai Jones, Mellish, Popplewell and George Thomson; reply 21 October 1955, P.99. Austen Albu to HG, 14 October 1955, P.97; Wilfred Fienburgh publicly appealed to HG to stand himself and not settle for the deputy leadership: Hunter (1959), p. 145. Anthony Benn thought that only ten of the Left MPs would now vote for Bevan and the rest for HG: reported n. 17*b*.

114 Hunter (1959), pp. 149–51; and n. 89*a*.

115 Interview, Roy Jenkins; his emphasis. HG told Asa Briggs the same. The lunch was probably on 7 November.

116 Hunter (1959), pp. 166–7; and n. 89*a*.

117 At lunch on Thursday 10 November: Hunter (1959), pp. 162–4.

118 Griffiths (1969), pp. 133, 145.

119 Hunter (1959), p. 164. Interview, Sir William Webber. Below, p. 366.

120 HG to Mrs Deane, 29 December 1955, P.101. Cf. Jack Brocklebank of the NUAW to HG, 11 December 1955, P.101 (on their talk before Margate, on 1 October). One other who did not want him to stand was Dora (interview).

121 File P.98.

122 Hunter (1959), pp. 162–3. HG to Arthur Schlesinger, 15 December 1955, P.192, cancelling the trip: 'I had no idea ... that Clem was going to retire before Christmas'.

123 *a*. Interview, A. Allen; *b*. the two were Allen and Crosland.

124 Interview, J. Parker (who with Callaghan was at Moyle's lunch table).

125 Foot (1973), p. 495 attributed Bevan's view to talks with Attlee in Malta in late October. Attlee had then expressed his dislike for these forces, which (strangely) seems to Foot 'the clearest proof of how unwilling Attlee was to go'. He ignores Hunter's evidence.

126 Dalton (1962): *a*. p. 418; *b*. pp. 430–1; *c*. p. 431; *d*. p. 429.

127 Crossman in *Tribune*, 30 December 1955; n. 92*b*. Of the three union leaders named by Foot as urging Attlee's retirement, two acted by arrangement with Morrison's friends in the unions, and so told Hunter (P.138). The third wrote just after HG offended some trade unionists by suggesting that the Budget would provoke new wage claims: *DT*, 3 and 4 November 1955.

128 Hunter (1959) assumes that Attlee meant to precipitate a decision. But his editor held up the story for a week and watered it down: pp. 161–2, 168–9.

129 *DT*, 1 and 8 December 1955; RCD, 2 December 1955.

130 Lords Gordon Walker and Moyle, F. Mulley, M. Stewart, Lady White and Sir Kenneth Younger thought so; Lords Pannell and Wigg and W. Wyatt did not; Lady Burton and D. Healey were unsure (interviews).

131 Crossman in *Daily Mirror*, 14 October 1955, cf. *Tribune*, 30 December 1955; GWD, 16 October 1955; HDD, 'End October 1955'; *The Times*, 8 December 1955; Driberg in *Reynolds News*, 11 December 1955.

132 Viscount Stuart of Findhorn, *Within the Fringe* (Bodley Head, 1967), p. 144; in 1955 he was Secretary for Scotland. (What would Foot have said if it had been HG who consulted a Tory?)

133 HDD, 3 November 1955 (he notes with malicious glee that Bevan paid!).

134 *a*. Lord Hale to author; *b*. he thinks no other Bevanites were told – cf. interview, Lord Shackleton; *c*. on Stokes, contrast n. 126*b*.

135 Shawcross to HG, 8 December 1955: P.99.

136 RCD, 2 and 16 December 1955; cf. Randolph Churchill, *Evening Standard*, 15 December 1955; and n. 126*b*.

137 Foot (1973), p. 494, gets the date wrong. Attlee had even told the

Chief Whip he could inform HG—but not Morrison! (In fact Bowden told both.) Interview, Lord Aylestone.

138 Dalton (1962), p. 431; Donoughue and Jones (1973), p. 540. Neither specifies a date but the contexts make it clear.

139 Seven signatories were over sixty, four over seventy: cf. nn. 64*j*, 89*e*.

140 Statement printed in Hunter (1959), pp. 173–4, and in Dalton (1962), p. 431.

141 Foot (1973): *a*. p. 496; *b*. pp. 494–5.

142 Mikardo recruited Hale: n. 134*a*.

143 Interviews: *a*. Lord Gordon Walker (who had been close to Morrison, and was among the twenty); *b*. A. Albu.

144 Donnelly to HG, 'Thursday 7.30 p.m.': P.101 (his italics).

145 *Daily Mirror*, 10 December 1955, cf. *Tribune*, 30 December 1955. RCD, 16 December 1955, quoting several others both at Westminster and in the Midlands.

146 Interviews.

147 Griffiths (1969), p. 145. Also Dalton (1962), pp. 431–2; political correspondents of the *ST*, 11 December 1955; *Observer*, 11 December 1955; *DT*, 15 December 1955.

148 *The Times*, 9 December 1955; E. L. Mallalieu MP, A. Crosland to HG, both P.101.

149 'Crossbencher' in *SE*, 11 December 1955.

150 Interview, Prof. S. G. Raybould.

151 Of the 275 Labour MPs, seven or eight were abroad. It had been thought that abstentions might reduce the total to 250: *Reynolds News*, 11 December 1955.

152 Lord Pakenham to HG, 18 December 1955; Lord Pethick-Lawrence to HG, 24 December 1955 ('quite perfect'): both P.114–1.

153 Interview, Lord Pannell.

154 Dalton (1962), pp. 432–3; Donoughue and Jones (1973), pp. 541–2. Cf. Hunter (1959), p. 167.

155 HG to Harold Clay, 2 January 1956: P.101.

156 All congratulations from P.101: Francis Drake-Briscoe (Norfolk); Richard Snedden (Balliol); Mr and Mrs P. H. Melliss (John Burns); Helen Mahoney (café).

157 Sub: interview, N. Mackenzie. WEA: *Yorkshire Evening Post*, 17 December 1955.

158 Fairlie (1968), p. 168.

159 The *Daily Mail* (14 December 1955) predicted 150–50–60; Hugh Dalton, 140–60–50; Jim Johnson, MP (from Africa), 140–60–40. Albert Roberts MP gave HG 150 to 160; Arthur Bottomley MP gave him 156. (Letters in file P.101, Johnson's in P. 114–1.)

160 Polling the first 10 Labour voters met in 50 constituencies, the *Sunday*

Dispatch (11 December 1955) found an identical majority: 293 for HG, 144 for Morrison, 63 for Bevan. Two months earlier the Gallup poll had found Labour voters equally split between Morrison and HG, with 23 per cent for Bevan: *The Economist*, 15 October 1955.

161 London: *SE*, 11 December 1955. North: Albert Roberts, 12 December 1955: P.101. Scots: John Taylor, the Scottish whip, 20 December 1955: P.101b.

162 W. Wyatt to HG, 13 October 1955, P.99.

163 W. R. Richardson to HG, telegram 14 December 1955: P.101.

164 Leslie Hunter in *DH*, 15 December 1955. A few weeks later HG said the labels Left and Right were dangerously imprecise: interview in *Observer*, 2 January 1956.

165 Interview, R. H. S. Crossman.

166 Crossman to HG, 'Thursday'; reply 'Boxing Day': filed with RCD. Their emphasis.

167 Wilson to HG, 16 December 1955: P.101.

168 Anthony Greenwood in *Labour's Northern Voice*, December 1955 (in file F.1b). Cf. Ben Parkin to HG, 10 December 1955, P.101; Marcus Lipton, Joe Reeves and Julian Snow, all P.114–1.

169 Hunter (1959), p. 177; Dalton (1962), p. 433.

170 RCD, 16 December 1955. The *MG* (12 December 1955) had remarked on 'the signs [of] Mr. Bevan['s] growing toleration towards Mr. Gaitskell'.

171 Hunter (1959), p. 180; Foot (1973), p. 499. Below, p. 408.

172 Attlee to HG, 16 December 1955, P.101. (Younger agreed about Bevan's vote: KYD, 23 December 1955.)

173 Interviews, D. Healey, Lord Pannell, P. Rosenstein-Rodan.

Chapter 13   Labour's New Champion

1 Williams (1970), p. 308.

2 Quoted in interview by Professor O. Morgenstern.

3 Arthur Allen: *a.* interview; *b.* to author.

4 Interview, M. Bonham Carter.

5 Interviews on this section: *a.* Lady Gaitskell and Mrs. McNeal (*née* Julia Gaitskell); *b.* Mrs Wasserman (*née* Cressida Gaitskell). Also, on his reading; *c.* Miss B. Woolgar; *d.* Mrs Gillinson.

6 Unique at the top of the Labour Party, said one MP at the time.

7 HG to Lady Plummer, 12 October 1953 (P.60b); and n. 8*a*.

8 HG to Julie: *a.* 20 February 1958; *b.* 23 June 1958; *c.* his emphasis; *d.* 12 June 1958, cf. 28 January 1958, 1 and 25 May 1958; *e.* n.d.,

probably 17 November 1958; *f.* 18 May 1959; *g.* 21 January 1959; *h.* 28 February 1961; *i.* 7 June 1959.

9 Interview, C. Plumb.

10 To Susan Barnes, *SE*, 30 September 1962.

11 Diary: *a.* 28 February 1956; *b.* 3 February 1956.

12 Interviews, Lady Bacon, Mrs George Murray.

13 On 'Press Conference', 21 September 1956: BBC; the transcript shows his embarrassment.

14 HG to Morgan Phillips, 30 October 1959: P.118x.

15 Interview, G. V. Keeling.

16 HG to Keeling, 3 March 1953, F.28; to Captain I. R. Maxwell, 20 January 1954, P.100A.

17 HG to J. B. Orrick, 21 October 1954: P.82.

18 See below, p. 753.

19 Interview, R. H. S. Crossman.

20 HG to George Martelli, 23 July 1959 (F.1a); to Frank Haley for profile in *Yorkshire Life*, December 1961; interview, J. B. Orrick; and n. 3*a*.

21 See above, p. 130 and n.

22 His tenant Jim Vale, the local taxi-man, still paid 6*s.* a week rent as in 1925; and the *Daily Mail* led the paper (11 June 1955) with HG's troubles over the house, wrongly suggesting that they were due to the Rent Restriction Acts. After the demolition order the Vales wrote him several most appreciative letters: 30 December 1954, 23 September 1955, 18 October 1955: all F.4.

23 Interviews: *a.* Lady Brook; *b.* and (almost identical) Professor A. Ranney; *c.* Miss B. Woolgar.

24 Jenkins (1974), p. 174.

25 Richard Argent, 15 November 1953 (P.67) and 28 December 1955, and HG's reply 2 January 1956 (P.101b). Mrs Ida Edwards, 15 December 1955 (P.101). Captain Derek Mason, 15 July 1953, 27 October 1953, 11 November 1953 (P.60b).

26 Cash to HG, 18 December 1953, and reply, P.60b.

27 Dr F. E. Budd to author.

28 RCD: *a.* 23 July 1952; *b.* 25 January 1957; *c.* 27 November 1958 (on Bevan too); *d.* 29 October 1958, 6 May 1959, 13 August 1959; *e.* 17 September 1957 (and n. 19); *f.* 16 December 1955.

29 L. Lyle (of the wartime Board of Trade) to HG, 6 November 1950; cf. W. Andrews (chairman of the RAC), 20 October 1950; both F.15.

30 B. W. Dale, a regular left-wing correspondent in 1954 (P.80 and 82) and 1955 (P.97); J. B. Kellar, 27 November 1954, P.82; Captain S. L Trevor, 5 October 1955, P.94-3; cf. above, Chapter 10 n. 76.

31 Peter Lewis in *Yorkshire Evening Post*, 26 September 1954; cf.

Birmingham Post political correspondent, 16 December 1955; *Washington Post*, 18 December 1955.

32 Quoted in *Observer*, 22 October 1950 by S. Haffner; reprinted in *Observer Profiles* (1954), p. 67.

33 670 *H.C. Deb.*, col. 48: 22 January 1963.

34 Interviews, W. T. Rodgers, Sir Kenneth Younger, Frank Hardie, Mrs Gillinson, Mrs Michael Stewart.

35 Interviews, Mrs McNeal (reporting Lord Pannell), Lord Greenwood, Lady White, Lady Wootton.

36 Interview, F. Hardie.

37 HG to Crosland, 16 January 1957: P.112–3.

38 Interviews: *a.* Mrs Jane Page (once Durbin's research assistant); *b.* Lady Donaldson; *c.* also J. Grimond, Mrs Skelly, Margaret Stewart; cf. N. Blewett to author (below, p. 756 and Chapter 26, n. 31).

39 Interviews, Lord Hirshfield, Mrs L. Middleton, R. Owen, H. Tout, Lord Willis; very appreciative letters from e.g. D. Rubinstein (a Highgate left-winger), 27 October 1954, P.82; R. Snedden (a Balliol Wykehamist), 15 December 1955 (P.101). Contrast interviews, Lord Briggs, Lord Greenwood.

40 Attached to C. B. Elbrick to R. Murphy, 21 May 1956: State Department no. 033.4111/5-2156 08/6.

41 *DT*: *a.* 19 May 1956; *b.* 16 January 1959.

42 Interview, J. Grimond.

43 Interviews, D. Healey, Mrs Sam Watson, W. Wyatt, and above, pp. 228, 234; cf. (in UK) RCD, 3 July 1956, 31 May 1957, and interviews, Lord Boothby, Lady Longford, H. Hutchinson, Miss B. Woolgar.

44 Hunter (1959), p. 219. Hunter's widow Margaret Stewart (now Lady Wilson) recalled getting an excellent interview from HG on the strength of the incident; but he blue-pencilled all the life and interest out of it: interview.

45 F. Williams in *DH*, 19 November 1957; Tom Hutchinson in *Illustrated*, 15 March 1958; and cf. interviews, J. Freeman, A. J. McWhinnie.

46 Interview, Mrs M. B. Skelly.

47 Interview, Alderman St J. Binns.

48 Interview, Mr and Mrs B. Gillinson.

49 Callaghan, Citrine, Diamond, Stanley Evans, Sir Donald Fergusson, Frank Hardie, when he became Chancellor; Dalton, Diamond, Jowitt, Paget, Strachey, when he became leader; many more at these and other times.

50 RCD, 21 January 1958, 29 October 1958, 22 June 1959; and fifteen interviews.

51 Crossman, working over a draft pamphlet on education, found that HG had already met three-quarters of his criticisms: RCD, 5 February 1959.

52 This paragraph is based on interviews, particularly with Lady Gaitskell, Lord Harris, Mrs Skelly, Mrs Crane, D. Ennals, D. Ginsburg, P. Morris, P. Shore.

53 Interview, P. Morris.

54 Alan Brien, *Sunday Dispatch*, 24 January 1960. Cf. interviews, A. Allen, M. Muggeridge.

55 HG to Nell Summerscale for her daughter Anne, 23 June 1955: P.49.

56 E.g. to William Connor, 26 November 1954; Donald Tyerman, 11 August 1956, P.110; Ian Trethowan, 10 December 1956, P.110; Henry Fairlie (see John Grigg in *Listener*, 6 April 1972); Donald Tyerman again (see his reply of 23 October 1962 in P.167b).

57 R. Rose, *Influencing Voters* (Faber, 1967), pp. 62–3, 66, 70, 201.

58 HG to Mayhew, 7 November 1958, P.114–3. Cf. below, pp. 388–9.

59 Interview, T. Driberg.

60 HG to P. Gordon Walker, 11 September 1959: P.114–3.

61 Cecil King in *ST*, 23 February 1969; and King (1969), p. 130.

62 Interviews, Lord Harris, D. Healey, P. Morris. HG to Crosland, 4 September 1960, P.183; to Kaldor, 21 March 1962, P.163–2 (below, Chapter 24, n. 197b). Lord Roberthall to author. Crossman to Sam Watson, 12 October 1960 (in RCD): 'he regarded me as a valuable propaganda expert who, however, should not try to contradict him on party strategy'.

63 *Socialist International Information*, 24 December 1955 (Chapter 1, n. 49).

64 'In the News', 9 December 1955, on Attlee: BBC. Also at Attlee's retirement dinner, 10 February 1956: P.191.

65 Bevan in *DT*, 3 December 1955 ('above all an imaginative sympathy').

66 Younger to HG, n.d. (4 April 1957, his emphasis) and reply, 8 April 1957: P.114–2. (Below, pp. 453–4).

67 Harold Hutchinson in *DH*, 22 September 1959.

68 HG to Crosland, 16 January 1957: P.112–3. Also in his Godkin lectures: Gaitskell (1957), p. 7; and in Briggs and Saville (1967), pp.18–19.

69 Fairlie, in *Spectator*: a. 9 December 1955; b. 22 January 1972.

70 Quoted by Nora Beloff, in *Observer*, 21 July 1974. Roth (1977), p. 286.

71 *New Statesman*, 13 February 1954.

72 In criticising the manuscript of Socialist Union's *Twentieth Century Socialism* (Penguin, 1956): 14 October 1955, P.107–4.

73 *FT*, 12 January 1973.

74 *Evening Standard*, 19 January 1963 (quoting Drew Middleton in that day's *New York Times*).

75 *LPCR*, 1955, p. 175.

76 Griffiths (1969), pp. 134–5.

77 Crossman, who drafted the Party policy statement on freedom, had

mistakenly thought him needlessly timid: RCD, 19 January 1956, 11 and 12 June 1956.

78 Interview, Lord Diamond.

79 See below, pp. 462–4.

80 Argued already in 'Public Ownership and Equality', *Socialist Commentary*, June 1955; and in his Fabian pamphlet, 'Socialism and Nationalisation'. ETU transcript: Chapter 6 n. 97.

81 HG to John Murray, P.99: *a*. 3 January 1955 (cf. above, p. 316); *b*. 9 March 1955.

82 Twenty years later the first experiment was attempted there.

83 To the Ottawa founding convention of the New Democratic Party on 4 August 1961: U.107.

84 Brown (1972), p. 241.

85 From Alastair Hetherington's memorandum of one off-the-record talk: AHD, 10 May 1961.

86 Interview in *Daily Mail*: *a*. 30 July 1959 (Henry Fairlie); *b*. 10 May 1957 (*ibid.*); *c*. 16 January 1961.

87 *a*. Interview, Lord Briggs; *b*. his first choice for chairman; *c*. on the television row see pp. 390–1, 669–70.

88 RCD, 19 March 1959. Cf. his letter from P. Donoghue (Chapter 12, n. 53).

89 HG to the chairman, Gerald Gardiner, 16 September 1959 (P.132) and *DT*, 17 September 1959.

90 Interview, Lord Willis.

91 The other members were Mark Abrams, Elaine Burton, Brian Copland, Alan Day, Nicholas Kaldor, Brian McCabe, Donald Macrae, Lord Peddie, Francis Williams and Richard Wollheim: *DH*, 23 March 1962.

92 Interview, S. C. Leslie.

93 *a*. Interview, A. Crosland; *b*. RCD, 19 September 1955.

94 HG's comment on a letter from R. Boothby to Maxwell Fyfe, 29 December 1953: F.39. HG to Greenwood, 10 September 1957 and 3 January 1958: P.114.

95 HG to A. J. P. Sellar, 10 March 1949: P.20.

96 HG to Hugh Cudlipp (whose phrase it was), 28 August 1959 (P.133c); cf. HG to Morrison, 29 January 1954 (P.100a); and n. 97*a*.

97 NEC-M: *a*. vol. 127, M.129; *b*. vol. 116, 24 January 1955, M.96; *c*. official report in *ibid.*, 23 February 1955, M. 126.

98 He endorsed Crosland's article in *Encounter*, November 1962 (reprinted in Crosland, 1962, Chapter 13): HG to Mayhew, 29 October 1962 (kindly supplied by him). Also interviews, C. Mayhew, Sir Vaughan Berry; HG to Driberg and Greenwood, 23 June 1959.

99 RCD, 26 March 1953; Crossman's question had been inspired by Cecil King's personal assistant.

100 Cmd. 1753 (June 1962). For its reception: E. G. Wedell, *Broadcasting and Public Policy* (Michael Joseph, 1968), pp. 94–8.

101 AHD, 10 July 1962. Other broadcasters quoted in *DE*, 10 July 1962.

102 ETU transcript, 28 June 1962 (Chapter 6, n. 97): *a.* p. 11; *b.* p. 15; *c.* p. 6; *d.* p. 14.

103 HG to Berry, 24 July 1962: P.163–2.

104 But when a Tory MP attacked the committee's composition, he at once retorted that no one had done so until they reported: 662 *H.C. Deb.*, col. 1512: 12 July 1962.

105 Interview, C. Mayhew (still a Labour MP when interviewed).

106 HG to Elaine Burton MP, 5 February 1954: P.80 (cf. *ibid.*, 4 and 9 November 1954).

107 To HG, 2 April 1955, P.96; interview, Lady Burton; RCD, 28 January 1955; and n. 97*b*.

108 Cf. *Tribune*, 25 February 1955; and n. 97*c*.

109 HG to P. Shore, 14 December 1962: P.168-B.

110 *LPCR*, 1959, p. 109; to the Society of Labour Lawyers: *The Times*, 20 March 1962 (HG's notes in U.117). Two years afterwards his successor (who claimed to take the matter more seriously than he) told the same audience that the Party was still considering the same solution – and made no commitment till July 1964. See W. P. Gwyn (who accepts Wilson's claim) in *Political Studies*, XIX. 4 (December 1971), pp. 399–401; and on the substance, Chapter 10 (by G. Marshall) of D. C. Rowat, *The Ombudsman* (Allen & Unwin, 1965).

111 HG to Martin Ennals, secretary of the NCCL, 17 May 1962; Richard Hayward (staff side, National Whitley Council) thanking HG, 21 September 1962: both P.163–2. The cautious advice was Gordon Walker's.

112 *Guardian*, 4 April 1962. (He also sympathised with those who felt that car owners never had to face a real economic choice: to W. J. White-head, 9 April 1962, P.182). Cf. above, pp. 188, 285; below, p. 660.

113 Interview, Lord Greenwood.

114 HG to Dr B. Stross MP, 7 November 1958: P.114–3. Also AHD, 22 April 1959.

115 *ST*, 29 July 1956.

116 *The Challenge of Coexistence*: see p. 970. His Foreword acknowledges help from Healey, Noel-Baker and Younger – and needless concern about appearing out of date: *a.* pp. 51–2; *b.* pp. 40–50, 71–2; *c.* pp. 54–8; *d.* pp. 35, 69–70; *e.* pp. 54–5, 70(Ho), 71–2, 77–8; *f.* p. 85; *g.* pp. 79–80; *h.* p. 89, cf. pp. 85–6; *i.* pp. 92–7; *j.* pp. 59–62.

117 Foot (1973), pp. 555, 582, 594.

118 HG to Crossman, 28 May 1958: P.148.

119 In opening the Congress for Cultural Freedom in Milan in September 1955 (U.85); and n. 116*f*.
120 In *Reynolds News*, 3 February 1957; and n. 116*j*.
121 Even Michael Foot gave backhanded approval: 'the ground is thick with buried hatchets', wrote 'John Marullus' in *Tribune*, 26 April 1957.
122 To Crosland (n. 93*a*) and Fairlie (nn. 69*b*, 86*b*).
123 Granada Television interview, 28 July 1961: U.87.
124 His own characterisation of Hugh Dalton: *Guardian*, 14 February 1962.
125 BBC microfilm, 1 April 1946.
126 HG to Strachey, 29 October 1950; cf. above, p. 207 and Ch. 7, n. 6*h*.
127 A. Allen MP to HG, 1 January 1958: P.118.

Chapter 14 Brief Honeymoon

1 *Birmingham Post, FT*, 15 December 1955.
2 R. T. McKenzie, *DT*, 15 December 1955.
3 Hunter (1959), p. 8.
4 Tom Hutchinson in *Illustrated*, 15 March 1958.
5 Henry Fairlie: *a. Daily Mail*, 6 February 1958; *b.* and 17 February 1958; *c.* and 30 July 1959 (HG interview); *d. Spectator*, 27 January 1956; *e.* and 10 February 1956; *f.* and 8 May 1956; *g.* cf. n. 31.
6 *Observer*, 5 February 1956: HG interview.
7 Interview, Sir Kenneth Younger.
8 On 'Press Conference', 2 August 1957: BBC transcript.
9 *a.* Mikardo in *Tribune*, 3 January 1958 (his italics); *b.* contrast his own earlier attack, and Michael Foot's continued hostility: *ibid.*, 24 February 1956, 15 August 1958, 27 March 1959.
10 On 2 January 1956: P.114–1.
11 *Daily Mail*, 3 October 1956; *DT*, 9 October 1957; cf. *ibid.*, 24 January 1956; 1 October 1956; *The Times*, 19 January 1957, 5 October 1957.
12 *DT*, 24 January 1956. Cf. *FT*, 7 February 1955, 25 April 1955; *Daily Mail*, 11 May 1955; *Sunday Dispatch*, 31 July 1955.
13 Robert Edwards: *a. SE*, 27 March 1959; *b.* quoted *Forward*, 26 May 1956.
14 Francis Williams, *DH*, 18 and 19 November 1957.
15 *Chartism* (WEA, 1928), p. 39.
16 He said so on 'In the News', 14 October 1955: BBC.
17 The same criticism was made of the Conservative Opposition under Heath, with whom HG was sometimes compared: see Malcolm Rutherford in *FT*, 16 December 1977.

18 But he disliked very precise public commitments: HG to Michael Stewart, 5 June 1957, on public schools; to Strachey, 2 September 1957, on armed forces pay; to Crossman, 30 January 1958, on indexed old age pensions (all P.114); to Marquand, 31 January 1957 (P.114) and to D. Ennals, 13 March 1959 (P.133), on foreign aid.

19 Diary: *a*. 9 January 1956; *b*. 28 February 1956; *c*. 14 February 1956; *d*. 11 March 1956; *e*. 21 January 1956; *f*. 24 February 1956; *g*. 3 April 1956; *h*. 14 July 1956; *i*. 16 January 1956; *j*. 23 February 1956; *k*. April 1956; *l*. 9 October 1956; *m*. 1 March 1956; *n*. 26 July 1956.

20 Punnett (1973), p. 69. On the pressure, RCD, 28 June 1955; cf. 15 July 1955.

21 *DT*: *a*. 29 June 1955, 29 July 1955; *b*. cf. 6 February 1956; *c*. 3 October 1956; *d*. 4 October 1956; *e*. 1 October 1956 (political correspondent).

22 Cf. George Hutchinson in *The Times*, 15 November 1975.

23 RCD, 9 February 1956, blames Wigg. (Cf. earlier comments: 15 October 1955, 2 and 16 December 1955.) Richard Stokes, Morrison's other main ally, was always loyal to HG.

24 John Murray to HG, n.d. but about 30 December 1955, P.187 (reporting Tony Greenwood). Also Diary, 28 February 1956, reporting Stokes (who was again friendly with Bevan) on Foot. *Tribune*, 23 December 1955 ('John Marullus'), 24 February 1956 (Mikardo).

25 George Gale in *DE*, 13 December 1955. 'Marullus' demanded a public denial.

26 So Bowden told HG who told Dalton: HDD, 27 October 1956 (Dalton's emphasis).

27 Hunter (1959), p. 180; Foot (1973), p. 499; interview, F. Mulley.

28 *a*. HDD, 2 February 1956; *b*. milder in HG's Diary, 3 February 1956.

29 Foot (1973), pp. 500–1. As usual Bevan was impulsive rather than calculating, and when Stokes asked why he had been 'such a b.f.', replied, 'Oh well, I can't help it': Stokes reported in n. 19*b*.

30 He 'was surprised and delighted' when all his friends approved. The Shadow Cabinet had given no advice but awaited his lead: n. 19*a, c*.

31 Who gave 'an almost verbatim account of my views': HG, n. 19*c*.

32 In 1970 Harold Wilson appointed 54, one-fifth of the PLP (compared to one-eighth under HG): Punnett (1973), Tables 46 and 50.

33 The press had expected Bevan to stay Shadow Minister of Labour, with little parliamentary scope: *DT*, 7 February 1956. That post went to George Brown.

34 So, contrary to Hunter (1959), p. 183, HG did not need persuading: n. 19*c*.

35 Cf. Eden (1960), p. 352; *The Times*, 19 March 1956.

36 Dalton to HG, 8 March 1956: P.118–6.

37 Quoted by Randolph Churchill in *The Rise and Fall of Sir Anthony Eden* (MacGibbon & Kee, 1959), p. 227.

38 Eden (1960), p. 320. HG specifically denied that they were hostile in his review: *ST*, 28 February 1960.

39 Diary, 24 February 1956; Macmillan (1971), pp. 12–14, 18 on his own threatened resignation, and on controls which, as HG knew, were favoured by Boyle the Economic Secretary.

40 RCD: *a.* 6 April 1956; *b.* 21 March 1956; *c.* 6 November 1957; *d.* 26 October 1956, reporting Sam Watson and Jack Cooper; *e.* 16 July 1956; *f.* 22 June 1956, 4 July 1956.

41 *MG*, 20 February 1956; *Leeds Weekly Citizen*, 9 March 1956.

42 549 *H.C. Deb.*, 20–21 February 1956: cols 59–80 (Wilson), 205–18 (Jay), 307–20 (HG).

43 Robert Carvel in *Star*, 24 January 1956.

44 HDD, 2 February 1956; HG to Donnelly (in the United States), 24 February 1956, P. 114–1. Carvel and Fairlie, *loc. cit.* (nn. 43, 5e).

45 HG's seven-page note of the conversations, on 29 and 30 March, is in P.118–4.

46 W. Leonhard, *The Kremlin since Stalin* (Oxford University Press, 1962), pp. 93–4.

47 This account is from HG's Diary, April 1956. See also Griffiths (1969), pp. 149–50; Brown (1972), pp. 65–70; Denis Healey in *New Leader*, 7 May 1956; H. Massingham in *Observer*, 29 April 1956; KYD, 24 May 1956. The verbatim report is in file P.105a.

48 In Rangoon on 6 December, Khrushchev had accused the Western powers of instigating their 'watchdog' Hitler to attack Russia.

49 Cf. Denis Healey, *New Leader*, 7 May 1956.

50 Confirmed by RCD, 8 May 1956; KYD, 24 May 1956.

51 HG took it for granted at this time that he would soon go to Moscow for serious talks: RCD, 13 March 1956. But when both the invitation and the acceptance were delayed, he was attacked from the Left for letting Macmillan get there first: below, p. 519.

52 Dr J. D. Cronin MP from Moscow to HG, 30 August 1962: P.118–7.

53 When HG unwisely referred on television to the Russians' provocative behaviour, Shinwell denied it: *DE*, 4 May 1956. Shinwell had not been there.

54 Interviews with William Pickles on May Day on the BBC (U.87) and with Percy Cudlipp, *NC*, 15 May 1956; RCD, 18 May 1956.

55 552 *H.C. Deb.*, cols 1751–60, 14 May 1956. HG was briefed by Shinwell's close ally Wigg, who did vote: Wigg (1972), p. 203 and interview.

56 Interview.

57 *Observer*, 20 May 1956; RCD, 18 and 31 May 1956; *ST*, 29 July 1956.

58 'Francis Flavius', *Tribune*, 25 May 1956. 'Crossbencher', quoted *Forward*, 14 September 1956, claiming that HG's leadership was a failure because Party membership was falling – on the basis of figures relating to Attlee's day.

59 *ST*, 20 May 1956; *Daily Worker*, 1 June 1956.

60 On these see Hunter (1959), Chapter 21; Foot (1973), pp. 509–13. HG lunched with Williamson on 1 March, and dined with the main union leaders on 4 April and 1 May: Diary.

61 Stokes to HG, 28 November 1956: 'When in July you asked me to stand aside in the debate on manpower, in order to let George Brown get the maximum publicity in view of his impending battle for the Treasurership ... ': P.114–1.

62 *The Times*, 6 October 1956. Cf. *DT*, 6 October 1956.

63 *LPCR*, 1956: *a.* pp. 81–2; *b.* p. 131; *c.* p. 132.

64 F. W. Mulley MP in *The Clerk*, November–December 1956.

65 KYD, 27 July 1956; Diary, 28 February 1956, 14 and 26 July 1956; *DT*, 18 May 1956.

66 KYD, 27 July 1956.

67 *New Statesman*, 28 July 1956.

68 In Stockholm; he sent the report to HG on 29 May 1956 (P.114–1).

Chapter 15 Suez

1 Diary, 30 January 1956. Cf. *The Economist*, 7 January 1956; RCD, 19 January 1956. See p. 407.

2 *People*, 29 January 1956.

3 RCD: *a.* 25 January 1956; *b.* 5, 14 and 28 September 1956; *c.* 5 September 1956; *d.* 28 September 1956; *e.* 26 October 1956; *f.* 7 November 1956; *g.* 21 November 1956; *h.* 16 May 1957.

4 549 *H.C. Deb.*, cols 2121–36: 7 March 1956.

5 Diary: *a.* 11 March 1956 (cf. above, p. 410); *b.* late July 1956; *c.* and n. 7*b.*; *d.* August 1956, his emphasis, dictated 12 and 22 August; *e.* 3 September 1956; *f.* 5 September 1956; *g.* 14 September 1956; *h.* 9 October 1956.

6 570 *H.C. Deb.*, 15–16 May 1957: *a.* col. 680; *b.* col. 690; *c.* col. 533; *d.* col. 685; *e.* cols 483–4 (A. Maude), 526–7 (B. Braine), 540–1 (Sir V. Raikes); *f.* col. 586.

7 See HG in 557 *H.C. Deb.*: *a.* cols 777–8, 27 July 1956; *b.* cols 1609–17, 2 August 1956.

8 Griffiths (1969): *a.* p. 151; *b.* p. 136; *c.* pp. 151–2; *d.* p. 153.

9 Interviews, Arthur Allen, Lords Harris and Jacobson, Alderman A. Tallant, Sir Harold Wilson; and n. 10*a.*

10 B. Reed and G. Williams, *Denis Healey and the Politics of Power* (Sidgwick & Jackson, 1971): *a.* Healey, p. 111; *b.* p. 112.

11 Diary, August 1956; KYD, 3 December 1956; cf. Hugh Thomas, *The Suez Affair* (Penguin, 1970), p. 64. Arthur Allen, HG's PPS, and Douglas Jay, also claimed credit for inserting this passage: interviews.

12 In Eden to HG, 6 August 1956, answering HG's letter of 3 August 1956: P.106.

13 Suggested by the Israeli Ambassador: n. 5*b.*

14 KYD: *a.* 16 September 1956; *b.* 30 December 1956; *c.* 17 March 1957.

15 HG to E. L. Mallalieu MP, 10 August 1956. Also to A. Blenkinsop MP, 10 August 1956 (both P.106); to D. Tyerman, 14 August 1956 (P.110); to Eden, 3 and 10 August 1956 (P.106). Cf. n. 8*b.*

16 Selwyn Lloyd, *Suez 1956* (Cape, 1978), pp. 83–6; cf. Thomas, pp. 63–4. On Eden's and Macmillan's earlier warnings to the Americans, Thomas, pp. 41, 56; Eden (1960), p. 428; R. Murphy, *Diplomat among Warriors* (Collins, 1964), pp. 462–3; cf. D. D. Eisenhower, *Waging Peace* (Heinemann, 1966), p. 40.

17 Interviews, Sir Robin Brook, Lord Harris, D. Jay.

18 HG to Cyril Robinson, 1 July 1958. On his confidence in Eden's assurances: interview, Sir Leslie Murphy; and n. 10*a.*

19 HG to Eden, 3 August 1956: P.106–1.

20 *Tribune*, 3 10, 17 and 24 August 1956; Shinwell (1963), p. 202; and e.g. R. Braddon, *Suez* (Collins, 1963), p. 53.

21 Thomas, pp. 64–5; L. D. Epstein, *British Politics in the Suez Crisis* (Pall Mall, 1964), pp. 66–7; R. Bowie, *Suez 1956* (Oxford University Press, 1974), p. 24. For contemporary evidence of its falsehood: n. 14*a.*

22 Interviews, Sir Isaiah Berlin (re Macmillan), A. Hetherington (re Hailsham). Braddon, p. 50 (re Thorneycroft).

23 Thomas: *a.* p. 65; *b.* p. 74; *c.* p. 136; *d.* p. 171.

24 Interview, E. Heath; cf. Kilmuir (1964), p. 269. D. Ayerst, *Biography of a Newspaper* (Collins, 1971), p. 622.

25 Elizabeth Monroe, *Britain's Moment in the Middle East* (Methuen edn, 1965), p. 204 (about other aspects of the crisis).

26 HG's review of Eden's memoirs in *ST*, 28 February 1960.

27 The letter was Jay's idea, but bringing Healey into it was HG's: n. 5*e.* Healey did not know that, for he wrote partly to influence HG: interview, and n. 10*a.*

28 HG to Eden, 10 August 1956, P.106–1; to Eirene White MP, 13 August 1956, P.106–2.

29 Jennie Lee signed, with 12 other Bevanites, 8 of the ILP-pacifist Left, and 3 others: *Tribune*, 10 August 1956.

30 *DT*, 9 August 1956; *ST*, 12 August 1956.

31 Griffiths to HG, 9 August 1956, P.106–1 (not 3 August, as in n. 8c). 'We saved him,' he claimed: interview.

32 HG to Mrs Skelly for Griffiths, 8 August 1956; Eden to HG, 6 August 1956: both P.106–1.

33 HG to Eden, 10 August 1956 (P.106–1) replying to Eden describing (9 August) the plans for a conference. HG again concluded that 'obvious aggression' by Nasser, or a UN condemnation of him, would change the situation.

34 Griffiths to HG, 10 August 1956, P.106–1; the underlining is in pencil, evidently by HG. Cf. n. 8d. On the conference, below, p. 428.

35 Panama was crucial for Dulles: H. Finer, *Dulles over Suez* (Heinemann, 1964), pp. 95–6. Cf. Lloyd, p. 100.

36 Foot (1973), pp. 519–20.

37 Interview, T. Driberg; and n. 23b.

38 Eden (1960), p. 492.

39 From the official American memorandum on the conversation, sent to HG (P.119–4) and coinciding with his own Diary account.

40 Also on the BBC: 'Press Conference', 21 September 1956.

41 *MG*, 31 August 1956; Diary, 3 September 1956; interviews, D. Ayerst, A. Hetherington, and n. 42; cf. Ayerst, pp. 622–3.

42 Interview, M. Arnold-Forster.

43 *Reynolds News*, 26 August 1956 (his heavy emphasis). Warning Eden now clearly took priority over keeping Nasser guessing.

44 So Morrison told HG: n. 5e. Cf. Donoughue and Jones (1973), p. 546.

45 *Observer*, 2 September 1956; *MG*, 3 September 1956; n. 42. (But cf. Thomas, p. 82; Finer, p. 191, on the TUC Right.)

46 Eden to Eisenhower, 6 September 1956 (Eden, 1960, pp. 464–7); Thomas, pp. 75–7, 80.

47 558 *H.C. Deb.*: *a.* 12–13 September 1956, Eden cols 11, 14; *b.* cols 15–32; *c.* cols 303–7; *d.* cols 27–9. *e.* 31 October 1956, HG col. 1454; *f.* cols 1458–9; *g.* cols 1461–2. *h.* 1 November 1956, col. 1569; *i.* Eden cols 1620–5, Head col. 1629; *j.* col. 1717; *k.* cols 1710–14, 1761, 1966. *l.* 3 November 1956 cols 1859, 1862, 1866, author's italics. *m.* 5 November 1956 col. 1967; *n.* Lloyd, cols 1975–6.

48 *New Statesman*: *a.* J. P. W. Mallalieu, 15 September 1956; *b.* and 15 December 1956; *c.* 13 October 1956; *d.* 10 November 1956 (and n. 3f); *e.* 31 January 1964; *f.* 8 December 1956.

49 Macmillan (1971): *a.* p. 125; *b.* p. 124; *c.* from his diary; *d.* pp. 171–3; *e.* p. 183; *f.* p. 236; *g.* p. 641; *h.* pp. 212, 238.

50 George Thomson in *Forward*, 21 September 1956; confirmed by RCD, 14 September 1956; KYD, 16 September 1956 (partially); cf. Macmillan (1971), p. 126; contrast Lloyd, Chapter 9.

51 *The Times*, 14 September 1956; *The Economist*, 22 September 1956; Macmillan (1971), pp. 126–7; Diary, 23 September 1956. Cf. n. 47*c*.

52 HG to Hugh Cudlipp, 14 September 1956, P.110; to Fred Lee MP, 18 September 1956, P.114–1; cf. KYD, 16 September 1956.

53 Nutting to the Canadian High Commissioner: T. Robertson, *Crisis* (Hutchinson, 1965, reflecting Lester Pearson's information), p. 174. Others: Thomas, p. 88. The plans were repeatedly postponed, though not abandoned: Lloyd, pp. 134–5; General Beaufre, *L'Expédition de Suez* (Paris, Grasset, 1967), pp. 67, 89, 91, 99.

54 Diary, 14 September 1956. On 24 September Monckton told Eden he must resign: n. 55*a*.

55 Birkenhead (1969): *a*. p. 308; *b*. Monckton's undated memorandum, pp. 307–8.

56 Birkenhead (1969), pp. 307–8; Lord Butler (1973), pp. 193–4, and in *Listener*, 22 July 1971, p. 108; Randolph Churchill, *The Rise and Fall of Anthony Eden* (MacGibbon & Kee, 1959), pp. 261, 287; Fisher (1973), p. 117; Lord Hailsham, *The Door Wherein I Went* (Collins, 1975), pp. 155, 175; Lloyd, pp. 183, 187, 190, 194; A. Nutting, *No End of a Lesson: The Story of Suez* (Constable, 1967), pp. 97–102; Robertson, pp. 124, 141, 145–6, 174, 179; Thomas, pp. 81–2, 113, 139n., 154. On the 1922 Committee, Churchill, pp. 252–3; Nicolson (1971), p. 284. On the Tory Foreign Affairs Committee: RCD, 14 September 1956, reporting Alec Spearman.

57 *a*. *Forward*, 12 October 1956; *b*. cf. n. 3*e*.

58 *The Economist*, 6 October 1956.

59 *LPCR*, 1956: *a*. p. 78; *b*. pp. 76–7, his emphasis.

60 But that optimism was not wholly wishful thinking, for Egypt's concessions at the UN appeared to satisfy Selwyn Lloyd himself: Nutting, pp. 50–1, 71–9. Cf. Robertson, pp. 141–6; T. Hoopes, *The Devil and John Foster Dulles* (Deutsch, 1974), p. 368; contrast Lloyd, pp. 169, 179.

61 Cf. *DT*, *Daily Mirror*, etc., 2 October 1956; grudgingly, *Spectator*, 5 October 1956; and nn. 48*c*, 57*a*.

62 HG's broadcast on 4 November: *Listener*, 8 November 1956.

63 Thomas, pp. 100–4; R. E. Neustadt, *Alliance Politics* (Columbia UP, 1970), pp. 20–1; Robertson, pp. 139–40.

64 Interview, T. A. K. Elliott (who argued with him at a dinner party on 10 October).

65 Lord Butler (1973), p. 190; cf. n. 66*a*.

66 Churchill: *a*. pp. 277–8; *b*. pp. 291–2; *c*. pp. 279–80; *d*. p. 307.

67 Hailsham, pp. 133–4.

68 Robertson: *a*. p. 124, quoting Monckton; *b*. cf. p. 225; *c*. pp. 219, 222.

69 Lawyers: Thomas, p. 139, Nutting, p. 95. Foreign Office: *ibid*. (Eden

insisted on secrecy). So only three knew: Sir Ivone Kirkpatrick the Permanent Secretary, Patrick Dean and, until early October, Geoffrey McDermott: McDermott (1972), pp. 112, 125.

70 Thomas, pp. 108–9, 132 (Tel Aviv), 140 (Cairo), 182 (Cairo, Moscow, Paris, the UN); Nutting, p. 111 (Washington), pp. 115–16 (Cairo).

71 Thomas, p. 115; Churchill, pp. 293–4; Robertson, pp. 168–71; Hoopes, pp. 372–3; Finer, pp. 335–6; Nutting, pp. 110–13.

72 Eden (1960), p. 526; Thomas, p. 133; Robertson, p. 182 (Canada); Churchill, p. 281 (Australia).

73 Thomas, p. 136; Robertson, pp. 183–4, 194–5; Churchill, pp. 257, 295. Lloyd later called the error about the United States the worst of many 'glaring miscalculations': Lloyd, p. 293. A charitable explanation is given in Neustadt, Chapter V.

74 Eden (1960), p. 526; cf. KYD, 30 December 1956; Eisenhower, p. 77.

75 Lloyd did: Lloyd, p. 183.

76 Eden (1960), p. 260. A. Head (Defence Minister during Suez), 597 *H.C. Deb.*, cols 1071–5: 16 December 1958.

77 Beaufre, pp. 83–5, 96, 109–10, 125, 221–2.

78 Nutting, p. 63 (at 13 September); cf. p. 40.

79 Lord Butler (1973), p. 193; Nutting, Chapter 10; Lloyd, pp. 173–5.

80 Pineau the French Foreign Minister, Dayan the Israeli Commander in Chief, Peres the director of their Defence Ministry, and others; summarised in Thomas, pp. 121–7, cf. pp. 93, 97; also in A. Moncrieff (ed.), *Suez Ten Years After* (BBC, 1967), pp. 90–5, 99–105; Robertson, pp. 139–40, 150–63; Beaufre, pp. 103–6; H. Azeau, *Le Piège de Suez* (Paris, Laffont, 1964), pp. 247–50; Frank Giles, *ST*, 24 October 1976. Cf. Lloyd's hints, reading pp. 181–2 with 188.

81 Lord Butler (1973), pp. 194–5; Eden (1960), p. 557; Lloyd, p. 210.

82 Interview, Malcolm Muggeridge: his strongest single memory of contacts with HG over a dozen years.

83 HG on 'Press Conference' (a US TV programme recorded on 21 November 1956). Cf. Thomas, p. 137; Griffiths (1969), p. 154 & n. 6c.

84 A. Hetherington to author.

85 HG quoted this comment soon after it was made: to Cyril Robinson, 1 July 1958.

86 In fact Australia and New Zealand voted with Britain, France and Israel.

87 Lloyd said truthfully that HMG had not incited Israel, and misleadingly that 'There was no prior agreement between us about it': n. 47h.

88 *DT*, 1 November 1956.

89 Consulted belatedly, the legal adviser to the Foreign Office told Ministers: 'We are in a state for which there is no legal precedent and

into which I hope my country will never again be plunged': Thomas, p. 155.

90 Grisewood (1968), pp. 198–201; Grace Wyndham Goldie, *Facing the Nation* (Bodley Head, 1977), pp. 183–6; contrast Dilks (1971), pp. 798–9.

91 At which HG was apparently furious, needlessly so according to Grisewood (1968), pp. 202–4. Others in the BBC sympathised with him: Stuart Hall in *Listener*, 28 March 1968. On the row, also *MG*, 5 November 1956; Goldie, pp. 174–6, 181–3.

92 *Ibid.*, p. 183. Mrs Goldie found him a private room away from his over-helpful entourage, and contrasted his calm and courtesy with Eden's near-hysterical tenseness: interview.

93 Thomas, p. 157; Braddon, p. 109; A. Howard in *New Statesman*, 12 January 1973. Cf. interview, Sir Arthur Gaitskell.

94 Albert Roberts to HG (from Beirut), 3 November 1956; Harry Hynd to HG, 3 December 1956: both P.114–1.

95 Interview, P. Clark. Cf. *Forward*, 1 March 1957 (John Harris), 21 March 1958 (Jeremy Isaacs), 11 April 1958 (A. N. Wedgwood Benn).

96 Interviews, Lord Boothby, Lord Boyle, Sir J. Foster, E. Heath, Sir Alec Spearman. Also *DT*, 5 November 1956; *MG*, 6 November 1956; RCD, 7 November 1956 (reporting Spearman); Nigel Nicolson in *People and Parliament* (Weidenfeld, 1958), p. 143; and in Nicolson (1971), pp. 289–90.

97 Interviews, Arthur Allen, Sir Hubert Ashton, Lord Butler.

98 Cf. Lord Butler (1973), p. 195; and in *Listener*, 22 July 1971, p. 110.

99 HDD, 3 November 1956, on all these points.

100 Crossman went further back, invoking the Whig supporters of American independence: *Daily Mirror*, 2 November 1956.

101 E.g. T. E. Utley in *DT*, 14 November 1956; and nn. 102, 103*a*.

102 Douglas Clark in *SE*, 11 November 1956.

103 561 *H.C. Deb.*, 3–5 December 1956: *a*. Lloyd, col. 887; *b*. col. 1570; *c*. col. 1471; *d*. cols 582, 1274–5, 1476; *e*. col. 128–2; *f*. col. 1302.

104 HDD, 3 November 1956, and Dalton to HG, 5 November 1956, P.115–6; letters in P.114–1; RCD, 16 May 1957. Jews: Epstein, Chapter 8.

105 Boyle to HG, 30 January 1957: P.114–2.

106 *National Newsletter*, no. 1063 of 5 December 1956, p. 585 (P.106).

107 Lady Violet to HG: *a*. 4 November 1956 (P.118–7); *b*. again, 10 Nov. 1956, praising his alpha-plus standard; *c*. 24 March 1959 (P.133–6).

108 Robertson, pp. 225–34; Thomas, p. 156; Lloyd, pp. 206–7.

109 Butler (1973), p. 195; Eden (1960) p. 556; Lloyd, pp. 209–11; Thomas, pp. 163–4; Robertson, pp. 262–4. Macmillan (1971), pp. 163– 7

claims that this was important but not decisive. Finer, pp. 427–9, says Butler, Monckton and Amory would have resigned if the cease-fire had been rejected. Hailsham and others told Crossman at the time of the violent Cabinet arguments: RCD, 7 and 9 November 1956.

110 Thomas, p. 159; Robertson, pp. 251–4.

111 In 1961 HG thought this speech – which covered much old ground – the best he had ever made. So, at the time, did Crossman: RCD, 7 November 1956.

112 560 *H.C. Dcb.*, 6 to 22 November 1956: *a.* cols 25–39 (quotes from cols 36, 39); *b.* cols 389–90, 399, 1946; *c.* col. 583.

113 Interview, Margaret Stewart (Hunter's widow).

114 Interview, Sir Arthur Gaitskell who was present. Cf. John Harris in *Forward*, 9 November 1956.

115 562 *H.C. Deb.*, 20 December 1956: *a.* col. 1518 (and n. 23*d*); *b.* col. 1402.

116 Some but not all are published in Epstein, pp. 142–3. (Liberals were particularly confused, approving Eden's handling of the situation by 46–31 per cent while opposing military action by 30–49 per cent in the same poll of 1–2 December.)

117 HG to Chuter Ede in the United States, P.114–1: *a.* 4 December 1956; *b.* 26 November 1956.

118 *DT*, 15 November 1956; RCD, 21 November 1956; Ian Trethowan to HG, 14 December 1956, P.110.

119 RCD, 21 November 1956; cf. HDD, 3 November 1956.

120 The passions persisted, and a respected historian ten years afterwards could misrepresent HG's speech of 2 August, dismiss his public warning, omit his private letters to Eden (by then publicly known), and suggest – ignoring HG's repeated explanations of the circumstances in which force would and would not be justified – that since Labour approved the Government's military precautions, they too envisaged using it: n. 121.

121 Robert Rhodes James in Moncrieff, pp. 111–12.

122 Interview, Lord Aylestone; and n. 123*a*, *b*.

123 Jenkins: *a*, Jenkins (1974), p. 175; *b*. in Rodgers (1964), pp. 123–4; *c*. *ibid.*, p. 122.

124 Hinted by *The Wykehamist*, 4 December 1956, and confirmed by two masters who were present.

125 In the poll of 1–2 December, people in non-manual occupations supported Eden by nearly 2 to 1; manual workers were evenly divided, and among Labour voters only, they were slightly *more* hostile to Eden than others.

126 In the House: Butler, nn. 47*j*, 103*b*; Macmillan, nn. 103*c*, 6*b*, 127*a*; and n. 49*d*. Also noted by Mallalieu, n. 48*b*; James, n. 121; Pannell,

Citizen, 10 May 1957; RCD, 18 December 1956, 11 and 25 January 1957; HDD, end 1956.

127 602 *H.C. Deb.*: *a.* col. 155; *b.* col. 140.

128 UN: nn. 112*b*, 103*d*. Tories: nn. 47*k*, 112*c*, 103*e*, 115*b*, 6*d*, 127*b*.

129 Henry Fairlie, *Daily Mail*, 10 May 1957; interviews, J. Callaghan, D. Healey, D. Ginsburg, S. Pearce, K. Robinson, Margaret Stewart, Sir Kenneth Younger; RCD, 28 September 1956; KYD, 30 December 1956; cf. Foot (1973), pp. 517–18; n. 123*c*.

130 As HG said on 'Press Conference' (US TV), recorded 21 November 1956: transcript, p. 10 (U.87). Also Griffiths (1969), p. 136, and interview; and n. 48*b*. Bevan even defended HG in private: RCD, 18 December 1956.

131 Hunter (1959), pp. 195–205. Cf. *Observer*, 28 October 1956; HDD, 27 October 1956, 2 November 1956.

132 He was thus less reluctant than Hunter believed. He may not yet have known of Bevan's feeler.

133 RCD, 2–16 December 1956; and nn. 48*f*, 113.

134 RCD, 4, 15 and 25 January 1957; Foot (1973), pp 539–40. Crossman thought the Shadow Cabinet favoured Bevan.

135 Sherman Adams, *Firsthand Report* (Harper, New York, 1961): *a.* pp. 267–70; *b.* Told of this reference in Oxford in 1962, HG was very disturbed at this evidence of United States intervention in British politics: interview, S. Rose.

136 Robens (from Italy) to HG, 21 January 1957: P.114–2.

137 RCD, 15 and 25 January 1957; *ST*, 21 January 1957; *DT*, 22 January 1957; *The Economist*, 26 January 1957; cf. n. 49*e*.

138 Macmillan (1971), p. 185. A 1922 Committee leader gave it less than three: P. Goodhart, *The 1922* (Macmillan, 1973), p. 176.

139 Jay to HG, 27 November 1956; Ede to HG, 29 November 1956: P.114–1. That was why Macmillan later said (*Listener*, 13 April 1971): 'they ought to have got us out'.

140 HG to Jay, 28 November 1956; to Ede, 4 December 1956: both P.114–1. Cf. his press conference in Washington: *DT*, 14 January 1957.

141 In the House (n. 47*d*); *LPCR*, 1956, p. 78; Foreign Press Association lunch on 17 September (text in *Socialist International Information*, 29 September 1956, P.106). Cf. Crossman's reluctant conclusion in RCD, 11 January 1957.

142 As many commentators have said he was; notably Robert Skidelsky in a sophisticated travesty of HG's position which condemns both Government and Opposition with a broad historical sweep without ever hinting at any alternative: in V. Bogdanor and R. Skidelsky (eds), *The Age of Affluence* (Macmillan, 1970), pp. 176–81. Cf. T. E. Utley in *DT*, 14 November 1956; RCD, 21 November 1956; and n. 121.

143 Selwyn Lloyd's former PPS, Lord Lambton, claimed that nearly half as much again could have been got by settling earlier: n. 144*a*.

144 620 *H.C. Deb.*, 16 March 1959: *a.* cols 123–5; *b.* cols 52–4, quoting Lambton on Lloyd; *c.* cols 152–5.

145 HG to Dingle Foot MP, 15 December 1958: P.114–3. RCD, 16 December 1958.

146 'John Marullus' (M. Foot) in *Tribune*, 6 February 1959. (Contrast *ibid.*, 11 January 1957.)

Chapter 16   Into Partnership with Bevan

1 To say one thing and do another, said Macmillan later, is 'a very common method' of Prime Ministers: to Nigel Lawson, *Listener*, 8 September 1966, p. 343 (quoted Sampson, 1967, p. 128).

2 To John Junor: quoted below, p. 786.

3 Jenkins (1974), p. 175, and in Rodgers (1964), p. 124; interview, Lady Gaitskell.

4 HG to John Beavan, 19 April 1961: P.166.

5 *Reynolds News*, 25 June 1957. Seven members were there named, of whom one died young. Harold Wilson made four of them Cabinet Ministers and one a Minister of State: Benn, Peart, Houghton, Mellish and Eirene White.

6 *a.* Interview with Harold Wilson on 8 May 1957 by Geoffrey Goodman who kindly lent it; *b.* Goodman there noted that most Labour leaders, Right and Left, said the same – and that all said HG was doing too much.

7 RCD, 3 May 1957, cf. 29 March 1957. He said so to HG, who replied: 'But there are only two others on the Executive to whom I can leave anything, you and Harold': 16 May 1957.

8 *Star*, 17 May 1957.

9 Fairlie in *Daily Mail*: *a.* 30 April 1957; *b.* 10 May 1957.

10 HDD, 'End 1956', reporting Sir Herbert Butcher.

11 RCD, 3 May 1957; cf. *ST*, 21 April 1957; *MG*, 30 April 1957; and n. 6*a*.

12 To Max Freedman in Washington, who so reported on 8 April 1957 to Alastair Hetherington (who kindly lent the letter). Cf. *ST*, 7 April 1957; and below, p. 454.

13 Cf. KYD, 30 December 1956.

14 Trevor Evans, *DE*, 3 October 1957.

15 Lord Pakenham, *Observer*, 6 October 1957.

16 H. B. Boyne in *DT*, 30 September 1957; *ST*, 6 October 1957. Cf. *The Times*, *DT*, 5 October 1957; and n. 17*a*.

17 *Observer* political correspondent: *a.* 6 Oct. 1957; *b.* 13 Sept. 1957.

18 Transcript of a taped discussion (HG, Harry Nicholas and John Murray) recorded in September 1957 by the Labour Party: P.118x.

19 *Public Enterprise* (Labour Party, 1957): see nn. 20, 21*a*.

20 Interview, D. Ginsburg.

21 RCD: *a.* 23 May 1957; *b.* 6 June 1955; *c.* 6 September 1957; *d.* 7 September 1957; *e.* 13 September 1957; *f.* 18 February 1958; *g.* 10 June 1959; *h.* 30 September 1957; *i.* 26 September 1957; *j.* 27 September 1957, reporting HG on their talk, 26 September; *k.* 4 October 1957; *l.* reporting Silverman; *m.* 3 May 1957.

22 As Fabian Tract no. 300; his foreword says it was written in 1953. Cf. HG in *Reynolds News*, 15 February 1953 (above, p. 316).

23 Crosland (1956): *a.* Chapters 22–3; *b.* pp. 492–3; *c.* p. 480.

24 R. M. Titmuss, *Income Distribution and Social Change* (Allen & Unwin, 1962).

25 *Tribune*: *a.* Crossman, 6 September 1957; *b.* e.g. Mikardo, 13 September 1957; *c.* Castle, 13 September 1957; *d.* editorial, 19 July 1957; *e.* cf. Mikardo, 26 July 1957.

26. *Keeping Left* (*New Statesman* pamphlet, January 1950), pp. 27–9. Mikardo as its draftsman: n. 25*a*.

27 Foot (1973), pp. 500–2; *ST*, 26 February 1956; *The Times*, 27 February 1956. Above, pp. 408–10.

28 Haseler (1969), pp. 107, 108n., says it had a right-wing majority, but gives six Left, five Right and three Centre names. Harold Wilson (Centre) was the 'highest common factor': n. 20.

29 Foot (1973), p. 557 (Bevan); RCD, 6 September 1957 (Castle).

30 Peter Shore, the research secretary concerned, reported n. 21*c*. Cf. *DT*, 22 July 1957.

31 NEC 25 June 1957, M.199; cf. 26 September 1957, M.281. Wilson in *Forward*, 19 July 1957; interviews, D. Ginsburg, Sir Harry Nicholas, W. Padley, R. Gunter (who said some members carefully left before the vote); and nn. 25*a*, *b*, 32*a*.

32 TUC Report, 1957: *a.* Peggy Herbison, p. 330; *b.* W. L. Heywood for the General Council, p. 461; *c.* but cf. nn. 21*d*, 25*c*.

33 Foot to Hugh Massingham on 15 July, reported in RCD, 20 September 1957. Bevan's unhappiness was short-lived.

34 Payment of shares as death duties had already been proposed in the previous year's pamphlet, *Towards Equality*.

35 *Industry and Society*: *a.* p. 58; *b.* p. 57; *c.* cf. n. 23*b*.

36 The phrase was already in Labour's 1951 manifesto.

37 *LPCR*, 1957, pp. 128–9, 158. Indeed HG had said that in his very first draft of his Fabian essay: to the Oxford University Labour Club on 23 May 1953 (U.181).

38 Wilson thought Bevan and HG might clash over that: n. 6*a*.

39 *Socialist Commentary*: *a*. editorial, October 1957 (its emphasis); *b*. August, September, October 1957.

40 Cf. Haseler (1969), pp. 110–11; Roth (1977), p. 219.

41 Interview, Lord Pannell.

42 *Forward*, 30 August 1957.

43 *FT*, 3 September 1957; cf. *Daily Mail*, 30 August 1957; *DT*, 2 September 1957.

44 *a*. Jay to HG, 4 September 1957, P.114–2, reporting Cousins telling Leslie Hunter that those assurances had decided his vote; *b*. reply, 6 September 1957; *c*. also n. 21 *c, e*.

45 Dalton to HG, 4 October 1957: P.118–6. Wilson in *LPCR*, 1957, pp. 129–30 (and n. 21*b*).

46 M. M. Postan in Rodgers (1964), p. 59; specifying aircraft, chemicals and urban land — interview.

47 Macmillan at Stockton: *DT*, 3 June 1957. Earlier, Randolph Churchill in *Evening Standard*, 26 August 1955; and *ST*, 24 June 1956.

48 HG to Stokes, P.114–2: *a*. 24 May 1957; *b*. 8 April 1957.

49 HG to John Murray, P.187: *a*. 9 October 1957; *b*. 9 March 1959; *c*. 10 April 1957.

50 A Gallup poll in March 1959 found that 17 per cent did so (to 33 per cent who saw it as the workers' or underdogs' Party; no other answer got more than 3 per cent). For Labour voters only the figures were 6 and 57 per cent; for all voters in 1951, 6 and 39 per cent. At the same period, more nationalisation was opposed by a small majority of Labour and a huge majority of Liberal and 'non-party' voters: n. 51*a*.

51 Butler and Rose (1960): *a*. pp. 244–5; *b*. p. 253.

52 Four times as much as the Conservatives spent on advertising in the same period, 14 times as much as Labour, and 40 per cent more than all candidates together spent in the election: n. 51*b*.

53 Letter to a friend, 10 February 1959.

54 AHD: *a*. 11 November 1958; *b*. 22 April 1959, 9 July 1959.

55 HG to Strachey, 4 May 1959: P.142–1. Cf. above, pp. 316, 318, and below, pp. 658–9.

56 Harrison (1960), pp. 156–8, 234–5.

57 H. B. Boyne in *DT*, 30 September 1957; and n. 17*a*.

58 Interview, G. Goodman (who was told so at the time): Goodman's forthcoming *Frank Cousins* (Davis-Poynter, 1979), Chapter 13.

59 *LPCR*, 1957, p. 129; Roth (1977), pp. 222–3.

60 *LPCR*, 1957: *a*. pp. 157–8; *b*. p. 128; *c*. p. 160; *d*. Bevan, p. 180; *e*. and p. 182; *f*. pp. 181–2.

61 RCD, 20 September 1957; *NC* 3 October 1957; and n. 44*a*.

62 Harrison (1960), pp. 145, 149, 177, 213, 234–5. Campbell's own

amendment was lost by 1,422,000 to 5,383,000; he had 865,000 union votes for it, and 700,000 against the main motion. The AEU later repudiated its delegation's vote.

63 Mulley to HG, 19 December 1957, P.114–3; and n. 15.

64 Dalton to HG, 4 and 9 October 1957: P.118–6. Cf. John Murray to HG, 4 October 1957: P.187.

65 Macmillan (1971): *a.* p. 235, cf. pp. 230, 231; *b.* pp. 261, 263; *c.* pp. 266, 297–9; *d.* from his diary.

66 568 *H.C. Deb.*, cols 45, 52–3, 68 (Macmillan); cols 71–3 (HG); cols 129–30 (Healey).

67 To Nigel Nicolson: Nicolson (1971), p. 306.

68 *DE*, 2 April 1957; *Evening News*, 2 April; *DT*, 3 April; *ST*, 7 April.

69 HG to Younger, 8 April 1957: P.114–2.

70 *DT*, 4 April 1957; *ST*, 7 April 1957.

71 *a.* KYD, 23 April 1957; *b.* and n. 48*b*.

72 Pannell to HG, 3 April 1957; other right-wing compromisers were Austen Albu and Lord Pakenham (all P.114–2).

73 Mayhew believed he would have carried the compromise proposal if HG had rejected it: interview. On his role, n. 70. Wilson privately claimed credit for the compromise: n. 6*a*.

74 The meeting lasted twelve minutes: *DT*, 4 April 1957 (also for Jennie Lee). For Brown, n. 71*a*. On the Right, Blyton, Shinwell and Stokes were critical, but others congratulated HG: Pannell, C. F. Grey and E. L. Mallalieu (also Kenneth Younger).

75 *ST*, 7 and 21 April 1957; *DT*, 17 April 1957; *MG*, 30 April 1957; and n. 9*a*.

76 Support for testing rose between early April and early May 1957 from 41 to 45 per cent (among Labour voters from 31 to 38 per cent); opposition to it fell from 44 to 39 (Labour, 55 to 45) per cent. By late May, 54 per cent were satisfied with Macmillan as Prime Minister (a figure he next reached in September 1958) while 41 per cent thought HG a good Labour leader, 3 per cent fewer than in December 1956.

77 Macmillan, minute to Charles Hill, Chancellor of the Duchy and Government publicity manager, 5 June 1957, and n. 65*c, d*

78 Foot (1973): *a.* p. 554–5; *b.* p. 568.

79 Duff (1971): *a.* pp. 70–1; *b.* p. 119; *c.* p. 74; *d.* p. 71.

80 According to the Minister responsible, his old friend G. R. Strauss: letter in *Encounter*, August 1963, and Oral History interview (Chapter 8, n. 63), p. 31. M. Gowing's authoritative *Independence and Deterrence* I (Macmillan 1974), Chapter 2 neither confirms nor denies.

81 Above, pp. 337–9; Duff (1971), p. 70.

82 D. E. Butler (1955), p. 90.

83 571 *H.C. Deb.*, cols 1080–3: 4 June 1957.

84 Transcript, 20 September 1957; P.124–1. Report to NEC, 24 July 1957 (Minutes, vol. 123).

85 *DT*, 10 and 11 July 1957.

86 On 24 September 1957: P.114–2.

87 Interview, G. Goodman (who heard it from both Bevan and Jennie Lee at the time). Bevan's speech also gave a strong hint: n. 60*e*. Cf. below, p. 520. Foot implies (1973, pp. 565–6) that the British bomb was not discussed in the Crimea.

88 RCD, 26 September 1957; NEC-M, 26 Sept. 1957, M. 266; Hunter (1959), p. 208. Foot (1973), pp. 567–8, follows Crossman's account, except in calling the office draft to which Bevan objected a 'Gaitskell-Morgan Phillips draft'; and in praising the Vienna resolution without mentioning either that HG strongly supported substituting it, or that he had been its original proponent in Vienna.

89 She was Vivienne Mendelson of Norwood; Foot (1973), p. 569, Hunter (1959), p. 209 omit her views.

90 RCD, 30 May 1957, reporting Watson; cf. Foot (1973), p. 581; Hunter (1959), p. 209.

91 Jennie Lee, *Observer Magazine*, 10 December 1972, pp. 54–5.

92 The subtitle of Krug's biography.

93 A common phrase of his: interview, Geoffrey Goodman.

94 T. Driberg in Bevan obituary programme, 3 October 1961 (BBC transcript, p. 26). Cf. Foot (1973), pp. 577, 581, 583–4; and n. 91.

95 Minute 70 of its BDG, 11 July 1957: 'An immediate cessation of H-Bomb tests by *all* Powers; Total abolition of the H-Bomb on a *universal basis* ... ' (my italics).

96 RCD, 4 October 1957. Cousins may have hoped to start a stampede which never came: *Spectator*, 11 October 1957. Goodman (n. 58), Chapter 13.

97 Most sources give the majority as 16 to 14, but others (quoted by Goodman) say it was even smaller.

98 Harrison (1960), pp. 237–8, estimates that of the minority, only 200,000 or 300,000 were union votes.

Chapter 17 Macmillan Ascendant

1 RCD, 24 October 1957; Hunter (1959), p. 210. In fact they had dined weekly with Cripps in 1948–50, and lunched together in October 1956.

2 Many letters in P.114–2, including HG to Bevan, 24 October 1957 and 26 November 1957. Cf. HG to Lord Faringdon, 13 November 1957, about arranging another social meeting after Bevan's return.

3 On 'Face the Nation', 3 November 1957, quoted Krug (1961), pp. 263–4. Cf. Sidney Lens in *Forward*, 15 November 1957.

4 HG to Crossman, 13 and 18 November 1957, and reply, 14 November: P.114–2.

5 Paget to HG, n.d. but 12 November 1957, reply 12 November (saying that it was Crossman's personal view): P.114–2.

6 *DT*, 26 April 1957; *MG*, 13 May 1957.

7 Summary by Michael Howard (11 November 1957) of HG's talk on 23 October 1957: P.107–3.

8 *DT*, 16, 17 and 24 October 1957; Randolph Churchill in *DE*, 17 October 1957.

9 Macmillan (1971): *a.* pp. 284–5; *b.* pp. 368, 372; *c.* pp. 716–18; *d.* pp. 719, 721 (and n. 37*b*); *e.* p. 419, all punctuation his; *f.* Chapter 17; *g.* p. 671; *h.* p. 695; *i.* p. 509; *j.* p. 506; *k.* pp. 516–20; *l.* p. 521; *m.* pp. 735–6; *n.* p. 737; *o.* p. 744; *p.* from his diary.

10 RCD: *a* 24 October 1957; *b.* 7 May 1958; *c.* 11 July 1958, reporting HG; *d.* 28 January 1958; *e.* 27 March 1953; *f.* 9 December 1958; *g.* and 21 January 1958; *h.* 17 February 1959; *i.* 4 May 1961; *j.* 21 May 1958; *k.* 19 June 1958; *l.* 18 February 1958; *m.* 19 October 1959; *n.* 19 March 1959; *o.* 26 November 1957; *p.* 28 February 1958; *q.* 8 October 1958; *r.* 18 July 1958; *s.* 27 November 1958; *t.* 25 March 1959; *u.* 18 December 1958; *v.* 14 May 1959.

11 Diary, 9 October 1956; RCD, 20 September 1957; HDD, 3–14 April 1958; HG to John Murray, 5 June 1957 (P.187), lamenting the lack of time for doing so; interviews, R. Crossman, D. Ginsburg, R. Jenkins, D. Wood.

12 574 *H.C. Deb.*, 25 July 1957: *a.* col. 718; *b.* cols 715–17.

13 Party political broadcasts: BBC. *a.* 27 October 1958; *b.* 29 November 1958; *c.* 21 April 1959.

14 John Murray to HG, P.187: *a.* 28 July 1957 and reply, 2 August 1957 (and nn. 15, 16); *b.* 5 April 1957 (he was a member); *c.* 31 August 1958; *d.* 19 and 28 July 1958.

15 HG on 'Press Conference', 2 August 1957: BBC.

16 *a.* Interview, David Ginsburg; *b.* who was present.

17 Thorneycroft in Washington (*The Economist*, 28 September 1957) and in the House, n. 18*a*. Dow (1970), pp. 101–2, 256.

18 581 *H.C. Deb.*, 3–6 February 1958: *a.* cols 859–60; *b.* cols 1093–1104, 1109; *c.* cols 1383–4.

19 Contrast HG's letter in *The Times*, 7 February 1958 and speech in the House (n. 18*b*) with Macmillan's bland omission of the points reflecting on his own actions (Macmillan, 1971, pp. 421–7).

20 For a similar, less important case: 566 *H.C. Deb.*, cols 40–130, 4 March 1957; Macmillan (1971), pp. 220–2.

21 *Political Quarterly*: *a*. October 1959, pp. 330–1, 335 (Arthur Butler); *b*. *ibid*., p. 329; *c*. Enoch Powell, p. 304; *d*. 1973, p. 202 (R. Bilski); *e*. January 1953, HG.

22 *The Times*: *a*. 18 September 1957; *b*. 5 May 1958; *c*. 9 February 1961; *d*. political correspondent, 17 July 1958; *e*. *ibid*., 21 July 1958; *f*. 24 November 1958; *g*. on the risks, see n. 9*k*.

23 HG to R. Boothby, 23 September 1957 (his italics). Cf. HG to A. Blenkinsop MP, 24 October 1957 (both P.114–2). Also in the House: nn. 24*a*, 25*a*.

24 HG in 577 *H.C. Deb.*, 5 and 12 November 1957: *a*. cols 784–97; *b*. cols 20–4, 789–800; *c*. cols 18–20.

25 HG in 580 *H.C. Deb.*, 23 January 1958: *a*. cols 1285–90; *b*. cols 1286, 1292–3.

26 Dow (1970), pp. 96–101; also nn. 27*a*, 28*a*, 29 *a*, *c*, *e*, *g*.

27 Shonfield (1959): *a*. pp. 230–4; *b*. pp. 124–7; *c*. pp. 246–8, and n. 29*e*; *d*. p. 250.

28 Brittan (1971): *a*. pp. 214–16; *b*. p. 215; *c*. p. 211 (cf. n. 27*b*); *d*. pp. 212–19; *e*. pp. 213–14, 217–18; *f*. pp. 224–6; *g*. p. 225 (cf. n. 29*b*, *f*).

29 Worswick and Ady (1962): *a*. Worswick, pp. 48–57; *b*. and pp. 65–7; *c*. Scott, pp. 222–3; *d*. and p. 226; *e*. Little, pp. 266–7; *f*. and p. 269; *g*. Kennedy, pp. 307–8; *h*. and p. 323.

30 Macleod rejecting a Whitley Council award to them. Cf. his and Thorneycroft's speeches (575 *H.C. Deb.*, cols 57, 236–7: 29 and 30 October 1957); and V. L. Allen, *Trade Unions and the Government* (Longmans, 1960), pp. 106–12.

31 At the pre-Conference Brighton demonstration, 28 September 1957 (U.92); in *Forward*, 1 November 1957; and in the House, nn. 24*b*, 25*b*.

32 His evidence is in vol. 3 at Questions 12324–74, on 18 December 1958.

33 Dow (1970), p. 100; cf. nn. 28*d*, 29*h*; contrast 27*d*.

34 Brittan (1971), pp. 209–10, 213; and n. 9*b*.

35 According to the Gallup poll, Conservatives only marginally preferred Macmillan (by 36 to 33), while Opposition voters favoured Thorneycroft heavily (Labour by 50 to 9, Liberals 66 to 9). Many in all parties thought Labour supported the ex-Chancellor. These bizarre results no doubt reflect attitudes to the Tory premier, rather than policy judgments.

36 HG to Don Chapman, 27 January 1958: P.114–3.

37 Fisher (1973): *a*. pp. 124–6; cf. G. Goodman's forthcoming biography of Cousins; *b*. p. 131.

38 Macmillan (1971), pp. 713–14 (from his diary, 29 April 1958), 719; Fisher (1973), p. 126; interviews, E. Heath, G. Goodman.

39 Stewart (1968): *a*. pp. 54–6, cf. n. 10*b*; *b*. pp. 57–8, cf. n. 9*c*.

40 Interviews: Sir William Webber, R. Gunter, W. Padley. Ted Hill (left-wing leader of the Boilermakers) to HG, who told Dalton: HDD, 18 June 1958.

41 Interviews, D. Ginsburg, R. Gunter.

42 Interviews, Sir Harry Nicholas (then Cousins's no. 2), Lord Jacobson.

43 HG to Julie: *a.* 1 May 1958; *b.* n.d., probably 17 November 1958, his emphasis; *c.* n.d., February 1958; *d.* 22 June 1958; *e.* 20 July 1958; *f.* 21 January 1959; *g.* 2 July 1958.

44 Against HG's better judgment, thought Crossman: RCD, 9 May 1958. 587 *H.C. Deb.*, cols 379–86, 719–26, 848–58.

45 *Ibid.*, cols 1452–3, 8 May 1958 (and Fisher, 1973, p. 128).

46 Allen, pp. 201–13.

47 HDD: *a.* 18 June 1958; *b.* 3–14 April 1958.

48 Cf. *DT*, 11 May 1958; H. Fairlie in *Daily Mail*, 19 May 1958. HG was warmly thanked by Cousins for his support (n. 49*a*) and later condemned by *Tribune* for not giving any (David Boulton, 13 October 1961).

49 *LPCR*, 1958: *a.* p. 166; *b.* pp. 169–70; *c.* p. 170; *d.* p. 85; *e.* pp. 201, 214; *f.* 1953, p. 172; *g.* 1956, p. 130.

50 594 *H.C. Deb.*: *a.* cols 23–4 (28 October 1958), 887–94 (4 November 1958), and *nn.* 49*b*, 51; *b.* cols 971–5, reply cols 1063–8 (5 November 1958).

51 *DE*, 14 January 1959; interview with A. Lejeune.

52 He consulted only Gordon Walker, Jay and Wilson, but the Shadow Cabinet retrospectively approved: *The Times*, 29 December 1958; *DT*, 1 January 1959; *ST*, 4 January 1959.

53 See Chapter 7, Section iv.

54 598 *H.C. Deb.*, 28 January 1959: *a.* cols 1093–6 (cf. n. 29*d.*); *b.* cols 1101, 1109–10, quoting the *Observer*'s economic editor.

55 On 29 April 1958: BBC; *The Economist*, 3 May 1958; interview, H. Hutchinson, a participant. (They differed in emphasis but it was not at all a 'confrontation', contrary to L. Panitch, *Social Democracy and Industrial Militancy*, Cambridge University Press, 1976, p. 46.)

56 RCD, 10 February 1958; interviews, R. Gunter, F. Mulley, W. Padley, Lady Phillips, Lady White; also J. Callaghan, Lord Cooper, I. Mikardo.

57 HG to John Murray, P.187: *a.* 9 October 1957; *b.* 24 July 1958; *c.* Crossman dissented: RCD, 6 September 1957.

58 HG to Cyril Robinson, 31 December 1953 (A.8) and 30 September 1955 (P.89). But he asked Rita Hinden (as a real question, not a negative rhetorical one): 'Are we going to go on with the comprehensive school?' in the next Labour government: 4 October 1955, P.107–4.

59 Interviews: *a.* Lady Gaitskell; *b.* Lady Bacon.

60 On 'Any Questions?', 29 April 1955: BBC transcript.

61 HG to Morrison: *a.* 29 January 1954; *b.* 25 June 1951.

62 F. L. Allen of Wallasey (the chairman) to HG, 13 October 1954: A.8.

63 Diary: *a.* 14 October 1954; *b.* 1 August 1956.

64 HG in *Reynolds News*, 8 May 1955; and for the whole paragraph.

65 HG to Diana Vernon, 19 October 1954; to R. O. F. Boyd, 7 October 1954 (P.80).

66 At Bilborough Grammar School, Nottingham: *The Times*, 6 April 1958. Cf. New Year Message in *Forward*, 2 January 1959; interview in *Daily Mail*, 16 January 1961.

67 *a.* HG to Cyril Robinson, 1 July 1958 (his italics); *b.* cf. *Observer*, 6 July 1958.

68 HG to C. Jordan, secretary of the Hornsea Labour Party, 12 January 1959.

69 M. Parkinson, *The Labour Party and the Organisation of Secondary Education 1918–65* (Routledge, 1970): *a.* p. 84; *b.* pp. 108–9; *c.* pp. 114–15; *d.* and R. Bilski, 'Ideology and the Comprehensive Schools', n. 21*d*.

70 19–30 January 1953: P.59 and P.60b.

71 *a.* Interview, G. Goodman; *b.* on HG in 1953; *c.* and n. 61*b*.

72 Brown (1972), p. 241; and nn. 49*f*, 69*b*.

73 HG to Alma Birk, 4 February 1955: P.97.

74 Interviews, Lady Bacon, D. Ginsburg, M. Stewart. Griffiths, p. 135.

75 He wrote to Michael Stewart, Labour's education spokesman, that preparatory school boys must not be eligible and that half was a minimum proportion, to be increased later: 5 June 1957, P.114–2. (The Fleming Report in 1944 had advocated up to 25 per cent free places.) Stewart vainly proposed such a scheme to the NEC: Re 375/April 1958, in the minutes for its special meeting, 14 May 1958. On HG's views: also nn. 49*f*, 67*a*.

76 RCD, 10 February 1958; *ST*, 5 January 1958, 18 May 1958.

77 *LPCR*, 1958, p. 113; it was moved by Fred Peart and supported by Frank Cousins. Cf. n. 69*c*. Dalton thought it could have cost Labour the election: HDD, 18 June 1958; Dalton to HG, 7 October 1958.

78 Surprisingly, Bevan too felt that very strongly: interview, G. Goodman (reporting both HG and Driberg on Bevan's view).

79 Lord Pethick-Lawrence's phrase: to HG, 24 December 1955 (P.114–1) covering many other issues. HG's reply 2 January 1956: 'I agree generally … ' But cf. HG in the *Star*, 14 January 1956 and in *Forward*, 28 January 1956, on subsidy cuts.

80 M. J. Barnett, *The Politics of Legislation: The Rent Act 1957* (Weidenfeld, 1969), Chapter 11.

81 HG's interview with Alan Wood, *NC*, 3 April 1957. Crossman agreed: n. 10*f*.

82 Interview, Lord Greenwood.

83 He got his way in 1961: RCD, 28 June 1961.

84 Above, p. 374.

85 Alf Robens's review of the Report in *Forward*, 9 May 1958.

86 MS message to *Cooperative News*, n.d. but about November 1958: P.112–3.

87 B. Smith and G. Ostergaard, *Constitutional Relations between the Labour and Cooperative Parties: an historical review* (Hansard Society, 1960), pp. 15–22; Roth (1977), p. 217; Carbery (1969), pp. 114–19. There was another minor clash in 1960 over boycotting South African goods: *ibid.*, pp. 241–2; *ST*, 24 January 1960.

88 Attlee thought abolition impracticable, and HG agreed: Diary, 1 August 1956.

89 *a.* HG's interview in *Observer*, 5 February 1956; *b.* and nn. 90, 91*a*.

90 HG to Lord Pakenham, 5 November 1957 (P.114–21).

91 582 *H.C. Deb.*, 12 February 1958: *a.* cols 419–20; *b.* col. 611; *c.* cols 608–9, 694–5; *d.* cols 414, 422.

92 HG's memorandum of their meeting, 17 January 1956 (P.118–4); Diary, 9 January 1956; and n. 89*a*.

93 HG to Benn, 5 Feb. 1958 (P.126B); and in the House, nn. 24*c*, 91*d*.

94 So he told the PLP later: *The Times*, 9 February 1961 (see next paragraph).

95 Interviews, Lord Shackleton, Lady Wootton. He succeeded: see Janet P. Morgan, *The House of Lords and the Labour Government 1964–70* (OUP, 1975), pp. 17–18.

96 Longford (1974), p. 29.

97 AHD, 26 April 1961 and 14 July 1961; *DT*, 29 April 1961, 17 May 1961, 20 July 1961; and in the House, 639 *H.C. Deb.*, cols 420–7; 430–1 (26 April 1961) and nn. 98*a*, 99*a*.

98 638 *H.C. Deb.*, 13 April 1961: *a.* cols 570–4; *b.* cols 583–4.

99 640 *H.C. Deb.*, 8 May 1961: *a.* cols. 84–97; *b.* cols 39–41.

100 Interview, Lord Pannell. Anthony Howard in *New Statesman*, 14 July 1961, and Pannell's letter 21 July.

101 AHD, 25 January 1962, 6 February 1962. *DT*, 1 February 1962; 656 *H.C. Deb.*, cols 1370–7 (28 March 1962). The *New Statesman* (12 January 1962) of course assumed HG had fallen into a Tory trap.

102 HG had suspected that dislike of that particular prospect explained the government's prolonged stonewalling: AHD, 14 July 1961, and n. 99*b*, cf. n. 98*b*.

103 *The Economist*: *a.* 4 October 1958; *b.* 21 June 1958.

104 'Crossbencher' in *SE*: *a.* 10 August 1958; *b.* 1 and 15 December 1957.

105 *Tribune*: *a.* 25 August 1958; *b.* 20 December 1957; *c.* 3 January 1958; *d.* 18 July 1958.

106 *Spectator*, 1 August 1958; and n. 21*c*.

107 Francis Williams in *DH*: *a.* 18 November 1957; *b.* 19 November 1957.

108 *DT*: *a.* 13 November 1957; *b.* 9 June 1959; *c.* 5 March 1958.

109 Henry Fairlie, *Daily Mail*: *a.* 6 February 1958, commenting on the debate on the bank rate affair; *b.* 19 May 1958, on continuing grumbles about the tea-room.

110 HG on 'Panorama', 3 March 1958 (blaming Tory propaganda).

111 Labour's lead was 6 per cent in August, 13 per cent in September, 10 per cent in October, 5 per cent in December – owing to Tory losses not Labour gains.

112 HG to Harold Wilson in the United States, 21 February 1958: P.129.

113 *ST*, 6 April 1958; *DT*, 14 June 1958; n. 10*k*. Cf. n. 114*a*.

114 *Sunday Dispatch*: *a.* 1 December 1957; *b.* 24 January 1960 (Alan Brien).

115 Foot (1973): *a.* p. 629; *b.* p. 609, delicately obscuring that the rebuke was addressed to himself.

116 612 *H.C.Deb.*, col. 960: 3 November 1959.

117 Interview, E. Heath.

118 *The Times*, 21 July 1958. Cf. *ST*, 5 July 1959; Crosland to HG, 4 May 1960 (P.183).

119 *MG*: *a.* 15 December 1958, political correspondent; *b.* 18 December 1959; *c.* 14 August 1959.

120 Gordon Walker, without telling HG (RCD, 10 November 1958) said government facilities had been used for party political propaganda: n. 50*b*.

121 602 *H.C. Deb.*, col. 443 (18 March 1959); cf. n. 10*n*.

122 For a scathing contemporary comment on Macmillan's treatment of HG at this time see Arthur Butler, n. 21*b*.

123 Roy Jenkins in Rodgers (1964), p. 124. AHD, 23 July 1959. Art Buchwald described HG's views in the *New York Herald Tribune* on 1 April 1959: 'Mr. Macmillan is an actor, and I think all this publicity is dragging British politics to its lowest level.' (HG repudiated the article, but it reflected his feelings.)

124 Interview, Lord Harris.

125 Macmillan in *Daily Mail* interview, January 1959, quoted Butler and Rose (1960), p. 32.

126 HG to Donnelly, 2 March 1955: P.97.

127 Bevan had told HG nothing much would happen: RCD, 26 November 1957 (reporting HG). But the meeting decided to install American missile bases in NATO countries, and Crossman had a point.

128 *Daily Mirror*, 3 December 1957; *DT*, 13 December 1957, for the

leaders rebuking him; RCD, 20 December; Crossman to HG, 23 December, P.114–3.

129 *The Times,* 23 December 1957; *SE,* 15 December 1957.

130 Anthony Greenwood to HG, 2 January 1958, HG's reply, n. 34*d*: P.114–3. Blackpool: above, p. 449.

131 Roy Mason to HG, 14 May 1957, F. Mulley to HG, 9 July 1957, D. Howell to HG, 18 July 1957: all P.114–2. (The Leader of the Opposition also received an increase which he had never suggested: *DT,* 5 July 1957.)

132 *Daily Mirror,* 5 July 1957; *The Times,* 17 and 25 December 1957. Brown and Crossman came to blows after another row in November: RCD, 15 November 1957. (HG patched it up.)

133 Reported to HG by his trade unionist PPS: n. 134. See I. Richter, *Political Purpose in Trade Unions* (Allen & Unwin, 1973), Chapters VII, VIII, for a critical account of the group's role.

134 Arthur Allen MP to HG, 24 December 1957: P.118–7.

135 For one such case (for once retracted) see *DE,* 27 November 1957 and 14 December 1957; Fred Lee MP to HG, 1 January 1958, and reply, 3 January 1958 (P.114–3); and n. 134.

136 RCD, 26 November 1957, 18 December 1957. Of those seven, three had – between them – visited Frognal Gardens three times in the previous year without ever meeting any of the others: *Spectator* diary, 20 December 1957.

137 See Chapter 25, Section i (p. 703).

138 *Observer, ST, SE,* 15 December 1957; *The Economist,* 28 December 1957; RCD, 18 December 1957; n. 134.

139 Dalton to HG, 31 December 1957, P.118–6. He blamed Brown or Wigg: HDD, 18 June 1958.

140 Brown to HG, 5 July 1957: P.118–6.

141 Crossman to HG, 23 December 1957: P.114–3.

142 See Chapter 18, Section i.

143 *ST,* 6 April 1958; and n. 47*b*.

144 *a. ST,* 2 March 1958; *b.* and nn. 10*p*, 110; *c.* cf. *The Economist,* 8 March 1958, 21 June 1958, 9 August 1958.

145 NEC, 26 February 1958, M.108; and n. 10*p*.

146 *NC,* 22 September 1958.

147 'John Marullus', 15 August 1958; Mikardo, 12 September 1958; David Ross, 7 November 1958 (attacking HG's unopposed re-election as leader and suggesting that he would be happier as a Liberal company director).

148 RCD, 18 December 1958, 23 March 1959, 26 June 1959.

149 Of whom Crossman said 'a friend of ours ... has the antennae of an elephant'. Thinking he meant HG, Bevan agreed and added 'and Ian

was nearly as bad': n. 10*p*. It was Bevan's first criticism of HG for six months.

150 'John Marullus', *Tribune*, 18 April 1958; *MG*, 14 April 1958; Foot (1973), pp. 600–3.

151 HG told Dalton he thought Foot was responsible for those attacks: HDD, 18 June 1958; cf. Dalton to HG, 29 June 1958, U.1.

152 *The Times*, 16 and 17 September 1958; HG to Soskice, 16 September 1958, P.114–3 (Soskice was among the many MPs who wrote in support); *Tribune*, 26 September 1958.

153 *a.* To Kenneth Harris on television, 1 October 1958, BBC; *b.* Harris, *ibid.*; *c.* cf. *MG, DT*, 2 October 1958; *Tribune*, 3 October 1958.

154 *Observer*, 5 October 1958. Also Dalton to HG, 7 October 1958 (U.1); Younger to HG, 'Sunday' i.e. 12 October 1958 (P.114–3).

155 *Evening Standard*, 13 March 1956: P.110. Also *MG*, 11 June 1956; 556 *H.C. Deb.*, col. 598, 11 July 1956; vol. 557 cols 723–4, 24 July 1956.

156 Interview, Mrs Duffield (*née* Brett).

157 F. Blackburn MP to HG, n.d. probably March 1956, P.103; R. Paget MP to HG, 14 July 1956, P.103; Jay to HG, 5 Sept. 1956, P.106–2.

158 RCD, 27 June 1958, on the pro-Turkish feeling among trade unionists.

159 Visiting Turkey, George Brown warned that the Turks' concern was entirely with military security, and that their threats of invasion if Britain left Cyprus were not bluff: Brown to HG, 8 January 1958, P.114–3.

160 D. Goldsworthy, *Colonial Issues in British Politics 1945–61* (OUP, 1971): *a.* pp. 353–7; *b.* pp. 356–7; *c.* pp. 319–20; *d.* p. 365.

161 MS note, n.d., but about 24 June 1958: P.103. (His punctuation: the note continues on the next page.)

162 Henry Fairlie in *Spectator*, 3 February 1956. The issue was the jamming of Greek broadcasts: see HG's memorandum of a talk with Grisewood, 8 February 1956, P.118–4.

163 HG to A. Lennox-Boyd the Colonial Secretary, 13 January 1958: P.103. Sir Hugh Foot, *A Start in Freedom* (Hodder & Stoughton 1964), p. 163.

164 Sir Hugh Foot to HG, P.103: *a.* 14 January 1958; *b.* (also to Bevan and Griffiths) 16 June 1958.

165 590 *H.C. Deb.*, cols 618–28: 26 June 1958.

166 Macmillan to HG, 19 June 1958 (P.103); and Macmillan (1971), p. 67.

167 He 'was obviously uneasy' in making the announcement: RCD, 20 February 1959. Cf. n. 9*h*.

168 600 *H.C. Deb.*, cols 622–4: 19 February 1959.

169 Cf. HG in *Listener*, 3 July 1958.

170 HG told Crossman so immediately after the interview: n. 10*k*. He later said so on the air: n. 169.

171 591 *H.C. Deb.*, 16 and 17 July 1958: *a.* HG, col. 1246; *b.* col. 1560; and n. 91*l*, *p.*

172 *a.* RCD, 16 July 1958; *b. DT, NC,* 16 July 1958; and n. 22*d, e.*

173 *DT,* 22 July 1958. Cf. *The Economist,* 19 July 1958; & n. 22*d, e.*

174 RCD, 25 July 1958, cf. 18 and 22 July. Also Pannell to HG, 20 July; A. Woodburn MP to HG, 21 July (both P.114–3); and n. 14*d.*

175 *Spectator,* 25 July 1958.

176 AHD: *a.* 6 August 1959; *b.* 22 April 1959; *c.* 9 July 1959; *d.* 23 July 1959.

177 W. P. Kirkman, *Unscrambling an Empire* (Chatto & Windus, 1966): *a.* p. 106; *b.* pp. 109, 126–30; *c.* p. 50, cf. p. 113; *d.* Keatley (1963), pp. 420–2, 426–30; *e.* and pp. 438–9.

178 *a.* Interview, Sir Arthur Gaitskell; *b.* cf. n. 160*c.* (Denis Healey thought Hugh's earlier views reflected Gordon Walker's influence: interview).

179 HG to Macmillan, P.139: *a.* 8 May 1959; *b.* 18 and 26 June 1959; cf. *DT,* 22, 23 and 26 June 1959.

180 HG to Arthur Gaitskell, 8 May 1959: P.133–6.

181 Macmillan (1972), pp. 136–7, from his diary—also complaining of HG's 'inflammatory speeches' in Ghana.

182 Welensky (1964): *a.* p. 146; *b.* pp. 145, 148, 153–5; *c.* pp. 146–7, 149–50, 157–60; *d.* p. 147, cf. p. 142 on Lord Home.

183 609 *H.C. Deb.*, 21–22 July 1959: *a.* col. 1074, also cols 1284–7, 1290–3, 1297; *b.* cols 1078, 1298–9; *c.* col. 1293.

184 Macmillan (1972), p. 137; and n. 182*b.*

185 Sir Robert Armitage the Governor to the author; and n. 9*n, p.*

186 Keatley (1963), p. 445; n. 160*d*; Griff Jones, *Britain and Nyasaland* (Allen & Unwin, 1964, an anti-Labour account), p. 248.

187 RCD, 27 November 1958. In drafting, Crossman had found HG niggling and timid; and Wilson praised it as 'the best political document he had ever read, apart from one or two ghastly concessions to the elector inserted by Hugh Gaitskell owing to his panic on the *Gallup Polls*': *ibid.*, 29 and 31 October 1958.

188 *New Statesman,* 29 November 1958.

189 *Forward,* 3 October 1958, was most defensive about it. Also e.g. *NC,* 20 and 22 September 1958.

190 Interview, Percy Clark (said spontaneously, not in answer to a question).

191 *Forward,* 17 October 1958 (George Thomson MP); *Spectator,* 21 February 1959 (Alan Brien); *Sunday Pictorial,* 22 February 1959.

192 HG to W. A. Wilkins MP, 31 January 1957: P.114–2. Labour's Scottish Council wrote a long report on 'A Scottish Parliament' in September 1958: NEC Minutes for December, in P.126–5.

193 626 *H.C. Deb.*, cols 1195–1210: 12 July 1960.

194 HG to Jay, 10 and 23 December 1958: P.114–3.

195 Some unilateralists had tried hard to lose the seat for Labour by persuading CND supporters to abstain: Driver (1964), pp. 68–9.

196 His first duty was to stay up late with Randolph Churchill, who was covering the tour as a journalist, so that the leader could get some sleep. Interview, Lord Harris. HG to Julie, 7 June 1959. Cf. HG to Dalton, 4 June 1959: U.1.

197 George Thomson (on Dundee); Alan Brien (on the North-east, saying HG made a far better personal impression than Macmillan in the same area just before): n. 191.

198 *ST*, 4 January 1959; cf. n. 51.

199 *Star*, 11 April 1957. *Observer*, 13 September 1957.

200 RCD, 29 October 1958; *The Times*, 28 October 1958; cf. *ST*, 2 November 1958.

201 *DT*, 22 April 1959, 5 May 1959; *Reynolds News*, 10 May 1959.

202 Mayhew to HG, 5 November 1958 and HG's reply, 7 November 1958: P.114–3. Cf. n. 43*f.*

203 Butler and Rose (1960): *a.* p. 29; *b.* p. 31.

204 Average of Gallup polls from October 1958 to July 1959.

205 In August, 37 and 38 per cent respectively; in September 32 and 43 per cent. October was much better and by December HG was back to 45 and 34 per cent. Pollsters thought he did badly in summer because he was out of the news.

206 Lord Hailsham, *The Door Wherein I Went* (Collins, 1975), pp. 155, 164.

207 On Labour morale: RCD, 2 February 1959, 25 March 1959, 14 May 1959, 5 June 1959.

208 HG to Dalton, U.1: *a.* 24 March 1959, agreeing with the latter's predictions; *b.* 4 June 1959.

209 On 3 April they told Macmillan that he would win by only 13: n. 9*o.*

210 HG to Ronald Harker of the *Observer*, 28 April 1959: P.133–H.

211 Even Bevan sometimes did that: RCD, 18 December 1958.

212 HG to Alan Rodway, 12 February 1959: P.134.

213 E.g. on television, 2 October 1958, 27 October 1958 (both referring to the responsibility the unions showed in 1945–51) and 21 April 1959: BBC.

214 Dow (1970), p. 106.

215 603 *H.C. Deb.*, cols 77 (HG), 207–8 (Wilson), 400 (Jay), 482–3 (Diamond), 485–91 (Roy Jenkins), 753–4 (Gordon Walker): 7–9 and 13 April 1959. The Chancellor replied at col. 764; no one else defended the delay.

216 HG to Anne Fleming, 10 February 1959; kindly supplied by Mrs Fleming.

217 He attacked the *Christian Science Monitor* at the May Day parade in London: *MG*, 4 April 1959; HG to Hetherington, 5 May 1959: P.134M. Cf. above, p. 441 and n.

218 Emmet J. Hughes, *The Ordeal of Power* (Atheneum, New York, 1963), pp. 289–90.

219 Brown, Castle, Greenwood, Mikardo and Wilson are specified in RCD, 14 May 1959, 3 July 1959. Cf. *ST*, 17 May 1959.

Chapter 18 The Campaign for Nuclear Disarmament

1 HG to A. Blenkinsop MP, 24 October 1957: P. 114–2.

2 Macmillan: *a*. (1971), pp. 321–4, 327, 494, 500; *b*. (1972), p. 76, from his diary, 8 July 1959.

3 *a*. HG to A. Woodburn MP, 25 February 1958: P.114–3; *b*. Cf. his Vienna speech, above p. 455.

4 Greenwood to HG, 2 and 6 January 1958; reply 3 January 1958; P.114–3.

5 Driver: *a*. Chapter 2; *b*. p. 91, saying HG objected.

6 *ST*, 2 March 1958; *DT*, 5 March 1958; n. 7*a*. On the VFS row, above, p. 476–7.

7 RCD: *a*. 28 February 1958; *b*. 28 January 1958; *c*. cf. n. 10*b*; *d*. 10 March 1958; *e*. reporting Strachey; *f*. 19 March 1958; *g*. 5 June 1959; *h*. 10 June 1959; *i*. 18 June 1959; *j*. 22 June 1959; *k*. 23 June 1959; *l*. 7 July 1959; *m*. 17 July 1959; *n*. 13 August 1959; *o*. reporting Dora; *p*. reporting Brown; *q*. 2 February 1959; *r*. 3 July 1959; *s*. cf. n. 9*c*.

8 For the TUC, G. Goodman's *Frank Cousins* (Davis-Poynter, 1979), Ch. 16. For HG: *ibid.*; and nn. 7*a*, 9*a*. For the NEC's protest, n. 10*a*.

9 AHD: *a*. 22 April 1959; *b*. 11 November 1958; *c*. 9 July 1959; *d*. 23 July 1959; *e*. his emphasis.

10 NEC-M: *a*. vol. 125, 26 February 1958, M.99; *b*. *ibid.*, M.98; *c*. 26 March 1958, M.121; *d*. 25 March 1959, M.133.

11 HG to Julie, 20 February 1958. Bevan: RCD, 18 December 1957, 28 and 29 January 1958.

12 RCD, 29 January 1958; and in the House: 580 *H.C. Deb.*, cols 755–9, 842–5 (20 December 1957); and nn. 13*a*, 14*a*. The Conservatives accused Bevan of ratting on his Brighton speech – quite wrongly: contrast Macmillan (1971), p. 472, with Bevan to Huw Edwards, 23 October 1957 (Foot, 1973, pp. 578–9).

13 582 *H.C. Deb.*, 19–20 February 1958: *a*. col. 1412; *b*. cols 1235–6.

14 583 *H.C. Deb.*, 26–27 February 1958: *a*. cols 412–16; *b*. cols 407–12, 650–7.

15 *a*. On 'Panorama', 3 March 1958 (saying that the delay would

influence the United States to accept summit talks); *b.* and in the House, n. 13*b.*

16 From the TUC's summary of the talks: I.C. Special 3/5 (1957/58), in NEC-M, vol. 125. Cf. above, p. 455. A Transport House draft in the same volume reports the conclusions but not the arguments.

17 Summary report of the joint meeting, NEC-M, vol. 125, papers for 26 March 1958: pp. 2, 3, 4, 5, 6, 7, 8, 11 (though on pp. 3, 9, 10, he seems to refer only to the H-bomb). Crossman stresses the change from Bevan's previous views: n. 7*d.* Foot (1973), pp. 595–8, obscures it, quoting the report extensively yet presenting HG as agreeing with the government, and omitting all Bevan's views on tactical atomic weapons. (On 13 February Bevan had dismissed pledges as 'academic and futile'.)

18 *DT*: *a.* 7 March 1958; *b.* 26 June 1959; *c.* quoted, 3 September 1959.

19 Mrs Castle and Crossman moved that the NEC should approve the foreword, but lost: n. 10*c.*

20 *MG*, 14 April 1958. Foot: above, p. 477.

21 *DT*, 3 April 1958. He told its author it would be a bad precedent: HG to Frank Tomney 2 April 1958 (P.114–3).

22 *a.* RCD, 2 April 1958; *b.* and 28 February 1958; *c.* also HDD, 2 April 1958, on unity; *d.* and 3–14 April 1958.

23 *Daily Mail*, 13 March 1958; *The Times*, 14 March 1958.

24 RCD, 2 April 1958, cf. 19 March 1958, 12 February 1960. On the Brown–Bevan alliance, n. 22*b, d.*

25 Wigg objected more violently but ineffectively: Wigg (1972), pp. 214–15; Wigg to HG, 17 March 1958, reply 18 March 1958 (P.148).

26 Crossman thought he had won HG over: RCD, 19 March 1958, 2 April 1958. But two months later HG still argued that tactical atomic weapons were necessary because Western democracies could never match the Russians in conventional (conscript) forces; he thought they would soon be available in sufficient quantities, and were – unlike the H-bomb – a real deterrent in minor wars: n. 27*a.*

27 HG to Crossman, P.148: *a.* 28 May 1958; *b.* 1 April 1958, enclosing the memorandum.

28 RCD, 2 April 1958; cf. 10 April 1958, for Bevan again advocating reliance on these weapons.

29 Cf. Bevan in *LPCR*, 1957, p. 182.

30 *LPCR*, 1958: *a.* p. 222; *b.* p. 189; *c.* p. 221 (on Quemoy, above, pp. 477–8); *d.* pp. 223–4; *e.* nn. 9*b*, 15*a.*

31 Foot's veiled reference to them mentions neither their outcome nor Bevan's alignment with the right wing: Foot (1973), p. 598. (He had access to Crossman's diaries.)

32 The unilateralist motion (no. 27) was defeated by 5,611,000 to 890,000, and a pure pacifist motion (no. 30) by 5,705,000 to 840,000: n. 30*d.*

33 586 *H.C. Deb.*, cols 1160–6: 24 April 1958. *DT*, 19, 26 and 27 March 1958.

34 *Spectator*, 1 August 1958.

35 *The Economist*, 15 March 1958.

36 HG was informed that the first result was 'a deliberate miscount': HG to Dan Jones MP, 2 May 1961, P.142–3.

37 HG to Professor Philip Reynolds, 21 July 1959: P.134–R.

38 Transport House brief (unsigned and undated, probably by David Ennals at the end of June) on press reactions to the new policy statement: P.113–R.

39 Interview, C. C. O'Brien. On the Irish proposals, *MG*, 7 May 1959, 25 August 1959, 15 September 1959 (the last quotes HG's views on it).

40 A. Hetherington to author. 214 *H.L. Deb.*, cols 71–187: 11 February 1959 (Russell spoke for Simon's motion).

41 HG to Lord Simon of Wythenshawe, 30 January 1959, P.134–S; to Alec Bagley, chairman of Oxford University CND, 10 February 1959, P.133–B.

42 HG in 608 *H.C. Deb.*, cols 1483–5: 8 July 1959.

43 HG to Pannell (in hospital), 29 June 1959: P.142–1. Also HG to Donnelly 9 June 1959 (P.142–1); and n. 9c.

44 *The Times*, 12 June 1959. Cf. *DT*, 15 June 1959; RCD, 12 June 1959.

45 a. *The Times*, 24 June 1959; b. and *DT*, 26 June 1959.

46 a. HG to Cousins, 30 June 1959, P.133C; b. and nn. 7j, 9c.

47 Foot (1973), p. 671, ignores Bevan's change of mind.

48 RCD, 18, 22, 23 and 29 June 1959, 7 July 1959; Crossman was furious that the statement was shown to Brown. Also *New Statesman*, 27 June 1959; protest letters to HG from Donnelly (8 June) and Pannell (27 June): P.146–1.

49 *ST*: a. 28 June 1959; b. 'an adroit conciliator'.

50 a. RCD, 29 June 1959; b. Crossman adds, wrongly in my view, that on the main issue HG had made a concession to Bevan. (Also n. 9c.)

51 *The Times*, 24 and 25 June 1959; RCD, 29 June 1959. (There was no vote in the PLP.)

52 Fairlie in *Daily Mail*: a. 26 June 1959; b. 30 July 1959.

53 RCD, 29 June 1959 (he may well have been wrong).

54 *DT* poll in fifty marginal seats: 16 July 1959. Among all voters, respectively 8, 12 and 67, with the rest Don't Knows. (The Gallup poll had reported a similar response just before the Labour Party statement.)

55 *The Times*, 25 June 1959; *ST*, 28 June 1959; 'At Home and Abroad', 17 July 1959 (BBC); *DT*, 18 July 1959.

56 a. Cousins to HG, 26 June 1959: P.133–C; b. and nn. 58b, 65a.

57 De Gaulle's most cherished project was for regular consultation

between the United States, the United Kingdom and France as the three NATO countries with overseas interests. HG favoured that (HG in *DT*, 21 January 1959), so that in office each would have had something to offer that the other deeply desired.

58 Minutes of the BDC of the T&GWU, 9 July 1959: *a.* M.55; *b.* M.56.
59 RCD, 29 June 1959 (reporting and agreeing with HG); in *Daily Mirror*, 14 July 1959.
60 Cousins always evaded an answer: n. 61*a*.
61 Stewart (1968): *a.* pp. 103–4; *b.* p. 60; *c.* p. 115.
62 At Workington, 11 July 1959.
63 'At Home and Abroad', 17 July 1959 (BBC); to Robert McKenzie.
64 *Daily Mail*, 18 July 1959; *MG*, 20 and 21 July 1959.
65 *a. New Statesman*, 18 July 1959; *b.* and n. 7*m*; *c.* and n. 7*i, j*.
66 *ST*, 5 and 19 July 1959; cf. *DT*, 8 and 14 July 1959; Dalton to HG, 20 July 1959, U.1.
67 *a.* Press Association report (in P. 133–C); *b. DT*, 10 July 1959.
68 Interview, Sir William Webber.
69 *DT*, 9 and 10 July 1959. There is no doubt of the genuineness of the debate.
70 On BBC television: *DT*, 11 July 1959 (which called his performance: 'the finest anti-Cousins propaganda Mr Gaitskell or Mr Bevan could have wished to devise').
71 On 9 July in the defence debate at his BDC: n. 67*a*.
72 *a.* Harry Urwin, a T&GWU official, reported in RCD, 17 July 1959; *b.* and n. 61*b*.
73 *a.* Interview, Geoffrey Goodman (Cousins's biographer); *b.* I have failed to trace it; perhaps Cousins meant the April 1958 broadcast, though he supported the leadership long after that.
74 Leslie Randall, *Daily Mail*, 23 July 1959; and n. 72*a*.
75 John Murray to HG, 16 June 1958 (P.187); HDD, 3/14 April 1958; interviews, G. Goodman, Lord Houghton, Margaret Stewart.
76 R. Churchill to HG, 14 July 1959, and reply, 20 July: P.133–C.
77 Wigg signed Shinwell's telegram; Morrison and Ellis Smith endorsed it.
78 He charitably added that Morrison was probably in the dumps because his constituency Party had just (privately) asked him to resign: n. 9*c*.
79 At the TUC: Report, 1959, p. 402; and n. 7*k*.
80 RCD, 29 June 1959 and 3 July 1959. In *Tribune*, 26 June 1959, Foot tried to foment all the 'pains and dissensions within the Party'; in Foot (1973), p. 617, he says they 'showed signs of subsiding', and ignores his own efforts to prevent that happening.
81 Parkin (1968), pp. 116–18.
82 Interview, Percy Clark, who tried and failed at Workington; cf. n. 74.
83 Interview, Lord Houghton.

84 Interviews, Roy Jenkins, David Wood; AHD, 9 July 1959. The Cousinses felt that and resented it: n. 61c.

85 To the Irish T&GWU at Galway: *Daily Mail*, 10 June 1960. Also in a press conference: *DT*, 3 June 1960.

86 As he said to George Brown a year later (below, p. 604).

87 As Crossman argued forcibly in *Daily Mirror*, 26 June 1959, and at Felixstowe on 11 July; and forgot in 1960–1.

Chapter 19　Gaitskell Abroad

1 To the Executive Club in Chicago, 16 May 1952: U.44.

2 James L. Wick of the *Freeman* to HG, 18 June 1953: V.4. Harlan Cleveland of *The Reporter* to Kay Daniels HG's secretary, 3 June 1953: U.154.

3 Willard Thorp, the conference organiser, to author.

4 HG to Brenda Woolgar, his former secretary, 11 August 1953. Kindly supplied by Miss Woolgar.

5 Al Friendly to HG, 11 September 1953: P.60b. HG to Thorp, 19 August 1953; kindly supplied by Professor Thorp.

6. Averell Harriman to HG, 21 September 1953: P.60b.

7 This account is from his Diary, May 1956; his talk on 'At Home and Abroad', 25 May 1956 (U.87); and his 'American Diary' in *Reynolds News*, 3 June 1956 (U.91).

8 Diary of D. E. Butler, then personal assistant to the British Ambassador; his emphasis.

9 HG to J. B. Orrick, 9 February 1961 (kindly supplied by Mr Orrick). Cf. above, pp. 394, 477–8.

10 Lord Pakenham in *World Affairs*, September/October 1957.

11 HG to Arthur Schlesinger, Jr, 6 February 1957: P.192.

12 R. B. Stewart, Dean of the Fletcher School to HG, 21 February 1957. Also from other campuses: RCD, 25 January 1957; *New Statesman*, 19 January 1957; and *Leeds Weekly Citizen*, 1 February 1957.

13 Denis Howell to HG from Harvard, 18 July 1957: P.114–2.

14 Gaitskell (1957), pp. 35, 90–3. *DT*, 14 and 17 January 1952.

15 Professor Lloyd Ulman to author; cf. Professor Walter Heller to HG, 6 June 1952 (U.85).

16 Interview, Professor A. Ranney.

17 Thomas E. Dewey to HG, 2 November 1961: P.163.

18 HG's letter in *The Reporter*, September 1953, replying to John Fischer.

19 HG in *DH*: *a*. 14, 15 and 16 September 1953; *b*. 9 January 1958 (and 19 January 1958, on South-east Asia).

20 'Francis Flavius' in *Tribune*, 25 May 1956.

21 HG to Gordon Walker, 6 January 1960: V.10–7.
22 Lecture to the American Society of Newspaper Editors on the role of the Opposition: *The Times*, 26 April 1960.
23 As he said at St Antony's, Oxford, on 16 March 1962: Professor N. Blewett to author, 7 August 1975.
24 Above, p. 382. On his attitude to the Kennedy Administration, below, pp. 685–6.
25 Interviews, D. Healey, D. Ennals, Mrs Sam Watson.
26 HG to Dr Bakaric, President of Croatia, 29 August 1960: V.10.
27 Interview, J. Kuehl.
28 Interviews, Mrs McNeal, Mrs Wasserman (Julie and Cressida).
29 AHD, 22 April 1959. Cf. below, p. 680.
30 HG to Julie: *a.* 18 May 1959; *b.* 18 March 1954; *c.* 13 December 1957, posted Calcutta; *d.* 22 June 1958; *e.* 21 January 1959.
31 He had visited Israel (and Jordan, Lebanon and Syria) in 1952 and wrote a diary (V.2 and U.146); though very impressed with the country's economic development and egalitarianism, he was already concerned about its problems of national integration and finding resources for investment.
32 *DT*, 22 May 1959.
33 HG to Dalton, 4 June 1959 (U.1); E. L. Mallalieu MP, to HG, 8 October 1961 (P.142–3) recalling the 'considerable clout' HG then gave him for his pessimism; HG to Geoffrey de Freitas, 17 January 1962 (P.182) on the 'incredible' fall of two leading Ghana Ministers.
34 Interview, Lord Gordon Walker.
35 HG broadcast, 20 April 1954 (BBC); to the Royal Institute of International Affairs (the sponsors) on 29 April 1954; to the Pakistan Society on 21 May 1954 (U.195–2).
36 *The Times*, 9 December 1957.
37 Letters to friends: *a.* December 1957; *b.* 29 May 1958; *c.* 21 February 1959.
38 Gunnar Fagnell to HG, 25 April 1959 (with drawings), reply 29 April: P.133–F.
39 RCD: *a.* 23 May 1957; *b.* 20 February 1959; *c.* 13 August 1959.
40 HG to Guy Hannaford (of the British Embassy), 3 March 1959: P.188.
41 HG to Crossman, 23 February 1959 (in RCD).
42 Interview.
43 On Cousins, see above, pp. 463–4.
44 HG to Jebb, by then Ambassador in Paris, 14 March 1958: P.114–3; and to Dalton, HDD, 18 June 1958.
45 HG's broadcast, 19 November 1957.
46 HDD, 18 June 1958; RCD, 19 June 1958 (both reporting HG); n. 30*d*.
47 Jules Moch had predicted a different reception: RCD, 2 February 1959, reporting HG.

48 RCD, 2 February 1959; Foot in *Tribune*, 6 June 1958 and (as 'John Marullus'), 23 January 1959; also in Foot (1973), pp. 604–5.

49 HG to Greenwood, 4 June 1958: P.114–3.

50 Macmillan to HG, 18 and 28 April 1958, reply 21 April: V.10–2.

51 Interview, Lord Noel-Baker; and n. 30*d*.

52 *Tribune* meeting, Conway Hall: *DT*, 6 November 1959. *Tribune*, 15 January 1960.

53 On television: *The Times*, 10 September 1959. At the TUC: Report, 1959, pp. 457–8. Cf. AHD, 6 August 1959.

54 Interview, D. Healey.

55 *LPCR*, 1960: *a*. Healey, p. 193; *b*. HG, p. 97.

56 AHD, 6 August 1959. Macmillan feared that the exchange might help Labour: (1972), pp. 79–80 (from his diary, 26 July 1959).

57 Foot (1973), p. 624; K. S. Karol (a journalist friend accompanying Bevan) in *L'Express* (Paris), 17 September 1959; and n. 54.

58 *a*. Interview, Lord Harris; *b*. HG in progamme on Bevan, 3 October 1961: BBC.

59 Foot (1973): *a*. p. 617; *b*. pp. 618–19.

60 D. Stuart, *A Very Sheltered Life* (Collins, 1970): *a*. p. 175; *b*. p. 180; *c*. p. 181; *d*. and n. 59*b*.; *e*. and interviews.

61 Impressions of the trip are from interviews with Lady Gaitskell, D. Ennals, D. Healey, Lord Jacobson and G. Goodman (with whom Bevan spent several weeks just afterwards, often chatting about it).

62 Foot (1973), pp. 619–20. Healey and Jacobson are sure no such scene occurred; Ennals does not recall it; Bevan never mentioned it to Goodman; Stuart's book omits it. Lady Gaitskell's account antedates Foot's by many years.

63 626 *H.C. Deb.*, 7 July 1960: *a*. col. 706 (and nn. 55*b*, 58*b*); *b*. col. 707, HG.

64 Interview, Lord Jacobson.

65 *DE*, 7 September 1959; cf. *The Times*, 7 September 1959; HG in *Daily Mirror*, 1 October 1959; Karol, *loc. cit.* n. 57.

66 D. Healey in obituary of HG, 18 January 1963: BBC.

67 Interview, D. Ennals (contradicting n. 60*b*).

Chapter 20 United We Fall

1 AHD: *a*. 9 July 1959; *b*. 6 August 1959; *c*. 29 October 1959.

2 RCD: *a*. 15 September 1959; *b*. 22 September 1959; *c*. 30 September 1959; *d*. 24 September 1959; *e*. 28 September 1959; *f*. 5 October 1959; *g*. 21 October 1959; *h*. 19 October 1959; *i*. 13 August 1959; *j*. 9 October 1959.

3 Interview, T. Driberg.

4 Macmillan (1972): *a.* p. 6; *b.* p. 8; *c.* p. 21; *d.* from his diary.

5 R. Rose, *Influencing Voters* (Faber, 1967): *a.* p. 42; over twenty-seven months they spent £468,000; *b.* pp. 63–4 (and n. 11*e*).

6 *DT*, 10 Sept. 1959; and n. 10*c*. It was not run by the electoral team.

7 George Woodcock, the general secretary, was horrified: n. 2*a*.

8 *Guardian, Daily Mail, NC,* 11 September 1959; and n. 10*c*. The T&GWU motion was lost by 5,133,000 to 2,795,000.

9 TUC Report, 1959, p. 460.

10 *Observer:* *a.* 20 Sept. 1959; *b.* 15 Nov. 1959; *c.* 13 Sept. 1959.

11 Butler and Rose (1960): *a.* pp. 46–7; *b.* pp. 51, 57; *c.* p. 59; *d.* p. 60; *e.* pp. 62–3; *f.* Chapter 12 (and n. 2*f*); *g.* summarised p. 105; *h.* p. 86; *i.* p. 103n. *j.* p. 254.

12 *NC,* 22 October 1959; *The Times,* 23 October; *ST,* 27 October on his success. He was less good on radio.

13 Morgan Phillips, reported n. 2*c*; cf. e.g. Eirene White to HG, 21 October 1959, P.131–3.

14 Robert Carvel in *Star,* 24 September 1959; cf. e.g. John Curtis, *Sunday Graphic,* 27 September 1959; n. 15*a*.

15 Walter Terry, *Daily Mail:* *a.* 28 September 1959; *b.* 13 March 1960.

16 Trevor Evans, *DE,* 25 September 1959; adding that 'the voluntary workers ... are now offering their services in droves'.

17 *a.* Butler and Rose (1960), pp. 58–9; *b.* Lord Hailsham, *The Door Wherein I Went* (Collins, 1975), p. 157.

18 *DT:* *a.* 26 September 1959; *b.* 7 October 1959.

19 Text in P.131–1.

20 *a.* Jenkins in Rodgers (1964), p. 125; *b.* Jenkins (1974), p. 176.

21 Francis Cassavetti, *DE,* 30 September 1959; adding that HG was far better than Macmillan on television.

22 Campaign Committee Report to the NEC of 28 October 1959 (GE/E/Sub. 2); in file P.131–1, and in NEC-M, vol. 127, p. 712: *a.* and n. 2*d*.

23 *a.* *The Times,* 30 September 1959; *b.* and n. 17*b*; *c.* and n. 11*d*; *d.* and *ST,* 4 October 1959.

24 For the 2*s*.6*d*. figure: RCD, 5 October 1959, Ivan Yates in *Reynolds News,* 4 October 1959; and nn. 22*a*, 11*c*, 15*b*. For the scare, but no figure mentioned: RCD, 30 September 1959 (from John Harris); AHD, 29 October 1959 (from HG); Bevan in his constituency, *DE,* 6 October 1959. Fifteen years later the Conservative Deputy Prime Minister told the author that it had been a possibility, but their chief whip denied such plans: interviews, Lord Butler, E. Heath. Standard rate was then 7*s*.9*d*.

25 *a.* Interview, Lord Harris; *b.* and n. 1*c*.

26 Interview, Sir Harold Wilson, who said he was 'against it for the wrong

reasons', because Labour would at once be asked about other taxes. Colleagues and pressmen who investigated at the time were all convinced that he had approved the pledge, and so was HG's personal assistant: interviews, T. Driberg, G. Goodman, Lord Harris, H. Hutchinson, D. Wood. *DT*, 24 October 1959 said that 'can be stated with certainty'. Crossman told David Butler so on 7 November 1959 (interview kindly shown me by Dr Butler) and told others later (John Cole in *Observer*, 9 October 1977); also RCD, 30 September 1959, 5 October 1959. Wyatt, who was on the television team, told Crossman that Wilson was intending to say on television on 1 October that Labour hoped to reduce taxes for all: *RCD*, 5 October 1959. The campaign committee report originally said Wilson had been consulted, but Ray Gunter got Crossman to delete that: *ibid.*, 22 October 1959.

27 He did not promise to reduce it (contrary to Hailsham, p. 157).

28 Interview, P. Morris; RCD, 5 October 1959; *ST*, 4 October 1959; *DT*, 24 October 1959; and n. 11*d*.

29 *a.* Shinwell (1963), p. 205; *b.* but in interview he blamed HG's 'inexperience'.

30 *The Times, NC*, 21 May 1955; *Observer*, 22 May 1955; above, p. 353.

31 Interview, *DE*, 19 January 1959.

32 In *Forward*, 15 May 1959 (based on a broadcast by him).

33 Interviews, Lady Gaitskell, D. Jay (also on costing); and n. 1*c*.

34 He was well aware how much more notice he now attracted: HG to Alan Williams, candidate for Poole, 22 October 1959: P.146.

35 Interviews, Mrs P. Crane (for Transport House); G. Goodman (for Bevan); J. Griffiths; A. J. McWhinnie (for Morgan Phillips and himself); R. Underhill (regional organiser).

36 A 'notable stage' in his career: Francis Boyd in *Guardian*, 6 October 1959. Also *ST*, 4 October 1959.

37 Of 200 whose replies were analysed at Transport House, 53 mentioned it as an adverse factor — apart from 56 who mentioned finance generally: n. 38*a*.

38 Morgan Phillips's report dated 22 October 1959 to NEC (from P. 131–1; and NEC-M, vol. 127, 28 Oct. 1959, p. 693): *a.* p. 43 and Appendix; *b.* conclusion, paragraph 9; and n. 22; *c.* p. 43; *d.* and nn. 11*i*, 42*b*; *e.* p. 40.

39 Interviews, Lady Burton, Lord Greenwood, Lord Pannell; Shinwell (1963) n. 29*a*.

40 RCD, 27 October 1959, also 9 October 1959; AHD, 29 October 1959; agreed by Hailsham, pp. 157, 164; interviews, Lord Boyle, J. Griffiths, E. Heath.

41 Interviews, Lord Butler, D. Jay, Michael Stewart.

42 Cf. J. Trenaman and D. McQuail, *Television and the Political Image* (Methuen, 1961): *a.* pp. 100–1; *b.* pp. 127–31.

43 All the polls on Wednesday 7 October and Thursday 8 October (polling day), but none earlier, showed a reversal of the trends.

44 So did the accompanying journalists, and also Hugh Dalton (to HG, 5 October 1959, U.1). Crossman thought it possible: n. 2*f*.

45 Interview, Lord Harris—who did not see it; also nn. 2*h*, 20*b*.

46 John Addey to HG, 14 October 1959, P.131–1.

47 Foot (1973), p. 629.

48 Interviews, R. Crossman, Lord Harris, Mrs McNeal, Mrs Skelly.

49 General Election Round-up, 9 October 1959 (BBC): *a*. Robert Kee, cf. n. 10*b*.; *b* HG in *ibid.*; and *Guardian*, 10 October 1959.

50 A. J. McWhinnie to HG, 11 October 1959, P.131–3; and n. 25*a*.

51 *Guardian*, 10 October 1959. Crossman claimed credit (n. 2*h*): 'I substituted ... a last sentence saying we shall fight, fight and fight again until we win, which he used straight away'. But HG had already said it at Leeds: *The Times*, 9 October 1959.

52 Sir Patrick Reilly to HG, 9 October 1959: P.131–3.

53 Interview, Lord Boyle.

54 Many admirers who wrote to him in 1960 (P.145) when he vowed to 'fight and fight again', said he had impressed them once before, when conceding defeat the previous year. Six of his obituaries also stressed the point.

55 *DT*, 27 November 1959; from a discussion among people they had polled during the election.

56 612 *H.C. Deb.*, cols 6–9 (HG), 11–14 (C. Pannell): 20 October 1959. Curiously, Macmillan blamed HG for Soskice's refusal: n. 4*c, d*.

57 See below, pp. 679–81.

58 Gallup Political Index, February 1960, p. 18.

59 *LPCR*, 1959: *a*. p. 117, Denis Howell; *b*. p. 83.

60 Mark Abrams in *Socialist Commentary*, July 1960, pp. 5 and 12; and in Abrams and Rose (1960), pp. 47–8. Of all 18–24s 52 per cent were Conservative, 43 per cent Labour, 5 per cent Liberal, 10 per cent with no opinion or inclination; Labour had 50 per cent of young workers, and 15 per cent of older middle-class people.

61 To Walter Nash the New Zealand Prime Minister, 20 October 1959 (P.134N); to Arthur Schlesinger, Jr, 20 October 1959 (P.192); to Stephen Spender, 27 October 1959 (P.131–3).

62 *a. Tribune*, 16 October 1959; *b*. Labour did very badly where unemployment was a fear not a reality (n. 22); *c*. cf. Foot (1973), p. 630.

63 HG thought Africa was an asset in Scotland: *Guardian*, 10 October 1959.

64 Wilfred Young (Eastern region) 9 October 1959: sent to HG and in P.131–3.

65 Letters to HG from A. J. Champion, George Thomson, Jack Diamond, George Murray, E. J. Milne, Horace King, Kenneth Younger,

Wilfred Fordham (all P.131–3); from Julian Richards, (P.146–1); RCD, 9 October 1959; Crossman and Barbara Castle in *New States-man*, 17 October 1959; *The Times*, 21 October 1959.

66 Barbara Castle to HG, 14 October 1959 (P.131–3), At least eight left-wingers were among the thirty-five candidates or prominent Labour figures who wrote to HG using adjectives like 'magnificent' (not counting the very many more less adjectival enthusiasts).

67 *New Statesman*: *a*. 17 October 1959; *b*. 24 October 1959; *c*. others agreed: Woodrow Wyatt in *DH*, 8 February 1960; Douglas Clark in *DE*, 20 February 1960.

68 Ernest Jones to HG, 13 October 1959: P.146–1. Harry Knight to HG, 9 October 1959: P.131–3.

69 Jim Raisin (Morrison's old agent in London) to HG, 9 October 1959: P.131–3.

70 Don Cook, *New York Herald Tribune*, 9 December 1959; cf. n. 10*b*.

71 *DT*, 9 and 23 October 1959; *Guardian*, 10 October 1959.

72 In *Daily Mail*, 12 October 1959.

73 Frau Lilo Milchsack to HG, 9 October 1959; cf. Strachey to HG, 12 October 1959: both P.131–3.

Chapter 21 Clause Four

1 Interview and memorandum, Lord Pannell: *a*. cf. AHD, 12 November 1959; *b*. and *DT*, 5 November 1959, reporting HG in the PLP.

2 AHD: *a*. 29 October 1959; *b*. 12 November 1959; *c*. 10 December 1959; *d*. 14 July 1960; *e*. 11 February 1960; *f*. 18 March 1960; *g*. put by AH, agreed by HG.

3 HG to Dalton, U.1: *a*. 10 November 1959; *b*. 1 December 1959; *c*. about 1 March 1960.

4 Foot (1973), pp. 632, 651. Similar wrong assumptions in Roth (1977), p. 233.

5 HDD: *a*. 16 October 1959; *b*. on the last point only; *c*. 11 October 1959; *d*. reporting HG; *e*. 4 May 1960.

6 Foot (1973): *a*. p. 630 (he gets the time wrong); *b*. pp. 631–2; *c*. pp. 637, 640n.; *d*. p. 638; *e*. pp. 641–50; *f*. pp. 650–1; *g*. p. 640; *h*. pp. 651–2; *i*. p. 555.

7 Interviews: *a*. Lord Aylestone (formerly Herbert Bowden); *b*. A. Crosland; *c*. Lord Gordon Walker; *d*. Lord Harris; *e*. D. Jay; *f*. R. Jenkins.

8 Jay soon came down against a Liberal pact.

9 Interview, Lady Brook, with whom first Jay, then the Gaitskells, stayed successive weekends: and n. 7*a*, *c*, *f*, on his dislike of it.

10 Interviews, Lord Harris, D. Jay. *Forward*, 16 October 1959; the old Glasgow left-wing weekly had become a Gaitskellite organ in 1956.

11 *a*. Interview D. Jay; *b*. HDD, 16 October 1959; RCD, 23 October 1959; AHD, 12 November 1959.

12 RCD, 19 October 1959. (Jenkins had spoken about it on 'Panorama' on the Monday night.)

13 RCD: *a*. 21 October 1959; *b*. 19 October 1959; *c*. 23 October 1959; *d*. 25 November 1959; *e*. 26 February 1960; *f*. 9 December 1959; *g*. 2 March 1960; *h*. reporting Strachey; *i*. and n. 56*b*.

14 Interview, A. N. W. Benn.

15 Interview, W. Wyatt.

16 *Forward*: *a*. 16 October 1959; *b*. 23 October 1959; *c*. 4 December 1959.

17 See below, pp. 696–8.

18 RCD, 19 Oct. 1959; omitted passages below, pp. 541, 543. A year later Crossman, by then hostile to HG, gave another and often contrary account of this conversation: Crossman to Sam Watson, 12 October 1960 – in RCD.

19 Jay's *Forward* article had proposed that too.

20 Interview, Sir Harry Nicholas.

21 *a*. Interview, D. Ginsburg; *b*. he was present, and in the light of later events came to assume, probably mistakenly, that Bevan was referring to Clause Four.

22 RCD, 19 October 1959; cf. Foot (1973), pp. 478, 625.

23 Henry Fairlie in *Daily Mail*: *a*. 12 October 1959, after two hours' talk with HG (and n. 13*b*); *b*. 19 October 1959; *c*. HG once wrote in his diary (16 February 1956) that Fairlie often misreported his views.

24 John Curtis, *Sunday Graphic*, 27 September 1959. HG was said to prefer Gordon Walker: *ibid.*, 4 October 1959, and 'Crossbencher', *SE*, 26 April 1959 and 24 October 1959. Jenkins (n. 29 below) and Jay (Roth, 1977, p. 234) were also named; Callaghan and Houghton were possible too.

25 Interview, Lord Harris.

26 Crossman does not say, or deny, that the suggestion came from himself: n. 13*b*.

27 *The Times*, 21 July 1958; *ST*, 5 July 1959, 15 November 1959, 13 December 1959; Crosland to HG, 4 May 1960 (P.183).

28 *ST*, 15 November 1959 (not naming but strongly hinting at Crossman); RCD, 9 December 1959, reporting Wilson on HG's hints to him. For the proposal, also Ivan Yates in *Reynolds News*, 22 November 1959.

29 Interview. Without denying that he was Wilson's source, the diarist wrote: 'I gather from Barbara today that Harold Wilson has convinced himself that I came as an emissary of Gaitskell's in order to put

Jenkins in his place. The idea that Gaitskell should send me as an emissary was a bit amusing': RCD, 27 October 1959. This contradicts Roth (1977), p. 234.

30 That post would be available when Bevan became deputy leader.
31 Lady Gaitskell (who was always loyal to Wilson as Party leader) remembered this incident, in identical terms, on five occasions spread over several years.
32 Crossman to David Butler, 7 November 1959 (kindly shown me by Dr Butler).
33 a. Interview, Sir Harold Wilson; b. cf. Roth (1977), p. 235.
34 AHD, 12 November 1959; they needed the Shadow Minister's permission and spoke from a back-bench; cf. RCD, 13 November 1959, DT, 24 October 1959.
35 A. J. McWhinnie, DH, 13 November 1959.
36 Punnett (1973), pp. 153–6.
37 Dalton to HG, U.1: a. 14 November 1959; b. 29 November 1959. F.17–7: c. 31 January 1960, his emphasis. P.120–5: d. 7 February 1960; e. 17 February 1960.
38 Interview, Mrs McNeal.
39 Lord Pannell (n. 1a); cf. Foot (1973), p. 637; DT, 8 November 1959. Crossman must have arrived late as usual, for he described HG's speech as 'so measured, so balanced, so indecisive that there was no suggestion of an ovation': n. 13a.
40 The Times: a. 22 October 1959; b. 23 November 1959; c. 15 February 1960; d. 16 March 1960, political correspondent.
41 DT, 23 October 1959 and 5 November 1959; Observer, 15 November 1959; and n. 13a. On 1950: above, p. 447.
42 a. Dalton to HG, n.d. but 18 November 1959 (P. 118–6); b. on its impact, also nn. 5a; 13a, b; 32.
43 Crossman reporting himself, Mikardo, Shore, Paul Johnson of the New Statesman and a dismayed Benn, all dining with Barbara Castle on 21 October 1959; and Bevan talking to Mikardo on 22 October: n. 13c.
44 RCD, 21 October 1959, reporting Ray Gunter. Also ibid., 30 October 1959, on NEC trade unionists; Trevor Evans in DE, 21 October 1959, on trade union leaders; The Times, 23 November 1959, Daily Mail, 27 November 1959, Evening Standard, 4 November 1959, Sunday Dispatch, 8 November 1959, on trade union MPs.
45 Observer political correspondent, 15 November 1959. Cf. Leslie Randall in Daily Mail, 27 November 1959; Robert Carvel in Star, 25 November 1959; Don Cook in Herald Tribune, 9 December 1959.
46 Spectator: a. 27 November 1959; b. Bernard Levin, 4 December 1959.

47 On 27 October 1959: P.131–3.

48 RCD, 3 July 1959 (above, p. 491), 25 November 1959; cf. Mikardo's Edmonton speech: *DT*, 3 December 1959.

49 625 *H.C. Deb.*, cols 1088–9: 27 June 1960.

50 HG to Cyril Robinson, 20 October 1959: P.131–3.

51 As he told the trade union group of MPs: *The Times*, 11 November 1959. Cf. *DT*, 21 October 1959. On the merits: nn. 2*a*, 13*b*.

52 'General Election Round-up', 9 October 1959 (BBC). Cf. below, p. 562.

53 *DT*, 21 October 1959; RCD, 30 October 1959; and n. 32.

54 Morgan Phillips's report on the election (Chapter 20, n. 38): *a*. p. 40 (and n. 55 below); *b*. p. 43 and Appendix.

55 These words are heavily marked in HG's copy (P.131–1); he marked very little else. But though 97 candidates out of 200 thought national-isation a liability, only 17 wanted the policy changed: n. 54*b*.

56 *ST*: *a*. 6 December 1959; *b*. Wilson in *ibid.*; *c*. 13 March 1960.

57 Foot (1973), pp. 622–8, quoting Geoffrey Goodman's notes of Bevan's conversations during the election.

58 In 1929 'workers' had replaced 'producers' and 'distribution and exchange' were added.

59 HG to J. B. Battle, 10 November 1952: C.6.

60 Interview, A. Crawley.

61 To the 1951 Society, Manchester: North of England Home Service, 31 October 1955 (BBC).

62 *DT*: *a*. 15 December 1955; *b*. 26 January 1960; *c*. 1 February 1960; *d*. 2 March 1960; *e*. 27 and 29 February 1960, 14 March 1960.

63 Interview, Arthur Allen.

64 The BBC programme 'At Home and Abroad', 4 October 1957: transcript in U.187.

65 Janosik (1968), p. 31.

66 Butler and Rose (1960), p. 255n.

67 *Observer*, 28 February 1960.

68 Griffiths (1969), p. 135.

69 HG to George Thomas MP, 26 January 1960: P.142–2.

70 *LPCR*, 1960, p. 219; HG to Lord Pethick–Lawrence, 23 March 1960, P.153; AHD, 14 July 1960.

71 F. S. Oliver, *The Endless Adventure* (Macmillan, 1930), pp. 46–8.

72 Interviews: *a*. P. Morris; *b*. W. Padley.

73 Watson in Rodgers (1964), p. 122; interviews, R. Prentice, Sir William Webber; Griffiths (1969), p. 135, and to author; n. 46*a*.

74 Interviews: W. Wyatt, with whom he and HG dined on 11 October; A. Crosland, who warned HG when helping with the speech in the House of Commons Library (also on 'The Day Before Yesterday',

Thames Television, 29 September 1970); Sir Kenneth Younger, to whom he talked in the train from Grimsby; Sir Harold Wilson.

75 Interview, Lord Gordon Walker. He had criticised Clause Four earlier, according to Frank Allaun: *Tribune*, 22 July 1955.

76 Interviews, A. J. McWhinnie, Lady Gaitskell.

77 It was not an example likely to appeal to them. RCD, 23 and 30 October 1959, reporting Anthony Howard.

78 In Oxford on 14 November he talked for a couple of hours about it with two prominent local Party leaders and a student activist (later an MP). They were surprised, cautious but not at all hostile: interviews, M. Lower, R. G. Owen, A. B. Walden, Mrs McNeal.

79 Murray to HG, 26 March 1690: P.187.

80 Dalton to HG, 1 Dec. 1959, U.1, quoting M. A. Hamilton, *Arthur Henderson* (Heinemann, 1938), p. 262. (The phrase, though in Henderson's draft, was perhaps Webb's: R. McKibbin, *The Evolution of the Labour Party 1910–24*, Oxford University Press, 1974, pp. 96–7.)

81 From Crosland (1962), pp. 120–1.

82 Pannell (n. 1); cf. n. 6c. Crossman confirms that Bevan saw it: n. 13*f*.

83 Pannell had failed two days earlier to get him to drop the whole idea.

84 A. Bevan, *In Place of Fear* (Heinemann, 1952), p. 118.

85 *LPCR*, 1959: *a*. pp. 83–6; *b*. p. 105; *c*. p. 105–14; *d*. p. 114; *e*. p. 122; *f*. pp. 125, 127, 131; *g*. pp. 136–7; *h*. pp. 143–4; *i*. pp. 151–5 (and n. 6*e*); *j*. p. 112.

86 J. H. Goldthorpe *et al.*, *The Affluent Worker: Political Attitudes and Behaviour* (Cambridge University Press, 1968), pp. 12–13.

87 Before the war a minimum of 10 per cent were out of work, from 1945 to 1959 a maximum of 3 per cent.

88 Foot contests that, with disingenuous references to Sections 6 and 7 of Clause Four (Foot, 1973, p. 640n.).

89 In fact the ILP had decided in 1893 to omit the word 'all' before 'the means of production, distribution and exchange': n. 72*b*.

90 Crossman lists Greenwood, Gunter, Mikardo and Eirene White, and says that he himself, Driberg and Bevan gave 'token applause': n. 13*f*. It was thin, wrote Bernard Levin, a keen supporter (n. 46*b*); 'a triumph' wrote James Margach in *ST*, 29 November 1959. For the contradictory press verdicts: Francis Williams in *New Statesman*, 5 December 1959.

91 Crossman thought him 'completely antediluvian': n. 13*f*. For his speech: n. 85*e*.

92 Interview, G. Goodman.

93 Interview, Lord Greenwood.

94 *The Economist*, 5 December 1959; *ST*, 6 December 1959.

95 HG to E. L. Mallalieu MP (from Nigeria) 8 February 1960: P.142-2.

96 HG to Leonard Cohen, 10 December 1959 (P.133C).

97 AHD, 10 December 1959. Perhaps HG thought he could have regained the treasurership, which Bevan would have had to give up at the next Conference.

98 *a.* Smith (1964), pp. 182–3; *b.* interviews, G. Goodman, I. Mikardo.

99 Interview, Michael Foot.

100 *a. Daily Mail*, 30 November 1959; *b. ST*, 6 December 1959, 'Crossbencher' in *SE*, 6 December 1959; *c. FT*, 30 November 1959.

101 Interviews, G. Goodman, Lord Harris; cf. n. 6*g.*

102 *The Economist*, 27 November 1959. Admitted by HG: to Crosland, 4 September 1960 (P.183).

103 *DT*, 22 March 1960. Cf. Memorandum, Lord Boyle.

104 Interview, Lord Moyle; cf. Griffiths (1969), p. 135.

105 Brown (1972): *a.* pp. 81, 82; *b.* p. 74.

106 Interview, D. Healey.

107 Strachey, in *ST*, 20 January 1963; Thomas (1973), p. 289.

108 Jenkins (1974), p. 177.

109 Malcolm Muggeridge (reviewing Rodgers, 1964) in *Evening Standard*, 21 January 1964. Also RCD, 25 November 1959, reporting Muggeridge; *Yorkshire Post*, 1 December 1959; *Guardian*, 26 February 1960.

110 *DT*, 24 and 30 December 1959, 20, 22 and 25 January 1960; correspondence in file V.10; appointments diaries; interviews, Mrs Fleming, Lord Walston.

111 Ian Mikardo, *DT*, 11 December 1959; cf. *New Statesman*, 5 December 1959.

112 *Tribune*: *a.* 29 January 1960; *b.* 19 February 1960.

113 'Panorama', 30 November 1959: BBC transcript, and *The Times*, 1 December 1959.

114 On 'Panorama', 18 January 1960; in *Tribune*, editorial 8 January 1960 and as 'John Marullus', 22 January 1960; in *DH*, 22 January 1960. On Russia, above, p. 519.

115 *DE*, 20 January 1960; *The Times*, 21 January 1960; *ST*, 24 January 1960.

116 *ST*, 17 January 1960, cf. 24 January 1960. The Bow Group were and are mildly progressive Tories.

117 Jay to HG, 23 January 1960: F.17–12. Cf. Dora to HG, 12 January 1960.

118 *DT*, 4 February 1960. The six were Foley, Rees, Richard, Rodgers, Taverne and Shirley Williams.

119 F. Boyd in *Guardian*, 26 February 1960.

120 To his local Party on 29 January 1960.

121 RCD, 9 December 1959; cf. *DT*, 4 December 1959; Roth (1977), pp. 235–6.

122 RCD, 12 February 1960; Roth (1977), p. 242.

123 *DT*, 11 February 1960. Also *The Times*, 11 and 15 February 1960.

124 HG's view. Crossman thought HG might have won by four votes: both n. 2*e*. Phillips was worried and offered to take over the proposal so as not to risk HG's prestige: n. 79.

125 George Darling MP in *Cooperative News*, 30 January 1960 (P.120–5); and to HG, 9 and 15 February 1960 and HG's reply, 16 February 1960: P.142–2.

126 His targets here were Wilson (in *ST*, 6 December 1959, and *The Times*, 11 February 1960) and Jennie Lee at the January NEC: RCD, 27 January 1960.

127 George Jeger; *DT*, 29 February 1960.

128 The Communist *Daily Worker* rightly replied next day that he had done nothing of the kind.

129 *Daily Mail*, 22 February 1960. Cf. *NC*, 22 January 1960.

130 HG to Sam Watson: *a*. 3 March 1960 (P.120–5); *b*. his italics; *c*. 23 September 1960 (P.118–7).

131 *a*. HG to Arthur Allen, 17 March 1960 (P.152); *b*. to Ernest Jones, 8 March 1960 (P.120–5); and to Dalton, 1 March 1960 (U.1).

132 *The Times*, 7 March 1960; *ST* and *Observer*, 13 March 1960. Pannell had urged it before Blackpool: n. 1. For Brown, n. 105*b*.

133 *The Times* political correspondent, 14 March 1960. Roth (1977, pp. 238–9) thinks the compromise would have been acceptable at the outset: a view reflecting badly on HG's critics, though he does not realise that.

134 Benn to HG, 28 October 1960, P.147–3, his emphasis. He referred back to the incident sixteen years later: interview.

135 But he had found Strachey, Stewart, Mulley and Ernest Popplewell, 'a Right-wing railwayman whip', all critical of HG: n. 13*e*.

136 See below, pp. 575–6.

137 Crossman to HG, 26 February 1960 (P.120–5) and n. 13*e*.

138 HG to Colin Jackson, 3 March 1960, P.153; to Crossman, 9 March 1960, P.120.

139 Driberg to HG, 14 March 1969: P. 120–5.

140 RCD, 22 March 1960, for this and the next paragraph. Crossman himself preferred Wilson to HG two months earlier, and four months later: RCD, 27 January 1960, 4 and 30 August 1960.

141 NEC-M, 16 March, 1960, M.80.

142 *The Times*, *Daily Mail*, 17 March 1960; RCD, 22 March 1960.

143 Pannell to HG, 19 March 1960; Jay to HG, 23 March 1960: P.142–2. Arthur Allen, Gordon Walker and Soskice were also fully satisfied; Crosland, Jenkins and John Murray not.

144 HG to Arthur Gaitskell, 14 April 1960: P.152. But he told Arthur Allen he was 'reasonably well satisfied': n. 131*a*.

145 Interview, Mrs Cressida Ridley.
146 *DT*, 14 July 1960; NEC–M, 13 July 1960, M.186. The 5 were Boyd of the AEU, who wanted the constitutional revision to go forward; Barbara Castle and Tony Greenwood from the CLP section, Nicholas and McGarvey among the trade unionists. (Cf. Crossman to T. Balogh, 12 July 1960, postscript 14 July 1960, in RCD.) Yet on 22 February, before HG had become vulnerable, Greenwood was willing 'to add anything within reason to the constitution'.
147 Phillips had suggested postponing a decision till 1962, in which HG saw no advantage.
148 *LPCR*, 1960, pp. 211, 214, 218–21. The voting was 2,310,000 to 4,153,000 and 4,304,000 to 2,226,000.
149 John Murray to Dora, 28 March 1960; cf. HG to Murray, 22 March, and replies 19 and 26 March: all P.187.

Chapter 22   'Ban the Bomb!'

1 The theme of Parkin (1968), Chapters 4–6.
2 Jackson (1968): *a*. pp. 176–7; *b*. p. 178n. (Judith Hart, Walter Monslow, Bert Oram).
3 RCD: *a*. 26 February 1960, 2, 4 and 15 March 1960 (and n. 5); *b*. 4, cf. 8, 15 and 22 March 1960.
4 *The Times, DT*: *a*. 3 March 1960 (and n. 5); *b*. 30 April 1960; *c*. 2 May 1960; *d*. 30 June 1960 (and n. 6).
5 A. Woodburn to HG, 2 March 1960: P. 142–2.
6 RCD: *a*. 4 March 1960; *b*. 18 July 1958; *c*. 8 March 1960; *d*. 15 March 1960; *e*. 2 March 1960; *f*. 3 May 1960, reporting Jenkins; *g*. 26 May 1960; *h*. 11 May 1960; *i*. typically, cf. above, pp. 507–8, below, p. 638; *j*. 30 May 1960; *k*. 1 June 1960; *l*. 12 May 1960; *m*. 22 June 1960; *n*. 4 August 1960; *o*. 29 June 1960; *p*. cf. 1 September 1960; *q*. 20 September 1960; *r*. 30 August 1960; *s*. 26 October 1956.
7 Wigg (1972); *a*. p. 226 (and *The Times*, 4 March 1960); *b*. cf. p. 127; *c*. p. 231.
8 *The Times*, 4 and 7 March 1960; Jackson (1968), p. 177 (who mistakenly names five other rebels).
9 AHD, *a*. 18 March 1960 (reporting HG); *b*. 22 June 1960; *c*. 14 July 1960; *d*. 15 November 1960; *e*. and n. 6*c*.
10 *The Times*, 15 March 1960; *Star*, 15 March 1960; *NC*, 16 March 1960. Crossman records with delight that he was the source of several other press stories: n. 6*d*.
11 Even Michael Foot conceded it was not HG who demanded sanctions: *Tribune*, 18 March 1960.

12 HG to Crossman; *a.* 10 March 1960, reply 11th (published *The Times*, 15 March 1960; personal letters in RCD); *b.* 27 September 1960.

13 HDD: *a.* 4 May 1960, reporting Roy Jenkins on what Crossman had said to him; *b.* 12 May 1960; *c.* 13 July 1960; *d.* reporting Brown.

14 *LPCR*, 1960; *a.* p. 156; *b.* p. 162; *c.* pp. 163–5; *d.* pp. 166–8; *e.* p. 171; *f.* p. 177; *g.* p. 180; *h.* p. 178; *i.* p. 200; *j.* pp. 195–200; *k.* p. 199; *l.* p. 201; *m.* p. 212 (Roy Jenkins).

15 In 1957 they had opposed unilateralism; by 1959 they were backing Cousins (A. J. R. Groom, *British Thinking about Nuclear Weapons*, Francis Pinter, 1974, p. 348; cf. Driver, 1964, p. 72); full, official support came only in May 1960 (Parkin, 1968, pp. 78–81).

16 Among Labour voters, 41 per cent. The shift was temporary.

17 Macmillan (1972): *a.* pp. 251–3; *b.* p. 232; from his diary, 19 and 30 June 1960.

18 618 *H.C. Deb.*, 1 March 1960: *a.* cols. 1143–4; *b.* cols 1136–9; *c.* cols 921–7, 1118–26, 1130–3.

19 *The Times*: *a.* 25 March 1960; *b.* 23 and 29 June 1960; *c.* 26 September 1960; *d.* and nn. 9*a*, 18*a*.

20 Cf. (e.g.) *LPCR*, 1958, pp. 222. Yet Foot told *Tribune* readers on 22 April 1960:

> Mr Gaitskell ... and the others ... have insisted on the absolute necessity of Britain maintaining her own independent deterrent – they ought now to insist that the Government should develop its own means of delivering the bombs, however astronomical they cost ... that is the logic of their earlier statements.

21 Crossman to A. Hetherington, 2 March 1960 (in RCD); RCD, 2 March 1960, 11 and 26 May 1960; fuller below, pp. 587–9.

22 As earlier over tests or 'first use': above, pp. 453–4, 499–502.

23 Gallup polls in Driver (1964), p. 99.

24 On the non-nuclear club, see Chapter 18, Section ii.

25 Nigel Birch, 29 February 1960, Sir Fitzroy Maclean and Sir Alexander Spearman, 1 March 1960: all in n. 18*c*. Antony Head and Aubrey Jones, n. 26*a*.

26 622 *H.C. Deb.*, 27 April 1960: *a.* cols 253–61, 280–8; *b.* cols 226–8; *c.* col. 329.

27 Weitzman, after abstaining on 1 March, wrote expressing admiration and support for HG: 2 March 1960, P.142–2.

28 *Observer*, 20 March 1960; on the political danger, cf. *New Statesman*, 19 March 1960; and n. 6*e*.

29 Crosland to HG, P.183: *a.* 4 May 1960; *b.* HG's marginalia; *c.* n.d. but 7 November 1960; *d.* 1 September 1960; *e.* HG's reply, 4 September 1960. All emphasis in originals.

30 Wigg (1972), p. 127, also quotes Brown's account, but believed HG's (interview).

31 *DT*, 21 and (on the TUC) 23 March 1960; and n. 19*a.*

32 *Guardian* political correspondent; *a.* 29 April 1960 (and n. 33); *b.* 26 October 1960; *c.* 4 October 1960.

33 *ST*, 1 May 1960.

34 HG to Tewson, 13 April 1960: P.146–B.

35 It was|broadly set out publicly by *The Times* political correspondent (n. 19*a*; cf. *DT*, 29 April 1960) and did not change in substance though the presentation was slightly modified (n. 36).

36 *a.* HG's original memorandum was sent to Tewson, Birch of USDAW and Carron of the AEU on 13 April. A copy, amended in his handwriting, is in file P.146–B; *b.* the amended version (in file P.148) was typed later that day. For the points of presentation where he had shifted, see p. 582 and n. 51.

37 Some of the criticism was petty. HG had told a press conference in New York that opinion polls reflected public views on the bomb better than numbers at demonstrations; Robert Willis of the TUC misquoted and denounced him for a 'gratuitous insult' to the Aldermaston marchers: *DH*, 20 April 1960; *The Times*, *Daily Mail*, 3 May 1960. Cf. the silly falsehood that he had forbidden a member of the Shadow Cabinet to march: *The Times*, 19 and 30 April 1960; *DT*, 16 and 19 April 1960; Greenwood to HG, 20 April 1960, P.142–2.

38 Carbery (1969), pp. 240–1; Groom, p. 423.

39 Its president Walter Padley thought (interview) that he might have swung the vote on defence if he had not had to speak on Clause Four instead. An orthodox executive motion passed by 62,000, the unilateralist one by 19,000.

40 On Gordon Walker's advice: n. 29*b.*

41 Wilson, n. 26*c.* He told Crossman there had been no discussion with HG, but he and Brown had agreed on a sharp switch – because of the huge CND demonstration, the USDAW vote, and the 'wind of change' in the Movement: RCD, 28 April 1960. Brown told Crossman that Wilson played no part: RCD, 30 May 1960. To the author years later, Brown said the same; Wilson said Brown had spoken without warning to him (interviews).

42 Interview, D. Ennals. HG's irritation with Brown was widely known after his return: interviews, A. Crosland, Lord Gordon Walker, R. Jenkins, Sir Harold Wilson (who briefed him at the airport); Smith (1964), p. 184. On 29 April 1960 he wrote from Haifa to a friend that

Brown's words would be misinterpreted, but implied no sensational change.

43 Interviews: Lord Gordon Walker, C. Mayhew, W. Wyatt, Sir Harold Wilson. Others thought he did not care about it much, or at all: Lord George-Brown, D. Healey, F. Mulley. Jenkins recalled that he had been difficult to budge; Crosland was not sure.

44 At Newcastle: *Observer*, 22 May 1960.

45 To the NUGMW conference at Great Yarmouth, 23 May 1960: *a.* Report, p. 343; *b.* p. 342; *c.* pp. 342–3; *d.* one reason was the misrepresentation – again – of his views by his opponents.

46 617 *H.C. Deb.*, cols 775–80: 11 February 1960.

47 Crossman had expected he would, and told Brown on feeble grounds that he did: RCD, 28 April 1960, 26 May 1960. J. P. W. Mallalieu said HG had 'adumbrated' but then dropped the idea: *New Statesman*, 28 May 1960. Cf. Wigg (1972), p. 228. Others did favour it: Mulley, briefly Brown, and perhaps Robens (RCD, 1 June 1960).

48 To Robin Day on 'At Home and Abroad' on 24 May 1960: BBC. Cf. n. 45*b*.

49 To William Clark on 'Right of Reply' (ATV: transcript in U.87) on 3 June 1960. Ennals apparently had told Crossman that HG thought a joint deterrent 'possible'; perhaps HG had been informing himself – from Robens? – about a plan which he never proposed and soon publicly disavowed.

50 At Newcastle: *The Times*, 22 May 1960. He expressed 'a great deal of doubt' about United States purchase to Mrs Helen Grant, 27 May 1960: P.152.

51 United States purchase was downgraded from 'obviously preferable' (to production at home) to 'hard to rule out altogether'. The redraft also introduced the first reference to sharing with the Europeans.

52 Crosland and Jenkins (interviews); Jav to HG, after talking to Gordon Walker, 14 May 1960, P.142–2; and n. 53*a*.

53 Dalton to HG, U.1: *a.* 30 April 1960; *b.* 4 April 1960; *c.* 30 June 1960; *d.* Crosland concurred: n. 13*c*.

54 As shown e.g. by *New Statesman*, 16 July 1960.

55 RCD, 26 May 1960, on NEC attacks on HG for this habit.

56 HG to Julie, 8 March 1958; interview, Mrs McNeal.

57 GWD, 12 May 1960.

58 *Commentary*, New York, May 1961, p. 376, quoted Groom, pp. 494–5.

59 *Tribune*; *a.* 'John Marullus', 29 April 1960; *b.* 24 June 1960.

60 *ST*, 1 May 1960; *DE*, 29 April 1960; cf. *Spectator*, 6 May 1960.

61 Deryck Winterton in *DH*, 5 May 1960.

62 Against Crosland's list of reforms (here omitted) HG scribbled: 'Because I tried to get these changes': n. 29*a, b*.

63 Walter Terry, *Daily Mail*, 16 March 1960.

64 Leslie Randall, *Daily Mail*, 3 May 1960; *DT*, 19 March 1960 and 5 May 1960 (Harry Boyne); *The Times* political correspondent, 9 May 1960. For some later ones see Francis Williams, *New Statesman*, 25 June 1960.

65 Trevor Evans, *DE*: *a.* 9 June 1960; *b.* 3 October 1960; *c.* 5 October 1960; *d.* 6 October 1960; *e.* & n. 151*b*; *f.* 8 October 1960.

66 RCD: *a.* 11 May 1960, reporting Wilson; *b.* 26 May 1960, reporting Brown on the evening of 12 May.

67 HG had told Dalton that same evening that the leadership and Front Bench which would succeed him 'wouldn't be impressive': HDD, 12 May 1960.

68 Letter to a friend, 15 May 1960.

69 HG's view: at Newcastle on 21 May 1960, and in 624 *H.C. Deb.*, cols 1012–20, 30 May 1960. (He suspected Chinese pressure, too.) Cf. M. Tatu, *Le Pouvoir en URSS* (Grasset, Paris, 1967), Part 1.

70 Cf. also HG to Lord Beaverbrook, 20 May 1960: P.153.

71 *a.* Crossman to HG, 2 June 1960; *b.* reply, 13 June 1960; *c.* Sam Watson was chairman of the international sub-committee.

72 *a.* Minutes in file P.146–B; *b.* numbers recorded there.

73 *DT*, *a.* 9 May 1960; *b.* 24 June 1960; *c.* 30 June 1960; *d.* 24 September 1960; *e.* 1 October 1960 (industrial correspondent).

74 *Sunday Dispatch*, 29 May 1960.

75 *The Times, NC, DE*, 25 May 1960.

76 Interview, G. Goodman (Cousins's biographer); and n. 77. RCD, 20 September 1960, recalls the meeting taking place 'after George Brown had persuaded Frank Cousins that our draft was OK'. (Harold Wilson later claimed he was partly responsible for the draft – 'which took my breath away': RCD, 27 October 1960.)

77 *Observer*, 5 June 1960.

78 Sam Watson had managed to have HG's name added: n. 6*k*.

79 Cousins made his opposition to it clear in his press conference: *DT*, 4 June 1960.

80 *Daily Mail*, 2 and 9 June 1960. Also Robert Carvel, *Star*, 9 June 1960 (who adds that Wilson was criticising HG's tactics). Roth (1977), p. 244, gives the Left version as usual.

81 He said there were 'fundamental differences', but no 'flaming row': press conference, *DT*, 4 June 1960.

82 HG to Sam Watson: *a.* P.146–B: 3 June 1960 (and n. 83); *b.* 23 June 1960; *c.* 29 June 1960, *d.* P.118–7: 16 September 1960; *e.* 23 September 1960; *f.* 30 August 1960 (and n. 6*r*).

83 Crossman's own account confirms the 'thirty-five-minute intermezzo

where the TUC members wrangled with each other, while we sat outside the ring as spectators': n. 6k.

84 He later recalled it differently: 'Gaitskell ... had deliberately picked a quarrel *with George Brown and myself* and destroyed any chance of agreement with Frank Cousins'; RCD, 20 September 1960, my italics.

85 623 *H.C. Deb.*, col. 641: 12 May 1960. To William Clark on ATV, 3 June 1960.

86 His handwritten amendments are on the drafts in file P.146–B. *Foreign Policy and Defence* (reprinted in *LPCR*, 1960, pp. 13–16) was finally passed 17 to 4 after three amendments from Barbara Castle, Greenwood and Nicholas received 3, 4 and 5 votes: n. 87a.

87 NEC: *a.* 22 June 1960, M.173; *b.* 13 July 1960, M.187–8; *c.* 27 July 1960, M.193–4; *d.* 2 October 1960, M.267; *e. ibid.*, M.264.

88 *Reynolds News*, 29 May 1960. He himself reported similar reactions in a letter to a friend, 1 June 1960.

89 *Observer*, 22 May 1960 (Newcastle): *Eastern Daily Press*, 24 May 1960 (Great Yarmouth); *The Times*, 28 May 1960 (Sheffield University); above, nn. 48 and 49, for the broadcasts.

90 Driver (1964), p. 95. The lowest unilateralist vote in 1959 was 139.

91 Ron Smith, their general secretary, wrote to tell HG, as the *Daily Herald* was anti-Gaitskell and did not report it: 23 May 1960, P.146–B.

92 HG to John Murray, 24 May 1960: P.187.

93 Needing TUC ratification, it was not published till July.

94 HG to Sam Watson (n. 82c). He rightly foresaw problems if the opposition motion was not strictly unilateralist but 'a more subtle one (such as the T & GW resolution)': n. 9b.

95 Interview, F. Mulley.

96 Dalton had expected to lose both unions on defence: HDD, 12 May 1960.

97 Haseler (1969): *a.* pp. 171–2; *b.* pp. 192–6 (cf. n. 9d).

98 HG to Dalton, 12 April 1960: U.1, his italics.

99 Greenwood as chairman of the Hampstead CLP let it 'lie on the table'. Its press officer (who was no Gaitskellite) resigned to protest at the leaking of the resolution and at the broken promises and 'appalling lack of courtesy and political responsibility' of her colleagues: Mrs Lawson to HG, 2 July 1960, P.152.

100 *DT*, 15 17 and 20 June 1960. Zilliacus liked the phrase and repeated it frequently.

101 *New Statesman*; *a.* 25 June 1960; *b.* 17 October 1959; *c.* editorial 28 June 1960, 16 July 1960, K. Martin 24 September 1960; *d.* letter, 9 July 1960; *e.* 1 October 1960, his emphasis.

102 *Evening Standard*, 26 June 1960.

103 Morgan Phillips at the NEC (RCD, 22 June 1960). Also (with no figure) from the Chief Whip's speech at the PLP: *DT*, 1 July 1960.

104 For the PLP meeting, see p. 596.

105 Unilateralists 2,884,000; multilateralists 1,904,000: *DT*, 8 and 23 July 1960.

106 *Daily Mail*: *a*. 25 July 1960; *b*. 9 June 1960.

107 By two-thirds of them (*DT*, 5 May 1960) or three-quarters (*DT*, 28 May 1960 & 8 July 1960).

108 John Murray to HG, 31 July 1960 (P. 187) summarising the attitude of six of them.

109 E.g., F. Boyd in *Guardian*, 6 October 1959; *DT*, 26 January 1960; *Evening Standard*, 2 March 1960; H. Boyne in *DT*, 5 May 1960; *Spectator*, 6 May 1960.

110 *The Economist*, 19 March 1960.

111 Roth (1977), p. 242. RCD, 12 May 1960.

112 Fuller below, p. 750.

113 It may have helped HG that the most recent Gallup poll gave him his best personal rating as leader: 56 per cent of all voters and 73 per cent of Labour voters found him a good one. (It did not last.)

114 The 7 were J. P. W. Mallalieu and 6 members of VFS: Harold Davies, Will Griffiths, Emrys Hughes, S. Silverman, Swingler and Zilliacus. Barbara Castle, Driberg and Shinwell abstained. The 53 absentees were not necessarily critics.

115 625 *H.C. Deb.*, col. 1557: 30 June 1960.

116 Strauss *et al.* to HG, 26 July 1960, P.147-3. All the signatories were past, present or future front-benchers, except for two members of the chairmen's panel. F. Blackburn, G. Chetwynd, R. Marsh, R. Mellish, F. Mulley, F. Peart, G. Reynolds, K. Robinson, W. Ross, M. Stewart, G. R. Strauss, W. R. Williams. One (G. Darling) approved later, and only one (Ungoed-Thomas) declined to sign.

117 Strauss's diary, kindly supplied by him.

118 *New Statesman*, 6 August 1960. He argued that the test of a Labour leader, as of an American President, was his ability to work the unworkable.

119 *Sunday Telegraph*, 2 October 1977. Cf. 26 September 1976.

120 626 *H.C. Deb.*, col. 1610: 14 July 1960.

121 At Hinckley in his constituency on 10 June 1960. The attack (though not the phrase) was instigated by HG, who was then taken aback by the furore it aroused: interview, W. Wyatt. A month later HG restrained him from following it up with a denunciation of the Clause Four retreat, of the annual NEC and PLP elections which encouraged candidates to trim, and of the influence of the Communist Party in certain unions: Wyatt to HG, 14 July 1960, P.142-2.

122 Robens had recently argued that Conference could decide that Labour was a pacifist Party, though he would not then speak for it: n. 106b.

123 HG to E. L. Mallalieu MP: 23 June 1960, P.142–2.

124 HG noted in the margin: 'all the difficulty!': annotated draft in Minutes, n. 87b file P.174.

125 Morgan Phillips, *Constitution of the Labour Party* (August 1960).

126 *The Times*, 29 July 1960. Crossman assumed that the press had been briefed in HG's favour: n. 6n.

127 From Mark Abrams's interviews in January and February 1960: *Socialist Commentary*, June 1960 and Abrams and Rose (1960), pp. 25–30. He proposed fifteen characteristics to his sample, from which the top two criteria chosen were 'strong leader' and 'strong enough to make unwelcome decisions'; among all voters 56 per cent chose the first and 47 per cent the second, among Labour voters 53 per cent and 43 per cent.

128 Understandably HG came somewhat behind Macmillan on this score even with Labour supporters, and behind by 3 to 1 among the Liberals and uncommitted.

129 Roth (1977), p. 249, apparently quoting Wilson.

130 HG to Arthur Gaitskell, 14 March 1960: P.152.

131 HG to the Yugoslav Ambassador, 29 August 1960: V.10.

132 *The Times*, 1 and 26 September 1960; *Guardian*, 23 September 1960; *DT*, 24 September 1960; appointments diary.

133 *New Leader* (New York), 3 October 1960; quoted Haseler (1969), p. 157, and Parkin (1968), p. 115.

134 Roy Jenkins and John Harris also disagreed: Harris to HG in Yugoslavia, 18 August 1960 (V.10). Crossman misjudged again: 'it is the tactic of Gaitskell now deliberately to bring the Conference into disrepute, as the TUC was brought into disrepute': RCD, 20 September 1960.

135 *a*. Houghton's report to HG on the TUC, 12 September 1960 (P.118–7); *b*. HG replied (14 September 1960) 'I entirely agree'.

136 TUC Report, 1960, p. 517.

137 RCD, 21 September 1960, reporting NEC trade unionists back from Douglas.

138 Interview, Lady Gaitskell.

139 Brown, *a*. to HG, and to Dora, both 29 September 1960 (P.118–7); *b*. to HG, 23 September 1960, his emphasis; *c*. and RCD, 20 September 1960.

140 Brown's memorandum is in RCD.

141 RCD, 20 September 1960. Admitting that the official policy differed from the T&GWU's over tactical atomic weapons, he claimed that Conference would dismiss the point as logic-chopping.

142 RCD, 21 September 1960. Sub-Committee Minutes, no. 10, M.53(a) amended by NEC, 29 September 1960, M.237. Brown's memorandum referred to the General Council's ruling, but Crossman had not noticed that. Roth (1977), p. 247, is sketchy.

143 RCD, 28 September 1960, contrasting it 'with Hugh's infuriated denunciation of George Brown on the phone a week ago and his stern reprimand to me ... for ... the most ridiculous and dangerous proposal he had ever heard'.

144 Interview, Lord George-Brown.

145 George Brown (reviewing Rodgers, 1964) in *Spectator*, 24 January 1964.

146 Interviews, A. N. W. Benn, Lady Gaitskell, G. Goodman, Lord Harris.

147 Earlier in private: HG to T. Heelas, 12 April 1960, P.152.

148 *DT*, 8 September 1960 (45 per cent); 21 September 1960 (40 per cent); *DE*, 27 September 1960 (50 per cent).

149 Interview, James Griffiths.

150 Interviews, Lady Bacon, Mrs Peggy Crane; and n. 151*a*.

151 Stewart (1968): *a*. p. 100; *b*. pp. 102–3.

152 *FT* diary, 5 October 1960.

153 *a*. *Guardian*, 3 October 1960; *The Economist*, 8 October 1960; *DT*, 3 October 1960; *b*. a minority, including most of the union's officials, objected to the breach of mandate: *DT* industrial correspondent, 7 October 1960.

154 *a*. James Margach, *ST*, 2 October 1960; *b*. and n. 65*b*. It was vain because the AEU delegation would not meet to decide their votes until the night before the defence debate.

155 *a*. interview, Lord Harris; *b*. mollified by the answers to his 23 September outburst, he had already sent both Gaitskells friendly replies: n. 139*a*.

156 The minority were Barbara Castle, Crossman, Driberg, Greenwood, Jennie Lee, Nicholas and Wilson: n. 87*d*.

157 Respectively by 19 to 11, 19 to 9, and unanimously; and by 21 to 11 for the whole package: *DT*, 5 October 1960. On the lobbying, by left-wing politicians like Norman Atkinson and Stan Orme, see Duff (1971), pp. 189–90.

158 Charles Pannell in *AEU Journal*, September 1961, p. 280; quoted Lord Windlesham, *Communication and Political Power* (Cape, 1966), p. 82n.

159 On 14 October 1960, *Tribune* published a letter on the subject from him and Harold Davies, Robert Edwards, Dick Kelley, Sydney Silverman, Warbey and Zilliacus; and on 23 October 1960 it published an anti-Gaitskell article by him. Years later he discredited himself, and it then wrote of him as always a Labour right-winger.

160 The votes were 3,586,000 to 1,874,000, and 767,000 to 5,627,000: n. 14*d*.

161 *DT*, 5 October 1960: 3,062,000. to 2,140,000.

162 'Labour Party Conference Report': BBC (cf. *The Times*, 6 October 1960).

163 Interview, Lady Gaitskell. Lord Harris also discussed the speech with him and thought the Chief Whip did, too. But the latter never saw the peroration: AHD, 15 December 1960 (quoting HG denying a report in *Tribune* that he had); Lord Aylestone to author (adding 'I agreed with it completely').

164 Press of 6 October 1960: *a*. Harold Hutchinson, *DH*; *b*. Geoffrey Goodman, *DH*, his emphasis; *c*. William Barkley, *DE*; *d*. *Guardian*; *e*. *The Times*; *f*. *DT*, political correspondents.

165 *a*. On them, n. 14*k*; *b*. cf. *Guardian*, 7 October 1960.

166 The resentment was lasting, and would have been greater still had HG not omitted two words—'and Communists'—on John Harris's advice: interview, Lord Harris.

167 *a*. *ST*, 9 October 1960; *b*. and nn. 65*d*, 164*a*, *b*, *c*, *e*, *f*.

168 Interview, Tom Jackson (1975). In 1960 he was a dissident in a strongly Gaitskellite trade union delegation.

169 Duff (1971), p. 191.

170 Before Cousins, the Left said they were crushed by union bosses with block votes; though probably the only important occasion when a CLP majority was overcome by a majority of union votes was over German rearmament in 1954: Harrison (1960), p. 229.

171 HG, reported *The Times*, n. 164*e*. 70 per cent: n. 164*f*. Two-thirds: n. 65*d*; of the uncommitted, n. 164*a*. Denis Healey went too far in claiming 80 per cent, and *Tribune* in conceding only 40 per cent after having, a year earlier (24 July 1959), claimed over 70 per cent for Cousins's resolution. Quite likely HG's speech caused some CLP delegates to abstain or even break their mandates; for many had arrived with a wholly false idea of the Executive's policy.

172 K. Hindell and P. Williams, 'Scarborough and Blackpool', *Political Quarterly*. 33. 3 (July 1962) give very full evidence. The percentage in the text corrects one error there: the Royal Arsenal Co-operative Society voted for the leadership in both years. (Isolated on its own in Table I in the article, alas it was missed in the very careful checking of the unions in Table II.)

173 Mrs N. Currie of Gateshead to HG, 7 October 1960; P.145–2.

174 Sam Watson in Rodgers (1964), p. 113.

175 HG to C. Shopland, 10 March 1960: P.153.

176 Interview, A. N. W. Benn (and above, p. 529).

177 For instance Lord Pakenham (*Observer*, 6 November 1960); Sam

Watson (RCD, 27 October 1960); the Chief Whip (interview, Lord Aylestone); David Marquand (*Encounter*, January 1961, p. 44).

178 A little later he rejected an American interviewer's suggestion that Communists caused the defence split: to the *Baltimore Sun*, 8 March 1961 (U.106).

179 Though when the Tory press attacked him, he was belaboured for that, too: e.g. *New Statesman*, 24 December 1960.

180 Above, pp. 577–8, 587, 590; below, n. 186.

181 ETU transcript, 28 June 1962 (Chapter 6, n. 97), p. 10.

182 The *New Statesman* on 1 October 1960 accused HG editorially of a 'splitting manoeuvre' for pointing out that the new policy was not unilateralist.

183 As one shrewd Tory saw from the start: Charles Curran, *Evening News*, 27 May 1960.

184 To HG, 20 June 1960: P.118–7.

185 *a.* Eirene White to HG, 18 October 1960; *b.* his reply, 20 October: P.145–6.

186 As shown in his eighty letters from friendly MPs in P.145–6. To one, Reginald Paget, he replied: 'I have gone to the limit in compromise – further, I know, than many people would have wished' (18 October 1960). Also AHD, 15 November 1960; and below, pp. 626–7, 631.

Chapter 23 'Fight and Fight Again'

1 GWD: *a.* 12 May 1960 (above, p. 585); *b.* 30 December 1960.

2 HDD, 13 July 1960, for Dalton; and n. 1*a*, for Gordon Walker.

3 *Guardian*, DT: *a.* 4 October 1960; *b.* 4 November 1960.

4 Interview, Lord Aylestone.

5 For Bowden: RCD, 19 October 1960. For both, AHD, 15 December 1960, reporting HG.

6 Donnelly (1968), p. 147, reporting Healey.

7 *Daily Mail* editorial, *DT*, *Evening News* political correspondent, all 6 October 1960; cf. n. 8*a*.

8 *The Times*: *a.* political correspondent, 7 October 1960; *b.* 3 March 1961; *c.* 1 May 1961; *d.* 3 May 1961; *e.* 5 May 1961; *f.* 15 February 1963.

9 Interview, Lady Gaitskell.

10 Interview, Lord Harris.

11 Lady Bacon in interview, and in *Leeds Weekly Citizen*, 25 January 1963.

12 Note in HG's handwriting, headed 'Objects': n.d. but before 13 October 1960, very likely at Scarborough (P.183).

13 Stewart (1968), p. 102; and n. 14.

14 Interview, G. Goodman.

15 Interview, Harold Hutchinson.

16 David Smawley to HG, 5 October 1960: P.146–2. 'Venom': John Cole in *Guardian*, 8 October 1960, blaming both sides; examples in Parkin (1968), p. 116n.

17 Reg Sorensen MP to HG, 23 Oct. 1960 (P.145–6); Mrs Ethel Shackleton, 6 October 1960 (P.147–1); Harold Campbell, n.d. but 5 October 1960 (P.152); David Warburton of Shipley CLP (*LPCR*, 1960, pp. 155–6, and n. 18*a*).

18 *Guardian*: *a.* 5 October 1960, F. Boyd; *b.* 6 and 10 October 1960; *c.* 14 and 15 October 1960; *d.* 27 October 1960; *e.* 26 October 1960; *f.* 6 May 1961.

19 Letters in files P.145, P.152, P.153, P.166.

20 F. Bealey, J. Blondel and W. P. McCann, *Constituency Politics* (Faber, 1965), pp. 282, 287 – on Newcastle-under-Lyme, whose MP was Stephen Swingler. They found 69 per cent liked HG for his character, 31 per cent for his policies.

21 Pakenham to HG, 20 June 1960, quoting a priest: P.118–7.

22 Griffiths (1969), p. 138.

23 *DH*: *a.* 10 October 1960; *b.* 14 January 1969; *c.* 11 March 1961; *d.* and n. 18*b*.

24 *The Times, DT*: *a.* 15 December 1960 (and n. 25*a*); *b.* 27 October 1960; *c.* 3 March 1961; *d.* 17 May 1961.

25 RCD: *a.* 14 December 1960; *b.* 20 October 1960; *c.* 13 October 1960; *d.* 23 November 1960; *e.* 13 February 1961; *f.* 26 October 1960, on Coventry; *g.* 8 December 1960; *h.* 27 January 1961, and n. 1*b*; *i.* on meetings of 8 and 9 February; *j.* 3 March 1961; *k.* 23 February 1961; *l.* and n. 93; *m.* quoting Foot and Greenwood; *n.* 21 March 1961; *o.* 24 April 1961; *p.* 4 May 1961; *q.* 14 June 1961; *r.* 8 March 1961; *s.* 24 March 1961; *t.* 28 March 1961; *u.* 11 May 1961; *v.* 17 May 1961.

26 The two dissenters were Emrys Hughes and Zilliacus himself. Contrast the strange account in Roth (1977), p. 255, with nn. 24*a*, 27*a*.

27 AHD: *a.* 15 December 1960; *b.* 11 January 1961; *c.* 15 November 1960; *d.* 25 January 1961; *e.* reporting HG; *f.* 21 March 1961; *g.* 26 April 1961; *h.* 10 May 1961; *i.* 24 June 1961; *j.* 21 September 1961.

28 RCD, 27 January 1960, 28 April 1960, on the early manoeuvres. Also Roth (1977), pp. 242–3.

29 *a.* HG to Crosland, 4 September 1960, P. 183; *b.* cf. *DT*, 7 July 1960, *ST*, 6 November 1960; *c.* his emphasis.

30 Watson to HG, 19 July 1960, and reply 21 July (P.118–7). Cf. *DT*, 5 May 1960, 7 July 1960; Trevor Evans, *DE*, 9 June 1960; *The Times*, 8 July 1960.

31 RCD, 27 January 1960, 30 August 1960, 1 September 1960; *DT*, 5 May 1960, 7 July 1960.

32 Douglas Clark, *DE*: *a*. 14 October 1960; *b*. 18 October 1960; *c*. and nn. 8*a*, 18*c*, 23*a*.

33 E. Kay, *Pragmatic Premier* (Frewin, 1967), pp. 112–13; cf. nn. 25*c*, 34.

34 Smith (1964), p. 187.

35 Interview, Lord Greenwood, who withdrew from the Shadow Cabinet rather than serve under HG: and n. 18*c*.

36 RCD, 19 October 1960; W. Wyatt, *Turn Again Westminster* (Deutsch, 1973), p. 133; and n. 32*b*.

37 RCD, 19 October 1960, referring to Sunday 16 October; cf. RCD, 8 February 1963. (Contrast Kay, pp. 113–14, who claims to have decided Wilson; Roth (1977), pp. 149–50.)

38 Sydney Silverman to HG, published in the press 19 October 1960.

39 He too wanted a new document to 'shift the basis of the debate away from Scarborough': n. 27*b*.

40 *The Times, Guardian*: *a*. 26 October 1960; *b*. 5 May 1961.

41 On 17 October 1960: P.145–1. King-Hall was friendly to HG on the Labour Party constitutional issue: his *Newsletter*, 29 September 1960, and private letter, n.d. but 5 October 1960: P.145–4.

42 Crosland's appeal to him to do so was made at this time: above, p. 582.

43 Estimates ranged up from 20 (*DT*, 20 and 21 October 1960) to 30 or 40 (*Guardian*, 6 October; *DE*, 21 October; *Spectator*, 28 October) or 50 (*The Economist*, 29 October) or 55 (*DH*, 21 October; his supporters, quoted *DE*, 24 October). Roth (1977), p. 251, says they were sure of 70.

44 Unilateralist parties were much less common in Labour constituencies than in Conservative ones, especially their safest. Among parties sending anti-leadership resolutions on defence to Conference, those in seats with a Tory majority above 10,000 outnumbered those from Labour seats in 1959, 1960, 1961 and (by 2 to 1) 1962: G. W. Jones in *Socialist Commentary*, October 1962, p. 13. In one sample of 134 CLPs at the 1961 Conference, 60 per cent of those in Tory strongholds (over 60 per cent Tory vote in 1959) were unilateralist; but only 44 per cent of CLPs from less safe Conservative seats, and 37 per cent of those with a Labour MP: K. Hindell and P. Williams, 'Scarborough and Blackpool', *Political Quarterly*, 33. 3, July 1962, p. 315; cf. A. J. R. Groom, *British Thinking about Nuclear Weapons* (Francis Pinter, 1974), p. 437.

45 Gallup polls, quoted Driver (1964), p. 99: among Labour voters 41, 31 and 28 per cent respectively.

46 Some thought this the dominant factor: Nora Beloff in *Observer*, 9 October 1960; and n. 47*a*.

47 *a*. W. Wyatt to HG, 11 October 1960, P.118-7; *b*. he listed 'our assets ... and liabilities' and counted the Parliamentary Committee – as well as the NEC – among the latter, though HG queried that.

48 524 *H.C. Deb.*, col. 592: 25 February 1954.

49 RCD, 27 October 1960. Crossman complained of HG's chairmanship at this meeting, but unjustifiably; and other critics of HG never felt that he abused his position as chairman: interviews, Lord Greenwood, A. N. W. Benn, Barbara Castle.

50 *DT*: *a*. 10 November 1960; *b*. 27 October 1960; *c*. 25 January 1961 (full report); *d*. 3 March 1961; *e*. 2 May 1961.

51 AHD, 5 November 1960, reporting HG. Her motion was rejected as 'palpably seeking tactical deception': RCD, 9 November 1960.

52 Quoted Kay, p. 112; *DT*, 4 October 1960.

53 Nora Beloff, *Observer*, 31 July 1966.

54 *a*. J. P. W. Mallalieu in *New Statesman*, 5 November 1960; *b*. also Roth (1977), p. 251, and n. 24*b*.

55 *Daily Mail*, 27 October 1960; Wigg (1972), p. 230; n. 54*a*.

56 Roth (1977), p. 252, says they cut their maximum from 110 to 90 after the PLP. Kay, p. 115, says Wilson hoped for 100 but expected only 70 (below any press estimate). Crosland to HG, n.d. but 21 October 1960: P.183. *Guardian*, 27 October 1960; *Spectator*, 28 October, for Wilson's supporters. (Crossman had Wilson's vote correct from the start, and HG's at the end; RCD 26 and 27 October 1960, 3 November 1960.)

57 *DT*, 21 and 27 October 1960; *DE*, 21 October 1690; RCD, 26 and 27 October 1960.

58 These four (and a fifth who was ill) were all strong Gaitskellites: David Logan to HG, 5 November 1960, P.153. One MP spoiled his ballot and a second abstained: n. 3*b*.

59 Then the right-wing vote was split, but the PLP was larger. Of the 18 Labour MPs under forty, 11 were known to be for HG and 3 against: *Reynolds News*, 6 November 1960.

60 Among his 'Objects' was 'A completely loyal Parly Cttee – thus the driving from the Cttee of Wilson, Greenwood, Lee': n. 12. But he expected Wilson to survive and thought Benn and Lee might both get on: n. 27*c*. If Wilson polled badly, HG thought of moving him to Colonies. But he did not do so, though Dalton proposed it too ('Wilson might take over "darkest Africa" ': n. 61*a*).

61 Dalton to HG, U.1.: *a*. 21 November 1960; *b*. 4 November 1960.

62 Not just because of the lower poll, for Gaitskellites gained: Healey by 46, Gordon Walker by 27. Wilson was 'shocked' at falling below third: Kay, p. 116.

63 Lee, a retiring vice-chairman, polled only 11, and Padley and Ness

Edwards also lost: *DT*, 2 November 1960 (cf. RCD, 3 November 1960). Two months later the PLP's defence group replaced Wigg by Paget as vice-chairman by 29 to 15: *DT*, 2 February 1961.

64 Macmillan (1972), p. 256; from his diary, 5 November 1960.

65 Interviews, Mrs P. Crane, M. Rees, P. Shore; and n. 25*c, d.*

66 At one Norwich rally Crossman thought 60 per cent of the 200 delegates were anti-CND, and 60 per cent anti-Gaitskell on these constitutional grounds: n. 25*e.*

67 Text in U.100C.

68 Interviews, Lady Gaitskell, Lord Aylestone, A. Crosland, Lord Gordon Walker, Lord Harris, D. Healey, R. Jenkins, T. Driberg — to whom he said so a year later. Jenkins was almost alone in thinking he would probably have gone out of politics entirely.

69 *Observer*, 6 November 1960.

70 *Daily Mail*, 24 October 1960.

71 HG to Mrs Helen Grant, 27 May 1960: P.152.

72 HG to Greenwood, 12 December 1960, P.142–2 (with note by Bowden); *The Times*, 15 December 1960 (reporting C. Mayhew); George Thomson in *Socialist Commentary*, January 1961 (fullest); n. 25a. (For earlier meetings, *DT*, 2, 3 and 10 November 1960.)

73 RCD, 14 December 1960; confirmed years later by an unnamed veteran quoted by H. B. Boyne in *DT*, 1 February 1958. Cf. above, p. 341 and n. 106; and below, p. 639.

74 In two Buckinghamshire seats on the same day, audiences of Labour activists favoured the leader by 120 to 5, and by 30 to 1: Robert Maxwell to *The Times*, 24 October 1960 and to HG, 26 October (P.145–4). In East Flint, Eirene White (no ardent Gaitskellite) found 2 unilateralists out of 50: to HG, 18 October 1960, P.145–6.

75 Archbishop to HG, 24 October 1960, P.145–4; Anne Noble, n.d., P.145–2; Cyril Robinson, 19 October, P.145–4.

76 J. Bradbury to HG, 6 October 1960: P.145–2.

77 They included old officials like Jim Middleton (once general secretary) or Mary Sutherland (women's organiser); ex-MPs like Philips Price; and several ordinary members who had belonged to the Party from the start.

78 In a T&GWU branch of BRS in South London unilateralists were 11 against 83 (with 16 Don't knows); at another in High Wycombe, 5 out of 220; in one engineering factory in Sheffield, 6 against 129; in another, 14 out of 400. Respectively, W. G. May to HG, 10 October 1960; J. D. Gunn, 7 October (both P.147–1); Andrew Lewis, 15 October (P.146–2); *The Times*, 8 November 1960.

79 Watson to HG: *a.* 5 January 1961 (P.118–7); *b.* 2 March 1961 (P.157B); *c.* 27 February 1961; *d.* reply, 28 February.

80 Following its old tradition, it declined to publish a letter signed among others by Professors A. J. Ayer, J. A. G. Griffith, H. L. A. Hart, Stuart Hampshire, and W. A. Robson, and by Dame Janet Vaughan: *The Times*, 11 October 1960, *Observer*, 16 October 1960.

81 HG to Dalton, 12 October 1960 (U.1). Cf. HG to Professor Arthur Schlesinger, Jr, 14 October 1960 (P.192); to Professor Leslie Lipton, 17 November 1960 (P.153).

82 GWD, 30 December 1960. The main sponsors were Blyton, Diamond, Irving, Mabon, Mayhew, Prentice and Reynolds, with Gordon Walker co-ordinating activities in the House, the constituencies and the unions. Other strong supporters were HG's Leeds colleagues Pannell, Healey and Alice Bacon; the old Party officials, Ginsburg, Woodburn and Carol Johnson; Keep Calmers like Strauss and Stewart; Douglas Houghton from the General Council; and HG's middle-class friends, Crosland, Jay, Jenkins and Soskice.

83 On CDS, Haseler (1969), Chapter 10; and n. 84*a*.

84 Lord Windlesham, *Communication and Political Power* (Cape, 1966): *a*. Chapters 4 and 5; *b*. p. 103; *c*. p. 135; *d*. p. 139.

85 Interviews, Sir William Webber, Lord Williamson, Lord Cooper; and n. 1*b*. Webber was chairman, Hayday secretary, and among the regulars were Birch, Carron, Collinson, Cooper, Sid Ford, Geddes, Greene, Ernest Jones, G. H. Smith, Ron Smith, and Williamson. George Brown came as deputy leader.

86 GWD, 30 December 1960. They met at Jenkins's house: Crosland, Harris, Jay, Mayhew, the host, the diarist and the leader. Gordon Walker thought if they lost again the Party would split. Crosland and Mayhew wanted simply to 'stand pat'.

87 NEC: *a*. 23 November 1960, M.43 (and n. 25*d*); *b*. 8 December 1960; *c*. Minutes of the joint meeting (Sec. no. 128) with the NEC papers for 22 February 1961 (and n. 50*c*); *d*. 23 January 1961, M.113; *e*. 22 March 1961, M.140.

88 On 8 December its representatives met those of the Shadow Cabinet, the respective chairmen Crossman and HG, after some absurd prior wrangling, each conspicuously avoiding sitting on the dais: *DT*, 9 December 1960, and nn. 87*b*, 25*g*.

89 Crossman says that only an accidental miscounting put Padley on instead of Wilson, and that HG at first wanted George Brinham instead of Driberg: RCD, 27 January 1961. Yet it was HG himself who proposed Driberg's name: n. 27*d*, *e*.

90 Characteristically Crossman frankly exposed his own motives and manoeuvres in his diary; equally characteristically he gave me free access to and permission to quote from it. Crossman the calculating politician would not have liked the use I have made of his generosity;

I think Crossman the candid political analyst would have approved.

91 To T. Balogh, 13 December 1960 (in RCD); also n. 25a.

92 RCD: a. 14 December 1960. (Privately Crossman thought Foot a bit embarrassed by CND.) b. 8 and 13 February 1961.

93 Crossman to Cousins, 10 February 1961 (in RCD).

94 All drafts (with HG's manuscript comments) are in file P.157B. Healey's was published in LPCR, 1961. Wilson: interview.

95 The renunciation was thus not sprung on him by Healey — contrary to Haseler (1969), p. 192, and to Thomas (1973), p. 287.

96 HG to Crosland, 28 February 1961: P.157B.

97 a. RCD, 8 February 1961; b. the dissidents had testified in the NEC to the amicable tone of all the meetings: n. 79b; c. HG confirmed that Cousins had said the same at Congress House (n. 27d, e); d. an impression shared by Strachey (n. 25j) and Driberg (interview).

98 Padley's amendments are in RCD; cf. n. 96. On his abstention: n. 99c.

99 W. T. Rodgers to HG, P.165: a. 28 February 1961; b. 2 March 1961; c. HG's reply, 1 March 1961.

100 One of the majority abstained in two previous votes.

101 DT, 24 February 1961; RCD, 3 March 1961 (a dozen abstained).

102 The minorities were: Castle, Driberg, Greenwood, Lena Jeger, McGarvey, Mikardo, Nicholas; plus Crossman, Eirene White, Wilson; plus Evans (NUR), Jennie Lee, Padley: Guardian, DT, 23 January 1961. Minutes: n. 87d.

103 E.g. Guardian, 23 February 1961 and 8 April 1961; DT, 23 February 1961, 4 and 6 March 1961; The Economist, 25 February 1961 and 25 March 1961.

104 Crosland to HG, n.d. (but 25 February 1961, 28 February 1961, 1 March 1961, respectively: P.157B, P.165, P.183) giving both his own and CDS views: also n. 99a. Crossman claimed that Strachey too would have agreed to his draft: n. 25j.

105 HG's interview with John Freeman in News of the World, 5 March 1961.

106 USDAW's 15th Annual Delegate Meeting: Report, a. p. 101 (and n. 50e); b. p. 94, cf. p. 108; (and n. 8d).

107 HG thought the differences between the drafts would be hard to explain to trade union conferences: n. 96.

108 HG on Brown and Callaghan, n. 99c; on Callaghan and Healey, n. 96. Crossman in RCD, 23 February 1961, on Brown in the NEC; 24 March 1951, on Callaghan in the PLP; cf. 29 December 1960 on 'Callaghan ... [saying] he would fight Gaitskell or anybody else who tried to work out a mere verbal compromise'. On 2 March 1961 HG told Freeman that Brown and Healey were 'far more prominent than

he in opposing the compromise': RCD, 8 March 1961, reporting Freeman.

109 RCD, 8, 13, 23 February 1961 and 3 March 1961. Crossman's draft had denied the need for conscription, but his account of the PLP meeting omits his old ally Wigg confirming HG's view: *DT*, 24 February 1961.

110 Interviews, G. Goodman, G. Woodcock.

111 RCD, 3 March 1961 (and, for Brown, 29 June 1961); n. 24*c*.

112 RCD, 21 February 1961, 21 March 1961; and n. 79*b, c, d*.

113 HG to Julie, 28 February 1961.

114 At one point the Chief Whip was canvassing for NEC support of the censure: RCD, 21 March 1961, reporting Mulley. Watson: n. 79*b*.

115 Press of 28 February 1961 (text in P.157B). Also n. 105.

116 HG too noted 'great indignation at his [Crossman's] behaviour': n. 113.

117 Crossman on a meeting the night before Cardiff: n. 25*j*.

118 *DT*, cf. *The Times, DH*, 11 March 1961; and n. 119*a*.

119 *Tribune*: *a*. 17 March 1961; *b*. 3 March 1961; *c*. 9 June 1961; *d*. 15 September 1961.

120 As John Cole (a Crossmanite) had already said forcibly in the *Guardian*, 8 April 1961. Cf. *Tribune*, 5 May 1961, 9 June 1961.

121 Editorial, 16 June 1961.

122 HG to Sam Watson, 28 January 1961 (P.157B); RCD, 21 February 1961; and below, pp. 657, 681.

123 AHD, 21 March 1961; RCD, 17 March 1961; *New Statesman*, 13 March 1961 (re Foot only); *The Economist*, 25 March 1961. (S. O. Davies voted in only one division, the others in two.) Jackson (1968), pp. 181, 185, 222–8.

124 One proscription list of fourteen MPs (Crosland's) included only one of the five (Davies) and only one prominent ex-Bevanite (Driberg): P.183. Also interview, Lord Harris; and p. 651.

125 *DT*, 21 and 22 March 1961; and interview, Lord Harris.

126 *Evening Standard*, 16 May 1961; Jackson (1968), p. 224 and n.; n. 24*d*.

127 HG told the ETU college on 28 June 1962 that for this reason the strongest pressure for discipline came from the back-bench loyalists, not from the leadership: transcript, p. 1.

128 Driver (1964), pp. 112–17; Duff (1971), pp. 170–8; Groom, pp. 384–6.

129 Driver (1964), p. 120.

130 Canon L. J. Collins, *Faith under Fire* (Frewin, 1960), especially p. 333. For recriminations between Labour and non-Labour supporters of CND: Parkin (1968), pp. 117–18; David Marquand in *Encounter*, January 1961.

131 Poll taken on 7-12 April 1961, just *before* Russell's statement.

132 *The Times, Guardian, DE,* 7 November 1960 (HG thought only 20 per cent and 30 per cent: *DH*).

133 Communists and Trotskyists—many with forged tickets—came to Derby from all over the Midlands: HG to P. Noel-Baker, 16 January 1961 (P.142-3), and nn. 10, 15.

134 HG to Don Chapman MP, 15 November 1960, P.142-2

135 Jenkins in Rodgers (1964): *a.* p. 119; *b.* p. 129.

136 HG's memorandum to John Beavan, editor of the *DH*, urging the paper to educate its readers about 'unity': 19 April 1961, P.166.

137 At a spring meeting at Crosland's flat which he could not date: interview.

138 RCD, 17 May 1961, reporting Martin's successor John Freeman.

139 RCD, 21 March 1961. They also voted 6 to 1 against withdrawal from NATO: *Guardian,* 16 March 1961. (Subscriptions had already dropped 40 per cent in 1960: above, p. 594.)

140 HG to Brewster Morris, 14 June 1961; P.166.

141 *a.* Interview, W. Padley; *b.* cf. nn. 84*c,* 142*a.*

142 Parkin (1968): *a.* p. 128; *b.* pp. 120-1; *c.* p. 118; *d.* pp. 119, 120, 124; *e.* p. 122; *f.* p. 132.

143 For, of 93,000 who voted unilateralist, 80,000 opposed Crossman–Padley and only 13,000 supported it—along with all the anti-unilateralists. Figures to the nearest thousand.

144 USDAW: n. 106*a.* AEU: n. 40*b.* For an excellent brief account of the different structures of the Big Six unions, Alan Fox, *Socialist Commentary,* February 1961.

145 Fox, *loc. cit.* In 1960 Bill Carron, the president, estimated 12 members and 6 to 8 allies: on BBC television, *The Times,* 6 October 1960.

146 See n. 40*b.* A majority (perhaps even three-quarters) of the non-Communist unilateralists must have switched.

147 *The Times, DH,* 5 May 1961. Two weeks later a pro-Gaitskell candidate for the AEU's seven-man executive defeated an opponent with Communist support by 5,800 to 4,200 on a 12 per cent poll (then high for that union).

148 *The Times,* 8 December 1960, 3 May 1961. Four left-wingers had been defeated meanwhile: n. 84*d.* The NUR vote would not be decided, however, till the evenly balanced national committee met in July.

149 Derek Marks, *Evening Standard,* 9 May 1961; his italics.

150 E.g. *New Statesman,* 3 March 1961 (cf. n. 142*b*).

151 In the latter the unilateralist vote was now down from 90 to only 16.

152 P.163. Watson could not, and they did not.

153 *New Dawn,* vol. 15, 24 June 1961, p. 386. HG wrote to thank Padley later.

154 In 1962 the NEC accepted Cousins's motion against testing; both in 1962 and 1963 Conference refused to find time for a defence debate.
155 Gordon (1969), p. 272. Cf. David Marquand in *Encounter*, December 1961, p. 4; and S. E. Finer, H. B. Berrington and D. J. Bartholomew, *Backbench Opinion in the House of Commons 1955–9* (Oxford University Press, 1961), p. 133.
156 Gordon (1969), pp. 275–7. He wrongly argues that minor concessions continued after Scarborough.
157 Above, p. 634.
158 Respectively, 61 per cent to 30 per cent and 37 per cent to 48 per cent: *DT*, 1 April 1961.
159 Memorandum to Fred Hayday and others, May 1962: P.163–2. He knew the PLP would support him over it: AHD, 10 July 1962.
160 Ian Aitken in G. Kaufman (ed.), *The Left* (Blond, 1966), p. 15. Cf. Gordon (1969), pp. 272–3; n. 142*e*.
161 'Given a little more time he would have had half his young unilateralist opponents standing on their heads': *Daily Mail*, 1 June 1961. Cf. *DH*, 2 June 1961; *New Advance*, July 1961; *DT*, 1 June 1962; AHD, 1 June 1962; R. Underhill, interview. Conferences: *Guardian*, 3 April 1961; *LPCR*, 1961, p. 15 (they voted 2 to 1 against NATO and for unilateralism, 3 to 2 for his resignation).
162 HG to Colin Smart, 11 April 1962; P.166–2.
163 Interview, Mr and Mrs D. Kennally. It was in Leeds town hall, probably on May Day 1960.
164 Interview, D. Healey.
165 He ticked this point on Wyatt's memorandum of 11 October 1960 (in P.118–7). See n. 47*a*.
166 *The Times*, 28 July 1961. The final vote was 70 to 18: *The Times*, *DT*, 14 December 1961.
167 Since 1945, every MP who lost the whip had (and has) regained it before the next election.
168 Instead, the NEC readmitted Zilliacus: Minutes, 29 September 1961, M.262, and 4 October 1961, M.3. Below, p. 690, for the one exception, a gesture against Bertrand Russell by the organisation sub-committee.
169 N. 27*c*. He thought perhaps fifteen MPs would go: n. 27*a*.
170 Crosland to HG, n.d. but 7 November 1960, and early July 1961, P.183; cf. nn. 1*b* (Gordon Walker) and 47*a* (Wyatt). The *New Statesman* and *Tribune* Left and the pacifists were explicitly excluded, and the highest figure suggested by anyone was twenty.
171 On 'Panorama', 2 October 1961: BBC. In June 1962 he saw no problem with neutralists who were 'not too aggressive' and accepted majority decisions: ETU transcript, p. 10.
172 *DH*, 6 July 1961. On the members' views, n. 148.

173 Scotland, South Wales and Kent, the strongholds of the Left, were joined by only three of the other seventeen area groups: Cumberland, Derbyshire and the craftsmen: *The Times*, 6 July 1961.

174 *a*. John Cole, *Guardian*, 14 July 1961; *b*. the view of most reporters, and his own, though *Tribune*, 21 July 1961, claimed 8 to 1.

175 Minutes of the BDG of the T&GWU, 13 July 1961, M.54, p. 30.

176 Respectively 5,733,000 to 2,003,000 and 5,570,000 to 2,048,000. It even voted for Polaris bases by 4,607,000 to 3,053,000.

177 *LPCR*, 1961, p. 173. Cf. *Tribune* editorials, 29 September 1961 and 13 October 1961.

178 John Cole, *Guardian*, 5 October 1961; also *The Times*, 5 October; *DE* (William Barkley), 5 October; *Daily Mirror* (Sydney Jacobson), 6 October; *Spectator* (Bernard Levin), 6 October.

179 All figures from Hindell and Williams (Chapter 22 n. 172), adjusted for the error there mentioned. That evidence demolishes Foot's claim that 75 per cent of the CLP vote was against HG: *Tribune*, 4 October 1961.

180 Duff (1971), p. 191. There were 30,000 'accidental' abstentions at Blackpool, where the CLPs cast 898,000 votes for the NEC and only 868,000 on defence. If that 'accidental' figure was the same in 1960, then there were 178,000 'political' abstentions at Scarborough, which if cast for the unilateralists would have given them 446,000 (48 per cent). They had 340,000 (39 per cent) in 1961.

181 HG to Sam Watson, 10 October 1961: P.118–7.

182 Gallup political index.

183 'Jim G.' to HG, 8 October 1961: P.118–7.

Chapter 24 Macmillan in Eclipse

1 HG interviews: *a*. with John Freeman in *News of the World*, 5 March 1961; *b*. in *Daily Mail*, 16 June 1961.

2 634 *H.C. Deb*.: *a*. cols 1025–36, 13 February 1961; *b*. col. 628, 9 February 1961.

3 *DT*, 16 and 17 February 1961; *Daily Mail*, 2 March 1961.

4 RCD: *a*. 23 November 1960; *b*. 11 May 1961; *c*. 24 April 1961; *d*. 15 May 1961; *e*. 17 May 1961; *f*. 14 June 1961; *g*. 29 June 1961; *h*. 28 June 1961; *i*. 13 July 1961; *j*. 28 November 1961; *k*. 2 March 1960; *l*. 20 October 1960; *m*. 8 February 1961, reporting Jacobson; *n*. 13 August 1959; *o*. 23 March 1960; *p*. 24 April 1961, reporting David Ennals; *q*. and n. 14*a*.

5 At the home policy sub-committee on 10 April: n. 4*c*.

6 On the NEC of 16 May and a private meeting the day before: n. 4*d*, *e*.

7 AHD: *a*. 10 May 1961; *b*. 22 June 1961; *c*. 15 November 1960;

d. 30 November 1961; *e.* 7 June 1962; *f.* 6 February 1962; *g.* 11 January 1961; *h.* 1 November 1961; *i.* 10 December 1959; *j.* 12 November 1959; *k.* 21 March 1961; *l.* 21 September 1961; *m.* 25 January 1961; *n.* 26 April 1961; *o.* cf. n. 94*i*; *p.* 25 January 1962; *q.* 17 May 1962; *r.* 1 June 1962; *s.* 17 April 1962; *t.* 10 April 1962; *u.* 21 November 1962; *v.* 5 November 1962; *w.* 23 October 1962; *x.* 29 October 1959; *y.* 26 July 1962, just before the debate.

8 M. Parkinson, *The Labour Party and the Organisation of Secondary Education* (Routledge, 1970), pp. 115–16; and nn. 7*b*, 4*b*, *c*, *d*.

9 RCD, 28 June 1961. A move to reaffirm total and immediate municipalisation was lost without a division in the NEC (n. 10*a*) and 'overwhelmingly' at Conference, without a card vote: *Guardian*, 3 October 1961.

10 NEC: *a.* 27 June 1961, M.199 at p. 17; *b.* 28 February 1962, M.107; *c.* 23 May 1962, M.168e, 27 June 1962, M.184 including the statement; *d.* organisation sub-committee, 20 March 1962, M.102, 104n; *e.* and 15 May 1962, M.140; 19 June 1962, M.151.

11 *a.* HG to Alderman George Hogkinson of Coventry (a left-winger), 11 April 1962 (P.166–2); *b.* Harold Wilson advocated it, too, but they were then on bad terms and had not consulted: Wilfred Sendall in *SE*, 26 June 1960; *c.* Interviews, R. Prentice, P. Shore.

12 627 *H.C. Deb.*, cols. 35, 44: 18 July 1960. At Durham (*The Times*, 20 June 1960): Hull (*Observer*, 26 June 1960, *The Times*, 27 June 1960); Cannock (*Observer*, 3 July 1960, *The Times*, 4 July 1960); Wolverton (*DH*, 3 September 1960).

13 *New Statesman*: *a.* 30 June 1961 (contrast n. 14*a*); *b.* 6 October 1961, editorial; *c.* 3 August 1962, A. Howard; *d.* 16 February 1962; *e.* 20 April 1962; *f.* 20 July 1962; *g.* 25 May 1962, 1 June 1962 (K. Martin); *h.* 23 February 1962; *i.* reported at length by Howard.

14 *The Economist*: *a.* 1 July 1961; *b.* 7 October 1961; *c.* 5 August 1961; *d.* 24 February 1962 (and n. 40*d*); *e.* 14 July 1962; *f.* and AHD, 10 July 1962.

15 ETU, 28 June 1962 (Chapter 6, n. 97); *a.* p. 18; *b.* p. 7; *c.* p. 11; *d.* p. 8; *e.* cf. pp. 12–13; *f.* using the same analogy.

16 Crosland to HG, P.183: *a.* n.d., probably July 1961; *b.* n.d., 7 November 1960.

17 To Robin Day on 'Panorama' (BBC): *a.* 2 October 1961; *b.* 26 February 1962.

18 *The Times*: *a.* 29 June 1961 (and n. 4*g*, *h*); *b.* 8 May 1961, political correspondent; *c.* 30 January 1961; *d.* 1 February 1962; *e.* 17 November 1961 (and n. 108*a*); *f.* 24 January 1961 (also *Guardian*); *g.* 20 February 1962 (and n. 31*b*).

19 Roy Jenkins in *Spectator*, 29 September 1961.

20 Official report to the Labour Party: U.87–4.

21 *DT, a.* 13 July 1961; *b.* 4 October 1961; *c.* 12 December 1961; *d.* 4 January 1962; *e.* 19 May 1962; *f.* 16 February 1962; *g.* 1 March 1962.

22 *LPCR,* 1961: *a.* pp. 148–9; *b.* p. 153; *c.* p. 154; *d.* p. 155; *e.* p. 252; *f.* pp. 150–1 (and n. 81*b*); *g.* pp. 192–3; *h.* pp. 165–6; *i.* 1962: pp. 126–30.

23 *Guardian: a.* John Cole, 4 October 1961; *b.* 3 October 1961; *c.* 5 October 1961; *d.* 2 October 1961, Cole; *e.* 27 October 1962; *f.* 3 November 1967; *g.* 4 October 1960.

24 It 'criticised Mr. Gaitskell for suggesting that his union's members played less part in Labour Party affairs than they should', referring to the T&GWU members on CLP delegations at Blackpool, and to Cousins's own electioneering efforts. It also hinted that HG's remark would encourage Tory pressures for 'contracting in': n. 23*b.*

25 *a.* S. Jacobson in *Daily Mirror,* 6 October 1961; *b.* and nn. 21*b,* 23*c.*

26 To John Freeman on 'Face to Face', 15 October 1961. The *New Statesman* would not print Denis Howell's letter quoting Cousins's 1958 speech; it is in *Campaign* (the CDS monthly), December 1961.

27 Respectively 1,611,000 to 4,531,000 and 2,453,000 to 3,759,000. (Ormskirk had sent the delegate who in 1959 was content to stay in opposition 'till 1964, 1974 or 1984'.)

28 Robert Carvel in *Evening Standard,* 5 October 1961.

29 HG to Oliver Woods, 9 October 1961: P.163.

30 In *Reynolds News,* 8 October 1961.

31 *Observer: a.* 15 October 1961 (Lord Longford); *b.* 11 March 1962; *c.* and n. 7*t.*

32 On becoming leader HG had endorsed Attlee's comment (above, p. 369), which echoed Roosevelt and typically left his hearers to decide for themselves what centre he meant.

33 On 'Ten O'Clock': BBC: *a.* 6 October 1961 to Geoffrey Goodman; *b.* 12 September 1961.

34 Before Scarborough he scored fewer than 44 per cent in half the Gallup polls taken (17 out of 35); after it only twice. Before that, he reached 50 per cent in only two monthly polls and approached it (47 per cent) in three more; afterwards, respectively 7 and 8 polls out of 23 (only one of the other 8 came after Blackpool). From mid-1960 fewer than 60 per cent of Labour voters thought him a good leader, over 20 per cent a bad one; but he was back to the old level of high approval in spring 1961, and of low disapproval a year later.

35 Ian Waller in *Sunday Telegraph,* 25 June 1961. Some of the 'Hampstead set' had strongly pressed him to do so: n. 16*b.*

36 Interviews: Sir Isaiah Berlin, Lords Diamond, Donaldson, Pannell and Rhodes, M. Stewart, W. Wyatt.

37 Smith (1904), p. 189; E. Kay, *Pragmatic Premier* (Frewin, 1967), p. 116.

38 Interviews: *a.* Lord Greenwood; *b.* M. Stewart; *c.* A. N. W. Benn; but HG in the end fully backed Benn in his battle to renounce his peerage.

39 But Wilson stressed the closeness of his co-operation with HG at this period: interview.

40 *The Times, DT: a.* 14 December 1961; *b.* 6 September 1958; *c.* 12 March 1960 (and n. 132*a*); *d.* 16 February 1962; *e.* 10 May 1962.

41 John Taylor and others to HG, 14 December 1961: P.118–7.

42 All did better than in 1960 (except Callaghan who lost 3), or in 1959 (except Lee who lost 25). The average increase was 24 since 1960, 41 since 1959.

43 Contrast his view of Bevan as Foreign Secretary and Wilson as Chancellor: p. 541.

44 Kenneth Younger, who did not stand in 1959, was followed out also by Chetwynd, de Freitas, Marquand, and Ungoed-Thomas.

45 Interview, Sir Ronald Edwards.

46 *a.* K. Robinson (unchallenged) in 631 *H.C. Deb.*, col. 722ff.: 2 December 1960; *b.* interview, Lord Jacobson.

47 RCD, 19 and 20 October 1960; HG to George Thomson MP, 24 October 1960, P.145–6. Also n. 46*b*, and interview, T. Driberg.

48 Correspondence in U.94.

49 *a.* Chancellor to HG, 26 April 1960 (U.94); *b.* Charles Forte to HG, 14 October 1960, reply 17 October (P.145–1); both 'Strictly Confidential' letters, cryptic in substance and conspiratorial in tone.

50 Hugh Cudlipp, *At Your Peril* (Weidenfeld, 1962): *a.* pp. 204–5; Chapters 21 and 23 for the *Mirror*'s battle for Odhams; *b.* pp. 227–9; *c.* pp. 232–3; *d.* pp. 228, 230.

51 He strenuously denies that he was influenced by being its paid industrial adviser: Brown (1972), p. 59. He scrupulously kept HG informed of all his dealings with the *Mirror* group.

52 Brown (1972), p. 59; Cudlipp, pp. 222, 229, 242 (wrongly saying the PLP critics were on the Left); correspondence from NUJ and John Harris in U.94.

53 Interviews, Sir Harold Wilson, Lord Jacobson; cf. HG in the House, 2*b*.

54 *a.* Interview, Mrs McNeal; *b.* and n. 46*b*, cf. n. 55*a*.

55 HG to Cudlipp (U.94): *a.* 14 December 1961, published n. 50*c*; *b.* June 1962.

56 H. Cudlipp, *Walking on the Water* (Bodley Head, 1976), on his own conflict with King.

57 Letters to friends: *a.* February 1961; *b.* 8 February 1961; *c.* 17 February 1959; *d.* n.d. but 13 February 1962.

58 E.g. HG to Surrey Dane, 28 March 1956; to Sir Vincent Tewson,

2H*

27 February 1958; to Douglas Machray, 18 December 1959; to Sir Christopher Chancellor, 7 April 1960. He was also absurdly suspicious of a new columnist on *Reynolds News*, who criticised the tactical wisdom of withdrawing the whip from Foot and his colleagues: Arthur Butler to HG, 5 April 1961. All U.94.

59 *DH*: *a.* 31 January 1962; *b.* 1 February 1962; *c.* 24 January 1961 (H. Hutchinson; also *The Times, Guardian*).

60 Cudlipp (now its chairman) asked it to do so as a result of the row: Cudlipp to HG, 1 February 1962. HG saw an improvement both immediate, as he told his old PPS, and long-term as he wrote to Cudlipp: nn. 61*a*, 55*b*.

61 HG to Arthur Allen: *a.* 6 February 1962; *b.* cf. n. 59*b*.

62 666 *H.C. Deb.*, 30 October 1962: *a.* cols 27, 30; *b.* cols 21–3; *c.* col. 19; *d.* cols 18–21; *e.* col. 714 (5 November 1962).

63 Interviews, M. Stewart, Professors W. A. Robson and W. Sayre; contrast n. 15*b*.

64 H. H. Wilson, *Pressure Group* (Secker & Warburg, 1961); Reginald Bevins (Postmaster-General in 1961), *The Greasy Pole* (Hodder & Stoughton, 1965), Chapters 10–13.

65 Correspondence kindly supplied by Mr Mayhew: *a.* Mayhew to HG, 1 May 1959; *b.* HG to Mayhew, 6 July 1962; *c.* and 11 July 1962, reply 12 July; *d.* Mayhew to George Brown, 5 July 1962; *e.* which refers to his having made the remark; *f.* reply.

66 Roth (1977), p. 261.

67 Interview, C. Mayhew.

68 Brown to HG, P.118–7: *a.* 'Monday' (i.e. 9 July 1962), reply 12 July; *b.* 'Wednesday', i.e. 11 July 1962; *c.* 24 July 1962; *d.* 31 August 1961, 11 September 1961, reply 13 September (cf. n. 73*e*); *e.* and n. 65*c*.

69 Howard in *New Statesman*, 27 July 1962 and 3 August 1962; *DT*, 29 July 1962. Mayhew to HG, 5 and 26 July 1962 and 24 October 1962; replies 6 and 27 July 1962, 29 October 1962 (all kindly supplied by Mr Mayhew). Mayhew wanted an immediate commitment; HG had a majority of only 3 votes for delay. (But he would unhesitatingly have accepted the majority view on Pilkington: n. 15*c*.)

70 *a.* Merlyn Rees's report, August 1962: NEC, September; *b.* interview, Lord and Lady Donaldson.

71 Interviews: *a.* Mr and Mrs B. Gillinson; *b.* Merlyn Rees; *c.* W. H. Goodwill.

72 Party political broadcast, 12 July 1961: U.87–4.

73 648 *H.C. Deb.*, 7 November 1961: *a.* col. 822; *b.* col. 820; *c.* cols 818–20; *d.* cols 807–8, 810, 819 (and n. 83*b*); *e.* col. 199 (Watkinson, Minister of Defence, 1 November 1961).

74 Also HG to Dan Jones MP on 5 May 1962 (P.142–4); and n. 7*e*.

75 657 *H.C. Deb.*, 3–10 April 1962: *a.* col. 1020; *b.* cols 1019–22; *c.* col. 1016; *d.* cols 719–33; *e.* cols 206–7; *f.* col. 1145; *g.* cols 647–50 (and n. 94*z*).

76 'Unsuccessful in substance', since the worst instability had occurred before it began: Sir Richard Clarke's report, analysed by Peter Jay in *The Times*, 27 June 1973; cf. n. 77*a.*

77 Brittan (1971), p. 261: *a.* he is a bit kinder to the policy; *b.* but he calls the White Paper 'a triumph of obscurity and an object of derision even in the Treasury corridors'.

78 To the Co-operative conference at Swanwick: *Guardian*, *DT*, 29 January 1962.

79 Like Brittan (1971, p. 258) he apparently thought a capital gains tax would have made pay restraint acceptable: AHD, 14 July 1961.

80 In the House: nn. 73*b*, 81*a.*

81 644 *H.C. Deb.*, 18 July 1961: *a.* cols 1074–5, 1082; *b.* cols 1069–72; *c.* col. 1080; *d.* col. 1082.

82 On TV, n. 17*a*; in the House, nn. 83*a*, 73*c*, 75*c*, 84*a.*

83 645 *H.C. Deb.*, 27 July 1961; *a.* col. 1718; *b.* cols 719–20; *c.* col. 723.

84 663 *H.C. Deb.*, 26 July 1962: *a.* col. 1742; *b.* cols 1744–5; *c.* col. 1821; *d.* col. 1818; *e.* cols 1750–1.

85 At Torquay: *Guardian*, 19 June 1962. Cf. speech at Nottingham on 27 January 1962.

86 The correspondence and his own notes for the debate are in file U.118. Cf. *LPCR*, 1962, pp. 126–30; Vig (1968), pp. 85–6.

87 HG to Callaghan, P.142–4: *a.* 19 June 1962 and 3 July 1962; *b.* reply, 29 June 1962; *c.* interview, Dr Jeremy Bray (Brown's PPS).

88 To R. T. McKenzie on 'Gallery', 19 July 1962: BBC.

89 At Derby on 14 January 1961: U.107 (the meeting wrecked by Trotskyites).

90 Walter Eltis in *ST*, 4 December 1977.

91 At Durham Miners' Gala, 15 July 1961: U.107.

92 Macmillan to Lloyd, 3 October 1961: in Macmillan (1973), p. 42.

93 For a full account, see Chapter 16 (by N. Deakin) in E. J. B. Rose (ed.), *Colour and Citizenship* (Oxford University Press, 1969).

94 Macmillan (1973): *a.* from his diary; *b.* pp. 75–7; *c.* p. 78; *d.* p. 82; *e.* pp. 299–301; *f.* p. 309; *g.* pp. 305–17; *h.* pp. 239–41; *i.* pp. 241–2 on it; *j.* pp. 243–4 (and n. 146*c*, *k*); *k.* pp. 172–5; *l.* pp. 146 and 152; *m.* pp. 153, 164, 173–4; *n.* pp. 153 and 168; *o.* pp. 153–66; *p.* p. 171; *q.* p. 177; *r.* pp. 123 and 335; *s.* p. 191, his italics; *t.* p. 195, his omission; *u.* pp. 187–9; *v.* p. 220; *w.* pp. 56, 63–4; *x.* p. 59; *y.* p. 108, his italics; *z.* pp. 424–5, 427; *aa.* p. 432.

95 649 *H.C. Deb.*, 14–16 and 23 November 1961: *a.* HG, col. 190; *b.* Butler, cols 689–91 (and n. 96*a*); HG, col. 797; *c.* Gordon Walker, cols 706–8;

d. Nigel Fisher, cols 779-80; *e*. cols 701-2; *f*. col. 32; *g*. col. 809; *h*. cols 1546-8; *i*. cols 188-91 and 1540-3; *j*. col. 794; *k*. col. 800; *l*. cols 792-803.

96 650 *H.C. Deb.*, 5-7 December 1961: *a*. Butler, col. 1183; *b*. cols 1433-6; *c*. col. 1495; *d*. col. 1173; *e*. Macmillan, col. 32, 31 October 1961; *f*. cols 1184-90; *g*. col. 1193; *h*. col. 1528; *i*. col. 1256; *j*. col. 1266; *k*. cols 1171-2.

97 As Jay pointed out (n. 96*b*) causing consternation on the Treasury bench (nn. 96*c*, 181*a*).

98 Gordon Walker's phrase (n. 95*c*) taken up by HG (n. 7*d*). Cf. Tory critics like Nigel Fisher (n. 95*d*), Sir John Vaughan-Morgan (n. 99*a*), Humphry Berkeley (n. 99b).

99 654 *H.C. Deb.*, 27 February 1962: *a*. col. 1205; *b*. cols 1222-8; *c*. col. 1276; *d*. Van Straubenzee, cols 1244-5; *e*. and cols 1246-7; *f*. col. 1271; *g*. cols 1532-4: 1 March 1962.

100 R. A. Butler, n. 95*e*; Attorney-General, n. 99*c*; cf. n. 99*a, d*.

101 HG speech, n. 96*d*. Cf. Macmillan (the Bill certainly would apply to them, 31 October 1961, n. 95*f*); Butler (it could not be done, 95*e*); Gordon Walker's reply (n. 95*c*); Hare (it might, n. 95*g*); HG and Thorpe on 'the complete muddle into which the Government have got' (n. 95*h*); Butler (it had been found quite impossible administratively but would be done if necessary, n. 96*f*; Grimond's reply, n. 96*g*); and Macmillan being embarrassed by HG at question time (n. 96*h*).

102 Paul Foot, *Immigration and Race in British Politics* (Penguin, 1965): *a*. p. 140 (cf. n. 99*e*); *b*. pp. 171-5; *c*. pp. 173-4.

103 Cf. Gordon Walker's comments, nn. 95*c*, 96*i*; and Tories attacking their excessive haste: e.g. John Harvey, n. 96*j*. (But cf. Rose, *op. cit.*, pp. 218-19.)

104 Minutes of the Jamaican Cabinet's special meeting on 11 January 1960: V.10.

105 HG in the House, n. 95*j*; in committee with figures, n. 96*k*. See Rose, *op. cit.*, Chapter 7.

106 Fisher (1973): *a*. p. 207; *b*. pp. 166-74 (and n. 94*g*).

107 *a*. HG to Percy Clark, 25 October 1962 (P.166), with a list of them; *b*. omitting this one.

108 *Tribune*: *a*. 24 November 1961 (and n. 18*e*); *b*. 28 April 1961; *c*. 12 May 1961; *d*. 25 May 1962; *e*. 11 May 1962 (and n. 13*g*).

109 Interview, Professor Austin Ranney (later President of the American Political Science Association). Both Michael Foot and Lord Noel-Baker thought it HG's best speech: interviews.

110 Dissidents numbered 25-30 (including old left-wingers like Marcus Lipton and Maurice Edelman) and doubters were perhaps in the majority: interviews, Lord Gordon Walker, R. Gunter, D. Jay, Caro

Johnson (then secretary of the PLP). Though George Brown felt as strongly as HG, the PLP put down a reasoned amendment instead of simply moving rejection, as HG would have preferred. See *DT*, 16 November 1961; and n. 102*b*.

111 It is therefore hard to understand why Sir Philip Allen, then deputy head of the Home Office, thought it might not have got through if it had been fought throughout with the same intensity: n. 112*a*, contrast n. 94*d*.

112 Butler (1973): *a*. p. 208; *b*. p. 234; *c*. pp. 232–4.

113 Some speculation in Chapter 27, Section iv.

114 Patrick Keatley quoting conversations with HG: *a*. in 1959, quoted Keatley (1963), p. 493; *b*. in December 1962, saying his first act in office (on Friday) would be to send troops to Lusaka (in n. 23*f*); *c*. also interviews, Sir Arthur Gaitskell, A. N. W. Benn, Lord Jacobson.

115 Interview, Lady Gaitskell.

116 612 *H.C. Deb.*, cols 62–3; 27 October 1959.

117 *The Times*, 25 November 1959, for Bevan's warning to the PLP, and for HG's anxiety to join. Bevan: also note 4*n*.

118 On HG's queries put to Macmillan, on 16 November 1959: n. 119*a*. Also in the House, n. 120*a*; and *DT*, 30 October 1959, 11 and 23 November 1959.

119 Macmillan to HG, P.139: *a*. 17 November 1959; *b*. 11 November 1959; *c*. 3 December 1959, answering HG's; *d*. 20 November 1959.

120 614 *H.C.* Deb., 24 November 1959: *a*. cols 211–12; *b*. cols 207–18.

121 Welensky (1964): *a*. pp. 153–5; *b*. p. 158 (Welensky's italics); *c*. pp. 158–61; *d*. pp. 171–4.

122 HG to Moffat, 24 November 1959: P.139.

123 Macmillan (1972): *a*. from his diary; *b*. pp. 141–2; *c*. p. 137; *d*. pp. 143–7 (and n. 121*d*); *e*. pp. 166–76, 295–300; *f*. p. 451; *g*. p. 457; *h*. pp. 449–53 (cf. Roth, 1977, p. 258); *i*. pp. 395–6 (and n. 143*b*); *j*. p. 401; *k*. p. 408, quoting telephone conversation with Kennedy; *l*. p. 404; *m*. 232.

124 Birkenhead (1969): *a*. p. 341; *b*. pp. 342–3; *c*. p. 347; *d*. pp. 357–60.

125 He had thanked HG during their talks for 'your obvious desire to cooperate if it is possible': n. 119*d*. Yet see n. 123*a*, *b*, *c*.

126 HG to Shawcross, 19 December 1959 (P.139); to another friend in the same month; and n. 7*i*.

127 615 *H.C. Deb.*, cols 1646–8: 17 December 1959.

128 See the long and anguished editorial in *DT*, 26 October 1960; n. 124*d*; cf. Macmillan in 629 *H.C. Deb.*, cols 29–31 (1 November 1960) and in n. 94*e*.

129 635 H.C. *Deb.*, cols 568–76: 22 February 1961.

130 655 *H.C. Deb.*: *a*. cols 1547–8 (15 March 1962); *b*. 5 March 1962:

PM, cols 31–4; *c.* cols 31–9; *d.* Gordon Walker, col. 63; Spearman, col. 292; Brown, cols 319–20.

131 Text of speech in U.100–C.

132 *DE*: *a.* 14 March 1960; *b.* 25 March 1960.

133 At Southsea, 6 April 1960; at Leeds, 1 May 1960: P.148 and U.100–C. For the NEC's performance, n. 4*o*.

134 Julius Nyerere, just appointed in Tanganyika, sent HG warm thanks for a stand 'very heartening to us in Africa': on 7 March 1961, U.107. For the Commonwealth Prime Ministers' views: n. 123*e*.

135 637 *H.C. Deb.*, 22 March 1961: *a.* HG, cols 449–57 (and nn. 7*k*, 136); *b.* PM, cols 442–6.

136 But he saw no case for her refusing UN supervision over South-West Africa (now Namibia), which she held under an old League of Nations mandate: 629 *H.C. Deb.*, cols 23–4 (1 November 1960).

137 At Leyton, 24 June 1961: U.100–C.

138 643 *H.C. Deb.*, 5 and 8 July 1961: *a.* cols 1457–67; *b.* col. 1466, on Angola.

139 Macmillan's voluminous memoirs contain no index reference to Angola and no relevant one to Portugal.

140 651 *H.C. Deb.*, 11 and 14 December 1961: *a.* col. 43; *b.* cols 736–47.

141 But HG too had doubts about the judgment of the UN representatives in the Congo: n. 7*l*. He almost certainly changed that view later.

142 Home had told him that the UN representative at Elizabethville was an 'American communist': n. 7*l*.

143 646 *H.C. Deb.*, 17 October 1961: *a.* cols 47–8; *b.* cols 38–9; *c.* 37–8 (and n. 149*a*); *d.* cols 35–46.

144 At Berwick-on-Tweed on 28 December 1961.

145 653 *H.C. Deb.*: 5 February 1962: *a.* col. 44; *b.* col. 51; *c.* col. 38; *d.* 8 February 1962: PM, cols 626–39; *e.* cols 630–2; *f.* 13 February 1962: cols 1120–2.

146 A. Schlesinger, Jr, *A Thousand Days* (Fawcett Crest edn, 1965): *a.* p. 273; *b.* pp. 354–66; *c.* pp. 476–8; *d.* pp. 449–59; *e.* p. 772; *f.* p. 458; *g.* pp. 775–6, 779–80; *h.* p. 746; *i.* pp. 747–8; *j.* p. 806. T. Sorensen, *Kennedy* (Pan edn, 1966): *k.* pp. 715–16; *l.* p. 684; *m.* pp. 682–90; *n.* p. 689.

147 At Leicester on 7 May 1961 (U.107) and n. 145*c*.

148 HG to Sir Geoffrey Vickers, 14 September 1961 (P.163–1); n. 146 *b* for the debate in Washington; n. 7*b* for HG's views.

149 HG's interview with CBS, 14 November 1961, transcript in U.87: *a.* p. 11; *b.* pp. 10–11, 14 (the fullest statement); *c.* pp. 12–13.

150 Optimistically, he hoped it might embarrass the Communists into getting rid of the Wall: n. 7*l*. Also HG to Herbert Morrison, 14 November 1961, P.163–1; and nn. 149*c*, 151.

151 *The Times*, 15 September 1961 (on the Shadow Cabinet's support for him); and nn. 33*b*, 22*g*, 143*d*.

152 He thought Cuba 'a disastrous error which is very well realised now', and blamed the China policy on American public opinion, not on the Administration itself: n. 22*g*.

153 HG, like Macmillan, still thought the West should open talks despite West German reluctance: n. 7*d, p*. Cf. his speech at the Socialist International: *The Times*, 25 October 1961.

154 McDermott (1972), pp. 225–8; Brandt in Rodgers (1964), pp. 137–8.

155 *a*. To the Socialist International in Oslo, 3 June 1962 (P.124–1); *b*. MS notes for his speech; *c*. he specified the Laotian Right, the Prime Minister of Thailand and 'some CIA agents' (cf. n. 94*h*); *d*. and n. 7*s*.

156 Including his present and former PPS, and the Chief Whip.

157 659 *H.C. Deb.*: *a*. cols 1530–2, 1551 (17 May 1962); *b*. col. 224 (8 May 1962).

158 For the United States view, n. 146*l*. For HG's, n. 7*s*. For the PM, nn. 94*k* and 159*a*.

159 658 *H.C. Deb.*: *a*. col. 693 (19 April 1962); *b*. cols 693–5; *c*. col. 1208 (3 May 1962); *d*. col. 814 (1 May 1962).

160 656 *H.C. Deb.*, 27–29 March 1962: *a*. col. 1558; *b*. col. 1017; *c*. and nn. 94*l*, 130*b*.

161 HG rightly denied that their reluctance was inconsistent with Labour's 1959 manifesto opposing any further testing by Britain: n. 17*b*. But it could be held inconsistent with Brown's speech, carelessly read (or carefully misread): n. 22*h*.

162 HG: *The Times*, 27 February 1962; nn. 7*f, s, t*, 17*b*, 149. PM: n. 94*m*. US: n. 146*d, m*.

163 HG: to the PLP, n. 21*f*; in the House, n. 145*e*; and n. 7*f*. PM: n. 94*a, n*.

164 HG: n. 7*s, t*, 17*b*. PM: n. 94*o*. In the House: nn. 145*f*, 99*g*, 160*b*, 75*e, f*, 159*b*.

165 HG: nn. 7*f*, 17*b*, 149. Brown was worried that opposing the British test but not the American would allow Macmillan to repeat his 'Lebanon' charge of 1958: n. 13*d*. But both men and all the NEC's international sub-committee agreed that the Party was so committed: its Minutes, 9 January 1962, M.13.

166 Sam Watson to HG, 21 December 1961, P.163–1; over a resolution drafted by David Ennals.

167 HG to Kennedy, 10 December 1962 (P.118–5) refers back to this letter.

168 Ben Bradlee, *Conversations with Kennedy*, reporting the President (Quartet Books, 1976), p. 62; and n. 146*f, n*.

169 Text of statement in P.167B. *Guardian, DH, DT*, 1 March 1962; and n. 10*b*.

170 AHD, 3 May 1962; and in the House, nn. 159*d*, 157*b*.

171 E.g. HG to J. C. Wells, 8 March 1962; to Colin Smart, 11 April 1962: P.163–2 (and above, pp. 498 and n. 41, 623, Chapter 22 n. 147).

172 HG to Brown, 25 January 1962: P.163–2.

173 Driver (1964), pp. 136–9; Duff (1971), pp. 237–9; contrast Canon L. J. Collins, *Faith Under Fire* (Frewin, 1960), p. 343, and Kingsley Martin, n. 13*f*.

174 HG, who was not on that sub-committee, would have been glad if Russell and Collins had left the Party, but was not for expulsion: n. 7*q*. Another who went to the congress, Lady Wootton, had known HG for over thirty years and thought him absurdly heavy-handed in conveying his displeasure: interview, and to HG, 21 June 1962, P.118–7. Minutes, n. 10*e*, *c*.

175 Driver (1964), p. 135; *DT*, 7 May 1962.

176 To Miss E. A. Strachan of Cheltenham, 26 June 1962; also to Michael Freeman of Hampstead, 16 May 1962: both P.163–2.

177 HG to Alan Thompson, 8 May 1962: P.142–4.

178 *SE*: *a*. 3 April 1962; *b*. 'Crossbencher', 18 November 1962; *c*. HG had feared the briefings were a device to silence him.

179 'Judgment and Control in Modern Warfare', *Foreign Affairs* (New York), 60. 2 (January 1962), pp. 196–212.

180 Interview, Lord Zuckerman; HG to Zuckerman, 26 December 1955: 'please consider yourself under contract for ... 1959 or 1960'.

181 652 *H.C. Deb.*, 25 January 1962: *a*. cols 474–5; *b*. cols 401–3.

182 The British government retorted that the Americans' new emphasis on conventional forces would make the deterrent less credible: n. 146*g*.

183 He welcomed it at Watford (*The Times*, 25 June 1962); A. J. R. Groom, *British Thinking about Nuclear Weapons* (Francis Pinter, 1974), p. 453, even suggests it had adopted many of his ideas. He underlined some similarities: to the ETU, n. 15*d*.

184 661 *H.C. Deb.*, cols 954–60: 26 June 1962.

185 *a*. At Huddersfield, n. 23*e*; *b*. and in the House, n. 62*b*. Privately he added that the fall of Krishna Menon, the Indian Defence Minister, was a welcome by-product of the attack: n. 7*u*.

186 *a*. AHD, 1 December 1962, reporting Kennedy; *b*. interview, Lady Berlin; *c*. at the White House, when she mentioned how worried HG had been, Kennedy replied: 'How does he think we felt?'

187 As he said an hour beforehand: n. 7*w*, n. 186*b*. For Macmillan's similar worries, n. 94*u*; for Washington's reaction to them, n. 146*h*.

188 Interview, D. Healey. HG took the Irish point from Hetherington, and used it in his lobby briefing; n. 7*w*.

189 Elie Abel, *The Missiles of October* (MacGibbon & Kee, 1966), p. 129; cf. n. 146*i*.

190 HG to Jean Mann, 8 November 1962: P.163–2. (That was true, but not the main point.)

191 File P.178: *a.* incoming letters; *b.* HG to J. Parsons, 29 October 1962; *c.* to Lady Snow, 29 October 1962.

192 From the election to June 1961 Macmillan's Gallup poll lead was always over 9 per cent, usually over 20 per cent; in the next year they were always within 3 per cent, HG usually ahead; in his last four months, HG averaged a 7 per cent lead. See below, p. 758.

193 627 *H.C. Deb.*, cols 1973–83: 28 July 1960.

194 Eden (1960), pp. 473–4.

195 On 10 March 1961: U.107 (cf. *DT*, 11 March 1961). Cf. 629 *H.C. Deb.*, col. 18 for another case: 1 November 1960.

196 Grimond to HG and reply, 7 December 1961, P.142–3; interview, J. Grimond.

197 *a.* HG to N. Kaldor, 21 March 1962 (P.163–2); *b.* ending: 'Honestly, you would do better to stick to economics!'; *c.* and n. 7*f.*

198 To Manchester University Labour Club, *Guardian*, 9 December 1961.

199 HG to Wyatt, P.170: *a.* 23 January 1962; *b.* 9 April 1962; *c.* and n. 7*f, t.*

200 Organisers: n. 7*f.* His papers contain no serious analysis distinguishing Labour, Conservative and marginal seats, or north and south, or inquiring whether defecting Tories would have gone Labour in the absence of a Liberal. The best studies are against him: H. Berrington in *Journal of the Royal Statistical Society*, series A, vol. 128, Part 1, 1965, pp. 45–8; M. Steed in Butler and Rose (1960), pp. 233–4; in Butler and King (1965), pp. 347–50; and in *New Outlook* no. 49, November–December 1965, pp. 8–10. HG relied heavily on the Gallup poll, which was tendentious on this subject.

201 HG to Julie, 24 August 1962, his emphasis.

202 They did not speak for months, but finally made it up: interview, W. Wyatt. *The Times*, 27 January 1962; HG to Arthur Allen, his old PPS and ex-MP for Bosworth, 6 February 1962 (kindly supplied by Mr Allen).

203 His memorandum to HG, 11 October 1960: P.118–7.

204 On average the Tory share of the poll again dropped by 19 per cent, Labour's by under 2 per cent. The mean drops in November 1961 were 19 per cent and 5 per cent; only once in the next spring did Labour drop over 5 per cent.

205 HG to S. Jacoby (a violently anti-Liberal Labour left-winger), 16 May 1962: P.163–2.

206 To Anthony Sampson on 13 November 1961 (in U.106: deleted by HG before the interview appeared in *Anatomy of Britain*, pp. 108–11). Cf. nn. 197*a*, 201.

207 HG to Crossman who was ill, 30 January 1962: P.142–4.

208 HG to J. Kuehl (an American friend of Julie's), 23 January 1962; P.163–2.

209 Interview, W. T. Rodgers (secretary of CDS, and the new MP for Stockton).

210 On 27 January 1962: U.100. He rather favoured nationalising chemicals: interview, Professor M. M. Postan.

211 Kilmuir (1964), p. 324. Macmillan had indeed foreseen a threat to his leadership: n. 94a, x.

212 Macmillan (1973), Chapters 2 and 4, especially pp. 63, 67–9, 89, 91, 99; and n. 112c. They show how shrewdly HG guessed at what had happened: n. 84b.

213 From a note written that evening (13 July 1962) by Bernard Gillinson, who kindly supplied it.

214 So Conservative MPs said in the lobbies: Charles Pannell, n. 84c. But then the Liberals would have tabled a motion, and the Left would have criticised HG: n. 14e.

215 E.g. Fred Bellenger to HG, 26 July 1962 (P.142–4). John Henderson, a Tory, describing its reception on the Labour benches: n. 84d.

216 So he told his daughter: interview, Mrs McNeal. For Macmillan's more favourable view of HG: interviews, A. Crawley, D. Ginsburg and Lord Harris (both quoting comments by well-informed officials), D. Wood (*The Times* political correspondent); cf. T. F. Lindsay, *Parliament from the Press Gallery* (Macmillan, 1967), p. 96.

217 Cf. 639 *H.C. Deb.*, cols 1609–18 (4 May 1961); 642, cols 211–15, 1683–8 (13 and 22 June 1961). 'Row': n. 7a.

218 Cf. 640 *H.C. Deb.*, cols 650–5 (11 May 1961); *DT*, 12 May 1961; and n. 7b.

219 'I felt strongly that not only should the truth be searched but the purveyors of lies should be punished': n. 94aa, and in the House, n. 220a.

220 667 *H.C. Deb.*, 13 and 14 November 1962: *a.* cols 191, 390–401; *b.* cols 401–11.

221 HG was prompted by Wigg, and legally advised by Arnold Goodman: Wigg (1972), pp. 238–9.

222 Interview, D. Ginsburg.

223 The Prime Minister later publicly contrasted his conduct with that of his colleagues: n. 94aa.

Chapter 25 The Common Market

1 Interview, Mrs McNeal: *a.* cf. n. 173e.

2 At W. T. Rodgers's house, where he met a group of CDS supporters

on 21 October 1962: *a.* Mr Rodgers's note, kindly supplied by him; *b.* and nn. 3*a*, 4; *c.* cf. n. 12*e*; *d.* and n. 12*m*.

3 Longford (1964): *a.* p. 243; *b.* p. 242; *c.* p. 238; *d.* pp. 233–4; *e.* pp. 234–5; *f.* pp. 240–1; *g.* p. 236; *h.* and nn. 113*a*, 155*a*; *i.* p. 232.

4 HG's speech to the World Parliamentary Association in Paris, 25 October 1962 (P.169) explains 'parochial'; cf. nn. 2*a*, 3*a*.

5 Private speech to the Commonwealth Parliamentary Association on 12 July 1962: transcript in P.167B: *a.* p. 3; *b.* p. 12; *c.* p. 5; *d.* p. 9; *e.* pp. 4, 11; *f.* p. 6; *g.* p. 10; *h.* pp. 7–8.

6 Lord Roberthall to author; *a.* without the analogy

7 State Department: *a* memorandum of his talk with David Linebaugh, the Labor Attaché, on 27 February 1953: no 741. 13/3–353; *b.* round table discussion chaired by Robert Murphy, 21 May 1956: no. 033. 4111/5–2156; *c.* William R. Tyler to Secretary of State, 14 February 1962: no. 64D 241 (BNA) Box 4033.

8 (*Manchester*) *Guardian*: *a.* 21 January 1957; *b.* 5 October 1960; *c.* in 14 September 1962; *d.* 21 September 1962; *e.* 4 October 1962 (John Cole); *f.* cf. n. 147*b*.

9 Interview, Lord Hirshfield.

10 Memorandum to President Kennedy, 11 December 1962, P.118–5 (of which Transport House had published a briefer version, which he gave on 3 December 1962 to the Anglo-American Press Association in Paris, paragraphs: *a.* 3; *b.* 8 and 9, his italics; *c.* 19; *d.* 22–5; *e.* 22; *f.* 39; *g.* 28; *h.* 30; *i.* 34; *j.* 33; *k.* 37–8; *l.* 48; *m.* 44, 50–4.

11 *DT*, 1 and 3 November 1956. Maurice Edelman to HG, 30 October 1957; HG to Wilson, 31 October 1957, and reply 4 November 1957; HG to Edelman, 7 November 1957: P.114–2.

12 AHD: *a.* 22 April 1959, 12 November 1959, 11 January 1961; *b.* 14 July 1960; *c.* 17 April 1962; *d.* 10 April 1962; *e.* 27 September 1962; *f.* 1 June 1962; *g.* 3 May 1962; *h.* 30 November 1961; *i.* 26 July 1962; *j.* 11 September 1962; *k.* cf. *The Times*, 10 September 1962; *l.* 23 October 1962; *m.* 5 November 1962, AH's italics; *n.* 1 December 1962; *o.* 21 November 1962; *p.* cf. n. 44.

13 645 *H.C. Deb.*, 2–3 August 1961: *a.* cols 1499–1500; *b.* Sandys, col. 1768, Foot, col. 1756, Harvey, col. 1579; *c.* col. 1496; *d.* cols 1662–3; *e.* col. 1508; *f.* cols 1501–2; *g.* col. 1503; *h.* cols 1505–6.

14 *a.* Interview, Harold Hutchinson; *b.* also (final phrase) n. 3*a*; *c.* reporting Brown.

15 Wilson's paper of 15 June 1960 is in P.167; Healey's, for the PLP on 26 June 1960, in P.149.

16 HG described these views in both Shadow Cabinet and PLP: AHD, 22 June 1960. A research department paper of 27 April 1961 argued against entry entirely on political grounds: P.157.

17 In the summer of 1961, Lord Longford recalls him saying half jokingly he was probably as favourable to it as Macmillan: n. 3*b*. Cf. Ian Waller in n. 18*a*, adding 'The Left suspect Mr. Gaitskell of being too enthusiastic'; Peregrine Worsthorne in n. 18*b*; Crossman, n. 19*a*; Sampson (1962, published July), p. 100 on Healey's view of HG; *DT*, 23 April 1961.

18 *Sunday Telegraph*: *a*. 26 June 1961; *b*. 16 July 1961; *c*. 27 September 1970 (Jay); *d*. 30 September 1962; *e*. 20 January 1963; *f*. 11 November 1962.

19 RCD: *a*. 13 July 1961; *b*. 17 May 1961; *c*. 14 June 1961; *d*. on HG rebuking him at a home policy sub-committee, contrast Roth (1977), p. 256.

20 HG to J. P. Nettl, 31 May 1961: P.163–1.

21 HG to Solly Pearce, editor of the *Leeds Citizen*, 21 June 1961: P.163.

22 Party political broadcasts, texts in P.167B: *a*. 8 May 1962; *b*. 21 September 1962.

23 661 *H.C. Deb.*, 6–7 June 1962, cols: *a*. 527; *b*. 513; *c*. 525; *d*. 521–2; *e*. 524–6; *f*. 524; *g*. 527; *h*. 780.

24 Miriam Camps, *Britain and the European Community 1955–63* (Oxford University Press and Princeton University Press, 1964): *a*. pp. 423–4; *b*. p. 424 and nn.; *c*. p. 468; *d*. p. 449; *e*. p. 451 (they did); *f*. pp. 499–504 (and n. 50*h*); *g*. pp. 468–71, 478–80, 503–4.

25 Cf. John Harvey (Conservative) on 'the sort of speech which must come down the right way however the future goes'; and Michael Foot: n. 13*b*.

26 HG to A. Albu: *a*. 10 August 1961 (P.142–3); *b*. 8 October 1962, answering Albu's of 4 October (kindly supplied by him).

27 In the same debate: n. 13*d*. For HG's view when Wilson did so again later: n. 70.

28 *LPCR*: *a*. 1961, p. 227; *b*. 1962, it is printed at pp. 245–51; *c*. pp. 154–65; *d*. pp. 193–4; *e*. p. 179; *f*. p. 174.

29 On his later shift to scepticism over the economic case: n. 3*b*.

30 On 'Ten O'Clock', BBC: *a*. 6 October 1961; *b*. 5 October 1962.

31 On 'Panorama', 2 October 1961: BBC.

32 *Observer*: *a*. 10 December 1961; *b*. 18 February 1962 (and *Reynolds News*, same day); *c*. 13 May 1962.

33 HG to Richard Marsh and Bert Oram, 12 December 1961, P.142–3. *DT*, 1 February 1962: cf. 19 February 1962, 7 and 8 March 1962.

34 HG to T. Cook of Ludlow CLP, 9 April 1962: P.163–2.

35 *a*. Roy Jenkins to HG, 1 May 1962; *b*. HG to Jenkins, 8 May 1962 (both P.167B); *c*. *ibid.*, 19 July 1962 (P.142–4).

36 *The Times*, 19 February 1962. The two new conditions were in his front-page *DH* article on 1 February 1962, but not when he talked on

TV about his United States trip, or in his question to the Prime Minister on 8 March 1962: 655 *H.C. Deb.*, col. 582.

37 Interviews: *a.* D. Jay (and n. 18*c*); *b.* Sir Robin Brook, Lord Diamond.

38 Interview, Sir Vaughan Berry.

39 Interviews, R. Jenkins, J. H. Lawrie, and n. 37*a*, *b*.

40 In Rodgers (1964), p. 130; interview; and n. 35*a*, suggesting that was the general view.

41 Interview, P. Shore.

42 *a.* To Pannell, 25 September 1962, kindly supplied by Lord Pannell; *b.* and nn. 2*a*, 10*c*, *d*, 12*e*, 43, 44.

43 To Strachey, 27 September 1962, P.167B (in Thomas, 1973, pp. 290–1).

44 To Brian Barder *et al.*, 31 October 1962, P.163–2.

45 Interviews (also with David Ginsburg, Fred Mulley and Lord Jacobson); and nn. 46*a*, *b*, 47*a*, 48*a*.

46 Macmillan (1973): *a.* from his diary; *b.* p. 122 (his italics); *c.* p. 62 (at Stockton, 2 April 1962); *d.* p. 65; *e.* pp. 119–21; *f.* pp. 121, 125; *g.* p. 129; *h.* and n. 50*j*; *i.* p. 134; *j.* p. 132, his omissions; *k.* p. 138, his italics; *l.* p. 130; *m.* p. 152; *n.* p. 139; *o.* pp. 347–8; *p.* p. 364; *q.* p. 128.

47 Brown (1972): *a.* p. 210; *b.* pp. 211–12; *c.* and interview.

48 Donnelly (1968): *a.* pp. 77–8; *b.* p. 82; *c.* p. 79; *d.* p. 81; *e.* p. 78.

49 Edward Heath's private statement reported to HG by 'Desmond' (Donnelly), 17 May 1962. Heath's earlier briefing was fully reported to HG by George Brown, 2 and 13 April 1962: both P.167B. Cf. n. 50*a*.

50 Nora Beloff, *The General Says No* (Penguin, 1963): *a.* pp. 133–4; *b.* p. 134; *c.* p. 168; *d.* p. 170; *e.* p. 140; *f.* pp. 140–1 (and n. 118*b*, *c*); *g.* p. 153; *h.* pp. 148–9, 156–61; *i.* pp. 150–2, 158–61; *j.* p. 136; *k.* p. 135.

51 Interview, Nigel Lawson.

52 E.g. *a.* to John Vaizey (anti), 8 February 1962, P.166; *b.* to Donnelly (pro), 5 December 1961; *c.* and 2 August 1962, both P.186.

53 HG to Cressida: *a.* 25 January 1962 (kindly supplied by Mrs Wasserman); *b.* 5 November 1962 (contrary to Roth, 1977, p. 263).

54 The international department's background paper no. 2, dated 3 July 1961 (P.167) has a manuscript note on it by G.B. attacking its tendentiousness; and HG forcefully said the same: n. 41. Cf. D. Ennals to HG, 12 July 1961 (P.119–2) and 20 July 1961 (P.167B).

55 In P.167B: *a.* HG to Shore, 29 May 1962; *b.* criticising it in detail as seriously overstating the restrictions on economic planning and measures against capital flight; *c.* cf. HG to William Pickles, 24 May 1962.

56 AHD, 1 June 1962, cf. 3 May 1962. It was by William Pickles, a right-wing Labour don at the LSE.

57 Neild to Callaghan, 27 March 1962 (P. 167B) with memorandum for HG. Meade's paper is in P.167.

58 *DT*: *a.* 13 April 1962; *b.* 9 May 1962 (cf. *Daily Mail*, same date); *c.* 26 September 1962; *d.* 19 September 1962; *e.* 1 October 1962; *f.* 29 September 1962; *g.* industrial staff; *h.* 4 October 1962; *i.* 30 September 1962; *j.* 8 November 1962.

59 At Fulham, 14 April 1962 (*ST*, 15 April): text in U.100.

60 Memorandum to be sent to Fred Hayday and others, attached to Hayday to HG, 7 May 1962: P.163–2 (his italics).

61 A month later he was again pessimistic about de Gaulle: n. 46*a, e.*

62 Interview, F. Mulley.

63 HG to Dan Jones MP, 25 September 1962: P.142–4.

64 Interview, Lord Longford.

65 HG in the House, n. 23*b*; and in nn. 12*f, g*, 66*a, b*; interviews, J. Meade, Lords Diamond, Longford and Roberthall; Cecil King in *ST*, 23 February 1969, reporting HG 'talking to a Professor Meade'.

66 HG to Hall, P.163–2: *a.* 15 October 1962; *b.* 30 October 1962.

67 *a.* But when asked after Brighton whether Labour's five conditions could be met, he sounded hesitant about the planning one; *b.* to Norman Hunt on 'The World Today', 4 October 1962: BBC.

68 On his concern with it, interviews: *a.* J. Callaghan; *b.* D. Ginsburg; *c.* Lord Kaldor.

69 HG to Thomas Balogh: *a.* 19 June 1962 (P.185); *b.* 19 October 1962 (P.167B).

70 Letter to a friend, 7 June 1962; AHD, 17 May 1962, 7 June 1962. On Wilson earlier: p. 706, n. 13*d.*

71 Thus it would be an 'outrageous' breach of a moral obligation to the poverty-stricken West Indies to sacrifice their sugar: n. 13*e.* And 'Lancashire might love it if we just followed the European terms, but it would be a betrayal of Hongkong': n. 12*d.*

72 But privately he saw 'not the slightest likelihood' of a break-up 'in the immediate future': to Dr Rita Hinden, 24 October 1962, P.166.

73 HG to Lady Rhys-Williams, 24 September 1962 (P.182), approving her letter to *The Times*, 20 September 1962. He later opposed any common currency arrangements on this ground in talking to Anthony Crosland: n. 74.

74 Undated note in Crosland's papers, probably on 20 December 1962: kindly supplied by Mrs Crosland.

75 To HG, 21 September 1962: P.182.

76 HG to Ray Steding, 20 September 1962, P.167B.

77 On this he was much influenced by Leonard Beaton of the *Guardian*: n. 1.

78 He told his old friend Marcus Fleming in the IMF that he had done so: 24 July 1962, P.167B. For the occasion: above, p. 689.

79 Interview, T. Driberg, who accompanied him to Oslo.
80 Publicly he called it 'silly' and 'foolish': n. 23*f*. 'Idiotic': n. 5*f*.
81 Griffiths (1969), pp. 135–6. Griffiths was a Marketeer.
82 Interview. For his suspicion of the Europeans, also: Sir Robin Brook, A. Crawley, R. Frost, Lord Kaldor, J. Meade, P. Rosenstein-Rodan, P. Shore, Mrs S. Williams, G. Thomson (reported by Sir Alexander Spearman). Crossman said (when promoting Wilson's leadership campaign after HG's death) that HG in December 1962 made Wilson chairman of a committee to assess whether the EEC might not become politically acceptable after de Gaulle and Adenauer went: Roth (1977), p. 269.
83 Interview, Professor Meade.
84 Added in his own writing to typed summary of speech in Oslo (P.124–1). Cf. *The Times*, 4 June 1962.
85 Interview, Barbara Castle; Crosland's note, n. 74; and in the House, nn. 13*g*, 23*e*.
86 He thought a veto for Britain plus two Scandinavian countries might do: nn. 12*f*, 5*c*. This was not a trivial change; when conceded by Heath in December 1962, it 'was very well received' by the Six: n. 24*c*.
87 To Reading University Socialist Society: *The Times*, 23 June 1962.
88 The four questions raised at Fulham related to colonial produce and manufactures, the CAP, and the veto: n. 59.
89 *The Times*, 9 May 1962; cf. *Guardian*, *DT*, and n. 32*c*.
90 *Newsbrief* no. 7 (June 1962), in P.169.
91 Mulley to HG, 5 June 1962: P.142–4.
92 So did Brown: n. 23*h*. HG: n. 12*f*.
93 AHD, 7 June 1962; letter to a friend, 7 June 1962. Both the press and later commentators thought it confirmed that he was mildly pro-entry: nn. 94*a*, *b*, 24*d*.
94 *The Economist*: *a*. 14 July 1962; *b*. 21 July 1962; *c*. 16 June 1962; *d*. 13 October 1962; *e*. 6 October 1962; *f*. for some other cynical errors, 7 October 1961, 12 May 1962.
95 *New Statesman*: *a*. 20 July 1962; *b*. Anthony Howard, 20 April 1962; *c*. and 28 September 1962; *d*. and 5 October 1962; *e*. 12 October 1962 (Barbara Castle).
96 AHD, 10 July 1962; also 26 July 1962, and n. 5*g*.
97 To R. T. McKenzie on 'Gallery', 19 July 1962: BBC transcript, P.10.
98 He, like Macmillan, thought Menzies not the Canadian Premier 'the key to the situation': n. 46*a*, *g*, and AHD, 10 July 1962.
99 HG to Arthur Calwell ('CONFIDENTIAL'): *a*. 3 August 1962, P.167B; *b*. 26 September 1962, P.142–4; *c*. 6 December 1962, P.169.
100 Lord Blyton; cf. n. 108.
101 At the Conservative Conference at Llandudno: *DT*, 15 October 1962.

102 He also mentioned those reactions to CDS on 21 October: n. 2*a*.

103 HG to Frau Lilo Milchsack, 7 September 1962, P.163–2; and interviews, Lady Gaitskell, Mrs McNeal, Sir Maurice Bowra.

104 Interviews: *a*. Sir Isaiah and Lady Berlin; *b*. Michael Foot.

105 Don Cook, who interviewed HG on 18 October 1962, in *New York Herald Tribune*, 21 January 1962; *a*. and nn. 104*a*, 106.

106 HG, after making up his mind, told David Wood, *The Times* political correspondent: 'There are no political advantages': interview.

107 *Guardian*, 16 July 1962; *DT*, 17 July. Norway was the prospective tenth.

108 HG to Robert Edwards MP, 25 July 1962: P.167B.

109 To John Murray, 18 September 1962: P.163–2.

110 *Observer*, 9 September 1962; *The Times*, 11 September; and nn. 12*j*, 111.

111 HG's interview with John Beavan: *Sunday Pictorial*, 16 September 1962.

112 For Nash: Brown, n. 47*b*, Sir Harold Wilson and Lord Pannell; for Lee, Denis Healey (interviews). For Lall, Roy Jenkins in *The Times*, 20 January 1973, in Jenkins (1974), p. 179, and interview; also interviews, A. Crosland, Lords Gladwyn, Harris and Roll, F. Mulley; and nn. 47*b*, 48*a*, 50*k*. Lee favoured British entry in principle, and Lall later came to do so.

113 David Wood (see n. 106) in Rodgers (1964); *a*. p. 156; *b*. p. 158; *c*. and *The Times*, 11 September 1962.

114 Interviews: *a*. Sir Harold Wilson; *b*. D. Healey.

115 HG to Dick Taverne MP, 25 September 1962: P.142–4.

116 Macmillan (1973), pp. 131–7; as usual he assumed that anyone who crossed him — in this case Menzies — was concerned solely with party politics.

117 From n. 44. Those thinking Macmillan's conduct a major influence on HG's also included Lord Pannell (n. 168), D. Ginsburg, K. Robinson, Mrs S. Williams (interviews); and n. 118*a*.

118 Henry Fairlie in *Spectator*: *a*. 28 September 1962; *b*. 12 October 1962; *c*. 4 January 1963 ('neutralism' retracted).

119 *a*. Interview, Lord Harris; *b*. HG was as suspicious of Macmillan as Macmillan was of everyone.

120 Lady Gaitskell in 323 *H.L. Deb.*, col. 471, 28 July 1971, and interview; and n. 48*b*.

121 HG to Tom Hockton (a Gaitskellite and former parliamentary candidate), 27 September 1962. Also to Kenneth May (another), 8 October 1962: both P.168.

122 Colin Gray to HG, 16 October 1962 and reply, 17 October 1962: P.163–2.

123 Above, p. 72. The result might well have been the same. John Stonehouse, secretary and organiser of the anti-Market MPs claimed 155 against 40 Marketeers: *DT*, 24 September 1962, and n. 95*c*. Privately, the Marketeers claimed 80 or 90 but thought only 20 really firm: n. 124*a*.

124 EEC diary of Austen Albu MP, kindly supplied by him: *a*. 18 and 19 September 1962; *b*. 21 September 1962; *c*. 16 September 1962; *d*. 27 September 1962; *e*. 'L.P. Confce'; *f*. 22 September 1962; *g*. 31 October 1962.

125 His interview with Beavan (n. 111): it had already *a*. proposed that course for these countries, the Africans and the West Indians; *b*. and used the final phrase.

126 Macmillan interpreted the next passage as indicating that HG was 'against going in on *any* terms', not mentioning that it was specifically about federation: n. 46*a*, *k*. At the Conservative Conference he called it 'prattle' and 'nonsense': n. 24*b*.

127 He was a little put out when Hetherington pointed out a few weeks later that during the Cuban missile crisis Kennedy called the senators from Texas and California to Washington: AHD, 5 November 1962.

128 *SE*: *a*. 23 September 1962; *b*. 30 September 1962.

129 Most letters in P.168. Cf. Driberg to HG 'Tuesday' (25th) on the reception of the broadcast: P.142–4. Many use phrases like 'a marvellous impression of deep sincerity and mastery' (J. Hills); the first politician who 'has given us a hint or clue' (C. F. Preston); 'That's the man for us' (E. F. R. Wilson, speaking for nine anti-Labour viewers).

130 On the *Herald*, interview, Lord Jacobson (above, p. 669).

131 Interviews, A. N. W. Benn, A. Crosland, Mrs S. Williams.

132 HG to Mrs J. P. Cannon, 26 September 1962 (P.167B); nn. 1, 68*c*.

133 *a*. HG to Bill Carron, 4 October 1962 (P.168); *b*. cf. n. 43.

134 To the CDS group on 21 October 1962 (n. 2*a*) and to Kennedy in December, quoting Brown and Jenkins (above, p. 724, and n. 10*d*).

135 Ian Aitken said fifteen would refuse so to vote: *DE*, 19 September 1962. Albu's friends thought twenty were firm.

136 So Jenkins told the Labour Marketeers: n. 124*d*. Also nn. 58*c*, 95*c*.

137 Shore consulted HG, whose copy (P.167) has innumerable scribbled amendments of his, removing many extreme passages. Cf. nn. 41, 58*d*, *e*.

138 Interviews: *a*. R. Gunter; *b*. W. Padley; *c*. and n. 124*e*.

139 James Margach, *ST*: *a*. 30 September 1962; *b*. and n. 58*f*, *g*; *c*. 7 October 1962; *d*. cf. *The Times*, political correspondent 4 October, labour correspondent 5 October; *e*. and n. 95*d*, *e*; *f*. and n. 95*d*.

140 Harold Wilson, chairman of the Party, was also reported to be a member: nn. 41, 124, 58*f*; but is not in NEC, n. 141*a*.

141 NEC–M: *a.* 28 September 1962, M.242; *b.* and M.245; *c.* 3 October 1962, M.8.

142 Driberg in *Sunday Citizen*, 30 September 1962. *DT*, 1 October 1962 mentions four abstentions, including Mikardo, who thought it 'hypocritical' to suggest the conditions could be met. Ian Waller (n. 18*d*) says Castle, Driberg, Greenwood and Mikardo abstained; if so, Nicholas the T&GWU member did not.

143 Sam Watson had cunningly flattered Crossman into drafting the pro-Market amendments: Longford, reporting both men, n. 3*c.*

144 Alan Watkins, n. 128*b*. Shore did not think the changes significant: interview.

145 Interviews, Lord George-Brown, R. Gunter, F. Mulley, Sir Harry Nicholas, W. Padley (for Watson), Lord Pannell, R. Underhill; and n. 58*e*.

146 Reported in interviews, J. R. L. Anderson, Lords Hirshfield, Pannell and Walston.

147 Interviews: *a.* Walter Padley; *b.* Sir William Webber; *c.* R. Gunter, Lord Hirshfield.

148 Interviews, P. Clark, F. Mulley, Sir Harry Nicholas, R. Underhill. For right-wing MPs and NEC trade unionists indignant at an alleged breach of a negotiated agreement: *The Times*, 4 and 5 October 1962.

149 Interviews, Mrs Sam Watson, Lady White; n. 48*c*. Barbara Castle, Lord Harris, Clark and Underhill recalled the charges but denied or did not vouch for them. Padley thought Watson did feel betrayed.

150 Interview, R. H. S. Crossman.

151 Challenged on that contradiction on television, HG replied that it was 'essential... to blow away the cobwebs' of propaganda: n. 67*b*.

152 Crosland's obituary of HG on BBC television, kindly supplied by Mrs Crosland.

153 William Barkley in *DE*, repeated in *Evening Standard*, 19 January 1963.

154 Beloff (who was present, and a passionate Marketeer), says the speech was 'tremendously popular with the rank and file': n. 50*e*.

155 *a.* Lord Pannell's memorandum; *b.* 'tide', also n. 14*a*.

156 *The Times*, 1 October 1962. Also nn. 133*a*, 67*b*.

157 Fitch to HG, 13 October 1962 (P.167B), answering a letter not in the Papers; and n. 26*b*.

158 E.g. HG to Postan, 8 October 1962, P.167B; and nn. 30*b*, 43.

159 Roy Jenkins in Rodgers (1964), p. 131; and nn. 3*f*, *a*, and 48*d*, *b*.

160 Ronald Stevens, *DT* industrial correspondent, 5 October 1962 on 'the suspicion that Mr Gaitskell has deserted his old friends in the knowledge that they will not desert him'. Cf. interviews, Lord Diamond, J. Callaghan.

161 HG to Cooper, 4 October 1962 (P.168); n. 133*a*; Webber's letter in his possession.

162 To F. V. Pickstock, chairman of CDS, 20 September 1962, P.167B; and nn. 2*a*, 44.

163 Beaverbrook to HG, 6 December 1962, and reply 12 December: P.118–7. Taylor (1974), p. 827: those suggestions may date from this period, though Macmillan's diary 6 June 1962 (Macmillan, 1973, p. 122) already refers to Montgomery's name being used. HG also reported that the Hon. Leo Russell was organising a committee: a list of people approached is in P.167B.

164 *DT*, 22 September 1962; and n. 124*f*. But it did provide half the votes for ASSET's demand for a general election.

165 Interview, Frank Cousins. (Lord Cooper and Sir William Webber wrongly supposed it had all been prearranged between them.)

166 *a*. Len Williams (by then general secretary of the Party) to HG, 11 October 1962 (P.167B); *b*. and n. 141*c*.

167 Interviews, G. Goodman (Cousins's biographer), Lady Gaitskell; Stewart (1968), p. 113; cf. n. 113*b*.

168 Pannell to HG, 26 September 1962: P.142–4.

169 *a*. Mayhew to HG, 24 October 1962; *b*. reply 29 October: P.142–4.

170 Cf. Trevor Evans, *DE*, 26 September 1962.

171 Hugh Massingham, n. 18*f*; cf. nn. 12*m*, 94*e* and *Topic*, 4 August 1962.

172 For a summary of their new intransigence, n. 173*a*; cf. 173 *b*. The same inference was drawn by HG, and Hetherington: n. 12*m*, *n*. It is broadly confirmed by Camps, pp. 462–8 and Beloff, pp. 142–7.

173 666 *H.C. Deb.*, 7 and 8 November 1962: *a*. Healey, col. 1101; *b*. cf. Brown, col. 1176; *c*. cols 1002–23; *d*. col. 1262; *e*. col. 1021; *f*. Heath, col. 1289; *g*. col. 1023.

174 Interviews, D. Ginsburg, F. Mulley (who thought he was concerned about American criticism); contrast nn. 3*f*, 114*b*.

175 To Donnelly, 29 October 1962, P.186; and n. 53*b*.

176 The speech was highly praised by Tories: Sir John Barlow called it his best (to HG, 7 November 1962, P.142–4) and Colin Welch described it as 'very, very brilliant ... an extraordinary performance': n. 58*j*.

177 In December he still thought such an election unlikely, since the voters had other interests: n. 10*a*.

178 Tyerman quoted these phrases in his first reply (n.d.), and then wrote (23 October 1962) to a quite unmollified HG: 'you still hate being called, or treated as, a politician ... [and] worse than being called an unsuccessful politician is to be called a successful one': P.167B.

179 Quotation from n. 124*d*. Cf. HG to I. R. Thomas 24 September 1962: P.181.

180 'We will take that hurdle when we come to it ... We won't pursue it ... no comment ... I really don't wish to discuss this matter now': n. 67*b*.

181 Macmillan's smear at Llandudno was quoted by Taverne (a Labour Marketeer) at n. 173*d*; for HG's repudiation, n. 173*e*. Fairlie made it n. 118*b*, withdrew it 118*c*, and finally (and inconsistently) assessed HG as 'the creature of an accumulation of political circumstances' which predetermined his choice: Fairlie (1968), pp. 79–80. Some of HG's strongest critics never believed it: n. 94*e*.

182 In the conclusion of his obituary in *Tribune*, 25 January 1963.

183 AHD, 1 December 1962, reporting Kennedy. Cf. A. Schlesinger, Jr, *A Thousand Days* (Fawcett Crest edn, 1965), pp. 772–3 for Kennedy's views (not all so helpful to HG).

184 Televised on 'Dinner Party' (with Lord Boothby as host): *The Times*, 16 October 1962. Press comments: e.g. *Washington Post* editorial (quoted *Guardian*, 26 September 1962); *New York Herald Tribune* editorial, 4 October 1962.

185 Acheson had raised a furore in Britain by saying at West Point on 5 December that she had 'lost an empire and not yet found a role'.

186 HG to Milton Katz, 9 October 1962: P.167B. Schlesinger, p. 774, on Ball and the pressure. Ball was to draft Kennedy's reply to the memorandum from HG, who died before the answer was ready: George Ball, *The Discipline of Power* (Bodley Head, 1968), p. 85.

187 Interview with an official.

188 T. Balogh to HG, 'secret', n.d. but early October 1962, reporting a contact in the Elysée. Interviews, D. Healey, Lady Gaitskell. Lord Longford says HG did not think British and French views could be reconciled (but did not expect a veto): n. 3*i*.

189 Interview, Lord Harris. Beloff, p, 156, is wrong to say he asked to see de Gaulle: E. Burin des Roziers, then Elysée Secretary-General, to the author.

190 From n. 10*l*. Couve kept no record and remembers only HG's hostility to British entry: letter to author. Lady Gaitskell recalls that it was Couve who convinced HG that France would keep Britain out, making the whole question academic. Cf. interview, G. Keeling.

191 Camps, p. 469n. HG is said to have told Pompidou that Labour would win the election, and would then negotiate associate status: interview, Professor Léo Hamon (an old friend of the present author, and in late 1962 a Gaullist deputy with excellent governmental contacts).

192 HG to J. A. Hands, 6 December 1962, P.163-2. Cf. nn. 46*o*, 24*g*, 50*i*, 173*a*; Sampson (1967), pp. 214–17; A. Grosser, *French Foreign Policy under de Gaulle* (Boston: Little, Brown, 1967), p. 89.

193 He had set up a committee to prepare for this with Wilson as chairman, Callaghan, Healey and Jay from the PLP, James Meade and John

Murray from outside, and Peter Shore as secretary: HG to Meade, 15 and 24 October 1962 (P.167B); to Murray, 19 October 1962 and 12 December 1962 (P.187); memorandum from Balogh in P.167B.

194 *Spectator*, 27 July 1962: and nn. 94*b*, 173*f*.

195 In the House: n. 173*g*. To Kennedy: n. 10*i*.

196 HG to A. B. Pinniger, 26 September 1962: P.167B.

197 Above, pp. 317–18, cf. pp. 218–20.

198 Interviews: *a*. Lord Harris, P. Shore; *b*. A. N. W. Benn, J. B. Orrick, Lord Kaldor and Lord Roberthall to author.

199 Interviews, A. N. W. Benn, J. Callaghan, R. Jenkins, Carol Johnson, Mrs McNeal and n. 198*a*.

200 Interviews, R. Jenkins, Lord Pannell.

201 Interviews, Lords Gordon-Walker, Jacobson and Shackleton, W. Wyatt; and n. 37*b*.

202 Interviews, F. Cousins, D. Healey, and nn. 198*a*, 169*a*.

203 They met, with Bill Carron and others, at Desmond Hirshfield's home on the evening of 18 October: n. 3*f*.

204 Ronald Butt, *ST*, 10 December 1977.

Chapter 26 In Sight of the Promised Land

1 This section was assisted by interviews with Mr and Mrs A. Allen, J. R. L. Anderson, Sir Isaiah Berlin, Lords Briggs, Diamond, Greenwood, Pannell, Rhodes and Walston; A. Crosland, R. Crossman, Lord and Lady Donaldson, Mrs Duffield, Sir Arthur Gaitskell, Lady Gaitskell, Mrs Gillinson, G. V. Keeling, Mrs McNeal, M. Muggeridge, R. Owen, R. Prentice, A. Ranney, M. Stewart, H. Tout, Mrs Sam Watson, Lady White, Mrs Shirley Williams, Miss B. Woolgar, Lady Wootton, W. Wyatt, Sir Kenneth Younger.

2 Muggeridge in *Evening Standard*, 21 January 1964.

3 *LPCR*, 1961, p. 194.

4 Jenkins (1974), p. 173.

5 Notably a deputation in 1962, led by Bertrand Russell and Alex Comfort.

6 Interview, Professor M. M. Postan; Roy Jenkins, reported RCD, 15 February 1963.

7 Interview, Lady Donaldson.

8 Interview, Mrs Skelly.

9 James Griffiths: *a*. to author, and interview; *b*. Griffiths (1969), p. 138.

10 Granada TV interview on 28 July 1961: in U.87.

11 Interview, Geoffrey Goodman.

12 Peter Walker in Oxford, November 1976.
13 Interviews: *a.* Lady Bacon; *b.* Lord Pannell; *c.* J. Callaghan, Sir Harry Nicholas, Mrs Skelly.
14 Interview, Mrs Grieveson; and n. 15*a*.
15 *DE*: *a.* 23 May 1962; *b.* 20 June 1962 (interview with Mrs Gaitskell and Mrs Butler); *c.* 19 August 1962; *d.* 26 September 1962 (Trevor Evans).
16 A. E. Skerry of Plymouth to HG, 8 February 1960: P.153. HG characteristically replied that he had only been an intermediary and the credit belonged to others.
17 Interview, R. Underhill.
18 Interview, Lord Briggs.
19 HG to Julie: *a.* 18 May 1959, his emphasis; *b.* 24 August 1962; *c.* 7 June 1959.
20 Interview, Professor A. Ranney.
21 *SE*, 28 September 1961.
22 Interview, T. Driberg.
23 Press of 27 April 1963.
24 Interviews: *a.* Lady Gaitskell; *b.* Sir Arthur Gaitskell; *c.* Sir Robin Brook.
25 Sampson (1962), p. 97.
26 To HG, n.d. but 7 November 1960 (P.183), and cautiously in public: Crosland (1962), p. 132. Wilson was also critical: RCD, 8 February 1963.
27 In *Guardian*, 14 February 1962.
28 HG to Mr and Mrs Jack Donaldson, n.d.
29 Letter to a friend, 8 February 1959, about 'good, intelligent argument' in an Oxford café until midnight.
30 Hugh Stephenson (that term's president) to author.
31 Professor Neal Blewett (the student chairman) to author.
32 Interview, Professor John Clive.
33 Longford (1964): *a.* p. 243; *b.* p. 242.
34 James Margach, *ST*, 7 October 1962; cf. n. 35*a*.
35 *Sunday Telegraph*: *a.* 6 January 1963 (on his 'towering presence'); *b.* in 19 January 1964.
36 E.g. H. B. Boyne in *DT*, 28 September 1962, 19 January 1963, 18 January 1964; Crossman in *Guardian*, 11 January 1963 and on BBC European Service, 19 January; *The Times* political correspondent, 19 January 1963; and n. 35*a*.
37 When naming three preferred candidates for office, over two-fifths omitted Macmillan from a Tory government but only one-eighth left Gaitskell out of a Labour one. He was named by over three times as many people as his six most favoured Labour critics put together, and

by more than his three leading colleagues—Brown, Wilson and Callaghan—combined.

38 HG naturally showed more enthusiasm over that victory than over Woodside; Ian Mikardo, unreconciled, insinuated (by pretending to deny it) that that was just prejudice against the Scot, a unilateralist: *Tribune*, 30 November 1962.

39 Foot in *Tribune*, 25 January 1963; Shinwell (1963), p. 215.

40 *Guardian*, 11 January 1963. Cf. Anthony Howard in *New Statesman*, 18 January 1963 on 'the most damaging allegation made against it— that it has virtually become a one-man party'.

41 Mr and Mrs G. M. Gammelien to HG, 25 September 1962: P.168.

42 Charles Curran in *Evening News*, 19 January 1963. Cf. T. F. Lindsay, *Parliament from the Press Gallery* (Macmillan, 1967), p. 96.

43 Dalton to HG, 18 December 1955 (P.101–2): omitted in Dalton (1962), p. 434.

44 Interviews, Lord Noel-Baker, R. Prentice, G. R. Strauss; and numerous letters.

45 Chapter 5, Section ii for his illness in 1945.

46 Interviews, Lord Aylestone, Lady Bacon, Lady Donaldson.

47 Interviews, A. N. W. Benn, Mrs Percy Clark, T. Driberg. Their recollections differ slightly, but confirm the incident, which alarmed them all.

48 Interview, Lady Brook; AHD, 17 May 1962.

49 HG to John Robertson MP, 9 October 1962; also to E. L. Mallalieu MP, 30 July 1962: both P.142–4.

50 His obituary, *Daily Mirror*, 19 January 1963.

51 Donnelly (1968), pp. 19–20; Sam Watson in Rodgers (1964), p. 113; Rodgers's note of the CDS meeting on 21 October 1962; interviews, Sir Hubert and Lady Ashton, Mrs Skelly, Lord Stow Hill; n. 9b; cf. *DT*, 19 January 1963.

52 Interview, Lord Harris.

53 On 19 December 1962: P.142–4.

54 To Mel Lasky, 21 December 1962 (P.163–2); to Dan Jones MP, 21 December 1962 (P.166); interview, Lady Ashton.

55 The account of his illness is based mainly on interviews with Drs Somerville, Colebourne, Kernoff and Ledingham, and with Percy Clark who dealt daily with the press.

56 HG to James Griffiths, 31 December 1962 (P.142–4); to Lord Walston and others.

57 A study published in 1971 listed forty-nine references, three-quarters published in the 1960s and most in the eight years after Gaitskell's death: D. Estes & C. Christian, 'The Natural History of Systemic Lupus Erythematosus by Prospective Analysis', *Medicine*, 50. 2, pp. 85–95.

58 Dr Somerville's statement in *SE*, 24 October 1971, and interview; n. 24*b*; on 1961 see A. Cockburn in *New Statesman*, 28 February 1978.

59 *Lancet*, 30 November 1974 (leading article, p. 1302); R. S. Schwartz in *New England Journal of Medicine*, 17 July 1975, pp. 132–6; cf. Estes and Christian, pp. 93–4.

60 D. L. Larson, *Systemic Lupus Erythematosus* (J. & A. Churchill, 1961), pp. 9–17; brief summary in *Lancet*, 2 February 1963. In 1971 Estes and Christian studied only patients suffering at least four manifestations.

61 In the 1971 study, 10 out of 150; but much more often nowadays.

62 The anti-nuclear factor is present in the vast majority of SLE cases (87 per cent in Estes and Christian, p. 88; 98 per cent according to two experienced doctors), but unless tested for seriously and early, it might be missed.

63 Hallucinations are quite common among SLE sufferers: Estes and Christian, p. 87.

64 Seventeen phoned the hospital: *DT*, 19 January 1963. One constituent was a miner who had once written to his MP with a problem; less than a week later he was surprised to see HG walking down his garden path to deal with it. Another, a decorator, wrote to HG's agent. *Yorkshire Evening Post*, 19 January 1963; interviews, Canon Hammerton, Mrs George Murray, Alderman A. Tallant.

65 Interviews, Michael Stewart, N. Ellis.

66 Archdeacon W. H. S. Purcell (former Vicar of Holbeck, who took the service) to author.

67 Interviews.

Chapter 27   The Last Irony

1 John Connell, *Sphere*, 2 February 1963.

2 *a*. Healey, *Leeds Weekly Citizen*, 1 February 1963; *b*. cf. Crosland's obituary on BBC television.

3 *a*. Humphrey in *Congressional Record*, 21 January 1964, pp. 690–1; *b*. Several experienced American political scientists then living in London felt unanimously that HG in Downing Street would have become the principal leader of the West: interview, Professor A. Ranney.

4 Above, p. 474; 670 *H.C. Deb.*, col. 42: 21 January 1963.

5 ETU transcript (Chapter 6, n. 97); *a*. pp. 5–6; *b*. p. 17; *c*. pp. 3–5 (his topic was the PLP).

6 Interview, D. Wood.

7 Obituary published by the WEA, *WEA News* November 1962, p. 6; cf. recorded broadcast, 12 May 1963: BBC.

8 A contrast noted in several profiles when he became leader: R. T. McKenzie, *DT*, 15 December 1955; *FT*, 15 December; *New York Times*, 15 December, *Birmingham Post* political correspondent, 16 December. It was also true of Asquith.

9 *Daily Mail*, 13 July 1959.

10 Addison (1975), Chapter 10.

11 The MP, Brigadier Smyth, quoted by Healey, n. 2*a*.

12 David Watt in *FT*, 12 January 1973.

13 In Briggs and Saville (1967), p. 19.

14 Healey's obituary on 'Panorama', 18 January 1963: BBC.

15 Interviews, Sir Ronald Edwards, Sir William Webber.

16 See Chapter 26, Section ii: p. 758

17 This summarises the views of 29 ex-Cabinet Ministers and 41 others; 53 were Labour (including 12 from the Left) and 17 were not. There were 9 don't knows (all Labour, 1 Left) and 9 who thought HG would have lost (including 6 of the Left, 1 other Labour man and 2 Tories).

18 AHD, 21 November 1962; interview, Mrs McNeal.

19 But he once told a Conservative MP that a Gaitskell Cabinet would include four newcomers—Crosland, Donnelly, Jenkins and Wyatt: *New Statesman*, 18 February 1977 and Rt Hon. Julian Amery to author.

20 On 10 February 1956: MS in P.191. At Leeds town hall: *MG*, 20 February 1956.

21 Lord Roberthall to author.

22 Interview, A. Crosland; a few stray references in the files. (Lord Harris associated it with 1959.)

23 Hirshfield to HG, 2 and 18 July 1962, 7 December 1962; HG's reply, 4 July 1962: P.163–2.

24 He never made a direct electoral appeal on that theme like Harold Wilson, though he hinted at it at the 1959 Conference: *LPCR*, 1959, p. 107. He told Hetherington that *Signposts for the Sixties* did not say much about it, 'but who has said anything to the point on this lately?' AHD, 22 June 1961.

25 Interviews, A. Albu, D. Ginsburg, Lord Zuckerman; Vig (1968), pp. 32, 85, and Albu's review of it in *Minerva*, vol. 8 (1970).

26 They said both to Crossman, who had become Shadow spokesman on science: RCD, 5 March 1963, 26 June 1963; cf. 8 Feb. 1963 (reporting Wilson); Vig (1968), pp. 4, 31–2, 38–42, 82–7; Roth (1977), p. 285.

27 He was keen on more scientists in the Civil Service: 629 *H.C. Deb.*, col. 1218, 10 November 1960.

28 Roy Jenkins, *The Labour Case* (Penguin, 1959), Chapter 5.

29 But not on 15 October 1964, the best time politically but unsuitable economically.
30 By Harold Wincott in *FT*, 17 January 1956; contrast HG replying in *ibid.*, 19 January, and reported in *The Times*, 18 September 1957.
31 Crosland (1956), p. 275.
32 See Vernon Bogdanor in *Oxford Journal of Education*, June–July 1977.
33 Above, p. 679.
34 RCD, 5 March 1963.
35 Janosik (1968), p. 29n.
36 Professor John Mackintosh MP in *The Times*, 22 July 1977.
37 P. Foot (1968), p. 127, quoting John Junor.
38 Joseph Kallenbach, *The American Chief Executive* (Harper & Row, 1966), pp. 257–67.

SELECT BIBLIOGRAPHY

Only books which are quoted throughout the text or in widely separated chapters are listed in this bibliography. Publication details for the remainder are given in full at the first mention within each chapter.

ABRAMS, M., and ROSE, R. *Must Labour Lose?* (Penguin, 1960).

ACHESON, DEAN, *Present at the Creation* (Macmillan, 1970).

ADDISON, PAUL, *The Road to 1945* (Cape, 1975).

AVON, see EDEN.

BIRKENHEAD, LORD, *Walter Monckton* (Weidenfeld & Nicolson, 1969).

BRIGGS, ASA, and SAVILLE, J. (eds), *Essays in Labour History in Honour of G. D. H. Cole* (Macmillan, 1967 edn).

BRITTAN, SAM, *The Treasury Under the Tories 1951–64* (Penguin, 1964).

—— *Steering the Economy* (Penguin, 2nd edn, 1971).

BROWN, LORD GEORGE-, *In My Way* (Penguin edn, 1972).

BUTLER, D. E., *The British General Election* (1) *of 1951* (2) *of 1955* (3) *of 1959* (with R. Rose) (4) *of 1964* (with A. King) (Macmillan, 1952, 1955, 1960, 1965).

BUTLER, LORD, *The Art of the Possible* (Penguin edn, 1973).

CARBERY, T. F., *Consumers in Politics* (Manchester University Press, 1969).

CROSLAND, C. A. R., *The Future of Socialism* (Cape, 1956).

—— *The Conservative Enemy* (Cape, 1962).

DALTON, HUGH, Memoirs I: *Call Back Yesterday* (Muller, 1953).

—— Memoirs II: *The Fateful Years* (Muller, 1957).

—— Memoirs III: *High Tide and After* (Muller, 1962).

DAVENPORT, N., *Memoirs of a City Radical* (Weidenfeld & Nicolson, 1974).

DILKS, D. (ed.), *The Diaries of Sir Alexander Cadogan* (Cassell, 1971).

DONNELLY, D., *Gadarene 68* (Kimber, 1968).

DONOUGHUE, B., and JONES, G. W. *Herbert Morrison* (Weidenfeld & Nicolson, 1973).

DOW, J. C. R., *The Management of the British Economy 1945–60* (Cambridge University Press, 1970).

DRIVER, C., *The Disarmers* (Hodder & Stoughton, 1964).

DUFF, PEGGY, *Left, Left, Left* (Allison & Busby, 1971).

DURBIN, E. F. M., *The Politics of Democratic Socialism* (Routledge, 1954 edn).

EDEN, ANTHONY (EARL OF AVON), *Full Circle* (Cassell, 1960).

FAIRLIE, HENRY, *The Life of Politics* (Methuen, 1968).

FISHER, NIGEL, *Iain Macleod* (Purnell, Deutsch, 1973).

FOOT, MICHAEL, *Aneurin Bevan,* I (Four Square, 1966); II (Davis-Poynter, 1973).

FOOT, PAUL, *The Politics of Harold Wilson* (Penguin, 1968).

GAITSKELL, HUGH, *Chartism* (WEA, 1929).

—— *The Challenge of Coexistence* (Methuen, 1957).

GOODMAN, G., *The Awkward Warrior: Frank Cousins, his Life and Times* (Davis-Poynter, 1979).

GORDON, M. R., *Conflict & Consensus in Labour's Foreign Policy* (Stanford University Press, 1969).

GRIFFITHS, JAMES, *Pages from Memory* (Dent, 1969).

GRISEWOOD, H., *One Thing at a Time* (Hutchinson, 1968).

HARRISON, MARTIN, *Trade Unions and the Labour Party since 1945* (Allen & Unwin, 1960).

HASELER, STEPHEN, *The Gaitskellites* (Macmillan, 1969).

HUNTER, LESLIE, *The Road to Brighton Pier* (Barker, 1959).

JACKSON, R. J., *Rebels and Whips* (Macmillan, 1968).

JANOSIK, E. G., *Constituency Labour Parties in British Politics* (Pall Mall, 1968).

JENKINS, ROY, *Nine Men of Power* (Hamish Hamilton, 1974).

KEATLEY, PATRICK, *The Politics of Partnership* (Penguin, 1963).

KILMUIR, EARL OF, *Political Adventure* (Weidenfeld & Nicolson, 1964).

KING, CECIL, *The Cecil King Diary 1965–70* (Cape, 1972).

—— *Strictly Personal* (Weidenfeld & Nicolson, 1969).

KRUG, M. M., *Aneurin Bevan: Cautious Rebel* (T. Yoseloff, New York & London, 1961).

LONGFORD, EARL OF (FRANK PAKENHAM), *Born to Believe* (Hutchinson, 1953).

—— *Five Lives* (Hutchinson, 1964).

—— *The Grain of Wheat* (Collins, 1974).

MCDERMOTT, GEOFFREY, *Leader Lost* (Frewin, 1972).

MACMILLAN, HAROLD, Memoirs III: *Tides of Fortune* (Macmillan, 1969).

—— Memoirs IV: *Riding the Storm* (Macmillan, 1971).

—— Memoirs V: *Pointing the Way* (Macmillan, 1972).

—— Memoirs VI: *At the End of the Day* (Macmillan, 1973).

MORRISON, HERBERT, *Autobiography* (Odhams, 1960).

NICOLSON, NIGEL (ed.), *Harold Nicolson Diaries III: 1945–62* (Fontana edn, 1971).

PAKENHAM, see LONGFORD.

PARKIN, FRANK, *Middle Class Radicalism* (Manchester University Press, 1968).

PUNNETT, R. M., *Front Bench Opposition* (Heinemann, 1973).

REES, G. L., *Britain and the Postwar Payments System* (University of Wales Press, 1963).

RODGERS, W. T. (ed.), *Hugh Gaitskell 1906–63* (Thames & Hudson, 1964).

ROTH, ANDREW, *Sir Harold Wilson— Yorkshire Walter Mitty* (Macdonald, 1977).

SAMPSON, ANTHONY, *Anatomy of Britain* (Hodder & Stoughton, 1962).

—— *Macmillan* (Penguin, 1967).

SHINWELL, EMANUEL, *The Labour Story* (Macdonald, 1963).

SHONFIELD, ANDREW, *British Economic Policy since the War* (Penguin, revised edn, 1959).

SMITH, LESLIE, *Harold Wilson* (Hodder & Stoughton, 1964).

STEWART, MARGARET, *Frank Cousins* (Hutchinson, 1968).

TAYLOR, A. J. P., *Beaverbrook* (Penguin edn, 1974).

THOMAS, HUGH, *John Strachey* (Eyre Methuen, 1973).

TRUMAN, HARRY S., Memoirs I *Year of Decisions* (Hodder & Stoughton, 1955).

—— Memoirs II *Years of Trial and Hope* (Hodder & Stoughton, 1956).

VIG, N. J., *Science and Technology in British Politics* (Pergamon, 1968).

'WATCHMAN' (VYVYAN ADAMS), *Right Honourable Gentlemen* (Hamish Hamilton, 1939).

WELENSKY, SIR ROY, *4000 Days* (Collins, 1964).

WIGG, LORD, *George Wigg* (Michael Joseph, 1972).

WILLIAMS, FRANCIS, *A Prime Minister Remembers* (Heinemann, 1961).

—— *Nothing So Strange* (Cassell, 1970).

WORSWICK, G. D. N., and ADY, P. (eds), *The British Economy: 1945–50* (Oxford University Press, 1952).

—— *The British Economy in the 1950s* (Oxford University Press, 1962).

ZUCKERMAN, SOLLY, *From Apes to Warlords* (Hamish Hamilton, 1978).

INDEX

Using the index

Main references are in **bold** type.

Organisations indexed by their initials come *first* in the relevant letter, e.g. 'AEU' before Abadan.

Most footnote references are identified by chapter and note number and come together *following* the last page reference, e.g. Abadan, Albu. Where the note follows directly from a page reference, the latter identifies it, e.g. Acheson. Sources in the notes are not normally indexed. Some long words are abbreviated by omitting the italicised letters, e.g. *commit*tees, *in*ternational, *nat*ionalisation; *q.v.* means *see that entry*. Relationships specified are to HG. Except for living persons, titles are normally those used during HG's career.